Law of Mortgage

Fisher and Lightwood's

Law of Mortgage

Eleventh edition

Co-ordinating editor and contributor

Wayne Clark LLB, BCL

Contributors

Katherine Astill BA, MPhil

Janet Bignell MA, BCL

Martin Dray LLB

Kim Lewison QC, MA

Paul Morgan QC, MA

Edward Peters MA

Adam Rosenthal BA

Anthony Tanney BA

Members of the LexisNexis Group worldwide

United Kingdom	Butterworths Tolley, a Division of Reed Elsevier (UK) Ltd, Halsbury House, 35 Chancery Lane, LONDON, WC2A 1EL, and 4 Hill Street, EDINBURGH EH2 3JZ
Argentina	Abeledo Perrot, Jurisprudencia Argentina and Depalma, BUENOS AIRES
Australia	Butterworths, a Division of Reed International Books Australia Pty Ltd, CHATSWOOD, New South Wales
Austria	ARD Betriebsdienst and Verlag Orac, VIENNA
Canada	Butterworths Canada Ltd, MARKHAM, Ontario
Chile	Publitecsa and Conosur Ltda, SANTIAGO DE CHILE
Czech Republic	Orac sro, PRAGUE
France	Editions du Juris-Classeur SA, PARIS
Hong Kong	Butterworths Asia (Hong Kong), HONG KONG
Hungary	Hvg Orac, BUDAPEST
India	Butterworths India, NEW DELHI
Ireland	Butterworths (Ireland) Ltd, DUBLIN
Italy	Giuffré, MILAN
Malaysia	Malayan Law Journal Sdn Bhd, KUALA LUMPUR
New Zealand	Butterworths of New Zealand, WELLINGTON
Poland	Wydawnictwa Prawnicze PWN, WARSAW
Singapore	Butterworths Asia, SINGAPORE
South Africa	Butterworths Publishers (Pty) Ltd, DURBAN
Switzerland	Stämpfli Verlag AG, BERNE
USA	LexisNexis, DAYTON, Ohio

A CIP Catalogue record for this book is available from the British Library.

ISBN 0 406 99975 9

Printed and bound in Great Britain by The Bath Press, Bath

Visit Butterworths LexisNexis *direct* at www.butterworths.com

Preface

A considerable time has passed since the 10th edition of this work and it comes as no surprise that there have been considerable developments in the law, although the major reform of land mortgages envisaged by the Law Commission's Working Paper No 99 on Land Mortgages has not found its way onto the statute book. There have been many important judicial and statutory developments, all of which we have endeavoured to incorporate into the text. Of particular note are the decision in *United Bank of Kuwait v Sahib,* holding that in light of the Law of Property (Miscellaneous Provisions) Act 1989 an equitable mortgage could no longer be created after 27 September 1989 by a simple deposit of title deeds, the very recent decision of the House of Lords in *Royal Bank of Scotland v Etridge* (undue influence and constructive notice by mortgagees of the claim of a signatory to set aside the mortgage) and the application of the Human Rights Act 1998 to a mortgagee's claims for possession of land.

Mr Tyler, the editor of several of the previous editions, expressed the view that the work was too much for one person. This is reflected in the fact that the work has required the efforts of nine members of Chambers. Although a long period has passed since the last edition, it is only recently that Chambers has been engaged upon the task of providing to the property world a new edition. In this edition, we have decided not to make major structural alterations. This will be a task for the not too distant future, as it is the intention to have new editions at more frequent intervals than has previously been the case. However, the work has not simply been updated. Although chapter titles will be familiar to readers of past editions, we have endeavoured to provide a comprehensive revision of the material, which in most cases has involved or necessitated a reorganisation of the existing text. We have, further, striven to render the text more reader friendly and it is presented in a more digestible form by the use of shorter paragraphs with the footnotes immediately following each paragraph. The new Civil Procedure Rules have, of course, been integrated into the work.

The preparation of this edition has been a substantial undertaking. Each member of the team has made a significant contribution to this edition and each has been unstinting in the time and effort devoted to revising the work which has competed with the demands of busy practices at the Bar. Chambers has been particularly productive when it comes to book writing. Our intention is that this edition is the beginning of a long-term relationship with *Fisher and Lightwood*. We trust that we have maintained its reputation for being accurate and trustworthy. Corrections or improvements are welcomed and appreciated and readers are encouraged to contact me, either directly or through the publishers. We shall continue to improve the work and its presentation in future editions. This edition will be the subject of cumulative supplements from time to time.

A particular debt of gratitude is owed to Chambers. Our clerks and fellow members have had to endure a quarter of its members diving head long into a time-consuming and demanding project, although its rewards will, we hope, be enjoyed by them all. We are grateful for their understanding and indulgence.

We are also grateful to the publishers for their tolerance in having to deal with the inevitable delays caused by the number of contributors and the vagaries of practice. We would like to thank everyone at Butterworths who has been involved in the project.

We have endeavoured to state the law as at 5 November 2001.

Wayne Clark
Falcon Chambers

5 December 2001

Contents

Table of statutes

References are to paragraph numbers.
Those paragraph numbers in **bold** type indicate where an Act is set out in full or in part.

Table of cases

PARA

A

B

PARA

PARA

PARA

C

PARA

D

E

F

PARA

G

PARA

H

PARA

I

J

PARA

Kelcey, Re, Tyson v Kelcey [1899] 2 Ch 530, 68 LJ Ch 472, 48 WR 59, 43 Sol Jo 720, sub nom Re Finn-Kelcey, Tyson v Kelcey 81 LT 354 .... 1.17
Kelday, Re, ex p Meston (1888) 36 WR 585, 4 TLR 478, CA 21.12
Keller (Samuel) (Holdings) Ltd v Martins Bank Ltd [1970] 3 All ER 950, [1971] 1 WLR 43, 22 P & CR 68, 114 Sol Jo 951, CA 19.2, 19.50, 20.51, 28.37, 28.51
Kelly v Selwyn [1905] 2 Ch 117, 74 LJ Ch 567, 53 WR 649, 93 LT 633 .... 24.94
Kelly & Co v Kellond (1888) 20 QBD 569, 57 LJQB 330, 36 WR 363, 58 LT 263, 4 TLR 290, CA; on appeal sub nom Thomas v Kelly (1888) 13 App Cas 506, 58 LJQB 66, 37 WR 353, [1886-90] All ER Rep 431, 60 LT 114, 4 TLR 683, HL 5.4, 5.6, 5.24, 5.27, 5.28, 5.32, 5.39
Kelo, The. See Kaukomarkkinat O/Y v Elbe Transport-Union GmbH, The Kelo
Kemmis v Kemmis (Welland intervening) [1988] 1 WLR 1307, [1988] 2 FLR 223, [1989] 3 LS Gaz R 43, CA 13.13, 24.31, 24.32
Kemmis v Stepney (1828) 2 Mol 85 .... 31.5
Kemp v Lester [1896] 2 QB 162, 65 LJQB 532, 44 WR 453, 40 Sol Jo 371, 74 LT 268, 12 TLR 292, CA 3.49
Kemp v Westbrook (1749) 1 Ves Sen 278 .... 20.3
Kemp v Wright [1895] 1 Ch 121, 59 JP 133, 64 LJ Ch 59, 7 R 631, 43 WR 213, 39 Sol Jo 43, 71 LT 650, CA 28.30
Kendle v Melsom (1998) 193 CLR 46 .... 18.7
Kennard v Futvoye (1860) 2 Giff 81, 29 LJ Ch 553, 6 Jur NS 312, 2 LT 30 .... 21.2
Kennedy v De Trafford [1896] 1 Ch 762, CA; affd [1897] AC 180, 66 LJ Ch 413, 4 5 WR 671, [1895-9] All ER Rep 408, 76 LT 427, HL 20.22, 20.31, 20.33, 35.17
Kennedy v General Credits Ltd (1982) 2 BPR 9456 .... 19.65
Kennedy v Green (1834) 3 My & K 699, [1824-34] All ER Rep 727 ..... 24.33, 24.44, 24.45
Kensington, ex p (1813) 2 Rose 138, 2 Ves & B 79 .... 1.18, 3.95, 3.98
Kensington (Baron), Re, Longford (Earl) v Baron Kensington [1902] 1 Ch 203, 71 LJ Ch 170, 50 WR 201, 46 Sol Jo 176, 85 LT 577, 18 TLR 89 .... 25.2
Kensington (Lord), Re, Bacon v Ford (1885) 29 Ch D 527, 54 LJ Ch 1085, 33 WR 689, 53 LT 19 .... 24.107
Kensington (Lord) v Bouverie (1852) 16 Beav 194 .... 22.11
Kensington (Lord) v Bouverie (1854) 19 Beav 39; on appeal (1855) 7 De GM & G 134, 24 LJ Ch 442, 3 Eq Rep 765, 1 Jur NS 577, 3 WR 469, 25 LT 169; affd (1859) 7 HL Cas 557, 29 LJ Ch 537, 6 Jur NS 105, [1843-60] All ER Rep 304, 34 LTOS 16 .... 19.65, 22.11, 27.4, 29.2, 35.22, 35.23, 35.26, 35.60, 35.63
Kent v Thomas (1856) 1 H & N 473 .... 28.45
Kent and Sussex Sawmills Ltd, Re [1947] Ch 177, [1946] 2 All ER 638, [1947] LJR 534, 91 Sol Jo 12, 176 LT 167, 62 TLR 747 .... 1.12, 7.3, 12.17
Kentish Homes Ltd, Re (1993) 91 LGR 592, [1993] BCLC 1375, [1993] BCC 212, [1993] 13 LS Gaz R 36, 137 Sol Jo LB 45 .... 18.4, 18.10, 18.13
Kenyon-Brown v Desmond Banks & Co (a firm) [2001] UKHL 44. See Kenyon-Brown v Banks & Co
Kepler, The (1861) Lush 201 .... 36.45
Ker v Ker (1869) 4 IR Eq 15, CA 26.4, 26.6
Kerford v Mondel (1859) 28 LJ Ex 303, 33 LTOS 289 .... 28.38
Kernohan Estates Ltd v Boyd [1967] NI 27 .... 20.22
Kerr's Policy, Re (1869) LR 8 Eq 331, 38 LJ Ch 539, 17 WR 989 .... 22.2, 35.40, 35.55
Kerrick v Saffery (1835) 7 Sim 317, 4 LJ Ch 162 .... 22.16
Kershaw v Kalow (1855) 1 Jur NS 974 .... 20.28
Kershaw v Kirkpatrick (1878) 3 App Cas 345 .... 28.49
Kestrel, The (1866) LR 1 A & E 78, 12 Jur NS 713, 2 Mar LC 472, 16 LT 72 .... 36.5
Ketley (A) Ltd v Scott [1981] ICR 241, [1980] CCLR 37 .... 10.86, 10.88, 10.91
Kettle's Gift, Re [1968] 3 All ER 88, [1968] 1 WLR 1459, 47 ATC 309, [1968] TR 279, 112 Sol Jo 706 .... 1.27
Kettlewell v Watson (1882) 21 Ch D 685, 51 LJ Ch 281, 30 WR 402, 46 LT 83; on appeal (1884) 26 Ch D 501, 53 LJ Ch 717, 32 WR 865, 51 LT 135, CA 24.26, 24.28, 24.44, 24.58, 24.59, 24.68, 31.14
Keys v Williams (1838) 3 Y & C Ex 55, 7 LJ Ex Eq 59, 2 Jur 611 .... 3.95
Kibble v Fairthorne [1895] 1 Ch 219, 64 LJ Ch 184, 13 R 75, 43 WR 327, [1891-4] All ER Rep 1356, 71 LT 755 .... 16.37, 16.43, 16.51, 16.52
Kidd, Re, Brooman v Withall [1894] 3 Ch 558, 63 LJ Ch 855, 13 R 101, 43 WR 51, 71 LT 481 .... 25.2

PARA

L

PARA

PARA

M

PARA

PARA

PARA

O

PARA

PARA

P

PARA

PARA

PARA

Q

R

PARA

PARA

PARA

S

PARA

PARA

PARA

T

PARA

V

W

PARA

Y

Z

PART I

MORTGAGES AND CHARGES

Chapter 1

Mortgages and other securities generally

SECURITIES GENERALLY

The nature and kinds of security

1.1 A creditor may be willing to rely solely on his debtor's personal credit for the fulfilment of the debtor's contractual obligations it is likely, however, that he will want something more than a mere contractual remedy to sue a debtor who defaults[1]. He obtains this by taking either personal or real security[2].

Personal security, or suretyship, consists of the contract of guarantee, whereby the guarantor promises to answer for the obligation of the debtor should the debtor default. The effect is to give the creditor a secondary contractual action against the guarantor in the event of default by the principal debtor. Such security does, however, have disadvantages from the creditor's point of view, as the efficacy of a guarantee depends upon the completeness of the form of the document itself and upon the continued solvency of the guarantor[3]. By contrast, real security gives the creditor rights over real or personal property appropriated to meet the debt or other obligation. For the creditor, the attraction of real security is that, if the debtor should become insolvent, the creditor may exercise his rights over the security in priority to the claims of the general creditors[4]. The most important form of real security is the mortgage.

1 In some cases, eg where the loan is by trustees, security will be *required* by the terms of the trust deed or statute.

2 'Security is created where a person ('the creditor') to whom an obligation is owed by another ('the debtor') by statute or contract, in addition to the personal promise of the debtor to discharge the debt, obtains rights exercisable against some property in which the debtor has an interest in order to enforce the discharge of the debtor's obligations to the creditor': *Bristol Airport plc v Powdrill* [1990] Ch 744 at 760C, [1990] 2 All ER 493, CA.

3 On guarantee generally, see 20 *Halsbury's Laws* (4th edn reissue), Guarantee and Indemnity; *Rowlatt on Principal and Surety* (5th edn).

4 Further, a secured creditor of an insolvent company is not required by Insolvency Rules 1986, r 4.90 to set off money owed by him to the company against the secured debt: *Re Norman Holding Co Ltd* [1990] 3 All ER 757, [1991] 1 WLR 10.

Real security

1.2 Real security may be created by contract or may arise by operation of law at common law, in equity or under certain statutes. When created by contract the security takes the form of mortgage, pledge or charge[1]; when created by operation of law the security is called a lien[2].

Real securities fall into three classes:

(a) those by which the creditor obtains proprietary rights over the subject matter of the security but which do not depend on the creditor obtaining possession of the property[3];
(b) those by which the creditor does not obtain proprietary rights over the property and which depend on him obtaining possession of the property[4]; and
(c) those which do not depend on the creditor obtaining either proprietary rights over or the possession of the property[5].

To each of the kinds of real security is incident:

(a) a right in the creditor to make the property which is subject to the security answerable for the debt or other obligation;
(b) a right in the debtor to redeem the property by paying the debt or performing the obligation; and
(c) a liability on the part of the creditor upon such payment or performance to restore the property to the owner.

1 Statutory charges do not arise out of agreement. For statutory charges, see Chapter 2. Charges created by will may also lack this element of agreement. See on estoppel, *Amalgamated Investment and Property Co Ltd v Texas Commerce International Bank Ltd* [1982] QB 84, [1981] 3 All ER 577, CA.
2 There is some looseness in the use of the terminology of real securities. In some works the word 'lien' includes charges arising out of contract.
3 Ie mortgage securities.
4 Ie pledge and the possessory lien.
5 Ie charges and non-possessory liens. This threefold classification is given by Willes J in *Halliday v Holgate* (1868) LR 3 Exch 299 at 302.

Mortgage

1.3 A mortgage is a form of security created by contract, conferring an interest in real or personal property[1] defeasible[2] upon performing the condition of paying a given sum of money, with or without interest, or of performing some other condition[3]. Such security depends upon a grant by the debtor or someone on the debtor's behalf, not upon a reservation[4].

A mortgage may be either legal or equitable[5]. A charge by way of legal mortgage of land has the same effect as a mortgage[6] without any legal estate being conferred on the mortgagee.

1 Mortgages of chattels are generally affected by bills of sale.
2 Ie annullable.
3 The classic description of a mortgage was given by Lindley MR in *Santley v Wilde* [1899] 2 Ch 474, CA in the following terms: 'A mortgage is a conveyance of land or an assignment of chattels as a security for the payment of a debt or the discharge of some other obligation for which it is given.' See also *Handevel Pty Ltd v Comptroller of Stamps (Vic)* [1984] VR 894; revsd [1986] ALJR 40, 157 CLR 177 at 192 and see *Doyle v Doyle* [1992] 3 NZLR 170 on the nature of a mortgage as both a contract creating a debt and a security. If there is no debt or other obligation the mortgage is of no effect: *Re GM Industries Pty Ltd* (1980) ACLC 34, 422.

4 *Re Bond Worth Ltd* [1980] Ch 228 at 252–256, [1979] 3 All ER 919 at 942–945; and see, generally, Goode, *Legal Problems of Credit and Security* (2nd edn) pp 2–5.
5 See **1.17** ff.
6 Law of Property Act 1925, s 87(1), and see *Downsview Nominees Ltd v First City Corpn Ltd* [1993] AC 295 at 311, PC and **1.5**. See also *London County and Westminster Bank Ltd v Tompkins* [1918] 1 KB 515, CA where the terms 'mortgage' and 'equitable charge' are discussed.

Pledge[1]

1.4 A pledge or pawn is a security created by contract and carried into effect by a bailment of a chattel to the lender to be kept by him until the debt is discharged. By its nature the pledge is, therefore, confined to physical assets. A pledge is incomplete without actual or constructive delivery of the goods to the lender.

The general property in the goods remains in the borrower although the lender has certain powers of sale[2]. On the sale of the pledged property, the pledgee holds any sum in excess of the debt on trust for the pledgor and is liable in equity to pay interest on the retained proceeds[3].

While the pledge is a powerful form of security interest, for a borrower the advantage of a mortgage as opposed to a pledge is that the borrower can keep possession of his property[4].

1 See, generally, 36(1) *Halsbury's Laws* (4th edn reissue), Pledges and Pawns. On the difference between pledge and charge see *Australia and New Zealand Banking Group Ltd v Curlett, Cannon & Galbell Pty Ltd* [1992] 2 VR 647.
2 See *Re Morritt* (1886) 18 QBD 222; *Re Cosslett (Contractors) Ltd* [1998] Ch 495 at 508, [1997] 4 All ER 115 at 126, CA, per Millett LJ.
3 *Matthew v T M Sutton Ltd* [1994] 4 All ER 793, [1994] 1 WLR 1455.
4 *Re Cosslett (Contractors) Ltd*, above.

Charge

1.5 A charge is the appropriation of real or personal property for the discharge of a debt or other obligation, without giving the creditor either a general or special property in, or possession of, the subject of the security[1]; for example, an order upon a third party to apply money in his hands to the discharge of a debt or a charge on realty for the payment of a specified amount. The creditor has a right of realisation by judicial process in case of non-payment of the debt. Where goods are so appropriated the transaction is sometimes called hypothecation[2]. Marine hypothecation may be by way of bottomry or *respondentia*[3].

Both 'mortgage' and 'charge' are often loosely used as a generic term for all species of security[4]. Indeed, the mortgage and charge have been gradually assimilated so that today, for practical purposes, there is little difference between them[5], though the fundamental difference in their nature remains[6].

1 *Re Cosslett (Contractors) Ltd* [1998] Ch 495 at 508 per Millett LJ; *Young v Matthew Hall Mechanical & Electrical Engineers Pty Ltd* (1988) 13 ACLR 399, SCWA. A charge involves some deduction from the right of ownership in the property, rather than a mere interference with possession.
2 The document setting out the terms of a pledge of documents of title is sometimes referred to as a letter of hypothecation but, nevertheless, the transaction is pledge.

3 See Chapter 6.
4 See *Re Bond Worth Ltd* [1980] Ch 228 at 250, [1979] 3 All ER 919 at 940. Also see generally (1978) 94 LQR 571, 574–576 (Jackson). Under the Law of Property Act 1925, mortgage includes charges and liens: s 205 (1) (xvi). In the construction of wills 'mortgage' includes charge and vice versa: see *Re Beirnstein, Barnett v Beirnstein* [1925] Ch 12. In the company context especially, mortgage and charge are often used as if there was no difference between them: see *Re Wallis and Simmonds (Builders) Ltd* [1974] 1 All ER 561. For a case where the distinction between 'mortgage' and 'charge' was expressly made by the claimant, see *Thames Guaranty Ltd v Campbell* [1985] QB 210 at 217, [1984] 1 All ER 144 at 148; affd [1985] QB 210, [1984] 2 All ER 585, CA.
5 The distinction is blurred by the 1925 legislation by the reference to a 'charge by way of legal mortgage': Law of Property Act 1925, ss 1(2)(c), 85(1). See *Grand Junction Co Ltd v Bates* [1954] 2 QB 160 at 168-169; *Regent Oil Co Ltd v J A Gregory (Hatch End) Ltd* [1966] Ch 402 at 431.
In the view of the Law Commission, the current law of mortgage is unnecessarily complex, confusing and artificial. As a result, the Law Commission, Transfer of Land — Land Mortgages, Law Com No 204, 13 November 1991 recommended that all existing methods of consensual mortgage and charge over land should be abolished and replaced by two new standardised forms of mortgage, the 'formal land mortgage' and 'the informal land mortgage'. No legislation giving effect to these proposals has been implemented.
6 See *Swiss Bank Corpn v Lloyds Bank Ltd* [1982] AC 584, [1980] 2 All ER 419, CA; affd [1982] AC 584, [1981] 2 All ER 449, HL. See also *United Travel Agencies Pty Ltd v Cain* (1990) 20 NSWLR 566 on the difference between an equitable charge and an equitable mortgage.

Lien[1]

1.6 A common law lien is a right conferred by law[2] upon a person to retain possession of, or to have a charge upon, the real or personal property of another, until certain demands are satisfied. The right is a mere passive right of retention giving no right to sell or otherwise deal with the property[3]. An equitable lien arises automatically under some doctrine of equity and is not intentionally created by contract[4]. In essence, an equitable lien is a species of equitable charge arising by implication of law[5]. The right is not dependent upon continued possession of the property[6] and, to this extent, resembles a mortgage. An equitable lien is also within the definition of 'mortgage' in the Law of Property Act 1925[7].

A statutory lien is dependent upon the terms of the statute under which it is created[8].

1 See generally, 28 *Halsbury's Laws* (4th edn), Lien. For the unpaid vendor's lien and loss thereof, see Chapter 2; also see *Hewett v Court* (1983) 149 CLR 639. For an insurer's proprietary lien or charge over damages recovered by the insured from the wrongdoer and the possible proprietary right of action for such damages, see *Lord Napier and Ettrick v Hunter* [1993] AC 713, [1993] 1 All ER 385, HL.
2 Ie not by contract: see *Re Bond Worth Ltd* [1980] Ch 228 at 250, [1979] 3 All ER 919 at 940—though the word 'lien' is sometimes used in practice to describe a right which arises by way of express contractual agreement.
3 *Mulliner v Florence* (1878) 3 QBD 484.
4 For example, a vendor of land has an equitable lien on it until the full purchase price is paid even if he has conveyed the land to the purchaser and put him in possession.
5 *Re Birmingham* [1959] Ch 523, [1958] 2 All ER 397.
6 *Wrout v Dawes* (1858) 25 Beav 369.
7 Section 205(1)(xvi).
8 See Chapter 2. For example, solicitors have been given such rights by s 73 of the Solicitors Act 1974.

MORTGAGES GENERALLY

Legal mortgage

1.7 Subject to the provisions of the Law of Property Act 1925, a legal mortgage is a conveyance or assignment of the whole or part of the estate or interest of the debtor in real or personal property of which he is the legal owner or of some legal estate or interest which he has the power to transfer[1]. Except in the case of a legal mortgage of land, the absolute assurance of the property is usually subject to a proviso that upon payment of the debt at a certain time the property should be reconveyed.

Under the Law of Property Act 1925, a legal mortgage of land must be created by demise for a term of years, or by charge by way of legal mortgage, subject to a provision for cesser on redemption[2]. The essence of the legal mortgage of land is the vesting of a legal estate in the mortgagee, together with an immediate right of possession (though this right to possession is now restricted in certain cases)[3]. On payment of the debt at the time fixed, the mortgagor may re-enter[4] and is entitled to a reconveyance[5].

1 *Santley v Wilde* [1899] 2 Ch 474, CA.
2 Law of Property Act 1925, ss 85, 86. A charge by way of legal mortgage is included in the definition of a legal mortgage: Law of Property Act 1925, s 205 (1) (xvi); and, although it does not actually create a legal estate, it gives the same powers and remedies as if it did; Law of Property Act 1925, s 87(1), see Chapter 3.
3 See Chapter 19.
4 Upon payment the mortgage term becomes a satisfied term and ceases: Law of Property Act 1925, ss 5 and 116 (see Chapter 28). In this respect the provision for cesser has the same effect as the former condition for defeasance (as to which, see below).
5 Notwithstanding the automatic cesser of the mortgage term on payment, the Law of Property Act 1925, provides for the surrender of the term: s 115 (see Chapter 28).

The development of mortgages of land before 1926[1]

1.8 Pledges of land are found in Anglo-Saxon times and in the Domesday Book. In Glanvill (c 1187) the rules relating to gage (or pledge) are dealt with as for movables and then applied by reference to immovables[2]. Possession would usually be given to the mortgagee[3], but he had only a special sort of seisin (*seisina ut de vadio*) which the law did not protect[4]. Such a pledge was called a mortgage (*mortuum vadium*) when the fruits or rent received did not tend to reduce the debt; it was called a *vivum vadium* when they were so applied[5]. The property became the mortgagee's on default of repayment on the appointed day, if it was so agreed, or if the mortgagor failed to redeem within a reasonable time after the court had ordered him to do so[6].

This early form of mortgage of land was succeeded by a form in which the mortgagee took an ordinary estate in the land entitling him to the usual remedies for recovering possession. In Bracton (c 1257) the mortgagee's estate appears as a term of years capable of being enlarged automatically into the fee simple on default of payment at the end of the term[7]. Later, when the treatment of estates had become more exact, this elasticity was not permitted as livery of seisin was essential for the creation of a fee simple and since there was no livery on the grant of the term a freehold estate would not arise afterwards[8]. As a result, it became necessary for the mortgagee to take the estate which was to become absolute on non-payment at the time named[9] at the outset. Mortgages might still be made by a lease at a nominal rent (the mortgagee having no right to the fee) and upon terms that the mortagee was to receive the rents and profits of the land in satisfaction of the debt, alternatively, in the case of freeholds, a mortgage might be made by a conveyance of the land in fee simple, subject to the condition either that the mortgagor might re-enter or that the conveyance should be void if the debt was unpaid by the appointed day[10]. Under this system the mortgagee did not necessarily go into possession and a new explanation of *mortuum vadium* and *vivum vadium* became necessary[11].

In or before the sixteenth century the form of the mortgage by conveyance had changed. The conditions mentioned above were replaced by the more convenient covenant for re-conveyance by the mortgagee on repayment by the appointed time[12]. This form of mortgage by conveyance became the usual form of legal mortgage of freeholds until the provisions of the Law of Property Act 1925 became operative on 1 January 1926 and it still remains the usual form of legal mortgage in other cases.

The alternative form of mortgage by lease continued to be generally used until the early nineteenth century. This form had advantages in that it could be used for a mortgage of both freehold and leasehold land and, since it created only a chattel interest, on the mortgagee's death this passed to his executors and not to his heir[13]. It had the disadvantage, however, that a reversion was left in the mortgagor, even if he defaulted. Moreover, there was doubt as to whether the mortgagee could call for the title deeds. As a result, the mortgage by lease fell into disuse[14], save for those circumstances where it was particularly useful, for example, for raising portions in family settlements[15].

1 See, generally, Holdsworth *History of English Law* (HEL); Pollock and Maitland *History of English Law* (P & M); Turner *Equity of Redemption;* Plucknett *Concise History of the Common Law* (5th edn) pp 603–608; (1952) 68 LQR 317 (Rabinowitz); (1967) 83 LQR 229 (Barton).
2 Book X, cc 6 to 11. See HEL vol II, pp 188 ff.
3 For the influence of the usury laws on mortgages, see HEL vol VIII, pp 100 ff.
4 HEL vol III, pp 128 ff; P & M vol II, p 120.
5 Glanvill, Book X, c 6.
6 Glanvill, Book X, cc 6 to 8.
7 F 20. See also P & M vol II, p 121; HEL vol III, p 129.
8 Littleton (c 1480), *Tenures*, s 349; Co Litt, pp 216 ff.
9 Litt, s 333.
10 HEL vol III, pp 129, 130. There were also statutory forms of real security (eg under Statutes Merchant and Staple) which were commonly used until the seventeenth century; see HEL vol III, p 132.
11 Litt, s 332. This was that the land was dead to the debtor if he did not pay at the appointed day, and the pledge was dead if he did pay. But Coke, in his comment on this, remarks that the mortgage, or *mortuum vadium*, is so called to distinguish it from the *vivum vadium* which he defines in Glanvill's sense (Co Litt 205a), though he carries out Littleton's idea by saying that if the creditor's estate is granted only till he has received his debt out of the issue and profits, neither money nor land dieth, or is lost; see also per Lord Eldon in *Fenwick v Reed* (1816) 1 Mer 114 at 124. The Usury Act 1545, permitted loans at interest, so that there was no longer any need for rents and profits to be taken in lieu of interest.
12 HEL vol V, pp 330, 331. The Court of Chancery would grant specific performance of this covenant. Moreover this change simplified proof of title which then depended on execution of the re-conveyance; see *Durham Bros v Robertson* [1898] 1 QB 765 at 772, CA. Although expressed as a covenant for reconveyance the proviso had the effect of a condition subsequent: see Hazeltine's Preface to Turner *Equity of Redemption* pp xi–xiv.
13 Co Litt 204b.
14 This mortgage device is still permitted today: Law of Property Act 1925, ss 85(1), 86(1). As to mortgages of leaseholds immediately prior to 1 January 1926, see Chapter 3.

It is convenient to mention here two other forms of mortgage now obsolete. Formerly a security was sometimes made in the form of a trust for sale, in case of non-payment of the debt at a certain time. This type of mortgage is referred to in the Law of Property Act

1925, ss 85 (3), 86 (3). This was in effect a mortgage and redeemable as such, the remedy of the mortgagee being under the trust for sale, instead of by foreclosure, though if the mortgagor commenced an action for redemption and failed to redeem he was foreclosed. See also (1984) 100 LQR 86, 87–90 (Anderson).

A Welsh mortgage was an assurance by which property was conveyed to the creditor without any condition for payment (as distinguished from a personal covenant), but upon the terms that the creditor was to receive the rents and profits in satisfaction of principal and interest or in lieu of interest. Since the assurance was without condition there could be no forfeiture; consequently there was no equity of redemption, which could be the subject of foreclosure. There was, however, a continuing right of redemption and the mortgagor could redeem at any time. See further Wylie *Irish Land Law* (2nd edn).

On both the above, see further the earlier editions of this work.

15 The term created did not disturb the limitations of the settlement.

The development of the equity of redemption[1]

1.9 Whatever form the mortgage took, at common law, upon non-payment by the appointed time the estate of the mortgagee became absolute and irredeemable unless the mortgage provided otherwise[2]. In the courts of equity, on the other hand, the mortgagee's estate was subject to a right called the equity of redemption, which arose from the court's consideration that the real object of the transaction was the creation of a security for the debt[3]. This entitled the mortgagor to redeem or recover the property even though he had failed to repay by the appointed time[4]. If the mortgagee retained possession, equity held him liable to account for the full rent to the mortgagor[5].

At first, the court would only intervene in cases of special hardship, but by the seventeenth century relief was given as a matter of course[6]. At the same time the mortgagee in possession became accountable to the mortgagor for rent[7]. The mortgagee was compensated for the special favour shown to the mortgagor by the right of foreclosure[8]: an order of the court, made on the mortgagee's application, declared that the equitable right to redeem was at an end, leaving the mortgagee with an unencumbered fee simple. If, however, the property was much more valuable than the debt, the court would order a sale of the property with the balance of the debt to be discharged from the proceeds, in order to prevent the remedy being used oppressively. Equitable rights became recognised in common law courts by the Judicature Act 1873.

Before 1926, when, by the usual method of freehold mortgage, the fee simple was vested in the mortgagee, the phrase 'equity of redemption' was used to denote the equitable interest of the mortgagor[9]: in equity the mortgagor was the owner of the land subject to the mortgage[10]. By contrast, under the present system, the legal estate in fee simple remains in the mortgagor and the phrase denotes the whole interest of the mortgagor in the land[11].

The equity of redemption arises as soon as the mortgage is made[12] and is an interest in the land which the mortgagor can transfer, lease or mortgage, just like any other interest. The equity of redemption may be disposed of *inter vivos* or by will and passes on intestacy[13]. Any attempted restriction on the equity of redemption beyond certain narrow limits is void[14]. The equity of redemption may be determined by release[15], lapse of time[16], sale[17] and foreclosure[18].

1 See Chapter 28.
2 See HEL vol II, pp 336, 579. And the mortgagor was still liable for the debt: see *Kreglinger v New Patagonia Meat and Cold Storage Co Ltd* [1914] AC 25 at 35, HL, per Lord Haldane.
3 *Sparrow v Hardcastle* (1754) 3 Atk 798 at 805, HL, per Lord Hardwicke; *Seton v Slade* (1802) 7 Ves 265, per Lord Eldon, and the court was, no doubt, anxious to increase its

jurisdiction. Moreover there had been a change in the usury laws: see HEL vol VIII, pp 100 ff.
4 See *Medforth v Blake* [2000] Ch 86 at 101, per Scott V-C.
5 *Holman v Vaux* (c 1616) Toth 133.
6 HEL vol V, pp 330–332; *Emanuel College v Evans* (1625) 1 Rep Ch 18. The Chancellor did not have everything his own way, but an ordinance to limit the right of redemption did not survive the Restoration.
7 *Holman v Vaux* (c 1616) Toth 133.
8 First mentioned in *How v Vigures* (1628) 1 Rep Ch 32.
9 See *Casborne v Scarfe* (1737) 1 Atk 603; *Thornborough v Baker* (1675) 3 Swan 628 at 630.
10 *Re Wells, Swinburne-Hanhan v Howard* [1933] Ch 29 at 52, CA and see the Australian cases of *Hyde Management Services Pty Ltd v FAI Insurances Ltd* (1983) 144 CLR 541; *Stock & Enterprises Pty Ltd v McBurney* (1977) 1 BPR 9251 at 9526.
11 The phrase equity of redemption is used in the Law of Property Act 1925: see s 115 (1) (b); but, in general, that Act uses the term right of redemption. The precise nature of the equity of redemption after 1925 is a matter of some controversy. It is said that since the mortgagor now retains a legal estate in the land the equity of redemption, as an equitable estate, must merge in the legal estate. No longer is the equity of redemption an equitable interest but merely a right attached to the mortgagor's legal estate: see *Abigail v Lapin* [1934] AC 491 at 501, PC; *British General Insurance Co Ltd v A-G* [1945] LJNCCR 113 at 122, 123. The better view is that there is no merger: *Re Wells, Swinburne-Hanham v Howard*, above.
12 *Kreglinger v New Patagonia Meat and Cold Storage Co Ltd* [1914] AC 25 at 48, HL.
13 See Chapter 28.
14 The right to redeem is an inseparable incident of the transaction of mortgage. See *Cheah v Equiticorp Finance Group Ltd* [1992] 1 AC 472 at 476, per Lord Browne-Wilkinson PC.
15 See Chapter 28.
16 See Chapter 28.
17 See Chapter 20.
18 See Chapter 21.

The equitable right to redeem

1.10 The equity of redemption should be distinguished from the equitable right to redeem, which it includes. The equitable right to redeem only arises when the contractual date of redemption has passed[1].

1 *Brown v Cole* (1845) 14 Sim 427. Also see *Twentieth Century Banking Corpn Ltd v Wilkinson* [1977] Ch 99, [1976] 3 All ER 361.

Legal charge

1.11 As stated above[1], a legal mortgage of land may be made, not only by the creation in the mortgagee of a legal estate, but by a charge expressed to be by way of legal mortgage[2]. Under such a mortgage the mortgagee has the same protection, powers and remedies (including the power of sale), as if it had been created by demise and, save that an actual legal estate is not created[3], a legal charge does not differ from any ordinary legal mortgage[4].

The charge becomes effective at law only when the chargee is entered as proprietor of the charge in the Charges Register of the chargor's title[5] and, until registration, the chargee holds only an equitable charge[6].

1 See **1.5**.
2 Law of Property Act 1925, ss 85 (1), 86 (1) (xvi).
3 The chargee has been said to take a statutory estate or interest as chargee or mortgagee simpliciter: *Lai v Beem Construction Ltd* [1984] 2 NZLR 278 at 285, per Somers J.

4 Law of Property Act s 87 (1); and see Chapter 3. For the statutory mortgage, see Chapter 3.
5 Land Registration Act 1925, s 26(1).
6 Section 106(2)(a). *E S Schwab & Co Ltd v McCarthy* (1976) 31 P & CR 196 at 201, 212; *Mortgage Corpn Ltd v Nationwide Credit Corpn Ltd* [1994] Ch 49 at 53–54.

SALES WITH RIGHT OF REPURCHASE

Mortgage or absolute conveyance

1.12 When a legal mortgage could be made in the form of an absolute conveyance of the property, it was sometimes doubtful, on the terms of the instrument, whether it was really a mortgage or an absolute conveyance. Under the present system of creating legal mortgages of land by demise, this can only happen in a very exceptional case[1], though the question may still arise on the assignment of an equitable interest or the disposition of property other than land.

As a general rule, the courts protect a purchaser in good faith[2], and will not lightly infer an intention to make a mere security if none is expressed[3]. The courts will, however, give effect to an intention to create a security, if proved[4], and will also take care that a borrower shall not suffer from the omission by fraud, mistake, or accident, of the usual requisites of a mortgage. An instrument which purports to be an absolute conveyance may, therefore, be construed as a mortgage where, according to the true intention of the parties, it was intended to be regarded as a mortgage[5]. This will be done where there is parol evidence of the non-execution, erasure or omission by mistake or fraud of an intended defeasance or proviso for redemption[6], or if a separate defeasance or agreement for a right of redemption has been made by the mortgagee or his duly authorised agent, either in writing or orally[7]; or, if it appears from recitals in, or by inference drawn from, the contents of other instruments, or from the payment of interest or other circumstances, that the conveyance was intended to be redeemable[8].

1 If the instrument purported to convey the legal fee simple and were held to be a mortgage, it would operate as a demise: Law of Property Act 1925, s 85(2). Similarly, in the case of leasehold, it would operate as a sub-demise: s 86 (2); and see *Grangeside Properties Ltd v Collingwoods Securities Ltd* [1964] 1 All ER 143, CA. See as to whether the transaction was an absolute assignment or an assignment by way of charge: *Chase Manhattan Asia Ltd v Official Receiver etc of First Bangkok City Finance Ltd* [1990] 1 WLR 1181, PC.
2 *Premier Group Ltd v Lidgard* [1970] NZLR 280.
3 *Cotterell v Purchase* (1734) Cas temp Talb 61.
4 *Mayfair London Bank Ltd v Workman* (1972) 225 Estates Gazette 989 (where the security was not proved). The burden of proof is on the party claiming that the apparent absolute conveyance is merely a security.
5 *Douglas v Culverwell* (1862) 4 De GF & J 20; *Re Duke of Marlborough, Davis v Whitehead* [1894] 2 Ch 133; *Grangeside Properties Ltd v Collingwoods Securities Ltd*, above; *Re Kent and Sussex Sawmills Ltd* [1947] Ch 177, [1946] 2 All ER 638; *Scottish and Newcastle Breweries Ltd v Liquidator of Rathbourne Hotel Co Ltd* 1970 SLT 313, ASCL 470 at 471; *Re Universal Management Ltd* [1983] NZLR 462, NZCA. On mortgages of chattels, see Chapter 5.
6 See Chapter 3. *Maxwell v Lady Montacute* (1719) Prec Ch 526; *England v Codrington* (1758) 1 Eden 169; *A-G v Crofts* (1788) 4 Bro Parl Cas 136; *Card v Jaffray* (1805) 2 Sch & Lef 374. A right of redemption may be implied in a purported assignment: *Coakley v Argent Credit Corpn plc* (4 June 1998, unreported).

The Statute of Frauds would not be allowed to be pleaded to cover what would amount to a fraud, unless perhaps the parties deliberately abstained from putting their meaning into writing: *Re Duke of Marlborough, Davis v Whitehead*, above, distinguishing and commenting on some earlier decisions.

7 *Clench v Witherly* (1678) Cas temp Finch 376; *Manlove v Bale and Bruton* (1688) 2 Vern 84; *Francklyn v Fern* (1740) Barn Ch 30; *Whitfield v Parfitt* (1851) 4 De G & Sm 240; *Lincoln v Wright* (1859) 4 De G & J 16.

8 *Maxwell v Lady Mountacute*, above; *Cripps v Jee* (1793) 4 Bro CC 472; *Sevier v Greenway* (1815) 19 Ves 413; *Allenby v Dalton* (1827) 5 LJOSKB 312; *Barton v Bank of New South Wales* (1890) 15 App Cas 379 (considered in *United Dominions Trust Ltd v Beech* [1972] 1 Lloyd's Rep 546; *Beattie v Jenkinson* [1971] 3 All ER 495); but see *Tull v Owen* (1840) 4 Y & C Ex 192.

Fraudulent or secret conveyance

1.13 If an absolute conveyance is made with a secret defeasance in order, by concealing the defeasance, to commit a fraud, the defeasance will be void as against a purchaser who had no notice of the defeasance[1]. If a mortgage has been fraudulently made to appear as an absolute conveyance it will not be corrected at the instance of those concerned in the fraud[2].

1 *Webber v Farmer* (1718) 4 Bro Parl Cas 170.

2 *Baldwin v Cawthorne* (1812) 19 Ves 166. A mortgage may be created by a deed duly executed, though it is retained by the debtor without communication with the creditor, unless it is shown that there was fraud in the execution, or that it was delivered as an escrow, and was intended to operate conditionally: *Exton v Scott* (1833) 6 Sim 31. For escrows, see Chapter 3.

Mortgage or conveyance with option of repurchase

1.14 Although, in certain cases, apparently absolute conveyances may be construed as mortgages, an absolute conveyance with an agreement for repurchase or an agreement that the conveyance shall be void upon payment of a certain fixed sum at a fixed time will create a mere right of repurchase to be exercised according to the strict terms of the power[1]. Such agreements will not, therefore, create such a right of redemption as is incidental to a mortgage[2] unless it is proved that the transaction was in the nature of a mortgage security and that the grantor and grantee were intended to have mutual and reciprocal rights to insist upon reconveyance of the estate and repayment of the consideration[3].

1 See *Thornborough v Baker* (1675) 3 Swan 628 at 631; *Barrell v Sabine* (1684) 1 Vern 268; *Joy v Birch* (1836) 4 Cl & Fin 57; *Pegg v Wisden* (1852) 16 Beav 239. Accordingly, where a limited time is fixed for repayment (*Williams v Owen* (1840) 5 My & Cr 303; *Acton v Acton* (1704) Prec Ch 237; but see *Waters v Mynn* (1850) 14 Jur 341); or where the agreement for repurchase is to be void on failure in punctual payment of the rent at which the land has been demised to the vendor (*Davis v Thomas* (1831) Russ & M 506; *St John v Wareham* (1635) cited in 3 Swan at 631) repurchase was refused on default in compliance with the condition; and see *Maclaine v Gatty* [1921] 1 AC 376, HL. In the case of a mortgage, the penalty or forfeiture is introduced for the purpose of security only and, in case of default in payment at the appointed time, the mortgagee is compensated by receiving interest, but in the case of a defeasible purchase, forfeiture is out of the question, the estate being absolutely vested in the grantee; and the power of repurchase, not arising from the nature of the contract, but being a special privilege given to one of the parties without any corresponding right in the other, must be strictly exercised. As to the strict observance of option terms, see also *Hare v Nicoll* [1966] 2 QB 130, [1966] 1 All ER 285, CA. By s 205 (1) (xvi) of the Law of Property Act 1925, 'right of redemption' includes an option to repurchase only if the option in effect creates a right of redemption.

2 *St John v Wareham*, above; *Barrell v Sabine*, above; *Ensworth v Griffiths* (1706) 5 Bro Parl Cas 184; *Perry v Meddowcroft* (1841) 4 Beav 197; *Tapply v Sheather* (1862) 7 LT 298; *Manchester, Sheffield and Lincolnshire Rly Co v North Central Wagon Co* (1888) 13 App Cas 554; *Beckett v Tower Assets Co* [1891] 1 QB 1 at 25.

3 *Goodman v Grierson* (1813) 2 Ball & B 274; *Alderson v White* (1857) 2 De G & J 97; *Shaw v Jeffery* (1860) 13 Moo PCC 432. Also see *Gurfunkel v Bentley Pty Ltd* (1966) 116 CLR 98; *Kreick v Wansbrough* (1973) 35 DLR (3d) 275.

Defeasible purchase of equity of redemption

1.15 The need for strict compliance with the conditions has been upheld even in transactions relating to securities. For example, where upon a release by the mortgagor to the mortgagee of the equity of redemption it had been agreed that the mortgagee should reconvey upon repayment to him within a fixed time of the original debt, with the money paid for the release and interest, and the outlay for repairs or improvements[1], it was held that no relief would be given in the case of default and the mortgagee was entitled to the whole of the original debt. Similarly, in circumstances where a creditor agreed to forgo part of his debt upon payment of the residue on a fixed day or to refrain from entering up judgment if an insurance was kept up, it was held that the creditor could take advantage of failure in the strict performance of the conditions[2].

1 *Ensworth v Griffiths*, above; *Gossip v Wright* (1863) 32 LJ Ch 648; *Sterne v Beck* (1863) 1 De G J & Sm 595; *Wallingford v Mutual Society* (1880) 5 App Cas 685; *Protector Endowment and Annuity Loan v Grice* (1880) 5 QBD 592.

2 *Ford v Earl of Chesterfield* (1854) 19 Beav 428; *Parry v Great Ship Co* (1863) 4 B & S 556; and see *Thompson v Hudson* (1869) LR 4 HL 1; *Tasburgh v Echlin* (1733) 3 Bro Parl Cas 265; *Ogden v Battams* (1855) 1 Jur NS 791; *King v Bromley* (1709) 2 Eq Cas Abr 595. Also see *Gilbert J McAaul (Aust) Pty Ltd v Pitt Club Ltd* (1957) 57 SRNSW 322; *Hall v Busst* (1960) 104 CLR 206; *Chase Manhattan Asia Ltd v Official Receiver of First Bangkok City Finance Ltd* [1990] 1 WLR 1181, PC.

Test for meaning of instrument

1.16 In every case the question is what, upon a fair construction, is the meaning of the instrument. For this purpose, the true nature, and not the form of the transaction, is to be regarded[1].

The inadequacy of the consideration to the value of the property, the taking by the grantee of immediate possession under the conveyance and the payment by him or by the grantor of the costs of the transaction, or of insurances and other outgoings of the property, will be taken into consideration, but will not be conclusive upon the question whether a doubtful instrument was intended to take effect by way of mortgage or by way of sale[2]. Circumstances of pressure upon the grantor — where he is insolvent or represented by the same solicitor as the grantee — will materially influence the court in construing an apparently absolute or conditional sale as a mortgage where, in the absence of such circumstances, the mere insufficiency of price would be given little weight. Weight will also be given to the circumstance that, in the peculiar position of the grantor, a mortgage might be beneficial to him when a sale would not[3].

1 *Re Watson, ex p Official Receiver in Bankruptcy* (1890) 25 QBD 27, CA; *Madell v Thomas* [1891] 1 QB 230, CA; *Salt v Marquess of Northampton* [1892] AC 1, HL; *Bradley v Carritt* [1903] AC 253, HL; *Lewis v Frank Love Ltd* [1961] 1 All ER 446; *Snook v London & West Riding Investments Ltd* [1967] 2 QB 786; *Alec Lobb (Garages) Ltd v Total Oil Great Britain Ltd* [1983] 1 All ER 944, [1983] 1 WLR 87; on appeal [1985] 1 All ER 303, [1985] 1 WLR 173, CA; *Lloyds v Scottish Finance Ltd v Cyril Lord Carpets Sales Ltd* [1992] BCLC 609, HL; *Welsh Development Agency v Export Finance Co Ltd* [1992] BCLC 148, [1992] BCC 270,

CA; *Re Row Dal Construction Pty Ltd* [1966] VR 249; *Automobile Association (Canterbury) Inc v Australasian Secured Deposits Ltd* [1973] 1 NZLR 417, NZCA; *Re Universal Management Ltd* [1983] NZLR 462, NZCA; *Arnal v Arnal* (1969) 6 DLR (3d) 245; *Hayes Securities Ltd v Banbury* (1991) ANZ Conv R 318, NZCA.

2 *Thornborough v Baker*, above at 632; *Davis v Thomas*, above; *Williams v Owen*, above; *Langton v Horton* (1842) 5 Beav 9; *Alderson v White*, above, *Douglas v Culverwell* (1862) 4 De GF & J 20.

3 *Fee v Cobine* (1847) 11 I Eq R 406, but it may be shown that the grantor entered into the contract with full knowledge of the consequences; *Bonham v Newcomb* (1683) 1 Vern 214, 231; *Langton v Horton*, above. As to mortgages by way of annuity deed and conditions for cesser of trust limitations, which were formerly, but are no longer, common securities, see **1.8**, n 14.

EQUITABLE MORTGAGES

Generally

1.17 An equitable mortgage is a contract that operates as a security and is enforceable under the equitable jurisdiction of the court. The court carries it into effect either by immediately giving the creditor the appropriate remedies or by compelling the debtor to execute a security in accordance with the contract[1].

Like any transaction by way of mortgage:

(a) a proprietary interest in the debtor's property is conferred or undertaken in a binding manner to be conferred by the debtor on the creditor;
(b) the creditor can procure the discharge of the debtor's liability to him by the realisation or appropriation of the proprietary interest; and
(c) the proprietary interest conferred upon the creditor is redeemable by the debtor, or the obligation to create it is defeasible, in the event of the debtor discharging his liability.

An equitable mortgage is applicable to all property of which a legal mortgage can be made, even where statute provides as, for example, in the case of land[2] and ships, a particular method for passing the legal property therein.

Whether a particular transaction gives rise to an equitable mortgage must depend upon the intention of the parties ascertained from what they have done in the then existing circumstances. The intention may be expressed or it may be inferred. Whether or not the parties appreciated the consequences of their acts, they will be presumed to intend those consequences[3]. If the debtor undertakes to segregate a particular fund or asset and to pay the debt out of that fund or asset, the inference may be drawn, in the absence of any contrary indication, that the parties' intention is that the creditor should have such a proprietary interest in the segregated fund or asset as will enable him to realise out of it the amount owed to him by the debtor. Where, however, the subject matter is precarious, this may be taken to be an indication that a security was not intended[4].

An equitable mortgage may be created by general words[5] (unlike a legal mortgage) and may even be created with regard to future acquired property[6].

An equitable mortgage of personalty, not being of an equitable interest[7] in personalty[8], is not required to be in writing[9]. It is, however, essential that an equitable mortgage be made by deed if the mortgagee is to have the power of sale and other powers conferred on a mortgagee by statute[10], or in writing if the mortgagee wishes to record an express agreement as to his remedies in the event of default.

1 *Ashton v Corrigan* (1871) LR 13 Eq 76; *Hermann v Hodges* (1873) LR 16 Eq 18.
2 As to which, see **1.18**.
3 *Swiss Bank Corpn v Lloyds Bank Ltd* [1982] AC 584 at 595–596, [1980] 2 All ER 419 at 426, per Buckley LJ; *Thames Guaranty Ltd v Campbell* [1985] QB 210 at 218, [1984] 1 All ER 144 at 149; affd [1985] QB 210, [1984] 2 All ER 585, CA.
4 *Swiss Bank Corpn v Lloyds Bank Ltd* [1982] AC 584 at 596–597, per Buckley LJ, [1980] 2 All ER 419 at 427, CA; affd [1981] 2 All ER 449, HL.
5 *William Brant's Sons & Co v Dunlop Rubber Co Ltd* [1905] AC 454 at 462, HL. The ordinary debenture of a limited company is a common example of this: *Elders Pastoral Ltd v Bank of New Zealand (No 2)* [1990] 1 WLR 1478, PC. See, however, in the case of land **1.18**.
6 A mortgage of all the mortgagor's 'real and personal property whatsoever and wheresoever' is not void for uncertainty, nor as being against public policy, if it is possible at the time when the charge is sought to be enforced to point out the property comprised in it: *Re Clarke, Coombe v Carter* (1887) 36 Ch D 348, CA; *Re Turcan* (1888) 40 Ch D 5, CA; *Tailby v Official Receiver* (1888) 13 App Cas 523, HL; *Re Kelcey, Tyson v Kelcey* [1899] 2 Ch 530 at 532–534; and see *Syrett v Egerton* [1957] 3 All ER 331 at 332, 334; cf *Barker v Barker* [1952] P 184 [1952] 1 All ER 1128, CA.

It is generally considered that a floating charge of all the stock in trade etc of an individual (as opposed to a company) is not possible and in any event would fall foul of the specificity required by the Bills of Sale Acts (see Chapter 5): see [1971] JBL 18 (Fitzpatrick); but compare agricultural floating charges (see Chapter 9). The Cork Report (Report of the Review Committee in Insolvency Law and Practice) 1982, Cmnd 8558, recommended that individuals should be able to create floating charges: see para 1569-69. A floating charge by an individual has been permitted in some jurisdictions, eg New Zealand: see *Philpott v NZI Bank Ltd* (1993) ANZ Conv R 242, referring to *Driver v Broad* [1893] 1 QB 744, CA.

For a mortgage of present and future property see *Corozo Pty Ltd v Total Australia Ltd* [1988] 2 QdR 366. For the difficulties of creating an enforceable mortgage of future property, see *Bridge Wholesale Acceptance Corpn (Australia) Pty Ltd v Fairstar Pty Ltd* [1991] ACL Rep 295, NSW 4; *ALH Australia Ltd v McGlinn* (1996) 7 BPR 15,179.
7 Equitable interest is defined in Law of Property Act 1925, s 205(1)(x) (amended by the Trusts of Land and Appointment of Trustees Act 1996, s 25(2), Sch 4).
8 Which is required to be in writing, see Law of Property Act 1925, s 53 (1) (c).
9 *Tibbits v George* (1836) 5 Ad & El 107; *Parish v Poole* (1884) 53 LT 35 at 38; *Brown, Shipley & Co v Kough* (1885) 29 Ch D 848 at 854, CA.
10 Ie under the Law of Property Act 1925, s 101; see Chapter 20.

Equitable mortgages of land

1.18 In the case of an agreement to create a mortgage of any interest in land after 27 September 1989, the provisions of s 2 of the Law of Property (Miscellaneous Provisions) Act 1989 must be satisfied.[1] The agreement must be made in writing and must incorporate all the terms which the parties have expressly agreed in one document or, where contracts are exchanged, in each[2]. The document incorporating the terms or, where contracts are exchanged, one of the documents incorporating them must be signed by or on behalf of each party to the contract[3].

Prior to 27 September 1989, a good security in equity could be created by the deposit of title deeds of freehold or leasehold property[4]. The deposit could be of the deeds alone or might be accompanied by a memorandum of the terms of the deposit or by an agreement to give a mortgage[5]. An equitable mortgage of land prior to 27 September 1989, not being by way of deposit of title deeds, required to be evidenced in writing or supported by a sufficient act of part performance[6].

Formerly, from the debtor's point of view there was an advantage in an equitable mortgage of land over a legal mortgage, in that an equitable mortgage usually did not appear in the title to the property and, in some circumstances, there was a stamp duty saving. Since mortgage stamp duty has been abolished[7] there is no advantage in an equitable mortgage, other than its relative informality, and a distinct disadvantage in the possible loss of priority if subsequent mortgages are created[8].

1 See **3.87**.
2 Law of Property (Miscellaneous Provisions) Act 1989, s 2(1), (6) (s 2(6) amended by the Trusts of Land and Appointment of Trustees Act 1996); *Firstpost Homes Ltd v Johnson* [1995] 4 All ER 355, [1995] 1 WLR 1567.
3 Sections 2(2), 2(3).
4 Since 29 September 1989 a deposit is insufficient: *United Bank of Kuwait plc v Sahib* [1997] Ch 107, [1996] 3 All ER 215.
5 *Russel v Russel* (1783) 1 Bro CC 269; *Ex p Kensington* (1813) 2 Ves & B 79; *Lister v Turner* (1846) 5 Hare 281.
6 Law of Property Act 1925, s 40; *Mounsey v Rankin* (1885) Cab & El 496.
7 Finance Act 1971, s 64.
8 See, eg, *McCarthy & Stone Ltd v Julian S Hodge & Co Ltd* [1971] 2 All ER 973; *Barclays Bank Ltd v Taylor* [1973] Ch 63, [1972] 2 All ER 752; and (1972) 116 Sol Jo 87 (Harris).

The classes of equitable mortgage

Mortgages of equitable rights

1.19 Mortgages by equitable owners of their equitable rights usually occur in the case of mortgages of interests by beneficiaries under a trust[1].

Prior to the commencement of the Law of Property (Miscellaneous Provisions) Act 1989[2], such a mortgage had either to be made in writing (not merely evidenced in writing) signed by the mortgagor, or signed by the mortgagor's agent authorised in writing or made by will[3]. If, of an interest in land, such a mortgage must now be made in accordance with the provisions of s 2 of the 1989 Act[4].

If the mortgage is not based on valuable consideration, it is essential that it should purport to operate by way of a complete assignment of all the mortgagor's equitable interest. Although equity will give effect to a completed voluntary assignment of equitable rights[5], it will not give effect to an incomplete assignment or one resting on an executory contract only[6].

The mortgagee should give notice in writing[7] to the trustees in whom the legal ownership is vested in order to preserve his priority[8] and in order to prevent the trustees from paying the mortgagor.

1 Before 1926 a mortgage of an equity of redemption, that is, a mortgage subsequent to a legal mortgage, was an equitable mortgage. As to the transitional provisions of the Law of Property Act 1925, see previous editions of this work.
2 27 September 1989.
3 Law of Property Act 1925, s 53 (1) (c).
4 See **1.18** and Chapter 3.
5 *Kekewich v Manning* (1851) 1 De GM & G 176.
6 *Re Earl of Lucan, Hardinge v Cobden* (1890) 45 Ch D 470.
7 Law of Property Act 1925, s 137 (3).
8 *Dearle v Hall* (1823–1828) 3 Russ 1; Law of Property Act 1925, ss 137, 138, J. de Lacy [1999] Conv 311 and see Chapter 24. Mortgages of a beneficial interest under a trust of land or strict settlement are not capable of registration under the Land Charges Act 1972: Land Charges Act 1972, s 2(4)(iii)(b). For mortgages of choses in action generally, see Chapter 7.

Equitable mortgages by legal owners

1.20 Equitable mortgages of the property of legal owners are created by some instrument or act which is insufficient to confer a legal estate or title, but which, being founded on valuable consideration, shows the intention of the parties to create a present security[1], or evidences a contract to do so[2].

A binding obligation that a particular fund shall be applied in a particular manner may found no more than an injunction to restrain its application in another way, but if the obligation entered is to pay a debt due by one party to the transaction to the other from a fund belonging to or being due to the debtor, this amounts to an equitable assignment pro tanto of the fund[3]. The distinction is, therefore, between a transaction which creates merely personal contractual rights (which may nevertheless be enforceable against third parties under the *De Mattos v Gibson*[4] rule) and a transaction which creates proprietary rights.

Examples of equitable mortgage have included:

(a) mortgages created prior to 27 September 1989[5] by deposit of title deeds, whether with or without a memorandum or other instrument of charge[6];
(b) circumstances where a formal legal mortgage has been attempted, but proves ineffective for some reason, such as some defect in execution or formality[7] or lack of title of the mortgagor[8];
(c) a written agreement to create a security in consideration of a debt due or an advance made[9];
(d) a document charging property with the debt and containing a declaration by the debtor that he holds the property in trust for the creditor[10];
(e) a written undertaking given in consideration of a loan to hold title deeds to the order of the lender[11];
(f) a written authority for a creditor to sell and retain a debt out of the proceeds[12];
(g) an assignment in writing of rent[13];
(h) a deposit of share certificates to secure a debt, or as cover, whether accompanied or unaccompanied by a transfer in blank as to the name of the transferee[14];
(i) any written instrument showing the parties' intention that it should create a security, although containing no general words of charge, for example, the appointment of a receiver to receive rents and pay an annuity from those rents[15];
(j) a power of attorney to a creditor to enter up judgment in his favour[16], or to receive rents and profits and apply them in payment of interest, or to repay himself out of the surplus proceeds of the sale of property in mortgage to the debtor, or to mortgage the debtor's land for payment of the debt[17].

1 See *Williams v Burlington Investments Ltd* (1977) 121 Sol Jo 424, HL.

2 See *National Provincial and Union Bank of England v Charnley* [1924] 1 KB 431 at 440, CA; *Swiss Bank Corpn v Lloyds Bank Ltd* [1982] AC 584 at 595, CA, per Buckley LJ (citing the 9th edn of this work), [1980] 2 All ER 419 at 425; *Thames Guaranty Ltd v Campbell* [1985] QB 210, [1984] 1 All ER 144; affd [1984] 2 All ER 585, CA. For cases where the intention could not be found, see *Travis and Arnold Ltd v Burnett* [1964] EGD 318; *Georgiades v Edward Wolfe & Co Ltd* [1965] Ch 487, [1964] 3 All ER 433; *Thomas v Rose* [1968] 3 All ER 765; *Swiss Bank Corpn v Lloyds Bank Ltd*, above.

3 *Swiss Bank Corpn v Lloyds Bank Ltd* [1982] AC 584 at 596, [1980] 2 All ER 419 at 426, CA; affd [1981] 2 All ER 449, HL.

4 (1859) 4 De G & J 276, considered in *Swiss Bank Corpn v Lloyds Bank Ltd*, above. On contractual rights and trusts, see *Mac-Jordan Construction Ltd v Brookmount Erostin Ltd* [1992] BCLC 350, CA; *Kingscroft Insurance Co Ltd v H S Weavers (Underwriting) Agencies Ltd* [1993] 1 Lloyds Rep 187; *Law Debenture Trust Corpn v Urals Caspian Oil Corpn Ltd* [1993] 2 All ER 355, [1993] 1 WLR 138.

5 Since 27 September 1989 the mere deposit of title deeds by way of security can no longer create a valid equitable mortgage unless it complies with the requirements of the Law of Property (Miscellaneous) Provisons Act 1989, s 2.

6 *Russel v Russel* (1783) 1 Bro CC 269. See Chapter 3.
7 See Chapter 3.
8 See Chapter 3.
9 *Eyre v M'Dowell* (1861) 9 HL Cas 619; *Parish v Poole* (1884) 53 LT 35; *Re Hurley's Estate* [1894] 1 IR 488; *Capital Finance Co Ltd v Stokes* [1969] 1 Ch 261.
10 *London and County Banking Co v Goddard* [1897] 1 Ch 642.
11 *Re Heathstar Properties Ltd* [1966] 1 All ER 628, [1966] 1 WLR 993.
12 *Re Cook, ex p Hodgson* (1821) 1 Gl & J 12.
13 *Ex p Wills* (1790) 1 Ves 162; cf *Re Whitting, ex p Hall* (1879) 10 Ch D 615, CA.
14 *Stubbs v Slater* [1910] 1 Ch 632, CA; *London and Midland Bank v Mitchell* [1899] 2 Ch 161.
15 *Cradock v Scottish Provident Institution* (1894) 70 LT 718.
16 *Cook v Fowler* (1874) LR 7 HL 27 at 35. See now Administration of Justice Act 1956, s 16.
17 *Spooner v Sandilands* (1842) I Y & C Ch Cas 390; *Abbott v Stratten* (1846) 3 Jo & Lat 603; *Re Cook, ex p Hodgson*, above; *Re Parkinson's Estate* (1865) 13 LT 26.

Specific performance of agreements for mortgages

1.21 Specific performance will not be ordered in respect of a contract to make or take a loan of money, whether or not the loan is to be on security[1], so long as the contract remains executory[2]. The parties will be left to their remedies in damages[3].

Specific performance of an enforceable contract to give security will be ordered where the loan has actually been made or the debt or other obligation incurred, because a mere claim to damages or repayment is obviously less valuable than a security in the event of the debtor's insolvency[4].

1 See Chapter 2. *Western Wagon and Property Co v West* [1892] 1 Ch 271.
2 *Hunter v Lord Langford* (1828) 2 Mol 272; *Rogers v Challis* (1859) 27 Beav 175; *Sichel v Mosenthal* (1862) 30 Beav 371; *Larios v Bonamy Y Gurety* (1873) LR 5 PC 346; *South African Territories v Wallington* [1898] AC 309, HL. A contract to take debentures in a limited company is an exception to this rule; see Companies Act 1985, s 195.
3 *Astor Properties Ltd v Tunbridge Wells Equitable Friendly Society* [1936] 1 All ER 531; *Manchester and Oldham Bank v Cook* (1883) 49 LT 674; *Trans Trust SPRL v Danubian Trading Co Ltd* [1952] 2 QB 297, [1952] 1 All ER 970, CA; *Cottrill v Steyning and Littlehampton Building Society* [1966] 2 All ER 295; *Wadsworth v Lydall* [1981] 2 All ER 401, [1981] 1 WLR 598, CA; *Popular Homes Ltd v Circuit Developments Ltd* [1979] 2 NZLR 642. It appears to have been more readily accepted in Australia that damages may not be an adequate remedy for breach of an agreement to grant a mortgage: *Wright v Haberdan Pty Ltd* [1984] 2 NSWLR 280; *Aziz v GIFC Ltd* (1988) ANZ Conv R 480; *Corpers (No 664) Pty Ltd v NZI Securities Australia Ltd* (1989) NSW ConvR 55-475; *Australia and New Zealand Banking Group Ltd v Widin* (1990) 26 FCR 21; *Bridge Wholesale Acceptance Corpn (Australia) Pty Ltd v Fairstar Pty Ltd* [1991] ACL Rep 295 NSW 4, and see *Pacific Industrial Corpn SA v Bank of New Zealand* [1991] 1 NZLR 368.
4 *Swiss Bank Corpn v Lloyds Bank Ltd* [1982] AC 584 at 595, [1980] 2 All ER 419 at 426, CA; affd [1982] AC 584, [1981] 2 All ER 449, HL; *Thames Guaranty Ltd v Campbell* [1985] QB 210, [1984] 1 All ER 144; affd [1985] QB 210, [1984] 2 All ER 585, CA. See *Parish v Poole*, above; *Loan Investment Corpn of Australasia v Bonner* [1970] NZLR 724, PC considering, amongst other cases, *Starkey v Barton* [1909] 1 Ch 284 and contracts for sale of land and loan. The distinction is between a genuine sale with loan attached and what is in substance a long-term secured loan.

Equitable charges

1.22 A transaction which creates proprietary rights will either be an equitable mortgage or an equitable charge. Under an equitable mortgage the intention is that the creditor shall have a transfer of the property, whereas under an equitable charge a transfer is not intended, but simply a present right to have the property appropriated to meet the debt in the event of default[1].

An equitable charge is created when real or personal property is expressly or constructively made liable, or specially appropriated, to the discharge of a debt or some other obligation without there being any change in ownership either at law or in equity[2]. It creates an equitable interest and confers on the chargee a right of realisation by judicial process[3].

1 For a comparison between an equitable charge and an equitable mortgage see *United Travel Agencies Pty Ltd v Cain* (1990) 20 NSWLR 566. On equitable charges see Chapter 2.
2 *Carreras Rothmans Ltd v Freeman Matthews Treasure Ltd* [1985] Ch 207 at 227; *Re Cosslett (Contractors) Ltd* [1998] Ch 495 at 508.
3 *Swiss Bank Corpn v Lloyds Bank Ltd* [1982] AC 584 at 595, [1980] 2 All ER 419 at 425, CA, per Buckley LJ, citing the 9th edn of this work.

COLLATERAL SECURITY

Collateral security

1.23 Collateral or additional security may be given by the principal mortgagor himself or by a third party. The most common example of the first type of collateral security is a mortgage by the principal mortgagor of a policy on his life, which is additional to and is to secure the same debt as that secured by the principal mortgage[1]. Examples of the second type of collateral security are a guarantee by a third party for the repayment of the principal mortgage debt[2] and a mortgage of land or other property by a third party to secure either a principal debt or his liability under a guarantee[3].

Collateral or additional security has special relevance in relation to building societies[4].

The advantage of taking additional real security from a third party to secure the principal debt is that in the event of the principal mortgagor's bankruptcy the collateral security need not go in reduction of proof[5].

1 See Chapter 7.
2 For form, see the Appendix.
3 See eg *Re Wallis & Simmonds (Builders) Ltd* [1974] 1 All ER 561. For forms see 28 *Forms and Precedents* (5th edn, 1999 reissue) Mortgages. Where stamp duty is relevant, there may be questions as to which of two or more documents is the primary security and which collateral: see eg *Stardawn Investments Pty Ltd v Comptroller of Stamps (Vic)* (1983) 15 ATR 180.
4 See Chapter 12.
5 See Chapter 23. For the Consumer Credit Act 1974, see Chapter 10. For an example of a collateral security given in breach of duty by one joint venturer, see *Brian Pty Ltd v United Dominions Corpn Ltd* [1983] 1 NSWLR 490, CA.

FOREIGN SECURITIES[1]

Mortgage of land situate abroad

1.24 In the case of such land the title to the land is generally governed by the *lex situs*[2] and to perfect his title a mortgagee must comply with the requirements, as to registration, etc, of the local law[3].

Even where the requirements of the local law have not been satisfied an English court may be able to enforce such a mortgage as if it were an effective equitable charge where the mortgagor and mortgagee are within the jurisdiction[4]; but it will not interfere with rights which have in the meantime been acquired under the foreign law[5].

1 It is recommended that the reader refers to specialist works on private international law to gain a full picture of the position at common law and under statutes and conventions.
2 See Dicey and Morris *Conflict of Laws* (13th edn) p 935; *Re Hoyles* [1911] 1 Ch 179, CA.
3 See *Dicey and Morris* p 935; Cheshire and North *Private International Law* (13th edn) p 925.
4 *Mercantile Investment and General Trust Co v River Plate Trust and Agency Co* [1892] 2 Ch 303; *Re Anchor Line (Henderson Bros) Ltd (No 2)* [1937] Ch 483, [1937] 2 All ER 823 (see now Companies Act 1985, ss 462 ff); *Richard West & Partners (Inverness) Ltd v Dick* [1969] 2 Ch 424, [1969] 1 All ER 289, 943, CA.
5 *Re Maudslay, Sons and Field, Maudslay v Maudslay, Sons and Field* [1900] 1 Ch 602.

Locality of debts[1]

1.25 A debt, like any other thing in action, has no tangible existence, and strictly has no locality, but for legal purposes it is deemed to possess an attribute of locality, arising from and according to its nature and in this respect there is a distinction between a debt by simple contract and a debt by specialty.

The locality of a simple contract debt is the place where the debtor resides, since it is there that the assets to meet it are presumably situate and it is there that he must be sued if the creditor requires to recover the debt at law. Hence when the creditor has died, inheritance tax will be leviable on simple contract debts owing to him according to the residence of the debtor at the time of his death.

A debt secured by an instrument under seal has been regarded as having a corporeal existence by which its locality may be reduced to a certainty — its place is where the instrument happens to be. Hence the incidence of inheritance tax has been determined by the place of the specialty at the creditor's death[2].

The rule that the locality of a simple contract debt is the residence of the debtor is in ordinary cases only an application of the wider principle that debt or choses in action generally are situate in the country where they are properly recoverable or can be enforced'[3]. For if, although the debtor is abroad at the time of the creditor's death, proceedings can be taken here which will directly result in an order for, and the enforcement of, payment of the debt, then the debt may, at any rate for some purposes, be treated as situate here[4].

1 Dicey and Morris *Conflict of Laws* (13th edn) pp 925 ff; Cheshire and North *Private International Law* (13th edn) p 955.
2 *A-G v Bouwens* (1838) 4 M & W 171 at 191; *Stamps Comr v Hope* [1891] AC 476 at 481, PC; *Re Maudslay, Sons and Field*, above; *New York Life Insurance Co v Public Trustee* [1924] 2 Ch 101, CA; *Re Helbert Wagg & Co Ltd* [1956] Ch 323, [1956] 1 All ER 129; but if the debtor resides in more than one country (eg a company with a principal and a branch office in different countries), the debt is situated in the country where the debt is payable: *F & K Jabbour v Custodian of Israeli Property* [1954] 1 All ER 145 at 152; *Re Russo-Asiatic Bank* [1934] Ch 720.
3 Dicey and Morris *Conflict of Laws* (13th edn); and see *New York Life Insurance Co v Public Trustee*, above, at 109, 119; *National Bank of Greece SA v Westminster Bank Executor and Trustee Co (Channel Islands) Ltd* [1971] AC 945, [1971] 1 All ER 233, HL.
4 For example, for the former probate duty: *A-G v Sudeley* [1896] 1 QB 354 at 360.

Mortgage debts

1.26 The mortgagee's interest under a mortgage consists of two elements:

(a) his contractual rights to sue for the debt; and
(b) his proprietary rights in the security.

English law has emphasised the latter aspect and classified the mortgagee's interest as immovable[1].

A mortgage debt is usually a specialty debt and, in accordance with the rule as to such debts, it is situate where the mortgage deed happens to be. Hence, for the purposes of inheritance tax, it is situate where the mortgage deed is at the death of the mortgagee. In the case of registered land this rule is, however, subject to variation and, if the mortgage is registered, and the mortgage deed retained in the registry, the mortgage debt will be regarded as situate at the registry[2].

1 *Re Hoyles*, above. Cf Australasian jurisprudence which, at least in the context of death duties, classifies the mortgagee's interest as a movable: see generally *Haque v Haque (No 2)* (1965) 114 CLR 98.
2 *Toronto General Trusts Corpn v R* [1919] AC 679, PC.

Shares

1.27 Similarly shares are situate where they can be effectively dealt with. If, therefore, they can only pass by registered transfer, they are situate where the registration office is[1].

1 See Dicey and Morris *Conflict of Laws* (13th edn) pp 932-933; Cheshire and North *Private International Law* (13th edn) p 970; *Brassard v Smith* [1925] AC 371; *R v Williams* [1942] AC 541, [1942] 2 All ER 95, PC; *Standard Chartered Bank Ltd v IRC* [1978] 3 All ER 644, [1978] 1 WLR 1160; and see *Re Kettle's Gift* [1968] 3 All ER 88, [1968] 1 WLR 1459.

Securities transferable by delivery

1.28 Where, however, debts are represented by bills of exchange or other marketable securities which are in fact in England and are saleable and transferable there by delivery only with or without endorsement, without its being necessary to do any act out of England in order to render the transfer valid, not only the bills themselves, but also the debts which they represent, are held to be situate in England, and this is so although the debts are owing by foreigners out of England[1]. Similarly, certificates of shares in a foreign company, on which a form of transfer and power of attorney has been endorsed and executed in blank, are treated as situate here if they are marketable in this country and pass by delivery[2].

1 Dicey and Morris *Conflict of Laws* (13th edn) pp 930-931; *A-G v Bouwens*, above: *A-G v Glendining* (1904) 92 LT 87; *Winans v R* [1908] 1 KB 1022; *Winans v A-G* [1910] AC 27, HL.
2 *Stern v R* [1896] 1 QB 211.

Judgment debts

1.29 Judgment debts are assets, for the purposes of jurisdiction, where they are recorded[1].

1 *A-G v Bouwens*, above, at 191, but see Dicey and Morris *Conflict of Laws* (13th edn), p 930.

Proper law of mortgage debt[1]

1.30 The proper law will be that chosen by the parties, expressly or by inference. Where an express choice is made, it must have some bona fide connection with the contract. An inference will be drawn from, amongst other matters, the form and terminology of the document, the nature and location of the subject matter and the residence of the parties[2].

The proper law of the deed is material to, amongst other things, the capacity of the parties, its validity, questions of priority[3] and the deductibility of tax from payments and interest made under the deed.

1 Dicey and Morris *Conflict of Laws* (13th edn), p 548 ff; Cheshire and North, *Private International Law* (13th edn), p 198 ff. See *Cripps Warburg Ltd v Cologne Investment Co Ltd* [1980] IR 321, where it was held that English law was the proper law of the loan agreement (see also *Bonython v Commonwealth of Australia* [1951] AC 201, PC; *The Assunzione* [1954] P 150, [1954] 1 All ER 278, CA) and Irish law the proper law of the mortgage, as the sale of Irish immovables was involved (see also *Grey v Manitoba and North Western Rly Co of Canada* [1897] AC 254, PC).
2 *Re Helbert Wagg & Co Ltd*, above; *Keiner v Keiner* [1952] 1 All ER 643.
3 For a case concerning priorities, to which the *lex fori* applies, see *Todd Shipyards Corpn v Altema Compania Maritima SA, The Ioannis Daskalelis* (1972) 32 DLR (3d) 571. See *Dicey and Morris* (10th edn) pp 1193, 1203; *Cheshire and North* (10th edn) p 704.

MORTGAGES AND TAXATION

1.31 See Chapter 37.

CONSUMER CREDIT SECURITIES

1.32 See in particular Chapter 10 and generally throughout the book, as appropriate.

MORTGAGES AND SOCIAL SECURITY BENEFITS

1.33 Where:

(a) mortgage interest[1] is payable to a qualifying lender[2] by a person ('the borrower') who is entitled, or whose partner[3], former partner or qualifying associate[4] is entitled, to income support or an income based jobseeker's allowance; and
(b) a sum in respect of that mortgage is or was brought into account in determining the applicable amount for the purposes of income support or an income-based jobseeker's allowance in the case of a borrower or the partner, former partner or qualifying associate[5], regulations may make provision:
    (i) requiring that, in prescribed circumstances, a prescribed part of any relevant benefits[6] to which the relevant beneficiary is entitled must be paid by the Secretary of State directly to the qualifying lender and applied

by that lender towards the discharge of the liability in respect of the mortgage interest;

(ii) for the expenses of the Secretary of State in administering the making of payments under the regulations to be defrayed, in whole or in part, at the expense of qualifying lenders, whether by requiring them to pay prescribed fees or by deducting and retaining a prescribed part of the payments that would otherwise be made to them under the regulations or by such other method as may be prescribed;

(iii) for requiring a qualifying lender, in a case where by virtue of head (ii) above the amount of the payment to him under the regulations is less than it would otherwise have been, to credit against the liability in respect of the mortgage interest (in addition to the payment actually made) an amount equal to the difference between the payment that would have been so made, apart from head (ii) above, and the payment actually made and, in any such case, for treating the amount so credited as properly paid on account of any benefit due to the relevant beneficiary;

(iv) for enabling a body which, or person who, would otherwise be a qualifying lender to elect not to be regarded as such for these purposes, other than the purposes of this head;

(v) for the recovery from any body or person of any sums paid to that body or person by way of payment under the regulations that ought not to have been so paid or of any fees or other sums due from that body or person by virtue of head (ii) above;

(vi) for cases where the same person is the borrower in relation to mortgage interest payable in respect of two or more different loans; and

(vii) for any person of a prescribed class or description who would otherwise be regarded for these purposes as the borrower in relation to any mortgage interest not to be so regarded, except for the purposes of this head;

but the Secretary of State must not make any regulations under head (ii) above unless he has consulted with such organisations representing qualifying lenders likely to be affected by the regulations as he considers appropriate[7].

For these purposes, regulations may make provision as to circumstances in which residential land is or is not to be treated as intended for occupation by the borrower as his home, or as to circumstances in which persons are to be treated as being or not being members of the same household[8].

The regulations governing the payment of income support for mortgage interest are the Income Support (General) Regulations 1987, SI 1987/1967 as amended. Essentially, income support equal to half mortgage interest is payable for the first 16 weeks of a claim and thereafter income support equal to the whole of the mortgage interest is payable[9].

1 For these purposes, mortgage interest means interest on a loan which is secured by a mortgage of or charge over land and which has been taken out to defray money applied for any of the following purposes: (a) acquiring any residential land which was intended, at the date of acquisition, for occupation by the borrower as his home; (b) carrying out repairs or improvements to any residential land which was intended, at the time of taking out the loan, for occupation by the borrower as his home; (c) paying off another loan; (d) or any prescribed purpose not falling within heads (a) to (c), but interest must be regarded as mortgage interest by virtue of head (d) only to the extent that interest on that other loan would have been regarded as mortgage interest for these purposes had the loan not

been paid off: Social Security Administration Act 1992, s 15A(4), added by the Social Security (Mortgage Interest Payments) Act 1992, s 1(2), Sch, para 1. 'Residential land' means any land which consists of or included a dwelling: Social Security Administration Act 1992, s 15A(4).

2 See Social Security Adminisration Act 1992, s 15A(3). The authorised institutions include: any authorised institution within the meaning of the Banking Act 1987 to which s 67 applies and any Building Society incorporated under the Building Societies Act 1986.

3 See Social Security Administration Act 1992, s 15A(4) for definition.

4 Section 15A(4).

5 Section 15A(1), amended by the Jobseekers Act 1995 Sch 2, para 40.

6 Section 15A(4), amended by the Jobseekers Act 1995: benefits as defined in the Social Security Contributions and Benefits Act 1992, s 122 (as amended); jobseeker's allowance and income support.

7 Section 15A(2) as added.

8 Section 15A(5) as added. As to the exercise of the payments conferred by s 15A (as added and amended) see the Social Security (Claims and Payments) Regulations 1987, SI 1987/1968, reg 34A (as added), Sch 9A (as added and amended).

9 Sch 3, para 7(3), as extensively amended.

CONTRACTS SUBJECT TO MORTGAGE, ETC

Generally

1.34 It was formerly not uncommon[1] for a contract to purchase land to be made 'subject to mortgage', 'subject to finance', etc[2]. Such conditions are rarely encountered today, at least where a formal contract is envisaged, because the purchaser's solicitor would insist on a firm offer from the proposed lender before allowing the purchaser to commit himself by signing the purchase contract[3]. However, such contracts are quite common in certain Commonwealth countries[4].

1 Some earlier forms of conditions expressly covered the point.

2 See Farrand *Contract and Conveyance* (4th edn) pp 26–28.

3 See *Buckland v Mackesy* (1968) 112 Sol Jo 841, CA.

4 See (1967) 8 Univ of Western Australia LR1; (1972) 36 Conv (NS) 317; (1976) 40 Conv (NS) 37 (Coote); [1979] Conv 285 (Callender); [1982] 35 CLP 151 (Oakley); [1984] Conv 243 (HWW); (1984) 58 ALJ 633, 690 (Swanton); [1985] Conv 90 (Wilkinson). And see *Graham v Pitkin* [1992] 2 All ER 235, [1992] 1 WLR 403, PC.

Certainty

1.35 Unless a subject to mortgage condition is sufficiently precise, it will be void for uncertainty. A condition that a sale was subject to the purchaser obtaining a satisfactory mortgage has been held to be too indefinite, rendering the condition itself and the whole contract void[1].

It would seem that if such a condition is to be effective it would be necessary to draft the condition to refer in detail to at least the appropriate time limit on obtaining the finance, the source of the finance and the amount of principal[2].

1 *Lee-Parker v Izzet (No 2)* [1972] 2 All ER 800. Cf *Lee-Parker v Izzet* [1971] 3 All ER 1099; *Janmohamed v Hassam* [1977] 1 EGLR 142, (1977) 241 Estates Gazette 609; *Brown v Gould* [1972] Ch 53 at 56–57, [1971] 2 All ER 1505 at 1507-1508; and the Commonwealth cases referred to in the above-mentioned articles.

2 (1976) 40 Conv (NS) 37.

Chapter 2

Charges

EQUITABLE CHARGES

Definition

2.1 A charge is a security whereby real or personal property is appropriated for the discharge of a debt or other obligation, but which does not pass either an absolute or a special property in the subject of the security to the creditor, nor any right to possession. In the event of non-payment of the debt, the creditor's right of realisation is by judicial process[1].

With the exception of the charge by way of legal mortgage[2], which is for all intents and purposes equivalent to a legal mortgage, and maritime hypothecations[3], charges are enforceable only in equity[4].

1 *Johnson v Shippen* (1703) 2 Ld Raym 982; *Stainbank v Fenning* (1851) 11 CB 51; *Stainbank v Shepard* (1853) 13 CB 418. See *Swiss Bank Corpn v Lloyds Bank Ltd* [1982] AC 584 at 595, [1980] 2 All ER 419 at 425, CA, citing the previous edition, [1982] AC 584, [1981] 2 All ER 449, HL; *Carreras Rothmans Ltd v Freeman Mathews Treasure Ltd* [1985] Ch 207 at 227, [1985] 1 All ER 155 at 169; *Re Charge Card Services Ltd* [1987] Ch 150 at 176; on appeal [1989] Ch 497, CA); *Re Bank of Credit and Commerce International SA (No 8)* [1998] AC 214, [1997] 4 All ER 568, HL; *Re Coslett Contractors Ltd* [1998] Ch 495 at 507-508, per Millett LJ.

2 See **1.3**.

3 See Chapter 6.

4 On the nature of equitable charges, see *Re Coslett Contractors Ltd* [1998] Ch 495.

Equitable charges distinguished from liens

2.2 Equitable charges arise out of agreement between the parties and in that respect differ from statutory charges[1] and equitable liens, which are rights given by law. Subject to the terms of the contract by which the agreement is effected and the special rights created by the contract, the rights created do, however, correspond with those that arise under actual liens.

The term 'lien' is often loosely used to include not only liens arising by operation of law, but also charges or hypothecations arising out of contract[2]. However, a charge, though expressed to be an agreement for a lien, will not confer an actual lien, and the rights of the parties will be limited by the terms of the express contract[3]. The express stipulation and agreement for a security excludes a lien and limits the rights by the extent of the express contract[4].

1 As to statutory charges, see **2.30-2.38**.

2 The distinction between lien and charge is especially important for registration under the Companies Act 1985; see *Re Wallis & Simmonds (Builders) Ltd* [1974] 1 All ER 561, [1974] 1 WLR 391; *Trident International Ltd v Barlow* [2000] BCC 602, CA and see Chapter 12.
3 *Gladstone v Birley* (1817) 2 Mer 401 at 404; *Re Leith's Estate, Chambers v Davidson* (1866) LR 1 PC 296 at 305. See **2.39-2.47**.
4 *Expressum facit cessare tacitum,* see *Gladstone v Birley* (1817) 2 Mer 401 at 404; *Re Leith's Estate, Chambers v Davidson* (1866) LR 1 PC 296 at 305.

Equitable charges distinguished from equitable mortgages

2.3 In relation to equitable charges on land, the assimilation of mortgages and charges[1] is illustrated by the older cases. It has been suggested both:

(a) that an express contract to create a charge is a contract to make a mortgage and that the case is within the rules of equitable mortgages[2]; and
(b) that where a security is intended and the land charged is specified an equitable mortgage will be created[3], provided that the instrument by which the charge is effected is not a will[4] or a voluntary settlement[5].

There is, however, a fundamental difference in the nature of an equitable charge and an equitable mortgage[6]. The remedies available to the equitable mortgagee are more extensive than those available to the equitable chargee; in particular, an equitable chargee does not have the remedy of foreclosure[7]. However, notwithstanding that the distinction between the equitable charge and equitable mortgage has been clearly drawn in some more recent cases[8], and it is submitted that the older cases must be treated with caution, the tendency of mortgage and charge to converge in practice is still evidenced by a judicial disinclination to separate the two[9].

1 See **1.5**. Also see *Jones v Woodward* (1917) 116 LT 378; *London County and Westminster Bank v Tompkins* [1918] 1 KB 515, CA.
2 See *Ex p Wills* (1790) 1 Ves 162; *Montagu v Earl of Sandwich* (1886) 32 Ch D 525; *Re Roberts, ex p Australian Telecom Employees Credit Co-operative Ltd v Taylor* (1982) 84 FLR 88; *Avco Financial Services Ltd v Commonwealth Bank of Australia* (1989) 17 NSWLR 679.
3 *Cradock v Scottish Provident Institution* (1893) 69 LT 380; affd 70 LT 718, CA. Cf *Matthews v Goodday* (1861) 31 LJ Ch 282; *Shea v Moore* [1894] 1 IR 158.
4 *Re Owen* [1894] 3 Ch 220.
5 *Balfe v Lord* (1842) 2 Dr & War 480; *Re Lloyd, Lloyd v Lloyd* [1903] 1 Ch 385, CA.
6 See **1.22**. In *Re Cosslett (Contractors) Ltd* [1998] Ch 495 at 508, Lillett LJ in distinguishing between a mortgage and an equitable charge said: 'The difference between them is that a mortgage involves a transfer of legal or equitable ownership to the creditor, whereas an equitable charge does not.' Also see Millett J's description of equitable charges in *Re Charge Card Services Ltd* [1987] Ch 150 at 175–179, [1986] 3 All ER 289 at 308–11 and Gough *Company Charges* (2nd edn) pp 38-39.
7 See Chapter 22.
8 See eg *Swiss Bank Corpn v Lloyds Bank Ltd* [1982] AC 584 at 594–597, [1980] 2 All ER 419 at 426, CA; affd [1982] AC 584, [1981] 2 All ER 449, HL; *Ladup Ltd v Williams & Glyn's Bank plc* [1985] 2 All ER 577, [1985]1 WLR 851, CA.
9 See Lord Hoffman in *Re Bank of Credit and Commerce International SA (No 8)* [1998] AC 214 at 225-227, [1997] 3 WLR 909 at 916-919 disapproving Millett J in *Re Charge Card Services Ltd* [1987] Ch 150 and see Palmer's *Company Law* vol 3, para 13.104.

Creation

2.4 An ordinary charge[1] may be created:

(a) by a charge or direction in a settlement, will, or other instrument, whereby real or personal property[2] is expressly or constructively made liable or specifically appropriated to the discharge of a debt, portion, legacy, or other burden, or declared to be subjected to a charge for securing the debt[3]; no debt is implied, but a right of realisation by judicial process is conferred and, in some cases, a power of distress; or

(b) by the appropriation to the discharge of a debt of specific things in action or chattels, which either are, at the time of appropriation, or may or will thereafter be in the hands of a third person[4].

The charge must be a present[5] charge of specified property either already in the chargor's possession or such as he may afterwards acquire or derive from a specified source[6]. An agreement for a future charge is not enforceable if it is voluntary[7], but if it is given for value the charge will attach to the chargor's property at the time agreed[8].

No special form is required to create a charge[9].

1 Ie not a maritime hypothecation.

2 An agreement to charge property which at the date of the agreement has been sold will bind the corresponding interest in the purchase money: *Re Selby, ex p Rogers* (1856) 8 De GM & G 271; and see *Byrne v Allied Irish Banks Ltd* [1978] IR 446. On the other hand, on the death of the chargor the charge will only affect the property of which he died possessed and not such as did not belong to him at his death, whether he had it at the date of the obligation or acquired it afterwards.

3 It is the absence of any immediate appropriation which prevents a negative pledge clause from creating any security interest until default. Whether such a clause can create a charge upon default is a matter of controversy: see Goode *Legal Problems of Credit and Security* (2nd edn) pp 19-23. The proprietary nature of negative pledge clauses was rejected in *Pullen v Abalcheck Pty Ltd* (1990) 8 ACLC 1087, 20 NSWLR 732 and *Bond Brewing Holdings Ltd v National Australia Bank* (1990) 8 ACLC 330. See further on negative pledge clauses [1991] NZLR 312 at 364, 411 (Stone).

4 See *Swiss Bank Corpn v Lloyds Bank Ltd* [1982] AC 584 at 596, [1980] 2 All ER 419 at 426, CA. For trust by way of security, see *Re Bond Worth Ltd* [1980] Ch 228 at 250, [1979] 3 All ER 919 at 940; cf *Carreras Rothmans Ltd v Freeman Mathews Treasure Ltd* [1985] Ch 207 at 227, [1985] 1 All ER 155 at 169.

5 See *Williams v Burlington Investments Ltd* (1977) 121 Sol Jo 424, HL.

6 *Metcalfe v Archbishop of York* (1836) 6 Sim 224; affd (1836) 1 My & Cr 547; *Buller v Plunkett* (1860) 1 John & H 441.

7 *Re Earl of Lucan, Hardinge v Cobden* (1890) 45 Ch D 470.

8 *Wellesley v Wellesley* (1839) 4 Myl & Cr 561.

9 *Cradock v Scottish Provident Institution* (1893) 69 LT 380; affd (1894) 70 LT 718, CA.

Equitable charges on land

2.5 An equitable charge on land or an interest in land must be in writing signed by the chargor or his agent[1]. An instrument which creates an equitable charge and contains an agreement to create a legal mortgage, but fails to comply with the formalities for an equitable mortgage on land[2], will still create a valid equitable charge[3]. Further, an oral agreement to mortgage a legal estate can generate a valid equitable charge if accompanied by additional detriment incurred by the lender in reliance on the verbal agreement[4]. Not even a charge will, however, be created where no particular land is mentioned in the agreement[5], or where the agreement is only for a personal security, with power to call for a real security[6], or where it otherwise appears to be intended to rely upon the agreement and not any security[7], or where the agreement is not based on valuable consideration[8].

1 Law of Property Act 1925, s 53(1)(c) and see Law of Property (Miscellaneous Provisions) Act 1989. See also *United Bank of Kuwait plc v Sahib* [1997] Ch 107, affd on different grounds [1997] Ch 107, [1996] 3 All ER 215, CA.
2 See *United Bank of Kuwait plc v Sahib*, above.
3 In such circumstances, equity looks on that as done which ought to be done and, in accordance with the doctrine in *Walsh v Lonsdale* (1882) 21 Ch D 9, treats the transaction as a valid equitable mortgage of the legal estate. See *Parker v Housefield* (1834) 2 My & K 419; *Murray v Guinness* [1998] NPC 79. Alternatively the formally defective mortgage can be said to be 'equitable in so far as it touches the conscience of the mortgagor': *Windella v Hughes* (1999) 9 BPR 17141, per Santow J.
4 See *Bankers Trust Co v Namdar* [1997] EGCS 20, per Peter Gibson LJ.
5 See *Re Clarke, Coombe v Carter* (1887) 36 Ch D 348 at 352, per Cotton LJ. See *Bridge Wholesale Acceptance Corpn (Aust) Ltd v Burnard* (Supreme Court of New South Wales, 31 May 1991, BPR Casenote 96206.
6 Cf a mere contract and a security interest: *Williams v Burlington Investments Ltd* (1977) 121 Sol Jo 424, HL.
7 *Collins v Plummer* (1708) 1 P Wms 104; *Berrington v Evans* (1839) 3 Y & C Ex 384.
8 *Re Earl of Lucan, Hardinge v Cobden* (1890) 45 Ch D 470.

Equitable charges of personalty

2.6 If the personal chattel charged falls within the definition of 'personal chattels' in s 4 of the Bills of Sale Act 1878[1], the charge will be a bill of sale and subject to the provisions of the Bills of Sale Acts 1878 and 1882[2]. The borrowing of money on mortgage or special agreement[3] is within the definition of bills of sale.

Amongst the exceptions to the definition of bills of sale are: bills of lading, warrants and orders for delivery of goods, any other documents used in the ordinary course of business as proof of the possession or control of goods, or authorising (either by indorsement or delivery) the possessor of such document to transfer or receive the goods[4]. Also excepted from the definition are: a letter of lien to a bank on goods in the process of manufacture[5], a letter of trust to a bank with respect to goods covered by bills of lading which has been redelivered by the bank for purposes of sale[6], and transfers of goods in the ordinary course of business of a trade or calling.

1 Goods, furniture, and other articles capable of transfer by delivery and (when separately assigned or charged) fixtures and growing crops, but not chattel interests in real estate, nor fixtures (except trade machinery as defined in the Act) when assigned together with a freehold or leasehold interest in any land or building to which they are affixed, nor growing crops when assigned together with any interest in the land on which they grow, nor shares or interests in the stock, funds, or securities of any government, or in the capital or property of incorporated or joint stock companies, nor choses in action, nor any stock or produce upon any farm or lands which by virtue of any covenant or agreement or of the custom of the country ought not to be removed from any farm where the same are at the time of making or giving of such bill of sale.
2 See Chapter 5. Also see *National Provincial and Union Bank of England v Lindsell* [1922] 1 KB 21.
3 *Tennant v Howatson* (1888) 13 App Cas 489, PC.
4 Bills of Sale Act 1878, s 4.
5 *Re Hamilton, Young & Co, ex p Carter* [1905] 2 KB 772 CA; *Official Assignee of Madras v Mercantile Bank of India Ltd* [1935] AC 53, PC.
6 *Re David Allester Ltd* [1922] 2 Ch 211.

Equitable charges of things in action

2.7 Charges of things in action[1] are often affected by an assignment of the property and will then be treated as equitable mortgages[2] with an implied equity of redemption[3]. A mere charge on a fund or debt operates as a partial equitable assignment[4].

While an absolute assignment of existing property is effectual though voluntary, an equitable assignment which merely gives a charge on property requires valuable consideration to support it[5]. The fund upon which the charge operates must be clear[6].

1 Such as debts or funds in the hands of trustees, including future choses in action and after acquired property: *Ryall v Rowles* (1750) 1 Ves Sen 348 at 364; *Syrett v Egerton* [1957] 3 All ER 331; *Elders Pastoral Ltd v Bank of New Zealand (No 2)* [1990] 1 WLR 1478, PC. It also seems that an equitable charge may be created over a bank deposit in favour of the bank: *Re Bank of Credit and Commerce International SA (No 8)* [1998] AC 214, [1997] 4 All ER 568, HL, but see *Re Charge Card Services Ltd* [1987] Ch 150.
2 As to which, see Chapter 7. For forms of charge, see 28 *Forms and Precedents* (5th edn, 1999 reissue) Mortgages; and the Appendix.
3 *Re Row Dal Construction Pty Ltd* [1966] VR 249 at 259; *Re National Westminster Finance Australia Ltd* [1991] 1 Qd R 130 at 135-136.
4 *Durham Bros v Robertson* [1898] 1 QB 765 at 769, CA; and see *Swiss Bank Corpn v Lloyds Bank Ltd*, above; *Colonial General Mutual Insurance Co Ltd v Banking Group (New Zealand) Ltd* [1995] 3 NZLR 1, 5 PC. Gough *Company Charges* (2nd edn) p 75.
5 *Re Earl of Lucan, Hardinge v Cobden* (1890) 45 Ch D 470.
6 See Chapter 7.

Registration of land charges

2.8 An equitable land charge should be registered as a C(iii) land charge[1] if it:

(a) is not registered in any other class of land charge;
(b) is not secured by a deposit of documents relating to the estate affected[2]; and
(c) does not arise, or affect an interest arising, under a trust of land or settlement[3].

Class C(iii) is a residuary class[4]. The Class includes equitable mortgages of a legal estate if not protected by a deposit of title deeds[5] and, if not, limited owner's charges. Equitable mortgages of an equitable interest under a settlement or a trust of land are excluded as they are overreached on a conveyance to a purchaser and no question of enforcing the charge against him can, therefore, arise.

If a charge is registrable and duly registered, its owner is protected and a purchaser can easily discover the existence of the charge. If a charge is registrable and not registered, the purchaser takes free from it and the owner's rights against the land are defeated.

In the case of registered land where the charge affects the legal estate, the charge should be registered by notice[6], caution[7] or restriction[8].

1 Land Charges Act 1972, s 2. See also **3.105-3.106**.
2 This excludes protected mortgages of a legal estate.
3 Land Charges Act 1972, s 2(4) as amended by s 25(1), Sch 3 para 12(1), (2) of the Trusts of Land and Appointment of Trustees Act 1996.
4 See Megarry and Wade *The Law of Real Property* (6th edn) pp 180-181.
5 Equitable mortgages by deposit of title deeds can now only take affect if there is a binding contract to create a mortgage: *United Bank of Kuwait plc v Sahib* [1997] Ch 107.
6 Land Registration Act 1925, s 49(1)(c).
7 Section 54.
8 Section 58(1). See also **4.36**.

Registration of company charges

2.9 Mortgages or charges by an incorporated company are excluded from the provisions of the Bills of Sale Act (1878) Amendment Act 1882[1] and are, consequently, excluded from the operation of the Bills of Sale Act 1878[2].

For the purposes of company charges registration, a charge over chattels is, however, made registrable according to whether it would be registrable as a bill of sale if given by an individual[3].

1 Section 17 of the Act.
2 Sections 3 and 15 of the 1882 Act and *Re Standard Manufacturing Co* [1891] 1 Ch 627, [1891-4] All ER Rep 1242, CA.
3 Companies Act 1985 s 395.

Remedies of chargee[1]

2.10 The principal remedies of the chargee are sale and the appointment of a receiver. If the charge is by deed the chargee will have the statutory powers in this respect[2]. Where the charge is not by deed the chargee must apply to the court for an order for sale[3] or for the appointment of a receiver[4].

In considering whether to order sale in the case of property subject to a trust of land, the court must have regard to the intentions of the person who created the trust, the purpose for which the property is held, the welfare of any child occupying the property as his home and the interests of any secured creditor of the beneficiary[5].

A mere equitable chargee is not entitled to possession[6] nor foreclosure[7].

1 See generally *Carreras Rothmans Ltd v Freeman Mathews Treasure Ltd* [1985] Ch 207 at 227, [1985] 1 All ER 155 at 169.
2 Law of Property Act 1925, ss 101 (1), 205 (1) (xvi).
3 Any person who has an interest in property subject to a trust of land may apply for an order for sale of the land: Trusts of Land and Appointment of Trustees Act 1996, s 14. An equitable chargee, including the holder of a charging order, of the share of a co-owner of the land may apply for an order for sale: *Tennant v Trenchard* (1869) 4 Ch App 537 at 542; *Midland Bank plc v Pike* [1988] 2 All ER 434; *Lloyds Bank plc v Byrne* [1993] 2 FCR 41; *Croydon (Unique) Ltd v Wright* [2000] 2 WLR 683 at 696.
Where shares are charged restrictions on the transfer of the shares may restrict sale: *Dalston Development Pty Ltd v Dean* [1967] WAR 176. See Chapter 21.
4 See Chapter 18.
5 Trusts of Land and Appointment of Trustees Act 1996, s 15.
Where an application was made before 1997 under the Law of Property Act 1925, s 30 (repealed), before the commencement of the Trusts of Land and Appointment of Trustees Act 1996, the interests of creditors would normally prevail over other beneficiaries of the trust: *Re Citro (a bankrupt)* [1991] Ch 142; *Lloyds Bank v Byrne* [1993] 2 FCR 41; *Zandfarid v Bank of Credit and Commerce International SA (in liquidation)* [1996] 1 WLR 1420; *Bank of Baroda v Dhillon* [1998] 1 FLR 524, CA, unless there was a collateral purpose of the trust other than the provision of a home for the chargor and his family: *Abbey National plc v Moss* [1994] 1 FLR 307, CA. Now, the interests of the secured creditor only represent one matter relevant to the exercise of the court's discretion: Trusts of Land and Appointment of Trustees Act 1996 s 15(1)(d). In *Bank of Ireland Home Mortgages Ltd v Bell* [2001] 3 FCR 134, CA Peter Gibson LJ stated that it was and ought to be, nevertheless, a powerful consideration whether the creditor is receiving proper recompense for being kept out of his money; *Mortgage Corpn v Shaire* [2001] 4 All ER 364, [2000] 1 FLR 973. See Gray and Gray *Elements of Land Law* pp 606-608.
6 *Garfitt v Allen* (1887) 37 Ch D 48 at 50.
7 *Tennant v Trenchard*, above; *Re Lloyd, Lloyd v Lloyd* [1903] 1 Ch 385 at 404, CA; *United Travel Agencies Pty Ltd v Cain* (1990) 20 NSWLR 566.

JUDGMENTS

Judgments generally

2.11 The distinction between a lien and a mortgage has already been referred to[1]. A lien is an obligation which by implication of law, and not by express contract, binds real or personal property for the discharge of a debt or other obligation. A judgment does not of itself create any lien or other security interest[2].

1 See **1.6**.
2 Note that an order for secured maintenance operates as an equitable charge which will be binding against, amongst others, the trustee in bankruptcy of the person ordered to give security: see *Platt v Platt* (1976) 120 Sol Jo 199; also *Hyde v Hyde* [1948] P 198, [1948] 1 All ER 362, 92 Sol Jo 98 (Steiner). A freezing injunction (formerly known as a mareva injunction) does not create a security over the assets subject to the injunction: *Hortico (Aus) Pty Ltd v Energy Equipment Co (Aus) Pty Ltd* (1985) 1 NSWLR 545 at 558-599, nor can it be registered as a 'writ or order affecting land' under the Land Charges Act 1972, s 6(1)(a): *Stockler v Fourways Estates Ltd* [1983] 3 All ER 501, [1984] 1 WLR 25. With registered land the Registrar will give effect to a freezing injunction by registering an inhibition, but this has no proprietary effect.

Charging orders[1]

2.12 Where, under a judgment or order of the High Court or a county court, a person ('the debtor') is required to pay a sum of money[2] to another person ('the creditor') then, for the purposes of enforcing that judgment or order, the appropriate court[3] may make an order, in accordance with the provisions of the Charging Orders Act 1979[4], imposing on any such property of the debtor as may be specified in the order a charge for securing the payment of any money due or to become due under the judgment or order[5].

In deciding whether to make a charging order the court shall consider all the circumstances of the case[6] and, in particular, any evidence before it[7] as to:

(a) the personal circumstances of the debtor; and
(b) whether any other creditors of the debtor would be likely to be unduly prejudiced by the making of the order[8].

A charging order may be made either absolutely or subject to conditions as to notifying the debtor or as to the time when the charge is to become enforceable, or as to other matters[9]. Additionally, the court has a statutory discretion to order an immediate sale of any co-owned land affected by a charging order[10].

1 See, generally, 17 *Halsbury's Laws* (4th edn), Execution. The Administration of Justice Act 1956 abolished writs of elegit and gave power to the court to impose by order a charge on any land or interest in land of the debtor: see Administration of Justice Act 1956, s 34; Administration of Justice Act 1965, s 34 (1), Sch 2. For a convenient short history of the matter, see The Law Commission Report on Charging Orders (Law Com No 74, 1976, Cmnd 6412). Most of the recommendations in this report were implemented by the Charging Orders Act 1979.
2 A charging order can only be made for an ascertained sum: *A & M Records Inc v Darakdjian* [1975] 3 All ER 983, [1975] 1 WLR 1610.
3 The appropriate court is (a) in a case where the property to be charged is a fund in court, the court in which the fund is lodged; (b) in a case where paragraph (a) above does not apply and the order to be enforced is a maintenance order of the High Court, the High Court or a county court; (c) in a case where neither paragraph (a) nor (b) above applies and the judgment or order to be enforced is a judgment or order of the High Court for a

sum exceeding the county court limit, the High Court or a county court; and (d) in any other case, a county court: Charging Orders Act 1979, s 1 (2); as amended (as regards paragraph (c) above) by the Administration of Justice Act 1982, s 37, Sch 3, Pt II, paras 2, 3 and County Courts Act 1984, s 148 (1), Sch 2, Pt V, para 71.

'Maintenance order' has the same meaning as in s 2(a) of the Attachment of Earnings Act 1971; 'county court limit' means the county court limit for the time being specified in an Order in Council under s 145 of the County Courts Act 1984: County Courts Act 1984, s 148 (1), Sch 2, Pt V, para 71. (The current limit is £5,000: County Courts Jurisdiction Order 1981, SI 1981/1123.)

4 Charging Orders Act 1979, s 1 (3).

5 Section 1 (1).

6 See *Roberts Petroleum Ltd v Bernard Kenny Ltd* [1983] 2 AC 192, [1983] 1 All ER 564, HL (the compulsory winding up of a company, or a resolution of a company in general meeting for voluntary winding up was, without more, a sufficient cause for not making a charging order nisi absolute).

7 The joint owner of a matrimonial home is entitled to be heard: *Harman v Glencross* [1985] Fam 49, [1984] 2 All ER 577; affd [1986] Fam 81, [1986] 1 All ER 545, CA.

Where a creditor applies for a charging order on the husband's share of the matrimonial home before the wife brings divorce proceedings, the wife has no competing claim to the husband's share and must seek to protect her rights of occupation under the Trusts of Land and Appointment of Trustees Act 1996 (previously under s 30 of the Law of Property Act 1925), but where the creditor applies for a charging order after the wife has petitioned for divorce, the court should consider whether it is proper to make the order before the wife's application for ancillary relief has been heard; see, generally, *Harman v Glencross* [1986] Fam 81, [1986] 1 All ER 545, CA. In *Austin-Fell v Austin-Fell* [1990] Fam 172, [1990] 2 All ER 455, Waite J stated that in balancing the claims of a spouse seeking ancillary relief and a judgment creditor the usual order would be to make the charging order absolute subject to it being unenforceable by an order for sale until the youngest child attained a certain age (a Mesher order). Only in very exceptional cases would the court refuse the creditor any form of security. In *Harman v Glencross* the Court of Appeal specifically approved the earlier decision of the Court of Appeal in *Llewellin v Llewellin* 30 October 1995 where the charging order was made absolute unconditionally on the ground that there was sufficient equity to satisfy both the wife and the judgment creditor (above) at 99 and 558-559.

8 Charging Orders Act 1979, s 1 (5). See *First National Securities Ltd v Hegerty* [1985] QB 850, [1984] 1 All ER 139; affd [1985] QB 850, [1984] 3 All ER 641, CA — wife not prejudiced by order as judgment creditors would need to apply for sale under s 30 of the Law of Property Act 1925 (now the Trusts of Land and Appointment of Trustees Act). For a difficult decision balancing the rights of a judgment creditor and a purchaser, see *Howell v Montey* (1990) 61 P & CR 18, CA; and see *Coughlan* [1990] Conv 392.

9 Charging Orders Act 1979, s 3 (1).

10 Trusts of Land and Appointment of Trustees Act 1996, s 14 (1)-(2).

Registration of writs and orders affecting land

2.13 The Land Charges Act 1972 and the Land Registration Act 1925 apply to charging orders as they apply to other writs or orders for the purpose of enforcing judgments[1].

1 Charging Orders Act 1979, s 3(2).

Unregistered land

2.14 In the case of unregistered land, a writ or order affecting land and issued for the purpose of enforcing a judgment should be registered in the register of writs and orders affecting land in the name of the estate owner or other person whose land is affected by the writ or order[1].

In this respect, the definition of 'land' in the Land Charges Act has not been changed and still specifically excludes an undivided share in land. As a result, while charging orders may be made in respect of beneficial interests in land subject to a trust of land, protection by registration is only possible under the Land Charges Act 1972 where the charging order is imposed on land held by the debtor beneficially or on land held by trustees.

Failure to register as a land charge renders the order void against a purchaser[2] of unregistered land for valuable consideration[3].

1 Land Charges Act 1972, s 6(1), (1A) (as inserted by the Trusts of Land and Appointment of Trustees Act 1996, s 25(1), Sch 3, para 12(3). A charging order over an interest in proceeds of sale is not registrable under the Land Charges Act 1972, s 6(1): *Perry v Phoenix Assurance plc* [1988] 3 All ER 60, [1988] 1 WLR 94.
2 This includes a mortgagee: Land Charges Act 1972, s 20 (8).
3 Land Charges Act 1972, s 7 (1).

Registered land

2.15 In the case of registered land, a charging order should be protected by a caution[1]. Alternatively, if the land certificate is available or there is a subsisting registered charge the order may be protected by a notice[2]. A notice cannot, however, be entered in respect of a charging order imposing a charge only on an undivided share in land.

A caution registered to protect a charging order confers no priority and the rule in *Dearle v Hall* does not relate to a judgment creditor[3].

Failure to protect by a caution or notice enables a purchaser of registered land in good faith[4] and for valuable consideration under a registered disposition to take free of any order[5].

1 Land Registration Act 1925, s 59 (1). See *Parkash v Irani Finance Ltd* [1970] Ch 101, [1969] 1 All ER 930; *Irani Finance Ltd v Singh* [1971] Ch 59, [1970] 3 All ER 199, CA. A charging order over an interest in the proceeds of sale of land can be protected by a caution: *Elias v Mitchell* [1972] Ch 652, [1972] 2 All ER 153.
2 Charging Orders Act 1979, s 3 (2). Under the Land Registration Act 1925, s 49 (1) (g) (added by the Charging Orders Act 1979, s 3 (3)).
3 *Clark v Chief Land Registrar* [1994] Ch 370; *United Bank of Kuwait plc v Sahib* [1997] Ch 107.
4 On good faith, see *Peffer v Rigg* [1978] 3 All ER 745, [1977] 1 WLR 285.
5 Land Registration Act 1925, s 59 (6).

Property which may be charged

2.16 The type of property which may be charged is described in s 2(1) of the Charging Orders Act 1979, which provides that:

'(1) Subject to subsection (3) below, a charge may be imposed by a charging order only on—
(a) any interest held by the debtor beneficially—
  (i) in any asset[1] of a kind mentioned in subsection (2) below, or
  (ii) under any trust[2]; or
(b) any interest held by a person trustee of a trust ('the trust'), if the interest is in such an asset or is an interest under another trust and—
  (i) the judgment or order in respect of which a charge is to be imposed was made against that person as trustee of the trust, or
  (ii) the whole beneficial interest under the trust is held by the debtor unencumbered and for his own benefit, or unencumbered and for their own benefit, or

(iii) in a case where there are two or more debtors all of whom are liable to the creditor for the same debt, they together hold the whole beneficial interest under the trust unencumbered and for their own benefit.

(2) The assets referred to in subsection (1) above are—

(a) land,

(b) securities of any of the following kinds—

(i) government stock,

(ii) stock of any body (other than a building society) incorporated within England and Wales,

(iii) stock of any body incorporated outside England and Wales or of any state or territory outside the United Kingdom, being stock registered in a register kept at any place within England and Wales,

(iv) units of any unit trust in respect of which a register of the unit holders is kept at any place within England and Wales, or

(c) funds in court[3].

(3) In any case where a charge is imposed by charging order on any interest in an asset of a kind mentioned in paragraph (b) or (c) of subsection (2) above, the court making the order may provide for the charge to extend to any interest or dividend payable in respect of the asset.

(4) In any case where a charge is imposed by a charging order on any interest in an asset of a kind mentioned in paragraph (b) or (c) of subsection (2) above, the court making the order may provide for the charge to extend to any interest or dividend payable in respect of the asset.'

1 A charging order can be imposed on an undivided share in land (ie the interest of a beneficial co-owner under a trust for land): *National Westminster Bank Ltd v Stockman* [1981] 1 All ER 800, [1981] 1 WLR 67; *Perry v Phoenix Assurance plc* [1988] 3 All ER 60. [1988] 1 WLR 940. Such an order cannot, however, itself be registered under the Land Charges Act 1972 s 17(1); see also the Land Charges Act 1972, s 6(1A), introduced by the Trusts of Land and Appointment of Trustees Act 1996, s 25(1), Sch 3, para 12(1), (3) and cannot, therefore, be noted in the Charges Register of a registered title: Land Registration Act 1925, s 49(1)(g).

2 *National Westminster Bank Ltd v Stockman* [1981] 1 All ER 800, [1981] 1 WLR 67; *First National Securities Ltd v Hegerty* [1985] QB 850.

3 The Lord Chancellor may by order made by statutory instrument amend s 2 (2) by adding to, or removing from, the kinds of asset for the time being referred to there, any asset of a kind which in his opinion ought to be so added or removed: Charging Orders Act 1979, s 3 (7).

Application for charging order[1]

2.17 An application by a judgment creditor for a charging order[2] in respect of a judgment debtor's beneficial interest[3] may be made without notice and any order made on such application shall, in the first instance, be an order to show cause, specifying the time and place for further consideration of the matter and imposing the charge in any event until that time[4].

The application must be supported by a witness statement or an affidavit:

(a) identifying the judgment or order to be enforced and stating the amount unpaid at the date of the application;

(b) stating the name of the judgment debtor and of any creditors of his whom the applicant can identify;

(c) giving full particulars of the subject matter of the intended charge including, in the case of securities other than securities in court, the full title of the securities, their amount and the name in which they stand and, in the case of funds in court, the number of the account; and

(d) verifying that the interest to be charged is owned beneficially by the judgment debtor[5].

On the making of an order to show cause[6], unless the court otherwise directs, notice of the order, together with a copy of the witness statement or affidavit in support, shall be served on the judgment debtor. Where the order relates to securities other than securities in court, copies of the order shall also be served on:

(a) in the case of government stock for which the Bank of England keeps the register, on the Bank of England;
(b) in the case of government stock to which (a) does not apply, on the keeper of the register;
(c) in the case of stock of any body incorporated within England and Wales, on that body or, where the register is kept by the Bank of England, on the Bank of England;
(d) in the case of stock of any body incorporated outside England and Wales or of any state or territory outside the United Kingdom, being stock registered in a register kept in England and Wales, on the keeper of the register; and
(e) in the case of units of any unit trust in respect of which a register of the unit holders is kept in England and Wales, on the keeper of the register.

Where the order relates to a fund in court, a copy of the order shall be served on the Accountant General at the Court Funds Office and where the order relates to an interest under a trust, copies of the order shall be served on such of the trustees as the court may direct[7].

Without prejudice to the above, the court may, on making the order to show cause, direct the service of copies of the order and of the witness statement or affidavit in support on any other creditor of the judgment debtor or on any other interested person as may be appropriate in the circumstances[8].

On the further consideration of the matter the court shall make the order absolute, with or without modifications, or discharge it[9].

1 See generally CPR Part 8 Practice Direction — Alternative Procedure for Claims, Section A applies to RSC Ord 50, Section B applies to CCR Ord 31.The application may be to enforce more than one judgment: Charging Orders Act 1979, s 1 (4); CPR, Sch 1; RSC Ord 50, r 1 (5).

2 For injunctions ancillary or incidental to charging orders, see CPR, Sch 1; RSC Ord 50, r 9.

3 For applications for a charging order against the interest of a trustee, see Charging Orders Act 1979, s 2 (1) (b); RSC Ord 50, r 4.

4 CPR, Sch 1; RSC Ord 50, r 1 (2). For the county court, see CCR Ord 31, r 1.

5 CPR, Sch 1; RSC Ord 50, r 1 (3). *Nightingale Mayfair Ltd v Mehta* (1999) 1 WTLR 901.

6 For the matters for consideration by the court on the application, see Charging Orders Act 1979, s 1 (5).

7 CPR, Sch 1; RSC Ord 50, r 2 (1).

8 CPR, Sch 1; RSC Ord 50, r 2 (1). Eg a spouse: *Harman v Glencross* [1985] Fam 49, [1984] 2 All ER 577; affd [1986] Fam 81, [1986] 1 All ER 545, CA. See also *Austin-Fell v Austin-Fell* [1990] Fam 172, [1990] 2 All ER 455 where a postponed enforcement order represented the fairest balance between competing claims of wife and creditor.

9 Documents to be served under this rule must be served at least seven days before the time appointed for the further consideration of the matter: CPR, Sch 1; RSC Ord 50, r 2 (3). Liquidation has been held to be a sufficient cause for refusing to make an order absolute: *Roberts Petroleum Ltd v Bernard Kenny Ltd* [1983] 2 AC 192.

Effect of charging order

2.18 Subject, where relevant, to the registration or protection of the order, a charging order has the like effect and is enforceable in the same courts and in the same manner as an equitable charge created by the debtor by writing under his hand[2]. An action to enforce a charging order is not an action to enforce a judgment, but an action to recover a sum due to the claimant as a secured creditor. As such, the claimant is not restricted to recovering only six years interest out of the proceeds of enforcing his security[3]. The costs of proceedings to enforce a charging order are payable out of the proceeds of sale of the property charged[4].

1 CPR, Sch 1; RSC Ord 50, r 3. For the county court, see CPR, Sch 1; CCR Ord 31, r 2.

2 Charging Orders Act 1979, s 3 (4). A charging order over an interest in the proceeds of sale is enforced by an application that the land should be sold under the Trusts of Land and Appointment of Trustees Act 1996 (previously under the Law of Property Act 1925, s 30. As to the remedies of a chargee, see **2.10**; accordingly foreclosure is not an appropriate remedy: see *Daponte v Schubert and Roy Nominees Ltd* [1939] Ch 958, [1939] 3 All ER 495; *United Travel Agencies Pty Ltd v Cain* (1990) 20 NSWLR 566. On sale, see CPR, Sch 1; RSC Ord 50, r 9A and Ord 88; CCR Ord 31, r 4.

The interest of a judgment creditor (whether he is with or without notice) in the property of his debtor is subject to every liability under which the debtor holds it: see *Langton v Horton* (1842) 1 Hare 549; *Whitworth v Gaugain* (1844) 3 Hare 416 at 427; affd (1846) 1 Ph 128; *Abbott v Stratton* (1846) 3 Jo & Lat 603; *Eyre v M'Dowell* (1861) 9 HL Cas 619; *Chung Khiaw Bank Ltd v United Overseas Bank* [1970] AC 767, PC.

An owner of a charging order holds an interest within s 138(9C) of the County Courts Act 1984 and is entitled to relief from forfeiture: *Bland v Ingrams Estates Ltd* [2001] 2 WLR 1638, CA; *Bland v Ingrams Estates Ltd (No 2)* [2001] 35 LS Gaz R 35.

3 *Ezekiel v Orakpo* [1997] 1 WLR 340, CA.

4 *Holder v Supperstone* [2000] 1 All ER 473 at 479-480.

Priority of charging order on insolvency

2.19 For the purposes of the provisions of the insolvency and companies legislation which restrict the rights of creditors under execution or attachment[1]:

(a) an execution against goods is completed by seizure and sale or by the making of a charging order under s 1 of the Charging Orders Act 1979;
(b) an attachment of a debt is completed by the receipt of the debt; and
(c) an execution against land is completed by seizure, by the appointment of a receiver, or by the making of a charging order under s 1 of the Charging Orders Act 1979[2].

1 See the Insolvency Act 1986, s 346 (formerly Bankruptcy Act 1914, s 40, then the Insolvency Act 1985, s 179) and the Insolvency Act 1986, s 183 (formerly the Companies Act 1948, s 325, then the Insolvency Act 1985, s 621).

2 Charging Orders Act 1979, s 4, adding a subsection in these terms to the Bankruptcy Act 1914, s 40 and the Companies Act 1948, s 325 (now repealed). The last part of the provision in effect reversed *Re Overseas Aviation Engineering (GB) Ltd* [1963] Ch 24, [1962] 3 All ER 12, CA. See Law Commission Report on Charging Orders (Law Com No 74, 1976, Cmnd 6412) paras 40, 41.

Discharge of charging order

2.20 The court by which a charging order was made may at any time, on the application of the debtor or of any person interested in any property to which the order relates[1], make an order discharging or varying the charging order[2]. The debtor cannot obtain a discharge of the charging order merely by paying the judgment debt but must also pay interest and costs as if he were seeking to redeem an equitable charge[3].

1 *Harman v Glencross* [1985] Fam 49, [1984] 2 All ER 577; affd [1986] Fam 81, [1986] 1 All ER 545, CA; *Banque Nationale de Paris plv v Montman Ltd* [2000] 1 BCLC 576 at 581.
2 Charging Orders Act 1979, s 3 (5). See CPR, Sch 1; RSC Ord 50, r 7; and see *Howell v Montey* (1990) 61 P & CR 18, [1990] Conv 392 (Coughlan). Where an order is made for the discharge or variation of a charging order in respect of funds in court, a copy of the order shall be served on the Accountant General at the Court Funds Office: CPR, Sch 1; RSC Ord 50, r 7 (4). Where an order is made for the discharge or variation of a charging order in respect of securities other than securities in court, a copy thereof shall be served on the Bank of England or on such other person or body specified (see CPR, Sch 1; RSC Ord 50, r 2(1)(b)) as may be appropriate, and the service of the order shall discharge or, as the case may be, vary, any stop notice in respect of such securities which may be in force pursuant to the original order: CPR, Sch 1; RSC Ord 50, r 7 (5).
For the vacating of land charge registrations, see the Land Charges Act 1972, ss 1 (6), 8. For the vacating of registered land entries, see the Land Registration Act 1925, s 56 (3); Land Registration Rules 1925, r 222 (withdrawal of caution); rr 16, 201 (cancellation of notices of land charges).
3 *Ezekial v Orakpo* [1997] 1 WLR 340, CA; *Re Drax, Savile v Drax* [1903] 1 Ch 781.

Appointment of receiver by way of equitable execution

2.21 The High Court and the county court may in appropriate circumstances appoint a receiver by way of equitable execution[1] in relation to personal property[2] and land and interests in land[3], including the interest of a co-owner under a trust for sale[4]. The power may be exercised in relation to an estate or interest in land, whether or not a charging order has been imposed on the land, and is in addition to and not in derogation of any power of the court to appoint a receiver in proceedings for enforcing a charge created by a charging order[5]. The court has jurisdiction to appoint a receiver by way of equitable execution in respect of future debts not yet accrued[6].

The appointment of a receiver does not create a charge on the property[7] and is subject to the rights of prior incumbrancers, but the judgment creditor's position is preserved by his being able to obtain an injunction to prevent the property being received by a subsequent assignee to his prejudice[8].

Because of the wide scope of charging orders, the appointment of a receiver by way of equitable execution is rarely necessary nowadays. In the case of an ordinary joint tenant or tenant in common it will nearly always be more just and convenient and more economic to impose a charging order than to appoint a receiver by way of equitable execution, as the charging order can be enforced by an order for sale. However, execution against life interests in trust funds or in land is more convenient by the appointment of a receiver.

1 See generally on the jurisdiction: *Bourne v Colodense Ltd* [1985] ICR 291, CA; *Maclaine Watson & Co Ltd v International Tin Council* [1988] Ch 1, [1987] 3 All ER 787, and on appeal [1989] Ch 253, [1988] 3 All ER 257, CA; affd [1990] 2 AC 418, [1989] 3 All ER 523, HL. A Master, the Admiralty Registrar, a district judge of the Family Division and a district judge still have power to make an order.
2 See CPR, Sch 1; RSC Ord 51, Receivers: Equitable Execution and RSC Ord 30, r 1 and rr 2-6 (which apply in relation to a receiver appointed by way of equitable execution as they apply in relation to a receiver appointed for any other purpose). The procedure is the same as that for the appointment of receivers generally. Application is made in accordance with CPR Part 23. Forms can be adapted to the needs of the case.
3 A power initially given by the Administration of Justice Act 1956, s 36, now replaced by Supreme Court Act 1981, s 37.

4 See *Levermore v Levermore* [1980] 1 All ER 1, [1979] 1 WLR 1277. (Note, after the Charging Orders Act 1979, a charging order on the husband's interest would be available.)
5 Supreme Court Act 1981, s 37 (4). See, generally, CPR, Sch 1; RSC Ord 51. 'Equitable execution is a process which the court allows for the purpose of enabling a judgment creditor to obtain payment of his debt, when the position of the legal estate is such that ordinary execution will not reach it': per Chitty J *Wills v Luff* (1888) 38 Ch D 197, 200.
6 *Soinco SACI v Novukuznetsk Plant* [1998] QB 406, [1997] 3 All ER 523.
7 *Re Potts, ex p Taylor* [1893] 1 QB 648 at 659, CA; *Re Pearce, ex p Official Receiver, The Trustee* [1919] 1 KB 354 at 363, 364, CA; *Giles v Kruyer* [1921] 3 KB 23.
8 *Ideal Bedding Co Ltd v Holland* [1907] 2 Ch 157 at 169, 170; *Stevens v Hutchinson* [1953] Ch 299, sub nom *Re No 39 Carr Lane, Acomb, Stevens v Hutchinson* [1953] 1 All ER 699.

Charging order on shares

2.22 A charging order may be made in respect of the appropriate interest in any of the securities specified in the Charging Orders Act 1979, s 2 (2) (b)[1].

1 For the appropriate interest, see s 2(1), **2.16**. For the effect of the order, see **2.23-2.24**; cf *Re Onslow's Trusts* (1875) LR 20 Eq 677.

Effect of order in relation to securities out of court

2.23 No disposition by the judgment debtor of his interest in any securities to which an order to show cause relates made after the making of that order shall, so long as that order remains in force, be valid as against the judgment creditor[1].

Until such order is discharged or made absolute, the Bank of England (or other appropriate person or body[2]) shall not permit any transfer of any of the securities specified in the order, or pay any dividend, interest or redemption payment in relation to the securites, except with the authority of the court and, if it does so, shall be liable to pay the judgment creditor the value of the securities transferred or, as the case may be, the amount of the payment made or, if that value or amount is more than sufficient to satisfy the judgment or order to which such order relates, so much of that value or amount as is sufficient to satisfy it[3].

If the court makes an order absolute, a copy of the order including a stop notice[4] shall be served on the Bank of England, or on such other specified[5] person or body as may be appropriate[6].

1 CPR, Sch 1; RSC Ord 50, r 5 (1).
2 As specified in CPR, Sch 1; RSC Ord 50, r 2 (2) (b); see **2.17**.
3 CPR, Sch 1; RSC Ord 50, r 5 (2).
4 As specified in CPR, Sch 1; RSC Ord 50, r 2 (2) (b); see **2.26**.
5 As provided in Form No 76 in Appendix A to the Rules.
6 CPR, Sch 1; RSC Ord 50, r 5 (3); and, save in the case of discharge or variation, the stop notice rules in CPR, Sch 1; RSC Ord 50, rr 11–14 shall apply to such notice.

Effect of order in relation to funds in court

2.24 Where an order to show cause has been made in relation to funds in court (including securities in court) and a copy of the order has been served on the Accountant General[1], no disposition by the judgment debtor[2] of any interest to which the order relates, made after the making of that order shall, so long as the order remains in force, be valid as against the judgment creditor[3].

1 In accordance with CPR, Sch 1; RSC Ord 50, r 2 (1) (c).

2 In the case of an order made under the Charging Orders Act 1979 s 2(1)(b)(ii) or (iii) charging an interest held by a trustee, 'trustee' should be substituted here for judgment debtor: CPR, Sch 1; RSC Ord 50, r 4(4).
3 CPR, Sch 1; RSC Ord 50, r 6 (1). If the court makes an order absolute, a copy of the order shall be served on the Accountant General at the Central Funds Office: RSC Ord 50, r 6 (2).

Charging partnership share

2.25 A writ of execution cannot issue against any partnership property except on a judgment against the firm[1], but the court may make an order under the Partnership Act 1890[2] charging the share of a partner who is a judgment debtor[3]. The effect of the order is the same as if the partner had executed a document charging his share with the debt[4].

1 Partnership Act 1890, s 23(1).
2 A charging order must be made under this provision and not under the Charging Orders Act 1979 because the assets which may be charged under the latter Act do not include a partnership share: Charging Orders Act 1979, s 2(2).
3 Section 23(2).
4 Section 23(2); and see *Peake v Carter* [1916] 1 KB 652; *Brown, Janson & Co v Hutchinson & Co* [1895] 2 QB 126 at 131, CA.

Stop notice

2.26 Any person claiming to be beneficially entitled to an interest in any securities of the kinds set out in s 2 (2) (b) of the Charging Orders Act 1979[1], other than securities in court, who wishes to be notified of any proposed transfer or payment of those securities, may obtain a stop notice from the High Court[2]. Where a stop notice has been served on the Bank of England or a company then, so long as the notice is in force, the Bank or company shall not register a transfer of the securities or take any other steps restrained by the stop notice until 14 days after sending notice of the stop notice, by ordinary first class post, to the person on whose behalf the notice was filed, but shall not by reason only of that notice refuse to register a transfer, or take any other step, after the expiry of that period[3].

1 See **2.16**.
2 CPR, Sch 1; RSC Ord 50, r 11. See, generally, notes to CPR, Sch 1; RSC Ord 50, rr 11–14.
3 CPR, Sch 1; RSC Ord 50, r 12. See further as to stop notices, Chapter 7.

Order prohibiting transfer, etc of securities

2.27 The court, on the application of any person claiming to be beneficially entitled to an interest in any securities of the kinds set out in s 2 (2) (b) of the Charging Orders Act 1979[1], may by order prohibit the Bank of England or other person or body concerned from registering any transfer of the securities or taking any other step to which s 5 (5) of that Act applies[2].

1 See **2.16**.
2 CPR, Sch 1; RSC Ord 50, r 15 (1). The application is made in the Chancery Division: r 15 (2). See generally, the notes to RSC Ord 50, r 15.

Stop order on funds in court

2.28 The court, on the application of any person:

(a) who has a mortgage or charge on the interest of any person in funds in court; or
(b) to whom that interest has been assigned; or
(c) who is a judgment creditor of the person entitled to that interest,

may make an order prohibiting the transfer, sale, delivery out, payment or other dealing with such funds, or any part thereof, or the income thereon, without notice to the applicant[1].

1 CPR, Sch 1; RSC Ord 50, r 10(1).

Garnishee proceedings

2.29 Where a person (the judgment creditor) has obtained a judgment or order for the payment by some other person (the judgment debtor) of moneys not being a judgment or order for the payment of money into court and any other person within the jurisdiction (the garnishee) is indebted to the judgment debtor, the court may order the garnishee to pay the judgment creditor the amount of any debt due or accruing due to the judgment debtor from the garnishee, or so much of the debt due as is sufficient to satisfy that judgment or order and the costs of the garnishee proceedings[1].

The judgment creditor does not become a creditor of the garnishee upon the making of the garnishee order nisi[2]. Nor does the order, whether nisi or absolute, effect a transfer of the debt to the judgment creditor[3].

1 CPR, Sch 1; RSC Ord 49, r 1(1); CCR Ord 30.
On the nature of garnishee proceedings and the effect of the order, see *Re Barrier Reef Finance and Land Pty Ltd* (1988) 13 ACLR 708, *Relwood Pty Ltd v Manning Homes Pty Ltd (No 2)* [1992] 2 QdR 197, FC; *M G Charley Pty Ltd v F H Wells Pty Ltd* [1963] NSWLR 22. On garnisheeing banks, see (1976) 126 New LJ 747. See further as to garnishee proceedings and how they affect surplus proceeds of sale of mortgaged property, Chapter 20.

2 *Norton v Yates* [1906] 1 KB 112; and see *Re Combined Weighing and Advertising Machine Co v Automatic Weighing Machine Co* (1889) 43 Ch D 99. On crystallisation of a floating charge the chargee has priority over the judgment creditor under a garnishee order nisi: *Relwood Pty Ltd v Manning Homes Pty Ltd (No 2)*, above.

3 See *Norton v Yates*, above; *Re Combined Weighing and Advertising Machine Co*, above; *Holmes v Tutton* (1855) 5 E & B 65; cf *Re Watts, ex p Joselyn* (1878) 8 Ch D 327.

STATUTORY CHARGES

Generally

2.30 In addition to the charging orders already mentioned in this chapter and the statutory charge created under the Improvement of Land Act 1864, dealt with in Chapter 12, a number of statutes provide for the creation of a charge over land for the recoupment of various kinds of liability incurred by the landowner. Such charges generally arise without the necessity of any deed and tend to constitute enforceable first legal charges.

Agriculture

2.31 Under the Agricultural Holdings Act 1986 a tenant has the ability to obtain a charge when his landlord has failed to pay compensation due[1] and the landlord has the ability to obtain a charge for the repayment of the payment of compensation by him to his tenant[2].

The charges are Class A land charges within the meaning of the Land Charges Act 1972 and, where applicable to unregistered land, should be registered accordingly[3]. If not so registered such a charge will be void against a purchaser for value[4] of the land charged[5].

It is provided by the Agricultural Holdings Act 1986[6] that tenants' charges[7] shall rank in priority to any other charge, however and whenever created or arising. A prospective mortgagee of an agricultural holding which is let should, therefore, bear in mind that a charge for compensation in favour of the tenant will have priority to his mortgage.

1 Agricultural Holdings Act 1986, s 85 (2).
2 Section 86.
3 Land Charges Act 1972, s 2 (2), Sch 2; Agricultural Holdings Act 1986, s 100, Sch 14, para 51.
4 This includes a mortgagee: Law of Property Act 1925, s 205 (1) (xvi).
5 Land Charges Act 1972, s 4 (2). For registered land, see **2.38**.
6 Agricultural Holdings Act 1986, s 87 (6).
7 Ie those created under s 85 (2) of the Agricultural Holdings Act 1986.

Business tenancies

2.32 Special provisions enable an order to be obtained charging on the holding a sum paid as compensation for improvements or the cost of executing an improvement after notice given in accordance with the Landlord and Tenant Act 1927[1].

Such a charge is obtained from the Minister of Agriculture, Fisheries and Food and may be registered as a Class A land charge[2].

Unlike the charge of a landlord of agricultural land mentioned above, there is no special provision for the priority of such a charge on business premises and therefore such a charge cannot rank in priority to a mortgage of the premises created before the charge.

1 Landlord and Tenant Act 1927, s 12, Sch 1, paras (1), (4).
2 Schedule 1, para (7).

Housing authorities

2.33 Where a housing authority carries out works following a failure to comply with a repair notice, the expenses and interest incurred in carrying out the work are a charge on the property, giving the authority the powers and remedies of a mortgagee, including the power to appoint a receiver from one month after the charge takes effect, which is when the demand becomes operative[1]. The charge takes priority over other mortgages and rent charges[2].

1 Housing Act 1985, s 193, Sch 10 para 7(1).
2 *Paddington Borough Council v Finucane* [1928] Ch 567; *Bristol Corpn v Virgin* [1928] 2 KB 622.

Street works

2.34 A street works authority may impose a charge upon premises owned by frontagers for expenses incurred in making up private streets[1].

Such a charge is registrable as a local land charge and, although failure to register no longer affects enforceability of the charge, it will give the purchaser a right to compensation in certain cases[2]. Further, if the charge is not registered it will not run with the land so as to be enforceable against a subsequent owner[3].

For the recovery of expenses charged on premises under s 212 of the Highways Act 1980, the local authority has, before registration of the charge, all the same powers and remedies under the Law of Property Act 1925, as if it were a mortgagee having powers of sale, of leasing and of appointing a receiver[4]. The authority, as chargee, is therefore given a power of sale in priority to earlier mortgages[5] or rent charges[6].

1 See, for example, Highways Act 1980, ss 212 and 305.
2 Local Land Charges Act 1975, s 10.
3 Section 10.
4 Highways Act 1980, s 212 (3). See *Dennerley v Prestwich UDC* [1930] 1 KB 334, CA; *Payne v Cardiff RDC* [1932] 1 KB 241; *Poole Corpn v Moody* [1945] KB 350, sub nom *Moody v Poole Corpn* [1945] 1 All ER 536, CA.
On registration of the charge under s 5 of the Local Land Charge Act 1975, the charge takes effect as a deed of charge by way of legal mortgage and the authority has the powers under ss 99–109 of the Law of Property Act 1925: Local Land Charges Act 1975, s 7.
5 *Paddington Borough Council v Finucane* [1928] Ch 567.
6 *Bristol Corpn v Virgin* [1928] 2 KB 622.

Legal Services Commission

2.35 Except so far as regulations otherwise provide[1], where services have been funded by the Legal Services Commission as part of the Community Legal Service, sums expended by the Commission in funding the services, and other sums payable by the individual by virtue of regulations, constitute a first charge on any property recovered or preserved by him (whether for himself or any other person) in any proceedings or in any compromise or settlement of any dispute in connection with which the services were provided[2].

Regulations may make provision about the charge, including provision as to whether it is in favour of the Commission or the body or person by whom the services were provided, and provision about its enforcement.

1 Access to Justice Act 1999, s 10.
2 Section 10(7) (formerly the Legal Aid Act 1988 s 16(6)); and see *Morgan v Legal Aid Board* [2000] 3 All ER 974, [2000] 1 WLR 1657. As to the statutory charge, see further the Community Legal Service (Financial) Regulations 2000, SI 2000/516, Pt III.

Solicitor's costs

2.36 Under the Solicitors Act 1974[1] the court is empowered to make a charging order as security for the solicitor's taxed costs[2] over real or personal property[3] recovered or preserved by the solicitor. The property recovered or preserved need not belong to the client[4].

Such a charge may give the solicitor priority over a mortgagee who had notice of the right to claim the order[5].

1 See generally *Cordery on Solicitors*.
2 Solicitors Act 1974, s 73. See generally 44 *Halsbury's Laws* (4th edn), Solicitors, paras 226

ff; and *Currie & Co v Law Society* [1977] QB 990, [1976] 3 All ER 832.
3 See Charging Orders Act 1979 s 2 for a list of the property which may be the subject of an application under the Act.
4 *Greer v Young* (1883) 24 Ch D 545.
5 *Ridd v Thorne* [1902] 2 Ch 344 at 349; *Newport v Pougher* [1937] Ch 214 at 224, 226, [1937] 1 All ER 276, 283, 285, CA. Also see *Wimbourne v Fine* [1952] Ch 869, [1952] 2 All ER 681.

Charge of patient's property

2.37 The Mental Health Act 1983 gives a general power of charging the patient's property[1] and the patient's property may be charged as security for money advanced for the permanent improvement or benefit of any property of the patient[2].

Statutory charges arise in a variety of circumstances. The precise nature of these and the precise nature of the powers conferred on the chargee depend on the terms of the statute conferring the charge.

1 Mental Health Act 1983, s 96 (1) (b).
2 Section 101 (5). Such a charge gives no right of sale or foreclosure during the patient's lifetime: s 101(6). Where the money is advanced out of the patient's general estate the charge should be made in favour of a person as trustee for the patient; s 101 (6).

Where registered land charged

2.38 Where the charge affects registered land and entitles the chargee to enforce it by realisation of the land charged, the chargee must be registered as proprietor of the charge before the land can be realised[1]. This substantive registration is in addition to registration in the local land charges registry, where appropriate, or of a notice or caution on the register of title[2].

While the priority of registered charges normally depends on the order in which they are entered on the register[3], a particular priority may be specified by the relevant statute in the case of certain statutory charges[4] and the register will reflect this[5].

1 See Ruoff & Roper *Registered Conveyancing*, Ch 24, Dispositions by Registered Chargees.
2 See *Rouff & Roper.*
3 Land Registration Act 1925, s 29.
4 See, for example, **2.31**.
5 See Land Registration Act 1925, s 34 (6); Land Registration Rules 1925, rr 157, 158.

VENDOR'S LIEN

Generally[1]

2.39 An equitable lien is an equitable right to a charge independent of contract and possession which arises automatically by operation of law[2]. It is founded on:

(a) the principle of equity that he who has obtained possession of property under a contract for payment of its value will not be allowed to keep it without payment[3]; or
(b) where there is a deposit of deeds creating a lien on the documents, supplementary remedies developed by the courts in such cases.

The unpaid vendor's lien operates as a form of equitable charge implied by law[4] giving the vendor full security in equity for full payment of the agreed purchase price. It confers a right to enforce the lien through a declaration of charge and a court order for sale[5] enabling the vendor to recover the unpaid moneys out of the sale proceeds.

An equitable lien is subject to all the usual conditions affecting equitable rights. Relief may, therefore, be refused where the conduct of the person claiming the right has been improper or where the retention of a lien is clearly inconsistent with the provisions of the contract or essence of the transaction[6].

1 As to liens generally, see 28 *Halsbury's Laws* (4th edn), Liens; Gough *Company Charges* (2nd edn) pp 500-505.
2 *Re Beirnstein, Barnett v Beirnstein* [1925] Ch 12 at 17-18, per Lawrence J; *Capital Finance Co Ltd v Stokes* [1969] 1 Ch 261 at 278, per Harman LJ; *Re Bond Worth Ltd* [1980] Ch 228 at 251, per Slade J; *Barclays Bank plc v Estates and Commercial Ltd* [1997] 1 WLR 415; *Hewett v Court* (1983) 149 CLR 639 at 663 (applied in *Shirlaw v Taylor* (1991) 5 ACSR 767).
3 *Mackreth v Symmons* (1808) 15 Ves 329. See also *Reliance Finance Corpn Pty Ltd v Heid* [1982] NSWLR 467, CA; sub nom *Heid v Reliance Finance Corpn Pty Ltd* (1984) 154 CLR 326.
4 *Hewitt v Court* (1983) 149 CLR 639 at 663.
5 *Re Stucley, Stucley v Kekewich* [1906] 1 Ch 67 at 76-77; *Hewett v Court* (1982) 149 CLR 639 at 663, per Deane J.
6 *Barclays Bank plc v Estates Commercial Ltd* [1997] 1 WLR 415 at 421, per Millett LJ. See also *Gracegrove Estates Ltd v Boateng* [1997] EGCS 103.

Cases in which a lien arises

2.40 Generally, a vendor has a lien for unpaid purchase money in respect of:

(a) freehold and leasehold land[1];
(b) trade machinery[2]; and
(c) choses in action and other personal property[3] where equity would decree specific performance but not goods[4], which are subject to the vendor's statutory lien under the Sale of Goods Act 1979[5].

A vendor's lien may also arise where the purchaser fails to perform acts, the obligation to perform which forms part of the consideration for the sale[6].

1 *Winter v Lord Anson* (1827) 3 Russ 488; *Lysaght v Edwards* (1876) 2 Ch D 499; *Re Birmingham, Savage v Stannard* [1959] Ch 523. See Gray *Elements of Land Law* (3rd edn) pp 609-611.
2 *Re Vulcan Ironworks Co* (1888) 4 TLR 312.
3 For lien in respect of shares, see *Musselwhite v C H Musselwhite & Sons Ltd* [1962] Ch 964, [1962] 1 All ER 201; *Langen and Wind Ltd v Bell* [1972] Ch 685, [1972] 1 All ER 296.
4 *Davies v Thomas* [1900] 2 Ch 462, CA (share of proceeds of sale of leaseholds); *Re Stucley, Stucley v Kekewich* [1906] 1 Ch 67, CA (reversionary interest in a trust fund). For solicitor's lien on title deeds, see *Caldwell v Sumpters* [1972] Ch 478, [1972] 1 All ER 567, CA; and for liens on chattels, eg innkeeper's lien, carrier's lien etc see 28 *Halsburys Laws* (4th edn).
5 See Sale of Goods Act 1979, s 41.
6 *Uziell-Hamilton v Keen* (1971) 22 P & CR 655.

Nature of the lien

2.41 The lien extends to the unpaid price and also to interest on it from the time the lien comes into existence[1]. The lien arises whether the whole or part of the purchase money is unpaid[2] and though a receipt may have been given for it[3] and whether the consideration is a sum in gross or is payable by instalments. The lien also extends to money advanced by the vendor to the purchaser for improvements[4].

1 *Rose v Watson* (1864) 10 HL Cas 672; *Re Stucley*, above.
2 *Elliot v Edwards* (1802) 3 Bos & P 181.
3 *Barclays Bank plc v Estates and Commercial Ltd* [1997] 1 WLR 415 at 420. See *London and Cheshire Insurance Co Ltd v Laplagrene Property Co Ltd* [1971] Ch 499, for the application of s 68 of the Law of Property Act 1925 to registered land.
4 *Re Baker and Harley, ex p Linden* (1841) 1 Mont D & De G 428.

Persons bound by the lien

2.42 The lien binds not only the purchaser and persons claiming under him as volunteers, but also persons having equitable interests and persons claiming under the original purchaser who acquired the legal estate with notice of the non-payment of the purchase money[1].

Where in the deed the consideration is expressed to be paid, but is in fact wholly or partly left unpaid, parol evidence may be given on the part of the purchaser of the actual transaction, because it is the vendor himself who, by claiming a lien, is the first to set up an equity against the written statement in the deed[2].

1 *Elliot v Edwards*, above; *Mackreth v Symmons*, above. This is subject to registration of the lien as a general equitable charge where appropriate (as to registration, see **2.43**).
2 *Winter v Lord Anson*, above.

Protection of the lien

2.43 It seems that a vendor who has such a lien is entitled to or to retain the title deeds[1].

Where the land is unregistered and the vendor does not hold the deeds the lien may be registered under the Land Charges Act 1972 as a Class C (iii) general equitable charge[2].

In the case of registered land, the lien can be protected by notice[3], caution[4] or substantive registration as a charge[5] and if the vendor is in possession his lien is an overriding interest[6].

1 See *Dryden v Frost* (1838) 3 My & Cr 670 at 672, 673.
2 See *Uziell-Hamilton v Keen*, above.
3 Under the Land Registration Act 1925, s 49 (1) (c).
4 Section 49 (1) (c).
5 Section 26.
6 *London and Cheshire Insurance Co Ltd v Laplagrene Property Co Ltd*, above; *UCB Bank Plc v Beasley and France* [1995] NPC 144; *Nationwide Anglia Building Society v Ahmed* (1995) 70 P & CR 381 at 386; *Gracegrove Estates Ltd v Boateng* [1997] EGCS 103.

Enforcement of the lien

2.44 A vendor's lien upon realty is enforceable by sale once the lien has been established by the court[1]. The court may also enforce a lien by appointing a receiver pending sale or by injunction operating to restore possession of the property. The lien of the unpaid vendor also gives him the alternative right to rescind the contract and recover possession[2], but he cannot enforce his lien by foreclosure[3].

1 See *Re Stucley, Stucley v Kekewich*, above.
2 *Lysaght v Edwards* (1876) 2 Ch D 499 at 506.
3 *Munns v Isle of Wight Rly Co* (1870) 5 Ch App 414; cf *Hughes v Griffin* [1969] 1 All ER 460, 461, CA.

Subrogation

2.45 If the unpaid vendor is paid off by a third party, the third party can claim the benefit of the lien by subrogation[1].

1 *Coptic Ltd v Bailey* [1972] Ch 446; *Orakpo v Manson Investments Ltd* [1978] AC 95.

Loss of lien

2.46 It is possible that a lien may never arise because the vendor takes a superior security, for example, where the vendor of property leaves the whole or part of the purchase money outstanding and secured by a mortgage of the property sold[1]. The lien may also be lost by waiver[2] or limitation[3].

1 See *Capital Finance Co Ltd v Stokes* [1969] 1 Ch 261, [1968] 3 All ER 625, CA; *Bank of Ireland Finance Ltd v Daly Ltd* [1978] IR 79; *Re Bond Worth Ltd* [1980] Ch 228 at 251, [1979] 3 All ER 919 at 941.
2 See Chapter 31.
3 See Limitation Act 1980, s 20 (1); *Re Stucley, Stucley v Kekewich* [1906] 1 Ch 67, CA.

Liens and invalid mortgages

2.47 By stipulating for and obtaining a valid mortgage or charge[1] the vendor abandons any claim to the unpaid vendor's lien (which, if it had continued to exist would have ranked in priority to any such mortgage or charge granted subsequently), because the vendor has got what he bargained for, namely a mortgage or charge which was valid and enforceable at its inception. If the mortgage or charge were void from the outset, the lien is not lost, for the vendor cannot be taken to have intended to give up his lien except on the basis of acquiring an effective mortgage or charge[2]. However, if the mortgage or charge were merely unenforceable, the lien is lost, because the lender obtained a valid security, albeit that it was unenforceable[3].

These principles apply also to persons, such as mortgagees advancing money for the purchase of the property to be mortgaged, succeeding to the vendor's lien by subrogation[4] and subsequent mortgagees whose advances are used to discharge prior mortgages, but there will be no lien if the intention was simply to create of an unsecured loan[5].

1 Even though it is later void for non-registration on the liquidation of the purchaser-company (see Chapter 12): *Re Molton Finance Ltd* [1968] Ch 325, [1967] 3 All ER 843, CA; *Capital Finance Co Ltd v Stokes*, above; *Burston Finance Ltd v Speirway Ltd* [1974] 3 All ER 735, [1974] 1 WLR 1648; cf *Coptic Ltd v Bailey* [1972] Ch 446, [1972] 1 All ER 1242, but see (1970) 33 MLR 131.
2 *Thurstan v Nottingham Permanent Benefit Building Society* [1902] 1 Ch 1, CA; on appeal

sub nom *Nottingham Permanent Benefit Building Society v Thurstan* [1903] AC 6, HL; *Orakpo v Manson Investments Ltd* [1978] AC 95, [1977] 3 All ER 1, HL. See also *Re Tramway Building and Construction Co Ltd* [1988] Ch 293, [1987] BCLC 632, sale avoided by Companies Act 1948, s 227 (now Insolvency Act 1986, s 127) and *Bowers v Woolwich Equitable Building Society* (3 February 1987, unreported Hoffman J).

3 *Orakpo v Manson Investments Ltd* [1978] AC 95 at 114, [1977] 3 All ER 1 at 15, 16, HL. Contrast *Bank of Ireland Finance Ltd v D J Daly Ltd* [1978] IR 79.

4 See *Boodle Hatfield & Co v British Films Ltd* [1986] PCC 176, [1986] NLJ Rep 117 where a firm of solicitors had made an unsecured advance to its client in order to facilitate the completion of a purchase before clearance of the client's cheque. Relying on *Orakpo v Manson Investements Ltd* [1978] AC 95, Nicholls J held the firm to have been subrogated to the vendor's lien. This outcome has been rejected in Australia, see *CID v Cortes* (1987) 4 BPR 9391 at 9393. It is also unclear whether *Boodle Hatfield* would have been decided in the same way if the Law of Property (Miscellaneous Provisions) Act 1989 s 2(1) had been in force.

5 See *Paul v Speirway Ltd* [1976] Ch 220, [1976] 2 All ER 587.

Chapter 3

Mortgages of unregistered land

LEGAL MORTGAGES

Generally

3.1 Since 1926 a legal mortgage can be made only by demise, sub-demise or charge by deed expressed to be by way of legal mortgage (hereinafter described, for shorthand purposes, as a 'legal charge')[1]. In practice, the use of a legal charge is nowadays almost invariable.

1 Law of Property Act 1925, s 85 (freehold land) and s 86 (leasehold land).

Mortgages of freehold land

Pre 1926

3.2 Before 1926[1] a mortgage of freehold land was usually made by conveyance subject to a proviso for redemption. Such proviso was originally in the form of a condition that the mortgagor might re-enter or the conveyance itself be void if the debt were repaid by the appointed day but later assumed the form of a covenant for re-conveyance by the mortgagee upon repayment of the debt by the mortgagor by the stipulated time. By such process the mortgagee took a legal estate in the land which became absolute if due repayment was not made, ie if the mortgage was not redeemed.

Further, since a freehold mortgage was made by conveyance, any second or subsequent mortgage was necessarily merely equitable because the mortgagor, not having retained his legal estate, could only mortgage his equity of redemption; there could only be one legal mortgage.

1 For an account of the historical background, see Chapter 1.

Post 1925

3.3 By the Law of Property Act 1925, s 85(1) a legal mortgage must now be made either by demise for a term of years absolute, subject to a provision for cesser on redemption, or by a legal charge[1]. Thus there are only two ways of creating a legal mortgage of freehold land.

Since 1926[2] any purported conveyance of a freehold by way of mortgage (which would, but for the statute, operate to vest the fee simple in the mortgagee subject to redemption) operates (to the extent of the estate of the mortgagor) as a demise of the land to the mortgagee for a term of years absolute, without impeachment for waste, but subject to cesser on redemption[3]. In that event, a first mortgagee takes a term of 3,000 years from the date of the mortgage and a second or subsequent mortgagee takes a term (commencing from the date of the mortgage) one day longer than the term vested in the first or other mortgagee whose security ranks immediately before that of such second or subsequent mortgagee[4]. This is so irrespective of whether the title to the land is registered or the mortgage is expressed to be made by way of trust for sale[5] or otherwise[6]. Since the mortgagor retains the legal estate, he can create second and subsequent mortgages, whether by demise[7] or legal charge, which are legal, as opposed to equitable, interests.

1 Legal charges are considered at **3.17**.
2 For the position before 1926, see **3.2**. The reintroduction of mortgaging by demise (a method which had fallen into desuetude long before the 1925 legislation) was advocated by Sir Arthur Underhill in his pamphlet *The Line of Least Resistance* (printed as an Appendix to the Fourth Report (1920) of the Acquisition of Land Committee) where the idea is attributed to Mr C P Sanger. The object was to keep the legal estate in the mortgagor, so that on a conveyance subject to the mortgage he should be able to transfer a legal estate and not an equitable interest. The difficulties formerly felt as to mortgages by demise are expressly provided against in the Law of Property Act 1925: as to the possession of title deeds by ss 85 (1), 86 (1) and as to sale and foreclosure by ss 88, 89.
3 Law of Property Act 1925, s 85(2).
4 Section 85(2).
5 As to mortgage by way of trust for sale (now trust of land), see **1.8**, n 14.
6 Law of Property Act 1925, s 85(3).
7 In relation to a succession of legal mortgages by demise see the Law of Property Act 1925, s 149(5).

Mortgages of leasehold land

Pre 1926

3.4 Before 1926 a mortgage of leasehold land might be made either by assignment of the term of the lease subject to a proviso for redemption or by way of sub-demise reserving to the mortgagor a nominal reversion out of the term[1]. A mortgage in either form was originally liable to destruction by forfeiture of the term for breach of covenant. Relief against forfeiture was later given by statute[2]. If the whole term was assigned to the mortgagee, he became personally liable to be sued by the lessor for the rent and also on the covenants, whether or not he had entered into possession[3]. Accordingly, of the two methods of making leasehold mortgages mentioned above, the usual and favoured practice was to make the mortgage by sub-demise, since the mortgagee thereby avoided direct liability to the lessor on the covenants in the lease. The sub-demise reserved a nominal reversion of one or more days to the mortgagor[4] and the mortgagor declared that he would hold this on trust for the mortgagee[5]. The mortgagee was usually also given power to remove the mortgagor from the trust and to appoint himself or any other person to be trustee in place of the mortgagor. This enabled the mortgagee, when necessity arose, to appoint himself or a purchaser from him to be trustee of the leasehold reversion and vest it by a vesting declaration[6].

1 The sub-demise would be for the term less one or more days. A mortgage by demise for a term concurrent with a term created by a first or other prior mortgage created a legal term under the subsequent mortgage, the mortgagee acquiring a legal reversion upon the term created by the first mortgage: *Re Moore and Hulm's Contract* [1912] 2 Ch 105; and see now Law of Property Act 1925, s 149 (5).
2 See **3.6** ff.
3 *Williams v Bosanquet* (1819) 1 Brod & Bing 238.
4 See *Bonner v Tottenham and Edmonton Permanent Investment Building Society* [1899] 1 QB 161, CA.
5 This did not render the mortgagee liable to the lessor under the lease: *Walters v Northern Coal Mining Co* (1855) 5 De GM & G 629.
6 *London and County Banking Co v Goddard* [1897] 1 Ch 642. An earlier device was to appoint the mortgagee the attorney of the mortgagor to convey the nominal reversion and sometimes mortgages contained both devices.

Post 1925

3.5 The Law of Property Act 1925, s 86 abrogated the method of effecting leasehold mortgages by assignment of the term and instead provided that the means of mortgaging leasehold land is now by sub-demise of the mortgagor's term of years absolute, less one day at least[1], and subject to a provision for cesser on redemption, or alternatively by legal charge. It thereby made the position analogous to that applicable to mortgages of freehold land. Thus there are only two ways of creating a mortgage of leasehold land. If the land is sub-demised, the term remains vested in the mortgagor, but, since statutory provision is also made for getting in the nominal reversion when the security has to be realised[2], the insertion in the mortgage of a trust of the reversion has become unnecessary.

Where, under the terms of the mortgagor's lease, licence to sub-demise by way of mortgage is required, such licence shall not be unreasonably refused[3].

Since 1926 any purported[4] assignment of a term of years absolute by way of mortgage (which would, but for the statute, operate to vest the term in the mortgagee subject to redemption) operates (to the extent of the estate of the mortgagor) as a sub-demise of the land to the mortgagee for a term of years absolute, but subject to cesser on redemption[5]. In that event, a first mortgagee takes a term ten days less than the term expressed to be assigned and a second or subsequent mortgagee takes a term one day longer than the term vested in the first or other mortgagee whose security ranks immediately before that of such second or subsequent mortgagee, if the length of the last mentioned term[6] permits, and in any case for a term less by one day at least than the term expressed to be assigned[7]. This is so irrespective of whether the title to the land is registered or the mortgage expressed to be made by way of trust for sale[8] or otherwise[9].

As with freehold mortgages, a mortgagor can create second and subsequent mortgages of leasehold land, whether by sub-demise[10] or legal charge, and such mortgages can create legal interests in such land.

Even today, a mortgage of leasehold land remains vulnerable to destruction by forfeiture of the mortgaged lease for breach of covenant. For this reason alone, a freehold presents a better security than a leasehold. Relief against forfeiture is discussed in the following paragraphs.

1 This is because if it were for the whole of the term of the lease it would take effect as an assignment thereof: *Beardman v Wilson* (1868) LR 4 CP 57.
The usual practice is to make the sub-term ten days shorter than the term of the lease, thereby catering for the possibility of second and subsequent mortgages. Failure to so provide is not fatal because a lease may take effect in reversion upon another lease of the same or greater length: Law of Property Act 1925, s 149(5).

2 Section 89. See **20.41**.
3 Section 89.
4 Though expressed as an absolute assignment of the term a document intended to be a mortgage operates by way of sub-demise: see *Grangeside Properties Ltd v Collingwoods Securities Ltd* [1964] 1 All ER 143, CA.
5 Law of Property Act 1925, s 86(2).
6 Ie that held by the immediately superior mortgagee.
7 Section 86(2).
8 As to mortgage by way of trust for sale (now trust of land), see **1.8**, n 14.
9 Law of Property Act 1925, s 86(3).
10 In relation to a succession of legal mortgages by sub-demise see the Law of Property Act 1925, s 149(5).

Relief against forfeiture of leasehold land

3.6 As previously stated, the liability of a mortgagee of leasehold property to lose his security by forfeiture[1] incurred by the mortgagor has been lessened by statute[2].

1 Where the benefit of a mortgage has become vested in the landlord, the evidence of forfeiture must be unequivocal: *Hone v Daejan Properties Ltd* (1976) 120 Sol Jo 488, CA. For protection from eviction, see Protection from Eviction Act 1977, ss 2 and 3.
2 Forfeiture for non-payment of rent might be avoided by the lender paying the rent and adding the amount to the security: see **16.5**. As to non-repair, the mortgage will usually give the lender the right to enter and repair and to add the cost to the security: see **3.43**.

Relief against forfeiture for breach of covenant except failure to pay rent

In cases of forfeiture by court action: High Court and county court

3.7 Where the lessor is proceeding, by action or otherwise, to enforce a right of re-entry or forfeiture, the court can, pursuant to s 146 of the Law of Property Act 1925, grant discretionary relief to the mortgagee either as 'lessee'[1] or as 'underlessee'[2] (which expressions include a mortgagee by demise or sub-demise and a legal chargee and anyone entitled to call for such a mortgage[3])[4]. However, relief under s 146 is not available to the holder of an equitable charge (as opposed to an equitable mortgagee)[5].

For the above purposes a lessor who seeks to forfeit by instituting a claim for possession is 'proceeding' to enforce his right of re-entry until the time when he actually recovers possession of the land pursuant to a lawfully executed judgment of the court. Consequently, the application for relief may be at any time before then. But once the lessor has so recovered the land, the jursidiction to grant relief is ousted[6].

Where relief is obtained under s 146(2), the lease (and any derivative interests, including mortgages) is retrospectively restored as if there had never been a forfeiture[7]. Therefore, no liability to pay mesne profits arises[8]. A further attraction, from the mortgagee's perspective, is (it is considered[9]) that the mortgagee assumes no direct liability to the lessor under the covenants in the lease.

On the other hand, where relief is obtained under s 146(4), a vesting order is made in favour of the successful applicant, eg the mortgagee[10]. The effect of such an order is to vest in the party in question a new lease for a term not exceeding that under his sub-lease[11], and upon such other terms as to payment of rent, compensation and otherwise as the court may think fit[12]. A mortgagee of part of the premises demised by the forfeited lease is eligible for relief under s 146(4)[13].

A vesting order in favour of a mortgagee binds the mortgagee directly to the lessor, but the relationship of mortgagor and mortgagee remains nevertheless, ie the new lease granted to the mortgagee is a substituted security and is subject to the mortgage[14]. Moreover, a vesting order under s 146(4) is not retrospective and does not operate to revive the original lease and derivative interests which were destroyed by the forfeiture[15]. Accordingly, the applicant may be required to pay, as a condition of relief, mesne profits for the period between the forfeiture and the making of the vesting order[16].

Where a mortgagee could obtain relief under s 146(2) or s 146(4), the court has a discretion as to which form of relief to grant[17]. The perceived unattractiveness of a lessor, who forfeits a long lease granted in return for a substantial premium on the basis of a minor breach[18], obtaining a perceived windfall by way of mesne profits at a rack rent level may well incline the court in favour of granting retrospective relief under s 146(2) in such circumstances[19].

The equitable jurisdiction of the High Court[20] to grant relief against forfeiture in respect of breaches of covenant except failure to pay rent has been wholly superseded by statute[21]. In such cases it is now the Law of Property Act 1925, s 146 which exclusively governs the granting of relief. Hence if the statutory jurisdiction does not apply, no relief can be granted.

Where relief is sought, it may be claimed in the proceedings brought by the lessor, if any, or in separate proceedings instituted by the applicant lessee or mortgagee for the purpose of securing relief. A claim for relief can be made within winding-up proceedings[22].

1 Under the Law of Property Act 1925, s 146(2): see *Escalus Properties Ltd v Robinson* [1996] QB 231, CA, not following *Nind v Nineteenth Century Building Society* [1894] 2 QB 226, CA. The decision, which went against orthodox opinion and came as a surprise to many, rests on the fact that the expression 'lessee' is afforded a wide definition by the Law of Property Act 1925, s 146(5)(b) as including an original or derivative underlessee and the persons deriving title under a lessee. It was described as a somewhat remarkable decision in *Bank of Ireland Home Mortgages v South Lodge Developments* [1996] 1 EGLR 91.

2 Under the Law of Property Act 1925, s 146(4).

3 See: *Re Good's Lease* [1954] 1 All ER 275, [1954] 1 WLR 309; *Grand Junction Co Ltd v Bates* [1954] 2 QB 160, [1954] 2 All ER 385; *Chelsea Estates Investment Trust Co Ltd v Marche* [1955] Ch 328, [1955] 1 All ER 195; *Belgravia Insurance Co Ltd v Meah* [1964] 1 QB 436, [1963] 3 All ER 828, CA (where the principles applicable to claims by an underlessee or mortgagee by sub-demise are fully dealt with); *Purley Automobile Co Ltd v Aldon Motors* (1968) 112 Sol Jo 482, CA; *Egerton v Jones* [1939] 2 KB 702, CA.

4 A mortgagee, as undertenant, can obtain relief under s 146(4) where the lease has been forfeited following a disclaimer of the same by the lessee's trustee in bankruptcy: *Barclays Bank plc v Prudential Assurance Co Ltd* [1998] 1 EGLR 44.

5 *Bland v Ingrams Estates Ltd* [2001] 2 WLR 1638, [2001] 24 EG 163, CA, a case concerned with the holder of a charging order (treated as an equitable chargee by s 3(4) of the Charging Orders Act 1979).

6 *Billson v Residential Apartments Ltd* [1992] 1 AC 494, HL.

7 *Dendy v Evans* [1910] 1 KB 263, CA.

8 *Escalus Properties Ltd v Robinson* [1996] QB 231, CA.

9 This view is based on the premise that the lease, when retrospectively revived, remains vested in the lessee and is not statutorily put into the hands of the mortgagee. If the position is otherwise, direct liability will necessarily be assumed by the mortgagee, although the consequences of such liability may be limited in the case of leases granted after the coming into force of the Landlord and Tenant (Covenants) Act 1995 (which abrogates original tenant liability).

The point does not seem to have been directly in issue in *Escalus Properties Ltd v Dennis* [1996] QB 231, CA where the real concern of the mortgagee was to avoid liability for payment of mesne profits. Such avoidance flows simply from the retrospective nature of relief under s 146(2), irrespective of the person (whether lessee or mortgagee) in whom the lease is so restored.

Support for the view expressed above is found in *Bland v Ingram's Estates Ltd* [2001] 2 WLR 1638, [2001] 24 EG 163, CA (a case concerned not with s 146 but with the inherent jurisdiction of the court) where Chadwick LJ, having referred to the reasoning in *Croydon (Unique) Ltd v Wright* [2001] Ch 318, [2000] 2 WLR 683, [1999] 4 All ER 257, CA, said (at para 70), 'There is no reason, in principle, why … the court should not make an order that restores the pre-existing lease—with the consequence that the former lessee remains liable under the covenants in that lease.' He then referred to the applicant for relief offering 'satisfactory indemnities to the lessee against the lessee's continuing liability under the restored lease—and, perhaps, to assume some liability to the landlord as surety for the performance of those covenants'. Further, at para 71 he spoke of 'a claim for relief in a form that restores or revives the pre-existing lease, under which the former lessee remains tenant …. The applicant claims to be entitled to make the application for relief that the lessee could have made, and to have relief in the form that would be granted upon an application by the lessee … The applicant does not claim a right to become tenant of the property under the restored lease'.

See also *Croydon (Unique) Ltd v Wright* (a case dealing with s 138 of the County Courts Act 1984): Sir Christopher Staughton appears at 693 to have contemplated that retrospective relief restores the original lease in the hands of the lessee, not the applicant mortgagee, hence his reference to the applicant thereafter applying for an order for sale.

Cf, however, *Bank of Ireland Home Mortgages v South Lodge Developments* [1996] 1 EGLR 91 in which Lightman J, commenting on the decision in *Escalus* in relation to s 138, said, 'a lease may be vested in the mortgagee with retrospective effect and accordingly the mortgagee is to be treated as lessee'.

10 Relief for underlessees under s 146(4) is not subject to the restrictions on relief contained in ss 146(8) and (9): Law of Property (Amendment) Act 1929, s 1. See *Grangeside Properties Ltd v Collingwoods Securities Ltd* [1964] 1 All ER 143, CA.

11 *Ewart v Fryer* [1901] 1 Ch 499 at 515, CA; *Factors (Sundries) Ltd v Miller* [1952] 2 All ER 630 at 634, CA. The Law of Property Act 1925, s 146(4) provides that the court may vest the demised premises in the underlessee for the whole term of the lease or any less term, but the underlessee shall not be entitled to require a lease to be granted to him for any longer term than he had under his original sub-lease. The above cases decided that the latter of these conflicting provisions prevails. See also *Chelsea Estates Investment Trust Co Ltd v Marche*, above, and *Belgravia Insurance Co Ltd v Meah*, above.

12 *Ewart v Fryer*, above; *Gray v Bonsall* [1904] 1 KB 601 at 604, CA.

13 Where the mortgage is of part of the demised premises relief may be given to the underlessee of the part on terms of his paying the whole of the arrears under the head lease: *Webber v Smith*(1689) 2 Vern 103; cf *Chatham Empire Theatre (1955) Ltd v Ultrans* [1961] 2 All ER 381, [1961] 1 WLR 817 (in which *Webber v Smith* was not considered) where it was held that the underlessee might have to pay only an apportioned part of the arrears.

14 *Chelsea Estates Investment Trust Co Ltd v Marche*, above.

15 *Hammersmith and Fulham London Borough Council v Top Shop Centres Ltd* [1990] Ch 237.

16 Pending any order, a receiver appointed by the mortgagee is not entitled to the rents of tenanted premises: *Official Custodian for Charities v Mackey* [1985] Ch 168, [1984] 3 All ER 689; and see also *Official Custodian for Charities v Mackey (No 2)* [1985] 2 All ER 1016, [1985] 1 WLR 1308.

The mortgagee could seek protection, eg against the reduction in the value of the property, during the intervening period: *Official Custodian for Charities v Mackey* [1985] Ch 168 at 189, [1984] 3 All ER 689 at 702.

17 *Escalus Properties Ltd v Robinson* [1996] QB 231, CA.

18 Eg a small sum of unpaid service charge (not reserved as rent).

19 *Escalus Properties Ltd v Robinson* [1996] QB 231, CA. Since it appears that relief under s 146(2) preserves the direct relationship between lessor and (recalcitrant) lessee (see n 9 above), such relief may, in the exercise of the court's discretion, be granted upon the application of a mortgagee solely for the purpose of enabling it thereafter to apply for an order for sale and on condition that it do so: *Croydon (Unique) Ltd v Wright* [2001] Ch 318, [1999] 4 All ER 257, CA.

20 The county court, being a creature of statute, has no inherent jurisdiction to grant relief: *Di Palma v Victoria Square Property Co Ltd* [1986] Ch 150, CA; *United Dominions Trust Ltd v Shellpoint Trustees Ltd* [1993] 4 All ER 310, CA.

21 *Billson v Residential Apartments Ltd* [1992] 1 AC 494, CA (unaffected by reversal by HL on another issue), following *Official Custodian for Charities v Parway Estates Developments Ltd* [1985] Ch 151, CA (a case concerned with s 146(10) which does not affect the operation

of s 146(4): see the Law of Property (Amendment) Act 1929, s 1), approving *Smith v Metropolitan City Properties* [1986] 1 EGLR 52 and overruling *Abbey National Building Society v Maybeech Ltd* [1985] Ch 190.

22 *Re Brompton Securities Ltd (No 2)* [1988] 3 All ER 677, [1988] 2 EGLR 95. Cf *Re Blue Jeans Sales Ltd* [1979] 1 All ER 641.

In cases of forfeiture by physical re-entry: High Court and county court

3.8 In such instances relief may be obtained under the Law of Property Act 1925, ss 146(2) and (4) as appropriate, subject to the matters and with the consequences outlined above.

However, the position of a lessor who has forfeited the lease by peaceable re-entry is markedly different from that of a lessor who has invoked the assistance of the court in enforcing his right of forfeiture for in such event the court's power to grant relief survives the physical recovery of the land[1] (since the lessor is viewed as still 'proceeding'[2] to enforce his right for the purposes of the Law of Property Act 1925, s 146) and thus there is no fixed period within which an application for relief must be brought, although relief will not be given in respect of stale claims[3].

As noted above, an equitable chargee is not entitled to relief under s 146[4]. Consequently, any entitlement to relief depends upon the inherent jurisdiction of the High Court[5]. But the High Court's inherent jursidiction to grant relief is restricted to cases where the applicant is entitled to possession or holds a legal estate or equitable interest in the land[6] and, consequently, an equitable chargee[7] (unlike an equitable mortgagee) is precluded from obtaining relief in his own right where the lessee does not himself claim relief. Moreover, it is uncertain whether an equitable chargee is entitled to seek relief indirectly, ie to require the former lessee to apply for relief[8], in cases of forfeiture for breaches other than non-payment of rent[9].

1 Law of Property Act, ss 146(2) and (4).
2 The language of s 146(2) and (4).
3 *Thatcher v C H Pearce & Sons (Contractors) Ltd* [1968] 1 WLR 748, CA.
4 *Bland v Ingrams Estates Ltd* [2001] 2 WLR 1638, [2001] 24 EG 163, CA.
5 The county court has no such inherent jurisdiction, being a creature of statute.
6 *Bland v Ingrams Estates Ltd* [2001] 2 WLR 1638, [2001] 24 EG 163, CA.
7 For example, the holder of a charging order.
8 Based upon the chargor's equitable duty (against a sufficient indemnity from the chargee) to take reasonable steps to preserve the security, as to which see *Bland v Ingrams Estates Ltd* [2001] 2 WLR 1638, [2001] 24 EG 163, CA.
9 The point was left open in *Bland v Ingrams Estates Ltd* [2001] 2 WLR 1638, [2001] 24 EG 163 at para 33, CA, per Nourse LJ.

Principles as to terms of relief granted

3.9 In general, the lessor is entitled, by the grant of relief against forfeiture, to be restored to the position in which he would have been had the forfeiture not been triggered, ie had there been no breach of covenant. Thus ordinarily, though not invariably, it will be a condition of relief that the underlying breach(es) be remedied and the landlord's costs both of the forfeiture and the grant of relief be paid. For detailed consideration of the factors relevant to the terms on which relief may be granted, see *Woodfall on Landlord and Tenant* vol 1, Chapter 17. In all instances, the granting of relief against forfeiture remains in the discretion of the court, although such discretion falls to be exercised consistently with principle.

Relief against forfeiture for non-payment of rent

Generally

3.10 The Law of Property Act 1925, s 146(2), as to which see **3.7**, does not apply where the forfeiture is based upon unpaid rent (or unpaid service charges reserved and payable as rent[1])[2].

1 *Escalus Properties Ltd v Robinson* [1996] QB 231, CA.
2 Law of Property Act 1925, s 146(11).

In cases of forfeiture by court action: High Court

3.11 Relief against forfeiture for non-payment of rent can be obtained under the Common Law Procedure Act 1852, s 212, such statutory right to relief being available to an underlessee (including a legal mortgagee or chargee)[1]. This section applies only where at least half a year's rent is in arrears[2]. Where, however, it does operate, if all the rent and the lessor's costs are paid to the lessor or into court before the trial of the claim, the forfeiture proceedings are automatically brought to an end.

Alternatively, relief is available to an underlessee (including a mortgagee by sub-demise or a legal chargee) under the Law of Property Act 1925, s 146(4), as to which see **3.7**. As noted above, such relief is only available before the lessor has recovered possession of the land pursuant to a court order[3].

Relief can also be obtained under the Supreme Court Act 1981, s 38[4]. By this provision in any proceedings brought by a lessor for forfeiture for non-payment of rent, the court is empowered to grant relief against forfeiture in a summary manner, subject to the same terms and conditions as to the payment of rent, costs or otherwise as could historically have been imposed by the Courts of Chancery.

Further, under the Common Law Procedure Act, s 210 a legal mortgagee or chargee is entitled as a person 'claiming or deriving [title] under the lease'[5] to relief on the same terms as the lessee[6] and accordingly he can obtain discretionary relief if he is willing, within six months after judgment enforcing the forfeiture, to pay all arrears, costs and damages, and to perform all covenants, unless in the meantime third parties have acquired rights which would be thereby infringed[7]. The section applies only where at least half a year's rent is in arrears and if this is not the case it affords the court no jurisdiction to grant relief. If relief is granted under s 210, the lessee holds the land accordingly to the old lease, without any new lease[8]. In other words, such relief retrospectively reinstates the lease as if there had been no forfeiture. However, after the lapse of six months following recovery of possession by the lessor, any claim for relief is barred[9]. This is, therefore, an important time-limit for a mortgagee to bear in mind.

Finally, it appears that the High Court retains its inherent jurisdiction and can grant relief in cases falling outside the Supreme Court Act 1981, s 38 and the Common Law Procedure Act 1852, s 210[10].

1 *Doe d Wyatt v Byron* (1845) 1 CB 623, a case on the Landlord and Tenant Act 1730, s 4, the statutory predecessor of ss 210 and 212, in which it was held that the word 'tenant' in this context includes an underlessee.
2 The words 'in all cases ... as often as it shall happen that one half year's rent shall be in arrear' appear not in s 212 but in s 210. However, they were held to apply also to s 212 in *Standard Pattern Co Ltd v Ivey* [1962] Ch 432.
3 *Billson v Residential Apartments Ltd* [1992] 1 AC 494, HL.
4 Previously the Supreme Court of Judicature (Consolidation) Act 1925, s 46 and before that the Common Law Procedure Act 1860, s 1. The statutes recognise the equitable

jurisdiction to grant relief for non-payment of rent, the proviso for re-entry being regarded as merely a security for rent: *Howard v Fanshawe* [1895] 2 Ch 581 at 588. See, generally, *Gill v Lewis* [1956] 2 QB 1, [1956] 1 All ER 844; and *Belgravia Insurance Co Ltd v Meah* [1964] 1 QB 436, [1963] 3 All ER 828, CA.

5 *Moore v Smee and Cornish* [1907] 2 KB 8, CA.

6 *Doe d Whitfield v Roe* (1811) 3 Taunt 402. A mortgagee may be required to pay the landlord's costs of the proceedings against the tenant: *Egerton v Jones* [1939] 2 KB 702, [1939] 3 All ER 889, CA.

7 *Hare v Elms* [1893] 1 QB 604; *Newbolt v Bingham* (1895) 72 LT 852, CA; *Howard v Fanshawe*, above; *Humphreys v Morten* [1905] 1 Ch 739. Note that there is no time limit where the landlord has re-entered peaceably without an order of the court.

8 Common Law Procedure Act 1852, s 212.

9 Section 210.

10 *Ladup Ltd v Williams & Glyn's Bank* [1985] 1 WLR 851 (in which Warner J refused to strike out a claim for relief against forfeiture made by an equitable chargee under the inherent equitable jurisdiction of the High Court). See also *Bland v Ingrams Estates Ltd* [2001] 2 WLR 1638, [2001] 24 EG 163, CA (in which the forfeiture had, in fact, been effected by peaceable re-entry).

In cases of forfeiture by court action: county court

3.12 As in the High Court, relief is available to an underlessee (including a mortgagee by sub-demise or a legal chargee) under the Law of Property Act 1925, s 146(4), as to which see **3.7**. As noted above, such relief is only available before the lessor has recovered possession of the land pursuant to a court order[1].

Also, in cases where the lessor is proceeding by action[2] to enforce a right of re-entry or forfeiture relief is available under the County Courts Act 1984, s 138 (as amended by the Administration of Justice Act 1985, s 55). Where the statute applies, relief may be granted to a mortgagee (including a mortgagee by demise or sub-demise and a legal chargee) either as 'lessee'[3] or as 'underlessee'[4]. An equitable chargee is also eligible for such relief[5].

Under s 138(2) if all the rent in arrear[6] and the costs of the proceedings are paid into court by the lessee at least five clear days before the return day, the claim ceases and the land is held according to the lease without any new lease, ie as if there had been no forfeiture[7]. If the proceedings do not cease then, by virtue of ss 138(3) and (5), if at trial the lessor's entitlement to enforce the right of re-entry is upheld by the court, relief to similar effect will automatically be obtained provided that, within the period specified by the possession order made by the court (which period must be at least four weeks[8] and may be extended at any time before possession is recovered pursuant to the order[9]), all the rent in arrear[10] and the costs of the proceedings (not merely the fixed issue costs)[11] are paid by the lessee into court or to the lessor.

In addition, s 138(9A) confers upon the lessee a further opportunity to obtain relief even where he has failed to avail himself of the chances afforded by ss 138(2) and (5). This takes the form of an entitlement to apply for relief within six months of recovery of the land by the lessor. Such period, unlike the time for payment specified in the possession order under s 138(3), is not extendable. Hence, this constitutes the lessee's final chance to obtain relief. However, whereas relief under ss 138(2) and (5) is automatic, the grant of relief under s 138(9A) is discretionary. If obtained though, the forfeited lease (and all derivative interests) is retrospectively revived[12].

The advantages, from a mortgagee's standpoint, of relief being obtained by the mortgagee in the shoes of the lessee are set out at **3.7**.

In the alternative, a legal mortgagee or chargee may seek relief in his own right under s 138(9C). The principles outlined above apply similarly in this respect—most notably, the six month time-limit from recovery of possession by the lessor—save that, if successful, the mortgagee obtains a vesting order which vests in him a new lease, held directly of the lessor, for the remainder of the term of the forfeited lease or for any lesser term. This form of relief thus mirrors that available under by the Law of Property Act 1925, s 146(4) as to which see **3.7**.

Where a mortgagee could obtain relief as 'lessee' under ss 138(5) or (9A) or (as 'a person with an interest under a lease of the land derived (whether immediately or otherwise) from the lessee's interest') under s 138(9C), the court has a discretion as to which form of relief to grant[13]. The perceived unattractiveness of a lessor, who forfeits a long lease granted in return for a substantial premium on the basis of small arrears, obtaining a perceived windfall in the form of mesne profits at a rack rent level may well incline the court in favour of granting retrospective relief under ss 138(5) or (9A) in such circumstances[14].

If a person fails to obtain relief against forfeiture under the provisions of the County Courts Act 1984, s 138, he is barred from all relief, whether in the county court or the High Court[15].

1 *Billson v Residential Apartments Ltd* [1992] 1 AC 494, HL.
2 As to the meaning of this expression see **3.7**.
3 Under the County Courts Act 1984, ss 138(2), (5) and (9A): see *United Dominions Trust Ltd v Shellpoint Trustees Ltd* [1993] 4 All ER 310, CA and *Escalus Properties Ltd v Robinson* [1996] QB 231, CA. The earlier decision rests on the fact that the expression 'lessee' is afforded a wide definition by the County Courts Act 1984, s 140 as including an original or derivative underlessee and the persons deriving title under a lessee.
4 Under the County Courts Act 1984, s 138(9C).
5 *Croydon (Unique) Ltd v Wright* [2001] Ch 318, [1999] 4 All ER 257, CA in which it was held that the holder of a charging order was entitled to apply under ss 138(9C) and that the relief available to such an applicant was not confined to relief under that subsection but also included relief under s 138(9A).
6 Which means all the rent in arrear at the date on which relief is to be obtained and so includes all rent falling due between the date of forfeiture and the granting of relief: *Maryland Estates Ltd v Joseph* [1999] 1 WLR 83, CA.
7 This is thus a similar, though not identical, provision to the Common Law Procedure Act 1852, s 212.
8 Section 138(3).
9 Section 138(4).
10 As to which see n 6.
11 *Sella House Ltd v Mears* (1988) 21 HLR 147; *Swordheath Properties Ltd v Bolt* [1992] 2 EGLR 68.
12 Since relief is retrospective, it can be obtained despite the lessor having re-let the land in the meantime: *Bank of Ireland Home Mortgages v South Lodge Developments* [1996] 1 EGLR 91. In that scenario, if relief be granted to the mortgagee, the reinstated lease may be vested in the mortgagee either in reversion upon the new lease or with priority to the same and, further, if it takes effect in reversion upon the new lease, the mortgagee will be entitled to any premium of rent paid by the new lessee to the lessor as moneys had and received.
13 *Escalus Properties Ltd v Robinson* [1996] QB 231, CA.
14 *Escalus Properties Ltd v Robinson*, above.
15 *Di Palma v Victoria Square Property Co Ltd* [1986] Ch 150, CA; *United Dominions Trust Ltd v Shellpoint Trustees Ltd* [1993] 4 All ER 310, CA; *Escalus Properties Ltd v Robinson* [1996] QB 231, CA. Section 138(7). This provision thus echoes the Common Law Procedure Act 1852, s 210.

In cases of forfeiture by physical re-entry: High Court

3.13 The High Court has power to grant relief under its inherent equitable jurisdiction where a lease has been forfeited for non-payment of rent by peaceable re-entry[1]. There is no prescribed period within which an application for such relief must be brought, although relief will not be given in respect of stale claims[2].

The High Court's inherent jursidiction to grant relief is restricted to cases where the applicant is entitled to possession or holds a legal estate or equitable interest in the land[3]. Consequently, an equitable chargee[4] (unlike an equitable mortgagee) is precluded from obtaining relief in his own right where the lessee does not himself claim relief. However, such a person is entitled to seek relief indirectly: the chargee can require the former lessee to apply for relief, there being an equitable obligation upon the chargor to do so (against a sufficient indemnity from the chargee) by virtue of the duty to take reasonable steps to preserve the security[5]. In that event, the lessee must be made a party for the purposes of the order for relief[6].

1 *Howard v Fanshawe* [1895] 2 Ch 581; *Lovelock v Margo* [1963] 2 QB 786, CA; *Ladup Ltd v Williams & Glyn's Bank* [1985] 1 WLR 851; *Billson v Residential Apartments Ltd* [1992] 1 AC 494, CA (unaffected by reversal on other grounds).
2 *Thatcher v C H Pearce & Sons (Contractors) Ltd* [1968] 1 WLR 748, CA.
3 *Bland v Ingrams Estates Ltd* [2001] 2 WLR 1638, [2001] 24 EG 163, CA.
4 For example, the holder of a charging order.
5 *Bland v Ingrams Estates Ltd* [2001] 2 WLR 1638, [2001] 24 EG 163, CA.
6 *Bland v Ingrams Estates Ltd*, above.

In cases of forfeiture by physical re-entry: county court

3.14 The county court may grant relief to a lessee or underlessee (including a legal mortgagee or chargee) at any time within six months of the date on which the lessor peaceably recovered possession of the land[1]. It seems that such relief is probably available to an equitable chargee, such as the holder of a charging order[2].

The county court, being a creature of statute, has no inherent jurisdiction to grant relief[3]. Consequently, after the expiry of the six month period, the county court is unable to grant relief in a case where the lessor has forfeited by peaceable re-entry for non-payment of rent.

1 County Courts Act 1984, s 139(2).
2 *Bland v Ingrams Estates Ltd* [2001] 2 WLR 1638, [2001] 24 EG 163, CA, per Chadwick LJ (at paras 63-67) and Hale LJ (at para 87)—both obiter, though applying the reasoning in *Croydon (Unique) Ltd v Wright* [2001] Ch 318, [1999] 4 All ER 257, CA (a case concerned with the County Courts Act 1984, s 138).
3 *Di Palma v Victoria Square Property Co Ltd* [1986] Ch 150, CA; *United Dominions Trust Ltd v Shellpoint Trustees Ltd* [1993] 4 All ER 310, CA.

Principles as to terms of relief granted

3.15 In cases where the precise terms of relief are not circumscribed by statute, it is nonetheless the almost invariable practice of the court, consonant with established principle, to require that all arrears of rent be paid to the lessor within a specified period. In addition, the applicant for relief will customarily have to pay the lessor's costs. For detailed consideration of the factors relevant to the terms on which relief may be granted, see *Woodfall on Landlord and Tenant*, vol 1, Chapter 17. Except where statute provides for mandatory relief, the granting of relief against forfeiture remains in the discretion of the court, although such discretion must be exercised consistently with the principle that the proviso for re-entry is merely a means of securing payment of the rent.

Surrender of leasehold land

3.16 A surrender of mortgaged leaseholds does not extinguish the mortgagee's interest and the mortgagee will thereupon be entitled to possession[1].

1 *Usher's Brewery Ltd v P S King & Co (Finance) Ltd* (1969) 113 Sol Jo 815; *E S Schwab & Co Ltd v McCarthy* (1975) 31 P & CR 196 at 209, CA. See also *London and County (A and D) Ltd v Wilfred Sportsman Ltd* [1971] Ch 764, [1970] 2 All ER 600, CA.

Legal charge of freehold or leasehold land

3.17 As noted in **3.1**, the alternative to creating a legal mortgage by demise of the fee simple (in the case of freehold land) or by sub-demise of a term of years (in the case of leasehold land) is to create it by a legal charge, ie 'a charge by deed expressed[1] to be by way of legal mortgage'. Such a charge does not create an actual or notional[2] term in the mortgagee, but it puts him in the same position as regards protection, powers and remedies (including the right to take proceedings to obtain possession from the occupiers and the persons in receipt of rents and profits, or any of them) as if a term (of 3,000 years, in the case of freehold land[3]) or a sub-term (equivalent to the term vested in the mortgagor less one day, in the case of leasehold land[4]) had been created in favour of the mortgagee[5]. It ranks as a legal interest[6] and in questions of priority it ranks as a legal estate[7]. The chargee of leasehold land may protect his charge by applying for relief against forfeiture[8].

The Law of Property Act 1925, ss 87 (2) and (3) deal with the conversion of mortgages existing on 1 January 1926 into legal charges upon a declaration in writing to that effect signed by the mortgagee.

1 The statement that the charge is made 'by way of legal mortgage' need not appear in a registered charge: Land Registration Act 1925, ss 25 and 27(1) and *Cityland and Property (Holdings) Ltd v Dabrah* [1968] Ch 166. The position in relation to unregistered land is less clear: in *Sopher v Mercer* [1967] CLY 2543, Cty Ct, it was held that the actual words were not necessary. *Sed quaere?*
2 *Weg Motors Ltd v Hales* [1962] Ch 49 at 73, 84, 77, [1961] 3 All ER 181 at 190, 192; *Cumberland Court (Brighton) Ltd v Taylor* [1964] Ch 29, [1963] 2 All ER 536; *Thompson v Salah* [1972] 1 All ER 530; and see *Edwards v Marshall-Lee* (1975) 119 Sol Jo 506. In *Ushers Brewery Ltd v P S King & Co (Finance) Ltd*, above, the legal charge was assumed to create a notional term.
3 As to which see the Law of Property Act 1925, s 85(2) and **3.3**.
4 As to which see the Law of Property Act 1925, s 86(2) and **3.5**.
5 Law of Property Act 1925, s 87(1). *Grand Junction Co Ltd v Bates* [1954] 2 QB 160 at 168, [1954] 2 All ER 385 at 388; *Belgravia Insurance Co ltd v Meah* [1964] 1 QB 436 at 443, [1963] 3 All ER 828 at 831; *Regent Oil Co Ltd v J A Gregory (Hatch End) Ltd* [1966] Ch 402 at 431, [1965] 3 All ER 673 at 681. Also see *Thompson v Salah* [1972] 1 All ER 530; (1978) 94 LQR 571 at 576–577 (Jackson).
6 Law of Property Act 1925, ss 1(2)(c) and (4).
7 *Caunce v Caunce* [1969] 1 All ER 722, [1969] 1 WLR 286.
8 See **3.7** ff.

Advantages of the legal charge

3.18 The legal charge has certain advantages over the mortgage by demise or sub-demise. The same document may conveniently be used for mortgaging both freeholds and leaseholds. The basic form of a legal charge is probably more intelligible to a mortgagor[1]. Where leasehold property is charged a legal charge probably does not amount to a breach of a covenant in the lease (if any) against sub-letting[2]. However, this last advantage is negligible nowadays since most leases contain restrictions on all forms of alienation including, specifically, the creation of charges.

There is, however, said to be an objection to the use of the legal charge. A legal charge need not contain a proviso for redemption[3]. Accordingly it is argued that the mortgagee cannot foreclose, since the date at which the mortgagor's right of redemption (and consequently the mortgagee's right to foreclose) is to arise is not fixed. However, it is clear from the Law of Property Act 1925, ss 87, 88 and 89 that the legal chargee has a right of foreclosure and it can be safely assumed that the right of the legal chargee to foreclose arises on the mortgagor's default in repaying at the date fixed in the covenant for repayment or if no date is fixed, on breach of, eg, the covenant to pay interest[4]. Moreover, in practice this problem remains theoretical because a proviso for redemption is generally included in a legal charge, thereby fixing the date when the chargee's rights become absolute and his entitlement to foreclose arises.

1 Maitland described the mortgage deed as 'one long *supressio veri* and *suggestio falsi*': Maitland *Equity* (2nd edn) p 182. And see the remarks of Lord MacNaghten in *Samuel v Jarrah Timber and Wood Paving Corpn Ltd* [1904] AC 323 at 326, HL.
2 *Gentle v Faulkner* [1900] 2 QB 267, CA; *Grand Junction Co Ltd v Bates* [1954] 2 QB 160 at 168; *Re Good's Lease* [1954] 1 WLR 309 (assumption made to this effect). Also see **13.59**. Where a licence to sub-demise is required, such licence must not be unreasonably withheld: Law of Property Act 1925, s 86(1) and the Landlord and Tenant Act 1927, s 19(1); **3.5**.
3 Indeed, the form (Form No 1) set out in the Law of Property Act 1925, Sch 5 does not contain such a proviso.
4 *Twentieth Century Banking Corpn Ltd v Wilkinson* [1977] Ch 99, [1976] 3 All ER 361.

Statutory mortgage

3.19 As a special form of charge by way of legal mortgage, a mortgage of freehold or leasehold land may be made by a deed expressed to be by way of statutory mortgage[1]. Such a mortgage must be in one of the Forms Nos 1 or 4 in Sch 4 to the Law of Property Act 1925, with such variations and additions, if any, as the circumstances may require. It implies a covenant to pay the mortgage debt with a half-yearly interest and a provision that the mortgagee will, on payment off, discharge the mortgaged property or transfer the benefit of the mortgage as the mortgagor directs[2]. In addition to the normal methods of transfer (eg by deed[3]) a statutory mortgage can be transferred in statutory form by use of Forms Nos 2, 3 or 4 in the said Schedule. The statutory mortgage is very rarely used today.

1 Law of Property Act 1925, s 117(1). This is in substitution for the Conveyancing Act 1881, s 26.
2 Section 117(2). For joint and several liability and joint benefit, see s 119.
3 Law of Property Act 1925, s 114. See Chapter 14.

Mortgage by estoppel

3.20 It sometimes arises that an otherwise perfectly good mortgage or charge is granted by a person who has no legal estate in the land in question. In this situation there arises the concept of a mortgage by estoppel. The basis of the estoppel is that, having entered into an agreement that constitutes a mortgage, the mortgagor cannot repudiate that incident or obligation[1]. Put another way, the common law principle precludes the mortgagor from disputing the validity or effect of his own deed[2]. Indeed, the principle operates to prevent both mortgagor and mortgagee from denying that the grant is ineffective to create the mortgage that it purported to create, notwithstanding that the mortgagor's title to the land was defective so that, as against third parties, he could create no interest in it[3]. It is the fact that the agreement between the parties constitutes a mortgage that gives rise to an estoppel in such circumstances; it is not the estoppel which gives rise to the mortgage[4].

The estoppel binds the mortgagor and all persons claiming under him whether or not for value, with the sole exception of a bona fide purchaser for value from the mortgagor without notice of the mortgage[5]. But the title of the mortgagor is precarious and cannot prevail over the title of the true owner of the land and those claiming under him. If, however, the mortgagor subsequently acquires the legal title from the true owner, the mortgagee's title becomes secure save against a bona fide purchaser as aforesaid.

Where there is in the mortgage an express recital or other clear and unequivocal representation of the mortgagor's title, the mortgagor is estopped from denying that he had the particular title which he had asserted and the estoppel is not excluded by the fact that he might own some lesser estate[6]. Furthermore, in that event the estoppel binds the world without exclusion with the consequence that if the mortgagor later acquires the legal estate which he had represented that he owned, the mortgagee obtains a title good against all and the estoppel is fed[7].

If, however, the mortgage contains no such recital or the like, the mortgagor is estopped only from denying that he had a legal title. Thus, no title by estoppel can arise if the mortgagor had *any* legal estate in the land at the date of the mortgage, even if that estate was insufficient to support the mortgage. In that event, the mortgagee obtains an estate in interest, although it cannot exceed the mortgagor's estate, which is not by estoppel. That being so, there is no estoppel which can be fed, with the result that if the mortgagee subsequently acquires a larger title capable of supporting the estate which he had mortgaged, this will not enure for the benefit of the mortgagee[8].

In the case of registered land, a legal charge cannot be registered until the chargor has acquired a legal estate and been registered as the proprietor, ie until the estoppel has been fed[9].

1 *Bruton v London and Quadrant Housing Trust* [1999] 3 WLR 150 at 157, per Lord Hoffmann.
2 *First National Bank plc v Thompson* [1996] Ch 231 at 237, CA, per Millett LJ.
3 *Wroe v Exmos Cover Ltd* [2000] 1 EGLR 66, CA.
4 *First National Bank plc v Thompson* [1996] Ch 231, CA; *Wroe v Exmos Cover Ltd* [2000] 1 EGLR 66, CA.
5 *Right d Jefferys v Bucknell* (1831) 2 B & Ad 278; *General Finance, Mortgage and Discount Co v Liberator Permanent Benefit Building* Society (1878) 10 Ch D 15; *First National Bank plc v Thompson* [1996] Ch 231, CA.
6 *First National Bank plc v Thompson* [1996] Ch 231, CA.
7 *First National Bank plc v Thompson*, above.
8 *Universal Permanent Building Society v Cooke* [1952] Ch 95; *First National Bank plc v Thompson* [1996] Ch 231, CA.
9 *First National Bank plc v Thompson* [1996] Ch 231, CA.

FORM AND CONTENTS OF MORTGAGE DEED

Form of mortgage deed

3.21 A legal mortgage can only be created by deed[1]. The mortgage or charge should be made by a separate deed; a combined form of conveyance and mortgage should not be used[2]. This applies especially where the transaction is one leading to first registration or is of already registered land because in that case the deed will be retained by HM Land Registry.

A mortgage which by reason of some formal defect fails to take effect as a legal mortgage may nevertheless be a valid equitable mortgage[3].

1 Law of Property Act 1925, ss 85 and 86.
2 Since in such cases there is a danger of the deed being inadvertently destroyed when the mortgage or charge is discharged.
3 See **3.89**.

Testatum

3.22 The testatum records that the mortgagee has advanced the agreed loan and that the mortgagor acknowledges receipt of such sum. The receipt is not conclusive as to the amount paid, at least as between the parties themselves[1]. Therefore, either party may prove that a different amount was loaned with the ensuing consequences in terms of redemption. A receipt for consideration money in the body of a deed is a sufficient discharge for the same to the person paying the same, without any further receipt for the same being endorsed on the deed[2].

But the receipt does operate to estop them from denying its truth as against third parties[3]. Further, where a solicitor produces a deed which has in the body thereof or indorsed thereon a receipt for consideration money or other consideration, the deed being executed or the indorsed receipt being signed by the person entitled to give a receipt for that consideration, the deed is a sufficient authority to the person liable to pay for his paying the same to the solicitor, without the solicitor producing any separate or other direction or authority from the person who executed or signed the deed or receipt[4].

1 *Mainland v Upjohn* (1889) 41 Ch D 126.
2 Law of Property Act 1925, s 67(1).
3 *Powell v Browne* (1907) 97 LT 854; *Bickerton v Walker* (1885) 31 Ch D 151.
4 Law of Property Act 1925, s 68(1), thereby operating in favour of a purchaser.

Covenant for repayment

3.23 It is usual in a mortgage to insert a covenant to repay the principal sum with interest, on a fixed day, and also to pay interest after default so long as the security shall subsist[1], but that is not, and never has been, a necessary part of a mortgage. For a mortgage in itself implies a loan, a promise to repay, and therefore a debt recoverable by court proceedings[2]. Moreover, it bears interest even though none is expressly reserved[3]. In the absence of a covenant or bond, the debt is only a simple contract debt[4] and whether the debt is a covenant or a simple contract[5] depends upon the true construction of the mortgage[6]. The principal secured by the mortgage and the interest thereon are distinct debts and may be separately recovered[7].

If no fixed date for repayment is specified by the mortgage deed the debt is repayable on demand. If a date for repayment, the legal date for redemption, is fixed by the mortgage deed—usually six months from the date of the mortgage[8]—on default of repayment on the day fixed the mortgagee may pursue his remedies, without having to serve a demand[9].

1 Where appropriate, the provision should deal with the rests, ie the intervals at which an account is struck for the purposes of determining interest (see **35.34** ff). Personal liability under the covenant may be negatived (where the mortgagors are trustees or personal representatives, see **12.116** and **12.124** or limited to interest (where the mortgagor is tenant for life, see **12.90**); and there may be no personal liability where a person charges his own property as collateral security for the debt of another: *Re Midland Bank Ltd's Application* [1941] Ch 350, sub nom *Franklin v Midland Bank Ltd* [1941] 2 All ER 135.

2 *Yates v Aston* (1843) 4 QB 182; *Sutton v Sutton* (1882) 22 Ch D 511 at 515, CA. Covenants to pay to both principal and interest are implied in registered charges: see **4.7**.

3 *Anon* (1813) 4 Taunt 876, Ex Ch; *Mendl v Smith* (1943) 112 LJ Ch 279; *NZI Capital Corpn Ltd v Child* (1991) 23 NSWLR 481; but see *Cityland and Property (Holdings) Ltd v Dabrah* [1968] Ch 166, [1967] 2 All ER 639; and see **35.40**.

4 *Ancaster v Mayer* (1785) 1 Bro CC 454 at 464; *Quarrell v Beckford* (1816) 1 Madd 269 at 278; *Sutton v Sutton*, above.

5 The distinction assuming significance for limitation purposes in view of the fact the applicable limitation period for recovery of the sums due is 12 years in the case of speciality debts but only six years in respect of simple contract debts: see the Limitation Act 1980.

6 *Sutton v Sutton*, above.

7 *Dickenson v Harrison* (1817) 4 Price 282. It is advisable, in the case of an express covenant, to word it so that the principal and interest are to be construed as two distinct debts, rather than a single debt.

8 By convention, being a reasonably short period before the mortgage is redeemable by the mortgagor and the mortgagee's default powers are exercisable, though it can be a different period. The significance of the legal date of redemption is simply that, in the absence of other provision in the mortgage deed, the mortgagee's statutory powers of sale etc do not arise until that date has passed.

9 See **17.6**.

What is repayable

3.24 In the simplest case, the covenant provides for the repayment of the sum advanced and interest thereon. Even here problems may arise as to what is meant by a particular expression used, eg 'principal', 'mortgage money', etc[1]. Alternatively, the mortgage may be an 'all money' security, ie to secure all moneys on all accounts owing from time to time by the borrower to the lender[2]. In any case where there is an issue as to what is repayable, it is a matter of construction to be determined in the light of the particular words used[3].

1 In *Davidson v Sydney County Council Employees' Credit Union Ltd* [1979] 1 NSWLR 41 it was held that 'principal' did not cover liability to repay money obtained by the borrower by fraudulent misappropriation. For the meaning of 'mortgage money', see Law of Property Act 1925, s 205 (1) (xvi); and see *Bevham Investments Pty Ltd v Belgot Pty Ltd* (1982) 149 CLR 494 ('money secured by the mortgage'); *Burnes v Trade Credits Ltd* [1981] 2 All ER 122, [1981] 1 WLR 805, PC ('advance'); *Mobil Oil Co Ltd v Rawlinson* (1981) 43 P & CR 221.

2 Bank mortgages are often in this form. See eg *Re Rudd & Son Ltd* [1991] BCLC 378n, (1988) 2 BCC 98, 955, CA. On the meaning of contingent liability see *Re Sutherland decd* [1963] AC 235, [1961] 3 All ER 855; *Estoril Investments Ltd v Westpac Banking Group* (1993) ACL Rep 295 NSW 24.

3 See eg *Re Clark's Refrigerated Transport Pty Ltd* [1982] VR 989 (did not include debts owing by the borrower to a parent company of the lender which had been assigned to the lender); *Catley Farms Ltd v ANZ Banking Group (NZ) Ltd* [1982] 1 NZLR 430 (included sums due

under guarantee); *Cambridge Credit Corpn Ltd v Lombard Australia Ltd* (1977) 136 CLR 608 (included sums due under guarantees); *Bank of India v Trans Continental Commodity Merchants Ltd* [1982] 1 Lloyd's Rep 506 (guarantee to cover banking facilities anywhere and on any account whatsoever extended to foreign exchange dealings). On construction see *Katsikalis v Deutsche Bank (Asia) AG* [1988] 2 QdR 641; *Estoril Investments Ltd v Westpac Banking Group* (1993) ACLRep 295 NSW 24. For a full review of the construction of 'all moneys' (in the USA called 'dragnet') clauses see the *Estoril* case, per Young J.

Repayment by instalments

3.25 Many mortgages today provide for repayment of the advance by instalments. Such mortgages may take the form of a covenant to repay at a fixed date, but with a proviso that if the specified instalments are punctually paid the mortgagee will not require payment in any other manner. Alternatively there may be a direct covenant to pay by instalments, with a proviso that in case of default in payment of any instalment the whole debt shall become immediately payable (in which event a demand is a necessary prerequisite to the bringing of a claim to recover the debt[1])[2]. The disadvantage of the direct covenant method for the mortgagee is that if he has to exercise his power of sale he will have to prove that the instalments are in arrears (with the fixed date method he merely has to show that that date has passed)[3]. The disadvantage for the mortgagor is that the form may operate to postpone redemption[4].

A provision that the whole loan (principal advanced and accrued interest) should become due on default is not bad as a penalty or otherwise[5]. The position would, however, be different if the mortgage provided that in addition interest for the full term of the loan was immediately payable upon default[6]. Provision may be made for the payment by the mortgagor of interest on the instalment[7] or a commission or fine in the event of an instalment being in arrear[8], but where a premium is added to the advance and it is provided that the whole of the premium should also become due on default that is a different matter. Where the premium is substantial the provision may be void as a penalty[9].

For the type of mortgage where the interest is calculated for a fixed term and added to the principal as a premium[10], the mortgage should provide for an early repayment discount[11]. The absence of such may result in the premium being void as an unreasonable collateral advantage[12]. For regulated agreements under the Consumer Credit Act 1974, regulations provide for a rebate on early settlement[13] and these provisions apply equally to any security provided in relation to a regulated agreement[14].

1 *Esso Petroleum Co Ltd v Alstonbridge Properties Ltd* [1975] 3 All ER 358, [1975] 1 WLR 1474.
2 See generally (1972) 122 New LJ 815 at 836.
3 See **20.6**.
4 See **28.6**.
5 *Sterne v Beck* (1863) 1 De G J & Sm 595; *Wallingford v Mutual Society* (1880) 5 App Cas 685, HL; *Protector Endowment Loan and Annuity Co v Grice* (1880) 5 QBD 592, CA; *Cityland and Property Holdings Ltd v Dabrah*, above. On acceleration clauses, see *O'Dea v Allstates Leasing System (WA) Pty Ltd* (1983) 152 CLR 359.
6 *Oresundsvarvet Aktiebolag v Marcos Diamantis Lemos, The Angelic Star* [1988] 1 Lloyd's Rep 122, CA.
7 *Belmore (C J) Pty Ltd v AGC (General Finance) Ltd* [1976] NSWLR 507.
8 *General Credit and Discount Co v Glegg* (1883) 22 Ch D 549.
9 *Cityland and Property (Holdings) Ltd v Dabrah*, above; *Wanner v Caruana* [1974] 2 NSWLR 301; and see **3.29**, n 6.

10 See **3.33**, n 1.
11 This is usually done by reference to a scheduled table or to the Rule of 78 (a formula under which a sum of interest is spread over the period of a loan so that, in general terms, the interest is at a constant rate over the period and reducing). It is not advisable to provide for a discount based simply on the proportion of the term expired, because, although the interest element will have been spread evenly over the term of the mortgage, the interest is in fact greater in the early part of the term. Note, however, the impact of the Unfair Terms in Consumer Contracts Regulations, as to which see **3.50**.
12 *Cityland and Property (Holdings) Ltd v Dabrah* [1968] Ch 166, [1967] 2 All ER 639; see **28.11-28.13**. Subject thereto there would appear to be no entitlement to a discount: see *Harvey v Municipal Permanent Investment Building Society* (1884) 26 Ch D 273, CA. The position is not like that in hire-purchase where the owner is claiming damages against the hirer on default: see *O'Dea v Allstates Leasing System (WA) Pty Ltd*, above.
13 Section 95. See **10.53**.
14 Section 113. See **10.66**. For a discussion on early settlement rebate in the consumer credit context, see the Crowther Report (1971) paras 5, 4, 4, and 6, 7, 6 ff.

Covenant not to call in the money

3.26 Unless fraud is proved, there is no objection to an agreement that the principal debt shall not be called in until a particular time, however long the postponement, and even though a period of six months is fixed for redemption[1]. If such an agreement is absolute, default in payment of interest pending the day for redemption will not entitle the mortgagee to foreclose[2] and, if the mortgage provides merely for repayment by instalments, this may prevent the lender calling in the money. However, if, as is usually the case, the covenant is expressed to be conditional on regular payment of interest, the right both to call in the principal and to foreclose arises on default in such payment[3]. If 'punctual payment' is required, this is construed strictly and the privilege of deferred repayment is lost even if the default be minor[4]. The mere receipt of interest after the due date is not a waiver of the right to sue[5], though it is a circumstance to be taken into account in determining whether there has been a waiver[6].

1 See **16.10**.
2 See **16.10**.
3 *Edwards v Martin* (1856) 25 LJ Ch 284; *Burrowes v Molloy* (1845) 2 Jo & Lat 521; *Re Theobold, ex parte Bignold* (1838) 3 Deac 151; *Seaton v Twyford* (1870) LR 11 Eq 591; *Tate v Crewdson* [1938] Ch 869, [1938] 3 All ER 43; and see *Clark v Vile* (1969) 209 Estates Gazette 169.
4 *Hicks v Gardner* (1837) 1 Jur 541; *Leeds and Hanley Theatre of Varieties v Broadbent* [1898] 1 Ch 343, CA; *Maclaine v Gatty* [1921] 1 AC 376, HL.
5 *Keene v Biscoe* (1878) 8 Ch D 201; *Re Taafe's Estate* (1864) 14 I Ch R 347.
6 *Seal v Gimson* (1914) 110 LT 583.

Provisions for payment of interest

3.27 It is standard for a mortgage deed to make express provision as to the payment of interest on the principal sum advanced by the mortgagee pending repayment of the same. However, as regards simple interest, it has been held that a mortgage bears interest even if interest is not specifically provided for in the deed[1].

1 *Farquhar v Morris* (1797) 7 Term Rep 124; *Anon* (1813) 4 Taunt 876, Ex Ch; *Ashwell v Staunton* (1861) 30 Beav 52, *Re Drax, Savile v Drax* [1903] 1 Ch 781, CA. See also *Lord Kilmurry v Geery* (1713) 2 Salk 538.

Further, covenants to pay to both principal and interest are implied in registered charges: see **4.7**.

See also *Al-Wazir v Islamic Press Agency Inc* [2001] EWCA Civ 1276, [2001] NPC 130, CA (a case concerned with an equitable charge): an award of equitable interest, running from the date on which repayment of the loans was due, can be made, even in the absence of a contractual obligation upon the debtor to pay interest. The interest is imposed upon the charged property.

Provisions to secure punctual payment (by preferential rate of interest)

3.28 It is a well settled, if not an intelligible rule, that if the mortgagee wishes to stipulate for a higher rate of interest in default of punctual payment he must reserve the higher rate as the interest payable under the mortgage, and provide for its reduction in case of punctual payment[1]. He cannot effect his object by reserving the lower rate and making higher the penalty for non-payment at the appointed time, because, it is said, an agreement of the latter kind, being a penalty, is relievable in equity[2].

A covenant to secure punctual payment, providing for a reduction in the rate of interest payable, is strictly construed and the mortgagor must pay the higher, full rate of interest unless he makes the payment by the stipulated date[3]. Moreover, the fact that the mortgagee once accepted the reduced rate of interest when payment was not made punctually does not preclude him from demanding the full rate in the event of a subsequent late payment by the mortgagor[4]. However, unless the covenant provides otherwise, late payment by the mortgagor on one occasion will not deprive him of the benefit of the covenant in respect of future payments[5].

It is, however, questionable quite how secure the above rule is (in view of the provisions of the Unfair Terms in Consumer Contracts Regulations 1999)[6].

1 *Strode v Parker* (1694) 2 Vern 316. As to the restriction on increasing the rate of interest under the Rent Act, see **16.25** ff.
2 *Wallingford v Mutual Society*, above. Also see **35.53**.
3 *Stanhope v Manners* (1763) 2 Eden 197; *Union Bank of London v Ingram* (1880) 16 Ch D 53; *Maclaine v Gatty* [1921] 1 AC 376, HL.
4 *Maclaine v Gatty* [1921] 1 AC 376, HL.
5 *Stanhope v Manners* (1763) 2 Eden 197.
6 See **3.30** and **3.50**. There seems to be little practical difference between (a) provision for a concessionary rate of interest as a discount for prompt payment and (b) provision for a higher rate of interest in the event of default. The Office of Fair Trading and the County Court Judge in *Falco Finance Ltd v Gough* (see **3.30**, n 10) have expressed the view that there is no valid distinction between such clauses, at least for the purposes of the 1999 Regulations.

Rate of interest allowed

3.29 The Consumer Credit Act 1974 contains provisions of general application to a credit agreement between an individual[1] debtor and any other person, giving the court power to rewrite the agreement, where it finds the agreement extortionate[2]. Among the factors to which regard shall be paid are prevailing contemporary interest rates[3]. For full consideration of the 1974 Act see **10.83** ff.

In other cases there is no restriction on the rate of interest which may be charged[4]. Equity does not reform mortgage transactions because they are unreasonable[5].

If some other provision in the mortgage relating to the interest could be set aside as an unreasonable collateral advantage, eg if all the interest calculated in advance became payable on early redemption, a lower rate of interest might be fixed by the court[6].

Where no rate of interest is fixed by the parties the court can fix it[7].

1 Which expression includes a partnership or other unincorporated body of persons not consisting entirely of bodies corporate: Consumer Credit Act 1974, s 189 (1).
2 Section 139; see **10.83** ff. Note the true cost of borrowing provision (s 20).
3 Compound interest may be agreed: *Clarkson v Henderson* (1880) 14 Ch D 348. See **35.48**. Interest arises on a day-to-day basis, unless otherwise agreed: see **35.40**.
4 The restrictions imposed by the Moneylenders Act 1927, s 10 (1)—namely, the presumption that interest exceeding 45 per cent was excessive and the court's powers to declare lower rates nonetheless excessive—were repealed as of 19 May 1985: see Consumer Credit Act 1974 (Commencement No 8) Order 1983/1551.
For the recommendations of the Law Commission for a general jurisdiction to set aside or vary terms of land mortgages see Part VIII of the Report *Transfer of Land—Land Mortgages*, 1991 (Law Com no 204).
5 *Knightsbridge Estates Trust Ltd v Byrne* [1939] Ch 441 at 457, [1938] 4 All ER 618 at 626, per Greene MR; *Multiservice Bookbinding Ltd v Marden* [1979] Ch 84, [1978] 2 All ER 489; but for undue influence and unconscionability see **13.22** ff. Note that the Unfair Terms in Consumer Contracts Regulations 1999, SI 1999/2083 do not apply to terms which are concerned with the adequacy of price or remuneration.
6 *Cityland and Property (Holdings) Ltd v Dabrah* [1968] Ch 166, [1967] 2 All ER 639 (7 per cent in place of 19 per cent or, as a premium, 57 per cent); and see *United Dominions Trust Ltd v Thomas* (1976) 120 Sol Jo 561.
7 *Re Drax* [1903] 1 Ch 781, CA (4 per cent); *Mendl v Smith* (1943) 169 LT 153 (5 per cent); *Al-Wazir v Islamic Press Agency Inc* [2001] EWCA Civ 1276, [2001] NPC 130, CA (judgment rate: 15 per cent, then 8 per cent).

Variation of interest rate

3.30 In the absence of express provision in that behalf, the rate of interest cannot be varied though, if the money can be called in, this fact will usually be sufficient to make the borrower agree a variation.

Most building society and commercial mortgages expressly provide for variation. An agreed power for the lender to vary the interest rate at will upon giving notice to the borrower is valid as a matter of contract law and does not contravene the provisions of the Consumer Credit Act 1974 governing the formalities for entry into regulated agreements.[1] Further, the Courts and Legal Services Act 1990, s 104(3)(b) implicitly recognises the validity of such a provision.

However, where a lender is given the power to set the prevailing interest rate from time to time, that entitlement is unlikely to be wholly unfettered.[2] In general, there is an implied term that the (apparently absolute) discretion to vary interest rates should not be exercised dishonestly, for an improper purpose[3], capriciously[4] or arbitrarily (for, in the absence of such a term, there would be nothing to prevent the lender from raising the rate demanded of the borrower to an exorbitant level).[5] Such a term is necessary in order to give effect to the reasonable expectations of the parties.[6]

Moreover, the implied term also requires that the lender will not set rates of interest unreasonably.[7] This too is necessary to give effect to the reasonable expectations of the parties.[8] However, this is of limited application: it means only that the lender must not exercise his discretion in a way that no reasonable lender, acting reasonably, would do[9]; it does not mean that the lender may not impose what might be regarded (by the borrower, at least) as 'unreasonable rates'.[10] Thus, there is no breach of the implied term where the level of interest rates set is motivated by purely commercial considerations[11].

Therefore, the variation should be subject to some ceiling (for otherwise it may be arguable that the power to vary is invalid as unreasonable)[12] or by reference to some external yardstick (such as the Retail Prices Index, the base rate from time to time of a named bank,[13] the London Interbank Offered rate, or the value of a foreign currency).[14]

In the absence of any implied term, the potential impact of the Unfair Terms in Consumer Contracts Regulations 1999, SI 1999/2083, must also be borne in mind.[15] For present purposes, the regulations apply in relation to unfair contractual terms in contracts concluded between a lender acting for purposes relating to his business (ie as a 'supplier') and a 'consumer', ie a person acting for purposes outside his business.[16] Therefore, loans by lending institutions to homeowners will generally fall within the purview of the regulations. In such cases a term permitting unilateral variation (by the lender) of the interest rate payable (by the borrower) which has not been individually negotiated[17] will be regarded as unfair if, contrary to the requirement of good faith, it causes a significant imbalance in the parties' rights and obligations arising under the contract to the detriment of the borrower.[18] The indicative and non-exhaustive list of terms which may be regarded as unfair, contained in Schedule 2 to the 1999 Regulations, suggests that a unilateral power of variation may be adjudged unfair unless such power is conferred for a good reason[19] which is specified in the agreement and/or unless the lender is obliged to notify the borrower of any variation at the earliest opportunity and the borrower is thereupon free to dissolve the contract immediately.[20]

A provision for a dual rate of interest, where the borrower is entitled to take advantage of a discounted rate if but only if all repayments are made on time, has been held to be an unfair term.[21]

The effect of the inclusion of such an unfair term is that it is not binding on the borrower.[22] However, the remainder of the parties' contract will, if it is capable of continuing in existence without the unfair term, continue to bind the parties.[23]

1 *Lombard Tricity Finance Ltd v Paton* [1989] 1 All ER 919, CA. For full consideration of the 1974 Act see Chapter 10.
2 Though, of course, the scope of any implied term depends on the circumstances of the particular contract.
3 For example, if the lender were to decide that the borrower was a nuisance, although not in breach of the loan agreement, and were to raise the interest rate to a level that it knew the borrower could not afford to pay: *Nash v Paragon Finance plc* [2001] EWCA Civ 1466 at para 31, CA, per Dyson LJ.
4 For instance, if the lender were to increase the interest rate because of the colour of the borrower's hair: *Nash v Paragon Finance plc* [2001] EWCA Civ 1466 at para 31, CA, per Dyson LJ.
5 *Nash v Paragon Finance plc* [2001] EWCA Civ 1466, CA, not following the obiter dicta in *Lombard Tricity Finance Ltd v Paton* [1989] 1 All ER 919, CA.
6 *Nash v Paragon Finance plc* [2001] EWCA Civ 1466 at para 36, CA, per Dyson LJ.
7 *Nash v Paragon Finance plc* [2001] EWCA Civ 1466 at para 42, CA, per Dyson LJ. See also *Abu Dhabi National Tanker Co v Product Star Shipping Ltd (The Product Star) (No 2)* [1993] 1 Lloyd's Rep 397 at 404, per Leggatt LJ: 'Where A and B contract with each other to confer a discretion on A, that does not render B subject to A's uninhibited whim. In my judgment, the authorities show that not only must the discretion be exercised honestly and in good faith, but, having regard to the provisions of the contract by which it is conferred, it must not b exercised arbitrarily, capriciously or unreasonably.'
8 *Nash v Paragon Finance plc* [2001] EWCA Civ 1466 at para 42, CA, per Dyson LJ.

9 It is unlikely that a lender who acted in that manner would not also be acting either dishonestly, for an improper purpose, capriciously or arbitrarily. Ie *Wednesbury* unreasonableness.

10 *Nash v Paragon Finance plc* [2001] EWCA Civ 1466, CA, per Dyson LJ at paragraph 41.

11 For example, if the lender encounters financial difficulties, is charged higher rates for lending by the money markets than other lenders and duly seeks to pass on those increased costs to its borrowers.

Nash v Paragon Finance plc [2001] EWCA Civ 1466, CA, per Dyson LJ at paragraphs 46 & 47. The mere fact that there is a divergence between the lender's rates and those charged by other lenders, especially lenders in another category, does not constitute a breach of the implied term: *Nash v Paragon.*

12 On the possibility of an unlimited clause being invalid, see also *ANZ Banking Group Ltd v Gibson* [1981] 2 NZLR 513. Cf Lingard *Bank Security Documents* para 7.37. See, generally, the Law Commission Report *Transfer of Land - Land Mortgages*, 1991, Law Com no 204, paras 6.33-6.41.

13 On the former Bank of England minimum lending rate, see (1981) 78 LS Gaz 1029, [1982] Conv 93, [1985] Conv 88. Bank rate and Bank of England minimum lending rate have been held to be the same thing: *First National Securities Ltd v Onwuegbuzie* (1976) 120 Sol Jo 458 (Lambeth County Court).

14 *Multiservice Bookbinding Ltd v Marden*, above; [1978] Conv 346 (Wilkinson); (1981) 55 ALJ 820 (Butt); *Nationwide Building Society v Registry of Friendly Societies* [1983] 3 All ER 296, [1983] 1 WLR 1226; and see *Charmelyn Enterprises Pty Ltd v Klonis* [1982] ACLD 106.

15 These regulations were, it seems, not in issue in *Nash v Paragon Finance plc* [2001] EWCA Civ 1466, CA.

16 The Unfair Terms in Consumer Contracts Regulations 1999, SI 1999/2083, regs 4(1) and 3(1).

17 A term shall always be regarded as not having been individually negotiated where it has been drafted in advance and the consumer has therefore not been able to influence the substance of the term. In other words, a pre-formulated standard contract is caught by the regulations. Further, it is for the supplier to prove that any given term was indeed individually negotiated. See regs 5(2) and (4).

18 Regulation 5(1).

19 For example, it is suggested, an associated change in base lending rates.

20 1999 Regulations, Sch 2, paras 1(j) and 2(b).

21 *Falco Finance Ltd v Gough* (1999) 17 Tr LR 526, [1999] CCLR 16 (Cty Ct): loan of £30,000 repayable over 25 years; monthly repayments £449 (13.99%) or £324 (8.99%). The dual rate scheme was remarkable in that the higher rate was triggered in the event of the most trivial default by the mortgagor and, moreover, the lower rate would not subsequently be restored, even if all the arrears were discharged.

It was held that the substantial differential between the basic interest rate and the higher rate was not based on the loss suffered by the lender through delayed receipt of the moneys. The term, which thus required the consumer who failed to fulfil an obligation to pay a disproportionately high sum in compensation, was unfair because it caused a significant imbalance in the parties' rights and obligations to the detriment of the consumer. Cf *Lordsville Finance plc v Bank of Zambia* [1996] 3 All ER 156, CA in which a modest 1% increase in the interest rate upon default was upheld.

22 1999 Regulations, reg 8(1).

23 1999 Regulations, reg 8(2).

Period during which contractual interest payable

3.31 Once a judgment is obtained and entered for a principal sum due to a creditor, the loan contract merges in the judgment and the principal becomes owed under the judgment and not under the contract. Further, if under the contract interest on any principal sum is due, generally the contractual interest provision is considered ancillary to the covenant to pay the principal, with the result that if judgment is obtained for the principal, the covenant to pay interest also merges in the judgment.

At common law, however, the parties may agree that a covenant to pay interest will not merge in any judgment for the principal sum and in that event interest may be charged under the contract on the principal sum due even after judgment for that sum, even if interest prescribed by statute is at a lower rate[1]. Moreover, the doctrine of merger does not apply where, as is customary, there is an independent covenant to pay interest, in which event the provision for contractual interest may continue to apply even after judgment[2].

It has been held that a term of a consumer credit agreement which provides for interest on sums outstanding to be charged both before and after judgment is susceptible to assessment under the Unfair Terms in Consumer Contracts Regulations 1999[3] (because it is not concerned with the adequacy of price or remuneration)[4]. However, such a term is not unfair within the meaning of those regulations[5] because it does not give rise to a significant imbalance in the parties' positions under the contract to the detriment of the consumer in a manner or to an extent which is contrary to requirement of good faith, notwithstanding that it enables the lender to recover post-judgment interest in circumstances where the County Courts Act 1984 and the County Courts (Interest on Judgment Debts) Order 1991[6] preclude this[7]. A stipulation for repayment of the principal in full with interest in full down to the date of actual repayment, even post-judgment, is not inherently unfair[8].

1 *Economic Life Assurance Society v Usborne* [1902] AC 147 applying *Re Sneyd, ex p Fewings* (1883) 25 Ch D 338; *Director General of Fair Trading v First National Bank plc* [2001] UKHL 52, [2001] 3 WLR 1297, HL.
2 *Ealing London Borough Council v El Isaac* [1980] 1 WLR 932 at 937; *Director General of Fair Trading v First National Bank plc* [2000] QB 672, [2000] 2 All ER 759, CA.
3 As to which see **3.50**.
4 *Director General of Fair Trading v First National Bank plc* [2001] UKHL 52, [2001] 3 WLR 1297, HL. The decision actually concerned the 1994 Regulations (SI 1994/3159) which were superseded by the 1999 Regulations.
5 *Director General of Fair Trading v First National Bank plc*, above.
6 SI 1991/1184.
7 *Director General of Fair Trading v First National Bank plc*, above.
8 See also **10.79** and **10.82** for discussion of the House of Lords' decision in relation to the court's powers (in relation to the enforcement of regulated agreements) under the Consumer Credit Act 1974.

Classification of legal mortgages of land according to method of repayment

3.32 Legal mortgages of land are today generally classified according to the method of repayment of the money advanced. There are four main classes[1], namely:

(1) Repayment, Annuity or Flat Rate mortgages;
(2) Fixed Instalment mortgages;
(3) Endowment (or Pension) mortgages;
(4) Interest-only (formerly known as Standing) mortgages.

There is a further class, namely mixed mortgages, which are a combination of class (1) and either class (3) or (4).

1 This classification was employed in the official guide to the option mortgage scheme. For the scheme, now repealed, see the previous edition of this work. There have been various proposals for new forms of repayment over the years, ie low start mortgages

(see (1975) 233 Estates Gazette 457); equitable half mortgage ((1975), Times, 22 April); never-never mortgages ((1969) 113 Sol Jo 645); and see (1969) 119 New LJ 327 (Aldridge); home reversions and annuity scheme (1978) 128 New LJ 1179 (Myers) etc.

Repayment mortgages

3.33 These take the form of repayment by fixed periodical instalments, comprised partly of principal and partly of interest, over a specified period (the term of the mortgage). Subject, of course, to interest rate fluctuations over the course of the mortgage, the amount of the instalments remains the same throughout the term, although the proportion of each instalment which is allocated to principal or interest varies, the amount allocated to principal increasing throughout the period[1].

1 This classification should not be confused with 'flat rate interest' mortgages, under which interest is calculated as a percentage of the advance over the term and usually added to the advance to form a lump sum (see eg *Cityland and Property (Holdings) Ltd v Dabrah* [1968] Ch 166, [1967] 2 All ER 639).

Fixed instalment mortgages

3.34 Under these a fixed amount of principal is a repaid each year of the term of the mortgage together with interest at the appropriate rate on the balance of principal for the time being outstanding. The amount of the instalments therefore varies, decreasing throughout the mortgage term (subject to interest rate changes).

Endowment (or pension) mortgages

3.35 Under these the principal is left outstanding until the end of the term, only the interest thereon being paid during the term. At the end of the term the intention is that principal is paid off in a single sum from the proceeds of an endowment policy taken out by the mortgagor on his own life and for a term equal to the term of the mortgage[1]. The taking out and maintenance of such a policy is a condition of this type of mortgage. However, there is no guarantee that the policy at its maturity date will yield a sum sufficient to discharge the capital initially advanced by the mortgagee. In that event, the mortgagor remains liable for the shortfall, which may be significant (though in some instances the possibility of a likely shortfall can be reduced by increased periodical payments into the policy during its currency). In the light of highly-publicised cases of the misselling and/or inadequacy of endowment plans, this method of repayment has recently fallen into disfavour.

A pension mortgage is similar to an endowment mortgage except that the mortgage is linked with a pension policy taken out by the mortgagor rather than an endowment policy. Specifically, the parties will be concerned with that part of the pension fund which can, upon the mortgagor's retirement at the term of the mortgage, be taken as a (tax-free) lump sum (rather than by way of annuity). Again, there is, of course, a risk that in any given case the proceeds of the pension policy may fail to meet the amount required to repay the mortgage in full, in which event the mortgagor must find the necessary resources from his own funds.

1 See *Bank of Scotland (Governor & Co) v Grimes* [1985] QB 1179, [1985] 2 All ER 254, CA; and, generally (1976) 126 New LJ 449 (Vann); (1976) 126 New LJ 1087. Further, the abolition of tax relief for life assurance premiums has made endowment mortgages less attractive.

For the duty of a solicitor acting for the mortgagor/mortgagee in respect of such a policy, see *McLellan v Fletcher* (1987) Times, 3 June, [1987] NLJ Rep 593, which was not followed in *Lynne v Gordon Doctors and Walton* (1991) 135 Sol Jo LB 29, (1991) 7 PN 170, (1991) Times, 17 June.

Interest-only mortgages

3.36 These take a form similar to endowment mortgages insofar as there is no provision for regular repayment of the principal, which is left outstanding until the end of the term with only interest being payable during the term. At the end of the term the principal is repayable from the mortgagor's own resources[1].

1 Where the term is the traditional six months, this is called the classic form of mortgage: see eg *Habib Bank Ltd v Tailor* [1982] 3 All ER 561 at 565, CA; *Centrax Trustees Ltd v Ross* [1979] 2 All ER 952; and the other cases referred to in the notes to **19.52**.

The demise or charge

3.37 Covenants for title are implied by statute in a mortgage. The terms of such covenants depend upon the date of grant of the mortgage, the capacity of the mortgagor and whether the title to the land is registered or unregistered. In any case, the demise or charge must be of specific realty[1].

1 For equitable mortgages of future property, see **1.17**. On the effect of the Law of Property Act 1925, s 63, see *Thames Guaranty Ltd v Campbell* [1985] QB 210, [1984] 1 All ER 144; affd [1985] QB 210, [1984] 2 All ER 585, CA.

Mortgage or charge before 1 July 1995

3.38 Where a mortgagor demised or charged the property as beneficial owner, the covenants implied by s 76 of, and Sch 2, Pts III and IV to, the Law of Property Act 1925[1] to be made by the mortgagor with the mortgagee were for the right to convey, for quiet enjoyment after default, for freedom from incumbrances and for further assurance. Further, where the mortgage was of leasehold land, there were additional covenants that the lease was valid and that the rents had been paid and the covenants performed and for the indemnity of the mortgagee in respect of future rents and the future performance of the leasehold covenants.

The implied covenants could be varied or extended by the mortgage deed and in that event operated accordingly, ie as if such variations or extensions were implied by the statute[2].

The benefit of the covenants went with the mortgagee's estate or interest and was capable of being enforced by every person in whom that estate or interest was from time to time vested[3].

1 See also (1964) 28 Conv NS 205 (Prichard); [1985] Conv 398 (Russell).
2 Law of Property Act 1925, s 76(7).
3 Section 76(6).

Mortgage or charge since 1 July 1995

3.39 By virtue of the Law of Property (Miscellaneous Provisions) Act 1994, in an instrument effecting or purporting to effect a mortgage or charge after 1 July 1995 and expressed to be made with full or limited title guarantee, there are implied covenants that the mortgagor has the right, with the concurrence or any other mortgagor, to dispose of the property as he purports to do[1] and that he will, at his own cost, do all that he reasonably can do to give the mortgagee the title he purports to give[2]. Further, in such an instrument, covenants are also implied that the mortgage is free from all charges and incumbrances and free from all third party rights save those which the mortgagor does not and could not reasonably be expected to know about and certain statutory charges which do not amount to defects in title[3].

Where only limited title guarantee is given, there is an implied covenant that the mortgagor has not, since the last disposition for value, created any charge or incumbrance or granted any third party rights which subsist at the date of the mortgage and, further, that he has not suffered anyone else to do so and is not aware that anyone else has done so[4].

The covenants can be expressly limited or excluded in their application[5] and do not impose liability to the extent that they are so limited or excluded in relation to any matter to which the mortgage is made subject or in respect of anything within the mortgagee's actual knowledge or which is a necessary consequence of facts known to him[6].

The benefit of the implied covenants goes with the mortgagee's estate or interest and is capable of being enforced by every person in whom that estate or interest is from time to time vested[7].

1 By s 2(3) of the 1994 Act the mortgagor is presumed to purport to dispose of (in the case of a mortgage of registered land) the whole of the registered title or (in the case of a mortgage or unregistered land) the fee simple or unexpired term, as the case may be.
2 Section 1(2).
3 Sections 1(2), 3(1), 3(2) and 5.
4 Sections 1(2) and 3(3).
5 Section 8.
6 Section 6(1) and (2).
7 Section 7.

Statutory mortgages

3.40 As to the covenants implied in a statutory mortgage, see **3.19**.

Proviso for cesser on redemption

3.41 The classical form of legal mortgage by demise follows the proviso for cesser which provides that if the mortgagor shall on a given day pay to the mortgagee the mortgage debt and interest the mortgage term shall cease[1]. In the case of a legal charge there may be included a similar proviso that on payment on the given day the mortgagee will discharge the security[2]. The date for redemption should be the same as the date fixed by the covenant for payment. The proviso for cesser or the proviso for discharge are not essential, since in the former case the term ceases and in the latter case the legal charge is discharged upon payment, but they are inserted, because, by specifying a date for redemption, the end of the legal right of redemption is fixed and, on default in payment on the date fixed, the right of foreclosure arises[3].

In the modern form of building society mortgage there is no express provision for redemption, the mortgage terms or conditions generally allowing repayment at any time on due notice and the right of foreclosure on default by the mortgagor being left to be implied.

Restrictions on the right of redemption are dealt with later[4].

1 Law of Property Act 1925, ss 85 (1) and 86 (1).
2 See **3.18**.
3 See Chapter 22.
4 See **28.6** ff. Certain rights ancillary to the land, such as goodwill or a licence to trade on the premises (eg a liquor licence), will need to be separately assigned. For goodwill, see **3.62**.

Other covenants by the mortgagor[1]

3.42 After the proviso for cesser follow various covenants by the mortgagor. These may include, for instance, covenants to repair and to insure or not to insure.

1 Where property is sold subject to a mortgage, it is usual, particularly where the mortgagee is a building society, for the mortgagee to release the original mortgagor from all future liability under the mortgage and for the purchaser to enter into new covenants with the mortgagee for payment of principal and interest and observance of the covenants in the mortgage. A deed containing such covenants is commonly called a deed of covenant(s). Such a deed may also be executed where the terms of the mortgage, eg as to the rate of interest, are varied. As to variation, see **3.79**.
See the Law Commission Report, Transfer of Land—Land Mortgages, 1991, on standard provisions (eg as to repair and insurance) for the proposed formal legal mortgage, Law Com no 204, Pts V and VI, especially paras 6.13-6.15. It is proposed that some of the standard terms should be overriding, ie incapable of variation.

Covenants to repair

3.43 There is no statutory obligation on a mortgagor to keep the property in repair. The mortgagor's position as tenant arising by virtue of possession of the mortgaged property with the permission of the mortgagee or of an attornment clause[1] imposes no obligation upon him to repair. However, the mortgagee is entitled to have the mortgaged property preserved from deterioration in the hands of the mortgagor or of any other person whose interest is inferior to that of the mortgagee and any moneys expended by him in preserving the property are allowed in taking the accounts[2]. In the absence of express provision difficulty may be experienced by the mortgagee in effecting repairs. Accordingly most mortgages contain a covenant by the mortgagor to keep the property in good repair and to repair on notice from the mortgagee and in case of default to permit the mortgagee to enter and effect repairs without becoming liable as mortgagee in possession, together with provision for the mortgagor to pay the cost thereof and a charge of such moneys on the mortgaged property.

1 See **3.49**.
2 See **16.4**.

Covenants relating to insurance

Insurance

3.44 As to insurance[1], where the mortgage is made by deed, the mortgagee has by virtue of the Law of Property Act 1925[2] the (limited) power, to the like extent as if it had been in terms conferred by the mortgage deed but not further, at any time after the date of the mortgage deed to insure and keep insured against loss or damage by fire any building, or any effects or property of an insurable nature, whether affixed to the freehold or not, being or forming part of the mortgaged property. However, the amount of an insurance effected by a mortgagee under the above power must not exceed the amount specified in the mortgage deed or, if no amount is therein specified, two thirds of the amount that would be required, in case of total destruction, to restore the property insured[3]. This is a not insignificant restriction on the value to the mortgagee of the statutorily conferred power to insure.

Further, the premiums paid for any such insurance are a charge on the mortgaged property or estate or interest, in addition to the mortgage money, and with the same priority and with interest at the same rate, as the mortgage money. But although the premiums are a charge, they cannot be recovered from the mortgagor as a debt, in the absence of a covenant to pay them.

Also, the statutory power cannot be exercised:

(a) where there is a declaration in the mortgage deed that no insurance is required;
(b) when an insurance is kept by or on behalf of the mortgagor in accordance with the mortgage deed;
(c) where the mortgage deed contains no stipulation respecting insurance, and an insurance is kept up by or on behalf of the mortgagor with the consent of the mortgagee to the amount to which the mortgagee is by the 1925 Act authorised to insure[4].

For the above reasons, a mortgage deed normally includes a covenant by the mortgagor to insure the property comprising the mortgagee's security. Indeed, a prudent mortgagee of property which consists wholly or partly of buildings will, of course, notwithstanding the statutory power, take care that his security contains the usual covenant for insurance by the mortgagor and for production of the policy and receipts for premiums, with a provision that the insurance so effected, or any insurance made by the mortgagee under the statutory power, shall be for a specified sum or for the full value of the buildings. The inclusion of an express covenant to insure by the mortgagor enables the mortgagee, in the case of default by the mortgagor, to recover premiums paid by him (the mortgagee) from the mortgagor as a debt and a breach of the covenant by the mortgagor[5]. Bank and building society mortgages of residential property may often provide that the society shall (and the mortgagor shall not) insure[6].

1 See (1986) 83 LS Gaz 343 (Murray) and the Law Commission Report, Transfer of Land—Land Mortgages, 1991, paras 6-9 to 6-12.
2 Section 101 (1) (ii). This power may be varied or extended by the mortgage deed; and the section applies only if and so far as a contrary intention is not expressed in that deed: sub-ss (3), (4). The provisions as to insurance in ss 101, 108 replace, with slight variations, the corresponding provisions of ss 19, 23 of the Conveyancing Act 1881.
3 Law of Property Act 1925, s 108(1).
4 Law of Property Act 1925, s 108(2).
5 As to the charging of premiums in an account, see above.
6 On tied agency provisions, see (1965) 62 LS Gaz 57.

Laying out of insurance moneys in reinstatement

3.45 All moneys received on an insurance of mortgaged property (against loss or damage by fire or otherwise) effected under the 1925 Act, or any enactment replaced by that Act, or on an insurance for the maintenance of which the mortgagor is liable under the mortgage deed shall, if the mortgagee so requires, be applied, by the mortgagor in making good the loss or damage in respect of which the money is received or (without prejudice to any obligation to the contrary imposed by law[1]) in or towards the discharge of the mortgage money[2].

If the policy is effected in the name of the mortgagee, he is entitled in law to the proceeds but his interest is merely to secure the mortgage debt and thus he is liable to both the mortgagor and subsequent mortgagees in respect of any surplus[3].

If the policy is in the name of the mortgagor pursuant to a covenant to insure, the mortgagor is entitled in law to the proceeds. However, in this event the mortgagee has an interest by way of charge in the proceeds in order to secure the mortgage debt[4]. The interest takes effect as a partial equitable assignment and is not prejudiced by a breach by the mortgagor of any of the terms[5] included in a standard insurance covenant for the protection of the mortgagee's interest[6]. It is, however, subject to the rule that notice must be given to the debtor (insurance company) for the mortgagee's interest as assignee to be protected[7].

On a joint insurance, if the policy moneys are received by one party they cannot be applied by him irrespective of the claims by the other party and may be ordered to be paid into court[8]. On the destruction of the security by fire, the right of the mortgagee to the policy money has priority over a garnishee order against the money[9].

1 Fires Prevention (Metropolis) Act 1774, s 83, gives persons interested the right to have insurance moneys expended in rebuilding. The Act is of general, and not merely of local, application and applies as between mortgagor and mortgagee: *Sinnott v Bowden* [1912] 2 Ch 414; *Portavon Cinema Co Ltd v Price and Century Insurance Co Ltd* [1939] 4 All ER 601 at 607. Cf Law Commission Working Paper no 99, Land Mortgages, para 3.28.

2 Law of Property Act 1925, ss 108(3) and (4). Note that these provisions are limited to insurance effected under the terms of the mortgage deed (or under the 1925 Act itself). Note also that a mortgagee is not entitled to the benefit of a further insurance effected by the mortgagor which is independent of the security: *Halifax Building Society v Keighley* [1931] 2 KB 248; and see *Myler v Mr Pussy's Note Club Ltd* (1979) unreported, extracted in Wylie *Casebook on Irish Land Law* p 445. A further problem may arise if the existence of another insurance policy entitles the insurer to limit the amount paid under the very policy in respect of which the mortgagee stands to benefit. Accordingly an express covenant for application of proceeds should include *any* insurance; and see (1953) 103 L Jo 230.

Where a capital sum is received by the owner of an asset under a policy of insurance of the risk of any kind of damage or injury to or loss or depreciation of an asset, there is deemed to be a disposal for the purposes of capital gains tax. This general principle does not apply in the case of a non-wasting asset if the sum is wholly applied in restoring the asset. A lease of land becomes a wasting asset when its duration does not exceed 50 years, but, by concession (Extra Statutory Concession D1), if the tenant of such a lease applies money received by him in discharging an obligation to restore the property the money will not be treated as such a capital sum as previously mentioned: see the Taxation of Chargeable Gains Act 1992, ss 22, 23 and 204.

These provisions have no application to the receipt of insurance money qua mortgagor or qua mortgagee.

3 *Colonial Mutual General Insurance Co Ltd v ANZ Banking Group (New Zealand)* [1995] 1 WLR 1140, [1995] 3 All ER 987, PC.

4 *Colonial Mutual General Insurance* etc, above.

5 For example, the requirement that the insurance be effected in the name of the mortgagee.

6 *Colonial Mutual General Insurance Co Ltd v ANZ Banking Group (New Zealand)* [1995] 3 All ER 987, [1995] 1 WLR 1140, PC, applying *Durham Bros v Robertson* [1898] 1 QB 765. In that case the mortgagor had insured in his name rather than, as he was obliged to do, in the mortgagee's name.

7 The rule in question is that in *Dearle v Hall* (1828) 3 Russ 1 (which applies to equitable assignments generally).

8 *Rogers v Grazebrooke* (1842) 12 Sim 557.

9 *Sinnott v Bowden*, above.

Covenants relating to mortgagor's statutory powers of leasing, etc

3.46 A mortgage deed frequently limits the mortgagor's statutory powers to grant and accept surrenders of leases[1], either by abrogating the same in their entirety or by making the same conditional upon the prior written consent of the mortgagee[2]. Conversely, the mortgagee's powers of leasing and accepting surrenders are often extended[3].

The exclusion or restriction of the statutory powers is possible because the powers are, except in respect of certain mortgages of agricultural land[4] or where any exclusion thereof would operate to prevent the carrying out of an order for the grant of a new business tenancy[5], subject to any contrary intention expressed in the mortgage deed[6].

Where a mortgagor has no power to lease the mortgaged property without the mortgagee's consent, the mortgagor is (in the absence of an express term) not entitled to assert that there is an implied term that the mortgagee must act reasonably in considering an application for licence to let the property[7]. Similarly, he cannot complain that consent has been unreasonably withheld[8]. Further, the mortgagee owes no duty in equity properly to consider any request for permission to let the mortgaged property[9]. Consequently, it seems that the mortgagee may simply consider his own interest; this is the protection of the security by the prevention of the mortgaged property becoming encumbered with an unwanted tenancy which may (particularly in the case of property in residential occupation) affect adversely his ability to exercise the remedies of possession and sale[10].

Neither a prohibition barring the mortgagor from letting the mortgaged property without the lender's prior consent nor a refusal of such consent contravene the right to freedom of movement for workers enshrined in EC law[11].

Failure to restrict or exclude the powers means that the mortgagor can, subject to compliance with the statutory requirements, grant and accept surrenders of leases so as to bind the mortgagee[12].

1 As to which see the Law of Property Act 1925, ss 99 and 100.

2 In the case of a lease granted by a mortgagor prior to 1 November 1993 which lease was not authorised as against the mortgagee, any extended lease granted under the Leasehold Reform, Housing and Urban Development Act 1993, s 56 will nonetheless be deemed to be authorised against the mortgagee and shall bind such person: s 58(1). However, an extended lease does not bind the mortgagee if the existing lease was not binding on the mortgagee and, further, was granted after 1 November 1993: s 58(2).

3 Law of Property Act 1925, ss 99(14) and 100(10).

4 Namely mortgages of agricultural land made after 1 March 1948 but before 1 September 1995: Law of Property Act 1925, s 99(13A). The same applies to any such mortgage made on or after 1 September 1995 but only if the tenancy in question is of an agricultural holding and is a tenancy to which the Agricultural Holdings Act 1986 applies: s 99(13A). See further Chapter 9.

5 Landlord and Tenant Act 1954, s 36(4).

6 Law of Property Act 1925, ss 99(13) and 100(7).

7 *Citibank International plc v Kessler* [1999] Lloyd's Bank 123, (1999) 78 P & CR D7, CA.

8 *Citibank International plc v Kessler*, above. The Court of Appeal observed that there is nothing in the Law of Property Act 1925, s 99 which qualifies the mortgagee's power to withhold consent: cf the Landlord and Tenant Act 1927, s 19(1) which applies as between landlords and tenants.

9 *Starling v Lloyds TSB Bank plc* [2000] 1 EGLR 101, CA, in which a claim to that effect was struck out on the ground that it did not advance any reasonable cause of action. The question whether, in an extreme case, the equitable duty of good faith might avail a mortgagor desirous of letting the mortgaged property was left open. However, bad faith is not established in the absence of evidence of dishonesty or improper motive: *Medforth v Blake* [2000] Ch 86, [1999] 3 All ER 97, CA.

10 *Citibank International plc v Kessler* [1999] Lloyd's Bank 123, (1999) 78 P & CR D7, CA.
11 *Citibank International plc v Kessler*, above.
12 See further **19.21** ff.

Miscellaneous

3.47 Other covenants by the mortgagor commonly found in mortgage deeds include a covenant to pay rent and observe covenants (in the case of leasehold land)[1], a covenant to observe the rules of the society (in the case of a building society mortgage), a covenant to observe and perform restrictive covenants to which the land is subject and to indemnify in respect of breaches thereof, a covenant to pay road charges, a covenant to personally occupy the premises, a covenant not to alter the premises, a covenant not to obtain a loan or grant creating a charge on the property without consent, a covenant to inform the mortgagee of all notices received, a covenant to observe the provisions of the Town and Country Planning Acts etc and, where appropriate, a covenant not to register the title under the Land Registration Act 1925, without the consent of the mortgagee.

Covenants entered into by the mortgagor are enforceable by the mortgagee and his successors against the mortgagor's successors, since the relationship of mortgagor and mortgagee is in effect that of landlord and tenant[2].

1 As noted at **4.7**, by s 28 of the Land Registration Act 1925 in the case of a charge of leasehold land the title to which is registered, there is implied, subject to any entry on the register to the contrary, a covenant by the proprietor of the land at the time the charge was created, or the persons deriving title under him, to pay the rent and to observe and perform the covenants and conditions contained in the registered lease and to indemnify the proprietor of the charge, and persons deriving title under him, against any claims, proceedings and expenses in respect thereof.
2 See (1966) 82 LQR 21 (PVB); **3.49**, n 10.

Other provisions

3.48 The mortgagee's statutory powers to sell and to appoint a receiver[1] are frequently varied[2], being commonly made exercisable after a default of a shorter period than that specified in the Law of Property Act 1925, s 103[3].

The mortgagee's right of consolidation[4] is generally reserved.

On a mortgage of one or more of several adjoining properties of the mortgagor it may be appropriate to include appurtenant and adverse rights of way etc and an agreement and declaration as to party walls.

1 Law of Property Act 1925, s 101, see **18.4**.
2 The statutory powers apply only so far as a contrary intention is not expressed in the mortgage deed: Law of Property Act 1925, s 101 (4).
3 See **20.5** and **20.12**. There is no implied obligation that the mortgagee will co-operate with the mortgagor to achieve the mortgagor's objectives: *Estoril Investments Ltd v Westpac Banking Group* (1993) ACL Rep 295 NSW 24.
4 See Chapter 27 and **11.9**, n 2. The Law Commission in its Report no 204 recommends the abolition of the doctrine of consolidation: see para 6.44.

Attornment clause[1]

3.49 This clause is found in mortgages where, in the case in a mortgage of a single private dwelling house, the mortgagor is already in possession and is to remain in possession. By the mortgagor attorning tenant to the mortgagee, in other words acknowledging that he is the tenant of the mortgagee, the relationship of landlord and tenant is created[2]. Although a legal charge does not create a term of years in the mortgagee an attornment clause in a legal charge makes the chargor tenant to the mortgagee[3]. The tenancy may be a tenancy at will, from year to year, or for the duration of the mortgage according to the terms of the mortgage deed. Formerly the attornment gave the mortgagee a right to distrain for the rent reserved. Attornment clauses are within the Bills of Sale Act 1878[4], and the mortgagee cannot now distrain, unless the clause has been registered as a bill of sale[5]. The clause also formerly enabled the mortgagee to obtain a summary judgment for possession qua landlord[6], a procedure which initially was not open to a mortgagee[7]. While summary judgment later became available to a mortgagee independently of attornment[8], the current position, following the introduction of the Civil Procedure Rules, is that summary judgment is available in any type of proceedings except (so far as material) proceedings for possession of residential premises against (a) a mortgagor or (b) a tenant or other person holding over at the end of his tenancy whose occupancy is protected by either the Rent Act 1977 or the Housing Act 1988[9].

The advantage in including an attornment clause in a mortgage deed is open to some doubt but it appears that it may have some use. The inclusion of an attornment clause enables restrictive covenants in the deed on the part of the mortgagor to be enforced against the mortgagor's successors in title on the basis of privity of estate[10].

The tenancy created by an attornment clause is commonly made determinable by re-entry by the mortgagee without notice after default by the mortgagor. The taking of proceedings for possession by the mortgagee is equivalent to re-entry and no notice terminating the tenancy is necessary before proceedings are begun[11], but if the attornment clause provides for notice of a particular length proceedings cannot be commenced until such a notice has been given and has expired[12]. In the case of a mortgage of leasehold property the tenancy created by an attornment clause passes on the assignment of the lease subject to the mortgage[13].

An attornment by the mortgagor to a second mortgagee is valid even though he has attorned tenant to the first mortgagee[14].

1 (1966) 30 Conv NS 30 (Miller); (1969) 22 CLP 129 (Ryder); Sykes *The Law of Securities* (4th edn) pp 85 ff.

2 As to the nature of the tenancy, see *Regent Oil Co Ltd v J A Gregory (Hatch End) Ltd* [1966] Ch 402, [1965] 3 All ER 673. But it is not a tenancy within the Rent Acts or Agricultural Holdings Act 1986, see, generally, *Steyning and Littlehampton Building Society v Wilson* [1951] Ch 1018, [1951] 2 All ER 452; *Alliance Building Society v Pinwill* [1958] Ch 788, [1958] 2 All ER 408; *Peckham Mutual Building Society v Registe* (1980) 42 P & CR 186.

The rent reserved under the attornment clause was formerly fixed at an amount equal to the mortgage interest. If so large as to be out of all proportion to the value of the estate for use and occupation the inference was that the intention was not to create a tenancy, but a device to give the mortgagee an additional security in case of the mortgagor's bankruptcy. This was a fraud on the bankruptcy law and the mortgagee was not allowed to distrain. Now the rent is nominal: *Woolwich Equitable Building Society v Preston* [1938] Ch 129. There is no point in making it other than nominal because any rent received is prima facie applicable to the discharge of principal and interest due: *Re Betts, ex p Harrison* (1881) 18 Ch D 127 at 136, CA.

If the clause relates to future acquired property it should be limited to property coming into possession within 21 years. A term limited to take effect more than 21 years from the date of the instrument purporting to create it and any contract to create such a term is void: Law of Property Act 1925, s 149 (3).

3 See *Regent Oil Co Ltd v J A Gregory (Hatch End) Ltd* [1966] Ch 402 at 430, 438, [1965] 3 All ER 673 at 678, 683.
4 Section 6. See further **5.22**. The exemption in s 189 (1) of the Law of Property Act 1925 is not applicable.
5 *Re Willis, ex p Kennedy* (1888) 21 QBD 384. Although void as a security, the clause still created the relationship of landlord and tenant: *Mumford v Collier* (1890) 25 QBD 279.
6 Under the Small Tenements Recovery Act 1838; repealed as from 1 October 1972 (SI 1972/1161).
7 *Mumford v Collier*, above; *Kemp v Lester* [1896] 2 QB 162, CA.
8 See, historically, RSC Ord 14, r 1 (2), Ord 88 and the County Courts Act 1984, s 21.
9 CPR Pt 24.3(2)(a). Mortgage possession proceedings in the High Court remain governed by RSC Ord 88, as applied by CPR Pt 50 and Sch 1.
10 *Regent Oil Co Ltd v J A Gregory (Hatch End) Ltd*, above, but see (1965) 81 LQR 341 (PVB) and (1966) 82 LQR 21 (PVB).
11 *Woolwich Equitable Building Society v Preston* [1938] Ch 129, 131, 132; *Portman Building Society v Young* [1951] 1 All ER 191.
12 *Hinckley and Country Building Society v Henny* [1953] 1 All ER 515, [1953] 1 WLR 352. The Protection from Eviction Act 1977, s 5, requiring four weeks notice to quit, will not apply to an attornment clause, unless, perhaps, the rent is a full rack rent or the mortgagor is required to reside on the premises: *Alliance Building Society v Pinwill*, above; *Peckham Mutual Building Society v Registe* (1980) 42 P & CR 186.
13 *Regent Oil Co Ltd v J A Gregory (Hatch End) Ltd*, above; but see (1965) 81 LQR 341.
14 *Re Kitchin, ex p Punnett* (1880) 16 Ch D 226, CA.

Unfair contract terms

3.50 The significant impact of the Unfair Terms in Consumer Contracts Regulations 1999, SI 1999/2083, must now be borne in mind. For present purposes, the regulations apply in relation to unfair contractual terms in contracts concluded between a 'supplier', ie a natural or legal person acting for purposes relating to his business (eg a commercial lender) and a 'consumer', ie a natural person acting for purposes outside his business[1]. Therefore, by way of example, loans by lending institutions to an individual homeowner, usually secured by mortgage granted by the consumer, will generally fall within the scope of the regulations.

In such cases a term which has not been individually negotiated[2] will be regarded as unfair if, contrary, to the requirement of good faith, it causes a significant imbalance in the parties' rights and obligations arising under the contract to the detriment of the borrower[3].

Schedule 2 to the 1999 Regulations comprises an indicative and non-exhaustive list of terms which may be regarded as unfair[4]. The assessment of whether or not a particular term is unfair is to take into account the nature of the services for which the contract was concluded and to have regard to all the circumstances surrounding the conclusion of the contract and to all the other terms of the contract or another contract on which it is dependent[5].

A provision for a dual rate of interest, where the borrower is entitled to take advantage of a discounted rate if but only if all repayments are made on time, has been held to be an unfair term[6]. So too the imposition of a 'flat' rate of interest, calculated not on the reducing balance of the loan but upon the assumption that the original sum advanced remained outstanding in full throughout the term of the loan, with no regard being had to any payments made[7]. The position has been held to be likewise as regards use of the Rule of 78 formula for calculating the rebate due upon early redemption[8].

However, insofar as it is in plain intelligible language, a term which defines the main subject matter of the contract or concerns the adequacy of the price or remuneration, as against the services supplied in exchange, is not to be the subject of any assessment of fairness[9]. But a term of a credit agreement which provides for interest on sums outstanding to be charged both before and after judgment is susceptible to assessment under the 1999 Regulations because it is not concerned with the adequacy of the price or remuneration[10]. Such a term has been held to be not unfair although it entitles the creditor to recover post-judgment interest in circumstances where the County Courts Act 1984 and the County Courts (Interest on Judgment Debts) Order 1991[11] do not[12].

The effect of the inclusion of such an unfair term is that it is not binding on the borrower[13]. However, the remainder of the parties' contract will, if it is capable of continuing in existence without the unfair term, continue to bind the parties[14].

1 Unfair Terms in Consumer Contracts Regulations 1999, SI 1999/2083, regs 4(1) and 3(1).
2 A term shall always be regarded as not having been individually negotiated where it has been drafted in advance and the consumer has therefore not been able to influence the substance of the term. Further, it is for the supplier to prove that any given term was indeed individually negotiated. See regs 5(2) and (4).
Even if certain terms in a contract have been individually negotiated, the regulations will nonetheless apply to the remainder of the contract if an overall assessment of the contract indicates that it is a standard form contract: reg 5(3).
3 Regulation 5(1).
4 For further discussion of the potential impact of the regulations in relation to mortgage terms see **3.30** and **3.53**.
5 Regulation 6(1).
6 *Falco Finance Ltd v Gough* (1999) 17 Tr LR 526, [1999] CCLR 16, Cty Ct: see **3.30**. Query also whether a provision of the type discussed in **3.25** might fall foul of the 1999 Regulations.
7 *Falco Finance Ltd v Gough. Sed quare?* It seems that the true cost of borrowing was apparent from the stated APR (19.4%). Nonetheless, it was held that the provision for a 'flat' rate of interest was not in plain intelligible language and was unfair.
8 *Falco Finance Ltd v Gough.* As to the Rule of 78 formula, see **3.25**, n 11. Where, however, the loan is regulated by the Consumer Credit Act 1974 (as to which see Chapter 10) such redemption terms would appear immune to challenge because they reflect the provisions of the Consumer Credit (Rebate on Early Settlement) Regulations 1983.
9 Regulation 6(2).
10 *Director General of Fair Trading v First National Bank plc* [2001] UKHL 52, HL. The decision actually concerned the 1994 Regulations (SI 1994/3159) which were superseded by the 1999 Regulations.
11 SI 1991/1184.
12 *Director General of Fair Trading v First National Bank plc*, above. The House of Lords held that a stipulation for the repayment of principal in full with interest down to the date of actual repayment (post-judgment) is not unfair.
13 Regulation 8(1).
14 Regulation 8(2).

CONSTRUCTION OF MORTGAGE DOCUMENTS

Nature of the transaction

3.51 Whether a transaction is a mortgage or a conveyance depends, as we have already seen[1], upon the construction of the documents or documents and the evidence surrounding the making of the transaction[2]. Parol evidence is admissible to prove the true nature of the transaction[3].

1 See **1.12**.
2 *Prenn v Simmonds* [1971] 3 All ER 237, [1971] 1 WLR 1381, HL; *Swiss Bank Corpn v Lloyds*

Bank Ltd [1982] AC 584, [1980] 2 All ER 419, CA, affd [1981] 2 All ER 449, HL. The nature of the transaction depends upon the construction of the relevant documents in the light of any admissible evidence, even though the parties may not have realised the consequence: *Swiss Bank Corpn v Lloyds Bank Ltd*, above.

3 *Barton v Bank of New South Wales* (1890) 15 App Cas 379, PC; *Gurfinkel v Bentley Pty Ltd* (1966) 116 CLR 98; *Wilson v Ward* (1930) 2 DLR 433; and see **1.12**, n 9. On the parol evidence rule generally, see Law Commission Report on the Parol Evidence Rule (Law Com no 154 (1986), Cmnd 9700).

Terms of the mortgage

At common law

3.52 The terms of the mortgage will be construed in their natural meaning[1]. Clerical and obvious mistakes may be amended by the court without the need for formal rectification[2]. Extrinsic evidence will be admissible to resolve any ambiguities[3]. If the document is silent on a point, eg interest periods, the practice of the parties may bind them. Many mortgages are made on printed forms and the blanks are often not filled in. In those circumstances the conduct of the parties may operate, as it were, to fill the blanks[4].

1 *Prenn v Simmonds*, above.

2 *Re United Pacific Transport Pty Ltd* [1968] Qd R 517 ('mortgagor' substituted for 'mortgagee'). For rectification, see **13.47**.

3 *Prenn v Simmonds*, above; *Western Bank Ltd v Schindler* [1977] Ch 1 at 9, [1976] 2 All ER 393 at 396; *Reardon Smith Line v Hansen-Targen* [1976] 3 All ER 570, [1976] 1 WLR 989; *Secured Income Real Estate (Australia) Ltd v St Martin's Investments Pty Ltd* (1979–80) 144 CLR 596; *Gilberto v Kenny* (1983) 48 ALR 620, HC; *Codelfa Construction Pty Ltd v State Rail Authority for New South Wales* (1982) 149 CLR 337; *National Bank of New Zealand v West* [1978] 2 NZLR 451, NZCA.

4 See, generally, *Amalgamated Investments Property Co Ltd v Texas Commerce International Bank Ltd* [1982] 1 QB 84, [1981] 3 All ER 577, CA.

Unfair Terms in Consumer Contracts Regulations 1999

3.53 As noted in **3.50**, the 1999 Regulations apply in relation to contracts concluded between a 'supplier', ie a natural or legal person acting for purposes relating to his business (eg a commercial lender) and a 'consumer', ie a natural person acting for purposes outside his business[1]. Thus, by way of example, loans by lending institutions to an individual homeowner, usually secured by mortgage granted by the consumer, will generally fall within the purview of the regulations.

A specific statutory requirement, of potential significance, is that a supplier (mortgagee) must ensure that any written term of a contract is expressed in plain, intelligible language[2]. This stipulation applies to all terms, irrespective of whether they were individually negotiated between the contracting parties or not. The provision is bolstered by the regulations providing that, if there is doubt about the meaning of a written term, the interpretation most favourable to the consumer (mortgagor) shall prevail[3]. To this extent, therefore, the common law rules governing construction of mortgage documents have been modified.

1 Unfair Terms in Consumer Contracts Regulations 1999, SI 1999/2083, regs 4(1) and 3(1).

2 Regulation 7(1).

3 Regulation 7(2).

THE EXTENT OF THE SECURITY

Fixtures passing by mortgage of land[1]

3.54 A legal mortgage of land, whether freehold or leasehold[2], comprises, without express mention, and subject to any contrary intention, all fixtures which at the date of the mortgage are, or at any time afterwards during its continuance may be, annexed to the land[3], whether or not they are removable as between landlord and tenant. Fixtures passing by a mortgage of land to the mortgagee will not pass to the trustee in bankruptcy of the mortgagor[4]. The rule applies also to equitable mortgages[5].

The general rule is unaffected by the Bills of Sale Acts, except when fixtures are the subject of a separate security distinct from the security in the land. When separately assigned or charged apart from the land, fixtures are 'personal chattels' within the Acts[6] though not for other purposes[7]; but not, except in the case of trade machinery, when conveyed or assigned together with a freehold or leasehold interest in any land or building to which they are affixed[8]. Fixtures are not deemed to be separately mortgaged merely because they are assigned by separate words or that power is given to sever them from the land or building to which they are affixed, without otherwise taking possession of, or dealing with, such land or building[9]. Consequently, a mortgage of fixtures is not a bill of sale of personal chattels unless the instrument specifically creates a mortgage of the fixtures apart from the land. The court will examine whether the instrument empowers the mortgagee to realise his security in the fixtures separately from his security in the land[10]. Of course, a mortgage of fixtures by an instrument dealing with them alone is a bill of sale. If, on its true construction, the security constitutes a mortgage of land and of fixtures separately as chattels, the mortgage of the latter is a bill of sale and, if not in proper form, is void in respect of the chattels[11] and the mortgagee cannot set up any title to the fixtures on the basis of the mortgage of the land[12]. In such cases the question is essentially one of construction[13].

Where, however, trade fixtures customarily belong to the tenant of the mortgagor, the mortgagee cannot claim them as against the tenant[14]. A mortgagor while in possession may permit trade fixtures to be put up and removed, so long as he does not either materially diminish the mortgagee's security, or commit a breach of some express stipulation in the mortgage[15]; the right of removal ceases when possession is taken by the mortgagee. The above-noted exception as to trade fixtures in favour of a tenant does not apply in the case of fixtures erected on the mortgaged premises under a hire-purchase agreement on the terms that, until paid for, they shall remain the property of the owner who supplied them. In such cases, if the mortgage is a legal mortgage and the mortgagee had no notice of the hire-purchase agreement[16], or the latter was made later than the mortgage, the title of the mortgagee will prevail over that of the owner by virtue of his legal title unless the mortgagee has acquiesced in their removal[17]. Where, however, the mortgage is an equitable mortgage, and is given after the hire-purchase agreement, then, even if the mortgagee takes without notice of it, his title is postponed to that of the owner[18].

1 For recent examples of what are fixtures see *Bank of Melbourne Ltd v CBFC Leasing Pty Ltd* [1991] ACL Rep 295 Qd 7 (air conditioner); *North West Trust Co v Rezyn Developments Inc* (1991) 81 DLR (4th) 751 (10 pin bowling alley); *TSB Bank plc v Botham* [1996] EGCS 149, [1996] NPC 133, sub nom *Botham v TSB Bank plc* 73 P & CR D1, CA (a decision on which household items, such as 'white goods', are fixtures).

2 *Meux v Jacobs* (1875) LR 7 HL 481; *Southport and West Lancashire Banking Co v Thompson* (1887) 37 Ch D 64, CA.
3 *Mather v Fraser* (1856) 2 K & J 536; *Walmsley v Milne* (1859) 7 CBNS 115; *Cullwick v Swindell* (1866) LR 3 Eq 249; *Longbottom v Berry* (1869) LR 5 QB 123; *Holland v Hodgson* (1872) LR 7 CP 328; *Smith v Maclure* (1884) 32 WR 459; *Tottenham v Swansea Zinc Ore* Co Ltd (1885) 52 Lt 738; *Monti v Barnes* [1901] 1 KB 205, CA; *Reynolds v Ashby & Son* [1904] AC 466, HL; *Ellis v Glover and Hobson Ltd* [1908] 1 KB 388, CA; *Vaudeville Electric Cinema v Muriset* [1923] 2 Ch 74; *Hulme v Brigham* [1943] KB 152, [1943] 1 All ER 204.
4 *Clark v Crownshaw* (1832) 3 B & Ad 804.
5 *Re Lusty, ex parte Lusty v Official Receiver* (1889) 60 LT 160.
6 *Climpson v Coles* (1889) 23 QBD 465. Agricultural charges on tenants' fixtures are excepted from the Bills of Sale Acts: Agricultural Credits Act 1928, s 8 (1); Agricultural Marketing Act 1958, s 15 (5).
7 *Meux v Jacobs* (1875) LR 7 HL 481.
8 Bills of Sale Act 1878, s 4.
9 Section 7.
10 *Re Yates, Batcheldor v Yates* (1888) 38 Ch D 112, CA.
11 As to personal chattels for the purposes of the Bills of Sale Acts and mortgages of chattels generally, see Chapter 5.
12 *Johns v Ware* [1899] 1 Ch 359.
13 Trade machinery (except fixed motive powers etc) is deemed to be personal chattels by s 5 of the Act of 1878. The courts have not interpreted ss 4 and 5 of the 1878 Act as excepting trade fixtures from the general rule that fixtures pass with a mortgage of land unless a contrary intention appears. Accordingly, for the Acts to apply the mortgage must show an intention that the machinery is to be dealt with separately as chattels or by conferring on the mortgagee an express power to sell the machinery separately: see *Re Yates, Batcheldor v Yate*, above; *Small v National Provincial Bank of England* [1894] 1 Ch 686; *Re Brooke, Brooke v Brooke* [1894] 2 Ch 600.
14 *Sanders v Davis* (1885) 15 QBD 218.
15 *Ellis v Glover and Hobson Ltd*, above. On the removal of fixtures and waste, see *Mancetter Developments Ltd v Garmanson Ltd* [1986] QB 1212, [1986] 1 All ER 449, CA; (1986) 136 NLJ 675 (Wilkinson).
16 *Re Samuel Allen & Sons Ltd* [1907] 1 Ch 575.
17 *Hobson v Gorringe* [1897] 1 Ch 182, CA, distinguishing *Cumberland Union Banking Co v Maryport Hermatite Iron and Steel Co* [1892] 1 Ch 415; *Gough v Wood* [1894] 1 QB 713, CA; *Reynolds v Ashby & Son Ltd*, above; *Lyon & Co v London City and Midland Bank* [1903] 2 KB 135.
18 *Re Samuel Allen & Sons Ltd* [1907] 1 Ch 575; *Re Morrison, Jones & Taylor Ltd* [1914] 1 Ch 50, CA. Where a hire-purchase agreement entitles the owner to enter and seize on default etc, the owner has an equitable interest in the land to which the fixture is attached: *Gough v Wood & Co* [1894] 1 QB 713 at 722, CA; *Hobson v Gorringe* [1897] 1 Ch 182 at 192, CA; *Reynolds v Ashby & Son Ltd*, above; *Kay's Leasing Corpn Pty Ltd v CSR Provident Fund Nominees Pty Ltd* [1962] VR 429 at 436. Such an interest does not appear to be registrable either as a land charge of Class C (iii), s 4, Land Charges Act 1972—general equitable charge—or under Class C (iv)—estate contract or under Class D (iii)—equitable easement, right or privilege: see *Poster v Slough Estates Ltd* [1969] 1 Ch 495, [1968] 3 All ER 257; *Shiloh Spinners Ltd v Harding* [1973] AC 691, [1973] 1 All ER 90, HL. See generally (1963) 27 Conv (NS) 30 (Guest and Lever) and also [1990] Conv 275 (McCormack). Further, the interest seems incapable of protection under the Land Registration Act 1925.

Fixtures not passing

3.55 The general rule as to fixtures is subject to qualifications arising out of the terms of the security. Thus, if two kinds of property are mortgaged, and the fixtures are expressly included in one of them, the principle *expressio unius est exclusio alterius* may exclude the fixtures annexed to the other[1]. The bare enumeration of specific fixtures in the mortgaged property will not rebut the inference that all fixtures were intended to pass[2]. Again, if it is the custom of the place that fixed machinery which can be removed without injury to the freehold should be so removed, and it has been treated between the parties as separate from the land and unaffected by the mortgage, such machinery may be held not to pass by a mortgage of the building and machinery[3].

1 See eg *Hare v Horton* (1833) 5 B & Ad 715. *Sed quaere* whether this would not be too refined a distinction to be followed now? Ultimately, the issue will always be one of the true construction of the deed(s) in question.
2 *Mather v Fraser* (1856) 2 K & J 536; and see *Hamp v Bygrave* (1982) 266 Estates Gazette 720 (QBD).
3 *Trappes v Harter* (1833) 2 Cr & M 153; cf *Whitmore v Empson* (1857) 23 Beav 313.

Loose parts of fixtures

3.56 With any fixture will pass, without any special mention, whatever (though accidentally detached from it, or not of its own nature a fixture) may be essential for the proper employment of the fixture (machine or fixed article) of which it forms part, even though it is more or less capable of use in a detached state[1]. The same rule is also applicable in the case of machinery not of a fixed kind[2]. On the same principle a mortgage of a ship at sea with its tackle and appurtenances will pass a chronometer then on board belonging to the owner of the ship[3].

1 *Place v Fagg* (1829) 4 Man & Ry KB 277; *Mather v Fraser*, above.
2 *Re Richards, ex parte Astbury, ex p Lloyd's Banking Co* (1869) 4 Ch App 630.
3 *Langton v Horton* (1842) 1 Hare 549.

Accretions to the security

3.57 Whatever the mortgagor adds to the property to improve its value is an accretion to the property for the benefit of the mortgagee[1] as also are additions made by a second or subsequent mortgagee[2]. Where a mortgagor acquires an interest in place of the interest mortgaged the mortgagee will be entitled to it for the purpose of the security[3].

1 *Re Kitchin, ex parte Punnett* (1880) 16 Ch D 226, CA.
2 *Maxwell v Ashe* (1752) 1 Bro CC 444n; *Landowners West of England and South Wales Land Drainage and Inclosure Co v Ashford* (1880) 16 Ch D 411 at 433. Similarly in the case of a mortgage of chattels: *Webster v Power* (1868) LR 1 PC 150 (sheep); and see *Tucker v Farm and General Investment Trust Ltd* [1966] 2 QB 421, [1966] 2 All ER 508, CA (a hire-purchase case).
3 See **3.66** and **3.58**.

New leases

3.58 Thus, in the case of a mortgage or charge upon leaseholds, if a new lease or other interest of a like nature is obtained by the mortgagor, either on a forfeiture (by any contrivance or otherwise) of the original lease, or by other means, the owner of the mortgage or charge will have the benefit of the new lease or interest for the purpose of the security[1].

On the other hand, if the mortgagee of a term obtains a renewal, the mortgagor will generally have the benefit of the new term, upon redemption because the term comes from the same root and is subject to the same equity of redemption[2]. Similarly, where a mortgagee has exercised an option contained in a lease to purchase the freehold, the mortgagor will have the benefit thereof upon redemption[3]. And where a mortgagee obtains a new lease by way of vesting order granted as relief from forfeiture under the Law of Property Act 1925, s 146 (4) (see **3.7**), the new lease is a substituted security and again subject to the mortgagor's right of redemption[4].

1 *Moody v Matthews* (1802) 7 Ves 174; *Hughes v Howard* (1858) 25 Beav 575; *Sims v Helling* (1851) 21 LJ Ch 76; *Leigh v Burnett* (1885) 29 Ch D 231; and see *Re Hill Pottery Co* (1866) 15 WR 97 (claim to additions by execution creditor subject to allowance for labour and costs).
2 *Rakestraw v Brewer* (1728) 2 P Wms 511; *Leigh v Burnett*, above; *Re Biss, Biss v Biss* [1903] 2 Ch 40 at 62, CA.
3 *Nelson v Hannam and Smith* [1943] Ch 59, [1942] 2 All ER 680, CA.
4 *Chelsea Estates Investment Trust Co Ltd v Marche* [1955] Ch 328, [1955] 1 All ER 195.

Enlargement of leases

3.59 Certain long leases may be enlarged into a fee simple[1]. The fee simple so acquired is subject to all the same covenants, provisions and obligations as the term would have been subject to if it had not been so enlarged[2]. A mortgage of the term will therefore upon enlargement of the term affect the fee simple so created.

1 Law of Property Act 1925, s 153. The provision extends to mortgage terms, where the right of redemption is barred: sub-s (3). See eg **28.94**.
2 Section 153 (8).

Leasehold enfranchisement

The 1967 Act

3.60 The Leasehold Reform Act 1967 entitles tenants of houses held on long leases[1] to acquire the freehold or an extended lease[2].

Where a tenant, whose interest is mortgaged, acquires the freehold[3] the existence of the mortgage will prevent the merger of the enfranchising tenant's leasehold and freehold estate[4] and the mortgagee's security will remain the lease, but if the enfranchising tenant and mortgagee agree (and this will often be the case particularly where the mortgagee is making a further advance for the purchase price of the freehold) the freehold estate may be substituted for the leasehold estate as the security and the lease merged in the freehold.

Where a tenant, whose interest is mortgaged, obtains an extended lease[5] and the new tenancy takes effect subject to the subsisting charge on the existing tenancy, then if at the time of the execution of the extended lease the mortgagee is entitled to possession of the title deeds relating to the existing tenancy, he is similarly entitled to possession of the title deeds relating to the new tenancy and the tenant must within one month of the execution of the extended lease deliver it to him, and the instrument creating or evidencing the charge shall apply in the event of the tenant failing to deliver the extended lease as if the obligation to do so were included in the terms of the charge as set out in that instrument[6].

1 A mortgage term is excluded and cannot be enfranchised (see ss 1(2) and 37(1)(f)), unless the term no longer subsists: *Re Fairview Church Street, Bromyard* [1974] 1 All ER 1233; *Re Pettifer's Application* (1974) 231 Estates Gazette 371.
2 For another example of enfranchisement, see the Places of Worship (Enfranchisement) Act 1920, amended by the Act of 1967. Here also a mortgage on the term will affect the fee simple created by enfranchisement: s 3.

3 See the Leasehold Reform Act 1967, ss 8–13. The tenant acquires the freehold subject to the tenancy and to tenant's incumbrances: s 8.
4 There can be no merger unless the leasehold and freehold estates are vested in the same person in the same right with no vested estate intervening. See further as to merger, Chapter 32. For a protracted correspondence about whether or not there will be a merger where the tenant-mortgagor acquires the freehold reversion, see (1972) 60 LS Gaz 469, 562, 1221 and correspondence in subsequent issues including (1973) 61 LS Gaz 1312.
5 See the Leasehold Reform Act 1967, ss 14–16.
6 Leasehold Reform Act 1967, s 14 (6). The new lease will generally be subject to the subsisting charge (see **3.58**, 'New leases', above). It will be so subject in the absence of a provision in the mortgage to the contrary and it is inconceivable to imagine a mortgage containing an exclusion of this rule. The mortgagee will be entitled to the new lease on request under general principles (see 'Custody of deeds', **3.69** ff) and the above provision goes further by requiring the mortgagor to deliver the new lease.

The 1993 Act

3.61 The Leasehold Reform, Housing and Urban Development Act 1993 confers on tenants of flats a right of collective enfranchisement (by which the freehold of their block is acquired on their behalf by a nominee purchaser) and an individual right to an extended lease[1].

Where the freehold is acquired, provision is made for the discharge of existing mortgages of that interest upon the transfer of the same to the nominee purchaser[2]. Safeguards are provided, whereby it is the duty of the nominee purchaser to apply the consideration payable for the acquisition of the freehold, in the first instance, in or towards the redemption of any such mortgage, according, if there are more than one, to their priorities[3]. Failure to comply with this requirement leads to the consequence that the mortgage is not discharged to the extent of the amount remaining unpaid to the mortgagee[4].

Of course, as above, if the mortgage is of one of the tenant's lease, the mortgagee's security will, in the absence of agreement to the contrary, remain the lease in question.

Where an individual lease, the subject of any mortgage, is extended, the new lease shall take effect subject to the mortgage in substitution for the existing lease; and the terms of the mortgage, as set out in the instrument creating or evidencing it, shall accordingly apply in relation to the new lease in like manner as they applied in relation to the existing lease[5].

Further, where a tenant, whose interest is mortgaged, obtains an extended lease and the new tenancy takes effect subject to the subsisting charge on the existing tenancy, then if at the time of the execution of the extended lease the mortgagee is entitled to possession of the title deeds relating to the existing tenancy, he is similarly entitled to possession of the title deeds relating to the new tenancy and the tenant must within one month of the date on which the lease is received from Her Majesty's Land Registry following its registration deliver it to him; and the instrument creating or evidencing the mortgage shall apply in the event of the tenant failing to deliver the extended lease as if the obligation to do so were included in the terms of the charge as set out in that instrument[6].

1 See the Leasehold Reform, Housing and Urban Development Act 1993, Pt I, Chs I and II respectively.
2 Leasehold Reform, Housing and Urban Development Act 1993, s 35 and Sch 8.
3 Schedule 8, para 2(1).
4 Schedule 8, para 2(2).
5 Section 58(4).
6 Sections 58(5) and (6).

Goodwill

3.62 All incidental rights[1], such as the goodwill of a business carried on, upon and inseparably connected with, and attaching to, the mortgaged property (and compensation for such goodwill when the property is taken compulsorily) will follow the security[2] unless the goodwill is owing to the personal skill, name and reputation of the mortgagor and is thus personal to him[3] or is excluded by the terms of the security[4]. A mortgagee of a public house and associated goodwill is entitled, as against the mortgagor, to an assignment of the licence[5].

1 Eg licence for abattoir: see *Daniels v Pynbland Pty Ltd (No 2)* [1985] ACLD 472.
2 *Chissum v Dewes* (1828) 5 Russ 29; *King v Midland Rly Co* (1868) 17 WR 113; *Pile v Pile, ex p Lambton* (1876) 3 Ch D 36, CA; *Re Kitchin, ex p Punnett* (1880) 16 Ch D 226, CA. The same rule is not to be applied to the equity of redemption: see *Re Bennett, Clarke v White* [1899] 1 Ch 316.
3 *Cooper v Metropolitan Board of Works* (1883) 25 Ch D 472, CA.
4 *Whitley v Challis* [1892] 1 Ch 64, CA; *Palmer v Barclays Bank Ltd* (1971) 23 P & CR 30.
5 *Rutter v Daniel* (1882) 30 WR 724 & 801; *Garrett v Middlesex Justices* (1884) 12 QBD 620.

Compensation money

3.63 There are special statutory provisions for the payment of compensation on the compulsory acquisition of mortgaged land[1]. In summary, both mortgagor and mortgagee are entitled to a notice to treat and the court will apportion between them any sum paid by the relevant authority into court in respect of both their interests. However, except in cases where the mortgagee is in possession, is it customary for the authority to deal with the mortgagor alone and to leave him to redeem the mortgage.

Compensation for the licence on the compulsory acquisition of a mortgaged public house belongs to the mortgagee as part of the mortgage security[2].

1 As to which, see **28.31**. As to claims by a mortgagee under a mortgage created before 1 July 1948, or after 31 December 1954, for compensation in certain cases where planning permission is refused or restricted, see Town and Country Planning Act 1990, ss 135, 136, 117(3) and 250; and for compensation for blight, ss 150 and 162.
2 *Law Guarantee and Trust Society Ltd v Mitcham and Cheam Brewery Co Ltd* [1906] 2 Ch 98; *Noakes v Noakes* [1907] 1 Ch 64; *Dawson v Braime's Tadcaster Breweries Ltd* [1907] 2 Ch 359.

Mortgage indemnity policy

3.64 It is not uncommon, especially where the loan to property value ratio is high, for a mortgagee to take out a mortgage indemnity policy with an insurance company. Such a policy will entitle the mortgagee to a sum in certain prescribed events, most typically upon the sale of the mortgaged property at a price insufficient to discharge the mortgagor's indebtedness to the mortgagee.

Although it is invariably the mortgagor who is required to pay the one-off premium in respect of the policy, usually by deduction from the monies advanced, it has been held that the proceeds of the policy belong to the mortgagee and, moreover, do not operate to discharge any part of the mortgage debt (which remains due in full less only the proceeds of sale).[1] The indemnity insurance is for the benefit not of the mortgagor but the mortgagee. Indeed, the insurance company, having paid out under the policy, is entitled to claim the money in the name of the mortgagee from the mortgagor.[2]

1 *Woolwich Building Society v Brown* [1996] CLC 625, [1996] The Independent Case Studies, 22 January. See also *Mortgage Corpn v McNicholas* 22 September 1992, unreported, CA in which Staughton LJ said, 'it seems to be inconceivable that any insurance company would be stupid enough to provide insurance in favour of individuals in the event of their not paying their debts. It would be a licence to claim money. So I do not accept that the mortgage indemnity policy provides any ground of appeal to [the mortgagor].'
2 *Woolwich Building Society v Brown*, above. In other words, it is subrogated to the mortgagee's rights.

Other rights

3.65 The benefit of some rights relating to the security, eg appurtenant easements, will pass automatically with the mortgage of the security. Other rights will have to be expressly assigned by a separate clause or provision in the mortgage deed[1].

1 Eg the benefit of certain covenants, such as road-making covenants (see Wurtzburg and Mills *Building Society Law* (14th edn) pp 204, 571). There is no need to expressly assign the benefit of an NHBC agreement: see (1980) 130 New LJ 171, 173 (Adams); Topping and Rolte *Guarantees for New Homes* (2nd edn) pp 199–200.

Security over proceeds of sale where mortgage not discharged upon sale

3.66 It sometimes happens that a mortgage is not protected by registration, for example as a land charge, when this is necessary in order to ensure that the mortgage binds third parties[1]. An unregistered land charge is void against a purchaser and upon a sale of the mortgaged property the interest in land created by the mortgage ceases to subsist because it cannot subsist without the property to which it attaches and is ousted by the absolute interest which the purchaser acquires[2].

However, the position as between the parties to the mortgage is unaffected by non-registration and upon any sale (where the mortgage is not discharged[3]) the mortgagee retains any proprietary right conferred on him by the general law[4].

Moreover, it follows, from both the simple and eminently fair proposition (above) that a mortgagee should be entitled to accretions to the mortgaged property or property received in substitution for it and, from common sense, that a mortgagee is entitled to a security interest in the fruits of the mortgaged property[5].

This proprietary security interest carries through to the proceeds of sale, in accordance with the equitable principle of tracing[6].

1 As to registration generally, see **3.105** ff.
2 *Barclays Bank plc v Buhr* [2001] EWCA Civ 1223, [2001] 31 EG 103 (CS), [2001] NPC 124, CA.
3 Of course, in most cases the mortgage will be protected by registration and the mortgagor will have to discharge the mortgage in order to effect a sale.
4 *Buhr v Barclays Bank plc*, above.
5 *Buhr v Barclays Bank plc*, above. In that case the registration of a second mortgage as a land charge was invalid. The property was sold and the first mortgagee repaid. The second mortgagee was held entitled to recover the balance of the proceeds of sale from the mortgagor's solicitors who, in the circumstances, held the moneys as constructive trustee (and had not been entitled to use the same to satisfy other debts of the mortgagor in priority to the second mortgagee's claim).
6 *Buhr v Barclays Bank plc*, above. There is, however, a risk that the security interest in the proceeds may be lost if the moneys reach the hands of other creditors who are unaware of the mortgagee's proprietary interest therein: *Buhr v Barclays Bank plc*.

MORTGAGES OF PARTICULAR KINDS OF LAND

Incorporeal hereditaments

3.67 Land includes easements, profits, rentcharges and other incorporeal hereditaments[1]. Those which can exist at law[2] can be the subject of a legal mortgage; otherwise, any mortgage will be equitable only.

Generally, as in the case of easements, a mortgage of the land together with which the right is enjoyed will include a mortgage of the right. Incorporeal hereditaments, such as manors, commons, rentcharges[3], and other property of a like nature existing in gross and apart from the ownership of corporeal property may also be the subject of a mortgage, unless prohibited by law[4].

1 Law of Property Act 1925, ss 201 (1), 205 (1) (ix).
2 Section 1.
3 The Rentcharges Act 1977 prohibits the creation of new rentcharges after its commencement date (22 August 1977): s 2.
4 As in the case of advowsons, see **12.153**.

Type of land

3.68 The type of land which forms the security, by which, in this context, is meant whether the land be freehold or leasehold and its use, whether for residential, agricultural or commercial purposes, is of particular relevance to the mortgagee when contemplating a mortgage security and is primarily a matter of valuation[1].

In this respect leaseholds are a less satisfactory security than freeholds in that the lease may be determined or forfeited[2] or surrendered[3], and if the term, or the residue of the term, is short the lease is a wasting asset. Some freehold securities, eg mines, are also wasting securities, and both freehold and leasehold land may be subject, or become subject, to statutory provisions affecting the mortgagee's security. For example, reference will be made in Chapter 9 to the charge for compensation of the tenant of agricultural land which will take priority to the mortgage[4], and where the property is let and the lease is binding on the mortgagee there may be, eg, restrictions on his right to recover possession[5] or to increase the mortgage rate of interest under the Rent Act[6].

The use of the land may affect the extent and form of the mortgage and it is intended to deal here very shortly with the mortgage problems which arise out of schemes for dealing with the common parts of flat and estate developments[7]. Where the stairs, passages, roads, gardens etc of a flat or estate development are not transferred with the individual flats or houses there are a number of ways in which these common parts may be dealt with to provide for their maintenance and for contributions to the cost thereof from the owners of parts of the development. The management company scheme, the trust scheme and the deed of covenant scheme will be considered[8].

Under the management company scheme the purchaser of a flat, maisonette or house may also be required to take a share in a company which will hold and manage the common parts of the development[9]. The articles of the company will generally provide that no person may hold such a share unless he is also the owner of a flat or house comprised in the development and that such a share may only be transferred on a disposition of the flat or house to the purchaser thereof. The agreement for the original sale of the flat or house or the original conveyance or the lease may contain provisions requiring the purchaser on any disposition of the property to transfer his share in the management company to a purchaser of the property. Such a scheme also generally involves a lease by the management company to the flat or house owner of amenity rights over the common parts held by it. Accordingly where such a flat or house is the subject of a mortgage it is imperative that the lease of the amenity rights (if separate from, and not contained in, the lease of the flat or house itself) should form part of the security, so that if the mortgagee has to exercise his power of sale of the property he will be able to transfer the rights of appurtenant to the property. The share in the management company should also be included in the security[10]. Alternatively, the mortgagor should give the mortgagee power of attorney to transfer the share on a sale by the mortgagee. While the enjoyment of the appurtenant easements is not generally conditional upon the holding of a share, without a share a purchaser would have no rights in the management company. However, the articles of the company may provide for a director or other person to be deemed to be the duly appointed attorney of a shareholder who refuses or neglects to transfer his share with power to execute a transfer, so that the failure to include the share in the security may be remedied in this way.

Under the trust scheme the common parts are transferred by the developer to trustees, who will generally be two, three or four of the purchasers of parts of the development, to hold the same upon trusts declared by a trust deed. Those trusts include trusts to maintain the common parts and discharge all liabilities in respect thereof (provision being made for contributions from the owners of the respective parts of the development) and subject thereto to hold the property for the owners of the separate parts of the development[11]. Whilst the conveyance or lease of each part of the development should include rights over the common parts, a mortgage of such a property should include in the security the benefit of the owner's rights under the trust deed, thus enabling any purchaser of the property from the mortgagee to enforce the rights thereunder in respect of the maintenance of the common parts.

In the case of a small development it may be convenient for the developer to retain the common parts and the responsibility for the maintenance thereof and provide for a contribution towards the expenses of maintenance from each owner of the respective parts of the development. The developer's obligation to maintain the common parts and the owner's obligation to contribute may be effectively secured by a deed of mutual covenants made between the developer and the owners and the owners between themselves and such a deed may contain a provision that on a disposition by an owner he will require the purchaser or transferee to execute the deed[12]. On a mortgage of an individual property the security should include the benefit (and the liability) of the covenants in the deed so that should the mortgagee come to sell he will be able to assign the benefit of such covenants. A scheme by way of deed of covenants may also be employed even where the developer does not retain any land.

Finally it may be mentioned that in some modern developments the garages for the respective flats or houses are disposed of separately from the house or flat. Accordingly on taking a mortgage of the house or flat a mortgage of the garage should not be overlooked[13].

1 The importance of planning searches should not be overlooked. For restrictions on resale of houses sold by local authorities, see Housing Act 1985, s 33 and see **12.59**.

On the liability of surveyors and valuers, see *Smith v Eric S Bush* [1990] 1 AC 831, [1989] 2 All ER 514, HL in which the House of Lords, affirming *Yianni v Edwin Evans &*

Sons [1982] QB 438, [1981] 3 All ER 592, held that a surveyor owes a duty of care in tort to a prospective purchaser who purchases in reliance upon a survey or valuation carried out by a surveyor or valuer instructed by the prospective mortgagee (at least in the case of a purchaser of relatively low value residential property for owner-occupation). See also *Merrett v Babb* [2001] EWCA Civ 214, [2001] 3 WLR 1, [2001] 1 EGLR 145 and, generally, Jackson and Powell *Professional Negligence* (3rd edn) paras 3-33 to 3-41.

On the liability of mortgage brokers, see *Herrington v Kenco Mortgage and Investments Ltd* (1981) 125 DLR (3d) 377 (BCSC).

2 As to relief from forfeiture, see **3.7** ff.

3 See **3.16**. For the landlord's consent to a sale by the mortgagee, see *Property and Bloodstock Ltd v Emerton* [1968] Ch 94, [1967] 3 All ER 321, CA; and see **20.41**, n 2.

4 See **9.5**.

5 *Dudley and District Benefit Building Society v Emerson* [1949] Ch 707, [1949] 2 All ER 252, CA, [1982] Conv 169 (JTF); and see **19.16** ff.

6 See **16.25** ff.

7 For the conveyancing difficulties in relation to freehold flats and maisonettes, and in particular the enforcing of positive covenants, reference should be made to the conveyancing precedent books and George and George *The Sale of Flats* (5th edn); and see Wurtzburg and Mills *Building Society Law* (14th edn) pp 146 ff; and see also Law Commission Report of Working Group *Commonhold, Freehold Flats* (1987, Cmnd 179).

8 The form of such schemes may differ from one development to another. All that it is intended to do here is to draw attention to the fact that the security ought perhaps to include more than the individual flat or house.

9 For management company schemes, see George and George *The Sale of Flats* pp 170 ff; and precedents (1967) 31 Conv NS 716 ff.

10 For mortgages of shares, see **7.21**.

11 For a form of trust scheme, see (1967) 31 Conv NS 679 ff.

12 For precedents of a deed of mutual covenants, see (1963) 27 Conv NS 681 ff; (1964) 28 Conv NS 672 ff (for where the developer does not retain any land).

13 See eg *King v AGC (Advances) Ltd* [1983] VR 682.

CUSTODY OF DEEDS

Mortgagee's right to custody of deeds

Generally

3.69 It is advantageous for a mortgagee to have custody of the title deeds because the absence of the title deeds in the hands of the legal owner puts a third party proposing to deal with the legal estate on notice that the estate has previously been mortgaged. In addition, the mortgagee's control of the deeds further protects his position by making it difficult for the legal owner to deal with the property (in a manner prejudicial to the mortgagee) without his concurrence.

Legal mortgagee

3.70 A first legal mortgagee, whether by demise or legal charge, of freehold property has the same right to possession of documents as if his security included the fee simple[1]. Similarly, a first legal mortgagee, whether by sub-demise or legal charge, of leasehold property has the same right to possession of documents as if his security had been effected by assignment[2]. Because ownership of the legal title carries with it the right to custody of the title deeds, the effect of these provisions (equating, as they do, the status of mortgagee with that of the legal owner) is to confer on the mortgagee the right to all the deeds relating to the mortgaged property[3].

Failure to take custody of deeds may lead to postponement to other incumbrancers[4].

As soon as the statutory power of sale has become exercisable the mortgagee can demand to recover from any person, other than a person entitled in priority to himself, all the documents of title which a purchaser under the power of sale would be entitled to recover from him[5].

1 Law of Property Act 1925, s 85 (1), proviso. Formerly the mortgagee in fee was entitled to hold the deeds, but the mortgagee by demise or sub-demise had no such right. He therefore had to obtain the deeds at the time of the mortgage or take a covenant for delivery. Their (improved) positions are now the same.
2 Section 86 (1), proviso.
3 *Newton v Beck* (1858) 3 H & N 220.
4 See Priorities, **24.48** ff.
5 Law of Property Act 1925, s 106 (4).

Equitable mortgagee

3.71 An equitable mortgagee, not having the legal estate, has no right to the deeds, unless (as is commonplace in the case of first equitable mortgages) the mortgage provides that he shall have such a right. However, an equitable mortgagee by deposit of deeds[1] is entitled to retain the deeds until payment or tender of the amount due on his security[2], assuming the mortgage is valid.

1 Since the coming into force of the Law of Property (Miscellaneous Provisions) Act 1989, s 2 it has become impossible to create a mortgage by deposit of deeds: see **3.100**.
2 See *Re Molton Finance Ltd* [1968] Ch 325 at 333, [1967] 3 All ER 843 at 845, CA. This right to retain the deeds is not a separate legal or common law lien. Cf (1970) 33 MLR 131 (Sunnucks).

Position in relation to settled land

3.72 In the case of settled land, the legal estate is vested in the tenant for life who holds it on trust for all entitled under the settlement[1] and who is thereby entitled to custody of the title deeds. A mortgagee of the beneficial (equitable) interest of a tenant for life of settled land is not entitled to possession of the documents of title relating to the settled land, nor is the tenant for life entitled to deliver any such documents to such a mortgagee, unless the mortgagee is also the mortgagee of the whole of the settled land to which such documents relate[2]. The mortgagee of the life interest has, however, the same rights with respect to such documents as if the tenant for life had given to him a statutory acknowledgment of his right to production and delivery of copies thereof[3].

1 Settled Land Act 1925, s 107(1).
2 Settled Land Act 1925, s 111, proviso.
3 Section 111, proviso.

Upon enfranchisement of the mortgaged interest

3.73 The right of a mortgagee to possession of the title deeds in the event of enfranchisement of a mortgaged leasehold interest is considered at **3.60** and **3.61**.

Production of deeds

By mortgagee

3.74 By virtue of the Law of Property Act 1925, s 96(1)[1], a mortgagor[2], as long as his right to redeem subsists, shall be entitled from time to time, at reasonable times, on his request, and at his own cost and on payment of the mortgagee's costs and expenses in this behalf to inspect and make copies or abstracts of or extracts from the documents of title relating to the mortgaged property in the custody or power of the mortgagee[3].

The mortgagee's liability for production is owed to the mortgagor and any person from time to time deriving title under the original mortgagor or entitled to redeem a mortgage, according to his estate, interest or right in the mortgaged property[4].

The section, which supersedes the common law rule that a mortgagor could only oblige the mortgagee to produce the deeds upon payment of all money owing under the mortgage[5], takes effect notwithstanding any stipulation to the contrary and applies to all mortgages created since 1 January 1882.

In the case of a partial redemption, where the mortgagee retains the deeds relating to the remainder of his security, he must covenant to produce these deeds or give an acknowledgment for production to the mortgagor[6].

In a claim for sale brought by a subsequent mortgagee against the mortgagor, the prior mortgagee will not be ordered to lodge the deeds in court if he is willing to produce them and let copies be taken under this provision[7].

The mortgagee of a beneficial interest of a life tenant of settled land, if he takes the deeds, is liable to produce them for the inspection of those remaindermen with a vested, but not with a contingent, interest[8].

1 Replacing Conveyancing Act 1881, s 16. Cf *Ex p McDougall* [1982] Qd R 553. The right to inspect the mortgage deed was established in *Patch v Ward* (1865) LR 1 Eq 436, as an exception to the general rule before the Act of 1881 that the mortgagee could refuse production of the deeds.
2 If there are several mortgagors, *quaere* whether all must make the request: see *Holley v Metropolitan Permanent Building Society* [1983] 2 Qd R 756; *Thames Guaranty Ltd v Campbell* [1985] QB 210, [1984] 1 All ER 144; affd [1985] 2 QB 210, [1984] 2 All ER 585, CA.
3 As to which deeds are in the power of the mortgagee, see *Fenwick v Reed* (1816) 1 Mer 114 and *Bligh v Benson* (1819) 7 Price 205 (in possession of solicitor); *Rogers v Rogers* (1842) 6 Jur 497 (sub-mortgagee); *Palmer v Wright* (1846) 10 Beav 234.
4 Law of Property Act 1925, s 205 (1) (xvi). For re-delivery of the deeds on redemption, see **28.79** ff.
5 *Browne v Lockhart* (1840) 10 Sim 420.
6 Law of Property Act 1925, s 64.
7 *Armstrong v Dixen* [1911] 1 IR 435.
8 *Noel v Ward* (1816) 1 Madd 322; *Pennell v Earl of Dysart* (1859) 27 Beav 542. Before 1926 the remainderman had a legal estate. Now he has an equitable interest, but the rule probably still applies, although the life tenant has the primary right.

To mortgagee by tenant for life

3.75 Under the former law the mortgagee of a remainderman who had a vested (but not one who had only a contingent)[1] interest, and whose title was clear and free from reasonable cause of litigation, might sue the tenant for life for production and inspection of the title deeds. If it was suggested that the production was required for an improper purpose, the burden of proving the assertion lay on the person who resisted the production[2]. The tenant for life now holds the deeds as estate owner and the remainderman has only an equitable interest. But since he may require the deeds in order to prove his title, it seems that this rule still holds.

1 *Noel v Ward*, above.
2 *Davis v Earl of Dysart* (1855) 20 Beav 405.

To equitable mortgagee by legal owner

3.76 The legal owner is obliged to produce the deeds to a mortgagee of an equitable interest in the land[1].

1 Law of Property Act 1925, s 137(9).

DELIVERY OF DEED AS ESCROW

Generally[1]

3.77 An intended deed[2] may be delivered on the condition[3] that it is not to take effect until the happening of some specified event[4]. In that scenario, the document is delivered as an escrow[5]. It only becomes a deed when the condition is fulfilled, whereupon it operates as a deed without further delivery[6] and takes effect as from the date of the original delivery[7].

1 See generally *Kingston v Ambrian Investment Co Ltd* [1975] 1 All ER 120, CA; *Glessing v Green* [1975] 2 All ER 696, CA; *London Freehold and Leasehold Property Co v Baron Suffield* [1897] 2 Ch 608, CA; *Wollam v Barclays Bank* [1988] Fam Law 381.
2 Since 31 January 1990 the formalities for the execution of a document as a deed have been prescribed by the Law of Property (Miscellaneous Provisions) Act 1989, s 1. See further [1990] Conv 85 (Clarke). For delivery of a deed by a company see the Companies Act 1985, s 36A(5) (introduced by the Companies Act 1989, s 130).
3 Which may be express or implied: *Kingston v Ambrian Investment Co Ltd* [1975] 1 WLR 161 at 168.
4 Whether an instrument is executed as an escrow upon a condition is a question of fact depending on intention: *Glessing v Green* [1975] 1 WLR 863 at 867. Thus, the onus of proving the existence of an intention to deliver a deed subject to a condition giving rise to an escrow rests with the party who executed the deed.
5 During the time between the execution of the escrow and the satisfaction of the condition subject to which it was so delivered, the maker of the escrow cannot withdraw but must await the event to see whether or not the condition is fulfilled: *Beesly v Hallwood Estates Ltd* [1961] Ch 105; *Vincent v Premo Enterprises (Voucher Sales Ltd)* [1969] 2 QB 609; *Kingston v Ambrian Investment Co Ltd* [1975] 1 WLR 161.
6 *Alan Estates Ltd v WG Stores Ltd* [1982] Ch 511, CA.
7 But only for such purposes as are necessary to give efficacy to the transaction: *Security Trust Co v Royal Bank of Canada* [1976] AC 503, [1976] 1 All ER 381, PC. See also *Terrapin International Ltd v IRC* [1976] 2 All ER 461, [1976] 1 WLR 665; *Alan Estates Ltd v W G Stores Ltd* [1982] Ch 511, [1981] 3 All ER 481, CA; *Ansett Transport Industries (Operations) Pty Ltd v Comptroller of Stamps* [1985] VR 70; *Manton v Parabolic Pty Ltd* [1985] 2 NSWLR 361; [1982] Conv 409 (Kenny).

Mortgage as escrow

3.78 It will rarely happen (under English conveyancing practice) that a mortgage will be delivered as an escrow[1]. One possible instance, however, is when a builder or developer mortgages a site, the mortgage being made on the basis that the site would be developed. In practice, the terms of the mortgage should cover the possibility of development not taking place by allowing the lender to enter and to complete the works himself. The same applies where the mortgage advance was offered on the terms that the borrower executes certain repairs to the property[2], but, in the absence of any covenant to execute the works or a right of entry in the mortgage, the lender may be able to claim that the mortgage deed was delivered as an escrow, though it will rarely be advantageous to claim the ineffectiveness of the mortgage and repayment of the advance. Another instance of delivery in escrow might be when a mortgage is delivered conditionally upon the discharge of an earlier mortgage.

1 See *AIB Group (UK) Ltd v Hennelley Properties Ltd* [2000] EGCS 63 in which Evans-Lombe J cited this passage with approval and observed that 'one can readily see why this should be so'. He rejected a claim that an escrow had been delivered on the implied condition that a bank would make advances in strict compliance with the terms of a facility letter (which spoke of the moneys being applied in two distinct ways). He remarked that, on the facts of that case, this would have led to the highly unlikely scenario of the bank agreeing to shoulder the risk of being unsecured after it had made the first payment but before it had made the second advance.

2 This regularly occurs on advances by building societies.

VARIATION OF THE MORTGAGE

Generally[1]

3.79 The provisions of a mortgage are frequently varied, eg the rate of interest or the length of the mortgage term may be increased when there is a general increase in interest rates[2]. But a variation can only be effected by agreement between the parties, either initially, so that the mortgage deed contains a provision for variation, or subsequently by mutual agreement between the parties. Without such agreement the mortgage cannot be varied unilaterally, though if there is nothing to restrict the lender from calling the loan in, he will be in a strong bargaining position to enforce a variation. Even where there is a provision for variation, the parties may prefer to completely replace the original mortgage with a new one. Care must be taken not to lose any priority[3]. However, it seems that when, as sometimes happens, an equitable mortgage is replaced by a legal mortgage, there will be no merger if that result is necessary to preserve priority[4].

1 For rectification, see **13.47**.

2 On variation of interest, see **3.30**. Building societies will usually give the borrower the option of extending the mortgage term.

3 For the effect of a variation upon a guarantee, see *Burnes v Trade Credits Ltd* [1981] 2 All ER 122, [1981] 1 WLR 805, PC; and Chapter 31.

4 *Bank of New Zealand v Farrier-Waimak Ltd* [1964] NZLR 9 at 19 (citing *Whiteley v Delaney* [1914] AC 132); see **32.12** ff; see also *Farrier-Waimak Ltd v Bank of New Zealand* [1965] AC 376, [1964] 3 All ER 657, PC; *E S Schwab & Co Ltd v McCarthy* (1975) 31 P & CR 196.

Form and effect of variation

Generally

3.80 Like any other contract, a mortgage may, as regards its contractual elements, be varied, provided the variation complies with the rules as to variation of contracts[1]. In sum, there must be an agreement to vary which is supported by consideration.

While at common law a contract contained in a deed, such as a mortgage, could only be varied or discharged by another deed and not by a written or oral agreement, the equitable position (which now prevails) was that a deed can be varied or discharged in such manner[2].

Where the terms of a registered charge are varied, the variation is authorised to be by deed and the completion of such an alteration must be effected by due registration[3]. However, it is thought that there is nothing in that provision to nullify the contractual effect in equity of an otherwise valid variation effected in writing (otherwise than by deed) or orally[4].

The simple variation of (the contractual terms of) a mortgage, effected on or after 27 September 1989[5], does not have to comply with the requirements relating to formalities[6] prescribed by the Law of Property (Miscellaneous Provisions) Act 1989, s 2 because that statutory provision governs only the making of executory contracts and does not have effect upon agreements varying an already executed contract (such as a mortgage)[7]. This is because a mortgage is not 'a contract for the disposition of an interest in land'[8] but, rather, is itself a disposition[9].

1 For unilateral alteration and the application of the rule in *Pigot's Case* (1614) 11 Co Rep 26b, 77 ER 1177, see *Armor Coatings (Marketing) Pty Ltd v General Credits (Finance) Pty Ltd* (1978) 17 SASR 259; *Mitchelson v Mitchelson* (1979) 24 ALR 522; *Canadian Imperial Bank of Commerce v Skender* [1986] 1 WWR 284 (BCCA).
2 Chitty on Contracts (28th edn), para 1-057. See eg *Target Holdings Ltd v Priestley* (1999) 79 P & CR 305.
3 Land Registration Act 1925, s 31. See **4.18**.
4 *Target Holdings Ltd v Priestley* (1999) 79 P & CR 305.
5 A variation prior to that date would similarly not have needed to comply with the (less onerous) provisions of the Law of Property Act 1925, s 40 which, together with the doctrine of part performance, was superseded by the Law of Property (Miscellaneous Provisions) Act 1989, s 2. In any event, non-compliance with the 1925 compliance merely rendered an agreement unenforceable as opposed to void.
6 Namely that the contract is in writing, incorporates all the terms which the parties have expressly agreed in one document (or, where contracts are exchanged, in each) and is signed by or on behalf of each party thereto (although such signatures need not appear on the same document where contracts are exchanged).
7 *Tootal Clothing Ltd v Guinea Properties Management Ltd* (1992) 64 P & CR 452, CA.
8 The words in the Law of Property (Miscellaneous Provisions) Act, s 2(1).
9 *Target Holdings Ltd v Priestley* (1999) 79 P & CR 305.

Rescission or variation

3.81 However, the issue may arise as to whether any given variation merely amends the original contract (mortgage) or, alternatively, rescinds and discharges the original contract and produces a new and different contract in its place. If the latter, the original contract will have gone and the new contract must satisfy any statutory requirement of form[1] to be effective.

For the reasons explained below, whether a purported variation of a mortgage takes effect as a mere variation on the one hand or the rescission of the mortgage accompanied by the creation of a new mortgage on the other depends upon, in some cases, the nature of the variation and, in most instances, the intention of the parties.

As regards the proprietary aspects of the mortgage, ie those which affect the fundamental nature and quality of the legal interest itself (such as the extent of the property mortgaged or, in the case of a mortgage by demise or sub-demise, an extension of the length of the term), any variation will require the appropriate disposition, ie release or mortgage, or an agreement therefor satisfying the necessary formalities[2]. Thus, the discharge of the original mortgage and its replacement by a new mortgage may be the only available course for consumer credit securities where the statutory formalities (eg the signing of the necessary agreement before the loan) allow of no other method of variation; and where the subject matter of the mortgage is changed, by adding additional property or substituting a different property or taking some property out of the mortgage, the appropriate charge or release will be necessary[3].

In most other cases, the question is one of the intention of the parties to the variation[4]. This is to be inferred from the terms of their agreement viewed against the relevant factual matrix. Between development companies and banks or other institutions the original mortgage is frequently varied as facilities are increased and in this context deeds of consolidation are frequently encountered[5]. It is submitted that it is perhaps unlikely that, in general, variations of basic contractual terms which have no proprietary consequence as such (eg those relating to payment of interest and liability for the principal debt) will, in the absence of cogent evidence indicating that this indeed was the parties' intention, be held to work a rescission followed by the creation of a new mortgage, particularly where so to hold would mean that the variation would prove ineffective for failure to comply with the requirements of the Law of Property (Miscellaneous Provisions) Act 1989, s 2[6]. If, however, this was the parties' intention, effect will be given thereto and care should be taken in order to avoid losing any priority.

1 Ie (since 27 September 1989) the Law of Property (Miscellaneous Provisions) Act 1989, s 2.
2 Section 2.
3 A variation, eg of the amount of the principal, may amount to a new mortgage, compounding the terms of the original mortgage plus the variation: see *Scarel v City Loan & Credit Corpn Pty Ltd* (1986) 4 BPR 9226, (1986) SCNSW (Eq Div 4653), citing *Re Goldstones Mortgage* [1916] NZLR 489, CA, and *Public Trustee v Martileman* [1928] NZLR 337, NZCA (all relate to Torrens system land).
4 See *Morris v Baron & Co* [1918] AC 1, HL; *New Hart Builders Ltd v Brindley* [1975] Ch 342, [1975] 1 All ER 1007.
5 For deeds of consolidation, see Chapter 27.
6 See *Target Holdings Ltd v Priestley* (1999) 79 P & CR 305. See also, by analogy, *Friends' Provident Life Office v British Railways Board* [1996] 1 All ER 336, CA (a decision relating to surrender and re-grant by the variation of an existing lease, in which it was confirmed that the court would strive to give effect to the discerned intention of the parties to a deed of variation).

Non-compliance

3.82 If any formalities required for the variation of a mortgage are not met, the original mortgage stands[1].

1 *Morris v Baron*, above.

Effect on subsequent incumbrances

3.83 Where the mortgage secures a fixed sum with interest at a fixed rate, a subsequent incumbrancer cannot be affected by an increase of the principal[1] or of the rate of interest. In such a case, where the equity is adequate, the subsequent incumbrancer will usually be willing to allow the increase and there will be a deed of postponement[2]. Where the prior mortgage provided for variation (eg being security for such sum as shall be owing from time to time, or providing for an increase in the rate of interest) a subsequent incumbrancer takes subject to those terms and the first mortgagee has priority consistent with such terms[3].

1 *Scottish and Newcastle Breweries Ltd v Liquidator of Rathbourne Hotel Co Ltd* 1970 SLT 313. For further advances, see **24.83** ff.

2 See **24.2**, nn 11, 12 and **24.123**.
3 The terms of an equitable mortgage usually provide for the execution of a legal mortgage by the mortgagor when called upon for such by the mortgagee (see **3.101**). The subsequent legal mortgage may cause the prior equitable mortgage to disappear, by the latter merging in the former (see Chapter 32). But assuming that the prior equitable mortgage was duly registered or protected on the register, where appropriate, it is not thought that there would be any loss of priority (see **3.79**).

EQUITABLE MORTGAGES

Generally

3.84 An equitable mortgage is a specifically enforceable contract to create a legal mortgage[1]. An equitable mortgage may be created by:

(a) an agreement to create a legal mortgage;
(b) a mortgage of an equitable (cf legal) interest;
(c) a defective legal mortgage, ie a mortgage which does not meet the requirements for the creation of a legal mortgage.

The various methods of creation of an equitable mortgage are considered in detail below. Historically, an equitable mortgage could also be created by a deposit of title deeds; however, since 27 September 1989[2] it has not been possible so to create an equitable mortgage[3].

An equitable mortgage, which may relate to any property which can be the subject of a legal mortgage, creates, by way of security, a charge on the property in question. Such charge is an equitable interest which thus gives rise to no legal interest in favour of the lender. However, the mortgagee may enforce the rights thereby conferred by bringing a claim for specific performance of the agreement to create a legal mortgage and the court can duly vest in him a legal term of years enabling him to realise his security.

1 *Swiss Bank Corpn v Lloyds Bank Ltd* [1982] AC 584, HL affirming CA.
2 By reason of the Law of Property (Miscellaneous Provisions) Act 1989, s 2.
3 *United Bank of Kuwait plc v Sahib* [1997] Ch 107, CA.

Agreement to create a legal mortgage[1]

Generally

3.85 The agreement must be for valuable consideration. A voluntary agreement to create a security will not be enforced[2]. The money must have been paid[3] or in the case of an antecedent debt there must be an agreement to forbear from suing[4]. A mere executory agreement to borrow or lend money on mortgage, not intended to create a present security, will not constitute an equitable mortgage and specific performance of such an agreement will not be ordered[5].

1 See **1.20**.
2 See **1.19**.
3 *Rogers v Challis*(1859) 27 Beav 175. Also see *Lucia Heights Pty Ltd v Comptroller of Stamps* [1985] VR 338.
4 Or an actual forbearance: *Alliance Bank Ltd v Broom* (1864) 2 Drew & Sm 289; *Fullerton v Provincial Bank of Ireland* [1903] AC 309, HL.
5 See **1.21**.

Form

Before 27 September 1989

3.86 An agreement to create a legal mortgage was not enforceable unless in writing or evidenced by a written note or memorandum[1] of the agreement, signed by the party to be charged therewith or some person thereunto by him lawfully authorised[2], or unless there had been part performance of the agreement[3].

1 *Fenwick v Potts* (1856) 8 De GM & G 506; *Warner v Willington* (1856) 3 Drew 523; *Liverpool Borough Bank v Eccles* (1859) 4 H & N 139; *Fullerton v Provincial Bank of Ireland* [1903] AC 309, HL; *Astor Properties Ltd v Tunbridge Wells Friendly Society* [1936] 1 All ER 531; *Williams v Burlington Investments Ltd* (1977) 121 Sol Jo 424, HL.

2 Law of Property Act 1925, s 40 (1). See *Mounsey v Rankin* (1885) 1 Cab & El 496.

3 The payment of money (by itself an equivocal act: see *Re Whitting, ex p Hall* (1879) 10 Ch D 615, CA) might, taken with other matters, be a sufficient act of part performance: see *Steadman v Steadman* [1976] AC 536, [1974] 2 All ER 977, HL; [1979] Conv 40 (Thompson).

Since 27 September 1989

3.87 By the Law of Property (Miscellaneous Provisions) Act 1989, s 2[1] a contract for a mortgage of (or charge on) land (or any interest in land) can only be made in writing[2]. A further requirement of the statute is that the contract incorporate all the terms which the parties have expressly[3] agreed in one single document[4] or, where contracts are exchanged[5], in each[6] and, moreover, the document so incorporating the terms, or where contracts are exchanged, one of the documents incorporating them (though not necessarily the same one) must be signed[7] by or on behalf of each party to the contract[8]. In this regard, terms may be incorporated in a document either by being set out therein or by a reference to another document containing such terms[9].

Consequently, neither an exchange of correspondence[10] nor a facility letter[11] will satisfy the statutory requirements.

The variation of a material term of a contract for the disposition of an interest in land (including, therefore, a contract for a mortgage) is similarly subject to the formalities requirements imposed by s 2[12]. However, s 2 does not apply to a collateral contract which is not itself a contract for the disposition of an interest in land[13].

Non-compliance with s 2 renders the purported contract or variation thereto (as the case may be) void[14].

Section 2 does not invalidate a document which creates an equitable charge[15], as distinct from an agreement to create to a legal mortgage, or (as the case may be) that part of a document which so operates (notwithstanding the invalidity of a severable part of the same document which purports to create an equitable mortgage)[16].

The 1989 Act, s 2 does not affect the validity of an equitable mortgage created before 27 September 1989[17].

Section 2 applies only to a contract to mortgage and not to a mortgage itself executed as a deed (which deed need not comply with the requirements of s 2)[18].

1 Section 2 of the 1989 Act repealed the Law of Property Act 1925, s 40 and, in so doing, abolished the doctrine of part performance.

2 The definition of 'disposition' contained in the Law of Property Act 1925, s 205(1)(ii), which includes mortgage, is incorporated into the Law of Property (Miscellaneous Provisions) Act 1989, s 2 by s 2(6).

3 It need not incorporate those implied by law: *Blackburn v Walker* [1920] WN 291.
4 Therefore, an agreement reached in correspondence, ie an exchange of letters constituting an offer and acceptance, which does not record the express terms of an agreement already reached between the same parties does not satisfy the conditions of s 2 of the 1989 Act (which are more stringent than those of its predecessor, the Law of Property Act 1925, s 40): *Commission for the New Towns v Cooper (Great Britain) Ltd* [1995] Ch 259, CA.
5 In *Commission for the New Towns v Cooper (Great Britain) Ltd* [1995] Ch 259, CA it was held that the expression 'exchange of contracts' is a well-recognised concept which has the following features:
(1) each party draws up or is given a document which incorporates all the terms which they have agreed, and is intended to record their proposed contract;
(2) the documents are called 'contracts' or 'parts of a contract'. They are intended to take effect as formal documents of title and must be capable, on their face, of being fairly described as contracts having that effect;
(3) each party executes his part in the expectation that the other party has executed or will execute a corresponding part incorporating the same terms;
(4) at the time of execution neither party is bound by the terms of the document which he has executed, it being their mutual intention that neither will be bound until the executed parts are exchanged;
(5) the act of exchange is a formal delivery by each party of its part into the actual or constructive possession of the other with the intention that the parties will become mutually bound when the exchange occurs, but not before;
(6) the manner of exchange may be agreed and determined by the parties, and may be either simultaneous (eg when across a table or by telephone) or sequential (eg when by post) in which event exchange does not occur until the second document to be dispatched has been received or posted.

The exchange of contracts has therefore been preceded by an express oral or written agreement (concluded by final acceptance of an offer in the ordinary way) which agreement (eg as made in correspondence) cannot itself be a legally binding contract by virtue of s 2 of the 1989 Act: s 2.
6 Law of Property (Miscellaneous Provisions) Act 1989, ss 2(1) and (6).
7 The requirement for a signature was not satisfied where the purchaser's name had been typed at the top of a document as addressee and he had not otherwise signed the letter: *Firstpost Homes Ltd v Johnson* [1995] 1 WLR 1567, CA.
8 Law of Property (Miscellaneous Provisions) Act 1989, s 2(3).
9 Section 2(2) and *Firstpost Homes Ltd v Johnson* [1995] 1 WLR 1567, CA in which it was held that a letter purporting to constitute a contract for the sale of land which referred to an enclosed plan was a separate document from the plan itself. Moreover, because the plan was incorporated in the letter (rather than the other way round), it was the letter and not the plan which the 1989 Act required to be signed, so that the purchaser's signature on the plan alone did not suffice to create a contract.
10 *Commission for the New Towns v Cooper (Great Britain) Ltd* [1995] Ch 259, CA, not following *Hooper v Sherman* [1994] NPC 153, CA.
11 *Lloyd's Bank v Bryant* [1996] NPC 31, CA.
12 *McCausland v Duncan Lawrie Ltd* [1997] 1 WLR 38, CA. (For the position in relation to the variation of an executed (cf executory) contract, ie a mortgage itself, see **3.80**.)
13 *Record v Bell* [1991] 1 WLR 853 (vendor's solicitor's letter to the purchaser's solicitor shortly before exchange of contracts informing recipient that sender was awaiting the original office copy entries from the Land Registry showing the vendor as registered owner of the property held to constitute an offer of a warranty as to the state of the title to induce him to exchange which offer had been accepted by exchanging contracts such as to give rise to an enforceable collateral contract). It is unclear whether parties can hive off parts of the terms of a composite bargain into two contracts, namely a written land contract within s 2 and a separate non-land contract incorporating the remainder of the terms (not all recorded in writing), in an attempt to side-step the affects of s 2: cf *Tootal Clothing Ltd v Guinea Properties Management Ltd* (1992) 64 P & CR 452, [1992] 2 EGLR 80, CA, and *Grossman v Hooper* [2001] EWCA Civ 615, [2001] 27 EG 135, CA.
14 Cf the Law of Property Act 1925, s 40 which formerly rendered a contract not meeting its requirements merely unenforceable.
15 As to equitable charges generally, see Chapter 2.
16 *Murray v Guinness* [1998] NPC 79; *De Serville v Argee Ltd* [2001] NPC 82. An equitable charge must, in order to be valid, comply with the requirements of the Law of Property Act 1925, s 53(1)(a).

17 Sections 2(7), 5(3) and (4).
18 *Eagle Star Insurance Co Ltd v Green* (8 August 2001, unreported), CA, Mummery LJ (application for permission to appeal).

Mortgage of an equitable interest

3.88 This type of equitable mortgage is self-explanatory: because the interest mortgaged is equitable only, the resultant mortgage can be equitable only, even if made by deed. Such a mortgage can be effected by assignment of the equitable interest by way of security, subject to a proviso for redemption. The assignment must be in writing and must comply with the requirements of the Law of Property Act 1925, s 53(1)(c).

Defective legal mortgage

3.89 A document, which for some defect of form (but which is otherwise valid), fails to take effect as a legal mortgage will, subject to what follows, be a good equitable mortgage[1]. The basis of this is the court's power specifically to perform a contract to create a legal interest in land[2].

However, for an informally executed legal mortgage made after 27 September 1989 to take effect as an equitable mortgage, it must nonetheless comply with the provisions of the Law of Property (Miscellaneous Provisions) Act 1989, s 2 in relation to the formalities required for the creation of an equitable mortgage (as to which see **3.87**). Moreover, as informally executed mortgages are frequently executed only by the mortgagor, this may result in many such mortgages not creating any contract and security interest at all[3].

A common example of a defective legal mortgage is where land is owned by two persons, usually husband and wife, and the mortgage is made by one of them only. In that instance, the attempt to mortgage what one cannot, namely both the legal title and beneficial interest, is (subject to the statutory requirements) effective to create an equitable mortgage[4] of the mortgagor's beneficial (equitable) interest[5].

However, the power specifically to perform contracts is discretionary and will not be exercised to prejudice the position of a third party, such as a co-owner of the land[6].

1 See *Taylor v Wheeler* (1706) 2 Salk 449; and see **1.20** and **3.21**.
2 See *Sugden on Vendor and Purchaser* (14th edn) p 317; *Basma v Weekes* [1950] AC 441, sub nom *Abdul Karim Basma v Weekes* [1950] 2 All ER 146.
3 To be an equitable mortgage, the instrument must comply with s 2 of the 1989 Act: *United Bank of Kuwait plc v Sahib* [1997] Ch 107, CA. This in turn means that the document must bear the signatures of both parties. Compliance with the requirements of the Law of Property Act 1925, s 53(1)(a), which demands only the signature of the mortgagor, is insufficient.
4 The mortgage can be equitable only for the reasons set out in **3.88**.
5 *William & Glyn's Bank v Boland* [1981] AC 487, at 507G, [1980] 2 All ER 408, at 415 overruling *Cedar Holdings Ltd v Green* [1981] Ch 129, [1979] 3 All ER 117 on this point. As to the possibility of the mortgage attaching to a beneficial share to which the mortgagor subsequently succeeds, see (1936) 9 ALJ 431.

Where a transfer was executed by one of two joint owners who forged the signature of his co-owner, the transfer was held to be effective, by virtue of the Law of Property Act 1925, s 63 (the 'all-estate clause'), to vest the beneficial interest of the person who had executed it in the purchaser: *Ahmed v Kendrick* (1988) 56 P & CR 120, CA. See also, to like effect, *First National Securities v Hegerty* [1985] QB 850; *Regent Indemnity Co v Fishley* [1987] CLY 471, Cty Ct and *Bowers v Woolwich Equitable Building Society* (3 February 1987, Hoffmann J, unreported). Note, however, the decision in *Wollam v Barclays Bank* [1988] Fam 381 where it was intended that a husband and wife would jointly guarantee the borrowings of the husband's company and that the guarantee would be secured by a mortgage over the jointly owned house. The husband signed the guarantee and charge but the wife refused. It was held by Knox J that in all the circumstances the husband was not bound (and his beneficial interest was not charged) because the guarantee and charge were intended to be binding only if both owners signed. Query whether the result would have been different had the bank advanced money on the strength of the husband's signature.

6 *Thomas v Dering* (1837) 1 Keen 729; *Thames Guaranty Ltd v Campbell* [1985] QB 210, [1984] 1 All ER 144; affd [1985] QB 210, [1984] 2 All ER 585, CA; *Cedar Holdings Ltd v Green* [1981] Ch 129 at 141–143, 146–147; [1979] 3 All ER 117 at 123–124, 127–128—it is submitted that the overruling of *Cedar Holdings Ltd v Green* by the House of Lords in *William & Glyn's Bank v Boland* [1981] AC 487, [1980] 2 All ER 408 does not affect the second ground for the decision of the Court of Appeal.

Mortgage by deposit of deeds

Before 27 September 1989

Generally

3.90 Until the coming into force of the Law of Property (Miscellaneous Provisions) Act 1989, s 2, the delivery to the creditor or his agent of deeds or other documents of title with intent to create a security thereon constituted an equitable mortgage[1]. The delivery need not have been of the debtor's own deeds, but of some third party's (ie to secure that person's indebtedness)[2]. The deposit of deeds was viewed as an imperfect mortgage or as a contract for a legal mortgage which conferred on the mortgagee all such rights as he would have possessed had the mortgage been completed[3].

The charge created by the deposit was contractual for, although it arose by presumption, it did not arise by operation of law[4].

1 *Russel v Russel* (1783) 1 Bro CC 269; *Bank of New South Wales v O'Connor* (1889) 14 App Cas 273, PC, 282. As to equitable mortgages, see also **1.17** ff.

2 *Re Wallis & Simmonds (Builders) Ltd* [1974] 1 All ER 561, [1974] 1 WLR 391. See collateral security, **1.23** . For co-owners, see **3.93**.

3 *Parker v Housefield* (1834) 2 My & K 419; *Pryce v Bury* (1853) 2 Drew 41; *Carter v Wake* (1877) 4 Ch D 605; *Harrold v Plenty* [1901] 2 Ch 314.

4 *Re Wallis & Simmonds (Builders) Ltd*, above; *Re Alton Corpn* [1985] BCLC 27. See (1970) 33 MLR 131 (Sunnucks).

Form of deposit

3.91 The deposit of the deeds could have been with or without a memorandum or other instrument of charge. In practice, the deposit was generally accompanied by a memorandum under seal, thus giving the mortgagee the powers granted by s 101 of the Law of Property Act 1925[1].

In the case of registered land, the proprietor of any land or charge could create a lien on the land by deposit of the land or charge certificate (as the case might be)[2]. Such a lien was equivalent to a lien created in the case of unregistered land by the deposit by a legal and beneficial owner of the documents of title[3]. (Note that any notice of such deposit entered on the register before 3 April 1995 will take effect as a caution under s 54 of the Land Registration Act 1925[4].)

Where there was no memorandum in writing, the charge created by the deposit was prima facie unenforceable[5], but its validity was recognised on the ground that the deposit of deeds implied an agreement to make a mortgage and also operated a part performance[6].

Consequently *actual* deposit of the deeds was essential[7] and in the absence of actual deposit the security had to rest on a document in writing signed by the mortgagor or his authorised agent[8].

The mortgage might have been valid if only some or one of the material documents of title to the property had been deposited[9], although a complete title was not thereby shown to the debtor's interest in the property[10]. It followed that if part of the material documents were deposited with one person, and part with another, each may had have a good security[11], unless there was evidence of a contrary intention[12].

An equitable mortgage could have been created by deposit of a receipt for purchase money, containing the terms of the agreement for sale, if there were no title deeds or conveyance in the depositor's possession[13], or even by a deposit of a map of the property[14], or by an agreement for lease[15], but not by the deposit of an unattested copy of a deed[16]. An equitable sub-mortgage of an equitable security could have been created by re-deposit of the deeds without a deposit of the memorandum given with the original security[17].

1 Ie the power to sell and appoint a receiver: see Part V. Where there was an accompanying document it was a question of construction whether the security was constituted by the deposit or the document: *Hari Sankar Paul v Kedar Nath Saha* [1939] 2 All ER 737, PC; and see *Re White Rose Cottage* [1965] Ch 940, [1965] 1 All ER 11, CA.

2 Land Registration Act 1925, s 66.

3 Section 66.

4 Land Registration Rules 1925, r 239 (as substituted by the Land Registration Rules 1995).

5 Ie for want of compliance with s 40 of the Law of Property Act 1925.

6 *Russel v Russel* (1783) 1 Bro CC 269; *Burgess v Moxon* (1856) 2 Jur NS 1059; *Dixon v* Muckleston (1872) 8 Ch App 155; *Re Wallis & Simmonds (Builders) Ltd* [1974] 1 All ER 561; [1974] 1 WLR 391; *Thames Guaranty Ltd v Campbell* [1985] QB 210, [1984] 1 All ER 144; affd [1985] QB 210, [1984] 2 All ER 585, CA.

Lord Eldon, in *Ex p Haigh* (1805) 11 Ves 403 and *Ex p Mountfort* (1808) 14 Ves 606, protested against the evasion of the Statute of Frauds 1677 (the forerunner of the Law of Property Act 1925, s 40) but the doctrine came to be well established.

In *Deutsche Bank v Ibrahim* (1991) Financial Times, 13 December, Mr David Neuberger QC sitting as a Judge of the High Court held that a deposit of documents of title to answer the debts of another was a guarantee and hence only enforceable if there had been compliance with the Statute of Frauds 1677, s 4. In doing so the judge did not follow the obiter dicta of Higgins J in H*arvey v Edwards, Dunlop & Co Ltd* (1927) 39 CLR 302 at 311. However, it is doubtful whether the Statute of Frauds applies to a charge which does not impose personal liability. See further Baughen [1992] Conv 330.

7 *Re Beavan, ex p Coombe* (1819) 4 Madd 249; *Re Ridge, ex p Hallifax* (1842) 2 Mont D & De G 544; *Bank of New South Wales v O'Connor* (1889) 14 App Cas 273, PC.

8 *Re Leathes, ex Leathes* (1833) 3 Deac & Ch 112. If there was such a document, the mortgage was good, even though the documents to be deposited pursuant to it were not executed at its date: *Re Carter and Justins, ex p Sheffield Union Banking Co* (1865) 13 LT 477.

9 *Re Daintry, ex p Arkwright* (1843) 3 Mont D & De G 129; *Lacon v Allen* (1856) 3 Drew 579.

10 *Ex p Wetherell* (1804) 11 Ves 398; *Roberts v Croft* (1857) 24 Beav 223; affd 2 De G & J 1.

11 *Roberts v Croft*, above.

12 *Re Price, ex p Pearse and Prothero* (1820) Buck 525.

13 *Goodwin v Waghorn* (1835) 4 LJ Ch 172.

14 *Simmons v Montague* [1909] 1 IR 87.

15 *Unity Joint-Stock Mutual Banking Association v King* (1858) 25 Beav 72; *Tebb v Hodge* (1869) LR 5 CP 73; *Re Buckland, ex p Reid* (1848) De G 600.

16 *Re Borrow, ex p Broadbent* (1834) 1 Mont & A 635.

17 *Re Hildyard, ex p Smith* (1842) 2 Mont D & De G 587.

Where deeds remained in debtor's custody

3.92 Where a document remained in the possession of a debtor, a memorandum annexed to it, purporting to appropriate the proceeds to satisfy the debt, would not generally of itself have created a charge[1]. However, a charge might have been created where the document was in the actual keeping of the debtor, if it was in the legal custody of the creditor, eg where the debtor held it as his solicitor[2], even though the creditor was not aware of the creation of the security[3]. A verbal direction to a third party who had possession of the deeds to hold for the creditor was not a part performance and would not create an equitable mortgage, but it was otherwise if there was a written memorandum[4].

1 *Adams v Claxton* (1801) 6 Ves 226.
2 *Middleton v Pollock, ex p Elliott* (1876) 2 Ch D 104; *Sharp v Jackson* [1899] AC 419, HL; *Taylor v London and County Banking Co* [1901] 2 Ch 231; *Re Pidcock, Penny v Pidcock* (1907) 51 Sol Jo 514.
3 *Re Beetham, ex p Broderick* (1887) 18 QBD 766, CA; *Ex p Coming* (1803) 9 Ves 115.
4 *Lloyd v Attwood* (1859) 3 De G & J 614.

Co-owners

3.93 Co-owners of land are trustees of the deeds no less than they are of the legal estate[1]. Trustees can only act with unanimity. One cannot part with custody of the deeds without the consent of the other. Accordingly a purported mortgage by deposit by one co-owner without the consent of the other was ineffective, in the absence of facts giving rise to an estoppel[2].

1 See **12.2**.
2 *Thames Guaranty Ltd v Campbell* [1985] QB 210, [1984] 1 All ER 144; affd [1985] QB 210, [1984] 2 All ER 585, CA.

Form of memorandum accompanying deposit

3.94 Where the memorandum accompanied a deposit of title deeds it ought to have referred to the deposit and stated that the deposit was made to the intent that the property should be equitably charged with the repayment of the moneys advanced[1]. Express reference should have been made to the fact that the land was charged with the payment of interest, although an equitable mortgage by deposit of title deeds carried interest even in the absence of such a provision[2].

Where the memorandum was by deed (thus giving the mortgagee the statutory power to appoint a receiver and to sell)[3] it should also have contained a declaration by the mortgagor that he held the property on trust for the mortgagee and, in addition or alternatively, a power of attorney for the mortgagee to convey the property in the name of the mortgagor. It now seems that, even without such power of attorney, the equitable mortgagee, on exercising the statutory power of sale, was able to convey the legal estate in the mortgaged property[4]. But the inclusion of the power of attorney made the lender's position certain on this point[5].

Every memorandum should also have contained an undertaking by the mortgagor to execute a legal charge when called upon to do so[6], although an equitable mortgagee was entitled to call for a legal mortgage even in the absence of such a provision (unless the right was specifically excluded)[7]. Upon the execution of such a legal mortgage, it seems that the equitable mortgage continued in existence (for the purposes of priority etc), notwithstanding the usual rule of merger of a lower in a higher security[8].

1 As previously mentioned (see **3.85**) for an equitable mortgage there must be consideration or forbearance.
2 *Re Drax, Savile v Drax* [1903] 1 Ch 781 at 794, 796, CA.
3 Law of Property Act 1925, s 101: see **18.4** and **20.6** ff.
4 See **20.43**.
5 Notwithstanding he sold in the name of the mortgager, he sold as mortgagee and subject to the duty to obtain a proper price; *Palmer v Barclays Bank Ltd* (1971) 23 P & CR 30.
6 This undertaking was registrable as a land charge of Class C (iv) under the Land Charges Act 1972, s 2 (4); see **24.4**.
7 *Birch v Ellames and Gorst* (1794) 2 Anst 427; *Parker v Housefield* (1834) 2 My & K 419 at 421.
8 See **31.12** ff.

Proof of intent to create equitable mortgage by deposit

3.95 The deposit of deeds did not, without more, create an equitable mortgage. For a security to arise it was necessary to demonstrate an intention to create such a mortgage.

The intent to create an equitable mortgage by deposit of documents could be established by writing alone, writing coupled with parol evidence[1], by parol evidence alone[2], or by inference arising from the deposit, where the possession of the documents by the holder could not be otherwise explained[3].

But an inference that the deposit was made by way of equitable mortgage would not be admitted in contradiction of a written statement[4] or correspondence[5], the terms of which governed the contract, where it was consistent with the security[6]; nor by reason of the possession by a solicitor of his client's deeds, or against a purchaser who did not enquire into the nature of the possession[7]; nor where there was no evidence as to the origin of the possession from which a contract might have been inferred[8].

An intention to create an equitable mortgage might have been inferred from a delivery of the documents to be held, or a direction to hold them, until the settlement of an account or the execution of a mortgage[9].

Where deeds were delivered merely for the purpose of enabling a solicitor to prepare a legal mortgage, an equitable mortgage by deposit was not created[10], unless there was an intention to give an immediate security by deposit (notwithstanding that a formal legal security was also contemplated)[11]. So where, before the money was advanced, the deeds were deposited with a view to preparing a future mortgage with no intention of giving an immediate security, the deposit would not be considered as an equitable mortgage by deposit, but there would be an equitable mortgage if there was an immediate advance or the deeds were deposited under a promise to forbear suing, even though they might have been deposited only for the purpose of preparing a future mortgage, for in such a case the deeds were given as part of the security[12].

1 *Casberd v A-G* (1819) 6 Price 411; *Ede v Knowles* (1843) 2 Y & C Ch Cas 172; *Burgess v Moxon*, above; *Re Boulter, ex p National Provincial Bank of England* (1876) 4 Ch D 241.
2 *Russel v Russel*, above; *Ex p Kensington* (1813) 2 Ves & B 79; *Ex p Haigh* (1805) 11 Ves 403; *Ex p Mountfort* (1808) 14 Ves 606.
3 *Edge v Worthington* (1786) 1 Cox Eq Cas 211; *Ex p Langston* (1810) 17 Ves 227; *Re Wallis and Simmonds (Builders) Ltd*, above; *Thames Guaranty Ltd v Campbell*, above. See *Re Alton Corpn* [1985] BCLC 27 (first transaction silent as to whether deposit as security for loan; second deposit expressed as security for loan showed intention that first deposit not intended as security).
4 *Ex p Coombe* (1810) 17 Ves 369.
5 *Thames Guaranty Ltd v Campbell*, above.

6 *Shaw v Foster* (1872) LR 5 HL 321 at 341; *Re White Rose Cottage* [1965] Ch 940, [1965] 1 All ER 11, CA.
7 *Bozon v Williams* (1829) 3 Y & J 150; *Lloyd v Attwood* (1859) 3 De G & J 614 at 651.
8 *Re Oliver, ex p Jones* (1837) 3 Mont & A 152 at 327; *Chapman v Chapman* (1851) 13 Beav 308; *Burgess v Moxon*, above; *Dixon v Muckleston* (1872) 8 Ch App 155.
9 *Fenwick v Potts* (1856) 8 De Gm & G 506; *Lloyd v Attwood*, above.
10 *Norris v Wilkinson* (1806) 12 Ves 192; *Lloyd v Attwood, Attwood v Lloyd*, above.
11 *Edge v Worthington*, above; *Ex p Wright* (1812) 19 Ves 255 at 258; *Ex p Bruce* (1813) 1 Rose 374, *Hockley v Bantock* (1826) 1 Russ 141. See further as to intent, **1.20**.
12 *Keys v Williams* (1838) Y & C Ex 55 at 61; and see *Sun Hung Kai Bank Ltd v A-G* [1986] HKLR 587, affd on appeal to PC, sub nom *Sun Tai Cheung Credits Ltd v A-G of Hong Kong* (1987) 131 Sol Jo 938.

Form of memorandum where no deposit

3.96 A memorandum showing an intention to deposit deeds by way of mortgage was sufficient even if no deeds were in fact deposited[1]. However, the intention to create an equitable mortgage must have been clear. The instrument should have contained a charge on the land of principal and interest. The memorandum should have been by deed if the mortgagee was to have the statutory powers (and the same requirements and provisions were applicable as where the memorandum accompanied a deposit).

1 *Re Carter and Justins, ex p Sheffield Union Banking Co* (1865) 13 LT 477.

Property affected by an equitable mortgage by deposit

3.97 An equitable mortgage by deposit prima facie affected the beneficial interest of the mortgagor in all the property comprised in the deposited documents[1], including accretions[2], but the agreement, if any (which could have been explained by other written evidence), was the measure of the security[3], both with respect to the particular property included in the security[4] and also in relation to the extent to which the interest of the mortgagor therein was to be affected[5]. And if the memorandum of deposit referred to deeds which were not shown to have been deposited, and other deeds were deposited, the actual deposit constituted the security[6].

1 *Ashton v Dalton* (1846) 2 Coll 565.
2 *Re Baker, ex p Bisdee* (1840) 1 Mont D & De G 333; *Re New, ex p Farley* (1841) 1 Mont D & De G 683; *Chissum v Dewes* (1828) 5 Russ 29; see **3.57**.
3 *Re Amner, ex p Hunt* (1840) 1 Mont D & De G 139; *Re Medley, ex p Glyn* (1840) 1 Mont D & De G 29.
4 *Re Leathes, ex p Leathes* (1833) 3 Deac & Ch 112; *Wylde v Radford* (1863) 33 LJ Ch 51. The security would not, as against prior incumbrancers, be extended to property not included in the deposited documents merely by reason of a false statement by the mortgagor to the mortgagee that such property was included therein: *Jones v Williams* (1857) 24 Beav 47.
5 *Pryce v Bury* (1853) 2 Drew 41.
6 *Re Moore, ex p Powell* (1842) 6 Jur 490.

Debt secured by equitable mortgage by deposit

3.98 An equitable mortgage was, prima facie, a security only for the debt specified in the agreement and did not include debts previously due from the mortgagor to the mortgagee[1]. But it could have included such debts if an intention that it should do so appeared from the circumstances[2]. An equitable mortgage by deposit, although accompanied by a written agreement, could, either by written or parol evidence[3] and also, it seems, by inference alone arising from possession of the deed[4], have been extended to further advances, even where changes had occurred in the depositee's firm[5]. A legal security cannot be extended by such means to subsequent advances made on a parol agreement for a further mortgage because, it has been said, the legal mortgagee holds his mortgage on a contract for conveyance only and not for deposit[6]; and it would seem that the leaving of the documents in the custody of each successive firm was constructively a re-deposit[7]. It could not, however, be shown by parol that the depositee held the documents as security both for his own debt and that of another person[8], though, if the depositee himself was not a creditor, but a trustee only, he might have been shown to hold them for another's benefit[9].

In order to connect a debt of long-standing with the possession of the debtor's deeds the creditor had to proceed upon a distinct allegation, supported by proper evidence, that they were delivered to him by way of security[10]. If the claimant's evidence of the deposit was defective at the hearing, the creditor was not entitled to an inquiry to enable him to establish his security, because a reference would not then be directed upon a matter which involved the very root of the claimant's title[11]. The rule in bankruptcy also required that evidence could be given of the intention to effect a security by deposit. The usual order for sale in cases of an equitable mortgage was refused after the lapse of 12 years from the date of the deposit, there being no memorandum and the bankrupt being dead[12]. However, an enquiry would sometimes have been directed in bankruptcy as to the circumstances attending a deposit of doubtful effect[13].

1 *Mountford v Scott* (1823) Turn & R 274; *Re Cowderoy, ex p Martin* (1835) 2 Mont & A 243.
2 *Re New, ex p Farley*, above; *Re Hildyard, ex p Smith* (1842) 2 Mont D & De G 587.
3 *Ex p Whitbread* (1812) 19 Ves 209; *Re Burkill, ex p Nettleship* (1841) 2 Mont D & De G 124.
4 *James v Rice* (1854) 5 De Gm & G 461; see *Barclays Bank Ltd v Taylor* [1974] Ch 137 at 140.
5 *Ex p Kensington* (1813) 2 Ves & B 79.
6 *Re Hopkins ex p Hooper* (1815) 19 Ves 477. Thus a person who has obtained a legal mortgage might, as to future advances, have been in a worse position than an equitable mortgagee by deposit.
7 *Ex p Kensington*, above; *Re Gye, ex p Smith* (1841) 2 Mont D & De G 314.
8 *Ex p Whitbread*, above.
9 *Ex p Whitbread*, above.
10 *Chapman v Chapman* (1851) 13 Beav 308; *Re McMahon, McMahon v McMahon* (1886) 55 LT 763.
11 *Holden v Hearn* (1839) 1 Beav 445 at 456; *Kebell v Philpott* (1838) 7 LJ Ch 237.
12 *Re Oliver, ex p Jones* (1837) 3 Mont & A 152, 327.
13 *Re Lindon, ex p Clouter* (1843) 7 Jur 135.

Equitable mortgage by deposit and lien mutually exclusive

3.99 When an equitable mortgage or charge was created by deposit of title deeds there was an implied contract that the mortgagee or chargee might retain the deeds until he was paid. This implied contract was part and parcel of the equitable mortgage or charge. It was not a separate legal or common law lien. It had no independent existence apart from the equitable mortgage or charge. If the mortgage or charge were avoided, eg for non-registration, then everything ancillary to it would be avoided also, so that the contractual right of retention would be avoided too[1].

1 *Re Molton Finance Ltd* [1968] Ch 325 at 332, 333, [1967] 3 All ER 843 at 845, CA; *Re Wallis and Simmonds (Builders) Ltd*, above. But note (1970) 33 MLR 131.

Since 27 September 1989

3.100 Since 27 September 1989[1] it has not been possible to create a valid equitable mortgage (ie an agreement to mortgage) by mere deposit of title deeds by way of security[2]. Although historically it was not necessary for there to be an express contract between the depositor of the title deeds and the person with whom they were deposited for an equitable mortgage so to arise, nonetheless the deposit was treated as (rebuttable) evidence of a contract to mortgage[3]. Consequently, the provisions of the Law of Property (Miscellaneous Provisions) Act 1989, s 2[4] apply to such a transaction. Necessarily, a deposit of deeds fails to meet the statutory requirements.

1 By reason of the Law of Property (Miscellaneous Provisions) Act 1989, s 2.
2 *United Bank of Kuwait plc v Sahib* [1997] Ch 107, CA. For a case of solicitor's negligence in failing to ensure the provision of a valid and effective security where deeds were deposited without the execution of a signed memorandum, see *Dean v Allin & Watts (a firm)* [2001] EWCA Civ 758, [2001] 2 Lloyd's Rep 249, CA.
3 *Dean v Allin & Watts*, above. See also *Re Wallis & Simmonds (Builders) Ltd* [1974] 1 WLR 391; *Re Alton Corpn* [1985] BCLC 27.
4 As to which see **3.87**.

Terms of equitable mortgages

Generally

3.101 In addition to the usual terms found in legal mortgages, eg covenants by the mortgagor[1] (insofar as the same may be applicable), every equitable mortgage should contain an undertaking by the mortgagor to execute a legal charge when called upon to do so[2] (although an equitable mortgagee is entitled to call for a legal mortgage even in the absence of such a provision (unless the right is specifically excluded)). Upon the execution of such a legal mortgage, it seems that the equitable mortgage continues in existence (for the purposes of priority etc), notwithstanding the usual rule of merger of a lower in a higher security[3].

The mortgage should refer to any deposit (of the title deeds) and state that the deposit is made to the intent that the property should be equitably charged with the repayment of the moneys advanced. Express reference should also be made to the fact that the land is charged with the payment of interest, although an equitable mortgage carries interest even in the absence of such a provision[4].

Where the mortgage is by deed[5] (thus giving the mortgagee the statutory power to appoint a receiver and to sell)[6] it should also contain a declaration by the mortgagor that he holds the property on trust for the mortgagee[7] and, in addition or alternatively, a power of attorney for the mortgagee to convey the property in the name of the mortgagor[8]. Even without such power of attorney, the equitable mortgagee, on exercising the statutory power of sale is, it seems, able to convey the legal estate in the mortgaged property but the inclusion of the power of attorney makes the mortgagee's position certain on this point[9].

1 As to which see **3.42** ff.
2 The undertaking should be to execute a mortgage in such form and containing such covenants and conditions as the mortgagee shall reasonably require. (A covenant for payment of principal and interest is reasonable: *Saunders v Milsome* (1866) LR 2 Eq 573.) This would not entitle the mortgagee to insist on the mortgage including, for example, a reservation of the right of consolidation: *Farmer v Pitt* [1902] 1 Ch 954 or an extension of the subject matter of the mortgage: *Whitley v Challis* [1892] 1 Ch 64, CA. The undertaking should expressly refer to such provisions.

3 See **32.12** ff.
4 *Re Drax, Savile v Drax* [1903] 1 Ch 781 at 794, 796, CA. See also *Al-Wazir v Islamic Press Agency Inc* [2001] EWCA Civ 1276, [2001] NPC 130, CA (equitable charge): the interest is imposed upon the charged property.
5 Eg in the case of a mortgage of an equitable interest.
6 Law of Property Act 1925, s 101: see **18.4** and **20.6** ff.
7 See further **3.102**.
8 See further **3.103**.
9 See **20.43**.

Trust of the legal estate[1]

3.102 The purpose of this provision is to enable the mortgagee on exercising the power to sell to vest the legal estate in the mortgaged property in himself or a purchaser. It consists of a declaration by the mortgagor that he holds the mortgaged property in trust for the mortgagee. Properly drafted, it makes the statutory power of appointing new trustees[2] exercisable by the mortgagee and persons deriving title under him and gives the mortgagee and those deriving title under him power to remove the mortgagor from the trusteeship and to appoint himself or themselves or any of them as trustees. On an appointment of new trustees the legal estate in the mortgaged property vests in the new trustees[3].

1 *London and County Banking Co v Goddard* [1897] 1 Ch 642.
2 Trustee Act 1925, s 36.
3 Section 40.

Power of attorney[1]

3.103 This may be included for the same purpose as the trust of the legal estate. The mortgagor irrevocably appoints the mortgagee and the persons deriving title under him the attorney or attorneys of the mortgagor and the persons deriving title under him in his or their name and on his or their behalf to vest the legal estate in the mortgaged property in any purchaser or other person in exercise of the statutory powers conferred on a mortgagee free and discharged from the mortgagor's right of redemption. Section 4 of the Powers of Attorney Act 1971 provides that where a power is expressed to be irrevocable and is given to secure a proprietary interest of the donee or the performance of an obligation owed to the donee then, so long as the donee has that interest or the obligation remains undischarged, the power shall not be revoked—(a) by the donor without the consent of the donee; nor (b) by the death, incapacity or bankruptcy of the donor, or, if the donor is a body corporate, by its winding up or dissolution. A power to secure a proprietary interest may be given to the person entitled to the interest and any persons deriving title under him and these persons shall be duly constituted donees of the power but without prejudice to any right to appoint substitutes given by the power. Where the mortgagee, in exercise of the statutory power of sale, conveys the mortgaged property pursuant to such a power of attorney, it seems that the purchaser will take the property free from subsequent incumbrances as well as the mortgage in respect of which the right of sale is being exercised[2].

1 It is desirable that the power should be expressed to be by way of security. If this is so then, unless the person dealing with the attorney knows that it was not in fact given by way of security, he is entitled to assume that the power is incapable of revocation except by the appointor acting with the attorney's consent and so the third person will be treated as having knowledge of the revocation only if he knows that the power has been revoked by the appointor acting with the attorney's consent: see s 5 (3).

2 *Re White Rose Cottage* [1965] Ch 940, [1965] 1 All ER 11, CA. For the effect of the statutory power of sale, see **20.40**.

Title against trustee in bankruptcy

3.104 An equitable mortgage of property which is valid between mortgagor and mortgagee is equally valid as between a trustee in bankruptcy of the mortgagor and the mortgagee[1].

1 As to the former position under the rules governing property in the reputed ownership of the bankrupt now abolished by the Insolvency Act 1986, see *Re Daintry, ex p Arkwright* (1843) 3 Mont D & De G 129; *Re Sketchley, ex p Boulton* (1857) 1 De G & J 163.

REGISTRATION OF MORTGAGES OF UNREGISTERED LAND[1]

Puisne mortgages and equitable charges

3.105 Provision is made by the Land Charges Act 1972 for the registration of certain legal and equitable mortgages in the Land Charges Register[2]. For this purpose a distinction is made between mortgages and charges depending on whether they are protected by a deposit of deeds or not. In this regard:

(a) there may be a succession of legal mortgages, with (usually) the first mortgagee holding the deeds, in which case all the other legal mortgages will be puisne mortgages[3]; alternatively,
(b) the deeds may be deposited by way of equitable mortgage[4]. In that event any legal mortgages that may exist will be puisne mortgages (for a 'puisne mortgage' is defined to be a 'legal mortgage not being a mortgage protected by a deposit of documents relating to the legal estate affected')[5]. And, further,
(c) there may be equitable mortgages not protected by deposit of documents. ('Protected' in this context means protected by a deposit of deeds at the time of the creation of the mortgage. Such a mortgage does not become registrable if the mortgagee parts with the deeds[6].)

Thus there are—for the purposes of registration—four kinds of securities:

(a) legal mortgages accompanied by title deeds;
(b) puisne mortgages, ie legal mortgages not accompanied by title deeds;
(c) equitable mortgages accompanied by title deeds[7];
(d) equitable mortgages[8] not accompanied by title deeds.

1 Registration of mortgages of registered land is considered in Chapter 4.
2 Section 2 (4); **24.4**. In the case of charges, capable of being registered as land charges, created by a company, registration under the Land Charges Act 1972 is required in addition to registration under the Companies Act, 1985, s 395 (as to this section, see **12.15** ff).
3 Before 1926 a puisne mortgage was a mortgage subsequent to the first mortgage. This, in freehold mortgages, carried the legal estate in fee simple and all subsequent mortgages were equitable.
4 Note that since 27 September 1989 an equitable mortgage cannot be created by mere deposit of deeds: see **3.100**.
5 Land Charges Act 1972, s 2 (4), Class C(i). Part of the deeds may be held by one mortgagee and part by another, see **3.91**. Quaere whether 'protected' under the Act means protected by all the deeds: see (1950) 13 MLR 534 (Hargreaves).

6 See (1941) 7 CLJ 249 (Megarry). See Law Commission Report Transfer of Land – Land Mortgages, 1991 (Law Com no 204, paras. 3.18-3.19, 3.30-3.34). As to the effect of the mortgagee failing to retain the deeds, see Chapter 24.
7 Although since 27 September 1989 an equitable mortgage cannot be created by mere deposit of deeds: see n 2, above.
8 Ie equitable mortgages not arising or affecting an interest arising under a trust for sale or a settlement and not included in any other class of land charge: Land Charges Act 1972, s 2 (4), Class C(iii).

Registration as land charges

3.106 Securities in division (a) do not require to be registered.

Securities in division (c) above probably do not require to be registered. However, it has been suggested that securities in division (c) are registrable as estate contracts[1]. An estate contract is a contract by an estate owner to convey or create a legal estate[2] and an equitable mortgage either includes an express agreement to create a legal mortgage or implies such an agreement[3]. Although an equitable mortgage accompanied with title deeds is expressly excluded from Class C (iii)—general equitable charge—it is not expressly excluded from Class C (iv)—estate contract. While the argument that a protected equitable mortgage is registrable as an estate contract is logically sound, such a construction would frustrate the policy behind the 1925 legislation which was to exempt all mortgages protected by deposit of deeds from registration, such deposit being a substitute for registration[4]. It is not the general practice of conveyancers to register an equitable mortgage as an estate contract unless there is an express (cf implied) agreement to create a legal mortgage. However, given the uncertainty of the legal position, it would be prudent to effect registration in all cases, although the better view is that a protected equitable mortgage is not registrable[5].

Securities in divisions (b) and (d) above require to be registered as land charges in Class C (i) (puisne mortgage) and Class C (iii) (general equitable charge respectively)[6]. Further, the priority of securities in division (d) depends on the order in which they are registered.

1 (1930) 69 LJ News 227 (Lightwood); (1941) 7 CLJ 250, 251 (Megarry); (1949) 10 CLJ 241 (Bailey); (1962) 26 Conv NS 446–449 (Rowley).
2 Land Charges Act 1972, s 2 (4), Class C (iv). See *Williams v Burlington Investments Ltd* (1977) 121 Sol Jo 424, HL. Where a legal charge executed pursuant to an agreement to execute a legal charge is an agreement for sale, which had to be registered as an estate contract, had priority to, though executed after, another legal charge executed after the sale.
3 See **3.95**, **3.96** and **3.100**, n 3.
4 For the arguments against such a construction, see 7 CLJ 252. Further, it was accepted in *United Bank of Kuwait plc v Sahib* [1997] Ch 107, CA that it was plainly not envisaged in the 1972 Act that a deposit of title deeds might fall within Class C(iv). It was recognised that it was part of the scheme of the legislation that all mortgages should be registered unless protected by deposit and acknowledged that it would be inconsistent with that scheme that a deposit of title deeds by way of security should be an estate contract registrable as a Class C(iv) land charge. An equitable charge which contains an ancillary agreement to execute a mortgage is likewise not registrable as an estate contract: *Property Discount Corpn Ltd v Lyon Cerasp Ltd* [1981] 1 WLR 300, CA.
5 If a Class C(iv) registration is necessary, any failure to register would avoid the contract to create the legal mortgage but presumably leave the mortgagee with the rights and remedies available to an equitable chargee: *Pryce v Bury* (1853) 2 Drew 41; *United Bank of Kuwait plc v Sahib* [1997] Ch 107, CA.
6 As to failure to register (which renders the unprotected mortgage void against a purchaser for value of any interest in the land), see **24.10** ff. Note, however, that an unregistered land charge is void only against a purchaser and the position as between the parties to

the charge is unaffected by non-registration if the mortgaged property is sold. Although the interest in land created by the charge ceases to subsist (because it cannot subsist without the property to which it attaches and is ousted by the absolute interest which the purchaser acquires) the mortgagee remains entitled to a security interest in the proceeds of sale: see *Barclays Bank plc v Buhr* [2001] EWCA Civ 1223, [2001] 31 EG 103 (CS), [2001] NPC 124, CA and **3.66**.

On a solicitor's liability for a failure to register a mortgage and the limitation period, see *Bell v Peter Browne & Co* [1990] 2 QB 495, CA.

Registration of mortgages by companies

3.107 Legal and equitable mortgages by a company must be registered in the Companies Register[1].

Those mortgages capable of registration under the Land Charges Act 1972 must also be registered under that Act[2].

1 See **12.15** ff.
2 Land Charges Act 1972, s 3 (7), (8).

TRANSITIONAL PROVISIONS AND COPYHOLD MORTGAGES

3.108 This topic is dealt with in detail in some earlier editions of this book. Problems on the transitional provisions are only rarely encountered nowadays and therefore this section has been excluded from this edition.

Chapter 4

Mortgages of registered land

REGISTERED CHARGES

Power of registered proprietor to create charges

4.1 By s 25(1) of the Land Registration Act 1925, the proprietor[1] of any registered land may[2] by deed:

(a) charge the registered land with the payment at an appointed time of any principal sum of money either with or without interest;
(b) charge the registered land in favour of a building society (within the meaning of the Building Societies Acts 1986)[3] in accordance with the rules of that society.

Notwithstanding that the above section only requires that the charge be by deed, it seems that an equitable charge may not be the subject of a substantive registration.[4]

1 The power is also conferred on: (a) a person entitled to be registered (eg pursuant to a registered disposition) before he is in fact registered: Land Registration Act 1925 s 37; (b) a person having the right to apply for registration as first proprietor before he is so registered: Land Registration Rules 1925, r 72. For the effect of a forged transfer, see *Argyle Building Society v Hammond* (1984) 49 P & CR 148, [1985] Conv 136 (Sydenham). For further proceedings in *Argyle Building Society v Hammond* see *Norwich and Peterborough Building Society v Steed* [1993] Ch 116, [1993] 1 All ER 330, CA.
2 Unless prevented from so doing by restriction, inhibition, notice or other entry: see Land Registration Act 1925, s 69 (4).
3 See now Building Societies Act 1986, Sch 18, para 2.
4 *Re White Rose Cottage* [1965] Ch 940 at 949, [1965] 1 All ER 11 at 14, per Lord Denning MR, CA. This appears to be the Registry practice: [1965] Ch at 954, [1965] 1 All ER at 17; and see Law Commission Working Paper No 67 (1976); and Land Registration Act 1925, s 27 (1) (see **4.4**, n 3). But cf Wilberforce J at [1964] Ch 483 at 490, [1964] 1 All ER 169 at 173; and see (1966) 19 CLP 26 (Ryder).

Form of charge

4.2 A charge may be in any form provided that:

(a) the registered land comprised in the charge is described by reference to the register or in any other manner sufficient to enable the registrar to identify the same without reference to any other document;[1]

(b) the charge does not refer to any other interest or charge affecting the land which would have priority over the same and is not registered or protected[2] on the register and is not an overriding interest.[3]

Thus, subject to the above requirements, the charge can be by deed in any form the mortgagee pleases.

1 As to description of registered land, see Land Registration Act 1925, s 76, and Rules, rr 272 and 285.
2 By notice, caution, inhibition or restriction.
3 As to overriding interests, see the Land Registration Act 1925, ss 3 (xvi) and 70. Section 25(2).

Terms of charge rendered void by statute

4.3 Any provision contained in a charge which purports to take away from the proprietor thereof the power of transferring it by registered disposition or of requiring the cessation thereof to be noted on the register or which affects any registered land or charge other than that in respect of which the charge is to be expressly registered, shall be void.[1]

1 Section 25(3); but this does not prevent the reservation of a right of consolidation: s 26 (2); and Land Registration Rules 1925, r 154.

Mode of mortgaging and time when charge or demise takes effect

4.4 The provisions[1] of the Law of Property Act 1925 as to the means of mortgaging freehold and leasehold land apply equally in relation to registered land.[2]

As regards registered land, a charge may contain, in the case of freehold land, an express demise and, in the case of leasehold land, an express sub-demise, subject to a provision for cesser on redemption. Otherwise, it will, subject to any provision to the contrary contained in the charge, take effect as a charge by way of legal mortgage.[3] (In the case of registered land, unlike the position governing unregistered land, the words 'by way of legal mortgage' are not required in a legal charge.[4])

A charge by way of legal mortgage, or a demise or sub-demise contained in a registered charge, takes effect from the date of delivery of the deed, but subject to the estate or interest of any person (except the proprietor of the land) whose estate or interest, whenever created, is registered and noted on the register before the date of registration of the charge.[5] Pending registration, the charge takes effect in equity only.[6]

1 Law of Property Act 1925, ss 85 and 86. See **3.3** and **3.5**.
2 Sections 85(3) and 86(3).
3 Section 27 (1), (2). The introduction of the mortgage by demise into the system of registration of title seems to have been unnecessary. The better course would have been to preserve the registered charge as a statutory charge only, but to have attached to its remedies, including the right to recover possession and to sue on the covenants in leases, incident to ordinary mortgages.
4 *Cityland and Property (Holdings) Ltd v Dabrah* [1968] Ch 166, [1967] 2 All ER 639. See also the Land Registration Rules 1925, r 139 and the Land Registration Act 1925, s 144(2).
5 Land Registration Act 1925, s 27(3).
6 Section 106 (as substituted).

Application for registration of charge

4.5 The application for registration of the charge must be on the appropriate form and accompanied, in a simple case, by the original charge and a certified copy thereof, the certificate of official search,[1] the land certificate,[2] any necessary consent or certificate under a restriction and a cheque for the fees.

1 Where an official search is obtained by a purchaser, any entries on the register made during the priority period of 15 days are postponed to the purchaser's application.
2 Which will be retained in the Land Registry until the charge is cancelled: Land Registration Act 1925, s 65.

Completion of charge by substantive registration

4.6 The charge is completed by the registrar entering on the Charges Register the person (or persons[1]) in whose favour it is made as proprietor of the charge and the particulars of the charge.[2] A charge certificate will then be prepared. The basic contents of the charge certificate are prescribed — it is to certify the registration of the charge and to contain:

(a) either the original or an office copy of the charge;
(b) a description (if none is contained in the charge) of the land affected;
(c) the name and address of the proprietor of the charge; and
(d) a list of the prior incumbrances, if any, appearing on the register.[3]

It must also bear the Land Registry's seal.[4] The precise form of the certificate will vary according to the circumstances. The charge certificate is issued to the chargee.[5]

The requirement, mentioned above, that the land certificate accompany the application may cause difficulty when there has been a prior mortgage by deposit of the land certificate.[6] Until registered, the mortgagee will not be able to exercise the statutory powers under the Land Registration Act 1925, s 34[7] (although he will have all the powers of an equitable mortgagee including those conferred by the Law of Property Act 1925, s 101). A caution will be the appropriate means of protecting the mortgage in this case.[8]

1 Where a charge is registered in the names of two or more proprietors (whether jointly or in undivided shares) the mortgage term implied or comprised in the charge vests in them as joint tenants and notwithstanding that the money is held in undivided shares, receipts may be given as if the money had been held on a joint account: Land Registration Act 1925, s 32: Land Registration Rules 1925, r 146.
2 Land Registration Act 1925, s 26 (1). Completion takes place as at the date and time of the delivery of the documents for registration: see Land Registration Rules 1925, r 85 (2) (as amended). Until such delivery the charge takes effect in equity only (*Woolwich Equitable Building Society v Marshall* [1952] Ch 1 at 6, [1951] 2 All ER 769 at 771; *Grace Rymer Investments Ltd v Waite* [1958] Ch 831, [1958] 2 All ER 777, CA) and, as a minor interest, will be overridden by a registered disposition for valuable consideration: Land Registration Act 1925, s 101. Until the entry is made the chargee's title is not perfected and he cannot exercise his statutory powers (as to which, see **4.13**; *Lever Finance Ltd v Needleman's Trustee* [1956] Ch 375, [1956] 2 All ER 378).
3 Land Registration Rules 1925, r 262 (as amended).
4 Rule 262.
5 Land Registration Act 1925, s 63, although it cannot be deposited in the registry if the chargee prefers.
6 Note, however, that a mere deposit of the certificate cannot, since 27 September 1989,

give rise to a valid charge: see the Law of Property (Miscellaneous Provisions) Act 1989, s 2, discussed in **4.30**.

7 *Lever Finance Ltd v Needleman's Trustee* [1956] Ch 375, [1956] 2 All ER 378.

8 See, generally, Law Commission Working Paper No 67 (1976).

Implied covenants in registered charge

4.7 Section 28 of the Land Registration Act 1925[1] makes the following provision as to covenants in a registered charge. Where a registered charge is created on any land there is implied on the part of the person being proprietor of such land at the time of the creation of the charge in the absence of any entry on the register negativing such implication, a covenant with the proprietor for the time being of the charge, to pay the principal sum charged, and interest, if any, thereon at the appointed time and rate, and a covenant, if the principal sum or any part thereof remains unpaid at such appointed time, to pay interest half-yearly at the appointed rate both before and after any judgment in respect of the charge is obtained on so much of the principal sum as for the time being remains unpaid.

It is not necessary (under the Land Registration Rules 1925, r 140) for there to be express words in the charge in order to negative the covenant otherwise implied by s 28; it is sufficient if the negativing be implicit in the instrument.[2]

Where the land charged is leasehold land, there is also implied in a registered charge, unless there is an entry on the register negativing the implication, a covenant by the proprietor of the land at the time the charge was created, or the persons deriving title under him, to pay the rent and to observe and perform the covenants and conditions contained in the registered lease and to indemnify the proprietor of the charge, and persons deriving title under him, against any claims, proceedings and expenses in respect thereof.

1 The implied covenants may be modified or negatived: Land Registration Rules 1925, r 140. They are in practice often varied. For example, there is no covenant for insurance or repair and a covenant for payment by trustees is usually restricted (see **12.116**). The registration of an instrument of charge negativing or modifying the provisions of this section shall be deemed a sufficient negative or contrary entry on the register: Land Registration Rules 1925, r 140.

2 *Fairmile Portfolio Management Ltd v Davies Arnold Cooper (a firm)* [1998] EGCS 149, Ch D, Mr M Mann QC.

MORTGAGES ON FIRST REGISTRATION

When registration required

4.8 The following dispositions of unregistered land now give rise to compulsory first registration:

(a) any conveyance of the freehold for valuable or other consideration, by way of gift or in pursuance of a court order;
(b) any grant of a lease for more than 21 years from the date of grant which is similarly for valuable or other consideration, etc;
(c) any assignment of a lease which on the date of such assignment has more than 21 years to run which is likewise for valuable or other consideration, etc;
(d) any disposition of the freehold or a lease with more than 21 years to run effected by an assent or vesting deed.[1]

Further, the requirement of compulsory registration also applies in relation to any disposition by the estate owner of unregistered land which is a legal mortgage of the freehold or a lease with more than 21 years to run where, on its creation, the mortgage takes effect as a mortgage to be protected by the deposit of documents relating to that estate or term of years and ranks in priority ahead of all other mortgages (if any) then affecting the same.[2]

1 Land Registration Act 1925, s 123(1) (as substituted by the Land Registration Act 1997, ss 1, 5(4)).
2 Section 123(2) (as substituted by the Land Registration Act 1997, ss 1, 5(4)).

By whom and when registration to be effected

4.9 Registration is to be effected by:

(a) in the first class of cases,[1] the transferee/grantee/assignee;
(b) in the second class of cases,[2] by the estate owner of the legal estate charged by the mortgage; or
(c) in either case, by that person's successor in title or assign.[3]

In any case, the application for first registration must be made within two months beginning with the date of the disposition in question, although the registrar may extend that period if satisfied that there is good reason for doing so.[4]

1 Those falling within s 123(1).
2 Those falling within s 123(2).
3 Section 123A(2) (as substituted by the Land Registration Act 1997, ss 1, 5(4)).
4 Section 123A(3) (as substituted by the Land Registration Act 1997, ss 1, 5(4)).

Position pending registration

4.10 Until an application has been made for the registration of the estate in question, no dealing, including a mortgage, relating to that estate can be accepted for registration.[1]

1 Land Registration Rules 1925, r 72(3).

Procedure upon application for registration

4.11 The procedure on the application is to be found in the registered conveyancing books.

Procedure upon registration

4.12 A legal mortgage will be registered with substantive registration[1] and on completion of the registration the charge certificate will be returned to the mortgagee with the deeds accompanying the application for first registration. The land certificate is kept at the Registry until the mortgage or charge is cancelled.[2]

An equitable mortgage will be protected by means of a notice on the register.[3]
Where there are two or more incumbrances prior to first registration of the land, their relative priorities are not affected by the registration of some or one of them only, or by the order in which such of them as are registered are entered in the register.[4]

1 Ie under Land Registration Act 1925, s 26, which apparently applies only to legal mortgages and charges. See **4.1**, n 4.
2 See Land Registration Act 1925, s 65.
3 Under the Land Registration Act 1925, s 49(1)(c). For the effect of notices, see the Land Registration Act 1925, s 52.
4 Land Registration Rules 1925, r 160 (2).

POWERS OF PROPRIETOR OF CHARGE (AND PROVISIONS ANCILLARY THERETO)

The same powers as a legal mortgagee of unregistered land

4.13 First and foremost, subject to any entry[1] on the register to the contrary,[2] the proprietor of a charge shall have and may exercise all the powers conferred by law on the owner of a legal mortgage.[3]

1 Eg a restriction against sub-charging.
2 The registration of an instrument of charge negativing or modifying the provisions of this section shall be deemed a sufficient negative or contrary entry on the register: Land Registration Rules 1925, r 140.
3 Land Registration Act 1925, s 34(1).

Power to bar right of redemption

4.14 Secondly, subject to any entry to the contrary on the register[1] and subject to the right of any persons appearing on the register to be prior incumbrancers, the proprietor of a charge may, after entry into possession and after having acquired a title under the Limitation Acts, execute a declaration in the prescribed form[2] that the right of redemption is barred and thereupon he shall be entitled, subject to furnishing any evidence which may be prescribed in support thereof,[3] to be registered as proprietor of the land, with the same consequences as if he had been a purchaser for valuable consideration of the land under the power of sale.[4]

1 The registration of an instrument of charge negativing or modifying the provisions of this section shall be deemed a sufficient negative or contrary entry on the register: Land Registration Rules 1925, r 140.
2 Form 52.
3 See the Land Registration Rules 1925, r 149.
4 Land Registration Act 1925, s 34(2).

Position on foreclosure

4.15 Thirdly, an order for foreclosure shall be completed by the registration of the proprietor of the charge (or such other person as may be named in the foreclosure order absolute for that purpose) as the proprietor of the land and by the cancellation of the charge and of all incumbrances and entries inferior thereto; and such registration shall operate in like manner and with the same consequences as if the proprietor of the charge or other person aforesaid had been a purchaser for valuable consideration of the land under a subsisting power of sale.[1]

1 Section 34(3).

Position where power of sale exercised

4.16 Fourthly, a sale by the court or under the power of sale shall operate and be completed by registration in the same manner, as nearly as may be (but subject to any alterations on the register affecting the priority of the charge), as a transfer for valuable consideration by the proprietor of the land at the time of the registration of the charge would have operated or been completed,[1] and, as respects the land transferred, the charge and all incumbrances and entries inferior thereto shall be cancelled.[2] Notwithstanding the creation of a term or sub-term, expressly or by implication, under this Act, such transfer shall (subject to any prior incumbrances or other entries on the register) operate to transfer the registered estate and the mortgage term or sub-term shall become merged, and any purported disposition of or dealing with the mortgage term or sub-term apart from the charge, and any process or act purporting to keep alive that term or sub-term after the cessation of the charge shall be void.[3]

1 See the Land Registration Act 1925, s 20, but see *Lyus v Prowsa Developments Ltd* [1982] 2 All ER 953, [1982] 1 WLR 1044, where the purchaser took subject to a constructive trust. Note, though, that purchasing land 'subject to' the rights of another does not, of itself, create a constructive trust: *Ashburn Anstalt v Arnold* [1989] Ch 1 at 24-25, [1988] 2 All ER 147, at 166, CA (decision unaffected despite being overruled and disapproved (on other points) in *Prudential Assurance Co Ltd v London Residuary Body* [1992] 2 AC 386, [1992] 3 All ER 504, HL and *Wallcite Ltd v Ferrishurst Ltd* [1999] Ch 355, [1999] 1 All ER 977, CA respectively).
2 Land Registration Act 1925, s 34(4).
3 Land Registration Act 1925, s 34(5).

Powers under Law of Property Act 1925, ss 99 and 100 when in possession

4.17 The proprietor of a charge, while in possession, or after a receiver has been appointed, or such receiver on his behalf, has all the powers conferred by ss 99 and 100 of the Law of Property Act 1925,[1] as extended by the instrument of charge or any instrument varying the terms thereof, but subject to any contrary intention expressed in any such instrument, a note of which intention shall, under an application to be made for that purpose, be entered in the register.[2]

1 See **19.21** et seq.
2 Land Registration Rules 1925, r 141(2).

Power to alter charge

4.18 The proprietor of a charge may by deed in the prescribed manner alter[1] the terms of the charge, with the consent of the proprietor of the registered land and of the proprietors of all registered charges (if any) of equal or inferior priority affected by the alteration.[2] The alteration must be completed by the registrar entering it on the register.[3] Where an alteration is executed between borrower and lender but no express consent is given thereto by a subsequent chargee, the alteration in question cannot bind the proprietor of the subsequent charge.[4]

1 The making of a further advance where the charge so provides is not an alteration of the charge.
2 Land Registration Act 1925, s 31(1); Land Registration Rules 1925, r 150. Form 51 is to be used.
3 Land Registration Act 1925, s 31(3).
4 *Ashfield Land (Bartlett Court) Ltd v B Ratcliffe (Gloucester) Ltd* (11 May 2000, unreported), Ch D, Mr K Lewison QC.

Power to transfer registered charge

4.19 The registered proprietor of a charge (or person entitled to be registered[1]) may, in the prescribed manner, transfer the charge to another person as proprietor.[2] (Note that any provision contained in a charge which purports to take away from the proprietor thereof the power of transferring it by registered disposition is void.[3])

The transfer is completed by the registrar entering on the register the transferee as proprietor of the charge transferred and the transferor is deemed to remain proprietor of the charge until the name of the transferee is entered on the register in respect thereof.[4]

A registered transferee for valuable consideration is not affected by any irregularity or invalidity in the original charge of which he did not have notice when it was transferred to him.[5]

On the registration of the transfer of the charge, any subsisting mortgage term or sub-term vests in the proprietor of the charge, notwithstanding anything to the contrary in the transfer or any other instrument.[6] In addition, subject to any entry to the contrary on the register, such vesting shall (subject to the right of redemption) have the same effect as if the proprietor of the charge had been registered as the transferee for valuable consideration of the term or sub-term.[7]

1 Land Registration Act 1925, s 37. A prospective purchaser can insist on the mortgagee procuring the registration of himself as proprietor of the charge: Land Registration Act 1925, s 110 (5).
2 Section 33(1); Land Registration Rules 1925, r 153. Form TR3 or TR4 is to be used, as the case requires.
3 Land Registration Act 1925, s 25(3).
4 Section 33(2).
5 Section 33(3). Further, nothing in the Consumer Credit Act 1974 affects the transferee who is the proprietor of a registered charge if he has no notice, or derives title through a person who had no notice of any defect in title arising under that Act: s 166 of the 1974 Act.
6 Section 33(4).
7 Section 33(5). Contrast s 33 with the Law of Property Act 1925, s 114 in relation to unregistered land where the position is that the transferee steps into the shoes of the transferor. Because in the registered land context, on registration of the transfer, the transferee is in the same position as a transferee for valuable consideration of the term or sub-term, it follows that, by virtue of the Land Registration Act 1925, s 23, the transferee may take free of incumbrances and other matters not protected on the register which bound the transferor, eg by estoppel, and thereby be in a better position than the transferor. *Quaere* whether the provisions of s 114 apply to the transfer of registered charges in so far as that section is not inconsistent with ss 23 and 33?

Power to sub-charge

4.20 For sub-mortgages of registered charges, see **15.4**.

POWERS OF PROPRIETOR OF LAND SUBJECT TO CHARGE

4.21 The proprietor of the land, while in possession, has all the powers of leasing and of accepting surrenders of leases conferred by ss 99 and 100 of the Law of Property Act 1925, as extended by the instrument of charge or any instrument varying the terms thereof, but subject to any contrary intention expressed in such instrument, a note of which intention shall, under an application to be made for that purpose, be entered on the register.[1] Subject as aforesaid all dispositions by the proprietor of the land shall, unless the proprietor of the charge concurs in the disposition, take effect subject to any charge registered at the time of the disposition.[2]

1 Land Registration Rules, r 141 (1).
2 Rule 141 (4).

TRANSMISSION OF REGISTERED CHARGE ON DEATH OR BANKRUPTCY

4.22 The personal representative(s) of (a) a deceased sole registered proprietor of a charge, or (b) the survivor of two or more joint registered proprietors of a charge is (are) entitled to be registered as the proprietor(s) in the place of the former proprietor.[1]

The trustee in bankruptcy of a registered proprietor of a charge which is comprised in the bankrupt's estate is similarly so entitled.[2] Such a person may deal with the charge before he is himself registered as proprietor.[3]

It should be noted that the fact of any person having become entitled to any charge in consequence of the death or bankruptcy of any registered proprietor has to be proved in the prescribed manner.[4]

Any person registered in place of a deceased or bankrupt proprietor holds the charge upon the trusts and for the purposes upon and subject to which the same is applicable by law and subject to any minor interests, subject to which the deceased or bankrupt proprietor held the same; but, save as aforesaid, he is in all respects (and in particular as respects any registered dealings with such land or charge), in the same position as if he had taken such land or charge under a transfer for valuable consideration.[5]

On the registration of any transmission of a charge, any subsisting mortgage term or sub-term vests without conveyance or assignment in the proprietor for the time being of the charge.[6] In addition, subject to any entry to the contrary on the register, such vesting shall (subject to the right of redemption) have the same effect as if the proprietor of the charge had been registered as the transferee for valuable consideration of the term or sub-term.[7]

1 Land Registration Act 1925, s 41.
2 Section 42.
3 Section 37; Land Registration Rules 1925, r 170.
4 Section 45; Land Registration Rules 1925, rr 168–185.
5 Land Registration Act, s 43.

6 Section 44(1).
7 Section 44(2).

PRIORITIES OF REGISTERED CHARGES

4.23 Subject to any entry to the contrary on the register,[1] registered charges on the same land, as between themselves, rank according to the order in which they are entered on the register, and not according to the order in which they are created.[2]

1 The registration of an instrument of charge negativing or modifying the provisions of this section shall be deemed a sufficient negative or contrary entry on the register: Land Registration Rules 1925, r 140.
2 Land Registration Act 1925, s 29. Priority may be determined by the relevant statute in the case of certain statutory charges and the register will reflect this: Land Registration Rules 1925, rr 157 and 158.

CHARGE FOR SECURING FURTHER ADVANCES

4.24 When a registered charge is made for securing further advances, the registrar will enter notice of this on the register and, before making a subsequent entry on the register which would prejudicially affect the priority of any further advance under the charge, he must give notice to the proprietor of the charge of the intended entry. The proprietor of the charge will not be affected, in respect of any further advance, by such a subsequent entry unless the advance is made after the date when the notice ought to have been received in the ordinary course of post.[1]

In a case where a registered chargee made further advances pursuant to an obligation which was not noted on the register, such advances nonetheless had priority over the subsequent chargee because they were made before the first chargee received notice from the registrar of the second charge.[2]

If the proprietor of the charge suffers loss in relation to a further advance by reason of any failure on the part of the registrar or the post office he is entitled to indemnity, unless the loss arises by reason of the proprietor's omission to amend his address for service on the register.[3]

Where the proprietor of a charge is under an obligation, noted on the register, to make a further advance, a subsequent registered charge takes effect subject to any further advance made pursuant to the obligation.[4]

The registrar shall add a note (of such an obligation to make further advances) to the entry of the charge in the register upon an application by the proprietor or intending proprietor of the charge in question.[5] The application must be made by a separate application[6] unless included in the instrument of charge or a deed of alteration of a registered charge.[7]

1 Land Registration Act, s 30(1). Notice is given by registered post or the recorded delivery service.
2 *Lloyd v Nationwide Anglia Building Society* [1996] EGCS 80.
3 Section 30(2).
4 Section 30(3), inserted by the Law of Property (Amendment) Act 1926, s 5; cf Law of Property Act 1925, s 94 (see **24.83** et seq).
5 Land Registration Rules 1925, r 139A(5) (added by the Land Registration (Charges) Registration Rules 1990, r 3(1)).
6 In Form 113: Land Registration Rules 1925, r 139A(3).

7 Land Registration Rules 1925, r 139A(3) and (4). The application cannot, however, be included in an incorporated document as defined in r 139.

LOST CHARGE CERTIFICATE

4.25 A new land or charge certificate may be issued in place of one lost.[1] Where it is proved to the satisfaction of the registrar that a certificate has been lost or destroyed, or that it is in the possession of a person out of the jurisdiction of the court or its production cannot be obtained without undue delay or expense, he may issue a new one after taking such indemnities as he may consider necessary and after giving such public notice in the *Gazette* and in such local or other newspapers (if any) and in such manner as shall appear to him sufficient in each case.[2]

1 Land Registration Act 1925, s 67.
2 Land Registration Rules 1925, r 271 (1).

DEPOSIT OF CERTIFICATE

BEFORE 27 SEPTEMBER 1989

Generally

4.26 Before 27 September 1989 the proprietor (or joint proprietors acting in concert[1]) of registered land or of a registered charge could (subject to overriding interests, any entry to the contrary on the register, and any estates, interests, charges or rights otherwise registered or protected on the register at the date of deposit) create a lien on the registered land or charge by deposit of the land (or charge[2]) certificate.[3] Such a lien was equivalent to a lien created in the case of unregistered land by the deposit of documents of title or of the mortgage deed by an owner entitled for his own benefit to the registered estate, or a mortgagee beneficially entitled to the mortgage, as the case might be.

This procedure afforded a simple and not uncommon method of securing a temporary loan.

The Land Registration Act 1925, s 66 probably envisaged a simple deposit of the certificate without any accompanying documentation. Where a security of this nature was taken, it could, prior to 3 April 1995, be protected by the creditor giving notice of the deposit[4] (or intended deposit[5]) to the Land Registry.[6] On receipt of the notice, the registrar would enter notice of the deposit in the Charges Register.[7] A notice of deposit entered on the register prior to 3 April 1995 operated (and continues to operate) as a caution under s 54 of the Land Registration Act 1925.[8] A caution[9] gives protection to the cautioner in that it gives notice of his interest, thereby ensuring that the cautioner can ensure that he is warned of any proposed dealing and given an opportunity to assert priority for his interest.[10] This method of protection was considered to be appropriate where the deposit did not itself create the security, eg where it accompanied a memorandum by way of equitable mortgage,[11] or even a legal mortgage.[12]

It will be noted that a substantive registration and an entry of notice of deposit or intended deposit could not be made on the same register because, if substantive registration had been effected no deposit would be possible since the land certificate would be lodged in the Registry[13] and if there had been a deposit it would not be possible to lodge the land certificate for the purpose of substantive registration. Further, a notice of deposit or intended deposit could not be entered while another such notice was on the register.[14] In such cases registration of a caution or entry of notice had to be sought.

1 Co-owners can only act with unanimity. One cannot part with custody of the deeds without consent of the other. So where a husband purported to charge the matrimonial home without his wife's knowledge and consent and deposited the land certificate with the lender without her consent, she was entitled to demand the return of the certificate: *Thames Guaranty Ltd v Campbell* [1985] QB 210, [1984] 1 All ER 144, affd [1985] QB 210, [1984] 2 All ER 585, CA.
2 In the case of a sub-charge by the proprietor of a charge.
3 Land Registration Act 1925, s 66(1).
4 Land Registration Rules 1925, r 239 (as originally enacted and as substituted).
5 Rule 240 (now revoked).
6 Or a notice or caution might be registered: *Re White Rose Cottage* [1965] Ch 940, [1965] 1 All ER 11, CA.
7 No notice of deposit or intended deposit could be entered while another such notice was on the register, nor as to part only of the land or charge to which the certificate related: Land Registration Rules 1925, r 243 (revoked by the Land Registration Rules 1995, r 4(4)).
8 Rule 239(1) (as substituted). (Formerly, the Land Registration Rules 1925, rr 239(4) and 242.)
9 Which can be warned off. On the nature of cautionable interests see (1971) 35 Conv (NS) 21 (Robinson).
10 See *Re White Rose Cottage* [1965] Ch 940 at 949 and 950, [1965] 1 All ER 11 at 14, CA; *Parkash v Irani Finance Ltd* [1970] Ch 101, [1969] 1 All ER 930; *Clark v Chief Land Registrar* [1993] Ch 294, [1993] 2 All ER 936 (Ferris J) and [1994] Ch 370, [1994] 4 All ER 96, CA.
11 *Re White Rose Cottage* [1965] Ch 940 at 955, [1965] 1 All ER 11 at 14–15, CA per Harman LJ. On this case generally, see (1966) 19 Current Legal Problems 26 (Ryder).
12 *Barclays Bank Ltd v Taylor* [1973] Ch 63, [1972] 2 All ER 752; revsd [1974] Ch 137, [1973] 1 All ER 752, CA.
13 Land Registration Act 1925, s 65.
14 Land Registration Rules 1925, r 243 (revoked by the Land Registration Rules 1995, r 4(4)).

Procedure

4.27 Where the depositor was a transferee the certificate had first to be sent to the Registry for the registration of the transfer before it could be deposited. A notice of intended deposit ought to have been given by the depositor in such a case.[1]

The effect of the entry of the notice of deposit or intended deposit was that the creditor was entitled to have notice and to be heard before any subsequent dealing was registered.[2]

1 Land Registration Rules 1925, r 240 (similarly revoked).
2 Land Registration Act 1925, s 55 and rr 218 and 219.

Priorities

4.28 There is no express provision in the Land Registration Act 1925 as to priorities where the charges are not registered charges. However, as the depositee had the land certificate, he could effectively prevent any subsequent charge being registered (since such subsequent chargee could not lodge the certificate with his application) and, moreover, notice of deposit gave him priority to a subsequent equitable charge or interest protected by caution.[1]

1 *Re White Rose Cottage* [1965] Ch 940; *Barclays Bank Ltd v Taylor*, above, in the Court of Appeal where it seems that the prior unregistered mortgage would have had priority, as the prior minor interest, even without the registration of the notice of deposit. In *Mortgage Corpn Ltd v Nationwide Credit Corpn* [1994] Ch 49, [1993] 4 All ER 623, CA it was held that the principles in *Barclays Bank Ltd v Taylor* (namely, that priority as between unregistered equitable interests depends upon time of creation) applied to regulate priorities between two mortgages of registered land neither of which had been substantively registered as a registered charge, the rule of priority contained in Land Registration Act 1925, s 29 being inapplicable to such mortgages. Thus, neither registration of a caution nor registration of a notice (under Land Registration Act 1925, s 49) gave any priority as between the mortgages which, by reason of s 106, took effect only in equity unless and until registered as charges. See also (1994) 137 Sol Jo 1113 (Council).

Powers of depositee

4.29 There is also no express provision as regards the powers of sale, etc, of someone other than the proprietor of a registered charge. A simple depositee under s 66 would have had no power of sale without an order of the court. Accordingly, it was desirable for a deposit to have been accompanied by a memorandum under seal or other deed in order to give the depositee the statutory power of sale.[1] However, the power of sale by itself would not be enough to enable the depositee to effect a sale for the Land Registration Act 1925, because s 110(5) enables the purchaser of registered land to insist on either the vendor's registration as proprietor of the charge under which he is selling or a sale by the proprietor of the land. Accordingly, the deeds ought to have been in the form previously mentioned,[2] incorporating a power of attorney and undertaking to execute a registered charge. The depositee would then be able to make a transfer under the power of attorney.

1 Where there was a deposit and a memorandum it was a question of construction which created a security (see *Re White Rose Cottage*, above) and the method of protection might vary depending upon whether the deposit alone was the security (ie only a s 66 situation) or the memorandum supported by the deposit was the security (protection by notice of deposit, caution or notice on the register).

2 See **3.101** and **3.103**.

SINCE 27 SEPTEMBER 1989

4.30 Since 27 September 1989 the mere deposit of a certificate has been ineffective to create a charge on the land.[1] Just as, in the case of unregistered land, the mere deposit of title deeds no longer creates a valid equitable mortgage, the position is mirrored in the registered land context.[2] It has been held that s 66 of the Land Registration Act 1925 does not confer validity on a purported mortgage by deposit because it simply begs the question what lien, if any, is created by the deposit of title documents in the case of unregistered land.[3] The section merely equates the registered land position with that applicable to unregistered land (which, as noted above, is that a mere deposit is incompatible with the Law of Property (Miscellaneous Provisions) Act 1989).[4]

Indeed, since 3 April 1995 a notice of deposit (or intended deposit) can no longer be registered.[5] An equitable mortgage should thus be protected by notice.[6]

Further, a notice of deposit will be cancelled in respect of an equitable mortgage created since 27 September 1989 which is not in writing.

1 By reason of the Law of Property (Miscellaneous Provisions) Act 1989, s 2. See *United Bank of Kuwait plc v Sahib* [1997] Ch 107, CA.
2 For a case based on alleged professional negligence in which promissory notes were purportedly secured by the deposit of title deeds for registered leasehold land, such security being ineffective because it was not recorded in writing in a document signed by the owners of the property (as required by the Law of Property (Miscellaneous Provisions) Act 1989, s 2), see *Dean v Allin & Watts (a firm)* [2000] Lloyd's Rep PN 469, [2000] EGCS 5 (unaffected by the reversal of the decision itself, as to which see [2001] EWCA Civ 758, [2001] 2 Lloyd's Rep 249, CA).
3 *United Bank of Kuwait plc v Sahib* [1997] Ch 107, CA.
4 Accordingly, the Land Registry will no longer entertain applications to enter a notice of deposit of a land or charge certificate.
5 Note the revocation of Land Registration Rules 1925, r 240.
6 Land Registration Act 1925, s 49(1) as amended.

MORTGAGES OFF THE REGISTER (UNREGISTERED MORTGAGES IN RESPECT OF REGISTERED LAND)

Creation, protection and registration generally

4.31 Whereas a registered charge, the subject of a charge certificate, derives its status and protection from the register, mortgages may nonetheless be created by transactions which obtain protection by the methods outlined below but are not registered. Such mortgages may be either unregistered legal mortgages, whether or not with deposit of certificate, or equitable mortgages, whether or not with deposit of certificate.

As regards mortgages effected off the register, it is statutorily provided that the proprietor of any registered land may, subject to any entry to the contrary on the register, mortgage, by deed or otherwise,[1] the land or any part thereof in any manner which would have been permissible if the land had not been registered and with the like effect.[2]

Unless and until the mortgage becomes a registered charge, it takes effect only in equity, and can be overridden — unless it is protected by notice under s 49, any such other notice as may be prescribed[3] or a caution under s 54.[4]

Further, although a charge which is so protected by a notice under s 49 will no longer be capable of being overridden, it will still only take effect in equity unless and until it becomes a registered charge.[5]

It seems that between mortgages or interests protected by caution, priority depends on the order in which the cautions are lodged.[6]

1 There *should* be a deed (thus giving the mortgage the statutory powers) or an instrument including a power of attorney and undertaking; see above.
2 Land Registration Act 1925, s 106(1) (as amended by the Administration of Justice Act 1977, s 26).
3 No other notice has been prescribed.
4 Land Registration Act 1925, ss 106(2) and (3) (as so amended). The 1977 amendments followed the proposals of the Law Commission in Working Paper No 67 (1976). The special mortgage caution of the 1925 Act was abolished. On the special mortgage caution, see *Barclays Bank Ltd v Taylor* [1973] Ch 63, [1972] 2 All ER 752; affd [1974] Ch 137, [1973] 1 All ER 752, CA.
5 *Mortgage Corpn Ltd v Nationwide Credit Corpn* [1994] Ch 49, [1993] 4 All ER 623, CA.

6 See per Denning MR, in *Re White Rose Cottage* [1965] Ch 940 at 949, [1965] 1 All ER 11 at 14; and see (1978) 94 LQR 571 at 583 (Jackson).

Protection by registration as land charge

4.32 Section 48 of the Land Registration Act 1925 provides for the registration of notice of a lease and s 49 provides for the extension of the provisions of that section to provide for notices of other rights, interests and claims (including land charges until the land charge is registered as a registered charge).[1] A land charge means a land charge of any class described in s 2 of the Land Charges Act 1972 or a local land charge.[2] Accordingly, a puisne mortgage[3] and general equitable charge[4] of registered land may be protected by notice under s 49 if the land certificate can be produced.[5] Also, it appears that an equitable charge protected by deposit of the land certificate[6] may perhaps be so protected.[7]

Where a charge is protected by a notice of this kind it means that every subsequent proprietor or incumbrancer is deemed to be effected with notice of the charge. A disposition takes effect subject to any estate, right or claim protected by notice but only if and so far as the same is valid and is not (independently of the Land Registration Act) overridden by the disposition.[8]

1 Land Registration Act 1925, s 49(1)(c). The extension was made by Land Registration Rules 1925, r 190. Form 59 is to be used.
2 Land Registration Act 1925, s 3 (ix), as substituted by Local Land Charges Act 1975, s 17, Sch 1.
3 Namely, a legal mortgage not protected by a deposit of documents. See **24.4** et seq.
4 Namely, any equitable charge similarly unprotected. See **24.4** et seq.
5 Land Registration Act 1925, s 64.
6 As to whether this constitutes an estate contract, see **3.106**, n 4.
7 Land Registration Act 1925, s 106 (3) covers any mortgage which is not a registered charge. Also see *Re White Rose Cottage*, above. *Sed quaere*, see (1966) 19 Current Legal Problems, pp 24, 35. The protection may be under s 49 (1) (f) and r 190 where an equitable charge by deed is protected by deposit: see Hayton *Registered Land* (3rd edn), pp 118–130.
8 Land Registration Act 1925, s 52.

Transfer of unregistered mortgages

4.33 A mortgage which is not a registered charge devolves and may be transferred, discharged, surrendered or otherwise dealt with by the same instruments and in the same manner as if the land had not been registered.[1] Transfer is effected in the usual way for unregistered land. The devolution of the title to the mortgage does not appear on the register.

If the mortgage is protected by caution a fresh caution should be lodged by the transferee and a withdrawal of the existing caution procured.[2] No further step is required when the mortgage is protected by notice on the register.

1 Land Registration Act 1925, s 106 (4) (as substituted).
2 Under the Land Registration Rules 1925, r 222. Form WCT should be used.

Mortgages of equitable interests in registered land

4.34 Such interests are minor interests and as such are not capable of being disposed of by registered dispositions. Thus they may be overridden by registered dispositions for valuable consideration.[1] Such interests may be disposed of off the register.[2] Priorities as between minor interests are regulated by ss 137 and 138 of the Law of Property Act 1925.[3]

1 Land Registration Act 1925, ss 3(xv) and 101(2).
2 Section 101(1).
3 Land Registration Act 1986, s 5 (which abolished the Minor Interests Index).

Floating charge over registered land

4.35 Such a charge may be protected by notice,[1] provided the land certificate can be produced.[2] Otherwise it can only be protected by caution.[3]

1 Land Registration Act 1925, s 49 (1) (f); Land Registration Rules 1925, r 190.
2 Section 64. For registration of company charges, see **12.15** et seq.
3 Under s 54.

Equitable charge of registered land

4.36 Such a charge is a minor interest capable of taking effect in equity only and capable of being overridden by registered dispositions for valuable consideration unless protected.[1] It may be protected by caution.[2]

1 Land Registration Act 1925, s 3 (xv).
2 Section 54.

REGISTERED CHARGES OF SETTLED LAND

4.37 The proprietor of settled land which is registered (and all other necessary parties, if any) shall, on the request and at the expense of any person entitled to an estate, interest, or charge conveyed or created for securing money actually raised at the date of such request, charge the land in the prescribed manner with the payment of money so raised, but so long as the estate, interest or charge is capable of being overridden under the Settled Land Act 1925, or the Law of Property Act 1925, no charge can be created or registered.[1]

1 Land Registration Act 1925, s 90.

DISCHARGE OF MORTGAGES OF REGISTERED LAND

4.38 For this topic, see **28.59**.

Chapter 5

Mortgages of chattels

MORTGAGES OR PERSONAL CHATTELS GENERALLY[1]

Generally

5.1 Personal chattels may be the subject of securities made either by legal or equitable mortgage or by pledge. No instrument in writing is necessary for the validity of such security[2].

A mortgage of chattels which is, however, made in writing, is (with certain exceptions, the most important of which is when the mortgagor is a company) subject to the provisions of the Bills of Sale Acts. Certain securities are also subject to the formalities prescribed by the Consumer Credit Act 1974 and regulations made under that Act[3].

A legal mortgage of chattels passes the property in the goods to the mortgagee, subject to redemption. Where the goods are already mortgaged or pledged, a second mortgage of them, in other words of the equity of redemption in them, is as good as it is in the case of land[4].

1 The third section of this chapter is merely an outline of the law relating to bills of sale. The complicated requirements of the Bills of Sale Acts (failure to observe which may invalidate the bill) make bills of sale unattractive to lenders and the requirements of registration of bills makes them unattractive to borrowers. There are approximately 8,000 registrations annually. Further reference should be made to 4 *Halsbury's Laws* (4th edn reissue), Bills and the Report of the Committee on Consumer Credit (Crowther Report) 1971, Cmnd 4596.

2 *Reeves v Capper* (1838) 5 Bing NC 136; *Flory v Denny* (1852) 7 Exch 581; and see *United Forty Pound Loan Club v Bexton* [1891] 1 QB 28n. But if the mortgage is in writing it is subject to the statutory provisions affecting bills of sale (unless within an exception thereto), as to which, see below. Writing will be necessary if the security relates to a regulated agreement under the Consumer Credit Act 1974 (as to which, see Chapter 10) and the security is not given by the debtor himself: Consumer Credit Act 1974, s 105 (6). On fixed charges on stock in trade, see Goode *Legal Problems of Credit and Security* (2nd edn), pp 54–5; Gough *Company Charges* (2nd edn), pp 630–631.

3 See Chapter 10.

4 *Usher & Co v Martin* (1889) 24 QBD 272.

Possession of the chattels

5.2 The possession of the creditor is not necessary for the validity of a legal mortgage of personal chattels[1], but an actual or constructive delivery of possession is essential for the validity of a pledge[2].

For many years it was considered fraudulent for the debtor to continue in possession of the mortgaged goods, since he was thereby invested with a delusive credit arising out of such possession[3]. That rule still holds good in the case of absolute bills of sale[4], but the continuance of the grantor in possession under a bona fide conditional bill of sale given by way of security only[5], when consistent with the deed, is no longer regarded as even prima facie evidence of fraud[6].

1 *Maugham v Sharpe* (1864) 17 CBNS 443.
2 See **1.4**.
3 In *Twyne's Case* (1602) 3 Co Rep 80, soon after the passing of the statute against fraudulent deeds and alienations, 13 Eliz 1, c 5 (1571) (subsequently the Law of Property Act 1925, s 172 and see now the Insolvency Act 1986, ss 238-241, 339-341), it was held that such possession was within the mischief aimed at by the Act.
4 A bill given otherwise than as security for the payment of money.
5 A bill given to secure a money payment.
6 *Pennell v Dawson* (1856) 18 CB 355; *Hale v Metropolitan Saloon Omnibus Co* (1859) 28 LJ Ch 777.

Provision for possession till default

5.3 A proviso that the mortgagor of goods shall remain in possession till default operates as a re-demise by the mortgagee, who cannot sue for the goods till default has been made, or until the expiration of the time limited, when notice for payment is to be given upon default. As a consequence, the mortgagor may maintain an action for interference with his possession during the term[1].

Such a proviso will not, however, prevent the mortgagee from exercising an express power to take possession on the happening of other contingencies, though no default has been made.

In the case of a bill of sale by way of security the grantee may only take possession on the statutory grounds. The re-demise entitles the mortgagor to the use of the chattels, but if he or his trustee in bankruptcy sells them during the term, it will be a disclaimer of the tenancy and the mortgagee or his assignees may sue in respect of the conversion[2]. There may, however, be an express or implied licence to the mortgagor to deal with the goods in the way of his trade and, so long as he does so, a bona fide purchaser from him will be protected. If not, the sale will be bad, despite the bona fides of the purchaser[3].

If there is an express right to make use of the goods, a licence to consume any perishable goods may be implied, but such goods cannot be sold or otherwise dealt with as if there had been no grant[4].

1 See Chapter 19.
2 *Fenn v Bittleston* (1851) 7 Exch 152; *Brierly v Kendall* (1852) 17 QB 937.
3 *National Mercantile Bank v Hampson* (1880) 5 QBD 177; *Payne v Fern* (1881) 6 QBD 620.
4 *Gale v Burnell* (1845) 7 QB 850.

Chattels not yet in existence

5.4 It is not necessary for the validity of a mortgage of chattels that the mortgagor should be aware of their exact nature[1]. He may even, subject, where appropriate, to the provisions of the Bills of Sale Acts[2], create a valid security upon personal property not yet in existence, provided he has an interest, actual or potential, in the source from which the property may arise[3].

1 *Re Beattie, ex p Kelsall* (1846) De G 352.
2 Chattels which are not yet in existence do not fall within the category of 'personal chattels', as defined in the Bills of Sale Acts, since they are not 'capable of complete transfer by delivery': *Brantom v Griffits* (1877) 2 CPD 212, CA; *Thomas v Kelly* (1888) 13 App Cas 506 at 518, HL, per Lord Macnaghten; but see the cases cited in 4 *Halsbury's Laws* (4th edn reissue) para 616, n 1, especially *Re Reis, ex p Clough* [1904] 2 KB 769 at 788.
3 See eg *Langton v Horton* (1842) 1 Hare 549. However, mortgages which are confined to after-acquired chattels and not, therefore, executed under the Bills of Sale Acts, appear to be wholly outside the provisions of the Acts and to be valid, provided that they conform with the equitable doctrine described below. For the difference between a chattel mortgage and a floating charge, see *Re Zegalski* (1972) 31 DLR (3d) 766.

Incomplete chattels

5.5 An incomplete chattel may be the subject of a security comprising a contract to complete it and to assign the materials appropriated for its completion and the chattel when finished[1].

1 *Woods v Russell* (1822) 5 B & Ald 942; *Reid v Fairbanks* (1853) 13 CB 692.

Future acquired property

5.6 An assignment of chattels not in the mortgagor's possession at the date of the assignment will, if there is a sufficiently specific[1] description of them, operate to transfer an equitable title as soon as the property is acquired by the assignor[2].

If future acquired chattels are included in a security bill of existing chattels, the validity of such document will, however, be affected. Section 9 of the Bills of Sale Act (1878) Amendment Act 1882 requires every security bill to be made in accordance with the statutory form and s 5 of that Act requires the grantor to be the true owner of the chattels at the time of the execution of the bill[3].

1 As to the meaning of 'specific', see *Tailby v Official Receiver* (1888) 13 App Cas 523, HL; and *Syrett v Egerton* [1957] 3 All ER 331. See also *King v Greig* [1931] VLR 413 (re sale of unascertained part of defined whole); *Re Wait* [1927] 1 Ch 606, CA.
2 *Holroyd v Marshall* (1862) 10 HL Cas 191. The equitable title relies on the possibility of a decree of specific performance of a contract to assign. See (1985) 6 Co Law 9 (Pennington).
3 In *Thomas v Kelly* (1888) 13 App Cas 506, HL it was held that such inclusion avoids the whole bill of sale, but if the reference to future acquired chattels occurs only in the schedule, the bill is void only in respect of the future acquired chattels; moreover, the bill is valid even in respect of them as between mortgagor and mortgagee: Bills of Sale Act (1878) Amendment Act 1882, ss 4, 5, 6.

EFFECT OF MORTGAGE ON FIXTURES

Fixtures passing by mortgage of land[1]

5.7 A mortgage of land[2] comprises, without express mention, and subject to any contrary intention, all fixtures which at the date of the mortgage are, or at any time afterwards during its continuance may be, annexed to the land[3], whether or not they are removable as between landlord and tenant[4]. Fixtures passing by a mortgage of land will not pass to the trustee in bankruptcy of the mortgagor[5].

The general rule is unaffected by the Bills of Sale Acts, except when fixtures are the subject of a separate security distinct from the security in the land. When separately assigned or charged, fixtures are 'personal chattels' within the Acts[6] though not for other purposes[7], and not, except in the case of trade machinery, when conveyed or assigned together with a freehold or leasehold interest in any land or building to which they are affixed[8].

1 See generally, as to fixtures, 27(1) *Halsbury's Laws* (4th edn reissue) paras 143 ff; and Megarry and Wade *The Law of Real Property* (6th edn) pp 928 ff.
2 Whether legal or equitable (see *Re Lusty, ex p Lusty v Official Receiver* (1889) 60 LT 160) and whether of freeholds or leaseholds (see *Meux v Jacobs* (1875) LR 7 HL 481; *Southport and West Lancashire Banking Co v Thompson* (1887) 37 Ch D 64, CA).
3 Law of Property Act 1925, s 62. *Mather v Fraser* (1856) 2 K & J 536; *Walmsley v Milne* (1859) 7 CBNS 115; *Longbottom v Berry* (1869) LR 5 QB 123; *Holland v Hodgson* (1872) LR 7 CP 328; *Smith v Maclure* (1884) 32 WR 459; *Reynolds v Ashby & Son* [1904] AC 466, HL; *Ellis v Glover and Hobson Ltd* [1908] 1 KB 388, CA; *Vaudeville Electric Cinema v Muriset* [1923] 2 Ch 74; *Hulme v Brigham* [1943] KB 152, [1943] 1 All ER 204; *TSB Bank plc v Botham* [1996] EGCS 149, *sub nom Botham v TSB Bank plc* (1996) 73 P & CR DI, CA; *Bank of Melbourne v CBFC Leasing Pty Ltd* [1991] ACL Rep 295 Qd 7; *North West Trust Co v Rezyn Developments Inc* (1991) 81 DLR (4th) 751. See generally Palmer and McKendrick *Interests in Goods*. As to the power of sale in relation to fixtures, see Chapter 20.
4 *Monti v Barnes* [1901] 1 KB 205; *Climie v Wood* (1869) LR 4 Exch 328 at 330.
5 *Clark v Crownshaw* (1832) 3 B & Ad 804 and see 3(2) *Halsbury's Laws of England* (4th edn reissue) para 404.
6 *Climpson v Coles* (1889) 23 QBD 465. Agricultural charges on tenants' fixtures are excepted from the Bills of Sale Acts, previously the Agricultural Credits Act 1928, s 8 (1); Agricultural Marketing Act 1958, s 15 (5).
7 *Meux v Jacobs* (1875) LR 7 HL 481.
8 Bills of Sale Act 1878, s 4. See also s 7. As to personal chattels for the purposes of the Bills of Sale Acts, see **5.23**.

Trade fixtures

5.8 Where trade fixtures customarily belong to the tenant of the mortgagor, the mortgagee cannot claim them as against the tenant[1]. A mortgagor while in possession may permit trade fixtures to be put up and removed, so long as he does not either materially diminish the mortgagee's security, or commit a breach of some express stipulation in the mortgage[2]. The right of removal ceases when possession is taken by the mortgagee.

The exception as to trade fixtures in favour of a tenant does not, however, apply in the case of fixtures erected on the mortgaged premises under a hire-purchase agreement on the terms that, until paid for, they shall remain the property of the owner who supplied them. In such cases, if the mortgage is a legal mortgage and the mortgagee either had no notice of the hire-purchase agreement[3] or the hire-purchase agreement was made later than the mortgage, the title of the mortgagee will prevail over that of the owner by virtue of his legal title unless the mortgagee has acquiesced in their removal[4]. Where, however, the mortgage is an equitable mortgage and is given after the hire-purchase agreement then, even if the mortgagee takes without notice of it, his title is postponed to that of the owner[5].

Before the Bills of Sale Act 1878, a grantee by bill of sale of fixtures annexed to mortgaged premises had no title against the mortgagee[6] and this appears still to be the law[7]. A mortgage of land which passes fixtures without mentioning them is not a bill of sale[8].

1 *Sanders v Davis* (1885) 15 QBD 218.
2 *Ellis v Glover and Hobson Ltd*, above. On the removal of fixtures and waste, see *Mancetter*

Developments Ltd v Garmanson Ltd [1986] QB 1212, [1986] 1 All ER 449, CA; (1986) 136 NLJ 675 (Wilkinson).

3 *Re Samuel Allen & Sons Ltd* [1907] 1 Ch 575.

4 *Hobson v Gorringe* [1897] 1 Ch 182, CA, distinguishing *Cumberland Union Banking Co v Maryport Hermatite Iron and Steel Co* [1892] 1 Ch 415; *Gough v Wood* [1894] 1 QB 713, CA; *Reynolds v Ashby & Son Ltd* [1904] AC 466, HL; *Lyon & Co v London City and Midland Bank* [1903] 2 KB 135.

5 *Re Samuel Allen & Sons Ltd* [1907] 1 Ch 575; *Re Morrison, Jones & Taylor Ltd* [1914] 1 Ch 50, CA.

Where a hire-purchase agreement entitles the owner to enter and seize on default etc the owner has an equitable interest in the land to which the fixture is attached: *Gough v Wood & Co* [1894] 1 QB 713 at 722, CA; *Hobson v Gorringe* [1897] 1 Ch 182 at 192, CA; *Reynolds v Ashby & Son Ltd*, above; *Kay's Leasing Corpn Pty Ltd v CSR Provident Fund Nominees Pty Ltd* [1962] VR 429 at 436. Such an interest does not appear to be registrable either as a land charge of Class C (iii), Land Charges Act 1972, s 4 (general equitable charge) or under Class C (iv) (estate contract) or under Class D (iii) (equitable easement, right or privilege): see *Poster v Slough Estates Ltd* [1969] 1 Ch 495, [1968] 3 All ER 257; *Shiloh Spinners Ltd v Harding* [1973] AC 691, [1973] 1 All ER 90, HL. See generally (1963) 27 Conv (NS) 30 (Guest and Lever). Where, however, the title is registered, the equitable right of entry can be protected by registration either as a notice if the land certificate is produced or as a caution if it is not: Land Registration Act 1925, s 49(1)(f). In *Poster v Slough Estates Ltd* [1969] 1 Ch 495 Cross J suggested to the contrary, but his attention was not drawn to s 49(1)(f). On hire-purchase agreements and fixtures, see also [1990] Conv 275 McCormack.

6 *Longbottom v Berry* (1869) LR 5 QB 123.

7 *Reynolds v Ashby & Son Ltd*, above.

8 *Meux v Jacobs* (1875) LR 7 HL 481, HL.

Fixtures not passing

5.9 The general rule as to fixtures is subject to qualifications arising out of the terms of the security. If two kinds of property are mortgaged, and the fixtures are expressly included in one of them, the principle *expressio unius est exclusio alterius* may exclude the fixtures annexed to the other[1]. The bare enumeration of specific fixtures in the mortgaged property will not rebut the inference that all fixtures were intended to pass[2]. Again, if it is the custom of the place that fixed machinery which can be removed without injury to the freehold should be so removed and it has been treated between the parties as separate from the land and unaffected by the mortgage, such machinery may be held not to pass by a mortgage of the building and machinery[3].

1 See eg *Hare v Horton* (1833) 5 B & Ad 715. But query whether this would not be too refined a distinction to be followed now.

2 *Mather v Fraser* (1856) 2 K & J 536; and see *Hamp v Bygrave* (1982) 266 Estates Gazette 720, QBD.

3 *Trappes v Harter* (1833) 2 Cr & M 153; cf *Whitmore v Empson* (1857) 23 Beav 313.

Loose parts of fixtures

5.10 Without any special mention, there will pass with any fixture any loose part of such fixture which, though accidentally detached from it, or not of its own nature a fixture, may be essential for the proper employment of the machine or fixed article of which it forms part. This will be the case even though that loose part is more or less capable of use in a detached state[1]. The same rule is also applicable in the case of machinery not of a fixed kind[2]. On the same basis, a mortgage of a ship at sea with its tackle and appurtenances will pass a chronometer on board belonging to the owner of the ship[3].

1 *Place v Fagg* (1829) 4 Man & Ry KB 277; *Mather v Fraser* (1856) 2 K & J 536.
2 *Re Richards, ex p Astbury, ex p Lloyd's Banking Co* (1869) 4 Ch App 630.
3 *Langton v Horton* (1842) 1 Hare 549.

The separation of chattels from land

5.11 As previously stated fixtures are personal chattels within the Bills of Sale Acts when separately assigned or charged apart from the land[1]. In the event that a mortgage of an interest in land specifically mentions fixtures, s 7 of the Bills of Sale Act of 1878 applies and provides that the fixtures are not to be deemed to be separately mortgaged merely because they are assigned by separate words or because power is given to sever them from the land or building to which they are affixed, without otherwise taking possession of, or dealing with, such land or building.

The combined effect of ss 4 and 7 of the 1878 Act is that a mortgage of fixtures is not a bill of sale of personal chattels unless the instrument specifically creates a mortgage of the fixtures apart from the land. The court will, therefore, examine whether the instrument empowers the mortgagee to realise his security in the fixtures separately from his security in the land[2]. In such cases the question is essentially one of construction and if, on its true construction, the security constitutes a mortgage of land and of fixtures separately as chattels, the mortgage of the latter is a bill of sale. If not in proper form, the mortgage will, therefore, be void in respect of the chattels. The mortgagee cannot set up any title to the fixtures on the basis of the mortgage of the land[3]. Fixtures may be separately assigned though other goods are assigned with them[4].

1 Bills of Sale Act 1878, s 4.
2 *Re Yates, Batcheldor v Yates* (1888) 38 Ch D 112, CA; *Small v National Provincial Bank of England* [1894] 1 Ch 686; *Re Brooke, Brooke v Brooke* [1894] 2 Ch 600.
3 *Johns v Ware* [1899] 1 Ch 359.
4 *Roberts v Roberts* (1884) 13 QBD 794.

THE EFFECT OF THE BILLS OF SALE ACTS

The Acts

5.12 The registration of bills of sale was introduced by the Bills of Sale Act 1854. By the Bills of Sale Act 1866, renewal of registration was required every five years. Following the repeal of these Acts, bills of sale are now regulated by the Bills of Sale Act 1878, commonly called the 'Principal Act', and the Bills of Sale Act (1878) Amendment Act 1882, generally called the 'Amending Act'. The Amending Act is to be construed as one with the Principal Act in so far as it is consistent with the tenor of the Principal Act.

It is the Amending Act that is most important for present purposes as it relates exclusively to bills of sale given by way of security for money and, therefore, governs the law of mortgage of personal chattels.

The Bills of Sale Act 1890, as amended by the Bills of Sale Act 1891, merely exempted certain commercial hypothecations from the operation of the Acts of 1878 and 1882.

Difference in objects of Act

5.13 The Bills of Sale Acts 1854 and the Principal Act of 1878 were intended to prevent credit being given to people allowed to remain in possession of goods which though apparently theirs were no longer in their ownership. The purpose of the Amending Act was, however, to prevent needy persons from being entrapped into signing complicated documents which they might often be unable to understand and so being subjected by their creditors to the enforcement of harsh and unreasonable provisions[1]. With this object in view, a particular form of words was insisted upon, which should plainly express the nature of the contract as to the loan and the security for the loan.

As a result, two classes of bills of sale have been created:

(a) absolute bills of sale, to which the Principal Act continues to apply; and
(b) bills of sale given to secure the payment of money, with respect to which the Principal Act and the Amending Act are to be construed together.

The operation of the Amending Act, like the operation of the Principal Act, is restricted to bills of sale whereby the holder or grantee has power, either with or without notice, and either immediately or at any future time, to seize or take possession of any personal chattels comprised in or made subject to such bill of sale[2].

1 *Manchester, Sheffield and Lincolnshire Rly Co v North Central Wagon Co* (1888) 13 App Cas 554 at 560, HL.
2 Bills of Sale Act 1878, s 3.

Bills of Sale Acts affect documents only

5.14 The Bills of Sale Acts affect documents and not transactions[1] and they do not apply where the possession of goods passes. Pledges[2] and liens[3], not depending on written documents, are outside the Acts altogether, even when accompanied by collateral instruments regulating the rights of the parties[4].

The Acts do not require that any transaction shall be put into writing, but they do require that if a transaction is put into writing, and is of a particular character it shall be registered[5]. If the real bargain between the parties is reduced into writing, the Bills of Sale Acts apply to the written contract[6]. If the bargain is complete without any writing, so that the property intended to be dealt with passes independently, the Acts have no application to a document referring to or confirming the transaction[7] and the fact that such a document is drawn up, and is not registered, does not invalidate the transaction.

Not every instrument which creates a security on personal chattels for the payment of money necessarily falls within the provisions of the Acts. To bring such an instrument within the Acts it must:

(a) be a bill of sale within the statutory definition; and
(b) relate to personal chattels within the statutory definition.

The Acts also exempt certain classes of bills of sale from their operation and the decisions of the courts have exempted certain other instruments.

1 *Manchester, Sheffield and Lincolnshire Rly Co v North Central Wagon Co* (1888) 13 App Cas 554, HL.

2 *Re Hardwick, ex p Hubbard* (1886) 17 QBD 690.
3 *Re Vulcan Ironworks Co* [1888] WN 37.
4 *Manchester, Sheffield and Lincolnshire Rly Co v North Central Wagon Co*, above.
5 *North Central Wagon Co v Manchester, Sheffield,and Lincolnshire Rly Co* (1887) 35 Ch D 191 at 216, per Fry LJ; *United Forty Pound Loan Club v Bexton* [1891] 1 QB 28n.
6 *Newlove v Shrewsbury* (1888) 21 QBD 41, CA.
7 *Ramsay v Margrett* [1894] 2 QB 18 at 23, CA, per Lord Esher MR.

Definition of a bill of sale

5.15 A bill of sale has been described as an instrument in writing whereby one transfers to another the property he has in goods or chattels, or as a document given with respect to the transfer of goods or chattels used in cases where possession is not intended to be given[1]. The Principal Act[2] declares that the expression 'bill of sale' shall, unless there is something in the subject or context repugnant to such construction, include:

(a) bills of sale;
(b) assignments;
(c) transfers;
(d) declarations of trust without transfer;
(e) inventories of goods with receipt attached or receipts for purchase money of goods;
(f) other assurances of personal chattels;
(g) powers of attorney, authorities, or licences to take possession of personal chattels as security for any debt; and
(h) any agreement, whether intended or not to be followed by the execution of any other instrument by which a right in equity to any personal chattels, or to any charge or security on personal chattels, shall be conferred[3].

1 *Johnson v Diprose* [1893] 1 QB 512 at 515, CA, per Lord Esher MR.
2 The term 'bill of sale' has the same meaning in the Bills of Sale Act (1878) Amendment Act 1882, except that the latter Act does not apply to bills of sale given otherwise than by way of security for the payment of money.
3 Bills of Sale Act 1878, s 4. Certain instruments conferring powers of distress are declared to be bills of sale by s 6; see **5.22**. See *Halsbury's Statutes* (4th edn).

Documents which are not bills of sale

5.16 The expression 'bill of sale' does not include the following:

(a) assignments for the benefit of the creditors of the person making or giving the same;
(b) marriage settlements;
(c) transfers or assignments of any ship or vessel[1] or any share thereof;
(d) transfers of goods in the ordinary course of business of any trade or calling;
(e) bills of sale of goods in foreign parts or at sea;
(f) bills of lading;
(g) India warrants;
(h) warehousekeepers' certificates;
(i) warrants or orders for the delivery of goods, or any other documents used in the ordinary course of business as proof of the possession or control of goods, or authorising or purporting to authorise, either by endorsement or

by delivery, the possessor of such document to transfer or receive goods thereby represented[2];

(j) an instrument charging or creating any security on, or declaring trusts of imported goods, given or executed at any time prior to their deposit in a warehouse, factory or store, or prior to their being re-shipped for export or delivered to a purchaser who did not give or execute the instrument[3].

Further, the Bills of Sale Acts do not apply to:

(a) any debentures issued by any mortgage, loan or other incorporated company and secured on the capital stock, or goods, chattels and effects of such company[4];

(b) mortgages and charges for the registration of which provision is made by the Companies Acts[5];

(c) an agricultural charge created by a farmer in favour of a bank on his farming stock and other agricultural assets[6];

(d) mortgages of registered aircraft and stores of spare parts for such aircraft[7].

1 For the difference between a ship or vessel and a mere boat, see *Gapp v Bond* (1887) 19 QBD 200, CA.

2 Bills of Sale Act 1878, s 4.

3 Bills of Sale Act 1890, s 1; Bills of Sale Act 1891, s 1.

4 Bills of Sale Act 1882, s 17.

5 See *NV Slavenburg's Bank v Intercontinental Natural Resources Ltd* [1980] 1 All ER 955, [1980] 1 WLR 1076. A memorandum of deposit of deeds, not containing an agreement for payment of a specific debt, is not a debenture within s 17: *Topham v Greenside Glazed Fire-brick Co* (1887) 37 Ch D 281; and the charges of societies registered under the Industrial and Provident Societies Act 1965 are excepted from the Acts if an application is made within 14 days to record the charge at the central office: Industrial and Provident Societies Act 1967, s 1.

6 Agricultural Credits Act 1928, ss 5, 8 (1). See also as to debentures issued by agricultural marketing boards (Agricultural Marketing Act 1958, s 15 (5)) and by societies registered under the Industrial and Provident Societies Act 1965, which, if registered as agricultural charges, are excluded from the statutory definition of bills of sale (Agricultural Credits Act 1928, s 14 (1)).

7 Mortgaging of Aircraft Order 1972 (SI 1972/1268) at r 16 (1).

Instrument must effect the transaction

5.17 An instrument, although within the statutory definition and given by way of security for money, is not necessarily a bill of sale within the Acts unless it was intended by the parties to be a document passing the property in the goods, or giving power to seize them, or to be a record of the transfer[1].

1 *Marsden v Meadows* (1881) 7 QBD 80; *Manchester, Sheffield and Lincolnshire Rly Co v North Central Wagon Co* (1888) 13 App Cas 554, HL; *Charlesworth v Mills* [1892] AC 231, HL; *Ramsay v Margrett* [1894] 2 QB 18, CA; *Koppel v Koppel* [1966] 2 All ER 187, [1966] 1 WLR 802, CA.

Instrument must be security for a debt

5.18 The Acts do not apply, for instance, to a power for a lessor to re-enter on default in the performance by a builder of his contract and to take as the lessor's own property the materials on the ground, no security for a debt being thereby created[1]. Under the former law of reputed ownership, the lessor was, however, defeated if he failed to enter before the builder's bankruptcy[2]. A mortgage by a lessee under a building lease providing that all building materials when brought in the premises should be considered as attaching to the land, with power to seize, etc, is void as a bill of sale[3].

1 *Brown v Bateman* (1867) LR 2 CP 272; *Reeves v Barlow* (1884) 12 QBD 436.
2 *Re Weibking, ex p Ward* [1902] 1 KB 713; *Re Fox, ex p Oundle and Thrapston RDC v Trustee* [1948] Ch 407, [1948] 1 All ER 849. See Gough *Company Charges* (2nd edn) pp 524-525.
3 *Climpson v Coles* (1889) 23 QBD 465; *Re Hawkins, ex p Emerson* (1871) 41 LJ Bcy 20; *Re Robertson, ex p Crawcour* (1878) 9 Ch D 419.

Hire-purchase agreements not bills of sale

5.19 The Bills of Sale Acts do not extend to an ordinary agreement for the hire or hire purchase of chattels which, until the stipulated payments have been made, are not the property of the hirer but rather the property of the owner who has simply temporarily parted with possession. While licences to seize are frequently inserted in hire-purchase agreements, such licences merely empower the owner to retake possession of his own property and are not bills of sale[1]. No security is created on the debtor's goods.

1 *McEntire v Crossley Bros Ltd* [1895] AC 457, HL. For a general discussion of hire-purchase agreements as bills of sale, see (1960) 23 MLR 399, 516 (Diamond) and see Gough *Company Charges* (2nd edn) p 518. See re dealer financing: *Pacific Motor Auctions Pty Ltd v Motor Credits (Hire-Finance) Ltd* [1965] AC 867, [1965] 2 All ER 105, PC.

Retention of title clauses

5.20 A retention of title clause which reserves the legal ownership in goods sold is not a bill of sale[1]. If, however, merely the equitable ownership is reserved[2] or the goods are mixed with other goods or used in the manufacture of other goods so that they cease to be identifiable, the agreement is a bill of sale[3].

Where, on the other hand, there is a sale of goods passing the immediate property to the purchaser and a provision for payment by instalments and interest is charged on the unpaid purchase money, the document is a bill of sale[4].

1 *Aluminium Industrie Vaassen BV v Romalpa Aluminium Ltd* [1976] 2 All ER 552, [1976] 1 WLR 676, CA; *Clough Mill Ltd v Martin* [1984] 3 All ER 982, [1985] 1 WLR 111, CA.
2 *Re Bond Worth Ltd* [1980] Ch 228, [1979] 3 All ER 919.
3 *Borden (UK) Ltd v Scottish Timber Products Ltd* [1981] Ch 25, [1979] 3 All ER 961, CA; *Re Peachdart Ltd* [1984] Ch 131, [1983] 3 All ER 204.
4 *Coburn v Collins* (1887) 35 Ch D 373, and see *Re Bond Worth Ltd* [1980] Ch 228, [1979] 3 All ER 919.

Substance of transaction

5.21 Whatever form the transaction may take, in deciding whether a document is within the terms of the Acts, the court looks at the real substance of the transaction[1] and determines the proper inference to be drawn from the facts[2].

Where the documents effecting a transaction are genuine documents and are not intended to cloak the true nature of the transaction, the legal rights and obligations flowing from the documents according to their true construction and effect are the substance of the transaction. If, as a result, the transaction is outside the scope of the Acts, the terms of the documents cannot be disregarded in order to bring the transaction within the scope of the Acts[3].

The court is, however, also entitled to look behind the documents and if it then appears that the documents are sham documents intended to conceal the fact that the transaction was a loan of money on security, the documents will be within the Acts[4].

A hire-purchase agreement will not be allowed to oust the Acts where it is used, together with a sham sale by the borrower to the lender, to disguise what is really, according to the intent of the parties, a security for a loan[5]. If, however, a sale is intended to be a genuine transaction and the hire-purchase agreement is executed by a person who is in law the true owner of the property, the transaction cannot be said to be merely a colourable cloak for the mortgage[6].

1 *Re Watson, ex p Official Receiver in Bankruptcy* (1890) 25 QBD 27, CA; *Madell v Thomas & Co* [1891] 1 QB 230, CA.
2 See *Johnson v Rees* (1915) 84 LJKB 1276. For a general discussion on sham hire-purchase agreements, see Gough *Company Charges* (2nd edn) Ch 21.
3 *Helby v Matthews* [1895] AC 471 at 476, HL, per Lord Herschell, LC; *Staffs Motor Guarantee Ltd v British Wagon Co Ltd* [1934] 2 KB 305; *Re Lovegrove* [1935] Ch 464, CA; *Stoneleigh Finance Ltd v Phillips* [1965] 2 QB 537, [1965] 1 All ER 513, CA; *Snook v London and West Riding Investments Ltd* [1967] 2 QB 786, [1967] 1 All ER 518, CA.
4 *Re Lovegrove* [1935] Ch 464, CA, at 495, 496, per Maugham LJ; *Polsky v S and A Services Ltd* [1951] 1 All ER 185 at 189; *affd* [1951] 1 All ER 1062n, CA.
5 *Re Walden, ex p Odell* (1878) 10 Ch D 76, CA; *Maas v Pepper* [1905] AC 102, HL; *North Central Wagon Finance Co Ltd v Brailsford* [1962] 1 All ER 502; *Mercantile Credit Co Ltd v Hamblin* [1965] 2 QB 242, [1964] 3 All ER 592, CA.
6 *Manchester, Sheffield and Lincolnshire Rly Co v North Central Wagon Co* (1888) 13 App Cas 554.

Attornment clauses subject to the Acts

5.22 Every attornment, instrument, or agreement, not being a mining lease, whereby a power of distress is given or agreed to be given by way of security for any present, future, or contingent debt or advance, and whereby any rent is reserved or made payable as a mode of providing for the payment of interest on such debt or advance, or otherwise for the purpose of such security only, is deemed[1] to be a bill of sale of any personal chattels which may be seized or taken under such power[2]. Any distress levied under such a clause is, therefore, unlawful unless the clause has been registered as a bill of sale. The validity of the mortgage and of the clause in other respects is, however, not affected[3].

1 It should be noted that the instrument is only 'deemed to be' a bill of sale of any personal chattels which may be seized or taken under the power of distress: *Green v Marsh* [1892] 2 QB 330 at 335, CA. It need not, therefore, be in the statutory form, not being in fact a bill of sale, though for the purpose of registration it is treated as one.
2 Bills of Sale Act 1878, s 6.The object of this provision was to prevent the practice, which had been adopted to avoid registration under the Act of 1854, of making securities upon chattels by assignment or demise of the interest of the debtor in the premises in which the chattels were placed and including a proviso that the premises should be held by the debtor as tenant from year to year at a rent which, with the tenancy itself, should cease upon payment of all moneys recoverable under the security; a power of entry without previous demand was also reserved on default in payment. Before the Principal Act came into force, this right of distress could be exercised, not only on the goods of the borrower, but on those of a stranger, *Kearsley v Philips* (1883) 11 QBD 621. Such a clause is now within s 6 of the 1878 Act, so as to render any distress under the clause unlawful unless the clause has been registered as a bill of sale.
3 See eg *Mumford v Collier* (1890) 25 QBD 279, DC.

Definition of 'personal chattels'

5.23 The Amending Act applies to forms of personalty defined in s 4 of the Principal Act as:

> 'Goods, furniture and other articles capable of complete transfer by delivery, and (when separately assigned or charged) fixtures and growing crops[1], but shall not include chattel interests in real estate, nor fixtures (except trade machinery as hereinafter defined), when assigned together with a freehold or leasehold interest in any land or building to which they are affixed, nor growing crops when assigned together with any interest in the land on which they grow, nor shares or interests in the stock, funds or securities of any government, or in the capital or property of incorporated or joint stock companies, nor choses in action[2] nor any stock or produce upon any farm or lands which by virtue of any covenant or agreement, or of the custom of the country, ought not to be removed from any farm where the same are at the time of making or giving of such bill of sale.'

The description of personal chattels in the Principal Act is applicable only for the purpose of the Bills of Sale Acts; it is, for instance, only for the purpose of the Acts that trade machinery is deemed to be personal chattels.

1 See Bills of Sale Act 1878, s 7.
2 But note that a general assignment of book debts requires registration as if it were an absolute bill of sale, otherwise it is void against the assignor's trustee in bankruptcy as regards any book debts which have not been paid at the commencement of the bankruptcy: Insolvency Act 1986, s 344. Specific assignments of specific book debts and assignments connected with a bona fide transfer of a business for value and a general assignment of assets for the benefit of creditors generally are not covered: IA 1986, s 344(3).
A reversionary interest in chattels is a chose in action and a mortgage of such an interest does not require to be registered as a bill of sale: *Re Thynne, Thynne v Grey* [1911] 1 Ch 282.

Restrictions on subject matter

5.24 In order that a bill of sale by way of security should have effect against persons other than the grantor, the personal chattels to which it relates should be capable of specific description and should be specifically described in the schedule annexed to the bill of sale[1]. If some of the chattels assigned are imperfectly described in the Schedule, the bill is good as regards those chattels against the grantor but void against all other persons[2]. The grantor should also be the true owner[3] of such personal chattels at the time of the execution of the bill[4]. There are exceptions in the case of growing crops, fixtures, plant and trade machinery[5].

1 Bills of Sale Act (1878) Amendment Act 1882, s 4.This section should be read with s 9.
2 *Kelly v Kellond* (1888) 20 QBD 569 at 574-576.
3 The legal owner may be the true owner although having no beneficial interest: *Re Sarl, ex p Williams* [1892] 2 QB 591.One beneficially entitled may be the true owner to the extent of his interest, although the legal title is in another: *Re Field, ex p Pratt* (1890) 63 LT 289.
4 Bills of Sale Act 1878, s 5. Avoidance is not against the grantor but against all other persons under this section.
5 Section 6.

Growing crops

5.25 Crops are not within the Bills of Sale Acts unless they are assigned or charged apart from the land on which they are growing or to which they are affixed[1]. An assignment of growing crops by separate words, or a power to sever and sell them apart from the land, does not of itself operate as a separate assignment if by the same instrument any freehold or leasehold interest in the land is also conveyed or assigned to the same person[2].

Crops which are separately assigned or charged which were actually growing at the time when the bill of sale was executed, are excepted from the provisions of the Amending Act, which, as against third parties, avoids a bill of sale given by way of security, in respect of chattels not specifically described in the schedule, or of which the grantor was not the true owner at the time when the bill of sale was executed[3].

When severed, growing crops become personal chattels in the ordinary sense and an assignment of them requires registration[4], unless made in the ordinary course of business[5] or contained in an agricultural charge.

1 Bills of Sale Act 1878, s 4.They may be separately assigned though other goods are assigned with them: *Roberts v Roberts* (1884) 13 QBD 794.
2 Section 7.
3 Bills of Sale Act (1878) Amendment Act 1882, ss 4, 5, 6.
4 *Re Phillips, ex p National Mercantile Bank* (1880) 16 Ch D 104.
5 *Stephenson v Thompson* [1924] 2 KB 240.

Trade machinery

5.26 For the purposes of bills of sale, trade machinery is deemed to be personal chattels[1]. Accordingly, trade machinery cannot ordinarily be made a security for money except by means of a bill of sale complying with the requirements of the Acts.

Fixed trade machinery may, however, without express mention, pass as part of mortgaged premises, whether freehold or leasehold, like other fixtures. In such circumstances, there is no disposition of trade machinery as such and registration is unnecessary[2]. If, however, no express power of separate sale is given, but an intention may be gathered from an instrument as a whole to give a power to sell trade machinery separately from the premises, the disposition will be a bill of sale as regards that trade machinery[3].

1 See Bills of Sale Act 1878, s 5. This section defines trade machinery.
2 *Re Yates, Batcheldor v Yates* (1888) 38 Ch D 112, CA.
3 *Small v National Provincial Bank of England* [1894] 1 Ch 686.

Conditions for validity of bill of sale

5.27 The following conditions are essential to the validity of a bill of sale. Breach of any of them makes the instrument void, not merely as against the grantor's creditors, but also as against the grantor himself. In the event of breach of the first two conditions, the bill is void in its totality. In the event of breach of the other conditions the bill will only be void as regards the personal chattels comprised within it.

(a) The bill must be in accordance with the form contained in the Schedule to the Act of 1882[1].
(b) The bill must be given by way of security for a sum not less than £30[2].
(c) The consideration for which the bill is given must be truly set out[3].

(d) The execution of the bill by the grantor must be attested by one or more credible witnesses, not being a party or parties to the bill[4].

(e) The bill must be registered within seven clear days after the making or giving of the bill (or, if executed out of England, within seven clear days after the time at which it would, in the ordinary course of post, have arrived in England if posted immediately after its execution)[5], or within such extended time as the court may (on being satisfied that the omission to comply with this provision was due to accident or inadvertence) direct[6].

A person wishing to register a bill of sale should produce at the Filing Department of the Royal Courts of Justice, Strand, London (Room E07):

(a) the original bill of sale 'with every schedule and inventory thereto annexed or therein referred to';

(b) a true copy of such bill, schedules and inventory and of every attestation of the execution of the bill;

(c) an affidavit of the execution and attestation of the bill of sale and of the time when it was made or given and a description of the residence and occupation of the person making or giving the same and of every attesting witness[7].

If the bill is given or made subject to any defeasance or condition or declaration of trust not contained in the body of the bill, such defeasance or condition or declaration of trust is to be deemed part of the bill and must be written on the same paper or parchment before registration and must be truly set out in the filed copy, otherwise the registration will be void[8].

Finally, such registration must be renewed every five years[9].

1 Act of 1882, s 9. It is sufficient if it is in substantial accordance with the form: *Thomas v Kelly* (1888) 13 App Cas 506; and see per Lord Fitzgerald at 516 as to the object of the form.

2 Section 12. See **5.34**.

3 Section 8. See **6.35**.

4 Act of 1882, ss 8 and 10.

5 Section 8; and Act of 1878, ss 8, 22.

6 Act of 1878, s 14; and see CPR Sch 1 RSC Ord 95, CPR 4PD-004 and the Queen's Bench Guide paras 12.4.1-12.4.12.

7 CPR Sch 1 RSC 95.1.2.

8 Act of 1878, s 10 (3). As to the effect of this, see *Heseltine v Simmons* [1892] 2 QB 547, CA.

9 Section 11. Omission to renew it avoids it even as against the grantor: *Fenton v Blythe* (1890) 25 QBD 417. There is no power under s 14 of the Act of 1878 to extend the time for renewed registration: *Re Emery, ex p Official Receiver* (1888) 21 QBD 405.

Compliance with the statutory form

5.28 A bill of sale made or given by way of security for the payment of money by the grantor of the bill is void[1] unless made in accordance with the form of the Schedule to the Amending Act[2]. This is so even though it purports to be an absolute bill[3]. This rule extends to all the instruments given by way of security which come within the definition of bills of sale in the Principal Act, but does not extend to those instruments giving powers of distress which are deemed to be bills of sale by the Principal Act[4]. Such instruments, although given by way of security, are not required to be in the statutory form[5].

If an instrument which comes within the description of a bill of sale cannot be reduced to the statutory form any security it purports to give will be void[6].

To be in accordance with the statutory form, a bill of sale must be substantially like it. Any addition or omission from the form which purports to give an effect greater or less than would result from the use of the form is substantial and material. To be valid, a bill of sale must, therefore, have the same legal effect as the exact statutory form[7]. Every word of the statutory form may not be imperative, but a bill of sale must not depart from any characteristic of that form, even where the same legal effect is produced[8]. The address and description of the attesting witness[9] and the description of the grantee[10] are material parts of the form and a bill of sale omitting them will be void. Moreover, the form was meant for the benefit of plain people and not experts[11] and nothing must destroy the simplicity which it was one of the objects of the Act to attain.

The mere fact, however, that two courts differ as to the proper construction of a bill is not of itself ground for avoiding it under this principle[12].

1 *Thomas v Kelly* (1888) 13 App Cas 506 at 516, per Lord Fitzgerald.
2 See Bills of Sale (1878) Amendment Act 1882, s 9 and Schedule.
3 *Madell v Thomas & Co* [1891] 1 QB 230, CA.
4 Section 6.
5 *Green v Marsh* [1892] 2 QB 330, CA.
6 *Re Townsend, ex p Parsons* (1886) 16 QBD 532, CA.
7 *Re Barber, ex p Stanford* (1886) 17 QBD 259, CA, where the majority of the court added that the bill must not be calculated reasonably to deceive those for whose benefit the statutory form is provided.
8 *Thomas v Kelly* (1888) 13 App Cas 506; *Re Trendent Industries Pty Ltd* [1983] 1 ACLC 980.
9 *Parsons v Brand, Coulson v Dickson* (1890) 25 QBD 110, CA.
10 *Altree v Altree* [1898] 2 QB 267.
11 *Furber v Cobb* (1887) 18 QBD 494.
12 See eg *Edwards v Marston* [1891] 1 QB 225.

The content of the statutory form

5.29 A bill of sale must be complete in itself and if it has to be read with some collateral agreement it is not in accordance with the statutory form[1].

In the case of a present advance the form requires the grantor's acknowledgment of receipt. It further requires that a fixed sum shall be secured.

A bill of sale cannot be given by way of indemnity, the amount ultimately payable being uncertain[2], nor can further advances be included[3]. The amount of interest payable and its time of payment must be certain[4]. The interest must be stated as a rate[5] and not as a lump sum[6]. A provision for payment of interest upon arrears of interest is contrary to the form[7] and so is a provision for payment of a bonus[8].

A bill of sale must contain an agreement to repay the principal sum at a certain stipulated time or times[9], though a time of payment fixed by reference to any known event is not necessarily uncertain. Payment cannot, however, be made to depend on the mere choice or volition of the grantee, so payment cannot be provided for on demand[10], or after demand[11]. The time for payment must not depend on a contingency[12]. A stipulation for payment at a specified time, providing that if the grantor should not commit breaches of the agreements in the bill of sale the grantee should accept payment by given monthly instalments, is in accordance with the form[13].

As to the mode of repayment, the general principle seems to be that if the time or times fixed for payment are certain, the manner of payment may be such as the parties agree, provided that the agreement is not misleading or contrary to the provisions of the Acts[14].

It is not necessary, though it is permissible, that principal and interest should be repayable together and it is a question of construction whether the agreement for payment is referable to both principal and interest together[15] or to principal or interest and, if so, as to which is payable first.

The statutory form also requires a proviso restricting the grantor's power of seizure to the events specified in s 7 of the Act of 1882.

1 See eg *Stott v Shaw and Lee Ltd* [1928] 2 KB 26, CA.
2 *Hughes v Little* (1886) 18 QBD 32, CA.
3 *Cook v Taylor* (1887) 3 TLR 800.
4 *Attia v Finch* (1904) 91 LT 70.
5 But it need not be expressed as a percentage: *Lumley v Simmons* (1887) 34 Ch D 698, CA.
6 *Blankenstein v Robertson* (1890) 24 QBD 543.
7 *Dresser v Townsend* (1886) 81 LT Jo 23.
8 *Myers v Elliott* (1886) 16 QBD 526, CA.
9 *De Braam v Ford* [1900] 1 Ch 142, CA.
10 *Hetherington v Groome* (1884) 13 QBD 789, CA.
11 *Sibley v Higgs* (1885) 15 QBD 619.
12 See *Hughes v Little* (1886) 18 QBD 32, CA.
13 *Re Coton, ex p Payne* (1887) 56 LT 571.
14 *Watkins v Evans* (1887) 18 QBD 386, CA.
15 *Goldstrom v Tallerman* (1886) 18 QBD 1, CA; *Edwards v Marston* [1891] 1 QB 225.

Maintenance or defeasance of security

5.30 A note appended to the statutory form expressly authorises the insertion of 'terms as to insurance, payment of rent, or otherwise, which the parties may agree to for the maintenance or defeasance of the security', and the following covenants and powers have been allowed:

(a) covenants to repair and replace[1];
(b) covenants not to remove the goods without consent[2];
(c) covenants not to assign or underlet the goods without consent[3];
(d) covenants to produce receipts for rent, rates and taxes[4];
(e) provisions for insurance and application of the insurance money in discharging the debt[5];
(f) power for the creditor, in case of default in insuring or repairing, to enter and insure and repair himself, and to charge all moneys so expended, with interest, on the goods[6];
(g) power if the grantee becomes entitled to seize the goods to enter the premises where the goods are[7];
(h) a covenant for further assurance, unless it is too wide[8].

A provision for defeasance of the security is one which limits the operation of the bill or stipulates for its discharge on stated events. If such a provision is not contained in the body of the bill it is deemed to be part of the bill and must be written on the same paper or parchment before registration and must be truly set out in the filed copy, otherwise the registration will be void[9].

1 *Furber v Cobb* (1887) 18 QBD 494, CA.

2 *Re Coton, ex p Payne* (1887) 56 LT 571.
3 *Seed v Bradley* [1894] 1 QB 319, CA; *Coates v Moore* [1903] 2 KB 140, CA.
4 *Furber v Cobb* (1887) 18 QBD 494, CA; *Cartwright v Regan* [1895] 1 QB 900.
5 *Neverson v Seymour* (1907) 97 LT 788.
6 *Topley v Crosbie* (1888) 20 QBD 350.
7 *Lumley v Simmons* (1887) 34 Ch D 698, CA.
8 *Re Cleaver, ex p Rawlings* (1887) 18 QBD 489.
9 Act of 1878, s 10 (3); but an agreement subsequent to the bill of sale, and made as a separate transaction, not to enforce the bill so long as certain conditions are complied with, is not a defeasance within s 10(3) and the bill is good: *Lester v Hickling* [1916] 2 KB 302.

Power of sale

5.31 Personal chattels assigned under a bill of sale are only liable to be seized or taken possession of by the grantee if the cause is listed in s 7 of the Amending Act[1]. On the goods being seized the grantee has an implied power to sell. As a result, the statutory power of sale under s 101 of the Law of Property Act 1925[2] is not incorporated in bills of sale[3] and a proviso excluding s 103 of the Law of Property Act 1925[4] is, therefore, superfluous and does not invalidate the bill. A power to sell goods by private treaty or public auction off the premises will also not invalidate the bill[5].

A provision that the grantee may retain out of the proceeds of sale the costs and expenses incurred in seizing and removing the chattels and his costs in defending and maintaining his rights under the bill and the expenses of sale is good[6], but where such a provision extends generally to costs and expenses incurred in relation to the security, it is too wide and the bill is void[7].

1 See Chapter 19.
2 See Chapter 20.
3 *Re Morritt, ex p Official Receiver* (1886) 18 QBD 222, CA; *Calvert v Thomas* (1887) 19 QBD 204, CA; cf *Watkins v Evans* (1887) 18 QBD 386, CA.
4 See Chapter 20.
5 *Bourne v Wall* (1891) 64 LT 530.
6 *Lumley v Simmons* (1887) 34 Ch D 698, CA; *Re Cleaver, ex p Rawlings* (1887) 18 QBD 489.
7 *Calvert v Thomas* (1887) 19 QBD 204, CA; *Macey v Gilbert* (1888) 57 LJQB 461.

Omissions from statutory form

5.32 A bill is invalid which omits the final proviso limiting the creditor's right to seize[1], or which omits the name or address or description of the attesting witness[2], or the acknowledgment of the receipt of the loan[3].

1 *Thomas v Kelly* (1888) 13 App Cas 506, HL, and see *Ex p Esanda Ltd* [1977] Qd R 162; *Ex p Citicorp (Aust) Ltd* [1983] 1 Qd R 509.
2 *Blankenstein v Robertson* (1890) 24 QBD 543.
3 *Davies v Jenkins* [1900] 1 QB 133; *Burchell v Thompson* [1920] 2 KB 80.

Collateral documents

5.33 It is not possible to avoid the statutory conditions by having a collateral deed containing covenants and provisions which would make the bill void if they formed part of it. In such cases, the two documents must be regarded as one and the bill will be void[1]. The collateral document may, however, be good[2].

Where the terms of a bill are varied by a collateral agreement, so that this operates as a defeasance of the security, the bill is void[3]. Further, a supplemental deed to a bill of sale, whether or not a defeasance, may so vary the bill that the bill no longer expresses the true interest of the parties. As a result, the true terms will not be included in the statutory form and the bill will be void[4].

1 *Sharp v McHenry* (1887) 38 Ch D 427; *Edwards v Marcus* [1894] 1 QB 587.
2 *Monetary Advance Co v Cater* (1888) 20 QBD 785.
3 *Smith v Whiteman* [1909] 2 KB 437.
4 *Cornell v May* (1915) 112 LT 1085. See 4 *Halsbury's Laws* (4th edn reissue), Bills of Sale.

Consideration

5.34 By s 12 of the Amending Act, a bill of sale by way of security made or given in consideration of any sum under £30 is void. Consideration means the whole consideration received by the grantor for the giving of the instrument[1].

1 *London and provinces Discount Co v Jones* [1914] 1 KB 147. The consideration may be past advances, but except to the extent to which the moneys have become repayable they cannot be included within the £30 sum for the purposes of s 12. As to past advances, see *Darlow v Bland* [1897] 1 QB 125, CA.

Necessity for correct statement of consideration

5.35 By s 8 of the Amending Act the consideration for which a security bill is given must be truly set out. If the consideration is misstated the bill will be void in respect of the personal chattels comprised within it[1]. Such a misstatement does not, however, amount to such a defect of form as to render the bill wholly void[2] and to nullify any personal covenant for payment contained in the bill[3].

The real consideration need not be set out with strict accuracy, but the facts as to the consideration must be stated with substantial accuracy, either as to their legal effect, or as to their mercantile and business effect[4]. It is not necessary to set out any arrangement relating to the mode of payment of the consideration or its application for the benefit of the borrower.

A statement of payment of the consideration to the borrower at the execution of the deed is consistent with its application in the payment of a bona fide debt due from him at the time of the transaction, either to the lender himself or to other persons[5]. The consideration must, however, be a debt actually payable at the time and it must be paid. The consideration must not be retained for rent or interest, or other debt, which has not yet become due, or which is not paid until after the execution of the deed[6]; nor for the costs of preparing and executing the bill, which, though properly payable by the mortgagor, are not due until the completion of the transaction after the execution of the bill[7].

If the consideration is stated as 'now paid' there must be a present payment in a legal or business sense[8]. The expression 'now paid' will, however, cover a payment made before execution of the bill, if it was made as part of the transaction[9].

1 Act of 1882, s 8.
2 Section 9; but a failure to insert any statement of consideration could amount to such a defect.

3 *Heseltine v Simmons* [1892] 2 QB 547, CA.
4 *Credit Co v Pott* (1880) 6 QBD 295, CA; and see *Roberts v Roberts* (1884) 13 QBD 794, CA, where the consideration was very inaccurately, but sufficiently, stated.
5 *Credit Co v Pott* (1880) 6 QBD 295, CA; *Thomas v Searles* [1891] 2 QB 408, CA.
6 *Parsons v Equitable Investment Co Ltd* [1916] 2 Ch 527, CA.
7 *Re Cowburn, ex p Firth* (1882) 19 Ch D 419, CA; *Richardson v Harris* (1889) 22 QBD 268, CA.
8 Eg within a few hours of the execution of the bill: *Henshall v Widdison* (1923) 130 LT 607. Cf *Re Spindler, ex p Rolph* (1881) 19 Ch D 98, CA (where the money was paid several days afterwards). Past advances cannot be now paid: *Davies v Jenkins* [1900] 1 QB 133.
9 *Re Chapman, ex p Johnson* (1884) 26 Ch D 338, CA; *Re Rouard, ex p Trustee* (1915) 85 LJ KB 393.

Attestation

5.36 The statutory form of bill of sale by way of security requires the execution of the bill to be attested by one or more credible witnesses who must not be a party or parties to the bill[1]. The name, address and description of each witness must be inserted. Failure to comply with these requirements will render the bill wholly void for want of form[2].

1 Act of 1882, s 10.
2 Act of 1882, s 9.

Schedule

5.37 The bill of sale must incorporate or have annexed to it a schedule containing an inventory of the personal chattels comprised in the bill. The bill will be effective only in respect of the personal chattels specifically described in the schedule and will be void, except as against the grantor, in respect of any personal chattels not so specifically described[1]. Furthermore, a bill of sale will be void, except as against the grantor, in respect of any personal chattels specifically described in the schedule to the bill and of which the grantor was not the true owner at the time of the execution of the bill of sale[2].

There are, however, excepted from these requirements:

(a) growing crops separately assigned or charged, where such crops were actually growing when the bill was executed;
(b) fixtures separately assigned or charged; and
(c) plant or trade machinery, where the fixtures, plant, and trade machinery are substituted for the same articles specifically described in the schedule[3].

The declaration in s 4 of the Amending Act that the bill of sale shall have effect only in respect of the personal chattels specifically described in the schedule to the bill is not consistent with the subsequent implication that the bill shall be good as against the grantor in respect of personal chattels not so specifically described. The effect of the section appears to be that the bill of sale will only affect persons other than the grantor in respect of those chattels specifically described and of which he was not then but may afterwards become the true owner. In respect of chattels only generally and not specifically described, the bill of sale will operate only as against the grantor.

1 Act of 1882, s 4.

2 Section 5.
3 Section 6.

What amounts to specific description

5.38 The scope and object of this requirement for specific description has been described as being to facilitate the identification of the articles listed in the schedule with those that are to be found in the possession of the mortgagor; that is to say, to render identification as easy as possible and to ensure that any dispute as to the intention of the parties is as rare as possible. In cases where a general description is used there is always the risk of fraud and controversy[1].

The goods must be described with the particularity usual in an inventory of chattels, in the ordinary business sense of the term[2]. Where in the ordinary course goods are frequently replaced or substituted, as in the case of stock of a business, more particularity is required than with articles, such as furniture in a dwellinghouse, which are not changed frequently[3].

1 *Carpenter v Deen* (1889) 23 QBD 566 at 574, CA, per Fry LJ.
2 *Witt v Banner* (1887) 20 QBD 114, CA.
3 *Davies v Jenkins* [1900] 1 QB 133; *Herbert's Trustee v Higgins* [1926] Ch 794.

True ownership

5.39 With regard to the question whether the grantor was the true owner of the chattels at the execution of the bill, s 5 of the Amending Act avoids, except as against the grantor:

(a) bills of sale of future acquired chattels; and
(b) bills of sale of chattels in which the grantor has no legal or beneficial interest.

A general assignment of future acquired chattels is, however, absolutely void even as against the grantor under s 9 of the Amending Act because such an assignment cannot be made in accordance with the statutory form[1].

A bill of sale of specific chattels which do not in fact belong to the grantor at the date of the deed, but which the grantor subsequently acquires, would be good as against the grantor by virtue of the doctrine of estoppel but would be void as against the grantor's creditors under s 5.

The grantor does not have to be the absolute or only owner for the purposes of s 5. It is sufficient if the grantor has a partial or equitable ownership. A bill of sale of the equity of redemption in chattels is, therefore, good[2]. A person beneficially interested in chattels is the true owner to the extent of his interest[3] and a bill of sale by a trustee is good, even though another person is equitably entitled[4].

1 *Thomas v Kelly* (1888) 13 App Cas 506, HL.
2 *Thomas v Searles* [1891] 2 QB 408, CA.
3 *Re Field, ex p Pratt* (1890) 63 LT 289.
4 *Re Sarl, ex p Williams* [1892] 2 QB 591.

How far the security is avoided

5.40 The Acts make a bill of sale void in its totality where it does not comply with the statutory form[1] and where the consideration is under £30[2].

The Acts only make a bill void in respect of any personal chattels comprised within the bill:

(a) when the consideration is not truly set out[3];
(b) when the bill is insufficiently attested[4];
(c) when the bill is not registered[5]; and
(d) when the bill is a successive bill of sale.

A successive bill of sale is a bill executed within, or on the expiration of, seven days after the execution of a prior unregistered bill of sale and given for the same or part of the same debt and comprising all or part of the same chattels[6].

As against creditors, though not as against the grantor, a bill of sale is void in respect of chattels which are not specifically described[7], or which were not the property of the grantor[8] at the execution of the bill.

The registration of a bill of sale is void and the bill is therefore void in respect of the personal chattels comprised within it if the bill is given subject to an unregistered defeasance, condition or declaration of trust[9], or if the registration is not renewed once at least every five years[10].

Even where a bill is void in its totality, this does not mean that the security of which it forms part is also void in its totality. If the security comprises personal chattels and also property which does not fall within that description and it is possible to sever the security on the personal chattels from the security on the other property, then the security will be void as to the personal chattels but good as to the other property[11]. A bill of sale will, however, be bad if it includes in the schedule property other than personal chattels[12].

Where a bill of sale is void for non-compliance with the statutory form, it is void, not only in respect of the assignment of personal chattels but also in respect of the personal covenant to pay principal and interest[13], however the grantor may be estopped from setting up the invalidity of the bill against the grantee[14].

1 Act of 1882, s 9.
2 Section 12.
3 Section 8.
4 Section 8.
5 Section 8.
6 Act of 1878, s 9.
7 Act of 1882, s 4, but note the exception in s 6.
8 Section 5, but note the exception in s 6.
9 Act of 1878, s 10 (3).
10 Section 11.
11 Eg where the same instrument comprises a bill of sale of personal chattels and a mortgage of freehold or leasehold property (*Re O'Dwyer* (1886) 19 LR Ir 19), or a bill of sale of personal chattels and also of trade machinery excepted under s 5 of the Act of 1878 (*Re Burdett, ex p Bryne* (1888) 20 QBD 310, CA).
12 *Cochrane v Entwistle* (1890) 25 QBD 116, CA, but the mortgage will be effective as regards the other property.
13 *Davies v Rees* (1886) 17 QBD 408; *Smith v Whiteman* [1909] 2 KB 437, CA, but the lender may recover his money, with reasonable interest, as money had and received: see *North Central Wagon and Finance Co Ltd v Brailsford* [1962] 1 All ER 502. (It is hard to see why, in this case, judgment was given for money had and received since, when a bill of sale is 'void' only for non-registration, the agreement for payment of principal and interest still stands: *Heseltine v Simmons* [1892] 2 QB 547, CA. *Davies v Rees* (1886) 17 QBD 408, cited in the instant case, is concerned with want of form, an avoiding defect which attracts different considerations from those attaching to non-registration.)
In *Bradford Advance Co Ltd v Ayres* [1924] WN 152, 5 per cent per annum was taken as the appropriate rate of interest.
14 *Comitti & Son Ltd v Maher* (1905) 94 LT 158.

REGISTRATION OF BILLS OF SALE

Registration[1]

5.41 Under the Principal Act an unregistered bill of sale was void as against execution creditors and against the grantor's trustee in bankruptcy, but not as between grantor and grantee. Under the Amending Act an unregistered bill of sale by way of security is void as regards the personal chattels comprised within it[2].

The effect of the registration provisions of the Amending Act appears to be that although seven days are allowed for registration, the necessity for registering the bill of sale cannot be avoided by taking possession before the expiration of the seven days. Not only does the bill of sale become void as to the chattels for want of registration, but the grantee is prevented by s 7 of the Amending Act from taking possession except by reason of defaults which would be unlikely to occur within the seven days without collusion. Failure to register does not avoid the personal covenant for payment[3].

1 Registration does not of itself constitute notice to third parties: *Joseph v Lyons* (1884) 15 QBD 280 at 286. See 4 *Halsbury's Laws* (4th edn reissue), para 751. For priorities, see Chapter 24.
2 Act of 1882, s 8.
3 *Heseltine v Simmons* [1892] 2 QB 547, CA.

The mode of registering bills of sale

5.42 The mode of registering both kinds of bills of sale is regulated by the Principal Act and is as follows. The bill of sale with every schedule or inventory annexed to the bill or referred to in the bill and a true copy of such bill and of such schedule or inventory and of every attestation of the execution of such bill of sale, together with an affidavit or witness statement in Form PF179 or PF 180 containing the particulars mentioned below[1], must be filed in Room E17 of the Royal Courts of Justice if made within the prescribed time[2].

1 See **5.44**.
2 Bills of Sale Act 1878, s 10(2). See the Queen's Bench Guide 12.4.As to the copies required for local registration, see the Administration of Justice Act 1925, s 23(2) and also ss 13 and 22. The omission of matters required to be stated in a bill makes the registration of the bill not a due registration: *Ex p Esanda Ltd* [1977] Qd R 162.

What is a sufficient copy?

5.43 The copy of the bill of sale, schedule or inventory and attestation to be presented to, and filed with, the Master, must be substantially a true copy, but need not be an exact copy, and clerical or verbal errors (including omission of date and omission of signature of grantor or that of a witness, etc) do not avoid registration.

Contents of statutory affidavit or witness statement[1]

5.44 The affidavit or witness statement presented to and filed with the Master must prove the following facts:

(a) the due execution and attestation of the bill of sale;
(b) the residence and occupation of the grantor and of every attesting witness; and
(c) the true date of the execution of the bill of sale[2].

The description should be of the grantor's and witnesses' residence and occupation at the time of registering the bill of sale, not at the time of its execution[3].

1 For forms, see Table 2 of Practice Direction (Forms) supplementing CPR Pt 4 (Forms).They may be modified as circumstances require.
2 Bills of Sale Act 1878, s 10 (2).
3 *Button v O'Neill* (1879) 4 CPD 354, CA.

Local registration

5.45 Where the residence of the grantor of the bill of sale or the person against whom the process is issued is outside the London insolvency district[1], or where the bill of sale describes the chattels as being in some place outside the London bankruptcy district, the Central Office will send copies of the bill of sale to the appropriate county court district judge[2].

Every copy of the bill of sale so transmitted must be filed, kept and indexed by the district judge of the county court in the manner prescribed by the rules[3] and any person may search, inspect and make extracts from and obtain copies of the bill of sale so registered, in the same way and upon the same terms as to payment or otherwise as may be the case with bills of sale registered by the Master under the Principal Act.

The provisions for local registration are directory and any default by the Master in transmitting the copy of the bill of sale to a county court does not avoid registration[4].

1 See Insolvency Act 1985, s 235, Sch 8, para 1.
2 Bills of Sale Act 1882, s 11 and Bills of Sale Registration Rules 1960.
3 Act of 1878, s 10 (2).
4 *Trinder v Raynor* (1887) 56 LJQB 422.

Extension of time for registering

5.46 By s 14 of the Principal Act, any judge of the High Court of Justice, or Master of the Supreme Court may, in his discretion, if satisfied that any failure to register within the prescribed time was accidental or due to inadvertence, order an extension of time for registration of a bill of sale or an affidavit of renewal. Such an order may be made on terms and conditions (if any) as to security, notice by advertisement or otherwise, or as to any other matter, as he thinks fit to direct[1].

Further, by s 14, any judge of the High Court of Justice or any Master of the Supreme Court may, in his discretion, if satisfied that any or the omission or misstatement of the name, residence or occupation of any person was accidental or due to inadvertence, order any omission or misstatement on the register to be rectified by the insertion in the register of the true name, residence or occupation of any person. Such an order may be made on terms and conditions (if any) as to security, notice by advertisement or otherwise, or as to any other matter, as he thinks fit to direct.

It should be noted that relief is limited to rectification of the register or an extension of time. An order cannot be made for an affidavit or witness statement to be filed correcting a mistake in the affidavit or witness statement made on registration[2]. Further, such an order will only be granted subject to rights which have already accrued to third persons[3].

1 See Queen's Bench Guide para 12.4.5 and 12.4.6 as to applications under this section.
2 *Crew v Cummings* (1888) 21 QBD 420, CA.
3 *Crew v Cummings*, above, and see *Re Parsons, ex p Furber* [1893] 2 QB 122, CA; and see Queen's Bench Guide, para 12.4.6. The order will be drawn up in Form PF 182.

Provisions as to keeping and inspecting register

5.47 Section 12 of the Principal Act provides for the Masters of the Queen's Bench Division to keep registers and an index containing particulars of the registration of bills of sale and the renewal of registrations of bills of sale, with an index[1].

Section 15 of the Principal Act provides that the Queen's Bench Masters may also order a memorandum of satisfaction to be written upon any registered copy of a bill of sale upon the prescribed evidence being given[2].

The register of bills of sale may be inspected either personally or by requisitioning an official search[3]. Any person is, upon payment[4], entitled to have an office copy or extract of any registered bill of sale and of the affidavit of execution filed with it or a copy of the bill and of any affidavit filed with it or of any registered affidavit of renewal. In all legal proceedings, any copy of a registered bill of sale and any affidavit purporting to be an office copy is admissible as prima facie evidence of the bill of sale and of the fact and date of registration shown[5].

1 Bills of Sale Act 1878, s 12, Sch B.
2 See CPR Sch 1 RSC 95.2 and PD 95.001 for the application procedure.See also Queen's Bench Guide para 12.4.7 and Form PF 183 containing precedents for evidence and forms of consent.
3 Bills of Sale Act (1878) Amendment Act 1882, s 16.
4 Bills of Sale Act 1878, s 16. See also CPR Sch 1 RSC 95.4, applications are to the Filing Department, Central Office (Room E07).For the prescribed fee see Supreme Court Fees Order 1999, Sch 1, Fee No 4.1.
5 Bills of Sale Act 1878, s 16.

Renewal of registration

5.48 The registration of a bill of sale must be renewed once at least every five years[1]. If a period of five years elapses from the registration, or renewed registration, of a bill of sale without renewal or further renewal, the registration becomes void.

A renewal of registration does not, however, become necessary by reason only of a transfer or assignment of a bill of sale.

The renewal of a registration is effected by filing in the Filing Department evidence in support stating the date of the bill of sale and of the last registration the names, residences and occupations of the parties as stated in the bill of sale and that the bill of sale is still a subsisting security[2]. The evidence must state the names, residences and occupations of the parties as stated in the bill of sale, even if they are stated incorrectly in the bill but the correct descriptions should also be added.

If these requirements of the Act are not complied with, the renewal of registration will be invalid[3]. Local registration of renewals is effected in the manner required by the Amending Act on registering a bill of sale. The court has jurisdiction under s 14 of the Principal Act of 1878 to extend the time for renewed registration[4].

1 Bills of Sale Act 1878, s 11.
2 Section 11. See CPR Sch 1 RSC 95.1.3 and for a form of evidence in support see PF181.
3 *Re Morris, ex p Webster* (1882) 22 Ch D 136, CA, and see *Ex p Esanda Ltd* [1977] Qd R 162.
4 See 4 *Halsbury's Laws* (4th edn) para 739; cf *Re Emery, ex p Official Receiver* (1888) 21 QBD 405.

Registration on transfer[1]

5.49 A transfer or assignment of a registered bill of sale need not be registered[2] A renewal of registration is also unnecessary by reason only of a transfer or assignment of a bill of sale[3]. A memorandum of charge by the transferee of a bill of sale, given by way of sub-mortgage and accompanied by a deposit of the bill of sale and transfer, need not be registered, even though the transferee afterwards acquires the grantor's equity of redemption[4].

1 For transfer of bills of sale, see Chapter 4.
2 Bills of Sale Act 1878, s 10.
3 Section 11.
4 *Re Parker, ex p Turquand* (1885) 14 QBD 636, CA. For priorities as between two or more holders of bills of sale, see **24.120**.

Chapter 6

Mortgages of ships and aircraft

SHIPS

Merchant Shipping Act 1995

6.1 Under the Merchant Shipping Act 1995 British ships[1] are entitled,[2] subject to certain detailed provisions,[3] to be registered in a central register maintained by the Registrar General of Ships and Seaman.[4]

Ships so registered are referred to in the 1995 Act as 'registered ships'.[5]

Schedule 1 to the 1995 Act (which makes provision relating to, among other things, the registration of mortgages over ships) applies to registered ships,[6] except:

(a) those excluded from its application by registration regulations,[7] namely small ships;[8]
(b) ships bareboat chartered-in by British charterers.[9]

1 For the definition of 'ship' see the Merchant Shipping Act 1995, s 313(1). For the definition of 'British ship' see s 1(1).
2 Registration is not compulsory.
3 As to which see the Merchant Shipping Act 1995, Pt II.
4 In relation to the register, see the Merchant Shipping Act 1995, s 8.
5 Section 23(1).
6 Merchant Shipping Act 1995, s 16(1).
7 Section 16(2).
8 Merchant Shipping (Registration of Ships) Regulations 1993, SI 1993/3138, reg 91. For the meaning of 'small ships' see the Merchant Shipping Act 1995, s 1(2).
9 Merchant Shipping Act 1995, s 17(7), disapplying 'the private law provisions for registered ships', as to which see s 16(6).

Mortgages of ships

Registered ships

6.2 A registered ship, or share in a registered ship, may be made a security for the repayment of a loan or the discharge or any other obligation.[1]

The instrument creating any such security (a 'mortgage') is required to be in the form prescribed by or approved under registration regulations.[2]

Where a mortgage executed in accordance with the foregoing is produced to the registrar, he must register the mortgage in the prescribed manner.[3] Such a mortgage is referred to in the 1995 Act as a 'registered mortgage'.[4]

Mortgages are registered in the order in which they are produced for registration.[5]

1 Merchant Shipping Act 1995, s 16(1) and Sch 1, para 7(1).
2 Merchant Shipping Act 1995, s 16(1) and Sch 1, para 7(2). As to 'registration regulations', see s 10. A mortgage produced for registration must be in a form approved by the Secretary of State, with appropriate attestation: the Merchant Shipping (Registration of Ships) Regulations 1993, SI 1993/3138, reg 57 (as amended). Under the similar requirements imposed by the (now repealed) Merchant Shipping Act 1894, it was held that the provision relating to the form of the mortgage is, however, directory only, and a mortgage is not invalid by reason of the detailed stipulations of the mortgage being contained in a separate instrument, and not appearing in the mortgage itself: *The Benwell Tower* (1895) 8 Asp MLC 13.
3 Merchant Shipping Act 1995, s 16(1) and Sch 1, para 7(3). See also the Merchant Shipping (Registration of Ships) Regulations 1993, SI 1993/3138, reg 58.
4 Merchant Shipping Act 1995, s 16(1) and Sch 1, para 14.
5 Section 16(1) and Sch 1, para 7(4).

Non-registered ships

6.3 If the ship is not registered a mortgage of it need not be in the statutory form. Further, it need not be registered either under the Merchant Shipping Act 1995 or under the Bills of Sale Acts.[1]

1 As to which see Chapter 5. See also *The Shizelle* [1992] 2 Lloyd's Rep 444, QBD: nothing in the Merchant Shipping Act 1894 which alters the common law position in relation to British ships which are not required to be registered and are not registered; an unregistered legal mortgage is valid in such circumstances.

Equitable mortgages

6.4 A deposit of a registered mortgage of a ship will create a valid security by way of equitable mortgage.[1] An equitable mortgage may also be created by the deposit of the builder's certificate of an unfinished ship.[2]

The court will enforce equities between the owner and the mortgagee and in estimating the rights of the mortgagee will not consider only the registered documents but all the transactions between the parties in relation to the mortgage.[3]

An unregistered legal mortgage takes effect as such and not as an equitable mortgage.[4]

1 *Lacon v Liffen* (1862) 4 Giff 75; affd (1863) 32 LJ Ch 315.
2 *Re Softley, ex p Hodgkin* (1875) LR 20 Eq 746.
3 *The Cathcart* (1867) LR 1 A & E 314.
4 *Re Shizelle* [1992] Lloyd's Rep 444, QBD.

Mortgagee not entitled to certificate of ship's registration

6.5 The certificate of registration of a British ship may be used only for the lawful navigation of the ship and shall not be subject to detention to secure any private right or claim.[1]

This provision covers a mortgage and, therefore, a pledge of the certificate is unlawful.

1 The Merchant Shipping Act 1995, s 13.

Registration under Companies Act 1985[1]

6.6 If the owner of a ship is a limited company, registration of a mortgage on the ship, or share in the ship, is also required under the Companies Act 1985.[2] Failure so to register renders the charge void as against a liquidator and any creditor,[3] though not as against the company (while it is a going concern) itself.[4] But this is without prejudice to any contract or obligation for repayment of the money secured by the charge; and when a charge becomes void under this provision, the money secured by it immediately becomes payable.[5]

1 The Companies Act 1989, ss 93-104, when in force, will substitute new ss 395-420 of the Companies Act 1985. However, at the date of writing, no order had been made bringing the sections into force.
2 Section 395(1), s 396(1)(h): 'a charge on a ship ..., or any share in a ship'.
3 Section 395(1). This means that the charge is void as against the company acting by its liquidator or administrator: *Smith (Administrator of Cosslett (Contracts) Ltd) v Bridgend County Borough Council* [2001] UKHL 58, HL.
4 *Buhr v Barclays Bank plc* [2001] EWCA Civ 1223, [2001] 31 EG 103 (CS).
5 Section 395(2).

Property passed by mortgage of ship

6.7 All articles necessary to the navigation of the ship or to the prosecution of the adventure, for example, oil in bunkers,[1] pass to the mortgagee under the word 'ship'.[2] Articles later substituted for the original ones also pass.[3] However, where the cargo belongs to the owner of the ship, it will not, in the absence of any special agreement, pass to the mortgagee.[4]

1 *The Span Terza (No 2)* [1983] 1 WLR 632; revsd on other grounds [1984] 1 WLR 27.
2 Although bunker oil was not included in the expression 'appurtenances' in *The Pan Oak* [1992] 2 Lloyd's Rep 36. As to whether bunkers pass to a mortgagee upon the true construction of the mortgage deed, see *Den Norske Bank A/S and Irish Intercontinental Bank v Owners of the Ships Eurosun and Eurostar and Euro Marine Carrier BV* [1993] 1 Lloyd's Rep 106.
3 *Coltman v Chamberlain* (1890) 25 QBD 328.
4 *Alexander v Simms* (1854) 18 Beav 80; affd 5 De GM & G 57; *Keith v Burrows* (1877) 2 App Cas 636.

Miscellaneous

6.8 In a ship mortgage the right of the mortgagee to insure and add the cost to the debt must be expressly stipulated.[1]

1 *The Basildon* [1967] 2 Lloyd's Rep 134. On insurance, see *Glafki Shipping Co SA v Pinios Shipping Co (No 1), The Mairia (No 2)* [1985] 1 Lloyd's Rep 300, CA; *Schiffshypothekenbank Lubeck AG v Norman Phillip Crompton, The Alexion Hope* [1987] 1 Lloyd's Rep 60.

Priority of mortgages of ships

Between registered and unregistered mortgages

6.9 The rights of an unregistered mortgagee are postponed to those of a registered mortgagee, even where the unregistered mortgage predates its registered counterpart.[1]

Equitable mortgages do not have priority over or equality with legal mortgages and their recognition does not introduce the equitable doctrines as to constructive notice into such transactions. Consequently, a legal registered mortgagee of a ship has priority over an earlier unregistered equitable charge, even though he had notice of that charge when he made his advance.[2]

1 *Coombes v Mansfield* (1855) 3 Drew 193, 3 Eq Rep 566, 2 LJ Ch 513. This provides a powerful incentive for both ships and mortgages thereof to be registered under the Merchant Shipping Act 1995.
2 *Black v Williams* [1895] 1 Ch 408. See also *Barclay and Co Ltd v Poole* [1907] 2 Ch 284.

Between registered mortgages

6.10 Registration confers priority over mortgages registered subsequently. Thus, where two or more mortgages are registered in respect of the same ship or share, the priority of the mortgagees between themselves is determined by the order in which the mortgages were registered and not by reference to any other matter, for example the dates of creation of the mortgages.[1]

However, registration regulations[2] may provide for the giving to the registrar by intending mortgagees of 'priority notices'[3] in prescribed form which, when recorded in the register, determine the priority of the interest to which the notice relates.[4]

1 Merchant Shipping Act 1995, s 16(1) and Sch 1, para 8(1).
2 See s 10.
3 As to which see the Merchant Shipping (Registration of Ships) Regulations 1993, SI 1993/3138, reg 59.
4 Merchant Shipping Act 1995, s 16(1) and Sch 1, para 8(2).

Transfer of registered mortgages

6.11 A registered mortgage may be transferred by an instrument made in the form prescribed by or approved under registration regulations[1] and, upon production of the instrument to the registrar, the transferee shall be registered in the prescribed manner.[2] However, an agreement to transfer a ship need not be registered, and may be enforced by the registered owner.[3]

1 Merchant Shipping Act 1995, s 16(1) and Sch 1, para 11(1). As to 'registration regulations', see s 10. A transfer of a registered mortgage must be in a form approved by the Secretary of State, with appropriate attestation: the Merchant Shipping (Registration of Ships) Regulations 1993, SI 1993/3138, reg 57 (as amended).
2 Merchant Shipping Act 1995, s 16(1) and Sch 1, para 11(2). See also the Merchant Shipping (Registration of Ships) Regulations 1993, SI 1993/3138, reg 61.
3 *Batthyany v Bouch* (1881) 4 Asp MLC 380.

Transfer of registered mortgage by operation of law

6.12 Where the interest of a mortgagee in a registered mortgage is transmitted to any person by any lawful means (except a transfer as above), the registrar must, on production of the prescribed evidence,[1] cause the name of that person to be entered in the register as mortgagee of the ship or share in question.[2]

1 As to which see the Merchant Shipping (Registration of Ships) Regulations 1993, SI 1993/3138, reg 60 (as substituted).
2 Merchant Shipping Act 1995, s 16(1) and Sch 1, para 12.

Remedies of mortgagees of ships

6.13 See **19.91** ff.

Registered mortgagee's power of sale

6.14 Every registered mortgagee has the statutory power, if the mortgage money or any part of it is due, to sell the ship or share in respect of which he is registered and to give effectual receipts for the purchase money.[1] However, the mortgagee is only empowered, not obliged, to sell.[2]

Where two or more mortgagees are registered in respect of the same ship or share, a subsequent mortgagee is not entitled to sell the ship or share without the concurrence of every prior mortgagee, except under an order of a court of competent jurisdiction.[3]

1 Merchant Shipping Act 1995, s 16(1) and Sch 1, para 9(1).
2 *European and Australian Royal Mail Co Ltd v Royal Mail Steam Packet Co* (1858) 4 K & J 676.
3 Merchant Shipping Act 1995, s 16(1) and Sch 1, para 9(2). As to priorities between registered mortgagees, see **6.10**.

Protection of registered mortgagees

6.15 Where a ship or share is subject to a registered mortgage then:

(a) except so far as may be necessary for making the ship or share available as a security for the mortgage debt, the mortgagee shall not by reason of the mortgage be treated as owner of the ship or share; and
(b) the mortgagor shall be treated as not having ceased to be owner of the ship or share.[1]

This means that, as regards third parties, the mortgagor remains in charge of the ship and the mortgagee is protected from associated liabilities.

1 Section 16(1) and Sch 1, para 10.

Discharge of registered mortgages

6.16 Where a registered mortgage has been discharged, the registrar shall, on production of the mortgage deed and such evidence of the discharge as may be prescribed,[1] cause an entry to be made in the register to the effect that the mortgage has been discharged.[2]

If for good reason the registered mortgage cannot be produced to the registrar, he may, on being satisfied that it has been properly discharged, record that the mortgage has been discharged.[3]

1 It appears that 'such evidence as satisfies [the registrar] that the mortgage has been discharged' will suffice: Merchant Shipping (Registration of Ships) Regulations 1993, SI 1993/3138, reg 62(1).
2 Merchant Shipping Act 1995, s 16(1) and Sch 1, para 13. A discharge of a registered mortgage must be in a form approved by the Secretary of State, with appropriate attestation: the Merchant Shipping (Registration of Ships) Regulations 1993, SI 1993/

3138, reg 57 (as amended). The registrar cannot erase the entry of the mortgage itself: *Chasteauneuf v Capeyron* (1882) 7 App Cas 127.
3 The Merchant Shipping (Registration of Ships) Regulations 1993, SI 1993/3138, reg 62(2).

Termination of registration of ship: effect on registered mortgages

6.17 Where the registration of any ship terminates by virtue of any provision of registration regulations,[1] the termination of that registration does not affect any entry made in the register so far as it relates to any undischarged registered mortgage of that ship or of any share in it.[2] Thus, such a mortgage continues in full force and effect, notwithstanding the fact that the ship herself has ceased to be registered.

1 As to which see the Merchant Shipping Act 1995, s 10.
2 Sections 16(4), (5).

Maritime liens, bottomry and respondentia

6.18 English law recognises maritime liens in respect of bottomry and *respondentia* bonds, salvage of property, seamen's wages and damage.

The master of a ship might, in circumstances of unforeseen necessity or distress, pledge the ship and freight to raise the necessary funds for the voyage, by a contract called 'bottomry'. The contract of bottomry usually took the form of a bond whereby the master stated the occasion for resorting to bottomry and pledged himself, the ship and the freight, and sometimes the cargo, for the repayment of the principal and interest on the safe arrival of the ship at the end of her voyage on such conditions as to risk as might be agreed upon.

Bottomry created a debt (which was generally treated as only nominal) against the master, but none against the owner.[1]

Respondentia was the separate hypothecation of the cargo alone as security for the repayment of a debt contracted about the necessary cost of transhipping[2] and forwarding the cargo to its destination.[3]

Bottomry and *respondentia* are obsolete in practice.[4]

1 *The Atlas* (1827) 2 Hag Adm 48; *The Mary Ann* (1865) LR 1 A & E 8 at 13.
2 Ie transferring the cargo to another vessel.
3 *The Atlas*, above. For a lien on sub-freight as an equitable mortgage, see *Re Welsh Irish Ferries Ltd* [1986] Ch 471.
4 But they remain part of the jurisdiction *in rem* and *in personam* of the Admiralty Court: Supreme Court Act 1981, s 20(2)(r) which speaks of 'any claim arising out of bottomry'.

AIRCRAFT

Civil Aviation Act 1982

6.19 Aircraft may be registered under the Civil Aviation Act 1982.[1] The register is maintained by the Civil Aviation Authority.

The Mortgaging of Aircraft Order 1972[2] (which makes provision relating to, among other things, the registration of mortgages over aircraft) applies to aircraft so registered.

1 Section 60 (regulation of civil aviation), as amended, and the Air Navigation Order 2000, SI 2000/1562, Art 3.
2 SI 1972/1268, as amended. The Order, which was made under s 16 of the Civil Aviation Act 1968, continues to have effect as if made under the s 86 of the Civil Aviation Act 1982, by virtue of the Interpretation Act 1978, s 17(2)(b).

Mortgages of aircraft

Registered aircraft

Generally

6.20 A registered aircraft, or such an aircraft together with any store or spare parts for it, may be made security for a loan or other valuable consideration.[1]

The mortgage of an aircraft is defined to include a mortgage which extends to any store of spare parts for that aircraft but does not otherwise include a mortgage created as a floating charge.[2]

There is no specified form of mortgage (except for securities created in Scotland[3]). Any such mortgage may be registered.[4] Registration is voluntary, not mandatory.[5]

All persons are at all times taken to have express notice of all facts appearing in the register, but the registration of a mortgage is not evidence of its validity.[6]

Mortgages of registered aircraft made after 1 October 1972, which would otherwise require registration under the Bills of Sale Acts,[7] are exempted from those Acts.[8]

1 Mortgaging of Aircraft Order 1972, SI 1972/971, Art 3.
2 Article 2(2).
3 Schedule 2.
4 Article 4.
5 But there is an obvious inducement to register since a registered mortgage has priority over an unregistered one, even where the unregistered mortgage was first in time: Art 14. See, further, **6.24**.
6 Article 13.
7 See Chapter 5.
8 Article 16(1).

Registration of mortgages: practice and procedure

6.21 Registration is effected by application for registration in the prescribed form[1] together with a certified copy of the mortgage and fee.[2] Where two or more aircraft are the subject of one mortgage, or where the same aircraft is the subject of two or more mortgages, separate applications for registration must be made in respect of each aircraft or mortgage.[3]

Changes in the registration particulars must be notified by or on behalf of the mortgagee in the prescribed form.[4]

The register may be rectified on an order of the High Court.[5]

The register of aircraft mortgages is open to the public on payment of the appropriate fee. Inspection may be made in person or by application for a certified copy of the entries in the Register. Application may also be made for notification as to whether or not there are any relevant entries in the Register.[6] Further, an official copy of an entry in the Register certified as a true copy by the Authority is admissible in evidence.[7]

1 Mortgaging of Aircraft Order 1972, SI 1972/971, Sch 1, Pt I.
2 Article 4.
3 Article 6.
4 Article 8 and Sch 1, Pt. III.
5 Article 10.
6 Article 11.
7 Article 11.

Unregistered aircraft

6.22 Mortgages of unregistered aircraft are not governed by the Mortgaging of Aircraft Order 1972 and remain subject to the Bills of Sale Acts, where appropriate.

Registration under the Companies Act 1985[1]

6.23 Whether or not the mortgage is registered, a mortgage of a registered aircraft made by a company is registrable under the Companies Act 1985.[2] Failure so to register renders the charge void as against a liquidator and any creditor,[3] though not as against the company (while it is a going concern) itself.[4] However, this is without prejudice to any contract or obligation for repayment of the money secured by the charge and when a charge becomes void under this provision, the money secured by it immediately becomes payable.[5]

1 Companies Act 1989, ss 93-104, when in force, will substitute new ss 395-420 of the Companies Act 1985. However, at the date of writing, no order had been made bringing the sections into force.
2 Companies Act 1985, ss 395(1) and 396(1)(h): 'a charge on [an] aircraft'. The Admiralty jurisdiction of the High Court does not extend to a claim in respect of a mortgage of an aircraft: *Re The Glider Standard Austria SH* [1965] P 463, [1965] 2 All ER 1022.
3 Section 395(1). This means that the charge is void as against the company acting by its liquidator or administrator: *Smith (Administrator of Cosslett (Contractors) Ltd) v Bridgend County Borough Council* [2001] UKHL 58, HL.
4 *Buhr v Barclays Bank plc* [2001] EWCA Civ 1223, [2001] 31 EG 103 (CS).
5 Section 395(2).

Priority of mortgages of aircraft

Between registered and unregistered mortgages

6.24 A registered mortgage of an aircraft has priority over any unregistered mortgage of that aircraft, even if the other mortgage was created before the registered mortgage.[1]

1 Mortgaging of Aircraft Order 1972, SI 1972/971, Art 14(1).

Between registered mortgages

6.25 Where two or more mortgages of an aircraft are registered, those mortgages as between themselves have priority according to the times at which they were respectively registered.[1] Therefore, as with ships, registration confers priority over mortgages registered subsequently, even if those mortgages were first in time.

A very limited exception to the above is that mortgages of an aircraft made before 1 October 1972 which were registered before 31 December 1972 have priority over any mortgages of that aircraft made on or after 1 October 1972 and as between themselves have the same priority as they would have had at common law.[2]

There is provision for a 'priority notice' to be served by a mortgagee or prospective mortgagee intending to register his mortgage.[3] Such a notice may afford priority from the time it was registered[4], which, when recorded in the register, determine the priority of the interest to which the notice relates.

The above priorities have effect notwithstanding any express, implied or constructive notice affecting the mortgagee.[5]

1 Mortgaging of Aircraft Order 1972, SI 1972/971, Art 14(2).
2 Article 14(2).
3 Article 5.
4 However, priority is only conferred if the contemplated mortgage is made and registered within 14 days of the entry of the priority notice: Art 5. For this purpose, days when the office is not open for registration are excluded: Art 14(3).
5 Article 14(4).

Transfer of registered mortgages of aircraft

6.26 There is no prescribed form of transfer of registered mortgage of an aircraft.

The Bills of Sale Acts[1] do not apply to registered mortgages of aircraft made on or after 1 October 1972.[2]

1 See Chapter 5.
2 Mortgaging of Aircraft Order 1972, SI 1972/971, Art 16(1).

Mortgagee's power of sale

6.27 Where the mortgage is by deed, the mortgagee of an aircraft has the usual statutory power to sell when the mortgage money has become due.[1]

1 Law of Property Act 1925, ss 101(1)(i), 205(1).

Discharge of registered mortgages

6.28 On receipt of the form set out in Pt IV of Sch 1 to the Order duly completed and signed by or on behalf of the mortgagee and of a copy of the document of discharge or receipt for the mortgage money, or of any other document which shows, to the satisfaction of the Civil Aviation Authority, that the mortgage has been discharged and on payment of the appropriate charge, the Authority is to enter the form in the register and mark the relevant entries 'Discharged' and, further, is required to notify the mortgagee, mortgagor and the owner that it has done so.[1]

1 Mortgaging of Aircraft Order 1972, SI 1972/971, Art 9 (as substituted).

Termination of registration of aircraft: effect on registered mortgages

6.29 Removal of an aircraft from the register[1] does not affect the rights of any mortgagee under any registered mortgage. Furthermore, in that event, entries shall continue to be made in the register in relation to the mortgage as if the aircraft had not been so removed.[2]

1 Ie that maintained under the Civil Aviation Act 1982, s 60.
2 Mortgaging of Aircraft Order 1972, SI 1972/971, Art 12.

Chapter 7

Mortgages of things in action

LEGAL AND EQUITABLE ASSIGNMENTS

By assignment

7.1 Insurance policies, shares, stocks, book and other debts, equitable interests in land[1] and personality, and other things in action[2], legal or equitable, are frequently mortgaged. Save where some special method of disposition is provided by statute, a mortgage of a thing in action is effected by an assignment of the thing[3]. The Bills of Sale Acts do not apply to mortgages of things in action[4].

At common law, things in action, with certain exceptions, notably negotiable instruments[5], were incapable of being assigned without the express or implied consent of the holder of the fund to apply it in accordance with the assignment[6]. As a consequence, except where particular classes of things in action were made assignable by statute, mortgages of even legal things in action were necessarily purely equitable. Equity regarding an assignment of a thing in action as valid and operating as an agreement to permit the assignee to sue for the thing in action in the name of the assignor[7].

1 These are not strictly things in action, but it is convenient to deal with these here as the same principles apply.

2 Things in action (formerly known as choses in action) are all personal rights of property which can only be claimed or enforced by action and not by taking physical possession: 2 Bl Com 396.

3 Rights can, however, be incapable of assignment under contracts which declare the rights to be incapable of assignment: *Linden Gardens Trust Ltd v Lenesta Sludge Disposals Ltd* [1994] 1 AC 85; *Circuit Systems Ltd v Zuken-Redac (UK) Ltd* [1996] 3 All ER 748, CA; *Oakdale (Richmond) Ltd v National Westminster Bank plc* [1997] 1 BCLC 63; *Hendry v Chartsearch Ltd* [1998] CLC 1382, CA. Rights can also be incapable of assignment if assignment is prohibited by statute or public policy: for example, under the Social Security Administration Act 1992, s187; if the assignment savours of maintenance: *Rees v de Bernardy* [1896] 2 Ch 437; and if the contract is personal: *Tollhurst v Associated Portland Cement Manufacturers Ltd* [1902] 2 KB 660. See further Chitty on Contracts (28th edn) Ch 20.

4 Bills of Sale Act 1878, s 4; see **5.16**.

5 See *Hopkinson v Forster* (1874) LR 19 Eq 74 at 76.

6 *Lampet's Case* (1612) 10 Co Rep 46b at 48a.

7 *Crouch v Crédit Foncier of England* (1873) LR 8 QB 374.

Statutory assignment

7.2 During the course of the nineteenth century the exceptions to the common law rule were extended[1] and a general form of statutory assignment was introduced by the Judicature Act 1873[2]. This is now contained in s 136 of the Law of Property Act 1925.

Section 136 provides:

> '**136.**(1) Any absolute assignment by writing under the hand of the assignor (not purporting to be by way of charge only) of any debt or other legal thing in action, of which express notice in writing has been given to the debtor, trustee or other person from whom the assignor would have been entitled to claim such debt or thing in action, is effectual in law (subject to equities having priority over the right of the assignee) to pass and transfer from the date of such notice—
> (a) the legal right to such debt or thing in action;
> (b) all legal and other remedies for the same[3]; and
> (c) the power to give a good discharge for the same without the concurrence of the assignor:
>
> Provided that if the debtor, trustee or other person liable in respect of such debt or thing in action has notice—
> (a) that the assignment is disputed by the assignor or any person claiming under him; or
> (b) of any other opposing or conflicting claims to such debt or thing in action;
> he may, if he thinks fit, either call upon the persons making claim thereto to interplead concerning the same, or pay the debt or other thing in action into court under the provisions of the Trustee Act 1925[4].
>
> (2) This section does not affect the provisions of the Policies of Assurance Act 1867[5].'

1 By the Companies Act 1862, shares, stocks and debentures in public companies were made freely assignable by registered transfer, and see now the Companies Act 1985, s 182(1) and the Stock Transfer Act 1963. Further see the Carriage of Goods by Sea Act 1992, in relation to bills of lading; Policies of Assurance Act 1867, s 1, in relation to policies of life insurance; Marine Insurance Act 1906, s 50(2), in relation to policies of marine insurance; Bills of Exchange Act 1882; Patents Act 1977, ss 30 and 32 and the Copyright Designs and Patents Act 1988, ss 90 and 94, in relation to patents and copyright. Furthermore, to protect the creditors of insolvent assignees, provision has been made for the registration of certain assignments: Insolvency Act 1986, s 344; Companies Act 1985, ss 395-398.

2 Section 25 (6).

3 Including rights of set-off: *Robbie (NW) & Co Ltd v Witney Warehouse Co Ltd* [1963] 3 All ER 613, CA. See also *Rother Iron Works Ltd v Canterbury Precision Engineers Ltd* [1974] QB 1, [1973] 1 All ER 394, CA; *George Barker (Transport) Ltd v Eynon* [1974] 1 All ER 900, [1974] 1 WLR 462, CA; *Security Trust Co v Royal Bank of Canada* [1976] AC 503, [1976] 1 All ER 381, PC; *Business Computers Ltd v Anglo-African Leasing Ltd* [1977] 2 All ER 741, [1977] 1 WLR 578. See Goode *Legal Problems of Credit and Security* (2nd edn) Ch V. Also Meagher Gummow & Lehane *Equity-Doctrines & Remedies* (3rd edn) Ch 37; *Tony Lee Motors Ltd v M S MacDonald & Son (1974) Ltd* [1981] 2 NZLR 281.

4 Section 63 amended by the Administration of Justice Act 1965, s 369(4), Sch 3; and s 63A, inserted by the County Courts Act 1984, s 148(1), Sch 2, Pt I, para 1.

5 See **7.14**.

Assignments within s 136 of the Law of Property Act 1925

7.3 In order that an assignment may be within the Act:

(a) it must be of a debt or other legal thing in action[1]. This definition includes equitable things in action[2] and legal should, therefore, be read as meaning 'enforceable in a court of justice'.

(b) the assignment must be in writing under the hand of the assignor, although no special form is necessary [3]. If the assignment is of an equitable interest, it must be in writing to be valid, in any event[4].

(c) the assignment must be absolute (as opposed to conditional) and not by way of charge only[5]. An assignment by way of security can still be a legal assignment if it is expressed to be an absolute assignment subject to a proviso for reassignment[6].

(d) the assignment must be of the whole of the thing in action, not part only[7].

(e) express notice in writing must be given to the assignor[8].

1 In *Stein v Blake* [1996] AC 243 the House of Lords held that if A and B have mutual claims against each other and A becomes bankrupt, the effect of s 323 of the Insolvency Act 1986 is that the debt due to A ceases on A's bankruptcy to exist as a thing in action and is replaced by a new thing in action: the claim to the net balance owing (approving *Farley v Housing and Commercial Developments Ltd* [1984] BCLC 442). Further, like any other thing in action, the right to the net balance can be assigned by the trustee in bankruptcy before it has been ascertained by the taking of an account between the trustee and B.

In *Investors Compensation Scheme Ltd v West Bromwich Building Society* [1998] 1 WLR 896, the House of Lords confirmed that a right to rescind a mortgage is not a thing in action or part of a thing in action and an owner cannot assign a right to rescission separately from his property. By contrast, a right to damages is a thing in action which can be assigned.

2 See *Torkington v Magee* [1902] 2 KB 427 at 430 to 431 (revsd on facts [1903] 1 KB 644); *Tolhurst v Associated Portland Cement Manufacturers Ltd* [1903] AC 414 at 424 per Lord Lindley; *Compania Colombiana de Seguros v Pacific Steam Navigation Co* [1965] 1 QB 101 and see Chitty on Contracts (28th edn) Ch 20. Assignments of future debts are capable of falling within the section: *Walker v Bradford Old Bank Ltd* (1884) 12 QBD 511; *G and T Earle Ltd v Hemsworth RDC* (1928) 44 TLR 605 at 609.

3 *Re Westerton* [1919] 2 Ch 104; *Curran v Newpark Cinemas Ltd* [1951] 1 All ER 295; *The Kelo* [1985] 2 Lloyds Rep 85 at 89.

4 Law of Property Act 1925, s 53(1)(c). This applies to personal as well as real equitable interests: *Grey v IRC* [1960] AC 1; *Oughtred v IRC* [1960] AC 206; *Vandervell v IRC* [1967] 2 AC 291. Section 53(1)(c) does not apply to the creation or operation of resulting, implied or constructive trusts: s 53(2). If the true effect of the assignment is the creation of a constructive trust, it need not, therefore, be in writing to be effective in equity: *Neville v Wilson* [1997] Ch 144, [1996] 3 All ER 171.

5 The mortgage of a debt or thing in action made in the ordinary form of an assignment with a proviso for redemption (express or implied) is an absolute assignment: *Tancred v Delagoa Bay Co* (1889) 23 QBD 239, CA; *Hughes v Pump House Hotel Co* [1902] 2 KB 190, CA. As is also an assignment by way of trust: *Comfort v Betts* [1891] 1 QB 737, CA. See also *Durham Bros v Robertson* [1898] 1 QB 765, CA. As to assignments which were held not to be absolute, see *Durham Bros v Robertson* [1898] 1 QB 765, CA; *Jones v Humphreys* [1902] 1 KB 10; *Re Kent and Sussex Sawmills Ltd* [1947] Ch 177, [1946] 2 All ER 638; *Re Interview Ltd* [1975] IR 382; *Contemporary Cottages (NZ) Ltd v Margin Traders Ltd* [1981] 2 NZLR 114; *Re Welsh Irish Ferries Ltd* [1986] Ch 471; (1985) 6 Co Law 224 (Milman). For an assignment which was held not to be a charge, see *Welsh Development Agency v Export Finance Co Ltd* [1991] BCLC 936. And see *Lloyds and Scottish Finance Ltd v Cyril Lord Carpet Sales Ltd* [1992] BCLC 609, 129 NLJ 366 Giddins. There must be an intention to transfer: *Coulls v Bagot's Executor and Trustee Co Ltd* (1967) 119 CLR 460.

6 *Tancred v Delagoa Bay and East Africa Railway Co* (1889) 23 QBD 239; *Durham Bros v Robertson* [1898] 1 QB 765; *Hughes v Pump House Hotel Co Ltd* [1902] 2 KB 190.

7 This does not authorise the legal assignment of part of a debt: *Forster v Baker* [1910] 2 KB 636; *Re Steel Wing Co Ltd* [1921] 1 Ch 349; but cf *Ramsey v Hartley* [1977] 2 All ER 673, [1977] 1 WLR 686, CA; but an assignment of part of the debt may be a good equitable assignment: *Walter and Sullivan Ltd v J Murphy & Sons Ltd* [1955] 2 QB 584, [1955] 1 All ER 843, CA, and see generally (1959) CLJ 99 (Hall); (1966) 30 Conv (NS) 286 (Cullity and Ford). See also *Camdex International Ltd v Bank of Zambia* [1996] 3 All ER 431, CA; *Re Steel Wing Co Ltd* [1921] 1 Ch 349; *Bank of Liverpool and Martins Ltd v Holland* (1926) 43

TLR 29; *Williams v Atlantic Assurance Co Ltd* [1933] 1 KB 81; *Walter v Sullivan Ltd v J Murphy & Sons Ltd* [1955] 2 QB 584, [1995] 1 All ER 843.

8 As to which, see **7.4**.

The statutory requirement of a notice in writing

7.4 Notice in writing is essential to enable the assignee to sue in his own name[1]. It may be given at any time before an action in respect of the thing has begun[2]. The notice is good if it indicates with sufficient certainty that the assignment has been executed and the name of the assignee is sufficiently disclosed if there is a reference to the deed of assignment[3]. If a date is stated, it must be correctly stated[4].

The notice may be given by either the assignor or the assignee or their successors in title[5]. In the case of joint debtors notice must be given to both[6]. The assignment takes effect on receipt of the notice by or on behalf of the debtor[7].

Quite apart from the statutory notice, it is necessary in all assignments of things in action to give notice of the assignment to the debtor, trustee or other person liable to pay the debt[8] or distribute the fund. This is:

(a) for the purpose of preventing such person from paying the debt or handing the fund to the assignor;
(b) to prevent a subsequent incumbrancer or purchaser without notice of the assignment from gaining priority over it[9]; and
(c) to prevent any equities or further equities arising.

1 Law of Property Act 1925, s 136 (1); and see also s 137 (3) (see **7.5**) for equitable interests. This is so even if the debtor is unable to read and other means are used to bring the assignment to his attention: *Hockley and Papworth v Goldstein* (1920) 90 LJKB 111. A payment on account does not estop the debtor from relying on the statutory requirement for notice in writing: *Hockley and Papworth v Goldstein* (1920) 90 LJKB 111.

2 *Bateman v Hunt* [1904] 2 KB 530, CA; *Compania Colombiana de Seguros v Pacific Steam Navigation Co* [1965] 1 QB 101 at 129, [1964] 1 All ER 216 at 235, 236.

3 *Denney, Gasquet and Metcalfe v Conklin* [1913] 3 KB 177; *Curran v Newpark Cinemas Ltd* [1951] 1 All ER 295; *Van Lynn Developments Ltd v Pelias Construction Co Ltd* [1969] 1 QB 607. Cf *James Talcott Ltd v John Lewis & Co Ltd* [1940] 3 All ER 592; *Herkules Piling Ltd v Tilbury Construction Ltd* (1992) 61 BLR 107, the disclosure to the debtor of a document of assignment on discovery in an action by the assignor was held to be insufficient notice for a legal or equitable assignment.

4 *Harrison (W F) & Co Ltd v Burke* [1956] 2 All ER 169, [1956] 1 WLR 419, CA. This case also suggests that the amount of the debt must be correctly stated. See (1956) 72 LQR 321 (REM), but a date need not be stated: *Van Lynn Developments Ltd v Pelias Construction Co Ltd* [1969] 1 QB 658, [1968] 3 All ER 824, CA.

5 *Bateman v Hunt* [1904] 2 KB 530, CA.

6 *Josselson v Borst* [1938] 1 KB 723, [1937] 3 All ER 722. If there are joint debtors and covenantors, notice to one who is bankrupt is unnecessary: Insolvency Act 1996, s 345(4). For the service of notices, see Chapter 20.

7 *Holt v Heatherfield Trust Ltd* [1942] 2 KB 1, [1942] 1 All ER 404; *Holwell Securities Ltd v Hughes* [1973] 2 All ER 476, [1973] 1 WLR 757.

8 *Amalgamated General Finance Co Ltd v C E Golding & Co Ltd* [1964] 2 Lloyds Rep 163.

9 *Spencer v Clarke* (1878) 9 Ch D 137. *Rhodes v Allied Dunbar Pension Services Ltd* [1988] 1 All ER 524. For priorities, see Chapter 24.

The priority of assignments

7.5 The priority of assignments is determined by the date of notice under the rule in *Dearle v Hall* as extended by s 137 (1) of the Law of Property Act 1925[1].

Section 137 preserves the rule governing assignments of things in action other than negotiable instruments[2], namely, that the assignee takes them subject to all equities, whether he has notice of the equities or not[3]. As a result, an assignee of shares or debentures takes them subject to all equitable claims of the company, such as the company's lien on the shares of its members, but this only extends to cover claims arising before notice of the assignment and the company cannot, after such notice, create fresh equities[4].

1 As amended by the Trusts of Land and Appointment of Trustees Act 1996, s 25(1), Sch 3. See Chapter 24; (1975) 39 Conv (NS) 261 (Kloss). For registration of company charges, see Chapter 12.

2 See *London Joint Stock Bank v Simmons* [1892] AC 201, HL; *Lloyds Bank v Swiss Bankverein* (1913) 108 LT 143.

3 See, generally, *Roxburgh v Cox* (1881) 17 Ch D 520; *Biggerstaff v Rowatt's Wharf Ltd* [1896] 2 Ch 93; *Popular Homes Ltd v Circuit Developments Ltd* [1979] 2 NZLR 642, but the parties may agree to the assignment being without set-off or counter-claim: see *First National Bank of Chicago Ltd v Moorgate Properties Ltd* (1975) Times, 21 October. A claim to damages for fraud in a contract is not prior to the claim of an assignee of the contract where the debtor is not in a position to rescind the contract: *Stoddard v Union Trust Ltd* [1912] 1 KB 181; cf *Lawrence v Hayes* [1927] 2 KB 111. Upon a claim by mortgagees in possession for rent, the tenant was not allowed to set off a claim for damages on a covenant by the mortgagor, since this claim was not an interest in the land by which the mortgagee was bound: *Reeves v Pope* [1914] 2 KB 284, CA; followed in *Citibank v Fredericks Pty Ltd* [1991] ACL Rep 295 Vic 3. For contractual exclusion of set-off see *Hong Kong Shanghai Banking Corpn v Kloeckner & Co AG* [1990] 2 QB 514, approved *Coca-Cola Financial Corpn v Finsat International Ltd* [1998] QB 43. For exclusion of set-off and the Unfair Contract Terms Act 1977 see *Stewart Gill Ltd v Horatio Myer & Co Ltd* [1992] QB 600 , applied *Esso Petroleum Co Ltd v Milton* [1997] 1 WLR 938, CA; *Skipkredittforeningen v Emperor Navigation* [1998] 1 Lloyds Rep 66.

4 *Bradford Banking Co v Briggs* (1886) 12 App Cas 29; and an assignee from a trustee-beneficiary can claim nothing from the trust estate until any default of the trustee has been made good: *Doering v Doering* (1889) 42 Ch D 203.

Difference between legal assignments and equitable assignments

7.6 In practice, the distinction between legal and equitable assignments makes little difference to the efficacy of an assignment[1]. An out and out equitable assignment and an equitable assignment which is intended to operate as a security resemble each other in most respects; indeed, a mere charge on a fund or debt operates as a partial equitable assignment[2].

Apart from some differences regarding the need for consideration, in that an equitable assignment which merely gives a charge on property[3] and an equitable assignment of property not yet in existence both require valuable consideration to support them (since they operate by way of contract) while an absolute assignment of existing property is effective although voluntary[4], the main distinction is procedural. An assignee under a legal assignment can sue the debtor without joining the assignor as a party to the action whereas, as a general rule, an equitable assignee must join the assignor[5].

An assignment which fails to fulfil the requirements of s 136 of the Law of Property Act 1925 may take effect as a good equitable assignment.

1 There are, however, some circumstances where the distinction can prove of importance. It has been held that an assignee of an option to renew a contract for service who had not given notice of the assignment to the other contracting party could not exercise the option as the assignment was equitable only: *Warner Bros Records Inc v Rollgreen Investments Ltd*

[1976] QB 430. Some aspects of the reasoning disapproved by a majority of the Court of Appeal in *Three Rivers District Council v Bank of England* [1996] QB 292, [1995] 4 All ER 312.

2 *Durham Bros v Robertson* [1898] 1 QB 765 at 769, CA.

3 *Re Earl of Lucan, Hardinge v Cobden* (1890) 45 Ch D 470; *Squib v Wyn* (1717) 1 P Wms 378.

4 *Squib v Wyn* (1717) 1 P Wms 378; *Nanney v Morgan* (1887) 37 Ch D 346; *German v Yates* (1915) 32 TLR 52; *Re Westerton* [1919] 2 Ch 104; *Holt v Heatherfield Trust Ltd* [1942] 2 KB 1, [1942] 1 All ER 404; *Re McArdle* [1951] Ch 669, [1951] 1 All ER 905, CA; *Re Wale* [1956] 3 All ER 280, [1956] 1 WLR 1346, *Corin v Patton* (1990) 169 CLR 540 and see (1943) 59 LQR 58, 208 (REM); (1943) 59 LQR 129 (Hollond); (1951) 67 LQR 295 (REM); (1955) 33 Can BR 284 (Sheridan).

5 See 7.7.

EQUITABLE ASSIGNMENT

Creation

7.7 An equitable assignment by way of security may be made, for example[1]:

(a) by an agreement between a debtor and his creditor that a specific thing in action which is, or will be, in the hands of or due from a third person and which belongs to the debtor, shall be applied in discharge of the debt[2]; or

(b) by an order given by the debtor whereby the holder of a fund is directed or authorised to pay it to the creditor[3].

The assignment may, generally, be made either by writing or orally[4], no particular words being necessary[5], provided that the intention is sufficiently expressed[6]. An equitable assignment of an equitable thing in action must, however, be in writing if it is caught by s 53(1)(c) of the Law of Property Act 1925[7].

1 See Chitty on Contracts (28th edn) Ch 20.

2 *Row v Dawson* (1749) 1 Ves Sen 331; *Brice v Bannister* (1878) 3 QBD 569; *Palmer v Carey* [1926] AC 703, PC. See *Swiss Bank Corpn v Lloyds Bank Ltd* [1982] AC 584, [1981] 2 All ER 449, HL; *Re Welsh Irish Ferries Ltd* [1986] Ch 471 and 7.7. For sub-mortgages, see Chapter 15.

3 *Row v Dawson* (1749) 1 Ves Sen 331; *Burn v Carvalho* (1839) 4 My & Cr 690; *Rodick v Gandell* (1851) 1 De GM & G 763 at 777; *Diplock v Hammond* (1854) 5 De GM & G 320; *Palmer v Carey* [1926] AC 703, PC; *Cotton v Heyl* [1930] 1 Ch 510; *Re Warren, ex p Wheeler v Trustee in Bankruptcy* [1938] Ch 725, [1938] 2 All ER 331; *William Brandt's Sons & Co v Dunlop Rubber Co* [1905] AC 454, HL. Such an equitable assignment will not be a bill of exchange: see *Brice v Bannister*, supra; *Tibbits v George* (1836) 5 Ad & El 107.

4 *Gurnell v Gardner* (1863) 4 Giff 626. It was suggested in *Re Richardson, Shillito v Hobson* (1885) 30 Ch D 396, that an assignment of a debt had to be effected in writing.

5 *William Brandt's Sons & Co v Dunlop Rubber Co* [1905] AC 454, HL, at 462; *IRC v Electric and Musical Industries Ltd* [1949] 1 All ER 120 at 126.

6 *William Brandt's Sons & Son v Dunlop Rubber Co* [1905] AC 454, HL, at 462; *Elders Pastoral Ltd v Bank of New Zealand (No 2)* [1990] 1 WLR 1478, PC.

7 A disposition of an equitable interest or trust subsisting at the time of the disposition, must be in writing, signed by the person disposing of the same, or by his agent thereunto lawfully authorised in writing or by will (the section replaces s 9 of the Statute of Frauds 1677).

Essentials of equitable assignment

7.8 An equitable assignment will not be valid, unless there is an obligation:

(a) to pay the debt owing by the assignor and to pay it out of a particular fund[1]; and
(b) to pay it to the person who claims under the assignment[2].

Therefore, the assignment of the benefit of a contract to make a loan is not good as an equitable assignment since there is no particular fund bound by the original contract[3]. It is not necessary, however, that the exact amount of the debt to be paid or of the fund out of which it is directed to be paid, should be ascertained[4]. The obligation that the particular fund shall be made liable to the debt must be clear[5].

The following will not take effect as equitable assignments:

(a) a promise to pay the debt out of the particular fund, if such an arrangement is countermandable[6];
(b) a direction to apply the fund where no consideration is proved[7], if such an arrangement is countermandable;
(c) an assignment created by giving an authority to a person without interest in the debt to receive it though he promises to pay it to the creditor of the person who gives the authority, as such a transaction comprises neither a direction to the person who owes the money, nor a direct agreement between the debtor and the creditor[8].

Further, a cheque is not an equitable assignment of the drawer's balance at his bankers, being in the nature of a bill of exchange[9]. If, however, there is a sufficient indication that the supposed assignee is to have the benefit of the fund or thing in action in addition to relying on the credit of the assignor or, as it is sometimes put, is to be paid 'out of the fund' as distinguished from 'when the assignor gets the fund', a valid equitable assignment is created, provided that the transaction is for value. The intention must be that the property shall pass[10].

1 *Watson v Duke of Wellington* (1830) 1 Russ & M 602 at 605; *Percival v Dunn* (1885) 29 Ch D 128; *Re Gunsbourg, ex p Trustee* (1919) 88 LJKB 479.
2 *Bell v London & North Western Rly Co* (1852) 15 Beav 548.
3 *Riccard v Prichard* (1855) 1 K & J 277. See *Swiss Bank Corpn v Lloyds Bank Ltd* [1982] AC 584, [1981] 2 All ER 449, HL.
4 *Western Wagon etc Co v West* [1892] 1 Ch 271; *May v Lane* (1894) 64 LJQB 236, CA.
5 *Brown, Shipley & Co v Kough* (1885) 29 Ch D 848, CA.
6 *Malcolm v Scott* (1843) 3 Hare 39.
7 *Re Whiting, ex p Hall* (1879) 10 Ch D 615, CA.
8 *Rodick v Gandell* (1851) 1 De GM & G 763.
9 *Hopkinson v Forster* (1874) LR 19 Eq 74.
10 *Gorringe v Irwell India Rubber etc Works* (1886) 34 Ch D 128, CA; *Re Casey's Patents, Stewart v Casey* [1892] 1 Ch 104, CA.

Effect of equitable assignment

7.9 An equitable assignment of a thing in action passes to the assignee the right to sue for its recovery[1]. If the thing in action is equitable and the assignment is absolute, the assignee can sue in his own name without making the assignor a party to the action[2]. All necessary parties must be before the court and, therefore, where part of a debt has been made the subject of an equitable assignment, neither the assignor nor the assignee can sue the debtor without joining the assignee or assignor as appropriate[3].

If the thing in action is legal, the assignor ought to be a party to the transaction either as claimant or defendant—even where the equitable assignment is absolute[4]. The non joinder as a party of the person in whom in law the thing in action is vested does not, however, render the action a nullity, though the equitable assignee will not be able to obtain damages or a permanent injunction without joining him as a party[5]. If the assignor does not commence the action himself, the assignee is entitled to do so in the name of the assignor on giving him a proper indemnity as to costs and charges consequent on the use of his name[6].

An equitable assignment of a thing in action would stand, though the assignor became bankrupt or died before the notice reached the holder of the fund or could otherwise be acted upon[7], since it was effective between assignor and assignee without notice[8] of the holder of the fund[9]. When a debtor has received notice of an equitable assignment of the debt he is bound to pay it to the assignee, although the latter refuses to give him indemnity[10]. It is no excuse for refusal and payment to the assignor that he has brought an action to which the debtor has no legal defence, for the court will indemnify him by making the wrongful claimant pay the costs. Equally, the fact that, after the assignment, the assignor has become bankrupt, or has made a composition with his creditors, makes no difference[11].

1 *Durham Bros v Robertson* [1898] 1 QB 765 at 769, CA.

2 *Cator v Croydon Canal Co* (1841) 4 Y & C Ex 593.

3 *Walter v Sullivan Ltd v J Murphy & Sons Ltd* [1955] 2 QB 584, CA.

4 *Durham Bros v Robertson* (as cited above); *Rumput (Panama) SA and Belzetta Shipping Co SA v Islamic Republic of Iran Shipping Lines, The Leage* [1984] 2 Lloyds Rep 259. Nor can the original creditor sue without joining he assignee: *Walter and Sullivan Ltd v J Murphy & Sons Ltd* [1955] 2 QB 584, [1955] 1 All ER 843, CA. See *Warner Bros Records Inc v Rollgreen Ltd* [1976] QB 430 at 435, [1975] 2 All ER 105, CA. See further *Chitty on Contracts* (28th edn) Ch 20.

5 The debtor may waive the requirement that the assignor be joined: *William Brandt's Sons & Co v Dunlop Rubber Co Ltd* [1905] AC 454, HL; a requirement that the assignor be made a party to the proceedings serves little useful purpose and may be dispensed with where the assignor retains no interest at all in the thing in action and the assignment only failed to be statutory for want of formality: *Weddell v JA Pearce & Major* [1988] Ch 26 (applied in *Grovewood Holdings plc v James Capel & Co Ltd* [1995] Ch 80); *Three Rivers District Council v Bank of England* [1995] 4 All ER 312, CA. CPR Pt 19 rr 1-2, provides that a court may also order a person to be added as a new party if this is desirable for the court to resolve all the matters in dispute or if there is an issue which requires such joinder.

6 *Wood v Griffith* (1818) 1 Swan 43 at 56, per Lord Eldon. See 6 *Halsburys Laws* (4th reissue) para 69.

7 *Smith v Everett* (1792) 4 Bro CC 64; *Burn v Carvalho* (1839) 4 My & Cr 690; *Gurnell v Gardner* (1863) 4 Giff 626; *Walker v Bradford Old Bank* (1884) 12 QBD 511.

8 Notice should, however, be given as it prevents a subsequent assignee from gaining priority by himself giving notice, prevents the holder of the fund from obtaining a good discharge by afterwards paying the fund to the assignor, and prevents any or further equities being set up against the assignee. Moreover the giving of notice in writing may give a right to sue at law under s 136 of the Law of Property Act 1925.

9 *Rodick v Gandell* (1852) 1 De GM & G 763; *Gorringe v Irwell India Rubber etc Works* (1886) 34 Ch D 128, CA. Notice is not necessary to complete the title of the assignee: *Ward v Duncombe* [1893] AC 369 at 392, HL.

10 *Magee v UDC Finance Ltd* [1983] NZLR 438, CA; and see *Barclays Bank plc v Willowbrook International Ltd* [1986] BCLC 45.

11 *Hutchinson v Heyworth* (1838) 9 Ad & El 375; *Jones v Farrell* (1857) 1 De G & J 208.

Stop notice

7.10 Where the mortgage is of a fund in court a stop order should be obtained, and this is equivalent to a notice given to the trustees[1]. Where government stock, or the stock or shares or debentures of any public company are equitably mortgaged a stop notice may be given instead of notice to the company[2].

1 *Pinnock v Bailey* (1883) 23 Ch D 497; *Montefiore v Guedalla* [1903] 2 Ch 26, CA, and see **2.28**. Express notice should also be given to the trustees.
2 A stop notice was formerly called a notice in lieu of distringas: see, further, **2.26**.

Subject to equities

7.11 Unless by the instrument creating the thing in action it is made assignable by the creditor free from equities between himself and the debtor, the assignee takes subject to rights of set-off and otherwise between the debtor and the assignor existing before notice of the assignment[1].

The equitable assignee of a debt is not in the same position as to the obligation of using diligence as the holder of a bill of exchange or promissory note; but, like a mortgagee in possession, he is chargeable with wilful default[2].

1 See **7.5**.
2 *Glyn v Hood* (1860) 1 De GF & J 334.

Expectancies and future things in action[1]

7.12 A mere expectancy (such as an expectancy under a will), not based on any existing legal right, is simply a future thing in action and cannot be assigned without consideration[2]. The assignment operates as a contract to assign property answering the description of the property mortgaged[3] when it comes into the mortgagor's possession and passes an interest which will attach to the property when acquired[4]. Until the property is acquired, there is only a liability on the contract, which is provable in the bankruptcy of the mortgagor and from which he is released by the order of discharge[5]. An expectant share in the estate of the living person transfers the share and does not impose a mere personal liability which is affected by the bankruptcy of the mortgagor[6].

1 As to future acquired property and bills of sale, see **5.6**. Also see *Chitty on Contract* (28th edn) Ch 20.
2 The assignment is unenforceable if purely voluntary: *Meek v Kettlewell* (1843) 1 Ph 342.
3 The property must be sufficiently described to be ascertainable: *Tailby v Official Receiver* (1888) 13 App Cas 523, Hl, and see **1.17**.
4 *Holroyd v Marshall* (1862) 10 HL Cas 191. Also see *Winn v Burgess* (1986) Times, 8 July.
5 *Collyer v Isaacs* (1881) 19 Ch D 342; *Wilmot v Alton* [1897] 1 QB 17; *Bank of Scotland v Macleod* [1914] AC 311, HL; *Re Collins* [1925] Ch 556.
6 *Re Lind, Industrial Finance Syndicate Ltd v Lind* [1915] 2 Ch 345, CA. As to the acquisition of expectancies at an undervalue, see the Law of Property Act 1925, s 174 (see Chapter 13).

Mortgage of interest in trust funds[1]

7.13 Such an interest is necessarily equitable. It has been held that equitable things in action are within s 136 of the Law of Property Act 1925, and capable of legal assignment[2]. The generally accepted view, however, is that a mortgage of an equitable interest must be an equitable mortgage. There is usually no need for any statutory assignment as, if the whole interest is assigned, the assignee can sue in his own name, without joining the original creditor[3].

The form of the assignment is governed by s 53(1)(c) of the Law of Property Act 1925[4]. Such a mortgage is, as a rule, created by a formal deed, and where it is desired to incorporate the statutory power of sale and other powers a deed is essential[5]. The mortgage takes the form of an assignment of the interest with a proviso for reassignment on payment of the loan. In view of the hazardous nature of such securities, the mortgagee will generally insist on the mortgagor effecting a policy of insurance on his own life and mortgaging the policy as collateral security.

Where there are several such mortgages their priority depends upon the rule in *Dearle v Hall*, as extended by the Law of Property Act 1925[6]. The mere giving of notice of the assignment does not constitute the taking of possession of the interest. To do that the notice must also require payment of the income to the mortgagee[7]. Where the interest in a fund is a reversionary one, the trustees may, when the interest falls into possession, pay the whole fund over to the mortgagee[8], but they are not bound to do so and they may pay over only so much as suffices to discharge the principle, interest and costs due on the mortgage[9].

1 For mortgages of equitable interests in registered land, see Chapter 5.
2 See **7.2**, *Re Pain* [1919] 1 Ch 38; cf *Torkington v Magee* [1902] 2 KB 427 at 430, 431.
3 *Performing Right Society Ltd v London Theatre of Varieties Ltd* [1924] AC 1, HL.
4 See **7.7** above.
5 See Chapter 20.
6 See Chapter 24.
7 *Re Pawson's Settlement, Higgins v Pawson* [1917] 1 Ch 541.
8 *Jones v Farrell* (1857) 1 De G & J 208.
9 *Re Bell, Jeffery v Sayles* [1896] 1 Ch 1, CA; *Hockey v Western* [1898] 1 Ch 350, CA.

ASSIGNMENTS UNDER PARTICULAR STATUTES

Mortgages of policies of life insurance

7.14 Mortgages of life insurance policies are principally effected as collateral security to mortgages of land. Building societies frequently insist on such collateral security[1].

Policies of life insurance are assignable either in equity[2] or under the Policies of Assurance Act 1867[3]. An equitable assignment of a policy of life insurance is subject to the rules governing equitable assignments generally[4]. An assignment under the Act of 1867 is a legal assignment subject to certain formalities. If these are observed the assignee can sue in his own name[5].

1 Endowment mortgages are now less popular: see **3.35**.
2 See 25 *Halsburys Laws* (4th edn reissue) Insurance paras 545-551.
3 The provisions of this Act are not affected by the Law of Property Act 1925, s 136; s 136(2). The Law of Property Act does, however, offer an alternative method of legal assignment and if a formal mortgage is made it will generally be made under that Act.
4 See **7.8**.
5 Section 1. The only effect of the Act is to enable the assignee to sue insurers in his own name. The Act does not affect the rights of the assignor and assignee between themselves.

Statutory formalities

7.15 The assignment must be in writing, either endorsed on the policy or by a separate instrument in the form given in the Schedule to the Act or in a similar form[1]. Written notice of the date and purport of the assignment must be given to the insurance company at their principal place of business[2]. The company must acknowledge receipt of a notice, if requested, and on payment of a fee not exceeding 25p[3]. An acknowledgment is conclusive evidence against the company of the receipt of the notice[3].

1 Section 5; cf *Crossley v City of Glasgow Life Assurance Co* (1876) 4 Ch D 421; *Spencer v Clarke* (1878) 9 Ch D 137.
2 Section 3. The policy must specify the places at which notices of assignment may be given: s 4. For service of notice, see Chapter 20.
3 Section 6, as amended; and see Decimal Currency Act 1969, s 10.

The form of the mortgage

7.16 The mortgage takes the form[1] of an assignment with a proviso for reassignment. It commonly includes covenants by the mortgagee not to permit the policy to become void, to pay premiums and produce the receipts for the payments to the mortgagee and a power, in case of default, for the mortgagee to pay premiums and for any such payments to be a charge on the policy[2]. The mortgage should also provide for a sale[3], surrender or exchange of the policy by the mortgagee and other powers.

The mortgagee will usually take possession of the policy[4].

1 A mandate conditional on the grantor predeceasing the person to whom it is given is not within the statutory provisions: *Re Williams, Williams v Ball* [1917] 1 Ch 1, CA.
2 There will be a right to keep the policy on foot and a charge even if there is not express provision: *Gill v Downing* (1874) LR 17 Eq 316, see Chapters 16 and 36.
3 The statutory power of sale (see Chapter 20) applies to mortgages by deed of policies and other choses in action.
4 *Spencer v Clarke* (1878) 9 Ch D 137.

Priorities

7.17 The assignee takes subject to equities[1]

If there are several mortgages their priority will be regulated by the order in which notice of the assignments was given[2], save that a second mortgagee with notice, whether actual, imputed or constructive[3], of a first mortgagee cannot gain priority over the first mortgage by giving notice before the first mortgagee[4].

1 Eg a contract of insurance is a contract *uberrimae fidei*, so that the policy may be avoided by the company if there has not been full disclosure by the insured.
2 Policies of Assurance Act 1867, s 3.
3 *Re Weniger's Policy* [1910] 2 Ch 291; cf *Re Lake, ex p Cavendish* [1903] 1 KB 151.
4 *Newman v Newman* (1885) 28 Ch D 674; *Re Wallis, ex p Jenks* [1902] 1 KB 719.

Insurance by the creditor

7.18 Where a mortgage of a life assurance policy is to be taken as collateral security an assignment is sometimes rendered unnecessary by the creditor taking out a policy on the life of the debtor[1]. In the absence of express contract, the policy will, on the discharge of the debt, belong to the mortgagor if he pays the premiums or is with his own knowledge charged with them in account[2]. In other cases the policy will belong absolutely to the mortgagee[3].

1 The policy should not be taken out by the borrower in the name of the creditor because the creditor would have no rights under the policy, not being a party thereto: see *Re Sinclair's Life Policy* [1938] Ch 799, [1938] 3 All ER 124.
2 *Morland v Isaac* (1855) 20 Beav 389; *Drysdale v Piggott* (1856) 8 De GM & G 546; *Freme v Brade* (1858) 2 De G & J 582; *Bruce v Garden* (1869) 5 Ch App 32; *Salt v Marquess of Northampton* [1892] AC 1, HL; and see Chapter 28.
3 *Bruce v Garden* (1869) 5 Ch App 32.

Avoiding the policy

7.19 Unless the terms of a life policy provide to the contrary, the policy will be avoided by the suicide of the insured[1]. It has not been decided whether, if the policy has been mortgaged, the security is avoided[2]. Express provision is usually made in the policy for it not to become void in such circumstances against the assignee. Where a policy contains a clause to the effect that it shall be valid notwithstanding the suicide of the assured, a mortgagee, whether legal or equitable, can enforce it against the company in that event, even where the mortgagee could recover the debt from another source and the company has no claim for indemnity or repayment against the estate of the assured[3]. This has been held to be the case even though the company is itself the mortgagee[4].

1 *Beresford v Royal Insurance Co Ltd* [1938] AC 586, [1938] 2 All ER 602, HL. The forfeiture rule applies to aiding and abetting suicides but the interests of justice may require that relief against forfeiture be granted: *Dunbar v Plant* [1998] Ch 412, [1997] 4 All ER 289.
2 *Beresford v Royal Insurance Co Ltd* [1938] AC 586 at 600, [1938] 2 All ER 602, HL, but see *Hardy v Motor Insurers' Bureau* [1964] 2 QB 745, [1964] 2 All ER 742, CA.
3 *Moore v Woolsey* (1854) 4 E & B 243; *Solicitors' Life Assurance Society v Lamb* (1864) 2 De GJ & Sm 251.
4 *White v British Empire Mutual Life Assurance Co* (1868) LR 7 Eq 394 and see *Royal London Mutual Insurance Society v Barrett* [1928] Ch 411.

Discharge of the policy

7.20 A legal mortgage of a policy is discharged by reassignment or receipt[1], an equitable mortgage by cancellation. The policy must be returned to the mortgagor or handed over to a subsequent mortgagee, if any. Notice of the discharge should be given to the company[1].

1 See Chapter 28.

Mortgages of shares

7.21 A shareholder may mortgage his shares by granting either a legal mortgage or an equitable charge or mortgage on them.

Legal mortgage of shares

7.22 A legal mortgage of shares is effected by a transfer of the shares to the mortgagee[1], subject to an agreement for their re-transfer on repayment of the loan[2].

The mortgagee is registered in the register of members as a fully entitled shareholder of the company[3], and not merely as mortgagee, because s 360 of the Companies Act 1985 prohibits entry on the register of notice of any trust[4]. As a result, from the point of view of the company, the transfer will operate as an out and out transfer and will give the mortgagee the rights and impose upon him the liabilities, where they exist, of a shareholder. During the time that the mortgagee is registered as a shareholder, the company will, therefore, pay to him all dividends and other moneys with respect to the shares, and he is entitled to vote[5]. Equally, if the shares are partly paid, the mortgagee will be personally liable for calls[6]. Any person inspecting the register or the share certificate issued to the mortgagee will be induced, if ignorant of the true facts, to treat the mortgagee as the absolute legal and equitable owner of the shares. The mortgagor may, therefore, be well advised to protect his equity of redemption by serving a 'stop notice' on the company[7].

A legal mortgage on shares has been described[8] as providing the best security which the mortgagee can obtain when a loan is secured on shares. Following registration, the mortgagee can be certain that his security cannot be defeated by fraud on the part of the mortgagor. Such a legal mortgage is, however, disadvantageous in relation to shares which are not fully paid up and stamp duty will also be payable twice: on the transfer and re-transfer[9].

1 In the case of shares and other securities held in uncertificated form under the CREST system a legal mortgage will be executed by a transfer from the stock account of the mortgagor to that of the mortgagee, which requires that the transferee be a member or sponsored member of CREST.
2 For forms of agreements, see 28 *Forms and Precedents* (5th edn, 1999 reissue) Mortgages.
3 See *Palmer's Company Law*, para 6.802 and *Gore Browne on Companies* vol 1, para 16.4.3.
4 Such registration would reveal notice of a trust, in particular of the equity of redemption in the mortgagor.
5 Where the shares have been transferred to the mortgagee, a mandatory injunction may be granted to enforce an agreement by him to vote in accordance with the wishes of the mortgagor: *Puddephatt v Leith* [1916] 1 Ch 200; *Musselwhite v C H Musselwhite & Son Ltd* [1962] Ch 964 at 981–984, [1962] 1 All ER 201 at 206–207.
6 *Re Land Credit Co of Ireland, Weikerman's Case* (1873) 8 Ch App 831.
7 See **2.26**.
8 *Palmer's Company Law*, para 6.802.
9 Currently 50 pence, stamp duty on shares is to be abolished under the Finance Act 1990 at a date to be appointed.

Equitable mortgage of shares

7.23 A mortgage of shares is most commonly effected by a deposit of the share certificates with the mortgagee[1], usually accompanied by a memorandum of deposit[2]. This is not a mere pledge[3], but affects a true equitable mortgage entitling the mortgagee to foreclosure[4].

Amongst other matters, the memorandum usually contains: a statement that the deposit is by way of security, a covenant for payment of principal and interest, a proviso for redemption, a power for the mortgagee to sell the shares[5], a covenant by the mortgagor not to incur a forfeiture and an undertaking by the mortgagor to execute a registered transfer[6].

1 *Harrold v Plenty* [1901] 2 Ch 314.
2 For example, *Barclay v Prospect Mortgages Ltd* [1974] 1 WLR 837. While the mortgagor remains the registered holder of the shares he must vote as the mortgagee directs: *Wise v Landsdell* [1921] 1 Ch 420.

3 On the difference between a pledge and a charge see *Askrigg Pty Ltd v Student Guild of the Curtin University of Technology* (1989) 18 NSWLR 738; *Re City Securities Pte, Ho Mun-Tuke Don v Dresdner Bank* [1990] 2 MLJ 257, on appeal sub nomen *Dresdner Bank AG v Mun-TokeDon* (1993) 3 MSCL 95, 875 Sing AC; *ANZ Banking Group Ltd v Curlett, Cannon & Galbell Pty Ltd* [1992] 2 VR 647; *Chase Manhattan Bank NA v Wong Tui San* (1993) ACSLR 600-737, (1993) 11 ACLC 3 at 112, Sing CA.

4 *Harrold v Plenty* [1901] 2 Ch 314; *Adelaide Building Co Pty Ltd v ABC Investments* (1990) 8 ACLC 445.

5 There is an implied power to sell on reasonable notice: *Stubbs v Slater* [1910] 1 Ch 632, (see Chapter 20) and an express power if the memorandum is under seal (Law of Property Act 1925, s 101). For foreclosure, see Chapter 21.

6 For forms, see 28 *Forms and Precedents* (5th edn, 1999 reissue) Mortgages; 4(1) *Forms and Precedents* (5th edn, 2000 reissue) Banking; and the Appendix, infra.

The mortgagee does not lose his security by handing over the shares to facilitate a takeover and the mortgagee is entitled to claim delivery of new shares: *UTC Ltd v NZI Securities Australia Ltd* (1991) 4 WAR 349, FC.

A mortgage of shares would not, it is submitted, extend to a bonus issue based on the original holding (cf accretions to the security in relation to mortgages of land, **3.57**). Accordingly the memorandum should contain an express provision extending the security to a bonus issue. Where a rights issue is offered, the mortgagee should consult the borrower. It is submitted that the mortgagee can only disclaim or sell the rights if the borrower refuses to pay the price of the shares or to allow the price to be added to the security (see *Waddell v Hutton* 1911 SC 575). It is further submitted that the mortgagee cannot on his own initiative take up the issue and add the shares and the price to the security.

Transfers in blank

7.24 Sometimes the deposit is accompanied by a form of transfer executed by the mortgagor, but leaving the name of the transferee and the date blank[1]. This method has the disadvantage that the transfer, if required to be by deed[2], cannot be validly completed without re-execution by the mortgagor[3] as an instrument containing blanks is not a deed[4]. A person who executes a deed of transfer in blank may, however, be estopped from denying its validity as against bona fide purchasers from the grantee without notice[5].

Where transfers are not required to be by deed, the mortgagor must be presumed to have authorised the mortgagee to act as his agent for the purposes of completing the transfer by delivering it to the mortgagee[6]. However, even in such cases, a person dealing with the mortgagee ought to make enquiries and, arguably, cannot claim the benefit of being purchaser for value without notice, so as to acquire a better right than the person from whom he received the instrument[7].

A blank transfer will be effective in the case of shares which are transferable by writing under hand only[8] and, when filled in, passes the legal property.

1 See eg *Barclay v Prospect Mortgages Ltd* [1974] 2 All ER 672, [1974] 1 WLR 837.

2 See now Stock Transfer Act 1963, under which fully paid up registered securities may, generally, be transferred by instrument under hand, notwithstanding anything to the contrary in the articles.

3 *Powell v London and Provincial Bank* [1893] 2 Ch 555, CA; *Ireland v Hart* [1902] 1 Ch 522. The principle has been applied to a mortgage of a ship in *Burgis v Constantine* [1908] 2 KB 484.

4 *Bradford Banking Co v Briggs, Son & Co Ltd* (1886) 12 App Cas 29, HL.

5 *Earl of Sheffield v London Joint Stock Bank* (1888) 13 App Cas 333; *Warehouse v Bank of Ireland* (1891) 29 LR Ir 384; *London Joint Stock Bank v Simmonds* [1892] AC 201, HL; *Fuller v Glyn Mills Currie & Co* [1914] 2 KB 168.

6 *Colonial Bank v Cady* (1890) 15 App Cas 267 at 286m HL. This will not be the case where the transfer is required to be by a deed, which can only be executed by an agent appointed

by instrument under seal: *Powell v London and Provincial Bank*; *Fitch Lovell Ltd v IRC* [1962] 3 All ER 685, [1962] 1 WLR 1325.

7 It has been suggested that the mere fact that the transferee sees that the transfer delivered by the transferor to the holder was in blank is enough to put the transferee on notice that an out and out transfer: *France v Clark* (1884) 26 Ch D 257, CA. This view has been doubted: *Fry v Smellie* [1912] 3 KB 282, CA and is probably not good law. See *Gore Brown on Companies* vol 1, para 16.5.

8 *Ortigosa v Brown Janson & Co* (1878) 47 LJ Ch 168; cf *France v Clarke* (1884) 26 Ch D 257, CA.

Notice

7.25 Notice of the deposit of share certificates should be given to the company. This is not for the purpose of priorities for no trust may be entered on the register of a company[1] and the rule in *Dearle v Hall*[2] does not apply to equitable mortgages of shares[3]. Nevertheless notice is advisable[4]. If the company has notice it will generally not register another person as owner while there are conflicting claims[5]. Further, while the mortgagee takes the shares subject to all equitable claims of the company, such as the company's lien on the shares of its members, this only extends to claims arising before notice of the mortgage and the company cannot, after such notice, create fresh equities[6].

The limited effect of notice could be overcome by giving the company a stop notice[7]. This entitles the mortgagee to notice from the company of an application to transfer and gives the mortgagee an opportunity of obtaining a restraining order or an injunction[8]. This procedure is rarely used, but provides a very valuable method for checking any anticipated or possible misappropriation of shares.

1 Companies Act 1985, s 360; *Société Générale de Paris v Walker* (1885) 11 App Cas 20, HL.

2 See **7.22**.

3 *Macmillan Inc v Bishopsgate Trust (No 3)* [1996] 1 All ER 585. Priorities of mortgages of shares are governed by the same rules of priority as applied to mortgages of land before 1926. As to which, see Pt VI, below.

4 Notice was not required to protect the mortgagee of shares against a claim by the mortgagor's trustee in bankruptcy under the reputed ownership clause (Bankruptcy Act 1914, s 38(c) repealed by Insolvency Act 1985, s 235, Sch 10, Pt III) since things in action, including shares (*Colonial Bank v Whinney* (1886) 11 App Cas 426; *Re Collins* [1925] Ch 556), other than debts due or growing due to the bankrupt in the course of his trade or business, were not deemed goods within the meaning of the clause.

5 See *Ireland v Hart* [1902] 1 Ch 522. *Roots v Williamson* (1888) 38 Ch D 485.

6 *Bradford Banking Co Ltd v Briggs & Co Ltd* (1886) 12 App Cas 29, HL; *Mackereth v Wigan Coal and Iron Co Ltd* [1916] 2 Ch 293; *Champagne Perrier-Jouet v H H Finch Ltd* [1982] 3 All ER 713, [1982] 1 WLR 1359.

7 CPR, Sch 1 sc50.11; and see **2.26**.

8 See *Société Générale de Paris v Tramways Union Co* (1884) 14 QBD 424 at 453, CA.

Mortgage of partnership share[1]

7.26 Under the Partnership Act 1890, s 31, an assignment by a partner of his share in the partnership[2], either absolute or by way of mortgage, does not, as against the other partners, entitle the assignee during the continuance of the partnership to interfere in the management of the partnership business or affairs[3] or to require accounts or inspection of books[4]. It only entitles the assignee to receive the assignor's share of the profits.

On a dissolution of the partnership, the assignee is entitled to receive the assignor's share of the assets and, for the purpose of ascertaining the share, he is entitled to an account as from the date of dissolution[5].

Under s 33 the partnership may, at the option of the other partners, be dissolved if any partner charges his share of the partnership property for his separate debt. Consequently, such mortgages, without the consent of the other partner, afford a very unsatisfactory security.

If the mortgage is by deed the mortgagee will have the statutory powers of sale and appointing a receiver[6] and, whether by deed or not, may enforce his security by foreclosure[7].

Notice of the mortgage should be given to the firm.

1 For forms, see 28 *Forms and Precedents* (5th edn, 1999 reissue) Mortgages. A mortgage of a share in a partnership is a mortgage of a chose in action and is not required to be registered as a bill of sale: *Re Bainbridge, ex p Fletcher* (1878) 8 Ch D 218. As to whether the partnership or any individual is the debtor, see *Custom Credit Corpn Ltd v Heard and Raphael* (1983) 33 SASR 45.
2 As to the nature of a partnership share see *United Builders Pty Ltd v Mutual Acceptance Ltd* (1980) 144 CLR 673.
3 See eg *Re Garwood's Trusts, Garwood v Paynter* [1903] 1 Ch 236. For a discussion of the nature and effect of an assignment of part of a partner's interest in a partnership see *Hadlee v IRC* [1993] AC 524, [1993] 2 WLR 696, PC.
4 *Bonnin v Neame* [1910] 1 Ch 732.
5 See *Watts v Driscoll* [1901] 1 Ch 294, CA.
6 See Chapters 18 and 20.
7 *Whetham v Davey* (1885) 30 Ch D 574.

Mortgage of debts[1]

7.27 Such a mortgage may be affected by either a legal or equitable assignment of the debt[2] with a proviso for redemption[3]. The mortgage should relieve the mortgagee of any liability should the debt become irrecoverable[4].

There cannot be a legal assignment of a future debt[5]. An assignment of a future debt, if made for valuable consideration, is treated as a contract to assign[6]. Accordingly, a mortgage of all the book debts due and owing, or which may, during the continuance of the security, become due and owing to the mortgagor, has been held to be sufficiently definite and to pass the equitable interest in book debts incurred after the assignment, whether in the business carried on by the mortgagor at the time of the assignment or in any other business[7].

Until notice of the mortgage is given to the debtor the assignment is merely equitable[8]. In the case of a mortgage of book debts the giving of such notice would, generally, be prejudicial to the mortgagor's credit. As a result, it will often be agreed that notice will not be given unless there is default and the mortgage will contain a provision whereby the mortgagor will appoint the mortgagee his attorney to collect the debts[9].

In the absence of notice, payment by the debtor to the mortgagor or a release by the mortgagor will be good as against the mortgagee[10].

The priority of such mortgages is governed by the date of the receipt by the debtor of notice of the mortgages[11].

1 See *Contemporary Cottages (N) Ltd v Margin Traders Ltd* [1981] 2 NZLR 114. Every sub-mortgage involves a mortgage of a debt: see Chapter 15.
2 See **7.2** and **7.7**. If the assignment is a legal assignment the mortgagee will be able to sue the debtor without joining the mortgagor. The assignee of a judgment debt has the same rights of enforcing the judgment as the assignor had: *Goodman v Robinson* (1886) 18 QBD

332; cf *Forster v Baker* [1910] 2 KB 636 at 642. An assignee of part of a judgment debt cannot issue execution for the part assigned to him: *Forster v Baker* [1910] 2 KB 636 at 642.

3 For forms, see 28 *Forms and Precedents* (5th edn, 1999 reissue) Mortgages; and see the Appendix. For prohibitions on the assignment of debts, see *Helstan Securities Ltd v Hertfordshire County Council* [1978] 3 All ER 262.

4 See *Ex p Mure* (1788) 2 Cox Eq Cas 63; *Williams v Price* (1824) 1 Sim & St 581.

5 See *Chitty on Contract* (28th edn) Ch 20.

6 *Holroyd v Marshall* (1862) 10 HL Cas 191.

7 *Tailby v Official Receiver* (1888) 13 App Cas 523, HL. For fixed charges over book debts, see *Siebe Gorman & Co Ltd v Barclays Bank Ltd* [1979] 2 Lloyd's Rep 142. Also see the Insolvency Act 1986, s 344 (1), whereby a mortgage by a person engaged in any business of existing or future book debts will be void against this trustee in bankruptcy, as regards any book debts not paid before the presentation of the bankruptcy petition, unless the mortgage has been registered as if it were a bill of sale under the Bills of Sale Act 1878, but this provision does not render void any assignment of book debts due at the date of assignment from specified debtors, or of debts becoming due under specified contracts, or any assignment of book debts included in either a transfer of a business made in good faith and for value, or on any assignment of assets for the benefit of creditors generally.

A mortgage of payments to become due under contracts entered into by the mortgagor, but not completed at the date of the commencement of the mortgagor's bankruptcy, is void against the mortgagor's trustee in bankruptcy: *Re Collins* [1925] Ch 556.

8 Law of Property Act 1925, s 136 (1).

9 See 28 *Forms and Precedents* (5th edn, 1999 reissue) Mortgages, and see the Appendix.

10 *Stocks v Dobson* (1853) 4 De GM & G 11.

11 See Chapter 24.

Profit-sharing loans

7.28 The book debts and goodwill of a business are sometimes mortgaged on the terms of the lender receiving a share of the profits in lieu of interest, or of the interest varying with the profits. Such arrangements must be treated with caution as an agreement which includes participation in profits is prima facie evidence of partnership[1]. The substance of the transaction will, therefore, be examined[2] and, if the transaction is in reality a partnership, 'no phrasing of it by dextrous draftsmen will avail to avert the legal consequences of the contract, namely, full liability for the debts of the firm'[3].

If the reality[4] is that a person is not taking a profit share as a return on a loan that he has made, then he is not a partner[5], provided that his arrangement to that effect is in writing and what he is making is a loan to the partners and not a purchase of a partnership share[6]. In all such transactions there must be a bona fide loan, one necessary ingredient of which is personal liability on the part of the borrower to repay the loan.

The following arrangements have been held to be partnerships:

(a) an arrangement by which the lender is only to be repaid out of the assets of the business[6];
(b) an arrangement where the lender takes an interest in or share of the capital of the business and becomes jointly interested in capital and profits, in effect becoming part owner of (ie partner in) the business;
(c) an arrangement where the lender's share of the profits varies in the proportion which his loan may from time to time bear to the rest of the capital, will not be regarded as lending his money on the security.

A provision for the return by the lender of a proportion of the profits received by him in one year, in case of subsequent losses, would also be an almost certain mark of partnership on the basis that no lender would in good faith submit to such a provision. For the same reason, arbitration clauses must be avoided[7] and clauses giving the lender a right to interfere or take part in the management of the business. Even a covenant by the borrower to employ the loan exclusively in the business is not to be lightly introduced[8].

If a lender is not a partner, he is not entitled to recover anything in respect of his loan or his share of profits in the event of a bankruptcy or insolvency of the borrower until all the claims of the other creditors have been satisfied[9], but if he has security he will nevertheless have his rights as a secured creditor[10].

1 Partnership Act 1890, s 2(3).
2 *McKie v Luck* (1925) 9 TC 511; *Keith Murphy Pty Ltd v Custom Credit Corpn Ltd* (1992) 6 WAR 332. And see Blackett-Ord *Partnership*, (1997) Ch 1.
3 *Adam v Newbigging* (1888) 13 App Cas 308, HL, per Lord Halsbury. An express declaration that no partnership is to be constituted is not conclusive: *Firth v Amslake* (1964) 108 Sol Jo 198; *Weiner v Harris* [1910] 1 KB 285, 290.
4 *Frowde v Williams* (1886) 56 LJQB 62; *Singleton v Knight* (1888) 13 App Cas 788. He may still be a lender although he has certain rights of a partner if those rights are for the protection of his interest as lender: *Hollom v Whichelow* (1895) 64 LJQB 170.
5 *Mollwo, March & Co v Court of Wards* (1872) LR 4 PC 419.
6 *Re Megevand, ex p Delhasse* (1878) 7 Ch D 511, CA.
7 See *Cox v Hickman* (1860) 8 HL Cas 268; *Syers v Syers* (1876) 1 App Cas 174, HL; *Pooley v Driver* (1876) 5 Ch D 458; *Re Howard, ex p Tennant* (1877) 6 Ch D 303, CA; *Davis v Davis* [1894] 1 Ch 393; *Re Young, ex p Jones* [1896] 2 QB 484.
8 See *Badeley v Consolidated Bank* (1888) 38 Ch D 238, CA. For forms of mortgage avoiding a partnership, see 28 *Forms and Precedents* (5th edn, 1999 reissue) Mortgages.
9 Partnership Act 1890, s 3, and see *Re Abenheim, ex p Abenheim* (1913) 109 LT 219 at 221.
10 *Badeley v Consolidated Bank* (1888) 38 Ch D 238, CA.

Mortgage of copyright

7.29 The copyright in every original literary, dramatic, musical or artistic work and in sound recordings, films, broadcasts, cable programmes and the typographical arrangement of published editions may be mortgaged.

A legal mortgage of copyright takes the usual form of a mortgage of a thing in action: a covenant to pay, an assignment of the copyright[1] with a proviso for redemption and the appropriate covenants and provisions[2]. The assignment must be in writing and signed by or on behalf of the assignor[3], but does not require to be expressed in any particular form of words and may be contained in letters[4]. Indeed, there is no requirement that the assignment should specifically mention copyright[5].

An equitable or informal mortgage may be created by agreement, express or implied[6].

A legal assignment of a copyright, or of any part of it, vests the right assigned in the assignee so that he becomes the owner of the right and may sue for infringements in his own name[7]. By contrast, an equitable assignee cannot sue for infringements in his own name, but must make the assignor a party to the action and his rights will be postponed to those of a subsequent assignee, unless such assignee acquired his rights with notice of the prior equitable assignment[8].

Where there has been a purported assignment of future copyright[9] then, if on the coming into existence of the copyright, the assignee or a person claiming under him would be entitled to require the copyright to be vested in him, the copyright, on its coming into existence, vests in the assignee or his successor in title without further assurance[10].

Where the author is the first owner and his rights to copyright arise before 1 June 1957, the benefit of an assignment by way of mortgage will endure for 25 years only after his death, the copyright for the remainder of its duration then reverting to the estate of the author[11].

1 Copyright is transmissible by assignment: Copyright, Designs and Patents Act 1988, s 90(1). See 9(2) *Halsbury's Laws* (4th edn reissue).
2 For a form, see 28 *Forms and Precedents* (5th edn, 1999 reissue) Mortgages.
3 Copyright, Designs and Patents Act 1988, s 90(3).
4 *London Printing and Publishing Alliance Ltd v Cox* [1891] 3 Ch 291, CA. In *Python (Monty) Pictures Ltd v Paragon Entertainment Corpn* [1998] EMLR 640 a provision for termination contained in a side letter was held to be binding on a sub-assignee.
5 *Murray v King* [1986] FSR 116.
6 *Grace v Newman* (1875) LR 19 Eq 623; *Performing Right Society Ltd v London Theatre of Varieties Ltd* [1924] AC 1, HL.
7 But a person who was not the owner of the copyright at the date of the issue of proceedings for an infringement cannot recover although during the proceedings he has taken an assignment which gave him the property necessary to maintain the action: *Cox v Cox* (1853) 11 Hare 118.
8 *Werdeman v Société Générale d'Electricité* (1881) 19 Ch D 246 at 252, CA; *Macdonald v Eyles* [1921] 1 Ch 631.
9 Copyright which will or may come into existence in respect of future work or class of works or on the occurrence of a future event.
10 Copyright, Designs and Patents Act 1988, s 91(1). Section 91 does not apply to an agreement made before 1 June 1957: s 170, Sch 1, para 26(1).
11 Copyright, Design and Patents Act 1988, Sch 1, para 27.

Rights of a person having recording rights

7.30 The rights conferred by the Copyright Designs and Patents Act 1988 Pt II (as amended) on a person having recording rights[1] are not assignable[2].

A person may, however, acquire the recording rights in a performance if he takes an assignment either of the benefit of the exclusive recording contract to which the performance is subject or the benefit of a licence from the person who has the exclusive recording contract[2].

1 Section 185(1).
2 Section 192B(1) added by the Copyright and Related Rights Regulations 1996, SI 1996/2927, regs 4, 21(2).

Design right

7.31 The provisions of the Copyright, Designs and Patents Act 1988 relating to assignment of design right are identical to those relating to copyright[1].

1 Part III of the Act, ss 222 and 223.

Mortgage of patents

7.32 A patent granted under the Patents Act 1977 is personal property, without being a thing in action, and may be assigned or mortgaged[1]. A mortgage of a patent is void unless made in writing and signed by or on behalf of the parties to the transaction or, in the case of a body corporate, is signed or is under the seal of that body[2]. In general, where two or more persons are proprietors of a patent, the mortgage of a share in the patent by one requires the consent of the other or others[3].

A legal assignment of a patent usually takes the form of an assignment of the patent by the registered proprietor to the lender with an undertaking for re-assignment on repayment[4]. An agreement in writing to assign a patent will take effect as an equitable mortgage of the patent[5]. A mortgage of a patent should be registered, as an unregistered mortgage is ineffective against a person who later acquires the patent or an interest in the patent and who does not know at the time of this acquisition of the unregistered mortgage or charge[6].

1 Patents Act 1977, s 30 (1), (2). Cf the Patents Act 1949, s 54 (5), under which a patent was a chose in action. Nevertheless, it is convenient to deal with patents here. 'Mortgage' includes a charge: Patents Act 1977, s 130 (1).
2 Patents Act 1977, s 30 (6).
3 Patents Act 1977, s 36 (3).
4 For form, see 21(1) *Forms and Precedents* (5th edn, 1997 reissue) Intellectual Property and 28 *Forms and Precedents* (5th edn, 1999 reissue) Mortgages.
5 Patents Act 1977, s 30 (6).
6 Patents Act 1977, s 33.

Mortgages of registered trade marks and designs

Registered trade marks

7.33 A registered trade mark is generally transmissible by assignment in the same way as other personal property[1]. It is transmissible either in connection with the goodwill of a business or independently[2].

An assignment of a registered trade mark is not effective unless it is in writing signed by or on behalf of the assignor or his personal representative. In a case where the assignor or personal representative is a body corporate, this requirement may be satisfied by the affixing of a seal[3]. A person who becomes entitled by assignment to a registered trade mark must apply for registration of his title[4]. The Trade Marks Act 1994 provides sanctions in the nature of deprivation of rights for failure to register any registrable transaction affecting a registered trade mark. Until an application has been made for registration of the prescribed particulars of a registrable transaction, the transaction is ineffective as against a person acquiring a conflicting interest in or under the registered trade mark in ignorance of it[5]. Further, where a person becomes the proprietor of a registered trade mark by virtue of a registrable transaction, unless an application for registration of the prescribed particulars of the transaction is made before the end of the period of six months beginning with its date or the court is satisfied that it was not practicable for such an application to be made before the end of that period and that an application was made as soon thereafter as possible, he is not entitled to damages or an account of profits in respect of any infringement of the registered trade mark occurring after the date of the transaction and before the prescribed particulars of the transaction are registered[6].

1 See 44 *Halsbury's Laws* (4th edn 2000 reissue).
2 Trade Marks Act 1994, s 24(1).
3 Section 24(3).
4 Trade Marks Act 1994, s 25 (2).
5 Trade Marks Act 1994, s 25 (1)(a).
6 Section 25(4).

Registered designs

7.34 In general, a registered design may be assigned by the registered proprietor, subject to any rights vested in any other person of which notice is entered in the register of designs kept at the Patent Office[1]. Where a person becomes entitled as mortgagee or otherwise to any interest in a registered design, he must apply to the registrar for registration of his title as proprietor or, as the case may be, of notice of his interest, in the register of designs[2]. There is no penalty for failure to register, although it is only a registered proprietor who may sue, and the registered proprietor must be joined in any action for infringement. Further, except for the purposes of an application to rectify the register, a document in respect of which no entry has been made in the register may not be admitted in any court as evidence of the title of any person to a registered design or share or interest therein unless the court otherwise directs[3]. Any equities in respect of the design may, however, be enforced in the same manner in respect of any other personal property[4].

1 Registered Designs Act 1949, s 19 (4). See 35 *Halsbury's Laws* (4th edn reissue).
2 Section 19 (1). For form of application, see 21(2) *Forms and Precedents* (5th edn, 1999 reissue) Intellectual Property.
3 Registered Designs Act 1949, s 19 (5).
4 Section 19 (4), proviso.

Chapter 8

Debentures

Generally[1]

8.1 A company may create ordinary mortgages[2] or borrow on the security of debentures. Debentures consist, basically, of an actual acknowledgment of indebtedness by the debtor company and a charge on the company's property[3]—generally, a fixed charge on specific assets[4], particularly the company's land, and a floating charge on the rest of its undertaking, including its trading assets.

Debenture stock is of the same nature as ordinary debentures except that instead of each debenture securing a definite and generally equal amount, the whole sum secured is treated as a single stock and certificates are issued in respect of multiples of the stock. The great advantage of debenture stock is its divisibility[5].

An issue of debentures or debenture stock is in substance a contributory mortgage[6] with a large number of contributors.

The term debenture is usually associated with companies[7] although it is also sometimes used in relation to an unincorporated club[8]. The term is not used in connection with individual traders[9].

1 See Gough *Company Charges* (2nd edn); 7(2) *Halsbury's Laws* (4th edn reissue) Companies; *Palmer's Company Law* Ch 13. For registration of company charges, see Chapter 12.

2 See eg *Knightsbridge Estates Trust Ltd v Byrne* [1940] AC 613, [1940] 2 All ER 401, HL. Such a mortgage is technically a debenture, but not usually so called.

3 The root meaning of 'debenture' is indebtedness, and to constitute a debenture the written acknowledgment of debt must be executed by or on behalf of the debtor: *Broad v Stamp Duties Comr* [1980] 2 NSWLR 40 at 52-54, per Lee J. The document must also be an actual acknowledgment of debt, as opposed to being mere evidence of debt: *Edmonds v Blaina Furnaces Co* (1887) 36 Ch D 215 at 219, per Chitty J; *Austral Mining Construction Pty Ltd v NZI Capital Corpn Ltd* (1991) 4 ACSR 57 at 58 and 65. There may be a debenture which is nothing more than an acknowledgment of indebtedness; see *Lemon v Austin Friars Investment Trust Ltd* [1926] Ch 1, CA, *Handeval Pty Ltd v Comptroller of Stamps (Victoria)* (1985) 157 CLR 177, but usually a debenture contains a charge of the property of the company and then it is a mortgage debenture.

The Companies Act 1985 defines a debenture as including debenture stock, bonds and any other securities of a company whether constituting a charge on the assets of the company or not: s 744. See further, for the meaning and nature of debentures: *Gough* Ch 24.

4 For the meaning of fixed assets see *National Bank of New Zealand v Comr of Inland Revenue* [1992] 1 NZLR 250, HC (NZ).

5 See *Palmer's Company Law* Ch 13.

6 As to which, see Chapter 20.

7 Debentures of incorporated companies are excepted from the application of the Bills of Sale Acts: Bills of Sale Act (1878) Amendment Act 1882, s 17; and see *Slavenburg's Bank*

NV v Intercontinental Natural Resources Ltd [1980] 1 All ER 955, [1980] 1 WLR 1076.

8 *Wylie v Carlyon* [1922] 1 Ch 51. As to a charge of future-acquired land by an individual, see **1.17**. A charge of chattels by an individual is subject to the Bills of Sale Acts. As to agricultural charges, see Chapter 9.

9 In *Handeval Pty Ltd v Comptroller of Stamps (Victoria)* (1985) 10 ACLR 207, 157 CLR 177; see also (1984) 15 ATR 672, it was assumed that debentures were only issued by companies.

Form[1]

8.2 A single instrument may be a mortgage debenture[2], but often a debenture will be one of a series of short contemporaneous instruments. It is usually, but not necessarily, under the company's seal[3].

1 For forms, see 10 *Forms and Precedents* (5th edn, 2001 Reissue) Companies; and the Appendix for a mortgage and general charge by a company.

2 *Edmonds v Blaina Furnaces Co* (1887) 36 Ch D 215 at 221; *Robson v Smith* [1895] 2 Ch 118.

3 *Lemon v Austin Friars Investment Trust Ltd* [1926] Ch 1, CA; *Re Burns* [1969] WAR 97 at 102.

The traditional form

8.3 The traditional form of debenture, which is still used when a company borrows from only a few lenders, contained:

(a) a covenant by the company to pay a named person or the registered holder[1] or sometimes the bearer of the debenture a specified sum on a specified day[2] or such earlier day as the debt might become payable under conditions specified in the instrument[3];

(b) a covenant to pay interest in the meantime at the specified rate[4];

(c) a charge of such payments on the company's undertaking and all its real and personal property[5], present and future, including (sometimes) uncalled capital, or on some specified property[6]; and

(d) a statement that it was issued subject to certain conditions endorsed on the debenture or otherwise annexed to it. For example:

  (i) that the debenture was one of a series, all of which were to rank *pari passu* as a first (or, as the case may be, a second or third) charge on the property charged without any preference or priority of one over another[7]; and

  (ii) (very generally) that such charge was to be a 'floating security'[8];

  (iii) that the money secured should become payable if default were made in payment of interest, or if an order were made, or an effective resolution passed, for the winding up of the company[9];

  (iv) (usually) that there was power to appoint a receiver[10];

  (v) provisions (in detail) for the assignment or transmission of the debenture, sometimes by registered assignment, sometimes by mere delivery[11];

  (vi) provisions for meetings of the debenture holders and for the validity of resolutions passed at such meetings, so as to bind a dissentient minority[12];

  (vii) the place of payment[13]; and

  (viii) provisions for the service of notices[14].

Contrary to the general rule that a mortgage cannot be made irredeemable, it is provided by the Companies Act 1985, s 193, that debentures shall not be invalid by reason only that they are made irredeemable, or redeemable only on the happening of a contingency, however remote, or on the expiration of a period, however long[15].

1 Where a debenture, not payable to bearer, is issued to a person with his name left blank, the debenture, as such, is void, but where it forms one of a series of debentures secured by a trust deed, the lender will have an equitable security and can share *pari passu* with the holders of valid debentures in the property comprised in the trust deed: *Re Queensland Land and Coal Co, Davis v Martin* [1894] 3 Ch 181.

2 Payment will nevertheless become due on a winding up before that date: *Wallace v Universal Automatic Machines Co* [1894] 2 Ch 547. Where the principal moneys have become immediately payable by reason of a winding up, the company or the guarantors of the loan are entitled to redeem and the debenture holders can only refuse payment if the conditions so provide: *Consolidated Goldfields of South Africa v Simmer and Jack East Ltd* (1913) 82 LJ Ch 214.

3 For the effect of the absence of a covenant for payment, see **3.23**.

4 *British India Steam Navigation Co v IRC* (1881) 7 QBD 165 at 173.

5 Property or assets includes goodwill: *Re Leas Hotel Co* [1902] 1 Ch 332. As to a charge on uncalled capital see 7(2) *Halsbury's Laws* (4th edn reissue) para 1245.

6 An exception of a certain class of assets means assets of the class from time to time and not only at the date of the debenture: *Imperial Paper Mills of Canada v Quebec Bank* (1913) 83 LJ PC 67. A debenture issued to a member of an unincorporated club by a committee acknowledging the receipt of advances does not create a charge on the assets of the club: *Wylie v Carlyon* [1922] 1 Ch 51.

7 Holders would, otherwise, rank in priority in order of issue of the individual debentures; ie the order of the respective charges. As to debentures ranking *pari passu*, see *Re Mersey Rly Co* [1895] 2 Ch 287. Where interest on some debentures has been paid to a later date than on others, the interest will not, in the absence of special provision, be equalised in a winding up, but the principal and interest due to each debenture holder will be calculated, and the assets distributed rateably according to the amounts due: *Re Midland Express Ltd* [1914] 1 Ch 41.

8 As to floating securities, see **8.8**.

9 For other specified events upon which the money becomes payable, see eg 10 *Forms and Precedents* (5th edn, 2001 reissue) Companies.

10 As to a receiver, see Chapter 18.

11 According to the ordinary form a registered debenture is legally transferable only by an instrument of transfer duly executed or signed and by registration in the company's books. A bearer debenture, being a negotiable instrument, is transferable by delivery, see **8.4**. For forms of transfer, see the Stock Transfer Act 1963 (as amended) and Regulations made thereunder. A debenture also usually provides for the transfer thereof to be free from equities: see *Re Palmer's Decoration and Furnishing Co* [1904] 2 Ch 743. As to the effect of this provision, see *Hilger Analytical Ltd v Rank Precision Industries Ltd* [1984] BCLC 301. As to equities, see **7.7**.

12 Such as a resolution modifying the rights of the debenture holders. Such a power must be exercised bona fide and must not amount to an oppression of the minority: *British America Nickel Corpn Ltd v MJ O'Brien Ltd* [1927] AC 369, PC. The power given to the court by the Companies Act 1985, s 425, to sanction schemes between a company and its creditors extends to debenture holders; and the court has jurisdiction to deprive them of their security and to force fully paid up shares on them in lieu thereof, if satisfied that the scheme is fair and equitable, but not otherwise: *Re Alabama, New Orleans etc, Rly Co* [1891] 1 Ch 213, but except under the provisions of the Act, or under the express conditions of the debentures themselves, no majority of the debenture holders can bind a dissentient minority even where the effect of their dissent is to ruin the securities: *Hay v Swedish and Norwegian Rly Co* (1889) 5 TLR 460.

13 See *Fowler v Midland Electric Corpn etc, Ltd* [1917] 1 Ch 656.

14 If there is no express provision, newspaper advertisement is sufficient: *Mercantile Investment and General Trust Co v International Co of Mexico* [1893] 1 Ch 484n, CA.

15 *Knightsbridge Estates Trust Ltd v Byrne* [1940] AC 613, [1940] 2 All ER 401, HL. As to the meaning of redeemable and irredeemable debentures, see *Re Joseph Stocks & Co Ltd* (1909) [1912] 2 Ch 134n. As to the conversion of redeemable into irredeemable debentures, see *Northern Assurance Co Ltd v Farnham United Breweries Ltd* [1912] 2 Ch 125. Otherwise the rules as to collateral advantages and clogs on the equity (see Chapter 28) apply to debentures.

Bearer debentures

8.4 Debentures payable to bearer are negotiable instruments, so as to pass the property in them by delivery to a holder for value in good faith[1]. As a result, the bearer can sue the company in his own name[2].

1 As opposed to registered debentures which are transferable only in the register of holders. See *Palmer's Company Law* paras 13.066-069; *Edelstein v Schuler & Co* [1902] 2 KB 144.
2 *Mowatt v Castle Steel and Iron Works Co* (1886) 34 ChD 58.

Trust deeds[1]

8.5 A series of secured or mortgage debentures is normally secured by means of a trust deed containing the actual charge, although each individual debenture in the series, though complete in itself, may also contain a charge as well. A trust deed is ordinarily used to secure debenture stock.

The advantage of employing a trust deed is to separate the debenture holders from the security holders, being the debenture trustees or trustee (generally a trust corporation). This separation is to the advantage of the company in that it will only have to deal with the trustees or trustee. The separation is also to the advantage of the debenture holders in that the trustees, who will generally have expert knowledge, can watch over their interests and will be able to take any steps necessary to protect the debenture holders' interests[2].

The typical form of trust deed contains:

(a) a covenant to repay the principal either on a fixed date, or on some earlier date, on the happening of certain specified events[3], or by instalments or by the sinking fund method[4];
(b) a covenant to pay interest in the meantime at a specified rate;
(c) a specific charge of the company's freehold or leasehold property[5] and a floating charge over all the company's other assets;
(d) rights for the trustees similar to those which each debenture holder would have in the case of ordinary debentures.

1 For forms, see 10 *Forms and Precedents* (5th edn, 2001 reissue) Companies.
2 See generally *State Superannuation Board v Trustees Executors and Agency Co Ltd* (1963) 38 ALJR 1 at 2, per Dixon CJ and see *Palmer's Company Law* para 13.148.
3 For example, winding up.
4 By provision out of the profits of the company (but the tax consequences must be considered) or by the company effecting a sinking policy with an insurance company.
5 On 'fixed assets' see *Tudor Heights Ltd v United Dominions Corpn Finance Ltd* [1977] 1 NZLR 532. In *Re Hi Fi Equipment (Cabinets) Ltd* [1988] BCLC 65 a company charged by way of a fixed charge its land, fixtures and 'fixed plant and machinery' and by way of a floating charge all its other assets. Harman J not following *Tudor Heights* held that the word 'fixed' qualified 'machinery' as well as 'plant' and that the phrase only referred to things physically attached to land.

Debenture trustees

8.6 The trustees should have no interest, whether as shareholders or otherwise, which might conflict with their duty as trustees[1]. The trust deed should provide for remuneration to the trustees[2]. In the absence of express provision the remuneration is not payable in priority to the claims of stockholders[3]. Any provision in a debenture trust deed exempting a trustee from or indemnifying him against liability for breach of trust where he fails to show the degree of care and diligence required of him as trustee is void[4], but a release is permissible[5].

1 *Re Dorman, Long & Co Ltd, Re South Durham Steel and Iron Co Ltd* [1934] Ch 635 at 670, 671. The trustees of such trust deeds are, generally, in much the same position as any other trustees: *Re Magadi Soda Co Ltd* (1925) 94 LJ Ch 217 at 219.
2 The trustees are entitled to the remuneration provided by the trust deed, notwithstanding the appointment of a receiver: *Re Anglo-Canadian Lands (1912) Ltd* [1918] 2 Ch 287; *Re British Consolidated Oil Corpn Ltd* [1919] 2 Ch 81.
3 *Re Accles Ltd, Hodgson v Accles Ltd* (1902) 51 WR 57. Normally this remuneration is a first charge on the proceeds of sale: *Re Piccadilly Hotel Ltd, Paul v Piccadilly Hotel Ltd* [1911] 2 Ch 534.
4 Companies Act 1985, s 192, but the trustee may claim protection under the Trustee Act 1925, s 61.
5 Section 192(2).

The charge

8.7 The charge created by the debenture may be either fixed or floating[1]. A debenture almost invariably creates a floating charge[2], but it may also or alternatively create a legal charge or a fixed equitable charge[3]. Where there is a power to create a charge and an intention to do so, a good equitable charge will be created notwithstanding any mistake in the attempt to effect it[4].

When the charge is fixed it is like an ordinary mortgage and affects the title to the property so that the company can only deal with it subject to the charge. When the charge is floating, the company may, in the ordinary course of business, deal with the property covered by the charge, mortgaging it so that the mortgage takes priority over the floating charge, selling or disposing of it free from the floating charge or using it before the charge attaches[5].

1 See Millett LJ in *Re Cosslett (Contractors) Ltd* [1998] Ch 495 at 510c for the difference between a floating and a fixed charge.
2 It should be noted, however, that the concept of a floating security exists quite independently of whether or not the document creating it might be described as a debenture: *Mercantile Bank of India Ltd v Chartered Bank of India, Australia and China and Strauss & Co Ltd (in liquidation)* [1937] 1 All ER 231 at 240, per Porter J.
3 On company charges relating to land, see [1982] Conv 43 (Hare and Flanagan).
4 *Re Strand Music Hall Co Ltd* (1865) 3 De GJ & Sm 147, 158; *Re Fireproof Doors Ltd, Umney v Fireproof Doors Ltd* [1916] 2 Ch 142 at 150. A charge on assets situated abroad in a country which does not recognise floating securities may nevertheless be a valid equitable charge according to English law: *Re Anchor Line (Henderson Bros) Ltd (No 2)* [1937] Ch 483 at 487, [1937] 2 All ER 823 at 827. See now as to floating charges created by an English company over assets in Scotland, the Companies Act 1985, ss 462 ff, [1984] JBL 255 (Gretton).
5 *Re Florence Land and Public Works Co* (1878) 10 Ch D 530, CA;

Floating charge[1]

8.8 Such a security is an immediate equitable charge on the assets of the company for the time being[2], but it remains unattached to any particular property and leaves the company at liberty to deal with its property in the ordinary course of its business, as it thinks fit, until stopped either by the appointment of a receiver[3] or by a winding up[4], or the company ceasing business[5], or the happening of some agreed event[6], when the charge becomes fixed to the assets[7] and crystallises[8] giving the debenture holder priority over the general creditors.

So long as the security remains a floating security, the property of the company may be dealt with and even a part of the property sold[9] in the ordinary course of business[10], as if the security had not been given. Any such dealing with a particular property will be binding on the debenture holders, provided that the dealing is completed before the charge ceases to be a floating security[11].

A purchaser or other mortgagee from the company will require evidence of non-crystallisation. This is generally supplied by a letter to this effect from some officer of the company or the company's solicitor[12].

1 See *Re Yorkshire Woolcombers Association Ltd, Houldsworth v Yorkshire Woolcombers Association Ltd* [1903] 2 Ch 284 at 294, CA, per Romer LJ; affd sub nom *Illingworth v Houldsworth* [1904] AC 355, HL; *Re Bond Worth Ltd* [1980] Ch 228, [1979] 3 All ER 919; *Siebe Gorman & Co Ltd v Barclays Bank Ltd* [1979] 2 Lloyd's Rep 142; *Clough Mill Ltd v Martin* [1984] 3 All ER 982, [1985] 1 WLR 111, CA; *Agnew v Comr of Inland Revenue* [2001] UKPC 28, [2001] 3 WLR 454.

2 The exact nature of a floating charge has caused much academic and judicial debate. See Gough *Company Charges* (2nd edn) pp 97-101 (but cf (1980) 1 Co Law 83 (Farrar)) and see Goode *Legal Problems of Credit and Security* (2nd edn) pp 47 ff and Lightman & Moss *The Law of Administrators and Receivers of Companies* (3rd edn) Ch 3. And see: *Re Atlantic Computer Systems plc* [1992] Ch 505; *Re Cimex Tissues Ltd* [1995] 1 BCLC 409; *Royal Trust Bank v National Westminster Bank plc* [1996] 2 BCLC 682; *Re Manurewa Transport Ltd* [1971] NZLR 909; *Landall Holdings Ltd v Caratti* [1979] WAR 97; *Hamilton v Hunter* (1983) 7 ACLR 295; *Torzillu Pty Ltd v Brynac Pty Ltd* (1983) 8 ACLR 52; *Re Margart Pty Ltd* (1985) 2 ACLR 709, [1985] BCLC 314; *Taxation Comr v Lai Corpn Pty Ltd* (1986) 83 FLR 63 (FCWA); *Tricontinental Corpn Ltd v FCT* [1988] 1 QdR 474, 73 ALR 433; *Re Bartlett Estates Pty Ltd (In Liquidation)* (1989) 14 ACLR 512 and *Fire Nymph Products Ltd v Heating Centre Pty Ltd* (1992) 7 ACSR 365. The traditional view is that while a floating charge creates a species of immediate equitable interest over the class of assets charged in favour of the chargee, it does not create an immediate proprietary interest in any specific assets.

3 *Re Panama, New Zealand and Australia Royal Mail Co* (1870) 5 Ch App 318; *Re Florence Land and Public Works Co, ex p Moor* (1878) 10 ChD 530, CA; and see *George Barker (Transport) Ltd v Eynon* [1973] 3 All ER 374; revsd [1974] 1 All ER 900, CA, but not merely taking steps to appoint a receiver: *Re Colonial Trusts Corpn, ex p Bradshaw* (1879) 15 ChD 465 at 472; *Government Stock and Other Securities Investment Co v Manila Rly Co* [1897] AC 81, HL.

4 *Wallace v Evershed* [1899] 1 Ch 891 at 894.

5 Or ceasing to be a going concern. In *Re Woodroffes (Musical Instruments) Ltd* [1986] Ch 366, [1985] 2 All ER 908, Nourse J appears to have accepted that crystallisation on the cessation of the company's business was well established. He also thought that the phrases 'ceasing to carry on business' and 'ceasing to be a going concern' were used interchangeably in the cases. See also *Hamilton v Hunter* (1983) 7 ACLR 295.

6 On automatic crystallisation, see Gough, *Company Charges* (2nd edn), Chapter 11 and pp 135-178 (implied crystallisation) (note his view on automatic partial crystallisation); Goode *Legal Problems of Credit and Security* [2nd edn] pp 69–76; (1976) 40 Conv (NS) 397 (Farrar); [1979] JBL 231 (Boyle). The principle has been accepted in England: *Re Woodroffes (Musical Instruments) Ltd* [1986] Ch 366, [1985] 2 All ER 908; *Re Brightlife Ltd* [1987] Ch 200, [1986] 3 All ER 673); *Re Permanent Houses (Holdings) Ltd* [1988] BCLC 563 (where Hoffman J followed his earlier decision in *Re Brightlife Ltd*); *William Gaskell Group Ltd v Highley* [1993] BCC 200; New Zealand: *Re Manurewa Transport Ltd* [1971] NZLR 909; Australia: *Re Obie Pty Ltd (No 2)* (1983) 8 ACLR 574; *Fire Nymph Products Ltd v Heating Centre Pty Ltd (In Liquidation)* (1988) 14 ACLR 274; and on appeal (1992) 10 ACLC 628, NSW CA (where the clause was expressed to effect crystallisation immediately prior to any dealing with the charged property other than in the ordinary course of business), (1989) 7 Co & Sec LJ 131 (Purcell), (1992) 20 ABLR 125 (Burns); but not in Canada: see *R v Consolidated Churchill Copper Corpn Ltd, Brameda Resources Ltd and Bank of Nova Scotia* [1978] 5 WWR 652, 90 DLR (3d) 357 (where it was rejected as a matter of policy and in any event would not have applied as a matter of construction). See also (1987) 8 Co Law 75 (Wilkinson).

7 Including future assets of the description of the assets charged which come into existence after the crystallisation of the charge: *Ferrier v Bottomer* (1972) 46 ALJR 148.

8 The charge does not crystallise on a demand for payment or on notice by the debenture holder to the company's bank: *Evans v Rival Granite Quarries Ltd* [1910] 2 KB 979, CA; cf *Re Permanent Houses (Holdings) Ltd* [1988] BCLC 563, it was held that the making of a demand for payment automatically crystallised a floating charge, but the debenture expressly provided that the making of a demand was 'an event of default' leading to crystallisation. *Re Bartlett Estates Pty Ltd (In Liquidation)* (1989) 14 ACLR 512 is to similar effect. On de-crystallisation see Lightman & Moss *The Law of Receivers and Administrators of Companies* (3rd edn) Ch 3.

9 *Re Vivian & Co, Metropolitan Bank of England and Wales v Vivian & Co* [1900] 2 Ch 654.

10 Gough *Company Charges* (2nd edn), Chapter 9; and see *Willmott v London Celluloid Co* (1886) 34 Ch D 147, CA; *Re Hubbard & Co Ltd, Hubbard v Hubbard & Co Ltd* (1898) 68 LJ Ch 54; *Reynolds Bros (Motors) Pty Ltd v Esanda Ltd* (1983–4) 8 ACLR 422; *Fire Nymph Products Ltd v Heating Centre Pty Ltd (In Liquidation)* (1992) 10 ACLC 629, NSW CA; *Julius Harper Ltd v F W Hagedorn & Sons* [1989] 2 NZLR 471 at 489-493; *Hospitality Management Consultants Ltd v Winchester* [1992] 6 NZCLC 67, 76 HC NZ.

11 *Robson v Smith* [1895] 2 Ch 118 at 124. For rights of set-off against the receiver, see *Biggerstaff v Rowatt's Wharf Ltd* [1896] 2 Ch 93, CA; *N W Robbie & Co Ltd v Witney Warehouse Co* [1963] 3 All ER 613, CA; *Rother Iron Works Ltd v Canterbury Precision Engineers Ltd* [1973] 1 All ER 394, CA; *George Barker (Transport) Ltd v Eynon* [1974] 1 All ER 900, CA; *Felt and Textiles of New Zealand Ltd v R Hubrich Ltd* [1968] NZLR 716. See Goode *Legal Problems of Credit and Security* (2nd edn) Ch VI.

12 See *Emmet on Title* (19th edn) para 10.186; Ruoff and Roper *Registered Conveyancing* paras 17-15, 17-40.

Priorities

8.9 Unless prohibited by the conditions of the debentures, the company's power of disposition extends to the creation of fixed charges[1], but not the creation of further general floating securities so as to give these priority[2]. In fact, it is usual to provide in the deed that no mortgage or charge ranking *pari passu* with or in priority to the debenture shall be created by the company[3].

The registration of the charge in the Companies Register will constitute constructive notice of the floating charge to a subsequent mortgagee[4]. The restriction may be noted amongst the filed particulars of the charge in the Companies Register[5] (though there is no express sanction for this practice under the Companies Act[6]), but while this may give someone who searches the Register actual notice of the restriction, it is generally accepted that such noting is not sufficient to give constructive notice of the restriction[7]. In the case of registered land, if the floating charge is noted[8] on the register, the entry will usually refer to the restriction and a subsequent mortgagee will take subject to the noted rights[9].

Where a company which has issued floating debentures purchases property with money advanced by a person who is to have a charge on the property, the purchase is, in effect, the purchase of an equity of redemption and the charge[10] has priority over the debentures[11].

The subsequent dealing, in order to confer rights prior to those of the holder of the floating security, need not be a voluntary act on the part of the company. A garnishee order gives no priority in itself[12] and the title of a receiver subsequently appointed under a debenture prevails over that of an execution creditor unless the money has been actually paid over under the garnishee order[13]. Payments made to the sheriff to get him out of possession have been held to be good as against debenture holders[14]. A distress levied by a landlord under a power in a lease, conferred either before the creation of the debentures or while they were still floating, and levied before the debenture ceased to be a floating charge is valid against the debenture holders[15].

1 *Re Florence Land and Public Works Co* (1878) 10 Ch D 530, CA; *Re Hamilton's Windsor Ironworks ex p Pitman and Edwards* (1879) 12 ChD 707; *Wheatley v Silkstone and Haigh Moor Coal Co* (1885) 29 ChD 715; *English and Scottish Mercantile Investment Co v Brunton* [1892] 2 QB 700, CA; *Re Valletort Sanitary Steam Laundry Co Ltd* [1903] 2 Ch 654. The priority of the subsequent fixed charge (whether legal or equitable) is not affected by notice of the floating charge, but the subsequent mortgagee, to gain priority, would need to obtain the title deeds or register his mortgage under the Land Charges Act 1972 or, where appropriate, register under the Land Registration Act 1925, besides registering under the Companies Act 1985. If a specific charge is postponed to a floating charge the doctrine of marshalling (see **26.8-26.12**) will apply.

2 *Re Benjamin Cope & Sons Ltd* [1914] 1 Ch 800, but where a company has reserved power to charge specified assets, it may create a floating charge on those assets in priority to the general floating charge: *Re Automatic Bottle Makers Ltd* [1926] Ch 412, CA.

3 See eg *Siebe Gorman & Co Ltd v Barclays Bank Ltd* [1979] 2 Lloyd's Rep 142. For a precedent, see 10 *Forms and Precedents* (5th edn, 2001 reissue) Companies and subsequent forms.

4 *Wilson v Kelland* [1910] 2 Ch 306. The abolition of the doctrine of deemed notice by the Companies Act 1989, s 142 (now Companies Act 1985, s 711A) does not apply to notice of registered charges: see, Companies Act 1985, s 146.

5 Notice of the restriction may also be effected by the registration of a special resolution referring to such a restriction under the Companies Act 1985, s 380 (as amended).

6 Query whether such a practice is legal, compare *R v Registrar of Companies, ex p Central Bank of India* [1986] QB 1114, [1986] 1 All ER 105, CA. See the practice in Scotland: Companies Act 1985, s 417 (3) (*e*).

7 See *Siebe Gorman v Co Ltd v Barclays Bank Ltd* [1979] 2 Lloyd's Rep 142, and *Welch v Bowater (Ireland) Ltd* [1980] IR 251; and *English and Scottish Mercantile Investment Co v Brunton* [1892] 2 QB 700, CA; *Re Castell and Brown Ltd* [1898] 1 Ch 315; *Re Valletort Sanitary Laundry Co Ltd* [1903] 2 Ch 654; *Re Standard Rotary Machine Co* (1906) 95 LT 829; *Wilson v Kelland* [1910] 2 Ch 306; *G and T Earle Ltd v Hemsworth RDC* (1928) 44 TLR 605, CA. These cases indicate that the subsequent mortgagee would only lose priority if he had actual notice of the restriction, but the earlier cases preceded the introduction of registration by the Companies Act 1900, s 14. On this point generally, see Goode *Legal Problems of Credit and Security* (2nd edn) pp 41-5. For an argument in favour of inferred knowledge, see (1974) 38 Conv (NS) 315 (Farrar), (1980) 1 Co Law 83 (Farrar).

8 Under the Land Registration Act 1925, s 49.

9 Land Registration Act 1925, s 52.

10 Assuming the chargee has the title deeds or registers.

11 *Re Connolly Bros Ltd (No 2), Wood v Connolly Bros Ltd* [1912] 2 Ch 25, CA; *Security Trust Co v Royal Bank of Canada* [1976] AC 503, [1976] 1 All ER 381, PC. Approved by the House of Lords in *Abbey National Building Society v Cann* [1991] 1 AC 56, [1990] 1 All ER 1085. See also *Composite Buyers Ltd v State Bank of New South Wales* [1991] ACL Rep 295, NSW 1; *Australian Guarantee Corpn (NZ) Ltd v Nicholson* [1996] 1 NZLR 167, HC (NZ).

12 *Cairney v Back* [1906] 2 KB 746; *Relwood Pty Ltd v Manning Homes Pty Ltd (No 2)* [1992] 2 QdR 197; *Haddad v AMH Import and Export Co Pty Ltd* (1993) ACL Rep 295 SA 1. See Gough *Company Charges* (2nd edn) pp 326-328; (1982) 10 NZULR 111 (Calnan); [1982] LMCLQ 57 (Hare and Milman).

13 *Robson v Smith* [1895] 2 Ch 118; *Norton v Yates* [1906] 1 KB 112; *Taunton v Sheriff of Warwickshire* [1895] 2 Ch 319, CA. The debenture holders have priority even if the debentures were irregularly issued: *Duck v Tower Galvanizing Co* [1901] 2 KB 314.

14 *Robinson v Burnell's Vienna Bakery Co* [1904] 2 KB 624; *Heaton and Dugard Ltd v Cutting Bros Ltd* [1925] 1 KB 655.

15 *Re Roundwood Colliery Co Ltd, Lee v Roundwood Colliery Co* [1897] 1 Ch 373, CA; *Re Bellaglade Ltd* [1977] 1 All ER 319; *Rhodes v Allied Dunbar Pension Services Ltd* [1989] 1 WLR 800, [1989] 1 All ER 1161, CA. For priorities, see further Ch 24, below.

Creation of floating securities

8.10 The use of the words 'floating security' is not essential to the creation of a security of this nature[1]—such a security has been created by a debenture purporting to bind all the company's 'estate property and effects'[2]. Where the debenture is a charge on specific assets, the words, which are commonly to be found in a floating charge, to the effect that the company is not to be at liberty to create any mortgage or charge in priority to the debentures, do not turn the specific charge into a floating charge[3]. Whatever label, if any, the parties may put upon the charge, its classification will depend upon what provisions, if any, there are in the charge document preventing the chargor from disposing of an unencumbered title to the subject matter of the charge[4]. The critical feature which distinguishes a floating from a fixed charge lies in the chargor's ability, freely and without the chargee's consent, to control and manage the charged assets and withdraw them from the security[5].

Uncalled capital may be charged if the documents of the company so permit, but where a company has by special resolution declared that a part of its capital shall only be capable of being called up for purposes of liquidation, it cannot create a charge on that part[6].

1 See, eg *Re Bond Worth Ltd* [1980] Ch 228, [1979] 3 All ER 919; *Siebe Gorman & Co Ltd v Barclays Bank Ltd* [1979] 2 Lloyd's Rep 142.

2 *Re Florence Land and Public Works Co* (1878) 10 Ch D 530, CA; *Re Panama, etc, Royal Mail Co* (1870) 5 Ch App 318; *National Provincial Bank of England Ltd v United Electric Theatres Ltd* [1916] 1 Ch 132. There has been an increase in the use of floating charges so that the lender can prevent the appointment of an administrator by the appointment of an administrative receiver. See (1990) 134 Sol Jo 32 (Simmonds).

3 *Grigson v Taplin & Co* (1915) 85 LJ Ch 75.

4 *Agnew v Comr of Inland Revenue* [2001] UKPC 28, [2001] 3 WLR 454.

In *Re ASRS Establishment Ltd (in administrative receivership and liquidation)* [2000] 2 BCLC 631 CA, the debenture document described the charge as fixed; it was held to be floating. The Court of Appeal placed particular emphasis on the fact that the company was free to deal with the property in the ordinary course of business without consent (confirming the first instance decision, [2000] 1 BCLC 727, Ch D). Similarly, in *Chalk v Khan* [2000] 2 BCLC 361, Ch D, the charge over the company's debts was held to be floating rather than fixed, despite its description. The much criticised decision in *Re New Bullas Trading Ltd* [1994] BCC 36 was not followed in either case. See Goode 'Charges over Book Debts: A Missed Opportunity' (1994) 110 LQR 592.

5 In *Agnew v Comr of Inland Revenue* [2001] UKPC 28, [2001] 3 WLR 454 the Privy Council considered a debenture dated 9 August 1995 by which the company created a charge, expressed to be 'fixed', in favour of the bank over its book debts arising in the ordinary course of business and their proceeds, but not over such proceeds as were received by the company before the bank required them to be paid into an account with itself, or before the charge crystallised or was enforced, whichever occurred first. Subject thereto the debenture created a charge, expressed to be 'floating', in respect of other assets of the company and, while prohibiting the company from disposing of its uncollected book debts, permitted it to deal freely in the ordinary course of trading with assets, including the proceeds of collected book debts, which were subject to the floating charge. The company went into receivership and the receivers applied for directions as to whether the book debts which were uncollected at the time of their appointment were subject to a fixed charge and so payable to the bank, or subject to a floating charge and so available for distribution to the preferential creditors. The Privy Council (upholding the Court of Appeal of New Zealand, *sub nom Re Brumark Investments Ltd, Comr of Inland Revenue v Agnew* [2000] 1 BCLC 353) held that since alienation and collection merely signified different ways of realising a debt, a restriction on disposal which permitted collection and free use of the proceeds enabled a debt to be withdrawn from the security by the chargor's act and was inconsistent with the nature of a fixed charge; and in consequence the prohibition on factoring or alienation of the book debts was insufficient to convert a floating into a fixed charge. Further, as a result of the drafting of the charge, as the company was left in control of the process by which the book debts were extinguished and replaced by the proceeds which were freely at its disposal, the charge over the uncollected debts was floating and not fixed. *Re Brightlife Ltd* [1987] Ch 200 and *Re Cosslett (Contractors) Ltd* [1998] Ch 495, CA applied. *Re New Bullas Trading Ltd* [1994] 1 BCLC 485, CA overruled. See Berg, The Journal of Business Law, Sept 2001, p 532.

6 *Re Mayfair Property Co, Bartlett v Mayfair Property Co* [1898] 2 Ch 28, CA; *Re Irish Club Co Ltd* [1906] WN 127.

Registered land

8.11 On first registration, if the applicant company has issued debentures, this fact must be disclosed on the application form and a certified copy of the trust deed or debenture must accompany the application. If the debenture creates a legal charge this will be registered as a charge[1]. If it creates a floating charge the trust deed or debenture will be noted in the Charges Register[2]. Where the land has already been registered, the debenture holder should apply for the registration of the debenture. Where a company is registered as proprietor the registrar is not concerned with any mortgage, charge, debenture etc created or issued by the company, whether or not registered under the Companies Act 1985[3], unless such incumbrance is registered or protected by caution or otherwise under the Land Registration Act 1925[4].

1 Under the Land Registration Act 1925, s 26: Land Registration Rules 1925, rr 72, 160.
2 Under the Land Registration Act 1925, s 49; and see Land Registration Rules 1925, r 40. A fixed equitable charge is similarly noted.
3 The charges registration provisions in Companies Act 1985, s 396(1)(a) include in the list of registrable charges a charge for the purpose of securing any issue of debentures (defined in s 744). Registration of a land charge for securing money under s 396 is sufficient in place of registration under the Land Charges Act 1972 and has effect as if the land charge had been registered under that Act: Land Charges Act 1972, ss 3(7), 3(8).
4 Land Registration Act 1925, s 60 (1). If a charge by a company, which requires registration, has not been registered in the Companies Register under s 395 of the Companies Act 1985, or no evidence of such registration is produced to the registrar, a note will be made on the register that the charge is subject to the provisions of that section: Land Registration Rules 1925, r 145 (2).

VOIDABLE CHARGES

Insolvency

8.12 In the event that an insolvency regime is imposed on a company, the Insolvency Act 1986 permits the office holder to revisit the creation of certain securities by the company[1].

1 See Goode *Principles of Corporate Insolvency Law* (2nd edn) pp 343-442. For a comparison of the English and Australian provisions, see Keay (1998) Journal of Business Law 515.

Preferences[1]

8.13 In a case where an administration order is made in relation to a company or the company goes into liquidation[2] and a company has at a relevant time given a preference to any person, the liquidator or administrator[3] may apply to the court for an order under s 239 of the Insolvency Act 1986 and the court shall, on such application, make such order as it thinks fit for restoring the position to what it would have been if the company had not given that preference[4].

A company gives a preference to a person if:

(a) that person is one of the company's creditors or a surety or guarantor for any of the company's debts or other liabilities; and

(b) the company does anything or suffers anything to be done which (in either case) has the effect of putting that person in a position which, in the event of the company going into insolvent liquidation, will be better than the position he would have been in if that thing had not been done[5].

The court shall not, however, make an order under s 239 in respect of a preference given to any person unless the company which gave the preference was influenced in deciding to give it by a desire to produce in relation to that person the effect mentioned[6].

The time at which a company gives a preference is a relevant time for the purposes of s 239 if the preference is given:

(a) in the case of a preference which is given to a person who is connected with the company[7], at a time in the period of two years ending with the onset of insolvency (see below); or
(b) in the case of a preference which is not such a transaction and is not so given, at a time in the period of six months ending with onset of insolvency; or
(c) in either case, at a time between the presentation of a petition for the making of an administration order in relation to the company and the making of such an order on that petition[8].

Where a company gives a preference at a time mentioned in (a) or (b) above, that time shall not, however, be a relevant time for the purposes of s 239 unless the company:

(a) is unable to pay its debts within the meaning of s 123 of the Insolvency Act 1986 at that time; or
(b) becomes unable to pay its debts within the meaning of that section in consequence of the preference[9].

For these purposes the onset of insolvency is:

(a) in a case where the section applies by reason of the making of an administration order or of a company's going into liquidation immediately upon the discharge of an administration order, the date of the presentation of the petition on which the administration order was made; and
(b) in a case where the section applies by reason of a company's going into liquidation at another time, the date of the commencement of the winding up[10].

A company which has given a preference to a person connected with the company[11] at the time the preference was given shall be presumed, unless the contrary is shown, to have been influenced in deciding to give it by such desire as aforesaid[12].

The fact that something has been done in pursuance of the order of a court shall not, without more, prevent the doing or suffering of that thing from constituting the giving of a preference[13].

1 For the former law see the Companies Act 1948, s 320(1), later the Companies Act 1985, s 615, repealed by the Insolvency Act 1985, s 235, Sch 10, Pt II. On the former law, see the 9th edition of this work, and see [1983] JBL 390 (Farrar); Report of the Review

Committee on Insolvency Law and Practice (1982), Cmnd 8558 (the Cork Report). For transactions at an undervalue, see the Insolvency Act 1986, s 238; for analogous provisions for bankrupts, see **13.10** and **13.11**.

2 Insolvency Act 1986, ss 238(1), 239(1).

3 The office holder as defined for the purposes of ss 238–245: Insolvency Act 1986, s 238 (1).

4 Insolvency Act 1986, s 239(3). See the standard company law textbooks.

5 Insolvency Act 1986, s 239(4).

6 Insolvency Act 1986, s 239(5).

In *M C Bacon Ltd* [1990] BCLC 324 a company was experiencing trading difficulties. The directors genuinely believed that the company could trade out of its difficulties. In order to continue trading the company required additional overdraft facilities from its bank, which would not be provided unless the company executed a debenture in favour of the bank. A debenture was duly executed and the company subsequently went into an insolvent liquidation. The court rejected an application by the liquidator to set aside the debenture as a preference. Millett J held that the desire to produce a preference was a subjective desire and that in the present case the directors were motivated solely by a desire to keep the company trading. See to the same effect *Re Beacon Leisure Ltd* [1991] BCC 213; *Re Fairway Magazines Ltd* [1993] BCLC 643, [1992] BCC 924 and *Re Ledingham-Smith* [1993] BCLC 635.

The date at which the 'desire' is to be considered is the date that the preference is in fact conferred: *Wills v Corfe Joinery Ltd* [1998] 2 BCLC 75. If the company has only one active director, it is his state of mind that must be examined: *Re Agriplant Services Ltd* [1997] 2 BCLC 598. Cf the former dominant intention test: *Peat v Gresham Trust Ltd* [1934] AC 252 at 260, HL; *Re F L E Holdings Ltd* [1967] 3 All ER 553, [1967] 1 WLR 1409; *Re F P & C H Matthews Ltd* [1982] Ch 257, [1982] 1 All ER 338, CA. The company must have a desire to prefer. Preference implies a freedom of choice. If the company is under pressure to pay or give security to a particular creditor, the choice may not be free and the requisite desire may not be present: *Sharp v Jackson* [1899] AC 419, HL; *Re Cutts* [1956] 2 All ER 537, [1956] 1 WLR 728, CA.

For payment or security given in satisfaction of an existing obligation, see *Re F & E Stanton Ltd* [1929] 1 Ch 180; cf *Re Jackson and Bassford Ltd* [1906] 2 Ch 467.

7 See n 11.

8 Insolvency Act 1986, s 240(1).

9 Section 240(2).

10 Section 240(3).

11 A person is connected with a company if—(a) he is a director or shadow director of the company or an associate of such a director or shadow director; or (b) he is an associate of the company: Insolvency Act 1986, s 249(1). Associate is defined in s 435. For the purposes of s 239 a person who is connected with a company by reason only of being its employee shall not be deemed to be connected with the company: s 239(6).

12 Insolvency Act 1986, s 239(6).

13 Section 239(7).

Orders under Insolvency Act 1986, s 239

8.14 Without prejudice to the generality of s 239 (3), an order under that section with respect to a preference given by a company may:

(a) require any property transferred in connection with the giving of the preference to be vested in the company;
(b) require any property to be so vested if it represents in any person's hands the application either of the proceeds of sale of property so transferred or of money so transferred;
(c) release or discharge (in whole or in part) any security given by the company;
(d) require any person to pay, in respect of benefits received by him from the company, such sums to the office holder[1] as the court may direct;

(e) provide for any surety or guarantor whose obligations to any person were released or discharged (in whole or in part) by the giving of the preference to be under such new or revived obligations to that person as the court thinks appropriate;
(f) provide for security for the discharge of any obligation imposed by or arising under the order, for such an obligation to be charged on any property and for such security or charge to have the same priority as a security or charge released or discharged (in whole or in part) by the giving of the preference; and
(g) provide for the extent to which any person whose property is vested by the order in the company, or on whom obligations are imposed by the order, is to be able to prove in the winding up of the company for debts or other liabilities which arose from, or were released or discharged (in whole or in part) under or by the giving of the preference[2].

The form of order that can be made is qualified, in that while an order under s 239 may affect the property of or impose any obligation on any person, whether or not he is the person to whom the preference was given, such an order:

(a) shall not prejudice any interest in property which was acquired from a person other than the company and was acquired in good faith, for value and without notice of the relevant circumstances, or prejudice any interest deriving from such an interest; and
(b) shall not require a person who received a benefit from the transaction or preference in good faith, for value and without notice of the relevant circumstances, to pay a sum to the office holder, except where the payment is to be in respect of a preference given to that person at a time when he was a creditor of the company[3].

The relevant surrounding circumstances, in relation to a preference, are (as the case may require):

(a) the fact that the company in question entered into the transaction at an undervalue; or
(b) the circumstances which amounted to the giving of the preference by the company in question; and
(c) sub-ss (3A)–(3C) of s 241 have effect to determine whether, for these purposes, a person has notice of the relevant proceedings[4].

The provisions of ss 239–241 of the Insolvency Act 1986 apply without prejudice to the availability of any other remedy, even in relation to a preference which the company had no power to give[5].

1 The office holder as defined for the purposes of ss 238–245: Insolvency Act 1986, s 238(1).
2 Insolvency Act 1986, s 241(1). See *Re M C Bacon Ltd* [1990] BCLC 324; *Re Fairway Magazines Ltd* [1993] BCLC 643, (1992) 109 LQR 371 (Prentice).
3 Insolvency Act 1986, s 241(2). A new s 241(2A) was added by the Insolvency (No 2) Act 1994, s 1 and sets out the test where a person has acquired an interest in property from a person other than the company in question or has received a benefit from the transaction or preference.
4 Insolvency Act 1986, s 241(3). Substituted for the original by the Insolvency (No 2) Act 1994.
5 Section 241(4).

Extortionate credit transactions[1]

8.15 Where a company is, or has been, a party to a transaction for, or involving, the provision of credit to the company, the court may, on the application of the liquidator or administrator[2], make an order with respect to the transaction if the transaction is or was extortionate and was entered into in the period of three years ending with the day on which the administration order was made or (as the case may be) the company went into liquidation[3].

In this context, a transaction is extortionate if, having regard to the risk accepted by the person providing the credit:

(a) the terms of it are or were such as to require grossly exorbitant payments to be made (whether unconditionally or in certain contingencies) in respect of the provision of the credit; or
(b) otherwise grossly contravened ordinary principles of fair dealing.

Further, it is presumed, unless the contrary is proved, that a transaction with respect to which an application is made under s 244 of the Insolvency Act 1986 is or, as the case may be, was extortionate[4].

1 For extortionate credit bargains under the Consumer Credit Act 1974, see **10.83-10.95**.
2 For the definition of office holder, see the Insolvency Act 1986, s 238 (1).
3 Insolvency Act 1986, s 244 (1), (2).
4 Insolvency Act 1986, s 244 (3).

Potential orders

8.16 If the court finds the credit transaction to be extortionate, any order made by the court may contain any one or more of the following provisions:

(a) provision setting aside the whole or part of any obligation created by the transaction;
(b) provision otherwise varying the terms of the transaction or varying the terms on which any security for the purposes of the transaction is held;
(c) provision requiring any person who is or was a party to the transaction to pay to the liquidator or administrator any sums paid to that person, by virtue of the transaction, by the company;
(d) provision requiring any person to surrender to the liquidator or receiver any property held by him as security for the purposes of the transaction;
(e) provision directing accounts to be taken between any persons[1].

1 Insolvency Act 1986, s 244 (4). The powers conferred by s 244 shall be exercisable in relation to any transaction concurrently with any powers exercisable in relation to that transaction as a transaction at an undervalue: s 244 (5).

Avoidance of certain floating charges[1]

8.17 A floating charge on the company's undertaking or property created at a relevant time is invalid[2] under s 244 of the Insolvency Act 1986, except to the extent of the aggregate of:

(a) the value of so much of the consideration for the creation of the charge as consists of money paid, or goods or services supplied[3], to the company at the same time as[4], or after, the creation of the charge;
(b) the value of so much of that consideration as consists of the discharge or reduction, at the same time as, or after, the creation of the charge, of any debt of the company[5]; and[6]
(c) the amount of such interest (if any) as is payable on the amount falling with (a) or (b) above in pursuance of any agreement under which the money was so paid, the goods or services were so supplied or the debt was discharged or reduced[6].

The provision does not invalidate the floating charge retrospectively by relation back to the beginning of the clawback period—if and when a liquidation occurs, s 244 merely invalidates it for the purposes of adjusting the claims of creditors in that liquidation[7]. Further, only the floating charge is invalidated, the covenant to pay is still valid[8].

If the sum secured is repaid before the onset of insolvency[11], the liquidator or administrator cannot recover the sum so paid unless the repayment is set aside as a preference[9]. Transactions effected under the authority of the charge which have been completed before the commencement of the winding up of the company are also unaffected. If, for example, a receiver appointed by the debenture holder realises the mortgaged property by sale before the onset of insolvency, he is not required to pay the proceeds to the liquidator[10].

The time at which a floating charge is created by a company is a relevant time for the purposes of the avoidance provision if the charge is created:

(a) in the case of a charge which is created in favour of a person who is connected with the company, at a time in the period of two years ending with the onset of insolvency[11];
(b) in the case of a charge which is created in favour of any other person, at a time in the period of 12 months ending with that date; or
(c) in either case, at a time between the presentation of a petition for the making of an administration order in relation to the company and the making of such an order on that petition[12].

Where a company creates a floating charge at a time mentioned in (b) above and the person in favour of whom the charge is created is not connected with the company[13], that time shall not be a relevant time for the purposes of this section unless the company:

(a) is unable to pay its debts within the meaning of s 123 of the Insolvency Act 1986 at that time; or
(b) becomes unable to pay its debts within the meaning of that section in consequence of the transaction under which the charge is created[14].

1 For the former law, see the Companies Act 1948, s 322 (1), later the Companies Act 1985, s 617, repealed by the Insolvency Act 1985, s 235, Sch 10, Pt II. On the former law, see the 9th edition of this work, and see the Report of the Review Committee on Insolvency Law and Practice (1982), Cmnd 8558 (the Cork Report) paras 1551–1566. Care must be taken in considering the previous authorities as there are some differences in the statutes.

2 The provision is intended to prevent a company in financial difficulty from giving an all assets floating charge to secure past debts or cash payments which do not swell the assets of the company and become available to creditors generally.

3 The value of any goods or services supplied by way of consideration for a floating charge shall be the amount in money which at the time they were supplied could reasonably have been expected to be obtained for supplying the goods or services in the ordinary course of business and on the same terms (apart from consideration) as those on which they were supplied to the company: Insolvency Act 1986, s 245 (6).

4 In *Re Shoe Lace Ltd* [1992] BCLC 636, Hoffmann J had to decide the meaning of 'at the same time as' in the Insolvency Act 1986, s 245(2)(a). Payments to the company were made in April, May, June and early July 1990. On 24 July 1992 the company executed an 'all monies debenture' to secure such advances. Hoffmann J held that the meaning of 'at the same time as' was a question of fact to be answered in a way in which a businessman knowing of the time limits imposed by the Insolvency and Company legislation would approach the matter. He had no hesitation in holding that all the payments had not been 'at the same time' as the execution of the debenture. The decision of Hoffmann J was affirmed by the Court of Appeal [1994] 1 BCLC 111, [1993] BCC 609. Sir Christopher Slade in giving the leading judgment of the Court of Appeal distinguished between two situations. In the first where the previous payment of money created an equitable security, s 245(2)(a) had no application upon the execution of a formal security instrument which took the place of the previous equitable security. In the second situation where there was no prior equitable security, to satisfy the test of s 245(2)(a) the interval between execution of the charge and payment of the money had to be de minimis. Sir Christopher Slade stated that in so far as *Re Columbian Fireproofing Co Ltd* and *Re F and E Stanton Ltd* put forward a test of payment being in consideration of the execution of the charge as opposed to a purely temporal test they were not to be followed. The Court of Appeal also rejected an argument that s 245 does not apply to a winding up by the Court (*Mace Builders (Glasgow) Ltd v Lunn* [1987] Ch 191 followed).

Re Shoe Lace Ltd was followed by Mummery J in *Re Fairway Magazines Ltd* [1993] BCLC 643, [1992] BCC 924; and see *Power v Sharp Investments Ltd* [1994] 1 BCLC 111: any delay whatsoever between the making of the advance and formal execution of the charge would invalidate it, unless the delay is so short as to be de minimis.

5 See *Re Columbian Fireproofing Co Ltd* [1910] 2 Ch 120, CA; *Re F and E Stanton Ltd* [1929] 1 Ch 180. Where a company has an overdrawn account with a bank, cheques paid into that account constitute cash paid to the company: see *Re Yeovil Glove Co Ltd* [1965] Ch 148, [1964] 2 All ER 849, CA, criticised in the Cork Report, paras 1560–1562.

The payment must not be illusory: *Re Orleans Motor Co Ltd* [1911] 2 Ch 41; *Re Destone Fabrics Ltd* [1941] Ch 319, [1941] 1 All ER 545, CA; *Re Fairway Magazines* [1992] BCC 924.

In *Re Fairway Magazines Ltd* [1993] BCLC 643, [1992] BCC 924 it was held that one of the payments allegedly secured by the debenture was not made 'to the company' because the company received no real benefit from a reduction in its overdraft (*Re Orleans Motor Co Ltd* [1911] 2 Ch 41 applies).

6 Insolvency Act 1986, s 245 (2).

7 *Mace Builders (Glasgow) Ltd v Lunn* [1987] Ch 191.

8 *Re Parkes Garage (Swadlincote) Ltd* [1929] 1 Ch 139; *Mace Builders (Glasgow) Ltd v Lunn* [1987] Ch 191, CA. See Gough *Company Charges* (2nd edn) p 1056.

9 (a) in a case where an administration order has been made, the date of the presentation of the petition on which the order was made; and (b) in a case where the company goes into liquidation, the date of the commencement of the winding up: Insolvency Act 1986, s 245 (5).

10 *Re Parkes Garage (Swadincote) Ltd* [1929] 1 Ch 139.

11 *Mace Builders (Glasgow) Ltd v Lunn* [1987] Ch 191, CA.

12 Insolvency Act 1986, s 245 (3).

13 See **8.13**, n 10.

14 Insolvency Act 1986, s 245 (4).

Transactions at an undervalue[1]

8.18 It should be noted that s 238 of the Insolvency Act 1986[2], which relates to transactions at an undervalue, has been held to have no application to a typical company charge given to a bank as a charge in consideration of the bank's forbearance in calling in an overdraft, making advances and honouring cheques[3]. Under s 238 the concept of consideration that the court is required to apply is restricted to a comparison of value received against value given[4]. As a result, unless the consideration can be valued in terms of money or money's worth the transaction falls outside the section. While the bank provides consideration in the usual sense by refraining from calling in an overdraft, making advances and honouring cheques, the company is merely making its assets or their proceeds available to the bank in priority to its other creditors and such a transaction does not result in a depletion or diminution in the value of the assets themselves.

A dealing with the borrower's equity of redemption may, however, be valued in the ordinary way[5].

1 See Gough *Company Charges* (2nd edn) Ch 41, p 1047ff.
2 A company enters into a transaction with another person at an undervalue if (a) it makes a gift to that person or otherwise enters a transaction with him on terms which provide for the company to receive no consideration or (b) it enters into a transaction with that person for a consideration the value of which, in money or money's worth, is significantly less than the value, in money or money's worth, of the consideration, provided by the company: Insolvency Act 1986, s 238(4).
3 *Re M C Bacon Ltd* [1990] BCLC 324.
4 See *National Westminster Bank plc v Jones* [2001] 1 BCLC 98; *Re Mistral Finance Ltd* (20 January 2000, unreported), Ch D.
5 *Re Kumar* [1993] BCLC 548.

REALISATION

Preferential creditors

8.19 In a winding up preferential debts[1], incurred before a floating charge has crystallised, rank before the claim of debenture holders under the floating charge[2]. In so far as the assets of the company available for payment of general creditors are insufficient to meet them—the costs and expenses of the winding up also rank before the claims of debenture holders[3].

Similarly, where a receiver is appointed on behalf of holders of any debentures of a company secured by a floating charge[4], or possession is taken by or on behalf of those debenture holders of any property comprised in or subject to the charge then, if the company is not at the time in the course of being wound up, the debts which in a winding up are preferential payments[5] and to be paid in priority to all other debts shall be paid out of assets coming into the hands of the receiver or other person taking possession[6], in priority to any claims for principal or interest in respect of the debentures[7]. This priority applies only to preferential claims accrued due by the date of the crystallisation of the charge[8].

Where the floating charge has crystallised before the making of a winding up order, the assets realised by a receiver are not 'assets' in the subsequent winding up[9].

1 As set out in the Insolvency Act 1986, ss 175, 386 and Sch 6.
2 Insolvency Act 1986, s 175 (2) (b).
3 *Re Barleycorn Enterprises Ltd* [1970] Ch 465, [1970] 2 All ER 155 was followed in *Re Portabase Clothing Ltd* [1993] Ch 388, [1993] 3 All ER 829 and *Re Leyland Daf Ltd* [2001] 1 BCLC 419. See also *Re Fairway Magazines Ltd* [1993] BCLC 643, (1993) 109 LQR 371 (Prentice).
4 See now Insolvency Act 1986, s 40 (2), ie a charge which, as created, was a floating charge: Insolvency Act 1986, s 40 (1) previously Insolvency Act 1985, Sch 6, para 15. Considerable

difficulties have been experienced with the definition of 'company' in the Insolvency Act 1986, s 40. Part III of the Insolvency Act 1986 does not define 'company' and accordingly 'except so far as the context requires' 'company' is to be defined in accordance with the Companies Act 1985, s 735.

In *Re International Bulk Commodities Ltd* [1993] Ch 77, [1993] 1 All ER 361, [1992] BCLC 1074 an issue arose as to whether a receiver appointed over the property of a foreign company not registered in England and Wales was an 'administrative receiver' within the Insolvency Act 1986, s 29(2). Mummery J held that such a receiver came within s 29(2) and stated that the 'company' in Part III of the Insolvency Act 1986 referred not only to the definition in the Companies Act 1985, s 735, but covered any company which could be wound up by the English Court. In *Re Devon and Somerset Farmers Ltd* [1993] BCC 410, Judge Hague QC sitting as a Judge of the High Court doubted and distinguished *Re International Bulk Companies Ltd* in holding that the Insolvency Act 1986, s 40, did not apply to the receiver appointed over a floating charge of a body incorporated under the Industrial and Provident Societies Act 1965.

5 As set out in the Insolvency Act 1986, ss 175, 386 and Sch 6.

6 It has been held that the duty to distribute first to preference creditors applies only in respect of debenture holders for whom the receiver is acting: *Griffiths v Yorkshire Bank plc* [1994] 1 WLR 1427. The better view is that the duty applies to all debenture holders with a floating charge: see *Re H & K (Medway) Ltd* [1997] 2 All ER 321, where Neuberger J declined to follow *Griffiths v Yorkshire Bank plc*. A debenture holder secured by a validly created floating charge has, however, priority over unsecured creditors in a winding up or otherwise.

7 Insolvency Act 1986, s 40, as regards appointment of receiver. Companies Act 1985, s 196, as amended and substituted by Insolvency Act 1986, s 439 (1), Sch 13, as regards taking possession. This section does not apply to a fixed charge: *Re Lewis Merthyr Consolidated Collieries Ltd* [1929] 1 Ch 498. Nor does it apply where there are both fixed and floating charges and the mortgagee appoints a receiver who sells under the Law of Property Act 1925, s 101 and has a surplus under s 105: *Re G L Saunders Ltd* [1986] 1 WLR 215; see Chapter 20. In *Re Portbase Clothing Ltd* [1993] Ch 388, [1993] 3 All ER 829 a company created a fixed charge and subsequently a floating charge. The chargee under the first fixed charge entered into a deed of postponement postponing its charge to the subsequent floating charge. The company went into liquidation and a dispute arose as to whether the preferential creditors and liquidation expenses, which were payable out of the property subject to the floating charge under the Insolvency Act 1986, ss 40(2) and 115, were payable in priority to the fixed charge. Chadwick J held that the deed of postponement postponed the fixed charge to the floating charge for all purposes and hence the preferential creditors and liquidation expenses had priority. In doing so Chadwick J followed *Re Camden Brewery Ltd* (1911) 106 LT 598n and *Waters v Widdows* [1984] VR 503 and rejected the argument put forward in Goode *Legal Problems of Credit and Security* (2nd edn) pp 97-98 that in such a case the priority agreement only operated to subrogate the floating chargee to the rights of the first fixed chargee. He did however state that it was possible for the parties to enter into a priority agreement which had that effect ([1993] Ch at 407, [1993] 3 All ER at 844).

8 *Re Christonette International Ltd* [1982] 3 All ER 225, [1982] 1 WLR 1245. As to the liability of the receiver for preferential payments, see *IRC v Goldblatt* [1972] Ch 498, [1972] 2 All ER 202.

9 *Re Griffin Hotel Co Ltd* [1941] Ch 129, [1940] 4 All ER 324; *Stein v Saywell* (1969) 121 CLR 529; *Re Woodroffes (Musical Instruments) Ltd* [1986] Ch 366, [1985] 2 All ER 908; *Re Brightlife Ltd* [1987] Ch 200, [1986] 3 All ER 673. *Re Griffin Hotel Co Ltd* was followed by the Privy Council in *Herde v Mahabirsingh* [1992] 1 WLR 869. See also *Re Portbase Clothing Ltd* [1993] Ch 388, where it was stated that the assets of a company available for distribution in this way include assets subject to a floating charge that has already crystallised. Presumably it would not, however, catch those already distributed.

Remedies of debenture holders[1]

8.20 Every debenture trust deed should contain provisions for the enforcement of the security without the aid of the court, for example, by the appointment of a receiver. In appropriate cases, the remedies of sale and foreclosure will also be available. Apart from such remedies the debenture holders may have remedies available with the aid of the court. Furthermore, a debenture holder whose interest is in arrear, or whose principal is due and unpaid may present a creditor's petition to wind up the company[2], but a debenture holder who is only a *cestui que trust* cannot petition to wind up a company[3].

1 See generally 7(2) *Halsbury's Laws* (4th edn reissue) paras 1154 ff; and see Goode *Legal Problems of Credit and Security* (2nd edn) pp 76-77.
2 Under the Insolvency Act 1986, s 122 (f) and see s 123.
3 *Re Dunderland Iron Ore Co Ltd* [1909] 1 Ch 446.

Action on covenant

8.21 A debenture holder may sue on the personal covenant, as may the trustees of a trust deed.

Appointment of receiver under trust deed

8.22 A trust deed will usually contain provisions for the appointment by the trustees of a receiver and manager and for the sale of the mortgaged property and, apart from such express provision, where the mortgage is by deed, the statutory power to appoint a receiver will apply[1].

1 See Chapter 18.

Sale and foreclosure

8.23 Where a debenture deed contains a mortgage of specific property the debenture holder has a mortgagee's powers of sale and foreclosure in respect of the property[1].

1 See Chapters 20 and 22, respectively. See 7(2) *Halsbury's Laws* paras 1364-1365.

Debenture holders' action

8.24 Where the company is in default as regards principal or interest the debenture holder may bring an action on behalf of all the rest of the debenture holders to realise the security[1]. The court will give leave to commence or continue such an action as a matter of course, notwithstanding winding up. The claim form in the action is indorsed with a claim for a receiver, or a receiver and manager, and immediately after issue of the claim form (or contemporaneously with it, by permission) an interim application for the appointment of a receiver is served[2]. Frequently it is agreed to treat the hearing of this application as the trial of the action and the usual order in a debenture holders' action is taken on the application.

1 *Re Dunderland Iron Ore Co Ltd* [1909] 1 Ch 446.
2 See generally 7(2) *Halsbury's Laws* (4th edn reissue) paras 1203 ff.

Chapter 9

Agricultural mortgages and charges

ORDINARY MORTGAGES AND CHARGES

GENERAL LAW APPLICABLE

9.1 The general law of mortgages and bills of sale applies to mortgages and charges of farms and stock.

SPECIFIC MATTERS

9.2 However, with regard to ordinary agricultural mortgages and charges there are several points to note.

Statutory power of leasing

Mortgages made between 1948 and 1995

9.3 The statutory power of leasing conferred by s 99 of the Law of Property Act 1925[1] cannot be excluded or restricted (by virtue of sub-s (13)) in the case of any mortgage of agricultural land[2] made after 1 March 1948 but before 1 September 1995[3].

1 See **19.21**.

2 Agricultural land includes land used for agriculture, fruit growing, dairy farming and livestock breeding. The definition of 'agricultural land' used is that in the Agriculture Act 1947: the Law of Property Act 1925, s 99(13B), inserted by the Agricultural Tenancies Act 1995, s 31.

3 Law of Property Act 1925, s 99(13A), inserted by the Agricultural Tenancies Act 1995, s 31. Previously, the prohibition of the exclusion of the powers conferred by s 99 of the 1925 Act was contained in the Agricultural Holdings Act 1986, s 100, and Sch 14, para 12 (and, before that, in the Agricultural Holdings Act 1948, Sch 7, para 2). For an example of a case in which the mortgagee was so precluded from relying on the terms of the mortgage (which purported to exclude the operation of s 99(13)), see *National Westminster Bank plc v Jones* [2001] 1 BCLC 98, [2000] BPIR 1093, [2000] EGCS 82, [2000] NPC 73, affd [2001] EWCA Civ 1541, [2001] 44 LS Gaz R 35.

Mortgages since 1995

9.4 A similar bar on any exclusion or restriction of the statutory power of granting a lease of an agricultural holding[1] to which, by virtue of s 4 of the

Agricultural Tenancies Act 1995, the Agricultural Holdings Act 1986 will apply, exists in relation to any mortgage of agricultural land made on or after 1 September 1995[2]. The provision is, however, of limited ambit because in most instances the 1986 Act will not apply in relation to mortgages of agricultural land made since September 1995[3]. Consequently, the general position is that the statutory power of leasing can be excluded as regards agricultural mortgages granted on or after 1 September 1995.

1 'Agricultural holding' means a holding within the 1986 Act: Law of Property Act 1925, s 99(13B).
2 Law of Property Act 1925, s 99(13A).
3 Section 4 of the Agricultural Tenancies Act 1995 provides for the continued application of the Agricultural Holdings Act 1986 in a limited number of transitional cases.

Charges for compensation

9.5 A tenant's charge for compensation at the termination of his tenancy obtained under s 85 of the Agricultural Holdings Act 1986 ranks in priority to any other charge, however and whenever created[1].

1 Agricultural Holdings Act 1986, s 87(6); and see **3.68**. See also the Improvement of Land Act 1864, s 59 (**12.110**).

Growing crops

9.6 A mortgagee who has not taken possession is not entitled to growing crops which have been removed by the mortgagor between the time of demand and recovery of possession, but he has a right to all crops growing on the premises when he takes possession, unless the mortgagor can claim them as emblements under an express contract of tenancy between the mortgagee and himself[1].

1 *Re Skinner, ex p Temple and Fishe* (1822) 1 Gl & J 216; *Bagnall v Villar* (1879) 12 Ch D 812; *Re Phillips, ex p National Mercantile Bank* (1880) 16 Ch D 104, CA. This applies also to an equitable mortgagee: *Re Gordon, ex p Official Receiver* (1889) 61 LT 299.

SPECIAL TYPES OF MORTGAGES AND CHARGES AVAILABLE TO FARMERS

AGRICULTURAL CHARGES

Power to charge

9.7 A farmer[1] may by instrument in writing create in favour of a bank[2] an agricultural charge on all or any of the farming stock[3] and other agricultural assets[4] belonging to him as security for sums advanced or to be advanced to him or paid or to be paid on his behalf under any guarantee by the bank and interest, commission and charges thereon[5]. A farmer who is the tenant of an agricultural holding[6] may make a charge notwithstanding any contrary provision in the contract of tenancy[7].

1 'Farmer' means any person (not being an incorporated company or society) who as tenant or owner cultivates an agricultural holding for profit: Agricultural Credits Act 1928, s 5(7).

2 For the definition of 'bank', see s 5(7), as amended.
3 'Farming stock' includes crops or horticultural produce, whether growing or severed, livestock, vehicles, machinery and plant, and fixtures: s 5(7).
4 'Other agricultural assets' means a tenant's right to compensation under the Agricultural Holdings Act 1986, except under ss 60(2)(b) or 62, for improvements, damage by game, disturbance or otherwise, a tenant's right to compensation under s 16 of the Agricultural Tenancies Act 1995, and any other tenant right: s 5(7), as amended.
5 Agricultural Credits Act 1928, s 5(1).
6 This expression is not defined in the 1928 Act; cf the Agricultural Holdings Act 1986.
7 Agricultural Credits Act 1928, s 13.

Form and effect: fixed and floating charges

9.8 An agricultural charge is not a bill of sale within the Bills of Sale Acts 1878 and 1882[1]. It is exempt from stamp duty[2]. An agricultural charge (although it must be in writing) may be in any form the parties desire[3].

An agricultural charge may be either a fixed charge or a floating charge or both[4].

A fixed charge must specify the property charged, but may include in the case of livestock any progeny thereof and in the case of the agricultural plant any plant which may whilst the charge is in force be substituted for the specified plant[5]. A floating charge covers all farming stock and other agricultural assets from time to time belonging to the farmer[6]. The sum secured may be either a specified amount or a fluctuating amount advanced on current account not exceeding at any one time such amount (if any) as may be specified in the charge, and in the latter case the charge shall not be deemed to be redeemed by reason only of the current account having ceased to be in debit[7].

An agricultural charge creating a floating charge has the same effect as if it had been created by a duly registered debenture issued by a company[8]. Therefore, irrespective of the terms of the charge itself, the charge will automatically become a fixed charge if the chargor ceases carrying on business, this being an inherent feature of a floating charge[9]. Moreover, it crystallises and becomes a fixed charge: (i) when a bankruptcy order is made against the farmer; (ii) on his death; (iii) on the dissolution of a partnership where the property charged is partnership property; or (iv) upon notice in writing to that effect being given by the bank to the farmer on the happening of any event which by virtue of the charge confers on the bank the right to give such a notice[10].

1 Ibid, s 8 (1).
2 Section 8 (8).
3 Agricultural Credits Act 1928, s 5(6).
4 Section 5(2).
5 Section 5(3).
6 Section 5(4).
7 Section 5(5).
8 Section 7(1).
9 *National Westminster Bank plc v Jones* [2001] 1 BCLC 98, [2000] BPIR 1093, [2000] EGCS 82, [2000] NPC 73; affd [2001] EWCA Civ 1541, [2001] 44 LS Gaz R 35, considering *Re Woodroffes (Musical Instruments) Ltd* [1986] Ch 366.
10 Section 7(1), amended by the Insolvency Act 1985, s 235, Sch 8, para 6. The events specified are usually the same as those giving rise to the right of seizure/possession. It is doubtful that the four specified circumstances identified in s 7(1)(a) of the 1928 Act are exclusive: see *National Westminster Bank plc v Jones* [2001] 1 BCLC 98, [2000] BPIR 1093, [2000] EGCS 82, [2000] NPC 73 (obiter).

Rights of parties under charge

Bank's right to possession and sell

9.9 A fixed charge confers on the bank the right to take possession of the property charged upon the happening of any event specified in the charge as being an event authorising the seizure of the property[1] and, after five clear days or such less time as may be allowed by the charge, to sell it either by auction or, if the charge permits, by private treaty, and either for a lump sum payment or payment by instalments[2]. The proceeds of any sale must be applied in the discharge of the money secured and the costs of seizure and sale, and any surplus must be returned to the farmer[3].

1 The usual events are breach of covenant to repay, breach of other covenants, death or bankruptcy of the farmer or his making a composition or arrangement with creditors, dissolution of partnership, distress or execution against the property charged, the removal or disposal by the farmer of any of the property charged otherwise than by way of sale in the ordinary way of trading as a farmer.
2 Agricultural Credits Act 1928, s 6(1).
3 Section 6(1).

Farmer's right to sell, subject to paying over the proceeds of sale

Fixed charge

9.10 The farmer is entitled to remain in possession of the property charged and to sell it. Unless otherwise agreed, in the case of a fixed charge, the proceeds of any sale must be paid to the bank to be applied towards the discharge of the sum secured[1]. The farmer is under the same obligation as to payment to the bank in respect of insurance moneys and compensation for destruction of livestock and crops[2].

A purchaser from the farmer and, in the case of a sale by auction, the auctioneer, is not concerned to see that the obligations as to payment over to the bank are complied with, notwithstanding that he may be aware of the existence of the charge[3]. Where any proceeds of sale, which in pursuance of the obligation ought to be paid to the bank, are paid to some other person, nothing in the 1928 Act confers on the bank a right to recover the proceeds from that other person, unless the bank proves that the other person knew that the proceeds were paid to him in breach of the obligation, but the other person is not deemed to have such knowledge by reason only that he has notice of the charge[4].

1 Agricultural Credits Act 1928, s 6(2)(a). A chargor who with intent to defraud fails to pay such sums or removes or suffers to be removed from his holding any property subject to the charge is liable to three years' imprisonment: s 11.
2 Section 6(2)(b).
3 Section 6(3).
4 Section 6(4).

Floating charge

9.11 A floating charge gives the bank the same right to receive from the farmer the proceeds of sale of any assets subject thereto, except that it is not necessary for the farmer to pay over such moneys if and so far as they are expended by him in the purchase of farming stock which on purchase becomes subject to the charge[1].

1 Agricultural Credits Act 1928, s 7(1), proviso (b).

Registration of agricultural charges

9.12 An agricultural charge must be registered under the Agricultural Credits Act 1928 at the Land Registry within seven days after execution[1]. Non-registration renders the charge void against any person other than the farmer, subject to the power of the High Court to extend the time for registration on proof that the omission to register within time was accidental or due to inadvertence[2]. Registration is effected by sending a memorandum of the charge together with the fee to the Land Registrar[3]. Provision is made for official searches and inspection of the register[4]. Registration is deemed to constitute actual notice of the charge and of the fact of such registration to all persons and for all purposes connected with the property charged[5]. Where, however, a charge in favour of a bank is expressly made for securing a current account or further advances, the bank in relation to such advances is not deemed to have notice of another charge by reason only that it is so registered if it was not registered when the first mentioned charge was created or when the last search, if any, by or on behalf of the bank was made, whichever last happened[6]. Provision is made for the cancellation of registration on the discharge of a charge and for the rectification of any entry in the register[7].

1 Days when the Registry is closed are excluded: Agricultural Credits Regulations 1928, SI 1928/667, reg 6(3).
2 Agricultural Credits Act 1928, s 9(1).
3 Section 9(3).
4 Section 9(4) and (5); Agricultural Credits Regulations 1928; Agricultural Credits Fees Order 1975. For restrictions on the publication of agricultural charges, see s 10.
5 Section 9(8).
6 Section 9(8), proviso.
7 Agricultural Credits Regulations 1928, regs 3, 4, and see Schedule for forms.

Priority of agricultural charges

9.13 Agricultural charges in relation to one another have priority in accordance with their respective dates of registration[1]. An agricultural charge creating a fixed charge or a bill of sale is void so far as it relates to property subject to a floating charge previously created and for so long as the floating charge remains in force[2].

The rights of a bank under an agricultural charge which includes growing crops have priority to those of a mortgagee of the land comprised in the holding (ie the farm) in respect of the crops, irrespective of the dates of the mortgage and the charge[3]. Nevertheless, an ordinary mortgage or charge of a farm should contain a provision that the borrower will not without the consent of the mortgagee include any growing crops in an agricultural charge. A breach of this covenant would bring the statutory power of sale[4] into operation.

1 Agricultural Credits Act 1928, s 8(2).
2 Section 8(3).
3 Section 8(6).
4 See **9.9**.

Supplementary provisions as to agricultural charges

9.14 A farmer was not for the purposes of bankruptcy law the reputed owner of farming stock subject to an agricultural charge[1], but if a charge to secure a sum then owing is made within three months of the presentation of a bankruptcy petition then, unless it is proved that the farmer was solvent immediately after the execution of the charge, the charge secures only advances made after the execution of the charge, although the bank's right to enforce any other security or claim payment of the sums due to the bank immediately prior to the giving of the charge as an unsecured debt is unaffected[2].

An agricultural charge does not protect the property charged from distress[3].

1 Agricultural Credits Act 1928, s 8(4) repealed by the Insolvency Act 1985, s 235, Sch 10, Pt III.
2 Section 8(5).
3 Section 8(7).

DEBENTURES ISSUED BY REGISTERED SOCIETIES

9.15 A debenture issued by an industrial or provident society creating in favour of a bank a floating charge on farming stock may be registered as an agricultural charge and notice of such registered charge must be sent to the central office established under the Friendly Societies Act 1974[1]. The charge, if so registered, is not a bill of sale for the purposes of the Bills of Sale Acts 1878 and 1882[2].

1 Agricultural Credits Act 1928, s 14(1). Such debentures are also exempted from the provisions of the Industrial and Provident Societies Act 1967: s 2(2) of the 1967 Act. By virtue of the 1967 Act an agricultural society may create a floating charge in favour of a lender other than a bank without such charge constituting a bill of sale if the provisions for registration are observed; see **5.16**.
2 Section 14(1).

DEBENTURES ISSUED BY AGRICULTURAL MARKETING BOARDS

9.16 An agricultural marketing board may create a floating charge on farming stock[1] owned by it in favour of a bank[2]. Such a debenture must be registered in the same way as an agricultural charge[3].

1 'Farming stock' has the same meaning as in the Agricultural Credits Act 1928. See **9.7**, n 3.
2 Agricultural Marketing Act 1958, s 15(5).
3 Section 15(5).

LONG TERM CREDITS

9.17 Part I of the Agricultural Credits Act 1928 provided for the establishment of a corporation for the purpose of making loans on mortgages of agricultural land and making loans under the Improvement of Land Acts 1864 and 1899 for agricultural purposes[1]. The Agricultural Mortgage Corporation Limited, a company limited by shares, which is the corporation established under the Act of 1928[2], has all the powers of a company incorporated under the Companies Acts to grant mortgages[3].

1 As to these Acts, see **12.107**.
2 See Pt 1 of the Act of 1928 and the Agricultural Mortgage Corporation Acts 1956 and 1958.
3 Sections 1 and 2 of the Agricultural Credits Act 1928 (which imposed maximum limits on the loan to value ratio and the period for repayment) were repealed by the Agriculture and Forestry (Financial Provisions) Act 1991, s 1(1) and Sch 1. On the availability of deeds and production for inspection by the borrower, see (1981) 78 LS Gaz 326.

SMALLHOLDINGS

9.18 The main statutory provisions relating to smallholdings are embodied in the Agriculture Act 1970. The Minister may make loans to tenants to provide working capital[1]. Such loans are unsecured and upon the condition, amongst other things, that the tenant will not borrow money from any other source.

1 Agriculture Act 1970, s 53.

Chapter 10

Consumer credit agreements and securities

INTRODUCTION TO THE SCOPE OF THE CONSUMER CREDIT ACT 1974

INTRODUCTION

10.1 The Consumer Credit Act 1974 represented the most radical and progressive reform ever effected in the fields of security and purchase financing. It emanated (with certain modifications[1]) from the report of the Crowther Committee on Consumer Credit[2]. A whole spectrum of transactions is covered by the Act, including hire purchase, moneylending, running-account credit, consumer hire agreements, pawning and bills of sale[3]. The Act also affects the law relating to land mortgages[4].

The Act contains provisions as to both the form and content of documentation in relation to regulated agreements and also as to the cancellation, termination, withdrawal from and enforcement of such transactions and securities provided in connection therewith. Further, the Act confers on the court the power to reopen extortionate credit bargains irrespective of whether the underlying credit agreement is a regulated agreement subject to the other provisions of the legislation.

In this book on mortgages it is only possible to give a general overview of the Act[5]. This chapter will concentrate upon providing an abbreviated survey of the Act in its more general aspects; individual provisions will be referred to elsewhere in the appropriate context.

1 For instance, the report had recommended the abolition of the legal anatomy of hire-purchase and its replacement by an immediate passing of title to goods acquired under deferred purchasing systems: Cmnd 4596, paras 5–21 ff. Cf the ensuing Government White Paper (Cmnd 5427, para 8) which decided in favour of preserving the traditional structure of hire-purchase.
2 Cmnd 4596 (1971).
3 The following statutes were repealed by the Act: Pawnbrokers Acts 1872–1960, Moneylenders Acts 1900–1927, Hire Purchase Act 1964, Hire Purchase Act 1965. In addition, one small amendment to the Bills of Sale Acts was made: see the Consumer Credit Act 1974, Sch 4, para 1.
4 Defined by s 189(1) of the Act as including 'any security charged on land'. The difficulties of this definition are discussed in (1975) 39 Conv (NS) 94, 96–97 (Adams) and at **10.28**, n 1. See also (1985) 274 Estates Gazette 33 (Fielding).
5 For specialised texts, see Guest and Lloyd, *Encyclopaedia of Consumer Credit Law*; Goode, *Consumer Credit Law and Practice*. See also *Chitty on Contracts* (28th edn), 1999 vol 2, Ch 38.

This chapter is an updated version of the chapter in a previous edition written by Professor N E Palmer.

CONTRACTING OUT FORBIDDEN

10.2 Contracting out of the Act is precluded. Thus, any term of a regulated agreement or linked transaction (or any term in any other agreement relating to an actual or prospective regulated agreement or linked transaction) is void insofar as it is inconsistent[1] with any provision of the Act (or regulation made thereunder) for the protection of the debtor or hirer or his relative or any surety[2].

1 A term is inconsistent with a provision of the Act if it purports to impose, directly or indirectly, a duty or liability additional to that specified by the provision in question: s 173(2).

2 Section 173(1). Note, however, s 173 (3) which provides that, notwithstanding s 173(1), an act which may be done in relation to a person pursuant only to an order of the court order (or the Director-General of Fair Trading) may nevertheless be validly done at any time with the consent of that person *given at that time*, but the refusal of such consent shall not give rise to any liability. (Therefore, an attempt to contract-out of the Act by the inclusion of a provision purportedly giving such consent in advance will fail.)
For criticism of sub-s (3), see Adams (1975) 39 Conv (NS) 94, 111.

AGREEMENTS WITHIN THE ACT

REGULATED AGREEMENT: DEFINITION

10.3 It is necessary to begin by looking at some definitions.

A 'regulated agreement' is a consumer credit agreement, or a consumer hire agreement, other than an exempt agreement[1]. These aspects of the regulated agreement will now be examined in turn.

In the Act, 'regulated' and 'unregulated' are to be construed accordingly[2].

1 Consumer Credit Act 1974, s 189(1).
2 Section 189(1).

REGULATED AGREEMENT: WHEN MADE

10.4 Any agreement made before 1st April 1977 is not a regulated agreement within the meaning of the Act[1].

1 Consumer Credit Act 1974, s 192(1), Sch 3, para 1(1) (as amended by the Consumer Credit Act 1974 (Commencement No 2) Order 1977, SI 1977/325).

CONSUMER CREDIT AGREEMENT

Primary definition

10.5 A 'consumer credit agreement' is a personal credit agreement by which the creditor provides the debtor with credit not exceeding £25,000[1].

1 Consumer Credit Act 1974, s 8(2) (as amended by the Consumer Credit (Increase of

Monetary Limits) Order 1983, SI 1983/1878, Art 4, Sch, Pt II and by the Consumer Credit (Increase of Monetary Limits) (Amendment) Order 1998, SI 1998/996, Art 2) and 189(1). The limit was £5,000 until 20 May 1985: see the 1983 Order. The limit was £15,000 until 1 May 1998: see the 1998 Order. The power to amend the monetary limit by statutory instrument is contained in s 181 of the Act.

Constituent elements of primary definition

Personal credit agreement

10.6 Continuing the definition trail, a 'personal credit agreement' is itself defined as an agreement between an individual[1]—'the debtor'[2]—and any other person[3]—'the creditor'[4]—by which the creditor provides the debtor with credit of any amount[5].

1 Which, under s 189(1), can extend to partnership, unincorporated associations and any other form of legal entity which is not a body corporate.
2 'Debtor' means the individual receiving credit under a consumer credit agreement. It also includes any person to whom the creditor's rights have been transferred by assignment or operation of law: Consumer Credit Act 1974, s 189(1).
3 Whether or not an individual.
4 'Creditor' means the person providing credit under a consumer credit agreement. It also includes any person to whom the creditor's rights have been transferred by assignment or operation of law: Consumer Credit Act 1974, s 189(1).
5 Section 8(1).

Credit

10.7 Further, 'credit' is liberally defined as including a cash loan or any other form of financial accommodation[1].

1 Consumer Credit Act 1974, ss 9(1) and 189(1): see further [1975] CLJ 79, 84–85 (Goode). For loans by Solicitors, see (1986) 130 Sol Jo 440 (Storry).

Monetary limit

10.8 The computation of the £25,000 ceiling is facilitated by a series of specific items which are to be disregarded in assessing whether the financial magnitude of the agreement lifts it beyond the realm of the Act.

Thus, down-payments (ie deposits) and credit-charges are to be excluded[1], as are other items which enter into the total charge for credit[2]. The financial limits are further amplified by s 18 of the Act which permits, in certain circumstances, the sub-division of multiple agreements ostensibly beyond its control into a series of lesser and therefore regulated agreements[3] and s 10(3) which offers guidelines for the assessment of credit provided under running accounts, irrespective (where necessary) of any stated superior limit which the debtor is in fact unlikely to reach[4].

1 Section 9 (3).
2 Section 9 (4): see the definition of 'total' charge for credit in s 20 (1).
3 See *National Westminster Bank plc v Story* [1999] Lloyd's Rep Bank 261, [1999] CCLR 70, [1999] PLSCS 123, CA (two facilities comprising of joint loans were properly regarded as one transaction, the object of which was to provide overall credit of £35,000; accordingly, the agreements were outside the Act and were not regulated).
4 See further s 171 (1) and Examples 5–7 and 9 contained in Sch 2 to that Act.

Supplementary

10.9 A 'consumer credit agreement' includes such an agreement which is cancelled under s 69(1) (which provides for a cooling-off period in respect of 'cancellable agreements'[1]) or becomes subject to s 69(2) (which provides for partial cancellation of certain agreements)[2].

1 See ss 67 and 189(1) in relation to the meaning of 'cancellable agreements'.
2 Consumer Credit Act 1974, s 189(1). As to cancellation, see **10.43**.

Summary

10.10 A consumer credit agreement is a regulated agreement for the purposes of the Act unless it is an exempt agreement[1]. Exempt agreements are considered below.

1 Sections 8(3) and 189(1).

CONSUMER HIRE AGREEMENT

Primary definition

10.11 For an agreement to constitute a 'consumer hire agreement' several conditions must be fulfilled:

(a) it must involve a bailment of goods and the hiring[1] must be to an individual (the 'hirer')[2];
(b) the agreement must not be a hire-purchase agreement[3];
(c) it must be capable of subsisting for more than three months[4]; and
(d) it must not require the hirer to make payments exceeding £25,000[5].

1 The concept of hiring is not defined in the Act.
2 Section 15(1).
3 Section 15(1)(a).
4 Section 15(1)(b).
5 Section 15(1)(c) (as amended by the Consumer Credit (Increase of Monetary Limits) Order 1983, SI 1983/1878, Art 4, Sch, Pt II and by the Consumer Credit (Increase of Monetary Limits) (Amendment) Order 1998, SI 1998/996, Art 2) and 189(1). The limit was £5,000 until 20 May 1985: see the 1983 Order. The limit was £15,000 until 1 May 1998: see the 1998 Order. The power to amend the monetary limit by statutory instrument is contained in s 181 of the Act.

Constituent elements of primary definition

Goods

10.12 The expression 'goods' has the meaning given to it by s 61(1) of the Sale of Goods Act 1979[1].

Thus, it includes all personal chattels other than things in action and money and, in particular, it includes emblements, industrial growing crops and things attached to or forming part of the land which are agreed to be severed before sale or under the contract of sale and includes an undivided share in goods.

Therefore, freehold and leasehold land is excluded from the concept as are contracts for the sale/letting of furnished premises where there is no separate rental of the furniture itself.

1 As amended by the Sale of Goods (Amendment) Act 1995, s 2. Consumer Credit Act 1974, s 189(1) as amended by the Sale of Goods Act 1979, s 63, Sch 2, para 18.

Hire-purchase agreement

10.13 A 'hire-purchase agreement' is an agreement, other than a conditional sale agreement[1], under which:

(a) goods are bailed in return for periodical payments by the person to whom they are bailed; and
(b) the property in the goods will pass to that person if the terms of the agreement are complied with and one or more of the following occurs –
  (i) the exercise of an option to purchase by that party;
  (ii) the doing of any other specified act by any party to the agreement;
  (iii) the happening of any other specified event[2].

1 A 'conditional sale agreement' is an agreement for the sale of goods or land under which the purchase price (or part of it) is payable by instalments and the property in the goods or land is to remain in the seller (notwithstanding that the buyer is to be in possession of the goods or land) until such conditions as to the payment of the instalments or otherwise as may be specified in the agreement are fulfilled: Consumer Credit Act 1974, s 189(1).
2 Section 189(1).

Commentary

10.14 A consumer hire agreement does not strictly involve the provision of credit, since the hirer will generally be paying in advance for the use of a chattel to which he never acquires a full title. However, many hiring agreements now represent a method of long-term disposition and bear a greater resemblance to deferred purchasing systems than to the ordinary bailment of goods. It is for this reason, no doubt, that special provision is made to assimilate them within the protection of the Act.

Summary

10.15 Unless qualifying as an exempt agreement, a consumer hire agreement is a regulated agreement within the meaning of the Act[1].

1 Sections 15(2) and 189(1).

EXEMPT AGREEMENT

Primary definition

10.16 An 'exempt agreement' is one specified by s 16 of the Act.
In general terms, for an agreement to be exempt:

(a) it must constitute a consumer credit agreement for the purposes of the Act[1];

(b) the creditor must be:
  (i) a local authority[2], or
  (ii) a body specified, or of a description specified, in a statutory instrument (being of a type prescribed by the Act itself)[3]; and (in any case)
(c) the agreement must be of a type prescribed by the Act[4].

These requirements will be examined in turn.

1 Section 16(1). If the agreement is not a 'consumer credit agreement' (whether because it affords credit exceeding £25,000 or otherwise), it will, of course, fall outside the purview of the Act (except, where applicable, those provisions in relation to extortionate credit bargains, namely ss 137-140) in any event.
2 Section 16(1).
3 Section 16(1).
4 Section 16(2). See also s 16(4), the significance of which is discussed at **10.26**.

Constituent elements of primary definition

Consumer credit agreement

10.17 The meaning of 'consumer credit agreement' has been considered at **10.5** ff.

Local authority

10.18 A 'local authority' means, in relation to England, a county council, a London borough council, a district council, the Common Council of the City of London, or the Council of Isles of Scilly[1].

1 Section 189(1) which also defines the expression in relation to Wales, Scotland and Northern Ireland.

Types of body prescribed by the Act

10.19 The list contained in s 16(1) (as amended) comprises:

(a) an insurance company[1];
(b) a friendly society[2];
(c) an organisation of employers or organisation of workers[3];
(d) a charity[4];
(e) a land improvement company[5];
(f) a body corporate named or specifically referred to in any public general Act[6];
(ff) a body corporate named or specifically referred to in an order made under ss 156(4), 444(1) or 447(2)(a) of the Housing Act 1985 or Art 154(1)(a) or 156AA of the Housing (Northern Ireland) Order 1981 or Art 10(6A) of the Housing (Northern Ireland) Order 1983[7];
(g) a building society[8]; or
(h) an authorised institution[9] or wholly-owned subsidiary (within the meaning of the Companies Act 1985) of such an institution[10].

It is to be noted that s 16 requires that (except as regards a local authority) the body in question be not only of a type listed therein but, in addition, be specified in a statutory instrument, ie an order made by the Secretary of State. Accordingly, a body does not have the ability to make exempt agreements merely because it falls within the list of bodies contained in s 16(1); rather, specification within a statutory instrument is crucial[11].

Such specification can, however, be effected in two ways: either a body may named specifically within the statutory instrument or it may be included within a generic class description, eg banks, contained therein.

In fact, the relevant statutory instrument[12] provides that *all* banks and building societies are bodies whose agreements (if of the specified description, as to which see **10.21** and **10.26**) are exempt agreements for the purposes of s 16[13]. The same position does not, however, obtain as regards other types of body, eg insurance companies, friendly societies and charities; these are not the subject of any general/blanket exemption, although many such bodies are exempted by being individually named in the statutory instrument[14]. It can thus be seen that the statutory instrument specifies a more limited group of bodies than is identified in s 16 itself.

To conclude: subject to the condition relating to the type of consumer credit agreement in question, agreements by both banks and building societies are exempt agreements for the purposes of the Act.

1 Consumer Credit Act 1974, s 16(1)(a). 'Insurance company' is defined in s 189(1) (as amended).
2 Section 16(1)(b). 'Friendly society' is defined in s 189(1) (as amended).
3 Section 16(1)(c).
4 Section 16(1)(d). 'Charity' is defined in s 189(1) (as amended).
5 Section 16(1)(e) (as amended). 'Land improvement company' is defined in s 189(1).
6 Section 16(1)(f). Notwithstanding the repeals of the statutory provisions governing the Agricultural Mortgage Corporation, that body is to be treated as falling within s 16(1)(f): see the Agriculture and Forestry (Financial Provisions) Act 1991, s 1(7).
7 Section 16(1)(ff)(added by the Housing and Planning Act 1986, s 22).
8 Section 16(1)(g) (added by the Building Societies Act 1986, Sch 18, Pt I, para 10). 'Building society' is defined in s 189(1) (as amended).
9 'Authorised institution' is defined in s 189(1) (as amended) and means an institution authorised under the Banking Act 1987, ie a bank. It also includes a European deposit-taker: see the Banking Coordination (Second Council Directive) Regulations 1992, SI 1992/3218.
10 Section 16(1)(h) (added by the Banking Act 1987, s 88).
11 The significance of the list of bodies contained in s 16(1) is to prescribe the ambit of any statutory instrument, for the Secretary of State cannot thereby confer the power to make exempt agreements on any body which is not of a type prescribed by the Act itself. The Act thus provides a framework for the all-important statutory instrument.
12 Consumer Credit (Exempt) Agreements Order 1989, SI 1989/869 (as amended).
13 Article 2(2).
14 Schedule 1.

Statutory instrument

10.20 The following relevant statutory instrument is the Consumer Credit (Exempt) Agreements Order 1989, SI 1989/869 (as amended on numerous occasions by various other statutory instruments).

Types of exempt agreement specified by the Act

10.21 As noted above, irrespective of the nature or identity of the creditor in question, the extent of the statutory exemption is confined to certain categories of consumer credit agreements[1].

The cases are where the agreement is:

(a) a debtor-creditor-supplier agreement financing the purchase of land or the

provision of dwellings on any land and is secured by a land mortgage on that land[2]; or
(b) a debtor-creditor agreement secured by any land mortgage[3]; or
(c) a debtor-creditor-supplier agreement financing a transaction which is a linked transaction[4] in relation to either:
    (i) an agreement falling within paragraph (a) above; or
    (ii) an agreement within paragraph (b) above financing the purchase of land or the provision of dwellings on any land,

and which, in both (i) and (ii), is secured by a land mortgage on either the land referred to in paragraph (a) or, as the case may be paragraph (ii), above[5].

1 Section 16(2).
2 Section 16 (2) (a).
3 Section 16 (2) (b).
4 As to which see s 19 and **10.42**, n 1.
5 Consumer Credit Act 1974, s 16(2)(c). This possible route to exemption has been described as 'obscure to the point of unintelligibility': see s 16 (2) (c): Goode *Consumer Credit Law and Practice* para 26.8, according to whom the subsection is designed to cover the case 'where a building society, pursuant to an arrangement with an insurance company, provides a larger purchase-money advance than it would ordinarily do (eg 90 per cent of the price instead of 80 per cent) against a bond from the insurance company on which payment of the premium charged to the purchaser is financed by the building society as part of the advance'.

Definitions of terms used in defining types of agreement specified by the Act

10.22 To understand the above limitations, it is necessary to resort to the vocabulary of the Act.

Restricted-use and unrestricted-use credit agreement

10.23 Although such expressions are not directly used in s 16(2), it is nevertheless necessary first to consider their meaning because they form central component parts in the definition of the terms 'debtor-creditor-supplier agreement' and 'debtor-creditor agreement'.

A 'restricted-use credit agreement' is defined by s 11(1). It is a regulated consumer credit agreement:

(a) to finance a transaction between the debtor and the creditor, whether forming part of that agreement or not[1];
(b) to finance a transaction between the debtor and a person (the 'supplier') other than the creditor[2]; or
(c) to refinance any existing indebtedness of the debtor, whether to the creditor or another person[3].

Despite the above, an agreement is not a restricted-use credit agreement if the credit is in fact provided in such a way as to leave the debtor free to use it as he chooses, even though certain uses would contravene that or any other agreement[4]. Therefore, if the money is advanced to the debtor who could (albeit contrary to the terms of the credit agreement) in practice use it however he liked, the agreement is not a restricted-credit agreement; the position is otherwise in cases where the creditor stipulates that the money must be paid by it direct to the supplier[5]. Indeed, an agreement will only be a restricted-use credit agreement if it contains an express or implied term that the loan will be used for the purpose in question[6].

Any regulated consumer credit agreement which is not a 'restricted-use credit agreement' is classed as an 'unrestricted-use credit agreement'[7].

1 Section 11(1)(a). An example in this category is a retail store's credit scheme, whereby finance is provided in order to enable the consumer to purchase goods from the store.
2 Section 11(1)(b). An agreement may fall within s 11(1)(b) although the identity of the supplier is unknown at the time the agreement is made: s 11(4). Examples in this category include loan agreements in respect of land purchases and credit card agreements (so far as they relate to the purchase of goods and not money advances).
3 Section 11(1)(c). This category of restricted-use credit agreement is not utilised in the definition of a 'debtor-creditor-supplier agreement' but is used in the definition of 'debtor-creditor agreement': see s 13(b).
4 Section 11(3).
5 See s 188 and examples 8 and 12 in Sch 2 to the Act.
6 *National Westminster Bank plc v Story* [1999] Lloyd's Rep Bank 261, [1999] CCLR 70, [1999] PLSCS 123, CA.
7 Section 11(2).

Debtor-creditor-supplier agreement

10.24 A 'debtor-creditor-supplier agreement' is defined by s 12. It includes the following kinds of agreement:

(a) a restricted-use credit agreement which falls within s 11(1)(a)[1];
(b) a restricted-use credit agreement which falls within s 11(1)(b)[2], although such an agreement qualifies as a debtor-creditor-supplier agreement *only* if made by the creditor under pre-existing arrangements, or in contemplation of future arrangements[3], between himself and the supplier[4];
(c) an *un*restricted-use credit agreement[5] which is made by the creditor under pre-existing arrangements[6] between himself and a person (the 'supplier') other than the debtor in the knowledge that the credit is to be used to finance the transaction between the debtor and the supplier[7].

1 Ie a regulated consumer credit agreement to finance a transaction between the debtor and the creditor. Section 12(a).
2 Ie a regulated consumer credit agreement to finance a transaction between the debtor and a person (the 'supplier') other than the creditor.
3 For the meaning of this expression, see s 187.
4 Section 12(b).
5 As to which see s 11(2).
6 As to the meaning of 'pre-existing or contemplated future arrangements', see s 187.
7 Section 12(c).

Debtor-creditor agreement

10.25 A debtor-creditor agreement, on the other hand, corresponds to what the Crowther Committee termed an 'unconnected loan'. The general feature of such agreements is that they involve the provision of credit by parties other than (a) the supplier of any goods or land intended to be purchased by the advance or (b) any creditor who acts under pre-existing arrangements (or in contemplation of future arrangements) with the supplier.

More specifically, a debtor-creditor agreement is one which falls within any of the following categories:

(a) a restricted-use credit agreement which falls within s 11(1)(b)[1], although (conversely to the debtor-creditor-supplier agreement identified in s 12(b)) such an agreement qualifies as a debtor-creditor agreement *only* if it is *not* made by the creditor under pre-existing arrangements, or in contemplation of future arrangements[2], between himself and the supplier[3];
(b) a restricted-use credit agreement which falls within s 11(1)(c)[4];
(c) an *un*restricted-use credit agreement[5] which is not made by the creditor under pre-existing arrangements[6] between himself and a person (the 'supplier') other than the debtor in the knowledge that the credit is to be used to finance a transaction between the debtor and the supplier[7].

1 Ie a regulated consumer credit agreement to finance a transaction between the debtor and a person (the 'supplier') other than the creditor.
2 As to which see s 187.
3 Section 13(a).
4 Ie a regulated consumer credit agreement made to refinance any existing indebtedness of the debtor, whether to the creditor or any other person. Section 13(b).
5 Section 11(2).
6 As to which see s 187.
7 Section 13(c).

Categories of exempt agreement specified by order

10.26 Section 16(2) is supplemented and amplified by the terms of the relevant regulations[1]. Before turning to consider the precise scope thereof, it should be noted that s 16(4) provides that any order relating to a body may be limited so as to apply only to agreements by that body of a description specified in the order. Consequently, the Secretary of State may restrict the ability of certain bodies to make exempt agreements to agreements of a narrower category than the types of agreement specified by s 16(2)[2]. As will be seen, this is indeed what has happened.

For instance, the order *could* have provided that any agreement made by a bank or building society would be an exempt agreement provided that it fulfilled the requirements of s 16(2). However, a less generous exemption has in fact been conferred by the regulations. This is set out below.

For the avoidance of doubt, local authorities are the most favoured type of creditor. Local authorities may enter exempt agreements provided simply that the agreements comply with s 16(2). The regulations do not apply to local authorities[3].

However, where the creditor is a building society or a bank (or a wholly-owned subsidiary thereof) or a body specified in Pt I of the Schedule to the Order[4], the agreement is exempt only if it is:

(a) a debtor-creditor-supplier agreement falling within s 16(2)(a) or (c) of the Act; or
(b) a debtor-creditor agreement secured by any land mortgage to finance:
    (i) the purchase of land;
    (ii) the provision of dwellings or business premises on any land; or
    (iii) the alteration, enlarging, repair or improvement of a dwelling or business premises on any land[5]; or
(c) a debtor-creditor agreement secured by any land mortgage to refinance any existing indebtedness of the debtor, whether to the creditor or another person,

under any agreement by which the debtor was provided with credit for any of the purposes specified in (i)-(iii) of paragraph (b) above[6].

It can be seen that the above criteria are more stringent and restrictive than those in s 16(2): the position in relation to debtor-creditor-supplier agreements is unaffected (since all such agreements are embraced by the regulations) but the range of exempt debtor-creditor agreements is narrowed for whereas s 16(2)(b) would, of itself, permit any 'debtor-creditor agreement secured by any land mortgage' to qualify as an exempt agreement, paras (b) and (c) in Art 2(2) of the Order provide that exemption will only occur where the money is used for certain specified purposes (each of which relates to, or is connected with, expenditure of the money advanced by the creditor on land, although the money need not be spent on the same land as that over which the security is taken.)[7]

Accordingly, the regulations do not allow a loan made by a bank or building society to a debtor for unrestricted purposes[8], albeit secured against property, to assume the status of an exempt agreement. On the contrary, such an agreement will be a regulated agreement.

In addition, as a separate point, the limited application of head (b)(iii)[9] means that, generally speaking, loans for home improvements and the like will be exempt only if made by way of further advance by an existing mortgagee who funded the original acquisition and holds an existing charge over the property[10].

Therefore, a second mortgage granted by a different lender, albeit for those prescribed purposes, would not qualify as an exempt agreement[11].

For the sake of completeness, the regulations also grant exemptions to certain categories of agreement made by various other bodies[12]. However, these bodies receive far less preferential treatment because these exemptions are far more limited than those applying to banks, building societies and the like. Consequently, these exemptions are not considered in detail in this work.

1 Consumer Credit (Exempt) Agreements Order 1989, SI 1989/869 (as amended).

2 The significance of the categories of agreements contained in s 16(2) is to prescribe the ambit of any statutory instrument, for the Secretary of State cannot thereby confer the power to make exempt agreements of types other than those prescribed by the Act itself. In this respect, the Act thus provides a framework for the all-important statutory instrument. See also **10.19**, n 11.

3 Because s 16(4) relates only to bodies specified in accordance with s 16(1).

4 Ie assorted named insurance companies, friendly societies, charities, agricultural corporations and one other body.

5 This head (b)(iii) only applies in limited circumstances: see the Consumer Credit (Exempt) Agreements Order 1989, SI 1989/869 (as amended), Art 2(3).

6 Consumer Credit (Exempt) Agreements Order 1989, SI 1989/869 (as amended), Art 2(2).

7 Cf the limitations inherent in s 16(2)(a) and (c).

8 Ie general borrowing for eg holidays, school fees, etc where the borrower is free to chose how he spends the money. In principle, the provision of credit on such basis might constitute an 'unrestricted-use credit agreement' (for the meaning of which, see s 11(2) and (3) and **10.23**) and, moreover, amount to a 'debtor-creditor agreement' within s 13(c) which, if secured by a land mortgage, would fall within s 16(2)(b).

9 See n 5.

10 The Consumer Credit (Exempt) Agreements Order 1989, SI 1989/869 (as amended), Art 2(3).

11 As Goode *Consumer Credit Law and Practice* para 26.27 puts it: 'the basic idea ... is to distinguish a further advance on a first or second mortgage from a second mortgage advance by a lender not involved in the financing (or refinancing) of the property over which the security for that advance is taken'.

12 Consumer Credit (Exempt) Agreements Order 1989, SI 1989/869 (as amended), Art 2(4) and (5).

Supplementary exclusions

10.27 Further noteworthy exemptions include:

(a) a consumer credit agreement where the creditor is a housing authority and the agreement is secured by a land mortgage[1]; and
(b) although of lesser importance in the context of mortgages, regulated agreements:
  (i) where the number of payments (excluding down-payments) does not exceed a specified number; or
  (ii) where the rate of the total charge for credit does not exceed a specified rate;
  (iii) which enjoy a connection with a country outside the UK[2];
  (iv) which comprise consumer hire agreements involving meters and metering equipment (or where the owner is a public telecommunications operator)[3].

The above list is not exhaustive and for full details of the various exemptions reference should be made to s 16 of the Act and the Consumer Credit (Exempt) Agreements Order 1989, SI 1989/869, both as amended[4].

1 Consumer Credit Act 1974, s 16(6A) (added by the Housing and Planning Act 1986, s 22).
2 Section 16(5). See, further, the Consumer Credit (Exempt) Agreements Order 1989, SI 1989/869 (as amended).
3 Section 16(6) (as amended). See, further, the Consumer Credit (Exempt) Agreements Order 1989, SI 1989/869 (as amended).
4 It will be noted that the definition of 'exempt agreement' focuses largely, though not exclusively, on exempting from the scope of the Act 'consumer credit agreements'. Thus, 'consumer hire agreements' are seemingly more likely to be embraced by the Act.

Commentary

10.28 A mortgagee who wishes to avail himself of the exempting provisions in s 16 is therefore confronted by three main requirements. First, he must qualify as one of the bodies or institutions specified in s 16(1) itself. Secondly, he must show that the agreement falls within one of the aforementioned categories; this involves mastering the telescopic glossary of agreements set out in the Act and the regulations and resolving the inevitable vagueness of such expressions as 'under pre-existing' or 'in contemplation of future' arrangements. Thirdly, he must surmount the problems of interpretation inherent in s 16(2), arising from the use of such expressions as 'land mortgage' and 'the provision of dwellings on any land'[1].

Nonetheless, it is evident that the ordinary first mortgage taken out by a house purchaser with a local authority, building society or bank will fall outside the scope of the Act[2] either on the ground that the relevant amount of credit exceeds £25,000[3] or because the agreement is an exempt agreement within s 16. The same is true of the situation where a mortgagee under a building society, bank or local authority mortgage makes a further advance to fund improvements to the mortgaged property. In both cases the agreement[4] is a debtor-creditor agreement secured by a land mortgage and satisfies the additional requirements of the regulations and is therefore exempt under s 16(2)(b) (as restrictively applied by the regulations)[5].

As has been noted above, however, the same result will *not* generally[6] follow when the party advancing credit on security of the land is a second or subsequent mortgagee[7].

It will be apparent that most mortgagees do not enter into mortgages under pre-existing arrangements, or in contemplation of future arrangements[8], with the 'supplier' of the land. However, such arrangements may exist between the mortgagee and a supplier of goods or services at whose suggestion (express or implied) the mortgagor takes out the mortgage. An example of this kind of transaction has been given by one commentator[9]. Where the owner of a house contracts with a builder for the extension of his property and at the builder's instigation obtains an advance[10] for the cost of construction from a mortgagee, the status of any resultant mortgage as an exempt agreement depends upon two principal questions.

The first question is whether there are any 'arrangements' (pre-existing or contemplated) between the builder and the mortgagee[11]. If not, the mortgage is a simple debtor-creditor agreement and will fall within the exemption conferred by s 16(2)(b) as outlined above[12].

If, however, there are such arrangements, the mortgage becomes a debtor-creditor-supplier agreement[13] and the second question arises, namely whether the agreement can be said to finance the purchase of land or the provision of dwellings on land[14]. In this context, it is doubtful as to whether the extension of existing premises[15] can be so classified[16]. If it does, the agreement will be exempt[17]. If (as seems more likely) not, the agreement will not be exempt but, rather, will constitute a regulated agreement subject to the Act[18].

Further, in those cases involving debtor-creditor-supplier agreements, it should be noted that an agreement qualifies as an exempt agreement under s 16(2)(a)[19] only when the mortgage in question is secured over the *same* land as that in respect of which the debtor-creditor-supplier agreement finances the purchase (or in relation to which the agreement finances the provision of dwellings)[20]. Therefore, if, for example, funds are advanced to enable a debtor to purchase certain land and a mortgage is taken to secure such advance but is secured on different land, the agreement is not exempt[21].

1 As for 'land mortgage', this term is defined in s 189(1) of the Act which provides that the concept includes 'any security charged on land'. In so doing, the Act raises questions as to whether the word 'security' in this context carries the same extensive meaning as the definition of security itself in s 189(1). This defines security, 'in relation to an actual or prospective consumer credit agreement, or any linked transaction', as 'a mortgage, charge, pledge, bond, debenture, indemnity, guarantee, bill, note or other right provided by the debtor or hirer, or at his request (express or implied) to secure the carrying out of the obligations of the debtor or hirer under the agreement'. The interrelationship between this and the word 'security' in the definition of 'land mortgage' is not easy to discern, and it may be that the definition of 'security' is material only to those cases in which the security, as thus defined, consists of a collateral agreement taken out in support of a primary regulated agreement, and not to these cases in which the 'security' and the regulated agreement are one and the same thing: Adams (1975) 39 Conv (NS) 94, 96. On balance, however, it is submitted that s 189(1) would seem to contemplate both species of mortgage security as within the compass of the statutory concept of security.

2 Except the provisions in relation to extortionate credit bargains: ss 137-139.

3 Section 8(2).

4 Assuming that it provides credit not exceeding £25,000.

5 In the case of a typical first mortgage, the credit agreement is to finance a transaction (namely the purchase of the property) between the debtor (purchaser) and a third party

(the vendor). It is thus a 'restricted-use credit agreement' within s 11(1)(b).

(It is most unlikely that s 11(3) would apply so as to render the agreement an unrestricted-use credit agreement: it would be a rare case in which a lender would advance funds directly to the prospective purchaser/mortgagor since there would be the very real risk of that party making off with the money and failing to complete the purchase, thereby leaving the lender unsecured, without any enforceable charge on the property. Indeed, for example, solicitors and licensed conveyancers who are members of the Council of Mortgage Lenders' conveyancing panel are required, under the terms of their instructions, to ensure that a fully enforceable first charge is obtained and to report to the lender if they will not have control over the payment of all the purchase money (eg if it is proposed that the borrower pays money to the seller direct). Moreover, they are only authorised to release the loan when they hold sufficient funds to complete the purchase and perfect the security. Pending completion the loan is held on trust for the lender and, if completion be delayed, it must be returned: see the *Council of Mortgage Lenders' Handbook* paras 5.8, 6.3.2 and 10.3.)

Because the loan is not usually made by the lender under pre-existing or envisaged arrangements between it and the vendor, the agreement assumes the status of a 'debtor-creditor agreement under' s 13(a). Being, of course, secured by a land mortgage, it is thus brought within s 16(2)(b). Further, because the loan is made to finance the purchase of land, it meets the requirements of Art 2(2)(b)(i) of the regulations.

A like position would obtain in relation to the further advance, provided that the use of the credit was restricted and the borrower was not free to use it as he chose. Being made to finance the improvement of a dwelling, the further advance would meet the requirements of Art 2(2)(b)(iii) of the regulations. (See also the restrictions imposed by Art 2(3).)

6 Though it might if, for instance, the second mortgage funded the provision of new dwellings on the land: see the Consumer Credit (Exempt Agreements) Order 1989, SI 1989/869, Art 2(2)(b)(ii).

7 See **10.26**.

8 As to the meaning of these expressions see s 187.

9 Adams (1975) 39 Conv (NS) 94.

10 It is assumed that the advance does not exceed £25,000.

11 'Arrangements' is not a defined term in the Act. In this context, the arrangements might include the giving of a warranties in relation to the construction of the extension.

12 Provided always that the advance is made by the mortgagee who funded the original acquisition and holds an existing charge over the property and not by a different lender (or the other requirements of the regulations are met): see the Consumer Credit (Exempt Agreements) Order 1989, SI 1989/869, Art 2(3), especially para (i)(a). See also **10.26**, n 11.

13 As in the previous example, it is assumed that the credit agreement is a 'restricted-use credit agreement' within s 11(1)(b). Furthermore, it is a 'debtor-creditor-supplier agreement' within s 12(b) if (for example) made by the mortgagee in contemplation of future arrangements between himself and the supplier (the builder). Its status, as an exempt agreement or otherwise, is thus governed by s 16(2)(a).

14 Section 16(2)(a)(i) and (ii).

15 Further, if the work in question did not relate to the building of an extension but was work of repair/improvement, such as the installation of double-glazing, such doubt would increase.

16 It is considered that the better view is that it does not; the language simply precludes it.

(Further, though not strictly relevant to the interpretation of s 16(2)(a), it is interesting to note that in the Consumer Credit (Exempt Agreements) Order 1989, Art 2(2)(b) a striking distinction is drawn between, on the one hand, the purchase of land and provision of dwellings and, on the other hand, the extension or improvement of premises.)

17 Under s 16(2)(a), as applied by the Consumer Credit (Exempt Agreements) Order 1989, Art 2(2)(a).

18 Consumer Credit (Exempt Agreements) Order 1989, Art 2(2)(b)(iii) would not assist a bank or building society mortgagee, despite the fact that the credit agreement would be financing the alteration, enlarging, repair or improvement of the dwelling, because that provision applies only to a debtor-creditor agreement: Art 2(2)(b)(iii).

19 A like position obtains as regards s 16(1)(c) of the Act.

20 See also **10.21** and **10.26**, n 7.

21 Although the likelihood of this scenario in a case where the debtor (borrower) is an individual, as opposed to a body corporate, is perhaps small. Of course, if the debtor were a company, the agreement would not be a regulated agreement in any event.

Summary

10.29 Notwithstanding the various difficulties identified above, the combined effect of s 16(1) and (2) and the £25,000 financial ceiling[1] is to make the majority of land mortgages exempt agreements beyond the general purview of the Act.

In addition, as noted above, where the debtor is a company, the statutory regime is also inapplicable[2].

1 Consumer Credit Act 1974, s 8(2) (as amended).
2 Sections 8(1) and (2) (as amended). Such transactions fall entirely outside the ambit of the Act and are not simply excluded (as exempt agreements) from the majority of its provisions.

Effect of classification as exempt agreement

10.30 Exempt agreements do not escape all the provisions of the Act[1], but because they are not regulated agreements they are substantially beyond its field of operation. It should, however, be noted that the powers of the court in relation to extortionate credit bargains (ss 137–140) apply even to exempt agreements[2].

1 For example, the rules as to advertising (see Pt IV of the Act) and linked transactions (s 19(1)) continue to apply.
2 Consumer Credit Act 1974, s 16(7).

OTHER CATEGORIES OF AGREEMENT

10.31 The Act describes a number of other categories of agreement for the purposes of particular reforms. Some of these[1] have already been encountered. Other classifications include small agreements[2], multiple agreements[3] and the concept of the linked transaction[4]. They will be considered as and when the agreements in question arise.

1 Such as restricted and unrestricted-use credit agreements, debtor-creditor agreements and debtor-creditor-supplier agreements.
2 Sections 17 and 189 (1).
3 Sections 18 and 189 (1).
4 Sections 19 and 189 (1); and see Adams (1975) 39 Conv (NS) 97–99.

THE SUBSTANTIVE CONTENT OF THE ACT

OUTLINE

10.32 A broad, and admittedly simplistic, division of the reforms effected by the 1974 legislation may be made between its 'transactional' provisions (ie those which relate per se to the rights of the parties and arise from the terms of their agreement) and 'non-transactional' provisions (ie those which represent controls upon such matters as the method of conducting business and the form of agreements). Although this classification will be adopted in the ensuing account, it must be observed that infringement of the non-transactional rules will often produce a fundamental effect upon the enforceability of the agreement itself. Indeed, therefore, the practical consequences of the non-transactional provisions may well far outweigh those stemming from the transactional provisions.

NON-TRANSACTIONAL PROVISIONS

Licensing

10.33 The Act introduced an elaborate and revolutionary[1] licensing structure as part of its general policy of control over consumer lending. This structure is contained in Pt II and is to be administered by the Director-General of Fair Trading[2].

Local authorities are exempt from the duty to acquire a licence[3], as are those bodies corporate which are empowered by public general Acts naming them to carry on a business[4]. Apart from this, licences are required by all those who carry on a consumer credit business[5], a consumer hire business[6] or an ancillary credit business[7]. Detailed rules as to the types of licence which may be granted, the authority they may confer, the circumstances in which they may be issued, varied, renewed, revoked or suspended and associated matters are contained in the remainder of Pt III of the Act[8].

Of particular relevance is s 40, which provides that, unless the Director-General makes an order to contrary effect, regulated agreements (other than non-commercial agreements[9]) made by an unlicensed creditor or owner are unenforceable against the debtor or hirer[10].

1 Prior to the Act, the main licensing requirements in force were those relating to moneylenders, which operated on a local basis: for criticisms of this see Cmnd 4596, paras 4.1.11, 6.3.2.
2 Section 1 (1).
3 Section 21 (2).
4 Section 21 (3). The exemption from the licensing requirement does not exclude the transactional provisions of the Act.
5 A 'consumer credit business' is defined as any business so far as it comprises or relates to the provision of credit under regulated consumer credit agreements: s 189(1).
6 A 'consumer hire business' is defined as any business so far as it comprises or relates to the bailment of goods under regulated consumer credit agreements: s 189(1).
7 Consumer Credit Act 1974, ss 21(1) and 147(1). As to the meaning of 'ancillary credit business' and exceptions to the general definition see ss 145 and 146.
8 Sections 22–42.
9 Which expression is defined as meaning a consumer credit agreement or a consumer hire agreement not made by the creditor or owner in the course of a business carried on by him: s 189(1). 'Business' is itself defined as including profession or trade (s 189(1)) but it is specifically provided that a person is not to be treated as carrying on a particular type of business merely because occasionally he enters into transactions belonging to a business of that type: s 189(2).
10 Section 40 does not apply to an ancillary credit business: s 147(1).

Seeking business

10.34 This area is regulated by Pt IV of the Act, which governs such classes of activity as advertisement[1], canvassing[2], quotations[3], compulsory display of information[4], and the conduct of business generally[5]. The relevant sections confine themselves to providing a framework for the operation of the orders by which the Act is supplemented, but there is a considerable degree of specificity as to the scope and method under which such orders shall take effect[6].

1 Sections 43–47. It is important to note that these sections apply to, amongst others, those who carry on business in the course of which they provide credit to individuals secured on land, irrespective of whether the operation of such business is confined to the entering into of agreements which are above the £25,000 ceiling or is otherwise exempted from the

Act under s 16: see eg s 43(2)(b) of the Act.

See also the Consumer Credit (Advertisements) Regulations 1989, SI 1989/1125, the Consumer Credit (Exempt Advertisements) Order 1985, SI 1985/621 and *R v Secretary of State for Trade and Industry, ex p First National Bank plc* [1990] CCLR 94, 154 JPN 266, CA (in which the requirement imposed by the regulations that advertisements carry a warning was held not to be ultra vires).

Likewise, s 50 of the Act (prohibiting the sending of circulars to minors) is not confined to the sending of those circulars which relate to facilities obtainable under regulated agreements

2 Sections 48–51.
3 Section 52.
4 Section 53.
5 Section 54.
6 See particularly s 43, which designates the types of advertisement to which Pt IV applies.

Entering into agreements

Generally

10.35 Again, the relevant provisions of the Act (contained in Pt V) are a framework, which has been clad with a detailed range of regulations governing most of the important aspects of the negotiation and conclusion of regulated agreements. However, the impact of these rules upon the validity of the agreement is wider and more immediate.

It should be noted that, with the exception of s 56, the non-transactional provisions which relate to entry into regulated agreements (including the provisions relating to the withdrawal from and cancellation of such agreements), ie those found in Pt V of the Act, do not apply to certain kinds of agreements, most notably non-commercial agreements[1]. The categories of excluded agreements are considered below[2].

1 For the definition of which, see **10.46**, n 1.
2 See **10.46**.

Disclosure of information before entry into regulated agreement

10.36 Thus, s 55 provides that regulations may require specific information to be disclosed in the prescribed manner to a debtor or hirer before the making of the agreement[1] and that, unless such regulations have been complied with, the agreement shall not have been properly executed[2]. In such circumstances, the agreement is enforceable against a debtor or hirer only by order of the court[3]. However, no such regulations have yet been made.

1 Section 55 (1).
2 Section 55 (2).
3 Section 65 (1). The principles according to which the court's discretion is to be exercised are set out in s 127 (see **10.70** ff). By s 65(2), a retaking of goods or land to which a regulated agreement relates is an enforcement of the agreement. Cf *Four-Maids Ltd v Dudley Marshall (Properties) Ltd* [1957] Ch 317 at 310, [1957] 2 All ER 35 at 36.

Form and contents of regulated agreement

10.37 Section 60 which obliges the Secretary of State to make regulations concerning the form and content of documents embodying regulated agreements[1]. The section particularises certain things which the Secretary of State shall ensure are brought to the debtor or hirer's attention by virtue of these regulations[2]. Compliance with s 60 (1) may in certain circumstances be waived by the Director upon application by a person conducting a consumer credit or consumer hire business if it appears impracticable for the applicant to comply with any requirement of the regulations but he may exercise this power only if satisfied that to do so would not prejudice the interests of debtors or hirers[3].

There is no specific provision within s 60 for the civil effects of a failure to conform with that section. However, s 61(1)(a), which deals with the signing of regulated agreements[4], provides that one of the conditions to be fulfilled before the agreement is properly executed for the purposes of the Act is that it should be in the form prescribed by s 60(1) and contains the prescribed terms and conforms to the regulations issued thereunder. Failure to comply with this requirement means that the agreement is enforceable against a debtor or hirer only by order of the court[5].

The relevant regulations in this context are the Consumer Credit (Agreements) Regulations 1983, SI 1983/1553, (as amended)[6].

1 Section 60 (1).
2 See further s 60 (2).
3 Section 60 (3), (4).
4 Also see (1975) 39 Conv (NS) 94, 104.
Under s 61(4), where the debtor or hirer is a partnership or other unincorporated body of persons, sub-s (1)(a) applies with the substitution of 'by or on behalf of the debtor or hirer' for the words 'by the debtor or hirer'.
5 Section 65 (1).
6 In *Lombard Tricity Finance Ltd v Paton* [1989] 1 All ER 918, CA it was held that an unsecured loan agreement made on terms which entitled the creditor to vary the interest rate at will upon giving notice did not infringe the Act or regulations made thereunder. It is unclear whether the existence of a provision in the agreement enabling the debtor to pay off the loan at any time without penalty was regarded as essential for the decision.

Signing of regulated agreement

10.38 By s 61(1) of the Act, a regulated agreement is not properly executed unless:

(a) a document in the prescribed form itself containing all the prescribed terms and conforming to regulations under s 60 (1) is signed in the prescribed manner both by the debtor or hirer and by or on behalf of the creditor or owner; and
(b) the document embodies all the terms of the agreement, other than implied terms; and
(c) the document is, when presented or sent to the debtor or hirer for signature, in such a state that all its terms are readily legible.

In addition[1], where the agreement is one to which s 58(1)[2] applies, the creditor or owner must, after supplying the copy of the prospective agreement, allow seven days to elapse before sending the unexecuted agreement to the debtor or hirer for his signature[3] and he must not during the ensuing consideration period[4] approach the debtor or hirer (whether in person or otherwise) except in response to a specific request on the part of the latter after the beginning of the consideration period[5]. Unless these conditions have been fulfilled and no notice of withdrawal by the debtor or hirer has been received by the creditor or owner before the sending of the unexecuted agreement[6], the agreement is not properly executed[7]. The consequence of this is that the agreement is unenforceable against the debtor or hirer except by order of the court[8].

1 The provisions of s 61(2) apply in addition to (and not in substitution for) those of s 61(1). They represent a powerful, and possibly over-protective, fortification against attempts by lenders to 'rail-road' consumers into taking out ill-considered mortgages: see Goode [1975] CLJ 79, 100.
2 As to which see **10.44**.
3 Section 61 (2) (b).
4 The 'consideration period' is defined by s 61 (3) as the period beginning with the giving of the copy under s 58 (1) and ending *either* at the expiry of seven days after the day on which the unexecuted agreement was sent, *or* on its return by the debtor or hirer after his signature thereto, whichever first occurs.
5 Section 61 (2) (c).
6 Section 61 (2) (d).
7 Section 61(2).
8 Section 65 (1).

Miscellaneous other circumstances where agreement not properly executed

10.39 Further sections within Pt V deal with the duty to give notice of cancellation rights[1] and the duty to supply copies of executed and unexecuted agreements[2]. Non-compliance with such provisions again means that the agreement in question is not properly executed and thus enforceable by the creditor or owner only pursuant to a court order.

1 Section 64; these rights do not generally apply to mortgages of land.
2 Sections 62 and 63. the expressions 'executed' and 'unexecuted' agreement are defined by s 189 (1). As to the potential difficulties of implementing these rules in relation to bank mortgages, see Adams (1975) 39 Conv (NS) 104–105. The same author points out that the provisions of Pt V generally could govern not only those cases in which the mortgagee is an institution which operates a business of providing credit but also those cases in which (for instance) an employer provides house loans for its staff or a solicitor takes a charge over a client's property as security for costs, unless exempt under s 16 (5) (see **10.27**).

Agreement to enter future agreement void

10.40 Other sections within Pt V are more total in their effect and state that their contravention shall render the agreement void. This is the case with s 59(1) under which an agreement is void 'if and to the extent that it purports to bind a person to enter as debtor or hirer into a prospective regulated agreement'[1].

1 Regulations made under s 59(2) exempt certain specified agreements from the operation of s 59 (1): see the Consumer Credit (Agreements to Enter Prospective Agreements) (Exemptions) Regulations 1983, SI 1983/1552.

Agreement providing that negotiator is agent of debtor void

10.41 Mention should also be made of s 56(3) which provides that an agreement is void if and to the extent that it purports in relation to an actual or prospective regulated agreement either to provide that a person acting as, or on behalf of, a negotiator is to be treated as the agent of the debtor or hirer, or to relieve a person from liability for acts or omissions of any person acting as or on behalf of a negotiator[1].

1 For the meanings of 'antecedent negotiation' and 'negotiator' and the circumstances in which a negotiator shall be deemed to be acting as agent for the creditor, see ss 56(1) and (2). For the time at which negotiations are to be deemed to commence, see s 56(4). For 'negotiator', see *Moorgate Mercantile Leasing Ltd v Isobel Gell and Ugolini Dispensers (UK) Ltd* [1986] CLY 371 (Cty Ct) and *Forthright Finance Ltd v Ingate* [1997] 4 All ER 99, CA.

Withdrawal and cancellation

Withdrawal

10.42 When the agreement is still at its negotiating stage, or where it has failed for any other reason to ripen into a contract, the debtor may of course withdraw at any time. Moreover, as we have seen, s 59 (1) enlarges this entitlement to include an agreement to enter a future agreement. The primary consequences of withdrawal are set out in s 57, which provides that withdrawal from a prospective regulated agreement may be either written or oral and shall cause the provisions of Pt IV to apply not only to the regulated agreement itself but also to any linked transaction[1], and to any other thing done in anticipation of the making of the agreement, as it would apply if the agreement had been made and cancelled under s 69 (as to which see below)[2].

1 As defined in s 19. A linked transaction is any transaction, *other than one for the provision of security*, which is entered into by the debtor or hirer under an actual or prospective regulated agreement and, while not forming part of the latter agreement itself, fulfils one of the three following conditions:
(a) is entered into in compliance with a term of the principal agreement;
(b) is financed, or to be financed, by the principal agreement where that principal agreement is a debtor-creditor-supplier agreement;
(c) is entered into by the debtor or hirer with a person specified in s 19 (2), and at the suggestion of such a person, for one of the following purposes:
(i) to induce the creditor or owner to enter into the principal agreement;
(ii) for another purpose related to the principal agreement; or
(iii) where the principal agreement is a restricted-use credit agreement, for a purpose related to a transaction financed, or to be financed, by the principal agreement: s 19 (1).

The persons specified by s 19(2) are the creditor or owner, or his associate (as defined by ss 189 (1), 184); a person who in the negotiation of the transaction, is represented by a credit broker (see ss 189 (1), 145 (2)) who is also a negotiator in antecedent negotiations for the principal agreement, and a person who, at the time the transaction is initiated, knows that the principal agreement has been made or contemplates that it might be made.

The exclusion from s 19 of transactions for the provision of security seems, as Adams (1975) 39 Conv (NS) 94, 98, remarks, to adopt a notion of security in this context as something collateral rather than integral to the regulated agreement. The illustration (no 11) given in Sch 2 to the Act, which refers to the charging of an insurance policy and the execution of a mortgage as being collateral security for a loan and thus as transactions for the provision of security, affords support for this view.

2 Infra. See further s 57 (3) (identifying the parties who shall be deemed to be agents for the creditor or hirer for the purpose of receiving a withdrawal notice) and s 57 (4) (s 57 (1) to apply although the agreement, if made, would not be a cancellable agreement). In relation to s 57 (3), see further s 175 (duty of persons deemed to be agents).

Cancellation

10.43 Cancellation becomes an issue once the regulated agreement has been entered into. It is dealt with under ss 67–73. The right of the debtor or hirer to cancel a regulated agreement arises if the antecedent negotiations included oral representations[1] made in the presence of the debtor or hirer by an individual as, or on behalf of, the negotiator[2] (although it does not exist where the unexecuted agreement was signed by the debtor or hirer at premises at which the creditor or owner was carrying on any business).

The ability to cancel does not, however, apply to agreements secured on land, restricted-use credit agreements[3] to finance the purchase of land, or agreements for bridging loans in connection with the purchase of land[4]. Consequently, a land mortgage cannot be cancelled in this way.

Taken in conjunction with the exemption of most land mortgages under s 16, the relevance of these sections to mortgages is therefore slight and they will not be discussed in detail.

However, since (as noted in **10.42**) s 69 applies by way of statutory analogy[5] to the withdrawal from prospective non-cancellable agreements[6], it is necessary to examine the consequences specified by that section in order to identify the rights of the parties after a withdrawal in accordance with s 57. These are as follows. A cancellation notice complying with s 69 operates to cancel the agreement and any linked transaction and to withdraw any offer by the debtor (or hirer) or his relative to enter into a linked transaction (unless in both cases a linked transaction is exempted by regulation)[7]. Further, an agreement or transaction so cancelled is to be treated as if it had never been entered into[8].

Where, however, the relevant agreement is a debtor-creditor-supplier agreement financing the doing of work or supply of goods in an emergency, or financing the supply of goods which have become incorporated[9] in any land or thing not itself comprised in the agreement or any linked transaction, the effect of cancellation (and thus of withdrawal under s 57) is less total. In such an event, the cancellation or withdrawal avoids only those provisions of the agreement or any linked transaction as relate to provision of credit, or require the debtor to pay an item in the total charge for credit, or subject the debtor to any obligation other than to pay for the doing of the work or the supply of the goods[10].

Where a regulated agreement is cancelled under s 69(1), or becomes subject to s 69(2), the court may make a declaration to that effect upon the application of an interested party[11].

1 For the meaning of 'representation' for the purposes of s 67, see *Moorgate Services Ltd v Kabir (t/a Shapla)* [1995] CCLR 74, CA.
2 'Negotiator' is defined in s 56: see **10.41**, n 1.
3 Defined by ss 11, 189 (1); see **10.23**.
4 Section 67(a).
5 Sections 57(1) and (4).
6 Ie those types of regulated agreements which cannot be cancelled by the debtor or hirer under s 67: see the definition of 'cancellable agreement' in s 189(1).
7 Sections 69(1) and (5). See also the Consumer Credit (Linked Transactions) (Exemptions) Regulations 1983, SI 1983/1560.
8 Section 69(4).
9 By act of the debtor or his relative.
10 Section 69 (2). So if, eg, the agreement or any linked transaction related to the installation of central heating, the debtor would have to pay the cost of installation but not the credit charges.
11 Section 142(2)(a).

Withdrawal from prospective land mortgage

10.44 The exclusion[1] of land mortgages from the rights relating to cancellation precipitated a special provision which grants the debtor or hirer under certain land-mortgage transactions a *locus poenitentiae* comparable to that enjoyed under ss 67–73. It is contained in s 58(1) which requires that, in a case where the prospective regulated agreement is to be secured on land, the creditor or owner shall give the debtor or hirer a copy of the unexecuted agreement containing a notice in prescribed form[2] indicating the right of the debtor or hirer to withdraw from the prospective agreement and how and when the right is exercisable, together with a copy of any other document referred to in the unexecuted agreement[3].

Section 58 does not, however, apply to a restricted-use credit agreement[4] to finance the purchase of the mortgaged land, or an agreement for a bridging loan in connection with the purchase of such land or other land[5]. Such agreements frequently require the rapid provision of finance and it was felt that the delays necessitated by s 58(1) would in many cases be counter-productive.

If, where they apply, the requirements of s 58(1) are not complied with, the agreement is not properly executed[6] with the result that it is unenforceable against the debtor or hirer except an order of the court is obtained[7]. Further safeguards in such cases are also provided by s 61(2), discussed above[8].

1 Prompted by the inconvenience which might arise from the registration (under the Land Charges Act 1972 or the Land Registration Act 1925) and almost immediate de-registration of mortgages if they were readily cancellable: Goode [1975] CLJ 79, 99.
2 The relevant form is prescribed by the Consumer Credit (Cancellation Notices and Copies of Documents) Regulations 1983, SI 1983/1557 (as amended).
3 Including, therefore, a copy of the complete, but unexecuted, mortgage.
4 Defined by s 11(1). See **10.23**.
5 Section 58(2).
6 Section 61(2)(a).
7 Section 65 (1).
8 See **10.38**.

Ancillary provisions in relation to withdrawal/cancellation

10.45 Further sections deal with the repayment of money paid by the debtor under a cancelled regulated agreement[1]; the repayment of credit in like circumstances[2]; the return of goods acquired by the debtor or hirer under certain kinds of regulated agreement[3]; and the recovery of goods given by him in part exchange[4]. Again the consequences specified in these sections apply *mutatis mutandis* on the withdrawal by the debtor from a non-cancellable agreement (such as a regulated agreement secured on land, ie a land mortgage).

1 Section 70.
2 Section 71. See also the Consumer Credit (Repayment of Credit on Cancellation) Regulations 1983, SI 1983/1559.
3 Section 72.
4 Section 73.

Exclusion of certain agreements from Pt V

10.46 As indicated above, various types of agreement, although falling within the general definition of a regulated agreement, are excluded either wholly or in part from the operation of Pt V. The primary source of exclusion is s 74(1), which provides as follows that Pt V (except s 56) does not to apply to:

(a) a non-commercial agreement[1]; or
(b) a debtor-creditor agreement[2] enabling the debtor to overdraw on a current account; or
(c) a debtor-creditor agreement to finance the making of such payments arising on, or connected with, the death of a person as may be prescribed[3].

Further, s 74(2) provides that Pt V (except ss 55 and 56) does not apply to a small debtor-creditor-supplier agreement[4] for restricted-use credit[5].

Further provisions are contained in s 74(3) and (3A)[6]. These limit the exclusion of those types of agreement mentioned in sub-ss 1(b) and (c) to cases where the

Director General of Fair Trading so determines. In addition, sub-s (4)[7] stipulates that if any term of an agreement falling within sub-ss (1)(c) or (2) is expressed in writing, the regulations made under s 60(1)[8] apply to that term (subject to s 60 (3)) as if the agreement were a regulated agreement not falling within sub-s (1) (c) or (2).

It will be recognised that s 74 itself does not operate to exempt the majority of those land mortgages which qualify as regulated agreements[9] from the provisions of Pt V.

1 Defined by s 189 (1) as 'a consumer credit agreement or a consumer hire agreement not made by the creditor or owner in the course of a business carried on by him'.
2 Defined by ss 13 and 189 (1).
3 See the Consumer Credit (Payments Arising on Death) Regulations 1983, SI 1983/1554.
4 Defined by ss 12, 17, 189 (1).
5 Defined by ss 11 (1), 189 (1).
6 Inserted by the Banking Act 1979, s 38(1).
7 As amended by the Banking Act 1979, s 38 (1).
8 Which section, as noted above, governs the form and content of regulated agreements. For the regulations made thereunder, see the Consumer Credit (Agreements) Regulations 1983, SI 1983/1533.
9 Ie those which involve the provision of credit of less than £25,000 (s 8(2)) and are not exempt agreements (s 16).

TRANSACTIONAL PROVISIONS

10.47 The extent to which the Consumer Credit Act intervenes to protect hirers and debtors from the civil consequences of unbridled freedom of contract is considerable and almost certainly unprecedented[1]. For instance, it enlarges the liability of a creditor under a debtor-creditor-supplier agreement for breaches of contract or misrepresentations on the part of the supplier[2] and, significantly, strictly circumscribes the courses of action which a creditor or owner may legitimately adopt in enforcing a regulated agreement.

1 Although consumer rights have since 1974 assumed a greater significance generally: see eg the Consumer Protection Act 1987 and the Unfair Terms in Consumer Contracts Regulations 1999, SI 1999/2083.
2 Section 75 (1): the agreement must be one falling within ss 12 (b) or (c) and must not be a non-commercial agreement (s 75(3)(a)). Further, s 75(1) does not apply to any claim so far as it relates to any single item to which the supplier has attached a cash price not exceeding £100 or more than £30,000 (s 75(3)(b): financial limits raised by the Consumer Credit (Increase of Monetary Limits) Order 1983, SI 1983/1878).
An example of a mortgage falling within this section, therefore rendering the creditor-mortgagee liable for breaches of contract committed by a supplier of goods or services for the payment of whose charges the mortgage was first taken out, would be that posited in **10.28** (if pre-existing or contemplated arrangements could be established between the mortgagee and the builder).

Enforcement (including termination) of regulated agreements

Duty of creditor or owner to give notice before taking certain action (non-default cases)

10.48 Where the right to enforce arises (other than upon a breach by the debtor or hirer[1]), s 76(1) provides that the creditor or owner is not entitled to enforce a term of a regulated agreement by:

(a) demanding earlier payment of any sum; or
(b) recovering possession of any goods or land; or
(c) treating any right conferred on the debtor or hirer by the agreement as terminated, restricted or deferred except by or after giving the debtor or hirer not less then seven days' notice of his intention to do so[2].

Notices given under s 76(1) must be in the prescribed form in order to be effective[3].

The subsection does not, however, prevent a creditor from treating the right to draw on any credit as restricted or deferred, or from taking necessary steps to implement such restriction or deferment[4]. Moreover, s 76(1) may be displaced by exempting regulations in the case of particular agreements[5].

Because, as noted above, it does not apply where the creditor's rights in question arise on default by the debtor (which, in practice, will ordinarily be the case), s 76 is unlikely to be of frequent application. It was no doubt included in the Act for the purpose of precluding avoidance of the procedures applicable in cases of default (as to which see **10.49**) by means of provisions enabling the creditor to exercise such rights irrespective of default by the debtor.

Further, a provision almost identical to s 76 is contained in s 98 of the Act. Indeed, the requirements of both sections are the same and it is therefore unclear why both sections were included in the Act.

1 Section 76(6). For example, upon the bankruptcy of the debtor or hirer.
2 This subsection is qualified to some extent by s 76 (2), which confines its operations to cases where a period for the duration of the agreement is specified therein and that period has not ended when the creditor or owner adopts the conduct in question. Moreover, where the enforcement (or the security) takes a form other than that specified in s 76(1), the only prior notification required of the creditor or owner seems to be that, if any, set out in the security instrument itself.
3 Section 76 (3). For the prescribed form, see the Consumer Credit (Enforcement, Default and Termination Notices) Regulations 1983, SI 1983/1561.
4 Section 76 (4).
5 Section 76 (5). See the Consumer Credit (Enforcement, Default and Termination Notices) Regulations 1983, SI 1983/1561. By virtue of these regulations, the duty does not apply to non-commercial agreements in relation to which no security has been provided.

Need for notice (default cases)

10.49 Under s 87(1), if the debtor or hirer is in breach of a regulated agreement, the creditor or owner must serve a 'default notice'[1] before he can terminate the agreement, demand earlier payment of any sum, repossess any goods or land, enforce any security or treat any rights of the debtor or hirer as terminated, restricted or deferred[2]. Broadly, the notice required must be in writing and must specify the breach and, in the case of a remediable breach, what action is required to remedy the same and the date before which that action is to be taken, which date must be at least seven days after the date of service of the notice[3].

The notice must specify with reasonable accuracy what sum of money the recipient was obliged to pay in order to remedy the breach and thus a default notice which substantially overstates the arrears is invalid[4].

The effect of a default notice differs radically from a notice given under s 76[5], insofar as s 89 provides that compliance by the debtor or hirer with the action specified by the notice as necessary to remedy the breach within the stipulated time means that the breach shall be treated as if it had never occurred.

1 For the prescribed form, contents and effect of such notices, see s 88 (modelled on the Law of Property Act 1925, s 146) and the Consumer Credit (Enforcement, Default and Termination Notices) Regulations 1983, SI 1983/1561 (as amended).
2 Section 87(2) and (4) corresponds substantially with ss 76(4) and (5), above. Thus, s 87(1) does not prevent a creditor from treating the right to draw on any credit as restricted or deferred, or from taking necessary steps to implement such restriction or deferment and s 87(1) may be displaced by exempting regulations in the case of particular agreements, as to which see the Consumer Credit (Enforcement, Default and Termination Notices) Regulations 1983, SI 1983/1561.
3 Section 88(1) and (2).
4 *Woodchester Lease Management Services Ltd v Swayne & Co* [1999] 1 WLR 263, CA.
5 Or under s 98 (termination other than by default): see **10.48**.

Re-taking of protected hire-purchase, etc goods

10.50 Where the creditor or owner wishes to repossess goods on default, he is further subject to the provisions of s 90 if the agreement in question is a regulated hire-purchase or conditional sale agreement[1].

This section (which is of course of merely marginal interest to mortgages) corresponds substantially to ss 33–44 of the Hire-Purchase Act 1965, in that it reintroduces the notion of protected goods into the superseding legislation. A court order is required for the recovery of possession of such goods. Recovery contrary to s 90 involves termination of the agreement, total release of the debtor from liability and the right on his part to recover all sums hitherto paid to the creditor[2]. Where a regulated agreement is so terminated, ie under s 91, the court may make a declaration to that effect upon the application of an interested party[3].

1 For the definitions of these terms, see **10.13**.
2 Section 91.
3 Section 142(2)(b).

Recovery of possession of goods or land in hire-purchase, etc cases

10.51 A court order is required before creditors under such agreements, or owners under regulated consumer hire-agreements[1] may enter premises to take possession of goods subject thereto[2]. Further, the recovery of possession of land is subject to the same restriction after the debtor is in breach of a regulated conditional sale agreement[3] relating to land[4]. Failure to obtain a court order may render the creditor or owner liable for breach of statutory duty[5].

1 For the definition of this term, see **10.3** and **10.11**.
2 Section 92 (1).
3 For the definition of this term, see **10.13**, n 1.
4 Section 92 (2).
5 Section 92 (3).

Interest not to be increased on default

10.52 The rate of interest payable under a regulated consumer credit agreement is not to be increased on default by the debtor[1].

1 Section 93. This may give rise to a problem in relation to interest free loans where it is desired to charge interest on default.

Right of debtor to early settlement (and associated consequences)

10.53 The Act acknowledges that debtors or hirers should be entitled, where appropriate, to accelerate their discharge from the agreement or to terminate that agreement before it has run its full course. Accordingly, s 94 confers on a debtor under a regulated consumer credit agreement the right to complete payments ahead of time: the debtor is entitled at any time, provided he gives statutory notice to that effect, to release himself from further liability by immediate discharge of all outstanding commitments under the agreement[1]. In this event he may be entitled to a rebate[2] and either he or any relative of his will generally be discharged from liability (except in respect of a debt which has already become payable) under any linked[3] transaction[4].

1 Section 94 (1).
2 Section 95. See also the Consumer Credit (Rebate on Early Settlement) Regulations 1983, SI 1983/1562 (as amended). For the interrelationship of an acceleration clause and a rebate under the regulations, see *Forward Trust plc v Whymark* [1990] 2 QB 670, [1989] 3 All ER 915, CA.
3 'Linked transaction' is defined in s 19(1): see **10.42**, n 1.
4 Section 96. See also the Consumer Credit (Linked Transactions) (Exemptions) Regulations 1983, SI 1983/1560 which exclude certain linked transactions from the operation of the section.

Termination by debtor of regulated hire-purchase, conditional sale or consumer hire agreement

10.54 As regards termination by the debtor under a regulated hire-purchase or conditional sale agreement[1], the provisions of the Act[2] are substantially those embodied in the Hire-Purchase Act 1965[3]. Equivalent provision is made for the termination of regulated consumer hire agreements[4].

1 For the definitions of these expressions, see **10.13**.
2 Sections 99 and 100.
3 Hire Purchase Act 1965, ss 27 and 28.
4 Section 101; see also s 132. For the definition of 'consumer hire agreement', see **10.11**.

Information and documentation

Duties imposed on creditor

10.55 Certain information and documents must in specified circumstances (eg upon request), and in accordance with prescribed time limits, etc be given to debtors and hirers during (or shortly after) the currency of the agreements. Such information includes:

(a) sums paid and payable under fixed-sum[1] and running-account[2] credit agreements[3];
(b) a breakdown of the sums payable under regulated consumer hire agreements[4];
(c) the amounts required to discharge the debtor's indebtedness under regulated consumer credit agreements[5]; and
(d) statements that the liability of a debtor or hirer under regulated agreements has been discharged[6].

In most cases a failure to comply will render the agreement unenforceable for the period of default and may, after a certain time, constitute an offence. Further, statements given in connection with the above requirements are generally binding[7] unless the court grants relief[8].

1 For 'fixed-sum credit', see ss 10 and 189(1).
2 For 'running-account credit', see ss 10 and 189(1).
3 Sections 77 and 78 respectively. See also the Consumer Credit (Prescribed Periods for Giving Information) Regulations 1983, SI 1983/1569 and the Consumer Credit (Running-Account Credit) Information Regulation 1983, SI 1983/1570.
4 For the definition of 'consumer hire agreement', see **10.11**. Section 79. See also the Consumer Credit (Prescribed Periods for Giving Information) Regulations 1983, SI 1983/1569.
5 Section 97. See also the Consumer Credit (Settlement Information) Regulations 1983, SI 1983/1564.
6 Section 103. See also the Consumer Credit (Prescribed Periods for Giving Information) Regulations 1983, SI 1983/1569.
7 Section 172 (1), (2).
8 Section 172 (3).

Duties imposed on debtors or hirers

10.56 Other provisions within Pt VI of the Act deal with the duty of debtors or hirers under regulated agreements to give information about the location of goods[1].

1 Section 80. This does not apply to non-commercial agreements.

Miscellaneous

10.57 The Act further contains provisions dealing with assorted matters including:

(a) the appropriation of payments made by debtors or hirers to the same person under two or more regulated agreements[1];
(b) the variation of regulated agreements[2];
(c) the debtor's liability for misuse of credit facilities or credit-tokens[3]; and
(d) the effect of the death of a hirer or debtor upon a regulated agreement[4].

1 Section 81.
2 Section 82. This section does not apply to non-commercial agreements: s 80(7). See also the Consumer Credit (Notice of Variation of Agreements) Regulations 1977, SI 1977/328 (as amended).
3 Sections 83 and 84. See also the Consumer Credit (Credit-Token Agreements) Regulations 1983, SI 1983/1555.
4 Section 86.

Security

10.58 The rules as to security are contained in Pt VIII of the Act.

'Security'

10.59 With the exception of s 105, Pt VIII appears to govern both primary and collateral securities. The sections in this Part speak generally in terms of 'any security'. Section 189 (1) defines 'security' as including 'a mortgage ... provided by the debtor or hirer, or at his request (express or implied), to secure the carrying out of [his] obligations ... under the agreement'. Although the matter is not free from doubt, the definition therefore seems to encompass both the mortgage which is given by way of reinforcement to, and the mortgage which itself constitutes, a regulated agreement.

Form and content of security instrument

10.60 All securities in relation to regulated agreements, other than those provided by the debtor or hirer[1], must be in writing[2], must adopt the prescribed form and must embody the prescribed contents[3].

Unless these and other formalities are observed[4] the security instrument is not properly executed[5]. The consequence is that the security, so far as provided in relation to a regulated agreement, is enforceable against the surety only on a court order[6].

1 Section 105(6). Such security may, of course, be covered by s 60 (**10.37**). See also s 105(9).
2 Section 105 (1).
3 Section 105(2). See the Consumer Credit (Agreements) Regulations 1983, SI 1983/1553 and the Consumer Credit (Guarantees and Indemnities) Regulations 1983, SI 1983/1556.
4 Section 105 (3); and see s 105 (5) (copies to sureties).
5 Section 105(4) and (5).
6 Section 105(7).

Ineffective security

Generally

10.61 If, for want of compliance with s 105 of the Act (as to which see **10.60**), a security is not properly executed and, moreover, an application (under s 105(7)) by the creditor to enforce the same against the surety is dismissed by the court, other than on technical grounds only, s 106 applies to the security in question[1].

Section 106 itself allows for the retrospective extinguishment of securities. It stipulates that, in relation to any security provided in relation to a regulated agreement, the following consequences shall follow:

(a) the security, so far as it is so provided, shall be treated as never having effect;
(b) any property lodged with the creditor or owner solely for the purposes of the security as so provided shall be returned by him forthwith;
(c) the creditor or owner shall take any necessary action to remove or cancel an entry in any register, so far as the entry relates to the security as so provided; and
(d) any amount received by the creditor or owner on realisation of the security shall, so far as it is referable to the agreement, be repaid to the surety.

The object of the section is to restore the position which obtained prior to the provision of the security, so far as can be done.

In addition to the above-mentioned instance, s 106 also applies (with like effect) in the following cases[2]:

(a) where a regulated agreement is cancelled under s 69 (1) or becomes subject to s 69 (2) (as to which see **10.43**)[3];
(b) where such an agreement is terminated under s 91 (as to which see **10.50**)[4];
(c) where the court dismisses otherwise than on technical grounds an application[5] to enforce an improperly executed regulated agreement or security[6];
(d) where a declaration is made by the court under s 142(1) of the Act (refusal of enforcement order) in respect of any regulated agreement[7].

1 Section 105(8).

2 Section 113(3)-(6).
3 Section 113(3)(a).
4 Section 113(3)(b).
5 Made under ss 40(2), 65(1), 124(1) or 149(2) of the Act.
6 Section 113(3)(c).
7 Section 113(3)(d).

Saving for registered charges

10.62 In any case, s 106 is, however, expressly subject to s 177 (saving for registered charges).

Section 177(1) provides that nothing in the Act is to affect the rights of a proprietor of a registered charge within the meaning of the Land Registration Act, provided that one of two conditions is fulfilled: (a) he became proprietor under a transfer for value without notice of any defect in title arising under the Act or (b) he derives title from such a proprietor. In addition, s 177(3) adds the condition that the proprietor must not carry on a business of debt-collecting for s 177(1) to apply[1].

This saving provision has occasioned considerable academic criticism. On one level it is said that s 177(1) does not go far enough, insofar as it does not apply to the second proprietor or holder of any other form of charge over registered land[2], or to any transferee of any mortgage over unregistered land[3]. On another level, the subsection is criticised for a lack of clarity, both in the area of 'defects of title' and again in the scope of protection which it purports to confer. Some have contended that the only defect in a mortgagee's title which arises under the Act is that emanating from s 106 (as applied by ss 105 (8) and 113 (3)), by virtue of which the mortgage is treated as never having had effect[4]. Elsewhere it is questioned whether the unsatisfied necessity to obtain a court order before enforcing an improperly executed mortgage, or the entry into a mortgage by unlicensed professional creditors without enforcement orders, can genuinely be said to constitute or procreate defects in title[5].

In any event, it would appear that notice of a breach of the Act does not necessarily impart notice of a defect in title and that a transferee protected by s 177(1) may be entitled to enforce the mortgage according to the ordinary law, thus averting, for instance, the operation of s 126[6] or s 105(7)[7].

Further subsections in s 177 provide that nothing in the Act affects the operation of s 104 of the Law of Property Act 1925[8] and that where, by virtue of s 177(1), a land mortgage is enforced which would otherwise have been unenforceable, the original creditor or owner shall be liable to indemnify the debtor or hirer against any loss suffered by him as a result[9].

1 This exception has been criticised on the ground that it could imperil 'rescue operations' in respect of finance companies, because any mortgage within the Act in which a finance company is mortgagee cannot be taken over by an institution within s 177 (3) without forfeiting s 177 (1): Adams (1975) 39 Conv (NS) 114.
2 Adams 113.
3 Adams 113–114.
4 It has been observed that the principal cases of such a defect arising are those where the court or the Director has refused to make an enforcement order under ss 30 (2), 65 (1), 105 (1), 124 (1) or 149 (2), or where the court has made a declaration under s 142(1), or where a cancellable agreement has been cancelled by the debtor under s 69 (1). Accordingly it has been contended that where the transferee of the mortgage has no notice, actual or constructive, of the making or refusing of the appropriate order, or of the cancellation of the agreement, the transferee is protected under s 177 (1).
5 Adams 114.
6 Which requires a court order before enforcement of a land mortgage securing a regulated

agreement. See **10.64**.
7 Which likewise requires a court order before an improperly executed security agreement is enforceable against a surety. See **10.60**.
8 Section 177 (2). Section 104 provides protection for a purchaser where a mortgagee exercises his power of sale.
9 Section 177 (4).

Need for notice (default and non-default cases)

10.63 Where there has been a breach of a regulated agreement, no security given in connection therewith can be enforced until a default notice conforming with s 87 has been given and has duly expired without the breach being remedied[1].

Further, s 76 governs non-breach situations and provides that no recovery of possession of goods or land shall occur without service and expiry of the customary seven-day notice.

Consideration has been given to ss 76 and 87 earlier in this chapter and the reader is referred to the relevant passages for full treatment of those provisions[2].

1 Sections 87 (1) and 88; see also s 112. The doing of an act by which a floating charge becomes fixed is no enforcement of a security: s 87 (3).
2 See **10.48** and **10.49** respectively.

Enforcement of land mortgages

10.64 Where the regulated agreement is secured by a land mortgage, however, that mortgage is enforceable (so far as provided in relation to the agreement) only on an order of the court[1].

This is, it is submitted, one of the most important provisions of the entire Act. However, it is remarkable that no sanction is specifically imposed to cater for its breach. Accordingly, it is thought that a mortgagee who, in contravention of s 126, obtains vacant possession and exercises a right of sale can pass a good title to the purchaser of the land[2]. Unless s 106 applies to the security, the debtor or hirer would appear to be limited to seeking an injunction or to proceeding for the withdrawal of the creditor's licence[3].

1 Section 126.
2 See also s 177(2) (**10.62**, n 8). *Quaere* whether the prospective purchaser could legitimately object to the mortgagee's title on the grounds of non-compliance with s 126.
3 See Goode [1975] CLJ 79, 113.

Redemption and realisation of pawns

10.65 This is dealt with under ss 116–121 of the Act.

Miscellaneous

10.66 The remainder of Pt VIII embraces an assortment of ancillary matters, many of them comparable to provisions in earlier Parts. Thus, there are rules relating to various information requirements[1] and a special section, s 112, enabling regulations[2] to be made providing for 'any matters relating to the sale or other realisation by the creditor or owner of property over which any right has been provided by way of security in relation to an actual or prospective regulated agreement other than a non-commercial agreement'[3].

In addition s 113 makes elaborate provision for ensuring that the Act may not be evaded by the taking of security and provides that no security provided in relation to an actual or prospective regulated agreement shall be enforced so as to benefit the creditor or owner, directly or indirectly, to a greater extent than would have been the case if the security had not been provided. The rules by which this policy is implemented are complex and abstruse and space does not permit a detailed discussion. However, in summary, the general tenor of s 113 is to treat securities given in relation to regulated agreements which are subject to some debilitating event—such as termination, cancellation (whether actual or notional[4]), or being enforceable only by order of the Court or the Director-General—in a manner equivalent to that applicable to the regulated agreement itself.

1 See ss 107 (duty to give information to surety under fixed-sum credit agreement); 108 (duty to give information to surety under running-account credit agreement); 109 (duty to give information to surety under consumer hire agreement); 110 (duty to give information to debtor or hirer under regulated agreements which are non-commercial agreements); 111 (duty to give surety copy of notices despatched under ss 76(1), 87(1) or 98(1). See also the Consumer Credit (Prescribed Periods for Giving Information) Regulations 1983, SI 1983/1569. In most cases a failure to comply will render the agreement unenforceable for the period of default and may, after a certain time, constitute an offence. Further, statements given in connection with the above requirements are generally binding unless the court grants relief: s 172.
2 No such regulations have been made.
3 This section is subject to s 121 which deals with the realisation of pawns.
4 See s 57; see also **10.42** ff.

Negotiable instruments

10.67 Finally, regard should be paid to the rules relating to negotiable instruments: these are contained in ss 123–125. The Crowther Committee reported considerable malpractice in the taking of such documents (particularly promissory notes) from consumers under deferred purchasing or work and labour transactions, and s 123[1] reflects the restrictive policy now adopted towards these and associated practices. It provides that:

(a) a creditor or owner shall not take a negotiable instrument[2], other than a bank note or cheque, in discharge of any sum payable:
  (i) by the debtor or hirer under a regulated agreement; or
  (ii) by any person as surety in relation to the agreement[3];
(b) the creditor or owner shall not negotiate a cheque taken by him in discharge of a sum payable as mentioned in (a) except to a banker (within the meaning of the Bills of Exchange Act 1882)[4];
(c) the creditor or owner shall not take a negotiable instrument as security for the discharge of any sum payable as mentioned in (a)[5].

Once s 123 has been contravened in relation to a sum payable as mentioned in (a), the agreement under which the sum is payable can be enforced against the debtor or hirer only upon an order of the court[6]. A similar restriction on enforcement is imposed in the case of contraventions of s 123 in relation to sums payable by sureties[7]. Further, the dismissal of any application for an order to enforce such a security (other than a dismissal on technical grounds alone) shall mean that s 106[8] applies so as retrospectively to extinguish the security[9].

While nothing in the Act is to affect the right of holders in due course[10], any person who takes a negotiable instrument in contravention of s 123(1) or (3) is a holder in due course or entitled to enforce the instrument[11]. In addition, a creditor or owner is bound to indemnify any debtor, hirer or surety against liability to a holder in due course when the instrument was originally taken by such creditor or owner in contravention of s 123(1) or (3) or taken and negotiated in contravention of s 123(2)[12].

1 Which does not apply where the regulated agreement is a non-commercial agreement: s 123(5). Further, see the Consumer Credit (Negotiable Instruments) (Exemption) Order 1984, SI 1984/435 for exemptions where the regulated agreement has a connection with a country outside the UK: s 123(6).
2 Doubt has been expressed as to the meaning of 'negotiable instrument' in s 123: see Goode [1975] CLJ 79, 114n. However, it seems to include a bill of exchange and a promissory note.
3 Section 123(1).
4 Section 123(2).
5 Section 123(3). A person takes a negotiable instrument as security for the discharge of a sum if the sum is intended to be paid in some other way, and the negotiable instrument is to be presented for payment only if the sum is not paid in that way: s 123(4).
6 Section 124 (1).
7 Section 124 (2). Section 189(1) defines 'surety' as 'the person by whom security is provided, or the person to whom his rights and duties in relation to the security have passed by assignment or operation of law'.
8 See **10.61**.
9 Section 124(3).
10 As to which see the Bills of Exchange Act 1832, ss 29 and 38. Section 125(4).
11 Section 125(1).
12 Section 124(3).

ENFORCEMENT OF THE ACT

10.68 Part XI of the Consumer Credit Act identifies the persons and institutions charged with its implementation and enforcement[1] and invests these bodies with a formidable array of sanctions and powers. It may be observed that s 168 contains a 'non-fault' defence not dissimilar to that contained in ss 24 (1) and (2) of the Trade Descriptions Act 1968 and s 25 (1) and (2) of the Fair Trading Act 1973[2].

1 Section 161.
2 Cf *Tesco Supermarkets Ltd v Nattrass* [1972] AC 153, [1971] 2 All ER 127, HL; *McGuire v Sittingbourne Co-operative Society Ltd* [1976] CLR 268.

JUDICIAL CONTROL OF REGULATED AGREEMENTS[1]

Part IX generally

10.69 There remains one further (and vitally important) Part of the Consumer Credit Act which sets out the principles upon which the court may adjust or administer agreements and contains wide powers of supervision and intervention. This Part (Pt IX) is of unprecedented latitude and specificity. It operates upon a varying spectrum of agreements through a number of different media.

1 As to the applicability of the ensuing provisions to 'rental purchase' schemes, see (1975) 39 Conv (NS) 343 (Hoggett), especially at 354; (1975) 39 Conv (NS) 94 (Adams), 112–113.

Enforcement orders in cases of infringement

General power of the court in relation to enforcement

10.70 It will be recalled that a number of sections within the Act have the effect, if contravened, of rendering the relevant agreement unenforceable unless the court orders to the contrary. Section 127(1) delineates the circumstances in which this discretionary power is to be exercised: in the event of an application for an enforcement order under ss 65(1)[1], 105(7)(a) or (b)[2], 111(2)[3], or 124(1) or (2)[4], the application shall be dismissed if, but only if, the court considers it just to do so; and in reaching its conclusion the court shall pay regard to:

(a) prejudice caused to any person by the relevant contravention, and the degree of culpability involved therein; and
(b) the powers conferred on the court by ss 127(2), 135 and 136[5].

This power is expressly subject, however, to the mandatory terms of s 127(3) and (4), as to which see below.

1 Improperly executed agreements: see, eg, **10.37**, n 5, **10.38**, n 8, **10.44**, n 7.
2 Improperly executed security instruments.
3 Failure to serve copy of notice on surety.
4 Taking a negotiable instrument contrary to s 123.
5 As to which see below.

Restriction on discretionary power of court where agreement improperly executed

Section 127(3)

10.71 Further conditions are attached to the making of enforcement orders under s 65(1), ie where the agreement was improperly executed for some or other reason.

In such cases an enforcement order shall *not* be made if:

(a) s 61(1)(a)[1] was not complied with (although an exception to this blanket prohibition exists where a document containing all the prescribed terms of the agreement has been signed by the hirer, even though the form and contents of that document did not comply with s 60(1) and despite the fact that the manner in which it was signed was other than that prescribed[2]); or
(b) in the case of a cancellable agreement[3]:
  (i) a provision of s 62[4] or s 63[5] was not complied with and the creditor or owner did not give a copy of the executed agreement and of any other document referred to in it to the debtor or hirer before the commencement of the proceedings in which the order is sought; or
  (ii) s 64(1)[6] was not complied with[7].

Where s 127(3) applies, it is of draconian consequence, particularly because, as has been seen, not only is the agreement itself rendered unenforceable but also any related security is similarly unenforceable[8].

1 Which deals with the signing of agreements: see **10.38**.
2 Section 127 (3); see further s 127 (5) which prescribes that where an enforcement order is made in such a case, the order may direct that the regulated agreement is to have

effect as if it did not include a term omitted from the document signed by the debtor or hirer.
3 For the definition of which expression: see s 189(1) and **10.43**, n 6.
4 Duty to supply copy of unexecuted agreement: see **10.39**.
5 Duty to supply copy of executed agreement: see **10.39**.
6 Duty to give notice of cancellation rights: see **10.39**.
7 Section 127 (4).
8 Sections 106 and 113: see **10.61** and **10.66**.

Section 127(3) declared incompatible with the Human Rights Act 1998

10.72 Following the coming into force of the Human Rights Act 1998, it has been held[1] that the absolute bar, imposed by s 127(3), to enforcement of an agreement which does not contain all the prescribed terms infringes the rights of a creditor in that it constitutes:

(a) a disproportionate restriction on the lender's right to have the enforceability of the loan agreement determined by the court, contrary to Art 6(1) of the European Convention on Human Rights;
(b) an interference with the creditor's peaceable enjoyment of its possessions[2], contrary to Art 1 of the First Protocol to the Convention.

It has been judicially observed that there is no discernible reason why, if it is appropriate to confer on the court the discretion permitted by s 127(1) and (2), it is proportionate to provide an absolute bar in a case to which s 127(3) applies[3]. Thus, although the policy aim of s 127(3), namely to ensure that particular attention is paid to the inclusion in the document to be signed by the debtor of certain prescribed terms, is a legitimate policy objective, the method by which such aim is achieved is not legitimate because the inflexible prohibition against the making of an enforcement order (in a case where the document signed by the debtor does not include the prescribed terms) infringes guaranteed Convention rights to an extent which is disproportionate to the policy aim[4]. There is no reason why that aim should not be achieved through judicial control, by empowering the Court to do what is just in the circumstances of the particular case[4].

Further, it is impossible to read and give effect to s 127(3) in a way which is compatible with the Convention Rights (as required by s 3 of the 1998 Act)[5].

Moreover, a declaration of incompatibility has been made, the Court of Appeal declaring that the provisions of s 127(3), in so far as they prevent the court from making an enforcement order under s 65(1) unless a document containing all the prescribed terms of the agreement has been signed by the debtor or hirer, are incompatible with the rights guaranteed to the creditor or hirer by Art 6(1) of the Convention and Art 1 of the First Protocol[6].

1 *Wilson v First County Trust Ltd (No 2)* [2001] EWCA Civ 633, [2001] 3 All ER 229, [2001] 3 WLR 42. (The Court of Appeal had adjourned the appeal in order to allow the Crown to be given notice under the Human Rights Act 1998, s 5 that the court was considering making a declaration of incompatibility under s 4 of that Act.) In that case the amount of credit had been incorrectly stated in the regulated agreement by a mere £250. Thus, the agreement lacked a term prescribed by s 60(1) and was accordingly improperly executed by virtue of s 61(1)(a). It was, therefore, unenforceable by reason of s 127(3): *Wilson v First County Trust Ltd* [2001] QB 407, [2001] 2 WLR 302, CA.
2 The money advanced by the creditor to the debtor being its 'possessions'. That money was lent on terms that it be repaid within a specified period. By operation of s 127(3), however, the creditor is deprived of its possessions without a fair balance being struck between the demands of the general community and the fundamental right of the

individual. In so holding, the Court of Appeal rejected an argument that non-compliance with the 1974 Act means that the creditor has no possessions. It noted that there is nothing in the 1974 Act which prevents an improperly executed regulated agreement from giving rise to contractual rights. The effect of the 1974 Act is limited to restricting the ability of the creditor to enforce such rights and any security.

3 *Wilson v First County Trust Ltd* [2001] QB 407, [2001] 2 WLR 302, CA at para 26; *Wilson v First County Trust Ltd (No 3)* [2001] EWCA Civ 633, [2001] 3 All ER 229, [2001] 3 WLR 42, CA at paras 38–39.

4 *Wilson v First County Trust Ltd* [2001] EWCA Civ 633, [2001] 3 All ER 229, [2001] 3 WLR 42, CA at para 39.

5 *Wilson v First County Trust Ltd* [2001] EWCA Civ 633, [2001] 3 All ER 229, [2001] 3 WLR 42, CA at paras 43 and 45.

6 *Wilson v First County Trust Ltd* [2001] EWCA Civ 633, [2001] 3 All ER 229, [2001] 3 WLR 42, CA at para 50. Permission to appeal was refused by the Court of Appeal.

The aftermath

10.73 The making by the court of a declaration of incompatibility does not affect the validity, continuing operation or enforcement of the provision in respect of which it is made[1]. Consequently, unless and until Parliament changes the law, s 127(3) continues to present an absolute bar to the enforcement of agreements and securities in those cases to which it applies.

However, a declaration of incompatibility provides a basis[2] for a Minister of the Crown to consider whether there are compelling reasons to make amendments to the legislation by remedial order[3] for the purpose of removing the incompatibility which the court has identified.

As at the time of writing, however, no remedial order has been made. It therefore remains to be seen whether Parliament will amend s 127(3) and, if so, how. Further, in view of the decision in relation to s 127(3), it is hard to see how s 127(4)[4], at least insofar as it relates to notice of cancellation rights, can be compatible with the Convention since a trifling error in the prescribed form of notice will deprive the creditor of power to enforce the agreement and an associated security.

1 Human Rights Act 1998, s 4(6).

2 Section 10(1)(a).

3 Under the Human Rights Act 1998, Sch 2. A remedial order can be retrospective: Sch 2.

4 As to which see **10.71**, n 7.

Ancillary powers where enforcement order granted

Power to reduce or discharge liability of debtor, hirer or surety

10.74 Section 127(2) permits the court, if it grants an enforcement order, to order an adjustment of the liabilities of the debtor, hirer or surety as an alternative to either total enforcement of the regulated agreement or nullity. Thus, the court may, if it appears just for it to do so, 'reduce or discharge any sum payable by the debtor or hirer, or any surety, so as to compensate him for prejudice suffered as a result of the contravention in question'.

Where, by reason of an infringement of the 1974 Act[1] by the creditor, a debtor (who subsequently enters a regulated agreement secured by a land mortgage) is deprived of the requisite seven-day cooling-off period and, consequently, the possibility of obtaining a loan from another source at a lower rate of interest during that period, compensation for the prejudice suffered by the debtor may be awarded in the form of a credit equivalent to a proportion of the interest claimed by the creditor[2].

In a case where the creditor failed to comply with s 60 and the regulations supplementary thereto, thereby omitting to bring to the attention of the hirer his liability to make accelerated payments in the event of breach of the regulated agreement, the discretion of the court was exercised by substantially reducing the claim for such accelerated payments[3].

1 Sections 58(1) and 61(2)(b): see **10.44**.
2 *National Guardian Mortgage Corpn v Wilkes* [1993] CCLR 1 (Cty Ct), following *Cedar Holdings Ltd v Jenkins* [1988] CCLR 34. The accrued interest was reduced by 40 per cent. It appears that reliance was also placed on the wide powers of the court under s 136 of the Act to vary regulated agreements: see **10.82**.
3 *Rank Xerox Finance Ltd v Hepple* [1994] CCLR 1 (Cty Ct). The reduction was from £5,444.36 to £500.

Power to impose conditions or suspend operation of order

10.75 The above power is supplemented by s 135, which entitles the court, if it considers it just to do so, in any order made by it in relation to a regulated agreement to include provisions:

(a) making the operation of any term of the order conditional on the doing of specified acts by any party to the proceedings;
(b) suspending the operation of any term of the order either:
 (i) until such time as the court subsequently directs, or
 (ii) until the occurrence of a specified act or omission[1].

1 See further s 135(2) (no suspension of term requiring delivery up of goods unless court satisfied that the goods are in his possession or control) and 135(3) (suspension in case involving consumer hire agreement not to extend the period for which the hirer is entitled to possession of the goods).

Enforcement order on death of debtor or hirer

10.76 Section 128 deals with the making of enforcement orders on the death of the debtor or hirer. Under s 86(2), a creditor or owner under an unsecured or partly secured regulated agreement may not do an act specified in s 87(1)[1] by reason of the death of the debtor or hirer unless he obtains an order of the court. The effect of s 128 is to prohibit the making of such an enforcement order unless the creditor or owner proves that he has been unable to satisfy himself that the present and future obligations of the debtor or hirer under the agreement are likely to be discharged.

1 As to which see **10.49**.

Exclusive jurisdiction of the county court in relation to enforcement

10.77 In England and Wales, *only* the county court (and no other court) has jurisdiction to hear and determine:

(a) any action by a creditor or owner to enforce a regulated agreement or any security relating to it;
(b) any action to enforce any linked transaction[1] against the debtor or hirer or his relative[2].

Where an action or application is brought in the High Court which ought, by virtue of the Act, to have been brought in the county court, it shall not be treated as improperly brought, but shall be transferred to the county court[3].

1 Defined by s 19(1). See **10.49**, n 1.
2 Section 141(1).
3 Section 141(2). In *Sovereign Leasing plc v Ali* [1992] CCLR 1 it was held that s 141(2) does not confer on the High Court a discretion to decide whether or not the case should continue in the High Court or be transferred to the county court. In *Automobile Financial Services v Docherty* (10 November 1987, unreported) it was held that the High Court must set aside any default judgment entered in such a case of its own initiative.

Power of court to grant declaration in relation to enforcement

10.78 Where:

(a) an application for an enforcement order is dismissed (except on technical grounds); or
(b) in circumstances in which an enforcement order is required by the creditor or owner to do some act, no such application has been made (or, if made, has been dismissed on technical grounds),

the court may, if it thinks it just to do so, make a declaration that the creditor or owner is not entitled to do the act in respect of which an enforcement order is required[1]. If such a declaration is made, no application for an enforcement order in respect of the act in question shall be entertained thereafter[1].

1 Section 142(1).

Time orders

10.79 Section 129 endows the court with wide powers for the making of time orders whereby (amongst other things) repayment of debt can be effectively rescheduled and rates of interest altered, or even extinguished, by the court in favour of the debtor or hirer.

Section 129(1) delineates the circumstances in which this discretionary power can be exercised, namely in the event of:

(a) an application by a creditor or owner an enforcement order[1];
(b) an application by a debtor or hirer under s 129(1) after service on him of:
 (i) a default notice[2], or
 (ii) a notice under s 76(1) or s 98(1)[3]; or
(c) an action brought by a creditor or owner to enforce a regulated agreement or any security, or recover possession of any goods or land to which a regulated agreement relates[4].

A time order may be made, if it appears to the court just to do so. A time order, if made, may provide for one or both of the following, as the court considers just:

(a) the payment by the debtor or hirer or any surety of any sum owed[5] under a regulated agreement or a security by such instalments, payable at such times as the court, having regard to the means of the debtor or hirer and any surety, considers reasonable[6];
(b) the remedying by the debtor or hirer of any breach of a regulated agreement (other than non-payment of money) within such period as the court may specify[7].

The position under s 129 is amplified by s 130 which contains supplemental provisions about time orders.

The following propositions have been judicially stated in relation to time orders[8]:

(a) When a time order is applied for, or a possession order sought of land to which a regulated agreement applies, the court must first consider whether it is just to make a time order. This involves consideration of all the circumstances and of the positions of the creditor as well as the debtor[9].
(b) When a time order is made it should normally be for a stipulated period on account of temporary financial difficulty. If, despite the giving of time, the debtor is unlikely to be able to resume payment of the total indebtedness by at least the amount of the contractual instalments, no time order should be made. In such circumstances it will be more equitable to allow the regulated agreement to be enforced[10].
(c) When a time order is made relating to the non-payment of money:
    (i) the 'sum owed'[11] means every sum which is due under the agreement[12], but where possession proceedings have been brought by the creditor that will normally comprise the total indebtedness[13], and
    (ii) the court must consider what instalments would be reasonable both as to amount and timing, having regard to the debtor's means.
(d) The court may include in a time order any amendment of the agreement which it considers just to both parties and which is a consequence of a term of the order[14]. If the rate of interest is amended, it is relevant that smaller instalments will result both in a liability to pay interest on accumulated arrears and, on the other hand, in an extended period of repayment[15]. However, to some extent the high rate of interest usually payable under regulated agreements already takes account of the risk that difficulties in repayment may occur.
(e) If a time order is made when the sum owed is the whole of the outstanding balance due under the loan, there will inevitably be consequences for the term of the loan or for the interest rate or both.
(f) If justice requires the making of a time order, the court should suspend any possession order that it also makes, so long as the terms of the time order are complied with.

It is thus clear that the court's powers in making a time order are not—at least in (the majority of) cases where the loan is secured by a land mortgage and the creditor has brought a possession action in exercise of his right to realise the total indebtedness secured by the charge on the property[16]—limited to rescheduling existing arrears (as distinct from sums not yet due but to become payable in the future). Indeed, the court's powers extend to altering the rate of interest payable by the debtor or hirer or even providing that no further interest should accrue[17].

1 Section 129(1)(a).
2 Ie a notice served under s 87(1), as to which see **10.49**.
3 The pre-enforcement notices served in cases not involving default: see **10.48**. Section 129(1)(b).
4 Section 129(1)(c).
5 For the meaning of this expression, see n 11.
6 Section 129(2)(a).
7 Section 129(2)(b).

8 *Southern & District Finance plc v Barnes* [1996] 1 FCR 679, 27 HLR 691, CA.
9 See also *First National Bank plc v Syed* [1991] 2 All ER 250, CA in which it was stated (by Dillon LJ at 256) that the court must take into account any previous history of default and of sporadic payments and the existence of real, as opposed to speculative, evidence of the ability of the debtor to make good the default.
10 Time orders extending over very long periods of time are usually better avoided. However, the Court of Appeal in *Southern and District Finance plc v Barnes* (1995) 27 HLR 691, CA upheld the decision of the trial judge to reschedule payments over a period of 15 years. Further, the broad language of s 129 should be so construed as to permit the county court to make such order as seems to it just in all the circumstances: *Director General of Fair Trading v First National Bank plc* [2001] UKHL 52, [2001] 3 WLR 1297, HL per Lord Bingham of Cornhill at para 28.
11 The expression used in s 129(2)(a).
12 Thus, the basic position (which, as will be seen, is significantly altered, where the loan is secured and possession is sought by the creditor) is that 'sums owed' in s 129(2)(a) refers *only* to sums which the lender is then entitled to recover by action, ie those presently payable (as opposed to in the future).
13 Because, as a matter of law as well as of common sense, when a creditor brings a possession action, he thereby demands payment of the whole of the sum outstanding under the charge, notwithstanding that he does not expressly call in the loan: *Southern & District Finance plc v Barnes* (1995) 27 HLR 691, CA, per Leggatt LJ at 697, applying *Smith v Smith* [1891] 3 Ch 550 at 552.
14 See s 136 as to power to vary regulated agreements, discussed at **10.82**.
15 Note, however, that the court can order that no additional interest should be payable beyond that which has already accrued: *Southern and District Finance plc v Barnes* (1995) 27 HLR 691, CA; *Director General of Fair Trading v First National Bank plc* [2001] UKHL 52, [2001] 3 WLR 1297, HL per Lord Bingham of Cornhill at para 29. See, further, **10.82,** n 3.
16 And also in cases involving a hire-purchase or conditional sale agreement only, in relation to which it is expressly provided that a time order may deal with sums which, although not payable by the debtor at the time the order is made, would if the agreement continued in force become payable under it subsequently: s 130(2).
17 The county court cases of *Ashbroom Facilities v Bodley* [1992] CCLR 31 and *J&J Securities Ltd v Lee* [1994] CCLR 44 (in both of which the loan was secured by a mortgage) were therefore wrongly decided. Cf *Cedar Holdings Ltd v Jenkins* [1988] CCLR 34 and *Cedar Holdings v Thompson* [1993] CCLR 7 (both county court).

Protection orders

10.80 The court, if invited to do so by the creditor or owner under a regulated agreement, is empowered to make such orders as it thinks just for the protection of any property belonging to the applicant, or of property subject to any security[1].

1 Section 131.

Special powers in relation to hire, hire-purchase and conditional sale agreements

10.81 If they fall within the definition of a regulated agreement, these transactions attract the operation of special powers of the court which are set out in ss 132[1] and 133[2].

1 Financial relief for the hirer under a regulated consumer hire agreement.
2 Containing equivalent provisions for cases of hire-purchase and conditional sale (return and transfer orders). See also s 134, which caters for evidence of adverse detention in cases of this kind.

Power to vary agreements and securities

10.82 Section 136 of the Act allows the court to vary or amend any agreement or security, in such manner as it considers just, in consequence of a term of *any* order made by it under the Act[1].

The phrase 'in consequence of a term' is of crucial importance: unless the contemplated amendment is truly a consequence of a term of the court's order and the making of it is also just, there is no power to make the variation[2]. Consequently, the power conferred by s 136 is not a general, freestanding one but, rather, is merely ancillary to the court's other powers under the Act[3].

1 Whether the order be an enforcement order under s 127, a time order under s 129 or otherwise.
2 *Southern & District Finance plc v Barnes* (1995) 27 HLR 691, CA, per Leggatt LJ at 698.
3 Provided, however, that the amendment is a consequence of an order, the court should be ready to include (in a time order under s 129, as to which see **10.79**) any provision amending the credit agreement which it considers just to both parties. Thus, the court can provide that no additional interest should be payable beyond that which has already accrued: *Southern and District Finance plc v Barnes* (1995) 27 HLR 691, CA; *Director General of Fair Trading v First National Bank plc* [2001] UKHL 52, [2001] 3 WLR 1297, HL per Lord Bingham of Cornhill at para 29. Indeed, unless such a variation is ordered, there may well arise the unacceptable scenario of a borrower duly paying all the instalments ordered by the court but nonetheless discovering that, because of a contractual interest provision, his indebtedness continues to mount.

Extortionate credit bargains[1]

Loan agreements subject to these provisions

10.83 Sections 137–140 empower the court to reopen extortionate credit bargains. These sections have been described as the most radical within Pt IX of the Act[2].

The sections operate by means of distinction between the concepts of 'credit-bargain' and 'credit agreements'.

A 'credit agreement' is defined as any agreement between an individual (the 'debtor'), and any other person ('the creditor') by which the creditor provides the debtor with credit of any amount[3]. It follows that the provisions relating to extortionate credit bargains are not subject to the £25,000 limit which is integral to the definition of a regulated agreement and which applies generally throughout the Act.

Credit bargains are more esoterically defined: where no transaction, other than the credit agreement (as defined above), is to be taken into account in computing the total charge for credit[4] 'credit bargain' means the credit agreement itself[5]; where, however, one or more other transactions are to be so taken into account, it means the credit agreement and these other transactions collectively[6].

Accordingly, ss 137-140 apply to all loans—of any amount, including (for the avoidance of doubt) regulated and exempt agreements[7], small agreements[8], non-commercial agreements[9]—and all forms of mortgage—provided in every case that the credit is taken out by an individual[10].

These provisions are retrospective and apply to credit bargains whenever made[11].

1 For the setting aside of extortionate credit transactions under ss 244 and 343 of the Insolvency Act 1986, see **8.15** and **23.44**.

2 Goode [1975] CLJ 79, 118.
3 Section 137 (2) (a).
4 As to the 'total charge for credit' see s 20 and the Credit (Total Charge for Credit) Regulations 1980, SI 1980/51. The effect of these provisions is that subsequent variations of the rate of interest are not taken into account in determining the total charge for credit.
Therefore, changes in the original interest rate levied at the date of the credit agreement are irrelevant to the question of whether the credit bargain is extortionate: *Nash v Paragon Finance plc* [2001] EWCA Civ 1466, [2001] 44 LS Gaz R 36, CA, per Dyson LJ at paras 63 and 64.
5 Section 137 (2) (b) (i).
6 Section 137 (2) (b) (ii).
7 As to which see **10.16** ff.
8 As to which see **10.31**, n 2.
9 As to which see **10.33**, n 9.
10 They do not, however, apply to hire agreements (whether qualifying as consumer hire agreements or not.) See (1980) 130 NLJ 749 (Wilkinson).
11 Ie whether before or after the coming into force of the sections on 16 May 1977: Consumer Credit Act 1974, Sch 3, para 42.

Overview of court's power in relation to extortionate credit bargain

10.84 The general discretion is stated in s 137(1): if the court finds a credit bargain extortionate it may reopen the credit agreement so as to do justice between the parties.

Procedure, burden of proof and limitation period

10.85 It seems that an allegation of extortionate credit bargain has to be made by the debtor or any surety and that the court cannot raise the point itself[1]. Indeed, the situations in which an extortionate credit bargain may be reopened are prescribed as follows:

(a) on an application for the purpose made by the debtor or any surety to the High Court, county court of sheriff court[2];
(b) at the instance of the debtor or a surety in any proceedings to which the debtor and creditor are parties, being proceedings to enforce the credit agreement, any security relating to it, or any linked transaction[3]; or
(c) at the instance of the debtor or a surety in other proceedings in any court where the amount paid or payable under the credit agreement is relevant[4].

If the debtor or any surety alleges that the credit bargain is extortionate, it is for the creditor to prove the contrary[5].

The limitation period for a claim to reopen a credit bargain under s 139(2) is 12 years[6].

1 Note s 138(2) which speaks of regard being had to evidence adduced.
2 For cases in which the application can only be made to a county court, see ss 139(5)–(7). Section 139(1)(a).
3 Section 139(1)(b). See s 19(1) and **10.42**, n 1.
4 Section 139(1)(c).
5 Section 171(7).
6 *Rahman v Sterling Credit Ltd* [2001] 1 WLR 496, (2001) 81 P&CR D4, CA, observing that the cause of action arises out of the provisions of the Act and is thus an action on a 'specialty' within the meaning of the Limitation Act 1980, s 8. In *Nash v Paragon Finance plc* [2001] EWCA Civ 466, [2001] 44 LS Gaz R 36, CA, the issue as to whether the decision in *Rahman* proceeded on the basis of an incorrect concession that a claim under s 139 is an action upon a specialty was left undecided.

Extortionate credit bargain: definition

10.86 Under s 138(1) a credit bargain is extortionate *either* if it requires the debtor (or a relative of his) to make unconditional or contingent payments which are grossly extortionate[1], *or* if it otherwise grossly contravenes ordinary principles of fair dealing.

1 Decisions under the Moneylenders Acts ('harsh and unconscionable'), for which see earlier editions of this work, do not assist : see *A Ketley Ltd v Scott* [1981] ICR 241; *Davies v Directloans Ltd* [1986] 2 All ER 783, [1986] 1 WLR 823.

Factors to be taken into account in determining whether credit bargain extortionate

10.87 Subsections (2) and (5) of s 138 set out the relevant factors in determining whether a credit bargain is extortionate[1]. In this context it is provided that regard shall be had by the court to such evidence as is adduced concerning:

(a) interest rates prevailing at the time the credit bargain was made[2];
(b) the factors mentioned in sub-ss (3)–(5);
(c) any other relevant considerations.

In turn, the factors specified in sub-ss (3)–(5) are:

(a) the age, experience, business capacity and state of health of the debtor[3]; and the degree to which, at the time of making the credit bargain, he was under financial pressure and the nature of that pressure[4];
(b) the degree of risk accepted by the creditor, having regard to the value of any security provided[5]; his relationship to the debtor[6]; and whether or not a colourable cash price was quoted for any goods or services included in the credit bargain[7];
(c) in relation to a linked transaction[8], how far the transaction was reasonably required for the protection of the debtor or the creditor, or was in the interest of the debtor[9].

It should be noted that the factors relevant in determining whether a credit bargain is extortionate are cumulative, not alternatives.

1 See, generally [1975] CLJ 79, 120–121 (Goode); (1975) 39 Conv (NS) 67, 111–112 (Adams); (1980) 130 NLJ 749 (Wilkinson); (1986) 136 NLJ 796 (Wilkinson); and Goode *Consumer Credit Law and Practice*; Guest and Lloyd *Encyclopaedia of Consumer Credit Law.*
2 Therefore, variations in rates of interest are not to be taken into account when deciding whether a credit bargain is extortionate; regard may only be had to the original interest rate: *Nash v Paragon Finance plc* [2001] EWCA Civ 466, [2001] 44 LS Gaz R 36, CA.
3 Section 138(3)(a).
4 Section 138(3)(b).
5 Section 138(4)(a).
6 Section 138(4)(b).
7 Section 138(4)(c).
8 See s 19(1) and **10.42**, n 1.
9 Section 138(5).

Prevailing interest rates

10.88 To enable a proper comparison of the rate of interest levied under the credit bargain in question and prevailing interest rates generally, it will invariably be necessary for the true rate of interest payable to be determined[1] and it will be usual to show the annual percentage rate (APR) calculated according to the appropriate statutory method as if (where it is not) the credit bargain were a credit agreement not exceeding £25,000[2]. In considering prevailing interest rates at the time when the credit bargain was made, like must be compared with like[3], so that interest rates appropriate to building society or bank loans will not necessarily be relevant to second mortgage finance company loans[4]. If the terms of the loan, including the interest rates, were the normal terms on which the borrower could obtain finance in the circumstances at the time, then the interest rate will not be extortionate[5]. The mere fact that the agreement provides for a variable rate of interest does not make the agreement extortionate[6]. It should be noted that, in order to fall foul of the 1974 Act, the interest rates levied must be grossly exorbitant. They are not merely required to be exorbitant. Therefore, the mere fact that rates may be high, even unreasonably high, is insufficient.[7]

A provision for a dual rate of interest, where the borrower is entitled to take advantage of a discounted rate if, but only if, all repayments are made on time, may grossly contravene the principles of fair dealing and thus represent an extortionate bargain if the rates themselves are relatively high and, further, the substantial differential between the discounted interest rate and the rate applicable in the event of default is not based on the loss suffered by the lender through delayed receipt of the monies[8].

The relationship between s 138 (1) (a) 'payments grossly exorbitant' and s 139(2) 'sums in excess of that fairly due and reasonable' is a matter of some debate[9] but it would seem to be a proper construction that a payment is not per se a grossly exorbitant one merely because it is in excess of what the court would consider fairly due and reasonable.

Because, as noted above, the factors of which account must be taken are cumulative, what might appear at first sight to be a grossly exorbitant rate of interest may in fact not be so in the light of the borrower's circumstances, the risk to the lender and the inadequacy of the security[10].

1 *Castle Phillips Finance Co Ltd v Singh* unreported (Cty Ct) referred to in the looseleaf texts mentioned in **10.87**, n 1.

2 See *Davies v Directloans Ltd* [1986] 2 All ER 783, [1986] 1 WLR 823, Ch D. See also the Consumer Credit (Total Charge for Credit) Regulations 1980, SI 1980/51 (as amended) and the Consumer Credit Tables.

3 *A Ketley Ltd v Scott* [1981] ICR 241; *Woodstead Finance Ltd v Petrou* [1986] FLR 158, [1986] NLJ Rep 188, CA; *Davies v Directloans Ltd* [1986] 2 All ER 783, [1986] 1 WLR 823, Ch D.

4 However the fact that the allegedly extortionate rate of interest was not far out of line with bank/building society rates will be relevant: see *Davies v Directloans Ltd* [1986] 2 All ER 783, [1986] 1 WLR 823, Ch D.

5 See *A Ketley Ltd v Scott* [1981] ICR 241 (48 per cent pa); *Woodstead Finance Ltd v Petrou* [1986] FLR 158, [1986] NLJ Rep 188, CA (42.5 per cent pa) (although in this case only the creditor adduced evidence of prevailing rates); *Condunell Ltd v Gallon* [1986] QB 1184, [1986] 1 All ER 429, CA (40 per cent pa); *Davies v Directloans Ltd* [1986] 2 All ER 783, [1986] 1 WLR 823, Ch D (21.6 per cent APR). In none of these cases was the rate held to be extortionate.

However, in *Shahabinia v Gyachi* (1988, unreported) unsecured loans of £3,000, £2,000 and £3,000 reserved rates of interest of 104 per cent, 78 per cent and 156 per cent respectively. It was found that there was a low risk of default and the loans were not made in a commercial context. The trial judge set a rate of 15 per cent but the Court of Appeal fixed the rate at 30 per cent.

Further, in *Castle Phillips & Co v Wilkinson* [1992] CCLR 83 (Cty Ct) a bridging loan of £21,000 for a period of between 4 and 6 months was made. The interest rate was at least 50 per cent. The borrowers were inexperienced in business, had no real independent advice and were not warned to obtain such advice. The loan was fully secured. The interest rate was reduced to 20 per cent, being the rate charged by a building society (15 per cent) plus one-third to reflect the short-term nature of the loan.

See also *Barcabe v Edwards* [1983] CCLR 11 (Cty Ct): 100 per cent interest reduced to 40 per cent.

6 *First National Securities Ltd v Bertrand* [1980] CCLR 5 (Cty Ct).

7 *Nash v Paragon Finance plc* [2001] EWCA Civ 1466, [2001] 44 LS Gaz R 36, CA, per Dyson LJ at para 69 (obiter). In that case the Court of Appeal would have held (if, contrary to its view, variations in interest rates could be taken into account in deciding whether a credit bargain is extortionate) that a disparity of 4 per cent between the rates charged by the lender in question and those charged by other lenders at the time was not such as to make the rates grossly exorbitant.

8 *Falco Finance Ltd v Gough* (1999) 17 Tr LR 526, [1999] CCLR 16 (Cty Ct): loan of £30,000 repayable over 25 years; monthly repayments £449 (13.99 per cent) or £324 (8.99 per cent). The dual rate scheme was remarkable in that the higher rate was triggered in the event of the most trivial default by the mortgagor and, moreover, the lower rate would not subsequently be restored, even if all the arrears were discharged.

9 *First National Securities Ltd v Bertrand* [1980] CCCR 5 (Cty Ct).

10 See *A Ketley Ltd v Scott* [1981] ICR 241; *Davies v Directloans Ltd* [1986] 2 All ER 783, [1986] 1 WLR 823, Ch D.

Other factors

10.89 The factors set out in sub-ss (3)–(5) of s 138 really speak for themselves. Those in sub-s (3) (ie age, health, experience, pressure etc) are all factors relevant to undue influence or unconscionable bargains[1]. For the aged or youthful borrower the lender will have to be more careful and give a full explanation. So long as the lender applies its standard terms to all borrowers (and these terms are reasonable) and does not seek to impose special terms on the particular borrower it is considered unlikely that the agreement will be upset on this ground alone.

1 For relevant cases on age etc see *Condunell Ltd v Gallon* **10.88**, n 5; *Davies v Directloans Ltd* **10.88**, n 2; and on pressure, see *Wills v Wood* [1984] CCLR 7, 128 Sol Jo 222, CA; *Davies v Directloans Ltd.*

Gross contravention of ordinary principles of fair dealing

10.90 Besides being extortionate because payments are grossly exorbitant, a credit bargain may be extortionate because it otherwise grossly contravenes ordinary principles of fair dealing[1]. 'Extortionate' is comprehensively defined by s 138 by reference to the matters therein set out and the test is not whether the creditor has acted in a morally reprehensible manner[2]. A bargain is not extortionate merely because the borrower has been unwise[3].

In the mortgage context it is uncertain whether this head goes beyond the existing grounds for invalidating a mortgage or a term thereof, eg penalties and unconscionable bargains etc or undue influence[4]. A possible example of where it might apply is if security were taken over a debtor's property with knowledge that the debtor was likely to default and that the creditor would then have resort to the security[5].

1 Section 138 (1) (b).

2 *Davies v Directloans Ltd* [1986] 2 All ER 783 at 789.

3 *Wills v Wood* (1984) 128 Sol Jo 222; [1984] CCCR 7, CA.

4 See **13.22**, et seq.

5 *Encyclopaedia of Consumer Credit Law*, note to s 138.

Discretion vested in the court

10.91 Section 137 (1) provides that if the court finds a credit bargain extortionate it *may* reopen the agreement. The court therefore has a residual discretion not to reopen the agreement. The court might refuse to reopen an extortionate credit bargain because, for example, of the delay in the borrower's application[1], his deceit in failing to disclose his true financial position[2] or his having obtained the credit by false representations[3].

1 The acceptance by the borrower of the terms of the loan for a long time may be a relevant consideration.
2 *A Ketley Ltd v Scott* [1981] ICR 241.
3 *First National Securities Ltd v Bertrand* [1980] CCCR 5 (Cty Ct) and *Premier Finance Co Ltd v Gravesande* [1985] CCLR 1 (Cty Ct).

Specific powers of court in reopening extortionate credit bargain

10.92 In reopening the agreement in question the court may adopt (by order) certain procedures for relieving the debtor or a surety from payment of any sum in excess of that fairly due and reasonable. These powers are set out in s 139(2) and comprise:

(a) the power to direct that accounts be taken between any person[1];
(b) the power to set aside any obligation (in whole or in part) imposed on a debtor or surety by the credit bargain or any related agreement[2];
(c) the power to require repayments by the creditor[3];
(d) the power to direct the return to the surety of any property provided as security[4]; and
(e) the power to alter the terms of the credit agreement or of any security instrument[5].

The court is not precluded from making an order reopening a credit bargain by the fact that the effect of its order is to place a burden on the creditor in respect of an advantage unfairly enjoyed by another person who is a party to a linked transaction[6]. However, an order made under s 139(2) cannot alter the effect of any judgment[7].

1 Section 139 (2) (a).
2 Section 139 (2) (b).
3 Section 139 (2) (c).
4 Section 139 (2) (d).
5 Section 139 (2) (e).
6 Section 139 (3).
7 Section 139(4). See *Cohen v Jonesco* [1926] 1 KB 119; revsd [1926] 2 KB 1, CA and *Rahman v Sterling Credit Ltd* [2001] 1 WLR 496, 81 P & CR D4, CA (possession order could not be set aside).

Miscellaneous: interpretation

10.93 Lastly, mention should be made of s 140 which provides that where the credit agreement in question is not a regulated agreement, expressions used in ss 137–139 which, apart from this section, apply only to regulated agreements, shall be construed as nearly as may be as if the credit agreement were a regulated agreement.

The object of this provision is to accommodate within ss 137–139, by way of analogy, certain concepts which are utilised within these sections but which the Act otherwise defines solely in terms of regulated agreements. Since ss 137–139 are not limited to regulated agreements, s 140 is necessary in order to permit analogous images of such concepts as the 'linked transaction' to operate within the sphere of these sections.

ANCILLARY CREDIT BUSINESSES

10.94 These are defined by s 145 and regulated by Pt X of the Act. Their relevance to the law of mortgage is oblique rather than immediate and the reader is referred to specialised works[1] for further information. However, it should be noted that a regulated agreement made by a debtor or hirer upon introduction by an unlicensed credit-broker[2] is enforceable against him only by order of the Director-General of Fair Trading[3].

1 Goode *Consumer Credit Law and Practice*; Guest and Lloyd *Encyclopaedia of Consumer Credit Law*.
2 As defined in ss 145 (2), (3) and (4).
3 Section 149 (1), (2); and for the procedure in making orders, see s 149(3), (4) and (5).

SUPPLEMENTAL PROVISIONS

10.95 Part XII of the Act embodies a whole assortment of supplemental rules, including such matters as: the prohibition on disclosure of information about individuals without their consent[1]; the duty of persons deemed to be agents[2]; the service of documents[3]; amplification of the powers the Secretary of State may exercise by statutory instrument[4]; clarificatory measures concerning 'associates'[5], certain multipartite agreements[6] and the meaning of pre-existing and contemplated arrangements between creditor and supplier[7] and definitions of the novel vocabulary used throughout the Act[8].

1 Such information being 'obtained under or by virtue of this Act': s 174 (1). For exceptions see s 174 (3), (4).
2 Section 175.
3 Section 176. Note that under s 176 (7), s 9 of the Administration of Estates Act 1925 is not to be construed as authorising service on the probate judge.
4 Sections 179 to 182.
5 Section 184.
6 Sections 185 (agreement with more than one debtor or hirer) and 186 (agreement with more than one creditor or owner).
7 Section 187. It will be recalled that whether or not such arrangements exist dictates whether any given agreement is a debtor-creditor-supplier agreement (s 12) or a debtor-creditor agreement (s 13): see **10.24** and **10.25**.
8 Sections 188 and 189.

Chapter 11

Second and subsequent mortgages

Historical position

11.1 Before 1926 there could only be one legal mortgage of freehold land and all subsequent mortgages of the same land were equitable[1].

In the case of leasehold land, where the first mortgage had been made by way of assignment, subsequent mortgages were also necessarily equitable. Where, however, the first mortgage of leasehold land had been made by sub-demise, subsequent legal mortgages could be made by further sub-demises, each generally being one day longer than the previous one.

1 See **3.2**.

Present position

11.2 Since 1925 the mortgagor of land retains a legal estate therein and therefore subsequent mortgages can now be legal in all cases, ie irrespective of whether the land is freehold or leasehold. Indeed, second equitable mortgages are now very rare.

Second and subsequent legal mortgages are, like first mortgages, created either by demise or sub-demise (as the case may be) or, more usually, by charge expressed to be by way of legal mortgage.

When made by demise or sub-demise each successive mortgage is generally for a term of years one day longer than the previous mortgage[1].

1 See the Law of Property Act 1925, ss 85(2)(b) and 86(2)(b); **3.3** and **3.5**.

Form

11.3 A second or subsequent mortgage should recite the mortgagor's title and the state of the prior mortgage debt or debts. This gives the mortgagee a remedy under the covenants for title implied by the mortgagor mortgaging as beneficial owner should a larger sum than that recited be owing. The mortgage should be made subject to the prior mortgage or mortgages. The statutory power of sale may be made exercisable in the event that interest under any prior mortgage is in arrears for a specified number of days. The mortgage should also include a power for the mortgagee to settle with prior mortgagees and to redeem their securities and to charge the costs of so doing upon the mortgaged property.

Protection: title deeds and registration

Unregistered land

11.4 The first (or other prior) mortgagee will usually have the title deeds, but if he does not then the second (or subsequent) mortgagee should obtain them. A second mortgagee has the right to inspect and make copies of title deeds in the custody of the first mortgagee[1].

If a prior mortgagee holds the deeds, the subsequent mortgage should be registered as a land charge. If it is legal, it will be a puisne mortgage (ie one unprotected by deposit of deeds) and falls to be registered as a Class C(i) land charge[2]. If, on the other hand, it is equitable, it should be registered as a Class C(iii) general equitable charge.

1 Law of Property Act 1925, ss 96(1) and 205(1)(xvi). He will, of course, generally have examined the deeds and the prior mortgage before completion.
2 Land Charges Act 1972, s 2(4). A priority notice should have been lodged at least 15 days prior to completion. See, further, **3.106** and **24.3**, et seq as to registration generally.

Registered land

11.5 If the prior charge has been registered, the land certificate will have been deposited at the Registry[1] and the second mortgage, if a legal mortgage, can be registered and a charge certificate in respect thereof will be issued. (For the priorities of/between registered charges, see **4.23** and **24.69** et seq.)

If, on the other hand, the prior mortgage was by way of deposit of the land certificate[2], this will be held by the depositee and, since the second mortgagee will not be able to deposit the land certificate at the registry, the second mortgage can only be protected by caution[3] or (if the prior mortgagee is content to make the land certificate available) notice[4].

The effect of protection by notice of deposit or ordinary notice is to give priority to the prior mortgage. But where the prior mortgage has not been protected by notice there is nothing in the Land Registration Act or Rules to indicate which has priority or whether actual notice is relevant[5]. It seems that if a subsequent mortgage is protected before a prior mortgage is protected by notice the subsequent mortgage has priority even where the subsequent mortgagee had actual notice of the prior mortgage.

1 Land Registration Act 1925, s 65.
2 Note, however, that since 27 September 1989 the mere deposit of a land certificate has been ineffective to create a charge and a purported mortgage by deposit is invalid: *United Bank of Kuwait plc v Sahib* [1997] Ch 107, CA; see also **3.100** and **4.30**.
3 Under the Land Registration Act 1925, s 54.
4 Under the Land Registration Act 1925, s 49(1)(c).
5 See *Re White Rose Cottage* [1964] Ch 483 at 492, [1964] 1 All ER 169 at 175; revsd [1965] Ch 940, [1965] 1 All ER 11, CA.

Notice

11.6 On completion, a second or subsequent mortgagee should give notice of the mortgage to the first and any other prior mortgagee. The purpose of such notice is to protect the second or subsequent mortgagee against tacking[1]. This is because (in the absence of agreement between the mortgagees in question) the right to tack exists only where the prior mortgagee had no notice of the subsequent mortgage when he made the further advance[2].

Although in the case of a second or subsequent mortgage of unregistered land registration as a land charge generally constitutes actual notice[3], a mortgagee under a mortgage made expressly for securing a current account or other further advances is not deemed to have notice of a mortgage merely by reason that it was registered as a land charge if it was not so registered at the time when the original mortgage was created or when the last search (if any) by or on behalf of the mortgagee was made, whichever last happened[4]. It is thus particularly important that in such cases the second or subsequent mortgagee gives notice of his mortgage to the prior mortgagee.

Furthermore, the giving of actual notice to a prior mortgagee who holds the title deeds will give him no excuse if, on the discharge of his mortgage, he delivers them to the mortgagor instead of to the subsequent mortgagee[5].

1 Namely, the right of a prior mortgagee to make further advances which rank in priority to subsequent mortgages (whether legal or equitable): see the Law of Property Act 1925, s 94 and **24.83** et seq. Section 94 does not apply to charges registered under the Land Registration Act 1925: s 94(4). These are instead governed by the Land Registration Act 1925, s 30 as to which see **24.88**.

2 As to unregistered land, see the Law of Property Act 1925, s 94(1)(b). There is an exception to this rule in cases where the prior mortgage imposes an obligation on the mortgagee to make further advances: s 94(1)(c). In this event neither registration nor actual notice of any subsequent mortgage denies the mortgagee the right to tack. It is, however, considered that this scenario is uncommon. As to registered land, see the Land Registration Act 1925, s 30(1); again, notice plays an important role in determining the priority of advances. Further, s 30(3) has an effect similar to s 94(1)(c).

3 See Law of Property Act 1925, s 198 and **24.8**.

4 Section 94(2), as amended by the Law of Property (Amendment) Act 1926, s 7, Sch.

5 Section 96(2). Registration of the second mortgage does not for this purpose amount to notice: s 96(2) (proviso added by the Law of Property (Amendment) Act 1926, Sch).

Remedies of second or subsequent mortgagee

11.7 A second or subsequent mortgagee has all the remedies of a first mortgagee[1], but except for a claim on the personal covenant he will not generally be able to exercise his remedies whilst the first or any other prior mortgagee is exercising the same remedies. So he cannot take possession if the first mortgagee is already in possession or has appointed a receiver[2], and if a subsequent mortgagee sells he must sell subject to prior mortgages[3], unless the prior mortgagees agree to join in the conveyance and receive part of the purchase moneys sufficient to discharge their respective mortgages[4]. Alternatively the second mortgagee can take a transfer of any prior mortgage.

1 For remedies, see Part V. The position of the second mortgagee is dealt with specifically in that part where it differs from that of a first mortgagee.

2 However the existence of an order for possession in favour of a prior mortgagee does not prevent a court from ordering possession in favour of a subsequent mortgagee: *Universal Showcards and Display Manufacturing v Brunt* (1984) 128 Sol Jo 581, [1984] LS Gaz R 1603, CA. See also *Cassel Arenz & Co v Taylor* (1968) 209 Estates Gazette 357: usual possession order made inserting the words "subject to the rights of the first mortgagee". See further *Berkshire Capital Funding Ltd v Street* (1999) 27 P&CR 321, D23, (2000) 32 HLR 373, [1999] 2 EGLR 92, CA: possession order made subject to the interests of the prior mortgagee, including the interests of that person as landlord in respect of a lease granted under the Law of Property Act 1925, s 99. In that case it was noted that a warrant of possession would probably not lie in respect of such an order.

3 But see the Law of Property Act 1925, s 50; **28.74**.

4 The first mortgagee will be entitled to rely on the six months' interest rule: see **28.34**.

Discharge

11.8 A second or subsequent mortgage is discharged in the same manner as a first mortgage[1].

1 See Part VIII.

Generally

11.9 The disadvantages of second and subsequent mortgages are generally stated to be the risks of tacking[1] and consolidation[2], the absence of the title deeds[3] and the fact that the first mortgagee may sell or foreclose the property.

However, in the case of an ordinary second or subsequent mortgage (eg of a private dwelling-house) the first risks are slight and, as explained above, the second or subsequent mortgagee of land can to a large extent protect his position by registering his mortgage and giving notice of his mortgage to the prior mortgagee. Further, the risks attendant on a sale of the property can be minimised by a proper valuation, proper searches and by ascertaining the amount due under a previous mortgage or mortgages. There may well be sufficient equity in the property in question to enable a second mortgage for an appropriate advance to be taken, with the second mortgagee adequately secured (even taking into interest accruing on the earlier mortgage)[4]. Finally, foreclosure is rarely employed as a remedy today and the rights of subsequent mortgagees where a prior mortgagee is claiming foreclosure are dealt with subsequently[5].

1 As to which see **11.6**, n 1.
2 Namely, the right of a prior mortgagee holding more than one mortgage created by the same mortgagor to consolidate the mortgages and insist that any redemption is of all the mortgages: see Chapter 27. By the Law of Property Act 1925, s 93 the right to consolidate must be expressly preserved in one or more of the mortgage deeds; otherwise the mortgagor who seeks to redeem any one mortgage is entitled to do so without paying any money due under any separate mortgage made by him, or by any person through whom he claims, solely on property other than that comprised in the mortgage which he seeks to redeem.
3 As to which see **11.4**.
4 On second mortgages see the Report of the Committee on the Enforcement of Judgment Debts (Payne Committee) 1969, paras 1345 ff; and the Report of the Committee on Consumer Credit (Crowther Report) 1971, 2. 4. 48–53; 6. 4. 22–25. It should not be forgotten that a prior mortgagee exercising a power of sale owes a duty of care to obtain the proper value of the property at the time he sells it: *Cuckmere Brick Co Ltd v Mutual Finance Ltd* [1971] Ch 949.
5 See Chapter 22. As to a further or subsequent security effecting a waiver of a prior security, see Chapter 31.

PART II

PARTIES TO MORTGAGES

Chapter 12

Parties to mortgages

ABSOLUTE OWNERS

Absolute owner

12.1 Generally an absolute owner of property, who is not under any incapacity[1] can, in exercise of the power of alienation incident to his ownership[2], mortgage the property[3]. The general rule is subject to exceptions which are dealt with elsewhere in this work. For example, government salaries and the like, and permanent maintenance of a former spouse after divorce cannot be mortgaged[4].

1 As to minors and mentally ill people, see **12.128–12.131** and **12.140–12.143**.
2 Co Litt 223a. For restrictions on alienation, see **13.56**.
3 For forms of mortgage by absolute owners, see 28 *Forms and Precedents* (5th edn, 1999 reissue) Mortgages, and the Appendix.
4 See further **13.54–13.55**.

Co-owners

12.2 Where more persons than one own land they may be beneficially interested in the land either jointly or as tenants in common, but in either case the legal estate in the land will be held by not more than four of the co-owners as joint tenants upon trust for the co-owners as joint tenants or tenants in common, as the case may be[1]. The co-owners can mortgage the land under the statutory powers of trustees[2]. However, where the same persons are both the trustees and the beneficiaries there is no need to rely on those powers as they can mortgage by virtue of their beneficial ownership[3].

Where a legal mortgage is made to several persons the legal estate vests in the mortgagees or the first four named as joint tenants upon trust[4]. In mortgages to several mortgagees made after 1881 to them jointly or in which the mortgage moneys are expressed to belong to them on a joint account, the mortgage moneys are, as between the mortgagees and the mortgagor, deemed to be and remain moneys belonging to the mortgagees on a joint account, unless a contrary intention is expressed in the mortgage[5]. Persons dealing in good faith with several mortgagees may assume, unless the contrary is expressed in the instruments relating to the mortgage, that the mortgagees are entitled to the mortgage moneys on a joint account[6].

1 Law of Property Act 1925, ss 35 and 36 as amended; Settled Land Act 1925, s 36 as amended; Trustee Act 1925, s 34 as amended. Where a co-owner is a minor, see Law of Property Act 1925, s 1(6) and Trusts of Land and Appointment of Trustees Act 1997, s 2(6), Sch 1, para 9(1) as well as the provisions first mentioned.
2 For the mortgage powers of trustees, see **12.112** ff.
3 For forms of mortgage by co-owners, see 28 *Forms and Precedents* (5th edn, 1999 reissue) Mortgages, and the Appendix. For mortgages of their beneficial interests, see **7.13**. A purported mortgage of the property by one co-owner may operate as a mortgage of the mortgagor's beneficial interest (see **3.89**) and in the case of a beneficial joint tenancy probably severs the joint tenancy: *Thames Guaranty Ltd v Campbell* [1985] QB 210, [1984] 1 All ER 144; affd [1985] QB 210, [1984] 2 All ER 585, CA; cf *First National Securities Ltd v Hegerty* [1985] QB 850, [1984] 1 All ER 139; affd [1985] QB 850, [1984] 3 All ER 641, CA; in Australia, see *Clark v Raymore (Brisbane) Pty Ltd* [1982] Qd R 479 and generally (1967) 41 ALJ 61.
4 See the provisions in n 1.
5 Law of Property Act 1925, s 111; and see **14.24**.
6 Law of Property Act 1925, s 113 (1) (a); and see **14.16**. For forms of mortgage to two or more persons, see 28 *Forms and Precedents* (5th edn, 1999 reissue) Mortgages; and the Appendix. A contributory mortgage is a mortgage to several persons who each advance distinct sums (as compared to a mortgage to several trustees advancing money on joint account). In practice a contributory mortgage often takes the form of an ordinary joint account mortgage, the rights of the parties being defined by a declaration of trust in the mortgage or by a separate document. Thus separate covenants for payment of each sum advanced, and separate power of sale, etc are avoided. For forms of contributory mortgages, see 28 *Forms and Precedents* (5th edn, 1999 reissue) Mortgages.

MORTGAGES UNDER POWERS GENERALLY

Power to mortgage

12.3 A power to mortgage may be conferred expressly by one person on another. This may be done formally, for example by a power of attorney or a settlement of land, or informally, as where a person is appointed a agent for another. A power to authorise the raising of money on mortgage should specify that it is intended that the power has that effect. Nevertheless, a mortgage may be made under a general power, such as a power of attorney, the terms of which are sufficiently extensive[1].

The donor of a power of doubtful sufficiency may, however, by direction as to its exercise, preclude himself from disputing the validity of a security made under the power[2].

1 *Willis v Palmer* (1860) 7 CBNS 340; see also *Mostyn v Lancaster* (1883) 23 Ch D 583, but the general words may be restricted by the particular purpose of the instrument: *Lewis v Ramsdale* (1886) 55 LT 179. A general power to sell, assign and transfer is not sufficient to authorise a mortgage: *Australian Auxiliary Steam Clipper Co v Mounsey* (1858) 4 K & J 733; *Jonmenjoy Coondoo v Watson* (1884) 9 App Cas 561. For enduring powers of attorney, see Enduring Powers of Attorney Act 1985; for delegations by trustees, see Trustee Act 1925, s 25 and Trustee Delegation Act 1999.
2 *Perry v Holl* (1860) 2 Giff 138, 2 De GF & J 38; and see *Davies v Bolton & Co* [1894] 3 Ch 678.

Powers of limited owners and corporations

12.4 When a person is not the absolute owner of a property, he can create a security on it to last beyond his own beneficial interest (if any), only under some power or authority conferred upon him. Such power or authority may be created by statute, or by the party beneficially entitled (under power of attorney), or by some will or settlement by which the property was and remains settled. Moreover, in the case of a corporation, unless the instrument by which it was founded, or some statute, either expressly or impliedly authorises a mortgage, it cannot create one.

Exercise of a power

12.5 The power, even where explicit, must be exercised subject to the general terms of the instrument in which it is contained[1]. Where a mortgage is made under a provision that all mortgages shall be on an equal footing an undue advantage cannot be given to a creditor by a security upon other property belonging to the donees of the power[2]. A power, whether special or general, must be exercised only for purposes consistent with the object of the trust or undertaking for the furtherance of which it was given. Thus, a building society can only exercise its borrowing powers for the legitimate purposes of the society[3].

A mortgage purporting to be executed according to, but which is in contravention of, statutory powers, will be good by estoppel in favour of a purchaser for value without notice of the infirmity[4].

A mortgage is not invalid only because it is made to secure a debt originally contracted on an improper security, provided it is clear that the mortgage is to secure the money and not to secure the invalid transaction. A security made in excess of power, but by which an estate passes, will be treated as valid in a foreclosure action and must be set aside, if at all, by an independent proceeding[5].

A special power to mortgage is not inconsistent with the existence of a general right to mortgage property if the donees of the power are not prohibited from so doing and if they hold the property in a capacity and mortgage it for purposes which do not affect the exercise or the objects of the power[6].

Upon the principle that in equity whatever is agreed to be done, is done, effect will be given to an intention to create a security where the maker is of capacity to contract the debt, notwithstanding any mistake in the manner of doing it[7], or that it was done informally[8].

1 So that, for example, a corporation, having a general power by statute to mortgage its land, cannot mortgage the land which by the same Act it is bound to sell within a limited time.
2 *De Winton v Brecon Corpn* (1859) 26 Beav 533.
3 *Sinclair v Brougham* [1914] AC 398, HL; see also as to improper exercise, *Rigall v Foster* (1853) 18 Jur 39; *Eland v Baker* (1861) 29 Beav 137. See now **12.73**.
4 *Webb v Herne Bay Comrs* (1870) LR 5 QB 642; *Re Romford Canal Co* (1883) 24 Ch D 85.
5 *Scott v Colburn* (1858) 26 Beav 276.
6 Thus the directors of a company who have power to borrow on mortgage to a certain amount may mortgage the property of the company by debenture or deposit of deeds to secure a past debt (*Re Patent File Co, ex p Birmingham Banking Co* (1870) 6 Ch App 83; *Re Inns of Court Hotel Co* (1868) LR 6 Eq 82; *Re General Provident Assurance Co, ex p National Bank* (1872) LR 14 Eq 507), or to secure payment of purchase money (*Seligman v Prince* [1895] 2 Ch 617, CA).
7 *Re Queensland Land and Coal Co, Davis v Martin* [1894] 3 Ch 181.
8 *Webb v Herne Bay Comrs* (1870) LR 5 QB 642 at 654.

Effect of unauthorised security

12.6 If the maker of the security is not of capacity to contract the debt, as where borrowing is expressly forbidden or is authorised only subject to the performance of certain conditions, which have not been performed, or within a certain limit which has been exceeded, no debt will arise at law[1]. However, money borrowed or contracted to be paid irregularly on behalf of, but shown to have been bona fide applied in payment of liabilities or, a corporation, may be treated as an equitable debt bearing interest. The principle is either that, as the money was applied in payment of recoverable debts, no addition is made to the liabilities of the corporation, or that the lender should stand by subrogation in the place of the creditor who was paid[2]. However, the advance will not be recognised in the absence of evidence, which must be adduced by the lender, that the money was so applied[3]. So if a trustee improperly raises money by mortgage, although the security will be void against a mortgagee with notice, the latter may nevertheless be a creditor on the proceeds of the trust property to the extent to which the money lent was properly applied in administration[4].

1 *Chambers v Manchester and Milford Rly Co* (1864) 10 Jur NS 700; *Re Pooley Hall Colliery Co* (1869) 18 WR 201; *Landowners West of England and South Wales Land Drainage and Inclosure Co v Ashford* (1880) 16 Ch D 411; *Firbank's Executors v Humphreys* (1886) 18 QBD 54, CA.
2 *Sinclair v Brougham* [1914] AC 398 at 441, HL; cf *Re Wrexam, Mold and Connah's Quay Rly Co* [1899] 1 Ch 440, CA.
3 *Re National Permanent Benefit Building Society, ex p Williamson* (1869) 5 Ch App 309; *Blackburn Benefit Building Society v Cunliffe, Brooks & Co* (1882) 22 Ch D 61, CA.
4 *Devaynes v Robinson* (1857) 24 Beav 86 (mortgage instead of selling); *Paul v Speirway Ltd* [1976] Ch 220, [1976] 2 All ER 587. For other cases of subrogation, see **14.22**. As regards mortgages under powers, see **12.113.**

CORPORATIONS

BORROWING POWERS

Distinction between trading and other companies

12.7 The powers of a company formed under the Companies Acts[1] are limited by reference to the objects and purposes specified in the memorandum of association[2], and this principle applies to all companies created by statute for a particular purpose[3].

Generally an express power to borrow is inserted in the company's memorandum of association, but it is not always essential that powers should be expressly given[4] and a power of borrowing may be implied from the objects of the company. Thus an ordinary trading or commercial company may borrow money for the purposes of its undertaking, unless positively prohibited[5], and may mortgage its property for the purpose of securing the money borrowed[6]. But a non-trading company can borrow only if and when it is expressly authorised to do so[7]. A company limited by guarantee cannot charge the amounts which the members have undertaken to contribute in the event of a winding up[8].

1 See generally, 7(2) *Halsbury's Laws* (4th edn) (1996 reissue) Companies, paras 1233 ff. As to the effect of a mortgage by a company struck off the register at the time of the mortgage but subsequently restored to the register, see *Re Boxco Ltd* [1970] Ch 442, [1970] 2 All ER 183n.
2 *Ashbury Railway Carriage and Iron Co v Riche* (1875) LR 7 HL 653.
3 *Baroness Wenlock v River Dee Co* (1885) 10 App Cas 354 at 360, HL. A corporation created by royal charter has, prima facie, the power to do with its property all such acts as an ordinary person can do: *Jenkin v Pharmaceutical Society* [1921] 1 Ch 392 at 398. A company incorporated by a special Act of Parliament has the powers conferred by the special Act

and the Companies Clauses Consolidation Act 1845, s 38: see that Act generally and the Companies Clauses Acts 1863 and 1869; 7(2) *Halsbury's Laws* (4th edn) (1996 reissue) Companies, paras 1599 ff.

4 *Rolled Steel Products (Holdings) Ltd v British Steel Corpn* [1986] Ch 246 at 287, [1985] 3 All ER 52 at 80, CA.

5 *General Auction Estate & Monetary Co v Smith* [1891] 3 Ch 432.

6 *Re Patent Ivory Manufacturing Co, Howard v Patent Ivory Manufacturing Co* (1888) 38 Ch D 156.

7 *Re Badger, Mansell v Viscount Cobham* [1905] 1 Ch 568; and see *Rosemary Simmons Memorial Housing Association Ltd v United Dominions Trust Ltd* [1987] 1 All ER 281, [1986] 1 WLR 1440.

8 *Re Irish Club Co Ltd* [1906] WN 127; cf *Re Mayfair Property Co, Bartlett v Mayfair Property Co* [1898] 2 Ch 28, CA. Nor can reserve capital created under ss 120 and 124 of the Companies Act 1985 be charged.

Extent of the powers[1]

12.8 A limited company usually has under its memorandum of association express power to borrow money[2] and to secure the repayment thereof in such manner as the company shall think fit[3], and by the articles of association the exercise of the power is usually delegated to the directors, generally with a limitation[4] on the amount which can be borrowed without the sanction of a general meeting[5].

1 On substantive objects and ancillary powers, see *Rolled Steel Products (Holdings) Ltd v British Steel Corpn* [1986] Ch 246 at 288, [1985] 3 All ER 52 at 81, CA.

2 Where a secured loan is deliberately made by way of overdraft that is borrowing: *Cunliffe Brookes & Co v Blackburn Benefit Society* (1884) 9 App Cas 857, HL. If there is no express power to borrow or only a limited power the memorandum or articles should be altered: see Companies Act 1985, ss 4–6, 9.

3 Such a power enables the company to give a mortgage to a surety by way of indemnity, even where the surety is a director of the company: *Re Pyle Works (No 2)* [1891] 1 Ch 173.

4 A transaction which was within the objects of a company or which was capable of being performed as reasonably ancillary or incidental to the objects is not ultra vires merely because the directors carried out the transaction for purposes which were not within the objects of the company: *Rolled Steel Products (Holdings) Ltd v British Steel Corpn* [1986] Ch 246 at 295, [1985] 3 All ER 52 at 85. This case clarifies the distinction between corporate capacity and excess of directors' powers; see (1985) 48 MLR 109 (Gregory); [1985] CLJ 39 (Sealy); (1985) 6 Co Lawyer 155 (Clark).

5 For forms, see 9 *Forms and Precedents* (5th edn, 2000 reissue) Companies and 10 *Forms and Precedents* (5th edn, 2001 reissue) Companies. For the power of a company to mortgage its uncalled capital see, generally, *Newton v Debenture Holders of Anglo-Australian Investment Co* [1895] AC 244, PC.

Company's capacity not limited by its memorandum

12.9 The doctrine of ultra vires which resulted in an apparent act of a company being a nullity if the act was outside the powers of the company has been substantially abrogated by statutory provisions[1]. The general rule now is that the validity of an act done by a company may not be called into question on the ground of the lack of capacity of the company by reason of anything in the company's memorandum[2]. A member of a company may bring proceedings to restrain the doing of an act which would otherwise be beyond the company's capacity, but no such proceedings lie in respect of an act to be done in fulfilment of a legal obligation arising from a previous act of the company[3]. It remains the duty of the directors to observe any limitations on their powers flowing from the company's memorandum and action by the directors which would otherwise be beyond the company's capacity may only be ratified by the company by special resolution. A resolution ratifying such action does not affect any liability incurred by the directors or any other person and relief from any such liability must be agreed to separately by separate resolution[4].

1 The doctrine was first eroded by European Communities Act 1972 s 9(1), re-enacted as Companies Act 1985, s 35. The current provisions are in Companies Act 1985, s 35 (substituted by Companies Act 1989, s 108 with effect from 4 February 1991 but without retrospective effect) and Companies Act 1985, ss 35A, 35B (inserted by Companies Act 1989, s 108 with effect from 4 February 1991 but without retrospective effect).
2 Companies Act 1985, s 35(1) as substituted by Companies Act 1989, s 108. The general rule is restricted in its operation in the case of companies which are charities (by Charities Act 1993, s 65(1) and Companies Act 1989, s 112(3)) and Companies Act 1985, s 322A (which deals with the invalidity of certain transaction to which directors or their associates are parties) has effect notwithstanding Companies Act 1985, s 35.
3 Companies Act 1985, s 35(2) as substituted by the Companies Act 1989, s 108.
4 Companies Act 1985, s 35(3) as substituted.

Powers of directors to bind company

12.10 In favour of a person dealing with a company in good faith, the general rule now is that the power of the board of directors to bind the company, or authorise others to do so, is deemed to be free of any limitation under the company's constitution[1]. For these purposes, a person 'deals with' a company if he is a party to any transaction or other act to which the company is a party. A person is not regarded as acting in bad faith by reason only of his knowing that an act is beyond the powers of the directors under the company's constitution[2]. A person is presumed to have acted in good faith unless the contrary is proved[3]. These provisions as to the effect of limitations on the directors do not, however, affect any right of a member of a company to bring proceedings to restrain the doing of an act which is beyond the powers of the directors, but no such proceedings lie in respect of an act to be done in fulfilment of a legal obligation arising from a previous act of the company[4]. Nor do these provisions affect any liability incurred by the directors, or any other person, by reason of the directors exceeding their powers[5].

1 Companies Act 1985, s 35A(1) substituted by Companies Act 1989, s 108. For these purposes, the references to limitations on the directors' powers under the company's constitution include limitations deriving: (a) from a resolution of the company in general meeting or a meeting of any class of shareholders; or (b) from any agreement between the members of the company or of any class of shareholders: Companies Act 1985, s 35A, as substituted. The operation of s 35A is restricted by Charities Act 1993, s 65(1) and Companies Act 1989, s 112(3) in relation to companies which are charities and Companies Act 1985, s 322A has effect notwithstanding s 35A: s 35A(6).
2 Companies Act 1985, s 35A(2).
3 Section 35A(2). *Barclays Bank Ltd v TOSG Trust Fund* [1984] BCLC 1, 18 ('reasonableness is not a necessary ingredient of good faith', per Nourse J at first instance); see also *International Sales and Agencies Ltd v Marcus* [1982] 3 All ER 551, 559.
4 Section 35A(4).
5 Section 35A(5).

No duty to inquire as to capacity of company or authority of directors

12.11 A party to a transaction (such as a mortgage) with a company is not bound to inquire as to whether it is permitted by the company's memorandum or as to any limitations on the powers of the board of directors to bind the company or authorise others to do so[1].

Where ss 35, 35A and 35B of the Companies Act 1985 do not apply[2], the mortgagee should bear in mind the following points. If there are restrictions on the amount which may be borrowed, the lender must see that the limit is not exceeded, unless the limit is imposed by the articles and they provide that only express notice of any excess will invalidate the loan[3]. Where there are no restrictions on the exercise of the borrowing powers conferred by the company's public documents, the lender is not bound to look beyond these (and the register of mortgages and charges at the Companies Registry) and, finding that the company is empowered to borrow, may assume that it has done any preliminary acts, such as the passing of resolutions, which its memorandum or articles require[4], but where the power expressly provides what shall be evidence of the preliminary acts[5], or where the security would, on the face of the articles, be in excess of the directors' powers, unless a power is extended by the shareholders[6], the lender must see that what is necessary has been done[7].

Where the borrowing powers of directors are limited to a certain amount they cannot borrow beyond that amount so as to bind the company[8]. If, however, the borrowing, though in excess of their own powers, is not in excess of the powers of the company, the borrowing may be ratified by the company[9] and the company may be bound if the borrowing was within the ordinary ambit of the directors' authority[10].

Still dealing with those cases outside ss 35, 35A and 35B of the Companies Act 1985, if a company borrows money in circumstances which render the borrowing ultra vires no debt arises either at law or in equity and the lender cannot recover the money in an action for money had and received[11]. Where the borrowing powers of a company are limited, any security given for any amount lent to the company beyond the limit is void, even though the limit is subsequently increased[12], but where the security is given in respect of a loan which is to be applied in paying off other loans properly made to the company the limit is not exceeded[13].

1 Companies Act 1985, s 35B substituted by Companies Act 1989, s 108. In the case of an unregistered company: (a) for references to the memorandum or articles of association of a company there must be substituted references to any instrument constituting or regulating the company; (b) s 35B has effect as though it were expressed to be without prejudice to any rule of law which gives to a person dealing with a company incorporated by letters patent or by royal charter any greater protection in relation to the capacity of such a company than that afforded by s 35B: Companies (Unregistered Companies) Regulations 1985, SI 1985/680, reg 6(a), (c) (amended by SI 1990/2571).

2 For example, where the mortgage is entered into before the coming into effect of the relevant provisions or by reason of the operation of provisions relating to companies which are charities: Charities Act 1993, s 65(1); Companies Act 1989, s 112(3).

3 *Chapleo v Brunswick Permanent Benefit Society* (1881) 6 QBD 696, CA.

4 *Royal British Bank v Turquand* (1856) 6 E & B 327. See, further, as to the rule in this case and subsequent cases, *Buckley on the Companies Acts* (14th edn) pp 241 ff, and 433 ff, and see (1966) 30 Conv (NS) 123, 163 (Nock). The rule applies even where the secretary of the borrowing company knew of the irregularity, he being also secretary of the lending company: *Re Hampshire Land Co* [1896] 2 Ch 743, but where a director of the borrowing company is the lender he will be taken to have notice of non-compliance with internal regulations: *Re Patent Ivory Manufacturing Co, Howard v Patent Ivory Manufacturing Co* (1888) 38 Ch D 156 at 170; cf *Re Fireproof Doors Ltd* [1916] 2 Ch 142.

The company may also be bound where a director or other agent exceeds his actual authority, but the act is one within the ordinary ambit of the authority of such a person: see *Freeman and Lockyer v Buckhurst Park Properties (Mangal) Ltd* [1964] 2 QB 480, [1964] 1 All ER 630, CA; *Hely-Hutchinson v Brayhead Ltd* [1968] 1 QB 549, [1967] 3 All ER 98;

cf *Armagas Ltd v Mundogas SA* [1986] AC 717, [1985] 3 All ER 795, CA; affd [1986] AC 717, [1986] 2 All ER 385, HL, and see *Kilgobbin Mink Ltd v National Credit Co* [1980] IR 173.

5 *Fountaine v Carmarthen Rly Co* (1868) LR 5 Eq 316.

6 *Irvine v Union Bank of Australia* (1877) 2 App Cas 366, PC.

7 For other exceptions to the rule in *Royal British Bank v Turquand*, see *Buckley on the Companies Acts* (14th edn) pp 433 ff.

8 *Re Pooley Hall Colliery Co* (1869) 21 LT 690. The directors may be personally liable for breach of warranty of authority: *Chapleo v Brunswick Permanent Benefit Society*, above; *Whitehaven Joint Stock Banking Co v Reed* (1886) 54 LT 360, CA.

9 *Irvine v Union Bank of Australia*, above.

10 See n 5, above.

11 *Sinclair v Brougham* [1914] AC 398 at 426, HL, and see *Re Introductions Ltd* [1970] Ch 199, [1969] 1 All ER 887, CA.

12 *Fountaine v Carmarthen Rly Co*, above.

13 *Re Harris Calculating Machine Co, Sumner v Calculating Machine Co* [1914] 1 Ch 920, and see **12.6**, for the effect of unauthorised security.

Pre-incorporation contracts

12.12 The subject of pre-incorporation contracts (including contracts made by deed) is now governed by s 36C of the Companies Act 1985[1]. A contract which purports to be made by or on behalf of a company at a time when the company has not been formed has effect, subject to any agreement to the contrary, as one made with the person purporting to act for the company or as agent for it, and he is personally liable on the contract accordingly. This provision applies to the making of a deed as it applies to the making of a contract. Although the section specifically refers to a person being liable on the contract, it has been held that the section allows a person purporting to act on behalf of a non-existent company to enjoy rights under the contract made with the assistance of s 36C and the section is not confined to imposing liabilities on such a person[2]. In the case of a signed written contract, normally the person 'purporting to act' is the person who signed for the company; it is not necessary or appropriate to inquire as to who was 'the controlling mind' behind the transaction[2]. In the case of a contract for the sale or other disposition of an interest in land (to which s 2 of the Law of Property (Miscellaneous Provisions) Act 1989 applies) s 2 of the 1989 Act is satisfied where the contract is signed by the person who has the rights and liabilities by reason of s 36C of the 1985 Act[2]. A contract for the grant of a mortgage is within s 2 of the 1989 Act.

1 Section 36C was introduced by Companies Act 1989, s 130(4). Earlier provisions dealing with pre-incorporation contracts were contained in European Communities Act 1972, s 9(2) and Companies Act 1985, s 36(4). See *Phonogram Ltd v Lane* [1982] QB 938, [1981] 3 All ER 182, CA (on the earlier provision contained in European Communities Act 1972, s 9(2)); this decision also considers the earlier cases as to whether on its true analysis a transaction involved a purported contract on behalf of a non-existent company or an actual contract by some other existing person.

2 *Braymist Ltd v Wise Finance Co Ltd* [2001] EGCS 35.

Specific loan not a company asset

12.13 Where a loan of money was made to a company for a specific purpose, but that purpose failed, the money was to be held on resulting trust for the lender and was not a general asset of the company[1].

1 *Barclays Bank Ltd v Quistclose Ltd* [1970] AC 567 applied in *Re EVTR Ltd* [1987] BCLC 646.

Form of mortgage

12.14 A mortgage by a company takes the usual form of mortgage by an absolute owner[1]. Such mortgages may also include a specific charge of future acquired freehold and leasehold property[2] and a floating charge over the company's other assets[3]. In the case of private companies the mortgagee will often require the directors of the company to guarantee repayment of the advance[4].

Unless the objects so provide, it is not usually legitimate for one company to charge its property with the debts of another company, eg its parent company[5].

1 For forms of mortgage by limited companies, see 10 *Forms and Precedents* (5th edn, 2001 reissue) Companies; 28 *Forms and Precedents* (5th edn, 1999 reissue) Mortgages; and the Appendix.
2 As to the effect of such a charge, see **1.17**.
3 See **8.8**. For restrictions on mortgage of assets of insurance companies, see Insurance Companies Act 1982, ss 29, 40.
4 Note that a director who has guaranteed an overdraft of or advance to the company of which he is director may be interested for the purposes of the Companies Act 1985, s 317, and Table A, regs 94, 95. See *Victors Ltd v Lingard* [1927] 1 Ch 323; *Rolled Steel Products (Holdings) Ltd v British Steel Corpn* [1986] Ch 246, [1985] 3 All ER 52, CA.
5 For a form of mortgage of properties of subsidiary companies to secure loan to holding company, see 28 *Forms and Precedents* (5th edn, 1999 reissue) Mortgages.

REGISTRATION OF COMPANY CHARGES

Introduction

12.15 The Companies Act 1985, as originally enacted, makes detailed provision for the registration of company charges[1]. These provisions will be repealed and replaced by new provisions under the Companies Act 1989 if the 1989 Act provisions are ever brought into force[2]. It has been doubted whether the 1989 Act provisions will ever be brought into force[3]. Accordingly, the relevant provisions of the 1985 Act will be considered in detail and the provisions of the 1989 Act which are not yet in force will be considered more briefly.

1 Companies Act 1985, Pt XII, ss 395-409 (in relation to England and Wales). For a more detailed consideration of company charges, see Gough *Company Charges* (2nd edn, 1996).
2 Companies Act 1989, ss 92-107.
3 See, for example, Megarry and Wade *Law of Real Property* (6th edn), para 5-108, fn 30.

Companies Act 1985, s 395

12.16 The Companies Act 1985[1], provides as follows:

> **395** (1) Subject to the provisions of this Chapter, a charge created[2] by a company registered in England and Wales and being a charge to which this section applies is, so far as any security on the company's property or undertaking is conferred by the charge[3], void against the liquidator or administrator and any creditor of the company, unless the prescribed particulars[4] of the charge together with the instrument (if any)[5] by which the charge is created or evidenced, are delivered to or received by the registrar of companies for registration in manner required by this Chapter within 21 days after the date of the charge's creation[6].
>
> (2) Subsection (1) is without prejudice to any contract or obligation for repayment of the money secured by the charge; and when a charge becomes void under this section the money secured by it immediately becomes payable[7].

1 Ie as enacted, subject to amendments made by Insolvency Act 1985, s 109(1), Sch 6, para 10 (to include a reference to an 'administrator') but before the amendments prospectively made by the Companies Act 1989.

2 Ie not arising by operation of law, eg a lien: see *London and Cheshire Insurance Co Ltd v Laplagrene Property Co Ltd* [1971] Ch 499, [1971] 1 All ER 766; in *Re Wallis & Simmonds (Builders) Ltd* [1974] 1 All ER 561, where the mortgage was by way of deposit of title deeds, it was held that the charge was not created by operation of law but by act of the parties; the deposit of title deeds was analysed as evidence of a contract to create a mortgage and in the case of land, such a contract was enforceable by reason of part performance (the deposit of the deeds); now, by reason of s 2 of the Law of Property (Miscellaneous Provisions) Act 1989, since 27 September 1989, a contract to create a mortgage must comply with the requirements of that section and it is no longer possible to create an equitable mortgage by the mere deposit of title deeds: *United Bank of Kuwait plc v Sahib* [1997] Ch 107. For liens, see **1.6**. Compare these provisions dealing with a charge 'created' with the provisions dealing with acquiring property subject to a charge, **12.24**.

To be registrable the charge must be a present existing charge, not an agreement for a future charge: *Williams v Burlington Investments Ltd* (1977) 121 Sol Jo 424, HL.

3 The charge will still be effective as regards any non-security aspects: *Re J and D Contracting Pty Ltd* [1970] QWN 40. However, in relation to security aspects, the charge and everything ancillary to the charge is rendered void. In *Re Molton Finance Ltd* [1968] Ch 325 , a mortgagee, who claimed an equitable charge by reason of the deposit of title deeds, could not on that charge being rendered void for non-registration, claim a common law lien on the deeds; and see **12.19**.

4 See Form No 395 in Sch 3 in the Companies (Forms) Regulations 1985, SI 1985/854. See Assistant Registrar's letter (1987) 137 NLJ 548. In *Grove v Advantage Healthcare (T10) Ltd* [2000] 1 BCLC 661, the application for registration wrongly stated the company registration number of the mortgagor and the charge was registered against the company (who was not the mortgagor) with that registration number; it was held that there was no failure to comply with s 395 as the registration number of the mortgagor was not a particular of the charge but a particular of the mortgagor.

5 An oral charge is registrable: *Re F L E Holdings Ltd* [1967] 3 All ER 553, [1967] 1 WLR 1409. On the meaning of 'instrument', see *R v Registrar of Companies, ex p Central Bank of India* [1986] QB 1114 ar 1174, 1179, CA; *Sun Tai Cheung Credits Ltd v A-G of Hong Kong* [1987] 1 WLR 948 at 954-955: an 'instrument' means any written document or documents, formal or informal, whereby rights or liabilities, legal or equitable exist or are confirmed.

6 The charge is created at the date of execution (*Esberger & Son Ltd v Capital and Counties Bank* [1913] 2 Ch 366) and, in the case of a trust deed to secure debentures, not when the debentures are issued thereunder (*Transport and General Credit Corpn Ltd v Morgan* [1939] Ch 531, [1939] 2 All ER 17). Where a charge is delivered (ie in the technical sense of one of the elements of execution) undated, it is created on the date of delivery, unless delivery is on terms (as an escrow, see **3.77-3.78**) that the deed is not to take effect until the happening of a specified event: see *Re C L Nye Ltd* [1971] Ch 442, [1970] 3 All ER 1061, CA; and *Security Trust Co v Royal Bank of Canada* [1976] AC 503, [1976] 1 All ER 381, PC.

For the rejection of the Registrar's previous practice of accepting 'explanations' of the particulars beyond the prescribed time limit, see *R v Registrar of Companies, ex p Central Bank of India* [1986] QB 1114, [1986] 1 All ER 105, CA; and see Department of Trade and Industry practice announcement in (1985) 135 NLJ 1066 (summarised in 7(2) *Halsbury's Laws* (4th edn) (1996 reissue) para 1300. See also *Sun Tai Cheung Credits Ltd v A-G of Hong Kong* [1987] 1 WLR 948.

7 For the liability of solicitors in this context, see *Re Foster* [1986] BCLC 307; *Bell v Peter Browne & Co* [1990] 2 QB 495.

Types of charge which require to be registered

12.17 The types of charge[1] which require to be registered are as follows:

(a) a charge for the purpose of securing any issue of debentures[2];
(b) a charge on uncalled share capital of the company;

(c) a charge created or evidenced by an instrument which, if executed by an individual, would require registration as a bill of sale[3];
(d) a charge on land, wherever situate, or any interest therein, but not including a charge for any rent or other periodical sum issuing out of land[4];
(e) a charge on book debts of the company[5] (not including the deposit for the purpose of securing an advance to the company of a negotiable instrument to secure payment of any book debts of the company[6]);
(f) a floating charge on the undertaking or property of the company;
(g) a charge on calls made but not paid;
(h) a charge on a ship or aircraft[7] or any share in a ship;
(i) and a charge on goodwill, or on any intellectual property; 'intellectual property' consists of any patent, trade mark, registered design, copyright or design right and any licence under or in respect of any such right[8].

A charge over a company's share in a chose in action does not require to be registered[9].

1 Companies Act 1985, s 396. 'Charge' includes 'mortgage': Companies Act 1985, s 396 (4). The provisions as to registration of charges cannot be evaded by making what is in fact a mortgage or charge in form an absolute assignment: *Re Kent and Sussex Sawmills Ltd* [1947] Ch 177, [1946] 2 All ER 638; *Re Welsh Irish Ferries Ltd* [1986] Ch 471; *Orion Finance v Crown Financial Management Ltd* [1996] 2 BCLC 78 and 382; compare *Lloyds and Scottish Finance Ltd v Cyril Lord Carpets Sales Ltd* (1979) [1992] BCLC 609. A charging order need not be registered: see *Re Overseas Aviation Engineering (GB) Ltd* [1963] Ch 24, [1962] 3 All ER 12, CA.

2 See *Levy v Abercorris Slate and Slab Co* (1887) 37 Ch D 260; *Automobile Association (Canterbury) Inc v Australian Secured Deposits Ltd* [1973] 1 NZLR 417.

3 An instrument does not fall within this head unless it creates or evidences a charge, as well as being an instrument which, if executed by an individual, would require registration as a bill of sale: *Stoneleigh Finance Ltd v Phillips* [1965] 2 QB 537, [1965] 1 All ER 513, CA. See also *Re Trendent Industries Pty Ltd (in liq)* (1983) 8 ACLR 115. The application of s 395 to a 'title retention' clause which was construed as creating a charge was considered in detail by Slade J in *Re Bond Worth Ltd* [1980] Ch 228 at 268-271; on the facts of that case, it was held that the charge was a floating charge within s 396(1)(f). In *Bordern (UK) Ltd v Scottish Timber Products Ltd* [1981] Ch 25, the Court of Appeal held that if the clause in that case had created a charge, it would have been a charge within s 396(1)(c) and would have been void for non-registration under s 395. There has now been a large number of reported decisions involving the construction of 'title retention' clauses; in the cases where the clause has been construed to involve the imposition of a charge, s 395 has been considered; see, for example, *Re Peachdart Ltd* [1984] Ch 131; *Specialist Plant Services Ltd v Braithwaite Ltd* [1987] BCLC 1; *E Pfeiffer v Arbuthnot Factors Ltd* [1988] 1 WLR 150; T*atung (UK) Ltd v Galex Telesure Ltd* (1988) 5 BCC 325; *Re Curtain Dream plc* [1990] BCLC 925; *Re Weldtech Ltd* [1991] BCLC 393; *Compaq Computer Ltd v Abercorn Group Ltd* [1993] BCLC 602; *Modelboard Ltd v Outer Box Ltd* [1993] BCLC 623. Foreign companies are excluded from the bills of sale legislation: see **5.16**.

4 The holding of debentures entitling the holder to a charge on land is not for the purposes of the section deemed to be an interest in land: Companies Act 1985, s 396 (3).

5 The 1985 Act does not define 'book debts'. The general law meaning is a debt connected with or arising in the course of trade of any business and due or growing due to the owner; it is not necessary that the transaction or debt be actually entered in a book. Book debts are debts which in the ordinary course of business, or as a matter of practice in a well-kept business, could be and commonly are entered in books: *Shipley v Marshall* (1863) 14 CBNS 566; *Independent Automatic Sales Ltd v Knowles and Foster* [1962] 1 WLR 974. For a detailed consideration of the meaning of 'book debts', see Gough *Company Charges* (2nd edn, 1996), Ch 26. For contingent debts, see *Paul & Frank Ltd v Discount Bank (Overseas) Ltd* [1967] Ch 348, [1966] 2 All ER 922; *Re Brush Aggregates Ltd* [1983] BCLC 320; both cases considered in (1983) 80 LS Gaz 2421 (Churchward); see also *Contemporary Cottages (NZ) Ltd v Margin Traders Ltd* [1981] 2 NZLR 114; *Byrne v Allied Irish Bank* [1978] IR 446. Despite an earlier decision to the contrary (*Re Charge Card Services Ltd* [1987] Ch

150), it is now established that there is no conceptual impossibility in having a charge over a debt where the chargor is the creditor and the chargee is the debtor: *Re Bank of Credit and Commerce International SA (No 8)* [1998] AC 214. A balance at a bank is not normally to be regarded as a book debt: see *Re Brightlife Ltd* [1987] Ch 200; *Northern Bank Ltd v Ross* [1991] BCLC 504; *Re Bank of Credit and Commerce International SA (No 8)* [1998] AC 214 at 227. A charge in favour of a landlord in relation to the tenant's interest in a deposit (in respect of rent) made by the tenant with the landlord was held not to be a charge on book debts in *Obaray v Gateway (London) Ltd* [2001] L & TR 223.

6 Companies Act 1985, s 396(2): there must be an actual deposit—*Chase Manhattan Asia v Official Receiver* [1990] 1 WLR 1181; the purpose of the exemption is to avoid prejudice to the negotiability of the instrument: at 1184.

7 See Mortgaging of Aircraft Order 1972, art 16 (2). A contractual lien on sub-freights was held to be a charge on book debts in *Re Welsh Irish Ferries Ltd* [1986] Ch 471, [1985] 3 WLR 610. In *Annangel Glory Compania Naviera SA v M Goldetz Middle East Marketing Corpn* [1988] 1 Lloyd's Rep 45 a lien on sub-freights was held to be registrable as a floating charge. See also *Care Shipping Corpn v Itex Itagrani Export SA* [1993] QB 1 for a consideration of the construction of a particular lien. However, the nature of a lien on sub-freights has been analysed by Lord Millett in the Privy Council in *Agnew v IRC* [2001] UKPC 28, [2001] 3 WLR 454 where the view was expressed that a lien on subfreights was not a charge at all: see [39]-[41].

8 'Intellectual property' is thus defined by Companies Act 1985, s 396(3A) inserted by the Copyright, Designs and Patents Act 1988, s 303(1), Sch 7, para 31(1),(2). The reference to 'trade mark' is to be construed as a reference to a trade mark within the meaning of the Trade Marks Act 1994, see s 106(1) and Sch 4, para 1 to that Act.

9 *Re Sugar Properties (Derisley Wood) Ltd* [1988] BCLC 146.

Effect of registration

12.18 The registrar of companies has a duty to keep, in respect of each company, a register in the prescribed form with the requisite particulars of all the charges requiring registration under these provisions[1]. The certificate of the registrar is conclusive that the requirements as to registration have been satisfied[2], even though all the required particulars have not been registered, or have been registered out of time[3]. As will be seen[4], the court has power to allow the registration out of time of a charge. In a case where the court made an order allowing registration out of time but that order was set aside on appeal, it was held that the certificate of the registrar that the charge was duly registered was conclusive evidence of that fact and was not affected by the subsequent removal of the charge following the order on appeal[5]. If a chargee knowingly makes a false statement as to the date of creation of a charge with the result that the charge is wrongly registered, then the registration can be set aside by the court as having been obtained by fraud[6].

1 Companies Act 1985, s 401(1). For a consideration of the extent to which the register constitutes constructive notice of its contents to persons subsequently interested, see *Constructive Notice and Company Charge Registration* [2001] 65 Conv 122 (de Lacy).

2 Companies Act 1985, s 401 (2) (b). On judicial review, see *R v Registrar of Companies, ex p Central Bank of India* [1986] QB 1114, [1986] 1 All ER 105, CA; rvsg sub nom *R v Registrar of Companies, ex p Esal (Commodities) Ltd* [1985] 2 All ER 79, QBD, and for judicial review where the registrar refused to register, see *Sun Tai Cheung Credits Ltd v A-G of Hong Kong* [1987] 1 WLR 948.

3 *Re C L Nye Ltd* [1971] Ch 442, [1970] 3 All ER 1061, CA.

4 See **12.26**.

5 *Exeter Trust Ltd v Screenways Ltd* [1991] BCLC 888.

6 *Sun Tai Cheung Credits Ltd v A-G of Hong* Kong [1987] 1 WLR 948 at 952-953, per Lord Templeman. If a chargee has fraudulently deceived the registrar, a creditor who has thereby suffered loss may be able to take proceedings *in personam*: per Russell LJ at [1971] Ch 475, [1970] 3 All ER 1073.

Effect of non-registration

12.19 It is the security only which is void against any creditor and the liquidator or administrator of the company for non-registration; the money itself becomes immediately repayable. The security is void against secured creditors of the company, even though they have notice of the unregistered security[1], but the security is valid against the company. Accordingly any steps taken by the mortgagee by way of enforcement of his security (eg by sale) are valid and cannot later be upset by a liquidator of the company subsequently appointed[2]. When a mortgage or charge is avoided as against the liquidator, everything by way of a security ancillary to it, such as a lien, is also avoided[3] but other contractual rights which are not by way of security and do not require registration remain unaffected[4]. The company itself cannot have a cause of action arising out of non-registration[5].

1 *Re Monolithic Building Co, Tacon v Monolithic Building Co* [1915] 1 Ch 643, CA; *Re Interview Ltd* [1975] IR 382.
2 See *Mercantile Bank of India Ltd v Chartered Bank of India, Australia and China and Strauss & Co Ltd, Chartered Bank of India etc v Mercantile Bank of India Ltd and Strauss & Co Ltd* [1937] 1 All ER 231; *Re Row Dal Constructions Pty Ltd* [1966] VR 249.
3 *Re Molton Finance Ltd* [1968] Ch 325, [1967] 3 All ER 843, CA, and see **2.47**.
4 *Re Cosslett (Contractors) Ltd* [1998] Ch 495; for later proceedings, see *Smith v Bridgend County Borough Council* [2000] 1 BCLC 775.
5 *Independent Automatic Sales Ltd v Knowles and Foster* [1962] 3 All ER 27, [1962] 1 WLR 974.

Registration otherwise than under the Companies Act

12.20 Charges of unregistered land (other than floating charges) created by a company on or after 1 January 1970 and which are capable of registration as a land charge should be registered under the Land Charges Act as well as under the Companies Act[1].

Registration under the Companies Act does not obviate the necessity for registration or protection of the charge under the Land Registration Act 1925, in so far as the charge relates to land the title to which is registered under that Act[2].

1 Land Charges Act 1972, s 3 (7), (8); see **24.5** ff.
2 See Chapter 4 and **8.11**.

Charges on foreign property

12.21 Where a charge is created in the United Kingdom but comprises property situate outside the United Kingdom, the instrument creating or purporting to create the charge may be sent for registration under the provisions of s 395 outlined above, despite the fact that further proceedings may be necessary to make the charge valid or effectual according to the law of the country in which the property is situate[1].

1 Companies Act 1985, s 398 (3). For charges created out of the United Kingdom comprising property situated outside the United Kingdom, see s 398 (1), (2). For charges comprising property situated in Scotland or Northern Ireland, see s 398 (4).

Registration of a series of debentures

12.22 Where a series of debentures containing, or giving by reference to another instrument, any charge to the benefit of which debenture holders of that series are entitled *pari passu* is created by a company, it is, for purposes of s 395, sufficient if there are delivered to or received by the registrar, within 21 days after the execution of the deed containing the charge (or, if there is no such deed, after the execution of any debentures of the series), the following particulars in the prescribed form[1]:

(a) the total amount secured by the whole series; and
(b) the dates of the resolutions authorising the issue of the series and the date of the covering deed (if any) by which the security is created or defined; and
(c) a general description of the property charged; and
(d) the names of the trustees (if any) for the debenture holders;

together with the deed containing the charge, or if there is no such deed, one of the debentures of the series[2]. Where more than one issue is made of debentures in the series, there must be sent to the registrar for entry in the register particulars in the prescribed form[3] of the date and amount of each issue, but any omission to do this does not affect the validity of the debentures issued[4].

1 See Form 397 in Sch 3 in the Companies (Forms) Regs 1985, SI 1985/854.
2 Companies Act 1985, s 397 (1).
3 Form 397a.
4 Companies Act 1985, s 397 (1).

Company's duty to register charges

12.23 It is the duty of a company to send to the registrar of companies for registration the particulars of every charge created by it and of the issues of debentures of a series requiring registration under ss 395 to 398 of the Companies Act 1985[1], but registration of any such charge may, however, be effected on the application of any person interested therein[2].

1 Section 399 (3) provides a penalty for non-compliance.
2 Section 399 (2), and that person may recover from the company the amount of any fees properly paid to the registrar on the registration: s 399 (2).

Charges existing on property acquired

12.24 Where a company registered in England and Wales acquires property which is subject to a charge of any such kind as would, if it had been created by the company after the acquisition of the property, have been required to be registered[1], the company must cause the prescribed particulars[2] of the charge, together with a copy (verified in the prescribed manner[3]) of the instrument (if any) by which the charge was created or is evidenced, to be delivered to the registrar of companies for registration in the manner required[4] within 21 days after the date on which the acquisition is completed[5].

1 Ie under Chapter I, Pt XII of the Companies Act 1985, s 399 (1).
2 See Form 400 in Sch 3 to the Companies (Forms) Regs 1985, SI 1985/854, as slightly amended by the Companies (Forms) (Amendment) Regulations 1987, SI 1987/752.

3 Previously it was prescribed that the certificate be signed by or on behalf of the person giving the verification and where this is given by a body corporate it must be signed by an officer of that body: Companies (Forms) Regulations 1985, reg 7 (3) (reg 7(1) was revoked by SI 1990/572 reg 4(4)).
4 See Companies Act 1985, s 401.
5 Section 400 (1), (2). See *Capital Finance Co Ltd v Stokes* [1969] 1 Ch 261, [1968] 3 All ER 625, CA; *Security Trust Co v Royal Bank of Canada* [1976] AC 503, [1976] 1 All ER 381, PC. If the property is situate and the charge was created outside Great Britain, the time for delivery of particulars etc is 21 days after the date on which the copy could in due course of post, and if despatched with due diligence, have been received in the United Kingdom: s 400 (3). Section 400 (4) provides for a penalty for non-compliance but the avoidance of the security imposed by s 395 in relation to charges created by the company does not apply to property acquired by the company subject to a pre-existing charge.

Substituted property

12.25 Where property subject to a mortgage is sold and the proceeds are invested in other property which is conveyed to the company, and then mortgaged by the company to the mortgagee, the latter mortgage requires registration[1]; but the registration of a trust deed securing debenture stock containing specific equitable charges on property is sufficient to cover subsequent legal mortgages of that property to complete the security and also mortgages of further property substituted under the powers of the deed for property comprised in the original charge[2].

1 *Cornbrook Brewery Co Ltd v Law Debenture Corpn Ltd* [1904] 1 Ch 103, CA; see also *Bristol United Breweries Ltd v Abbot* [1908] 1 Ch 279, for a situation in which registration would now be required under s 400 of the Companies Act 1985.
2 *Cunard Steamship Co Ltd v Hopwood* [1908] 2 Ch 564. This was a case under the Companies Act 1900, s 14 (4), but subsequent legislation is similar with the addition of the words 'for the purposes of this section'. It is doubted, however, whether this addition makes s 397 inapplicable to mortgages of substituted property which would otherwise require registration under the Companies Act 1985, s 400. In any case, failure to comply with the latter section does not affect the validity of the charge; cf s 395.
For the endorsement of the certificate of registration on debentures issued by the company, see Companies Act 1985, s 402.

Extension of time for registration and rectification of register

12.26 The court, on being satisfied that the omission to register a charge within the time required[1], or that the omission or misstatement of any particular with respect to any such charge or in a memorandum of satisfaction:

(a) was accidental; or
(b) was due to inadvertence; or
(c) was due to some other sufficient cause; or
(d) is not of a nature to prejudice the position of creditors or shareholders of the company; or
(e) on other grounds it is just and equitable to grant relief;

may[2], on the application of the company or any person interested[3] and on such terms and conditions as seem to the court just and expedient, order that the time for registration be extended or, as the case may be, that the omission or misstatement be rectified[4]. The court should be fully informed of the circumstances giving rise to the application and the evidence should not merely state that the matter was accidental or due to inadvertence[5]. The court will not as a rule, on an application for extension of time for registration, decide the question whether a charge requires registration[6], nor will late registration usually be permitted where the company is in liquidation[7]. The fact that a liquidation is 'imminent' although the procedures for liquidation had not commenced is a relevant factor but the court retains a discretion even in such a case to extend the time for registration[8]. But where a company was in administration and liquidation was regarded as 'inevitable', an extension of time should be refused[9]. An order granting an extension of time for registration is usually made without prejudice to any rights acquired prior to actual registration[10] against the persons entitled to the mortgage or charge[11]. Subject to any order the court may make, the registration out of time renders the charge valid *ab initio*[12].

1 See **12.16**, as to time within which application should be made.
2 The power is discretionary; see, in particular, *Re Ashpurton Estates Ltd* [1983] Ch 110 and the cases cited below as to the exercise of the discretion.
3 The application is made by a claim form pursuant to CPR Pt 8: see CPR Pt 49 PD—Applications under the Companies Act 1985 and the Insurance Companies Act 1982. For form of application, see 9(1) *Atkin's Court Forms* (2nd edn, 2000 issue) Forms 164 ff.
4 Companies Act 1985, s 404 (1), (2). This provision does not confer power on the court to grant interim relief: *Re Heathstar Properties Ltd* [1966] 1 All ER 628, [1966] 1 WLR 993. Nor to order the deletion of the whole registration: see *Re C L Nye Ltd* [1971] Ch 442 at 474, 477, [1970] 3 All ER 1061 at 1073, 1075, CA.
5 *Re Kris Cruisers Ltd* [1949] Ch 138, *Re Heathstar Properties Ltd* [1966] 1 All ER 628, [1966] 1 WLR 993 and *Re Heathstar Properties Ltd (No 2)* [1966] 1 All ER 1000, [1966] 1 WLR 993.
6 *Re Cunard Steamship Co Ltd* [1908] WN 110. See also *Re Heathstar Properties Ltd (No 2)* [1966] 1 All ER 1000, [1966] 1 WLR 993.
7 *Re Ashpurton Estates Ltd* [1983] Ch 100 sub nom *Victoria Housing Estates Ltd v Ashpurton Estates Ltd* [1982] 3 All ER 665, CA; *Re Resinoid and Mica Products Ltd* [1983] Ch 132n, *Re RM Arnold & Co Ltd* [1984] BCLC 535, [1986] JBL 282 (McCormack); *Wilde v Australian Trade Equipment Co Pty Ltd* (1980) 145 CLR 590; *Bloodstock Air Services of Australia Pty Ltd v Roadrunner Equipment Pty Ltd* (1985) 10 ACLR 36; *Re Guardian Securities Ltd* (1983) 8 ACLR 822.
8 *Re Braemar Investments Ltd* [1989] Ch 54; *Barclays Bank plc v Stuart Landon Ltd* [2001] 2 BCLC 316.
9 *Re Barrow Borough Transport Ltd* [1990] Ch 227; and see *Re Chantry House Developments Ltd* [1990] BCLC 813 and *Re Telomatic Ltd* [1994] 1 BCLC 90.
10 Ie between the end of the 21 days period and actual registration: *Watson v Duff Morgan and Vermont (Holdings) Ltd* [1974] 1 All ER 794, [1974] 1 WLR 450.
11 For forms of order, see 9 (1) *Atkin's Court Forms* (2nd edn, 2000 issue) Forms 171 ff, and *Watson v Duff Morgan and Vermont (Holdings) Ltd*, above. See also *Re Braemar Investments Ltd* [1989] Ch 54 at 60 and *Exeter Trust Ltd v Screenways Ltd* [1991] BCLC 888 at 895-896 (where the order extending time was set aside on appeal.
12 *Ram Narain v Radha Kishan* (1929) LR 57 Ind App 76, PC. See now *Watson v Duff Morgan and Vermont (Holdings) Ltd*, above (second debenture created on same day as that registered late, first had priority); cf *Re Monolithic Building Co, Tacon v Monolithic Building Co* [1915] 1 Ch 643 (second mortgage created after end of 21 days period, second had priority); in *Re Fablehill Ltd* [1991] BCLC 830, there were three charges, the first was not duly registered but the second and third were; the court allowed registration out of time of the first charge but with the third charge (but not the second charge) having priority over it; see also *Re Telomatic Ltd* [1994] 1 BCLC 90.

Registration of charges at company's registered office

12.27 Provision is made for the keeping by the company at its registered office of copies of instruments creating charges requiring registration and of a register of charges and for the entering therein of all charges specifically affecting property of the company and all floating charges on the undertaking or any property of the company[1].

Provision is also made for the inspection of such copies and of the register[2].

1 Companies Act 1985, ss 406, 407 (1). Subsection (2) provides for a penalty for non-compliance.

2 Section 408. A penalty is prescribed if inspection is refused: s 408 (3); and the court may by order compel an immediate inspection in relation to a company registered in England: s 408 (4).

There is no statutory requirement that a company must keep a register of debenture holders but provision is made by the Companies Act 1985 for the location of such a register, if kept, and for inspection of copies of debentures and of the register: ss 190, 191 as amended by Companies Act 1989, ss 143(4), 212, Sch 24.

Evidence of registration under the Companies Act on registration under the Land Registration Act

12.28 On an application under the Land Registration Act 1925, to register a charge, which requires to be registered under the Companies Act 1985, unless evidence is produced to the registrar that the charge has been registered under s 395 of the Companies Act 1985, a note will be made on the register that the charge is subject to the provisions of that section[1].

1 Land Registration Rules 1925, r 145 (2).

Entry of satisfaction or release from charge

12.29 Provision is made by the Companies Act 1985 for the registrar to enter on the register a memorandum of satisfaction or of the fact of the release of the property upon the appropriate evidence thereof[1].

1 Section 403. For form of declaration, see Form No 403b in Sch 3 to the Companies (Forms) Regulations 1985 as amended by SI 1987/752.

For cancellation where the charge is registered or protected under the Land Registration Act 1925, see **28.59**.

Foreign companies

12.30 The company charge registration provisions are extended to charges on property in England and Wales which are created, and to charges on property in England and Wales which is acquired, by a company[1] incorporated outside Great Britain which has an established place of business in England and Wales[2].

Whether a company has an established place of business in England and Wales is not always easy to determine. Prior to the *Slavenburg* case[3] the practice of the Companies Registry was not to require the registration of a charge by a foreign company unless the company were registered as an overseas company under what is now Pt XXIII of the Companies Act 1985. Now a charge will not be registered unless an address of the company's established place of business is given in the prescribed particulars[4]. A decision has therefore to be made by the charging company or the chargee as to whether or not the company has an established place of business in England and Wales[5].

A foreign company without an established place of business in England and Wales is not required to register a charge on property in England and Wales nor is it required to register charges created before the company had an established place of business in England and Wales, but a foreign company which has an established place of business in England and Wales which creates a charge over property not then in England and Wales must register the charge if the property is later brought into England and Wales (eg a ship or aircraft)[6].

1 Whether a company within the meaning of the Companies Act 1985 or not: Companies Act 1985, s 409 (1). In the Act a 'company' means a company formed and registered under the Act or an existing company (ie a company formed under certain earlier Companies Acts): s 735 (1).
2 Companies Act 1985, s 409 (1). Copies of charges and the company's register of charges must be kept at the company's principal place of business in England and Wales: s 409(2).
3 *Slavenburg's Bank NV v Intercontinental Natural Resources Ltd* [1980] 1 All ER 955, [1980] 1 WLR 1076.
4 See, generally, the Law Society's Standing Committee on Company Law paper, published in (1981) 78 LS Gaz 921.
5 *South India Shipping Corpn Ltd v Export-Import Bank of Korea* [1985] 2 All ER 219, [1985] 1 WLR 585, CA; *Re Oriel Ltd* [1985] 3 All ER 216, [1986] 1 WLR 180, CA; *Re Alton Corpn* [1985] BCLC 27; (1985) 6 Co Lawyer 187 (Milman); cf *Luckins v Highway Motel Pty Ltd* (1975) 133 CLR 164, (1979) 123 Sol Jo 560 (Milman).
6 *Slavenburg's Bank NV v Intercontinental Natural Resources Ltd*, above. See (1981) 125 Sol Jo 294 (Milman) and *Re Alton Corpn*, above.

Prospective amendment of the provisions as to registration of company charges

12.31 As explained in the introduction at **12.15**, the existing provisions of the Companies Act 1985 (which have been described in detail above) are subject to the prospect of amendment in accordance with the provisions of the 1989 Act as and when those provisions are brought into force. The 1989 Act provisions are contained in Part IV (ss 92-107) of the 1989 Act. These provisions were based partly upon a Department of Trade and Industry Report by Professor Diamond, *A Review of Security Interests in Property*. It should be stressed again that the 1989 Act amendments are not yet in force.

Charges requiring registration

12.32 The 1989 Act amendments only apply to 'charges'. A 'charge' is defined as:

> 'any form of security interest (fixed or floating) over property, other than an interest arising by operation of law'.[1]

The 1989 Act does not define 'security interest'.

The various kinds of charges requiring registration are[2]:

(a) a charge on land or any interest in land, other than (in England and Wales) a charge for rent or any other periodical sum issuing out of the land;[3]
(b) a charge on goods or any interest in goods, other than a charge under which the chargee is entitled to possession either of the goods or of a document of title to them;[4]
(c) a charge on intangible movable property of any of the following descriptions:
    (i) goodwill;
    (ii) intellectual property;[5]

(iii) book debts (whether book debts of the company or assigned to the company);[6]

(iv) uncalled share capital of the company or calls made but not paid;

(d) a charge for securing an issue of debentures; or

(e) a floating charge on the whole or part of the company's property.[7]

1 Companies Act 1989, s 93 inserting s 395(2) into the 1985 Act. 'Property' includes future property: the 1989 Act, s93 inserting s 395(2) into the 1985 Act.

2 Companies Act 1989, s 93 inserting s 396 into the 1985 Act.

3 This is a rewording of s 396(1)(d) of the orginal 1985 Act. For charges on debentures which are secured by a charge on land or an interest in land, see the substituted s 396(2)(a) of the 1985 Act.

4 'Goods' are defined to mean 'tangible movable property other than money: the 1989 Act, s 93, inserting s 396(2)(b) into the 1985 Act. For charges on debentures which are secured by a charge on goods or on an interest in goods, see the substituted s 396 (2)(a). A charge is not excluded from s 396(1)(b) because the chargee is entitled to take possession in case of default or on the occurrence of some other event: the substituted s 396(2)(c).

5 This is defined by the substituted s 396(2)(d) in the same terms as the existing s 396(3A) of the 1985 Act.

6 A debenture which is part of an issue or series is not treated as a book debt: the substituted s 396(2)(e). The deposit by way of security of a negotiable instrument given to secure the payment of book debts is not treated as a charge on book debts: the substituted s 396(2)(f). A shipowner's lien on sub-freights is not treated as a charge on book debts: the substituted s 396(2)(g); compare *Re Welsh Irish Ferries Ltd* [1986] Ch 471.

7 A shipowner's lien on sub-freights is not treated as a floating charge for the purposes of the substituted s 396(1)(e): see the substituted s 396(2)(g); compare *Annangel Glory Compania Naviera SA v M Goldetz Middle East Marketing Corpn* [1988] 1 Lloyd's Rep 45.

Procedural requirements

12.33 The procedure under the new legislation is similar to that under the existing legislation. The registrar of companies is obliged to keep a register for each company[1]. The primary duty to register remains with the company[2]. The time limit of 21 days from the date of creation of the charge or the date of acquisition of property subject to a charge remains[3]. There is now a statutory definition of the date of creation of a charge[4]. Unless the Secretary of State makes regulations to the contrary, there is no longer a requirement to deliver the original charge to the registrar[5].

1 The substituted s 397(1) of the 1985 Act.

2 The substituted s 398(1) of the 1985 Act.

3 The substituted s 398(1)(b) of the 1985 Act.

4 The substituted s 414 of the 1985 Act.

5 The substituted ss 398(1) and 413(2) of the 1985 Act.

The conclusiveness of the registrar's certificate

12.34 The certificate of the registrar of companies is to be conclusive evidence that the specified particulars or other information were delivered to the registrar no later than the date specified in the certificate; it is to be presumed, unless the contrary is proved, that they were not delivered earlier than that date[1].

1 The substituted s 397(5) of the 1985 Act. This provision removes much of the practical effect of *R v Registrar of Companies, ex p Central Bank of India* [1986] QB 1114. The change in the law is partly explained by the removal of the requirement to deliver the original charge to the registrar.

Consequences of non-registration

12.35 A charge which is not duly registered is void against a liquidator or administrator of the company and against any person who for value acquires an interest in or right over property subject to the charge, where the relevant event occurs after the creation of the charge, whether before or after the end of the 21 day period for registration[1]. The 'relevant event' in this context is the beginning of the insolvencyproceedings (in the case of voidness against a liquidator or administrator) or the acquisition of the interest in or right over property the subject of the charge (in the case of voidness against a person acquiring such an interest or right)[2]. Where the relevant event occurs on the same day as the charge is created, it is presumed to have occurred after the charge is created, unless the contrary is proved[3]. There are special provisions restricting the extent of the voidness of the unregistered charge against subsequent charges[4]. Further, the unregistered charge is not void as against a person acquiring an interest in or right over property where the acquisition is expressly subject to the charge [5]. Nor is the unregistered charge void by reason of a relevant event which occurs after the company which created the charge has disposed of the whole of its interest in the property[6]. There are also provisions to protect a purchaser from the chargee exercising a power of sale[7]. Where a charge becomes void to any extent by virtue of non-registration, the whole of the sum secured by the charge is payable forthwith on demand; this applies notwithstanding the fact that the sum secured by the charge is also the subject of other security[8].

1 The substituted s 399(1) of the 1985 Act.
2 The substituted s 399(2) of the 1985 Act.
3 The substituted s 399(3) of the 1985 Act.
4 The substituted s 404 of the 1985 Act.
5 The substituted s 405(1) of the 1985 Act.
6 The substituted s 405(2) of the 1985 Act.
7 The substituted s 406 of the 1985 Act.
8 The substituted s 407 of the 1985 Act.

Late delivery of particulars of a charge

12.36 The existing law allows registration out of time only upon an order of the court and the consequences of such late registration are largely to be dealt with in the court order. The substituted s 400 of the 1985 Act enables registration out of time without a court order and prescribes the consequences of late registration. Such a charge is void against a liquidator or administrator (but not a purchaser) if:

(a) the company is at the date of delivery of the particulars unable to pay its debts, or subsequently becomes unable to pay its debts in consequence of the transaction under which the charge is created; and
(b) insolvency proceedings begin before the end of the relevant period beginning with the date of delivery of the particulars.

'Unable to pay its debts' is construed in accordance with the Insolvency Act 1986[1]. The 'relevant period' is defined as being two years for a floating charge in favour of a 'connected person', one year for any other floating charge and six months in any other case[2]. The new sections have extensive provisions for the delivery of further particulars and for the treatment of errors and omissions[3].

1 The substituted s 400(3)(a) adopting the definition in Insolvency Act 1986, s123.
2 The substituted s 400(3)(b) of the 1985 Act.
3 The substituted ss 401 and 402 of the 1985 Act.

Notice arising from the registration of a charge

12.37 The issue of constructive notice arising from the registration of company charges is dealt with by the substituted s 416 of the 1985 Act which provides that:

(a) a person taking a charge over a company's property is taken to have notice of any matter requiring registration and disclosed on the register at the time the charge is created;
(b) otherwise, a person is not taken to have notice of any matter by reason of its being disclosed on the register or by reason of his having failed to search the register in the course of making such inquiries as he ought reasonably to have made[1].

1 This is confirmed by s 711A of the 1985 Act, to be inserted by s 142 of the 1989 Act, which abolishes the doctrine of deemed notice.

Registration of events crystallising floating charges

12.38 As with the existing legislation, there is a duty to register the appointment of a receiver or manager appointed either by the court or under a power in the charge[1]. The Secretary of State has power to make regulations for the registration of such events as may be prescribed affecting the nature of the security under a floating charge and setting out the consequences of a failure to register, including the postponement of crystallisation until registration[2].

1 The substituted s 409 of the 1985 Act.
2 The substituted s 410 of the 1985 Act.

Registration of events over the property of foreign companies

12.39 Sections 703A-703N of the 1985 Act[1] make extensive provision for the registration of charges on foreign companies. The principal change in the law is the reversal of the decision in the *Slavenburg*[2] case so that a duty to register charges only arises when an overseas company is registered under s 691 of the 1985 Act.

1 Inserted by s 105 of and Sch 15 to the 1989 Act.
2 *Slavenburg's Bank NV v Intercontinental Resources Ltd* [1980] 1 All ER 955, [1980] 1 WLR 1076.

Commencement and transitional provisions

12.40 The amendments made by the 1989 Act to the system of registration of company charges will only come into force on the day appointed in an order made by the Secretary of State[1]. To date no such order has been made and it has been doubted whether the provisions will ever be brought into force[2].

1 Pursuant to s 215(2) of the 1989 Act.
2 See the introduction at **12.15**.

LENDING POWERS

Generally

12.41 A company may have an implied power to lend money and allow credit in the ordinary course of its business and for the furtherance of the objects of the company. Generally the objects of the company will include an express power to make advances and that any money due to the company may be secured by mortgage[1].

1 As to prohibitions of loans to directors, see Companies Act 1985, ss 330 ff.

PUBLIC AUTHORITIES

The National Assembly for Wales

12.42 Many statutory functions previously vested in Ministers of the Crown are now exercisable in relation to Wales by the National Assembly for Wales. Functions transferred include functions under Acts whose provisions are discussed below, including: the Housing Act 1985; the Housing Associations Act 1985; the Local Government and Housing Act 1989 (with specified exceptions); the Leasehold Reform, Housing and Urban Development Act 1993; and the Housing Act 1996 (with specified exceptions).

BORROWING POWERS

Local authorities[1]

12.43 The power of local authorities to borrow is generally conferred by statute[2], but it may be implied where the borrowing is necessary to execute statutory powers[3]. The purposes for which money may be borrowed are those for which the power was granted by the relevant Act or is implied. Under the Local Government and Housing Act 1989, a local authority may borrow money for any purpose relevant to its functions under any enactment[4]. Borrowing is limited to three methods (except with the approval of the Secretary of State[5]): overdraft or short term from the Bank of England or a bank which is an authorised institution within the meaning of the Banking Act 1987; from the National Debt Commissioners or Public Works Loan Commissioners; or by means of a loan instrument[6].

All money borrowed by a local authority together with any interest thereon is charged indifferently on all the revenues of the authority[7]. A local authority has no other power to mortgage or charge any of its property as security for money borrowed or otherwise owing by it and any security purporting to be given in contravention of that provision is unenforceable[8].

Borrowing without statutory authority is ultra vires and may be restrained by injunction[9].

A person lending money to a local authority is not bound to inquire whether the authority has power to borrow the money and shall not be prejudiced by the absence of such a power[10].

All securities created by a local authority rank equally without any priority, subject to any priority existing on 1 June 1934[11] or any right to priority conferred by a security created before that date[12].

1 See 29(1) *Halsbury's Laws* (4th edn reissue) Local Government, paras 594 ff; 29 *Halsbury's Laws* (4th edn) London Government, paras 71–73.
2 See eg Highways Act 1980, ss 272 (6), 279.
3 *Baroness Wenlock v River Dee Co* (1883) 36 Ch D 675n, CA.
4 Local Government and Housing Act 1989, s 43(1).
5 In Wales, by the National Assembly of Wales.
6 Local Government and Housing Act 1989, s 43(2).
7 Section 47(1).
8 Section 47(1) and s 47(7). These provisions replace the corresponding provisions of the Local Government Act 1972 whereby loans could be raised by mortgages, stocks, bonds etc: Sch 13, para 2.
9 *A-G v Oldham Corpn* [1936] 2 All ER 1022.
10 Local Government Act 1989, s 44(6).
11 The date of the coming into force of the Local Government Act 1933.
12 Local Government and Housing Act 1989, s 47(2) and 47(3). For loans by the Public Works Loan Commissioners for the construction and improvement of houses, see Housing Act 1985, s 45(1).

Other public authorities

12.44 The powers of other public authorities are contained in the statutes creating them[1].

1 For the public utility authorities, see the statutes creating the relevant authority. For burial authorities, see 10 *Halsbury's Laws* (4th edn) Cremation and Burial, para 1010 ff; for the National Trust, see 34 *Halsbury's Laws* (4th edn reissue) Open Spaces and Historic Buildings, para 106; for water authorities, see 49(2) *Halsbury's Laws* (4th edn reissue) Water, para 144.

LENDING POWERS OF LOCAL AUTHORITIES

For housing purposes generally

Loans for housing purposes generally

12.45 A local authority may[1] advance money for the purpose of acquiring, constructing, altering, enlarging, repairing or improving houses, for converting buildings into houses or flats, for acquiring houses for that purpose or for paying off a loan for such purposes[2]. Before making an advance the local authority must be satisfied that the resultant house will be fit for human habitation or, in the case of a house to be acquired, is or will be made fit[3]. The amount of the advance must not exceed the value of the mortgaged security in the case of a house or houses[4] to be acquired or, in any other case, the value which it is estimated the mortgaged security will bear when the construction, conversion, alteration, enlargement, repair or improvement has been carried out[5]. The advance together with interest must be secured by a mortgage on the property[6]. The mortgage must provide for repayment of the principal either by instalments (of equal or unequal amounts) beginning either on the date of the advance or a later date or at the end of a fixed period (with or without a provision allowing the authority to extend the period) or on the happening of a specified event before the end of that period, and for the payment of instalments of interest[7] throughout the period beginning on the date of the advance and ending when the whole of the principal is repaid[8]. In either case, the balance outstanding is repayable on demand if there is a breach of any of the conditions of the advance and the borrower may repay on any of the usual quarter days, after giving a month's notice of his intention[9]. Advances may be made in addition to other assistance given by the local authority in respect of the same house under any other Act or any other provisions of the Housing Act 1985[10]. A local authority may for the assistance of a housing association subscribe for share or loan capital of the association. A local authority may make a loan to an unregistered self-build society for the purpose of enabling it to meet the whole or part of the expenditure incurred or to be incurred by it in carrying out its objects[11].

1 Subject to any restraints on local authority lending imposed from time to time for economic reasons.
2 Housing Act 1985, s 435. The borrower's estate in the mortgaged property must be not less than a term of years absolute for a period ten years in excess of the time fixed for repayment: s 436 (2) (b).
3 Section 439.
4 If the effect of the advance is to meet the borrower's housing needs, part may be used otherwise than as a dwelling: s 435 (2).
5 Section 436 (3). There must be a valuation on behalf of the local authority: s 436(3). Except in cases of advances for acquiring houses, the advance may be made by instalments as the works proceed: s 436 (4).
6 Section 436 (2).
7 For interest, see Housing Act 1985, s 438 and Sch 16.
8 This is subject to s 441 (waiver or reduction of payments in case of property requiring repair or improvement) and s 446 (1) (b) (assistance for first time buyers: part of loan interest-free for up to five years): s 436 (5).
9 Section 436 (6). For forms of mortgage, see 28 *Forms and Precedents* (5th edn, 1999 reissue) Mortgages; *Precedents for the Conveyancer* 7–15.
10 Section 435 (4). Eg under ss 143-153B as amended by the Leasehold Reform, Housing and Urban Development Act 1993: right to acquire on rent to mortgage terms.
11 In the case of housing associations which are not registered social landlords, this power is given by Housing Associations Act 1985, s 58 as substituted, and in the case of housing associations which are registered social landlords by s 22 of the Housing Act 1996. For housing associations see **12.65**.

For the acquisition of small dwellings

12.46 The Small Dwellings Acquisition Acts 1899 to 1923 have been repealed by the Housing (Consequential Provisions) Act 1985. Schedule 18 of the Housing Act 1985 contains provisions applicable to any existing mortgages made under the repealed legislation[1].

1 Housing Act 1985, s 456. References are made, where appropriate, elsewhere in this work to the provisions of Sch 18.

Secure tenant's right to a mortgage

Secure tenant's right to buy

12.47 A secure tenancy is a tenancy of a dwelling-house[1] which is let as a separate dwelling and in respect of which the statutory landlord condition and tenant condition are satisfied[2]. The landlord condition is that the interest of the landlord belongs to one of a specified list of authorities or bodies[3]. The tenant condition is that the tenant is an individual and occupies the dwelling-house as his only or principal home; or, where the tenancy is a joint tenancy, that each of the joint tenants is an individual and at least one of them occupies the dwelling-house as his only or principal home[4].

A secure tenant has a right to buy, that is, the right, in the circumstances and subject to the conditions and exceptions stated in ss 118 ff of the Housing Act 1985:

(a) if the dwelling-house is a house and the landlord owns the freehold, to acquire the freehold of the dwelling-house;
(b) if the landlord does not own the freehold or if the dwelling-house is a flat (whether or not the landlord owns the freehold), to be granted a lease of the flat[5].

The reader is referred to texts on the housing legislation[6] for details of the right to buy—the qualifying period[7], the exceptions to the right to buy[8], the circumstances in which the right cannot be exercised[9], the procedure for exercising the right[10] and the purchase price[11].

1 In this context 'dwelling-house' means a house or part of a house: Housing Act 1985, s 112 (1). For land let together with a dwelling-house, see s 112 (2).
2 Housing Act 1985, s 79.
3 Ie a local authority, a new town corporation, a housing action trust, an urban development corporation or a housing co-operative with whom a housing co-operative agreement was made: Housing Act 1985, s 80 (1), (2) as amended and s 27B.
4 Section 81.
5 Section 118 (1). Where a secure tenancy is a joint tenancy then, whether or not each of the joint tenants occupies the dwelling-house as his only or principal home, the right to buy belongs jointly to all of them or to such one or more of them as may be agreed between them; but such an agreement is not valid unless the person or at least one of the persons to whom the right to buy is to belong occupies the dwelling-house as his only or principal home: s 118 (2).
6 See eg *Encyclopedia of Housing Law and Practice*.
7 Housing Act 1985, s 119.
8 Section 120, Sch 5, as amended by the Housing and Planning Act 1986, s 1.
9 Section 121.
10 Sections 122–125, as amended by the Housing and Planing Act 1986, s 4.
11 Sections 126–131, as amended by the Housing and Planning Act 1986, s 2.

No right to a mortgage or a shared ownership lease

12.48 Formerly, a secure tenant who had the right to buy[1] had the ancillary rights, subject to the relevant provisions of the Housing Act 1985:

(a) to leave the whole or part of the amount to be secured outstanding on the security of a first mortgage of the dwelling-house; or
(b) if the landlord was a housing association, to have the whole or part of that amount advanced to him on that security by the Housing Corporation[2]; and
(c) to a shared ownership lease in accordance with the relevant provisions of the Housing Act 1985.

Those rights have now been abolished[3], except where the tenant served a notice claiming the right before 11 October 1993[4].

1 For change of secure tenant after notice claiming right to buy, see Housing Act 1985, s 136 as amended. For change of landlord, see s 137 as amended.

2 Housing Act 1985, s 132 (1), repealed.
3 Leasehold Reform, Housing and Urban Development Act 1993, s 107(a).
4 Leasehold Reform, Housing and Urban Development Act 1993 (Commencement and Transitional Provisions No 1 Order, SI 1993/2134.

Right to acquire on rent to mortgage terms

12.49 The former rights to a mortgage and to acquire a shared ownership lease have been replaced by the right to acquire on rent to mortgage terms[1]. A secure tenant acquires this right where (a) he has claimed to exercise the right to buy; and (b) his right to buy has been established and his notice claiming to exercise it remains in force[2].

A secure tenant claims to exercise the right to acquire on rent to mortgage terms by written notice to that effect served on the landlord. On service of the notice, any notice to complete served by the landlord[3] is deemed to have been withdrawn and no such notice may be served whilst a notice claiming to exercise the right remains in force[4]. The tenant's notice may be withdrawn at any time by notice to the landlord in writing; and where a notice is withdrawn, the tenant may complete the transaction pursuant to the right to buy provisions[5].

As soon as practicable after the tenant has served a notice, the landlord must serve on the tenant a written notice either admitting the right and informing the tenant of various matters[6] or denying the right and giving reasons for the denial[7].

Within 12 weeks[8] of the landlord's notice being served on him, the tenant must serve a further notice on the landlord stating that:

(a) he intends to pursue the claim and the amount of the initial payment he proposes to make; or
(b) he withdraws the claim but intends to pursue the claim to exercise the right to buy; or
(c) he withdraws both claims[9].

If the tenant fails to serve a notice of intention within the specified period, the landlord may upon its expiry serve a notice in default on the tenant. If the tenant does not comply the notice claiming the right to acquire on rent to mortgage terms is deemed to be withdrawn[10].

The landlord is under a duty to convey the freehold or grant a lease, as appropriate[11].

1 The right to acquire on rent to mortgage terms was created by amendments to the Housing Act 1985 by the Leasehold Reform, Housing and Urban Development Act 1993.
2 Housing Act 1985, s 143(1) The right is excluded where it has been determined that the tenant is or was entitled to housing benefit in respect of any part of the relevant period or a claim for housing benefit in respect of any part of that period has been made, or is treated as having been made by or on behalf of the tenant and has not been determined or withdrawn: s 143A(1). The relevant period means the period beginning 12 months before the day on which the tenant claims to exercise the right to acquire on rent to mortgage terms and ending on the day on which the conveyance or grant is executed in pursuance of that right: s 143A(2) The right is also excluded if the minimum initial payment exceeds the maximum initial payment: s 143B(1). For calculation of minimum initial payment see s 143B(2) and (3).
3 Under Housing Act 1985, s 140 or 141.
4 Section 144(3).
5 Section 144(2) and (4).
6 Section 146(1)(a) and s 146(2).
7 Section 146(1)(b).
8 Section 146A(2).

9 Section 146A(1).
10 Section 146B. The landlord may at any time before the expiry of the notice in default extend or further extend the period of the notice. If at any time before the end of that period, the circumstances are such that it would not be reasonable to expect the tenant to comply with the notice, the period must be extended until 28 days after the time when those circumstances no longer obtain: s 146B(3).
11 Section 150 as amended.

Terms and effect of the conveyance or grant

12.50 A conveyance of the freehold or grant of a lease executed in pursuance of the right to acquire on rent to mortgage term must conform with the relevant provisions applicable to conveyances or leases pursuant to the right to buy and the provisions relating to charges apply to such a conveyance or lease as they apply in a conveyance or lease executed pursuant to the right to buy[1].

1 Housing Act 1985, s 151.

Redemption of landlord's share

12.51 The conveyance or grant must contain:

(a) a covenant binding on the secure tenant and his successors in title to make a final payment, ie a payment of the amount required to redeem the landlord's share[1], immediately after the making of certain disposals[2] or the expiry of one year beginning with a relevant death[3];
(b) provision entitling the secure tenant and his successors in title to make a final payment at any time[4];
(c) provision entitling the secure tenant and his successors in title at any time to make the landlord an interim payment[5].

A provision of the conveyance or grant is void insofar as it purports to enable the landlord to charge the tenant or his successors in title a sum in respect of or in connection with the making of a final or interim payment[6]. The conveyance or grant may include such covenants and provisions as are reasonable in the circumstances[7]. The Secretary of State[8] may by order prescribe matters for which the mortgage must make provision and terms which must be contained in the deed[9]. The deed may contain such other provisions as are agreed between the mortgagor and the mortgagee, or as may be determined by the county court to be reasonably required by the mortgagor or the mortgagee[10].

1 The landlord's share is determined by a formula set out in s 148.
2 Ie a relevant disposal which is not an excluded disposal. A disposal is an excluded disposal if it is a further conveyance of the freehold or assignment of the lease by one spouse to another; or a vesting in a person taken under a will or intestacy; or a disposal pursuant to the Matrimonial Causes Act 1973 or the Inheritance (Provision for Dependants) Act 1975; and in all those cases, an interest to which the provisions relating to right to acquire on rent to mortgage terms applies, subsists immediately after the disposal: Housing Act 1985, Sch 6A, para 1(2).
3 Section 151A and Sch 6A, para 1(1) A relevant death is the death of a person who immediately before his death was the person, or as the case may be, the last remaining person entitled to an interest to which the Housing Act 1985, Sch 6A, para 1 applies: Sch 6A, para 13.
4 Section 151A, Sch 6A, para 2(1). When a final payment is made by two or more persons who include the secure tenant, or one of the secure tenants or a qualifying person, the person or persons making the payment are entitled to a final discount equal to 20 per cent of the landlord's share: Sch 6A, paras 4(1). However, the discount is not available

if the final payment is made after the end of the protection period, ie the period of two years beginning with the time when there ceases to be an interest to which the right applies: Sch 6A, 4(2) and 12(1). Further provisions relating to the final discount are contained in Sch 6A paras 4 and 5.
5 An interim payment is a payment which is less than the amount required to redeem the landlord's share but not less than 10 per cent of the value of the dwelling house agreed or determined: Housing Act 1985, Sch 6A, para 6(1). For calculation of the landlord's reduced share after the making of an interim payment, see Sch 6A, para 7.
6 Schedule 6A, para 15.
7 Schedule 6A, para 11.
8 Or the National Assembly for Wales: see **12.42**.
9 Section 151B(8).
10 Section 151B(9).

Mortgage for securing redemption of landlord's share

12.52 The liability which may arise under the covenant for the redemption of the landlord's share[1] must be secured by a mortgage[2]. The mortgage has priority immediately after any legal charge securing an amount advanced to the secure tenant by an approved lending institution[3] for the purpose of enabling him to exercise the right to acquire on rent to mortgage terms[4]. Where there is an advance which is made otherwise than for the purpose of enabling the tenant to exercise the right to acquire on rent to mortgage terms and is secured by a legal charge having priority to the mortgage or any other advance which is so secured, it will rank in priority to the mortgage only if the landlord has given his written consent[5]. The landlord must give his consent if the purposes of the advance is an approved purpose. The landlord may at any time postpone the mortgage to any advance which is made by an approved lending institution to the tenant and is secured by a legal charge not having priority to the mortgage and the landlord must so postpone the mortgage if the purposes of the advance is an approved purpose[6].

1 See **12.51**.
2 Housing Act 1985, s 151B(1).
3 The approved lending institutions are listed at s 151B(5).
4 Section 151B(2).
5 Section 151B(3). The approved purposes are set out at s 151B(6).
6 Section 151B(4) The approved purposes are set out at s 151B(6).

Completion

12.53 The Housing Act 1985 contains detailed provisions as to the period for completion, notices to complete and the tenant's rights in case of delay by the landlord[1].

1 Housing Act 1985, s 152 (landlord's first notice to complete), s 153 (landlord's second notice to complete), s 153A (tenant's notices of delay), s 153B (payment of rent attributable to purchase price).

Registration of title

12.54 On the grant of a lease under the right to buy or the right to acquire on rent to mortgage terms, s 123 of the Land Registration Act 1925 (compulsory registration of title) applies[1].

Where the landlord's title to the dwelling-house is not registered, the landlord must give the tenant a certificate in the form approved by the Chief Land Registrar stating that the landlord is entitled to convey the freehold or make the grant subject only to such incumbrances, rights and interests as are stated in the conveyance or grant or summarised in the certificate[2]. Such certificate is to be accepted by the Chief Land Registrar as sufficient evidence of the facts stated in it[3].

1 Housing Act 1985, s 154 as amended by Land Registration Act 1997. As amended, s 154 applies to dispositions made on or after 1 April 1998. Under the unamended section, the requirement for compulsory registration extended to the acquisition of the freehold interest by a tenant.
2 Section 154 (2), (4).
3 Section 154 (5). The landlord must indemnify him if a claim is successfully made against him under s 83 of the Land Registration Act 1925, as amended.

Repayment of discount on early disposal

12.55 If a purchaser under the right to buy or the right to acquire on rent to mortgage terms disposes[1] of the dwelling-house or his share within three years of the acquisition, the purchaser must repay the discount, reduced by one third[2] for each complete year which has elapsed since the acquisition[3]. The liability to repay is a charge on the dwelling-house, taking effect as if it has been created by deed expressed to be by way of legal mortgage[4].

The charge takes priority as follows:

(a) where it secures the liability that may arise under the covenant to repay discount on an early disposal in the case of a conveyance or grant in pursuance of the right to buy, immediately after any legal charge securing any amount advanced to the secure tenant by an approved lending institution[5] for the purpose of enabling him to exercise the right to buy;
(b) where it secures the liability that may arise under the covenant to repay discount on an early disposal in the case of a conveyance or grant in pursuance of the right to acquire on rent to mortgage terms, immediately after any legal charge securing an amount advanced to the secure tenant by an approved lending institution for the purpose of enabling him to exercise the right to acquire on rent to mortgage terms[6].

An advance made for any other purpose than those two aforementioned which is secured by a legal charge having priority to the charge and any further advance which is so secured will rank in priority to that charge only if the landlord consents and the landlord must consent if the purpose of the advance is an approved purpose. The landlord may postpone the charge to any advance made by an approved lending institution to the tenant and must do so if the purpose of the advance is an approved purpose[7].

1 For relevant disposals, see Housing Act 1985, s 159.
2 In the case of a conveyance or grant pursuant to the right to acquire on rent to mortgage terms. The discount is the discount to which the tenant was entitled on the making of the initial payment, or any interim payment made before the disposal or the final payment if so made: s 155(3).
3 Section 155 as amended by Leasehold Reform, Housing and Urban Development 1993. For exempted disposals, see Housing Act 1985, s 160.
4 Section 156 (1). Such charge is a land charge for the purposes of s 59 (2) of the Land Registration Act 1925; Housing Act, s 156 (3).
5 Section 6A.
6 Section 156(2).
7 Section 156(2A) and (2B).

Local authority assistance in connection with mortgages

Indemnity agreements

12.56 A local authority may, with the approval of the Secretary of State, enter into an agreement with a person or body making an advance on the security of a house[1] (or a building to be converted into a house), whereby, in the event of default by the mortgagor, and in the circumstances, and subject to conditions specified in the agreement, the authority binds itself to indemnify the mortgagee in respect of the whole or part of the mortgagor's outstanding indebtedness and any loss or expense falling on the mortgagee in consequence of the mortgagor's default[2]. The local authority may only enter into the agreement if the advance is for one or more of the specified purposes[3].

The agreement may also, if the mortgagor is made party to it, enable or require the authority in specified circumstances to take a transfer of the mortgage and assume rights and liabilities under it; the mortgagee is then discharged in respect of those rights and liabilities[4].

1 This includes a flat: Housing Act 1985, s 457.
2 Section 442 as amended by Housing Act 1996.
3 Section 442(1A) added by Housing Act 1996. The specified purposes are acquiring a house; constructing a house; converting another building into a house or acquiring another building and converting it into a house; or altering, enlarging, repairing and improving a house, or for the purpose of facilitating the repayment of an amount outstanding on a previous loan made for any of those purposes. The advance may be made notwithstanding that it is intended that some part of the premises will be used, or continue to be used, otherwise than as a dwelling if it appears to the authority that the principal effect of making the advance would be to meet the applicant's housing needs: s 435.
4 Section 442(2).

Contributions to mortgage costs

12.57 A local authority may contribute towards costs incurred by a person in connection with a legal charge which secures costs incurred by a person in connection with a legal charge which secures, or a proposed legal charge which is intended to secure, a relevant advance[1] made or proposed to be made to him by any person or body[2].

1 Ie where the advance is made to a person whose interest in the house (or building to be converted into a house) on the security of which the advance is made is or was acquired by virtue of a conveyance of the freehold or a grant or assignment of a long lease by a housing authority: s 444 as amended by the Housing Act 1996.
2 Section 443, as amended by the Housing Act 1996.

Assistance for first-time buyers

12.58 The scheme whereby the Secretary of State could make advances to recognised lending institutions[1] enabling them to provide an additional advance to a first-time buyer has been wound up[2].

1 Housing Act 1985, s 447, as amended by Building Societies Act 1986, s 120, Sch 18, para 18 (3).
2 Sections 445 ff. Local Government and Housing Act 1989, s 171(a), Home Purchase Assistance (Winding Up of Scheme) Order 1990, SI 1990/374 and the Home Purchase Assistance (Commutation of Repayments) Order 1994, SI 1994/548: no account has been taken of any application for assistance under this legislation since 1 April 1993.

Disposal of land held for housing purposes

12.59 A local authority may dispose of land held for housing purposes (without prejudice to the right to buy)[1] and, under its powers to advance money referred to above, leave part of the purchase money outstanding on mortgage. On a sale of such land there will not usually be a right of pre-emption reserved to the local authority[2], but there will be a covenant for repayment of discount on early disposal[3]. The Housing Act 1985 contains provisions for the vesting of the house in the local authority by court order[4] as a result of difficulties encountered under the earlier legislation where the local authority sold as mortgagee[5].

1 Housing Act 1985, s 32 as amended by the Housing Act 1988 and Housing Act 1996.
2 Section 33.
3 Section 35. the liability to repay is a charge on the premises: s 36 as amended. For disposals, see ss 38–40.
4 Section 452 and Sch 17.
5 *First National Securities Ltd v Chiltern District Council* [1975] 2 All ER 766, [1975] 1 WLR 1075; *Williams v Wellingborough Borough Council* [1975] 3 All ER 462, [1975] 1 WLR 1327, CA.

Grants for works of improvement, repair and conversion

Generally

12.60 Discretionary grants are available from local housing authorities towards the cost of works required for:

(a) the improvement or repair of dwellings, houses in multiple occupation or the common parts of buildings containing one or more flats;
(b) the provision of dwellings or houses in multiple occupation by the conversion of a house or other building; and
(c) the provision of facilities for disabled persons in dwellings and in the common parts of buildings containing one or more flats[1].

Applications for some types of grants are means tested[2]. Grants are also available for home repair assistance[3]; and for improvement of energy conservation in certain dwellings[4].

1 Housing Grants, Construction and Regeneration Act 1996, s 1(1).
2 1996 Act, s 30.
3 Section 76.
4 Social Security Act 1990, s 15.

Assistance for owners of defective housing

Generally

12.61 The Housing Act 1985 contains provisions for assistance, by way of reinstatement grant or by way of repurchase, for eligible persons who have purchased defective systems built dwellings from local or public authorities[1]. These provisions have now been extended to mortgagees of such defective dwellings[2].

1 Housing Act 1985, s 527 ff.
2 Defective Dwellings (Mortgagees) Regulations 1986, SI 1986/797 made under s 568 of the Housing Act 1985.

REGISTERED SOCIAL LANDLORDS AND HOUSING ASSOCIATIONS

The National Assembly for Wales

12.62 See **12.42**.

The Housing Corporation

12.63 The Housing Corporation, which is a body corporate[1], was established by Part I of the Housing Act 1964, and its functions extended by subsequent legislation, now contained in the Housing Associations Act 1985 and the Housing Act 1996. Its functions are to promote and assist the development of registered social landlords, to maintain a register of social landlords and to exercise supervision and control over such persons, to promote and assist the development of self-build societies (other than registered social landlords) and to facilitate the proper performance of the functions and to publicise the aims and principles of such societies and to undertake to such extent as the Corporation considers necessary, the provision (by construction, acquisition, conversion, improvement or otherwise) of dwellings for letting or for sale and of hostels and the management of dwellings and hostels so provided[2]. The Housing Corporation may also provide an advisory service[3].

1 Housing Associations Act 1985, s 74 and Sch 6.
2 Section 75 as amended by the Housing Act 1996.
3 Section 77.

Registered social landlords

12.64 A landlord which is registered with the Housing Corporation is a registered social landlord. The following bodies are eligible for registration: a registered charity which is a housing association; a society registered under the Industrial and Provident Societies Act 1965 as an industrial and provident society[1] which satisfies specified conditions; or a company registered under the Companies Act which satisfies the specified conditions[2]. The specified conditions are that the body is non-profit making[3] and is established for the purpose of or has among its objects or powers the provision, construction, improvement or management of houses to be kept available for letting, houses for occupation by members of the body where the rules of the body restrict membership to persons entitled or prospectively entitled (as tenants or otherwise) to occupy a house provided or managed by the body, or hostels and that any additional purposes or objects are among those specified[4].

1 See **12.80** ff.
2 Housing Act 1996, s 2(1).
3 For definition of non-profit making see Housing Act 1996, s 2(3).
4 Section 2(2). The specified additional purposes or objects are contained in s 2(4).

Housing associations[1]

12.65 A housing association is a society, body of trustees or company established for the purposes of, or amongst whose objects or powers are included those of, providing, constructing, improving or managing, or facilitating or encouraging the construction or improvement of, housing accommodation, which does not trade for profit or whose constitution or rules prohibit the issue of any capital with interest or dividend exceeding the rate for the time being prescribed by the Treasury, whether with or without differentiation as between share and local capital[2].

Every housing association which was registered in the register kept by the Corporation under Part I of the Housing Associations Act 1985 had to be registered as a social landlord on 1 October 1996[3].

1 As to the history and the various sorts of housing associations, see (1959) 23 Conv (NS) 3 (Craddock).
2 Housing Associations Act 1985, s 1 (1). In the Act 'fully mutual', in relation to a housing association, means that the rules of the association (a) restrict membership to persons who are tenants or prospective tenants of the association, and (b) preclude the granting or assignment of tenancies to persons other than members; and 'co-operative housing association' means a fully mutual housing association which is a society registered under the Industrial and Provident Societies Act 1965, s 1 (2). In the Act 'self-build society' means a housing association whose object is to provide, for sale to, or occupation by, its members, dwellings built or improved principally with the use of its members' own labour: s 1 (3). In the Act 'housing trust' means a corporation or body of persons which (a) is required by the terms of its constituent instrument to use the whole of its funds, including any surplus which may arise from its operations, for the purpose of providing housing accommodation, or (b) is required by the terms of its constituent instrument to devote the whole, or substantially the whole, of its funds to charitable purposes and in fact uses the whole, or substantially the whole, of its funds for the purposes of providing housing accommodation: s 2. The appropriate rates are set out in 19 *Halsbury's Laws* (3rd edn) 703, fn (s).
3 The commencement date of s 1 of the Housing Act 1996.

Borrowing powers

12.66 The Housing Corporation may, within specified limits[1], borrow from the Secretary of State[2] or, with his consent, from other specified bodies or persons[3].

1 Housing Associations Act 1985, s 93.
2 In Wales, the National Assembly of Wales: see **12.42**.
3 Section 92.

Lending powers

12.67 The Housing Corporation may lend to a registered social landlord, an unregistered self-build society, any subsidiary of the Corporation or any other body in which it holds an interest for the purpose of enabling the body to meet the whole or part of expenditure incurred or to be incurred by it in carrying out its objects[1]. It may also lend to an individual for the purpose of assisting him to acquire from the Corporation or any of the bodies previously mentioned a legal estate or interest in a dwelling which he intends to occupy[2].

Where the Corporation makes a loan to an unregistered self-build society and it has an interest in land belonging to the society under a mortgage to secure the loan, it may, with the consent of the Secretary of State[3], give the society directions with respect to the disposal of the land, including a direction that the society transfer its interest in the land to the Corporation[4].

Where the Corporation has left outstanding or advanced any amount in the case of disposal on a shared ownership lease, other than under the right to buy provisions of the Housing Act 1985[5], it may make further advances for the purpose of assisting the tenant to purchase further portions of the equity[6].

1 Housing Associations Act 1985, s 79 (1) as amended by Housing Act 1996. Any such loan may be by way of temporary loan or otherwise. The terms may prevent repayment before a specified date without the Corporation's consent: s 79 (3).
2 Section 79 (2). The terms may not prevent early repayment: s 79 (3).
3 In Wales, the National Assembly for Wales: see **12.42**.
4 Section 80.
5 See **12.47**.
6 Housing Associations Act 1985, s 81.

Power to guarantee loans

12.68 The Housing Corporation may, with the consent of the Secretary of State[1] given with the approval of the Treasury, guarantee the repayment of the principal of, and the payment of interest on, sums borrowed by registered social landlords, unregistered self-build societies, or other bodies in which the Corporation has an interest[2].

1 In Wales, the National Assembly for Wales: see **12.42**.
2 Housing Associations Act 1985, s 83. There is a limit on the outstanding amount guaranteed of £300m or such greater sum not exceeding £500m as the Secretary of State may specify by order made with the approval of the Treasury: s 83 (3), (4).

Indemnity agreements

12.69 The Corporation may, with the approval of the Secretary of State[1], enter into an agreement with (a) a building society lending on the security of a house, or (b) a recognised body making a relevant advance[2] on the security of a house, whereby, in the event of default by the mortgagor, and in circumstances and subject to conditions specified in the agreement, the Corporation binds itself to indemnify the society or body in respect of the whole or part of the mortgagor's outstanding indebtedness and any loss or expense falling on the society or body in consequence of the mortgagor's dafault[3].

1 Or National Assembly for Wales: see **12.42**.
2 Housing Associations Act 1985, s 85.
3 Section 84 (1). The agreement may provide for the Corporation to take a transfer of the mortgage: s 84 (2), (3).

Power to acquire land

12.70 The Housing Corporation may acquire land by agreement for the purpose of (a) selling or leasing it to a registered social landlord or an unregistered self-build society, or (b) providing dwellings (for letting or for sale) or hostels, and may be authorised by the Secretary of State[1] to acquire land compulsorily for any such purpose[2]. The Corporation may provide or improve dwellings or hostels on land belonging to it[3]. Land which the Corporation has not developed under these powers may be disposed of to a registered social landlord, an unregistered self-build society, a subsidiary of the Corporation, or any other body in which the Corporation holds an interest[4].

1 Or National Assembly for Wales: see **12.42**.
2 Housing Associations Act 1985, s 88 (1).
3 Section 89 (1).
4 Section 90 (1).

Registered social landlord finance

12.71 Registered social landlords are principally financed by grants made by the Housing Corporation[1]. The Corporation, acting in accordance with such principles as it may from time to time determine, must specify in relation to grants:
(a) the procedure to be followed in relation to applications for grant; (b) the circumstances in which the grant is or is not to be payable; (c) the method for calculating, and any limitations on, the amount of grant, and (d) the manner in which, and time or times at which grant is to be paid[2].

The Corporation has power in certain circumstances to reduce any grants payable by it, suspend or cancel any instalments of a grant or recover a grant[3].

Local authorities may promote the formation of bodies to act as registered social landlords and may subscribe for their share or loan capital. Local authorities may also make grants or loans to registered social landlords or guarantee or join in guaranteeing the payment of the principal of, and interest on, money borrowed by them (including money borrowed by the issue of loan capital) or of interest on share capital issued by the landlord[4].

In addition a local authority may promote the formation or extension of or assist a housing association[5].

1 For loans by the Public Works Loan Commissioners to registered social landlords, see Housing Act 1996, s 23.
2 Housing Act 1996, s 18.
3 Section 27(1), (2).
4 Section 22.
5 Housing Associations Act 1985, s 58 (1).

Registered social landlords: disposal of land

12.72 Subject to the consent of the Housing Corporation[1], registered social landlords have power to dispose of land[2].

1 Housing Act 1996, s 9 and s 10 for exceptions thereto.
2 Section 8. Unregistered housing associations may also dispose of land, subject to the consent of the Housing Associations: Housing Associations Act 1985, ss 9 and 10, as amended.

BUILDING SOCIETIES

GENERALLY

Purposes of building societies

12.73 The Building Societies Act 1986[1] permits the establishment of societies under the Act whose purpose or principal purpose is that of making loans which are secured on residential property, are funded substantially by its members and whose principal office is in the United Kingdom[2]. If a building society fails to comply with those requirements at any time after its establishment, then certain powers conferred on the Buildings Societies Commission[3] become exercisable in relation to it, but the failure does not affect the validity of any transaction or other act by the building society[4].

A society is established under the Act on compliance by the person establishing it with the scheduled requirements[5] and is incorporated under the Act as from the date of registration by the central office of friendly societies[6]. A society incorporated under the Act is referred to in the Act as a building society[7]. Certain societies incorporated under the earlier building societies legislation are deemed to be registered and accordingly incorporated under the 1986 Act[8].

The Building Societies Acts 1986 and 1997 have conferred extensive powers on building societies to compete in the financial services market and the regime is, by virtue of the 1997 Act, now generally permissive, and prohibitive of specified activities, whereas previously it was permissive only of specified activities. The following are prohibited. A building society must not (and must secure that each of its subsidiary undertakings does not):

(a) act as a market maker in securities, commodities or currencies;
(b) trade in commodities or currencies; and
(c) enter into any transaction involving derivative investments[9].

A building society must do all that is reasonably practicable to secure that neither it nor any of its subsidiary undertakings:

(a) hold more than 5 per cent of the issued share capital; or (b) is at any time entitled to exercise or control the exercise of more than 5 per cent of the voting power at any general meeting of an undertaking which is, at that time, doing any of the things which the society is prohibited from doing[10] or an undertaking whose subsidiary undertaking is at that time doing any of those things[11].

A building society must not create a floating charge on the whole or part of its undertaking or property[12].

The Financial Services and Markets Act 2000 which is intended to come into force no later than 30 November 2001[13] will make further changes to the statutory regime affecting building societies in relation to financial services generally. In particular, all the functions of the Building Societies Commission are to be transferred to the Financial Services Authority; a unified statutory process will be put in place authorising financial institutions including banks, building societies, insurance companies and investment firms; and a single financial services compensation scheme and ombudsman scheme will be established.

1 The 1986 Act has been substantially amended by the Building Societies Act 1997.
2 Building Societies Act 1986, s 5 (1) as amended.
3 Power to direct restructuring of business etc power to make prohibition orders and power to petition for winding up etc: see Building Societies Act 1986, ss 36, 36A and 37. The Building Societies Commission was established in the 1986 Act for the purpose of supervising building societies: ss 1-4 and 36-57. These powers have been prospectively transferred to the Financial Services Authority by the Financial Services and Markets Act 2000, which has yet to have effect in this respect.
4 Building Societies Act 1986, s 4A, inserted by the Building Societies Act 1997.
5 Section 5 (8), Sch 2.
6 Section 5 (2).
7 Section 5 (3).
8 Section 5 (4).
9 Section 9A(1). A transaction which contravenes the section is not invalid.
10 Ie under s 9A(1).
11 Section 9A(6).

12 Section 9B(1). A transaction which contravenes the section is void: s 9B(2).
13 At the date of writing, some provisions of the Act have been brought into force by various statutory instruments.

RAISING FUNDS AND BORROWING

Generally

12.74 A building society may not raise money from members or accept deposits of money unless authorised to do so by the Building Societies Commission[1].

A building society's power to issue shares is a power:

(a) to issue shares of one or more denominations whether in sterling or another currency; and
(b) to issue them either as shares paid up in full or as shares to be paid by periodical or other payments, and (in either case) with accumulating or other interest;

and funds so raised may be repaid when they are no longer required for the purposes of the society[2]. In the case of deferred shares, the power includes the power to issue shares at a premium[3]. A building society may not:

(a) accept a deposit from an individual;
(b) raise funds from an individual otherwise than by issue of shares; or
(c) raise funds from a body corporate or from a bare trustee for a body corporate or for persons who include a body corporate otherwise than by the issue of deferred shares[4].

The acceptance of deposits (including the issue of debt securities) does not constitute the raising of funds[5].

A building society must secure that the percentage of its value held in shares by or on trust for bodies corporate does not exceed a prescribed maximum[6].

1 Subject to certain exceptions: Building Societies Act 1986, s 9(1) and (3). Authorisation will be granted unconditionally or subject to conditions as set out in s 9(4) and (5): s 9(2). These provisions have been prospectively repealed by the Financial Services and Markets Act 2000.
2 Section 8(5).
3 Section 8(6).
4 Section 8(1).
5 Section 8(8).
6 Section 7.

LENDING POWERS

Generally

12.75 At least 75 per cent[1] of the assets of a building society must be held in loans fully secured on residential property[2]. A loan which is secured on residential property is fully secured on the land where the principal of and interest accrued on the land do not exceed the value of the security and there is no more than one prior mortgage of the land. This definition must be satisfied at the time when the loan is made or acquired[3].

1 This percentage may be reduced to no less than 60 per cent by order of the Treasury: Building Societies Act 1986, s 6(6).
2 The assets of the society are: the total assets of the society and subsidiary undertakings *minus* liquid assets and fixed assets and certain insurance funds *plus* provision for bad debts: s 6(1) and (2). This formula was introduced by the 1997 Act and replaces the lending structure set out in the 1986 Act, ss 10 and 11 which have been repealed. For an account of them, see the previous edition of this work.
3 Building Societies Act 1986, s 6B. Section 6A defines 'loans secured on land' as a loan secured by a mortgage of a legal estate in land in England and Wales or Northern Ireland or a qualifying security over land in an European Economic Area country or territory. The Commission (after implementation of Financial Services and Markets Act 2000, the Financial Services Authority) may with the consent of the Treasury by order provide for any provisions of the 1986 Act to have effect in relation to loans secured on land outside the EEA with appropriate modification: s 6A(2).

Duties of building society on sale

12.76 The general law rule that a mortgagee must take reasonable care to obtain the true market value or the best price reasonably obtainable at the time when selling a mortgaged property in possession applies to building societies[1].

1 Building Societies Act 1997, s 12 and *Reliance Permanent Building Society v Harwood-Stamper* [1944] Ch 362, [1944] 2 All ER 75 and **20.23**.

Discharge of mortgages

12.77 A building society may discharge a mortgage by:

(a) statutory receipt in the prescribed form signed by any person acting under the authority of the board of directors; or
(b) reconveyance of the mortgaged property to the mortgagor or reconveyance to such persons of full age and on such trusts as the mortgagor may direct[1].

In the case of unregistered land the receipt is issued pursuant to Law of Property Act 1925, s 115[2]. In the case of registered land, discharge is pursuant to the usual rules.

1 Building Societies Act 1986, s 6C, Sch 2A, para 1(1) as added by the Building Societies Act 1997.
2 Building Societies Act 1986, Sch 2A, para 1(2). For Law of Property Act 1925, s 115 see **28.57**.

Loans for mobile homes

12.78 Subject to the limits of its lending powers set out above, a building society may make mobile home loans[1]. Such a loan will rarely be secured on land, as the mobile home owner will be a mere licensee of the site[2].

1 This is the position following the amendments made by the 1997 Act. Under the 1986 Act, building societies were expressly authorised to make such loans: Building Societies Act 1986, s 15, repealed.
2 See generally on mobile homes, the Mobile Homes Act 1983.

Form of mortgage

12.79 There is no special form of mortgage or charge to a building society. Subject to the specific matters mentioned above, the general law of mortgages applies to mortgages taken by a building society[1]. The usual provisions of a mortgage are dealt with elsewhere[2] and in this work reference is made, where appropriate, to any special characteristics in relation to building societies. The principal difference between a building society mortgage and any other is the incorporation in a building society mortgage of the rules of that society[3]. The mortgage usually provides that any alteration of the rules will be binding on the mortgagor. A society has power to alter its rules[4]. The effect of the incorporation of the rules of the society in the mortgage on the transfer of the mortgage is considered elsewhere[5]. The transfer, realisation and discharge of a building society mortgage are also considered elsewhere[6].

1 *Provident Permanent Building Society v Greenhill* (1878) 9 Ch D 122; *Bell v London and South Western Bank* [1874] WN 10.
2 See **3.21** ff.
3 For further details as to the special features of building society mortgages, see Wurtzburg and Mills *Building Society Law* (15th edn) Ch 6, especially paras 6.26–6.28 on the relationship of the society's rules to the mortgage.
4 Building Societies Act 1986, s 5 (8), Sch 2, paras 3, 4; under the former law, see *Rosenburg v Northumberland Building Society* (1889) 22 QBD 373, CA; *Bradbury v Wild* [1893] 1 Ch 377.
5 See **14.14**.
6 See **14.14**, **20.22–20.23**, **28.57**.

INDUSTRIAL AND PROVIDENT SOCIETIES

BORROWING POWERS

Generally

12.80 The rules of the society must provide whether the society may contract loans or receive money on deposit from members or others and, if so, under what conditions, on what security and to what limits of amount[1]. Mortgages and charges of industrial and provident societies do not require registration with the Chief Registrar of Friendly Societies[2]. A mortgagee is not bound to inquire as to the authority for the mortgage, and the society's receipt is a good discharge for all moneys arising from such transaction or in connection therewith[3].

Industrial and provident societies may create charges on their personal chattels free from the provisions of the Bills of Sale Acts, 1878 and 1882, if an application is made within 14 days to record the charge at the central office established under the Friendly Societies Act 1896[4].

1 Industrial and Provident Societies Act 1965, s 1, and Sch 1. As to housing associations, see **12.65**. The Act 1965 consolidated the Industrial and Provident Societies Acts 1893 to 1961.
2 As to debentures issued under the Agricultural Credits Act 1928, see **9.12**.
3 Industrial and Provident Societies Act 1965, s 30 (1).
4 Section 1.

LENDING POWERS

Generally

12.81 The rules of a registered industrial and provident society may provide for advances of money to members:

(a) on the security of real or personal property or, in Scotland, of heritable estate; or
(b) if the society is registered to carry on banking business, in any manner customary in the conduct of such business[1].

Agricultural, horticultural or forestry societies may make advances to members for agricultural, horticultural or forestry purposes without security[2].

1 Industrial and Provident Societies Act 1965, s 21. For a form of mortgage, see 28 *Forms and Precedents* (5th edn, 1999 reissue) Mortgages.
2 Section 12.

Discharge of industrial and provident society mortgage

12.82 Special provision is made for the discharge of mortgages to industrial and provident societies[1].

1 See **28.54**.

CREDIT UNIONS

BORROWING POWERS

Generally

12.83 A credit union[1] may borrow money from an authorised bank[2] or temporarily from another credit union or an association of credit unions but the amount so borrowed and not repaid shall not at any time exceed in the aggregate one half of the total paid-up share capital[3].

1 'Credit union', generally, means a society registered under the Industrial and Provident Societies Act 1965 by virtue of s 1 of the Credit Unions Act 1979: Credit Unions Act 1979, s 31 (1). To be registered under s 1 of the Act the society must have as its objects only those of a credit union and the admission to membership must be restricted in the manner appropriate to a credit union so that in consequence a common bond exists between the members: Credit Unions Act 1979, s 1 (2). The objects of a credit union are set out in s 1 (3) (the promotion of thrift among the members etc). The qualifications for admission to membership which are appropriate to a credit union are set out in s 1 (4). For matters to be provided for in the rules of a credit union, see Credit Unions Act 1979, s 4 (1), Sch 1, paras 1–14.
2 See Credit Unions Act 1979, s 31 (1) for the meaning of 'authorised bank'. For calling in of a loan when an institution ceases to be an authorised bank, see s 13 (3).
3 Credit Unions Act 1979, s 10 (1). A person dealing with a credit union shall not be obliged to satisfy himself or to inquire whether the borrowing limit has been or is being observed, but if a person who lends money to a credit union or takes security in connection with such a loan has, at the time when the loan is made or the security is given, actual notice of the fact that the limit has been or is thereby exceeded, the debt or security shall be unenforceable: s 10 (3).

LENDING POWERS

Generally

12.84 Subject to certain provisions, a credit union may make to a member who is of full age a loan for a provident or productive purpose, upon such security (or without security) and terms as the rules of the credit union may provide[1]. The maximum period of a secured loan is five years and two years for an unsecured loan[2]. A credit union may charge interest on loans, but such interest shall be at a rate not exceeding 1 per cent per month[3] on the amount of the loan outstanding and such interest shall be inclusive of all administrative and other expenses incurred in connection with the making of the loan[4].

Where a credit union makes a loan to a member of the credit union and at the time the loan is made, the member's paid-up shareholding in the credit union is equal to or greater than his total liability (including contingent liability) to the credit union, on the application of the member to the credit union, the loan shall be treated as a secured loan[5].

A credit union may hold land for the purpose of conducting its business thereon and may mortgage such land[6]. A credit union may hold any interest in land so far as is necessary for the purpose of making loans to its members on the security of an interest in land and of enforcing such security[7].

1 Credit Unions Act 1979, s 11 (1).
2 Section 11 (4); until any other period shall be specified.
3 Or such other rate as may from time to time be specified.
4 Section 11 (5).
5 Section 11A.
6 Section 12 (1). No person shall be bound to inquire as to the authority for any dealing with land by a credit union: s 12 (6).
7 Section 12 (3).

FRIENDLY SOCIETIES

EXISTING FRIENDLY SOCIETIES

Borrowing powers

Generally

12.85 A registered society or branch may borrow on the mortgage of land and buildings if the rules provide that the society or branch may hold land[1].

1 Friendly Societies Act 1974, s 53 implies power to borrow; and see s 23 (2). As to deposits of members, see s 49.

Lending powers

Generally

12.86 The Friendly Societies Act 1974 makes provision for loans to members out of a separate loan fund[1]. The trustees of a registered society or branch may, with the consent of the committee or of a majority of the members present and entitled to vote in a general meeting, invest the funds of the society or branch or any part thereof, inter alia, upon any security expressly directed by the rule of the society or branch, not being personal security, except as in the Act of 1974 authorised with respect to loans[2], and in any investments authorised by law for investment of trust funds[3].

1 Friendly Societies Act 1974, s 49. The lending of money to members is not generally a purpose in respect of which a society can be registered, but provision is made for specially authorised societies with that purpose: s 7, Sch 1.
2 Sections 48, 49.
3 Section 46 (1) (d), (e). As to powers of trustees to invest in mortgages, see **12.118–12.119**.

Discharge of friendly society mortgage

12.87 Special provision is made for the discharge of mortgages to friendly societies[1].

1 See **28.54**.

INCORPORATED FRIENDLY SOCIETIES

12.88 The Friendly Societies Act 1992 creates a new type of institution called an incorporated friendly society, which has corporate status. After the commencement of the 1992 Act, no further friendly societies can be registered under the 1974 Act[1] and a registered friendly society can be registered and incorporated as an incorporated friendly society[2].

An incorporated friendly society may borrow on the mortgage of land or buildings, subject to the provisions of its memorandum and rules, so far as it is incidental or conducive to the carrying out of its purposes or the activities specified in Sch 5[3].

Any incorporated friendly society may invest its funds in the purchase of land or the erection of buildings therein, in any other security directed by the rules of the society other than personal security, or in other investments which trustees are authorised to make[4].

1 Friendly Societies Act 1992, Sch 16, para 4(c).
2 Schedule 4, s 6.
3 Section 7(4). For definition of 'its purposes' see s 5(2).
4 Section 14(1).

TENANTS FOR LIFE AND STATUTORY OWNERS

GENERALLY

No new strict settlements

12.89 No settlement created after 1 January 1997 is a settlement for the purposes of the Settled Land Act 1925; no settlement is deemed to be made under that Act after that date[1]. Where someone purports to grant an entailed interest in real or personal property, the instrument is not effective to grant an entailed interest[2]. Strict settlements existing on 1 January 1997 continue to exist until there is no relevant property[3]. The following discussion applies to existing settlements.

1 Trusts of Land and Appointment of Trustees Act 1996, s 2(1).
2 Section 2, Sch 1, para 5(1)(a). The effect of the instrument is to operate as a declaration that the property is held in trust absolutely for the person to whom an entailed interest in the property was purported to be granted: Sch 1, para 5(1)(b).
3 Section 2(4) 'Relevant property' is defined as land and personal chattels to which the Settled Land Act 1925 s 67(1) applies: s 2(4).

POWER TO MORTGAGE

Mortgages for purposes of the settled estate

12.90 The tenant for life or statutory owner[1] has power, by a legal mortgage[2], to raise money for certain specified purposes. The tenant for life has power to raise money which is required[3] for certain purposes on the security of settled land or any part of it by a legal mortgage. The money raised by the mortgage is capital money and may be paid or applied accordingly. The purposes for which money may be raised include (s 71):

(i) discharging an incumbrance[4] on the settled land or part thereof;
(ii) paying for any improvement authorised by this Act or by the settlement[5];
(iii) equality of exchange;
...[6]
(ix) payment of the costs of any transaction authorised by section 71 or either of section 69 or section 70.[7]

The tenant for life may raise the money so required, on the security of the settled land, or any part thereof, by a legal mortgage[8] and the money so raised shall be capital money for that purpose, and may be paid or applied accordingly[9].

Subsequent Acts have added further purposes, namely:

(a) satisfying any claim under the Landlord and Tenant Act 1927, for compensation for an improvement[10];
(b) paying a coast protection charge or expenses incurred in carrying out work under a works scheme under the Coast Protection Act 1949[11];
(c) paying certain expenses and making payments under the Landlord and Tenant Act 1954[12];
(d) paying certain sums recoverable under the Town and Country Planning Act 1990[13];
(e) paying expenses incurred by a tenant for life or statutory owner in connection with proceedings for enfranchising leaseholds or obtaining extensions of leases under the Leasehold Reform Act 1967 and paying of compensation in connection with the exercise of certain overriding rights of a landlord under the Act[14].

Furthermore, the court may direct that any costs, charges, or expenses to be paid out of the property subject to a settlement be raised and paid by means of a legal mortgage of the settled land or any part thereof[15].

1 For tenant for life, see Settled Land Act 1925, ss 19, 20 as amended, 117 (1) (xxviii). For a statutory owner, see ss 23, 26, 117 (1) (xxvi).
2 Or charge by way of legal mortgage: Settled Land Act 1925, s 117 (1) (xi), and see s 72 (1). For forms, see 28 *Forms and Precedents* (5th edn, 1999 reissue) Mortgages. The covenant for payment by a tenant for life will usually be limited to interest only. Where a tenant for life executes a mortgage as absolute owner in favour of a mortgagee without notice the charge is void: *Weston v Henshaw* [1950] Ch 510; doubted in *Re Morgan's Lease* [1972] Ch 1, [1971] 2 All ER 235; see (1971) 87 LQR 338 (Elliott); [1981] Conv 19 (Clayton); [1985] Conv 377, 381 (Warrington).
3 'Required' means reasonably required having regard to the circumstances of the settled land: *Re Clifford, Scott v Clifford* [1902] 1 Ch 87.
4 This includes local charges: *Re Pizzi, Scrivener v Aldridge* [1907] 1 Ch 67. Incumbrance in this section does not include any annual sum payable only during a life or lives or during a term of years absolute or determinable: s 71 (2).
5 For improvements authorised by the Act, see s 83 and Sch 3. The settlement can confer on the tenant for life additional or large powers: s 109.
6 The purposes specified in (iv) and (v) which relate to the extinguishment of manorial incidents are now spent. The purposes in (vi), (vii) and (viii) rarely arise.
7 That is, s 69 (shifting incumbrances); s 70 (varying rate of interest, etc): see **12.91**.
8 For tenant for life, see Settled Land Act 1925, ss 19, 20, 117 (1) (xxviii). For a statutory owner, see ss 23, 26, 117 (1) (xxvi).
9 For this purpose it must be paid to the trustees of the settlement: s 75.
10 Landlord and Tenant Act 1927, s 13 (2) as amended by Trusts of Land and Appointment of Trustees Act 1996.
11 Coast Protection Act 1949, s 11 (2) (a) as amended by Trusts of Land and Appointment of Trustees Act 1996.
12 Landlord and Tenant Act 1954, Sch 2, para 6.
13 Town and Country Planning Act 1990, s 328.
14 Leasehold Reform Act 1967, s 6 (5) as amended by Trusts of Land and Appointment of Trustees Act 1996, Sch 2, para 9 (1).
15 Settled Land Act 1925, ss 92, 114.

Shifting incumbrances and varying interest

12.91 Under s 69 of the Settled Land Act 1925, an incumbrance affecting any part of the settled land (whether capable of being overreached on the exercise by the tenant for life of his powers under the Act or not), may, with the consent of the incumbrancer, be charged on any other part of the settled land, or on capital moneys, whether already charged therewith or not, in exoneration of the first mentioned part and the tenant for life may by a legal mortgage or otherwise make provision accordingly.

By s 70 where an incumbrance[1] affects any part of the settled land, the tenant for life may, with the consent of the incumbrancer, vary the rate of interest charged and any other provisions of the instrument, if any, creating the incumbrance and, with the like consent, charge the incumbrance on any other part of the settled land, whether already charged therewith or not, or on capital money, by way of additional security or of consolidation of securities, and by a legal mortgage or otherwise make provision accordingly.

1 'Incumbrance' in this section includes any annual sum payable during a life or lives or during a term of years absolute or determinable, but in any such case an additional security must be effected so as only to create a charge or security similar to the original charge or security: s 70 (2).

Substituted security

12.92 The Settled Land Act 1925 also provides that land acquired by purchase or in exchange or otherwise under the powers of the Act may be made a substituted security for any charge from which the settled land or any part thereof has theretofore been released on the occasion and in order to[1] the completion of a sale, exchange or other disposition[2]. On land being so acquired, any person who, by the direction of the tenant for life, so conveys it as to subject it to any legal estate or charge by way of legal mortgage, is not concerned to inquire whether or not it is proper that it shall be so subjected[3].

1 Some word or words are missing in the Act.
2 Settled Land Act 1925, s 82 (1), but where the charge does not affect the whole of the settled land, the land acquired is not to be subjected, unless it is acquired with the proceeds of sale of the land which was subject to the charge; with a corresponding provision for the case of exchange: s 32 (1). For a form of charge by way of substituted security by a tenant for life, see 28 *Forms and Precedents* (5th edn, 1999 reissue) Mortgages.
3 Section 82 (2).

Payment of capital money to trustees

12.93 Since money raised under the statutory powers is capital money it must be paid to not fewer than two persons as trustees of the settlement, unless the trustee is a trust corporation[1]. The tenant for life must also give notice to the trustee of his intention to mortgage or charge the land[2]. This must be a notice of each specific transaction contemplated[3]. However, a lender dealing in good faith with the tenant for life is not concerned to inquire concerning the giving of the notice[4].

1 Settled Land Act 1925, s 94. It may be applied, inter alia, in discharge of incumbrances: s 73 (1) (ii). Though the advance is paid to the trustees the tenant for life should be the member, when the advance is made by a building society, because he holds the legal estate in the property.
2 Section 101 (1).
3 *Re Ray's Settled Estates* (1884) 25 Ch D 464. Section 101 (2), which allows a general notice in certain cases, does not extend to mortgages.
4 Section 101 (5).

Overreaching effect of mortgage

12.94 A legal mortgage by the tenant for life under the statutory powers is effectual to give the mortgagee a title free from the limitations of the settlement and from all estates, interests, and charges subsisting or to arise thereunder, except legal estates and legal charges having priority to the settlement and such estates and charges created for securing money actually raised at the date of the deed[1].

1 Settled Land Act 1925, s 72 (2).

Additional powers

12.95 The settlement may confer powers to mortgage additional to or larger than the statutory powers and such powers are exercisable by the tenant for life as if they were conferred by the Act[1]. The Act contains a general power for the tenant for life to effect any transaction under an order of the court[2].

1 Settled Land Act 1925, s 109 (1), (2), and any power conferred on the trustees will be exercisable by the tenant for life as if it were an additional power conferred on him: s 108 (2).

2 Section 64; Settled Land and Trustee Acts (Court's General Powers) Act 1943, ss 1, 2 as amended by Trusts of Land and Appointment of Trustees Act 1996; Emergency Laws (Miscellaneous Provisions) Act 1953, s 9, and see *Re White-Popham Settled Estates* [1936] Ch 725, [1936] 2 All ER 1486, CA.

Restrictions on powers

12.96 The statutory power to mortgage is not capable of restriction[1].

1 Settled Land Act 1925, ss 104 (1), (2), 106.

Tenant for life as trustee

12.97 A tenant for life, in exercising any power under the Act, must have regard to the interests of all parties entitled under the settlement and is, in relation to the exercise of such powers by him, deemed to be in the position and to have the duties and liabilities of a trustee for those parties[1].

1 Settled Land Act 1925, s 107 (1). See *Hampden v Earl of Buckinghamshire* (1893) 2 Ch 531, CA; *Re Charteris, Charteris v Biddulph* [1917] 2 Ch 379; *Re Gladwin's Trust* [1919] 1 Ch 232. This provision does not affect the title of a mortgagee. but affects the tenant for life personally with liability as a trustee: *Re Marquis of Ailesbury's Settled Estates* [1892] 1 Ch 506 at 535, 536, CA.

Mortgage to tenant for life

12.98 A mortgage or charge of the settled land may be made to the tenant for life. In that case the trustees of the settlement have, in addition to their powers as trustee, all the powers of a tenant for life as to negotiating and completing the transaction[1].

1 Settled Land Act 1925, s 68. For a form, see 28 *Forms and Precedents* (5th edn, 1999 reissue) Mortgages.

Mortgages to give effect to the beneficial interests

12.99 Where any principal sum is required to be raised on the security of the settled land, by virtue of any trust, or by reason of the exercise of an equitable power affecting the settled land, or by any person or persons who under the settlement is or are entitled or together entitled to or has or have a general power of appointment over the settled land, whether subject to any equitable charges or powers of charging subsisting under the settlement or not; or the settled land is subject to any equitable charge for securing money actually raised and affecting the whole estate the subject of the settlement then the estate owner shall be bound, if so requested in writing[1], to create such legal estate or charge by way of legal mortgage as may be required for raising the money or giving legal effect to the equitable charge[2].

This is subject to the proviso that, so long as the settlement remains subsisting, any legal mortgage so created shall take effect and be expressed to take effect subject to any equitable charges under the settlement which have priority to the interest of the person by or on whose behalf the money is required to be raised, unless the persons entitled to the prior charges consent in writing to the same being postponed, though such consent need not be expressed in the mortgage[3].

It is further provided by s 16 that where a mortgage or charge is expressed to be made by an estate owner pursuant to this section[4] then, in favour of the mortgagee or chargee and persons deriving title under him, the same shall take effect in priority to all the trusts of the settlement and all equitable interests and powers subsisting or to arise under the settlement except those to which it is expressly made subject, and shall so take effect whether the mortgagee or chargee has notice of such interests or powers or not, and the mortgagee or chargee shall not be concerned to see that a case has arisen to authorise the mortgage or charge, or that no more money than was wanted was raised[5].

A tenant for life, as estate owner, can also create a legal mortgage for the purpose of giving effect to an agreement for a mortgage, or a charge or lien, whether or not arising by operation of law, if the agreement, charge or lien ought to have priority over the settlement[6].

1 Where a tenant for life has power to raise a sum for his own benefit, the request should not be made by himself to himself, but should be made by the person who advances the money: *Re Egerton Settled Estates* [1926] Ch 574.
2 Settled Land Act 1925, s 16. Under this provision money can be raised for portions. See also Land Registration Act 1925, s 90; Land Registration Rules 1925, r 144.
3 Settled Land Act 1925, s 16 (1) (iii), proviso, and see Land Registration Rules 1925, r 156.
4 NB to have the overreaching effect of this subsection the mortgage must be expressed to be made pursuant thereto.
5 For a form of mortgage under s 16, see 28 *Forms and Precedents* (5th edn, 1999 reissue) Mortgages.
6 Settled Land Act 1925, s 16 (4), and see s 16 (5), (7), for mortgage under order of the court.

Mortgage of land subject to family charges

12.100 The Settled Land Act 1925 extended the meaning of settled land to include not only the ordinary case of land limited in trust for persons by way of succession but various other cases where land is not vested in some person absolutely and beneficially[1]. In particular, land is settled land where it is subject to family charges[2]. In such a case the estate owner can only create a legal mortgage free from the charges if the Settled Land Act procedure as to the appointment of trustees and the execution of a vesting deed are observed[3].

By the Law of Property (Amendment) Act 1926, a beneficial owner in fee simple subject to such family charges as would constitute the land settled land may execute a legal mortgage or charge by way of legal mortgage subject to such family charges as if the land had not been settled land and without compliance with the Settled Land Act procedure[4].

1 Settled Land Act 1925, s 1 (1) as amended by Trusts of Land and Appointment of Trustees Act 1996.
2 Section 1 (1) (v) as amended.
3 Section 13.
4 Section 1.

Mortgage by trustees where tenant for life has ceased to have a substantial interest

12.101 If it is shown to the satisfaction of the court that a tenant for life who has by reason of bankruptcy, assignment, incumbrance, or otherwise ceased in the opinion of the court to have a substantial interest in his estate or interest in the settled land or any part thereof, has unreasonably refused to exercise any of the powers conferred on him by the Settled Land Act 1925, or consents to such an order as is hereinafter mentioned, the court may, upon the application of any person interested in the settled land or the part thereof affected, make an order authorising the trustees of the settlement to exercise, in the name and on behalf of the tenant for life, any of the powers of a tenant for life under the Settled Land Act 1925, in relation to the settled land or the part thereof affected, either generally and in such manner and for such period as the court may think fit, or in a particular instance[1].

1 Settled Land Act 1925, s 24. See *Re Thornhill's Settlement* [1941] Ch 24, [1940] 4 All ER 83; affd [1941] Ch 24, [1940] 4 All ER 249, CA. A person dealing with the tenant for life is not affected by such an order, unless it is for the time being registered under the Land Charges Act 1972, as an order affecting land: see Land Charges Act 1972, s 6 as amended.

Mortgage of tenant for life's beneficial interest

12.102 For mortgages of beneficial interests in trust funds, see **7.1** ff.

Mortgage of tenant in tail's equitable interest

12.103 Where the tenant in tail is tenant in tail in possession he will generally have the legal estate in the entailed property vested in him as estate owner[1] and as such he will have the power of mortgaging of a tenant for life[2]. As regards his equitable interest in entailed lands the tenant in tail has special statutory powers of disposing of such interest[3] apart from the general powers of disposition conferred on limited owners under the Settled Land Act 1925[4]. If the tenant in tail is in possession he may execute by deed a mortgage in the form of a conveyance of his equitable interest in fee simple or any less interest[5]. If he is not in possession, unless the mortgage is made with the consent of the protector of the settlement, it will convey to the mortgagee only an equitable interest in the nature of a base fee.

1 Settled Land Act 1925, ss 4 (2), 6 (b), 7 (1)–(4), 9 (2), 20 (1) (i), 117 (1) (xxviii). If he is in a position to bar the entail and become absolute owner he will, of course, be able to mortgage as such.
2 **12.90**.
3 Under the Fines and Recoveries Act 1833, s 15, and see Law of Property (Amendment) Act 1924, s 9, Sch 9.
4 By Pt II (ss 35–72).
5 Fines and Recoveries Act 1833, ss 15, 40. Enrolment was abolished by the Law of Property Act 1925, s 133 (now repealed spent by Statute Law (Repeals) Act 1969).

Mortgages by charity trustees

12.104 Land held on charitable, ecclesiastical or public trusts was formerly deemed to be settled land but is now held on a trust of land. Charitable trustees have all the powers of an absolute owner, subject to certain statutory restrictions[1].

A mortgage of land held by or on trust for a charity other than an exempt charity[2] cannot be granted without an order of the court of the Charity Commissioners unless the charity trustees have obtained and considered proper advice before granting the mortgage[3]. 'Proper advice' is the advice of a person who is reasonably believed by the charity trustees to be qualified by his ability in and practical experience of financial matters and who has no financial interest in the making of the loan in question. It may constitute proper advice albeit that the person giving it does so in the course of his employment as an officer or employee of the charity or of the charity trustees[4].

Such advice must be given in writing on:

(a) whether the proposed loan is necessary in order for the charity trustees to be able to pursue the particular course of action in connection with which the loan is sought by them;
(b) whether the terms of the proposed loan are reasonable having regard to the status of the charity as a prospective borrower; and
(c) the ability of the charity to repay on those terms the sum proposed to be borrowed[5].

The terms of the charity trust deed may also require the observance of certain conditions before any disposition.

1 Trusts of Land and Appointment of Trustees Act 1996, ss 1, 2(6) and 6(8).
2 For exempt charities see 5(2) *Halsbury's Laws* (reissue) paras 293 and 346.
3 Charities Act 1993, s 38(1) and (2) See further 5(2) *Halsbury's Laws* para 346.
4 Section 38(4).
5 Section 38(3).

Form of mortgage by charity trustees[1]

12.105 The mortgage must contain a statement that the land is held by or on trust for a charity and indicating whether the statutory restrictions apply[2] and, if they apply, the mortgage must include a certificate indicating that the statutory requirements have been complied with[3]. Such a certificate raises a conclusive presumption in favour of a person who acquires an interest in the land for money or money's worth, (whether under the mortgage or afterwards) that the facts were as stated in the certificate[4]. Where no such certificate is given, the mortgage is valid in favour of such a person acting in good faith[5].

1 See further 5(2) *Halsbury's Laws* para 347.
2 Charities Act 1993, s 39(1), (1A), (1B).
3 Section 39(2).
4 Section 39(3).
5 Section 39(4).

Universities and colleges

12.106 Universities and their colleges are, as corporations and charities, subject to restrictions in dealing with their lands. Oxford, Cambridge and

Durham and the colleges therein are no longer subject to the further restrictions imposed by the Universities and College Estates Act 1925[1].

1 See Universities and College Estates Act 1964, especially Sch 1, Pt 1, para 6.

MORTGAGES FOR IMPROVEMENTS

Under the Improvement of Land Acts[1]

12.107 As previously stated[2] power to borrow money for improvements is conferred on tenants for life by the Settled Land Act 1925. Powers of improvement had been given to landowners generally[3] by the Improvement of Land Act 1864 and it may still be desirable to make use of the 1864 Act.

The 1864 Act gave in s 9 a list of improvements which were to be within the Act[4] and subsequent Acts[5] extended that list. Section 9 of the 1864 Act is in effect superseded, and the improvements which can be dealt with under the 1864 Act are those which are authorised by the Settled Land Act 1925[6] and a number of other Acts[7]. The authorised improvements also extend to any operation incident to or necessary or proper in the execution of the specifically authorised works, or necessary or proper for carrying into effect any of the specifically mentioned purposes, or for securing the full benefit of any of those works or purposes[8].

In order that an improvement may be sanctioned it must be shown that it will effect a permanent increase of the yearly value of the land exceeding the yearly amount to be charged thereon[9].

1 See generally, 1(2) *Halsbury's Laws* (4th edn reissue) Agriculture, paras 513 ff.
2 See **12.90**.
3 For the definition of landowner, see Improvement of Land Act 1864, ss 3, 10, 20, 24, 30.
4 These improvements were of an agricultural nature.
5 Eg Settled Land Act 1882, s 30 as amended; Agricultural Credits Act 1923, s 3 (4).
6 The whole of the Settled Land Acts 1882 to 1890, with the exception of s 30 of the Act of 1882, were repealed, and their provisions, with the amendments made by the Law of Property Act 1922, and the Law of Property (Amendment) Act 1924, consolidated in the Settled Land Act 1925.
7 See Public Health Act 1936, s 33 (sewage works for agricultural purposes) as amended; Limited Owners Residence Act (1870) Amendment Act 1871; District Councils (Water Supply Facilities) Act 1897; Improvement of Land Act 1899.
8 Settled Land Act 1925, s 83.
9 Improvement of Land Act 1864, s 25.

Charge for improvements

12.108 In the case of improvements to which the 1864 Act applies the Minister, when satisfied that the improvements or part thereof have been properly executed, may execute a charge on the land or some sufficient part thereof, for the sum, by the provisional, or other sanctioning, order, expressed to be chargeable (or for a proportional part thereof if only part of the improvement has been executed), together with interest, and for the amount which shall have been paid in respect of the purchase of adjoining lands, or of any easement or right affecting adjoining lands, with interest[1].

1 Improvement of Land Act 1864, s 49. As to charges for public improvements, see ss 57, 58.

Absolute order by way of rentcharge

12.109 The charge is created by an absolute order and by way of rentcharge, payable half-yearly, for the term of years fixed by the provisional or other sanctioning order[1]. The charge should be registered under the Land Charges Act 1972 as a land charge in Class A[2].

1 Improvement of Land Act 1864, s 51.
2 Note s 4 (1), (4) of the Land Charges Act 1972, re-enacting the Law of Property Act 1969, s 27, which exempted such charges made after the commencement of the 1969 Act from the provisions of s 11 of the Land Charges Act 1925, so that they no longer ranked as mortgages; and if a charge was then already registered building societies and other bodies might advance money on land subject to such charge. Where the land is registered the charge is protected by notice under the Land Registration Act 1925, s 49 (1) (c): see Land Registration Act 1925, s 59 (2); Land Registration Rules 1925, r 155.

Effect and priority of charge

12.110 From the date of the absolute order, the grantee has a charge upon the lands for the principal money from time to time remaining undischarged by payment of the rentcharge, with interest, at the dates expressed, and with priority over every other then existing and future charge and incumbrance affecting the lands or estates and interests, whether created under the powers of any Act of Parliament or otherwise, except charges under any Act authorising advances of public money for improvement of land, and charges created under the 1864 Act, or of prior date created under any other existing Act authorising the charging of lands with the expense of and incident to their improvement[1]. In view of the priority given to such rentcharges in appropriate cases the mortgage should contain a clause prohibiting the obtaining of loans under the Improvement of Land Acts. The person entitled to a rentcharge may assign it to a third party, either absolutely or by way of security[2].

1 Improvement of Land Act 1864, s 59. The charge created under the Limited Owners Residence Act (1870) Amendment Act 1871 does not take priority over an incumbrance affecting the land charged at the time when the charge was created: see s 9 of the 1870 Act; *Provident Clerks' Mutual Life Assurance Association v Law Life Assurance Society* [1897] WN 73.
2 Improvement of Land Act 1864, s 65.

Loans by Agricultural Mortgage Corporation Ltd

12.111 The Agricultural Mortgage Corporation has identical powers to mortgage as a company incorporated under the Companies Act[1].

1 Agriculture and Forestry (Financial Provision) Act 1991, s 1(1) and Sch 1. For powers of corporation to mortgage see **12.7** ff.

TRUSTEES

GENERALLY

12.112 The Trusts of Land and Appointment of Trustees Act 1996 ('TOLATA') applies to all trusts comprising or including land with the exception of land which prior to 1997 was settled land and land subject to the Universities and College Estates Act 1925[1]. TOLATA came into force on 1 January 1997. From that date, no new settlements, trusts for sale and bare trusts can be created and any trust of property which consists of or includes land is a 'trust of land' within the meaning of TOLATA[2].

1 Trusts of Land and Appointment of Trustees Act 1925, s 1. For settled land, see **12.90** ff. For Universities and College Estates Act 1925, see **12.106**.
2 TOLATA, s 1.

BORROWING POWERS

Power of trustees to mortgage

12.113 Trustees have no power to raise money on mortgage unless they are expressly or implicitly authorised to do so by the instrument creating the trust, or unless power is conferred on them by statute. Trustees empowered to mortgage may also raise the incidental costs by mortgage of the same property[1].

A power for trustees to mortgage has sometimes been implied in a power to sell[2] where an absolute conversion of the land is not necessary for the purpose of effecting the object of the power, such as the raising of money to satisfy a particular charge, but a mortgage cannot, apart from statute, be made under an absolute trust for sale[3] and if the raising of a charge by sale is forbidden, the prohibition extends also to raising it by mortgage, since this may cause the loss of the land by sale or foreclosure[4]. A power to mortgage may also be implied from powers of management which necessitate the expenditure of capital[5].

When trustees are empowered to raise money for particular purposes at their absolute discretion, the court will not interfere with their discretion as to the occasion, or the manner of exercising the power, or the refusal to exercise it in any particular manner, though they are bound to effect the general purpose[6].

1 *Armstrong v Armstrong* (1874) LR 18 Eq 541.
2 *Mills v Banks* (1724) 3 P Wms 1; *Stroughill v Anstey* (1852) 1 De GM & G 635.
3 *Devaynes v Robinson* (1857) 24 Beav 86. See *Re Suenson-Taylor's Settlement, Moores v Moores* [1974] 3 All ER 397, [1974] 1 WLR 1280.
4 *Bennett v Wyndham* (1857) 23 Beav 521.
5 *Re Bellinger, Durrell v Bellinger* [1898] 2 Ch 534.
6 *Tempest v Lord Camoys* (1882) 21 Ch D 571, distinguished in *Re Courtier, Coles v Courtier* (1886) 34 Ch D 136.

Statutory powers of mortgaging

Trusts to which the Trusts of Land and Appointment of Trustees Act 1996 applies

12.114 A trustee of land has all the powers of an absolute owner including the power to mortgage[1]. However, the power to mortgage is restricted by the following statutory provisions. First, the power to mortgage is subject to any restrictions upon it in the instrument creating the trust[2]. Second, the trustees' powers may not be exercised in contravention of any enactment, or rule of law or equity[3]. Third, the power may not be exercised without obtaining any consent provided for in the disposition[4]. Fourth, the trustees must consult the beneficiaries who are of full age and beneficially entitled to an interest in possession in the land and give effect to the wishes of those beneficiaries or the majority of them, so far as consistent with the general interest of the trust[5].

1 TOLATA, s 6.
2 Section 8.
3 Section 6(6).
4 Section 8(2).
5 Section 8(2).

Other trusts

12.115 Powers of mortgaging are conferred on trusts to which TOLATA does not apply as follows. Where trustees are authorised by the instrument, if any, creating the trust or by law to pay or apply capital money subject to the trust for any purpose or in any manner, they shall have and shall be deemed always to have had power to raise the money required by sale, conversion, calling in, or mortgage of all or any part of the trust property for the time being in possession[1]. This provision applies notwithstanding anything to the contrary contained in the instrument, if any, creating the trust, but does not apply to trustees of property held for charitable purposes, or to trustees of a settlement for the purposes of the Settled Land Act 1925, not being also statutory owners.[2] These provisions apply, with the exceptions mentioned above, to trustees generally, and enable them to raise money for any purpose to which, under the trust instrument or by law, capital money can be applied[3].

1 Trustee Act 1925, s 16 (1).
2 Section 16(2).
3 The statutory power does not permit the mortgaging of the trust fund to raise moneys for the purchase of further investments: *Re Suenson-Taylor's Settlement, Moores v Moores*, above.

Form of mortgage[1]

12.116 A trustee or other fiduciary owner who mortgages the trust estate does not usually covenant to pay the money borrowed. If there is such a covenant it should be limited to payment only out of money coming into the trustee's hands as trustee[2]. A covenant by a trustee to pay out of a trust fund prevents a personal liability being implied[3].

However, where the trustees are also the persons beneficially entitled the mortgage will take the same form as a mortgage by an absolute owner and accordingly they will then covenant to pay and demise or charge the property as beneficial owners. Where the trustees are not the same persons as those beneficially entitled the mortgage should contain a provision excluding their personal liability[4], for the demise or charge is in itself sufficient to imply personal liability unless the mortgage negatives it[5]. A trustee may not permit the inclusion in the mortgage of a consolidation clause extending to mortgages other than those made by him as trustee[6]. A trustee is under no obligation to exclude the statutory power of sale which is an implied provision in every mortgage[7].

1 For forms of mortgage by trustees, see 28 *Forms and Precedents* (5th edn, 1999 reissue) Mortgages.
2 *Re Robinson's Settlement, Gant v Hobbs* [1912] 1 Ch 717 at 729, CA.
3 *Mathew v Blackmore* (1857) 1 H & N 762.

4 For forms of mortgage by trustees, see 28 *Forms and Precedents* (5th edn, 1999 reissue) Mortgages.
5 *Yates v Aston* (1843) 4 QB 182.
6 *Thorne v Thorne* [1893] 3 Ch 196; and see *Cruickshank v Duffin* (1872) LR 13 Eq 555.
7 *Thorne v Thorne,* above.

Protection of mortgagee

12.117 In all cases where trustees raise money by mortgage and the mortgage purports to be made under a trust or power vested in them, the mortgagee is not concerned to see that the money is wanted, or that no more than is wanted is raised, or otherwise as to the application thereof[1]; or to see that the trustees have consulted the beneficiaries and given effect to the wishes of the majority of them[2].

A mortgagee of registered land is not affected with notice of an express, implied or constructive trust[3]. In relation to a mortgage granted since 1 January 1997, a mortgagee of unregistered land need not be concerned to see that the trustees have had regard to the rights of the beneficiaries[4]; and such a mortgage is not invalidated by any exclusion, limitation or restriction of the trustees' powers unless the mortgagee had actual notice thereof[5].

Since the mortgage money is capital money, the mortgagee must not pay it to fewer than two trustees, unless the trustee is a trust corporation[6]. A mortgage of a legal estate for value overreaches the interests of the beneficiaries if the mortgage is made by trustees of land and any capital monies are advanced to at least two trustees[7]. The beneficiaries' interests will be overreached in those circumstances even if they have an overriding interest by virtue of their actual occupation[8].

1 Trustee Act 1925, s 17. A mortgagee is not concerned even if he has actual notice that the purpose of the borrowing is unauthorised.
2 TOLATA, ss 11(1), 16.
3 Land Registration Act 1925, s 74.
4 TOLATA, s 6(6), (8), 8, 16.
5 TOLATA, s 10.
6 Trustee Act 1925, s 14.
7 Law of Property Act 1925, s 2 (as amended), s 27(2) as substituted and amended.
8 *City of London Building Society v Flegg* [1988] AC 54.

LENDING POWERS

Power to lend money on mortgage

12.118 At present[1], trustees must either have express power under the trust to lend money on mortgage[2], or rely on the statutory power under the Trustee Investments Act 1961. That Act authorises trustees to invest in mortgages of freehold property in England and Wales or Northern Ireland and of leasehold property in those countries of which the unexpired term at the time of the investment is no less than 60 years and in loans on heritable security in Scotland[3]. Mortgages are narrower range investments requiring advice[4]. The Trustee Act 1925[5] and the 1961 Act[6] impose duties on trustees in the exercise of their powers of investing in mortgages.

Trustees must not lend trust money to one of themselves on mortgage[7].

1 The Trustees Investment Act is prospectively repealed from a date to be appointed by the Trustee Act 2000. Section 3 of the Trustee Act 2000 will give trustees a general power of investment including the advance of monies secured on land.

2 See generally *Lewin on Trusts* (17th edn) paras 35-157 as to powers of investment on mortgage under the Trustee Act 2000.
3 Trustee Investments Act 1961, s 1 (1), and Sch 1, Pt II, para 13 and Pt IV, para 5. For the definition of mortgage, see s 17 (4), and Trustee Act 1925, s 58 (7). For the relationship between the 1961 Act and other powers of investment, see Trustee Investments Act 1961, s 3.
4 Trustee Investments Act 1961, ss 1, 6.
5 Sections 8, 9.
6 Section 6.
7 *Stickney v Sewell* (1835) 1 My & Cr 8, 14, 15; *Francis v Francis* (1854) 5 De GM & G 108; *Fletcher v Green* (1864) 33 Beav 426.

Form of mortgage[1]

12.119 A mortgage to trustees should generally be a first legal mortgage. The Trustee Investment Act 1961, which authorises trustees to invest in mortgages, makes no distinction between the types of mortgage in which trustees may invest[2] and it may be that the former restrictions against second, equitable and contributory mortgages no longer apply[3].

A mortgage to trustees generally takes the usual form as for a mortgage to a single mortgagee with only those variations necessitated by there being more than one mortgagee. So it is not usual to disclose the trusts and, indeed, any person dealing in good faith with the mortgagee, or mortgagor if the mortgage has been wholly or partially discharged, is not concerned with any trust at any time affecting the mortgage money[4]. It is the practice to recite that the mortgage money has been advanced on joint account. This gives no notice of the trusts[5] and enables the survivor to give a good receipt for the mortgage money[6].

It is not a breach of trust for the trustees to agree to the exclusion of the statutory power of sale[7].

1 For a form of mortgage to trustees, see 28 *Forms and Precedents* (5th edn, 1999 reissue) Mortgages; and the Appendix.
2 Cf Trustee Act 1925, s 1.
3 See generally *Lewin on Trusts* (17th edn) para 35.181. Investment in sub-mortgages was permitted: *Smethurst v Hastings* (1885) 30 Ch D 490. Trustees could only join in a contributory mortgage if expressly empowered to do so: *Webb v Jonas* (1888) 39 Ch D 660; *Re Dive* [1909] 1 Ch 328; and *Re MacPherson's Will* [1963] NSWR 268.
4 Law of Property Act 1925, s 113. See **14.16**.
5 See the cases in **14.16**, n 2.
6 Law of Property Act 1925, s 111. It is not strictly necessary that this recital be made, since in the absence of express provision s 111 (1) (b) will apply.
7 *Farrar v Barraclough* (1854) 2 Sm & G 231.

PERSONAL REPRESENTATIVES

Power to mortgage personal estate

12.120 An executor or administrator has always had power, by virtue of his office, to raise money, by sale or mortgage of the personal property of the testator, including leaseholds, for payment of debts and other purposes of administration[1]. The power is codified in statute[2]. The power enables an executor to mortgage even property specifically bequeathed, but it ceases as to property specifically bequeathed as soon as the executors have assented to the bequest, even though the bequest is to the executors themselves as trustees[3]. A mortgagee from an executor need not have any recital of the purpose for which the money is raised[4] and is equally protected whether the mortgage be legal or equitable[5]. The power of disposition is not affected by a mere administration order if no receiver has been appointed nor any injunction granted to restrain the personal representative from dealing with the assets[6].

1 *Mead v Lord Orrery* (1745) 3 Atk 235; *Scott v Tyler* (1788) 2 Dick 712; *Vane v Rigden* (1870) 5 Ch App 663.
2 Administration of Estates Act 1925, s 39(1)(i) as amended by TOLATA.
3 *Attenborough v Solomon* [1913] AC 76; *Wise v Whitburn* [1924] 1 Ch 460.
4 *Bonney v Ridgard* (1784) 1 Cox Eq Cas 145.
5 *Scott v Tyler*, above.
6 *Berry v Gibbons* (1873) 8 Ch App 747; *Re Barrett, Whitaker v Barrett* (1889) 43 Ch D 70; Administration of Estates At 1925, s 2 (1).

When mortgage invalid

12.121 Prima facie, when a personal representative is raising money on the property of the deceased, the presumption is that the money is required to pay debts or for some other purpose of administration[1] and, if there are no circumstances to raise an inference to the contrary[2] and the transaction is consistent with the duty of a personal representative, it will be supported[3]; but if the nature of the transaction affords intrinsic evidence that the executor is not acting in the execution of his duty, but is committing a breach of trust, as where the mortgage is given to secure a personal debt of the executor, the mortgagee, being a party to the breach of trust, does not hold the property discharged from the trusts, but it remains subject to the requirements of administration just as in the hands of the executor[4], and it is the same in the case of an advance made for the private purposes of the executor if notice of the fact is brought home to the mortgagee[5]; but a mortgage of the estate to secure the private debt of an executor who is beneficially interested will be good to the extent of his beneficial interest, provided the security is effected in terms which show an intention to charge that interest and not to mortgage in his representative capacity[6], though, if the executor is indebted to the estate, the mortgagee will be postponed to the claim of the estate[7]. If the executor, on borrowing the money, represents that 'part of it' is required for executorship purposes the onus of showing how much was so required is on the borrower[8].

1 *Re Venn and Furze's Contract* [1894] 2 Ch 101; *Re Henson, Chester v Henson* [1908] 2 Ch 356.
2 *Ricketts v Lewis* (1882) 20 Ch D 745.
3 *Nugent v Gifford* (1738) 1 Atk 463; *Mead v Lord Orrery*, above; *Bonney v Ridgard*, above; *Scott v Tyler*, above; *M'Leod v Drummond* (1810) 17 Ves 712; *Keane v Robarts* (1819) 4 Madd 332; *Re Whistler* (1887) 35 Ch D 561.
4 *M'Leod v Drummond*, above; *Keane v Robarts*, above.
5 *Bonney v Ridgard*, above; *Scott v Tyler*, above; *M'Leod v Drummond*, above, and circumstances of gross negligence on the part of the mortgagee are sufficient to defeat his mortgage, though there is no direct fraud: *Hill v Simpson* (1802) 7 Ves 152, but the claim to set aside the mortgage will be barred after a great length of time: *Bomney v Ridgard*, above.
6 *Farhall v Farhall* (1871) 7 Ch App 123.
7 *Cole v Muddle* (1852) 10 Hare 186.
8 *Carter v Sanders* (1854) 2 Drew 248.

Power to mortgage real estate

12.122 The Administration of Estates Act 1925 extends over real estate the same powers of disposition which personal representatives had at common law in regard to personal estate[1]. It is further provided that the personal representatives have as respects real estate all the functions conferred on them by Part I of TOLATA[2].

1 Section 2 (1). Before the Land Transfer Act 1897, there was no power to mortgage the deceased's real estate for payment of his debts, unless by his will he created a charge of debts, which gave the executors a power of sale of the charged property. This gave rise to difficulties because it was necessary on a sale of the property charged either to obtain the concurrence of both executors and devisee, or, if a title was taken from a devisee, for the purchaser to satisfy himself that the debts were paid, or to procure the executor's authority for payment of the purchase money to the devisee. After that Act real estate devolved on the deceased's personal representatives and they had over it the same powers for the purposes of administration as with regard to personal estate.
2 Administration of Estates Act 1925, s 39(1)(ii) as amended by TOLATA.

Protection of mortgagee

12.123 A conveyance of a legal estate made after 1925 by a personal representative to a purchaser for money or money's worth is not invalidated by reason only that the purchaser may have notice that all debts, liabilities etc have been discharged or provided for[1]. A written receipt of a personal representative for any money payable to him is a sufficient discharge to the person paying the money and effectually exonerates him from seeing to the application or being answerable for any loss or misapplication thereof[2].

A mortgagee dealing with a personal representative is not concerned to see that the money advanced on the mortgage is wanted, or that no more than is wanted is raised, or otherwise as to the application thereof[3].

A mortgagee taking a legal title from a personal representative must see that no memorandum of an assent or of a previous conveyance is indorsed on the grant of probate or letters of administration and must see that a memorandum of his own mortgage is indorsed[4].

1 Administration of Estates Act 1925, s 36 (8), (11), (12). This applies to a mortgage and a charge by way of legal mortgage, and purchaser includes a mortgagee: Administration of Estates Act 1925, s 55 (1) (iii), (xviii).
2 Trustee Act 1925, ss 14 (1), 68 (17).
3 Sections 17, 68 (17).
4 Administration of Estates Act 1925, s 36 (5), (6).

Form of mortgage[1]

12.124 A mortgage made by personal representatives should generally be a first legal mortgage or legal charge[2]. Personal representatives may grant a building society mortgage for purposes of administration[3], but such a mortgage is unusual[4]. As in the case of a mortgage by trustees[5] the usual form of mortgage by personal representatives will contain a limited covenant by the personal representatives for payment, unless they are also beneficiaries. A covenant by the personal representatives as such will not enable the mortgage to prove against the estate for the debt where the personal representative exceeds his powers[6], but the personal representative will be personally liable[7].

1 For forms, see 28 *Forms and Precedents* (5th edn, 1999 reissue) Mortgages.
2 See the Administration of Estates Act 1925, s 39 (1), above.
3 *Cruickshank v Duffin* (1872) LR 13 Eq 555; *Thorne v Thorne* [1893] 3 Ch 196.
4 See Wurzburg and Mills *Building Society Law* (15th edn) para 6.03.
5 See **12.116**.
6 *Farhall v Farhall* (1871) 7 Ch App 123.
7 See **12.116**.

PERSONS ACCOUNTABLE FOR DEATH DUTIES

Mortgage for estate duty

12.125 Estate duty has now been abolished[1]. Formerly, a person authorised or required to pay the estate duty in respect of any property had power to raise the amount of the duty and any interest and expenses properly paid or incurred by him in respect thereof by the sale or mortgage of, or a terminable charge, on the property or any part thereof[2], and a person having a limited interest in the property, who paid the estate duty, was entitled to the like charge as if the duty had been raised by means of a mortgage to him[3].

By the Law of Property Act 1925, a personal representative was accountable for all death duties which may become leviable or payable on the death of a decreased owner in respect of land (including settled land) which devolves upon him by virtue of any statute or otherwise; for the purpose of raising the duty and the costs of raising the same, the personal representative has all the powers which are by any statute conferred for raising duty[4].

1 See **12.126**.
2 Finance Act 1894, s 9 (5), but a tenant for life must keep down interest on charges and he cannot throw interest on estate duty on the land, unless there are special circumstances showing that it has been properly incurred by him: *Re Earl of Egmont's Settled Estates, Lefroy v Egmont* [1912] 1 Ch 251.
3 Here the charge is limited to the duty paid and does not include expenses, though it may include interest demanded by the revenue: *Re Earl Howe's Settled Estates, Earl Howe v Kingscote* [1903] 2 Ch 69.
4 Law of Property Act 1925, s 16 (1), (3).

Mortgage for inheritance tax

12.126 The above provision of the Law of Property Act 1925 was repealed as to persons dying on or after 13 March 1975[1], when capital transfer tax replaced estate duty. Capital transfer tax is now renamed as inheritance tax[2]. Any person liable, otherwise than as transferor[3] for inheritance tax has, for the purposes of paying the tax or raising the amount of it when paid, power, whether or not the property is vested in him, to raise the amount of tax by the sale or mortgage of, or a terminable charge on, the property or any part thereof[4]. A person having a limited interest in any property who pays any inheritance tax attributable to the value of that property is entitled to the like charge as if the tax attributable had been raised by means of a mortgage to him[5].

1 Finance Act 1975, s 59 (5), Sch 13.
2 Finance Act 1986, s 100, and the Capital Transfer Tax Act 1984 may be cited as the Inheritance Tax Act 1984.
3 Or as transferor's spouse to whom the property has been transferred by another transfer: see Capital Transfer Tax Act 1984, s 203 (1).

4 Capital Transfer Tax Act 1984, s 212 (1).
5 Capital Transfer Tax Act 1984, s 212 (2).

Inland Revenue charge

12.127 Unless a land charge in respect of estate duty or capital transfer tax has been registered as a land charge[1], the mortgagee is not required to see to the application of the mortgage money[2].

1 See Land Charges Act 1972, s 2 (5) Class D (i); Law of Property Act 1925, ss 16 (7), 17; Land Registration Act 1925, s 73 (1); Capital Transfer Tax Act 1984, ss 237, 238.
2 Law of Property Act 1925, s 17; Capital Transfer Tax Act 1984, s 199 (3).

MINORS

BORROWING POWERS

Loans and mortgages unenforceable

12.128 The law of contracts by minors[1] has been substantially altered by the Minor's Contracts Act 1987[2] which applies to all contracts coming into being after 9 June 1987[3]. This Act repeals the Infants Relief Act 1874 and the Betting and Loans (Infants) Act 1892[4] and essentially restores the common law position before 1874. At common law a loan to an infant could not be enforced against an infant[5], unless for necessaries, but the infant could upon attaining his majority ratify the contract. Further, s 3 (1) of the new Act gives the court a discretionary power to enable the other party to a contract with a minor which is unenforceable against him or which he has repudiated to order that 'any property or property representing property'[6] which has passed as a result of the contract to be returned.

A minor cannot hold an estate in land[7] and, therefore, he cannot be a legal mortgagor. An equitable mortgage made by a minor is unenforceable, but the minor can ratify it upon attaining his majority[8]. An equitable mortgage to secure a loan for the purchase of necessaries is voidable[9].

Where a minor is beneficially entitled to any property, the court may direct the trustees to raise money for his maintenance, education or benefit by mortgage of the property[10]. Personal representatives have powers of mortgaging during the minority of a beneficiary[11]. Powers of management of a minor's lands are conferred on the trustees appointed for this purpose, or if there are none so appointed then the trustees of the settlement under which the minor is entitled, and these powers may include a power to mortgage[12]. The court has no jurisdiction to direct a disentailing deed of a minor's estate to be made by way of mortgage even for providing maintenance for the minor[13], or to authorise a mortgage of a contingent interest coupled with a policy of assurance on the minor's life[14]. A minor may be a member of a building society, unless the rules provide otherwise, and may give all necessary receipts, but cannot vote or hold office[15].

1 The Family Law Reform Act 1969 reduced the age of majority to 18 (s 1). For the use of the word 'minor' in place of 'infant', see s 12.
2 The Act was essentially the result of Law Commission Report no 134 *Law of Contract: Minors' Contracts* (1984) which rejected the more radical proposals of Law Commission

Working Paper no 81 *Law Commission: Minors' Contracts* and essentially adopted the earlier proposals of the Latey Committee's Report on the Age of Majority (1967) Cmnd 3342, Pt IV. For the previous law, see the 9th edn of this work at pp 214–216.

3 Section 5 (2).

4 Section 1.

5 As to the position at common law see textbooks on the law of contract.

6 According to the Law Commission Report no 134 the words 'property representing property' are to be interpreted as referring to the principles of tracing.

7 Law of Property Act 1925, s 1 (6). An attempted conveyance to an infant in the case of transactions before 1 January 1997 formerly operated as a contract by the intending transferor to make a settlement under the Settled Land Act 1925, the parties in the meantime holding the land on trust for the minors. Since 1 January 1997, such a contract is void and the conveyance operates as a declaration that the land is held on trust of land for the minors: see Law of Property Act 1925, s 19 and Settled Land Act 1925, s 27, both now repealed; and TOLATA, Sch 1, para 1(3) and s 1(2).

8 See *Gardner v Wainfur* (1919) 89 LJ Ch 98.

9 *Martin v Gale* (1876) 4 Ch D 428.

10 Trustee Act 1925, s 53.

11 Administration of Estates Act 1925, s 33.

12 Settled Land Act 1925, s 102. The specified powers do not include a power to mortgage, but the power generally to deal with the land in a proper and due course of management may comprehend such a power. The interest of any principal sum charged on the land is to be kept down out of the income of the land (sub-s (3)). If the trustees are statutory owners they will have the powers of such. Trustees of land have these powers of management, even though there is no minority: TOLATA, s 6.

13 *Re Hambrough's Estate, Hambrough v Hambrough* [1909] 2 Ch 620.

14 *Cadman v Cadman* (1886) 33 Ch D 397.

15 Building Societies Act 1986, s 5, Sch 2, para 5 (3); *Nottingham Permanent Benefit Building Society v Thurstan* [1903] AC 6.

Method of securing advance for benefit of minor

12.129 As stated above a minor cannot hold a legal estate in land. Where a minor desires to purchase real estate and to raise the money therefor on the security of the property the following procedure is generally adopted. The property should be conveyed to trustees of land to hold upon the trusts declared by a contemporaneous trust deed. The advance will be made to the trustees who will execute a mortgage or charge of the property in favour of the lender. The trusts upon which the trustees hold the property will be to apply the rents and profits of the property pending sale until the minor attains full age in keeping down the mortgage payments and subject thereto in trust for the minor and upon the minor attaining full age to transfer the property to him[1]. In practice the minor will occupy the property and discharge the mortgage payments. If the minor defaults in making the payments the trustees should execute the trust for sale and discharge the mortgage.

1 In the case of a husband and a wife, where one is of full age and the other a minor, the one of full age should be one of the trustees. Upon the minor attaining full age he or she may then be appointed a trustee with the other spouse, the third party retiring from the trust. Alternatively the trustees may, on the minor attaining full age, transfer the property to the husband and wife.

In the event of a transfer to the former minor alone or the former minor and his or her spouse the mortgagee should be joined to release the trustees from the liability under the mortgage and a new covenant entered into by the grantee or grantees. Similarly on the appointment of the former minor as a trustee the mortgagee should release the retiring trustee from the liability under the mortgage and take a new covenant from the new trustee.

LENDING POWERS

Loans by minors

12.130 The repeal of the Infants Relief Act 1874 by the Minors' Contracts Act 1987 has removed any doubt that a contract of loan can be enforced by a minor[1]. A person who is a minor may, if the rules of a building society do not otherwise provide, be admitted as a member of the society and give all necessary receipts[2].

1 See the textbooks on the law of contract.
2 Building Societies Act 1986, s 5, Sch 2, para 5 (3) (a).

Mortgages to minors

12.131 As previously stated[1] a minor cannot hold a legal estate in land and therefore cannot be a legal mortgagee of land. Prior to 1 January 1997, an attempt to grant or transfer a legal mortgage or charge to an infant had the effect of an agreement for value to execute a mortgage or transfer when the infant attains its majority and in the meantime to hold the infant's beneficial interest in the mortgage debt in trust[2]. A grant or transfer made to an infant together with a person of full age operated to vest the legal estate in the person of full age subject to the infant's beneficial interest. Since 1 January 1997, any such contract ceased to have effect and the conveyance operates as a declaration that the land is held in trust for the minors[3].

An attempted conveyance to a minor jointly with a person of full age formerly vested the legal estate in the person of full age on statutory trust for sale for himself and the minor[4]. On 1 January 1997, any such trust became a trust of land[5].

In the case of attempted conveyances since 1 January 1997, the conveyance operates as a declaration that the transferor holds the land in trust for the minors[6]. An attempted conveyance to one or more minors together with one or more persons of full age vests the land in the adult transferees in trust for all the transferees[7].

An infant may, however, acquire an interest in property other than a legal estate.

1 See **12.128**.
2 Law of Property Act 1925, s 19(4), (6) repealed by TOLATA.
3 TOLATA, Sch 1, para 1(3).
4 Law of Property Act 1925, s 19(2), repealed by TOLATA.
5 TOLATA, s 1(2).
6 TOLATA, s 2(6), Sch 1, para 1(1).
7 TOLATA, Sch 1, para. 1(2).

SPOUSES[1]

FAMILY LAW ACT 1996[2]

Rights of occupation

12.132 Where one spouse is entitled to occupy a dwelling-house by virtue of a beneficial estate or interest or contract, any enactment giving that spouse the right to remain in occupation and the other spouse is not so entitled, the spouse not so entitled has certain rights called 'matrimonial home rights' in the house, namely:

(a) if in occupation, a right not to be evicted or excluded from the dwelling-house or any part of it by the other spouse except with the leave of the court; or
(b) if not in occupation, a right with the leave of the court to enter into and occupy the house[3].

A spouse who has an equitable interest in a dwelling house or in the proceeds of sale thereof, but who has no legal estate therein, is to be treated for the purpose only of determining whether he or she has rights of occupation under the Act as not being entitled to occupy the house by virtue of the interest[4].

1 See earlier editions for the development of the separate property of a married woman. A married woman is now capable of acquiring, holding and disposing of any property in all respects as if she were a *femme sole*: see Law Reform (Married Women and Tortfeasors) Act 1935. There is now no practical difference between male and female mortgagors; that equality is enshrined in the Sex Discrimination Act 1975, s 29. An endowment policy taken out by a husband as collateral security for a mortgage by himself and his wife is not part of settled funds for the purposes of a property adjustment order: *Meldrum v Meldrum* [1970] 3 All ER 1084, [1971] 1 WLR 5.

2 For the so-called deserted wife's equity and its rejection (other than as a personal right against the husband), see *National Provincial Bank Ltd v Ainsworth* [1965] AC 1175, [1965] 2 All ER 472, HL. The Matrimonial Homes Act 1983 repealed the Matrimonial Homes Act 1967. This legislation greatly increases the importance of making a land charges search before completion. Where a property is vested in a husband's sole name his wife may have a beneficial interest therein by virtue of a contribution to the purchase price: but see *Winkworth v Edward Baron Development Co Ltd* [1987] 1 All ER 114, [1986] 1 WLR 1514, HL. As to whether this interest will bind a mortgagee, see *Caunce v Caunce* [1969] 1 All ER 722, [1969] 1 WLR 286; *Hodgson v Marks* [1971] Ch 892, [1971] 2 All ER 684, CA; *Williams & Glyn's Bank Ltd v Boland* [1981] AC 487, [1980] 2 All ER 408, HL; *Kingsnorth Trust Ltd v Tizard* [1986] 2 All ER 54, sub nom *Kingsnorth Finance Co Ltd v Tizard* [1986] 1 WLR 783; cf *Bristol and West Building Society v Henning* [1985] 2 All ER 606, [1985] 1 WLR 778, CA. For rights of occupation of registered land, see *Williams & Glyn's Bank v Boland*, above. A wife's beneficial interest is overreached under s 27 (2) of the Law of Property Act 1925 where the purchase money is paid to two trustees: see *City of London Building Society v Flegg* [1988] AC 54, HL. The HL reversed the CA which had held there to be no overreaching under s 27 (2), s 14 of the Law of Property Act 1925 preventing the overreaching provisions having effect. This decision of the CA was severely criticised: see eg (1986) 132 NLJ 208 (Hayton); [1986] Conv 131 (Hayton); [1986] Conv 379 (Swadling); (1986) 6 Legal Studies 140 (Thompson). On the HL decision, see (1987) 137 NLJ 470 (Bridge). On the investigation of title by the mortgagee, see the standard conveyancing textbooks. The Matrimonial Homes Act 1983 is repealed and replaced by the Family Law Act 1996.

3 Family Law Act 1996, s 30(1). See *Barnett v Hassett* [1982] 1 All ER 80, [1981] 1 WLR 1385. Nothing occurring in the period beginning with the day of the presentation of the petition for a bankruptcy order and ending with the vesting of the bankrupt's estate in a trustee will be taken as having given rise to matrimonial home rights under the Family Law Act 1996 in relation to a dwelling house comprised in the bankrupt's estate: Insolvency Act 1986, s 336 (1). An application for an order in connection with matrimonial home rights where the other spouse is adjudged bankrupt is to be made to the court having jurisdiction in relation to the bankruptcy: Insolvency Act 1986, s 336 (2) (b). For the factors to be taken into account on any such application to the bankruptcy court, see Insolvency Act 1986, s 336 (4), (5).

4 Section 30 (9). Where a spouse is entitled to rights of occupation by reason of an interest of the other spouse under a trust, sub-ss (3)–(5) apply in relation to the trustees as they apply in relation to the other spouse: s 30(6).

Rights of occupation as a charge on the house

12.133 The matrimonial home rights of a spouse are a charge on the estate or interest of the other spouse who is entitled to occupy the house by virtue of some beneficial estate or interest[1]. Such charge has the like priority as if it were an equitable interest created at whichever is the latest of the following dates, that is to say (a) the date when the spouse so entitled acquired the estate or interest; (b) the date of the marriage; and (c) the commencement of the Matrimonial Homes Act 1967[2].

1 Family Law Act 1996, s 31(1) and (2).
2 Section 31(3). The commencement date was 1 January 1968. When a spouse's matrimonial home rights are a charge on the interest of the other spouse under a trust and there are, apart from either of the spouses, no persons, living or unborn, who are or could become beneficiaries under the trust, then the matrimonial home rights shall be a charge also on the estate or interest of the trustees of the other spouse, having the like priority as if it were an equitable interest created on the date when it arises: s 31(4), (5) and (6). Where a spouse's matrimonial home rights are a charge on the estate or interest of the other spouse or of trustees for the other spouse and the other spouse is adjudged bankrupt, the charge will continue to subsist notwithstanding the bankruptcy and will bind the trustee of the bankrupt's estate and persons deriving title under that trustee (Insolvency Act 1986, s 336 (2) (a)).

Registration of charge

Unregistered land

12.134 If title to the land over which the spouse has matrimonial home rights is unregistered, then the charge may be registered as a Class F land charge[1]. The charge created by the Act will be void as against a purchaser[2] of the land charged therewith, or of any interest in such land, unless the land charge is registered in the appropriate register before the completion of the purchase[3]. The charge may be registered, where it arises out of the right not to be evicted etc as soon as the spouse is in occupation[4] or, where it arises out of the right to enter and occupy, even before the court has given leave to enter and occupy[5].

1 Land Charges Act 1972, s 2(1), (7).
2 This includes a mortgagee: Land Charges Act 1972, s 17 (1).
3 Land Charges Act 1972, s 4 (8). See *Miles v Bull* [1969] 1 QB 258, [1968] 3 All ER 632; *Miles v Bull (No 2)* [1969] 3 All ER 1585; *Wroth v Tyler* [1974] Ch 30, [1973] 1 All ER 897.
4 See *Miles v Bull*, above.
5 See *Watts v Waller* [1973] QB 153, [1972] 3 All ER 257, CA. Where a spouse is entitled to a registrable charge in respect of two or more dwelling-houses only one of those charges shall be registered at any time: Family Law Act 1996, Sch 4, para 2.

Registered land

12.135 Where the title to the legal estate by virtue of which a spouse is entitled to occupy a dwelling-house[1] is registered under the Land Registration Act 1925, registration of a land charge affecting the dwelling-house by virtue of the 1996 Act shall be effected by registering a notice under the 1925 Act and the spouse's matrimonial home rights shall not be an overriding interest under that Act notwithstanding the spouse is in actual occupation of the dwelling-house[2].

1 Including any legal estate held by trustees for that spouse.
2 Family Law Act 1996, s 31(10).

Generally

12.136 Where a spouse's rights of occupation are a charge on the estate or interest of the other spouse, and that estate or interest is the subject of a mortgage, then if, after the date of creation of the mortgage the charge is registered as a land charge for the purposes of the Law of Property Act 1925, the charge shall, for the purposes of s 94 of that Act (which regulates the rights of mortgagees to make further advances ranking in priority to subsequent mortgages) be deemed to be a mortgage subsequent in date to the first-mentioned mortgage[1].

1 Family Law Act 1996, s 31(12).

Release of matrimonial home rights and postponement of priority of charge

12.137 A spouse entitled to matrimonial home rights may by a release in writing release those rights or release them as respects part only of the dwelling-house affected by them[1]. The registration of the charge may be cancelled by the spouse entitled to rights of occupation[2]. Where a contract is made for the sale of an estate or interest in a house, or for the grant of a lease or underlease thereof and the house is affected by a charge registered under s 31(10) of the Family Law Act 1996 or s 2 of the Land Charges Act 1972[3], the matrimonial home rights constituting the charge shall be deemed to have been released upon the first of (a) the delivery to the purchaser or lessee or his solicitor upon completion of the contract of an application by the spouse entitled to the charge for the cancellation of the registration of the charge; or (b) the lodging of such an application at the Land Registry[4].

A spouse entitled to a charge may agree in writing that any other charge on, or interest in, that estate or interest shall rank in priority to the charge to which that spouse is entitled[5]. Where a prospective mortgagee ascertains that a Class F land charge is registered[6], he should therefore require the spouse entitled to the charge to release the rights (and apply for the cancellation of the registration) or postpone the priority of the charge.

1 Family Law Act 1996, Sch 4, para 5(1). For a form of release, see the Appendix. Otherwise the charge is ended by the death of the other spouse or the termination of the marriage: s 31(8).
2 Land Charges Act 1972, s 16 (1) and see *Holmes v Kennard* (1984) 49 P & CR 202, CA; [1985] Conv 293 (Price).
3 See **12.134–12.135**.
4 Family Law Act 1996, Sch 4, para 5(2).
5 Schedule 5, para 6. For a form, see the Appendix.
6 Or a priority notice lodged in respect of the charge to arise on completion.

Payments under mortgages by spouse entitled to matrimonial home rights

12.138 Where a spouse is entitled to matrimonial home rights, any payment or tender made or other thing done by that spouse in or towards satisfaction of the liability of the spouse in respect of, inter alia, mortgage payments shall, whether or not it was made or done in pursuance of an order of the court, be as good as if made or done by the other spouse[1]. In respect of mortgage payments, the person to whom the payment is made may treat it as having been made by the other spouse, but that shall not affect any claim of the spouse making the payment against the other spouse to an interest in the house by virtue of the payment[2].

1 Family Law Act 1996, s 30(3).
2 Section 30(5).

Dwelling house subject to mortgage

12.139 In determining whether a spouse or former spouse is entitled to occupy a dwelling house by virtue of an estate or interest, there shall be disregarded any right to possession conferred on a mortgagee under or by virtue of his mortgage, whether the mortgagee is in possession or not; but the spouse's rights of occupation do not give that spouse any greater right against the mortgagee to occupy the house than the other spouse has, unless those rights were duly registered and thereby have priority[1]. This provision does not apply if the relevant rights are a charge affecting the mortgagee on the estate or interest mortgaged[2].

Where a mortgagee of land which consists of or includes a dwelling-house brings an action in any court for the enforcement of his security, and the circumstances are that:

(a) a spouse[3] is enabled to meet the mortgagor's liabilities under the mortgage;
(b) the spouse has applied to the court before the action is finally disposed of in that court; and
(c) the court sees no special reason against his being made a party and is satisfied:
  (i) that he may be expected to make such payments or do such other things in or towards satisfaction of the mortgagor's liabilities or obligations as might affect the outcome of the proceedings; or
  (ii) that the expectation of it should be considered under s 36 of the Administration of Justice Act 1970;

the spouse may apply to be made a party to the action[4].

Where a mortgagee of land which consists or substantially consists of a dwelling-house brings an action for the enforcement of his security and at the relevant time a spouse with rights of occupation has duly registered or protected those rights, then notice of the action must be served by the mortgagee on that spouse[5].

1 Family Law Act 1996, s 54(1) and (2).
2 Section 54(4).
3 Or former spouse, cohabitant, or former cohabitant: Family Law Act 1996, s 54(5) and s 55(4).
4 Section 55.
5 Section 56(1) and (2).

PERSONS SUFFERING FROM MENTAL DISORDER[1]

Capacity to contract

12.140 The validity of a contract entered into by a person who was apparently of sound mind, but who in fact was suffering at the time of the contract from such mental disorder as rendered him incapable of entering into the contract, is to be judged by the same standards as a contract made by a person of sound mind[2]. If the contract is to be avoided the person or persons denying its validity must prove that the person alleged to be mentally disordered at the time of the contract was so disordered as to be incapable of contracting and that the other party was aware or ought to have been aware of that fact[3]. The contract is not avoided by unfairness, unless such unfairness amounts to equitable fraud[4]. A contract made by a person mentally disordered during a lucid interval is binding upon him, whether or not the other party knew of his intermittent incapacity[5].

1 See generally, 30 *Halsbury's Laws* (4th edn reissue) Mental Health.
2 *Hart v O'Connor* [1985] AC 1000, [1985] 2 All ER 880, PC.
3 *Hart v O'Connor*, above; *Broughton v Snook* [1938] Ch 505, [1938] 1 All ER 411.
4 *Hart v O'Connor*, above.
5 *Selby v Jackson* (1844) 6 Beav 192.

Capacity of disposition

12.141 The deed of a person suffering from such mental disorder as to render him incapable of understanding the effect of the deed is void[1]. A deed made by a mentally disordered person during a lucid interval, the nature and effect of which he understood[2], is binding upon him, unless a receiver has been appointed for him[3].

1 *Price v Berrington* (1849) 7 Hare 394 at 402.
2 *Towart v Sellers* (1817) 5 Dow 231, HL.
3 See *Re Marshall, Marshall v Whateley* [1920] 1 Ch 284.

Mortgages on behalf of persons mentally disordered

12.142 Part VII of the Mental Health Act 1983 confers the modern statutory jurisdiction for the management of the property and affairs of patients. Without prejudice to the general functions of the judge[1] he may, inter alia, make orders or give directions and authorities for the charging of the patient's property[2].

Where the judge has ordered, directed or authorised the expenditure of money for the carrying out of permanent improvements on, or otherwise for the permanent benefit of any property of the patient, he may order that the whole or any part of the money expended or to be expended shall be a charge upon the property whether with or without interest at a specified rate[3]. The charge may be made in favour of such person as may be just and in particular, where the money charged is paid out of the patient's general estate, in favour of a person as trustee for the patient[4]. Where an order has been made charging property with the cost of permanent improvements, the order may also provide for excluding or restricting the provisions for preservation of the interests of other persons in the patient's property[5].

The mortgage in such cases will be made by the patient's receiver or, if he has none, some person authorised in that behalf pursuant to the order of the court and it must be settled and approved by the court[6].

1 See Mental Health Act 1983, s 95. The authority to mortgage will generally be an order of the Court of Protection.
2 Section 96 (1) (b).

3 Section 101 (5). See *A-G v Marquis of Ailesbury* (1887) 12 App Cas 672, HL; *Re Gist* [1904] 1 Ch 398.
4 Section 101 (6); but no charge under sub-s (5) shall confer any right of sale or foreclosure during the lifetime of the patient: s 101 (6).
5 Section 101 (5). The provisions for preservation of interests are in s 101 (1).
6 Court of Protection Rules 1994, SI 1994/3046. For forms of mortgage on behalf of mentally disordered persons, see 28 *Forms and Precedents* (5th edn, 1999 reissue) Mortgages.

Loans on behalf of patients

12.143 The court has in the past authorised the committee or receiver of a person of unsound mind to lend the patient's money upon mortgage[1]. Where the patient is tenant for life of settled land money may be raised out of the patient's free estate on the security of the settled land. The authority of the Court of Protection is required only for the receiver to raise the money and in this case the receiver will not be the mortgagor[2].

1 *Re Ridgeways* (1825) Hog 309.
2 The mortgage will be made by the trustees of the settlement in the name and on behalf of the patient under the Settled Land Act 1925, s 68 (see **12.98**). The receiver will of course be a party to the mortgage as mortgagee.

BANKRUPTS

Mortgages by bankrupts[1]

12.144 Where a person is adjudicated a bankrupt his property, with certain exceptions, passes to his trustee in bankruptcy, so that the bankrupt cannot mortgage such property or redeem it if already mortgaged[2]. However, the bankrupt may mortgage the excepted property which remains vested in him[3] and property acquired after the commencement of his bankruptcy, if the trustee has not intervened to exercise his right thereto[4].

A mortgage by a bankrupt will be effective against his trustee in favour of the mortgagee acting in good faith without notice of an available act of bankruptcy where the receiving order or bankruptcy petition has not been registered pursuant to the Land Charges Act 1972[5], where the mortgage is of an equitable chose in action and the trustee has not perfected his title by notice[6], and where the trustee has stood by and allowed the mortgagee to advance his money on the supposition that the bankrupt could dispose of the property[7].

1 For aircraft mortgages, see **6.19** ff.
2 Insolvency Act 1986, s 306. For transactions effected before the date of the bankruptcy order, see **13.2** ff.
3 Insolvency Act 1986, s 283 (2); see *Bird v Philpott* [1900] 1 Ch 822.
4 *Cohen v Mitchell* (1890) 25 QBD 262; Insolvency Act 1986, s 307 (4).
5 Land Charges Act 1972, ss 6, 7, 8, 17.
6 *Stuart v Cockerell* (1869) LR 8 Eq 607; *Palmer v Locke* (1881) 18 Ch D 381, CA.
7 *Troughton v Gitley* (1766) Amb 630; *Tucker v Hernaman* (1853) 4 De Gm & G 395.

Mortgages by trustee in bankruptcy

12.145 The trustee in bankruptcy, with the consent of the creditors' committee, may mortgage any part of the property of the bankrupt which has passed to him under the bankruptcy for the purpose of raising money for the payment of the bankrupt's debts[1].

1 Insolvency Act 1986, s 314 (1) (a), Sch 5, para 4.

AGENTS

Authority of agent to mortgage

12.146 As a general rule, an agent who is placed in temporary control of his principal's property has no authority to pledge or mortgage it. Thus a solicitor cannot, without authority (express or to be implied from strong circumstances) do anything to prejudice the estate or interest of his client[1].

Where a principal hands his title deeds to an agent to raise a specific sum, and the agent uses them for the purpose of raising a larger sum, the principal will not be able to redeem without paying the entire sum for which they were pledged, for the authority to pledge in fact existed and the pledge was not aware of the limitation on it[2].

Exceptions to the rule in so far as it relates to goods and documents of title thereto and to negotiable instruments have arisen from necessity and by the custom of trade[3].

1 *Cory v Eyre* (1863) 1 De GJ & Sm 149 at 168.
2 *Brocklesby v Temperance Permanent Building Society* [1895] AC 173, HL.
3 See the Factors Act 1889 and the powers of bankers to pledge customers' negotiable instruments and stockbrokers to pledge customers' negotiable securities.

PARTNERS

BORROWING POWERS

Agency of partners[1]

12.147 The Partnership Act 1890 provides that every partner is an agent of the firm and his other partners for the purpose of the business of the partnership and the acts of any partner who does any act for carrying on in the usual way business of the kind carried on by the firm of which he is a member bind the firm and his partners, unless the partner so acting has in fact no authority to act for the firm in the particular matter, and the person with whom he is dealing either knows that he has no authority, or does not know or believe him to be a partner[2].

1 Only ordinary partners are dealt with here. A limited partner does not have power to bind the firm: Limited Partnership Act 1907, s 6 (1).
2 Section 5.

General power to mortgage personal property

12.148 Accordingly one of several partners may make a security affecting the personal property of the partnership for a loan or debt contracted for the ordinary purposes of the undertaking, where there is no notice of fraud or want of authority[1]. This power continues after the dissolution of the partnership, for the purposes of winding up its affairs and of completing contracts entered into during its continuance[2]. The partnership will not be bound by a security given by one of the firm to a person who knowingly makes advances for extraordinary purposes, such as raising additional capital for payment of the share of a deceased partner, or making new arrangements for carrying on the business[3] and, a fortiori, one member of the firm cannot bind the others by a security for the payment of his separate debt, unless the creditor can prove a direct assent by the other partners, or circumstances from which such assent may reasonably be inferred. The presumption is that such a security was known by the creditor to have been given without the authority of the firm and he takes the onus of proving the authority[4]. If such a security is made by a partner knowing his firm is insolvent it is a fraud on the creditors of the firm and an act of bankruptcy[5].

1 *Re Litherland, ex p Howden* (1842) 2 Mont D & De G 574.
2 *Butchart v Dresser* (1853) 4 De GM & G 542; *Re Bourne, Bourne v Bourne* [1906] 2 Ch 427, CA.
3 *Fisher v Tayler* (1843) 2 Hare 218.
4 *Snaith v Burridge* (1812) 4 Taunt 684; *Leverson v Lane* (1862) 13 CBNS 278.
5 *Re Douglas, ex p Snowball* (1872) 7 Ch App 534 at 542.

Mortgage of real property

12.149 Where partners hold the legal estate in freehold or leasehold property, they necessarily hold it as joint tenants[1]. A single partner cannot give a legal mortgage on the property without express authority given under seal so to do[2], but where the mortgage does not require to be effected by deed or, for instance, in the case of an equitable mortgage made by deposit of the deeds, whether with or without a memorandum in writing, it seems that the same rule applies as in the case of any other transaction entered into by a partner on behalf of the firm, and the mortgage is valid and binds the firm, provided it is effected for carrying on in the usual way business of the kind carried on by the firm[3], and after the death of a partner, the surviving partners have power to mortgage the partnership property, whether real or personal, to secure a partnership debt, and such mortgage takes priority over the lien of the personal representatives of the deceased partners on the partnership assets[4].

1 Law of Property Act 1925, ss 34, 36; Settled Land Act 1925, s 36 (4); both as amended by the Trusts of Land and Appointment of Trustees Act 1996.
2 *Steiglitz v Egginton* (1815) Holt NP 141.
3 Partnership Act 1890, s 5; see **12.147**. A mortgage by deposit of deeds is no longer possible after the commencement of the Law of Property (Miscellaneous) Provisions Act 1989, s 2.
4 *Re Bourne, Bourne v Bourne* [1906] 2 Ch 427.

Mortgage of partnership share

12.150 An assignment by a partner of his share in the partnership, either absolute or by way of mortgage, does not, as against the other partners, entitle the assignee during the continuance of the partnership to interfere in the management of the partnership business or affairs[1], or to require accounts or inspection of books[2]. It only entitles the assignee to receive the partner's share of profits[3], but on the dissolution the assignee is entitled to receive the assignor's share of the assets and, for the purpose of ascertaining the share, he is entitled to an account as from the date of dissolution[4]. If any partner suffers his share of the partnership property to be charged under the Partnership Act 1890, for his separate debt, the partnership may, at the option of the other partners, be dissolved[5].

1 See eg *Re Garwood's Trusts, Garwood v Paynter* [1903] 1 Ch 236.
2 *Bonnin v Neame* [1910] 1 Ch 732, and see *United Builders Pty Ltd v Mutual Acceptance Ltd* (1980) 144 CLR 673. As to whether the debt is a partnership debt or the debt of a partner or partners, see *Custom Credit Corpn Ltd v Heard and Raphael* (1983) 33 SASR 45 (FC).
3 Partnership Act 1890, s 31. See **7.26**.
4 *Watts v Driscoll* [1901] 1 Ch 294, CA.
5 Partnership Act 1890, s 33.

LENDING POWERS

Partner's power to lend on mortgage

12.151 A partner has authority to lend the moneys of the firm on mortgage, when such a transaction is part of the ordinary business of the firm[1].

1 *Re Land Credit Co of Ireland, Weikersheim's Case* (1873) 8 Ch App 831; *Niemann v Niemann* (1889) 43 Ch D 198, CA.

MORTGAGES OF ECCLESIASTICAL PROPERTY

Powers to mortgage ecclesiastical property

12.152 In addition to the powers conferred by the Improvement of Land Act 1864[1], mortgages of glebe land may be made by incumbents under the Clergy Residences Repair Act 1776 and the Acts by which that Act has been amended and extended, for the purpose of providing or repairing parsonage houses[2].

Since mortgages of ecclesiastical property are generally made to the Church Commissioners, who will supply all the necessary forms, nothing further will be said of them here.

1 See **12.107** ff. Where the land is held in right of any church, chapel, or other ecclesiastical benefice, the consent of the patron and of the bishop is essential: Improvement of Land Act 1864, s 20; and see Improvement of Land (Ecclesiastical Benefices) Act 1884.
2 See generally 14 *Halsbury's Laws* (4th edn) paras 1146–1152. By the Glebe Exchange Act 1815, powers were given to incumbents to purchase additional land for the glebe, and, for that purpose, to make limited mortgages of the profits of the benefice. Provisions for raising money for dilapidations are contained in the Ecclesiastical Dilapidations Measures 1923 to 1951.

Advowson

12.153 An advowson cannot now be mortgaged[1].

1 Benefices Act 1898, ss 1 (1) (b), 7; Benefices Act 1898 (Amendment) Measures 1923, s 4.

PART III

VOID OR IMPERFECT SECURITIES

Chapter 13

Void or imperfect securities

INTRODUCTION

13.1 There is discussion elsewhere in this work of the requirements of the Bills of Sale Acts 1878–1882 and the requirements as to registration of charges under the Companies Act 1985 and under the Land Charges Act 1972 or the Land Registration Act 1925. There is also discussion elsewhere of the requirements of s 2 of the Law of Property (Miscellaneous Provisions) Act 1989 in relation to purported contracts to create a mortgage or charge. This present chapter collects together a large number of miscellaneous statutory provisions and rules of common law and equity, which may be relevant in particular circumstances and which may invalidate a mortgage or charge or render it liable to be set aside.

GENERAL STATUTORY PROVISIONS AS TO THE SETTING ASIDE OF TRANSACTIONS

TRANSACTIONS AT AN UNDERVALUE AND PREFERENCES

Power to restore position

13.2 Sections 339 and 340 of the Insolvency Act 1986 contain provisions whereby, where an individual is adjudged bankrupt and he has at a relevant time entered into a transaction with any person at an undervalue or given a preference to any person, his trustee in bankruptcy may apply to the court for such order as the court thinks fit to restore the position to what it would have been had that individual not entered into the transaction or, as the case may be, not given that preference[1].

1 Sections 339 and 340 replace ss 42 and 44 of the Bankruptcy Act 1914 (as to which see previous editions of this work). For a criticism of these Bankruptcy Act provisions, see the Cork Report (Cmnd 8558) Ch 28. For analogous provisions in respect of companies, see Insolvency Act 1986, ss 238, 239; see **8.12** ff.

Relevant time

13.3 The time at which an individual enters into a transaction at an undervalue or gives a preference is a relevant time for the purposes of these provisions if the transaction is entered into or the preference is given:

(a) in the case of a transaction at an undervalue, at a time in the period of five years ending with the day of the presentation of the bankruptcy petition on which that individual is adjudged bankrupt;
(b) in the case of a preference which is not a transaction at an undervalue and is given to a person who is an associate of that individual, at a time in the period of two years ending with that day; and
(c) in any other case of a preference which is not a transaction at an undervalue, at a time in the period of six months ending with that day[1].

Where an individual enters into a transaction at an undervalue or gives a preference at a time mentioned in (a), (b) or (c) above, not being, in the case of a transaction at an undervalue, a time less than two years before the end of the period mentioned in (a), that time shall not be a relevant time for the purposes of these provisions unless the individual:

(a) is insolvent at that time; or
(b) becomes insolvent in consequence of the transaction or preference;

but this requirement shall be presumed to be satisfied, unless the contrary is shown, in relation to any transaction at an undervalue which is entered into by an individual with a person who is an associate[2] of his (otherwise than by reason only of being his employee)[3].

For the above purposes an individual is insolvent if:

(a) he is unable to pay his debts as they fall due; or
(b) the value of his assets is less than the amount of his liabilities, taking into account his contingent and prospective liabilities[4].

1 Insolvency Act 1986, s 341 (1). Cf s 240 (1), **8.13**.
2 For the meaning of associate, see s 435.
3 Insolvency Act 1986, s 341 (2).
4 Section 341 (3). Cf s 240 (2), **8.13**.

Transactions at an undervalue

13.4 An individual enters into a transaction with a person at an undervalue if:

(a) he makes a gift to that person or he otherwise enters into a transaction with that person on terms that provide for him to receive no consideration;
(b) he enters into a transaction with that person in consideration of marriage[1]; or
(c) he enters into a transaction with that person for a consideration the value of which, in money or money's worth, is significantly less than the value, in money or money's worth, of the consideration provided by the individual[2].

The giving of security for a pre-existing debt which does not involve an overall depletion of assets of the debtor is not a transaction at an undervalue: the granting of a debenture by a company to secure existing borrowings is neither a gift, nor made without consideration, since the creditor forbears to call in the company's overdraft[3]. Where a mortgagee sells mortgaged property under its power of sale, this is not a sale by the mortgagor and the mortgagor has not 'entered into a transaction' in relation to the sale for the purposes of s 339[4]. Where a mortgagor sells mortgaged property, the value of the consideration provided by the mortgagor is the value of the land free from the mortgage and not the value of the equity of redemption[5]. A wife's assumption of sole liability for a mortgage was a transfer at an undervalue where the value of the wife's consideration was significantly less than that provided by her husband[6].

1 See *Re Densham* [1975] 3 All ER 726, [1975] 1 WLR 1519.
2 Insolvency Act 1986, s 339 (3).
3 *Re MC Bacon Ltd* [1990] BCLC 324 at 340–341, per Millett J (a decision on ss 238 and 239) approved in *Menzies v National Bank of Kuwait* [1994] BCC 119, CA (considering s 423) and applied in *Agricultural Mortgage Corpn plc v Woodward* [1995] 1 BCLC 1, CA (considering s 423), *Re Brabon* [2001] 1 BCLC 11 (considering ss 339 and 423) and *Re Mistral Finance Ltd* [2001] BCC 27 (considering ss 238 and 239); see also *Phillips v Brewen Dolphin* [2001] UKHL 2, [2001] 1 WLR 143 at 151.
4 *Re Brabon* [2001] 1 BCLC 11.
5 *Re Brabon* [2001] 1 BCLC 11 at 36, per Jonathan Parker J considering and applying *Re MC Bacon Ltd*. Where there is negative equity and the bankrupt mortgagor will not receive any proceeds of sale either if the property is sold for its full value or if it is sold for less than its full value, it was said that the question of whether the sale was at an undervalue or not was academic so far as the trustee in bankruptcy was concerned: *Re Brabon* [2001] BCLC 11 at 37.
6 *Re Kumar (a bankrupt) ex p Lewis v Kumar* [1993] 2 All ER 700, [1993] 1 WLR 224.

Preferences

13.5 An individual gives a preference to a person if:

(a) that person is one of the individual's creditors or a surety or guarantor for any of his debts or other liabilities; and
(b) the individual does anything or suffers anything to be done which (in either case) has the effect of putting that person into a position which, in the event of the individual's bankruptcy, will be better than the position he would have been in if that thing had not been done[1].

The court shall not make an order in respect of a preference given to any person unless the individual who gave the preference was influenced in deciding to give it by a desire to produce in relation to that person the effect mentioned in (b) above[2].

An individual who has given a preference to a person who, at the time the preference was given, was an associate[3] of his (otherwise than by reason only of being his employee) shall be presumed, unless the contrary is shown, to have been influenced in deciding to give it by such a desire as aforesaid[4].

The fact that something has been done in pursuance of the order of a court shall not, without more, prevent the doing or suffering of that thing from constituting the giving of a preference[5].

1 Insolvency Act 1986, s 340 (3).
2 Section 340 (4). For discussion of the case of *Re M C Bacon Ltd* [1990] BCLC 324 on the analogous provision relating to companies, see **8.13**. See also *Re Mistral Finance Ltd* [2001] BCC 27 (considering s 239).
3 For the meaning of associate, see s 435.
4 Insolvency Act 1986, s 340 (5).
5 Section 340 (6). A transaction entered into or preference given by a person who is subsequently adjudged bankrupt on a petition under s 264 (1) (d) of the Insolvency Act 1986 (criminal bankruptcy) shall be treated as having been entered into or given at a relevant time for the purposes of ss 339 and 340 if it was entered into or given at any time

on or after the date specified for the purposes of this subsection in the criminal bankruptcy order on which the petition was based: s 341 (4), but no order shall be made under ss 339 or 340 by virtue of sub-s (4) of this s where an appeal is pending (within the meaning of s 277 of the Act) against the individual's conviction of any offence by virtue of which the criminal bankruptcy order was made: s 341 (5). The power to make criminal bankruptcy orders was abolished with effect from 3 April 1989 (Criminal Justice Act 1988, s 101(1); Criminal Justice Act 1988 (Commencement No 7) Order 1989, SI 1989/264. The repeal does not affect any pre-existing orders: s 101(2).

Orders under ss 339–340

13.6 Without prejudice to the generality of ss 339 (2) or 340 (2) (power of the court to make an order restoring the position), an order under either of those sections with respect to a transaction or preference entered into or given by an individual who is subsequently adjudged bankrupt may:

(a) require any property transferred as part of the transaction, or in connection with the giving of the preference, to be vested in the trustee of the bankrupt's estate as part of that estate;
(b) require any property to be so vested if it represents in any person's hands the applications either of the proceeds of sale of property so transferred or of money so transferred;
(c) release or discharge (in whole or in part) any security given by the individual;
(d) require any person to pay, in respect of benefits received by him from the individual, such sums to the trustee of his estate as the court may direct;
(e) provide for any surety or guarantor whose obligations to any person were released or discharged (in whole or in part) under the transaction or by the giving of the preference to be under such new or revived obligations to that person as the court thinks appropriate;
(f) provide for security for the discharge of any obligation imposed by or arising under the order, for such an obligation to be charged on any property and for such security or charge to have the same priority as a security or charge released or discharged (in whole or in part) under the transaction or by the giving of the preference; and
(g) provide for the extent to which any person whose property is vested by the order in the trustee of the bankrupt's estate, or on whom obligations are imposed by the order, is to be able to prove in the bankruptcy for debts or other liabilities which arise from or were released or discharged (in whole or in part) under or by, the transaction or the giving of the preference[1].

An order under s 339 or s 340 may affect the property of, or impose any obligation on, any person whether or not he is the person with whom the individual in question entered into the transaction or, as the case may be, the person to whom the preference was given, but such an order:

(a) shall not prejudice any interest in property which was acquired from a person other than that individual and was acquired in good faith and for value or prejudice any interest deriving from such an interest; and
(b) shall not require a person who received a benefit from the transaction or preference in good faith and for value to pay a sum to the trustee of the bankrupt's estate, except where he was a party to the transaction or the payment is to be in respect of a preference given to that person at a time when he was a creditor of that individual[2].

Where:

(a) a person has acquired an interest in property from a person other than the individual in question, or has received a benefit from the transaction or preference, and at the time of that acquisition or receipt either had notice of the relevant surrounding circumstances[3] and of the relevant proceedings; or

(b) was an associate[4] of or was connected with, either the individual in question or the person with whom that individual entered into the transaction or to whom that individual gave the preference,

then, unless the contrary is shown it is presumed that the interest was acquired or the benefit received otherwise than in good faith[5].

Any sums required to be paid to the trustee in accordance with an order under s 339 or s 340 shall be comprised in the bankrupt's estate[6].

(a) the fact that the individual in question entered into the transaction at an undervalue; or

(b) the circumstances which amounted to the giving of the preference by the individual in question: s 342(4).

A person has notice of the relevant proceedings if he has notice:

(a) of the fact that the petition on which the individual in question is adjudged bankrupt had been presented; or

(b) of the fact that the individual in question had been adjudged bankrupt: s 342(5).

The definition of connected persons in s 249 applies.

1 Insolvency Act 1986, s 342 (1). See for the analogous provisions for companies, Insolvency Act 1986, s 241.

2 Section 342 (2).

3 The relevant surrounding circumstances are:
(a) the fact that the individual in question entered into the transaction at an undervalue; or
(b) the circumstances which amounted to the giving of the preference by the individual in question: s 242(4).
A person has notice of the relevant proceedings if he has notice:
(a) of the fact that the petition on which the individual in question is adjudged bankrupt had been presented; or
(b) of the fact that the individual in question has been adjudged bankrupt: s 342(5).
The definition of connected persons in s 249 applies.

4 As defined by s 435.

5 Section 342(2A) as added by Insolvency (No 2) Act 1994.

6 Insolvency Act 1986, s 342 (3).

Dispositions without notice of bankruptcy

13.7 Where a person is adjudged bankrupt, any disposition of property made by that person in the period beginning with the day of the presentation of the petition for the bankruptcy order and ending with the vesting of the bankrupt's estate in a trustee shall be void, except to the extent that it is or was made with the consent of the court, or is or was subsequently ratified by the court[1]. The above provision does not apply, however, against any person in respect of any property or payment which he received before the commencement of the bankruptcy in good faith, for value and without notice that the petition had been presented or any other person claiming through such person[2]. An order transferring property made under the Matrimonial Causes Act 1973 after the presentation of the bankruptcy petition is a relevant disposition[3].

1 Insolvency Act 1986, s 284 (1), (3).
2 Section 284 (4), and for the protection of bankers, see Insolvency Act 1986, s 284 (5). For the commencement of bankruptcy, see Insolvency Act 1986, s 278. For the former law, see Bankruptcy Act 1914, s 45; *Re Simms* [1930] 2 Ch 22. For the analogous provision on a winding up of a company, see Insolvency Act 1986, s 127; **20.44**.
3 See *Re Flint (a bankrupt)* [1993] Ch 319. Mr Nicholas Stewart QC sitting as a judge of the High Court also held that the county court judge had acted within his discretion in refusing to ratify the transfer of property order under s 284(1). The wife had not sought to rely upon s 284(4)(a) which has protected some wives in similar situations. Note, however, the discussion and contrary view expressed in *Muir-Hunter on Personal Insolvency* para 3.4482-3.

After-acquired property of bankrupt

13.8 The Insolvency Act 1986 enables a trustee in bankruptcy to claim after-acquired property for his bankrupt's estate by means of a notice to that effect[1]. Where, whether before or after the service of such a notice, a person acquires property in good faith, for value and without notice of the bankruptcy[2] the trustee shall not in respect of that property or transaction be entitled to any remedy against that person[3] or any person whose title to any property derives from that person[4]. The specific provisions of s 307 take priority over the general provisions of the Married Women's Property Act 1882[5].

1 Insolvency Act 1986, s 307 (1), (3).
2 And also where a banker enters into a transaction in good faith and without such notice.
3 Or banker.
4 Insolvency Act 1986, s 307 (4). For the former law, see Bankruptcy Act 1914, s 47.
5 *Rooney v Cardona* [1999] 1 WLR 1388 at 1397, CA.

TRANSACTIONS DEFRAUDING CREDITORS

Power to restore position

13.9 Section 423 of the Insolvency Act 1986 contains provisions whereby when a person has entered into a transaction at an undervalue and the court[1] is satisfied that the transaction was entered into for the purpose of putting assets beyond the reach of a person who is making, or may at some time make, a claim against the relevant person or of otherwise prejudicing the interests of such a person in relation to the claim which he is making or may make, the court may make such order as it thinks fit for restoring the position to what it would have been if the transaction had not been entered into and for protecting the interests of persons who are victims of the transaction[2].

Where the transaction is alleged to be for the purpose of putting assets beyond the reach of a person making a claim, it is not necessary to prove any element of dishonesty on the part of the person entering into the transaction[3]. The intention to put assets beyond the reach of a creditor must be the dominant purpose of the transaction — it need not be its only purpose[4]. The intentions of the transferor only are relevant — lack of any improper intent by the transferee is not relevant[5]. The fact that the transaction was effected upon legal advice is also irrelevant[6].

An application for an order under this section shall not be made in relation to a transaction except:

(a) in a case where the debtor (the person entering into the transaction) has been adjudged bankrupt or is a body corporate which is being wound up or in relation to which an administration order is in force, by the official receiver, by the trustee of the bankrupt's estate or the liquidator or administrator of the body corporate or, with the leave of the court, by a victim of the transaction;
(b) in a case where a victim of the transaction is bound by a composition or scheme approved under the Insolvency Act 1986[7] by the supervisor of the composition or scheme or by any person who (whether or not so bound) is such a victim; or
(c) in any other case, by a victim of the transaction;

and an application made under any of the preceding paragraphs in relation to a transaction shall be treated as made on behalf of every victim of the transaction[8].

1 'The court' means the High Court or:
(a) if the person entering into the transaction is an individual, any other court which would have jurisdiction in relation to a bankruptcy petition relating to him.
(b) if that person is a body capable of being wound up under Part IV or V of the Insolvency Act 1986, any other court having jurisdiction to wind it up: Insolvency Act 1986, s 423(4).

2 Insolvency Act 1986, s 423 (2), replacing s 172 of the Law of Property Act 1925 (as to which see earlier editions of this work). For criticism of s 172, see the Cork Report (Cmnd 8558) Ch 28. A victim of a transaction is a person who is, or is capable of being, prejudiced by it: Insolvency Act 1986, s 423 (5).

3 *Arbuthnot Leasing International Ltd v Havelet Leasing Ltd (No 2)* [1990] BCC 636.

4 *Chohan v Saggar* [1993] BCLC 661; on appeal [1994] BCC 134, [1994] BCLC 706, CA; and *Midland Bank plc v Wyatt* [1995] 1 FLR 697, [1997] 1 BCLC 242 where a husband declared a trust of his joint beneficial tenancy of the matrimonial home in favour of his family ostensibly with the motive of providing for them. The transaction was in breach of his covenant in the charge on the property and prejudiced the mortgagee. It was held voidable under s 423. See also the decision of the Court of Appeal on an interlocutory application in *Royscott Spa Leasing Ltd v Lovett* [1995] BCC 502, CA where the test of 'substantial purpose' was used and considered to be a lower test. In *Re Brabon*, above, Jonathan Parker J adopted 'substantial purpose' but noted that there was in his view little distinction between dominant and substantial purpose.

5 *Moon v Franklin* (1990) [1996] BPIR 196.

6 *Arbuthnot Leasing International Ltd v Havelet Leasing Ltd (No 2)*, above.

7 See Insolvency Act 1986, ss 1–7 (company voluntary arrangement), ss 252–263 (individual voluntary arrangement).

8 Section 424 (1), (2). For 'the debtor' see s 423 (5).

Transactions at an undervalue

13.10 A person enters into a transaction with another person at an undervalue if:

(a) he makes a gift to that other person or he otherwise enters into a transaction with that other person on terms that provide for him to receive no consideration;

(b) he enters into a transaction with that other person in consideration of marriage[1];
(c) he enters into a transaction with that other person for a consideration the value of which in money or money's worth is significantly less than the value, in money or money's worth, of the consideration provided by himself[2].

Where a property is mortgaged for a sum well above its realisable value, its transfer for the sum of £1 is not a transaction at an undervalue[3]. Where a transaction is alleged to fall within sub-s (1)(c), the court in weighing up the considerations moving between the parties must look at the totality of the transaction, examining it realistically and taking into account the real value of the benefits and advantages accruing to either side in the context of the purpose with which the transaction is found to have been done[4].

1 See *Re Densham* [1975] 3 All ER 726, [1975] 1 WLR 1519.
2 Insolvency Act 1986, s 423 (1).
3 *Pinewood Joinery v Starelm Properties Ltd* [1994] 2 BCLC 412: such a transfer does not deplete the assets of the disponor. See discussion of the parallel provisions in s 342 in *Re Brabon* [2001] 1 BCLC 11 and **13.4**.
4 *Agricultural Mortgage Corpn v Woodward* [1994] BCC 688: a farmer in financial difficulties gave his wife an agricultural tenancy of his mortgaged farm at a full market rent. The purpose of the transaction was to prevent the mortgagee from obtaining possession. The wife took the benefit of security of tenure, the continuation of the farming business and the surrender value of the tenancy. The totality of the transaction was held to constitute a transaction at an undervalue. See also *Barclays Bank plc v Eustice* [1995] 4 All ER 511, [1995] 1 WLR 1238 CA and *National Westminster Bank plc v Jones* [2001] 1 BCLC 98, [2001] EWCA Civ 1541.

Form of order

13.11 Without prejudice to the generality of s 423, an order made under that section with respect to a transaction may:

(a) require any property transferred as part of the transaction to be vested in any person, either absolutely or for the benefit of all the persons on whose behalf of the application for the order is treated as made;
(b) require any property to be so vested if it represents in any person's hands the application either of the proceeds of sale of property so transferred or of money so transferred;
(c) release or discharge (in whole or in part) any security given by the relevant person;
(d) require any person to pay to any other person in respect of benefits received from the debtor such sums as the court may direct;
(e) provide for any surety or guarantor whose obligations to any person were released or discharged (in whole or in part) under the transaction to be under such new or revised obligations as the court thinks appropriate;
(f) provide for security[1] for the discharge of any obligation imposed by or arising under the order, for such an obligation to be charged on any property and for such security or charge to have the same priority as a security or charge released or discharged (in whole or in part) under the transaction[2].

An order under s 423 may affect the property of, or impose any obligation on, any person whether or not he is the person with whom the debtor entered into the transaction, but such an order:

(a) shall not prejudice any interest in property which was acquired from a person other than the debtor and was acquired in good faith, for value and without notice of the relevant circumstances[3], or prejudice any interest deriving from such an interest; and
(b) shall not require a person who received a benefit from that transaction in good faith, for value and without notice of the relevant circumstances to pay any sum unless he were a party to the transaction[4].

The order need not restore the position of the victim to what it would have been had the transaction not been made[5].

1 'Security' means any mortgage, charge, lien or other security: Insolvency Act 1986, s 425(4).
2 Insolvency Act 1986, s 425 (1).
3 The relevant circumstances in relation to a transaction are the circumstances by virtue of which an order under s 423 may be made in respect of the transaction: s 425 (3).
4 Insolvency Act 1986, s 425 (2). The whole of property purchased with a loan from the bankrupt by a person benefiting from a right to buy discount vested in the trustee in bankruptcy, notwithstanding a lack of evidence of the borrower's state of mind: *Ashe (trustee in Bankruptcy of Henry Samuel Mumford) v Mumford* [2000] All ER (D) 1452, CA. For an example of the flexibility of the remedies available under s 423, see *Chohan v Saggar*, above.
5 *Moon v Franklin*, above; *Chohan v Saggar*, above.

Conveyances in fraud of subsequent purchasers

13.12 Every voluntary disposition of land made with intent to defraud a subsequent purchaser is voidable at the instance of that purchaser. However, no voluntary disposition, whenever made, is deemed to have been made with intent to defraud by reason only that a subsequent conveyance for valuable consideration was made, as long as the subsequent conveyance was made after 28 June 1893[1]. Thus, to avoid a settlement, conveyance or security under this provision, actual intent to defeat or defraud subsequent purchaser is essential[2].

1 Law of Property Act 1925, s 173.
2 *Moore v Kelly* [1918] 1 IR 169.

AVOIDANCE OF TRANSACTIONS TO PREVENT OR REDUCE FINANCIAL RELIEF

Generally

13.13 Section 37 of the Matrimonial Causes Act 1973 entitles a spouse to make an application to the court to prevent the other spouse from disposing of or dealing with property with the intention of defeating any claim by the other spouse for financial relief[1] for himself or for the benefit of any child of the family; further, the court may set aside a disposition made with that intention[2]. The court cannot make any order in respect of any disposition made for valuable consideration (other than marriage) to a person who, at the time of the disposition, acted in relation to it in good faith and without notice of any intention on the part of the disposing spouse to defeat the other spouse's claim for financial relief[3].

Section 10 of the Inheritance (Provision for Family and Dependants) Act 1975 provides analogous, but somewhat more extensively expressed, powers in the court to set aside dispositions intended to defeat a claim for family provision[4] which are not made for full valuable consideration and are made less than six years before the disposer's death.

1 On intention, see *Whittingham v Whittingham* [1979] Fam 9, [1978] 3 All ER 805, CA; *Kemmis v Kemmis* [1988] 1 WLR 1307; and note the presumption in Matrimonial Causes Act 1973, s 37 (5); and *K v K* (1982) 4 FLR 31, CA.
As to reviewable dispositions, see s 37 (6); *Whittingham v Whittingham*, above. A disposition made by a company is not reviewable: *McGladdery v McGladdery* [2000] 1 FCR 315, CA.
For the definition of 'financial relief', see Matrimonial Causes Act 1973, s 37 (1).
2 Matrimonial Causes Act 1973, s 37 (2).
3 Section 37 (4). On 'good faith', see *Whittingham v Whittingham*, above. If the disposition cannot be set aside under s 37 (1) and (2) the court cannot use its power to make consequential directions under s 37 (3) to defeat the statutory defence under s 37 (4): *Green v Green* [1981] 1 All ER 97, [1981] 1 WLR 391, and on notice see *Kemmis v Kemmis* [1988] 1 WLR 1307; *Sherry v Sherry* [1991] 1 FLR 307.
4 On registration as pending actions of claims for property adjustment orders under the Matrimonial Causes Act 1973, see *Whittingham v Whittingham* [1979] Fam 9, [1978] 3 All ER 805; *Sowerby v Sowerby* (1982) 44 P & CR 192; *Perez-Adamson v Perez-Rivas* [1987] Fam 89, [1987] 3 All ER 20.
See Tyler's *Family Provision* (2nd edn) pp 217 ff, and note *Cadogan v Cadogan* [1977] 3 All ER 831, [1977] 1 WLR 1041, CA as to an applicant's claim under s 172 of the Law of Property Act (now repealed, see **13.9**, n 2).

SECURITIES OF AN OPPRESSIVE NATURE

CLOGGING THE EQUITY[1]

13.14 A mere security for a debt cannot be forfeited for non-payment on the day stipulated in the mortgage; and any stipulation to the contrary either in or contemporaneously[2] with a mortgage is invalid[3]. Further, any attempt to clog or fetter the right of redemption by a provision which encumbers the property or gives the mortgagee a beneficial interest in it after redemption is void. Collateral advantages to the mortgagee are, however, permissible in certain circumstances. This matter is dealt with subsequently[4] in relation to redemption.

1 See further **28.6** ff.
2 See *Reeve v Lisle* [1902] AC 461, HL where an agreement made subsequently to the mortgage giving the mortgagee an option to purchase was upheld; and *Jones v Morgan* [2001] EWCA Civ 995, [2001] NPC 66 where an agreement made subsequently to the mortgage but which was not substantially independent of the original bargain was set aside by the Court of Appeal.
3 This doctrine was developed in the courts of equity on the basis of the principle: once a mortgage always a mortgage.
4 See further **28.6** ff.

SECURITIES BY EXPECTANT HEIRS[1]

Securities granted by expectant heirs and reversioners

13.15 In the exercise of its equitable jurisdiction, the court will interfere with regard to securities taken from expectant heirs or reversioners, or persons in great straits for money, especially if in weak health[2]. The courts have thus gone far beyond the original principle of protecting young and improvident persons whose expectations made them subject to impositions[3]. Where inadequate consideration was given, a mortgage will be reduced to a security for the actual advance, with interest[4], although the expectant heir with whom the transaction was made was of full, and even of mature age, and was independently advised and understood the nature of the bargain. The mortgagee bears the onus of showing that the transaction was reasonable and provident[5].

1 See further Withers on *Reversions* (2nd edn) pp 401 ff.
2 See *Croft v Graham* (1863) 2 De GJ & Sm 155.
3 See remarks of Lord Hardwicke LC in *Walmesley v Booth* (1741) 2 Atk 25.
4 In the older cases at the rate of 5 per cent per annum: *Croft v Graham*, above; *Miller v Cook* (1870) LR 10 Eq 641; *Tyler v Yates* (1871) 6 Ch App 665; *Beynon v Cook* (1875) 10 Ch App 389. No doubt a higher rate would be awarded nowadays; see **35.55**.
5 *Davis v Duke of Marlborough* (1819) 2 Swan 108 at 139; *Emmet v Tottenham* (1865) 12 LT 838; *King (J) Ltd v Hay Currie* (1911) 28 TLR 10.

Inequitable sale treated as a mortgage

13.16 Where the transaction takes the form of a sale, the conveyance will be directed to stand as a security for the amount actually found due, with interest, and in ordinary cases with costs, on the footing of a mortgage[1]. A security under the like circumstances will be ordered to stand for the sums actually advanced to, or for the benefit of, the owner of the expectancy; but where the case is tainted with fraud and misrepresentation, and it is not shown that the money was applied for the claimant's benefit, the security may be set aside unconditionally[2].

1 *Davis v Duke of Marlborough*, above; *Douglas v Culverwell* (1862) 4 De GF & J 20.
2 *Smith v Kay* (1859) 7 HL Cas 750. For a further discussion as to fraud and misrepresentation see **13.45** ff. For the principles relating to undue influence, see **13.22** ff.

Statutory protection for dealings with reversions

13.17 The acquisition of a reversionary interest at an undervalue is not a ground for setting the transaction aside[1]. However, the court's jurisdiction to set aside or modify unconscionable bargains is not affected by s 174[2] and undervalue is a material element in proving an unconscionable bargain[3].

An exorbitant rate of interest agreed to be paid by a young and needy man on the security of an indefeasible reversionary interest shows unfair dealing[4]. The doctrine as to heirs and reversioners does not apply, however, to mere cases of a high rate of interest where extraordinary risk is incurred. The risk justifies the taking of a security for interest beyond the usual rate, and even for a much larger principal sum than was really lent, the surplus being treated as a bonus[5]. The doctrine does not apply to the ordinary case of a loan by a moneylender[6].

1 Law of Property Act 1925, s 174(1).
2 Section 174(2). s 174 re-enacts the Sales of Reversions Act 1867 and s 174(2) incorporates a restriction placed upon that Act by the court in *Earl of Aylesford v Morris* (1873) 8 Ch App 484.
3 *Brenchley v Higgins* (1900) 70 LJ Ch 788.
4 *Tyler v Yates*, above: in such a case the charge will stand as security only for the sums actually advanced and interest at 5 per cent per annum: *Beynon v Cook*, above. The jurisdiction of the court was not affected by repeal of the usury laws: *Croft v Graham* above; *Miller v Cook*, above.
5 *Potter v Edwards* (1857) 26 LJ Ch 468; *Mainland v Upjohn* (1889) 41 Ch D 126; see now *Cityland and Property (Holdings) Ltd v Dabrag* [1968] Ch 166, [1967] 2 All ER 639.
6 *Gordon v Fowler* (1901) 17 TLR 243.

UNFAIR DEALING WITH THE POOR AND IGNORANT

13.18 A contract, including a mortgage, may be set aside at law if one party lacked mental capacity and that fact was known to the other party[1]. A contract, including a mortgage, may be set aside in equity if one party lacked sufficient mental capacity, even where that lack of capacity was unknown to the other party but where there is in the conduct of the latter unfairness amounting to equitable fraud which would have entitled the former to rescind the contract even if he had had mental capacity[2]. While equity will not set aside a transaction, merely on the ground that it is improvident, equity will set aside a purchase from a poor and ignorant vendor at a considerable undervalue, where the vendor has acted without independent advice, unless the purchaser satisfies the court that the transaction was fair, just and reasonable[3]. It has been said that 'poor and ignorant' may now be understood as 'member of the lower income group' and 'less highly educated', the latter requirement being applied in particular to the person's understanding of property transactions[4]. The jurisdiction will not be exercised unless the purchaser was guilty of unconscionable conduct; it is not sufficient that the parties had unequal bargaining power or that the terms of the bargain were more favourable to one party than to another[5]. The principle has been applied in Canada to a case of a mortgage[6].

1 *Manches v Trimborn* (1946) 115 LJKB 305.
2 *Hart v O'Connor* [1985] AC 1000. For drunkenness, see *Peeters v Schimanski* [1975] 2 NZLR 328.
3 *Fry v Lane* (1888) 40 Ch D 312 at 322.
4 *Cresswell v Potter* (1968) [1978] 1 WLR 255n at 257, 258, per Megarry J. Compare *Backhouse v Backhouse* [1978] 1 WLR 243. See, also, *Watkin v Watson-Smith* [1986] CLY 424. See generally [1973] 24 NILQ 171 (Lawson); (1971) 121 NLJ 1159 (Ross-Martyn); (1976) 39 MLR 369 (Waddams); (1986) 6 Oxford J of Legal Studies 123 (Beale).
5 *Boustany v Pigott* (1993) 69 P&CR 298; *Portman Building Society v Dusangh* [2000] 2 All ER (Comm) 221.
6 *Morrison v Coast Finance Ltd* (1965) 55 DLR (2d) 710. For the Canadian law in general see (1966) 44 Can Bar Rev 142 (B E Crawford) and (1972) 50 Can Bar Rev 296 (I Davis) but see *Portman Building Society v Dusangh* [2000] 2 All ER (Comm) 221.

ABUSE OF CONFIDENCE

13.19 Persons in fiduciary positions owe a duty to those who repose confidence in them to take care and skill in the management of their affairs. Thus an action may lie against a solicitor for loss sustained by his client through a misrepresentation made to his client in breach of his duty without fraudulent intent[1]. A transaction in which a person in a fiduciary positions procures a benefit for himself will be set aside[2]. The principles of undue influence and abuse of confidence overlap but do not coincide. Sometimes a transaction will engage both principles. Sometimes, the facts will engage one set of principles, but not the other. There is no requirement that the transaction will only be set aside if it is manifestly disadvantageous in a case of abuse of confidence[3].

1 *Nocton v Lord Ashburton* [1914] AC 932.
2 See *Snell's Equity* (30th edn) paras 11-68 ff. For the position of a solicitor who takes a security from his client, see **13.41** ff.
3 *Bank of Credit and Commerce International SA v Aboody* [1990] 1 QB 923 at 962-964; *CIBC Mortgages plc v Pitt* [1994] 1 AC 200 at 209; *Barclays Bank plc v Coleman* [2000] 3 WLR 405 at 414-416; on appeal to the House of Lords, reported as *Royal Bank of Scotland v Etridge (No 2)* [2001] UKHL 44 at [282]–]293], [2001] 4 All ER 449.

CONSUMER CREDIT SECURITIES

Unenforceable agreements and securities, reopening extortionate credit bargains, etc

13.20 See generally Chapter 10[1].

1 For extortionate credit transactions in company liquidation, see **8.15**. For analogous provisions on bankruptcy, see Insolvency Act 1986, s 343, and **23.44**.

UNFAIR TERMS IN CONSUMER CONTRACTS

Unfair Terms in Consumer Contracts Regulations 1999

13.21 These are discussed at **3.28, 3.30, 3.50** and **3.53**.

SECURITIES MADE UNDER UNDUE INFLUENCE[1]

Undue influence

13.22 A mortgagor may have the right to have the mortgage set aside in whole or in part on the ground that it was induced by undue influence. In considering the circumstances in which someone who has granted a mortgage may be able to have the mortgage set aside in whole or in part on this ground, it is important to bear in mind that there are important differences in the analysis required where one is dealing with a two party situation and where one is dealing with a three party situation. A two party situation arises where the undue influence was practised by the mortgagee upon the mortgagor. A three party situation is where the mortgagee did not itself practise any undue influence upon the mortgagor but, nonetheless, the mortgagor granted the mortgage to the mortgagee by reason of undue influence practised by another. An obvious example of a three party situation is where a wife agrees to join in a mortgage of the jointly owned matrimonial home in favour of a bank which has lent money to the husband or to the husband's company and where the wife's agreement to the mortgage was induced by the husband's undue influence. In the discussion which follows, the word 'complainant' will be used to refer to the person who has executed a mortgage but who now wishes to be relieved from it by reason of undue influence; the word 'wrongdoer' will be used to describe the person who has practised or is presumed to have practised the undue influence on the complainant; the words 'third party' will be used to describe the mortgagee. These descriptions are used in one of the leading cases.[2]

Thus in the typical three party situation described above, the wife will be the complainant, the husband will be the wrongdoer and the bank will be the third party.

1 For a general treatment of the principles relating to undue influence, see *Snell's Equity* (30th edn) paras 38-09 ff.
2 *Royal Bank of Scotland plc v Etridge (No 2)* [1998] 4 All ER 705, CA; [2001] UKHL 44, [2001] 4 All ER 449 (hereinafter called *Etridge (No 2)*).

Classification of cases of undue influence[1]

13.23 Cases of undue influence can be classified into two categories. Class 1 consists of cases of actual (or express) undue influence. In these cases, it is necessary for the complainant to prove affirmatively that she entered into the impugned transaction not of her own free will but as a result of actual undue influence.

Class 2 consists of cases where there is a recognised relationship from which the law presumes a relationship of trust and confidence; in such a case it is not necessary for the complainant to prove actual trust and confidence. These recognised relationships include that of parent and child, solicitor and client and medical advisor and patient. They do not include husband and wife nor, more generally, cohabiting persons of the same sex or different sexes. They do include engaged couples[2]. They do not include banker and customer[3]. The existence of these relationships does not of itself give rise to a presumption of undue influence, it depends on the nature of the transaction. In some cases, the transaction will be readily explicable without any suggestion of undue influence; examples are a Christmas or birthday gift from child to parent and the payment of reasonable fees by client to solicitor. However, if there is a Class 2 relationship and the transaction is not readily explicable by that relationship, then the complainant has shifted the evidential burden to the other party. In a case where both sides give evidence, the court should decide on all the evidence whether there was undue influence.

The relationship of husband and wife or other cohabiting or sexual relationship is not within Class 2. In the past there were decisions which discussed a possible Class 2B in which one could place such relationships if there was proven to be actual trust and confidence[4]. That approach is not considered helpful. In a case of husband and wife, or other cohabiting or sexual relationships, the complainant may have the benefit of certain evidential presumptions. If the complainant proves a relationship of trust and confidence and that the transaction is not readily explicable by reference to that relationship then, in the absence of rebutting evidence, the court is able to infer that the transaction was procured by undue influence. However, it is not open to a court to hold that there was no actual undue influence but there was presumed undue influence. In the type of mortgage case involving husband and wife, described in **13.22** above, in the ordinary case, the transaction is not one which is explicable only on the basis that the wife's involvement has been procured by the undue influence of the husband. Such transactions do not, in the ordinary case, constitute prima facie evidence of undue influence. However, there will be cases where the fact of the wife joining in the mortgage does call for explanation.

1 *Etridge (No 2)* .
2 *Re Lloyds Bank Ltd* [1931] 1 Ch 289; *Etridge (No 2)* at 719; cf *Zamet v Hyman* [1961] 3 All ER 933, [1961] 1 WLR 1442.
3 *National Westminster Bank Ltd v Morgan* [1985] AC 686; *Cornish v Midland Bank plc* [1985] 3 All ER 513; Cf *Lloyds Bank Ltd v Bundy* [1975] QB 326, [1974] 3 All ER 757.
4 *Barclays Bank plc v O'Brien* [1994] 1 AC 180.

Unconscionability[1]

13.24 The equitable doctrine of undue influence is not confined to cases of abuse of trust and confidence but is also concerned to protect the vulnerable from exploitation. It is brought into play where one party has acted unconscionably in exploiting the power to direct the conduct of another which is derived from the relationship between them. This conduct is often described in terms of domination by the wrongdoer of the mind and will of the complainant so that 'the mind of the latter became a mere channel through which the wishes of the former flowed'[2]. Importunity and pressure, if carried to the point at which the complainant can no longer exercise a will of her own, amounts to undue influence, but pressure is neither always necessary nor always sufficient. Legitimate commercial pressure brought by a creditor, however strong, coupled with proper feelings of family loyalty and a laudable desire to help a husband or son in financial difficulty, may be difficult to resist. That may be sufficient to induce a reluctant wife or mother to agree to charge her home by way of collateral security, particularly if they are accompanied by family pressure or emotional scenes. But they are not enough to justify setting aside the transaction unless they go beyond what is permissible and lead the complainant to execute the charge not because, however reluctantly, she is persuaded that it is the right thing to do, but because the wrongdoer's importunity has left her with no will of her own.

1 *Etridge (No 2)* at 712, CA, and HL at [32]–[33].
2 *Tufton v Sperni* [1952] 2 TLR 516 at 532, per Morris LJ.

Manifest disadvantage[1]

13.25 'Manifest disadvantage' was the label applied to the requirement in a Class 2 case that the transaction was not readily explicable by the relationship between the parties. The label has caused difficulty, particularly in husband and wife cases where the transaction was to some extent advantageous to the wife yet in other respects disadvantageous to her. The label may be misleading if it is used to describe the requirement that the transaction is not readily explicable. However, the presence or absence of manifest disadvantage is a powerful evidential factor when considering the other matters which must be shown to establish undue influence between the complainant and the wrongdoer and can be relevant also in considering whether the third party (in a three party situation) has or is to be taken to have notice of the undue influence so that the third party is affected by it. The more disadvantageous the transaction to the complainant the easier it is for her to establish that it has been procured by improper means and the more difficult it is for the wrongdoer to rebut the inference. Thus (in addition to the requirement that the transaction is not readily explicable in a Class 2 case), the fact that a transaction is manifestly disadvantageous to the complainant has a dual significance: (a) it assists the complainant in establishing her claim against the wrongdoer; and (b) it may be relevant to the way in which transaction appears to a third party (in a three party situation) and assists her in establishing that the third party had constructive notice of the impropriety.

1 *Etridge (No 2)* at [21]–[31], HL.

Rebutting the presumption[1]

13.26 As Class 2A can give rise to a presumption of undue influence, the presumption may be rebutted. However, the presumption is not rebutted merely by evidence that the complainant understood what she was doing and intended to do it. To rebut the presumption it must be shown that the complainant was either free from the influence of the alleged wrongdoer or had been placed, by the receipt of independent legal advice, in an equivalent position. The problem is not lack of understanding but lack of independence. The burden is on the wrongdoer to prove that the complainant entered into the transaction as the result of the free exercise of her independent will. The most obvious, though not the only, way to prove this is by showing that the complainant entered into the transaction only after the nature and effect of it were explained by some independent and qualified person fully informed of the material facts so completely as to satisfy the court that the complainant was acting independently of any influence from the wrongdoer and with the full appreciation of what she was doing. References to the complainant's freedom of action are references to her freedom from undue influence or illegitimate pressure. Where the transaction is one of gift or other bounty, the donor must be shown to have acted voluntarily in the fullest sense of the word. Any sign of reluctance on her part may indicate that improper pressure is being brought to bear. Where the transaction is a commercial one, the case is different. Reluctance to enter into a contract of guarantee or a collateral security is not necessarily indicative that any improper pressure is being brought to bear.

1 *Etridge (No 2)* at 714-715, CA, at [20], [153], HL.

Independent legal advice[1]

13.27 This paragraph focuses principally on the position between the wife and the solicitor. The mortgagee's position, the extent to which it is affected by what transpires between the wife and her solicitor and how matters appear to the mortgagee is separately considered. In identifying the solicitor's responsibilities to his client, the starting point is his retainer. In the type of case referred to in **13.22**, the involvement of the solicitor will often arise because the mortgagee has required to be satisfied that a solicitor has advised the wife and brought home to her the risks involved in the proposed transaction. In such a case, the solicitor needs to explain to the wife the purpose for which he has become involved. He needs to explain that should it become necessary, the mortgagee will rely on his involvement to counter any suggestion that the wife was overborne by her husband or that she did not fully understand the implications of the transaction. The solicitor will then need to obtain confirmation from the wife that she wishes him to act in the matter and to advise her on the legal and practical implications of the proposed transaction. The precise advice, which is appropriate, will depend on all the circumstances. The following are the typical core minimum requirements of the solicitor:

(a) He will need to explain the nature of the documents and the practical consequences these will have for the wife if she signs them.
(b) He will need to point out the seriousness of the risks involved. The wife should be told the amount of the proposed facility, the amount and principal terms relating to it, that, for example, the mortgagee might increase the amount of the facility, or change its terms, or grant a new facility, without reference to her. She should be told the amount of any guarantee. The solicitor should discuss the wife's financial means, including her understanding of the value of the mortgaged property and the availability of other assets for the purposes of repayment of indebtedness.
(c) The solicitor will need to state clearly that the wife has a choice. Explanation of that choice will call for a discussion of the financial position.
(d) The solicitor should check whether the wife wishes to proceed and whether she is content that the solicitor should write to the mortgagee confirming that he has explained to her the nature of the documents and the practical implications they may have for her, or whether, for instance, she would prefer him to negotiate with the mortgagee on the terms of the transaction. The solicitor should not give any confirmation to the mortgagee without the wife's authority.

The solicitor should explain these matters at a face to face meeting and in non-technical language. The solicitor should obtain from the mortgagee the information he needs. If the mortgagee fails to provide the necessary information, the solicitor should not give the requested confirmation to the mortgagee that he has explained matters to his client. It is not for the solicitor to veto the transaction. If the solicitor considers that the transaction is not in the wife's best interests, he will advise the wife accordingly. The general rule is that, at the end of the day, the decision to proceed is the wife's and not the solicitor's. However, there may be exceptional cases where it is glaringly obvious that the wife is being grievously wronged.

Whether the solicitor can act for the wife as well as for the husband and for the mortgagee (in a ministerial capacity) depends on whether the solicitor is satisfied that this is in the wife's best interests and will not give rise to conflicts of duty or interest. If the solicitor does act for the wife and for the husband and/or the mortgagee, his duty in relation to his advice to her is to her alone. If it emerges that that there is a real risk that other interests and duties inhibit his advice to the wife, he should cease to act for her.

1 *Etridge* at [58]–[74] and [352]–[374]; for earlier claims in negligence against solicitors see: *Northern Rock Building Society v Archer, Archer v Hickmotts* (1998) 78 P & CR 65, CA; *Etridge v Pritchard Englefield* [1999] PNLR 839, CA; *Quinn v Challinor Roberts Cooksey* [1999] PLSCS 119, CA; *Butigan v Negus-Fancey* [2000] EGCS 67.

The position between complainant and third party[1]

13.28 A transaction may be set aside for undue influence whether it was procured by the undue influence of the party seeking to uphold the transaction or that of a third party. Until the decision of the House of Lords in *Barclays Bank plc v O'Brien*[2] the basis upon which a transaction could be set aside as against a third party who was not himself guilty of any impropriety was obscure. Two principal theories competed for supremacy. One was based on agency, the other on notice. If the wrongdoer could be regarded as the agent of the third party when procuring the complainant to enter into the transaction, then the third party could not be in a better position than its agent, the wrongdoer. This theory is now almost wholly discredited. Usually, the wrongdoer is acting on his own behalf and not as agent for the third party; the husband is a principal debtor of the bank and it is artificial to regard him as agent for the creditor in procuring the further security from the wife. It will now be rare, in a case where the third party is a bank, for it to be appropriate to treat the wrongdoer as the agent of the third party. It is doubtful if it will ever be possible to treat the wrongdoer as the agent of the third party bank where he or his company is the principal debtor of the bank in relation to the transaction. Nonetheless, applying the notice theory, where a person has been induced into a transaction by undue influence, that person has an equity to have the transaction set aside and that equity is enforceable against third parties including third parties who have given value, where the third party has notice, actual constructive or imputed, of the equity.

1 *Etridge (No 2)* at [34]–[43], [139]–[150], HL.
2 [1994] 1 AC 180, [1993] 4 All ER 417.

Actual notice

13.29 Actual notice requires the third party actually to know the essential facts which found the claim of undue influence.

Imputed notice

13.30 The notice of the agent is normally imputed to his principal. This principle needs consideration where the same solicitor acts for the third party and for the wrongdoer. The third party is not, however, affected by notice of anything which its solicitor has discovered unless he was acting as the bank's solicitor at the time when he discovered it[1].

1 Law of Property Act 1925, s 199(1)(ii)(b); *Halifax Mortgage Services Ltd v Stepsky* [1996] Ch 207; *Woolwich plc v Gomm* (1999) 79 P & CR 61; *Etridge (No 2)* at [75]–[78] and [264], HL.

Constructive notice

13.31 The law relating to constructive notice has been developed in relation to matters of title in vendor and purchaser transactions. Where there is a standard procedure for investigating title, a purchaser is fixed with constructive notice of everything which he would have discovered if he had followed the standard procedure. The doctrine of constructive notice is, however, wider than this[1]. It also applies whenever a party is put on inquiry as to the existence of another's rights. If he makes no inquiry he is fixed with constructive notice of whatever he would have discovered if he had made reasonable inquiry.

1 Law of Property Act 1925, s 199(1)(ii)(a); *Etridge (No 2)* at [33]–[43], [143]–[150], HL.

In what circumstances is the third party put on inquiry?[1]

13.32 In applying the law of constructive notice in the present context of undue influence, the key question is as to the circumstances in which a third party is put on inquiry of the possibility of the transaction being induced by undue influence. Strictly speaking a reference to being 'put on inquiry' is a misnomer. The third party is not strictly required to make inquiries. However, it is a convenient term to use given that the *O'Brien* principles have involved a development of the principles of constructive notice where this is the relevant question. After considerable doubt on this question, the House of Lords has now settled on a clear simple rule. The third party is put on inquiry in every case where someone stands surety for the debt of another and the relationship between the surety and the debtor is non-commercial. In this context, a 'surety' is someone who provides a guarantee or who mortgages his or her property (whether solely or jointly owned) in relation to the debt of another. The first thing to notice is that this threshold is set much lower than the test for what is required to satisfy a court that, failing contrary evidence, the court may infer that the transaction was procured by undue influence. The test applies to cases involving husband and wife. The test also applies in the case of unmarried couples, whether heterosexual or homosexual, where the third party is aware of the relationship — cohabitation is not essential. The third party is not expected to probe the emotional relationship between the two individuals. However, the test applies yet more widely. It applies to cases of parent and child (a Class 2 relationship) but is equally not confined to Class 2 relationships. In these circumstances, the House of Lords decided that there was no rational line to be drawn other than the line between commercial relationships and non-commercial relationships[2].

In a case where the wife stands 'surety' for the debt of her husband, the position is straightforward, as described above. On the other side of the line is a case where the mortgagee advances money to the husband and wife jointly. In such a case, the mortgagee is not put on inquiry unless it knows that the loan is being made solely for the husband's purposes rather than for their joint purposes[3]. Less clear cut is the case where the wife enters into the transaction in respect of the debts of a company whose shares are held by her and her husband. Her shareholding may be nominal, or a minority stake or an equal stake to that of her husband's. For the sake of a clear simple rule, the House of Lords has decided that where the debt is that of the company and the wife enters into the transaction in her personal capacity, the mortgagee is put on inquiry, even where the wife is a director or the secretary of the company.

1 *Etridge (No 2)* at [44]–[49] and [82]–[89].
2 And see *Crédit Lyonnais Bank Nederland NV v Burch* [1997] 1 All ER 144.
3 For cases where this was not shown, see *CIBC Mortgages plc v Pitt* [1994] 1 AC 200; *Leggatt v National Westminster Bank plc* (2000) 81 P & CR 432.

What steps should the third party take if he is put on inquiry?[1]

13.33 If a the third party is put on inquiry, he needs to know what steps he ought to take to ensure that he does not have constructive notice of any undue influence that (it might later transpire) was practised on the wife. In *Barclays Bank plc v O'Brien*[2], the House of Lords indicated that the steps which a bank ought reasonably to take to avoid being fixed with constructive notice were to warn the wife, at a private meeting not attended by her husband, of the amount of the potential liability she was undertaking and of the risks involved and to advise the wife to take independent advice; a personal interview was regarded as essential to avoid the risk of written warnings being unread or even being intercepted by the husband[3]. Notwithstanding this advice, banks concerned in transactions following the *O'Brien* case (and necessarily many banks before the advice given in that case was available) did not arrange a personal interview with the wife but instead required the wife to obtain independent legal advice. The banks were concerned that statements made by their staff at such meetings would be relied upon as misrepresentations or as giving rise to estoppels. Accordingly, in *Etridge (No 2)* the House of Lords has reviewed the entire question.

1 *Etridge (No 2)* at [50]–[57], [79]–[80], [119]–[122] and [163]–[165].
2 [1994] 1 AC 180, [1993] 4 All ER 417.
3 For the requirement of a personal interview, see *Wright v Cherry Tree Finance Ltd* (2001) 82 P & CR D20.

The effect of legal advice[1]

13.34 The giving of legal advice to the wife may have two effects. The first effect is that the advice may in fact remove the effect of any undue influence. This relates to the circumstances between the complainant and the alleged wrongdoer. If the transaction was not procured by undue influence, on all the facts of the case, it is not necessary to investigate further the question of constructive notice. If, conversely, undue influence has been found, there arises the necessary question as to how matters appeared to the bank and whether the bank had constructive notice of the undue influence or whether it is to be treated as having made appropriate inquiries to avoid constructive notice. This second question depends on how matters appear to the bank. The bank should be able to rely on settled practice sanctioned by the decisions of the courts in this area. The matter ought not to turn on over-fine distinctions. The steps required of the mortgagee are as follows:

(a) The mortgagee should check directly with the wife the name of the solicitor she wishes to act for her. The mortgagee should communicate directly with the wife informing her that for its own protection it will require written confirmation from a solicitor acting for her to the effect that the solicitor has fully explained to her the nature of the documents and the practical implications they will have for her. She should be told that the purpose of this requirement is that thereafter she should not be able to dispute that she is legally bound by the documents once she has signed them. She should be asked to nominate a solicitor whom she is willing to instruct to advise her, separately from her husband, and act for her in giving the necessary confirmation to the bank. The solicitor may be the same solicitor as the solicitor acting for her husband or, if she prefers, a different solicitor. The mortgagee should not proceed until it has received an appropriate response directly from the wife.
(b) The mortgagee must provide the wife's solicitor with the information he needs to advise her. What is required will depend on the facts of the case: it is likely to include the purpose of the loan, the amount of the current indebtedness and the amount and terms of the proposed loan and mortgage. The mortgagee should supply a copy of any application for the loan. The mortgagee may need the husband's consent — if this is not forthcoming, the transaction will not be able to proceed.
(c) Exceptionally, there may be a case where the mortgagee believes or suspects that the wife has been misled by her husband or is not entering into the

transaction of her own free will. In such a case, the mortgagee must inform the wife's solicitors of this belief or suspicion.

(d) The mortgagee must obtain from the wife's solicitor a written confirmation to the above effect.

These steps are applicable to transactions which occur after the decision of the House of Lords in *Etridge (No 2)*. In relation to earlier transactions, the mortgagee will ordinarily be regarded as having discharged its obligations if a solicitor who was acting for the wife in the transaction gave the mortgagee confirmation to the effect that he had brought home to the wife the risks she was running by entering into the transaction.

It is neither desirable nor practicable for the mortgagee to be required to attempt to discover for itself whether the wife's consent is being procured by the undue influence of her husband. The steps set out above do not wholly eliminate the risk of undue influence but they do mean that the wife will enter into the transaction with her eyes wide open as to the basic elements of the transaction.

In the ordinary case, it will be reasonable that the mortgagee should be able to rely upon confirmation from the wife's solicitor that he has advised the wife appropriately. The position will be otherwise if the mortgagee knows that the solicitor has not duly advised the wife or if the mortgagee knows facts from which it ought to realise that the wife has not received the appropriate advice; in such a case, the mortgagee proceeds at its own risk[2].

Although the above commentary has referred to independent legal advice being given by a solicitor, responsibility for giving such advice may properly be, and frequently is, delegated to a legal executive[3].

1 *Etridge (No 2)* at [50]–[57], [79]–[80], [119]–[122] and [163]–[165].
2 *Northern Rock Building Society v Archer* (1998) 78 P&CR 65.
3 *Barclays Bank plc v Coleman* [2001] QB 20, [2000] 1 All ER 385, upheld by the House of Lords; see *Etridge (No 2)* at [292], HL.

The burden of proof

13.35–13.36 Whether a transaction was procured by undue influence is a question of fact. He who asserts a wrong must prove it. The evidence required depends on the nature of the alleged undue influence, the personality of the parties, their relationship, the extent to which the transaction cannot readily be accounted for by the ordinary motives of ordinary persons in that relationship and all the circumstances of the case. Proof that the complainant placed trust and confidence in the other party in relation to the management of the complainant's financial affairs (which can be presumed in Class 2 relationships), coupled with a transaction which calls for explanation, will normally be sufficient, failing satisfactory evidence to the contrary, to discharge the burden of proof. The evidential burden then shifts to the alleged wrongdoer. It is for him to produce evidence to counter the inference which should otherwise be drawn[1]. In order to prove that the mortgagee is put on inquiry of the possibility of undue influence, the complainant must show that the mortgagee knew that the transaction, in which she stood surety for the debt of another, was not a commercial transaction[2].

1 *Etridge (No 2)* at [13]–[19], HL; and see *Barclays Bank plc v Boulter* [1999] 1 WLR 1919.
2 See **13.32**.

The availability of relief

13.37 Where the third party is held to have notice of the wrongdoer's undue influence, then subject to the usual discretionary bars such as affirmation[1], delay or acquiescence, the complainant who has gained no benefit from the transaction is entitled to have it set aside[2]. Because the complainant has received no benefit from the transaction, the complainant is not required to restore anything to the third party under a suggested application of the requirement of *restitutio in integrum*. There may, however, be exceptional cases where it is possible to separate the part of the transaction vitiated by undue influence from other parts not so vitiated[3]. Where the complainant has received a benefit from the transaction, then rescission will be available on the usual basis that the complainant makes counter restitution[4]. Thus where the wrongdoer husband applied part of a loan from the third party to discharge an earlier mortgage of the matrimonial home to which the complainant wife had been a willing party, the third party was subrogated to that earlier mortgage[5]. Where rescission is impossible, it has been suggested that the court might order the third party to make a monetary payment to the complainant[6]. Where a lender's claim for possession against a husband and wife, who were both parties to the mortgage, failed because the mortgage was not binding on the wife by reason of undue influence, it was not an abuse of the process of the court for the lender to bring a money claim against the husband alone[7].

1 For an example, see *Barclays Bank plc v Goff* [2001] EWCA Civ 635, [2001] NPC 48.
2 *TSB Bank plc v Camfield* [1995] 1 WLR 430; relief was refused in circumstances where the wife had approbated the existence of the charge in ancillary relief proceedings brought against her husband: *First National Bank plc v Walker* [2001] NPC 4. Compare the specific agreement between a wife (who had asserted the charge was not binding on her) and the lender as to a sale of the charged property pending resolution of this issue in *Davies v Norwich Union Life Insurance Society* (1998) 78 P & CR 119.
3 *Barclays Bank plc v Caplan* [1998] 1 FLR 532.
4 *Dunbar Bank plc v Nadeem* [1998] 3 All ER 876 at 884.
5 *Castle Phillips Finance v Piddington* [1995] 1 FLR 783.
6 Megarry & Wade, *The Law of Real Property* (6th edn) para 19-175.
7 *Alliance & Leicester plc v Slayford* [2001] 1 All ER (Comm) 1.

ECONOMIC PRESSURE

Securities obtained by threats

13.38 The court may grant relief when the security has been obtained from the mortgagor by threat of physical violence[1].

1 See *Barton v Armstrong* [1976] AC 104, [1975] 2 All ER 465, PC; *Dandoroff v Rogozinoff* [1988] 2 NZLR 588.

Economic compulsion

13.39 This principle has been extended to economic compulsion where the pressure is such that the victim's consent to the contract was not a voluntary act on his part[1]. Duress includes two elements: first, pressure amounting to compulsion of the will of the victim[1]; and secondly, the illegitimacy of the pressure exerted[2].

1 *Pao On v Lau Yiu Long* [1980] AC 614, [1979] 3 All ER 65, PC, particularly on coercion of the will; *Crescendo Management Pty Ltd v Westpac Banking Corpn* (1988) 19 NSWLR 40; *Equiticorp Financial Services Ltd (NSW) v Equiticorp Financial Services (NZ)* (1992) 29 NSWLR 260.
2 For the rejection of the overborne will theory of duress in criminal law, see (1982) 98 LQR 197; (1983) 99 LQR 353 (Atiyah); cf (1983) 99 LQR 188 (Tiplady).

Duress

13.40 The practical effect of pressure is compulsion or the absence of choice. It is not that the weaker party cannot make a choice at all, but the victim's intentional submission arising from the realisation that there is no other practical choice open to him[1]. Inequality of bargaining power is not enough[2]. Commercial pressure, in some degree, exists wherever one party to a commercial transaction is in a stronger bargaining position than the other, but even though such pressure amounts to coercion of the will of a party in the weaker bargaining position, it may not be treated as illegitimate and, therefore, not give rise to any legal right of redress[3].

1 *Universe Tankships Inc of Monrovia v International Transport Workers Federation* [1983] 1 AC 366 at 400, [1982] 2 All ER 67 at 88, per Lord Scarman.
2 See also **13.18**. In Australia a wider concept of unconscionable dealing appears to be accepted: see *Commercial Bank of Australia Ltd v Amadio* (1983) 151 CLR 447; and generally (1984) 4 Oxford J of Legal Studies 275 (Hardingham); (1986) 60 ALJ 87 (Cope), but see *Behan v Obelon Pty Ltd* (1985) 157 CLR 326 as to the duty of a creditor to a co-surety. See generally Meagher, Gummow and LeHane *Equity Doctrines and Remedies* (3rd edn).
3 *Universe Tankships Inc of Monrovia v International Transport Workers Federation* [1983] 1 AC 366 at 384, [1982] 2 All ER 67 at 76, per Lord Diplock, and see *National Westminster Bank plc v Morgan* [1985] AC 686 at 707–708, [1985] 1 All ER 821 at 830, per Lord Scarman; *Alec Lobb (Garages) Ltd v Total Oil (GB) Ltd* [1985] 1 All ER 303 at 312–313, per Dillon LJ. The standard is impropriety not technical unlawfulness: *CTN Cash & Carry Ltd v Gallagher Ltd* [1994] 4 All ER 714 at 718; per Steyn LJ. Duress was not established in *Jones v Morgan* [2001] NPC 66, CA. For consumer credit securities, see Chapter 10. Cf *Commercial Bank of Australia Ltd v Amadio* (1983) 151 CLR 447; *Hayward v Bank of Nova Scotia* (1984) 7 DLR (4th) 135. See generally Finn (ed) *Essays in Equity* Ch 1, Unconscionable Dealing (Hardingham). For examples of illegitimate commercial pressure amounting to duress, see *B & S Contracts and Designs Ltd v Victor Green Publications Ltd* [1984] ICR 419; *Atlas Express Ltd v Kafco (Importers & Distributors) Ltd*[1989] QB 833, [1989] 1 All ER 641. To threaten to exercise one's contractual rights is not illegitimate: *Enimont Overseas AG v RO Jugo Tanker Zadar, The Olib* [1991] 2 Lloyd's Rep 108.

SECURITIES TO SOLICITORS

No advantage must be taken

13.41 The relationship between a solicitor and his client is presumed to be one of trust and confidence. In the case of a transaction between solicitor and client that is not readily explicable by reference to that relationship, the court will infer undue influence by the solicitor in the absence of rebutting evidence[1]. Hence if a solicitor purchases, or obtains a benefit, from his client, the solicitor must show that he has taken no advantage of his professional position, but has given every information and advice and has protected his client's interests in the same manner as if he had dealt with a stranger. The information disclosed must be sufficient for the client to give informed consent[2]. In default of such proof the deed will only stand as a security for the amount found to be due[3]. A gift or a security for a gift from client to solicitor is subject to the same principles[4]. An assignment by a client to his solicitor of a bare right to sue is good when it is made by way of security[5].

1 See *Royal Bank of Scotland v Etridge (No 2)* [2001] UKH 44 at [18], [24], [2001] 4 All ER 449.
2 *Sims v Craig Bell & Bond* [1991] 3 NZLR 535, CA.
3 *Tomson v Judge* (1855) 3 Drew 306; *Wright v Carter* [1903] 1 Ch 27, NZCA; *Demarara Bauxite Co Ltd v Hubbard* [1923] AC 673, PC; *McMaster v Byrne* [1952] 1 All ER 1362, PC; *Hanson v Lorenz & Jones* [1986] NLJ Rep 1088, CA.
4 *Liles v Terry* [1895] 2 QB 679; *Wright v Carter*, above, but, in the absence of bad faith, trifling gifts are not within this rule: *Rhodes v Bate* (1866) 1 Ch App 252.
5 *Wood v Downes* (1811) 18 Ves 120; *Anderson v Radcliffe* (1858) EB & E 806; affd 29 LJQB 128.

Conditions for validity of security

13.42 For a security given by a client to his solicitor to be valid, it is necessary that the money secured shall have been advanced, or shall otherwise be actually due[1]; that the amount, if not ascertained at the time, shall be capable of being ascertained (the onus of the inquiry being on the solicitor); and that there are no unusual provisions by which the client may be injured or kept in the solicitor's hands[2]. If any greater advantage is given to the solicitor than the law would give him (such as interest on his costs), the client must first have been informed of his rights[3].

The security may be for costs or advances, the amount of which has not been fixed, or where bills for the costs have not been delivered; and the amount due on such securities for costs will be ascertained by taxation[4]. Although a solicitor cannot commence an action for his charges until a month after his bill of costs has been delivered[5], this does not prevent his enforcing a security for his costs though no bill has been delivered[6]. A solicitor may take security for his future charges and disbursements, to be ascertained by taxation or otherwise[7].

1 *Nelson v Booth* (1857) 27 LJ Ch 110.
2 *Cockburn v Edwards* (1881) 18 Ch D 449, CA; but where the mortgage is to secure costs it may include special provisions: *Pooley's Trustee v Whetham* (1886) 33 Ch D 111, CA, and see Law Society's Digest, Opinions Nos 352 to 364.
3 *Lyddon v Moss* (1859) 4 De G & J 104.
4 An agreement to give security for costs to be ascertained by taxation is not required to be in writing: *Jonesco v Evening Standard Co* [1932] 2 KB 340, CA.
5 Solicitors Act 1974, s 69 (1).
6 *Thomas v Cross* (1864) 11 LT 430. See (1984) 100 LQR 86, 91 (Anderson). And see for a solicitor's right to serve a statutory demand under the Insolvency Act 1986 within one month of the delivery of the bill: *Re A Debtor No 88 of 1991* [1993] Ch 286, [1992] 4 All ER 301.
7 Solicitors Act 1974, s 65 (1) (contentious matters); s 56(1) and the Solicitors' (Non-Contentious Business) Remuneration Order 1994, SI 1994/2616, art 12(3) (non-contentious matters).

Security must not be oppressive

13.43 Where the debt is bona fide, the security will not be invalid because it was made under pressure from the solicitor[1]. If the mortgage is oppressive in form, as by an unreasonable postponement of the time for redemption, the mortgagor will have the general rights of a mortgagor[2] and where there has been a concealment or misrepresentation in obtaining or framing the security, the mortgage will be valid only for so much as, on taking the accounts, shall appear to be actually due[3]. So: where the power of sale omitted the usual conditions precedent to its exercise and the solicitor mortgagee who had not explained the omission to his client was not allowed to sell, even when interest was three months in arrear[4]. These older authorities should now be read in the light of the more recent developments of the law relating to undue influence[5].

Where a mortgagee, being a solicitor for the mortgagor, neglects his duty towards him as by omitting to register the mortgage when it requires registration by statute, he will not be allowed to avail himself of it, even though it is not avoided by the non-registration[6].

1 *Johnson v Fesenmeyer* (1858) 25 Beav 88; *Pearson v Benson* (1860) 28 Beav 598.
2 See **28.6** ff.
3 *Cowdry v Day* (1859) 1 Giff 316.
4 *Cockburn v Edwards* (1881) 18 Ch D 449, CA; *Cradock v Rogers* (1884) 53 LJ Ch 968; affd [1885] WN 134, CA
5 See **13.22** ff.
6 *Re Patent Bread Machinery Co, ex p Valpy and Chaplin* (1872) 7 Ch App 289. For negligence in relation to mortgages, see *Whiteman v Hawkins* (1878) 4 CPD 13 (failure to call for production of title deeds and consequent non-disclosure of prior equitable mortgage); *Cooper v Stephenson* (1852) 16 Jur 424 (failure to search in bankruptcy); *Bean v Wade* (1885) Cab & E 519; on appeal 2 TLR 157, CA (failure to give notice of mortgage).

Loss of lien

13.44 If a solicitor takes a security for his costs, this is, in the absence of evidence of a contrary intention, an abandonment of his lien[1], but the fact of his taking a security on the documents, by way of securing an advance, does not prejudice his lien[2].

1 *Re Taylor, Stileman and Underwood* [1891] 1 Ch 590, CA; *Re Douglas Norman and Co* [1898] 1 Ch 199. See **2.46**.
2 *Re Harvey's Estate* (1886) 17 LR Ir 165.

MISREPRESENTATION AND MISTAKE

Misrepresentation[1]

13.45 In general, either party to a mortgage transaction who is induced to enter into that transaction by reason of the misrepresentation of the other party, is entitled to have the transaction set aside[2]. This will generally[3] be so whether the misrepresentation is fraudulent[4] or innocent[5], and such person may also or alternatively be entitled to damages[6]. Questions of misrepresentation may arise not only in a two party situation, where the mortgagee is alleged to have made a misrepresentation to the mortgagor (or vice versa) but also in the three party situation where the three parties are the mortgagor, the representor and the mortgagee. Such a situation can arise where a wife enters into a mortgage in favour of a lender to provide a collateral security for the debts of her husband and there is alleged to have been a misrepresentation by the husband to the wife which induced the mortgage. In such a case, although the mortgagee did not itself make any representation, the mortgage may be capable of being set aside for misrepresentation against the mortgagor where the representor acted as agent for the mortgagee or where the mortgagee has actual, or constructive or imputed notice of the representation. The cases discussed above in relation to mortgagee's notice of undue influence practised on the mortgagor can be applied. In particular the decision of the House of Lords in *Royal Bank of Scotland plc v Etridge (No 2)*[7] discusses the principles not only relating to undue influence but also misrepresentation or other vitiating factor.

1 The provisions in the Building Societies Act 1962, s 30, whereby a building society warranted that the purchase price was reasonable, but which were always excluded in practice, were not re-enacted in the Building Societies Act 1986. Detailed provisions regarding valuations to be undertaken by building societies before making any advance secured on land are found in the Building Societies Act 1986, s 13.

2 See generally, 31 *Halsbury's Laws* (4th edn reissue) Misrepresentation and Fraud.

3 There can be no rescission where innocent third parties have acquired rights in the property. In *Barclays Bank v Waterson* [1989] CLY 2505 the mortgagor alleged that the mortgagee had misrepresented the condition and value of the property and sought rescission of the mortgage. It was held by the county court judge that this was an arguable claim. In *Leeds Permanent Building Society v Kassai* [1992] CLY 3156 a mortgagor alleged that a survey prepared by the building society had been negligently prepared and constituted a misrepresentation. The county court judge held that the mortgagor had no claim for rescission of the mortgage because on the facts *restitutio in integrum* was not possible, the current value of the property plus the value of the damages claim being insufficient to repay the mortgage advance *and interest*, the mortgagor having no other assets and because the mortgagor had affirmed the mortgage after knowledge of the right to rescind.

4 *Lee v Angus* (1866) 15 LT 380. See *Bloomfield v Blake* (1833) 6 C & P 75; *Lake v Brutton* (1856) 8 De GM & G 440 (untrue misrepresentation that representor liable as representee's surety). Where the mortgagor was induced to enter into the mortgage by the fraudulent misrepresentation of a broker who was not authorised to give advice on behalf of the mortgagee, the mortgagor is not entitled to have the transaction set aside: *National Home Loans Corpn v Yaxley* unreported; and where a mortgagor obtained mortgages by fraudulent misrepresentation, the mortgagee is not entitled to retain the balance of the proceeds of sale: *Halifax Building Society v Thomas* [1996] Ch 217, CA. Nor is the fraudulent mortgagor's solicitor so entitled; and a defence of illegality to a claim for such monies by the mortgagor will not succeed: *MacDonald v Myerson* [2001] EWCA Civ 66, [2001] 06 LS Gaz R 47.

5 Before the Misrepresentation Act 1967, there could be no rescission for an innocent misrepresentation not forming part of the contract once the contract was completed by conveyance or execution (the rule in *Seddon v North Eastern Salt Co Ltd* [1905] 1 Ch 326). s 1 of the 1967 Act removed this bar, but damages may be awarded in lieu of rescission in this situation: Misrepresentation Act 1967, s 2 (2). Where the innocent misrepresentation forms part of the contract the representee is also entitled to rescission, see Misrepresentation Act 1967, s 1, in addition to his common law rights for breach of contract.

6 Damages are available for fraudulent misrepresentation and for innocent misrepresentation where the misrepresentation forms part of the contract and, by s 2(1) of the Misrepresentation Act 1967, damages are available for an innocent misrepresentation not forming part of the contract, unless the representor can prove that he had reasonable ground to believe and did believe that the facts represented were true.

7 [2001] UKHL 44, [2001] 4 All ER 449. The result of that case may make it harder for wives to establish undue influence and in the future there may be more allegations of misrepresentation rather than undue influence.

Non est factum

13.46 In certain situations, where a person has mistakenly signed a document which turns out to be radically different from that which the signor thought he was signing, the document will be set aside. The defence of the person who signed the document to any action on the document is *non est factum*[1]. The doctrine will only rarely be established by a person of full capacity. Although it is not confined to the blind and illiterate, any extension of the scope of the plea will be kept within narrow limits. In particular it is unlikely that the plea will be available to a person who signed a document without informing himself of its meaning[2]. The distinction formerly drawn between the character and the contents of the document has been rejected[3]. For the plea to succeed there must be a radical (fundamental, serious or very substantial) difference between what the party signing signed and what he thought he was signing[4].

1 See generally, 9(1) *Halsbury's Laws* (4th edn reissue) para 687; 32 *Halsbury's Laws* (4th edn reissue) para 12; *Saunders v Anglia Building Society* [1971] AC 1004, [1970] 3 All ER 961, HL; and see *Petelin v Cullen* (1975) 132 CLR 355; *PT Ltd v Maradona Pty Ltd* (1992) 25 NSWLR 643.
2 The party raising the plea must have acted with reasonable care. Carelessness or negligence will preclude him from later pleading *non est factum*, but this is not an instance of negligence operating by way of estoppel: see generally *Saunders v Anglia Building Society*, above; *United Dominions Trust Ltd v Western* [1976] QB 513, [1975] 3 All ER 1017, CA (document incomplete when signed) and see *Avon Finance Co Ltd v Bridger* [1985] 2 All ER 281, CA. On lack of care precluding *non est factum* in the context of a power of attorney, see *Norwich and Peterborough Building Society v Steed* [1993] Ch 116, [1993] 1 All ER 330. A plea of non est factum succeeded in *Lloyds Bank plc v Waterhouse* [1993] 2 FLR 97, [1991] Fam Law 23 and failed in *Hambros Bank v British Historic Buildings Trust* [1995] NPC 179, CA.
3 See *Saunders v Anglia Building Society*, above.
4 There may be no binding contract where there has been a unilateral mistake known to the other party: see *Watkin v Watson-Smith* [1986] CLY 424.

Mistake and rectification

13.47 Rectification is an equitable remedy by which the court will change the terms of a written instrument in order to give effect to the intention of the parties to it[1]. A mortgage may be rectified on the basis of a mutual mistake: where both parties believe that the document expresses their consensus but both are mistaken that on its true construction, it does not carry out their common intention[2]. Alternatively, a mortgage may be rectified where there is a unilateral mistake: one party knows that the other party mistakenly believes that the document expresses that other's intention; realises that the mistake may operate to the other's disadvantage; but says nothing and executes the instrument[3].

1 See generally Snell *Equity* (30th edn) Ch 43.
2 See *Vaudeville Electric Cinema Ltd v Muriset* [1923] 2 Ch 74 at 80; also *Coote on Mortgages* (9th edn) p 84.
3 *Riverlate Properties Ltd v Paul* [1975] Ch 133, [1974] 2 All ER 656, CA; *Leighton v Parton* [1976] 1 NZLR 165; *Merbank Corpn Ltd v Cramp* [1980] 1 NZLR 721 and *Commission for the New Towns v Cooper (GB) Ltd* [1995] Ch 259, [1995] 2 All ER 929, CA.

FORGERIES[1]

Generally

13.48 A forged mortgage will generally be of no effect between the parties to it (but for a forged legal mortgage by a co-owner taking effect as an equitable mortgage of his share, see below). For what it is worth, there may be a right of action against the recipient of the money for the money advanced and, in appropriate cases, the payer may be able to rely on estoppel against the true owner (because of his conduct)[2], or a lien on the deeds of the property[3]. Registration vests the legal estate in a transferee, notwithstanding a forgery, though an innocent third party may be entitled to indemnity where the register is rectified because a document was forged[4].

1 See (1975) 119 Sol Jo 690 (Greene); (1984) 81 LS Gaz 641 (Kenny).
2 See *Re Cooper, Cooper v Vesey* (1882) 20 Ch D 611, CA; *Re De Leeuw, Jakens v Central Advance and Discount Corpn Ltd* [1922] 2 Ch 540.
3 Eg if the moneys are used on the property.
4 See Land Registration Act 1925, s 83 (4). See Land Registration Act 1925, s 69 (1); *Argyle Building Society v Hammond* (1984) 49 P & CR 148, CA. For further proceedings in the case of *Argyle Building Society v Hammond*, see *Norwich and Peterborough Building Society v Steed* [1993] Ch 116, [1993] 1 All ER 330 where there is an authoritative discussion of rectification under the Land Registration Act 1925. In *Commercial Acceptances Ltd v Sheikh* [2001] NPC 83, although the chargor's signature was forged, rectification of the register to remove the charge was refused, as a matter of discretion.

Husband and wife cases

13.49 It not uncommonly happens that where a husband and wife are co-owners of property the husband will raise a loan on the property without telling his wife and forging her signature. The mortgage is usually a second or subsequent mortgage where the lender does not bother to investigate title. (If such a lender took the trouble to investigate the title, a comparison of the relevant signatures on the disposition to the would-be borrowers and a first mortgage with those on the letter of acceptance would often disclose the true position.) Where there is such a forgery, the mortgage will, generally not be binding on the wife[1]: the legal title and the wife's beneficial interest will remain unaffected by the mortgage. The mortgage may, however, operate as a mortgage of the husband's beneficial interest[2]. In appropriate cases, for example where the wife was party to the earlier negotiations, she may be estopped from relying on the forgery. In some cases the husband may be deemed to have acted as agent for both himself and his wife, so that the mortgage could be treated as an effective equitable mortgage or equitable charge by both of them. Where the money has been used to purchase property, or for a permanent and substantial improvement to property, if the mortgage is ineffective, the lender may be able to claim a lien or equitable charge over the property purchased or improved[3].

1 Under Australian Torrens systems, see *Australian Guarantee Corpn Ltd v De Jager* [1984] VR 483 (mortgagee knew wife's signature unattested). See also *Rogers v Resi-Statewide Corpn Ltd* (1991) 101 ALR 377, SCSA. Whether or not the mortgage will be binding on the wife will turn on the particular wording of the relevant legislation. For a full review of the Australian authorities see Australian edition of *Fisher and Lightwood*; and see (1993) 67 ALJ 535 (Butt).
2 *First National Securities Ltd v Hegerty* [1985] QB 850, [1984] 1 All ER 139, CA; *Thames Guaranty Ltd v Campbell* [1985] QB 210, [1984] 1 All ER 144, affd [1985] QB 210, [1984] 2 All ER 585; cf *Cedar Holdings Ltd v Green* [1981] Ch 129, [1979] 3 All ER 117, CA (dictum of Lord Wilberforce in *Williams & Glyn's Bank Ltd v Boland* [1981] AC 487 at 507, [1982] 2 All ER 408, HL, explained in *Thames Guaranty Ltd v Campbell*, above); *Bankers Trust Co v Namdar* [1997] NPC 22, CA; *Mortgage Corpn v Shaire* [2000] 1 FLR 973 at 985. See also **3.89** and **12.2**. There may be a remedy available against a witness who knew or ought to have known of the forgery on the ground of warranty that the wife had signed when clearly she had not.
3 See **2.47**.

UNLAWFUL CONSIDERATION

IMMORAL OR ILLEGAL CONSIDERATION

Generally

13.50 A mortgage which is given in respect of a debt or other obligation arising out of an illegal transaction is not enforceable by a party who was also a party to the illegal transaction and who would be unable to enforce that transaction[1]. The security is tainted by the illegality of the original transaction[2]. So too where the mortgage secures a loan to discharge an illegal transaction[3], but a party to a security may be able to enforce his rights thereunder if at the time of the execution of the security he had no knowledge of the illegality of the original transaction[4]. Where the original transaction is not wholly unenforceable, the security will be unenforceable only in so far as it is related to or connected with the original transaction; if, for example, there are distinct considerations, it may be possible to sever the considerations[5].

1 *Fisher v Bridges* (1853) 3 E & B 642. For illegal contracts, see 9(1) *Halsbury's Laws* (4th edn reissue) paras 839 ff. See also *Selanger United Rubber Estates Ltd v Cradock (No 3)* [1968] 2 All ER 1073 at 1149 ff; *Heald v O'Connor* [1971] 2 All ER 1105; *Belmont Finance Corpn Ltd v Williams Furniture Ltd* [1979] Ch 250, [1979] 1 All ER 118, CA; *Belmont Finance Corpn Ltd v Williams Furniture Ltd (No 2)* [1980] 1 All ER 393, CA; *Patterson v Roden* (1972) 223 Estates Gazette 945; *Sidmay v Whettam Investments* (1967) 61 DLR (2d) 358; *Williams v Fleetwood Holdings Ltd* (1974) 41 DLR (3d) 636; on financial assistance for the purchase of shares (formerly Companies Act 1948, s 54, now Companies Act 1985, ss 151–158), see *Buckley on the Companies Acts* (14th edn) pp 157–158. *Firmin v Gray & Co Pty Ltd* [1985] 1 Qd R 160; *Field v Abduraham* [1984] 3 NSWLR 402.

2 *Cannan v Bryce* (1819) 3 B & Ald 179; but see *Carney v Herbert* [1985] AC 301, [1985] 1 All ER 438, PC (severance of guarantee from illegal mortgages); *Carney v Herbert* was applied in *Pont Data Australia Pty Ltd v ASX Operations Pty Ltd* (1990) 93 ALR 523.

3 *Spector v Ageda* [1973] Ch 30, [1971] 3 All ER 417, considering *Fisher v Bridges*, above, and *Cannan v Bryce*, above.

4 *Cannan v Bryce*, above; *Spector v Ageda*, above, at 45 and 427; *Re Mortgage Management Ltd* [1978] 1 NZLR 494. Knowledge of the facts is sufficient, it is not necessary to know of their illegal consequences: *Ninety Five Pty Ltd v Banque Nationale de Paris* [1988] WAR 132 at 177-178. See also *Williamson v Diab* [1988] 1 QD R 210.

5 *Sheehy v Sheehy* [1901] 1 IR 239; see *Robinson v Marsh* [1921] 2 KB 640. See also on illegal transactions, *Shackell v Rosier* (1836) 2 Bing NC 634; *Williams v Bullmore* (1863) 33 LJ Ch 461; *Re Onslow's Trusts* (1875) LR 20 Eq 677; *Herman v Jeuchner* (1884) 15 QBD 561; *Moulis v Owen* [1907] 1 KB 746 at 753, CA.

GAMING TRANSACTIONS

Gaming securities

13.51 Under the Gaming Act 1835, s 1, every note, bill or mortgage, the whole or part of the consideration for which is money or other valuables won by gaming, or playing at or betting on any games, or for the repayment of money knowingly lent for such gaming or betting, or at the time or place of such play, to any person gaming or betting, is deemed to have been made for an illegal consideration[1].

1 As to the loan itself, see *Carlton Hall Club Ltd v Laurence* [1929] 2 KB 153; cf *CHT Ltd v Ward* [1965] 2 QB 63 at 86, [1963] 3 All ER 835 at 842, 843, CA; Gaming Act 1968, s 16. See *Crockfords Club Ltd v Mehta* [1992] 2 All ER 748, [1992] 1 WLR 355, CA.

Wagering securities

13.52 Under the Gaming Act 1845, s 18, all contracts or agreements by way of gaming and wagering are null and void and no action may be brought or entertained in any court of law or equity for recovering any sum of money or valuable thing alleged to be won upon any wager, or which has been deposited in the hands of any person to abide the event on which any wager has been made. The effect of this provision was only to make a contract which is within it void, but not to make it illegal, so that money paid for one who lost a wager, at his request was recoverable, but by the Gaming Act 1892, losses paid by an agent are not recoverable from the principal[1].

1 Section 1.

Loan for payment of bets

13.53 If a loan is made by a lender to a borrower under an agreement that bets should be paid out of the loan, any security for the repayment of the loan will be bad[1], but such a security will be good if the borrower can dispose of money lent as he pleases[2].

1 *Hill v Fox* [1859] 4 H & N 359; *MacDonald v Green* [1951] 1 KB 594, CA.
2 *Re O'Shea* [1911] 2 KB 981 at 987–988, CA; *MacDonald v Green*, above, at 605, 606.

SECURITIES AFFECTED BY THE NATURE OF THE SECURITY

PUBLIC PAY AND PENSIONS

Public offices

13.54 A public office is deemed to be a position of public trust and the sale or other assurance of such offices is, even apart from statute[1] by which such assurances are declared to be void, contrary to public policy[2].

1 See Sale of Offices Act 1551; Sale of Offices Act 1809; Criminal Law Act 1967, s 1.
2 *Stackpole v Earle* (1761) 2 Wils KB 133.

Officers' pensions and pay

13.55 The assignment of the pay or half-pay of public officers is contrary to public policy[1]. This applies to officers in the Armed Forces[2], civil servants[3] etc, but to come within the rule the pay must come out of national and not out of local funds[4].

By statute the alienation of naval, military and air pensions[5] and the pensions of many other people, such as police officers, firemen, school teachers, etc is prohibited[6], but pensions given entirely as compensation for past services are assignable[7], unless this is prohibited by the statute under which they are paid[8].

1 *Flarty v Odlum* (1790) 3 Term Rep 681; *Stone v Lidderdale* (1795) 2 Anst 533. A mortgage of the profits of a college fellowship is not contrary to public policy: *Feistel v King's College Cambridge* (1847) 10 Beav 491; cf *Berkeley v King's College Cambridge* (1830) 10 Beav 602.

2 *Stone v Lidderdale*, above.
3 See *Lucas v Lucas* [1943] P 68, [1943] 2 All ER 110.
4 *Re Mirams* [1891] 1 QB 594. And see *Lynch v Subjic* (1987) Times, 18 May (assignment of dentist's salary paid out of public funds not illegal).
5 See Army Act 1955, s 203; Air Force Act 1955, s 203; Naval and Marine Pay and Pensions Act 1865, s 4.
6 As is alienation of the old age pension. See generally, 6 *Halsbury's Laws* (4th edn) para 84.
7 *Willcox v Terrell* (1878) 3 Ex D 323.
8 Eg under the Army Act 1955, s 203. See *Walker v Walker* [1983] Fam 68, [1983] 2 All ER 909, CA; *Roberts v Roberts* [1986] 2 All ER 483, [1986] 1 WLR 437; *Michael v Michael* [1986] 2 FLR 389, [1986] Fam Law 334.
Maintenance is not assignable unless secured: see 6 *Halsbury's Laws* (4th edn) para 85. Nor are national insurance benefits, child benefits etc alienable (see under the respective Acts providing for the benefit). As to family allowance as security, see *R v Curr* [1968] 2 QB 944, [1967] 1 All ER 478, CA; *Ranson v Ranson* [1988] 1 WLR 183, CA (pension already received assignable); *Bank Mellat v Kazmi* (1988) Times, 27 December, CA; *Cotgrave v Cotgrave* [1992] Fam 33, [1991] 4 All ER 537, CA (naval pension assignable).

PROPERTY FORBIDDEN TO BE INCUMBERED

Restraint on alienation

13.56 Property cannot be given to a person beneficially with a proviso that he shall not have the power of alienating or incumbering it. Such a proviso would be repugnant to the gift and void[1].

1 See *Caldy Manor Estate Ltd v Farrell* [1974] 3 All ER 753; but cf *Re Leahy's Estate* [1975] NSWLR 246. *Caldy Manor* may be considered dubious. The Court of Appeal in its brief judgments did not consider the issue in any great depth and it was not referred to in *Hall v Busst* (1960) 104 CLR 206 where Dixon CJ and others gave a rather more thorough review of the principles involved. *Re Leahy's Estate, Hall v Busst* was preferred to *Caldy Manor Estate*; also in *Johnston and Halliday v Halliday* (1984) ANZ Conv R 652, SCSA; and see *Reuthlinger v MacDonald* (1976) 1 NSWLR 88; affd [1977] ACLD 069.

Forfeiture on alienation

13.57 Although a person cannot be restrained from alienating property which is his, property may be settled in trust for him until he alienates or incumbers it, or attempts to do so, or becomes bankrupt or the like, and then in trust for another person or class of persons[1], but a person cannot settle his own property so as to confer on himself an interest determinable on his own bankruptcy and, if he becomes bankrupt, the forfeiture clause is void against his trustee in bankruptcy[2]. However, a clause defeating the settlor's interest takes effect in the event of voluntary alienation[3].

1 'Protective trusts' received statutory recognition in the Trustee Act 1925, s 33, but this does not validate trusts which apart from this recognition would be invalid: sub-s (3).
2 See *Mackintosh v Pogose* [1895] 1 Ch 505; *Re Brewer's Settlement, Morton v Blackmore* [1896] 2 Ch 503; *Re Burroughs-Fowler* [1916] 2 Ch 251; *Money Markets International Stockbrokers Ltd (in liquidation) v London Stock Exchange Ltd* [2001] 4 All ER 223.
3 *Brooke v Pearson* (1859) 27 Beav 181, and it has been held that it takes effect in the event of voluntary alienation at the instance of a particular creditor: *Re Detmold, Detmold v Detmold* (1889) 40 Ch D 585, but notwithstanding the decision, it appears still open to contend that the settlement is void as a fraud upon creditors: *Re Holland, Gregg v Holland* [1902] 2 Ch 360.

When forfeiture is incurred

13.58 Where the prohibition extends to an attempt to incumber, forfeiture is only operative if the act would, but for the prohibition, have the effect of an assignment or security upon the property. An offer to give a security will not create a forfeiture, much less the expression of a desire to create an incumbrance, and the taking of advice as to the power to do so[1].

1 *Graham v Lee* (1857) 23 Beav 388; *Jones v Wyse* (1838) 2 Keen 285, and as to 'attempting' to assign, see *Re Porter* [1892] 3 Ch 481; *Re Tancred's Settlement* [1903] 1 Ch 715.

Restraints on alienation in leases

13.59 Restraints on alienation in respect of leasehold property are frequently imposed by a covenant in the lease against sub-letting, assigning or parting with the property[1]. Such a covenant is broken by a mortgage by sub-demise[2]; but not by a deposit of the lease by way of equitable mortgage, the object of the covenant being only to restrain the alienation of the legal interest[3]. Similarly a mortgage by way of legal charge is probably not a breach of a covenant against sub-letting[4].

Where the covenant is against 'charging' the property, any mortgage or fixed charge, will be a breach of such covenant. There is no authority as to whether such a covenant prohibits the grant of a floating charge in respect of the company which is the lessee. This may be because the typical company charge will include both a fixed charge and a floating charge. It is arguable that the grant of a floating charge alone over the undertaking of the company which is the lessee but without a fixed charge of the lease will not necessarily result in the subsequent creation of a charge over the lease and so is not contrary to the covenant. However, if and when the floating charge subsequently crystallises, the result will be a charge over the lease; nonetheless the floating charge may have crystallised without any specific conduct on the part of the lessee and it may still be argued that the lessee has not acted contrary to the terms of the lease.

1 The covenant is often a covenant not to assign, etc without the consent of the lessor, such consent not to be unreasonably withheld. The qualification is implied by the Landlord and Tenant Act 1927, s 19 (but it will not be implied where the prohibition is absolute). s 89 (1) of the Law of Property Act 1925 provides that where a licence to sub-demise by way of mortgage is required, consent is not to be unreasonably withheld (presumably this means 'required by the terms of the lease'). As to whether the taking of possession by the mortgagee is a breach of a covenant not to part with possession, see **19.7**.

2 *Serjeant v Nash, Field & Co* [1903] 2 KB 304, CA.

3 *Doe d Pitt v Hogg* (1824) 4 Dow & Ry KB 226 at 229; *Ex p Drake* (1841) 1 Mont D & De G 539. A covenant against assigning is not broken by a mortgage by sub-demise: *Crusoe d Blencow v Bugby* (1771) 3 Wils 234; *Grove v Portal* [1902] 1 Ch 727.

4 *Gentle v Faulkner* [1900] 2 QB 267, CA. *Grand Junction Co Ltd v Bates* [1954] 2 QB 160 at 168, [1954] 2 All ER 385 at 388, on the basis that no term is created.

PART IV

TRANSFER AND DEVOLUTION OF MORTGAGES

Chapter 14

Transfer and devolution of mortgages

TRANSFER

Generally

14.1 A mortgagee is entitled to transfer his security[1] either absolutely or by way of sub-mortgage and, in general[2], with or without the concurrence of the mortgagor.

1 *Re Tahiti Cotton Co, ex p Sargent* (1874) LR 17 Eq 273 at 279; *France v Clark* (1883) 22 Ch D 830; affd (1884) 26 Ch D 257, CA. See **14.2**, but after a mortgagee has been in possession he will remain liable even after a transfer, unless that transfer is by the direction of the court.

2 The consent of the mortgagor is required in the case of a local authority mortgage, see Local Government Act 1986, ss 7-9 and Local Authorities (Disposal of Mortgages) Regulations 1986, SI 1986/1028; see **14.15**; for local authority mortgages, see **12.45** ff.

Concurrence of mortgagor

14.2 It is, however, always desirable that the mortgagor should be a party to a transfer[1] because, in his absence, the transferee is bound by the state of accounts between the mortgagor and the transferor[2]. The transferee is so bound nothwithstanding any contrary representations by the transferor to the transferee, or the fact that he has no notice of the discharge of any part of the debt[3]. As the amount of the debt and not the nature of the estate—which is only the security for it—is in this context the relevant consideration, the possession by the transferee of the legal estate does not strengthen his position[4]. If the mortgage was created in circumstances which call for inquiry, the transferee is bound, if he has notice of those circumstances, to inquire whether the advance was made and cannot recover more than the actual advance[5]. Where, however, the mortgagor has enabled the transferor to deceive the transferee, he will be estopped from denying it as against the transferee: for instance, by allowing it to be stated in the mortgage deed that a larger sum was advanced than was actually the case[6]. Arrears of interest can be capitalised where the transfer is made with the concurrence of the mortgagor, but not otherwise[7].

1 Where he is a party he usually enters into a new covenant for payment of the mortgage debt and interest with the transferee, although the transferee will have a right to sue under the Law of Property Act 1925, s 114 (1) (b), below. One advantage of the new

covenant is that it may extend time for the purposes of the Limitation Act 1980 (see **16.29** ff). A new covenant which is inconsistent with the covenant in the original covenant extinguishes the latter. A fresh covenant for payment at a new date with corresponding proviso for redemption amounts to a new mortgage: *Bolton v Buckenham* [1891] 1 QB 278, CA. A surety should also join in any new covenant: *Bolton v Buckenham*. When the mortgagor has not created further incumbrances the transfer may also contain a new demise or charge thus implying new covenants for title (as to which, see **3.38** and **3.39**).
2 *De Lisle v Union Bank of Scotland* [1914] 1 Ch 22, CA; *Parker v Jackson* [1936] 2 All ER 281.
3 See **35.18**. But the transferee may apparently rely on the face value of the mortgage where in fact a lesser sum was advanced; see *Elders Rural Finance Ltd v Westpac Banking Corpn* (1988) 4 BPR 9383.
4 *Chambers v Goldwin* (1804) 9 Ves 254.
5 *Bateman v Hunt* [1904] 2 KB 530, CA.
6 *Bickerton v Walker* (1885) 31 Ch D 151; *Powell v Browne* (1907) 97 LT 854.
7 See **35.51**.

Form of transfer[1]

14.3 The transfer of a mortgage consists of the assignment of the debt and the conveyance of the mortgagee's estate which is the security for the debt. Formerly these two parts of the transfer were separate. Thus it was usual in the deed of transfer first to assign the debt absolutely and then to convey the property subject to the equity of redemption. The separate assignment of the debt and the mortgagee's estate was rendered unnecessary by the Law of Property Act 1925, under which a deed merely purporting to transfer the mortgage has the effect of transferring at once the entire package of mortgagee's rights. In such a case, the deed will transfer, in the absence of a contrary intention expressed therein, the right to demand, sue for, recover and give receipts for the mortgage money or the unpaid part thereof and any interest due; the benefit of all securities for the debt, the right to sue on all covenants with the mortgagee, and the right to exercise all powers of the mortgagee; and all the estate and interest in the mortgaged property vested in the mortgagee subject to redemption or cesser subject to the equity of redemption[2]. There is a statutory form of transfer which may be used with necessary variations and additions[3]. The provisions do not apply to a transfer of a bill of sale of chattels by way of security[4].

1 See 28 *Forms and Precedents* (5th edn, 1999 reissue) Mortgages; and the Appendix. As to the costs of transfer, see **36.31**. For transfers of registered charges on registered land, see **4.19**.
2 Law of Property Act 1925, s 114(1).
3 Section 114(3).
4 Section 114(5).

Necessity for deed

14.4 A transfer of a mortgage must be made by deed in order for the legal estate to pass to the transferee[1] and in order to acquire the benefit of s 114 of the Law of Property Act 1925[2]. In the case of the mortgage of an equitable interest in either land or personalty the transfer must be in writing[3]. In the case of both equitable and legal morgages, the right to sue at law for the mortgage debt can only be transferred by writing under the hand of the transferor accompanied by notice to the debtor[4]. Where the transfer is a voluntary transfer, all formalities necessary for the complete transfer of the mortgage at law must be complied with, otherwise the transfer will be an incomplete gift, and void, even where the deeds have been handed over[5]. Where, however, there has been valuable consideration for the transfer, the fact that legal formalities have not been complied with will be immaterial, as between transferor and transferee, inasmuch as equity in such cases treats the transaction as an enforceable agreement to make over the benefit of the mortgage. For a contract to transfer the benefit of a mortgage (in so far as one is concerned with the interest in land) made after 27 September 1989 to be specifically enforceable and hence capable of acting as an equitable assignment, the contract must satisfy the requirements of s 2(1) of the Law of Property (Miscellaneous Provisions) Act 1989. A contract which does not satisfy those requirements is void.

1 Law of Property Act 1925, s 52 (1).
2 See **14.3**.
3 Section 53 (1) (c).
4 Section 136. See **7.2**.
5 *Re Richardson, Shillito v Hobson* (1885) 30 Ch D 396, CA.

Transfer of equitable mortgage by deposit

14.5 A contract for the transfer of an equitable mortgage (in so far as one is concerned with the interest in land) must now comply with s 2 of the Law of Property (Miscellaneous Provisions) Act 1989. If the contract does not satisfy the statutory formalities, it will be void. Accordingly, a contract to transfer an equitable mortgage which was created at an earlier time when this was still possible by deposit of the deeds must satisfy s 2; it is not sufficient merely to deliver the deeds to the transferee[1]. An agreement between the parties may nonetheless be enforceable on the basis of a constructive trust, which is imposed where the agreement is relied upon by the claimant and it would be unconscionable for the other party to disregard the claimant's rights[2]. Further, a transferee who pays off the mortgagee and takes delivery of the deeds without any assignment in writing may be subrogated to the rights of the mortgagee[3]. A voluntary transfer of an equitable mortgage must be in writing[4].

1 Formerly, delivery of the deeds was sufficient: *Brocklesby v Temperance Permanent Building Society* [1895] AC 173 at 182, 183 HL.
2 Law of Property (Miscellaneous Provisions) Act 1989, s 2(5); *Yaxley v Gotts* [2000] Ch 162.
3 See **14.22**.
4 In order to comply with the Law of Property Act 1925, ss 53(1)(c) and 136.

Transfer of statutory mortgage

14.6 A transfer of a statutory mortgage may be made by a deed expressed to be by way of statutory transfer of mortgage in either of the three forms (Nos 2, 3 and 4) given in the Fourth Schedule to the Law of Property Act 1925, with the variations adapted to the particular case[1]. A transfer in any of these forms vests in the person to whom the benefit of the mortgage is expressed to be transferred, the right to demand, sue for, recover and give receipts for the mortgage money or the unpaid part thereof, and the interest due and to become due, and the benefit of all securities for the same, and the benefit of and the right to sue on all covenants with, and to exercise all powers of the mortgagee. All the term and interest, if any, subject to redemption, of the mortgagee in the mortgaged lands vests in the transferee, subject to redemption[2].

1 Law of Property Act 1925, s 118.
2 As to the covenants implied, see s 118; as to when the covenants in the case of joint mortgagors are joint and several, see s 119.

Transfer by endorsed receipt

14.7 Where by the receipt the money appears to have been paid by a person who is not entitled to the immediate equity of redemption, the receipt operates as if the benefit of the mortgage had by deed been transferred to him, unless it is otherwise expressly provided or unless the mortgage is paid off out of capital money, or other money in the hands of a personal representative or trustee properly applicable for the discharge of the mortgage and it is not expressly provided that the receipt is to operate as a transfer[1].

If the receipt is to operate as a transfer, it must appear by the receipt that the person making the payment is not entitled to the immediate equity of redemption. A statement to that effect in the receipt will suffice but the fact may be indicated otherwise[2].

The operation of the statutory receipt as a transfer does not affect the right of any person to require a transfer to be executed in lieu of a receipt[3]. The receipt does not operate as a transfer when there is no right to keep the mortgage alive; and the mortgagor cannot keep the mortgage alive as against subsequent incumbrancers[4]. Accordingly, the receipt does not operate as a transfer to the mortgagor where there are subsequent incumbrancers; and the mortgagee cannot safely transfer the mortgage to the mortgagor or his nominee if he has notice of mesne incumbrancers without their consent[5].

1 Law of Property Act 1925, s 115 (2); see **28.54**.
2 *Simpson v Geoghegan* [1934] WN 232; *Pyke v Peters*[1943] KB 242.
3 There is a statutory form of transfer which avoids the difficulties which may arise by transfer by endorsed receipt: s 114(3), Sch 3, Form 1.
4 Law of Property Act 1925, s 115(3). See also *Cumberland Court (Brighton) Ltd v Taylor* [1964] Ch 29, [1963] 2 All ER 536 and *Otter v Lord Vaux* (1856) 6 De GM & G 638.
5 *Re Magneta Time Co Ltd, Molden v Magneta Time Co Ltd* (1915) 84 LJ Ch 814.

Transfer in lieu of discharge

14.8 A mortgagor, and a subsequent incumbrancer, is entitled to require a mortgagee to transfer the mortgage to a third party instead of re-conveying or surrendering[1].

1 Law of Property Act 1925, s 95; and see **28.52**. These provisions do not apply in the case of a mortgagee of land being or having been in possession: s 95(3).

Transfer of registered charges

14.9 As to transfer of registered charges, see **4.19**.

Transfer of sub-mortgages

14.10 As to transfer of sub-mortgages, see **15.5**.

Transfer of registered mortgages of ships

14.11 As to transfer of registered mortgages of ships, see **6.11** and **6.12**.

Transfer of bills of sale

14.12 The provisions of the Law of Property Act 1925, s 114, do not apply to a transfer of a security bill of sale[1]. A registered bill of sale can be transferred so as to constitute a valid security in favour of the transferee. The transfer need not be registered[2] and a renewal of registration does not become necessary by reason only of the transfer or assignment[3]. The transfer is usually effected by deed[4]. An equitable assignment by delivery of the bill is possible[5]. If the bill is unregistered, the transfer, in order to create an effective security, requires the same formalities as an original bill of sale[6].

1 Law of Property Act 1925, s 114 (5).
2 Unless the terms are varied: Bills of Sale Act 1878, s 10; and see *Marshall and Snelgrove Ltd v Gower* [1923] 1 KB 356.
3 Bills of Sale 1878, s 11.
4 For forms, see 4(1) *Forms and Precedents* (5th edn, 1999 reissue) Bills of Sale.
5 *Re Parker, ex p Turquand* (1885) 14 QBD 636.
6 *Jarvis v Jarvis* (1893) 63 LJ Ch 10.

Transfer of part of mortgage

14.13 A mortgage transaction has two aspects—the contractual, ie the covenant to pay, and the proprietary, ie the mortgage or charge. The debt and the security may be transferred together in whole or in part, or they may be transferred separately and independently. Where the whole of the security and the whole of the debt are transferred together no particular difficulty arises.

A transfer of the security without an assignment of the debt, in the absence of provision to the contrary (which would be unlikely), carries the benefit of the debt, so far as it is charged on the mortgaged property: the mortgagor cannot redeem without paying the debt to the transferee, but the transferee cannot sue on the covenant[1].

If the whole or part of the debt is assigned without the transfer of any of the security for the debt, the assignor remains the person entitled to exercise the powers and remedies qua mortgagee. He is a trustee of those powers and remedies and must hand over to the assignee the appropriate part of any moneys he receives by exercising them[2].

Since the mortgagee's remedies qua mortgagee are indivisible (otherwise the mortgagor might have to face a multiplicity of actions) a transfer of part of the mortgage security cannot be satisfactorily effected by a direct transfer of part thereof. In practice, the transaction will be effected either:

(a) by the mortgagee declaring himself a trustee, or transferring the security to a trustee, for himself and the transferee of the part in their respective shares; or
(b) by joinder of the mortgagor and the consequent severance of the mortgage into two or more separate mortgages; or
(c) by sub-mortgage[3].

There may be a valid equitable assignment of part of a debt[4], but the assignee will have to sue in the name of the assignor. Accordingly, a transfer of part of a mortgage debt is usually effected by the mortgagee declaring himself a trustee of such of the debt as is intended to be assigned or by the assignor assigning the benefit of the whole debt to a trustee for himself and the assignee of part.

1 *Jones v Gibbons* (1804) 9 Ves 407. See **24.101**.
2 *Morley v Morley* (1858) 25 Beav 253.
3 See **15.1** ff.
4 See **7.7** ff, and generally *Falconbridge on Mortgages* (7th edn) Ch 11.

Transfer of building society mortgages

14.14 In the case of a building society mortgage, the special relation existing between the mortgagor as a member of the society and the society, and the special form of the mortgage, may prevent the mortgage from being transferable like an ordinary mortgage. A transfer will not be possible even if there are indications in the mortgage that it is intended to be transferable[1], unless special provision is made, or the mortgagor consents[2]. Without special provision or the mortgagor's concurrence it may be that the society can only assign the mortgage debt[3]. Even if a transfer is possible the transferee may not be able to exercise the power of sale[4] and will not be in the same position as the society for the purpose of exercising the mortgagee's rights generally[5]. This difficulty can be met by making special provision in the mortgage defining the rights of a transferee[6]. However, if the loan is made by a mortgagee acting for the purposes of its business to a consumer, a term which gives the mortgagee the possibility of transferring his rights and obligations under the contract without the mortgagor's consent is presumed to be unfair, where this may serve to reduce the guarantees for the mortgagor[7].

1 For example, a definition of 'the society' to include its 'successors and assigns': *Sun Permanent Benefit Building Society v Western Suburban and Harrow Road Permanent Building Society* [1920] 2 Ch 144 at 157.
2 A transfer may be made under an amalgamation or transfer of engagements between societies and the mortgagor will be bound by the rules of the united or transferee society, see Building Societies Act 1986, ss 93 (4), 94 (8); and see also the power to transfer business from a building society to a commercial company, Building Societies Act 1986, s 97.
3 *Re Rumney and Smith* [1897] 2 Ch 351 at 359, CA.
4 *Re Rumney and Smith*, above.
5 *Sun Permanent Benefit Building Society v Western Suburban and Harrow Road Building Society* [1921] 2 Ch 438 at 459, 467, CA.
6 See Wurtzburg and Mills, *Building Society Law* (15th edn) paras 6.75-6.83.
7 See the Unfair Terms in Consumer Contracts Regulations 1999, SI 1999/2083, reg 5(5), Sch 2 para 1(p). 'Consumer' means a natural person who is acting for purposes which are outside his trade, business or profession: reg 3(1).

Transfer of local authority mortgages

14.15 A local authority must not dispose of its interest as mortgagee of land without the prior written consent of the mortgagor (or, if there is more than one mortgagor, all of them) specifying the name of the person to whom the interest is to be transferred[1]. A disposal made without this consent is void[2]. The Secretary of State may by regulations:

(a)[3] require a local authority to give to a mortgagor whose consent is sought such information as may be prescribed;
(b) prescribe the form of the document by which a mortgagor's consent is given;
(c) require a local authority making a disposal to secure that notice of the fact that the disposal has been made is given to the mortgagor; and
(d) prescribe the form of that notice and period within which it must be given.

Consent given for these purposes may be withdrawn by notice in writing to the authority at any time before the disposal is made[4]. It also ceases to have effect if the disposal is not made within six months after it is given[5]. If consent is withdrawn or ceases to have effect, the authority must return to the mortgagor any document in its possession by which he gave his consent[6]. If consent has been given and the local authority certifies in the instrument effecting the disposal that the consent has not been withdrawn or ceased to have effect, then disposal is valid notwithstanding that the consent had in fact been withdrawn or ceased to have effect[7]. In such a case, any person interested in the equity of redemption may, within six months of the disposal, by notice in writing served on the local authority, require the local authority, the transferee and any person claiming under the transferee, to undo the disposal on such terms as may be agreed between them or determined by the court, and execute any documents and take any other steps necessary to vest back in the local authority the interest disposed of by them to the transferee[8].

1 Local Government Act 1986, s 7(1); this applies to disposals on or after 24 July 1985 of a local authority's interest as mortgagee under a housing mortgage and to disposals on or after 1 April 1986 of such interest under any description of mortgage, except in either case where the disposal is carried out pursuant to a contract entered into before the relevant date: s 7(8).
2 Section 7(3).
3 Section 7(6). The current regulations are the Local Authorities (Disposal of Mortgages) Regulations 1986, SI 1986/1028, which came into force on 21 July 1986.
4 Local Government Act 1986, s 7(2)(a).
5 Section 7(2)(b).
6 Section 7(2).
7 Section 7(4).
8 Section 7(5).

Transfer of trust mortgages

14.16 In the case of a mortgage to trustees, it is the usual and convenient practice to take and transfer the mortgage without disclosing the trusts. In particular, on the appointment of new trustees, the transfer to the new trustees is made by a separate deed. Where no trust is disclosed and all that appears is that the mortgage money has been advanced on a joint account[1], this gives no notice of a trust[2]. The purchaser is not required to satisfy himself that the trustee has been properly appointed. Section 113 of the Law of Property Act 1925 relieves a purchaser of the need to satisfy himself that a trustee has been properly appointed, where a trust was disclosed in the course of examination of title[3]. It provides that a person dealing in good faith with a mortgagee, or with the mortgagor if the mortgage has been wholly or partially discharged, released or postponed, shall not be concerned with any trust at any time affecting the mortgage money or the income thereof, whether or not he has notice of the trust[4], and may assume, unless the contrary is expressly stated in the instruments relating to the mortgage and without investigating the equitable title to the mortgage debt or the appointment or discharge of trustees in reference thereto, that:

(a) the mortgagees (if more than one) are or were entitled to the mortgage money on a joint account[5]; and
(b) the mortgagee has or had power to give valid receipts for the purchase money or mortgage money and the income thereof (including any arrears of interest) and to release or postpone the priority of the mortgage debt or any part thereof or to deal with the same or the mortgaged property or any part thereof.

Section 113 does not affect the liability of any person in whom the mortgage debt is vested for the purpose of any trust to give effect to that trust.

1 See **12.119**.
2 *Re Harman and Uxbridge and Rickmansworth Rly Co* (1883) 24 Ch D 720; *Re Balen and Shepherds' Contract* [1924] 2 Ch 365.
3 Formerly, the purchaser had to satisfy himself that the trustee had been properly appointed: *Re Blaiberg and Abrahams' Contract* [1899] 2 Ch 340.
4 The Law of Property Act 1925, s 112 provides that the fact that a transfer bears only a 10s stamp, although the ad valorem stamp would exceed that sum, does not give notice of a trust. Stamp duty payable under the heading 'Mortgage, Bonds, etc' was abolished by Finance Act 1971, s 64.
5 Consequently the survivor can give a valid receipt for the mortgage money: s 111.

Transfer on appointment of new trustee

14.17 On an appointment of a new trustee the trust property in many cases automatically vests in the new and continuing trustees under the provisions of s 40 of the Trustee Act 1925. However, land conveyed by way of mortgage for securing money subject to a trust (except land conveyed on trust for securing debentures or debenture stock) is excluded from the operation of this section[1], but the mortgage debt itself is not so excluded. It is convenient on the appointment of a new trustee for the mortgage debt to be excluded from the implied vesting declaration and transferred together with the mortgaged land by a separate transfer of the benefit of the mortgage.

1 Trustee Act 1925, s 40 (4) (a). For forms of such transfer, see the Appendix.

Transfer of collateral securities

14.18 Where the mortgage or the benefit of it is transferred by deed, the transfer operates to transfer collateral securities for the mortgage debt unless a contrary intention is expressed[1]. If the collateral security is a negotiable instrument and the mortgagee indorses the instrument to a holder for value in good faith after a transfer of the mortgage alone for full value, the holder is able to recover on the instrument. The transferor holds the securities in trust for the mortgagor upon being paid off in full by the transferee, unless he has agreed to hold the securities for the transferee[2].

1 See Law of Property Act 1925, s 114(1)(b) and **14.3** and **14.4**. For notice to insurance offices, see **7.15**.
2 See *Glasscock v Balls* (1889) 24 QBD 13, CA.

Notice of transfer

14.19 Notice of the transfer should be given to the mortgagor by the transferee so that payment of the mortgage interest will be made to him[1]. After notice the mortgagor will only get a good discharge of the mortgage by paying the transferee[2]. Where the transfer takes the form of an express assignment of the mortgage debt, if the assignment is to be legal, notice must be given[3]. If the mortgage is of an equitable interest in settled land, capital money or securities representing capital money, notice should be given to the trustees of the settlement; if the mortgage is of an equitable interest in land subject to a trust of land or the proceeds of the sale of such land, notice should be given to the trustees; where the mortgage is of an equitable interest in land, notice should be given to the estate owner of the land[4]. If the mortgage is of an equitable interest in land or personalty the notice should be in writing[5]. In other cases the notice should be in the form required by the mortgage deed[6] or, in the absence of express provision, in the statutory form[7].

1 Notice to a solicitor is notice to his client: *Magee v UDC Finance Ltd* [1983] NZLR 438 CA.
2 *Dixon v Winch* [1900] 1 Ch 736; *Turner v Smith* [1901] 1 Ch 213. See **24.101**.
3 Law of Property Act 1925, s 136; see **7.4**.
4 Section 137 (2) as amended by the Trusts of Land and Appointment of Trustees Act 1996, s 25(1), Sch 3, para 4(1), (15). The provisions of the Law of Property Act 1925, s 113, have no effect on priorities: *Beddoes v Shaw* [1937] Ch 81.
5 Law of Property Act 1925, s 137 (3) and see **24.111**.
6 For forms, see 28 *Forms and Precedents* (5th edn, 1999 reissue) Mortgages and the Appendix.
7 Law of Property Act 1925, s 196. See **20.16**.

Effect of transfer

14.20 The rights of the transferee upon a transfer of the mortgage or the benefit thereof are set out in s 114 of the Law of Property Act 1925[1].

1 See **14.3**. See also ss 106 (1), 205 (1) (xvi). As to the effect of a transfer on an order for possession, see *Chung Kwok Hotel Co Ltd v Field* [1960] 3 All ER 143.

Position of transferee

14.21 In general, the transferee steps into the shoes of the transferor and he cannot stand in a better position than the transferor[1]. In relation to the mortgage debt, the transferee is bound by such equities and accounts as would bind the transferor[2]. Further, if the mortgagor has a claim by way of set off or mutual credit in relation to the mortgage debt against the mortgagee, it can also claim the benefit of the set off or mutual credit against the transferee. Leaving aside the effect of the charge being substantively registered as a charge at the Land Registry, the transferee is also in no better position than the mortgagee, when the mortgage deed is absolutely void from the beginning. However, if the charge has been substantively registered at the Land Registry, then the ability of the registered proprietor of the land to have the registration of the charge cancelled will depend on being able to persuade the court to rectify the relevant parts of the register[3]. In one case, the court refused to rectify the register to effect the cancellation of a charge even where the purported execution of the charge by the registered proprietor of the land was a forgery[4]. There is authority for the proposition that where a security is voidable and the mortgagor has an equity to set aside the security, a transferee for value of the security has a better equity and is entitled to his security[5]. In the case of unregistered land, the position should depend on whether the transferee of the security was a bona fide purchaser for value without notice of the equity. In the case of registered land, the position should depend on whether the equity is binding on the transferee and, ultimately, on the availability of rectification of the register[6]. A fraudulent mortgagee who knows his deed is absolutely void is liable to the transferee unless he discloses the fact[7].

1 *Ashenhurst v James* (1745) 3 Atk 270.
2 *Earl of Macclesfield v Fitton* (1683) 1 Vern 168; *Matthews v Wallwyn* (1798) 4 Ves 118; *Williams v Sorrell* (1799) 4 Ves 389; *Turner v Smith* [1901] 1 Ch 213; *Magee v UDC Finance Ltd* [1983] NZLR 438, CA; *Elders Rural Finance Ltd v Westpac Banking Corpn* (1988) 4 BPR 9383 and Law of Property Act 1925, s 136.
3 Under the Land Registration Act 1925, s 82; see, generally, *Norwich and Peterborough Building Society v Steed* [1993] Ch 116.
4 *Commercial Acceptances Ltd v Sheikh* [2001] NPC 83.
5 See *Judd v Green* (1875) 45 LJ Ch 108; *Nant-y-glo and Blaina Ironworks Co v Tamplin* (1876) 35 LT 125 ; but see the comment in 32 *Halsbury's Laws* (4th edn Reissue) para 581, n 1.
6 For the possibility of such an equity being an overriding interest under Land Registration Act 1925, see the discussion (but not the ultimate decision which turned on other considerations) in *Collings v Lee* [2001] 2 All ER 332.
7 *Marnham v Weaver* (1899) 80 LT 412.

Subrogated rights of person paying off mortgage debt

14.22 A person has a remedy in subrogation where he confers a benefit upon another (usually in the form of a money payment) and it is just in all the circumstances that he is allowed to succeed to rights and assets, either of the other person or of a third party, in order to prevent the other person's unjust enrichment[1]. Thus, although there has been no actual transfer, a person who advances money to a mortgagor which is used to pay off the mortgage, and whose money is so applied, is subrogated to the rights under the security against the mortgagor and subsequent encumbrancers[2]. The remedy is sought most usually where the mortgagor is insolvent and the lender seeks priority over the general creditors.

Entitlement to subrogation (as a restitutionary remedy) does not depend upon the intention of the parties[3] (although the remedy is not available where the parties intended that the loan be unsecured[4]), nor upon the lender showing that the mortgagor was at fault. The remedy will not be denied because the lender failed to take reasonable steps to protect his position[5].

Where the money advanced by the lender is used in partial discharge of a first charge, the lender is subrogated to the rights of the first chargee as against a second chargee; but the first chargee retains priority over the lender[6].

If the lender later takes a mortgage of part of the property, he remains subrogated to the rights under the security discharged with his funds, and the mortgage does not merge with the charge: the remedy given by the later mortgage is not co-extensive with the remedy of subrogation[7].

The effect of subrogation is to treat the relationship between the lender and the mortgagor as if the benefit of the security had been assigned to the lender. But the lender is not to be treated as an assignee in relation to someone who would not be unjustly enriched[8]. A claimant is entitled to enforce the subrogated security to recover payment of the secured debt together with interest at the rate which would have been payable under it up to the rate which the claimant agreed to accept[9]. An order for possession should not be made without determining what would have been due under the subrogated security. The court may have to consider what repayments should be attributed to the subrogated security; and the effect of subsequent events such as an agreement to extend time for or vary the amount of repayments[10].

A secured creditor whose debt has been repaid by another owes a duty to the payer not to prejudice the payer's remedy in subrogation. The creditor is liable to pay compensation for any loss caused to the payer by a breach of that duty[11].

1 See Goff and Jones *The Law of Restitution*, (5th edn), Ch 3.
2 *Banque Financière de la Cité v Parc (Battersea) Ltd* [1999] 1 AC 221, [1998] 1 All ER 737 HL; *Boscawen v Bajwa* [1995] 4 All ER 769, [1996] 1 WLR 328, CA. *Chetwynd v Allen* [1899] 1 Ch 353; *Butler v Rice* [1910] 2 Ch 277; *Ghana Commercial Bank v Chandiram* [1960] AC 732 at 744, 745, [1960] 2 All ER 865 at 870, 871, PC; *Paul v Speirway Ltd* [1976] Ch 220; *Financial and Investment Services for Asia Ltd v Baik Wha International Trading Co Ltd* [1985] HKLR 103; *Re H & S Credits Ltd, Tucker v Roberts* [1969] Qd R 280; cf *Re Peake's Abattoirs Ltd* [1986] BCLC 73; and see *Cochrane v Cochrane* (1985) 3 NSWLR 403 (payment made by co-owner—no subrogation); *Re Tramway Building and Construction Co Ltd* [1988] Ch 293, [1987] BCLC 632.
3 Thus a lender may be subrogated to the rights of a prior mortgagee over jointly owned property where one of the co-owners is unaware of the discharge: *National Guardian Mortgage Corpn v Roberts* [1993] NPC 149, CA.
4 *Banque Financière de la Cité v Parc (Battersea) Ltd*, per Lord Hoffmann at 234.
5 *Banque Financière* etc, above.
6 *Banque Financière* etc, above, per Lord Hoffmann at 236.
7 *Chetwynd v Allen* [1899] 1 Ch 353.
8 *Banque Financière* etc, above.
9 *Western Trust Savings Ltd v Rock* [1993] NPC 89, CA; *Halifax Mortgage Services Ltd v Muirhead* (1997) 76 P & CR 418, CA.
10 *Halifax Mortgage Services Ltd v Muirhead.*
11 *Faircharm Investments Ltd v Citibank International plc* [1998] Lloyd's Bank Rep 127, CA.

DEVOLUTION OF MORTGAGES ON DEATH OR BANKRUPTCY OF MORTGAGEE

Devolution on death

14.23 If the mortgage has been specifically bequeathed, then the executors, when they are ready to assent, will vest both the debt and the mortgage term (if any) in the beneficiary[1]. Otherwise the mortgage will be disposed of as part of the residuary personalty[2]. On intestacy[3] the mortgage will be subject to the statutory trust[4], and dealt with according to the statutory provisions[5].

The personal representatives for the time being are deemed to be the heirs and assigns of the mortgagee within the meaning of all trusts and powers[6] and can therefore exercise all powers conferred on the mortgagee, his heirs and assigns in mortgages made before 1926. As the definition of mortgagee includes any person from time to time deriving title under the original mortgagee[7], the personal representatives can exercise the statutory powers of the mortgagee.

1 Usually this is done by transfer. For forms, see the Appendix.
A personal representative may assent to the vesting of any estate or interest in land: Administration of Estates Act 1925, s 36(1). An executor may assent at common law to the vesting of personalty and on an assent of the mortgage term or charge the debt may pass also: see *Re Carter*, but a beneficiary can only sue for the debt in his own name if the assent operates as a transfer under s 114 of the Law of Property Act 1925 (see **14.3**) or as an assignment under s 136 of that Act (see **7.2** ff).

2 Previously to the Conveyancing Act 1881, the mortgagee's interest in mortgaged land, in the absence of testamentary disposition by the mortgagee, devolved upon his death on his heir or personal representative, depending upon whether it was freehold or leasehold respectively; but since the interest of the mortgagee lay substantially in the money, the mortgage debt went as part of his personal estate: *Thornborough v Baker* (1675) 1 Cas in Ch 283, 3 Swan 628 at 630. In the case of a mortgage of freehold land, the heir was regarded as a trustee thereof for the personal representative: *Re Loveridge, Drayton v Loveridge* [1902] 2 Ch 859. This separation of the land from the money was avoided in practice by inserting in wills a general devise of mortgaged properties to the executors. It was provided by s 30 of the Conveyancing Act 1881 that mortgaged freehold should, notwithstanding any testamentary disposition, devolve on the personal representative as if it were a chattel real vesting in him. Thereupon the devise of mortgaged properties became unnecessary and mortgaged freeholds devolved (as mortgaged leaseholds did) with the mortgage debt on the personal representatives. After the Land Transfer Act 1897, all property, whether real or personal, vested in the personal representatives in the same way as leaseholds had previously thereto. The provisions of the Acts of 1881 and 1897 are now replaced as to deaths after 1925 by the Administration of Estates Act 1925, ss 1(1), 3(1)(ii).

3 The doctrine of assent does not, apart from statute, apply to intestacy. So a transfer is needed to pass the debt. See n 1.

4 Administration of Estates Act 1925, s 33 as amended by the Trusts of Land and Appointment of Trustees Act 1996. For deaths prior to 1 January 1997, the relevant trust was a trust for sale; for deaths after 1 January 1997, the estate is held on trust with power to the personal representatives to sell.

5 See Administration of Estates Act 1925, as amended by the Intestates' Estates Act 1952, the Family Provision Act 1966, the Family Law Reform Act 1969 and the Family Law Reform Act 1987.

6 Section 1 (2), reproducing s 30 (1) of the Conveyancing Act 1881.

7 Law of Property Act 1925, s 205 (1) (xvi).

Death of one of several mortgagees

14.24 Where there are several mortgagees the mortgage deed will usually either expressly state that they advanced money on a joint account, or this will be implied by statute as between the mortgagor and the mortgagees in the absence of a contrary provision in the mortgage or transfer[1]. Accordingly, a receipt by the survivor is a complete discharge for all money or money's worth for the time being due, notwithstanding any notice to the payer of a severance of the joint account[2]. Such a provision (which is intended to facilitate the discharge of the mortgage) does not by itself affect the rights of the mortgagees inter se (as long as they are in fact entitled to the money as tenants in common)[3]. Accordingly, as between the mortgagees themselves, on the death of one of several mortgagees his personal representatives are prima facie entitled to his share or interest in the mortgaged property.

1 Law of Property Act 1925, s 111.

2 Section 111(1).

3 *Re Jackson, Smith v Sibthorpe* (1887) 34 Ch D 732.

Bankruptcy

14.25 On the bankruptcy of the mortgagee, all his interest in the property vests in his trustee[1] and the trustee can exercise his remedies under the mortgage, including the right to sue for foreclosure[2].

1 Insolvency Act 1986, s 306.

2 *Waddell v Toleman* (1878) 9 Ch D 212.

Death and bankruptcy of proprietors of registered charge

14.26 This is dealt with at **4.22**.

Dissolution of company mortgagee

14.27 On the dissolution of a company all property and rights whatsoever vested in or held on trust for the company immediately before its dissolution (including leasehold property, but not including property held on trust for any other person), is deemed to be bona vacantia and belongs to the Crown, or to the Duchy of Lancaster, or the Duke of Cornwall for the time being, as the case may be[1].

1 Companies Act 1985, s 654, formerly s 354 of the Companies Act 1948. See Ing *Bona Vacantia* Pt III and see *Re Wells, Swinburne-Hanham v Howard* [1933] Ch 29, CA; *Re Strathblaine Estates Ltd* [1948] Ch 228, [1948] 1 All ER 162.

Chapter 15

Sub-mortgages

Generally[1]

15.1 A sub-mortgage is a mortgage of a mortgage. A sub-mortgage for £600 of a mortgage for £1,000 consists in substance of a covenant to pay £600 and interest and a transfer of the mortgage for £1,000, subject to redemption on payment of £600 and interest. A mortgagee has, by implication of law, the right to mortgage his security without an express agreement to that effect[2].

A sub-mortgage is the easiest way of effecting a transfer of part of a debt[3] together with the security in respect of it.

1 (1948) 12 Conv (NS) 171 (Woodhouse). There would seem to be nothing in principle to prevent a sub-mortgage of part of the head mortgage debt and property (subject to the problems mentioned at **14.13**).
2 *Re Tahiti Cotton Co, ex p Sargent* (1874) LR 17 Eq 273; *Frances v Clark* (1884) 26 Ch D 257, CA.
3 See **14.13**.

Form of sub-mortgage[1]

15.2 Where the principal mortgage is a charge by way of legal mortgage or an equitable mortgage, a sub-mortgage is achieved (using the example given above) by:

(a) a covenant to pay £600 and interest;
(b) an assignment of the debt of £1,000 subject to redemption on payment of £600 and interest; and
(c) a conveyance or assignment of the mortgaged property subject to the subsisting right of redemption on payment of £1,000 and interest under the mortgage and also subject to redemption on payment of £600 and interest under the sub-mortgage[2].

Where the mortgage is a legal mortgage by demise, the sub-mortgagor has a term of years absolute. Consequently, he can only mortgage this by sub-demise or legal charge[3]. Hence the sub-mortgage should consist of three clauses, namely:

(a) a covenant to pay £600 and interest;
(b) an assignment of the debt of £1,000 subject to redemption under the sub-mortgage; and

(c) a sub-demise (or a legal charge) of the mortgaged premises subject to redemption under the sub-mortgage[4].

A sub-mortgage of several properties should not be effected by a single deed, as such a deed would be brought onto the title of each mortgagor. A sub-mortgage of each mortgage may be made and each sub-mortgage should contain a provision allowing consolidation. Alternatively each mortgage may be transferred accompanied by a collateral deed by way of sub-mortgage, regulating the rights of sub-mortgagor and sub-mortgagee between themselves[5].

A contract to create a sub-mortgage must comply with s 2 of the Law of Property (Miscellaneous Provisions) Act 1989 and may no longer be effected by deposit or redeposit of the mortgage deeds[6].

As the sub-mortgagee is in the position of transferee of the mortgage debt, he takes that debt subject to equities[7]. Notice of the sub-mortgage should be given to the mortgagor to prevent fresh equities, which arise after the sub-mortgage, being enforceable against him[8]. If the mortgage is of an equitable interest notice in writing of the sub-mortgage should be given to the trustees[9].

1 See 28 *Forms and Precedents* (5th edn, 1999 reissue) Mortgages, and see also forms of transfer, **14.3** ff.
2 It may be that advantage can be taken of Law of Property Act 1925 s 114 (see **14.3**) in order to effect the sub-mortgage by (a) a covenant to pay £600 and interest; and (b) a transfer of the benefit of the mortgage for £1,000 subject to redemption on payment of £600 and interest. It may be, however, that s 114 is restricted to a transfer under which a transferee will become absolutely entitled to the mortgage debt. In any event, the practice is for there to be an express transfer of the debt.
3 Law of Property Act 1925, s 86; see **3.5**. Although the effect of the statutory transfer under s 114 is the same, ie it operates as a sub-demise: sub-s (2), but it is undesirable to leave it to this provision to cure an inaccuracy in drafting.
4 The sub-mortgage term is made subject to redemption under the sub-mortgage only; the reversion of the sub-mortgage term, ie the mortgage term, is outstanding, and it is this that is subject to the right of redemption under the mortgage.
5 For form, see 28 *Forms and Precedents* (5th edn, 1999 reissue) Mortgages.
6 Although in appropriate circumstances, a constructive trust may be imposed: *Yaxley v Gotts* [2000] Ch 162. For creation of equitable mortgages see **3.84** ff.
7 *De Lisle v Union Bank of Scotland* [1914] 1 Ch 22, CA; *Parker v Jackson* [1936] 2 All ER 281.
8 *Reeve v Whitmore, Martin v Whitmore* (1863) 4 De GJ & Sm 1 at 19; *Bateman v Hunt* [1904] 2 KB 530, CA; *UTC (Ltd) v NZI Securities Australia Ltd* (1991) 4 WAR 349 FC; and see *Popular Homes Ltd v Circuit Developments Ltd* [1979] 2 NZLR 642 at 660. At the same time, or, preferably, before completion, the mortgagor should be asked to confirm the amount due under the principal mortgage.
9 Law of Property Act 1925, ss 136, 137. See **7.4** ff.

Effect of sub-mortgage

15.3 The effect of a formal sub-mortgage is to put the sub-mortgage in the position of the transferee of the principal mortgage[1]. He may exercise rights under the principal mortgage or under the sub-mortgage. He may exercise the power of sale under the principal mortgage, on default being made thereunder. In that case he extinguishes both the right of redemption under that mortgage and the right of redemption under the sub-mortgage. He can then dispose of the fee simple or lease under ss 88 (5) and 89 (5) of the Law of Property Act 1925[2], or he may exercise the power of sale under the sub-mortgage on default being made thereunder and sell the mortgage debt and the security for that debt[3]. If the sub-mortgagee receives the principal mortgage money he must reconvey to the principal mortgagor[4] and, after satisfying his own debt, he must account to the sub-mortgagor for the surplus[5]. Since the mortgagee is liable to the sub-mortgagee for the debt due to the latter he can require him to sue for the mortgage debt[6], but every well-drawn sub-mortgage should contain a provision that the sub-mortgagee shall be under no obligation to take steps to enforce the security and shall not be liable for any loss arising from any omission on his part to take any such steps.

1 See **14.21**.
2 See **20.40, 20.41**. The original mortgagee's power of sale is suspended during the continuance of the sub-mortgage.
3 Formerly a doubt appears to have existed as to whether a sub-mortgagee could exercise an express power of sale contained in the principal mortgage: *Cruse v Nowell* (1856) 25 LJ Ch 709, but it seems clear that if (as in most well-drawn powers and as in the case of the statutory power) the power is expressly made exercisable by any person entitled to give a receipt for the mortgage debt, the sub-mortgagee would be capable of exercising it, and see *Re Burrell, Burrell v Smith* (1869) LR 7 Eq 399.
An informal sub-mortgagee, whose sub-mortgage is not by deed, will generally have to seek an order for sale from the court. For the power of sale of an equitable mortgagee, see **20.43**.
4 For the sub-mortgagee's power to execute a vacating receipt, see 12 Conv (NS) at 177–179.
5 Law of Property Act 1925, ss 105, 107 (2); see **20.46**.
6 Cf *Gurney v Seppings* (1846) 2 Ph 40.

Sub-charges of registered charge

15.4 A proprietor of a registered charge may charge the mortgage debt with the payment of money in the same manner as a proprietor of the land may charge the land and such charges are referred to as sub-charges[1]. The sub-charge must be completed by registration[2]. The sub-chargee will then be entered as a proprietor of the sub-charge and be issued with a sub-charge certificate[3]. The proprietor of the sub-charge has, subject to any entry to the contrary in the register, the same powers of disposition, in relation to the land, as if he had been registered as proprietor of the principal charge[4]. A sub-charge is required to be completed, transferred, and discharged in the same form and manner as a charge[5]. Subject to any entry in the register to the contrary:

(a) a sub-charge, as against the person creating it, implies the same covenants and, as against that person and all persons over whose interests the charge confers power, confers the same powers and has the same effect as a charge and
(b) registered sub-charges on the same charge or incumbrance, as between themselves, rank accordingly to the order in which they are entered on the register and not according to the order in which they are created[6].

Section 66 of the Land Registration Act 1925 states that the proprietor of a registered charge may create a lien on the registered charge by deposit of the charge certificate and such lien is to be equivalent to a lien created in the case of unregistered land by the deposit of the mortgage deed by a mortgagee beneficially entitled to the mortgage. Before the coming into force of the Law of Property (Miscellaneous Provisions) Act 1989 on 27 September 1989, it was possible to create an equitable sub-charge by a deposit of the mortgagee's deeds with a sub-mortgagee. However in the light of *United Bank of Kuwait v Sahib*[7], it is now clear that it is not possible to create such a sub-mortgage merely by deposit of deeds. It would seem to follow that the mere deposit of a charge certificate does not create an equitable sub-charge. There needs to be compliance with s 2 of the 1989 Act in order to create a valid contract for a sub-charge and, consequentially, an equitable sub-charge. This understanding of the effect of s 2 of the 1989 Act has led to a change in the Land Registration Rules[8].

1 Land Registration Act 1925, s 36; Land Registration Rules 1925, r 163 (1). For a form of sub-charge (there is no prescribed form), see 28 *Forms and Precedents* (5th edn, 1999 reissue) Mortgages.
2 Land Registration Rules 1925, r 164 (1). Application should be made on Form AP1 accompanied by the sub-charge, a certified copy thereof, and the charge certificate (r 165).
3 Land Registration Rules 1925, r 166.
4 Rule 163 (2).
5 Rule 164 (1).
6 Rule 164 (2).
7 [1997] Ch 107, [1996] 3 All ER 215.
8 Land Registration Rules 1925, rr 239-243, as originally made were replaced by a new r 239 (and rr 240-243 were revoked) by Land Registration Rules 1995, r 4 with effect from 3 April 1995. The Land Registry's understanding in relation to notice of deposit of the land certificate between 27 September 1989 and 3 April 1995 is given in Ruoff and Roper *The Law and Practice of Registered Conveyancing* at paras 25-06 and 25-08.

Transfer of sub-mortgage[1]

15.5 Where the principal mortgage is a charge by way of legal mortgage or an equitable mortgage, the sub-mortgage is transferred by an assignment of the benefit of the legal charge or equitable mortgage. Where the principal mortgage is a legal mortgage by demise the conveyance is an assignment of the sub-mortgage term subject to the redemption under the sub-mortgage. However, whether the sub-mortgage is a security on an equitable mortgage or a legal charge, or is a security on a legal mortgage by demise, it is now sufficient to rely on s 114 of the Law of Property Act 1925[2] and simply to transfer the benefit of the sub-mortgage[3]. Notice of the transfer should be given to the sub-mortgagor and the principal mortgagor[4].

1 As to transfer of sub-charges, see transfer of charges, **4.19**.
2 See **14.3**.
3 For forms of transfer of sub-mortgage, see 28 *Forms and Precedents* (5th edn, 1999 reissue) Mortgages.
4 See **14.9** and see Chapter 14 as to transfers generally.

Discharge of sub-mortgage[1]

15.6 A legal sub-mortgage is generally discharged by a statutory receipt[2]. It has been suggested that a statutory receipt may be inappropriate, because in such a receipt a covenant by the mortgagee is implied that he has not incumbered[3]. Moreover the reassignment of the debt is involved[4]. Nevertheless the practice is to use a statutory receipt, where appropriate. If the mortgagee insists on a re-assignment, and reconveyance or, where there has been a sub-demise, reassignment and surrender, his wishes should be deferred to.

An informal sub-mortgage may be discharged by re-delivery if there is no accompanying document, or where there is an accompanying document by re-delivery and cancellation[5].

Notice of the discharge should be given to the mortgagor under the principal mortgage.

1 As to discharge of sub-charges, see discharge of charges, **28.59**. As to discharge of the principal mortgage by the sub-mortgagee, see **15.3**.
2 As to which, see **28.54**.
3 Law of Property Act 1925, s 115 (6).
4 As to whether or not a statutory receipt should be used for a thing in action, see **28.66**.
5 Or by receipt. For the discharge of equitable mortgages generally, see **28.61**.

PART V

THE MORTGAGEE'S REMEDIES

Chapter 16

The mortgagee's remedies

16.1 The mortgagee's principal remedies concern, first, the right to preserve his security and, secondly, recovery of the debt from the mortgagor personally and by enforcing the security. The security may be enforced by foreclosure or sale, by taking possession or by the appointment of a receiver.

THE MORTGAGEE'S RIGHT TO PRESERVE HIS SECURITY

COMPLETION OF THE SECURITY

16.2 If the agreement was for a legal, rather than an equitable mortgage, but the mortgagor has initially conveyed only an equitable title, the mortgagee is entitled, at any time up to the day of payment fixed in a redemption claim, to compel the creation in his favour of a legal estate at the mortgagor's cost[1]. Where the title conveyed to the mortgagor was defective, the mortgagee can likewise call for his security to be perfected where that is, or comes within, the mortgagor's power[2]. The mortgagee is entitled to sue for specific performance of the agreement for the purpose of enforcing his security[3].

1 *National Provincial Bank of England v Games* (1886) 31 Ch D 582, CA. See **3.84** ff. This is so even after notice or tender, if improper notice or insufficient notice is given: *Grugeon v Gerrard* (1840) 4 Y & C Ex 119; *Malone v Geraghty* (1843) 3 Dru & War 239; see also *Sporle v Whayman* (1855) 20 Beav 607.
2 *Smith v Osborne* (1857) 6 HL Cas 375 at 390; see also *Seabourne v Powell* (1686) 2 Vern 11; *Taylor v Debar* (1675) 1 Cas in Ch 274; *Smith v Baker* (1842) 1 Y & C Ch Cas 223.
3 *Browne v London Necropolis, etc Co* (1857) 6 WR 188.

RIGHT TO CUSTODY OF THE TITLE DEEDS

16.3 A mortgagee's right to custody of the title deeds, in certain circumstances an important means of protecting his rights under the security, has been considered[1].

1 See **3.69**.

PRESERVATION OF THE MORTGAGED PROPERTY

Right to preserve the mortgaged property

16.4 In order to preserve the sufficiency of his security, the mortgagee is entitled, from the time of the mortgage, to have the mortgaged property preserved from deterioration or diminution in value, either at the hands of the mortgagor, or of any other person whose interest is inferior to that of the mortgagee.[1] That applies whether he is in or out of possession. When in possession, the mortgagor may also, in some circumstances, be liable as the tenant of the mortgagee[2]. However, the mortgagee is under no duty to preserve his security unless and until he takes possession of it.[3]

1 See *Standared Chartered Bank v Walker* [1992] 1 WLR 561 at 567, [1992] BCLC 603 at 608, per Vinelott J: 'I myself feel no doubt that the courts of equity do have jurisdiction to restrain conduct which would destroy property over which a debtor has given a charge in appropriate, and no doubt rare, circumstances'. *Usborne v Usborne* (1740) 1 Dick 75; *Hippesley v Spencer* (1820) 5 Madd 422; *Hampton v Hodges* (1803) 8 Ves 105; *King v Smith* (1843) 2 Hare 239 at 243; *Simmins v Shirley* (1877) 6 Ch D 173. *Partridge v Bere* (1822) 5 B & Ald 604 and *Hitchman v Walton* (1838) 4 M & W 409 suggest that the mortgagor in occupation also has responsibilities as a quasi-tenant; but cf **19.3**, n 2 as to the true nature of relationship between mortgagor and mortgagee.

2 See **19.5**.

3 *AIB Finance Ltd v Debtors* [1998] 2 All ER 929, [1998] 1 BCLC 665.

Instances of the right

16.5 There are many instances of acts the mortgagee is entitled to undertake to preserve the mortgaged property. He can pay an insurance premium to keep a policy on foot[1], and take possession to prevent vandalism[2]. A mortgagee in possession can expend money on necessary maintenance works to the mortgaged property.[3] The mortgagee can restrain such acts as mining under buildings, so as to endanger their stability[4]. He is entitled to restrain acts which lessen its value such as to threaten the sufficiency of the security, such as the removal of valuable fixtures[5] or the cutting of timber[6]. The mortgagee of tolls on a turnpike road can restrain the trustees of the road from reducing the tolls[7]. If the company's assets are endangered, for instance by threatened executions by unsecured creditors[8], a debenture holder may obtain the appointment of a receiver before the debentures fall due. Where a company mortgaged a call upon its shareholders and, before it was received, made another call, it could not prejudice the mortgagees by getting in the second call at the expense of the first[9]. In the case of leasehold property, the mortgagee is entitled to pay rent to prevent forfeiture; or to apply for relief from forfeiture.[10] While an equitable chargee under a charging order cannot directly apply for relief from forfeiture, equity will intervene to protect for his benefit the charged leasehold property by entitling him to pursue an 'indirect' claim in proceedings to which the lessee is joined as a party.[11] A person claiming a lien for unpaid purchase money was entitled to restrain the liquidator of a company from selling part of the property, where its destruction or removal would have affected the claimant's interest[12]. The Admiralty Court will order the arrest of a mortgaged ship before the debt falls due if the mortgagor is using her for a purpose likely to injure the security[13].

1 See **36.34**. For the mortgagee's right to insure against fire at the mortgagor's expense, see **16.6**.

2 *Western Bank Ltd v Schindler* [1976] 2 All ER 393 at 396.
3 *Sandon v Hooper* (1843) 6 Beav 246; on appeal 14 LJ Ch 120.
4 *Dugdale v Robertson* (1857) 3 K & J 695 and see *Metropolitan Life Assurance Co v McQueen* [1924] 2 DLR 942.
5 *Ackroyd v Mitchell* (1860) 3 LT 236; *Gough v Wood & Co* [1894] 1 QB 713, CA; *Huddersfield Banking Co Ltd v Henry Lister & Son Ltd* [1895] 2 Ch 273, CA: *Ellis v Glover and Hobson Ltd* [1908] 1 KB 388, CA.
6 *Usborne v Usborne* (1740) 1 Dick 75; *Hampton v Hodges* (1803) 8 Ves 105; *Hippesley v Spencer* (1820) 5 Madd 422; *Humphreys v Harrison* (1820) 1 Jac & W 581; *King v Smith* (1843) 2 Hare 239 at 243; *Simmins v Shirley* (1877) 6 Ch D 173; *Harper v Alpin* (1886) 54 LT 383.
7 *Lord Crewe v Edleston* (1857) 3 Jur NS 128, 1061; 1 De G & J 93.
8 *Wildy v Mid-Hants Rly Co* (1868) 16 WR 409; *Re Carshalton Park Estate Ltd, Graham v Carshalton Park Estate Ltd* [1908] 2 Ch 62; *Higginson v German Athenaeum Ltd* (1916) 32 TLR 277.
9 *Re Humber Ironworks Co* (1868) 16 WR 474 at 667.
10 Law of Property Act 1925, s 146; County Courts Act 1984, ss 138, 139; *Barclays Bank plc v Prudential Assurance Co Ltd* [1998] 1 EGLR 44; *Bank of Ireland Home Mortgages v South Lodge Developments* [1996] 1 EGLR 91; *Sinclair Garden Investments (Kensington) Ltd v Walsh* (1995) 28 HLR 338; *Rexhaven Ltd v Nurse* (1995) 28 HLR 241; *Purley Automobile Co v Aldon Motors* (1968) 112 Sol Jo 482; *Chelsea Estates Investment Co v Marche* [1955] Ch 328; *Re Good's Lease* [1954] 1 WLR 309; *Grand Junction Co v Bates* [1954] 2 QB 160. A mortgagee in possession is entitled to serve a counternotice under s 1 of the Leasehold Property (Repairs) Act 1938: *Target Home Loans Ltd v Iza Ltd* [2000] 1 EGLR 23. For a detailed consideration of the right of a mortgagee to apply for relief from forfeiture, see Woodfall *The Law of Landlord and Tenant*, Ch 17.
11 *Bland v Ingram's Estates* [2001] 2 WLR 1638, CA.
12 *Blakely v Dent* (1867) 15 WR 663.
13 *The Blanche* (1887) 58 LT 592.

Insurance against fire at mortgagor's expense

16.6 Where the mortgage is made by deed, the mortgagee has the power at any time after the date of the deed, as if it were conferred by the terms of the mortgage, to insure against loss or damage by fire any building, or any effects or property of an insurable nature (whether or not affixed to the freehold), which are subject to the mortgage[1]. The premiums paid for such insurance are a charge on the mortgaged property, as an addition to the mortgage money, and with the same priority and with interest payable thereon at the same rate[2]. The power may be varied or extended by the mortgage deed and applies only if and so far as a contrary intention is not expressed therein[3]. The amount of insurance must not exceed the amount specified in the mortgage deed, or if no amount is specified, two thirds of the amount that would be required to restore the property in the event of its total destruction[4]. The mortgagee may not effect insurance under the statutory power if:

(a) there is a declaration in the mortgage deed that no insurance is required;
(b) insurance is kept up by or on behalf of the mortgagor in accordance with the mortgage deed; or
(c) the mortgage deed contains no stipulation respecting insurance, and insurance is kept up by or on behalf of the mortgagor, with the consent of the mortgagee to the amount to which the mortgagee is authorised to insure under the Act[5].

All money received under an insurance policy effected under the Act, or insurance for which the mortgagor is liable under the mortgage deed must, if the mortgagee requires, be applied by the mortgagor in making good the loss or damage in respect of which the money is received[6]. A mortgagee may require that all money received under such insurance is applied in or towards the discharge of the mortgage money[7]. Where the mortgagor insures neither under the provisions of the Act nor under the mortgage deed, the mortgagee has no right to monies paid under the policy[8]. However, where the mortgagor insures pursuant to a covenant in the mortgage, the covenant gives the mortgagee an interest by way of charge in the proceeds of the insurance policy, to ensure that if the value of the security is depreciated by the occurrence of a fire or other insurable risk, the proceeds of the policy will provide a fund to make up the shortfall. If the policy is in the name of the mortgagee, he is entitled in law to payment of the proceeds, but his interest remains by way of charge to secure the mortgage debt, and he will be accountable to subsequent mortgagee or the mortgagor for any surplus. If the policy is effected in the name of the mortgagor, the mortgagee has an interest by way of partial equitable assignment; to protect his interest, the mortgagee should give notice to the insurer[9].

1 Law of Property Act 1925, s 101(1)(ii). Sections 101 and 108 replace, with some variations, ss 19 and 23 of the Conveyancing Act 1881. See also **3.44**.
2 Section 101(1)(ii). They cannot be recovered form the mortgagor as a debt under the personal covenant, unless the mortgage deed provides otherwise.
3 Law of Property Act 1925, s 101(3), (4).
4 Section 108(1).
5 Section 108(2).
6 Section 108(3).
7 Section 108(4).
8 *Halifax Building Society v Keighley* [1931] 2 KB 248; and see *Myler v Mr Pussy's Nite Club Ltd* (1979, unreported, extracted in Wylie *Casebook on Irish Land Law* p 445; also (1953) 103 L Jo 230. See also **3.45**. The subsection has effect without prejudice to any obligation to the contrary imposed by law. In that context, s 83 of the Fires Prevention (Metropolis) Act 1774, which is of general application, and applies between mortgagor and mortgagee, gives interested persons the right to have insurance money extended in rebuilding: *Sinnott v Bowden* [1912] 2 Ch 414; *Portavon Cinema Co Ltd v Price and Century Insurance Co Ltd* [1939] 4 All ER 601 at 607.
9 *Colonial Mutual General Insurance Co Ltd v ANZ Banking Group (New Zealand) Ltd* [1995] 3 All ER 987, [1995] 1 WLR 1140.

Right to preserve the property as against third parties

16.7 The mortgagee is entitled, as against third parties, to protect his own or the mortgagor's title to the mortgaged property, for instance where its title is impeached[1]. Thus an equitable mortgagee is entitled to prevent a third party with inferior or uncertain title from disposing of the legal estate.[2] A mortgagee in possession can sue a third party in trespass; and since, after entry, his right to possession relates back to the time when his legal right to enter accrued, a claim can be brought for a trespass committed prior to his taking possession.[3] He may also have the right to sue in trespass if he has an immediate right to possession.[4] Where the mortgaged property is let, the right of a mortgagee in possession to enforce the covenants in the lease are considered below[5]. A mortgagee in possession, or with the immediate right to possession, of goods is entitled to claim for the recovery of the goods, or claim for trespass or conversion.[6] The mortgagee can claim for the full value of the goods, and, where required, account to the mortgagor subsequently for any surplus.[7] A prior mortgagee can restrain a judgment creditor from taking possession of the property under a charging order, even before the mortgage debt has become due[8]. A prior mortgagee, and a receiver appointed by him, can be restrained from breaching the equitable duty they owe to a subsequent mortgagee and the mortgagor.[9] A mortgagee is justified in interfering with, or procuring the breach of, a contract between the mortgagor and a third party where that is necessary for the defence and protection of the right to be repaid the secured debt.[10] Where mortgaged property is compulsorily acquired, notice to treat must be served on the mortgagee as well as on the mortgagor, and provision made for the mortgagee's interest[11]. If the mortgaged property comprises licensed premises, the mortgagee may take part in proceedings to obtain a renewal of the licence[12].

1 *Godfrey v Watson* (1747) 3 Atk 517; *Sandon v Hooper* (1843) 6 Beav 246. For costs of litigation, see **36.33**.
2 *London & County Banking Co v Lewis* (1882) 21 Ch D 490. The position prior to s 149(2) of the Law of Property Act 1925 was that the mortgagee could not sue in trespass before he had entered on the land: *Wheeler v Montefiore* (1841) 2 QB 133 at 142; *Doe d Parsley v Day* (1842) 2 QB 147 at 156.
3 *Ocean Accident & Guarantee Corpn v Ilford Gas Co* [1905] 2 KB 493.
4 *Harper v Charlesworth* (1825) 4 B & C 574 at 583; *Geary v Bearecroft* (1667) 1 Lev 202.
5 See **19.59**.
6 *Gordon v Harper* (1796) 7 Term Rep 9; *Sewell v Burdick* (1884) 10 App Cas 74; *Bristol and West of England Bank v Midland Rwy Co* [1891] 2 QB 653. The position is otherwise where, under the terms of the mortgage, the mortgagee is not yet entitled to possession: *Bradley v Copley* (1845) 1 CB 685; as to where goods are mortgaged by assignment to the mortgagor on trust to allow the mortgagor to remain in possession until payment is demanded, see *White v Morris* (1852) 11 CB 1015; *Barker v Furlong* [1891] 2 Ch 172.
7 *Brierly v Kendall* (1852) 17 QB 937 at 943; *The Winkfield* [1902] P 42 (overruling *Claridge v South Staffordshire Tramway Co* [1892] 1 QB 422.
8 *Legg v Mathieson* (1860) 2 Giff 71; *Wildy v Mid-Hants Rly Co* (1868) 18 LT 73, 16 WR 409. The cases themselves deal with elegit, which was abolished and replaced by charging orders by the Administration of Justice Act 1956. See **2.12**, n 1.
9 *Downsview Ltd v First City Corpn Ltd* [1993] AC 295, [1993] 3 All ER 626.
10 *Edwin Hill & Partners v First National Finance Corpn plc* [1988] 3 All ER 801, [1989] 1 WLR 225.
11 See further **28.31**. For consumer credit protection orders, see **10.80**.
12 *Garrett v St Marylebone Middlesex Justices* (1884) 12 QBD 620; Licensing Act 1964, s 21(1).

THE MORTGAGEE'S REMEDIES FOR RECOVERY OF THE DEBT

FORMS OF REMEDY

16.8 The mortgagee's remedies for the recovery of the debt are either:

(a) against the mortgagor personally, that is a claim on the debt[1]; or
(b) by enforcement of the security[2].

The security may be enforced by:

(a) the appointment of a receiver[3];
(b) taking possession[4];
(c) sale[5]; and
(d) foreclosure[6].

The right to sell or the right to appoint a receiver can generally be exercised by the mortgagee out of court, under the provisions of statute or the terms of the mortgage, although each may be ordered by the court in certain circumstances[7]. By contrast, enforcement of the personal covenant and foreclosure require proceedings to be brought[8]. A mortgagee may take possession himself if he can do so peaceably, but proceedings will usually be necessary[9]. Sale and foreclosure are the main remedies for recovering the principal debt and, subject to the right to recover any shortfall under the personal covenant, put an end to the transaction[10]. By sale he can realise the security;[11] by foreclosure, he can deprive the mortgagor of his equity of redemption and himself become the owner of the property.[12] Sale will often be ordered by the court in lieu of foreclosure[13]. The appointment of a receiver and taking possession are the main remedies for recovering interest out of the rents and profits of the property, as they allow the mortgage to continue, although possession will often be sought in conjunction with sale or foreclosure. In general, the mortgagee is entitled to enter into possession of the security immediately upon the execution of the mortgage;[14] by appointing a receiver, he can receive repayment out of the rents and profits without exposing himself to the liabilities of a mortagee in possession[15].

1 Usually the mortgage contains a covenant for payment and the remedy against the mortgagor personally is a claim is on the covenant. See Chapter 17.
2 For the meaning of 'enforcement' of the security, see **10.64** and **19.9**. On the defects in the enforcement of mortgages, see Law Commission Working Paper No 99, Land Mortgages, paras 3.46 ff.
3 See Chapter 18.
4 See Chapter 19.
5 See Chapters 20 and 21.
6 See Chapter 22.
7 See **18.2**, **18.16**, **20.1**.
8 See **17.1**, **22.1**.
9 See **19.1**, **19.7**.
10 See **20.38**, **20.40–20.41** and **20.58–20.59**.
11 See Chapter 20.
12 See Chapter 21.
13 See **22.47**.
14 See **19.1**.
15 See **18.1**, **19.65**.

WHEN THE REMEDIES ARISE

When the debt is due[1]

16.9 The purpose of the mortgage is to secure the repayment of the mortgagor's debt at the time agreed between the parties. Thus, the mortgagee's entitlement to exercise his remedies to claim for the debt, to appoint a receiver, to sell the security, or to foreclose do not arise until the debt has become due and the mortgagor has defaulted[2] in paying the mortgage debt[3]. (By contrast, the mortgagee is prima facie entitled to take possession as soon as the mortgage is executed[4].) Where a time is fixed for payment, the mortgagor defaults by non-payment on that day; where no time is fixed for payment, he defaults by non-payment on demand[5]. The mortgage may also provide for the mortgagee to be entitled to exercise his remedies upon some other breach of the terms of the mortgage. If 'punctual' payment is required, that is construed strictly[6]. The mere receipt of interest after the due date is not a waiver of the right to bring a claim[7], although it is a circumstance to be taken into account in determining whether there has been a waiver[8]. A covenant not to call in the money also affects the right to sue in respect of any moneys to which the mortgagee becomes entitled in that character, but not in respect of injury to the security[9]. Even when the debt has become due, there are restrictions on the mortgagee's right to sell the security or appoint a receiver[10].

1 See further **17.6**.
2 *Bonham v Newcomb* (1683) 1 Vern 231. It was allowed to be shown by parol evidence that an omission to pay did not amount to default within the meaning of the deed, the consent of the person entitled to payment to enlarge the time, though made without consideration, being held to show that there was no default: *Albert v Grosvenor Investment Co* (1867) LR 3 QB 123, but in *Williams v Stern* (1879) 5 QBD 409, the Court of Appeal held that a consent so given was no evidence of waiver of the mortgagee's rights to take possession at any time. On waiver of remedies, see *Barns v Queensland National Bank Ltd* (1906) 3 CLR 925 at 937–938.
3 *Burrowes v Molloy* (1845) 2 Jo & Lat 521, *Wilkes v Saunion* (1877) 7 Ch D 188.
4 See **19.1**.
5 Cas & Op II, 51; Glanv Lib 10, c 8. For implied demand, see *The Halcyon Skies (No 2)* [1977] 1 Lloyd's Rep 22. See further **17.6**.
6 *Leeds and Hanley Theatre of Varieties v Broadbent* [1898] 1 Ch 343, CA; *Maclaine v Gatty* [1921] 1 AC 376, HL.
7 *Keene v Biscoe* (1878) 8 Ch D 201.
8 *Seal v Gimson* (1914) 110 LT 583.
9 *Dugdale v Robertson* (1857) 3 K & J 695.
10 See **20.11–20.12** and **18.5**.

When the right to foreclosure arises[1]

16.10 Foreclosure consists of depriving the mortgagor of his equitable right to redeem the mortgage, and results in the mortgagee himself becoming owner of the property[2]. The mortgagor has two rights of redemption. First, he has a legal right of redemption until the day fixed for payment arrives and, where there is an express proviso for redemption, he cannot be deprived of this[3]. Secondly, on default in payment on that day, his legal right to redeem ceases, and thenceforth he has only an equitable right of redemption.

In the classical form of mortgage, the date for legal redemption is specified in the proviso for redemption—usually six months from the date of the mortgage and the same date as the date fixed by the covenant for payment. On default in payment on the specified date, the right of foreclosure arises. However, the parties can subsequently agree upon a later date for payment, with a consequent postponement of foreclosure. The effect is the same where, although the period of six months is fixed for redemption, there is a stipulation that the money will not be called in until a later date.[4] If the proviso for redemption contains a postponement, expressed in terms that there is a right to redeem on payment of principal at a future date, with interest to be paid in the meantime, the failure to pay interest periodically does not accelerate the right to foreclosure. That is the case even where there is a covenant to pay interest periodically, for the proviso for redemption is treated as independent of the covenant[5]. However, where the condition for periodical payment is contained in the proviso itself, for example where the proviso is for redemption on payment of principal with interest half-yearly in the meantime, or on payment of principal and interest in accordance with the covenant for payment, the right of foreclosure arises upon a failure to pay interest[6]. In the modern form of instalment mortgage there is generally no provision for redemption, but it seems to be accepted that the right of foreclosure nevertheless arises when the mortgage moneys become due, on default or otherwise[7]. Where a proviso for early redemption in the usual form is accompanied by a covenant that the money shall not be called in until a later date[8] then, if the covenant is absolute, default in payment of interest pending the day for redemption will not entitle the mortgagee to foreclosure[9], but if, as is usually the case, the covenant is expressed to be conditional on regular payment of interest, the right to foreclose arises on default in such payment[10].

1 See further **22.2**.
2 The mortgagee thereupon acquires a new title as owner: see *Heath v Pugh* (1881) 6 QBD 345, CA; on appeal sub nom *Pugh v Heath* (1882) 7 App Cas 235, HL. The remedies are equally available to a subsequent mortgagee: *Westpac Banking Corpn v Daydream Island Pty* [1985] 2 Qd R 330. See further **22.58–22.59**.
3 *Twentieth Century Banking Corpn Ltd v Wilkinson* [1977] Ch 99, [1976] 3 All ER 361.
4 Such a postponement is to the advantage of the mortgagor and since the mortgagee does not require the same protection as the mortgagor, it is not subject to the same restriction as a postponement of the right to redeem. Thus, for example, there is no objection to an agreement that the debt shall not be called in during the lifetime of any particular person: *Bonham v Newcomb* (1683) 1 Vern 231 and unless fraud is proved, no objection probably would be made to a postponement whatever its length.
5 *Re Turner, Turner v Spencer* (1894) 43 WR 153; *Williams v Morgan* [1906] 1 Ch 804.
6 *Burrowes v Molloy* (1845) 2 Jo & Lat 521 at 526; *Edwards v Martin* (1856) 25 LJ Ch 284; *Kidderminster Mutual Benefit Building Society v Haddock* [1936] WN 158; *Twentieth Century Banking Corpn Ltd v Wilkinson* above. And see *Mohamedali Jaffer Karachiwalla v Noorally Rattanshi Rajan Nanji* [1959] AC 518, [1959] 1 All ER 137, PC.
7 *Twentieth Century Banking Corpn Ltd v Wilkinson* [1977] Ch 99, [1976] 3 All ER 361.
8 It has been held that such a covenant by the second mortgagee prevents him from redeeming the first mortgage, because he cannot bring the mortgagor before the court: *Ramsbottom v Wallis* (1835) 5 LJ Ch 92, but this seems to be straining a technicality too far.
9 *Burrows v Molloy* (1845) 2 Jo & Lat 521.
10 *Stanhope v Manners* (1763) 2 Eden 197; *Seaton v Twyford* (1870) LR 11 Eq 591. For a form, see the Appendix.

MORTGAGEE'S OPTION TO EXERCISE ALL OR ANY OF THE REMEDIES CONCURRENTLY

16.11 Once the mortgagee has become entitled to exercise his remedies (and subject to restrictions imposed by statute or the terms of the mortgage deed), he is entitled to pursue any or all of them concurrently against the debtor, his assets, or the incumbered estate[1]. As a departure from the general rule that a person is not liable to be harassed by a multiplicity of claims, it is the right of the mortgagee, or other secured creditor, to pursue any or all of his remedies at the same time, for so long as any part of the debt remains unpaid, or until the mortgagee acts in such a way as to amount to an election[2]. Hence the mortgagee can at the same time, and in the same claim, claim for payment on the covenant to pay principal and interest, for possession of the mortgaged property, and for foreclosure. A mortgagee can obtain a possession order and a money judgment at the same time.[3] A mortgagee who has sold the property under his power of sale, or where there has been a sale by the court[4], can sue the mortgagor for any shortfall[5]. A mortgagee who has taken possession can appoint a receiver[6]. A mortgagee is not obliged to exhaust a claim for foreclosure before attempting to collect the debt in other ways[7].

There are, however, certain restrictions on the combination of remedies. Thus, a mortgagee who has obtained an order nisi for foreclosure, which has not yet been made absolute, cannot sell without the leave of the court[8]. If the mortgagee sues on the personal covenant after foreclosure absolute, that will open the foreclosure[9]. A mortgagee who has sold the property after foreclosure cannot sue on the personal covenant[10]. If the mortgagor chooses to sue the mortgagor on his personal covenant and obtains a money judgment, abandons his security and brings bankruptcy proceedings, he cannot thereafter exercise remedies as a secured creditor[11]. Once the whole debt has been repaid, the mortgagor is entitled to have any unsold security reconveyed to him[12].

Since a mortgage is entitled to pursue all his remedies, the court will not interfere with a claim by him on the personal covenant, simply because he has made a draft contract to sell the mortgaged property for a larger sum than is due on the mortgage[13]. Nor will the court interfere with the mortgagee's right to recover possession, simply because, after contracting to sell, he has brought a claim on the covenant, and has compromised it on payment of a sum of money by another person whom the original mortgagee afterwards redeemed for the purpose of completing his contract for sale[14]. The court also declined to interfere with a mortgagee's proceedings where an order had been made in another claim, but in his absence[15]. Where there are collateral securities, the mortgagee will be advised to realise those first, and foreclose in respect of the outstanding sums.[16] A prior incumbrancer may also bring a claim after a judgment has been obtained in another claim by the owner of a later charge, for he is not bound to come in under that judgment at the risk of losing his rights by the suspension of the proceedings in the later incumbrancer's claim[17].

1 *Lockhart v Hardy* (1846) 9 Beav 379; *Paynter v Carew* (1854) Kay App xxxvi; *Palmer v Hendrie* (1859) 27 Beav 349 at 351; *Cheltenham & Gloucester Building Society v Grattridge* (1993) 25 HLR 454; *Alliance & Leicester Building Society v Slayford* [2001] 1 All ER (Comm) 1. See also *China & South Sea Bank Ltd v Tan Soon Gin* [1990] 1 AC 536, [1989] 3 All ER 839; *Re McCann* [1985] 2 Qd R 381; *Cheah Theam Swee v Equiticorp Finance Group Ltd* [1992] 1 AC 472, [1991] 4 All ER 989; *Royal Trust Corpn of Canada v Northdale Development Co Ltd* [1994] 1 WWR 68 (CAN).

2 *Alliance & Leicester Building Society v Slayford* above. If he had been paid all that he claimed in a claim, he could not sue in equity for a further sum unclaimed by mistake in the claim: *Darlow v Cooper* (1865) 34 Beav 281. Nor can a building society who have in error given the usual statutory receipt: *Harvey v Municipal Building Society* (1884) 26 Ch D 273; see **28.58**.

3 *Cheltenham & Gloucester Building Society v Grattridge* (1993) 25 HLR 454. If the court suspends the order for possession under s 36 of the Administration of Justice Act 1970, as amended, it should also stay execution of the money judgment under s 71(2) of the County Courts Act 1984. On the effect of the money judgment on contractual interest, see (1993) 143 NLJ 1451 (Manley).

4 *Gordon Grant & Co Ltd v Boos* [1926] AC 781, PC.

5 *Rudge v Richens* (1873) LR 8 CP 358.

6 *Refuge Assurance Co Ltd v Pearlberg* [1938] Ch 687, [1938] 3 All ER 231.

7 *Royal Trust Corpn of Canada v Northdale Development Co Ltd* [1994] 1 WWR 68 (CAN).

8 *Stevens v Theatres Ltd* [1903] 1 Ch 857. See *Marshall v Miles* (1971) BDLR (3d) 158; cf *Petranick v Dale* (1973) 33 DLR (3d) 389 (where the foreclosure order had not been entered up); and see **20.7** and **22.47**.

9 *Perry v Barker* (1806) 13 Ves 198. See **22.69**.

10 *Lloyds and Scottish Trust Ltd v Britten* (1982) 44 P & CR 249 and see **17.7** and **22.69**.

11 *Alliance & Leicester Building Society v Slayford* [2001] 1 All ER (Comm) 1.

12 *Cheah Theam Swee v Equiticorp Finance Group Ltd* [1992] 1 AC 472, [1991] 4 All ER 989; *Lockhart v Hardy* (1846) 9 Beav 379.

13 *Willes v Levett* (1847) 1 De G & Sm 392.

14 *Davies v Williams* (1843) 7 Jur 663.

15 *Crowle v Russell* (1878) 4 CPD 186.

16 *Dyson v Morris* (1842) 1 Hare 413.

17 *Arnold v Bainbrigge* (1860) 2 De GF & J 92.

RESTRICTIONS ON BRINGING A CLAIM

RESTRAINT OF PROCEEDINGS IN GENERAL

Restrictions imposed by statute or the terms of the mortgage

16.12 There are certain statutory restrictions, and there will usually also be restrictions imposed by the terms of the mortgage, as to the mortgagee's entitlement to exercise his remedies.[1]

1 See **17.6** (personal remedy); **18.4–18.5** (appointment of a receiver); **19.2** and **19.51** (possession); **20.11–20.12** (sale); **22.2** (foreclosure); and Chapter 23 (insolvency).

Restraint of inequitable claim

16.13 In certain cases, incumbrancers will be restrained from pursuing one or more of their remedies[1]. Powers conferred on a mortgagee must be exercised in good faith for the purpose of obtaining repayment of the debt although, subject to that rule, powers conferred on a mortgagee may be exercised even though the consequences may be disadvantageous to the borrower.[2] Thus a possession claim has been dismissed where the right to possession was being exercised improperly[3]. It seems that a mortgagee who genuinely seeks payment of sums due will not be defeated merely because he has an additional improper motive.[4] The court has the power to make an order for possession against one of two mortgagors, however, it will not generally consider it appropriate to do so where that would be of no benefit to the mortgagee, particularly where the mortgagors are spouses.[5] Where a second or subsequent mortgagee claims an order for possession, it must respect the interests of the prior mortgagee, including his interests as landlord.[6]

1 As to restraining sale, see **20.34** ff. The inherent jurisdiction has been considered more in New Zealand than elsewhere: see *Clark v National Mutual Life Association of Australasia Ltd* [1966] NZLR 196; *Development Consultants Ltd v Lion Breweries Ltd* [1981] 2 NZLR 258, NZCA; and generally Croft *Mortgagee's Power of Sale* p 123.
2 *Downsville Nominees Ltd v First City Corpn Ltd* [1993] AC 295 at 312, [1993] 3 All ER 626 at 635 per Lord Templeman. See also *Medforth v Blake* [2000] Ch 86 at 98, 103; *Yorkshire Bank v Hall* [1999] 1 WLR 1713 at 1728; *Abbey Home Loans v Massey* [1997] 2 All ER 609; *Palk v Mortgage Services Funding plc* [1993] Ch 330; *Bank of New Zealand v Essington* (1990) 9 ACLC 1039; *Quennell v Maltby* [1979] 1 WLR 318; and see further **18.6** and **20.22**.
3 *Quennell v Maltby* [1979] 1 All ER 568, [1979] 1 WLR 318, CA; see also *Sadiq v Hussain* [1997] NPC 19, CA. Such a claim was rejected in *Ashley Guarantee plc v Zacaria* [1993] 1 All ER 254 at 260, [1993] 1 WLR 62 at 69. For criticism of *Quennell v Maltby*, see (1983) 127 Sol Jo 431 (Davey) and (1989) 139 NLJ 251. See also **19.9.**
4 *Ashley Guarantee plc v Zacaria* [1993] 1 All ER 254 at 260, [1993] 1 WLR 62 at 69.
5 *Albany Home Loans v Massey* [1997] 2 FLR 305, [1997] 2 All ER 609, CA.
6 *Berkshire Capital Funding Ltd v Street* (1999) 78 P & CR 321, CA.

Incumbrancer not bound to pursue simplest remedy

16.14 As stated above[1], subject to exercising his remedies in good faith and for the purpose of securing the repayment of the mortgage debt, the mortgagee is entitled to choose which remedies he wishes to exercise[2]. Thus, an incumbrancer is not generally prevented from using such remedies as are open to him, on the ground that he has easier mode of relief, or on the ground of interference with the rights of other persons claiming under the same security (though this may be a ground for staying execution[3]), unless the pursuit of the remedy in question would be contrary to the spirit and intention of the contract and in breach of good faith[4]. Thus a mortgagee of shares was entitled to refrain from exercising his power of sale and instead to sue the surety on his personal covenant, even though at the time of the mortgagor's default the value of the mortgaged shares exceeded the value of the security[5].

1 See **16.11** and **16.13**.
2 *Medforth v Blake* [2000] Ch 86; *Downsview Ltd v First City Corpn Ltd* [1993] AC 295; *Yorkshire Bank v Hall* [1999] 1 WLR 1713; *China and South Sea Bank Ltd v Tan Soon Gin* [1990] 1 AC 536, [1989] 3 All ER 839. Cf *Palk v Mortgage Services Funding plc* [1993] Ch 330 at 341, [1993] 2 All ER 481 at 489, per Sir Donald Nicholls V-V; *Gomba Holdings (UK) Ltd v Minories Finance Ltd (No 2)* [1993] Ch 171 at 177, [1992] 4 All ER 588 at 601.
3 *Bolckow v Herne Bay Pier Co* (1852) 1 E & B 74.
4 *Sherborn v Tollemache* (1863) 13 CBNS 742, and there would be similar impropriety in a claim by a mortgagee on his security after proving for his whole debt, when the estate was to be divided as in bankruptcy: *Kingsford v Swinford* (1859) 4 Drew 705. Cf *Quennell v Maltby* [1979] 1 All ER 568, [1979] 1 WLR 318, CA.
5 *China and South Sea Bank Ltd v Tan Soon Gin* [1990] 1 AC 536, [1989] 3 All ER 839.

No claim on the debt where mortgagee cannot return the security

16.15 The mortgagor is entitled to have the security reconveyed upon payment of the mortgage debt. Thus if the mortgagee sues for the debt and the mortgagor satisfies the judgment, he is entitled to have the security returned to him. Accordingly, if a mortgagee has improperly disposed of the security, and cannot return it to the mortgagor, he is not entitled to have judgment for the debt[1]. Where the title deeds were out of the mortgagee's power, so that he was unable effectually to reconvey the estate, his proceedings on his collateral security were restrained; it was ordered that the amount due should be ascertained and paid into the bank, to remain there until the title deeds could be secured, to enable a reconveyance[2]. A mortgagee who has foreclosed and sold the property cannot reconvey it and cannot therefore sue on the personal covenant[3]. A mortgagee who has foreclosed one mortgage and afterwards sold the property comprised in it properly, but for less than was due under the mortgage, will not be allowed to proceed on his collateral securities, since the sale has made it impracticable for the foreclosure to be reopened[4]. For the same reason, where a mortgagee transfers the mortgage without the collateral securities, he cannot sue the mortgagor on the latter[5]. Where shares deposited as security with a broker have been wrongfully sold, the broker cannot sue for the balance due, except where the shares are readily purchasable and their money value can be substituted[6]. Where a mortgagee holds bills of exchange as collateral security and retains them when he transfers the mortgage, he is not entitled to sue on them pending a claim for redemption[7]. However, a mortgagee who has sold the property under his power of sale, or under an order of the court, can sue the mortgagor for the deficiency, since the sale was a proper dealing with the security[8]. The mortgagee is also entitled to sue if he is unable to return the security to the claims of a third party, for example, where a landlord forfeits leasehold property, but not as a result of any default by the mortgagee[9].

1 *Ellis & Co's Trustee v Dixon-Johnson* [1925] AC 489, HL.
2 *Schoole v Sall* (1803) 1 Sch & Lef 176.
3 *Lloyds and Scottish Trust v Britten* (1982) 44 P & CR 249.

4 *Lockhart v Hardy* (1846) 9 Beav 349.
5 *Walker v Jones* (1866) LR 1 PC 50. Similarly, if the mortgagee joins with the transferee of the equity of redemption in a sale and allows the transferee to receive the purchase money, the mortgagee, since he is no longer able to reconvey the estate will not be allowed to sue the mortgagor on his covenant to pay: *Palmer v Hendrie* (1859) 27 Beav 349.
6 *Ellis & Co's Trustee v Dixon-Johnson* [1925] AC 489, HL.
7 *Walker v Jones* (1866) LR 1 PC 50.
8 *Rudge v Richens* (1873) LR 8 CP 358; *Gordon Grant & Co v Boos* [1926] AC 781, PC; *Coast Realities Ltd v Nolan* (1970) 20 DLR (3d) 96; *Re McHenry, McDermott v Boyd Barker's Claim* [1894] 3 Ch 290, CA.
9 *Re Burrell, Burrell v Smith* (1869) LR 7 Eq 399.

Conditional agreement not to sue

16.16 The mortgagee may be prevented from enforcing his remedies by a collateral agreement not to enforce the security if, and for so long as, the debtor observes certain conditions. However, if the debtor has failed to observe such conditions, the creditor will not be prevented from enforcing the security on that basis[1]. Thus a mortgagee was not restrained from exercising his remedy under a mortgage on the ground that there had been an agreement that it should contain a clause postponing the mortgagee's right to call in the money, where a corresponding condition for punctual payment of interest had not been observed by the mortgagor[2].

1 *Parry v Great Ship Co* (1863) 4 B & S 556.
2 *Seaton v Simpson* [1870] WN 261.

Cause of action estoppel and abuse of process

16.17 A party is not, in the absence of special circumstances, entitled to raise a ground of claim or defence which could have been, but was not, raised in earlier proceedings.[1] Thus a mortgagee who has obtained a judgment for possession and sums expressed to be due under the mortgage is not entitled to bring a subsequent claim for sums due under a guarantee which were also secured by the mortgage.[2] However, a judgment in possession proceedings does not itself give rise to an estoppel so as to prevent a claim under the personal covenant. Thus, a mortgagee who brought a claim for possession and payment, but obtained an unopposed order for possession alone was, following the sale of the security, entitled to bring a claim for payment of a shortfall on the personal covenant.[3] In such circumstances, consideration should be given as to why the money claim was not originally pursued to judgment. The maintenance of a second claim which could have been part of an earlier claim is not of itself an abuse of process—an additional element must be found, the onus being on the party alleging the abuse[4]. Where a mortgee's claim for possession has failed due to a defence of undue influence on the part of the mortgagor's spouse, it is not an abuse of process for the mortgagee to sue the mortgagor on his personal covenant with a view, as an unsecured creditor, to bankrupting him, even though that may lead to an application by the trustee in bankruptcy for the sale of the property in which the spouse has an equitable interest[5]. Where a mortgagee's claim for repayment of a loan by two guarantors had been struck out for delay, it was an abuse of process to commence a second claim for payment, but the mortgagee was entitled to bring claims to enforce its security over the guarantors' property by sale and possession, which were not (and did not need to be) raised in earlier proceedings[6].

1 See eg *Arnold v Westminster Bank plc* [1991] 2 AC 93, [1991] 3 All ER 41; *Talbot v Berkshire County Council* [1994] QB 290, [1993] 4 All ER 9, CA; *Yorkshire Bank v Hall* [1999] 1 All ER 879, [1999] 1 WLR 1713.
2 *Lloyds Bank v Hawkins* [1998] 3 EGLR 109.
3 *UCB Bank v Chandler* (1999) 79 P & CR 270, CA.
4 *Bradford and Bingley Building Society v Seddon* [1999] 4 All ER 217, [1999] 1 WLR 1482.
5 *Alliance & Leicester plc v Slayford* [2001] 1 All ER (Comm) 1. For the trustee's power to seek sale in such circumstances, see **21.17**; for the mortgagee's entitlement to seek an order for sale in such circumstances, see **21.18** ff and **21.13** ff.
6 *Securum Finance Ltd v Ashton* [2001] Ch 291, [2000] 3 WLR 1400.

Rights of third parties

16.18 The mortgagee will be restrained from doing acts in disregard of the rights of third persons which are superior to his own[1]. The mortgagee will be compelled to respect rights which have been acquired by third persons from the mortgagor since the date of the security, if he has acted in such a manner as to have amounted to an acknowledgement of such rights, or if the security was taken with the knowledge that the granting of such rights was incident to the purposes to which the property was devoted[2]. Where the mortgagor of land had employed a firm of architects to act in relation to its development and, when the mortgagor defaulted on the sums due to the mortgagee, the mortgagee only agreed to extend further finance to the mortgagor on condition that the mortgagor dismissed the firm of architects, the mortgagees were not liable to the architects for damages for interference with their contract with the mortgagor. The mortgagee would have been entitled to exercise its power of sale or the appointment of a receiver, which would equally have interfered with the contract, but would not have been claimable; the mortgagee could not become liable because he chose another method of protecting his security[3].

1 A mortgagee of a ship has been restrained from so dealing with her as to prevent the performance of a charter party of which he had notice: *De Mattos v Gibson* (1859) 4 De G & J 276; *Lord Strathcona Steamship Co Ltd v Dominion Coal Co Ltd* [1926] AC 108, PC; cf *Port Line Ltd v Ben Line Steamers Ltd* [1958] 2 QB 146, [1958] 1 All ER 787 and see *Swiss Bank Corpn Ltd v Lloyds Bank Ltd* [1982] AC 584, [1980] 2 All ER 419, CA; affd [1982] AC 584, [1981] 2 All ER 449, HL. The right of a receiver appointed under the Drug Trafficking Offences Act 1986 to sell prevails over the rights of a mortgagee: *Re M (Rrestraint Order)* [1992] QB 377, [1992] 1 All ER 537. The mortgagee may apply for the discharge of the receiver under s 8(5).
2 *Mold v Wheatcroft* (1859) 27 Beav 510.
3 *Edwin Hill and Partners v First National Finance Corpn plc* [1989] 1 WLR 225, [1989] BCLC 89.

Staying proceedings on payment or tender

16.19 The court will stay proceedings under its inherent powers, if the defendant incumbrancer pays or tenders to the claimant the principal debt, interest, and costs and brings into court a sum sufficient to cover the costs of any other defendants, so far as the claimant is liable to them, until the amount of such costs has been ascertained[1], or if the mortgagee has neglected to furnish a proper account and has refused a proper and sufficient tender[2]. Thus a mortgagee's claim for possession was stayed (on security being given to redeem) on the ground of entangled accounts, where a claim for an account was also pending against the mortgagee and it was considered beneficial to all parties to keep the possession in suspense in the meantime[3]. The owner of property subject to a charge, upon paying the amount of it with interest into court in a claim to raise the charge, has been protected by injunction from proceedings by the mortgagee of the charge to obtain possession of the land[4]. However, the court will refuse to make such an order where it would affect the interests of the other defendants, such as by interfering with questions as to priorities of the incumbrances, or where it would interfere with an order of the court made in another claim relating to the same securities. In such a case, though, the court will anticipate the order at the hearing by directing inquiries as to the priorities of, and the amounts due to, the incumbrancers and, if proper, by directing a sale[5]. The court can also, under its inherent powers, make such an order before the hearing as it might have made at the hearing[6], such as for accounts and for foreclosure in default of payment on a given day[7].

1 See form of order in *France v Cowper* [1871] WN 76.
2 *Herries v Griffiths* (1854) 2 WR 72.
3 *Booth v Booth* (1742) 2 Atk 343.
4 *Duncombe v Greenacre* (1860) 28 Beav 472.
5 *Paine v Edwards* (1862) 6 LTOS 600.
6 *Aberdeen v Chitty* (1839) 3 Y & C Ex 379 at 382.
7 Or for a stay with a proviso that on default of payment it should be deemed that no order had been made on the application: *Jones v Tinney* (1845) Kay App xlv.

Proof of the security

16.20 The mortgagee must be able to prove the mortgage deed or security to enable him to have relief from the court[1].

1 *Jacobs v Richards* (1854) 18 Beav 300. For early nineteenth century authorities on proving the mortgage or the security see the 10th edition of this work, pp 303–305. For the modern law of evidence, see *Phipson on Evidence* (15th edn, 2000).

INSOLVENCY

16.21 The restrictions on a mortgagee enforcing his security where the mortgagor has been adjudged bankrupt, or is subject to winding up proceedings or an administration order are considered in Ch 23.

UNDER THE RENT ACT 1977[1]

Where the protection of the Act applies

16.22 Part X of the Rent Act 1977 imposes certain restrictions upon the rights and remedies of a mortgagee. It applies to mortgages which (a) were created before the relevant date, and (b) are regulated mortgages as defined under the Act.

1 As amended by the Housing Act 1980, s 152, Schs 25, 26.

Mortgages created before the relevant date

16.23 The restrictions of the Rent Act 1977 apply only to mortgages created before the relevant date. In essence, this confines the protection to mortgages created before the Rent Acts applied to the tenancy, when the mortgagor as landlord was not affected by their operation. In most cases, the relevant date is 8 December 1965[1]. There are three exceptions. First, where a long tenancy has been converted into a regulated tenancy under the Leasehold Reform Act 1967, s 39, the relevant date is 28 November 1967[2]. Secondly, where a furnished tenancy was converted into a regulated furnished tenancy under the Rent Act 1974, the relevant date is 14 August 1974[3]. Thirdly, where a tenancy became a regulated tenancy under the Counter-Inflation Act 1973, the relevant date is 22 March 1973[4].

1 Rent Act 1977, s 129 (1) (a).
2 Rent Act 1977, s 129(2)(a). Under s 152(1) of the Rent Act 1977 a long tenancy is 'a tenancy granted for a term of years certain exceeding 21 years, whether or not subsequently extended by act of the parties or by any enactment'.
3 Being the day on which such tenancies became regulated tenancies. See Rent Act 1974, Sch 1, para 10; Rent Act 1974, s 17(5); Rent Act 1977, s 129(2).
4 Being the date when that Act came into force. See Rent Act 1977, s 129 (2)(b).

Regulated mortgages

16.24 For the restrictions to apply, the mortgage must also be a regulated mortgage within the meaning of s 131 of the Rent Act 1977. To be a regulated mortgage, six requirements must be fulfilled:

(a) it must be a legal mortgage[1];
(b) it must be of land consisting of or including a dwelling-house[2];
(c) the dwelling-house must be let on or subject to a regulated tenancy[3];
(d) the regulated tenancy must be binding on the mortgagee[4];
(e) the rateable value of the dwelling-house which falls within the mortgage or, if there is more than one such dwelling-house comprised in the mortgage, the aggregate of the rateable values of those dwelling-houses, must on the appropriate day[5] not be less than one-tenth of the rateable value on the appropriate day of the whole of the land comprised in the mortgage[6];
(f) the mortgagor must not be in breach of covenant, but for that purpose a breach of the covenant for the repayment of the principal money otherwise than by instalments shall be disregarded[7].

1 Rent Act 1977, s 131(1)(a). 'Legal mortgage' in relation to regulated mortgages includes any charge registered under the Land Registration Act 1925: Rent Act 1977, s 136 (b). 'Mortgagee' and 'mortgagor' include any person from time to time deriving title under the original mortgagee or mortgagor: s 136 (a).
2 Section 131(1)(a). For discussion of the meaning of 'dwelling-house', see *Megarry on The Rent Acts* (11th edn, 1988) vol 1, pp 109 ff.
3 Section 131(1)(a). For regulated tenancies see the Rent Act 1977, s 18, as amended by the Housing Act 1980, s 152, Sch 25, para 35 and Sch 26 and s 18A (controlled tenancies converted into regulated tenancies) inserted by the Housing Act 1980, s 152, Sch 25, para 35 and Rent Act 1977, Sch 17, as amended by the Housing Act 1985, Sch 25, para 59 and Sch 26; and *Megarry on The Rent Acts* (11th edn 1988) vol 1.
4 Section 131 (1).
5 See ss 25 (3), 152 (1). In relation to land consisting of or including a dwelling-house which on 22 March 1973 was subject to a tenancy which became a regulated tenancy by virtue of s 14 of the Counter-Inflation Act 1973, the appropriate day is 7 March 1973: Rent Act 1977, s 131(3).
6 Section 131 (2) (a).
7 Section 131 (2) (b).

Powers of court to mitigate hardship to mortgagors under regulated mortgages

When the powers of the court become exercisable

16.25 The powers of the court in relation to regulated mortgages become exercisable only if the mortgagor applies within 21 days, or such longer time as the court may allow, after the occurrence of one of the following events:

(a) if the rate of interest payable under such a mortgage has been increased; or
(b) if a rent for a dwelling-house comprised in the mortgage is registered under Pt IV of the Rent Act 1977 and the rent so registered is lower than the rent which was payable immediately before the registration[1]; or
(c) if the mortgagee[2] (not being a mortgagee in possession on the relevant date[3]) demands payment of the principal money secured by the mortgage or takes any steps for exercising any right of foreclosure or sale or for otherwise enforcing his security[4].

The appropriate court is the county court, except where an application is made in pursuance of any step taken by the mortgagee in the High Court[5].

1 Ground (2) does not apply to a case where, on 22 March 1973, land consisting of or including a dwelling-house was subject to a tenancy which became a regulated tenancy by virtue of s 14 of the Counter-Inflation Act 1973: Rent Act 1977, s 132(1).
2 'Legal mortgage' in relation to regulated mortgages includes any charge registered under the Land Registration Act 1925: Rent Act 1977, s 136 (b). 'Mortgagee' and 'mortgagor' include any person from time to time deriving title under the original mortgagee or mortgagor: s 136 (a).
3 As to which, see above: generally, 8 December 1965.
4 Rent Act 1977, s 132 (1), as amended by the Housing Act 1985, s 152, Sch 25, para 49.
5 Section 132(6).

The powers of the court

16.26 If the court is satisfied on any application under these provisions, that by reason of the event in question and of the operation of the Act the mortgagor would suffer severe financial hardship unless relief were given, then it may by order make such provision as it thinks appropriate, by:

(a) limiting the rate of interest;
(b) extending the time for repayment of the principal money;
(c) or otherwise varying the terms of the mortgage or imposing any limitation or condition on the exercise of any right or remedy in respect of the mortgage[1].

1 Rent Act 1977, s 132 (2). Such an order may be revoked or varied: Rent Act 1977, s 132 (5).

Apportionment

16.27 When the court makes an order in relation to a mortgage which comprises other land as well as a dwelling-house or dwelling-houses subject to a regulated tenancy, the order may, if the mortgagee so requests, make provision for apportioning the money secured by the mortgage between that other land and the dwelling-house or dwelling-houses[1]. Where such an apportionment is made, the other provisions of the order made by the court shall not apply in relation to such other land and the money secured by such other land and the mortgage shall have effect for all purposes as two separate mortgages of the apportioned parts[2].

1 Rent Act 1977, s 132 (3).
2 Section 132 (4).

UNDER THE CONSUMER CREDIT ACT 1974[1]

16.28 The Consumer Credit Act 1974 contains restrictions on the entitlement of a creditor to enforce any security or recover possession of any goods or land. These have been considered in Chapter 10.

1 See, generally, Chapter 10.

LIMITATION OF CLAIMS[1]

THE PERSONAL REMEDY ON THE COVENANT FOR PAYMENT

16.29 Section 5 of the Limitation Act 1980 provides that a claim founded on a simple contract[2] shall not be bought after the expiration of six years from the date on which the cause of action accrued[3]. Section 8 of the Limitation Act 1980 provides that a claim upon a speciality shall not be bought after the expiration of 12 years from the date on which the cause of action accrued[4]. Accordingly, so far as the mortgagee's remedy in simple contract, as distinct from enforcement of the charge, is concerned, a claim on the mortgagor's covenant for payment of the principal money secured by the mortgage may not be brought after 12 years from the date when the cause of action accrued[5], if the mortgage is by deed, or after six years if the mortgage is not by deed[6]. Where a mortgagee has repossessed and sold the security and is seeking to recover the shortfall, then depending on the source and precise terms of the contractual provisions under which the mortgagee is claiming, it may be that his claim is in simple contract[7]. However, where the shortfall was being claimed under a provision in a mortgage deed under seal which specifically addressed the situation where the mortgagee has realised the security and there is a shortfall, the claim was on a speciality and could not be categorised as a claim in simple contract[8].

1 See, generally, 28 *Halsbury's Laws* (4th edn reissue) paras 401 ff; Preston and Newsom *Limitation of Claims* (4th edn, 1989).
2 The word simple is used to exclude an action upon a speciality: *Westdeutsche Landesbank v Islington London Borough Council* [1994] 4 All ER 890 at 942; *Global Financial Recoveries Ltd v Jones* [2000] 02 LS Gaz R 30.
3 This section shall not bar the right of claim on a contract of loan to which s 6 applies, ie any contract of loan which does not provide for repayment of the debt on or before a fixed date; and does not effectively (whether or not it purports to do so) make the obligation to repay the debt conditional on a demand for repayment made by or on behalf of the creditor or on any other matter (see **17.6**), except where in connection with taking the loan the debtor enters into any collateral obligation to pay the amount of the debt or any part of it on terms which would exclude the application of s 6 to the contract of loan if they applied directly to repayment of the debt: s 6 (2). Where a demand in writing for repayment of the debt under a contract of loan to which s 6 applies is made by or on behalf of the creditor (or, where there are joint creditors, by or on behalf of any one of them) s 5 shall

thereupon apply as if the cause of action to recover the debt had accrued on the date on which the demand was made: s 6 (3).

4 A claim to enforce a contractual right or obligation arising under a contract under seal is an action upon a speciality: *Collin v Duke of Westminster* [1985] QB 581 at 601-603, CA; *Aiken v Stewart Wrightson Agency* [1995] 1 WLR 1281 at 1290-1291; *Global Financial Recoveries Ltd v Jones* [2000] 02 LS Gaz R 30. Subsection (1) does not affect any claim for which a shorter period is prescribed by any other provision of the Act: s 8 (2). Other relevant sections are s 20 (see **16.30**) and those sections either extending the period, eg in the case of disability, or postponing the period in case of fraud etc (see **16.54** ff and **16.56** ff).

5 As to when the right of claim arises, see **17.6**.

6 Where, eg, the property has been sold by the mortgagee and he is suing for the balance, the debt is still a speciality debt although the security has gone. The Act contains general and particular provisions suspending the running of time and effecting a fresh accrual of a right of claim: see **16.44** ff.

7 *John Hopkinson v Tupper* [1997] 6 CL 462, CA; *Global Financial Recoveries Ltd v Jones* [2000] 02 LS Gaz R 30.

8 *Global Financial Recoveries Ltd v Jones* above.

CLAIMS TO RECOVER MONEY CHARGED ON PROPERTY

Principal

Period of limitation

16.30 Section 20(1) of the Limitation Act 1980 provides that no claim shall be brought to recover (a) any principal sum of money secured by a mortgage or other charge on property (whether real or personal[1]), or (b) proceeds of the sale of land[2], after the expiration of 12 years from the date on which the right to receive the money accrued[3].

1 There had, previously to the Limitation Act 1939, been no statutory provision for personalty. Ships, which had been specifically excluded from the analogous provision in the 1939 Act, are no longer excluded.

2 'Land' includes corporeal hereditaments, tithes and rentcharges and any legal or equitable estate or interest therein, but in general not an incorporeal hereditament: Limitation Act 1980, s 38(1).

3 Nothing in this section shall apply to a foreclosure claim in respect of mortgaged land, but the provisions of this Act relating to claims to recover land shall apply to such a claim: s 20 (4).

Charge on property[1]

16.31 A charge on property is a burden imposed upon it: it will include a payment which has to be made in respect of the property, where the property can only be enjoyed subject to its payment, even though there is no direct remedy against the property itself[2]. The charge may be one imposed by statute[3]. A vendor's equitable lien for purchase money on the sale of real or personal property is such a charge.[4] The claim on the covenant has been held to be a claim to recover money charged on land[5], even when the covenant is contained in a separate deed[6]. Section 20 cannot apply after realisation of the mortgaged property[7].

1 For an example of a charge on property other than land, see *Re Compania de Electricidad de la Provincia de Buenos Aires Ltd* [1980] Ch 146, [1978] 3 All ER 668 (company bearer bonds).

2 *Payne v Esdaile* (1888) 13 App Cas 613.

3 Eg *Poole Corpn v Moody* [1945] KB 350, [1945] 1 All ER 536, CA (charge on property in repect of street works expenses; now under the Highways Act 1980, s 212, for which it seems the limitation period is six years; s 305(5)); *Hornsey Local Board v Monarch Investment Building Society* (1889) 24 QBD 1, CA (repairs to a dangerous structure near a highway); and see also charges on property for the recovery of local authority expenses of carrying out pubic health works (Public Health Act 1936, s 291); and charges on property for the recovery of local authority expenses of carrying out works to houses in multiple occupation (Housing Act 1985, s 193, Sch 10, para 7).
4 *Toft v Stephenson* (1851) 1 De GM & G 28; *Stucley v Kekewich* [1906] 1 Ch 67.
5 *Sutton v Sutton* (1882) 22 Ch D 511, CA. If this is so, s 20 (5) (see **16.33**) applies to a claim on the personal covenant as regards interest.
6 *Re Powers* (1885) 30 Ch D 291 at 297, CA.
7 *John Hopkinson v Tupper* [1997] 6 CL 462, CA; *Global Financial Recoveries Ltd v Jones* [2001] 02 LS Gaz R 30.

Date from which time runs

16.32 Time begins to run from the date when the right to receive the money accrued[1]. This probably means the same as the expression 'a present right to receive' as used in the Real Property Limitation Act 1874[2], being an immediate right which is not dependent upon the happening of some future event[3]. It is different from the right to enforce payment, and is distinct from the accrual of a cause of action[4]. Thus there can be a present right causing time to start running, notwithstanding there may be no means of immediately enforcing it[5]. The requirement that notice shall be given before suing does not postpone the running of time[6]. The right to receive any principal sum of money secured by a mortgage or other charge shall not be treated as accruing so long as the mortgaged property comprises any future interest or any life insurance policy which has not matured or been determined[7]. With a lien for unpaid purchase money, the right to receive the money accrues at the time for completion or, if subsequent to that, the time when title is accepted.[8] An amendment in a possession claim to claim a money judgment is not necessarily a new cause of action and such an amendment will be permitted after the expiry of the limitation period if no new factual issues are raised.[9]

1 Section 20 (1); *Cotterell v Price* [1960] 3 All ER 315, [1960] 1 WLR 1097, see **16.30**.
2 In s 8 of that Act.
3 *Farran v Beresford* (1842) 10 Cl & Fin 319 at 334.
4 Which is the event which starts time running under other sections of the Limitation Act.
5 *Hornsey Local Board v Monarch Building Society* (1889) 24 QBD 1; *Dennerley v Prestwich UDC* [1930] 1 KB 334, CA.
6 *Hervey v Wynn* (1905) 22 TLR 93.
7 Section 20 (3).
8 *Toft v Stephenson* (1851) 1 De GM & G 28; *Stucley v Kekewich* [1906] 1 Ch 67.
9 *Lloyds Bank plc v Rogers (No 2)* [1999] 3 EGLR 83, CA.

Arrears

Period of limitation

16.33 Section 20(5) of the Limitation Act provides that, subject to the exceptions dealt with below, no claim to recover arrears of interest payable in respect of any sum of money secured by a mortgage or other charge[1] or payable in respect of proceeds of the sale of land, or to recover damages in respect of such arrears[2] shall be brought after the expiration of six years from the date on which the interest became due. There are two exceptions:

(a) Where:
  (i) a prior mortgage or other incumbrancer has been in possession of the property charged; and
  (ii) a claim is brought within one year of the discontinuance of that possession by the subsequent incumbrancer, then the subsequent incumbrancer may recover by that claim all the arrears of interest which fell due during the period of possession by the prior incumbrancer or damages in respect of those arrears, notwithstanding that the period exceeded six years[3].

(b) Where:
  (i) the property subject to the mortgage or charge comprises any future interest or life insurance policy; and
  (ii) it is a term of the mortgage or charge that arrears of interest shall be treated as part of the principal sum of money secured by the mortgage or charge[4],

then interest shall not be treated as becoming due before the right to recover the principal sum of money has accrued or is treated as having accrued.

Where under a loan agreement the lender's right to bring a claim for interest accrued at a different date from the date upon which the interest became due, time was held to run from the date when the right to bring a claim accrued[5]. Once the mortgagee's right to the principal is limitation barred, so too is his right to bring a claim for interest[6]. It is not clear whether 12 years' interest are recoverable from a guarantor, under a speciality, of a payment of interest given that the money due from the guarantor is not secured by a charge[7]. The position in cases of redemption and foreclosure is considered below.

1 Eg interest on expenses incurred by a local authority in respect of street works and charged on property: see *Poole Corpn v Moody* [1945] KB 350; see now Highways Act 1980, s 212.
2 Where there is no covenant for payment of interest arrears are given by way of damages: *Mellersh v Brown* (1890) 45 Ch D 225; Law Reform (Miscellaneous Provisions) Act 1934, s 3. See **35.41**.
3 Limitation Act 1980, s 20(6). 'Incumbrancer' includes a judgment creditor: *Henry v Smith* (1842) 2 Dr & War 381 at 390. The section does not enable the recovery of arrears of interest due for any period preceding the prior incumbrancer's possession: *Montgomery v Southwell* (1843) 2 Con & Law 263.
4 For capitalisation of interest, see **35.48** ff.
5 *Barclays Bank v Walters* (1988) Times, 20 October, CA.
6 *Elder v Northcott* [1930] 2 Ch 422, [1930] All ER Rep 398.
7 See *Re Powers, Lindsell v Philips* (1885) 30 Ch D 291; *Re Frisby, Allison v Frsiby* (1889) 43 Ch D 106.

The mortgagee's right to retain limitation-barred arrears of interest

16.34 There are circumstances where the mortgagee may be able to obtain arrears of interest, even though he would be limitation-barred from bringing a claim for their recovery. Thus, where the mortgagee has sold the mortgaged property under his power of sale and has the proceeds in his hands, he can retain any arrears of interest[1]. In taking accounts between a mortgagor and mortgagee where the mortgagee has been in possession, all interest accrued would have to be taken into account[2]. Where money is held in court on behalf of all interested parties, the mortgagee will be restricted to six years of interest if he applies for payment out[3]; but if the mortgagor applies, he will only be entitled to the balance after the mortgagee has received his principal and full arrears of interest[4]. Where, however, the mortgage debt is barred and the mortgagee's title extinguished, the mortgagee will not be entitled to claim either principal or interest on that basis[5]. If the mortgagee sells after being in possession of the mortgaged land for 12 years he may keep the whole of the proceeds of sale, for the title of the mortgagor and those claiming under him is barred[6].

A receiver appointed by the mortgagee under the statutory power[7] is the agent of the mortgagor[8]. Hence, in applying rents and profits received by him in payment of the interest accruing due, he cannot pay interest which is statute barred. Equally, if the receiver pays the rents and profits to the mortgagee, the mortgagee is not entitled to appropriate such payments to arrears of interest which are time barred. In such circumstances the doctrine of retaining full arrears does not apply[9].

1 *Edmunds v Waugh* (1866) LR 1 Eq 418; *Banner v Berridge* (1881) 18 Ch D 254; *Holmes v Cowcher* [1970] 1 All ER 1224, [1970] 1 WLR 834.
2 Given that a mortgagee must account for all rents and profits received during the time when he was in possession, however long that was: *Hood v Easton* (1856) 2 Jur NS 729.
3 *Re Stead's Mortgaged Estates* (1876) 2 Ch D 713; *Re Owen Lewis' Estate* [1903] 1 IR 348, but see *Matthews (C & M) Ltd v Marsden Building Society* [1951] Ch 758 at 768–769, [1951] 1 All ER 1053 at 1059.
4 *Re Lloyd* [1903] 1 Ch 385, CA.
5 *Re Hazeldine's Trusts* [1908] 1 Ch 34, CA.
6 *Re Statutory Trusts Declared by Section 105 of the Law of Property Act 1925 affecting the Proceeds of Sale of Moat House Farm, Thurlby* [1948] Ch 191, sub nom *Young v Clarey* [1948] 1 All ER 197.
7 See the Law of Property Act 1925, s 101 (1) (iii); see also **18.4**.
8 Section 109 (2). See **18.8**.
9 *Hibernian Bank v Yourell (No 2)* [1919] 1 IR 310.

Trust of surplus sale moneys for subsequent incumbrancers

16.35 A first mortgagee who has sold the mortgaged property under his statutory power of sale is under a statutory obligation[1] to hand the surplus sale monies remaining after satisfying his own claim to a second mortgagee. On receipt of the surplus monies, the second mortgagee is in turn entitled to exercise his own rights of retention. Thus the first mortgagee is not entitled to pay the second mortgagee his principal and six years' arrears of interest only and hand the remainder to the mortgagor or a third mortgagee. A claim by the second mortgagee to have his rights determined is in substance a claim for the execution of the trusts of the surplus proceeds[2], and not a claim for the recovery of interest in respect of money secured by a mortgage or charge[3].

1 By virtue of the Law of Property Act 1925, s 105. See **20.46**.
2 *Re Thompson's Mortgage Trusts, Thomson v Bruty* [1920] 1 Ch 508.
3 Ie not a claim within the Limitation Act 1980, s 20 (5)–(7).

FORECLOSURE

Period of limitation

16.36 The provisions of the Limitation Act 1980 relating to claims to recover land[1] apply to a foreclosure claim in respect of mortgaged land and the provisions of s 20 do not apply to such claims[2]. Accordingly no foreclosure claim may be brought after the expiration of 12 years from the date on which the right of action accrued[3]. Longer periods are prescribed for claims by the Crown or any spiritual or eleemosynary corporation sole[4]. Foreclosure claims in respect of mortgaged personal property are barred after 12 years from the date on which the right to foreclosure accrued[5]. Thus, in a foreclosure claim the account taken will be of the whole of the arrears. In a redemption claim, the mortgagee is not seeking to recover his mortgage debt and interest and there is no limit to the arrears which the mortgagor must pay as a condition of redeeming[6].

1 Ie s 15 and Sch 1.
2 Section 20 (4).
3 Section 15 (1).
4 See Pt II of Sch 1 to the Act.
5 Section 20 (2). Personal property does not include chattels real: s 38(1). There had formerly been no limitation bar on foreclosure claims on mortgages of personal property: *London and Midland Bank v Mitchall* [1899] 2 Ch 161.
6 *Dingle v Coppen* [1899] 1 Ch 726; *Holmes v Cowcher* [1970] 1 All ER 1224, [1970] 1 WLR 834, and the same applies where the mortgagee has instituted proceedings for foreclosure and the mortgagor counterclaims for redemption.

Date from which time runs

16.37 Time generally begins to run upon default of payment of the principal on the date fixed for legal redemption of the mortgage[1]. However, if the principal is payable on demand and, on a proper construction of the terms of the mortgage, the sum is not recoverable until it has been demanded, time runs from the date of the demand[2]. Where the mortgagee has been in possession of the mortgaged property after the right of action has accrued, the right is deemed not to have accrued until the mortgagee has been dispossessed or has discontinued his possession[3].

1 The claim is to recover the equity of redemption. See *Samuel Johnson & Sons Ltd v Brock* [1907] 2 Ch 533 at 536; *Purnell v Roche* [1927] 2 Ch 142. *Kibble v Fairthorne* [1895] 1 Ch 219 at 225.
2 At least where the security is collateral: *Lloyds Bank Ltd v Margolis* [1954] 1 All ER 734 at 737, 738; and see *Re Brown's Estate, Brown v Brown* [1893] 2 Ch 300 and *Wakefield and Barnsley Union Bank Ltd v Yates* [1916] 1 Ch 452, CA. See also *Re Turner, Turner v Spencer* (1894) 43 WR 153; *Hamill v Matthews* (1909) 44 ILT 25. See **17.6**.
3 See Sch 1, para 1 (land) and s 20 (2), proviso (personalty).

Future interests in personalty

16.38 The right to foreclose in respect of mortgaged personalty is deemed not to accrue so long as the mortgaged property comprises any future interest or any life insurance policy which has not matured or been determined[1].

1 Section 20 (3).

Future interests in land

16.39 Where the interest mortgaged is an estate or interest in reversion or remainder or any other future estate or interest in land and no person has taken possession of the land by virtue of the estate or interest claimed, time does not start to run for the purpose of barring a foreclosure claim until the date on which the estate or interest falls into possession by the determination of the preceding estate or interest[1]. An estate in fee simple which is subject to a lease is an estate in possession and not an interest in reversion or remainder or other future estate or interest[2]. In those circumstances, where the person entitled to the preceding estate or interest (not being a term of years absolute)[3] was not in possession of the land on that date, claims in relation to the succeeding estate or interest are barred after the expiration of 12 years from the date on which the right of action accrued to the person entitled to the preceding interest, or six years from the date on which the right of action accrued to the person entitled to the succeeding right or interest, whichever period last expires[4].

1 Limitation Act 1980, Sch 1, para 4. See *Hugill v Wilkinson* (1888) 38 Ch D 480 (concerning s 2 of the Real Property Limitation Act 1874, a predecessor of Sch 1, para 4), where the property charged was a future interest in property subject to a trust, which would not come into the possession of the mortgagor until the death of the life tenant.

2 *Wakefield and Barnsley Union Bank Ltd v Yates* [1916] 1 Ch 452, CA (where freehold property was mortgaged in fee simple and at the date of the mortgage the property was subject to a 21 year lease with 20 years left to run). This is a relic of the feudal principle that a freeholder whose land is subject to a term of years has an interest vested not only in interest but also in possession, since for feudal purposes a lease was not considered to be an estate and thus did not deprive the lessor of seisin: see *Wakefield* at 460; and *Megarry and Wade on the Law of Real Property* (6th edn 2000) para 7-010. Thus, for the purposes of the Law of Proprty Act 1925, 'possession' is defined as including not only physical possession of the land, but also the right to receive, or the receipt of, any rents or profits: s 205(1)(xix). And see *Re Witham* [1922] 2 Ch 413.

3 In relation to limitation with regard to a reversioner on a lease when the tenant has been dispossessed, see *Chung Ping Kwan v Lam Island Development Co Ltd* [1997] AC 38.

4 Limitation Act 1980, s 15 (2).

POSSESSION

Period of limitation

16.40 Section 15(1) of the Limitation Act 1980 provides that no claim shall be brought by any person to recover any land after the expiration of 12 years from the date on which the right of action accrued to him or, if it first accrued to some person through whom he claims, to that person. By s 38(7), a right of action to recover land includes a right to enter into possession of land. Accordingly the right of a mortgagee to enter upon the mortgaged land or to bring a claim for possession will be barred 12 years after the right of action accrued to him or, if it first accrued to some person through whom he claims, to that person[1].

1 See *Wright v Pepin* [1954] 2 All ER 52, [1954] 1 WLR 635; *Cotterell v Price* [1960] 3 All ER 315, [1960] 1 WLR 1097. This is, of course, only where there had been no acknowledgment, part payment, etc; as to which, see **16.44** ff.

Date from which time runs

16.41 Since a legal mortgagee prima facie has a right of entry on the execution of the mortgage, time prima facie begins to run from the execution of the mortgage. However, the mortgagee's right to possession will frequently be qualified. Thus there may be a provision that the mortgage shall not be called in until the expiration of a given term and that until default in payment it shall be lawful for the mortgagor peaceably to enjoy and receive the rents. This amounts to a re-demise by the mortgagee to the mortgagor during the term fixed[1]. In that case, the mortgagee's right to possession arises upon default in payment on the date fixed for payment and time will begin to run from the date of the default. An equitable mortgagee has no right to possession without an order of the court, unless his mortgage expressly gives him such a right[2].

1 *Wilkinson v Hall* (1837) 3 Bing NC 508. See **19.5**.
2 See **19.6**.

Foreclosure gives new title

16.42 An order absolute for foreclosure vests in the mortgagee the entire ownership and beneficial interest in the fee simple or the leasehold interest of the mortgaged land for the first time. Accordingly a new right to the possession the land accrues to the mortgagee at the date of the order. Thus, the mortgagee is entitled to bring a claim for the recovery of the land within 12 years of the date of the order, irrespective of how long before the date of the order the mortgage was created or the mortgagor last paid principal or interest[1].

1 *Heath v Pugh* (1881) 6 QBD 345, CA; on appeal 7 App Cas 235, HL.

SUCCESSIVE MORTGAGES

16.43 Where there are two successive mortgages and no payment is made by the second mortgagee, time runs against him[1]. That is so even though the first mortgagee is in possession[2].

1 *Kibble v Fairthorne* [1895] 1 Ch 219.
2 *Johnson (Samuel) & Sons Ltd v Brock* [1907] 2 Ch 533. In *Re Bermingham's Estate* (1870) IR 5 Eq 147, it was considered that on the first mortgagee taking possession, the second mortgagee ceased to have a right of entry and his interest became for the purpose of Limitation Acts a future interest, but he can enter if he pays off the first mortgagee and in any case he has an immediate right of foreclosure.

ACKNOWLEDGMENT AND PART PAYMENT

Fresh accrual of right of action on acknowledgment or part payment

16.44 Where any right of action (including a foreclosure claim) to recover land, or any right of a mortgagee of personal property to bring a foreclosure claim in respect of the property, has accrued, then if the person in possession of the land or personal property acknowledges the title of the person to whom the right of action has accrued, the right is treated as having accrued on and not before the date of the acknowledgment[1]. In the case of a foreclosure or other claim by a mortgagee, if the person in possession of the land or personal property in question, or the person liable for the mortgage debt, makes any payment in respect of the debt (whether of principal or interest) the right is treated as having accrued on and not before the date of the payment[2]. Where any right of action has accrued to recover any debt or other liquidated pecuniary claim and the person liable or accountable for the claim acknowledges the claim or makes any payment in respect thereof, the right is treated as having accrued on and not before the date of the acknowledgment or the last payment[3]. A payment of a part of the rent or interest due at any time does not extend the period for claiming the remainder then due, but any payment of interest is treated as a payment in respect of the principal debt[4].

1 Limitation Act 1980, s 29(1).
2 Section 29(3).
3 Section 29(5).
4 Section 29(6).

By whom the payment may be made

16.45 In the case of foreclosure or other claim by a mortgagee, the payment must be made by the person in possession of the mortgaged land or personal property, or by the person liable for the mortgage debt[1]. In the case of a claim on the personal covenant the payment must be made by the person liable or accountable for the mortgage debt[2]. The payment must be made to the person, or the agent of the person, in respect of whose claim or entitlement the payment is being made, that is the mortgagee or his agent[3].

Thus payment of rent by a tenant of the mortgaged property in pursuance of a notice by the mortgagee will not preserve the mortgagee's right of action[4]. Where a mortgagee enters into possession, the payment of rent to him by the tenant of the mortgaged property is not a payment in respect of the mortgage debt[5]; nor will the right of action be preserved by a mere voluntary payment by a third person[6]. However the right of action will be preserved by payment by a person interested to pay[7]; a payment by a person entitled to pay, such as a surety[8]; and a payment by a person, such as a trustee[9], who is bound to pay as between himself and the mortgagor[10]. Payment by a devisee for life of interest on the testator's specialty debt will keep alive the right of action against the remainderman[11], and payment of interest in respect of a simple contract debt of the testator by a tenant for life preserves the right of action for the debt against the remainderman[12].

Payment may be made by an agent, such as a solicitor with authority to make an acknowledgment[13]. However, it must be shown that the agency was continuing at the time of payment[14]. A tenant is not the implied agent of the mortgagor to make acknowledgments or payments to the mortgagee[15]. A receiver, whether appointed by the court[16], or by the mortgagee under the power conferred on him by the mortgage[17] or by statute[18], is treated as the agent of the person liable to pay, and payment by him preserves the right of action. On the other hand, the realisation, after the expiration of the 12 years, of a policy of assurance which forms a collateral security is not a part payment of principal or interest so as to revive a title to land which the Act has previously extinguished[19]. Nor is there an effective payment when a beneficiary mortgages his interest in a trust fund and the trustees make a payment to the mortgagee[20]. Where a mortgagor has assigned the equity of redemption and the assignee has paid interest on the mortgage, he has been held to be the agent of the mortgagor[21]. Where the mortgagor has parted with the equity of redemption, payment by him will still be effectual to keep alive the mortgage against the land[22].

1 Limitation Act 1980, s 29(3).
2 Section 29(5).
3 Section 30(2); *Barclay v Owen* (1889) 60 LT 220; *Purnell v Roche* [1927] 2 Ch 142.
4 *Harlock v Ashberry* (1882) 19 Ch D 539.

5 *Cockburn v Edwards* (1881) 18 Ch D 449; *Harlock v Ashberry* (1882) 19 Ch D 539; *Wrigley v Gill* [1906] 1 Ch 165.
6 *Chinnery v Evans* (1864) 11 HL Cas 115; *Harlock v Ashberry* above; *Newbold v Smith* (1889) 14 App Cas 423. Not even where it is paid by the third party to conceal his own fraud: *Thorne v Heard* [1895] AC 495, HL.
7 *Roddam v Morley* (1857) 1 De G & J 1.
8 *Lewin v Wilson* (1886) 11 App Cas 639.
9 *Alston v Mineard* (1906) 51 Sol Jo 132.
10 *Bradshaw v Widdrington* [1902] 2 Ch 430.
11 *Roddam v Morley* above; *Barclay v Owen* (1889) 60 LT 220.
12 *Re Hollingshead* (1888) 37 Ch D 651; *Re Chant* [1905] 2 Ch 225.
13 *Wright v Pepin* [1954] 2 All ER 52, [1954] 1 WLR 635.
14 *Newbould v Smith* above.
15 *Harlock v Ashberry* above, but a payment by a tenant to the mortgagee on the mortgagor's express instructions will make him an agent.
16 *Chinnery v Evans* above.
17 *Re Hale* [1899] 2 Ch 107, CA.
18 Law of Property Act 1925, ss 101 (1) (iii), 109 (2). See **18.4** and **18.8**.
19 *Re Clifden (Lord), Annaly v Agar-Ellis* [1900] 1 Ch 774. See also *Staley v Barrett* (1856) 26 LJ Ch 321; *Re Irwin* [1907] 1 IR 357; and cf *Re Conlan's Estate* (1892) 29 LR Ir 199.
20 *Re Edward's Will Trusts* [1937] Ch 553, [1937] 3 All ER 58.
21 *Forsyth v Bristowe* (1853) 8 Exch 716; *Dibb v Walker* [1893] 2 Ch 429. It is no longer necessary to treat him as such; see s 29 (3).
22 *Chinnery v Evans* above; *Bradshaw v Widdrington* above. The contrary seems to have been assumed by the Court of Appeal in *Newbould v Smith* (1886) 33 Ch D 127. The House of Lords reserved their opinion on this point (1889) 14 App Cas 423.

Acknowledgment

Nature of acknowledgment

16.46 To be effective, an acknowledgment must be in writing and signed by the person making it[1], or by his agent[2]. It must be made to the person, or his agent, whose title or claim is being acknowledged, or in respect of whose claim the payment is being made[3]. The acknowledgment must contain a sufficiently clear admission, whether express or implied, of the title or claim being acknowledged[4], but otherwise need not be in any particular form[5]. The court is entitled to look at all the circumstances in construing whether the document constitutes a sufficient acknowledgment[6]. There need not be any reference to the amounts outstanding on the mortgage. Thus, where a mortgagor's solicitors wrote a letter which the court regarded as making sense only if the title of the mortgagee's was valid, that amounted to a sufficient acknowledgment[7]. A denial of a claim or title cannot constitute an acknowledgment[8].

1 Section 30.
2 Section 30(2)(a).
3 Section 30(2).
4 *Kamouh v Associated Electrical Industries Ltd* [1980] QB 199; *Surrendra Overseas Ltd v Government of Sri Lanka* [1977] 1 WLR 565. See also *Wright v Pepin* [1954] 2 All ER 52, [1954] 1 WLR 635; *Good v Parry* [1963] 2 QB 418, [1963] 2 All ER 59, CA; *Dungate v Dungate* [1965] 3 All ER 393; *Edginton v Clark* [1964] 1 QB 367, [1963] 3 All ER 468, CA; *Re Gee & Co (Woolwich) Ltd* [1975] Ch 52, [1974] 1 All ER 1149 (balance sheet); *Re Compania de Electricidad de la Provincia de Buenos Aires Ltd* [1980] Ch 146, [1978] 3 All ER 668; *Re Overmark Smith Warden* [1982] 3 All ER 513, [1982] 1 WLR 1195; and *Stage Club Ltd v Millers Hotels Pty Ltd* (1982) 150 CLR 535.
5 *Stansfield v Hobson* (1853) 3 De GM & G 620; *Thompson v Bowyer* (1863) 9 Jur NS 863 (both concerning acknowledgments by mortgagees of the right to redeem).
6 *Trulock v Robey* (1841) 12 Sim 402 at 406.

7 *Agricultural Mortgage Corpn plc v Williams* (15 May 1995, unreported), CA.
8 *Re Flynn* [1982] 1 All ER 882; *Horner v Cartwright* (11 July 1989, unreported), CA.

By whom the acknowledgment may be made

16.47 Where the claim is against the security, the acknowledgment must be made by the person in possession of the mortgaged property[1]. Where the claim is on the personal covenant, it must be made by the person liable or accountable for the debt[2]. The acknowledgment may also be made by the agent of the person by whom it is required to be made[3]. The acknowledgment will also be sufficient if made by a trustee of the estate, whether he is devisee in trust for the debtor[4], or a trustee appointed by the court[5].

1 Section 29 (2).
2 Section 29 (5).
3 Section 30 (2) (a); and see *Waters v Lloyd* [1911] 1 IR 153.
4 *St John v Boughton* (1838) 9 Sim 219.
5 *Toft v Stephenson* (1851) 1 De GM & G 28.

Joint obligations

16.48 Part payment by one co-debtor binds all persons liable in respect of the debt[1]. An acknowledgment by one co-debtor binds only the person making it and his successors[2]. A payment by one of two mortgagors who covenant jointly and severally to pay the mortgage debt prevents time running in favour of the other mortgagor[3]. A surety is a person liable in respect of the debt[4] which he has guaranteed and a payment of interest by the principal debtor makes the cause of action accrue afresh against the surety[5]. Payment of interest by the surety makes the cause of action accrue afresh against the principal debtor[6].

1 Section 31 (7).
2 Section 31 (6).
3 *Baillie v Irwin* [1897] 2 IR 614; and see *Re Earl Kingston's Estate* (1869) 3 IR Eq 485.
4 Within s 31 (7).
5 *Re Powers, Lindsell v Phillips* (1885) 30 Ch D 291, CA; *Re Frisby, Allison v Frisby* (1889) 43 Ch D 106, CA.
6 *Re Seager's Estate, Seager v Aston* (1857) 26 LJ Ch 809.

Dual role of person making the acknowledgment

16.49 Where an acknowledgment is made by a person who has a dual character, such as an executor and a beneficial devisee of the debtor, the acknowledgment will be of general effect and bind both the personal estate and the land devised to him[1]. However, if a person is the executor of a debtor, but is also himself personally a debtor in respect of the same debt, an act constituting an acknowledgment which he was bound to make in his personal capacity, will not prima facie be considered to have been made also in his role as executor[2].

1 *Fordham v Wallis* (1853) 10 Hare 217.
2 *Thompson v Waithman* (1856) 3 Drew 628.

Effect of payment and acknowledgment

Persons upon whom the payment or acknowledgement is binding

16.50 An acknowledgment of the title to land or mortgaged personalty by any person in possession of it binds all other persons in possession during the ensuing period of limitation[1]. A payment in respect of a mortgage debt by the mortgagor or any person in possession of the mortgaged property shall, so far as any right of the mortgagee to foreclose or otherwise to recover the property is concerned, bind all other persons in possession of the mortgaged property during the ensuing period of limitation[2]. An acknowledgment of any debt or other liquidated pecuniary claim binds the acknowledgor and his successors[3] but not any other person[4]. A payment made in respect of any debt or other liquidated pecuniary claim binds all persons liable in respect thereof[5]. An acknowledgment or a payment by a personal representative in respect of any claim against the estate of the deceased is binding upon the estate.[6]

1 Section 31 (1).
2 Section 31 (2).
3 'Successor' is defined by s 31 (9), in relation to any person liable in respect of any debt or claim, as meaning his personal representatives, and any other person on whom the rights under the mortgage or the rights in respect of the debt or claim devolve (whether on death or bankruptcy or the disposition of property or the determination of a limited estate or interest in settled property or otherwise).
4 Section 31 (6).
5 Section 31 (7). Eg sureties, see *Re Powers, Lindsell v Phillips* (1885) 30 Ch D 291, CA.
6 Section 31(8).

Timing of acknowledgment or payment

16.51 At the expiration of the period prescribed by the Act for any person to bring a claim to recover land the title of that person to the land is extinguished[1]. Accordingly a payment or acknowledgment made after the expiration of the period of limitation does not revive the right of the mortgagee of land against the security[2]. However, there is no corresponding provision in the Act extinguishing the title of the mortgagee of personalty[3].

A current period of limitation may be repeatedly extended by further acknowledgments or payments[4], but a right of action, once barred by the Limitation Act, is not revived by any subsequent acknowledgment or payment[5]. However, a payment of a part of the interest due at any time will not extend the period for claiming the remainder then due, but any payment of interest is treated as a payment in respect of the principal debt[6].

1 Section 17. See *Lewis v Plunket* [1937] Ch 306, [1937] 1 All ER 530. The mortgagor is then entitled to recover the mortgage and other title deeds. A second mortgagee whose rights against the mortgagor are barred cannot claim to redeem a prior incumbrancer: *Cotterell v Price* [1960] 3 All ER 315, [1960] 1 WLR 1097.
2 *Sanders v Sanders* (1881) 19 Ch D 373, CA; *Kibble v Fairthorne* [1895] 1 Ch 219; *Nicholson v England* [1926] 2 KB 93, DC.
3 Notwithstanding s 3, dealing with conversion of chattels and the extinction of title thereto.
4 *Busch v Stevens* [1963] 1 QB 1, [1962] 1 All ER 412.
5 Section 29 (7).
6 Section 29 (6).

Where a stranger is in possession

16.52 Where, after the creation of the mortgage, a stranger begins adverse possession of the land, so that time is running in his favour as against both mortgagor and mortgagee, payment of interest by the mortgagor keeps alive the right of the mortgagee[1]. However, if at the date of the mortgage time was already running against the mortgagor, payment of interest will not give the mortgagee a new right of entry and so stop time running[2].

1 Section 29 (3); *Consolidated Agencies Ltd v Bertram* Ltd [1965] AC 470; *Doe d Palmer v Eyre* (1851) 17 QB 366; *Ludbrook v Ludbrook* [1901] 2 KB 96, CA. *Kibble v Fairthorne* [1895] 1 Ch 219. Cf *Re Gee & Co (Woolwich) Ltd* [1975] Ch 52, [1974] 1 All ER 1149.
2 *Thornton v France* [1897] 2 QB 143, CA.

CONSTRUCTIVE PAYMENT OF INTEREST

16.53 For so long as the hand to pay and the hand to receive are the same, that is where the person entitled to the income from the mortgaged land is in substance the same person who is obliged to pay the mortgage interest, time does not run[1]. Thus where the mortgagee is himself entitled to the rents of the mortgaged property, for example where he is tenant for life of the equity of redemption, time does not run against the mortgage title. Since it is his duty as owner in possession of the land to keep down the interest, he is deemed to pay himself the interest out of the rents and profits and this is a sufficient payment to prevent time running[2]. The principle applies where the same person is beneficially entitled as tenant for life to the land and the charge, notwithstanding that the land and the charge are vested in different sets of trustees[3]; and also where a wife is mortgagee of her husband's property[4]. However, where the owner of the charge is the owner of only a share in the proceeds of sale of the land under a trust for sale affecting the entirety of the land, there is no constructive payment to keep the charge alive against the land[5].

Where a tenant for life of land pays off a charge on the land the presumption is that he intends to keep it alive for his own benefit, and it is thus saved from merger[6]. Accordingly, as stated above, so far as the charge on the land is concerned, the tenant for life is presumed to pay himself the interest on the charge and time will not run. However, so far as the personal remedy is concerned, the tenant for life will not normally be under a legal liability to pay the interest and thus time will not be prevented from running. Thus, where under a settlement A was tenant for life of money secured by a covenant of the settlor and charged on his land, and the settlor devised the land to A, the constructive payment of interest prevented time from running so far as the charge on the land was concerned, but did not prevent the remedy on the covenant from becoming limitation barred[7]. Equally, the principle of constructive payment will not apply unless there is an actual charge on the land[8].

1 *Hodson v Salt* [1936] 1 All ER 95.
2 *Burrell v Earl of Egremont* (1844) 7 Beav 205; *Re Drax, Savile v Drax* [1903] 1 Ch 781, CA; but see *Carbery (Lord) v Preston* (1850) 13 I Eq R 455.
3 *Topham v Booth* (1887) 35 Ch D 607.
4 *Re Hawes, Re Burchell, Burchell v Hawes* (1892) 62 LJ Ch 463; *Re Dixon, Heynes v Dixon* [1900] 2 Ch 561, CA.
5 *Re Finnegan's Estate* [1906] 1 IR 370.
6 See **32.4**.
7 *Re England, Steward v England* [1895] 2 Ch 820, CA. No new settlements under the Settled Land Act can be created after 1 January 1997: Trusts of Land and Appointment of Trustees Act 1996; see **12.89** ff.
8 *Re Allen, Bassett v Allen* [1898] 2 Ch 499.

DISABILITY

Generally

16.54 A person is deemed to be under a disability for the purposes of the Limitation Act 1980 while he is an infant[1] or of unsound mind[2]. If on the date when any right of action accrued for which a period of limitation is prescribed by the Act the person to whom it accrued was under a disability[3], the claim may be brought at any time before the expiration of six years from the date when the person ceased to be under a disability or died (whichever first occurred) notwithstanding that the period of limitation has expired[4]. If at the time when one disability ceases another disability has already supervened, time does not begin to run until the latter disability ceases[5]. However, when a right of action which has accrued to a person under a disability accrues, on the death of that person while still under a disability, to another person under a disability, no further extension of time is allowed by reason of the disability of the second person[6]. Where a person becomes subject to a disability after a right of action has accrued to him, that will not stop time running.[7]

1 The age of majority is 18 years: Family Law Reform Act 1969, s 1.
2 Section 38 (2). A person is of unsound mind if he is a person who, by reason of mental disorder within the meaning of the Mental Health Act 1983, is incapable of managing and administering his property and affairs: s 38 (3); *Kirby v Leather* [1965] 2 QB 367; *Penrose v Mansfield* (1971) 115 Sol Jo 309. It is for the claimant to prove that he was so incapable: *Dawson v Spain-Gower* (18 October 1988, unreported), CA. A person shall be conclusively presumed to be of unsound mind (a) while he is liable to be detained or subject to guardianship under the Mental Health Act 1983 (otherwise than by virtue of s 35 or 89); and (b) while he is receiving treatment as an in-patient in any hospital within the meaning of the Mental Health Act 1983 or mental nursing home within the meaning of the Nursing Homes Act 1975 without being liable to be detained under the 1983 Act (otherwise than by virtue of ss 35 or 89), being treatment which follows without any interval a period during which he was liable to be detained or subject to guardianship under the Mental Health Act 1959, or the Act of 1983 (otherwise than by virtue of ss 35 or 89), or by virtue of any enactment repealed or excluded by the Mental Health Act 1959, (4).
3 Ie the person to whom the right of claim has accrued must be under a disability at the date of the accrual of the right of claim. There is no extension if he subsequently becomes disabled and see s 28 (2), whereby the section shall not affect any case where the right of claim first accrued to some person (not under a disability) through whom the person under a disability claims.
4 Section 28 (1).
5 *Borrows v Ellison* (1871) LR 6 Exch 128.
6 Section 28 (3).
7 *Purnell v Roche* [1927] 2 Ch 142; *Murray v Watkins* (1890) 62 LT 796; *Garner v Wingrove* [1905] 2 Ch 233; *Owen v De Beauvoir* (1847) 16 M & W 547.

Recovery of land and money charged thereon

16.55 No claim to recover land or money charged on land shall be brought by virtue of the section extending the limitation period in the case of disability[1] by any person after the expiration of 30 years from the date on which the right of action accrued to that person, or some person through whom he claims[2].

1 Ie s 28.
2 Section 28 (4).

FRAUD AND MISTAKE

16.56 Where in the case of any claim for which a period of limitation is prescribed by the Limitation Act 1980, either:

(a) the claim is based upon the fraud[1] of the defendant; or

(b) any fact relevant to the claimants' right of action has been deliberately concealed from him by the defendant[2]; or
(c) the claim is for relief from the consequences of a mistake[3];

the period of limitation does not begin to run until the claimant has discovered the fraud, concealment or the mistake (as the case may be) or could with reasonable diligence have discovered it[4]. However, those provisions do not enable any claim to be brought to recover, or recover the value of, any property, or to enforce any charge against, or set aside any transaction, to be brought against the purchaser of the property or any person claiming through him in any case where the property has been purchased for valuable consideration by an innocent third party since the fraud or concealment or (as the case may be) the transaction in which the mistake was made took place[5]. A purchaser is an innocent third party for the purposes of these provisions:

(a) in the case of fraud or concealment of any fact relevant to the claimant's right of action, if he was not a party to the fraud or (as the case may be) to the concealment of that fact and did not at the time of the purchase know or have reason to believe that the fraud or concealment had taken place; and
(b) in the case of mistake, if he did not at the time of the purchase know or have reason to believe that the mistake had been made[6].

1 *Beaman v ARTS Ltd* [1949] 1 KB 550 at 558, [1949] 1 All ER 465 at 467, CA; *Clark v Woor* [1965] 2 All ER 353 at 355, 356; *RB Policies at Lloyds v Butler* [1950] 1 KB 76.
2 *Eddis v Chichester Constable* [1969] 2 Ch 345, [1969] 2 All ER 912, CA; *Bartlett v Barclays Bank Trust Co Ltd* [1980] Ch 515, [1979] 1 All ER 139; *King v Victor Parsons & Co* [1973] 1 WLR 29; *E Clarke & Sons (Coaches) Ltd v Axtell Yates Hallett* (1989) 30 Con LR 123.
3 *Re Jones' Estate* [1914] 1 IR 188; *Phillips-Higgins v Harper* [1954] 1 QB 411 at 420, [1954] 2 All ER 51n, CA.
4 Section 32 (1). References to the defendant include references to the defendant's agent and to any person through whom the defendant claims and his agent: s 32(1), and see *Thorne v Heard* [1894] 1 Ch 599, CA.
5 Section 32 (3). For the case of an innocent purchaser contracting through an agent who is ware of the fraud see: *Vane v Vane* (1873) 8 Ch App 383; *Eddis v Chichester Constable* [1969] 2 Ch 345; *Applegate v Moss* [1971] 1 QB 406; *Gawthrop v Boulton* [1979] 1 WLR 268.
6 Section 32 (4). See also *Westminster City Council v Croyalgrange Ltd* [1986] 1 WLR 674; *Mallon v Allon* [1964] 1 QB 385; *Taylor's Central Garages (Exeter) Ltd v Roper* [1951] WN 383; *Nakkuda Ali v Jayaratne* [1951] AC 66; *London Computator v Seymour* [1944] 2 All ER 11; *R v Harrison* [1938] 3 All ER 134. For the position of an innocent purchaser contracting through an agent who was aware of the fraud see: *Vane v Vane* (1873) 8 Ch App 383; *Eddis v Chichester Constable* [1969] 2 Ch 345; *Applegate v Moss* [1971] 1 QB 406; *Gawthrop v Boulton* [1979] 1 WLR 268.

HUMAN RIGHTS[1]

HUMAN RIGHTS ACT 1998

16.57 The Act makes it unlawful for a public authority to act, or fail to act, in a way which is incompatible with Convention Rights[2], unless it is compelled to do so by primary legislation[3]. 'Public authority' includes a court as well as any person 'certain of whose functions are of a public nature'[4]. So far as possible, legislation should be read and given effect to in a way which is compatible with

Convention rights[5] and where primary legislation is incompatible with a Convention right, the court[6] may make a declaration of that incompatibility[7]. Thus the Act potentially affects the process of judicial decision-making and the orders a court should make in relation to enforcement of a mortgagee's remedies. It will also be relevant to the actions of a court-appointed receiver, who as an officer of the court is a public authority[8], and mortgagees who are public authorities, for instance local authorities or housing associations[9].

1 This section only considers certain aspects of Human Rights Law. For further consideration, see eg Starmer *Blackstone's Human Rights Digest* (1st edn., 2001); Clayton and Tomlinson *The Law of Human Rights* (1st edn, 2000); Luba *Housing and the Human Rights Act* (1st edn, 2000); Rook *Property Law and Human Rights* (1st edn, 2001); Harpum *Property Law—The Human Rights Dimension* 1999 Blundell Memorial Lecture).
2 Section 6(1). 'Convention rights' includes Arts 6 and 8 of the Convention and Art 1 of the First Protocol: s 1(1). The remedies available to a victim of an unlawful act are set out in ss 7–9.
3 Section 6(2).
4 Section 6(3).
5 Section 3. The materials which a court must take into account in determining a question which has arisen in connection with a Convention Right are listed in s 2.
6 That is, the High Court and above: s 4(5)
7 Section 4(4). Such a declaration does not affect the validity of the legislation, nor is it binding on the parties to the proceedinmgs in which it is made: s 4(6).
8 See **18.6** and **18.25**.
9 *Southwark Borough Council v Saint Brice* [2001] EWCA Civ 1138, [2001] 35 LS Gaz R 34; *Castle Vale Housing Action Trust v Gallagher* [2001] EWCA Civ 944; for the powers of such bodies to grant mortgages, see **12.54** ff and **12.65** ff.

ARTICLE 1 OF THE FIRST PROTOCOL

16.58 Article 1 of the First Protocol states that:

> 'Every natural or legal person is entitled to the peaceful enjoyment of his possessions. No one shall be deprived of his possessions except in the public interest and subject to the conditions provided for by law and by the general principles of international law.
>
> The preceding provisions shall not, however, in any way impair the right of a State to enforce such laws as it deems necessary to control the use of property in accordance with the general interest or to secure the payment of taxes or other contributions or penalties.'

The article contains a general principle as to the right to the peaceful enjoyment of property[1]; and, as particular instances of interference with that right, provides that any deprivation of property can only take place subject to certain conditions and that the state nevertheless has the right to control the use of property in the general interest[2]. It is concerned with protecting property against the activities of the state, not private individuals, and is not directed against matters which are essentially ones of private law[3]. Thus, insofar as the exercise of the mortgagee's remedies deprives the mortgagor of his property (for instance, by foreclosure), it is unlikely that would amount to a breach of the article, since the deprivation will have come about as a result of a private agreement between the parties[4]. Further, by entering the mortgage the mortgagor will have consented to the mortgagee being entitled to exercise his various remedies as part of the contractual relationship between the parties and it seems such consent would be another reason why the exercises of those remedies would not constitute a breach of the article[5]. To the extent that a mortgagor is deprived of his possessions by the exercise of the mortgagee's remedies, that is in any event likely to be in the public interest in ensuring payment of contractual debts and thus within the exception to the protocol, so long as it is carried out in accordance with the conditions provided by law[6].

There are various statutory controls on a mortgagee's rights and remedies in relation to his interest in the mortgaged property, notably the restrictions imposed by s 36 of the Administration of Justice Act 1970 on a mortgagee's right to possession[7]. In assessing whether such controls fall within the proviso to the protocol, as being within the general interest, the court must determine whether a fair balance has been struck between the interest of the community and the protection of the individual's rights[8]. The control must have a legitimate aim and there must be a reasonable degree of proportionality between the aim and the means used to achieve it[9]. The court allows states a wide margin of appreciation in determining what is in the public interest, particularly in the field of housing[10]. The suspension of possession orders to reduce the prospect of the occupiers becoming homeless has been recognised as a legitimate aim in the public interest[11] and it seems unlikely that, applying the wide margin of appreciation allowed, the balance struck by the courts between the interests of mortgagor and mortgagee in their application of s 36[12] could be said to be unfair[13].

The operation of the Limitation Act 1980 in regard to the rights of mortgagor or mortgagee will not amount to the deprivation, or an interference with the peaceful enjoyment of, their interest in the mortgaged property; it simply removes their right to access to the courts where they have delayed bringing a claim and is essentially a matter of private law[14]. In any event, such provisions are likely to be justified as being in the public or general interest of achieving legal certainty, especially given the margin of appreciation allowed to states in setting limitation periods[15].

1 That is, in substance, guarantees the right of property: *Marckx v Belgium* (1979) 2 EHRR 330.
2 See *Sporrong and Lönnroth v Sweden* (1982) 5 EHRR 35; *James v United Kingdom* (1986) 8 EHRR 123 at 140; *Family Housing Association v Donellan* [2001] 30 EG 114 (CS), Park J, unreported).
3 *Bramelid and Malmström v Sweden* (1982) 5 EHRR 249 at 255; *AGOSI v United Kingdom* (1986) 9 EHRR 1; *Family Housing Association v Donellan* above.
4 See by analogy, the reasoning in *App. No 11949/86* (1988) 10 EHRR 149, concerning forfeiture of a lease for non-payment of service charges.
5 See *App No 11949/86* (1988) 10 EHRR 149; *Holy Monasteries v Greece* (1994) 20 EHRR 1.
6 *Wood v United Kingdom* (1997) 24 EHRR CD 69 (mortgagee exercising right to possession and sale).
7 See **19.51** ff.
8 *Sporrong and Lonnroth v Sweden* (1982) 5 EHRR 35; *Stran Greek Refineries and Stratis Andreadis v Greece* (1994) 19 EHRR 293.
9 See *Mellacher v Austria* (1989) 12 EHRR 391; *Baner v Sweden* No 1176/85, 60 DR 128, 142 (1989); *Chassagnou v France* (1999) 7 BHRC 151.
10 *Mellacher v Austria* (1989) 12 EHRR 391, para 45; *Immobilaire Safi v Italy* (1999) 7 BHRC 256, para 49; *GL v Italy* (3 August 2000, unreported), ECHR.
11 *Spadea v Italy* (1995) 21 EHRR 482; *Immobilaire Safi v Italy* above; *GL v Italy* above.
12 See **19.54** ff.
13 Consider also *James v UK* (1986) 8 EHRR 123 (leasehold 'reform'); *Kilbourn v United Kingdom* (1986) 8 EHRR 81 (rent control).
14 See cases concerning adverse possession: *J A Pye (Oxford) Ltd v Graham* [2001] EWCA Civ 117; [2001] 2 WLR 1293 at 1309–1310; *Family Housing Association v Donellan* [2001] 30 EG 114 (CS), Park J.
15 *Stubbings v United Kingdom* (1996) 23 EHRR 213; *J A Pye (Oxford) Ltd v Graham* above, at 1309-1310.

ARTICLE 8

16.59 Article 8 provides that:

> '1. Everyone has the right to respect for his private and family life, his home and his correspondence.
>
> 2. There shall be no interference by a public authority with the exercise of this right except such as is in accordance with the law and is necessary in a democratic society in the interests of national security, public safety or the economic well-being of the country, for the prevention of disorder or crime, for the protection of health or morals, or for the protection of the rights and freedoms of others.'

Where the mortgaged property is the mortgagor's home, a possession order if made and executed will constitute an interference by a public authority with the right conferred by Art 8[1]. The court will need to give the wording of s 36 of the Administration of Justice Act 1970 an effect consistent, so far as possible, with Art 8. A possession order may nevertheless be made if permitted by law in order to protect the rights and freedoms of others, including the mortgagee's property rights, or in the interests of the economic well-being of the country, including ensuring payment of contractual debts, and thus ensuring a continuing willingness to lend[2]. In each case, the court will need to balance the rights of the mortgagor in relation to his home and the impact of an eviction on his individual circumstances, against those legitimate aims[3]. Any possession order, and any terms imposed, should be necessary and proportionate to meet those other needs. However, the courts have already balanced such factors when applying s 36[4] and it seems unlikely that in practice Art 8 should make any real difference to the way in which the court will approach the question of whether to make, adjourn or suspend a possession order[5].

1 See *Southwark Borough Council v Saint Brice* [2001] EWCA Civ 1138, [2001] 35 LS Gaz R 34; *Castle Vale Housing Action Trust v Gallagher* [2001] EWCA Civ 944; *Poplar Housing and Regeneration Community Association Ltd v Donoghue* [2001] EWCA Civ 595 [2001] 4 All ER 604. See also *Larkos v Cyprus* (1999) 7 BHRC 244.

2 See *Southwark Borough Council v Saint Brice* above; *Castle Vale Housing Action Trust v Gallagher* [2001] EWCA Civ 595; *Wood v United Kingdom* (1997) 24 EHRR CD69; *Birmingham Midshires v Sabherwal* (1999) 80 P & CR 256 at 264 (possession order necessary to protect mortgagee's rights as secured lender and in accordance with the law). See also (1988) 10 EHRR 149 at 155, 156.

3 *Southwark Borough Council v Saint Brice* above; *Castle Vale Housing Action Trust v Gallagher* [2001] EWCA Civ 595; *Wood v United Kingdom* (1997) 24 EHRR CD69; *Chapman v United Kingdom* (2001) 10 BHCR 48.

4 See **19.54** ff.

5 *Castle Vale Housing Action Trust v Gallagher* above; *Birmingham Midshires v Sabherwal* (1999) 80 P & CR 256 at 264. See eg *Albany Home Loans v Massey* (1997) 29 HLR 902, where the court refused to make a possession order which would have brought no practical benefit to the mortgagee, and thus, in terms of Art 8 would have been neither necessary or proportionate for the protection of the rights of the mortagee or in the general economic interest. Although the court was referred 'in passing' to Art 8, and considered its decision to be in line with the requirements of the Article, the decision was based (at 906) on the application of the existing principles that powers conferred on a mortgagee must be exercised in good faith and for the purposes of obtaining repayment: see eg *Downsview Ltd v First City Corpn Ltd* [1993] AC 295 at 312; *Quennell v Maltby* [1979] 1 WLR 318 at 322. See **16.13**.

ARTICLE 6

16.60 Article 6 provides that:

'In the determination of his civil rights and obligations... everyone is entitled to a fair and public hearing within a reasonable time by an independent and impartial tribunal established by law....'

Severe delays in the determination of mortgage claims, for instance for possession, will amount to a breach of Art 6, in relation to both the rights of the mortgagor and mortgagee[1]. That may raise questions as to the validity of the court's current practice, where the mortgagor has paid off all the arrears, of adjourning the possession claim generally, with permission to apply, rather than dismissing the claim (although that practice is generally in the mortgagor's interest so far as costs are concerned)[2]. The issue of a possession warrant and its execution where the terms of a suspended possession order have been breached does not require a further hearing in order to comply with Art 6—it is purely an administrative act which does not involve a determination of the occupier's civil rights and obligations[3]. It has been suggested that the mortgagee's right, in certain circumstances, to take possession of the mortgaged property without a court order[4] 'appears to be a particularly clear breach of Article 6'[5]. However, it is submitted that in entering peaceably into possession the mortgagee is simply enjoying one aspect of his interest in the mortgaged property[6], which does not involve a determination of the civil rights and obligations of either mortgagor or mortgagee. If the mortgagor wishes to allege that the mortgagee had no right to enter and remain in possession, it is open to him to bring a claim for the determination of that issue by the court.

1 See *Di Mauro v Italy* (28 July 1999, unreported), ECHR (possession proceedings hanging over private sector tenant for 13 years); *GL v Italy* (3 August 2000, unreported), ECHR (delay in determining landlord's claim).
2 *Greyhound Guaranty v Caulfield* [1981] CLY 1808, 78 LS Gaz R 958; *Halifax plc v Taffs* [1999] CLY 4385; see **19.50**.
3 *Southwark Borough Council v Saint Brice* [2001] EWCA Civ 1138, [2001] 35 LS Gaz R 34.
4 *Ropaigealach v Barclays Bank plc* [2000] 1 QB 263, [1999] 4 All ER 235; see **19.8**.
5 Clayton and Tomlinson *The Law of Human Rights* (1st edn, 2000) para 11.318; see also Rook *Property Law and Human Rights* (1st edn, 2001), 8.4.1.3.
6 See **19.1**.

Chapter 17

The personal remedy

THE COVENANT TO PAY

Principal and interest

17.1 Every mortgage implies a loan, and every loan implies a debt, for which the borrower is personally liable. There will usually be an express covenant to pay. Where there is no express obligation to repay, that will normally be implied from receipt of the loan[1]. A covenant for payment will be implied by an admission of the debt coupled with an agreement to execute a security which would create a speciality debt[2]. It will also be implied by a mere admission of liability in a deed, provided that an intention to enter into an engagement to pay appears on the face of the deed (although not where the acknowledgment appears to have been made solely for a collateral purpose, such as by way of recital in an appointment of new trustee)[3].

Where a registered charge is created on any land there is implied on the part of the proprietor of the land at the time of the creation of the charge (unless there is an entry on the register negativing such implication):

(a) a covenant with the proprietor for the time being of the charge to pay the principal sums charged, and interest, if any thereon, at the appointed time and rate; and
(b) a covenant, if the principal sum or any part thereof is unpaid at the appointed time, to pay interest half-yearly at the appointed rate, both before and after any judgment obtained in respect of the charge, on so much of the principal sum as for the time being remains unpaid[4].

However, such an implication will be readily rebutted where the mortgagor had put up his property as security for a loan to a third party[5]. Where a registered charge is created on leasehold land, the proprietor of the land at the time of the creation of the charge is additionally under an implied covenant with the proprietor for the time being of the charge (unless there is an entry on the register negativing such implication) that the person being proprietor of such land at the time of the creation of the charge, or those deriving title under him, will

(a) pay, perform and observe the lessee's covenants and conditions as to rent and otherwise, in the registered lease; and
(b) will keep the proprietor of the charge, and those deriving title under him,

indemnified against all proceedings, expenses and claims arising from non-payment of rent or the breach of any such covenants or conditions[6].

The debt will be in the nature of a simple contract only, unless there is a bond or an express or implied covenant to give it the character of a specialty[7]. The principal secured by the mortgage, and the interest thereon, are distinct debts, thus they may be separately recovered[8]. The mortgagee can only bring a claim on the covenant for principal and interest and any other sums which the mortgagor has covenanted to pay and not for expenses incurred by the mortgagee outside the covenant (although he may be entitled to these in a redemption or foreclosure action)[9]. It is quite common to find a provision in the mortgage by which a certificate of some officer of the lender as to the amount due shall be conclusive. Such clauses are not contrary to public policy and in the absence of good evidence of mistake binding[10].

1 *Sutton v Sutton* (1882) 22 Ch D 511, CA.
2 *Saunders v Milsome* (1866) LR 2 Eq 573.
3 *Courtney v Taylor* (1843) 6 Man & G 851; *Jackson v North Eastern Rly Co* (1877) 7 Ch D 573. Where the mortgage contains no covenant for payment the mortgagee may sue for the debt if the security is collateral to it and was not taken in satisfaction of an existing debt: *Yates v Aston* (1843) 4 QB 182, but if it was so taken, the contract will have merged in the security which is of a higher nature as (under like circumstances) the remedy on simple contract will merge in a bond or covenant: *Price v Moulton* (1851) 10 CB 561; and see **32.12**.
4 Land Registration Act 1925, s 28(1).
5 *Fairmile Portfolio Management Ltd v Davies Arnold Cooper* [1998] EGCS 149; see also *Re Midland Bank Ltd's Application* [1941] Ch 350.
6 Land Registration Act 1925, s 28(2).
7 *Meynell v Howard* (1696) Prec Ch 61; *King v King* (1735) 3 P Wms 358; *Sutton v Sutton* (1882) 22 Ch D 511, CA. The limitation period will be different where there is a covenant (12 years) and where there is no covenant (6 years).
8 *Dickenson v Harrison* (1817) 4 Price 282.
9 *Re Sneyd, ex p Fewings* (1883) 25 Ch D338.
10 See *Bache & Co (London) Ltd v Banque Vernes et Commerciale de Paris SA* [1973] 2 Lloyd's Rep 437, CA: *Dobbs v National Bank of Australasia Ltd* (1935) 53 CLR 643; *ANZ Banking Group (NZ) Ltd v Gibson* [1981] 2 NZLR 513 at 524; *Papua and New Guinea Development Bank v Manton* [1982] VR 1000. The debtor who suffers any loss by virtue of such a certificate may have a claim against the maker. Consider also in the landlord and tenant context: *Re Davstone's Leases* [1969] 2 Ch 378; *Concorde Graphics v Andromeda Investments SA* [1983] 1 EGLR 53; *Nikko Hotels (UK) v MEPC* [1991] 2 EGLR 103; *Mercury Communications Ltd v Director General of Telecommunications* [1996] 1 All ER 575, [1996] 1 WLR 48; *British Shipbuilders v VSEL* [1997] 1 Lloyds Rep 106.

Mortgage of insurance policy

17.2 In the case of a mortgage of an insurance policy, where the insurers are the mortgagees, and the mortgagor covenants with them to keep up the policy, or in default that the insurers may pay and add the premiums to the mortgage debt, but where there is no covenant to repay them the premiums, the mortgagees are only entitled to nominal damages in an action against the mortgagor for breach of the covenant to keep up the policy; the addition of the premiums to the debt is the remedy provided. However, under a covenant to repay, the amount paid would be given as damages[1].

1 *Browne v Price* (1858) 4 CBNS 598. It has been held that a covenant 'not to do or suffer anything whereby the policy may become voidable or void' is not broken by the mortgagor

allowing the insurance company to take over a fully paid-up policy at surrender value: *Sapio v Hackney* (1907) 51 Sol Jo 428.

WHO CAN CLAIM

17.3 The mortgagee and all those who claim the mortgage security under him can make a claim on a covenant for payment in the mortgage deed. In the case of a transfer inter vivos, the right to sue on the covenant vests in the transferee on his giving notice in writing of the transfer to the mortgagor. If the requirements of s 136 of the Law of Property Act 1925 are fulfilled the transferee can then sue in his own name otherwise he must join the original mortgagee[1]. Where the mortgagee has died, his personal representatives will be entitled to claim on the covenant; where he has bequeathed the mortgage, the right to claim on the debt will vest in the legatee upon the executors giving their assent to the bequest, or transferring it under the statutory form[2]. On the bankruptcy of the mortgagee, his trustee can exercise all his remedies under the mortgage. On the dissolution of a mortgagee company, its rights under the mortgage vest in the Crown (or the Duchy of Lancaster or the Duchy of Cornwall as the case may be) as bona vacantia[3]. Where the mortgagees are trustees the right of action is in the trustees, unless it appears that the beneficiaries were to have the benefit of the contract of mortgage[4], the same applies to debenture trustees.

1 Law of Property Act 1925, s 136. For transfers of mortgages generally, see Chapter 14.
2 Law of Property Act 1925, s 118, Sch 4. For devolution upon death, see the Administration of Estates Act 1925, ss 1(1), 3(1)(ii), 36; and generally **14.23**.
3 Companies Act 1985, s 654.
4 *Gandy v Gandy* (1885) 30 Ch D 57, CA.

AGAINST WHOM CAN A CLAIM FOR PAYMENT BE MADE

17.4 The claim on the covenant can be maintained against any covenantor, whether principal or surety[1]. However, the covenant can be qualified so as to imply that there is no personal contract for repayment upon which a claim can be brought; for example, where the covenantor is a trustee and covenants for repayment only of money which he receives as trustee[2], or where a person merely agrees to charge his property as collateral security for the debt of another[3].

1 *Evans v Jones* (1839) 5 M & W 295. *Esso Petroleum Co Ltd v Alstonbridge Properties Ltd* [1975] 3 All ER 358, [1975] 1 WLR 1474.
2 *Mathew v Blackmore* (1857) 1 H & N 762; *Re Robinson's Settlement* [1912] 1 Ch 717; *Williams v Hathaway* (1877) 6 Ch D 544. But where there is an absolute covenant for payment, a clause excluding personal liability is repugnant and therefore void: *Watling v Lewis* [1911] 1 Ch 414; *Re Tewkesbury Gas Co* [1912] 1 Ch 1, CA, and where, although the covenant is absolute in form, the mortgage was really given to secure the balance of a current account, that fact may be proved and only so much as is due on the account can then be recovered: *Trench v Doran* (1887) 20 LR Ir 338.
3 *Re Midland Bank Ltd's Application* [1941] Ch 350, *sub nom Franklin v Midland Bank Ltd* [1941] 2 All ER 135; see also *Fairmile Portfolio Management Ltd v Davies Arnold Cooper* [1998] EGCS 149.

Assignment of equity of redemption[1]

17.5 The mortgagor cannot, without the mortgagee's consent, relieve himself of his liability under the covenant by transferring the equity of redemption[2]. Since the burden of the covenant for payment does not run with the equity of redemption, the mortgagee cannot sue the assignee of that equity either for principal or interest[3] nor prove for them in his bankruptcy[4]. However, the assignee will be liable to indemnify the mortgagor[5]—usually the assignment contains an express proviso to this effect and the express covenant then excludes implied liability[6]. While it has been held that the benefit of the covenant of indemnity is not assignable, it is submitted that a covenant of indemnity is as assignable as any other covenant[7]. The assignee may make himself directly liable by entering into a fresh covenant with the mortgagee[8], but such liability is not implied from the mere payment of interest[9]. Whilst upon assignment the mortgagor ceases to be entitled to redeem, his right to do so revives if he is sued for the mortgage debt. He is then, in effect, a surety for the assignee, and he may redeem notwithstanding that the assignee has created fresh charges in favour of the mortgagee[10].

1 And see **28.3**.
2 *West Bromwich Building Society v Bullock* [1936] 1 All ER 887.
3 The mortgagor remains liable: *Hall v Heward* (1886) 32 Ch D 430, CA; and see *Foster v Woolvett* (1963) 39 DLR (2d) 532, but liability under a running account is limited to the amount outstanding at the date when the mortgagee had notice of the change of ownership. Accordingly, the purchaser of the equity of redemption in a farm was liable for the price of goods supplied after that date and not the original mortgagor: *Edwards v Ottawa Valley Grain Products Ltd* (1970) 11 DLR (3d) 137. For a conveyance where a husband's interest in the mortgaged property is transferred under s 24 of the Matrimonial Causes Act 1973, see *Practice Direction* [1971] 1 All ER 896, [1971] 1 WLR 224 and the Appendix.
4 *Re Errington, ex p Mason* [1894] 1 QB 11.
5 *Waring v Ward* (1802) 7 Ves 332; *Simpson v Forrester* (1973) 47 ALJR 149, and this liability survives assignment: *Re Windle, ex p Trustee of Bankrupt v Windle* [1975] 3 All ER 987 at 995. So the survivor of joint tenants must indemnify the estate of the deceased joint tenant.
6 *Mills v United Counties Bank Ltd* [1912] 1 Ch 231, CA.
7 It was held that the covenant was not assignable in *Rendell v Morphew* (1914) 84 LJ Ch 517. However, that case turned upon the inability of executors of an insolvent estate to assign the benefit of an indemnity covenant (see *British Union and National Insurance Co v Rawson* [1916] 2 Ch 476 at 483, CA) and even on that point it is wrongly decided: see *Butler Estates Co v Bean* [1942] 1 KB 1, [1941] 2 All ER 793.
8 *Shore v Shore* (1847) 2 Ph 378. See *Esso Petroleum Co Ltd v Alstonbridge Properties Ltd* [1975] 3 All ER 358, [1975] 1 WLR 1474.
9 *Re Errington* above.
10 *Kinnaird v Trollope* (1888) 39 Ch D 636, and see **28.15**.

WHEN THE RIGHT TO CLAIM ARISES

17.6 This depends on the terms of the covenant for payment[1] and whether there is a pre-existing debt[2]. Where the covenant fixes a date for repayment, the right of action arises upon non-payment on that date[3]. Where the covenant is to pay on or after a certain date, the mortgagee cannot sue until after a demand for payment has been made[4]. If the principal is payable on demand, and there is no express or implied provision for notice to be given, the right of action generally accrues on the execution of the mortgage[5], with two exceptions. First, where the covenant is collateral, for example to secure the debt of another, or to secure a current account between the covenantor and the covenantee, a demand must first be made[6]. Secondly, in the case of an instalment mortgage, where the balance of the money due becomes payable on default, a demand is necessary before the right of action accrues, because of the nature of the debtor's obligation is changed from instalments to lump sum[7]. If the covenant provides expressly or impliedly for notice to be given, an actual demand in writing must be made before the right of action arises[8]. Any other condition prescribed as a preliminary to suing on the covenant must also be observed[9]. The notice given must be sufficient to allow the mortgagor a reasonable time to implement the mechanics of payment[10]. An effective demand is made by any clear communication that payment is required[11]. A notice is still an effective demand even if it does not state the amount due[12], or if it overstates the amount due[13], in which case the true amount due is recoverable; however, it is invalid if what is claimed is not in fact due[14]. Any mode of service is sufficient which brings home to the mortgagor the fact that the demand has been made[15].

1 As to the form of the covenant, see **3.23**. As to instalment mortgages, see **3.25**. See also **16.9**.
2 *D & J Fowler (Australia) Ltd v Bank of New South Wales* [1982] 2 NSWLR 879.
3 *Bolton v Buckenham* [1891] 1 QB 278, CA, and the mortgagee cannot sue before that date or exercise the power of sale: *Twentieth Century Banking Corpn Ltd v Wilkinson* [1977] Ch 99, [1976] 3 All ER 361. See also *Sinton v Dooley* [1910] 2 IR 163 at 165.
4 *Re Tewkesbury Gas Co* [1911] 2 Ch 279; affd [1912] 1 Ch 1, CA. For an example of implied demand, see *The Halcyon Skies (No 2)* [1977] 1 Lloyd's Rep 22.
5 *Evans v Jones* (1839) 5 M & W 295; *Re Brown's Estate, Brown v Brown* [1893] 2 Ch 300 at 304; *Esso Petroleum Co Ltd v Alstonbridge Properties Ltd* [1975] 3 All ER 358; *Lakshmijt v Sherani* [1974] AC 605 at 617–618 PC; *Young v Queensland Trustees Ltd* (1956) 99 CLR 560 at 566; *Golding v Russell* [1983] Qd R 53.
6 *Birks v Trippet* (1666) 1 Wms Saund 28; *Re Brown's Estate* above; *Lloyds Bank Ltd v Margolis* [1954] 1 All ER 734, [1954] 1 WLR 644; *Habib Bank Ltd v Tailor* [1982] 3 All ER 561, [1982] 1 WLR 1218, CA.
7 *Esso Petroleum Co Ltd v Alstonbridge Properties Ltd* above, and *Murphy v Lawrence* [1960] NZLR 772.
8 *Lloyds Bank Ltd v Margolis* above. The issue of proceedings does not continue a demand: *Esso Petroleum Co Ltd v Alstonbridge Properties Ltd* above.
9 *Rogers & Co v British and Colonial Colliery Supply Association* (1898) 68 LJQB 14.
10 *Bank of Baroda v Panessar* [1987] Ch 335, [1986] 3 All ER 751; and see *Brighty v Norton* (1862) 3 B & S 305; *Massey v Sladden* (1868) LR 4 Exch 13; *Fitzgerald's Trustees v Mellersh* [1892] 1 Ch 385 at 390; *Cripps (Pharmaceuticals) Ltd v Wickenden* [1973] 2 All ER 606, [1973] 1 WLR 994, cf *Ronald Elwyn Lister, Ltd v Dunlop Canada Ltd* (1982) 135 DLR (3d) 1; *ANZ Banking Group (NZ) Ltd v Gibson* [1981] 2 NZLR 513; *Bunbury Foods Pty Ltd v National Bank of Australasia Ltd* (1984) 58 ALJR 199; *Mister Broadloom Corpn (1968) Ltd v Bank of Montreal* (1984) 4 DLR (4th) 74. In *NRG Vision Ltd v Churchfield Leasing Ltd* [1988] BCLC 624 a receiver under a debenture could be appointed upon a demand being made. The debenture holder made a demand in writing coupled with an offer to accept weekly instalments of the monies due (which offer was not accepted). Knox J held that the demand was not invalidated by it being coupled with an offer to accept weekly instalments. For Canadian cases allowing the mortgagor more time to find the money due than under the rule in *Bank of Baroda v Panessar*, see *Picarda on the Law Relating to Receivers, Managers and Administrators* (13th edn), pp 80–84.
11 *Re Colonial Finance, Mortgage, Investment & Guarantee Corpn Ltd* (1905) 6 SRNSW 6; *Re a Company* [1985] BCLC 37.
12 *Bank of Baroda v Panessar* above; *Bunbury Foods Pty Ltd v National Bank of Australasia Ltd* above.
13 *Fox v Jolly* [1916] 1 AC 1, HL; *Campbell v Commercial Banking Co of Sydney* (1879) 40 LT 137, PC; *Clyde Properties Ltd v Tasker* [1970] NZLR 754; *National Australia Bank Ltd v Zollo* (1992) 59 SASR 76; *Stanley v Auckland Co-operative Terminating Building Society* [1973] 2 NZLR 673; *Bunbury Foods Pty Ltd v National Bank of Australasia Ltd* above; *Bank of Baroda v Panessar* above. See also *Clare Morris Ltd v Hunter BNZ Finance Ltd* [1988] ACLD 416, (1990) 64 ALJ 135 (Butt); *Parker v Rock Finance Corpn Ltd* [1981] 1 NZLR 488; *Commodore Pty Ltd v Perpetual Trustees Estates Agency Co of New Zealand Ltd* [1984] 1 NZLR 324, CA; *Websdale v S & J Investments Pty Ltd* (1991) 24 NSWLR 573, not following *MIR Bros Projects Pty Ltd v 1924 Pty Ltd* [1980] 2 NSWLR 907; *Mediservices International Pty Ltd v Stocks*

and Realty (Security Finance) Pty Ltd [1982] 1 NSWLR 516; *Clarke v Japan Machines (Australia) Pty Ltd* [1984] 1 Qd R 404; *Network Finance Ltd v Lane* (1984) ANZ Conv Rep 571; *Indrisie v General Credits Ltd* [1985] VR 251. On acquiescence in the notice by the borrower, see *Orr v Ford* (1989) 167 CLR 316. In *Lombard North Central plc v Stobart* [1990] CCLR 53 a finance company was held to be bound by its settlement figures. For the effect of a vacating receipt made for the wrong amount, see **28.58.** For the binding effect of statements given under the Consumer Credit Act 1974, see s 172 of that Act and **10.55.**

14 *Jaffe v Premier Motors Ltd* [1960] NZLR 146. Where there is a facility letter subject to normal banking terms and conditions, this does not of itself make the loan repayable on demand: see *Cryne v Barclays Bank plc* [1987] BCLC 548; *Williams and Glyn's Bank v Barnes* [1981] Com LR 205 (see discussion in *Lingard on Bank Security Documents* (3rd edn) p 7.10.

15 *Worthington & Co Ltd v Abbott* [1910] 1 Ch 588.

LOSS OF THE RIGHT TO CLAIM

17.7 Upon repayment of the debt secured by the mortgage, the mortgagor is entitled to have the mortgaged property reconveyed to him. Thus, where the mortgagee cannot reconvey the mortgaged property, the right to sue on the covenant may be lost[1]. A mortgagee will be restrained from suing on the covenant if, by his own conduct, he cannot hand back the title deeds, or because he has parted with the mortgaged property, for instance because a solicitor had a lien on the property[2]. He is not prevented from suing if his inability to restore the property is due to the intervention of a third party, such as where leasehold property has been forfeited by the lessor, not due to the mortgagee's default[3]. A mortgagee who has foreclosed and subsequently sold the property is precluded from suing on the covenant[4]. However, the mortgagee will not lose the right to sue where he has sold the property under his power of sale[5] or under an order of the court[6], since the sale was a proper dealing with the security. The right to sue is not prejudiced by a subsequent mortgagee submitting to a judgment for foreclosure at the suit of a prior mortgagee[7]. An action on the covenant after foreclosure reopens the foreclosure[8]. This principle applies also to personalty. So where shares have been deposited as security with a broker, and he wrongfully sells them, he cannot sue for the balance due[9].

1 *Schoole v Sall* (1803) 1 Sch & Lef 176; and see also **16.15.**

2 *Walker v Jones* (1866) LR 1 PC 50.

3 *Re Burrell, Burrell v Smith* (1869) LR 7 Eq 399.

4 *Lloyds and Scottish Trust Ltd v Britten* (1982) 44 P & CR 249. See **22.69.**

5 *Schoole v Sall* (1803) 1 Sch & Lef 176; *Rudge v Richens* (1873) LR 8 CP 358; *Re McHenry, McDermot v Boyd, Barker's Claim* [1894] 3 Ch 290, CA; *Scandinavian Pacific Ltd v Burke* (1991) 5 BPR 11846.

6 *Gordon Grant & Co v Boos* [1926] AC 781, PC.

7 *Worthington v Abbott* [1910] 1 Ch 588.

8 See **22.69.**

9 *Ellis & Co's Trustee v Dixon-Johnson* [1925] AC 489, HL. Though if the shares are readily purchasable their money value may be substituted and the mortgagee then entitled to sue on the covenant.

PROCEDURE[1]

17.8 In claims for payment, the High Court and the county court have concurrent jurisdiction[2]. This chapter considers the procedural requirements where the claim is for payment only; consideration is given elsewhere to the requirements where the claim is also for possession[3], sale[4], or foreclosure[5].

1 See 28 *Atkin's Court Forms* (1997 issue).
2 See County Courts Act 1984, s 15(1).
3 See **19.28** ff.
4 See Chapter 21.
5 See **22.4** ff.

HIGH COURT, CHANCERY DIVISION

Allocation

17.9 The former provisions of CPR Sch 1, RSC Ord 88 as to the allocation of mortgage claims to the Chancery Division have been revoked from 15 October 2001[1].

1 For case law on RSC Ord 88, see the 10th edn of this book, p 310; see also *National Westminster Bank v Kitch* [1996] 4 All ER 495, CA.

Form of claim

17.10 The claim should normally be brought by a Pt 8 claim form[1], although a Pt 7 claim form should be used where it is known that there is likely to be a substantial dispute of fact; for example, where the intended defendant is alleging that the mortgage deed is a forgery, or was obtained by undue influence[2].

1 Prior to the revocation of CPR Sch 1, RSC Ord 88 (from 15 October 2001) that was required by CPR 813PD–006, A.3, Table 1. Mortgage claims would have been sought by originating summons before 26 April 1999: CPR 8B PD, A.1(3). See also Chancery Guide 21.3.
2 CPR 8.1(2). Where interest is claimed, the particulars of claim must also comply with the requirements of CPR 16.4.

Evidence

17.11 An order for payment in a mortgage claim is a final order[1]. Prior to its revocation from 15 October 2001, CPR Sch 1, RSC Ord 88 contained certain requirements for a witness statement or affidavit in support of a mortgage claim in the Chancery Division for payment of moneys secured by the mortgage. The former requirements remain a useful guide to good practice as to the contents of such a statement[2]. The witness statement should exhibit a true copy of the mortgage or charge and the original mortgage or charge or the charge certificate must be produced at the hearing of the claim. Most mortgages taken by building societies or former building societies now incorporate standard mortgage conditions; in such cases, those should also be exhibited. Some standard forms of mortgage are now so abbreviated that they give no particulars of the amount of the advance, the terms of the loan, the rate of interest or the amount of the instalments, all such matters instead being defined by reference to the offer letter. Where the offer letter is in effect incorporated into the mortgage by reference, it should also be exhibited. Where a bank mortgage is qualified by an offer or side letter providing for the repayment of the advance by instalments, that should also be exhibited. The witness statement must show how the claim is calculated, including:

(a) the amount of the advance and the amount and dates of any periodic repayments and any interest claimed;
(b) the amount which would have to be paid (after taking into account any adjustment for early settlement) in order to redeem the mortgage at the date of commencement of the proceedings and at a stated date not more than 14 days after the date of commencement of the proceedings, specifying the amount of the solicitor's costs and administrative charges which would be payable; and
(c) the dates between which a particular rate of interest applied, the number of days in that period, and the capital; on which the interest was calculated.

Where the claimant's claim includes a claim for interest to judgment, the witness statement should state the amount of a day's interest and the claimant should bring a computation of interest to the hearing. The witness statement should set out full particulars of the mortgage (including its nature, date, parties, rate of interest, any relevant covenants or stipulation (eg as to notices or demands to be made) and all transfers and devolutions.

1 *Nationwide Building Society v Bateman* [1978] 1 All ER 999, [1978] 1 WLR 394.
2 See CPR Sch 1, RSC Ord 88, r 5(1), in Civil Procedure, Autumn 2001 edn and Chancery Guide, ch 21.

Service of evidence

17.12 CPR 8.5 provides that in a Pt 8 claim the evidence in support should be filed and served at the same time as the claim form. The court will generally consider it sufficient if the claimant serves his evidence with the notice of appointment rather than the claim form, whether or not the defendant acknowledges service. The court will usually fix a time for the hearing at the same time as it issues the claim form[1].

1 Chancery Guide, 1–135, 21.4.

Failure to file an acknowledgment of service

17.13 Where the defendant fails to file an acknowledgment of service, and the time for doing so has expired, he may attend the hearing, but not take part in it, unless the court gives permission. In a claim for money secured by a mortgage, the claimant is not entitled to a judgment in default without the permission of the court, notwithstanding a failure to file an acknowledgment of service or a defence[1].

1 CPR Pt 12PD-001, 1.2(3). The rule refers to RSC Ord 88, CPR Sch 1, which was revoked from 15 October 2001.

The hearing

17.14–17.15 The initial hearing will usually be before a Master[1]; difficult cases may be referred to the judge. Although CPR 8.5 requires a defendant who wishes to rely on oral evidence in answer to file and serve it when he serves his acknowledgment of service, in practice the Master will usually consider oral representations made at the hearing, particularly where the litigant is acting in person[2]. Since the Masters do not normally give any preliminary consideration to mortgage claims, the claimant should take an appointment of sufficient length before the Master for the hearing of the claim as soon as the claim form has been served[3].

1 Chancery Guide, Ch 21.
2 Chancery Guide, 1-135, 21.10.
3 Chancery Guide, 1-135, 21.11.

COUNTY COURT

Jurisdiction

17.16 The county court has unlimited jurisdiction to determine any action founded on contract[1]. Proceedings for the recovery of moneys secured by a mortgage or charge on land may be commenced only in the county court for the district in which the land or any part of the land is situated[2].

1 County Courts Act 1984, s 15(1).
2 CPR Sch 2, CCR Ord 4, r 3.

Form of claim

17.17 The claim should normally be brought by a Pt 8 claim form[1], although a Pt 7 claim form should be used where it is known that there is likely to be a substantial dispute of fact, for example, where the intended defendant is alleging that the mortgage deed is a forgery, or was obtained by undue influence[2]. In a claim in the county court for money secured by a mortagage, the claimant is not entitled to obtain default judgment, notwithstanding that no acknowledgment of service or defence has been filed, unless it obtains the permission of the court[3].

1 CPR 8BPD-007, B.1, (3), on the basis that prior to 26 April 1999 it would, in the county court, usually have been brought by originating application.
2 CPR 8.1(2).
3 CPR Pt 12PD-001, 1.2(3).

Particulars of claim

17.18 Where a claimant claims as mortgagee payment of moneys secured by a legal or equitable mortgage or charge of real or leasehold property, he should state the following information in his particulars of claim[1] (where there is more than one loan secured by the mortgage, he should state the required information in respect of each loan agreement):

(a) the date of the mortgage or charge;
(b) state whether or not the loan which is secured by the mortgage is a regulated consumer credit agreement and, if so, specify the date on which any notice required by s 76 or s 87 of the Consumer Credit Act 1974 was given and, if appropriate, details that show the property is not one to which s 141 of the Consumer Credit Act 1974 applies;
(c) show the state of account with particulars of:

(i) the amount of the advance, and of any periodic repayment and any payment of interest required to be made;
(ii) the amount which would have to be paid (after taking into account any adjustment for early settlement) in order to redeem the mortgage at a stated date not more than 14 days after the commencement of proceedings specifying the amount of solicitor's costs and administrative charges which would be payable;
(iii) where the loan which is secured by the mortgage is a regulated consumer credit agreement, the total amount outstanding under the terms of the mortgage;
(iv) the rate of interest payable:
(1) at the commencement of the mortgage;
(2) immediately before any arrears referred to in sub-para (v) accrued; and
(3) where it differs from that provided under (2) above, at the commencement of the proceedings; and
(v) the amount of any interest or instalments in arrear at the commencement of the proceedings;

(d) any previous steps which the claimant has taken to recover the moneys secured by the mortgage and, in the case of court proceedings:
(i) the date when proceedings were commenced and concluded; and
(ii) the dates and terms of any orders made.

Where the claim is based upon a written agreement, a copy of the contract or documents constituting the agreement should be attached to or served with the particulars of claim and the original(s) should be available at the hearing[2]. Where interest is claimed, the particulars of claim must also comply with the requirements of CPR 16.4.

1 Such information was required by CPR Sch 2, CCR Ord 6 which was revoked from 15 October 2001. Although the similar requirements now contained in CPR 55 PD 2.5 only apply to possession claims by mortgagees, it is submitted it will remain good practice to include such information in a claim on the debt.
2 CPR 16PD-008, para 8.3(1).

SUSPENDED ORDER FOR PAYMENT

17.19 Where a mortgagee claims possession in addition to a money judgment and the possession order is suspended on terms that the arrears are paid by instalments a suspended order for payment should be made on the same terms[1].

1 *Cheltenham and Gloucester Building Society v Grattridge* (1993) 25 HLR 454; *Cheltenham and Gloucester Building Society v Johnson* (1996) 28 HLR 885.

COSTS

17.20 Where the mortgagee has a contractual right to recover costs out of the mortgage sums, he is not required to apply for an order for those costs and the court is not required to assess such costs[1]. However, where the contract entitles a mortgagee to require a mortgagor to pay those costs, the mortgagor may make an application for the court to direct that an account of the mortgagee's costs be taken[2]. The mortgagor may then dispute an amount in the mortgagee's account on the basis that it has been unreasonable incurred or is unreasonable in amount[3]. Where a mortgagor disputes an amount, the court may make an order that the disputed costs are assessed under CPR 48.3[4].

CPR 48.3 provides that where the court does assess costs which are payable under the terms of the mortgage, then, unless the mortgage provides otherwise, the costs are to be presumed to be costs which (a) have been reasonable incurred, and (b) are reasonable in amount, and the court will assess them accordingly[5]. In assessing costs payable under a mortgage, the court will apply the following principles[6]:

(a) An order for the payment of costs of proceedings by one party to another is always a discretionary order[7].
(b) Where there is a contractual right to the costs, the discretion should ordinarily be exercised so as to reflect that contractual right.
(c) The power of the court to disallow a mortgagee's costs sought to be added to the mortgage security is a power that derives from the power of the courts of equity to fix the terms on which redemption will be allowed, and not from s 51 of the Supreme Court Act 1981.
(d) A decision by a court to refuse costs in whole or in part to a mortgagee litigant may be—
    (i) a decision in the exercise of the s 51 discretion;
    (ii) a decision in the exercise of the power to fix the terms on which redemption will be allowed;
    (iii) a decision as to the extent of a mortgagee's contractual right to add his costs to the security; or
    (iv) a combination of two or more of those things. The statements of case in the proceedings or the submissions made to the court may indicate which of the decisions has been made[8].
(e) A mortgagee is not to be deprived of a contractual or equitable right to add costs to the security merely by reason of an order for payment of costs made without reference to the mortgagee's contractual or equitable rights and without any adjudication as to whether or not the mortgagee should be deprived of those costs.

1 CPR 48PD, para 50.2.
2 CPR 48PD, para 50.4(1). The court may direct that a party file an account: CPR 25.1.(1)(n).
3 CPR 48PD, para 50.4(2).
4 CPR 48PD, para 50.4(3).
5 CPR 48.3(1).
6 CPR 48PD, para. 50.3. As to the mortgagee's contractual entitlement to costs, see also *Gomba Holdings (UK) Ltd v Minories Finance Ltd (No 2)* [1993] Ch 171, [1992] 4 All ER 588.
7 Supreme Court Act 1981, s 51.
8 CPR 48PD, para. 50.3.

Chapter 18

The appointment of a receiver[1]

Reasons for appointing a receiver

18.1 The appointment of a receiver is a means by which the mortgagee can ensure that the mortgaged property is efficiently managed and that the net rents and profits are paid first towards the interest due under the mortgage. A receiver may be appointed by a mortgagee out of court under an express or statutory power[2], or by the court itself[3]. The advantage for the mortgagee of appointing a receiver, rather than taking possession, is that the mortgagee will not be liable to account on the basis of wilful default, since the receiver is not normally the agent of the mortgagee[4]. The converse disadvantage is that a mortgagee who has appointed a receiver cannot obtain title to the land by limitation, unlike a mortgagee in possession[5].

1 This chapter only covers particular aspects of receivership. On receivership generally see: *Picarda on The Law Relating to Receivers, Managers and Administrators; Lightman & Moss on The Law of Receivers and Administrators of Companies* and *Kerr on Receivers and Administrators;* 39(2) *Halsbury's Laws* (Receivers). On the appointment of a receiver in relation to the Law Commission's proposed land mortgage and protected land mortgage, see Law Commission Report *Transfer of Land – Land Mortgage* 1991 (Law Com no 204, paras 7.39–7.46).

2 See **18.2** ff.

3 See **18.16** ff.

4 Where the receiver is appointed under the statutory or an express power, he is deemed to be the agent of the mortgagor; where the receiver is appointed by the court, he acts as an officer of the court: see **18.8** and **18.25**. As to the liability of a mortgagee in possession, see **14.65** ff.

5 See *Re Hale, Lilley v Foad* [1899] 2 Ch 107, CA, and **19.85**.

THE APPOINTMENT OF A RECEIVER BY THE MORTGAGEE

ADVANTAGE OF APPOINTING RECEIVER OUT OF COURT

18.2 Where a mortgagee has the power to appoint a receiver himself, under an express or the statutory power, he will usually prefer to take that course, rather than seeking an appointment by the court. Appointing a receiver out of court will normally be a faster and less expensive process, and the mortgagee will also have more control over the choice of the receiver and the scope of his duties.

An appointment by the court will generally only be sought where the express or statutory power is for some reason not exercisable.

EXPRESS AND STATUTORY POWERS OF APPOINTMENT

Historical origin[1]

18.3 As a result of the harsh liabilities imposed upon a mortgagee in possession, mortgagees sought to obtain the advantages of possession without its drawbacks, an aim with which the courts were generally sympathetic. Mortgagees began to insist upon the mortgagor appointing a receiver at the time of the mortgage and as part of the security to receive the income, keep down the interest on incumbrances and hold the surplus, if any, for the mortgagor. In due course, mortgagees started to stipulate by the terms of the mortgage that they should themselves have power to appoint the receiver, but that he should nevertheless be the agent of the mortgagor. Whilst the forms of appointment of receivers and their powers of management gradually became more extensive, in form, if not in substance, the receiver continued to be deemed agent of the mortgagor[2]. The practice of appointing receivers by agreement between the parties became so common that a statutory power to the mortgagee to appoint a receiver to be agent of the mortgagor was introduced, first, to a limited extent by Lord Cranworth's Act[3], and later more generally by the Conveyancing Act 1881[4] and now the Law of Property Act 1925[5]. In each case the power could be excluded by agreement.

1 See generally *Gaskell v Gosling* [1896] 1 QB 669 at 691–692; *Medforth v Blake* [2000] Ch 86 at 93–94.
2 *Jefferys v Dickson* (1866) 1 Ch App 183 at 190 per Lord Cranworth.
3 The Trustees, Mortgagees, etc, Powers Act 1860, 23 & 24 Vict c 145, ss 11–30.
4 Sections 19 (1) (iii), 20 and 24.
5 Section 101(1)(iii).

The statutory power

18.4 Section 101(1)(iii) of the Law of Property Act 1925 provides a mortgagee[1] with the power to appoint a receiver of the income of the mortgaged property, or any part thereof, provided that the mortgage was made by deed and the mortgage money has become due, to the same extent as if it had been conferred by the mortgage deed[2]. If the mortgaged property consists of an interest in income, or of a rentcharge or an annual or other periodical sum, the mortgagee has the like power to appoint a receiver of that property or any part thereof[3]. Since the statutory power is to appoint a receiver of the income of the mortgaged property[4], the receiver has no power of sale unless the statutory power is extended[5]. The provisions of the statutory power may be varied or extended by the mortgage deed[6] and, as so varied or extended, will, as far as may be, operate as if the variations or extensions were contained in the Act[7]. The section applies only if and as far as a contrary intention is not expressed in the mortgage deed and has effect subject to the terms and provisions of that deed[8]. An equitable mortgagee was always entitled to seek the appointment of a receiver by the court in a proper case[9], and he is now entitled to appoint a receiver under the statutory power where his mortgage is by deed.

1 Including a chargee by way of legal mortgage and a person from time to time deriving title under the original mortgagee: s 205 (1) (xvi).
2 For consideration of when the mortgage money becomes due, see **17.6**, see also **3.23** and **3.25**.
3 Law of Property Act 1925, s 101(1)(iii).
4 *Re Manchester and Milford Rly Co* (1880) 14 Ch D 645 at 653; *Marshall v Cottingham* [1982] Ch 82, [1981] 3 All ER 8. On the limited powers of a receiver to manage the property, see *Marshall v Cottingham* and *North City Developments, ex p Walker* (1990) 20 NSWLR 286. On the 'company doctor' role of the receiver, see *Duffy v Super Centre Development Corpn Ltd* (1967) 1 NSWLR 382.
5 In which case the power of sale is an express power, rather than an extension of the statutory power: *Phoenix Properties v Wimpole Street Nominees* [1992] BCLC 737. For an implied power of sale, see *Re JB Davies Enterprises Pty Ltd (In Liq)* [1990] 2 Qd R 129.
6 For express powers of appointment, see 28 *Forms and Precedents* (5th edn, 1999 reissue) Mortgages and the Appendix. The statutory power may be so varied that it is for all practical purposes, for instance as to construction, an express power: *Isherwood v Butler Pollnow Pty Ltd* (1986) 6 NSWLR 363. For an example of a substantial extension of the statutory powers, see *Re Kentish Homes Ltd* [1993] BCC 212 at 219.
7 Section 101 (3).
8 Section 101 (4).
9 See **18.16**.

When the power is exercisable

18.5 The mortgagee is entitled to appoint a receiver under the statutory power when he is entitled to exercise the statutory power of sale[1], that is when:

(a) notice requiring payment of the mortgage money has been served on the mortgagor[2], or one of two or mortgagors and default has been made in payment of the mortgage money, or of part thereof, for three months after such service; or
(b) some interest under the mortgage is in arrear and unpaid for two months after becoming due; or
(c) there has been a breach of some provision contained in the mortgage deed or the Act, which should have been observed or performed by the mortgagor or some other person who concurred in making the mortgage, other than a covenant for payment of the mortgage money or interest thereon[3].

Where the mortgage debt is repayable on demand[4], the debtor must be given a reasonable time following the demand to implement the mechanics of payment[5]. However, the mortgage deed will very often provide for the power to be exercisable whether or not those conditions are fulfilled. A person paying money to a receiver need not inquire whether the power to appoint a receiver had become exercisable[6]. In the case of a registered charge, the mortgagee cannot exercise the statutory power to appoint a receiver until the charge has been registered or, in the case of an assignment, he is registered as proprietor[7]. The fact that the mortgagee has taken possession does not prevent him form appointing a receiver[8]. The appointment of a receiver does not prevent the mortgagee bringing a claim on the personal covenant[9]. Where the mortgagee is relying on an express power to appoint a receiver, or upon an express variation of the statutory power, he may exercise the power upon the events specified in the mortgage deed. Where there were a number of express provisions in a mortgage deed designed to protect the mortgagee's security, a term could not be implied that the mortgagees would have the right to appoint a receiver if their security was in jeopardy[10]. An appointment will be valid if although it was made on an incorrect ground, the power was in fact exercisable on another basis[11]. The right to appoint a receiver may be waived[12].

1 Section 109(1).
2 It need not be served on later mortgagees: *Manton v Parabolic Pty Ltd* [1985] 2 NSWLR 361.
3 Section 103 (see further **20.12**). As to interest being in arrear when the mortgagee is in possession, and has received rents to an amount sufficient to keep down the interest, he cannot be allowed to say that interest is in arrear: see *Wrigley v Gill* [1906] 1 Ch 165 at 172, CA.
4 A demand prior to the appointment of receiver is not necessary, unless the mortgage deed requires one: *Cripps (Pharmaceuticals) Ltd v Wickenden* [1973] 2 All ER 606, [1973] 1 WLR 944; cf *Windsor Refrigeration Co Ltd v Branch Nominees Ltd* [1961] Ch 375, [1961] 1 All ER 277, CA.
5 *Bank of Baroda v Panessar* [1987] Ch 335, [1986] 3 All ER 751; *Cripps (Pharmaceuticals) Ltd v Wickenden* above; *Williams and Glyn's Bank Ltd v Barnes* [1981] Com LR 205; cf *Shamji v Johnson Matthey Bankers Ltd* [1986] BCLC 278. For the different approaches taken in Commonwealth jurisdictions see: *Ronald Elwyn Lister Ltd v Dunlop Canada Ltd* [1982] 1 SCR 726, (1982) 135 DLR (3d) 1, SCC; *Bunbury Foods Pty Ltd v National Bank of Australasia Ltd* (1984) 153 CLR 491, 51 ALR 609; *ANZ Banking Group (NZ) Ltd v Gibson* [1986] 1 NZLR 556; *Whonnock Industries Ltd v National Bank of Canada* (1987) 42 DLR (4th) 1; *Housing Corpn of New Zealand v Maoi Trustee (No 2)* [1988] 2 NZLR 708; *Bond v Hong Kong Bank of Australia Ltd* (1991) 25 NSWLR 286; *Royal Bank of Canada v W Got & Associates Electric* (1999) 178 DLR (4th) 385; *Australia and New Zealand Banking Group v Pan Foods Co Importers and Distributors* [1999] 1 VR 29. See also Lingard *Bank Security Documents*, (3rd edn) pp 7-10; (1986) 1 Banking & Finance Law Review 1 (Marantz). An appointment is not invalid merely because an incorrect sum is specified in a prior demand: *NRG Vision v Chesterfield Leasing Ltd* [1988] BCLC 624. See further **17.6** (including the form and service of a demand).
6 Section 109(4).
7 *Lever Finance Ltd v Needleman's Trustee* [1956] Ch 375. Similarly an assignee of a debenture cannot appoint a receiver until the assignment is completed: *Harris & Lewin (in liquidation) v Harris & Lewin (Agents)*(1975) ACLC 28, 279. See also the Companies Act 1985, s 396 as to the requirements to register charges created by a company.
8 *Refuge Assurance Co Ltd v Perlberg* [1938] Ch 687, [1938] 3 All ER 231, CA; (1989) 5 Banking Law Bulletin (Sutherland); (1989) 4 BLB 77 (Powers).
9 *Lynde v Waithman* [1895] 2 QB 180; see **16.1** and **17.7**.
10 *Cryne v Barclays Bank plc* [1987] BCLC 548. See also *McMahon v State Bank of New South Wales* (1990) 8 ACLC 315; *Canberra Advance Bank Ltd v Benny* (1992) 9 ACSR 179, Fed Ct.
11 *Byblos Bank SAL v Al-Khudhairy* [1987] BCLC 232; *Retail Equity Pty Ltd v Custom Credit Corpn Ltd* (1991) 9 ACLC 404; *Canberra Advance Bank Ltd v Benny* (1992) 9 ACSR 179, Fed Ct. On estoppel of the borrower from objecting to the appointment of a receiver, see *Bank of Baroda v Panessar* [1987] Ch 335.
12 *Butler Pollnow Pty Ltd v Garden Mews St Leonards Pty Ltd* (1988) 13 ACLR 656; *Canberra Advance Bank Ltd v Berry* (1992) 9 ACLR 179; cf *NRG Vision Ltd v Churchfield Leasing Ltd* [1988] BCLR 624.

No duty of care owed in deciding whether to appoint receiver

18.6 A mortgagee is given the power to appoint a receiver to protect his own interests. Thus, once the power to appoint a receiver is exercisable, in deciding whether to exercise that right the mortgagee owes no duty of care to the mortgagor, nor to guarantors or other creditors, and his decision to exercise it cannot be challenged except on grounds of bad faith[1]. A mortgagee who appoints a receiver knowing the receiver intends to exercise his powers for improper purposes, or who fails to revoke the receiver's appointment when he knows the receiver is acting improperly, may himself be in breach of his duty of good faith[2]. A mortgagee who appoints a receiver when he has no right to do so will risk being found liable for damages for breach of contract[3].

1 *Re Potters Oils (No 2)* [1986] 1 All ER 890, sub nom *Re Potters Oils Ltd* [1986] 1 WLR 201; and see *Shamji v Johnson Matthey Bankers Ltd* [1986] BCLC 278. A debenture holder owes a company no duty of care in exercising his rights to appoint a receiver: *Williams and Glynn's Bank Ltd v Barnes* [1981] Com LR 205; *Downsville Nominees Ltd v First City Corpn Ltd* [1993] AC 295 at 312, [1993] 3 All ER 626 at 635.
2 *Downsview Nominees Ltd v First City Corpn Ltd* [1993] AC 295.
3 *Cryne v Barclays Bank plc* [1987] BCLC 548.

APPOINTMENT OF A RECEIVER[1]

18.7 When the statutory power is exercisable, the mortgagee may appoint, in writing, such person as he thinks fit to be receiver[2]. The mortgagee may, in writing, from time to time remove the receiver, or appoint a new receiver[3]. The mortgagee may choose to exclude certain of the mortgaged property from the scope of the receiver's appointment[4]. Unless the mortgage contains an indication of a contrary intention, the mortgagee will be entitled to appoint more than one person as receiver[5]. The appointment takes effect once the written appointment has been given to the receiver and he has accepted the appointment[6]. Acceptance may be inferred from the actions of the receiver[7]. Where a receiver is appointed over the property of a company, under powers contained in an instrument, it is of no effect unless it is accepted by the receiver before the end of the business day next following that on which the instrument of appointment is received by him or on his behalf and, subject to that, is deemed to be made at the time at which the instrument of appointment is received[8]. A person appointing a receiver of a company's property must within seven days of the appointment give notice of the fact to the registrar of companies[9]. Where an administrative receiver[10] is appointed, the receiver must forthwith send to the company notice of his appointment in the prescribed form[11]. Where there are two or more mortgagees, and each wishes to appoint a receiver, their right to do so will depend on the construction of their respective instruments of charge and on questions of priority between them; the court may resolve such a dispute by appointing a receiver itself[12].

The mortgagee may owe a duty in the manner in which he exercises the right, for instance to take reasonable care not to appoint an incompetent[13]. Subject to that, there are, in general, few restrictions on who may be appointed as receiver[14]. A body corporate may not be a receiver of the property of a company[15]; where a corporation is appointed as receiver, the appointment is void[16] and the corporation is liable to a fine[17]. If an undischarged bankrupt acts as receiver of the property of a company on behalf of debenture holders, he is liable to imprisonment or a fine[18].

The validity of the acts of the receiver depend upon the validity of his appointment, so that if it is invalid he will be at risk against the mortgagor, the mortgagor's trustee in bankruptcy or liquidator, as appropriate, and other interested parties, such as other mortgagees. Thus, it is very much in the receiver's interests to check carefully that the power to appoint him as receiver has arisen[19]. However, where the appointment of a person as the receiver or manager of a company's property under the powers contained in an instrument is discovered to be invalid (whether by virtue of the invalidity of the instrument or otherwise), the court may order the person by whom or on whose behalf the appointment was made to indemnify the person appointed against any liability which arises solely by reason of the invalidity of the appointment[20].

1 For forms, see 28 *Forms and Precedents* (5th edn, 1999 reissue) Mortgages.

2 Law of Property Act 1925, s 109(1). There may be contractual requirements as to the form and method of appointment, which must be strictly observed: *Wright's Hardware Pty Ltd v Evans* (1988) 13 ACLR 631. Whether a receiver of a company is appointed under seal will affect his powers to execute deeds on behalf of the company: *Phoenix Properties Ltd v Wimpole Street Nominees Ltd* [1992] BCLC 737; in the case of an administrative receiver, see Insolvency Act 1986, s 42. On the appointment of a receiver by a negative pledge lender, see [1991] 10 JBL 405.

3 Law of Property Act 1925, s 109(5). There are restrictions on the removal and replacement of an administrative receiver: Insolvency Act 1986, s 45.

4 See eg *Re Griffin Hotel Co Ltd* [1941] Ch 129.

5 Law of Property Act 1925, s 61(c); *Wrights Hardware Pty Ltd v Evans* (1988) 13 ACLR 631; *NEC Information Systems Australia Pty Ltd v Lockhart* (1991) 9 ACLC 658; *Gwembe Valley Development Co Ltd v Koshy (No 2)* [2000] 2 BCLC 705 (which also considers whether such receivers may act severally as well as jointly). See also *Kendle v Melsom* [1998] 193 CLR 46. Where dual or multiple appointments are provided for, the terms of the appontment must be strictly observed: *Wrights Hardware Pty Ltd v Evans* (above); *NEC Information Systems Australia Pty Ltd v Lockhart* (1991) 22 NSWLR 518.

6 *Windsor Refrigerator Co Ltd v Branch Nominees Ltd* [1961] Ch 375, [1961] 1 All ER 277, CA.

7 *Cripps (Pharmaceuticals) Ltd v Wickenden* [1973] 2 All ER 606, [1973] 1 WLR 944; *Re Gabriel Control Pty Ltd* (1982) 6 ACLR 684.

8 Insolvency Act 1986, s 33 (1). Those provisions apply to the appointment of joint receivers: s 33 (2).

9 Companies Act 1985, s 405.

10 See **18.12**.

11 See generally Insolvency Act 1986, s 46. For notice of the appointment which must be given to the registrar of companies by the appointor, see Companies Act 1985, s 405. For notification of the appointment in the company's documents, see Insolvency Act 1986, s 39.

12 *Gwembe Valley Development Co Ltd v Koshy (No 2)* [2000] 2 BCLC 705; *Bass Breweries Ltd v Delaney* [1994] BCC 851.

13 *Shamji v Johnson Matthey Bankers Ltd* [1991] BCLC 36 at 42.

14 Only an insolvency practitioner may be appointed as an administrative receiver: see Insolvency Act 1986, ss 230, 389, 390,. For the recommendations of the Law Commission as to the qualifications of receivers, and receives in general, see *Transfer of Land – Land Mortgages* 1991 (Law Com no 204, para 7.39–7.47).

15 Insolvency Act 1986, s 30, replacing Companies Act 1985, s 489.

16 *Portman Building Society v Gallwey* [1955] 1 All ER 227, [1955] 1 WLR 96.

17 Insolvency Act 1986, s 30.

18 Insolvency Act 1986, s 31. That does not apply to a court-appointed receiver.

19 The validity of the mortgage by which the power to appoint a receiver is given requires attention as well as the appointment itself; if the mortgage is invalid, the appointment is necessarily so. For the consequences of an invalid charge, see: *Burston Finance v Speirway* [1974] 3 All ER 735, [1974] 1 WLR 1648 at 1657; *Food & Carter Ltd v Midland Bank Ltd* (1979) 129 NLJ 543; *Rolled Steel Products (Holdings) Ltd v British Steel Corpn* [1986] Ch 246, [1985] 3 All ER 52, CA; and **12.7** ff. See generally Lingard *Bank Security Documents* Ch 3 and p 132. For the effect of the forfeiture of mortgaged leasehold premises, see *Official Custodian for Charities v Mackay (No 2)* [1985] 2 All ER 1016, [1985] 1 WLR 1308. For the right of a receiver appointed under an invalid mortgage for reasonable remuneration for acts done for the benefit of the company, see *Monks v Poynice Pty Ltd* (1987) 8 NSWLR 662; *Moodmere Pty Ltd (In Liq) v Waters* [1988] VR 215.

20 Insolvency Act 1986, s 34. See also *Re B Johnson & Co (Builders) Ltd* [1955] Ch 634 at 647–648.

Receiver is agent of the mortgagor

18.8 Section 109(2) of the Law of Property Act 1925 provides that a receiver appointed under the statutory power is deemed to be agent of the mortgagor[1], and the mortgagor is solely responsible for the receiver's acts or defaults unless the mortgage deed otherwise provides[2]. An administrative receiver[3] of a company is deemed to be the agent of the company unless and until the company goes into liquidation[4]. A receiver appointed under an express power is generally expressed to be, or expressly deemed to be, the agent of the mortgagor by the terms of the power[5]. The mortgagor will thus be liable for the receiver's acts and defaults[6]. However, if the receiver appointed under an express power and is not expressed to be the agent of the mortgagor, he will be the agent of the mortgagee and the mortgagee will be responsible for his acts, defaults and remuneration[7]. The receiver will not be deemed to be the mortgagor's agent if the mortgagee represents otherwise, or directs or interferes with his actions[8].

The agency of the receiver for the mortgagor has been expressed to be a real one[9], but it is nevertheless of an unusual, special and limited nature[10]. The relationship set up by the appointment of a receiver is tripartite, involving the receiver, mortgagor and mortgagee[11]. This is apparent from the nature of the duties owed by a receiver[12]. Although nominally the agent of the mortgagor, his primary duty is to realise the assets of the mortgagor in the interests of the mortgagee[13]. In practical terms the receiver has a close association with the mortgagee and the mortgagor cannot instruct the receiver how to act in the conduct of the receivership[14]. Since a receiver acts as agent for the mortgagor, where a receiver as agent for a company causes the company to breach its contract with a third party, the receiver will not be liable for the tort of inducing or procuring a breach of contract[15].

Where the mortgagor has granted a tenancy of the mortgaged property which is not binding on the mortgagee, if the tenant pays rent to the receiver that will not create a tenancy binding on the mortgagee, since the receiver is deemed the agent of the mortgagor[16]. However, a tenancy binding on the mortgagee was created where both mortgagee and receiver 'remained in blissful ignorance of the effect of s 109(2)' and thus both believed the receiver was collecting rent on behalf of the mortgagee[17]. If a receiver is the agent of the mortgagee, the demand and receipt of rent by him may amount to the recognition of a tenancy not otherwise binding on the mortgagee, or the creation of a new tenancy[18].

The receiver ceases to be the agent of a mortgagor company upon that company being wound up, but the receiver does not thereupon automatically become the agent of the mortgagee[19] and the liquidation does not affect the receiver's power to hold and dispose of the company's property comprised in the mortgage[20]. A receiver who was originally appointed by the mortgagee, but is subsequently appointed by the court, ceases to be agent of the mortgagor[21]. Where a mortgagee takes possession after the appointment of a receiver, the receiver thereupon becomes agent of the mortgagee[22].

1 Including any person from time to time deriving title under the original mortgagor, or entitled to redeem the mortgage: s 205 (1) (xvi). See also *Re London Iron and Steel Co Ltd* [1990] BCLC 372; *Welsh Development Agency v Export Finance Co Ltd* [1992] BCLC 148, CA. As to the position of a receiver under the statute, see *White v Metcalf* [1903] 2 Ch 567. For the receiver's position on a sale, see **20.9** and **20.22**, n 2. For the position of a receiver appointed by the court, see **18.25**.

2 See *Hibernian Bank v Yourell (No 2)* [1919] 1 IR 310 (statute barred debts paid by receiver); *Portman Building Society v Gallway* [1955] 1 All ER 227, [1955] 1 WLR 96. As to sale, see **20.9** and **20.22**, n 2, but the receiver must account to the mortgagee: *Leicester Permanent Building Society v Butt* [1943] Ch 308, [1943] 2 All ER 523. As to the date from which a receiver appointed by a second mortgagee must account to a receiver subsequently appointed by a first mortgagee, see *Re Belbridge Property Trust Ltd, Swale Estates Ltd v Belbridge Property Trust Ltd* [1941] Ch 304, [1941] 2 All ER 48.

3 An administrative receiver under the Insolvency Act 1986 means (a) a receiver or manager of the whole (or substantially the whole) of a company's property appointed by or on behalf of the holders of any debentures of the company secured by a charge which, as created, was a floating charge, or by such a charge and one or more other securities; on (b) a person who would be such a receiver or manager but for the appointment of some other person as the receiver of part of the company's property: Insolvency Act 1986, s 29

(2). On the nature of the powers of an administrative receiver see *Re Atlantic Computer Systems plc* [1992] Ch 505, [1992] 1 All ER 476, CA.

4 Insolvency Act 1986, s 44 (1) (a). See also *Thomas v Todd* [1926] 2 KB 511.

5 For form, see 28 *Forms and Precedents* (5th edn, 1999 reissue) Mortgages and see generally (1981) 44 MLR 658 (Milman); *Gaskell v Gosling* [1896] 1 QB 669 at 692, CA; *Re Johnson & Co (Builders) Ltd* [1955] Ch 634, [1955] 2 All ER 775, CA; *Standard Chartered Bank Ltd v Walker* [1982] 3 All ER 938, [1982] 1 WLR 1410, CA; *American Express International Banking Corpn v Hurley* [1985] 3 All ER 564; *Visbord v Federal Comr of Taxation* (1943) 68 CLR 354; *Expo International Pty Ltd v Chant* [1979] 2 NSWLR 820, and see Law Commission Working Paper no 99, Land Mortgages, para 3.49.

6 See *Cully v Parsons* [1923] 2 Ch 512; *George Barker (Transport) Ltd v Enyon* [1974] 1 All ER 900, [1974] 1 WLR 462;

7 *Re Vimbos Ltd* [1900] 1 Ch 470; *Robinson Printing Co Ltd v Chic Ltd* [1905] 2 Ch 123; *Deyes v Wood* [1911] 1 KB 806, CA; *American Express International Banking Corpn v Hurley* [1985] 3 All ER 564; *Circuit Systems Ltd v Zuken-Redac (UK) Ltd* [1997] 1 WLR 721 at 739. Subject to the provision as to an administrative receiver mentioned above.

8 *Chatsworth Properties Ltd v Effiom* [1971] 1 All ER 604, [1971] 1 WLR 144; *American Express International Banking Co v Hurley* [1985] 3 All ER 564 at 571; see also *Nijar v Mann* (1998) 32 HLR 223.

9 *Ratford v Northavon District Council* [1987] QB 357, [1986] 3 All ER 193, CA; see also *Brown v City of London Corpn* [1996] 1 WLR 1070.

10 See *Gomba Holdings UK Ltd v Minories Finance Ltd* [1988] 1 WLR 1231, [1989] 1 All ER 261, CA; *Telematrix plc v Modern Engineers of Bristol* [1985] 1 BCC 99, 417 at 99, 420; *Expo International Pty Ltd v Chant* [1979] 2 NSWLR 820. For instance, the receiver is appointed whether the mortgagor likes it or not and cannot be dismissed by his principal: *Gomba Holdings UK Ltd v Minories Finance Ltd* (at 1233); *Telematrix plc v Modern Engineers of Bristol* (above) at 99, 420; and the mortgagor's death does not revoke the power to appoint a receiver: *Re Hale* [1899] 2 Ch 107 at 117, CA. For the duty of the receiver of a company to provide accounts or other information to the company, see *Re B Johnson & Co (Builders) Ltd* [1955] Ch 634 at 644-645; *Smiths Ltd v Middleton* [1979] 3 All ER 842; *Gomba Holdings UK Ltd v Homan* [1986] 3 All ER 94, [1986] 1 WLR 1301.

11 *Gomba Holdings UK Ltd v Minories Finance Ltd* [1988] 1 WLR 1231 at 1233.

12 See **18.9**.

13 *Lathia v Dronsfield Bros Ltd* [1987] BCLC 321; *Gomba Holdings UK Ltd v Minories Finance Ltd* [1988] 1 WLR 1231 at 1233; *Shamji v Johnson Matthey Bankers Ltd* [1991] BCLC 36, CA; *Downsview Nominees Ltd v First City Corpn Ltd* [1993] AC 295.

14 *Gomba Holdings UK Ltd v Minories Finance Ltd* (above) at 1233.

15 *Lathia v Dronsfield* [1987] BCLC 321; *Welsh Development Agency v Export Finance* [1992] BCC 270, CA. Cf the position where the receiver is appointed by the court: *Telematrix plc v Modern Engineers of Bristol* (1985) 1 BCC 99,417.

16 *Nijar v Mann* (1998) 32 HLR 223; see **19.27**.

17 *Nijar v Mann* (above) at 232, per Ward LJ, who also noted (at 228): 'I confess, with hardly a tinge of shame, that until I read the papers in this case I was also one of that merry ignorant band. So, I assume, was the judge."

18 See *Lever Finance Co Ltd v Needleman's Property Trustee* [1956] Ch 375, [1956] 2 All ER 378; *Chatsworth Properties Ltd v Effiom* [1971] 1 All ER 604, [1971] 1 WLR 144, CA; *Baring Bros & Co Ltd v Hovermarine Ltd* (1971) 219 Estates Gazette 1459; and see (1976) 120 SJ 496 (Markson); *Commonwealth Bank of Australia v Baranyay* [1993] 1 VR 589. On the circumstances in which a tenancy may become binding on the mortgagee, see further **19.19** ff.

19 *Gosling v Gaskell* [1897] AC 575 at 591, HL; *Thomas v Todd* [1926] 2 KB 511 at 516; *Goughs Garages Ltd v Puglsey* [1930] 1 KB 615; *Expo International Pty Ltd v Chant* [1979] 2 NSWLR 820; *Mercantile Credits Ltd v Atkins (No 1)* (1985) 9 ACLR 757, (1985) 1 NSWLR 670; affd (1985) 10 ACLR 153; *Moodmere Pty Ltd (In Liq) v Waters* [1988] VR 215. If he continues to act, he does so as principal, in a position similar to a receiver appointed by the court, until and unless the mortgagee acts such as to constitute him his agent: Meagher, Gummow and Lehane *Equity: Doctrines and Remedies* (3rd edn) p 2842; *American Express International Banking Corpn v Hurley* [1985] 3 All ER 564. In the case of an administrative receiver, see Insolvency Act 1986, s 44(1)(a).

20 *Sowman v David Samuel Trust Ltd* [1978] 1 All ER 616, [1978] 1 WLR 22; *Re Leslie Homes (Aust) Pty Ld* (1984) 8 ACLR 1020; *Mercantile Credits Ltd v Atkins* (1985) 1 NSWLR 670; affd (1985) 10 ACLR 153.

21 *Hand v Blow* [1901] 2 Ch 721 at 732, CA. Cf *Lever Finance Co Ltd v Needleman's Property Trustee* above.

22 *North American Trust Co v Consumer Gas Co* (1997) 147 DLR (4th) 645.

DUTIES OWED BY RECEIVER

18.9 The power to appoint a receiver is given to the mortgagee as a means of securing the repayment of his debt. Thus, the primary duty of the receiver is to the mortgagee who appointed him, not to the mortgagor[1], and he can exercise his powers even though they may be disadvantageous to the latter[2]. However, the mortgage is simply security for the repayment of that debt and the performance of the mortgagor's other obligations. Thus, a receiver appointed by the mortgagee must exercise his powers in good faith and for the purposes of obtaining repayment of the debt owed to the mortgagee[3]. While the receiver owes no general common law duty of care to the mortgagor or subsequent incumbrancers[4], he is under duties imposed by equity to ensure that, whilst discharging his duties to manage the property, he deals fairly and equitably with the mortgagor and others interested in the equity of redemption, and takes account of their interests[5]. The extent and scope of his duties are not inflexible; what he must do to discharge them depends on the particular facts of the case[6]. In exercising his powers of management his primary duty is to try and bring about a situation in which interest on the secured debt can be paid and the debt itself is repaid. Subject to that primary duty, the receiver owes a duty to manage the property with due diligence. While due diligence does not oblige the receiver to carry on a business previously carried on the mortgaged premises by the mortgagor, if he does so he should take reasonable steps in order to try to do so profitably[7]. Likewise, a receiver is under no duty to exercise a power of sale[8], but if he does exercise it he owes the same specific duties as the mortgagee, in particular to obtain the best price reasonably obtainable[9]. Thus a receiver may not purchase the property of which he is receiver without the leave of the court[10]. The receiver is more than a mere rent-collector: he is under a duty to act so as to safeguard the value of the mortgaged property, for instance by serving rent review notices at the required time[11]. Where appropriate, a receiver should seek specialist advice[12]. An administrative receiver is under a number of specific statutory duties[13].

1 *Downsview Nominees Ltd v First City Corpn Ltd* [1993] AC 295 at 313–315. See also *Gomba Holdings UK Ltd v Minories Finance Ltd* [1989] 1 All ER 261, [1988] 1 WLR 1231.

2 *Downsview Nominees Ltd v First City Corpn Ltd* (above) at 312; see also *China and South Sea Bank v Tan Soon Gin* [1990] 1 AC 536.

3 *Downsview Nominees Ltd v First City Corpn Ltd* (above) at 312; *Medforth v Blake* [2000] Ch 86 at 98, 102; *Bank of New Zealand v Essington* (1990) 9 ACLC 1039. See also *Quennell v Maltby* [1979] 1 All ER 568, [1979] 1 WLR 318; *Yorkshire Bank plc v Hall* [1999] 1 WLR 1713 at 1728. Only conduct which is dishonest or otherwise tainted by bad faith will amount to a breach of the receiver's duty of good faith: *Medforth v Blake* (above) at 103; on the meaning of dishonesty, see also *Royal Brunei Airlines v Tan* [1995] 2 AC 378; *BCCI v Akindele* [2001] Ch 437, CA; on the meaning of good faith see also *Mogridge v Clapp* [1892] 3 Ch 382.

4 *Downsview Nominees Ltd v First City Corpn Ltd.* [1993] AC 295 at 315. Cf *Pollnow v Garden Mews St Leonards Pty Ltd* (1985) 9 ACLR 82. See also *Medforth v Blake* (above) at 102, per Scott V-C: 'I do not ... think it matters one jot whether the duty is expressed as a common law duty or as a duty in equity. The result is the same. The origin of the receiver's duty, like the mortgagee's duty, lies in equity, and we may as well continue to refer to it as a duty in equity'; [2000] Camb LJ 31 at 33 (Sealy). The nature of the duty does, however, affect the ability to exclude or limit a receiver's duty, since the Unfair Contract Terms Act 1977 will have no application: *Raja v Lloyds TSB Bank Ltd* [2001] EWCA CIV 210 82 P & CR 191; cf [2000] 63 MLR 413 (Frisby). Clauses attempting to limit liability will be strictly construed: see *Bishop v Bonham* [1988] 1 WLR 742; see also [1975] JBL 23 (Farrar); *Expo International Pty Ltd v Chant* [1979] 2 NSWLR 820 and **20.22**.

5 *Medforth v Blake* (above) at 101; (2000) 63 MLR 413 (Frisby); see also *Palk v Mortgage*

Services Funding plc [1993] Ch 330 at 337-338. Those interested in the equity of redemption include subsequent mortgagees: *Midland Bank Ltd v Joliman Finance Ltd* (1967) 203 Estates Gazette 1039; *Alliance Acceptance Co Ltd v Graham* (1975) 10 SASR 220; and guarantors of the debt: *ENT Pty Ltd v McVeigh* (1996) 6 Tas R 202. (Cf *Standard Chartered Bank v Walker* [1982] 3 All ER 938, [1982] 1 WLR 1410 and *American Express International Banking v Hurley* [1985] 3 All ER 564, where the duty to guarantors was put on the basis of a duty of care. See also *Canadian Imperial Bank of Commerce v Haley* (1979) 100 DLR (3d) 470). A receiver only owes his duties in equity to those interested in the equity of redemption, thus, he owes no duty to a director, shareholder, employee or guarantors of unsecured debt of the mortgagor company: *Burgess v Auger* [1998] 2 BCLC 478 (see also *Watts v Midland Bank plc* [1986] BCLC 15); nor to unsecured creditors: *Northern Developments (Holdings) Ltd v UDT Securities* [1977] 1 WLR 1230; *Lathia v Dronsfield Bros Ltd* [1987] BCLC 321 at 324 *Standard Chartered Bank Ltd v Walker* [1982] 1 WLR 1410 at 1415, 1416, at CA; (cf *Expo International Pty Ltd v Chant* [1979] 2 NSWLR 820; nor to beneficiaries under a trust of the mortgaged property: *Parker Tweedale v Dunbar Bank plc* [1991] Ch 12.

6 *Medforth v Blake* (above) at 102.

7 *Medforth v Blake* (above) at 102.

8 *Routestone Ltd v Minories Finance Ltd* [1997] BCC 180 at 187G.

9 *Downsview Nominees Ltd v First City Corpn Ltd* (above) at 315; *Medforth v Blake* (above) at 98, 99. See eg *American Express International Banking Corpn v Hurley* [1985] 3 All ER 564 (sale of specialist equipment; receiver failing to obtain advice, or to properly advertise sale). As to the duties owed by a mortgagee when exercising his power of sale, see further **20.22**.

10 *Nugent v Nugent* [1908] 1 Ch 546 (sale by mortgagee out of court); *Watts v Midland Bank plc* [1986] BCLC 15 (receiver may not sell to a solicitor acting for it). The same applies where the receiver is acting as agent of the mortgagee: *Martinson v Clowes* (1882) 21 Ch D 857; affd (1885) 52 LT 706, CA; *Hodson v Deans* [1903] 2 Ch 647.

11 *Knight v Lawrence* [1993] BCLC 215, cited with approval (save as to the duty lying in equity, rather than at common law) in *Medforth v Blake* (above) at 99–100. See also [1992] Conv 161 (Adams).

12 *American Express International Banking Corpn v Hurley* [1985] 3 All ER 564 (sale of unusual equipment)

13 See eg Insolvency Act 1986, s 47 (statement of affairs to be submitted); Insolvency Act 1986, s 48 (compiling of report); Insolvency Rules 1986, r 3.32 (abstract of receipts and payments).

POWERS OF RECEIVER

Receiver appointed under the statutory power

18.10 A receiver appointed under the statutory power has the power to demand and recover all the income of which he is appointed receiver, by bringing proceedings, by distress or otherwise[1]. He may do so in the name of either the mortgagor or the mortgagee[2], and to the full extent of the estate or interest which the mortgagor could dispose of. He may give effectual receipts for such income[3]. He can also exercise any powers delegated to him by the mortgagee under the Law of Property Act 1925, such as the powers of leasing or accepting surrenders[4]. Where those powers of leasing have not been delegated, he is not entitled to grant leases without the sanction of the court[5]. The receiver must, if directed in writing by the mortgagee, insure any mortgaged property of an insurable nature to the extent to which the mortgagee might have insured it against loss or damage by fire, out of the money received by him[6]. The mortgage will very often provide the receiver with extensive additional powers[7]. Thus, the mortgage may empower the receiver to carry on a business operated on the mortgaged property by the mortgagor, to borrow money on the security of the mortgaged property, or to sell any part of the property[8]. Such an extension of the receiver's powers will normally take effect as an express power, rather than an extension of the statutory powers[9]. Any attempt by the mortgagor to interfere with the receiver's collection of the income (for instance, by distraining on the tenants) will be restrained[10].

1 Law of Property Act 1925, s 109(3). For the position where the lease over which the receiver is appointed is forfeited, see *Official Custodian for Charities v Mackey (No 2)* [1985] 2 All ER 1016, [1985] 1 WLR 1308. On the limited powers of a receiver to manage the property of the borrower, see *North City Developments ex p Walker* (1990) 20 NSWLR 286. On the receiver's power to continue litigation after the appointment of a liquidator, see *Kelaw Pty Ltd v Catco Developments Pty Ltd* (1989) 15 NSWLR 589.
2 He cannot normally bring a claim in his own name: *Re Sacker* (1888) 22 QBD 179. Where the mortgagor has died, the receiver may be able to bring a claim in the name of his personal representatives, if he gives a suitable indemnity: *Fairholme and Palliser v Kennedy* (1890) 24 LR Ir 498.
3 See above.
4 See above. See ss 99 (19), 100 (13), 109 (3). For the delegated power of sale, see further **20.44**.
5 *Re Cripps* [1946] Ch 265. Where a receiver is appointed under an express power, care should be taken in drafting the power that the receiver's power to lease is not dependent on the mortgagee having taken possession.
6 Law of Property Act 1925, s 109(7). For the powers of the mortgagee to insure the property, see s 108 and **16.6** and **3.44–3.45**.
7 For an example of a substantial extension of the statutory powers, see *Re Kentish Homes Ltd* [1993] BCC 212 at 219.
8 See eg *Medforth v Blake* [2000] Ch 86 at 89. For an implied power of sale, see *Re J B Davies Enterprises Pty Ltd (In Liq)* [1990] 2 Qd R 129. See further **20.44**.
9 *Phoenix Properties v Wimpole Street Nominees* [1992] BCLC 737 (power of sale).
10 *Bayly v Went* (1884) 51 LT 764.

Receiver appointed under an express power

18.11 Where a receiver is appointed under an express, rather than the statutory, power, the extent of his powers will be determined by the terms of the instrument under which he was appointed[1]. A receiver appointed with the power to do something also has an incidental power to do what is necessary to effect that object[2]. A receiver appointed under powers contained in an instrument is personally liable on any contract entered into by him in the performance of his functions, but he is entitled to an indemnity in respect of that liability out of the assets and he may also limit his liability[3]. Where a receiver is given the power to carry on a business on the mortgaged property previously carried on by the mortgagor, he is not obliged to do so[4]. A receiver of the property of a company appointed under powers contained in an instrument may apply to the court for directions in relation to any particular matter arising in connection with his duties, and the court may give such directions as it thinks fit[5].

A receiver appointed by debenture holders usually has an express power of sale under the debenture but, unless there is a specific legal charge, when the debenture holders can sell under the statutory power of sale[6] (or the receiver as their agent), on a sale by a receiver the mortgaging company will have to be a party, as the property will remain vested in it. Accordingly the debenture should appoint the debenture holders (or their receiver) attorneys of the company[7]. Often, of course, the company will be in liquidation and the liquidator will be able to assist in the sale[8].

1 Thus he must expressly be given the power to repair or insure the mortgaged property: *Visbord v Comr of Taxation* (1943) 68 CLR 354 at 382.
2 *M Wheeler & Co Ltd v Warren* [1928] Ch 840, CA; see also *Pole v Leask* (1860) 28 Beav 562;

Merchant Service Guild of Australasia v Commonwealth Steamship Owners' Association (1913) 16 CLR 664 at 688. On the residual powers of the board of directors after a receiver has been appointed, see *Newhart Developments Ltd v Co-operative Commercial Bank Ltd* [1978] QB 814, [1978] 2 All ER 896, CA, doubted and distinguished in *Tudor Grange Holdings Ltd v Citibank* [1992] Ch 53, [1991] 4 All ER 1.

3 Insolvency Act 1986, s 37; see s 44(1)(b) in the case of an Administrative Receiver.

4 *Medforth v Blake* [2000] Ch 86.

5 Insolvency Act 1986, s 35.

6 See **20.6**.

7 For forms, see 10 *Forms and Precedents* (5th edn, 2001 reissue) Companies. On the form of execution, see *Industrial Development Authority v Moran* [1978] IR 159.

8 See, generally, *Williams on Title* (4th edn) pp 226, 227.

Administrative receivers

18.12 An administrative receiver has the following general powers, except in so far as they are inconsistent with any of the provisions of the debenture under which the receiver is appointed[1]:

(a) power to take possession of, collect and get in the property of the company and, for that purpose, to take such proceedings as may seem to him expedient;
(b) power to sell or otherwise dispose of the property of the company by public auction or private contract or, in Scotland, to sell, feu, hire out or otherwise dispose of the property of the company by public roup or private bargain;
(c) power to raise or borrow money and grant security therefor over the property of the company;
(d) power to appoint a solicitor or accountant or other professionally qualified person to assist him in the performance of his functions;
(e) power to bring or defend any action or other legal proceedings in the name and on behalf of the company;
(f) power to refer to arbitration any question affecting the company;
(g) power to effect and maintain insurances in respect of the business and property of the company;
(h) power to use the company's seal;
(i) power to do all acts and to execute in the name and on behalf of the company any deed, receipt or other document;
(j) power to draw, accept, make and endorse any bill of exchange or promissory note in the name and on behalf of the company;
(k) power to appoint any agent to do any business which he is unable to do himself or which can more conveniently be done by an agent and power to employ and dismiss employees;
(l) power to do all such things (including the carrying out of works) as may be necessary for the realisation of the property of the company;
(m) power to make any payment which is necessary or incidental to the performance of his functions;
(n) power to carry on the business of the company;
(o) power to establish subsidiaries of the company;
(p) power to transfer to subsidiaries of the company the whole or any part of the business and property of the company;
(q) power to grant or accept a surrender of a lease or tenancy of any of the property of the company and to take a lease or tenancy of any property required or convenient for the business of the company;
(r) power to make any arrangement or compromise on behalf of the company;

(s) power to call up any uncalled capital of the company;
(t) power to rank and claim in the bankruptcy, insolvency, sequestration or liquidation of any person indebted to the company and to receive dividends, and to accede to trust deeds for the creditors of any such person;
(u) power to present or defend a petition for the winding up of the company;
(v) power to change the situation of the company's registered office;
(w) power to do all other things incidental to the exercise of the foregoing powers.

An administrative receiver is personally liable on any contract entered into by him in the performance of his functions, but he is entitled to an indemnity in respect of that liability out of the assets, and he may also limit his liability[2]. A receiver acting as agent of a company cannot act outside the powers conferred by the company's memorandum and articles of association[3]. However, a person dealing with the administrative receiver in good faith and for value is not concerned to inquire whether the receiver in acting within his powers[4].

An administrative receiver may also apply to the court for power to dispose of charged property as if it were not subject to the security. Section 43 of the Insolvency Act 1986[5] provides that where, on an application by the administrative receiver, the court is satisfied that the disposal (with or without other assets) of any relevant property[6] which is subject to a security would be likely[7] to promote a more advantageous realisation of the company's assets than would otherwise be effected, the court may by order authorise the administrative receiver to dispose of the property as if it were not subject to the security. The court may not make such an order in the case of any security held by the person by or on whose behalf the administrative receiver was appointed, or of any security to which a security so held has priority[8]. It must be a condition of such an order that: (a) the net proceeds of the disposal, and (b) where those proceeds are less than such amount as may be determined by the court to be the net amount which would be realised on a sale of the property in the open market by a willing vendor, such sums as may be required to make good the deficiency, must be applied towards discharging the sums secured by the security[9]. Where such a condition relates to two or more securities, that condition must require the net proceeds of the disposal and, where applicable, such sums as are required to make good the deficiency as compared to the market value, to be applied towards discharging the sums secured by those securities in the order of their priorities[10]. An office copy of such an order must be sent by the administrative receiver to the registrar of companies within 14 days[11].

1 Insolvency Act 1986, s 42 (1); the powers are set out in Sch 1 to the Insolvency Act 1986. For the property to which the powers apply and the effect of an appointment of a receiver by a prior chargee, see s 42 (2) (b).
2 Insolvency Act 1986, s 44(1)(b).
3 *Lawson v Hosemaster* [1966] 2 All ER 944 at 951, [1966] 1 WLR 1300 at 1315.
4 Insolvency Act 1986, s 42 (3). On the meaning of good faith, see **20.22**.
5 This section is based on recommendations in the Cork Report, paras 1510–1513. Cf an administrator's powers under the Insolvency Act 1986, s 15; see **23.8**. The purpose of these provisions is to induce the prior secured creditor to participate in a rescue scheme. For the procedure where the receiver applies to dispose of charged property, see the Insolvency Rules 1986, r 3.31.
6 'Relevant property', in relation to the administrative receiver, means the property of which he is or, but for the appointment of some other person as the receiver of part of the company's property, would be the receiver or manager: Insolvency Act 1986, s 43(7).
7 See *Re Harris Simons Construction Ltd* [1989] 1 WLR 368, [1989] BCLC 202.
8 Insolvency Act 1986, s 43(2).
9 Section 43(3).

10 Section 43(4).
11 Section 43(5). If the administrative receiver without reasonable excuse fails to comply with that duty, he is liable to a fine and, for continued contravention, to a daily default fine: s 43(6).

APPLICATION OF RECEIPTS

18.13 A receiver appointed under the statutory power must apply all money received by him[1] in the following order[2]:

(a) in discharge of all rents, taxes[3], rates[4], and outgoings whatever affecting the mortgaged property[5];
(b) in keeping down all annual sums or other payments and the interest on all principal sums having priority to the mortgage under which he was appointed receiver;
(c) in payment of his commission[6]; and of the premiums on fire, life, or other insurances, if any, properly payable under the mortgage deed or under the Act of 1925[7]; and the cost of executing necessary or proper repairs directed in writing by the mortgagee[8];
(d) in payment of all interest accruing due in respect of any principal money due under the mortgage[9]; and
(e) in or towards discharge of the principal money if so directed in writing by the mortgagee;
(f) he must pay the residue, if any, of the money received by him to the person who, but for the possession of the receiver, would have been entitled to receive the income of which he is appointed receiver, or who is otherwise entitled to the mortgaged property.

Those provisions take effect subject to the provisions in the Act as to the application of money paid out under insurance policies[10]. The terms of the mortgage may extend the receiver's powers as to the application of the income, such as to pay an unsecured debt by instalments[11]. The duty imposed on the receiver to apply the receipts in that order is owed to the mortgagor, mortgagee and puisne incumbrancers[12]. Thus if the receiver refuses to account to the mortgagee for money coming into his hands, the mortgagee can bring a claim against him for an account[13]; and a mortgagor can compel the receiver to comply with the provisions of the section[14]. The mortgagor, mortgagee and other incumbrancers can agree to vary the order in which the receipts are applied[15]. Where a receiver is appointed, but the mortgagor is subsequently allowed to receive some of the income from the mortgaged property, the mortgagee's rights are not affected, except as to later incumbrancers of whose claim he had notice[16]. Upon removal from office, the receiver is entitled to retain monies payable to preferential creditors, in order to discharge his personal liability in that respect[17]. Where a receiver appointed over the property of a company vacates office, (a) his remuneration any expenses properly incurred by him, and (b) any indemnity to which he is entitled out of the assets of the company, must be charged and paid out of the company which is in his custody or under his control at that time in priority to any charge or other security held by the person by or on whose behalf he was appointed[18].

1 For the position where the lease over which the receiver is appointed is forfeited, see *Official Custodian for Charities v Mackey (No 2)* [1985] 2 All ER 1016, [1985] 1 WLR 1308.
2 Law of Property Act 1925, s 109(7).

3 See *Re John Willment (Ashford) Ltd* [1979] 2 All ER 615, [1980] 1 WLR 73; *Re Liverpool Commercial Vehicles Ltd* [1984] BCLC 587 at 592. Tax includes VAT on rent paid to the receiver: *Sargent v Customs and Excise Comrs* [1994] 1 WLR 235; varied [1995] 1 WLR 821, CA.

4 See *Liverpool Corpn v Hope* [1938] 1 KB 751, [1938] 1 All ER 492, CA. For the liability of a receiver for rates, see *Ratford v Northavon District Council* [1987] QB 357, [1986] 3 All ER 193.

5 For the nature of this power, see *Liverpool Corpn v Hope* above; *Re John Willment (Ashford) Ltd* above. Its purpose is to preserve the property in the interest of both the mortgagee and the mortgagor by ensuring that the normal outgoings are discharged: *Sargent v Customs and Excise Comrs* [1994] 1 WLR 235 at 241; varied [1995] 1 WLR 821, CA. For the liability of the receiver to the mortgagor for failure to pay tax, see *Visbord v Federal Comr of Taxation* (1943) 68 CLR 354.

6 See **18.14**. The mortgage may provide for the receiver to have his costs, charges and expenses separately: *Marshall v Cottingham* [1982] Ch 82.

7 See Law of Property Act 1925, s 108 and **16.6**.

8 See *White v Metcalf* [1903] 2 Ch 567.

9 This extends to arrears of interest due at the time of the appointment of the receiver and not merely to interest accruing due afterwards: *National Bank v Kenney* [1898] 1 IR 197. Consent to the alteration of the order of the application of the surplus may be inferred from the facts: *Yourell v Hibernian Bank* [1918] AC 372, HL.

10 Law of Property Act 1925, s 109(8); for the provisions as to the application of insurance money, see s 108; and **16.6**.

11 *Hale, Re Lilley v Foad* [1899] 2 Ch 107 at 118–119.

12 But not to third parties to whom the payments should be made: *Yourell v Hibernian Bank Ltd* [1918] AC 372 at 387; *Leicester Permanent Building Society v Butt* [1943] 1 Ch 308; *Re Kentish Homes Ltd* [1993] BCC 212 at 219–221 (overruled on other grounds in *Re Toshoku Finance UK Plc* [2000] 1 BCLC 683, CA). See also *Visbord v Federal Comr of Taxation* (1943) 68 CLR 354.

13 *Leicester Permanent Building Society v Butt* (above).

14 *Re Kentish Homes Ltd* (above).

15 *Yourell v Hibernian Bank Ltd* (above).

16 *Juggeewundas Keeka Shah v Ramdas Brijbookundas* (1841) 2 Moo Ind App 487.

17 *IRC v Goldblatt* [1972] Ch 498.

18 Insolvency Act 1986, s 37(4).

REMUNERATION

18.14 A receiver appointed under the statutory power is entitled to retain out of any money received by him, for his remuneration, and in satisfaction of all costs, charges, and expenses incurred by him as receiver[1], a commission at such rate, not exceeding 5 per cent on the gross amount of all money received, as is specified in his appointment. If no rate is specified in his appointment, he is entitled to a commission at 5 per cent on that gross amount, or alternatively he may apply to the court, for the court to fix such rate as it thinks fit[2]. The remuneration allowed to a receiver appointed under an express power should be specified in the mortgage or on his appointment; in the absence of such express provision, he will be entitled to a proper remuneration as a *quantum meruit*[3]. On the application of a liquidator of a company, the court may fix the amount to be paid by way of remuneration to a person who, under powers contained in an instrument, has been appointed receiver of the company's property[4].

1 Costs of realisation should be made payable by the mortgage deed out of the proceeds of sale, not out of the receiver's commission: *Marshall v Cottingham* [1982] Ch 82, [1981] 3 All ER 8.

2 Law of Property Act 1925, s 109(6). An application is only necessary if the receiver wishes to obtain some other, in practice, a higher rate: *Marshall v Cottingham* [1982] Ch 82, [1981] 3 All ER 8. Doubts have been expressed (see, generally, Picarda *The Law Relating to Receivers and Managers* (3rd edn), pp 278–279) as to whether a rate higher than 5 per cent can be

provided for in the mortgage deed pursuant to s 101 (3) by way of an extension of the statutory power of appointing a receiver. There seems no reason why this general power of variation or extension should be limited in this way, but to be safe it may be better to expressly provide for the appointment of a receiver in the mortgage deed, rather than to rely on the statutory power, and to include a provision for remuneration in accordance with a professional scale. See the Appendix. Note Insolvency Act 1986, s 36 whereunder a liquidator may apply to the court to fix the rate of remuneration and an order made thereunder may prevail over the terms of the mortgage deed or the appointment. On this section, generally, see *Re Potters Oil Ltd (No 2)* [1986] 1 All ER 890, sub nom *Re Potters Oils Ltd* [1986] 1 WLR 201. For the right of a receiver appointed under an invalid mortgage to reasonable remuneration for acts done for the benefit of the company, see *Monks v Poynice Pty Ltd* (1987) 8 NSWLR 662; *Moodmere Pty Ltd v Waters* [1988] VR 215. The court has no power to order that the receiver's costs and expenses and remuneration be paid in priority to secured creditors: *Choudhri v Palta* [1992] BCC 787, CA. On a receiver's lien for liabilities incurred personally in the business of the company see *National Australia Bank v Composite Buyers Ltd* (1991) 6 ACSR 94. For an injunction to restrain a sale by a receiver merely to provide for his remuneration where that is in dispute, see *Rottenberg v Monjack* [1993] BCLC 374, [1992] BCC 688.

3 *Re Vimbos Ltd* [1900] 1 Ch 470.

4 Insolvency Act 1986, s 36(1). The court can fix the rate of remuneration for the period prior to the order, and order the receiver to account for any excess remuneration that he has already received: s 36(2).

TERMINATION OF RECEIVERSHIP

18.15 The mortgagee may, in writing, from time to time remove the receiver[1]. Although the receiver is deemed the agent of the mortgagor, the latter may not dismiss him[2]. An administrative receiver can only be removed by court order[3]. A receiver appointed under a subsequent incumbrance will be displaced by a receiver subsequently appointed by a prior incumbrancer. A receiver may not resign without the consent of the mortgagee, unless the terms of the mortgage or his appointment provide otherwise; an administrative receiver may resign on notice[4]. The appointment may be terminated by mutual agreement between the mortgagee and the receiver, which, where it takes place before any realisation of assets, is sometimes called the 'uplifting' of the receivership. An administrative receiver must vacate office immediately he ceases to be qualified to act as an insolvency practitioner[5], or where an administration order is made[6]. The receivership will be terminated by the receiver's death[7].

A receiver has discharged his duty, and his authority comes to an end, once he has paid any preferential or other debts ranking ahead of the debt secured by the charge under which he was appointed and he has discharged all monies secured by the charge under which he was appointed[8]. He is then under a duty to terminate the receivership and hand over any surplus assets to the mortgagor or next subsequent incumbrancer[9]. When an administrative receiver vacates office on completion of the receivership, or because he ceases to be qualified as an insolvency practitioner, he must forthwith give notice of his doing so: (a) to the company or, if it is in liquidation, the liquidator, and (b) to the members of the creditors' committee (if any)[10].

1 See Law of Property Act 1925, s 109(5) in relation to a receiver appointed under the statutory power. The same applies in the case of a receiver appointed under an express power, unless the mortgage or the appointment provides otherwise. There are restrictions on the removal and replacement of an administrative receiver: Insolvency Act 1986, s 45.

2 *Gomba Holdings UK Ltd v Minories Finance Ltd* [1988] 1 WLR 1231 at 1233; *Telematrix plc v Modern Engineers of Bristol* [1985] 1 BCC 99, 417 at 99, 420. Likewise, the mortgagor's death does not revoke the power to appoint a receiver: *Re Hale, Lilley v Ford* [1899] 2 Ch 107 at 117, CA.

3 Insolvency Act 1986, s 45 (1). On the basis on which the court may intervene, see *Re Neon Signs (Australasia) Ltd* [1965] VR 125.
4 Insolvency Act 1986, s 45 (1) and see Insolvency Rules 1986, r 3.33 for notification of the resignation.
5 Insolvency Act 1986, s 45 (2). See the Insolvency Rules 1986, r 3.35.
6 Insolvency Act 1986, s 11(1)(b). He is not then obliged to give notice to the company: Insolvency Rules 1986, r 3.35, as amended.
7 For notification on the death of an administrative receiver, see the Insolvency Rules 1986, r 3.34.
8 *Expo International Pty Ltd v Chant* [1979] 2 NSWLR 820.
9 *Rottenberg v Monjack* [1992] BCC 688. As to the distribution of the surplus monies, see Law of Property Act 1925, s 105; and **20.46**. For notification of the vacation of office by an administrative receiver, see the Insolvency Rules 1986, r 3.35.
10 Insolvency Rules 1986 r 3.35.

THE APPOINTMENT OF A RECEIVER BY THE COURT

POWER OF COURT TO APPOINT RECEIVER

18.16 Prior to 1873, the court's power to appoint a receiver was limited. The court would not generally appoint a receiver in favour of a legal mortgagee, on the basis that the legal mortgagee's general right against the income of the mortgaged property was to take possession[1]. The court would, however, appoint a receiver where the security was at risk[2], or where the mortgagee would face difficulties in exercising the usual remedy[3]. Since an equitable mortgagee or chargee was not entitled to take possession, he was generally entitled to the appointment of a receiver by the court[4]. Since the Judicature Act 1873, the court has had the jurisdiction to appoint a receiver in all cases where it appears to the court to be just and convenient to do so[5]. Thus a receiver may now be appointed on the application of a legal mortgagee, where it is just and convenient[6].

The statutory power of a mortgagee to appoint a receiver out of court and the inclusion of express powers in mortgage documentation has made this jurisdiction one that is rarely exercised today[7]. The appointment of a receiver by the court is likely to be a slower and more expensive process than an appointment by the mortgagee out of court. The mortgagee will also have less control over the identity and actions of the receiver. When selecting the receiver and giving him directions, the court will have regard not only to the interests of the mortgagee, but also to all other parties, including the mortgagor. The receiver must similarly act fairly in the interests of both mortgagee and mortgagor[8]. As an officer of the court, a court-appointed receiver will be a public authority for the purposes of the Human Rights Act 1998, with consequent restrictions on his activities[9]. However, there are circumstances in which a receiver appointed by the court will nevertheless be a useful remedy. Thus, the security may be at risk, when the express or statutory power to appoint a receiver has not yet arisen. There may be a dispute about the mortgagee's power to appoint a receiver, or a claim pending, making it desirable that a court appointed receiver should be able to act so as to be binding on both parties regardless of the outcome[10]. The powers available to a receiver appointed by the mortgagee might be insufficient for the particular circumstances.

1 *Berney v Sewell* (1820) 1 Jac & W 647; *Ackland v Gravener* (1862) 31 Beav 482; *Sollory v Leaver* (1869) LR 9 Eq 22; *Re Pope* (1886) 17 QBD 743; *Re Prytherch, Prytherch v Williams* (1889) 42 Ch D 590.
2 *Stevens v Lord* (1838) 2 Jur 92.

3 *Ackland v Gravener* (1862) 31 Beav 482.
4 *Berney v Sewell* (1820) 1 Jac & W 647; *Re Pope* (1886) 17 QBD 743.
5 Judicature Act 1873, s 25(8), replaced by the Supreme Court of Judicature (Consolidation) Act 1925, s 45; now under the Supreme Court Act 1981, s 37, and County Courts Act 1984, s 38. Courts and Legal Services Act 1990: the county court has unlimited jurisdiction to appoint a receiver. See generally CPR Sch 1, RSC Ord 30 (r A1: applicable to proceedings in both the High Court and the county court). The power may be exercised by a Master of the Chancery Division: *Practice Direction* [1975] 1 All ER 255, [1975] 1 WLR 129. See also generally *Chancery Guide* para 22.6. On unsecured creditors and court appointed receivers, see (1991) 107 LQR 551 (Chandler & Martin).
6 *Truman v Redgrave* (1881) 18 Ch D 547; *Re Pope* (1886) 17 QBD 743.
7 For appointment of a receiver to manage blocks of flats, see *Hart v Emelkirk Ltd* [1983] 3 All ER 15, [1983] 1 WLR 1289; *Clayhope Properties Ltd v Evans* [1986] 2 All ER 795, [1986] 1 WLR 1223, CA; *Daiches v Blue Lake Investments Ltd* (1985) 51 P & CR 51. And see now Landlord and Tenant Act 1987, s 24; (1987) 137 NLJ 843 (Madge); *Howard v Midrome* [1991] 3 EG 135.
8 *Re Newdigate Colliery Ltd, Newdigate v Newdigate Colliery Ltd* [1912] 1 Ch 468.
9 See **16.57** ff.
10 *Tillett v Nixon* (1883) 25 Ch D 238.

WHEN THE POWER MAY BE EXERCISED

18.17 The court should only exercise its power in aid of some legal or equitable right, which will usually take the form of a cause of action[1]. The applicant should have some interest in the mortgaged property[2]. Thus, the court cannot at the instance of a secured creditor appoint a receiver of the secured property and other unsecured property, with a view to the sale of the whole, where the secured creditor has no interest in relation to the uncharged property[3]. Subject to that, the court has a wide discretion as to whether or not to appoint, to be governed by the whole circumstances of the case. The mortgagee may apply for the appointment of a receiver where the security is in jeopardy, whether or not there has been any breach of the terms of the mortgage, or where the property is derelict[4]. A receiver may also be appointed where the mortgagor breaches any of his obligations[5], such as payment of interest[6] or the principal debt[7]. Where the mortgagee is for the time being unable to enforce the usual mortgagee's remedies, for instance if he has covenanted not to call in the mortgage debt for a certain period[8], a receiver may be appointed to ensure the interest is paid. An equitable mortgagee is generally entitled to a receiver[9], provided the court is satisfied of the existence of the equitable right in the applicant[10]. The appointment may be made on the application of a mortgagee in possession, even where he has surplus income from the property[11]. However, the court will not, in general, assist a mortgagee in possession to get rid of his liabilities by appointing a receiver[12]. The fact that in a claim for foreclosure the costs of the receiver will be borne by the mortgagee may influence the court in thinking it just to appoint a receiver[13]. The court has refused to appoint a receiver on the mortgagee's application even where the mortgagor consented[14]. The appointment will be made primarily for the protection of the mortgaged property and does not affect the ultimate rights of the parties to the action. Thus where a receiver is appointed in an administration action the appointment is also for the benefit of the mortgagees if they avail themselves of it[15]. It has been suggested that the court may appoint a receiver on the application of the mortgagor where a mortgagee in possession has mismanaged the property and there is insufficient margin in the debt to allow the mortgagor's position to be protected in the taking of accounts[16]. A receiver will not be appointed where it would put the security at risk (for example, putting the property at risk of forfeiture), or where it would serve no useful purpose, such as where the property is of no value[17]. The fact that the mortgagee could appoint a receiver out of court under an express or the statutory power is not a bar to the court exercising its own power[18]. The court may even appoint a receiver where a mortgagee has already done so, for instance where two mortgagees with equal priority had each appointed their own receivers[19].

A receiver will not normally be appointed unless a claim is pending[20]. Normally the claim form should be issued prior to the application being made[21]; but a receiver has been appointed before service of the claim form, where the residence of an absconding defendant was unknown[22], and where he was out of the jurisdiction[23]. The court will not appoint a receiver on a without notice application, save in unusual circumstances[24]. After a claim has been commenced, a receiver may be appointed, either at the final hearing or by interim order[25] (which may be either before or after final judgment[26]). Where a receiver is appointed on an interim basis, the court may require a cross-undertaking in damages[27]. A receiver may be appointed at the hearing, even though such relief was not sought, if the facts are sufficient to justify the appointment[28]. A receiver may also be appointed after judgment[29] in cases of urgency, without any supplemental claim being brought[30], for example where a third party has been in possession for such a long period without accounting that there was a danger of his acquiring a title by adverse possession[31]. An appointment may also be made after judgment if the circumstances would have entitled the party to the appointment of a receiver at the hearing[32]. The appointment will not be made after foreclosure absolute, even where the mortgagor remains in possession pending the settlement of the proper form of conveyance[33].

1 See Lightman and Moss *The Law of Receivers and Administrators of Companies* (3rd edn) para 22-003.
2 *A-G v Day* (1817) 2 Madd 246.
3 *Britannia Building Society v Crammer* [1997] BPIR 596.
4 *Wildy v Mid-Hants Rly Co* (1868) 18 LT 73; *McMahon v North Kent Ironworks Co* [1891] 2 Ch 148; *Re London Pressed Hinge Co Ltd* [1905] 1 Ch 576; *Higginson v German Athenaeum Ltd* (1916) 32 TLR 277. In the case of debentures see: *Re Victoria Steamboats* [1897] 1 Ch 158; *Re New York Taxi Cab Co Ltd* [1913] 1 Ch 1; *Re Tilt Cove Copper Co Ltd* [1913] 2 Ch 588; *Cryne v Barclays Bank Plc* [1987] BCLC 548.
5 *Stevens v Lord* (1838) 2 Jur 92; *Re New Publishing Co Ltd* (1897) 41 Sol Jo 839; *Re Carshalton Park Estate Ltd, Graham v Carshalton Park Estate Ltd* [1908] 2 Ch 62.
6 *Bissill v Bradford Tramways Co Ltd* [1891] WN 51; *Strong v Carlyle Press* [1893] 1 Ch 268.
7 *Curling v Marquis of Townshend* (1816) 19 Ves 628; *Hopkins v Worcester and Birmingham Canal Proprietors* (1868) LR 6 Eq 437; *Re Crompton* [1914] 1 Ch 954.
8 *Burrowes v Molloy* (1845) 2 Jo & Lat 521 and see **3.26**.
9 *Berney v Sewell* (1820) 1 Jac & W 647. So too a chargee.
10 *Davis v Duke of Marlborough* (1819) 2 Swan 108 at 138; *Greville v Fleming* (1845) 8 I Eq 201, 2 Jo & Cat 335.
11 *Mason v Westoby* (1886) 32 Ch D 206.
12 *Re Prytherch, Prytherch v Williams* (1889) 42 Ch D 590. Cf *Gloucester County Bank v Rudry Merthyr Steam and Colliery House Coal Colliery Co* [1895] 1 Ch 629.
13 *Tillett v Nixon* (1883) 25 Ch D 238; *Mason v Westoby* (1886) 32 Ch D 206; *Re Prytherch, Prytherch v Williams* (1889) 42 Ch D 590.
14 *London Pressed Hinge Co Ltd* [1905] 1 Ch 576.
15 *Bainbrigge v Blair* (1841) 3 Beer 421; *Gresley v Adderley* (1818) 1 Swan 573.
16 *Hayward v Martin* (1883) 9 VLR (E) 143.
17 *Colter v Osbourne* (1909) 19 Man LJ 145; *J Walls v Legge* [1923] 2 KB 240.
18 *Fripp v Chard Rly Co* (1853) 11 Hare 241; *Bord v Tollemache* (1862) 1 New Rep 177; *Tillett v Nixon* (1883) 23 Ch D 238; *Re Prytherch* (1889) 42 Ch D 590; *McMahon v North Kent Iron Works Co* [1891] 2 Ch 148; *Gloucester County Bank v Rudry Merthyr Steam and Colliery*

House Coal Colliery Co [1895] 1 Ch 629; *Britannia Building Society v Crammar* [1997] BPIR 596.
19 *Re Slogger Automatic Feeder Co Ltd* [1915] 1 Ch 478; *Bass Breweries v Delaney* [1994] BCC 851.
20 *Ex p Mountfort* (1809) 15 Ves 445; *Taylor v Emerson* (1843) 6 LR Eq 224; *Salter v Salter* [1896] P 291; and see *Gasson and Hallaghan Ltd v Jell* [1940] Ch 248; *Re Fawsitt, Galland v Burton* (1885) 30 Ch D 231, CA (originating summons).
21 *Stratton v Davidson* (1830) 1 Russ & M 484; *Brown v Blount* (1830) 2 Russ & M 83.
22 *Pitcher v Helliar* (1781) 2 Dick 580; *Dowling v Hudson* (1851) 14 Beav 423.
23 Absence beyond the jurisdiction is not by itself a reason for appointing a receiver before service of the writ, since an order may be made for service out of the jurisdiction.
24 Such as where there is extreme urgency, where giving notice to the mortgagor might defeat the object of the application, or where the mortgagor cannot be found. See *Taylor v Eckersley* (1876) 2 Ch D 302; *Hicks v Lockwood* [1883] WN 48; *Daw v Herring* (1892) 35 Sol Jo 752; *Re Connolly Bros* [1911] 1 Ch 731; see also *Don King Productions v Warren (No 3)* [2000] BCC 263.
25 SCA 1981, s 37; *Campbell v Lloyds Barnetts and Basanquet's Bank Ltd* (1889) [1891] 1 Ch 136n; expl in *Whitley v Challis* (1892) 1 Ch 64; *Gloucester County Bank v Rudry Merthyr Steam and House Coal Colliery Co* [1895] 1 Ch 629, CA
26 *Smith v Cowell* (1880) 6 QBD 75; *Anglo-Italian Bank v Davies* (1878) 9 Ch D 275, CA.
27 See in relation to cross-undertaking for benefit of third parties *Allied Irish Bank v Ashford Hotels Ltd* [1997] 3 All ER 309, CA. See also *Bond Brewing Holdings Ltd v National Australia Bank Ltd* (1990) 8 ACLC 330; on appeal sub nom *National Australia Bank Ltd v Bond Brewing Holdings Ltd* (1990) 1 ACSR 722.
28 *Malcolm v Montgomery* (1824) 2 Mol 500; *Osborne v Harvey* (1841) 1 Y & C Ch Cas 116; *Bowman v Bell* (1844) 14 Sim 392; *Re Lloyd, Allen v Lloyd* (1879) 12 Ch D 447 (permission to amend); but see *Wright v Vernon* (1855) 3 Drew 112. See also CPR 16.2(5).
29 See the cases in n 26.
30 *Thomas v Davies* (1847) 11 Beav 29; *Wright v Vernon* (1855) 3 Drew 112.
31 *Thomas v Davies* above and see *Hiles v Moore* (1852) 15 Beav 175.
32 *A-G v Galway Corpn* (1829) 1 Mol 95 at 105; *Harris v Shee* (1844) 6 Ir Eq R 543. Contrast *Wright v Vernon* above .
33 *Wills v Luff* (1888) 38 Ch D 197; see also *Pedwell v Wright* (1972) 23 DLR (3d) 198.

When manager appointed

18.18 A receiver of the property of a limited company can be appointed at the instance of debenture holders or other secured creditors, but a manager is only appointed where the security includes the business of the company and then only for the purpose of selling the business as a going concern[1]. A receiver and manager of mines may be appointed at the instance of a mortgagee, even although the business was not expressly mortgaged, because of the peculiar nature of the property, a mine being considered in this respect to be in the nature of a trade[2].

1 *Whitley v Challis* [1892] 1 Ch 64 at 69, 70, CA. As to the distinction between a receiver and manager, see *Re Manchester and Milford Rly Co, ex p Cambrian Rly Co* (1880) 14 Ch D 645 at 653, CA; *Re B Johnson & Co (Builders) Ltd* [1955] Ch 634, [1955] 2 All ER 775, CA; *Australian Industry Development Corpn v Co-operative Farmers and Graziers Direct Meat Supply Ltd* [1978] VR 633; and as to the duties of a receiver and manager in regard to contracts made by the company, see *Re Newdigate Colliery Ltd* [1912] 1 Ch 468, CA.
2 *Strong v Carlyle Press* [1893] 1 Ch 268, CA.

APPOINTMENT ON APPLICATION OF SUBSEQUENT INCUMBRANCER

18.19 A receiver may be appointed on the application of a subsequent incumbrancer, where no prior incumbrancer has taken possession or appointed a receiver[1]. The right of an equitable mortgagee to the appointment of a receiver was formerly subject to the general principle that the appointment was made without prejudice to the rights of the prior legal incumbrancer[2]. The same principle probably now applies to successive legal mortgages, so that the appointment of a receiver at the instance of a later incumbrancer, whether legal or equitable, is without prejudice to the rights of prior incumbrancers. Hence, where a prior mortgagee is not in possession, the appointment is made subject to his right to take possession[3]. Where such a provision has been included in the order, the prior mortgagee can take possession without the permission of the court and notify the tenants that they should pay their rents to him[4]. However, it would be usual to make an application for permission[5] and such an application must be made where the order contains no express reservation of the prior mortgagee's rights[6].

When a prior mortgagee is in possession a receiver will not be appointed, so long as he can show that something remains due to him[7]. A receiver can be appointed on the application of a subsequent incumbrancer where he pays off the prior incumbrancer's debt[8], or where the prior incumbrancer refuses to accept what is due, or cannot show by proper accounts that he is owed anything[9]. If the prior mortgagee has kept his accounts in an incomplete state, so that he cannot say whether anything remains due to him, the court may give him time to compile evidence of the amount of the debt[10].

1 *Re Metropolitan Amalgamated Estates* [1912] 2 Ch 497.
2 *Davis v Duke of Marlborough* (1819) 2 Swan 108; *Berney v Sewell* (1820) Jac & W 647.
3 *Cadogan v Lyric Theatre Ltd* [1894] 3 Ch 338, CA.
4 *Underhay v Read* (1887) 20 QBD 209 at 219, CA; *Engel v South Metropolitan Brewing and Bottling Co* [1891] WN 31.
5 *Preston v Tunbridge Wells Opera House Ltd* [1903] 2 Ch 323.
6 *Re Henry Pound, Son, and Hutchins Ltd* (1889) 42 Ch D 402 at 422, CA.
7 *Berney v Sewell* above; *Quarrell v Beckford* (1807) 13 Ves 377.
8 *Berney v Sewell* above; *Rowe v Wood* (1822) 2 Jac & W 553. An incumbrancer who is in possession, not in that character, but as tenant, cannot set up his possession as tenant as a reason against the appointment of a receiver: *Archdeacon v Bowes* (1796) 3 Anst 752.
9 *Berney v Sewell* above; *Hiles v Moore* (1852) 15 Beav 175; and see *Rowe v Wood* above.
10 *Codrington v Parker* (1810) 16 Ves 469; *Hiles v Moore* (1852) 15 Beav 175. It has been intimated that where by reason of the negligent mode of keeping the accounts, neither party can ascertain what is due, the court may assume that nothing is due: *Codrington v Parker* (1810) 16 Ves 469.

FORM OF APPLICATION

18.20 An application for the appointment of a receiver made in existing proceedings must be made in accordance with CPR Pt 23[1]. An application for an injunction ancillary or incidental to an order appointing a receiver may be joined with the application[2].

1 And the associated Practice Direction.
2 CPR Sch 1, RSC Ord 30, r 1. See further Chancery Guide, para 22.6.

IDENTITY OF RECEIVER

18.21 The court will normally appoint the nominee of the applicant incumbrancer, so long as he is suitably qualified and there are no other objections to his selection[1]. However, a proposal from another party will be entertained so long as the candidate is suitable[2]. The court will avoid appointing a receiver who would have some conflict of interest[3]. A mortgagee may be appointed as receiver[4], although normally without payment[5].

1 *Bowersbank v Colasseau* (1796) 3 Ves 164; *Wilkins v Williams* (1798) 3 Ves 588; *Anderson v Kemshead* (1852) 16 Beav 329.
2 *Thomas v Dawkin* (1792) 1 Ves 452 (nominee of mortgagor accepted where value of equity of redemption as great as mortgage debt); *A-G v Day* (1817) 2 Madd 246; *Lespinasse v Bell* (1821) 2 Jac & W 436; *Bord v Tollemache* (1862) 1 New Rep 177.
3 *Garland v Garland* (1793) 2 Ves 137; *Fripp v Chard Rly Co* (1853) 11 Hare 241; *Re Lloyd, Allen v Lloyd* (1879) 12 Ch D 447.
4 *Re Prytherch, Prytherch v Williams* (1889) 42 Ch D 590.
5 *Sayers v Whitfield* (1829) 1 Knapp 133; *Davis v Barrett* (1844) 13 LJ Ch 304; *Cummins v Perkins* [1899] 1 Ch 16.

SECURITY

18.22 A judgment or order directing the appointment of a receiver may include such directions as the court thinks fit as to the giving of security by the person appointed. Where a receiver is required to give security, he must give security approved by the court duly to account for what he receives as receiver and to deal with such receipts as the court directs. The security will normally be by guarantee[1]. The court will not generally dispense with security, even by consent of the interested parties[2]. Until the receiver has complied with his obligation to provide security, he is not legally clothed with, or able to perform the duties of, his office (thus it is not a contempt to interfere with the property before that point)[3]. However, the receiver is frequently permitted to act at once, before completing his security, if the applicant undertakes to be responsible for his actions.

1 CPR Sch 1, RSC Ord 30, r 2.
2 *Manners v Furze* (1847) 11 Beav 30; *Tylee v Tylee* (1853) 17 Beav 583; and see *Bainbrigge v Blair* (1841) 3 Beav 421.
3 *Edwards v Edwards* (1876) 2 Ch D 291.

OF WHAT PROPERTY A RECEIVER MAY BE APPOINTED

18.23 In the case of a secured creditor, the appointment will relate to the security; thus a receiver will not appointed with the power to sell uncharged property along with charged property on the application of the secured creditor[1]. A receiver will not be appointed over a business operated from the mortgaged property, where the business itself is not included within the security[2]. It must be shown that a valid mortgage or charge has been made over the relevant property or, where the security was by way of assignment, that the property was properly assignable. A receiver may also be appointed of property where the validity of a mortgage or charge over it is in dispute. Where the appointment is made on the ground that the security is at risk, the appointment may be confined to the vulnerable property. A receiver may generally be appointed over any property, real or personal, which may be taken in execution[3] (on the analogy of which remedy the mortgagee's right to a receiver is founded[4]). Where the property consists of payments, such as tolls, a receiver may be appointed if the payments are fixed[5]; but not, however, if they have still to be assessed. If the payments are made out of a fund, as might be the case where the property was a pension[6], the fund out of which the payments are made must be certain[7]. Holders of debentures of companies formed for carrying out public undertakings, such as waterworks and the like, are entitled to the appointment of a receiver, this being the only remedy open, the right of sale or foreclosure usually having been denied in the public interest[8]. The appointment of a receiver does not supersede the statutory powers where an undertaking is carried on under statutory powers[9]. A receiver may be appointed over personal property and the rents and profits of realty, outside the United Kingdom, if the owner is within the jurisdiction[10].

1 *Britannia Building Society v Crammer* [1997] BPIR 596.
2 *Whitley v Challis* [1892] 1 Ch 64. The position may be otherwise if the security would be at risk if the business were not continued.
3 *Hope v Croydon and Norwood Tramways Co* (1887) 34 Ch D 730. For a detailed consideration of what property may be assigned, see *Picarda on The Law Relating to Receivers, Managers and Administrators* (3rd edn, 2000) Ch 24.
4 *Davis v Duke of Marlborough* (1819) 2 Swan 108 at 83.
5 *Lord Crewe v Edleston* (1857) 1 De G & J 93; *De Winton v Brecon Corpn* (1859) 26 Beav 533.
6 Which may be lawfully assigned.
7 *Cooper v Reilly* (1829) 2 Sim 560; and see *Clydesdale v McManus* (1934) 36 WALR 89. For the appointment of a receiver over a right of action, see *Bourne v Colodense Ltd* [1985] 1 ICR 291; *Garden Mews St Leonards Pty Ltd v Butler Pollnow Pty Ltd* (1984) 9 ACLR 117.
8 *Blaker v Herts and Essex Waterworks Co* (1889) 41 Ch D 399.
9 *Marshall v South Staffordshire Tramways Co* [1895] 2 Ch 36, CA.
10 *Mercantile Investment and General Trust Co v River Plate Trust, Loan, and Agency Co* [1892] 2 Ch 303; *Ballabil Holdings Pty Ltd v Hospital Produvts Ltd* (1985) 1 NSWLR 155.

RIGHTS, POWERS, DUTIES AND LIABILITIES

When the receiver has power to act

18.24 The receiver has power to act from the date of the order appointing him, subject to him providing any security which has been ordered[1]. A copy of the judgment or order appointing the receiver must be served by the party with conduct of the proceedings on the receiver and all other parties[2]. To be binding on third parties, the appointment of a receiver in respect of land or an interest in land should be protected by registration as a land charge in the case of unregistered land[3] or by lodging a caution or notice in the case of registered land[4]. Notice of an order for the appointment of a receiver or manager of a company's property must be given to the registrar of companies, who will enter the fact of the appointment in the register of charges[5].

1 *Edwards v Edwards* (1876) 2 Ch D 291; *Morrison v Skerne Ironworks Co Ltd* (1889) 60 LT 588; *Re Clarke* [1898] 1 Ch 336.
2 CPR Sch 1, RSC Ord 30, r 4.
3 Land Charges Act 1972, s 6 (1) (b), which applies to any receivership of land: *Clayhope Properties Ltd v Evans* [1986] 2 All ER 795, [1986] 1 WLR 1223, CA.
4 Land Registration Act 1925, ss 54 (1), 55, 59 (1), (5), and see *Clayhope Properties Ltd v Evans* above.
5 Companies Act 1985, s 405 (1) and for notice of ceasing to act: s 405 (2).

Status of court receiver appointed by the court

18.25 A receiver appointed by the court is an officer of the court. He is appointed for the benefit of all parties and is neither agent nor trustee for any of the parties[1].

Interference with the receiver's possession[2] or the performance of the receiver's duties[3] may constitute a contempt of court. The court uses its powers of committal sparingly and only when it is necessary to vindicate its authority. Thus, the court refused to commit for contempt where an application was made long after the disturbance of the receiver's possession complained of and where the real motivation for the application was to compel payment of the receiver's expenses after the question relating to the possession was settled[4]. The court has power by making an order of release and discharge to protect a receiver, acting as its officer, from liability for acts done in the course of its duties[5].

A person who is not a party to the claim in which the receiver was appointed (for example, a tenant of the mortgaged property) is not entitled to bring a claim to restrain a receiver from acting outside his authority[6]. Nor, in general, can a non-party apply for the payment of money in the hands of the receiver which is due to him[7]. The court may give leave to a person who claims an interest in real or personal property paramount to that of the receiver to bring a claim to establish his right, or for an inquiry to be directed as to his interest in the property, and that of the claimant in the proceedings in which the receiver was appointed[8]. If a person claiming a prior interest has already brought proceedings, or otherwise interfered with the receiver's possession without leave of the court, the court may restrain such actions, but by the same order direct similar inquiries[9].

1 *Angel v Smith* (1804) 9 Ves 335; *Bacup Corpn v Smith* (1890) 44 Ch D 395; *Paterson v Gaslight & Coke Co* [1896] 2 Ch 476; *Re Flowers & Co* [1897] 1 QB 14, CA; *Boehm v Goddall* [1911] 1 Ch 155; *Re Newdigate Colliery Ltd, Newdigate v Newdigate Colliery Ltd* [1912] 1 Ch 468, CA; *Parsons v Sovereign Bank of Canada* [1913] AC 160, PC; *Channel Airways v Manchester Corpn* [1974] 1 Lloyd's Rep 456.

2 *Angel v Smith* (1804) 9 Ves 335; *Broad v Wickham* (1831) 4 Sim 511; *Russell v East Anglian Rly Co* (1850) 3 Mac & G 104; *Ames v Birkenhead Docks Trustees* (1855) 20 Beav 332; *Defries v Creed* (1865) 6 New Rep 17; *Re Mead, ex p Cochrane* (1875) LR 20 Eq 282.

3 *Searle v Choat* (1884) 25 Ch D 723. It has been held that even a libel on the business carried on by a receiver and manager is a contemp. *Whadcoat v Shropshire Rly Co* (1893) 9 TLR 589.

4 *Ward v Swift* (1848) 6 Hare 309. The proper course was to make a direct application for the costs. See also *McIntyre v Perkes* (1987) 15 NSWLR 417.

5 *IRC v Hoogstraten* [1985] QB 1077; *Clarke v Heathfield* [1985] ICR 203.

6 *Wynne v Lord Newborough* (1790) 1 Ves 164.

7 *Brocklebank v East London Rly Co* (1879) 12 Ch D 839.

8 *Angel v Smith* (1804) 9 Ves 335; *Walker v Bell* (1816) 2 Madd 21; *Re Henry Pound, Son and Hutchins* (1889) 42 Ch D 402; *Lane v Capsey* (1891) 3 Ch 411. *Potts v Warwick and Birmingham Canal Navigation Co* (1853) Kay 142. As to such a person's entitlement to monies received by the receiver, if their claim is made out, see: *Walker v Bell* (1816) 2 Madd 21; *Re Hoare, Hoare v Owen* [1892] 3 Ch 94; *Preston v Tunbridge Wells Opera House Ltd* [1903] 2 Ch 323.

9 *Johnes v Claughton* (1822) Jac 573.

General powers and duties

18.26 The powers of the receiver will be determined by the terms order under which he is appointed. Generally, he will be appointed to collect, get in, receive and take charge of any outstanding parts, and the rents and profits, and to see to the management of the mortgaged property, applying the moneys received according to the directions of the court and accounting to the court for such application. A receiver appointed by the court will generally be under the same general duties as a receiver appointed out of court: for example, to act in good faith and to avoid any conflict of interest[1] and, where he sells property with the consent of the court[2], to obtain the best price reasonably obtainable[3]. As an officer of the court, the receiver must adopt high standards of honesty and straightforward dealing[4].

1 *Re Gent* (1892) 40 WR 267; *Newdigate Colliery Ltd, Re, Newdigate v Newdigate Colliery Ltd* [1912] 1 Ch 468. See also *Mirror Group Newspapaers plc v Maxwell* [1998] 1 BCLC 638 at 648 as to the receiver's fiduciary duty to protect, get in, realise and ultimately pass on assets and property to the creditors or other beneficiaries.
2 See **18.30**.
3 *Telsen Electric v J J Eastick* [1936] 3 All ER 266; *Procopi v Maschakis* (1969) 211 Estates Gazette 31.
4 *Re Condon, ex p James* (1874) Ch App 609; *Re Tyler, ex p Official Receiver* [1907] 1 KB 865. He is also under certain obligations under the Human Rights Act 1998: see **16.57** ff.

Receiver's right to apply to the court

18.27 The receiver ought not to originate any proceedings in the claim in which he was appointed, except in cases of necessity[1]. If an application to the court becomes necessary, the receiver should apply to the party having the conduct of the claim, who is the proper person to bring any difficulty before the court[2]. If the person with conduct of the claim fails to apply to the court and the receiver remains unrelieved from his difficulty, he may apply himself, and will then be entitled to his costs. There are, however, cases in which receivers have applied to the court without any objection having been made[3]. If a party to an action is appointed a receiver he does not lose his privileges as a party and may apply to the court as if he did not hold office[4]. In some cases it may be necessary that the receiver should join in the proceedings[5]. A receiver may at any time request the court to give him directions and should state in writing to the court the directions that are required[6].

1 *Comyn v Smith* (1823) 1 Hog 81; *Parker v Dunn* (1845) 8 Beav 497; *Ward v Swift* (1848) 6 Hare 309; *Re Sacker, ex p Sacker* (1888) 22 QBD 179.
2 *Windschuegl v Irish Polishes Ltd* [1914] 1 IR 33.
3 *Mills v Fry* (1815) Coop G 107; *Wickens v Townshend* (1830) 1 Russ & M 361; *Shaw v Rhodes* (1826) 2 Russ 539.
4 *Scott v Platel* (1847) 2 Ph 229.
5 *Chater v Maclean* (1855) 3 WR 261.
6 CPR Sch 1, RSC Ord 30, r 8.

The receiver's right to possession and receipt of rents

18.28 Once the receiver has power to act, he is entitled to possession of the property to which is appointment extends[1], subject to the rights of any prior incumbrancer in possession[2]. Where the property is let, he is entitled to receipt of the rents. Usually the order will make express provision to that effect, including that the tenants should attorn[3] to the receiver. Notice should be given to tenants to attorn to the receiver[4]; upon doing so, the receiver is entitled to receive all rents in arrear at the date of his appointment[5]. Prior to the tenants having notice that the rents should be paid to the receiver, they are entitled to continue to pay the rent to their landlord[6]. Where the person in possession does not hold as a tenant, the court will order that possession be given to the receiver[7] and, if it is refused, the receiver will be put into possession by the ordinary process of the court[8]. If it is unclear whether the person in possession is a tenant or not, the question may need to be brought before the court for determination[9]. If the mortgagor is in possession, the order may direct him to pay an occupation rent to the receiver, in which case the liability commences from the date of the order and the receiver may not demand a rent in respect of any preceding period[10], otherwise he will be liable to pay rent once it is demanded by the receiver[11]. The court may itself determine the appropriate amount of rent[12]. There is no privity of estate or contract between a landlord and the debenture holders or receiver where the demised premises are included in a floating charge and the landlord is not entitled to occupation rent out of the proceeds of goods sold by the receiver while in occupation[13]. A person who admits a sum of money to be due from him to the estate may not dispute the receiver's right to collect it[14]. The receiver is not liable for rent even when he has not complied with terms on which the lessor's judgment for rent and possession has been stayed[15].

The receiver is entitled to arrears of rent remaining due at the date of the order appointing him[16]. A receiver may distrain without the permission of the court, if (generally) he does so in the name of the landlord[17]. If, as is the regular course, the tenants have been made to attorn[18] to the receiver, the distress may then be made in his name[19]; a direction that the tenants attorn to the receiver is usually contained in the order appointing him[20]. The attornment creates a tenancy by estoppel between the tenant and the receiver only, and none between the tenant and the mortgagor[21]. The landlord is still entitled to distrain if he has the permission of the court or of the receiver[22].

The possession of the receiver is the possession of the court[23], without whose authority no one may interfere with the receiver, or with property of which he has taken or has been directed to take, possession[24], by any proceedings, whether of an ordinary kind or authorised by statute[25]. Where, however, the receiver is expressly appointed subject to the rights of prior incumbrancers, a prior incumbrancer may exercise his rights without the leave of the court[26], although a first mortgagee is not entitled to rents collected by a receiver prior to his application to take possession[27]. A claimant will be restrained from prosecuting his claim if he has not first obtained the permission of the court[28], whether or not he knew of the appointment of a receiver and no matter how clear his title; if he has commenced proceedings without permission, he may be obliged to discontinue them and commence fresh proceedings with the permission of the court[29]. If the receiver is informed that the mortgagor has interfered with the rents, he should seek an attachment[30]. The interference of the mortgagor with the rents does not exempt the receiver from being charged with the whole amount; he must discharge himself by showing what the owner received, or hindered him from getting[31].

1 See eg *McDonnell v White* (1865) 11 HL Cas 570; *Underhay v Read* (1887) 20 QBD 209. Cf *Re Watkins* (1879) 13 Ch D 252. The order of appointment must be so distinct on the face of it that it may be known of what property the receiver is in possession: see *Crow v Wood* (1850) 13 Beav 271. The appointment should be over the rents of the particular property and should be followed by a direction to the owner to deliver possession, or that the tenants should attorn: *Davis v Duke of Marlborough* (1819) 2 Swan 108 at 116.

2 If there are two receivers, both acting under the authority of the court, one of them ought not to take possession against the other; but he, or those at whose instance he was appointed, should seek the directions of the court: *Ward v Swift* (1848) 6 Hare 309.

3 That is, acknowledge that they are his servants: see **3.49**. For forms requiring attornment, see 33 *Atkin's Court Forms* (1997 issue).

4 *Mitchel v Duke of Manchester* (1750) 2 Dick 787; *Hobhouse v Hollcombe* (1848) 2 De G & Sm 208.

5 *Codrington v Johnstone* (1838) 1 Beav 520; *Re Ind Coope & Co Ltd, Fisher v Ind Coope & Co Ltd* [1911] 2 Ch 223.

6 *Brown v O'Connor* (1828) Hog 77; *Codrington v Johnstone* (1838) 1 Beav 520; *McDonnel v White* (1865) 11 HL Cas 570.

7 *Davis v Duke of Marlborough* above, at 116.
8 See *Wyman v Knight* (1888) 39 Ch D 165.
9 *Re Burchnall, Walter v Burchnall* [1893] WN 171.
10 *Lloyd v Mason* (1845) 2 My & Cr 487; *Re Burchnall, Walter v Burchnall* [1893] WN 171.
11 *Yorkshire Banking Co v Mullan* (1887) 35 Ch D 125.
12 *Re Burchnall, Walter v Burchnall* [1893] WN 171.
13 *Re J W Abbott & Co, Abbott v J W Abbott & Co* (1913) 30 TLR 13.
14 *Wood v Hitchings* (1840) 2 Beav 289.
15 *Re Westminster Motor Garage Co, Boyers v Westminster Motor Garage Co* (1914) 84 LJ Ch 753.
16 *Codrington v Johnstone* (1838) 1 Beav 520; *Hobson v Sherwood* (1854) 19 Beav 575.
17 *Pitt v Snowden* (1752) 3 Atk 750; *Bennett v Robins* (1832) 5 C & P 379. Cf *Brandon v Brandon* (1821) 5 Madd 473, suggesting he may only distrain for up to a year's rent in arrear without the court's permisson.
18 See n 3.
19 See *Pitt v Snowden* (1752) 3 Atk 750; *Brandon v Brandon* (1821) 5 Madd 473; *Bennett v Robins* (1832) 5 C & P 379.
20 Dan Ch Pr (8th edn) 1476; for form of order, see Seton (7th edn) pp 725, 762, and see *Hobhouse v Hollcombe* (1848) 2 De G & Sm 208 (where tenants properly opposed a motion to enforce the direction).
21 *Evans v Mathias* (1857) 7 E & B 590.
22 *Sutton v Rees* (1863) 9 Jur NS 456.
23 *Russell v East Anglian Rly Co* (1850) 3 Mac & G 104.
24 *Ames v Trustees of Birkenhead Docks* (1855) 20 Beav 332.
25 See *Angel v Smith* (1804) 9 Ves 335; *Evelyn v Lewis* (1844) 3 Hare 472; *Tink v Rundle* (1847) 10 Beav 318; *Hawkins v Gathercole* (1855) 1 Drew 12; *De Winton v Brecon Corpn (No 2)* (1860) 28 Beav 200.
26 *Underhay v Read* (1887) 20 QBD 209 at 218; *Engel v South Metropolitan Brewing and Bottling Co* [1891] WN 31.
27 *Re Metropolitan Amalgamated Estates Ltd, Fairweather v Metropolitan Amalgamated Estates Ltd* [1912] 2 Ch 497. As to the first mortgagee obtaining possession against the receiver, see **19.10**.
28 *Evelyn v Lewis* (1844) 3 Hare 472.
29 *Lees v Waring* (1825) 1 Hog 216; *Potts v Warwick and Birmingham Canal Navigation Co* (1853) Kay 142 (lessor restrained from proceeding to enforce a forfeiture without the leave of the court).
30 It is sufficient if he swears that he had the information from the tenants and that he believes it: *Anon* (1824) 2 Mol 499.
31 *Hamilton v Lighton* (1810) 2 Mol 499.

Letting

18.29 The receiver ought not to let without the consent of the court[1]. The order appointing the receiver may provide for him to have powers of leasing otherwise an application to the court should be made for directions[2]. The court can approve a letting by a receiver after it has begun[3]. Where the receiver has power to let, he should do so as advantageously as possible[4]. The receiver should not terminate tenancies except where the court has authorised him to do so[5], nor should he accept a surrender without the permission of the court[6].

1 *Wynne v Lord Newborough* (1790) 3 Bro CC 88; *Swaby v Dickon* (1833) 5 Sim 629; *Stamford, Spalding and Boston Banking Co v Keeble* [1913] 2 Ch 96; *Re The Liabilities (War-Time Adjustment) Act 1941* and *Re Cripps* [1946] Ch 265.
2 CPR Sch 1, RSC Ord 30, r 8.
3 *Re The Liabilities (War-Time Adjustment) Act 1941* and *Re Cripps* [1946] Ch 265.
4 *Wynne v Lord Newborough* (1790) 3 Bro CC 88.
5 *Wynne v Lord Newborough* above; *Doe d Mann v Walters* (1830) 10 B & C 626. The receiver may have implied authority to determine leases where he has been authorised to grant tenancies: *Doe d Marsack v Read* (1810) 12 East 57; *Doe d Manvers v Mizem* (1837) 2 Mood & R 56.
6 *Davidson v Armstrong* (1837) Sau & Sc 135.

Sale by receiver

18.30 A receiver appointed by the court can only sell the property of which he is appointed receiver by order of the court[1]. The receiver may purchase the property himself with the consent of the court[2].

1 *Re Henry Pound, Son and Hutchins Ltd* (1889) 42 Ch D 402, CA; and see *Australian Industry Development Corpn v Co-operative Farmers and Graziers Direct Meat Supply Co* [1978] VR 633.
2 *Nugent v Nugent* [1908] 1 Ch 546.

Expenditure and borrowing

18.31 The order appointing the receiver should deal with the scope of his powers to manage the property and to incur expenditure relating to it. As a general rule, the receiver should not act in such a way as to involve the estate in expense without the sanction of the court[1]. He cannot, therefore, on his own authority enter into contracts relating to the property. If he does so, he is not acting as agent of either party so as to bind them and is personally liable[2]. A receiver being an officer of the court appointed on behalf of all parties, the person at whose instance he is appointed is not (in the absence of an express undertaking) liable for his debts[3]. He must strictly observe the terms of his appointment and not incur liability on his own responsibility, only later seeking the sanction of the court[4]. The court may, however, retrospectively authorise expenditure, allowing the receiver to include it in his accounts, where the court considers it was justifiable[5]. The test of whether a receiver has acted properly in undertaking a particular task at a particular cost is whether a reasonably prudent man, faced with the same circumstances in relation to his own affairs, would lay out or hazard his own money in doing what the receiver has done. It is not sufficient for the receiver to say that what he has done is within the scope of the duties or powers conferred upon him. He is expected to deploy commercial judgment, not act regardless of expense. Transactions carried out at a high cost in relation to the benefit received, or expensive failures, will be subjected to close scrutiny[6]. In general, a receiver will be authorised to discharge necessary outgoings on the mortgaged property, such as rent or rates[7], or minor and necessary repairs[8]. He may also expend money on keeping the property insured[9]. The receiver should not borrow without the consent of the court, nor in excess of borrowing limits set by the court[10]. The court will need to be satisfied that the borrowing will be of general benefit. In an emergency, where it is genuinely necessary for the preservation of the property, the court has jurisdiction to authorise a receiver to raise money by mortgage of the property, even where all parties are not before the court[11].

1 *Fletcher v Dodd* (1789) 1 Ves 85; *A-G v Vigor* (1805) 11 Ves 563.
2 *Burt, Boulton and Hayward v Bull* [1895] 1 QB 276, CA; and see *Re Ernest Hawkins & Co Ltd, Brieba v Ernest Hawkins & Co Ltd* (1915) 31 TLR 247.
3 *Gosling v Gaskell* [1897] AC 575, HL, where, however, the receiver was appointed by the mortgagees. see also *Evans v Claystone Properties Ltd* [1988] 1 All ER 444, [1988] 1 WLR 358.
4 *Blunt v Clitherow* (1802) 6 Ves 799; *Re Wood Green and Hornsey Steam Laundry Ltd, Trenchard v Wood Green and Hornsey Steam Laundry Ltd* [1918] 1 Ch 423.
5 See eg in the context of repairs: *Tempest v Ord* (1816) 2 Mer 55; *Macartney v Walsh* (1830) Hayes 29n; *Whitley v Lowe* (1858) 25 Beav 421; *Re Gomersall, ex p Gordon* 20 (1875) LR Eq 291; *Re Graham, Graham v Noakes* [1895] 1 Ch 66.

6 *Mirror Group Newspapers plc v Maxwell (No 2)* [1998] 1 BCLC 638 at 649.
7 *Jacobs v Van Boolen, ex p Roberts* (1889) 34 Sol Jo 97; *Re Mannesmann Tube Co Ltd* [1901] 2 Ch 93.
8 *Blunt v Clitherow* (1802) 6 Ves 799; *A-G v Vigor* (1805) 11 Ves 563; *Thornhill v Thornhill* (1845) 14 Sim 600; *Re Graham, Graham v Noakes* [1895] 1 Ch 66; *Practice Direction* [1970] 1 All ER 671, [1970] 1 WLR 520 (a receiver appointed by the court may without leave effect small repairs, estimated to cost not over £150 in any one accounting period; a higher limit may be provided for on application to the Master); the current practice is to allow repairs of £1,000 in any accounting period without permission.
9 *Re Graham, Graham v Noakes* [1895] 1 Ch 66.
10 *Re British Power, Traction and Lighting Co Ltd* [1906] 1 Ch 497.
11 *Securities and Properties Corpn Ltd v Brighton Alhambra Ltd* (1893) 62 LJ Ch 566; *Greenwood v Algeçiras (Gibraltar) Rly Co* [1894] 2 Ch 205; *Re Thames Ironworks, Shipbuilding and Engineering Co Ltd* (1912) 106 LT 674.

Litigation

18.32 A receiver should not bring a claim for possession, or any other claim in relation to the property of which he has been appointed receiver, without the consent of the court[1]. Where it is necessary for proceedings to be brought, the application for the court's consent should normally be made by the party with the conduct of the claim and only by the receiver where that is for some reason not possible[2]. Where a receiver has granted leases with the authority of the court, or where he is entitled to receive rents, he may bring a claim in his own name for arrears, or otherwise as landlord, with the consent of the court[3]. It is not proper for the receiver to defend claims brought against him in respect of the estate, without the sanction of the court, especially if they arise out of acts improperly done by the receiver on his own authority; if he is unsuccessful, he will not be allowed an indemnity for the costs of such claims[4]. However, if he successfully defends a claim, and might have applied to the court for his own security, but did not do so, with consequent saving of expense on the part of the estate, he has the same right to be indemnified as if he had applied to the court[5]. Again, where it is necessary to defend proceedings, an application for the court's consent should normally be sought by the party with conduct of the proceedings in which the receiver was appointed, rather than the receiver himself.

1 *Wynne v Lord Newborough* (1790) 3 Bro CC 88; *Re Sartoris's Estate* [1892] 1 Ch 11; *Viola v Anglo-American Cold Storage Co* [1912] 2 Ch 305. For form of application to the court, see 33 *Atkin's Court Forms*.
2 *Comyn v Smith* (1823) 1 Hog 81; *Parker v Dunn* (1845) 8 Beav, 497; *Ward v Swift* (1848) 6 Hare 309; *Re Sacker, ex p Sacker* (1888) 22 QBD 179. See **18.27**.
3 *Dancer v Hastings* (1826) 4 Bing 2.
4 *Swaby v Dickon* (1833) 5 Sim 629.
5 *Bristowe v Needham* (1847) 2 Ph 190.

Contracts

18.33 Where a receiver is appointed of a company not in liquidation, the appointment does not generally affect the validity of the contracts of the company, since the persona of the contracting company remains legally interact, albeit under the control of the receiver[1]. A receiver and manager will not be authorised to repudiate contracts where this will damage the goodwill, which it is his duty to preserve[2]. However, the court will not sanction the borrowing of money to complete the contract, where the completion will produce no profit, direct or indirect[3]. The appointment of a receiver by the court operates as a dismissal of the employees of the mortgagor company[4].

1 *Parsons v Sovereign Bank of Canada* [1913] AC 160, PC.
2 *Re Newdigate Colliery Ltd, Newdigate v Newdigate Colliery Ltd* [1912] 1 Ch 468, CA.
3 *Re Thames Ironworks, Shipbuilding and Engineering Co Ltd, Farrer v Thames Ironworks etc, Co* (1912) 106 LT 674.
4 *Reid v Explosives Co Ltd* (1887) 19 QBD 264; *Nicoll v Cutts* [1985] BCLC 322, CA; cf where the receiver is appointed out of court. The court's receiver does not operate on behalf of the company, but adversely to it.

REMUNERATION

18.34 A person appointed receiver will be allowed such proper remuneration, if any, as the court may authorise[1]. The court will normally direct that such remuneration is by reference to appropriate rates of professional charges, or (in rare cases) by assessment by a costs judge on the standard basis[2]. The receiver is only entitled to discharge his remuneration from the assets of which he is appointed receiver; he cannot seek payment from a party personally, in the absence of any guarantee from them[3]. Where a mortgagee is appointed as receiver[4], he will normally be required to act without payment[5].

1 CPR Sch 1, RSC Ord 30, r 3(1). See *Mellor v Mellor* [1992] 4 All ER 10, [1992] 1 WLR 517; *Clark Equipment Credit Pty Ltd v Como Factors Pty Ltd* (1988) 14 NSWLR 552.
2 CPR Sch 1, RSC Ord 30, r 3(2). See also *Alliance & Leicester Building Society v Edgeshop* [1995] 2 BCLC 506; *Mirror Group Newspapers plc v Maxwell (No 2)* [1998] 1 BCLC 638.
3 *Boehm v Goodall* [1911] 1 Ch 155; *Alliance & Leicester Building Society v Edgeshop* [1995] 2 BCLC 506; *Re Andrews* [1999] 2 All ER 751, [1999] 1 WLR 1236.
4 See *Re Prytherch, Prytherch v Williams* (1889) 42 Ch D 590.
5 *Sayers v Whitfield* (1829) 1 Knapp 133; *Davis v Barrett* (1844) 13 LJ Ch 304; *Cummins v Perkins* [1899] 1 Ch 16.

LIABILITY TO ACCOUNT AND THE APPLICATION OF MONIES RECEIVED

18.35 It is a fundamental duty of a receiver to account for the way in which he exercises his powers and for all property dealt with and monies received by him[1]. In order to properly discharge that duty, he must keep proper records of what he has done and why he has done it[2]. He must submit accounts to the parties and on the dates ordered by the court[3]. A party may bring an objection to any item in the accounts before the court for examination[4]. The court may fix the amounts and frequency of payments into court to be made by the receiver[5]. If the receiver fails to submit proper accounts or to make the required payments into court, the court may give such directions as it thinks fit, including his discharge, or a disallowance of his remuneration[6].

Where a receiver has been appointed in a foreclosure action at the instance of the claimant, then money which comes into the receiver's hands belongs in the first instance (unless particular directions have been given for its application) to the claimant, who will be entitled to receive it on the dismissal of the claim[7]. If, following an inquiry, the court is satisfied that a person is a prior mortgagee, he is entitled to have possession from the receiver or sequestrator and to have any rents and profits received by the latter applied in payment of their mortgage debt, after paying the receiver's or sequestrator's costs and the costs of the application[8].

1 *Hamilton v Lighton* (1810) 2 Mol 499; *Re Skerretts* (1829) 2 Hog 192; *Mirror Group Newspapers plc v Maxwell (No 2)* [1998] 1 BCLC 638 at 648.
2 *Mirror Group Newspapers plc v Maxwell (No 2)* [1998] 1 BCLC 638 at 649.
3 CPR Sch 1, RSC Ord 30, r 5(1). There is provision for an interested party to inspect the papers etc. relating to the accounts on reasonable notice to the receiver: CPR Sch 1, RSC Ord 30, r 5(2).
4 CPR Sch 1, RSC Ord 30, r 5(4).
5 CPR Sch 1, RSC Ord 30, r 6.
6 CPR Sch 1, RSC Ord 30, r 7.
7 *Paynter v Carew* (1854) 23 LJ Ch 596; *Wright v Mitchell* (1811) 8 Ves 293; *Re Hoare, Hoare v Owen* [1892] 3 Ch 94.
8 *Walker v Bell* (1816) 2 Madd 21; *Re Hoare, Hoare v Owen* [1892] 3 Ch 94; *Preston v Tunbridge Wells Opera House Ltd* [1903] 2 Ch 323.

Chapter 19

The mortgagee's right to possession

MORTGAGEE'S RIGHT TO POSSESSION OF LAND[1]

LEGAL MORTGAGEE'S RIGHT TO POSSESSION

Right to immediate possession

19.1 The general rule is that, subject to contractual or statutory limitations, a mortgagee under a legal charge is entitled to seek possession of the mortgaged property at any time after the mortgage is executed, by virtue of the estate vested in him[2]. A second or subsequent mortgagee is similarly entitled to possession, except as against prior mortgagees[3]. This also applies to a legal charge[4] and to a registered charge[5]. The mortgagee is entitled to possession without notice or demand[6] and, subject to statutory or contractual restrictions, without a court order[7].

1 See Transfer of Land Mortgages (1991), (Law Com No 204) paras 7.28–7.38.

2 There is no requirement for default on the part of the mortgagor: *Birch v Wright* (1786) 1 Term Rep 378; *Doe d Roylance v Lightfoot* (1841) 8 M & W 553; *Four-Maids Ltd v Dudley Marshall (Properties) Ltd* [1957] Ch 317, [1957] 2 All ER 35; *Western Bank Ltd v Schindler* [1977] Ch 1, [1976] 2 All ER 393; *Mobil Oil Co Ltd v Rawlinson* (1981) 43 P& CR 221; *Barclays Bank plc v Tennet* [1985] CLY 130; *National Westminster Bank plc v Skelton* [1993] 1 All ER 242, [1993] 1 WLR 72. See, generally, (1961) 25 Conv (NS) 278 (Rudden), (1957) 73 LQR 300 (Megarry); (1969) 22 Current Legal Problems 129 (Ryder); [1979] Conv 266 (Smith); [1982] Conv 453 (Jackson); (1983) 133 NLJ 247 (Wilkinson); (1983) 127 Sol Jo 431 (Davey).

Section 95(4) of the Law of Property Act 1925 provides that nothing in the Act affects prejudicially the right of a mortgagee of land, whether or not his charge is secured by a legal term of years absolute, to take possession of the land.

3 See *Universal Showcards and Display Manufacturing Ltd v Brunt* (1984) 128 Sol Jo 581, CA; (1985) 136 NLJ 120. The order may be made subject to the rights of the prior incumbrancer or alternatively there may be a declaration of entitlement to possession with liberty to apply. A guarantor of a mortgage debt who has paid off the debt and to whom the benefit of the mortgage has been transferred is entitled to possession of the mortgaged property: *Spector v Applefield Properties Ltd* (1968) 206 Estates Gazette 537.The assignment of rights under a mortgage to a sub-mortgagee does not destroy the right of the head mortgagee to go into possession: *Owen v Cornell* (1967) 203 Estates Gazette 29.

4 Law of Property Act 1925, s 87 (1).

5 Land Registration Act 1925, s 34 (1); *Cityland and Property (Holdings) Ltd v Dabrah* [1968] Ch 166 at 171, 172, [1967] 2 All ER 639 at 649, 641.

6 *Birch v Wright*, above; *Doe d Roby v Maisey* (1828) 8 B & C 767.

7 *Ropaigealach v Barclays Bank Plc* [2000] 1 QB 263; [1983] Conv 293 (Clarke); see **19.8**. A mortgagor who refuses to give up possession has the status of a trespasser: *Birch v Wright* (1786) 1 Term Rep 378; *Jolly v Arbuthnot* (1859) 4 De G & J 224; see **19.3**. Where the

mortgagee cannot take physical possession because the land is subject to a tenancy which is binding on him (see **19.16** and **19.19** ff), he is entitled to possession by receiving the rents: *Moss v Gallimore* (1779) 1 Doug KB 279; *Horlock v Smith* (1842) 6 Jur 478; and see further **19.11**.

Express or implied restrictions on right to possession

19.2 Where the advance is repayable by instalments the mortgage deed usually provides that the mortgagee will not be entitled to possession until default[1] and such a provision may be implied, for example from the terms and circumstances of the mortgage; however, the court will not lightly restrict the mortgagee's right[2]. The fact that the secured moneys were payable only on demand did not imply that the right to possession arose only on demand, rather than on execution of the mortgage[3]. Where the right of entry is to arise only on default on payment on demand, a reasonable time must be given to the mortgagor to comply with the demand before the right is exercised. If the demand is made by an agent the mortgagor must be given a reasonable time to ascertain if the agent is duly authorised to receive the money[4]. A right to retain possession is sometimes specially secured to the mortgagor, by him becoming tenant of the mortgagee[5]. Restrictions on the right to possession are also imposed by statute[6]. The existence of a counterclaim, whether a mere counterclaim, or a cross-claim for unliquidated damages, which if established would give rise to an equitable set-off, does not by itself defeat the mortgagee's right to possession, even if it exceeds the amount of the mortgage debt[7]. It seems the right to possession must also be exercised in good faith and for the purposes of preserving or enforcing the security[8]. Thus the court will not normally order possession against one of two joint mortgagors, where the other has a defence to the claim, given that it would be of no benefit to the mortgagee[9].

1 See **3.25**.
2 *Birmingham Citizens Permanent Building Society v Caunt* [1962] Ch 883 at 890, [1962] 1 All ER 163 at 168; *Esso Petroleum Co Ltd v Alstonbridge Properties Ltd* [1975] 3 All ER 358 at 367; *Western Bank Ltd v Schindler*, above; *Ashley Guarantee plc v Zacaria* [1993] 1 All ER 254, [1993] 1 WLR 62; [1979] Conv 266 (Smith). If there is any restriction an injunction restraining the mortgagee from taking possession contrary thereto will be granted: *Doe d Parsley v Day* (1842) 2 QB 147, and the right is, of course, only exercisable so long as an action to enforce it may be brought; see *Wright v Pepin* [1954] 2 All ER 52 and **16.40** ff.
3 *National Westminster Bank plc v Skelton* [1993] 1 All ER 242; [1993] 1 WLR 72n.
4 *Toms v Wilson* (1862) 4 B & S 442; *ANZ Banking Group (NZ) Ltd v Gibson* [1981] 2 NZLR 513.
5 *Moore v Shelley* (1883) 8 App Cas 285, PC; *Cripps (Pharmaceuticals) Ltd v Wickenden* [1973] 2 All ER 606, [1973] 1 WLR 944; *ANZ Banking Group (NZ) Ltd v Gibson*, above; cf *Ronald Elwyn Foster Ltd v Dunlop Canada Ltd* [1982] 1 SCR 726.
6 The wording of the implied statutory covenants for title in Sch 2, Pt III of the Law of Property Act 1925, seems to assume that such a right is given. The right may also be secured by an attornment clause (as to which see **3.49**, or by the mortgagor becoming tenant of the mortgagee, in which case the mortgagor's tenancy must be terminated in the manner provided: see **19.5**.
7 Administration of Justice Act 1970, s 36 as amended (**19.51** ff); Rent Act (**16.22** ff); Protection from Eviction Act 1977 (**19.8**); Consumer Credit Act 1974, s 126 (**10.64**).
8 *Mobil Oil Co Ltd v Rawlinson* (1981) 43 P&CR 221; *Citibank Trust Ltd v Ayivor* [1987] 1 WLR 1157; *Samuel Keller (Holdings) Ltd v Martins Bank Ltd* [1971] 1 WLR 43; *Midland Bank plc v McGrath* [1996] EGCS 61; *Albany Home Loans v Massey* [1997] 2 All ER 609, [1993] Conv 459. The question of whether there may be an exception in the case of an equitable right of set-off equal to or in excess of the mortgage debt has not been decided: see *National Westminster Bank plc v Skelton* [1993] 1 All ER 242, [1993] 1 WLR 72n; *Ashley Guarantee plc v Zacaria* [1993] 1 All ER 254, [1993] 1 WLR 62. The existence of such a

claim may, however, be taken into account by the court in deciding whether to exercise its statutory powers for adjournment or suspension of an order for possession of a dwelling-house. *National Westminster Bank plc v Skelton*, above; *Ashley Guarantee plc v Zacaria*.

10 *Quennell v Maltby* [1979] 1 WLR 318; *Palk v Mortgage Services Funding plc* [1993] Ch 330; *Downsview Nominees Ltd v First City Corp. Ltd* [1993] AC 295 at 312, 3 All ER 626 at 635; *Albany Home Loans Ltd v Massey* [1997] 2 All ER 609; Cf Gray *Elements of Land Law* (3rd edn 2001) pp 414-415.

11 *Albany Home Loans Ltd v Massey*, above.

POSITION OF MORTGAGOR UNTIL LEGAL MORTGAGEE TAKES POSSESSION

Mortgagor allowed to remain in possession

19.3 Until the legal mortgagee seeks possession of the property, the mortgagor may remain in possession of it. After the execution of the mortgage, the mortgagor is usually allowed to do so, until he default in payments under the mortgage, and the mortgagee finds it necessary to use the remedies given him by the security[1].

The relationship between mortgagor and mortgagee whilst the mortgagor remains in occupation is best described simply in those terms; the mortgagor is not, as he has sometimes been called, the tenant at will or by sufferance of the mortgagee[2]. Although the mortgagor in possession has parted with his immediate estate, he remains in possession at the pleasure, and consistently with the right, of the grantee. He is entitled to exercise the ordinary rights of property. Thus he is not liable to pay any occupation rent until a demand or order for possession has been made[3]. He is entitled to receive rents for his own use and is not obliged to account to the mortgagee for them[4]. He can bring actions in respect of the mortgaged property against anyone save the mortgagee[5]. Subject to certain restrictions, he can grant leases[6]. However, his rights are limited by the grant he made and in particular are subject to the mortgagee's right to take possession at any time[7].

Whilst in possession the mortgagor may not diminish or prejudice the security, for example by committing waste (by felling timber or pulling down a house); he can be sued by the mortgagee for injuring the property[8] and conduct putting the security at risk will be restrained by injunction[9]. Upon the mortgagee taking possession, the mortgagor is not entitled to the crops growing on the land at the time the mortgagee takes possession, nor to rents in arrear or accruing[10].

1 A mortgagee might want to take possession before the power of sale has arisen, eg to prevent vandalism to the property: see *Twentieth Century Banking Corpn Ltd v Wilkinson* [1977] Ch 99, [1976] 3 All ER 361, and see *Western Bank Ltd v Schindler* [1977] Ch 1, [1976] 2 All ER 393, CA. However, he will generally be reluctant to do so because of the liability of a mortgagee in possession to account: see **19.65**. Generally, see (1977) 41 Conv (NS) 76 and Law Commission Working Paper no 99, *Land Mortgages*, paras 3.23–3.24. And Law Commission Report *Transfer of Land – Land Mortgages* 1991 Law Com no 204, para 6.16.

2 See (1969) 22 Current Legal Problems 129 (Ryder); *Doe d Higginbotham v Barton* (1840) 11 Ad & El 307 at 314; *Doe d Jones v Williams* (1836) 5 Ad & El 291 at 297; *Birch v Wright* (1786) 1 Term Rep 378 at 383. Cf, however per Lord Mansfield, *Moss v Gallimore* (1779) 1 Doug KB 279 at 282; the former CPR Sch 2, Ord 88, r 5 (5) (revoked from 15 October 2001), which may be interpreted as supposing the relationship to be that of tenancy at will; also *Keech v Hall* (1778) 1 Doug KB 21; *Moore v Shelley* (1883) 8 App Cas 285; *Thunder d Weaver v Belcher* (1803) 3 East 449; *Doe d Roby v Maisey* (1828) 8 B & C 767; *Bagnall v Villar* (1879) 12 Ch D 812; *Heath v Pugh* (1881) 6 QBD 345 at 359.

3 *Heath v Pugh* (1881) 6 QBD 345 at 359, CA, affd sub nom *Pugh v Heath* (1882) 7 App Cas 235, HL; *Yorkshire Banking Co v Mullan* (1887) 35 Ch D 125.
4 *Moss v Gallimore*, above; *Rogers v Humphreys* (1835) 4 Ad & El 299; *Re Ind, Coope & Co Ltd, Fisher v Ind, Coope & Co* [1911] 2 Ch 223; *Birch v Wright*, above; and see **19.4**.
5 *Sellick v Smith* (1826) 11 Moore CP 459; Law of Property Act 1925, s 98 and see **19.4**.
6 Law of Property Act 1925, s 99 and see **19.21**.
7 See **19.1**.
8 *King v Smith* (1843) 2 Hare 239; *Bagnall v Villar* (1879) 12 Ch D 812.
9 See **16.4–16.5**.
10 *Re Gordon, ex p Official Receiver* (1889) 61 LT 299; *Ex p Temple* (1822) 1 Gl & J 216, where the mortgagor was held entitled to the crops as tenant at will by express contract; *Doe d Roby v Maisey*, above; *Doe d Griffith v Mayo* (1828) 7 LJOSKB 84; *Jolly v Arbuthnot* (1859) 4 De G & J 224; *Re Gordon, ex p Official Receiver*, above.

Mortgagor's statutory right to sue for rents or in trespass

19.4 Where the mortgage is of land subject to a lease, the entire reversion in the land, together with the right to receive future rents, is vested in the mortgagee[1]. However, before the mortgagee has taken possession, the mortgagor has a statutory right to sue in his own name for possession or damages for trespass. Section 98 of the Law of Property Act 1925 provides that a mortgagor for the time being entitled to the possession or receipt of the rents and profits of any land, as to which the mortgagee has not given notice of his intention to take possession or to enter into the receipt of the rents and profits thereof, may sue for such possession, or for the recovery of such rents or profits, or to prevent or recover damages in respect of any trespass or other wrong relative thereto, in his own name only, unless the cause of action arises upon a lease or other contract made by him jointly with another person[2]. That does not prejudice the power of a mortgagor independently of that section to take proceedings in his own name only, either in right of any legal estate vested in him or otherwise[3]. The mortgagor is also entitled to sue on the covenants in any lease[4], which entitle him to enforce the covenants so long as he is for the time being entitled to the rents and profits under the tenancy[5].

Thus so long as the mortgagor is allowed to remain in possession, he may recover the rents and as against trespassers may recover possession or obtain an injunction without joining the mortgagee[6]. However, the mortgagor is not entitled to do things which might prejudicially affect the mortgagee's interests. Thus the mortgagor is not entitled to forfeit a lease under a proviso for re-entry for breach of covenant[7], nor to enforce a right which would involve the taking of accounts in which the mortgagee is interested[8]. If in any such case the mortgagee refuses to be a claimant, he may be made a defendant; but in that case, it seems, the mortgagor must offer to redeem[9]. The mortgagor's right to grant a tenancy is considered below[10].

1 As to the vesting of the reversion in the mortgagee, see **19.17**.
2 Law of Property Act 1925, s 98(1). The section applies whether the mortgage was made before or after the commencement of this Act: s 98(3).
3 Law of Property Act 1925, s 98(2).
4 Under s 141 of the Law of Property Act 1925 in respect of leases granted before after 1 January, 1996 and under s 15 of the Landlord and Tenant (Covenants) Act 1995 in respect of tenancies granted after 1 January, 1996.
5 The references in sub-s 141(1) to the severance of the reversionary estate suggest that the provision was aimed primarily at the difficulties formerly caused by such severance, but while this is one effect, the subsection is not restricted to cases of severance and it enables a mortgagor in possession to sue in his own name on the covenants in the lease whether

the lease is by deed or not and whether made before or after the commencement of the Act: see *Turner v Walsh* [1909] 2 KB 484, CA.

6 *Fairclough v Marshall* (1878) 4 Ex D 37.

7 *Matthews v Usher* [1900] 2 QB 535; see *Molyneux v Richard* [1906] 1 Ch 34.

8 *Van Gelder, Apsimon & Co v Sowerby Bridge United District Flour Society* (1890) 44 Ch D 374 at 392, CA.

9 See *Hughes v Cook* (1865) 34 Beav 407.

10 See **19.20**, **19.21** ff.

Mortgagor as tenant of mortgagee[1]

19.5 The mortgagor may become tenant to the mortgagee by implication of a provision in the mortgage qualifying the mortgagee's right to possession. Thus a tenancy was created where there was a provision that the mortgage should not be called in until the expiration of a given term and that until default in payment it should be lawful for the mortgagor peaceably to enjoy and receive the rents; that amounted to a re-demise by the mortgagee to the mortgagor during the term fixed[2]. However, no tenancy was created where the mortgage deed provided that the mortgagee could enter after default; it was held that that did not imply that the mortgagor could remain in possession until default, but rather that until default the mortgagee could rest upon his title under the mortgage, and afterwards also rely on the benefit of the covenant[3]. Even if the words used imply some right to possession in the mortgagor, they will not amount to a re-demise to him unless some certain time is fixed during which the mortgagor is to hold[4]. Thus no tenancy was created by a covenant that the mortgagee should not sell or lease without a month's notice demanding payment and default thereon. The creation of a tenancy will not be implied where the effect would be inconsistent with the general object of the deed[5].

A tenancy is also created where the mortgagor, being in occupation, attorns tenant to the mortgagee[6]. Such attornment clauses were commonly inserted in mortgage deeds. In certain circumstances, a tenancy at will which existed before the mortgage will not be determined by the mortgage[7].

Where the mortgagor is tenant to the mortgagee, the nature of the tenancy will depend upon the intention of the parties, particularly the language and intention of the deed. Given the relationship of mortgagor and mortgagee, the courts may be more willing to imply that the mortgagor is simply a tenant at will rather than a yearly tenant. Thus a tenancy at will was created in the following circumstances: where the tenancy was nominally created for a term of years, but the mortgagee had the power to enter at any time without notice[8]; where the mortgagor agreed to pay a yearly rent as tenant at will, in return for the mortgagee giving a covenant for quiet enjoyment, with a proviso that no possession should be taken till the expiration of 12 months after notice of such intention to the mortgagor[9]; and where the mortgagor agreed to become tenant during the will and pleasure of the mortgagee, at a rent payable on certain days in every year[10]. Where the mortgagor is tenant at will he cannot determine the tenancy by transferring his interest to another, without notice to the mortgagee[11], but the death of the mortgagor determines it and his successor is not tenant to the mortgagee[12]. Notwithstanding the existence of apt words for the creation of a tenancy, the mortgagee may retain his ordinary power as mortgagee to take possession, and eject the mortgagor, if his ordinary rights are reserved[13].

1 See (1969) 22 Current Legal Problems 129 (Ryder).

2 *Wilkinson v Hall* (1837) 3 Bing NC 508.

3 *Doe d Roylance v Lightfoot* (1841) 8 M & W 553.
4 *Doe d Parsley v Day* (1842) 2 QB 147; and see *Clowes v Hughes* (1870) LR 5 Exch 160; *Wilkinson v Hall*, above.
5 *Walker v Giles and Fort* (1848) 6 CB 662; *Pinhorn v Souster* (1853) 8 Exch 763; *Thorn v Croft* (1866) LR 3 Eq 193.
6 See **3.49**.
7 *Doe d Goody v Carter* (1847) 9 QB 863.
8 *Morton v Woods* (1869) LR 4 QB 293; but see *Re Threlfall, ex p Queen's Benefit Building Society* (1880) 16 Ch D 274.
9 *Doe d Dixie v Davies* (1851) 7 Exch 89.
10 *Doe d Bastow v Cox* (1847) 11 QB 122.
11 *Pinhorn v Souster* (1853) 8 Exch 763.
12 *Scobie v Collins* [1895] 1 QB 375.
13 *Doe d Garrod v Olley* (1340) 12 Ad & El 481; *Doe d Snell v Tom* (1843) 4 QB 615.See also *Doe d Parsley v Day* (1842) 2 QB 147.

RIGHT OF EQUITABLE MORTGAGEE TO POSSESSION

19.6 An equitable mortgagee, has no legal estate and thus no legal right to the mortgaged land[1]. It has thus often been said that he has no inherent right to possession against the mortgagor, and those claiming under the mortgagor[2]. However, he can be given a right to possession by an express provision in the mortgage deed[3], or the permission of the mortgagor, or the appointment of a receiver[4], and may seek an order of the court entitling him to possession[5]. However, a mortgagee who has taken possession may defend his possession[6] and may keep rents paid to him by the mortgagor's tenants[7]. An equitable chargee has no right to possession without a court order[8].

While, today, possession is rarely taken under any mortgage without an order of the court[9], the existence or non-existence of such a right is of some significance. First, if there is a right, on an application to the court an order for possession is a matter of course, subject to the powers of suspension and adjournment where they apply[10]. Secondly, the equitable mortgagee's entitlement to rents will depend on his right to possession[11].

Where a mortgage contains a recital that the mortgagor is seised in fee simple this operates as an estoppel in favour of the mortgagee. If the mortgagor, having then only an equitable interest, for instance, under a contract to purchase, subsequently acquires the legal estate, this will feed the estoppel and the mortgagee's estate will become legal[12]. However, in the absence of such a precise averment the mortgagee will not obtain the legal estate and the mortgagor can create a legal estate in favour of a subsequent mortgagee, so that, if such subsequent mortgagee took without notice[13], he will have priority[14].

1 See *Vacuum Oil Co Ltd v Ellis* [1914] 1 KB 693 at 703, CA.
2 See eg *Barclays Bank v Bird* [1954] Ch 274 at 280; *Royal Bank of Canada v Nicholson* (1980) 110 DLR (3d) 763; *Ladup Ltd v Williams & Glynn's Bank plc* [1985] 1 WLR 851 at 855; *Ashley Guarantee plc v Zacaria* [1993] 1 WLR 62 at 69; *Zanzoul v Westpac Banking Corp* (1995) 6 BPR 14142. The rationale for the equitable mortgagee not having a general right to possession was based on the ground that a person with an equitable title only could not bring ejectment: see Waldock *Law of Mortgages* (2nd edn) p 55; but it has been argued that even before the Judicature Acts this was not always so: (1955) 71 LQR 204, 216; and see *Ex p Bignold* (1834) 4 Deac & Ch 59; *Re Gordon* (1889) 61 LT 299; *Tichborne v Weir* (1892) 67 LT 735; *Antrim County Land Building and Investment Co Ltd and Houston v Stewart* [1904] 2 IR 357, CA; *Maio v Piro* [1956] SASR 233 at 239; *Spencer v Mason* (1931) 75 Sol Jo 295) and that this reason cannot have survived the Judicature Acts, reliance being placed on *Walsh v Lonsdale* (1882) 21 Ch D 9, CA (see (1954) LQR 161 (Megarry); (1955) 71 LQR 204; Sykes *The Law of Securities* (5th edn) pp 161-162; Croft *Mortgagee's Power of Sale* p 47; and *Antrim County Land Building and Investment Co Ltd and Houston v Stewart*

[1904] 2 IR 357, CA; *Maio v Piro* [1956] SASR 233 at 239; *General Finance Mortgage and Discount Co v Liberator Permanent Benefit Building Society* (1878) 10 Ch D 15; *Re O'Neill* [1967] NI 129; *Mills v Lewis* (1985) 3 BPR 9421 NSW, CA).In *Spencer v Mason* (1931) 75 Sol Jo 295 the mortgage contained an express right to a legal mortgage, the mortgagor apparently let the mortgagee into possession and this was held to be effective against a successor in title of the mortgagor.

3 *Vacuum Oil Co Ltd v Ellis*, above at 703; *Ocean Accident and Guarantee Corpn v Ilford Gas Co* [1905] 2 KB 493, CA; *Mercantile Credits Ltd v Archbold* [1970] QWN 9. However an equitable mortgagee is entitled to call for a legal mortgage (see **3.84** ff), so an equitable mortgagee could obtain a right to possession by enforcing his right to a legal mortgage, but until such mortgage were executed, it would seem that he would have no right to possession *qua* legal mortgagee.

4 *Vacuum Oil Co Ltd v Ellis* [1914] 1 KB 693 at 703, 708, CA (by the court or out of the court).

5 *Barclays Bank Ltd v Bird* [1954] Ch 274, [1954] 1 All ER 449; *Re Postle, ex p Bignold* (1835) 4 Deac & Ch 259.Both *Re Gordon, ex p Official Receiver* (1889) 61 LT 229 and *Ocean Accident and Guarantee Corpn Ltd v Ilford Gas Co*, above, give some support to those who argue that the equitable mortgagee has the same right to possession as a legal mortgagee. For a criticism of *Barclays Bank Ltd v Bird*, above, and generally of the view as expressed above, see *Croft* pp 44–48; (1954) 70 LQR 161 (REM), (1955) 71 LQR 204 (Wade).

6 Relying on *Walsh v Lonsdale*, above.

7 *Finck v Tranter* [1905] 1 KB 427. For the equitable mortgagee's right to rents, see **35.13**. For the right of the equitable mortgagee in possession to growing crops, see *Re Postle, ex p Bignold*, above; and **35.14**.

8 An equitable chargee has no right to possession without a court order: *Garfitt v Allen* (1887) 37 Ch D 48; see **2.10**. North J appears to have wrongly equated equitable charges with equitable mortgages in this case: see Croft *Mortgagee's Power of Sale* p 45; (1955) 71 LQR 204 (Wade). Irish courts have reached the same conclusion: see *National Bank Ltd v Hegarty* (1901) 1 NIJR 13; *Northern Banking Co Ltd v Devlin* [1924] 1 IR 90; Ch D; *Bank of Ireland v Faney* [1930] IR 457.

9 See **19.8**. See though, *Repaigealach v Barclays Bank plc* [2000] QB 263, [1999] 3 WLR 17, [1999] 4 All ER 235, CA; [2000] 1 WLR 1034, HL (pet. dismissed).

10 See **19.51** ff.

11 See **19.11**.*Re Pearson* (1838) 3 Mont & A 592; *Finck v Tranter* [1905] 1 KB 427; *Vacuum Oil Co Ltd v Ellis* [1914] 1 KB 693 at 703, CA.

12 *Doe d Christmas v Oliver* (1829) 10 B & C 181. Cf *Heath v Crealock* (1874) 10 Ch App 22; *Onward Building Society v Smithson* [1893] 1 Ch 1.

13 Registration under the Land Charges Act 1972 constitutes notice: Law of Property Act 1925, s 198 (1); and see **24.8**.

14 *Right d Jefferys v Bucknall* (1831) 2 B & Ad 278.

EXERCISE OF THE MORTGAGEE'S RIGHT TO POSSESSION

Exercising the right

19.7 Where the mortgagor is in possession (and he is not a tenant of the mortgagee[1]), the right is exercised by taking physical possession of the land, if that can be done peaceably[2], or by bringing an action for possession[3]. The same applies where a tenant of the mortgagor, whose tenancy is not binding on the mortgagee[4], is in possession. The mortgagee need not give notice either before entering[5] or commencing proceedings[6]. If a tenant of the mortgagor, whose tenancy is binding on the mortgagee[7], is in possession, the right is exercised by notice to the tenant to pay the rent to the mortgagee[8]. Since no one is allowed to dispute a title which he himself has granted, the mortgagor cannot set up as against his mortgagee the title of a third person, even though such third person may have a right to possession[9]. In the case of leasehold property, the mortgagee should consider whether by taking possession it would breach any covenant in the lease against the mortgagor as tenant parting with possession[10].

1 See **19.5**.
2 The right to the peaceable recovery of possession is not restricted by the Administration of Justice Act 1970 (as amended); *Ropaigealach v Barclays Bank plc* [2000] 1 QB 263, [1999] 3 WLR 17, [1999] 4 All ER 235, CA; [2000] 1 WLR 1034, HL (pet. dismissed).See [1983] Conv 293 (Clarke); [1999] CLJ 281 (Dixon); [1999] Conv 263 (Dunn); (1999) 143 Sol Jo 206 (Grant).
3 See **19.28** ff.
4 See **19.18**. As to the rights of occupation of a spouse, see **12.132** ff.
5 *Birch v Wright* (1786) 1 Term Rep 378 at 383.
6 *Jolly v Arbuthnot* (1859) 4 De G & J 224 at 236.
7 See **19.16, 19.19** ff.
8 *Horlock v Smith* (1842) 6 Jur 478; *Davies v Law Mutual Building Society* (1971) 219 Estates Gazette 309. For forms, see 28 *Forms and Precedents* (5th edn, 1999 reissue) Mortgages.
9 *Doe d Bristowe v Pegge* (1785) 1 Term Rep 758n.
10 Leases often contain a covenant by the tenant against sub-letting, assigning or parting with possession of the demised property, such covenant being either absolute or qualified by the requirement of consent. Where the covenant is qualified, the position on an assignment on sale by the mortgagee is covered by a part of s 89 (1) of the Law of Property Act 1925. This provides that where a licence to assign is required on a sale by a mortgagee, such licence shall not be unreasonably refused. It is submitted that a parting of possession by the mortgagor arising on the sale of the property by the mortgagee with such licence is not a breach of a covenant against parting with possession. Where the mortgagee himself takes possession prior to a sale (as will usually be the case) or for a longer period it is submitted that the landlord cannot complain where the mortgage is valid against him, ie if by sub-demise and licence were given or by legal charge (It is assumed that a legal charge in itself cannot be a breach of the covenant). For, if the mortgage itself is valid against him, a fortiori, any power exercisable thereunder. The position may be the same for an absolute covenant. It is not certain precisely what the part of s 89 referred to above is intended to cover. There are three possibilities. First, it may be referring to a covenant in the lease which expressly requires a licence to assign on a sale by a mortgagee. This is unlikely. Leases rarely, if ever, have or have had such a provision. Secondly, it may be referring to the situation where there is a qualified covenant in the lease against assignment etc. Thirdly, it may be referring to the situation where, as a matter of face, rather than the terms of any covenant, licence is required. This latter construction would include the case where there was an absolute covenant. It is submitted that this third construction is not correct, since to hold that it was correct would mean that where there was an absolute covenant and there had been a mortgage without the landlord's approval and he could be forced to accept a new tenant by virtue of the exercise of the mortgagee's power of sale. It is submitted that the second alternative is the correct construction. This means that, where there is an absolute covenant, an assignment on sale by a mortgagee by demise will involve a breach of the covenant. So too a legal charge, for, although the charge itself may be effective against the landlord, the assignment and parting with possession to the purchaser from the chargee will be a breach. As regards the mortgagee's own possession, if the mortgage itself is in breach of covenant, a fortiori, the taking of possession by the mortgagee. (If the legal charge is not a breach, it can be argued that the mortgagee's own possession is also not in breach.) Sometimes an absolute covenant is qualified only to allow mortgaging. In that case the mortgagee's own possession and the assignment to and possession of a purchaser from the mortgagee are, it is submitted, unobjectionable. By allowing the mortgage, the landlord allows all that the mortgage entails. The matter is, it is submitted, one of estoppel or implied licence. (See Wolstenholme and Cherry's *Conveyancing Statutes* (13th edn) p 182 (repeating the statement in earlier editions) for support of this view, but no reasons are given there.)Furthermore, it is well established that there is no breach of a covenant against assignment etc unless the disposition is voluntary and, where the mortgage is valid against the landlord, it can be argued that any potential breach of covenant occurring through the exercise of the mortgagee's powers for enforcing the security is a result of an involuntary disposition or act by the mortgagor-tenant (but see *Re Wright, ex p Landau v Trustee* [1949] Ch 729, [1949] 2 All ER 605).

Taking peaceable possession

19.8 If physical possession is to be taken, it must be taken peaceably. If violence is used to secure entry, the mortgagee may be liable to prosecution under the criminal law[1], although the mortgagor will have no civil remedy against the mortgagee[2]. Violence need not only be against the person, but may also be in the manner of entry[3], as by breaking open the doors of a house[4]. Consequently, save where the mortgagor consents to the mortgagee taking actual possession, which will be rare[5], the occasions where a physical taking of possession is possible will be rare. It will generally only be possible where the mortgagor (and any tenant of the mortgagor)[6] has abandoned the premises[7].

1 Criminal Law Act 1977, as amended by the Criminal Justice and Public Order Act 1994. The 1977 Act repealed the Forcible Entry Acts: s 13. Also the Protection from Eviction Act 1977 applies in relation to tenants of the mortgaged property; *Bolton Building Society v Cobb* [1966] 1 WLR 1. On self help generally, see Croft *Mortgagee's Power of Sale* pp 57–59. Also the Protection from Eviction Act 1977 applies in relation to tenants of the mortgaged property; *Bolton Building Society v Cobb* [1966] 1 WLR 1.
2 *Beddall v Maitland* (1881) 17 Ch D 174; *Hemmings v Stoke Poges Golf Club* [1920] 1 KB 720, CA; *Aglionby v Cohen* [1955] 1 QB 558, [1955] 1 All ER 785; *McPhail v Persons (Names Unknown)* [1973] Ch 447, [1973] 3 All ER 393 at 398.
3 Criminal Law Act 1977, s 6 (4). The offence is committed only when the accused knows that there is another person on the premises when he uses or threatens violence and knows that he is opposed to the entry: s 6 (1) (a), (b). The fact that a person has an interest or right in the property does not constitute lawful authority to use or threaten violence to secure entry: s 6 (2).
4 *Hemmings v Stoke Poges Golf Club*, above.
5 See eg *Hughes v Waite* [1957] 1 All ER 603 at 604.
6 *Bolton Building Society v Cobb* [1966] 1 WLR 1.
7 For an example, see *Ropaigealach v Barclays Bank plc* [2000] 1 QB 263.

Claims for possession

19.9 A claim for possession alone is simply a claim for the recovery of land[1] and is not proceedings for enforcing the mortgage[2]. An order for possession might not be made if there were a substantial question as to the validity or right to enforcement of the mortgage[3], or if the right to possession were being exercised improperly[4].

1 See **16.40**.
2 *Esso Petroleum Co Ltd v Alstonbridge Properties Ltd* [1975] 3 All ER 358 at 365; *Western Bank Ltd v Schindler* above; both *Quennell v Maltby* [1979] 1 All ER 568, [1979] 1 WLR 318, CA, and *Mobil Oil Co Ltd v Rawlinson*, above, assume that the claim for possession was an enforcement of the mortgage; and see *Martin v Watson and Egan* [1919] 2 IR 534. Mortgages sometimes refer to the lender being able to enforce the mortgage or security on default etc.
3 *Mobil Oil Co Ltd v Rawlinson* (1981) 43 P & CR 221.
4 See cases cited in **16.13**, n 3.

Where receiver in possession

19.10 If a receiver appointed by the court is in possession, and the rights of prior incumbrancers have not been preserved[1], the mortgagee wishing to go into possession must apply in the action in which the receiver was appointed for the discharge of the receiver[2], or for leave to bring an action for the recovery of the land[3]. If the rights of prior incumbrancers are preserved, as they usually will be, the mortgagee is entitled to possession as against the receiver and accordingly should give the tenant notice to pay rent to him[4].

1 See **18.19**.

2 *Thomas v Brigstocke* (1827) 4 Russ 64; *Searle v Choat* (1884) 25 Ch D 723, CA; *Custom Credit Corpn Ltd v Heard and Raphael* [1982] 31 SASR 101; see **18.28**.
3 *Doe d Roby v Maisey* (1828) 8 B & C 767.
4 *Underhay v Read* (1887) 20 QBD 209 at 219, CA.

What constitutes possession

19.11 Where the mortgagee has taken actual possession of the whole of the property that certainly constitutes possession. Entry on to part of the mortgaged property, where it has a defined area or is a unit, will be regarded as entry on the whole[1], although the mortgagee may limit his possession to part[2]. The mortgagee's intention is also clear when he gives notice to the mortgagor's tenants to pay rent to him or his agent, as that is equivalent to taking possession[3]. However, the mere fact that the mortgagee is in receipt of the rents does not necessarily make him accountable as a mortgagee in possession. The question depends on whether he has taken out of the mortgagor's hands the power and duty of managing and controlling the mortgaged property and dealing with the tenants[4]. Thus where the mortgagee received from the mortgagor's agent a sum equal to the rents which the agent has to collect, but the agent had not served on the tenants any notice on behalf of the mortgagee, the mortgagee was not chargeable as a mortgagee in possession[5]. Where, though, a receiver appointed by the court was discharged and thereafter paid the rents to the mortgagee, his possession was treated, as from his discharge, as the possession of the mortgagee[6]. Where the mortgage deed creates a tenancy under which the mortgagor holds from the mortgagee at a rent, that does not result in the mortgagee being in possession and he is not thereby liable to account to the mortgagor on that basis[7].

1 *Low Moor Co v Stanley Coal Co Ltd* (1876) 34 LT 186, CA; *Lord Advocate v Young* (1887) 12 App Cas 544, 556, HL.
2 *Soar v Dalby* (1852) 15 Beav 156; *Simmins v Shirley* (1877) 6 Ch D 173.
3 As to acts which amount to taking possession, see *Noyes v Pollcok* (1886) 32 Ch D 53; *Kirby v Cowderoy* [1912] AC 599, PC; *Davies v Law Mutual Building Society* (1971) 219 Estates Gazette 309. The mere demand for rent without obtaining payment is not sufficient: *Ward v Carttar* (1865) LR 1 Eq 29. Notice to a tenant not to pay rent to the mortgagor suffices: *Heales v M'Murray* (1856) 23 Beav 401.
In the case of a mortgage by assignment of an interest in personalty, giving notice to the trustees is not equivalent to going into possession, unless the notice also requires payment of income to the mortgagee: *Re Pawson's Settlement, Higgins v Pawson* [1917] 1 Ch 541. See **19.98**.
4 *Noyes v Pollock*, above; *Ward v Carttar* (1865) LR 1 Eq 29; *Mexborough UDC v Harrison* [1964] 2 All ER 109. See also *Elders Rural Finance Ltd v Westpac Banking Corpn* (1990) 5 BPR 11790 at 11702-11703; *North American Trust Co v Consumer Gas Co* (1997) 147 DLR (4th) 645.
5 *Noyes v Pollock*, above.
6 *Horlock v Smith* (1842) 11 LJ Ch 157.
7 *Re Betts, ex p Harrison* (1881) 18 Ch D 127; *Stanley v Grundy* (1883) 22 Ch D 478; *Re Knight ex p Isherwood* (1882) 22 Ch D 384 at 392.Cf though *Re Stockton Iron Furnace Co* (1879) 10 Ch D 335 at 356; *Re Kitchen, ex p Punnett* (1880) 16 Ch D 226; *Green v Marsh* [1892] 2 QB 330 at 336.

Capacity in which possession taken

19.12 A mortgagee who is in possession of the mortgaged property will not be liable to account as mortgagee in possession unless he entered as mortgagee.

The court will not treat possession as being held by the mortgagee as such unless it is satisfied that he took possession in his capacity of mortgagee without reasonable grounds for believing himself to hold in another capacity[1].

1 *Gaskell v Gosling* [1896] 1 QB 669 at 691; *Vacuum Oil Co Ltd v Ellis* [1914] 1 KB 693; *Re Colnbrook Chemical and Explosives Co, A-G v Colnbrook Chemical and Explosives Co* [1923] 2 Ch 289.

Effect of taking possession

19.13 The point at which the mortgagee is treated as having taken possession of the property will determine the point at which he assumes the liabilities of a mortgagee in possession[1]. The taking of possession also allows the mortgagee to treat the mortgagor as a trespasser, even if it was done forcibly and constituted a criminal offence[2].

1 As to which, see **19.65**.
2 *Lows v Telford* (1876) 1 App Cas 414; *Harvey v Brydges* (1845) 14 M & W 437, on appeal 1 Ex Ch 261; *Beddall v Maitland* (1881) 17 Ch D 174.

Giving up possession

19.14 Once a mortgagee has taken possession as such and thereby assumed the liabilities of a mortgagee in possession he cannot easily give up possession and will remain liable as a mortgagee in possession even after he has transferred the mortgage, unless the transfer is by order of the court[1]. While he is not prevented from appointing a receiver under an express or the statutory power[2], in the absence of special circumstance the court will not assist him to give up possession[3].

1 *Hall v Heward* (1886) 32 Ch D 430, CA.
2 See **18.5**.
3 *Refuge Assurance Co Ltd v Pearlberg* [1938] Ch 687, [1938] 3 All ER 231, CA.

POSSESSION WHERE ADVANCES MADE UNDER SMALL DWELLINGS ACQUISITION ACTS[1]

19.15 Where default is made in complying with the statutory condition as to residence, the local authority may take possession of the house, and where default is made in complying with any of the other statutory conditions, whether or not the statutory condition as to residence has or has not been complied with, the local authority may either take possession of the house or order the sale of the house without taking possession[2]. In the case of the breach of any condition other than that of punctual payment of the principal and interest of the advance, the authority shall, previously to taking possession or ordering sale, by notice in writing delivered to the house and addressed to the proprietor, call on the proprietor to comply with the condition, and if the proprietor (a) within 14 days after delivery of the notice gives an undertaking in writing to the authority to comply with the notice, and (b) within two months after the delivery of the notice complies with it, the authority shall not take possession, or as the case may be, order sale[3].

Where a local authority takes possession of a house, all the estate, right, interest and claim of the proprietor in or to the house vest in and become the property of the local authority and that authority may retain the house under their own management or sell or otherwise dispose of it as they think expedient[4]. Where a local authority takes possession of such a house they must pay the proprietor either (a) such sum as may be agreed upon, or (b) a sum equal to the value of the interest in the house at the disposal of the local authority, after deducting the amount of the advance then remaining unpaid and any sum for interest[5]. The taking of possession by a local authority operates as an immediate and irrevocable foreclosure of the proprietor's interest, subject only to his right to be paid such sum as aforesaid[6]. Where the local authority are so entitled to take possession of a house, possession may[7] be recovered in a county court, whatever the annual value of the house for rating[8]. The proprietor remains personally liable for the payment of any sum due in respect of the advance, after allowing for the sum agreed or the value of the proprietor's interest[9].

1 The Acts were repealed by the Housing (Consequential Provisions) Act 1985, s 3(1), Sch 1, Pt 1; and see **12.46** and **20.54**.
2 Housing Act 1985, s 456, Sch 18, para 5 (1). For the definition of 'residence' and 'proprietor' see para 9 (1), (3). The local authority has the same rights of possession or sale in the case of the bankruptcy of the proprietor or in the case of his estate being administered in bankruptcy and in these cases must exercise their rights except in pursuance of some agreement to the contrary with the trustee in bankruptcy: para 5 (3).
3 Paragraph 5 (2).
4 Paragraph 6 (1) and see *Mexborough UDC v Harrison* [1964] 2 All ER 109, [1964] 1 WLR 733.
5 Paragraph 6 (2). The value of the interest, in the absence of a sale and in default of agreement, shall be settled by a county court judge as arbitrator or, if the Lord Chancellor so authorises, by a single arbitrator appointed by the county court judge: para 6(2). The sum so payable to the proprietor shall if not paid within three months after the date of taking possession carry interest at the rate of 3 per cent per annum from the date of taking possession: para 6 (3). All costs of or incidental to the taking possession, sale or other disposal of the house (including the costs of the arbitration, if any) incurred by the local authority, before the amount payable to the proprietor has been settled either by agreement or arbitration, shall be deducted from the amount otherwise payable to the proprietor: para 6 (4). See generally *Mexborough UDC v Harrison*, above.
6 For sale without taking possession, see para 7 (1) (see **20.54**). See generally, *Alnwick RDC v Taylor* [1966] Ch 355 at 361, [1966] 1 All ER 899.
7 *Quaere*, must be recovered: see *Alnwick RDC v Taylor*, above.
8 Housing Act 1985, Sch 18, para 6 (5).
9 Paragraph 4 (1) and see *Mexborough UDC v Harrison*, above.

THIRD PARTY TENANCIES AND THE MORTGAGEE'S RIGHT TO POSSESSION[1]

TENANCY GRANTED BEFORE THE MORTGAGE

Tenancy binding on the mortgagee

19.16 A lease by the mortgagor made before the mortgage is generally binding on the mortgagee[2]. However, where a tenant consents to the grant of the mortgage, or estops himself from asserting that his tenancy has priority, the mortgagee will not be bound by the tenancy, except where the tenancy has statutory protection[3]. Where the mortgagee obtained from the mortgagor's tenants an express agreement that their rights of occupation were to be subject to the mortgagee's right to possession, that was binding between the mortgagee and the tenants as persons; however, it had no effect on the property or charges register in the Land Registry, and did not preclude the tenants being entitled to an overriding interest in the absence of a provision to that effect in the register[4]. If the mortgagor himself is in possession of the mortgaged property under a lease made to him before the mortgage, he is not estopped from setting up the lease merely because in a conveyance of the legal estate in fee simple of the mortgaged property it was recited that he was seised in unincumbered fee simple in possession[5]. Where a second charge is executed after the mortgagor has granted a tenancy, but is in reality merely varying the terms of a first charge pre-dating the tenancy, the mortgagee will not be bound by it[6].

Where a purchaser purports to grant a legal tenancy before completion, when he only has an equitable interest, the tenancy will subsist by estoppel and on completion the estoppel will be fed so that the tenancy will be treated as having been legal from its grant[7]. Such a tenancy will therefore bind a mortgagee of a charge executed after completion of the purchase[8]. However, where (as is commonly the case) the charge is granted simultaneously with the completion of the purchase, the two elements of the transaction are indivisible in time, thus the legal estate never vests in the purchaser free of the charge and a legal tenancy purportedly granted prior to completion will not bind the mortgagee[9]. In the case of registered land, the mortgagee does not obtain a legal estate until his charge is registered, thus a legal tenancy granted after the execution of a charge, but before its registration, will bind the mortgagee. That applies even if the mortgagor granted the tenancy in breach of the terms of the charge[10].

1 See Law Com no 204, *Transfer of Land Mortgages* (1991) paras. 7.54–7.59.

2 *Moss v Gallimore* (1779) 1 Doug KB 279 at 283; *Skipton Building Society v Clayton* (1993) 66 P & CR 223; *Woolwich Building Society v Dickman* [1996] 3 All ER 204. Where a tenancy is binding on a mortgagee he is an owner for the purpose of the Protection from Eviction Act 1977, sections 3, 8 (protection from eviction without due process of law): see *Bolton Building Society v Cobb* [1965] 3 All ER 814. The position is otherwise in the case of a legal charge of registered land, where there has been a mere oral agreement for a lease and the prospective tenant has not taken possession: *City Permanent Building Society v Miller* [1952] Ch 840; see also *Hughes v Waite* [1957] 1 WLR 713.

3 *Skipton Building Society v Clayton* (1993) 66 P & CR 223; *Woolwich Building Society v Dickman* [1996] 3 All ER 204. In *District Bank Ltd v Webb* [1958] 1 WLR 148, [1958] 1 All ER 126 the mortgagors were not estopped from remaining in possession under a lease granted prior to the mortgage merely because they had recited in their conveyance of the freehold to a third party that they were seised in fee simple in possession.

4 *Woolwich Building Society v Dickman* (1996) 28 HLR 661.

5 *District Bank Ltd v Webb* [1958] 1 All ER 126, [1958] 1 WLR 148.

6 *Walthamstow Building Society v Davies* (1989) 60 P & CR 99, 22 HLR 60, CA.

7 See generally (1964) 80 LQR 370 (Prichard); *Cuthbertson v Irving* (1859) 4 H & N 742; *First National Bank v Thompson* [1996] Ch 231, [1996] 1 All ER 140; *Iron Trades Employers Insurance Association Ltd v Union Land and House Investors Ltd* [1937] Ch 313, [1937] 1 All ER 481; *Commonwealth v Orr* (1982) 58 FLR 219; *Webb v Austin* (1844) 7 Man & G 701 at 724. (See also (1954) 18 Conv (NS) 723 and(1957) 101 Sol Jo 438, 439, 822–824 (LHE).)

8 Cf the position where both tenancy and mortgage are granted before completion: *Rust v Goodale* [1957] Ch 33, [1956] 3 All ER 373.

9 *Abbey National Building Society v Cann* [1991] 1 AC 56, [1990] 1 All ER 1085 (overruling *Church of England Building Society v Piskor* [1954] Ch 553, [1954] 2 All ER 85. See also *Re Connolly Bros Ltd (No 2)* [1912] 2 Ch 25;*Rust v Goodale* [1957] Ch 33, [1956] 3 All ER 373 (and see (1956) 20 Conv (NS) 444 (Crane)); *Coventry Permanent Building Society v Jones* [1951] 1 All ER 901; *Nationwide Anglia Building Society v Ahmed* (1995) 70 P & CR 381.

10 *Barclays Bank plc v Zaroovabli* [1997] Ch 321, [1997] 2 All ER 19.

Reversion vests in the mortgagee

19.17 Under former freehold mortgages the entire reversion in the land subject to the lease passed to the mortgagee, and with it the right to receive the future rents, and the other rights incident to the estate which theretofore belonged to the mortgagor[1]. The position remains the same now that the mortgage is made by demise or legal charge, for the mortgage operates as a concurrent lease and carries the reversion upon the existing term with the rights and the liabilities incident thereto[2]. However, until the mortgagee gives notice to the tenant to pay rent to him and while the mortgagee allows the mortgagor to receive the rents, the tenant may nevertheless safely pay the rent to the mortgagor without incurring liability for breach of any covenant for non-payment of rent[3] (provided it is rent due and not a payment in anticipation on account of rent[4]). However, if the tenant pays rent to the mortgagor after notice to pay to the mortgagee and is afterwards compelled to pay the latter, the payment, being voluntary, cannot afterwards be recovered from the mortgagor[5]. If the mortgagee goes into possession and gives notice to the tenant, the tenant cannot set off against the rent a personal claim he has against the mortgagor[6].

The right of the mortgagor to sue on the covenants of a lease before the mortgagee has taken possession have been considered[7]. The rights of the mortgagee and the mortgagor once the mortgagee has taken possession, or given notice to tenant to pay the rent to him, are considered below[8].

1 *Rogers v Humphreys* (1835) 4 Ad & El 299 at 314; *Trent v Hunt* (1853) 9 Exch 14. Arrears of rent do not pass without express words: *Salmon v Dean* (1851) 3 Mac & G 344.
2 See also *Neale v Mackenzie* (1836) 1 M & W 747; *Harmer v Bean* (1853) 3 Car & Kir 307; *Rhodes v Allied Dunbar Pension Services Ltd* [1989] 1 All ER 1161, [1989] 1 WLR 800; for a charge by way of legal mortgage, see the Law of Property Act 1925, s 87(1). For tenancies granted prior to 1 January 1996, see Law of Property Act 1925, s 141; and Law of Property Act 1925, s 142 (1) (replacing 32 Hen 8, c 34 (1540) (Grantees of Reversions), s 2, and the Conveyancing Act 1881, s 11 (1)).For tenancies granted after 1 January 1996, see Landlord and Tenant (Covenants) Act 1995, s 15.
3 Law of Property Act 1925, s 151 (1).
4 *De Nicholls v Saunders* (1870) LR 5 CP 589; *Cook v Guerra* (1872) LR 7 CP 132, but if at the time of the mortgage he has paid rent in a lump sum in advance under an arrangement with the mortgagor, this binds the mortgagee, since he should inquire as to the terms on which the tenant holds: *Green v Rheinberg* (1911) 104 LT 149; *Grace Rymer Investments Ltd v Waite* [1958] Ch 831 at 847, [1958] 2 All ER 777 at 781, 782, CA.
5 *Higgs v Scott* (1849) 7 CB 63.
6 *Reeves v Pope* [1914] 2 KB 284.
7 See **19.4**.
8 See **19.59**.

TENANCY GRANTED AFTER THE MORTGAGE

Unauthorised lease by mortgagor not binding on mortgagee

19.18 The mortgagor is unable to confer upon another a greater right than he himself possesses. Thus, in the absence of a statutory or express power of leasing, where, after the mortgage, the mortgagor purports to grant a lease without the privity of the mortgagee, the tenancy will subsist by estoppel between mortgagor and tenant[1], but be void against the mortgagee[2]. Such a tenant is liable, like his lessor, to be ejected without notice[3]. His only remedy is against the mortgagor[4]. By contrast, a tenancy granted by a first mortgagee will bind a second mortgagee, even where the second mortgage prohibited the grant of a tenancy without the second mortgagee's prior consent[5]. Where a mortgage is granted of a property subject to a subsisting tenancy and the mortgagor grants a further tenancy to the same tenant without the authorisation of the mortgagee, then as between the mortgagor and the tenant the grant of the second tenancy will operate as a surrender of the original tenancy by operation of law; however, because the second tenancy is void as against the mortgagee, the mortgagee will continue to be bound by the original tenancy[6].

As stated above, although a lease made after the mortgage is void against the mortgagee, it subsists between the tenant and the mortgagor by estoppel[7]. The mortgagor's interest by estoppel can be inherited, or purchased by an assignee, and the heir or assignee would be entitled to sue the tenant on the covenants in the lease[8]. There was no estoppel where the lease disclosed that the land was mortgaged and that the lessor had only an equity of redemption — the lessee's covenants were then only in gross and could not be sued upon by the assignee of the mortgagor[9]. Where a mortgagor granted a lease in breach of the mortgage, a notice from the mortgagee addressed to 'the occupier' was sufficient to constitute an eviction or threat of eviction; accordingly, when the sub-lessee subsequently purchased the property from the mortgagee, he was not estopped from denying the validity of the lessee's lease, and was entitled to an order for possession against the lessee[10].

1 *Alchorne v Gomme* (1824) 2 Bing 54; *Cuthbertson v Irving* (1860) 6 H & N 135; *Hartup & Co v Bell* (1883) Cab & El 19. The mortgagor's power to grant a lease binding between himself and the tenant is not affected by the statutory leasing provisions (as to which, see **19.21**: *Iron Trades Employers Insurance Association Ltd v Union Land and House Investors Ltd* [1937] Ch 313, [1937] 1 All ER 481. A tenant under such a lease does not obtain the benefit of the Rent Act: *Dudley and District Benefit Building Society v Emerson* [1949] Ch 707, [1949] 2 All ER 252, CA.

2 *Keech v Hall* (1778) 1 Doug. KB 21; *Pope v Biggs* (1829) 9 B & C 45; *Trent v Hunt* (1853) 9 Ex Ch 14; *Rust v Goodale* [1957] Ch 33; *Taylor v Ellis* [1960] Ch 368, [1960] 1 All ER 549; *Sadiq v Hussain* [1997] NPC 19, CA. Cf the position where the mortgagee is acting in bad faith and in collusion with the lessor: *Quennell v Maltby* [1979] 1 All ER 568, [1979] 1 WLR 318.The mere fact a tenancy has statutory protection under the Rent Act 1977 does not make it binding on the mortgagee: *Britannia Building Society v Earl* [1990] 2 All ER 469, [1990] 1 WLR 422 (and see also in that context *Bolton Building Society v Cobb* [1965] 3 All ER 814; *Jessamine Investment Co v Schwartz* [1978] QB 264, [1976] 3 All ER 521, CA; *Moore Properties (Ilford) Ltd v McKeon* [1977] 1 All ER 262; (1977) 41 Conv (NS) 197 (Smith); [1978] Conv 9, 322–323; *Quennell v Maltby*, above; (1983) 127 Sol Jo 432 (Davey); (1986) 83 LS Gaz 3331 (McConnell); *Barclays Bank v Zaroovabli* [1997] Ch 321).

3 See eg *Dudley and District Benefit Building Society v Emerson* [1949] Ch 707, [1949] 2 All ER 252, CA; *Parker v Braithwaite* [1952] 2 All ER 837; *Taylor v Ellis* [1960] Ch 368, [1960] 1 All ER 549; *Stroud Building Society v Delamont* [1960] 1 All ER 749; *Baring Bros & Co Ltd v Hovermarine Ltd* (1917) 219 Estates Gazette 1459; *Commonwealth Bank of Australia v Baranyay* [1993] 1 VR 589; *Quennell v Maltby* [1979] 1 All ER 568, [1979] 1 WLR 318, CA, but he is entitled to redeem the mortgage: *Tarn v Turner* (1888) 57 LJ Ch 452; affd 39 Ch D 456, CA.

4 *Keech v Hall* (1778) 1 Doug KB 21; *Rogers v Humphreys* (1835) 4 Ad & El 299; *Trent v Hunt* (1853) 9 Exch 14. *United Starr-Bowkett Co-operative Building Society (No 11) Ltd v Clyne* (1967) 68 SR NSW 331, 338. Such a lease is binding on the mortgagor by estoppel, and the tenant is estopped from disputing the mortgagor's tile. The lessee may also redeem the mortgage: *Tarn v Turner* (1888) 39 Ch D 456, CA.

5 *Berkshire Capital Funding Ltd v Street* [1999] 2 EGLR 92, (1999) 32 HLR 373.

6 See *Barclays Bank Ltd v Stasek* [1957] Ch 28, [1956] 3 All ER 439.

7 *Trent v Hunt* (1853) 9 Exch 14. After the mortgagee has obtained payment of the rent, the tenant, in defending himself against a subsequent action by the mortgagor, was still not allowed to deny the mortgagor's title. He must admit it and then show that it had been determined and that he had been compelled to make the payment to the mortgagee: *Underhay v Read* (1887) 20 QBD 209, CA.

8 *Cuthbertson v Irving* (1859) 4 H & N 742.
9 *Pargeter v Harris* (1845) 7 QB 708; *Saunders v Merryweather* (1865) 3 H & C 902, but cf *Morton v Woods* (1869) LR 4 QB 293 at 303, referring to *Jolly v Arbuthnot* (1859) 4 De G & J 224.
10 *Sadiq v Hussain* [1997] CLY 4247, [1997] NPC 19, CA.

Leases which bind the mortgagee

19.19 There are, however, four circumstances where a tenancy granted after the mortgage will be effective against the mortgagee:

(a) if it was granted under an express power of leasing in the mortgage deed;
(b) if it was granted under the statutory power of leasing;
(c) if the mortgagee expressly consents to the grant of the lease; and
(d) if the mortgagee treats the tenant as his own.

Additionally, a new lease granted under the Leasehold Reform Act 1967 or under the Leasehold Reform, Housing and Urban Development Act 1993 is generally deemed to be authorised by the mortgagee, notwithstanding that the lease is not authorised by him, and that the existing lease was not authorised and not binding on him[1].

1 The exceptions are where (a) under the 1967 Act, the existing lease was granted after 27 October 1967 and would not otherwise bind the mortgagee (s 14), and (b) under the 1993 Act, the existing lease was granted after 1 November 1993, and would not otherwise bind the mortgagee (s 58). See generally Hague *Leasehold Enfranchisement* (3rd edn 1999) paras 7-48, 32-10.

Express power of leasing

19.20 The mortgagor and mortgagee can agree by the terms of the mortgage deed that the mortgagor have the power to grant leases binding on the mortgagee[1]. Any conditions for the exercise of such powers (for instance, prior approval by the mortgagee of the terms of the tenancy) must be adhered to by the mortgagor, or the mortgagee will not be bound by the tenancy[2].

1 *Carpenter v Parker* (1857) 3 CBNS 206.
2 For cases where the mortgagee's consent is required, see cases under the similarly modified statutory power: **19.22**.

Statutory power of leasing[1]

19.21 Section 99 of the Law of Property Act 1925[2] gives the mortgagor of any mortgage made after 31 December 1881 statutory powers to grant leases binding against the mortgagee. The section applies only if and so far as a contrary intention is not expressed in the mortgage deed (or otherwise in writing) and has effect subject to the terms of the deed (or of any such writing)[3]. It provides that a mortgagor[4] of land while in possession[5] has, as against every incumbrancer, the power to make from time to time any such lease of the mortgaged land, or any part thereof[6], as is authorised by the section[7]. Likewise, a mortgagee of land while in possession[8] has, as against all prior incumbrancers, if any, and as against the mortgagor, the power to make from time to time such a lease[9]. The leases which the section authorises are: (a) agricultural or occupation[10] leases for any term not exceeding 21 years, or, in the case of a mortgage made after the commencement of the Act, 50 years; and (b) building lease[11] for any term not exceeding 99 years, or, in the case of a mortgage made after the commencement of the Act, 999 years[12]. Every such lease must be made to take effect in possession not later than 12 months after its date[13]; must reserve the best rent that can reasonably be obtained, regard being had to the circumstances of the case[14], but without any fine being taken[15]; and must contain a covenant by the lessee for payment of the rent and a condition of re-entry on the rent not being paid within a time therein specified not exceeding 30 days[16]. Every person making a lease under s 99 may execute and do all assurances and things necessary or proper in that behalf[17]. A counterpart of every such lease must be executed by the lessee and delivered to the lessor, of which execution and delivery the execution of the lease by the lessor shall, in favour of the lessee and all persons deriving title under him, be sufficient evidence[18].

Where a lease fails to comply with the above terms, if it was made in good faith and the lessee has entered thereunder, it takes effect in equity as a contract for the grant, at the request of the lessee, of a valid lease of like effect as the invalid lease, subject to such variations as may be necessary in order to comply with the terms of the power[19]. The mortgagor and mortgagee may, by agreement in writing, whether or not contained in the mortgage deed, reserve or confer on either party, or both, any further or other powers of leasing or having reference to leasing, but without prejudice to the rights of other mortgagees, and these will be exercisable, so far as may be, as if they were conferred by the Act[20].

1 See Law Com no 204, *Transfer of Land Mortgages* para 7-47.
2 Following s 18 of the Conveyancing Act 1881.
3 Section 99 (13), but the statutory power cannot be modified or excluded in a mortgage of agricultural land made after 1 March 1948: Agricultural Holdings Act 1986, Sch 14, para 12. Nor can it be modified or excluded so as to prevent the carrying out of an order for a grant of a new tenancy of business premises: Landlord and Tenant Act 1954, Pt II, s 36 (4). A clause excluding the statutory leasing powers does not deprive the mortgagor of his power of creating a lease valid as between himself and the tenant by estoppel: *Iron Trades Employers Insurance Association Ltd v Union Land and House Investors Ltd* [1937] Ch 313, [1937] 1 All ER 481; *Rust v Goodale* [1956] 3 All ER 373; *Bolton Building Society v Cobb* [1965] 3 All ER 814, [1966] 1 WLR 1; *Commonwealth v Orr* (1982) 58 FLR 219; *Commonwealth Bank of Australia v Baranyay* [1993] 1 VR 589. A mortgagor who has bound himself not to exercise the statutory power of leasing cannot authorise a second mortgagee to do so. Section 99 does not confer on a mortgagee rights which the mortgagor does not himself have: see *Julian S Hodge & Co Ltd v St Helen's Credit Ltd* [1965] EGD 143.
4 For the purposes of this and the next section only 'mortgagor' does not include an 'incumbrancer' deriving title under the original mortgagor (sub-s (18) and s 100 (12), that is, a subsequent incumbrancer: cf s 205 (1) (xvi)).
5 A prospective purchaser, who is also a prospective mortgagor, is not in possession: *Hughes v Waite* [1957] 1 All ER 603, [1957] 1 WLR 713.
6 *Rhodes v Dalby* [1971] 2 All ER 1144, [1971] 1 WLR 1325, was a case where a part of premises was involved.
7 Law of Property Act 1925, s 99(1).
8 This includes in receipt of rents and profits: Law of Property Act 1925, s 205 (1) (xix). If the mortgagor is in possession he has the statutory powers (unless they are excluded) to the exclusion of the mortgagee and vice versa, see *Meah v Mouskos* [1964] 2 QB 23 at 40, [1963] 3 All ER 908 at 914, CA.
9 Law of Property Act 1925, s 99(2). A mortgagee (which expression includes a legal chargee: Law of Property Act 1925, s 205 (1) (xvi)), who has appointed a receiver under his statutory powers can exercise the powers of leasing as if he were in possession and may by writing delegate any of the powers to the receiver: sub-s (19). Leases may be granted under the statute in the name of the estate owner: s 8 (1). A legal chargee has no legal estate in the mortgaged property and must grant a lease under s 8. The immediate reversion on such a lease is in the chargor, not the chargee: see *Weg Motors Ltd v Hales*

[1961] Ch 176 at 194, 195, [1960] 3 All ER 762 at 771, 772; affd [1962] Ch 49, [1961] 3 All ER 181, CA. See also **19.6**.

10 The inclusion in the lease of chattels and sporting rights over other land comprised in the mortgage, but not in the lease, does not take a lease out of the description of 'an occupational lease': *Brown v Peto* [1900] 2 QB 653.

11 Ie the lessee must be obliged to erect, improve or repair buildings on the land within five years. As to building leases, see sub-ss (9), (10).

12 Law of Property Act 1925, s 99(3).

13 Law of Property Act 1925, s 99(5).

14 *Coutts & Co v Somerville* [1935] Ch 438.

15 Law of Property Act 1925, s 99(6).The rent must be paid annually or oftener. A lump sum for future years will not do: *Municipal Permanent Investment Building Society v Smith* (1888) 22 QBD 70, CA; *Green v Rheinberg* (1911) 104 LT 149, CA; *Rust v Goodale* [1957] Ch 33, [1956] 3 All ER 373; *Hughes v Waite* [1957] 1 All ER 603, [1957] 1 WLR 713; *Grace Rymer Investments Ltd v Waite* [1958] Ch 831, [1958] 2 All ER 777, CA; *Quaere* whether the rent can be left to be fixed by a valuer later: *Lloyds Bank v Marcan* [1973] 3 All ER 754 at 761.

16 Law of Property Act 1925, s 99(7). It seems that a condition of re-entry is not required in the case of an oral tenancy agreement. See *Rhodes v Dalby* [1971] 2 All ER 1144; cf *Pawson v Revell* [1958] 2 QB 360, [1958] 3 All ER 233, CA, and see Wolstenholme and Cherry *Conveyancing Statutes* (13 edn) vol 1, p 198.

17 Law of Property Act 1925, s 99(4).

18 In the case of a lease by the mortgagor, he shall, within one month after making the lease deliver to the mortgagee, or, where there are more than one, to the mortgagee first in priority, a counterpart of the lease duly executed by the lessee, but the lessee shall not be concerned to see that this is complied with: sub-s (11). The provision that the lessee shall not be concerned to see that the provision for delivery of the counterpart lease is complied with applies also to a lease granted under an extended statutory power: *Public Trustee v Lawrence* [1912] 1 Ch 789. Failure to deliver a counterpart to the mortgagee does not invalidate the lease, although it would cause the statutory power of the sale to become immediately exercisable: *Public Trustee v Lawrence*, above. The provisions of the section referring to a lease shall be construed to extend and apply, as far as circumstances admit, to any letting, and to an agreement whether in writing or not for leasing or letting: sub-s (17); but the provision as to a counterpart lease does not apply to an oral tenancy; *Rhodes v Dalby*, above; cf *Pawson v Revell*, above.

19 Law of Property Act 1925, s 152 (1). See *Pawson v Revell*, above; *Rhodes v Dalby*, above; (1971) 87 LQR 338 (Elliott).

20 Subsection (14).

Modification or exclusion of statutory powers

19.22 In practice, the mortgagor's powers of leasing under the section are generally restricted or excluded by the mortgage deed[1]. Where the powers are not excluded, the mortgage will usually require the consent of the mortgagee before the statutory powers can be exercised[2]. Where the statutory powers have been modified to require such consent, the mortgagee is not under an implied obligation not to refuse consent unreasonably; although in extreme cases there may be scope for a complaint based on a refusal made in bad faith[3]. Where the mortgage prohibits the letting of property without the prior consent of the lender, a refusal of consent does not contravene the right to freedom of movement of workers under EC law[4]. If the mortgage permits the mortgagor to exercise the statutory leasing powers with the consent of the mortgagee, the onus is on the lessee to prove that the mortgagee gave his consent[5]. If the mortgage deed provides that an intending lessee shall not be concerned to inquire as to such consent, the mortgagee is estopped from denying the lease was made with his consent[6]. Furthermore, if a lease is made without consent and the mortgagee then accepts the lessee as his own, the lease will be binding on him[7]. Besides restricting or excluding the statutory powers it is not uncommon for the deed to expressly exclude all powers of leasing and any parting with possession (though, of course, leases not made under statutory or express powers would not generally be binding on the mortgagee anyway)[8]. The statutory powers of leasing cannot be excluded in the case of a mortgage of agricultural land made after 1 March 1948[9].

The statutory powers are fairly restrictive and are thus sometimes extended. For example, they are only exercisable by a mortgagee when he is in possession[10] and accordingly may be modified such that they are exercisable by the mortgagee without going into possession[11]. The statutory powers do not permit the taking of premiums[12], and in suitable cases, as in the mortgage of a building development, the mortgagee's powers of leasing should be extended so as to enable him to grant leases at ground rents taking a premium[13].

1 It is so common that the Northern Ireland Land Law Working Party (1971) proposed that any new provision in NI should be to the effect that any lease granted by the mortgagor would not be binding on the mortgagee unless made with his consent. The exclusion of the mortgagor's powers are more important since the Leasehold Reform Act 1967. It is also particularly important in the case of building leases. Without a check on the statutory powers there would be nothing to prevent a reckless mortgagor from making the security valueless by granting building leases to persons of insufficient means and throwing the property upon the mortgagee's hands covered with half-finished buildings. For forms of modification of the statutory power, see 28 *Forms and Precedents* (5th edn, 1999 reissue) Mortgages. As to the extent of the restriction, see *Westbourne Park Building Society v Levermore* [1955] CLY 1703.

2 If consent is not obtained there will be a breach of the terms of the mortgage. Where there is a provision that the statutory power shall not be exercised without the mortgagee's consent and the mortgagor leases without consent, such lease is a lease outside the statute and there is therefore no breach of the above-mentioned provision: *Iron Trades Employers Insurance Association Ltd v Union Land and House Investors Ltd* [1937] Ch 313 (unless, as is usually the case nowadays, the mortgage expressly makes it a breach), and this is not a defective exercise of the statutory power which the Law of Property Act 1925, s 152, above, will cure, and see *Commonwealth v Orr* (1982) 58 FLR 219; *ANZ Bank Ltd v Sinclair* [1968] 2 NSWLR 26; *Commonwealth Bank of Australia v Barranyay* [1993] 1 VR 589.

3 Breach of an implied term that the mortgagee's consent would not be unreasonably withheld would not give rise to a claim for damages: *Citibank International plc v Kessler* [1999] Lloyd's Bank LR 123; *Starling v Lloyds TSB Bank plc* [2000] 1 EGLR 101.

4 *Citibank International plc v Kessler* [1999] Lloyd's Bank LR 123, CA (Art 48).

5 *Taylor v Ellis* [1960] Ch 368, [1960] 1 All ER 549; *Re O'Rourke's Estate* (1889) 23 LR Ir 497; *Barclays Bank v Kiley* [1961] 1 WLR 1050.See also (1994) 2 APLJ 290-300 (Redfern).

6 *Lever Finance Ltd v Trustee of Property of LN and HM Needleman (Bankrupts) and Kreutzer* [1956] Ch 375, [1956] 2 All ER 378; see also *Brittania Building Society v Earl* [1990] 2 All ER 469, [1990] 1 WLR 422.

7 *Stroud Building Society v Delamont* [1960] 1 All ER 749, [1960] 1 WLR 431. See **19.27**.

8 In *Rhodes v Dalby* [1971] 2 All ER 1144, a 'gentleman's agreement' was not a letting and therefore no breach.

9 Agricultural Holdings Act 1986, Sch 14, para 12.

10 Law of Property Act 1925, s 99 (2).

11 See 28 *Forms and Precedents* (5th edn, 1999 reissue) Mortgages.

12 See s 99 (6).

13 See the Appendix.

Surrender of lease

19.23 Under the Law of Property Act 1925[1], a mortgagor[2] or mortgagee in possession is also given the power to accept a surrender of a lease to enable another lease to be granted[3]. Section 100 of the Act provides that for the purpose only of enabling a lease authorised under s 99, or under any agreement made pursuant to that section, or by the mortgage deed ('an authorised lease') to be granted, a mortgagor of land while in possession has, as against every incumbrancer, the power to accept from time to time a surrender of any lease of the mortgaged land or any part thereof comprised in the lease[4]. An exception may be made in respect of all or any of the mines and minerals in the mortgaged land, and, on a surrender of the lease so far as it comprises part only of land or mines and minerals leased, the rent may be apportioned[5]. For the same purpose, a mortgagee of land while in possession has, as against all prior or other incumbrancers, if any, and as against the mortgagor, power to accept from time to time any such surrender[6]. No surrender is rendered valid by s 100 unless:

(a) an authorized lease is granted of the whole of the land or mines and minerals comprised in the surrender to take effect in possession immediately or within one month after the date of the surrender; and
(b) the term certain or other interest granted by the new lease is not less in duration than the unexpired term or interest which would have been subsisting under the original lease if that lease had not been surrendered; and
(c) where the whole of the land mines and minerals originally leased has been surrendered, the rent reserved by the new lease is not less than the rent which would have been payable under the original lease if it had not been surrendered; or where part only of the land or mines and minerals has been surrendered, the aggregate rents respective remaining payable or reserved under the original lease and the new lease are not less than the rent which would have been payable under the original lease if no partial surrender had been accepted[7].

Section 100 only applies if and so far as a contrary intention is not expressed by the mortgagor and mortgagee in the mortgage deed, or otherwise in writing, and has effect subject to the terms of the mortgage deed or of any such writing and to the provisions contained therein[8]. The mortgagor and mortgagee may, by agreement in writing (whether or not contained in the mortgage deed), reserve or confer on the mortgagor or mortgagee, or both, any further or other powers relating to the surrender of leases and any further or other powers so conferred or reserved are exercisable, as far as may be, as if they were conferred by the Act and with all the like incidents, effects and consequences. However, the powers thereby reserved or conferred will not prejudicially affect the rights of any mortgagee interested under any other mortgage subsisting at the date of the agreement, unless that mortgagee joins in or adopts the agreement[9]. The powers of accepting surrenders conferred by s 100 are exercisable, after a receiver of the income of the mortgaged property or any part thereof has been appointed by the mortgagee, under the statutory power, and so long as the receiver acts, by such mortgagee instead of by the mortgagor, as respects any land affected by the receivership, in like manner as if such mortgagee were in possession of the land; and the mortgagee may, by writing, delegate any of such powers to the receiver[10].

1 A surrender of a lease granted under the statutory power could not before the Conveyancing Act 1911 be made to the mortgagor without the joinder of the mortgagee: *Robbins v Whyte* [1906] 1 KB 125. Section 100 of the Law of Property Act 1925 replaces s 3 of the Conveyancing Act 1911.

2 For the purpose of s 100, 'mortgagor' does not include an incumbrancer deriving title under the original mortgagor: s 100(12) Law of Property Act 1925. A subsequent mortgagee who exercises the statutory powers of leasing and accepting surrenders of leases exercises the powers as mortgagee and not because he derives title under the mortgagor. See **19.25**, n 1.

3 *Barclays Bank Ltd v Stasek* [1957] Ch 28, [1956] 3 All ER 439; 73 LQR 14 (REM). As to the effect on a surrender of an invalid fresh grant, see *Rhyl UDC v Rhyl Amusements* [1959] 1 All ER 257 at 267, 268.

4 Law of Property Act 1925, s 100(1).
5 Section 100(1).
6 Section 100(2). Subsection (3) deals with variation of the lease on a surrender of part and provides that the value of the lessee's interest shall be taken into account in determining the rent and covenants under the new lease. Subsection (4) provides that if a consideration is given for the surrender, the consent of prior incumbrancers is required.
7 Section 100(5). Subsection (6) provides that a contract to make or accept a surrender may be enforced by or against every person on whom the surrender, if completed, would be binding.
8 Section 100(7). Subsection (8) applies the section to mortgages made after 31 December 1911, but the provisions of the section may by agreement in writing made after that date between mortgagor and mortgagee be applied to a mortgage made before that date, without prejudice to the interests of persons not parties to or adopting such agreement.
9 Section 100(10). Subsection (9) extends the provisions of the section to any letting and agreement for a lease. Subsection (11) provides that the statutory powers do not authorise a surrender which could not have been accepted by the mortgagor with the concurrence of all the incumbrancers before 1 January 1912.
10 Section 100(13).

Registered land and charges

19.24 In the case of registered land, its proprietor, while in possession, has all the powers of leasing and of accepting surrenders of leases conferred by ss 99 and 100 of the Law of Property Act 1925, as extended by, but subject to any contrary intention expressed in, the instrument of charge or any instrument varying its terms. Application can be made for a note of any such intention to be entered in the register[1]. The proprietor of the charge, while in possession, or after a receiver has been appointed, such receiver on his behalf, has the like powers[2]. Subject to that, all dispositions by the proprietor of the land authorised by ss 18 and 21 of the Land Registration Act 1925[3] take effect, unless the proprietor of the charge concurs in the disposition, subject to any charge registered at the time of the disposition[4].

1 Land Registration Rules 1925, r 141 (1). Land Registration Act 1925, s 34 (1).
2 Rule 141 (2).
3 Section 18 (powers of disposition of registered freeholds); s 21 (powers of disposition of registered leaseholds).
4 Land Registration Rules 1925, r 141 (4). Rule 141 has effect without prejudice to s 104 of the Land Registration Act 1925 (protection of leases granted under statutory powers by persons other than registered proprietor and restriction on power); r 141 (5).

Effect of leases under statutory powers

19.25 A lease granted under s 99 of the Law of Property Act 1925 has the same effect as if both mortgagor and mortgagee were parties to it. Thus if a mortgagor grants such a lease, the assignees of the mortgagee cannot obstruct the lessee's rights[1]. A lease under the statutory power is not invalidated by reason of its containing an option for determination or renewal, however, it is invalidated as against the mortgagee by the inclusion of other land not comprised in the mortgage at a single rent[2].

1 *Wilson v Queen's Club* [1891] 3 Ch 522; *Turner v Walsh* [1909] 2 KB 484, CA.
2 *King v Bird* [1909] 1 KB 837; cf *Dundas v Vavasour* (1895) 39 Sol Jo 656.

Express consent of mortgagee

19.26 Where the lease is not granted under the statutory or some other power of leasing, the mortgagee can be a party to the lease and expressly consent to its grant. In the case of a mortgage by demise, that will operate as a demise by the mortgagee and a confirmation by the mortgagor[1] and, in the case of a charge by way of legal mortgage, as a demise by the mortgagor and a confirmation by the mortgagee. To make the lessee's covenants run with the reversion, they should be with the owner of the immediate reversion, that is with the mortgagee in the case of a mortgage by demise but, it would seem, with the mortgagor in the case of a charge by way of legal mortgage[2].

The mortgagee can also consent after the grant of the lease[3]. Although a lease made after the mortgage is void against the mortgagee, it subsists between the tenant and the mortgagor by estoppel[4]. The mortgagee can consent to the tenant's interest by estoppel being converted into a lease in interest, with the effect that the tenant becomes the mortgagee's tenant under a new tenancy[5]. In those circumstances, a purchaser from the mortgagor, making a conveyance in which the mortgagee concurred, would have a remedy against the lessee on his covenants[6].

1 *Doe d Barney v Adams* (1832) 2 Cr & J 232. For a form see 28 *Forms and Precedents* (5th edn, 1999 reissue) Mortgages.
2 *Webb v Russell* (1789) 3 Term Rep 393.
3 Expressly, or impliedly: *Stroud Building Society v Delamont* [1960] 1 WLR 431 at 434; *Mann v Nijar* (1998) 32 HLR 223.
4 *Trent v Hunt* (1853) 9 Exch 14: see **19.27**. After the mortgagee has obtained payment of the rent, the tenant, in defending himself against a subsequent action by the mortgagor, was still not allowed to deny the mortgagor's title. He must admit it and then show that it had been determined and that he had been compelled to make the payment to the mortgagee: *Underhay v Read* (1887) 20 QBD 209, CA.
5 *Stroud Building Society v Delamont* [1960] 1 WLR 431 at 434; *Mann v Nijar* (1998) 32 HLR 223.
6 *Webb v Austin* (1844) 7 Man & G 701.

Mortgagee treating tenant as his own: implied consent or estoppel

19.27 The mortgagee may treat the mortgagor's tenant as his own, such as to preclude him from saying that he has not consented to the tenant as his own. That may arise not only by express agreement, but also by implied agreement or estoppel[1]. The question may be formulated in these terms: looking at all the facts in order to get a picture as a whole, has the mortgagee accepted the tenant as his own?[2] Once the mortgagee recognises the occupier as his own tenant, he cannot afterwards treat him as a trespasser[3]; and once the relationship of landlord and tenant has been established between them (although not before), the mortgagee can distrain or bring an action for rent and is entitled to arrears of rent due at the date of his taking possession. The main means by which a tenancy between the tenant and the mortgagee can be created is by the actual payment of rent to the mortgagee[4]. Such tenancy will usually be a yearly or periodic one and not necessarily on the terms of the old tenancy[5]. A change in the tenant's position will also be effected if the mortgagee, or his agent, calls on the mortgagor's tenant to pay, and he actually pays, the interest of the mortgagee instead of rent to the mortgagor[6]. Where a tenant of the mortgagor pays rent to a receiver that will not create a tenancy binding on the mortgagee, since the receiver is deemed the agent of the mortgagor under s 109(2) of the Law of Property Act 1925. However, that does not preclude a mortgagee from consenting to accept the tenant as its own whilst the receiver remains in office.[7]

However, a tenancy between mortgagee and tenant will not be created by a mere notice to the tenant requiring him to pay rent to the mortgagee in the absence of an attornment or other evidence of consent by the tenant. Nor will such a tenancy be created by an authority to the tenant from the mortgagor to pay rent to the mortgagee, even if it is communicated to and acted upon by the tenant[8]. Thus nor will a subsequent attornment by the tenant set up the mortgagee's title by relation from the time at which a previous notice was given[9]. No change of tenancy will be established simply by showing that interest was paid, as such, by the person in possession of the land[10].

1 *Iron Trades Employers Insurance Association Ltd v Union Land and House Investors Ltd* [1937] 1 Ch 313 at 318-319; *Parker v Braithwaite* [1952] 2 All ER 837 at 841; *Mann v Nijar* (1998) 32 HLR 223.See also *Rancho Holdings Pty Ltd v Impact Developments Pty Ltd* [1994] Vic Con Rep 54-501.
2 *Mann v Nijar* (1998) 32 HLR 223, per Ward LJ.
3 *Birch v Wright* (1786) 1 Term Rep 378. For the effect of the recognition is not to set up the lease made by the mortgagor, but to create a new tenancy: *Corbett v Plowden* (1884) 25 Ch D 678 at 681, 682, CA. Where the tenancy of a dwelling-house is effective against the mortgagee, the Protection from Eviction Act 1977 will apply: see **19.8**.
4 *Keith v R Gancia & Co Ltd* [1904] 1 Ch 774, CA; *Parker v Braithwaite* [1952] 2 All ER 837; *Stroud Building Society v Delamont* [1960] 1 All ER 749; *Chatsworth Properties Ltd v Effiom* [1971] 1 All ER 604, CA; *Baring Bros & Co Ltd v Hovermarine Ltd* (1917) 219 Estates Gazette 1459. See (1976) 120 Sol Jo 497 (H Markson); (1978) 128 NLJ 773 (Waite).
5 *Keith v R Gancia & Co Ltd*, above.
6 *Doe d Whitaker v Hales* (1831) 7 Bing 322. As to evidence of the recognition of the tenancy, see *Keech v Hall* (1778) 1 Doug KB 21; *Smith v Eggington* (1874) LR 9 CP 145. As to a lease contemporaneously with the mortgage, see *Rogers v Humphreys* (1835) 4 Ad & El 299 and see *Kitchen's Trustee v Madders* [1949] Ch 588, [1949] 2 All ER 54.
7 *Mann v Nijar* (1998) 32 HLR 223 (where both the mortgagee and the receiver 'remained in blissful ignorance of the effect of s 109(2)', and believed the receiver was collecting rent on behalf of the mortgagee).
8 *Evans v Elliot* (1838) 9 Ad & El 342; *Towerson v Jackson* [1891] 2 QB 484, CA.
9 *Evans v Elliot*, above.
10 *Doe d Rogers v Cadwallader* (1831) 2 B & Ad 473.

PROCEEDINGS FOR POSSESSION

19.28 Before proceedings are commenced it should be confirmed that the right to possession has arisen and any necessary notice given[1].

1 Eg notice to quit might be necessary if the mortgagor had attorned tenant, depending on the wording of the clause (see **34.9**, **19.5**). Possession should not be sought before the power of sale has arisen. Usually possession is merely a preliminary to a sale and in that case, because of the liability imposed on a mortgagee in possession (see **19.65**), there is no point in having an order for possession before the power of sale has arisen. A subsequent mortgagee, intending to apply for possession, should give notice of intention to any prior mortgagee. There used to be a *Practice Direction* ([1968] 1 All ER 752, [1968] 1 WLR 442) requiring this but it has been cancelled (*Practice Direction* [1970] 1 All ER 671, [1970] 1 WLR 520). Nevertheless the practice of informing any prior mortgagee is a useful one. Often the subsequent mortgagee will want to take a transfer of any prior mortgage: see Chapter 14. It may also be necessary to serve a notice under the Consumer Credit Act 1974, s 76; see **10.63**.

THE COUNTY COURT[1]

County court the normal court

19.29 Possession claims[2] should normally be brought in the county court, except where it does not have jurisdiction. Only exceptional circumstances justify starting a claim in the High Court[3]. Circumstances which may, in an appropriate case, justify starting a claim in the High Court include: (a) if there are complicated disputes of fact; and (b) if there are points of law of general importance[4]. The value of the property and the amount of any financial claim may be relevant circumstances, but those factors alone will not normally justify starting the claim in the High Court[5]. The Chancery Guide, prior to the coming into force of CPR Pt 55, provided that in the case of mortgage possession claims for dwelling houses in Greater London, where the High Court has concurrent jurisdiction with the county court[6], lenders could take block bookings of such claims in the Chancery Division, timed at 12 an hour (or six a half-hour), and could book a whole day (or two whole days) at a time, enabling a lender to deal with all its Greater London claims at one time and one place, with consequent costs savings[7]. Given that one of the overriding objectives of the CPR is saving expense[8], it may be that would remain a valid reason for bringing such claims in the High Court although it is doubtful whether such circumstances could be described as 'exceptional'. To start a claim in the High Court, the claimant must file with his claim a certificate stating the reasons for bringing the claim in that court, verified with a statement of truth in accordance with CPR 22.1(1)[9]. If a claimant starts a claim in the High Court and the court decides that it should have been started in the county court, the court will normally either strike the claim out or transfer it to the county court of its own initiative. That is likely to result in delay and the court will normally disallow the costs of starting the claim in the High Court and of any transfer[10].

1 See 28 *Atkin's Court Forms* (1997 issue).
2 As defined in CPR 55.1 and 55.2: this includes a claim for possession by a mortgagee, including a legal or equitable mortgagee and a legal or equitable chargee.
3 CPR PD55, para 1.1.
4 Paragraph 1.3.
5 Paragraph 1.4.
6 See **19.30**.
7 Chancery Guide, para 21.1.
8 CPR 1.1(2)(b).
9 CPR 55.3(1), (2).
10 CPR PD55, para 1.2.

Jurisdiction

19.30 The county court has jurisdiction to hear and determine any action for the recovery of land[1] and a claim for possession by a mortgagee is such an action[2]. For claims for possession of a dwelling-house the county court has, with certain exceptions, exclusive jurisdiction. Where a mortgage of land consists of or includes a dwelling-house[3] and no part of the land is situated in Greater London, then any action for possession by a mortgagee can only be brought in the county court[4]. In Greater London the High Court has concurrent jurisdiction with the county court in mortgage possession claims for dwelling houses[5]. Possession proceedings within the exclusive jurisdiction of the county court cannot be transferred by the county court to the High Court, and the High Court has no jurisdiction even if such an order for transfer has been made[6]. However, a defendant to a High Court action may counterclaim for possession of a dwelling-house outside Greater London, and the High Court may determine that counterclaim[7].

The county court does not have exclusive jurisdiction where there is a genuine claim for foreclosure or sale in which a claim for possession is also made[8]. Foreclosure or sale must genuinely be the relief sought, rather than added simply as a formal or colourable device to take the proceedings outside the county court's exclusive jurisdiction[9]. While it is commonplace to claim payment, possession, foreclosure or sale and other relief in the same proceedings, the mere claim for foreclosure or sale does not make the action one for foreclosure or sale: the test is what the claimant is genuinely seeking[10].

Where the mortgage secures an agreement which is a regulated agreement within the meaning of the Consumer Credit Act 1974, s 21 of the County Courts Act 1984 does not apply[11] and the county court has exclusive jurisdiction[12]. Possession may be recovered in the county court of any dwelling subject to a mortgage made under the Small Dwellings Acquisition Acts[13]. The court's powers in respect of regulated mortgages[14] are exercisable by the county court, except where the mortgagee has claimed possession, or taken any other relevant step, in the High Court[15].

1 County Courts Act 1984, s 21 (1).
2 *Re v Judge Dutton Briant, ex p Abbey National Building Society* [1957] 2 QB 497 at 498, [1957] 2 All ER 625 at 626; *West Penwith RDC v Gunnell* [1968] 2 All ER 1005, [1968] 1 WLR 1153, CA; *Esso Petroleum Co Ltd v Alstonbridge Properties Ltd* [1975] 3 All ER 358 at 365; cf *Redditch Benefit Building Society v Roberts* [1940] Ch 415 at 420, [1940] 1 All ER 342 at 345, CA.
3 Dwelling-house includes any building or part thereof which is used as a dwelling: County Courts Act 1984, s 21 (7). The fact that part of the premises is used as a shop or office or for a business trade or professional purposes does not prevent the dwelling-house from being a dwelling-house for the purposes of this provision: County Courts Act 1984, s 21 (8).
4 County Courts Act 1984, s 21 (3), (4).
5 Section 21 (3); Chancery Guide Ch 21.
6 *Yorkshire Bank v Hall* [1999] 1 WLR 1713.
7 *Maria St George (London) Ltd v Burlington Investments Ltd* 14 October 1977, Oliver J, unreported (noted at The Supreme Court Practice, 1999, vol 1, p 1575).
8 County Courts Act 1984, s 21(4).
9 *Manchester Unity Life Insurance Collecting Society Trustees v Sadler* [1974] 2 All ER 410, [1974] 1 WLR 770; cf *Lord Marples of Wallasey v Holmes* (1975) 31 P & CR 94.
10 *Manchester Unity Life Insurance Collecting Society Trustees v Sadler*, above. Whether a possession claim is heard in the county court or the High Court, the court will have the powers of adjournment, etc, given by the Administration of Justice Acts 1970 and 1973 (see **19.51** ff).Historically, the High Court may have been less favourable to the mortgagor than the county court: see (1970) 120 NLJ 808, 829.
11 County Courts Act 1984, s 21 (9).
12 Consumer Credit Act 1974, ss 21(9), 141, 189.
13 See now Housing Act 1985, s 456, Sch 18, para 6(5); and **12.46** and **19.15**.
14 See **16.22** ff.
15 Rent Act 1977, Part X, s 132.

The appropriate county court

19.31 The appropriate county court is the one for the district in which the land is situated[1]. If proceedings have been brought in the wrong county court, a judge may, on an application made in the court where the claim is proceeding, order that the proceedings (a) be transferred to the county court in which they ought to have been started; (b) continue in the county court in which they have been started; or (c) be struck out[2].

1 CPR 55.3(1). For the appropriate court in the case of a charging order, see CPR Sch 2, Ord 31, r 4 (2). For the limits on the powers of a court officer where the claimant is seeking to issue in the wrong county court, see: *Gwynedd County Council v Grunshaw* [1999] 4 All ER 304.
2 CPR 30.2(2), 30.2(3).

Parties

19.32 The principles as to the choice of defendants are the same in the county court and the High Court. A mortgagee's application for an order for possession is simply an order for the recovery of land and is not proceedings for enforcing the mortgage[1]. Hence an order for possession can be made against a complete stranger to the title who happens to be in actual possession in the total absence of the mortgagor[2]. Thus, while the mortgagor for the time being should always be joined if he is in occupation, after the original mortgagor has parted with the property, he should not be a defendant in a claim for possession[3]. If there are several mortgagors, they should all be joined; but, if they are not all in occupation and it is not possible to effect service[4] on any or all of those not in occupation, only those in occupation and the others on whom service can be effected without difficulty need be served[5]. The trustee in bankruptcy of a bankrupt mortgagor should only be joined as a defendant if the court so directs[6].

Any person, other than the mortgagor, who has an independent right to remain in occupation[7] should also be made a defendant. It will generally be advisable to join every person who may assert a claim. Thus a tenant of the mortgagor should be joined, even where it is uncertain whether or not his tenancy is binding on the mortgagee[8]. A spouse of the mortgagor is not entitled to be joined merely because he or she is the spouse of the mortgagor[9]. A spouse who is entitled to occupy a dwelling house which is a matrimonial home under s 30 of the Family Law Act 1996 is entitled to be joined as a defendant if there is a reasonable prospect of her being able to pay the monies due under the mortgage, but not if her joinder would merely amount to a tactic to stall the obtaining of a possession order[10]. Where the mortgagor is the only defendant, and he dies after proceedings have been commenced but before the hearing, or after the order has been made but before it has been served, any occupants should be joined as defendants and the proceedings pursued against them[11]. If there are no occupants, proceedings will have to be continued against the estate; alternatively, physical possession could be taken without continuing the proceedings.

1 *Esso Petroleum v Alstonbridge Properties* [1975] 3 All ER 358, [1975] 1 WLR 1474 at 1481.
2 *Esso Petroleum v Alstonbridge Properties*, above; *Alliance Building Society v Shave* [1952] Ch 581.
3 *Esso Petroleum Co Ltd v Alstonbridge Properties Ltd* above.
4 For the rules on service, see CPR Pt 6.
5 *Alliance Building Society v Yap* [1962] 3 All ER 6n, [1962] 1 WLR 857.
6 *Alliance Building Society v Shave* [1952] Ch 581.
7 *Brighton and Shoreham Building Society v Hollingdale* [1965] 1 All ER 540, [1965] 1 WLR 376; *Williams & Glyn's Bank Ltd v Boland* [1981] AC 487, [1980] 2 All ER 408, HL.
8 For tenancies binding on the mortgagee, see **19.16**, **19.19**. A former tenant cannot be evicted from a dwelling without a court order: Prosecution from Eviction Act 1977, ss 2, 3, but nothing in the Act affects the jurisdiction of the High Court in proceedings to enforce a mortgagee's right of possession in a case where the tenancy is not binding on the mortgagee: Protection from Eviction Act 1977, s 9 (3); and see *Bolton Building Society v Cobb* [1965] 3 All ER 814, [1966] 1 WLR 1. In *Midland Bank Ltd v Monobond* [1971] EGD 673 it was doubted whether the summary procedure under RSC Ord 113 (see now CPR Pt 55) could

be used to evict 'tenants' of a mortgagor letting without consent; and see *London Goldhawk Building Society v Emener* (1977) 242 Estates Gazette 462, (1976) 126 NLJ 1193.

9 *Brighton and Shoreham Building Society v Hollingdale*, above; *Hastings and Thanet Building Society v Goddard* [1970] 3 All ER 954, [1970] 1 WLR 1544, CA.

10 *Hastings and Thanet Building Society v Goddard*, above.

11 See also *Barclays Bank Ltd v Kiley* [1961] 2 All ER 849, [1961] 1 WLR 1050 (in this case the mortgagor was dead and no personal representatives had been constituted).

Claim form and particulars of claim

19.33 The requirements for the claim form and particulars of claim in a claim for possession by a mortgagee in the county court are contained in CPR 55.4 and the Part 55 Practice Direction and CPR Pt 16. The appropriate claim form is N5 (possession of property)[1].

Where a claimant claims as mortgagee possession of land which consists of or includes residential premises, the particulars of claim must be in the prescribed form, N120[2], which will contain most of the information required by the rules[3]. There is one exception: although there is no specific provision in the prescribed form for such information, the claimant must also state any previous steps which the claimant has taken to recover the money secured by the mortgage or the mortgaged property and, in the case of court proceedings, the dates when the claim started and concluded and the dates and terms of any orders made[4].

Where the land does not consist of or include residential premises, the particulars of claim should be drafted to contain the following information specified by the CPR Part 55 Practice Direction. Where there is more than one loan secured by the mortgage, the following information should be provided in respect of each loan agreement. The particulars must state the date and give full details of the mortgage[5], and state the ground on which possession is claimed[6]. The particulars of claim must identify the land to which the claim relates and which is sought to be recovered[7]. The particulars must state whether or not the claim relates to residential property[8]. The particulars must give details of every person who, to the best of the claimant's knowledge, is in possession of the property[9]. The particulars must state whether or not the loan which is secured by the mortgage is a regulated consumer credit agreement and, if so, specify the date on which any notice required by s 76 or s 87 of the Consumer credit Act 1974 was given[10]. If appropriate, the particulars should give details to show that the property is not one to which s 141 of the Consumer Credit Act 1974 applies[11]. The particulars must show the state of the mortgage account between the claimant and the defendant, by including:

(a) the amount of the advance and of any periodic repayment and any payment of interest required to be made;
(b) the amount which would have to be paid (after taking into account any adjustment for early settlement) in order to redeem the mortgage at a stated date not more than 14 days after the commencement of the proceedings specifying the amount of solicitor's costs and administrative charges which would be payable;
(c) where the loan which is secured by the mortgage is a regulated consumer credit agreement, the total amount outstanding under the terms of the mortgage;
(d) the rate of interest payable—
    (i) at the commencement of the mortgage;

(ii) immediately before any arrears referred to in paragraph (e) below accrued; and

(iii) where it differs from the rate in (ii) above, at the commencement of proceedings;

(e) if the claim is brought because of failure to pay the periodic payments when due—

(i) in schedule form, the dates when the arrears arose, all amounts due, the dates and amounts of all payments made and a running total of the arrears;

(ii) give details of:

(1) any other payments required to be made as a term of the mortgage (such as for insurance premiums, legal costs, default interest, penalties, administrative or other charges);

(2) any other sums claimed and stating the nature and amount of each such charge; and

(3) whether any of those payments is in arrear and whether or not it is included in the amount of any periodic payment[12].

The particulars must state any relevant information about the defendant's circumstances, in particular (a) whether the defendant is in receipt of social security benefits, and (b) whether any payments are made on his behalf directly to the claimant under the Social Security Contributions and Benefits Act 1992[13]. The particulars must give details of any tenancy entered into between the mortgagor and mortgagee (including any notices served)[14]. The particulars of claim must state any previous steps which the claimant has taken to recover the moneys secured by the mortgage or the mortgaged property and, in the case of court proceedings, state (a) the dates when proceedings were commenced and concluded, and (b) the dates and terms of any orders made[15]. Copies of all relevant documentation should be annexed[16]. The particulars of claim must contain a statement of truth[17].

Where possession is sought of different properties all charged by the same mortgage, all the claims for possession can properly be included in a single claim form[18]. A copy of the charge certificate should be attached to or served with the particulars of claim, and the original made available at the hearing[19]; under s 113 of the Land Registration Act 1925 office copies of the register and of documents filed in the Land Registry, including original charges, are admissible in evidence to the same extent as the originals[20].

1 CPR 55.3(5); CPR 55PD1.5.
2 The new form N120 replaced the old form N120 with effect from 15 October 2001.
3 See CPR 55PD. In relation to the old form N120 it was held that variations from the prescribed form should not preclude an order for possession: *Nationwide Building Society v Shillibeer* [1994] CLY 3295 CC.
4 CPR 55PD, para 2.5(8).
5 CPR 55PD, para 2.1(4).
6 CPR 55PD, para 2.1(3).
7 CPR 55PD, para 2.1(1).
8 CPR 55PD, para 2.1(2).
9 CPR 55PD, para 2.1(5).
10 CPR 55PD, para 2.5(4).
11 CPR 55PD, para 2.5(5).
12 CPR 55PD, para 2.5(3).
13 CPR 55PD, para 2.5(6).
14 CPR 55PD, para 2.5(7).
15 CPR 55PD, para 2.5(8).

16 CPR 16PD, para 8.3(1).
17 CPR Pt 22.
18 *First National Bank v Virdi* [1993] 5 CLY 3192.
19 CPR 16PD, para 8.3.
20 A provision to which attention is drawn by CPR 55PD, para 5.5. See also Land Registration Act 1925 s 68 re land and charge certificates.

Service

19.34 The court will fix a date for the hearing when it issues the claim form[1]. The hearing date will be not less than 28 days from the date of issue of the claim form; according to CPR 55.5 the standard period between the issue of the claim form and the hearing will be not more than eight weeks[2]. The claim form must be served not less than 21 days before the hearing date[3]. Where the claimant serves the claim form, he must serve notice of the hearing date at the same time, unless it is specified in the claim form[4]. The particulars of claim must be filed and served with the claim form[5]. In the case of a mortgagee's claim for possession of a dwelling house, a copy of the particulars of claim should be served on a person with matrimonial homes rights under Pt IV of the Family Law Act 1996[6]. Where the claimant serves the claim form and particulars of claim he must produce at the hearing a certificate of service of those documents[7].

1 CPR 55.5(1). See CPR 55PD, paras 3.1 and 3.2 as to circumstances in which the court may shorten the time until the hearing.
2 CPR 55.5(1), (3).
3 CPR 55.5(3)(c). See CPR 55PD paras 3.1 and 3.2 for the court's power to order an earlier hearing and shorten the periods for service, where violence or damage to property is apprehended.
4 CPR 8BPD, para B.11.
5 CPR 55.4.
6 Or previous matrimonial legislation: see CPR 55PD, para 2.5(1).
7 And CPR 6.14(2)(a) will not apply: CPR 55.8(6).

Notice to occupiers

19.35 After the issue of the claim form in a mortgagee's claim for possession of land which consists of or includes a dwelling-house, the claimant must not less than 14 days before the hearing send to the address of the property sought to be recovered a notice addressed to 'the occupiers', which:

(a) states that possession proceedings have been commenced in respect of the property;
(b) shows the name and address of the claimant, of the defendant and of the court which issued the claim form; and
(c) gives details of the claim number and of the hearing date.[1] The claimant must produce at the hearing a copy of the notice and evidence that he has served it[2]. The purpose of this rule is to allow occupiers of the property who are unaware that they are in peril of being evicted, such as tenants of the mortgagor, the opportunity to make representations to the court. The court will insist on strict compliance with the rule, in view of its purpose and importance.

1 CPR 55.10.
2 CPR 55.10.

Response by the defendant

19.36 The defendant is not required to serve an acknowledgment of service[1]. The general rule is that a defence must be served 14 days after service of the particulars of claim or, where the defendant has filed an acknowledgement of service, 28 days after service of the particulars of claim[2]. However, if, in a possession claim, the defendant does not file a defence within that time, he may still take part in the hearing. The court may, though, take into account his failure to file a defence when deciding what order to make about costs[3]. Thus the defendant will be well advised to complete form N11M (the court's Form of Reply (mortgaged property))[4] and, if he intends to defend the claim, to file and serve a defence in advance of the hearing. That will also reduce the chances of the claim being dealt with summarily on the first hearing. The claimant is not entitled to obtain a default judgment in a possession claim[5].

1 CPR 55.7; CPR Pt 10 does not apply.
2 CPR 15.4.
3 CPR 55.7(3).
4 CPR 55PD, para 1.5 (the new form N11M superseded the old form N11M with effect from 15 October 2001). It should be sent out with the claim form, together with Form N7, Notes for Defendant).
5 CPR 55.7(4).

The hearing

19.37 A mortgagee's claim for possession will generally be heard in private and in those circumstances the facts which need to be proved can be proved by evidence in writing (except where the claim is allocated to the fast or multi-track, or the court orders otherwise)[1]. Each party should wherever possible include all the evidence he wishes to present in his statement of case, verified by a statement of truth and copies of all relevant documentation should be annexed[2]. If possible the arrears in the particulars of claim should extend to the date of the hearing by specifying the relevant daily rate of arrears and interest; if necessary, such evidence can be brought up to date orally or in writing at the hearing[3]. Any additional information which needs to be proved should be included in a witness statement, which must be filed and served at least two days before the hearing[4]. In the case of residential premises, a witness statement will need to be prepared to exhibit the notice served on 'the occupiers' of the premises and evidence of its service[5]. Where necessary, there should be evidence confirming that the requirements as to service have been complied with. The original charge certificate, or an office copy of it, should be brought to the hearing[6]. If relevant the defendant should give evidence of:

(a) the amount of any outstanding social security or housing benefit payments relevant to mortgage arrears; and
(b) the status of
    (i) any claims for social security or housing benefit about which a decision has not yet been made; and

(ii) any applications to appeal or review a social security or housing benefit decision where that appeal has not yet concluded[7].

The claim may be heard by a district judge or a judge[8]. A claim by a mortgagee against one or more individuals for an order for possession of land must, in the first instance, be listed by the court as a hearing in private[9]. On the initial hearing date, the court may decide the claim, or give case management directions[10]. The court cannot give summary judgment in a claim for possession of residential premises against a mortgagor[11]. If the defendant has filed a defence, and the claim is genuinely disputed on grounds which appear to be substantial, such case management directions will include the allocation of the claim to a track, or directions to enable the claim to be allocated[12]. In allocating the claim, the court will have regard to the amount of arrears of mortgage instalments, the importance of vacant possession to the claimant, the importance to the defendant of retaining possession, and the various matters specified in CPR 26.8; the court will not give particular weight to the value of the property and may allocate the claim to the fast track even if its value exceeds £15,000[13]. If the maker of a witness statement does not attend a hearing, and the other party disputes material evidence contained in his statement, the court will normally adjourn the hearing so that oral evidence can be given[14]. The court's general powers of adjournment are dealt with below[15].

On the hearing of the claim originating summons the judge may order that additional persons be joined and served (though this will usually be when a non-party has asserted a claim after the proceedings have been commenced and has applied to be joined, in which case there should be no difficulty about service). Where a person has not been joined who should have been, the order for possession may be set aside, but only as against such person[16].

1 CPR 55.8(3); CPR 39PD, para 1.15.The general rules as to the giving and proving of such evidence are contained in CPR r 32.2.
2 CPR 55PD, para 5.1; CPR 16PD, para 8.3(1).
3 CPR 55PD 5.2.
4 CPR 55.8(4).
5 CPR 55.10.
6 CPR 16PD, para 8.3. The charge certificate is admissible as evidence of its contents: Land Registration Act 1925, s 68.Office copies of the register and of documents filed in the Land Registry, including original charges, are admissible in evidence to the same extent as the originals: Land Registration Act 1925, s 113; CPR 55PD, para 5.5.
7 CPR 55PD, para 5.3.
8 CPR 2.4, 2BPD, para 11.1(b).
9 CPR 39PD, para 1.5(1), CPR 39.2(3)(c).
10 CPR 55.8(1); CPR 8BPD, para B.13.
11 CPR 24.3(2).
12 CPR 55.8(2).
13 CPR 55.9(1); CPR 55PD, para 6.1.
14 CPR 55PD para 5.4.
15 See **19.50** ff.
16 *Brighton and Shoreham Building Society v Hollingdale* [1965] 1 All ER 540, [1965] 1 WLR 376.

Costs

19.38 The mortgagee will normally wish to add the costs of the proceedings to the mortgage debt, under the terms of the mortgage and will seek no order for costs in the proceedings. Accordingly, the CPR provides that where the mortgagee has a contractual right to recover costs out of the mortgage sums he is not required to apply for an order for those costs and the court is not required to assess such costs[1]. Moreover, a mortgagee is not to be deprived of a contractual nor equitable right to add costs to the security merely by reason of an order for payment of costs made without reference to the mortgagee's contractual or equitable rights, and without any adjudication as to whether or not the mortgagee should be deprived of those costs[2].

However, where the contract entitles a mortgagee to:

(a) add the costs of litigation relating to the mortgage to the sum secured by it; or
(b) require a mortgagor to pay those costs; or
(c) both,

the mortgagor may make an application for the court to direct that an account of the mortgagee's costs be taken[3]. The mortgagor may then dispute an amount in the mortgagee's account on the basis that it has been unreasonably incurred or is unreasonable in amount[4]. Where a mortgagor disputes an amount, the court may make an order that the disputed costs are assessed under CPR 48.3[5].

CPR 48.3 provides that where the court does assess costs which are payable under the terms of the mortgage, then, unless the mortgage provides otherwise, the costs are to be presumed to be costs which (a) have been reasonably incurred, and (b) are reasonable in amount, and the court will assess them accordingly[6]. In assessing costs payable under a mortgage, the court will apply the following principles[7]:

(a) an order for the payment of costs of proceedings by one party to another is always a discretionary order[8];
(b) where there is a contractual right to the costs, the discretion should ordinarily be exercised so as to reflect that contractual right;
(c) the power of the court to disallow a mortgagee's costs sought to be added to the mortgage security is a power that derives from the power of the courts of equity to fix the terms on which redemption will be allowed, and not from s 51 of the Supreme Court Act 1981;
(d) a decision by a court to refuse costs in whole or in part to a mortgagee litigant may be—
    (i) a decision in the exercise of the s 51 discretion;
    (ii) a decision in the exercise of the power to fix the terms on which redemption will be allowed;
    (iii) a decision as to the extent of a mortgagee's contractual right to add his costs to the security; or
    (iv) a combination of two or more of those things. The statements of case in the proceedings or the submissions made to the court may indicate which of the decisions has been made.
(e) A mortgagee is not to be deprived of a contractual or equitable right to add costs to the security merely by reason of an order for payment of costs made without reference to the mortgagee's contractual or equitable rights and without any adjudication as to whether or not the mortgagee should be deprived of those costs[9].

1 CPR 48PD, para 50.2. On costs generally, see further Chapter 36.

2 CPR 48PD, para 50.3(5).
3 CPR 48PD, 50.4(1).The court may direct that a party file an account: CPR 25.1(1)(n).
4 CPR 48PD, 50.4(2).
5 CPR 48PD, 50.4(3).
6 CPR 48.3(1).
7 CPR 48PD, para 50.3. As to the mortgagee's contractual entitlement to costs, see also *Gomba Holdings (UK) Ltd v Minories Finance Ltd (No 2)* [1992] 4 All ER 588.
8 Supreme Court Act 1981, s 51.
9 CPR 48PD, para 50.3.

HIGH COURT[1]

County court the normal court

19.39 Only exceptional circumstances justify starting a possession claim in the High Court rather than the county court. The grounds upon which a claim may be brought in the High Court have been considered above[2].

1 See 28 *Atkin's Court Forms* (1997 issue).
2 See **19.29**.

Jurisdiction

19.40 The cases in which the county court has exclusive jurisdiction have been considered in detail above[1]. In summary, the High Court has no jurisdiction:

(a) where a mortgage of land consists of or includes a dwelling-house[2] and no part of the land is situated in Greater London[3], except where the claim for possession is made as an additional claim in a genuine claim for foreclosure or sale[4]; and
(b) where the mortgage secures an agreement which is a regulated agreement within the meaning of the Consumer Credit Act 1974[5].

Possession proceedings within the exclusive jurisdiction of the county court cannot be transferred by the county court to the High Court, and the High Court has no jurisdiction even if such an order for transfer has been made[6]. However, a defendant to a High Court action may counterclaim for possession of a dwelling house outside Greater London, and the High Court may determine that counterclaim[7].

1 See **19.30**.
2 Dwelling-house includes any building or part thereof which is used as a dwelling: County Courts Act 1984, s 21 (7). The fact that part of the premises is used as a shop or office or for a business trade or professional purposes does not prevent the dwelling-house from being a dwelling-house for the purposes of this provision: s 21 (8).
3 Section 21 (3), (4).
4 Section 21(4).
5 Section 21 (9); Consumer Credit Act 1974, ss 21(9), 141, 189.
6 *Yorkshire Bank v Hall* [1999] 1 WLR 1713.
7 *Maria St George (London) Ltd v Burlington Investments Ltd*, 14 October 1977, Oliver J, unreported (noted at The Supreme Court Practice, 1999, vol 1, p 1575).

19.41 The former provisions for the assignment of a mortgagee's claim for possession to the Chancery Division have been revoked from 15 October 2001[1].

1 Formerly contained in CPR Sch 1, RSC Ord 88, r 2.

Parties

19.42 The principles as to whom it is appropriate to join as defendants are the same as with proceedings in the county court and have been considered above[1].

1 See **19.32**.

Claim form and particulars of claim

19.43 The requirements for the claim form and particulars of claim in a claim for possession by a mortgagee in the High Court are contained in CPR 55.4 and the Part 55 Practice Direction and CPR Pt 16.The appropriate claim form is N5 (possession of property)[1]. The property should be sufficiently described in the claim form to enable an adequate description to be carried forward into any possession order made and any subsequent writ of possession[2]. The particulars of claim must contain a statement of truth[3]. To start a claim in the High Court, the claimant must file with his claim a certificate stating the reasons for bringing the claim in that court, verified with a statement of truth in accordance with CPR 22.1(1)[4]. A claim for possession by a mortgagee is a claim for the recovery of land.[5]

Where a claimant claims as mortgagee possession of land which consists of or includes residential premises, the particulars of claim must be in the prescribed form, N120[6], which will contain all the information required by the rules[7], with the exception of the required information as to any previous steps which the claimant has taken to recover the money secured by the mortgage or the mortgaged property[8].

Where possession is claimed of land which does not consist of or include residential premises, the particulars of claim must be drafted so as to:

(a) identify the land to which the claim relates;
(b) state whether the claim relates to residential property;
(c) state the ground on which possession is claimed;
(d) give full details about any mortgage or tenancy agreement; and
(e) give details of every person who, to the best of the claimant's knowledge, is in possession of the property[9].

They must also set out the state of the mortgage account by including:

(a) the amount of:—
 (i) the advance;
 (ii) any periodic payment; and
 (iii) any payment of interest required to be made;
(b) the amount which would have to be paid (after taking into account any adjustment for early settlement) in order to redeem the mortgage at a stated

date not more than 14 days after the claim started specifying the amount of solicitor's costs and administration charges which would be payable;

(c) if the loan which is secured by the mortgage is a regulated consumer credit agreement, the total amount outstanding under the terms of the mortgage; and

(d) the rate of interest payable—
   (i) at the commencement of the mortgage;
   (ii) immediately before any arrears of periodic instalments accrued;
   (iii) at the commencement of the proceedings[10].

If the claim is brought because of failure to pay the periodic instalments when due, the particulars must state:

(a) in schedule form the dates when the arrears arose, all amounts due, the dates and amounts of all payments made, and a running total of the arrears;

(b) give details of—
   (i) any other payments required to be made as a term of the mortgage (such as for insurance premiums, legal costs, default interest, penalties, administrative or other charges);
   (ii) any other sums claimed, and stating the nature and amount of each such charge; and
   (iii) whether any of those payments is in arrear and whether or not it is included in the amount of any periodic payment[11].

The particulars must state whether or not the loan which is secured by the mortgage is a regulated consumer credit agreement and, if so, specify the date on which any notice required by s 76 or s 87 of the Consumer Credit Act 1974 was given[12]. If appropriate, the particulars should give details to show that the property is not one to which s 141 of the Consumer Credit Act 1974 applies[13]. The particulars must give details of any tenancy entered into between the mortgagor and mortgagee (including any notices served)[14]. The particulars of claim must state any previous steps which the claimant has taken to recover the moneys secured by the mortgage or the mortgaged property and, in the case of court proceedings, state:

(a) the dates when proceedings were commenced and concluded; and
(b) the dates and terms of any orders made[15].

Copies of all relevant documentation should be annexed[16]. The particulars of claim must contain a statement of truth[17].

1 CPR 55.3(5); CPR 55PD1.5; CPR 8BPD, B.1(2)(a), B.8(2), CPR Pt 4, Table 3.
2 See *Thynne v Sarl* [1891] 2 Ch 79; and see CPR 55 PD 2.1(1)
3 CPR Pt 22.
4 CPR 55.3(1), (2); for the grounds for bringing a claim in the High Court, see **19.29**.
5 *Esso Petroleum Co Ltdv Alstonbridge Properties* Ltd [1975] 1 WLR 1474 at 1481; CPR 55.1, 55.2.
6 The new form N120 became applicable to possession claims in the High Court with effect from 15 October 2001.
7 CPR 55PD.
8 Which should be added: see CPR 55PD, para 2.5(8).
9 CPR 55PD, para 2(1).
10 CPR 55PD, para 2.5(3).
11 CPR 55PD, para 2.5(3).

12 CPR 55PD, para 2.5(4).
13 CPR 55PD, para 2.5(5).
14 CPR 55PD, para 2.5(7).
15 CPR 55PD, para 2.5(8).
16 CPR 16PD, para 8.3(1).
17 CPR Pt 22.

Service of the claim and notice to occupiers

19.44 The court will fix a date for the hearing when it issues the claim form[1]. The hearing date will be not less than 28 days from the date of issue of the claim form; according to CPR 55.5 the standard period between the issue of the claim form and the hearing will be not more than eight weeks[2]. The claim form must be served not less than 21 days before the hearing date[3]. The particulars of claim must be filed and served with the claim form[4]. Where the claimant serves the claim form and particulars of claim he must produce at the hearing a certificate of service of those documents[5]. In possession claims relating to mortgaged residential property, not less than 14 days before the hearing the claimant must send a notice to the property addressed to 'the occupiers'. The notice must:

(a) state that a possession claim for the property has started; and
(b) show the name and address of the claimant, the defendant and the court which issued the claim form; and
(c) give details of the hearing.

The claimant must produce at the hearing (a) a copy of that notice, and (b) evidence that he has served it[6]. If someone other than the defendant is known to be in occupation, a possession order will not be made unless that person has been given notice of the hearing[7].

1 CPR 55.5(1). See CPR 55PD, paras 3.1 and 3.2 as to circumstances in which the court may shorten the time until the hearing where violence or damage to property is apprehended.
2 CPR 55.5(1), (3).
3 CPR 55.5(3)(c). See CPR 55PD, paras 3.1 and 3.2 as to circumstances in which the court may shorten the time limits. It should be served on the mortgagor and any other person in possession claiming a right to possession against the mortgagee: see *Alliance Building Society v Yap* [1962] 1 WLR 857; *Brighton and Shoreham Building Society v Hollingdale* [1965] 1 WLR 376.
4 CPR 55.4.
5 And CPR 6.14(2)(a) will not apply: CPR 55.8(6).
6 CPR 55.10.
7 Chancery Guide, para 21.6.

Response by defendant

19.45 The defendant is not required to serve an acknowledgment of service[1]. The general rule is that a defence must be served 14 days after service of the particulars of claim or, where the defendant has filed an acknowledgment of service, 28 days after service of the particulars of claim[2]. However, if, in a possession claim, the defendant does not file a defence within that time, he may still take part in the hearing (as has long been the practice of the Masters)[3]. The court may, though, take into account his failure to file a defence when deciding what order to make about costs[4]. Thus the defendant will be well advised to complete form N11M (the court's Form of Reply (mortgaged property))[5] and, if he intends to defend the claim, to file and serve a defence in advance of the hearing. That will also reduce the chances of the claim being dealt with summarily on the first hearing. The claimant is not entitled to obtain a default judgment in a possession claim[6].

1 CPR 55.7. CPR Pt 10 does not apply.
2 CPR 15.4.
3 Chancery Guide, para 21.6, 21.7.
4 CPR 55.7(3).
5 CPR 55PD, para 1.5 (the new form N11M became applicable to possession claims in the High Court from 15 October 2001). It should be sent out with the claim form, together with Form N7, Notes for Defendant.
6 CPR 55.7(4); CPR 12PD, para 1.2(3).

Evidence

19.46 Any fact that needs to be proved by the evidence of witnesses at the hearing may be proved by evidence in writing (except where the case is allocated to the multi-track or the court orders otherwise)[1]. Each party should, wherever possible, include all the evidence he wishes to present in his statement of case, verified by a statement of truth[2], to which copies of all relevant documentation should have been annexed[3]. Any mortgage arrears should, if possible, be stated up to date to the date of the hearing, if necessary by specifying a daily rate of arrears and interest. However, such evidence can be brought up to date orally or in writing on the day of the hearing if necessary[4].

1 CPR 55.8(3).
2 CPR 55PD, para 5.1.
3 CPR 16PD, para 8.3(1). Office copy entries of Land Registry documents are admissible in evidence to the same extent as the originals: CPR 55 PD, para 5.5
4 CPR 55PD, para 5.2.

The hearing

19.47 The hearing will generally be before a Master. A claim by a mortgagee against one or more individuals for an order for possession of land must, in the first instance, be listed by the court as a hearing in private[1]. The Masters give no preliminary consideration to mortgage possession cases, and thus the claimant should take an appointment of sufficient length for the hearing of the claim as soon as the claim form has been served[2]. In the case of mortgage possession claims for dwelling houses in Greater London, lenders can take block bookings of such claims in the Chancery Division, timed at 12 an hour (or six a half-hour) and may book a whole day (or two whole days) at a time, which will enable a lender to deal with all its Greater London claims at one time and one place, with consequent costs savings[3].

On the initial hearing date, the court may decide the claim, or give case management directions[4]. The Master may order further parties to be joined or notified of the proceedings, or require further evidence to be filed. If the maker of a witness statement does not attend a hearing and the other party disputes material evidence contained in his statement, the court will normally adjourn the hearing so that oral evidence can be given[5]. Where the claim is genuinely disputed on grounds which appear to be substantial, case management directions will include directions as to allocation[6]. The court cannot give summary judgment in a claim for possession of residential premises against a mortgagor[7]. The court's general powers of adjournment are dealt with below[8]. If an order for possession is made, the practice is to order possession 28 days after service of the order on the defendant. An order for immediate possession will not ordinarily be made. This practice is the same for dwelling-houses and other premises. If the defendant is in default of acknowledgment of service[9] and does not attend the hearing, the order will be for possession 28 days after personal service upon him of the order. Otherwise the order will be for possession 28 days after postal service of the order. If it proves impossible to serve the order personally, an order for service by another method will be made[10].

1 CPR 39PD, para 1.5(1), CPR 39.2(3)(c).
2 Chancery Guide, para 21.6, 21.7.
3 Chancery Guide, para 21.1.Whilst the provisions in the Chancery Guide predate the coming into force of CPR Pt 55, with its restrictions on bringing possession claims in the High Court, it would seem that that overriding objective of saving expense may remain a good reason for claims being brought in the High Court in such circumstances: see **19.29**.
4 CPR 55.8.
5 CPR 55PD, para 5.4.
6 CPR 55.8(2).
7 CPR 24.3(2).
8 See **19.51** ff.
9 He is not required to file an acknowledgement: CPR 55.7(1).
10 See also: *Barclays Bank Ltd v Bird* [1954] Ch 274 at 282, [1954] 1 All ER 449 at 453; *Four-Maids Ltd v Dudley Marshall (Properties) Ltd* [1957] Ch 317, [1957] 2 All ER 35; *London Permanent Benefit Building Society v De Baer* [1969] 1 Ch 321, [1968] 1 All ER 372. For issue of a writ of possession upon non-compliance with the order, see CPR Sch 1, RSC Ord 46. If the mortgagor afterwards gets back into possession a writ of restitution (see RSC Ord 46, r 3 and *Abbey National Building Society v Morris* (1978) 128 NLJ 999) or, more rarely, committal for contempt should be sought: *Alliance Building Society v Austen* [1951] 2 All ER 1068, *Wiltshire County Council v Frazer* [1986] 1 All ER 65, [1986] 1 WLR 109. Leave to issue execution on a suspended order for possession must not be given without allowing the defendant an opportunity to be heard. See *Fleet Mortgage and Investment Co Ltd v Lower Maisonette, 46 Eaton Place, Ltd* [1972] 2 All ER 737; *Practice Direction* [1972] 1 All ER 576.

Costs

19.48 The principles applicable to the mortgagee's entitlement to the costs of the proceedings are the same as those applying to claims in the county court[1].

1 See **19.38**.

EFFECT OF THE LIMITATION ACT

19.49 Under the Limitation Act 1980 a mortgagee's right to bring an action for possession is barred after 12 years from the date when repayment became due and his title to the land is extinguished[1]. A mortgagee does not lose his right to bring an action for the possession of the mortgaged land until the expiration of 12 years from the date when repayment became due[2].

1 See **16.40**.
2 See **16.41**. This period prevails over those for fixed or periodic tenancies in the Limitation Act 1980, s 15 (6) and Sch 1, paras 4, 5 and 6.

THE COURT'S POWERS OF ADJOURNMENT[1]

INHERENT JURISDICTION TO ADJOURN

19.50 Generally, the court has no inherent jurisdiction to adjourn a claim for possession to which there is no arguable defence[2], whether on terms of keeping up payments or paying arrears, unless the mortgagee agrees[3]. An alleged counterclaim or set-off is no ground for adjournment[4], unless the validity of the mortgage agreement is itself attacked, in which case the court should not prejudge that issue in any way[5]. The court also has a limited jurisdiction to adjourn or postpone the ordering of possession where there is a reasonable prospect of the mortgagor being able to pay off the mortgage in full within a short time, such as where the mortgagor has entered or is about to enter into a contract for the sale of the property at a price which will enable that to be achieved, or where the mortgage can be paid off from another source[6]. Where the claim is for arrears and possession and the arrears have been paid the court may adjourn the possession claim generally, with permission to apply, so that if there are further arrears the action can be reinstated rather than fresh proceedings being instituted[7]. That is a desirable procedure since it prevents the need for payment of further court fees by the mortgagee, which would normally be added to the debt under the terms of the mortgage[8]. The restrictions on the discretion of the court in making orders for possession of land contained in s 89 of the Housing Act 1980 does not apply to any order made in an action by a mortgagee for possession[9].

1 See (1997) LS 483 (Haley).
2 The existence of a triable defence is, of course, likely to be a good reason for not ordering possession: for instance, where there is a substantial question as to the existence or enforceability of the mortgage (see eg *Mobil Oil Co Ltd v Rawlinson* (1982) 43 P & CR 221, referred to *Lidco Investments Ltd v Hale* (1971) 219 Estate Gazette 715 (a decision under the former Moneylenders Acts); *Patterson v Roden* (1972) 223 Estates Gazette 945 (where the mortgage was alleged to form part of a fraud on the Revenue); or if the default has been waived (see eg *Hughes v Birks* [1958] EGD 341; *Ushers Brewery v Alro Club Holdings Ltd* (1970) 213 Estates Gazette 1537); or some estoppel can be raised against the mortgagee (see eg *Manson Finance v Oliso-Emosingoit* [1975] CLY 273; *Mobil Oil Co Ltd v Rawlinson*, above.) See also *Household Mortgage Corpn v Pringle* (1997) 30 HLR 250. Where a defence based upon a claimed equitable interest failed, the court refused to stay the warrant for possession pending the outcome of an application to the ECHR: *Locobail Ltd v Waldorf Investments Ltd* (2000) Times, 13 June.
3 *Birmingham Citizens Permanent Building Society v Caunt* [1962] Ch 883, [1962] 1 All ER 163; *Mobil Oil Co Ltd v Rawlinson* (1982) 43 P & CR 221. For the historical position in the QB Division, see *Redditch Benefit Building Society v Roberts* [1940] 1 Ch 415 at 420-421. See also *Roberts v Cilia* [1956] 1 WLR 1502; *Braithwaite v Winwood* [1960] 1 WLR 1257 and **19.52**, n 1.
CPR Sch 1, RSC Ord 45, r 11 does not confer on the court any power to grant a stay of execution of an order for possession: *London Permanent Benefit Building Society v De Baer* [1969] 1 Ch 321, [1968] 1 All ER 372.
4 *Mobil Oil Co Ltd v Rawlinson*, above. *Barclays Bank plc v Tennet* [1985] CLY 130, [1984] CA Transcript 242; *Citibank Trust Ltd v Ayivor* [1987] 3 All ER 241. Even an admitted liquidated claim which exceeds the mortgage does not per se discharge the mortgage and is no reason for adjourning the application: *Samuel Keller (Holdings) Ltd v Martins*

Bank Ltd [1970] 3 All ER 950, [1971] 1 WLR 43, CA. See also *Inglis v Commonwealth Trading Bank of Australia* (1972) 126 CLR 161; *United Dominions Corpn Ltd v Jaybe Homes Pty Ltd* [1978] Qd R 111 (where the sums alleged due to the mortgagor arose out of a transaction independent of the mortgage). See the disapproval in *Mobil Oil Co Ltd v Rawlinson*, above, of the statement made at this point in the previous edition and the note on that case and comment on the statement in the previous edition in [1982] Conv 453 (Jackson).

5 *Household Mortgage Corpn v Pringle* (1997) 30 HLR 250, CA; *Leeds Permanent Building Society v Kassai* [1992] CLY 3156 (CC); *Barclays Bank v Waterson* [1989] CLY 2505 CC.

6 *Royal Trust Co of Canada v Markham* [1971] 3 All ER 433, [1975] 1 WLR 1416, CA; *Cheltenham & Gloucester plc v Booker* (1996) 73 P & CR 412, 29 HLR 634, CA; (1997) LS 483 (Haley).'In proper cases the wind was tempered to the shorn lamb', per Clauson LJ, *Redditch Benefit Building Society v Roberts* [1940] Ch 415 at 420.

7 *Greyhound Guaranty v Caulfield* [1981] CLY 1808, (1981) 78 LS Gaz 958.

8 *Halifax plc v Taffs* [1999] CLY 4385.

9 Section 89 (2) (a).

STATUTORY POWERS OF ADJOURNMENT, SUSPENSION AND POSTPONEMENT[1]

Statutory powers of adjournment where mortgage of a dwelling houses

19.51 The Administration of Justice Act 1970, as amended, gives the court certain powers to adjourn the proceedings, stay the order or postpone the date for delivery of possession[2]. Section 36 of the Act provides that where the mortgagee[3] under a mortgage[4] of land which consists of or includes a dwelling-house[5] brings an action in which he claims possession of the mortgaged property, other than an action for foreclosure in which a claim for possession of the mortgaged property is also made, the court may exercise any of the powers conferred on it by sub-s 36(2), if it appears to the court that in the event of its exercising the power the mortgagor[6] is likely to be able within a reasonable period to pay any sums due under the mortgage[7], or to remedy a default consisting of a breach of any other obligation arising under or by virtue of the mortgage[8]. The powers conferred by s 36(2) give the court the power to:

(a) adjourn the proceedings, or
(b) on giving judgment, or making an order, for delivery of possession of the mortgaged property, or at any time before the execution of such judgment or order[9], to—
  (i) stay or suspend execution of the judgment or order, or
  (ii) postpone the date for delivery of possession,

for such period or periods as the court thinks reasonable[10].

Any such adjournment, stay, suspension or postponement may be made subject to such conditions with regard to payment by the mortgagor of any sum secured by the mortgage or the remedying of any default[11] as the court thinks fit[12]. The court may from time to time vary or revoke any such condition imposed[13]. The court's powers under s 36 cease once a possession order has been executed, unless the execution of the warrant amounts to an abuse of process or oppression[14]. However, where a mortgagor's application for a suspension of a possession warrant has been made and refused by a district judge before its execution, and the warrant is then executed, a circuit judge on a subsequent appeal can make any order the district judge would have made; he is entitled to set aside execution of the warrant and restore possession to the mortgagor[15].

Section 36 does not restrict the mortgagee's common law right to take peaceable possession without a court order[16]. The powers do not apply to an agreement regulated under the Consumer Credit Act 1974[17]. The court's powers to suspend an order for possession or make a time order in respect of such a mortgage have already been considered[18]. Section 36 will also not apply to a claim simply for an order for sale[19], event though, if the mortgagee is successful, the order made will include an order for possession. A tenant has no right to apply for relief under s 36 against a possession claim[20].

1 Although the marginal note to s 36 refers to *additional* powers, the court's inherent powers of adjournment outside the section are very limited: see **19.50**.

2 These powers are not dependent upon default by the mortgagor: see per Buckley LJ and Scarman LJ (but contra Goff LJ) in *Western Bank Ltd v Schindler* [1977] Ch 1, [1976] 2 All ER 393, CA (where there was default only under a collateral mortgage of a policy); see (1977) 40 MLR 356(Harpum).

3 'Mortgagee' and 'mortgagor' include any person deriving title under the original mortgagee or mortgagor: Administration of Justice Act 1970, s 39(1).

4 Which includes a charge: Administration of Justice Act 1970, s 39(1).

5 Dwelling-house includes any building or part thereof which is used as a dwelling: Administration of Justice Act 1970, s 39(1). The fact that part of the premises is used as a shop or office or for a business, trade or profession does not prevent the dwelling-house from being a dwelling-house for the purposes of the section: s 39 (2). See for the problems of mixed use, [1979] Conv 266, 270–271 (Smith).The land must consist of or include a dwelling-house at the time when the claim is brought: *Royal Bank of Scotland v Miller* (2001) 82 P & CR 31, CA.

6 While 'mortgagee' and 'mortgagor' include any person deriving title under the original mortgagee or mortgagor (Administration of Justice Act 1970, s 39(1)) that does not include a statutory tenant of a mortgagor: *Britannia Building Society v Earl* [1990] 2 All ER 469, [1990] 1 WLR 422, CA.

7 As to which, the court can order its own inquiry: *Shirlstar Container Transport Ltd v Re-Enforce Trading Co Ltd* [1990] NPC 76. For the meaning of 'sums due under the mortgage' see **19.52**.

8 Administration of Justice Act 1970, s 36(1). Eg subletting without the consent of the mortgagee: *Britannia Building Society v Earl* [1990] 2 All ER 469, [1990] 1 WLR 422, CA. 'Any other obligation' is not confined to obligations affecting the mortgagor's security.

9 The court's jurisdiction ceases once the judgment or order has been executed, or once the mortgagor's equity has been extinguished by the mortgagee: *National & Provincial Building Society v Ahmed* [1995] 2 EGLR 127, [1995] NPC 88.

10 Which may not be for an indefinite period: *Royal Trust Co of Canada v Markham* [1975] 1 WLR 1416, [1975] 3 All ER 433; *Bristol & West Building Society v Ellis* (1996) 73 P & CR 158, 29 HLR 282.As to what constitutes a 'reasonable period', see **19.54**.

11 Where the mortgagor has breached the terms of the mortgage by unlawfully subletting, the remedy is the removal of the subtenants: *Britannia Building Society v Earl* [1990] 2 All ER 469, [1990] 1 WLR 422, CA.

12 Administration of Justice Act 1970, s 36(3).

13 Section 36(4). 1970. In the application of this section to Northern Ireland, 'the court' means a judge of the High Court in Northern Ireland and in sub-s (1) the words from 'not being' to 'made' shall be omitted: s 36 (6).For time orders and regulated agreements under the Consumer Credit Act 1974, see **10.79** and Chapter 10 generally. On setting aside an order or judgment where the mortgagor did not attend the hearing, see *National Counties Building Society v Antonelli* [1995] NPC 177.

14 *Cheltenham & Gloucester Building Society v Obi* (1994) 28 HLR 22; *National & Provincial Building Society v Ahmed* [1995] 2 EGLR 127; *Hammersmith and Fulham London Borough Council v Hall* (1994) 27 HLR 368;*Cheltenham and Gloucester Building Society v Ebbage* [1994] CLY 3292; *Leicester Building Society v Aldwinkle* (1992) 24 HLR 40. On oppression, see *Lambeth v Hughes* [2001] 33 HLR 33; *Hammersmith and Fulham London Borough Council v Lemeh* (2000) 33 HLR 231.

15 *Hyde Park Funding v Ioannou* [1999] CLY 4382 CC.

16 *Ropaigealach v Barclays Bank Plc* [2000] 1 QB 263, [1999] 3 WLR 17, CA; (pet. dismissed) [2000] 1 WLR 1034, HL; [1999] CLJ 281 (Dixon); (1999) 143 Sol Jo 206 (Grant); [1999] Conv 263 (Dunn).

17 Administration of Justice Act 1970, s 38A. Cf *First National Bank plc v Syed* [1991] 2 All ER 250, decided per incuriam: (1994) 110 LQR 221 (Hickman).
18 See **10.79** and Chapter 10 generally.
19 See Chapter 21.
20 *Britannia Building Society v Earl* (1990) 22 HLR 98.

Meaning of 'sums due under the mortgage', where principal sum payable by instalments or otherwise deferred, but with provision for earlier payment in the event of any default or demand by the mortgagor

19.52 In determining what sums are due under the mortgage, s 36 was modified[1] by s 8 of the Administration of Justice Act 1973, which provides that where by a mortgage[2] of land which consists of or includes a dwelling-house, or by any agreement between the mortgagee under such a mortgage and the mortgagor, the mortgagor is entitled, or is to be permitted[3], to pay the principal sum secured by instalments, or otherwise to defer payment of it in whole or in part, but provision is also made for earlier payment in the event of any default by the mortgagor, or of a demand by the mortgagee or otherwise, then for purposes of s 36 of the Administration of Justice Act 1970 a court may treat as due under the mortgage, on account of the principal sum secured and of interest on it, only such amounts as the mortgagor would have expected to be required to pay if there had been no such provision for earlier payment[4]. However, the court may not exercise the powers conferred by s 36[5] unless it appears to the court that not only is the mortgagor likely to be able within a reasonable period to pay any amounts thereby regarded as due on account of the principal sum secured, together with the interest on those amounts, but also that he is likely to be able by the end of that period to pay any further amounts that he would have expected to be required to pay by then on account of that sum, together with interest on it, if there had been no provision for earlier payment on default or demand[6].

Section 8 of the 1973 Act applies to instalment mortgages and all other mortgages where the payment of the whole or part of the principal is deferred (including an endowment mortgage[7]), but provision is also made for earlier repayment on default of the mortgagor or demand by the mortgagee[8]. All the terms of the mortgage document and any agreement between the mortgagee[9] and the mortgagor must be considered to see if the mortgagor is entitled or is to be permitted to defer payment[10]. In order for s 8(1) to apply there must be a contractually binding or otherwise legally enforceable agreement that the mortgagor may pay by instalments or otherwise defer payment. Thus s 8(1) will not apply where a deferral is granted as a mere indulgence by the mortgagee, lacking contractual force, unless it is enforceable by estoppel[11]. The words of the section, 'where … the mortgagor is to be permitted … to defer payment', presuppose an existing liability to pay which was deferred by the terms of the mortgage or the covenant or some subsequent agreement between mortgagor and mortgagee. Thus, s 8 has no application to a mortgage or charge securing an overdraft payable on demand, where no demand has been made; there can be no agreement to defer a payment until it has become due[12]. However, the section was held to apply to an endowment mortgage where the mortgage moneys were repayable on demand, but the prior loan agreement referred to the period of the loan as 25 years and contained a provision making the mortgage moneys immediately payable upon default (as therein defined)[13]; giving the section a purposive construction, the agreement could be read as containing a provision for deferred payment[14].

In those cases where s 8 applies, the court may treat as due under the mortgage, on account of the principal sum secured and of interest on it, only such amounts as the mortgagor would have expected to be required to pay if there had been no such provision for earlier payment[15]. A court shall not exercise the powers conferred by s 36 of the 1970 Act unless it appears to the court, not only that the mortgagor is likely to be able within a reasonable period to pay any amounts regarded (under s 8 (1)) as due on account of the principal sum secured, together with interest thereon, but also that he is likely to be able, by the end of that period, to pay any further amounts that he would have expected to be required to pay by then[16].

1 The need for the modification arose for the following reasons. Section 36 followed (in most respects) a recommendation in the Report of the Payne Committee (Report of the Committee on the Enforcement of Judgment Debts, 1969, Cmnd 3909, pp 355 ff), which intended to authorise and extend the practice of masters and registrars (now district judges) of adjourning possession applications to allow the mortgagor to solve his financial difficulties on the terms of paying off arrears and keeping up current payments (for this practice, see eg (1961) 77 LQR 351, 352 (Master Ball). This practice had become somewhat restricted as a result of *Birmingham Citizens Permanent Building Society v Caunt* [1962] Ch 883, [1962] 1 All ER 163. The object of the section was to give the mortgagor an opportunity to make good his default if there were a reasonable prospect that he could do so, but the draftsman overlooked the fact that most mortgages and, in particular, most instalment mortgages, were drafted on the basis that upon default the whole of the mortgage moneys became due (On Homer nodding, see [1984] Conv 91 at 92–93 (Tromans) and see (1970) 120 NLJ 829 (the editor). While the mortgagor might be likely to be able to pay off arrears within a reasonable period, he was less likely to be able to pay off the whole of the mortgage money within such a period. Not long after the section came into effect (on 1 February 1971: Administration of Justice Act 1970 (Commencement No 3) Order 1970) this oversight was confirmed in the decision of *Halifax Building Society v Clark* [1973] Ch 307; [1973] 2 All ER 33, in which it was conceded that any sums due under the mortgage meant the redemption moneys (although that interpretation was not universally accepted: see *First Middlesborough Trading and Mortgage Co Ltd v Cunningham* (1974) 28 P & CR 69 at 72–75, where Scarman LJ (with whom Davies LJ agreed) thought that 'any sums due' should be limited to arrears of instalments only). See [1979] Conv 266 (Smith) and [1984] Conv 91 (Tromans); also (1973) 89 LQR 171 (Baker); (1973) 36 MLR 550 (Jackson); (1973) 37 Conv (NS) 213 (Crane). The intended effect of s 36 was restored by the Administration of Justice Act 1973. On the history of the defect and its remedy, see also *Habib Bank Ltd v Tailor* [1982] 1 WLR 1218 at 1222, CA. With regard to s 8, it is clear that it is to be given a purposive construction (see both Sir John Arnold P and Davies LJ in *Bank of Scotland v Grimes* [1985] 2 All ER 254 at 256, CA, and Goulding J in *Centrax Trustees Ltd v Ross* [1979] 2 All ER 952 (a reasonably liberal interpretation) and it is probably a fruitless exercise seeking technical deficiencies in the wording of the section. (See generally on the section [1979] Conv 266 (Smith); [1984] Conv 91 (Troman); [1983] Conv 80 (Kenny).

2 While there is some uncertainty as to the meaning of 'a mortgage' in this context (does the expression mean the mortgage document, or does it, as Sir John Arnold P suggested in *Bank of Scotland v Grimes* [1985] 2 All ER 254 at 256, CA, have a wider scope to include the whole mortgage transaction?) because of the inclusion of any agreement between the mortgagee and the mortgagor, the point is probably of little practical significance.

3 What is the difference between 'entitled' and 'permitted'? In *Bank of Scotland v Grimes*, above, Sir John Arnold P stated that he was wholly unable to come to any conclusion as to any possible meaning of 'is to be permitted'; if it were something which was short of a contractual obligation or a contractual right which was intended to be referred to, the words 'is to be' were peculiarly unsuitable; if it were something distinct from being entitled, then it was wholly obscure. 'Is to be permitted', as compared to 'is entitled', suggests an element of futurity and the possibility that the entitlement has to be found in the original agreement between the parties, rather than in an agreement made subsequently. This

raises the question whether there can be an agreement, effective for the purposes of s 8, made subsequently to the mortgage. In principle, there would seem to be no reason why the parties should not be able to vary the original terms in the relevant respect.

4 Administration of Justice Act 1973, s 8(1). Section 8 came into force on 18 May 1974: s 20 (1) (b) of the 1973 Act.

5 Of the Administration of Justice Act 1970.

6 Administration of Justice Act 1973, s 8(2).

7 On the application of s 8 to such mortgages, see [1984] Conv 91 at 96–99 (Tromans); [1985] Conv 407 (JEM).

8 The section does not apply where there is no provision for acceleration: *Peckham Mutual Building Society v Registe* (1980) 42 P & CR 186.

9 'Mortgagor' and 'mortgagee' are to be construed in the same way as in relation to the Administration of Justice Act 1970, s 36 (as to which, see **19.51**, n 3): Administration of Justice Act 1973, s 8 (4).

10 See eg *Centrax Trustees Ltd v Ross* [1979] 2 All ER 952.

11 *Rees Investments Ltd v Groves* (Neuberger J, Chancery Division, 27 June 2001, unreported); see also *Centrax Trustees Ltd v Ross*, above, at 955.

12 *Rees Investments Ltd v Groves*, above; *Habib Bank Ltd v Tailor* [1982] 3 All ER 561, [1982] 1 WLR 1218, CA. Cf re s 36, *Western Bank Ltd v Schindler* [1977] Ch 1 at 13, 19.

13 *Bank of Scotland (Governor & Co) v Grimes* [1985] 2 All ER 254 at 258.

14 *Bank of Scotland (Governor & Co) v Grimes*, above. *Habib Bank Ltd v Tailor*, above was distinguished on the facts and as being 'a rather different case from an overdraft, at least socially, in regard to the purpose of the legislation'. *Grimes* was followed in *Royal Bank of Scotland v Miller* (2001) 82 P & CR 96, CA.

15 Section 8 (1).

16 Section 8 (2). Cf s 36 of the 1970 Act on the construction of that section by Scarman LJ in *First Middlesborough Trading and Mortgage Co Ltd v Cunningham* (1974) 28 P & CR 69 at 72–75. See [1979] Conv 266, 274–275 (Smith).

Application of statutory powers to claims for foreclosure

19.53 Section 36 provides that its powers apply to an action in which the mortgagee claims possession of the mortgaged property, with the exception of a claim for foreclosure in which a claim for possession of the mortgaged property is also made. In relation to mortgages to which s 8 of the Administration of Justice Act 1973 applies, s 8(3) modifies s 36 so as to provide that s 36 applies to a foreclosure action, whether it is with or without a claim for possession, as if there was a claim only for possession, except that s 36(2)(b) is to apply only in relation to any claim for possession. The effect of this amendment appears to be that, in relation to mortgages to which s 8 applies, if the only claim is for foreclosure, the only statutory power is adjournment; whereas if the claim is for foreclosure and possession, there is power to adjourn the foreclosure claim and to adjourn the possession claim, or stay or postpone any order for possession.

A claimant for foreclosure need not also claim possession — delivery of possession will generally be ordered as part of the foreclosure order, even though possession is not expressly sought in the relief claimed. Where the mortgage is not within the provisions of s 8, the powers under s 36 do not apply to a claim simply for foreclosure. Thus a foreclosure action will avoid the statutory powers of adjournment, suspension and postponement[1]. The meaning of 'an action for foreclosure' is therefore of some importance[2]. For s 36 not to apply, the foreclosure must not be a disguise for what in reality is a claim for payment and/or possession[3]. If the claimant has claimed foreclosure in his claims and pursues his remedy of foreclosure at the hearing (in which case his evidence will be somewhat different from that on a claim simply for possession[4]) the action will be a foreclosure action and s 36 will not apply[5].

1 An action for foreclosure or sale, even where possession is expressly claimed, is also excluded from s 37 of the 1970 Act (exclusive jurisdiction of the county court).
2 See generally on the point in the article by the editor of the 10th edn in (1970) 120 NLJ 808, 829.
3 *Manchester Unity Life Insurance Collecting Society Trustees v Sadler* [1974] 2 All ER 410, [1974] 1 WLR 770.As with s 37 of the 1970 Act.
4 Compare **19.33**, **19.46** and **22.25**.
5 See *Lord Marples of Wallasey v Holmes* (1975) 31 P & CR 94.

EXERCISE OF THE STATUTORY POWERS: WHETHER MORTGAGOR LIKELY TO BE ABLE TO PAY WITHIN A REASONABLE PERIOD[1]

Payment within a reasonable period

19.54 For the purposes of s 36, it is, in the absence of unusual circumstances, the remaining term of the mortgage which should be the starting point for determining what is a reasonable period[2]. The question is whether it is likely that the mortgagor will be able to pay off both the current instalments and the accrued arrears over that period[3]. To answer that question, the court should at the outset resolve disputes over the calculation of the amount of arrears and the assessment of future instalments for their payment-off. In particular, the court should determine which items should be attributed to the mortgagor's current interest payment obligations and which to his ultimate liability on capital account. The Court of Appeal has suggested[4] the following as a practical summary of the considerations which would be relevant when determining the 'reasonable period':

(a) How much can the borrower reasonably afford to pay, both now and in the future?
(b) If the borrower has a temporary difficulty in meeting his obligations, how long is the difficulty liable to last?
(c) What was the reason for the arrears which have accumulated?
(d) How much remains of the original term?
(e) What are the relevant contractual terms, and what type of mortgage is it, ie when is the principal due to be repaid?
(f) Is it a case where the court should exercise its power to disregard accelerated payment provisions (s. 8 of the Act of 1973)?
(g) Is it reasonable to expect the lender, in the circumstances of the particular case, to recoup the arrears of interest (i) over the whole of the original term, or (ii) within a shorter period, or even (iii) within a longer period, ie by extending the repayment period?
(h) Is it reasonable to expect the lender to capitalise the interest or not ?
(i) Are there any reasons affecting the security which should influence the length of the period for payment?

In all cases, the value or future value of the security will be relevant; if the future value of the security may be threatened by postponing payments over too long a period, that will be a circumstance justifying a departure from treating the remaining term of the mortgage as a reasonable period. Expert evidence may be required to see if and when the lender's security may be put at risk[5]. In the light of the answers to the above, the court can proceed to exercise its overall discretion, taking into account also any further factors which may arise in the particular case. It may be appropriate to take into account the nature of the mortgagee and mortgagor: thus in the case of a lender who is a private individual, as opposed to an institutional lender, the reasonable period may be shorter. Where the mortgagor has a counterclaim, which he claims would enable him to pay the sums due, the court should determine whether the prospects of it succeeding are such that can be viewed as enabling such sums to be paid within a reasonable time[6]. If there is no prospect of the mortgagor being able to pay within a reasonable period, the court has no discretion to suspend an order for possession under s 36, however hard the circumstances[7].

Likelihood is a question of fact to be determined by the judge on the evidence before him[8]. It may be that there is no, or inadequate, information before the court to enable it to make a decision to adjourn or suspend[9]. However, the court has a discretion as to whether or not to require sworn evidence from the mortgagor as to his ability to pay and is also entitled to infer from the mortgagor's previous payment record, or past broken promises, that he is unlikely to make the required payments in the future[10]. The fact that the mortgagor is unemployed at the time of the hearing is not fatal for him, since his mortgage repayments may be met by the social security authorities[11].

1 Administration of Justice Act 1970, s 36 (1). See generally [1979] Conv 266 (Smith).

2 *Cheltenham and Gloucester Building Society v Norgan* [1996] 1 All ER 449 , [1996] 1 WLR 343; (1996) Conv 118 (Thompson); (1996) 112 LQR 553 (Morgan); (1996) 146 NLJ 252 (Wilkinson); see also *Bristol & West Building Society v Ellis* (1996) 73 P & CR 158, 29 HLR 282; *Western Bank Ltd v Schindler* [1976] 2 All ER 393, [1976] 3 WLR 341, CA; *First Middlesborough Trading and Mortgage Co Ltd v Cunningham* (1974) 28 P & CR 69, CA (see also [1979] Conv 266 at 273). Cf the position in Northern Ireland: *National & Provincial Building Society v Lynd* [1996] NI 47.A mortgagee will be at risk of costs if it now contends that the arrears should be discharged over a shorter period: *Abbey National plc v Acharya* [1996] CLY 4979 (CC).The Payne Committee in its Report (at para 1388) had in mind a period of six months in the usual case, while considering that in some cases a longer period might be appropriate. In the past a period of five years has been suggested: see (1971) 69 LS Gaz 268 (Wareham) and letters at 377, 427. Until disapproved in *Cheltenham & Gloucester Building Society v Norgan*, many courts had adopted the practice of taking a short period of two or so years: see eg the facts in *Citibank Trust Ltd v Ayivor* [1987] 1 WLR 1157. A mortgagee will be at risk of costs if it contends that the arrears should be discharged over a shorter period: *Abbey National plc v Acharya* [1996] CLY 4979 CC.

3 *First National Bank v Syed* [1991] 2 All ER 250, [1991] CCLR 37; *Town & Country Building Society v Julien* (1991) 24 HLR 312; *Abbey National Mortgages plc v Bernard* (1995) 71 P & CR 257.

4 Per Evans LJ, in *Cheltenham and Gloucester Building Society v Norgan* [1996] 1 WLR 343 at 357-358.

5 *Cheltenham & Gloucester Building Society v Norgan* [1996] 1 WLR 343 at 354.

6 *National Westminster Bank plc v Skelton* [1993] 1 All ER 242, [1993] 1 WLR 72n; *Ashley Guarantee plc v Zacaria* [1993] 1 WLR 62, [1993] 1 All ER 254. The court declined to take into account, for the purposes of s 36, the mortgagor's claim for damages pending its resolution in: *Citibank Trust Ltd v Ayivov* (1987) 19 HLR 463; *Household Mortgage Corpn plc v Pringle* (1997) 30 HLR 250; *Albany Home Loans plc v Massey* (1997) 29 HLR 902; *National Home Loans Corpn plc v Yaxley* (1997) 73 P & CR D41.

7 *Abbey National Mortgages v Bernard* [1995] CLY 3597, [1995] NPC 118, CA.

8 *Royal Trust Co of Canada v Markham* [1975] 3 All ER 433 at 438, CA; *Western Bank Ltd v Schindler* [1977] Ch 1, [1976] 2 All ER 393, CA; *Cheltenham and Gloucester Building Society v Grant* (1994) 26 HLR 703.

9 See eg *Royal Trust Co of Canada v Markham*, above; *Peckham Mutual Building Society v Registe* (1980) 42 P & CR 186. For an example, see *Halifax plc v Purvis* (1998) 77 P & CR D29, CA.

10 *Cheltenham and Gloucester Building Society v Grant* (1994) 26 HLR 703; *Abbey National v Mewton* [1995] CLY 3598, CA; *Halifax Plc v Purvis* (1998) 77 P & CR D29, CA. In *Town & Country Building Society v Julien* (1991) 24 HLR 312, CA the court took into account the

fact that previous promises as to the likelihood of obtaining employment had failed to bear fruit.

11 Cf where the arrears accrued before the application for income support was made: *Town & Country Building Society v Julien* (1991) 24 HLR 312, CA.

Payment of moneys due by sale of the property

19.55 There may be circumstances where the mortgagor is only likely to be able to repay the whole of the mortgage moneys if he can sell the property. The court can exercise its powers under s 36 to suspend or adjourn a possession claim in such circumstances, if the prospects of a sale, or a sale at a higher price, would be more favourable with the mortgagor in occupation, than if the house were repossessed[1]. The court should consider the likelihood of a sale being achieved within a reasonable period. In contrast to the position where the arrears are to be discharged by periodic payments, the outstanding term of the mortgage should not be taken as the starting point for determining reasonableness. Rather, the question of what constitutes a reasonable period depends on all the circumstances; there should be evidence as to the prospects, and likely time-scale, of a sale before the court[2]. When considering whether to exercise its powers, the court should take into account the value of the security compared to the size of the debt, and whether any delay pending a sale would reduce the extent to which the debt remained secured[3]. If the sale proceeds would not discharge the whole of the mortgage moneys, the court should not exercise its powers under s 36, unless other moneys would be available to repay the balance[4]. If the court is satisfied that the proceeds of sale will discharge the debt, and that the necessary period for sale is reasonable, it should, if it decides to suspend the order for possession, identify the period in its order[5].Where a sale of part of the property would discharge the mortgage in a reasonable time, but one of two joint owners and mortgagors refuses to consent to a sale, it may be appropriate for the court to suspend the possession proceedings to allow the other owner to apply for an order for sale under s 14 of the Trusts of Land and Appointment of Trustees Act 1996[6].

1 *Royal Trust Co of Canada v Markham* [1975] 3 All ER 433; *Western Bank Ltd v Schindler* [1976] 2 All ER 393; *Citibank Trust Ltd v Ayivor* [1987] 3 All ER 241, [1987] 1 WLR 1157; *National & Provincial Building Society v Lloyd* [1996] 1 All ER 630, 28 HLR 459; *Target Home Loans v Clothier* [1994] 1 All ER 439.

2 Six months to one year is likely to be the normal maximum period. *Cheltenham and Gloucester Building Society v Johnson* (1996) 73 P & CR 293, 28 HLR 885; *Bristol & West Building Society v Ellis* (1996) 73 P & CR 158, 29 HLR 282; *National & Provincial Building Society v Lloyd* [1996] 1 All ER 630, 28 HLR 459; *Mortgage Services Funding v Steele* (1996) 29 HLR 597; [1998] Conv 25 (Thompson).

3 *Bristol & West Building Society v Ellis*, above.

4 *Cheltenham & Gloucester Building Society v Krausz* [1997] 1 All ER 21, [1997] 1 WLR 1558, (1996) 29 HLR 597.

5 *Bristol & West Building Society v Ellis*, above.

6 *Abbey National plc v Powell* (1999) 78 P & CR D16, CA. As to an order for sale under the 1996 Act, see: **21.13** ff.

Postponing possession pending completion of sale by mortgagee

19.56 The court may postpone possession so as to allow the mortgagor to remain in occupation pending completion of the sale by the mortgagee, if the court is satisfied that:

(a) possession would not be required by the mortgagee pending completion of the sale, but only by the purchasers on completion;
(b) the presence of the mortgagor pending completion would enhance, or at least not depress, the purchase price; and
(c) the mortgagor would co-operate in effecting the sale.

In practice, it is seldom likely those conditions will be satisfied and the jurisdiction should be used sparingly and with great caution; it is unlikely to be appropriate to take that course if the mortgagee does not consent[1].

1 *Cheltenham & Gloucester Building Society v Booker* (1996) 73 P & CR 412, 29 HLR 634.

Choice of powers[1]

19.57 The court's discretion under s 36 is to adjourn the proceedings, to stay or suspend execution of the order, or to postpone the date for delivery of possession[2]. It is submitted that adjournment (other than for further evidence etc) is only likely to be appropriate in such cases as a prospective sale by the mortgagor, or temporary illness or unemployment[3]. The adjournment will be for a fairly short period to see whether the circumstances may have changed. Thus, an adjournment for six months was granted where the mortgagee's evidence was that her employment prospects would by that time be greatly improved; the court was not able to say at the date of the hearing that there was a likelihood that the arrears would be cleared within a reasonable time, but would be able to consider that question on the adjourned hearing[4]. In appropriate cases there may be several adjournments. There is no jurisdiction to adjourn indefinitely[5]. Otherwise a possession order should be made and suspended. The suspension must be for a fixed period[6]. There is no jurisdiction to suspend indefinitely[7].Where the court suspends an order for possession on terms that the mortgagor pays the arrears by instalments, the mortgagee is entitled to a money judgment suspended on the same terms. The former practice of adjourning the money claim generally, with permission to restore, should now only be followed in special circumstances, such as where the mortgagor provides evidence that sale of the property would take place within a reasonable time[8]. The court has jurisdiction to make an order under s 36 even where it has previously refused an application in the same terms, for instance where the mortgagor's circumstances have changed, although it can reject what amounts to a repeat application if it amounts to an abuse of the process[9].

Can the court exercise its powers when the defendant mortgagor has not asked it to do so? There is no burden of proof imposed by the relevant sections one way or the other. It is for the court to decide whether or not to exercise the additional powers on such evidence as it has before it. Often the defendant will not file any evidence on which the court can reach a view, or which would enable it to exercise any of its additional powers[10]. However, there may be enough of the background in the plaintiff's evidence to enable the court to make a suspended order, thus the court may be able to make inferences from the mortgagor's previous payment record[11].

It has been argued that a tenant of the mortgagor may be able to rely on these statutory powers[12]. However, if the tenancy is binding on the mortgagee[13] there will be no need to rely on the powers. If the tenancy is not binding on the mortgagee[14], it seems rather strange that such tenant could rely on the circumstances relevant to another, that is the mortgagor[15].

1 See [1979] Conv 266 (Smith).
2 Administration of Justice Act 1970, s 36 (2).
3 See *Williams & Glyn's Bank Ltd v Boland* [1979] Ch 312, [1979] 2 All ER 697, CA; affd [1981] 1 AC 487, [1980] 2 All ER 408, HL.
4 *Skandia Financial Services Ltd v Greenfield* [1997] CLY 4248 CC.
5 See *Western Bank Ltd v Schindler* [1976] 2 All ER 393.
6 See *Centrax Trustees Ltd v Ross* [1979] 2 All ER 952, where the arrears had already been paid and the suspension was conditional on payment of current instalments and costs.
7 *Royal Trust Co of Canada v Markham* [1975] 3 All ER 433; *Cheltenham and Gloucester Building Society v Ensor* (31 August 1992, CA, unreported); *National Westminster Bank plc v Skelton* [1993] 1 WLR 72 at 81.
8 *Cheltenham and Gloucester Building Society v Grattridge* (1993) 25 HLR 454, CA; *Cheltenham and Gloucester Building Society v.Johnson* (1996) 28 HLR 885, CA.
9 *Abbey National Mortgages plc v Bernard* [1995] CLY 3597, [1995] NPC 118, CA.
10 *Royal Trust Co of Canada v Markham*, above.
11 *Cheltenham and Gloucester Building Society v Grant* (1994) 26 HLR 703; *Abbey National v Mewton* [1995] CLY 3598; cf *Town & Country Building Society v Julien* (1991) 24 HLR 312, CA (record of past broken promises had the opposite effect).
12 See (1979) 129 NLJ 457 (Waite).
13 See **19.16**, **19.19** ff.
14 See **19.18**.
15 Quaere whether such tenant could be said to derive title under the mortgagor within s 39 (1) of the Administration of Justice Act 1970 (see **19.51**, n 3).

ORDER FOR POSSESSION AGAINST ONE JOINT MORTGAGOR

19.58 Where a mortgagee applies for possession of a jointly owned and jointly mortgaged property, and whilst one mortgagor has no defence to the claim, the other has a defence or an arguable defence, the court should in general adjourn the proceedings against the mortgagor who has no defence, with permission to restore if the other mortgagor leaves the property or has an order for possession made against her. Alternatively, the court can make an order for possession against the first mortgagor, upon the mortgagee giving an undertaking not to enforce the order until the other mortgagor leaves or has an order for possession made against her[1].

1 *Albany Home Loans v Massey* (1997) 29 HLR 902.

RIGHTS OF MORTGAGEE IN POSSESSION

RIGHT TO RENTS AND PROFITS AND THE BENEFIT OF COVENANTS

19.59 The mortgagee in possession is entitled to the rents and profits of the mortgaged property, by virtue of the legal or equitable ownership which the mortgage confers on him. The legal mortgagee is the reversioner expectant on any lease granted out of the mortgaged property and a legal chargee is placed in a similar position by s 87 of the Law of Property Act 1925[1]. Where a mortgagee takes possession of land with the benefit of a milk quota, the mortgagee is entitled to the benefit of 'rents' from a 'lease' of the quota[2].

Where the tenancy was created before the mortgage, or is otherwise binding on the mortgagee, he will take possession by giving notice to the tenant requesting payment of the rent to himself[3]. His title thereupon relates back to the date when his right first accrued, that is (unless the mortgage deed provides otherwise) on the grant of the mortgage. Thus, he can sue a trespasser for a trespass committed before he took possession[4]. He also becomes entitled to and may distrain or sue for any rent in arrear at the date of his taking possession, and any arrears which have accrued since the mortgage, and also for any rent which subsequently falls due[5]. He may sue a tenant claiming under an agreement for a lease made by the mortgagor[6]. If, after the mortgage, the rent has been varied by agreement between the tenant and the mortgagor, the mortgagee is entitled to recover for the additional as well as the original rent[7]. He will have priority over persons to whom, after the mortgage, the mortgagor assigned the rents[8].

The tenancy may be in respect of a furnished house, where the rent is payable in respect of both the property and the furniture, but where although the mortgagee has a claim to possession of the property, he has no right in respect of the furniture. In such circumstances, if the tenant after notice from the mortgagee pays him the whole rent, then the tenant may be liable to be sued again by a party who has an interest in the furniture (for example, the mortgagor's trustee in bankruptcy) for the use of the furniture in which the mortgagee had no interest. The appropriate course for the tenant would be to apportion the rent[9].

After the mortgagee has taken possession, the mortgagor has no remedy against the tenant in respect of rent alleged to be due from him[10]. That is the case even where the mortgagee has refused to ask for it[11]. In the latter case, his only remedy is against the mortgagee on taking the accounts[12]. Where rent falls due after the mortgagee has taken possession, but the tenant paid it prematurely to the mortgagor before it fell due, when the mortgagee goes into possession he may demand payment again[13]. However, the position is otherwise where the advance payment was made before the mortgage: the payment then binds the mortgagee, since he should have inquired as to the terms on which the tenant was in occupation[14]. The tenant cannot set off against the rent claimed by the mortgagee in possession a personal claim he had against the mortgagor[15].

Where the tenancy is not binding on the mortgagee, the mortgagee is not entitled to demand rents as such, nor any arrears of rent under such a tenancy due at the date of his taking possession[16]. He can create a new tenancy under the mortgage. Alternatively, after notice from the mortgagee, the tenant should pay the rent to him, since the mortgagee will in any case be entitled to an equivalent amount as mesne profits[17]. After the mortgagee takes possession (or receives judgment for possession), his right of possession relates back to the time that right accrued, that is (unless the mortgage deed provides otherwise) on the grant of the mortgage[18]. Accordingly, the mortgagee will be entitled to mesne profits within that period, subject to the limitation period of six years[19].

1 *Cockburn v Edwards* (1881) 18 Ch D 449 at 457, CA; *Municipal Permanent Investment Building Society v Smith* (1888) 22 QBD 70, CA; *Re Ind Coope & Co Ltd* [1911] 2 Ch 223 at 231-232; *Rhodes v Allied Dunbar pension Services* [1989] 1 All ER 1161 at 1166. In relation to mortgaged property which is subject to a lease granted before 1 January 1996, the mortgagee is entitled to the benefit of every covenant which touches and concerns the land, and to exercise any right of re-entry: see s 141 of the Law of Property Act 1925. In relation to mortgaged property which is subject to a lease granted after 1 January 1996, under s 15 of the Landlord and Tenant(Covenants) Act 1995 a mortgagee in possession is entitled to enforce any tenant covenant or right of re-entry which is enforceable by the mortgagor. See **19.17**.

2 *Harries v Barclays Bank plc* [1997] 2 EGLR 15.

3 See *Horlock v Smith* (1842) 6 Jur 478; *Heales v M'Murray* (1856) 23 Beav 401; cf *Kitchen's Trustee v Madders* [1949] Ch 588, aff'd [1950] Ch 134. It has been held that he cannot charge as mortgagee's costs for the expense of drafting more than one notice, however many tenants there may be: *Re Tweedie's Taxation* (1908) 53 Sol Jo 118.

4 *Ocean Accident and Guarantee Corpn v Ilford Gas Co* [1905] 2 KB 493, CA.
5 *Moss v Gallimore* (1779) 1 Doug KB 279; *Rogers v Humphreys* (1835) 4 Ad & El 299, 314.
6 *Rawson v Eicke* (1837) 7 Ad & El 451, where damages for use and occupation were awarded (a case decided before *Walsh v Lonsdale* (1882) 21 Ch D 9).
7 *Burrowes v Gradin* (1843) 1 Dowl & L 213.
8 *Re Ind Coope & Co Ltd* [1911] 2 Ch 223; and see *Rhodes v Allied Dunbar Pension Services* [1989] 1 All ER 1161.
9 *Salmon v Matthews* (1841) 8 M & W 827; see *Hoare (Charles) & Co v Hove Bungalows Ltd* (1912) 56 Sol Jo 686.
10 *Underhay v Read* (1887) 36 WR 75, affd 36 WR 298 and 20 QBD 209.
11 *Salmon v Dean* (1849) 14 Jur 235; see on appeal at (1851) 3 Mac & G 344.
12 Where the mortgagee will be liable on the basis of wilful default: see **19.65**.
13 *Reeves v Pope* [1914] 2 KB 284, CA; followed in *Re Arrows Ltd (No 3)* [1992] BCLC 555, [1992] BCC 131.
14 *De Nicholls v Saunders* (1870) LR 5 CP, 589; *Green v Rheinberg* (1911) 104 LT 149.
15 *Green v Rheinberg* (1911) 104 LT 149, CA.
16 *Corbett v Plowden* (1884) 25 Ch D 678; *Kitchen's Trustee v Madders* [1950] Ch 134, [1949] 2 All ER 1079, CA.
17 *Ocean Accident and Guarantee Corpn v Ilford Gas Co* [1905] 2 KB 493, CA.
18 *Ocean Accident and Guarantee Corpn v Ilford Gas Co* [1905] 2 KB 493, CA.
19 *Barnett v Earl of Guilford* (1855) 11 Exch 19; *Harris v Mulkern* (1875) 1 Ex D 31; *Ocean Accident and Guarantee Corpn v Ilford Gas Co* [1905] 2 KB 493, CA. Cf *Turner v Cameron's Coalbrook Steam Co* (1850) 5 Exch 932.

LEASING

19.60 A mortgagee in possession of land has the same statutory power of leasing, and of accepting surrenders of leases, as a mortgagor in possession[1]. Such a lease by a mortgagee in possession binds all prior incumbrancers and the mortgagor himself[2]. A mortgagee who has appointed a receiver has, while the receiver is acting, the same powers, and may delegate the power of leasing to the receiver[3].

1 This has been considered fully at **19.21**, n 8 ff. Law of Property Act 1925, ss 99 (2), 100 (2). See also *Berkshire Capital Funding Ltd v Street* (1999) 32 HLR 273. If the mortgagor's statutory power of leasing has been excluded a second mortgage in possession will not have the statutory powers. Subsection (13) of s 99 applies as much to sub-s (2) as to (1): *Julian S Hodge & Co Ltd v St Helen's Credit Ltd* [1965] EGD 143.
2 Law of Property Act 1925, s 99 (2), but for the purposes of s 99 'mortgagor' does not include an incumbrancer deriving title under the original mortgagor: sub-s (18). However, a lease made by a mortgagee in circumstances where it is not made under the statutory power, nor under any express power in the mortgage, nor with the consent of the mortgagor, will not bind the mortgagor upon redemption. In such circumstances the mortgagor should be made a party to the lease, consenting to the mortgagee's grant: see *Chapman v Smith* [1907] 2 Ch 97; *Saunders v Merryweather* (1865) 3 H & C 902; *Franklinski v Ball* (1864) 33 Beav 560; *Doe d Barney v Adams* (1832) 2 Cr & J 232; *Smith v Pocklington* (1831) 1 Cr & J 445; *Webb v Russell* (1789) 3 Term Rep 393; *Hungerford v Clay* (1722) 9 Mod Rep 1.
3 Law of Property Act 1925, s 99 (19).

CARRYING ON OF BUSINESS

19.61 Where the mortgaged property includes a business carried on upon mortgaged premises the mortgagee in possession is entitled to carry on the business with a view to a sale[1]. The terms of the mortgage in such a case should provide for this eventuality[2], although usually the mortgagee will prefer to appoint a receiver to run the business. The mortgagee has the same powers to operate the business as the mortgagor enjoyed[3]. The mortgagee is entitled to exercise his power even if that is disadvantageous to the mortgagor, although he is under a duty to exercise it in good faith and for the purpose of repaying the mortgage debt[4]. He is entitled to be recouped from losses not attributable to his negligence out of the proceeds of sale of the business[5].

1 *Cook v Thomas* (1876) 24 WR 427; *Gloucester County Bank v Rudry Merthyr Steam and House Coal Colliery Co* [1895] 1 Ch 629; *Mercantile Credits Ltd v Atkins (No 1)* (1985) 9 ACLR 757. As to his position, see *Chaplin v Young* (1864) 33 Beav 330. Because of the liability of the mortgagee in possession (see **19.65**), it will usually be more convenient to appoint a receiver who will be agent of the mortgagor (see **18.1** and **18.8**); see generally (1976) 120 Sol Jo 497.
2 See 28 *Forms and Precedents* (5th edn, 1999 reissue) Mortgages.
3 *Chaplin v Young* (1864) 33 Beav 330 at 337.
4 *Downsview Nominees Ltd v First City Corpn Ltd* [1993] AC 295, [1993] 3 All ER 626; *AIB Finance Ltd v Debtors* [1998] 2 All ER 929, [1998] BCLC 665; *Medforth v Blake* [2000] Ch 86.
5 *Bompas v King* (1886) 33 Ch D 279, CA.

CHATTELS ON THE PREMISES

19.62 When the mortgagee takes possession, either by taking physical possession or under an order of the court, there may be chattels of the mortgagor's (or his tenant's) left on the premises. Where the mortgagee takes possession under an order of the court, the order for possession means vacant possession[1]. Thus if furniture and other effects are left on the premises, the mortgagee may obtain an order for their removal[2]. If the mortgagor fails to obey such an order he may be committed or attached for contempt. Alternatively, if an order for payment under the personal covenant is obtained and not satisfied, execution may be levied against the furniture. This may be in conjunction with taking possession or separately from it. It is submitted that the mortgagee who goes into possession without an order of the court[3] has the same right to vacant possession and accordingly is entitled to an order for removal.

Since the presence of the chattels on the premises constitutes an impediment to the mortgagee's possession, a mortgagee who has taken possession, whether by court order or otherwise, is not obliged to look after chattels left on the premises pending their removal[4]. He is entitled to take self-help steps to remove that impediment, including removal and disposal of the chattels[5]. The mortgagee would be entitled to recover the cost of removal from the mortgagor as damages[6], and thus, it is submitted, would be entitled to include such costs in the account[7]. While the mortgagee could alternatively arrange for the property to be stored, the expenses of removal and storage would have to be justified before they could properly be added to the mortgage debt. However, if there is or will be an outstanding balance of the proceeds of sale of the premises, the storage expenses could, it is submitted, be paid out of these where the balance has not been paid into court[8].

1 *Norwich Union Life Insurance Society v Preston* [1957] 2 All ER 428, [1957] 1 WLR 813.
2 See *Norwich Union Life Insurance Society v Preston*, above. See also, in the landlord and tenant context, *Cumberland Consolidated Holdings Ltd v Ireland* [1946] KB 264; and on notice before removal *Hanistis v Dimitriou* [1983] VR 498 at 503.
3 See **19.8**.
4 See *Jones v Foley* [1891] 1 QB 730.
5 *Cumberland Consolidated Holdings Ltd v Ireland* [1946] KB 264, [1946] 1 All ER 284 ; *Norwich*

Union Life Insurance Society v Preston [1957] 2 All ER 428, [1957] 1 WLR 813. Cf *Hynes v Vaughan* (1985) 50 P & CR 444, concerning outdoor rubbish.

6 *Cumberland Consolidated Holdings Ltd v Ireland* [1946] KB 264, [1946] 1 All ER 284.

7 These difficulties may be provided for by the terms of the mortgage deed, but unless carefully drawn such a provision may infringe the Bills of Sale Acts. For form, see the Appendix.

8 Under s 63 of the Trustee Act 1925. See **20.48**, n 4.

REPAIRS, IMPROVEMENTS, MINING AND CUTTING TIMBER

19.63 The mortgagee's rights and liabilities to carry out repairs[1] and improvements[2], to work mines[3] and to cut timber[4] are considered below.

1 See **19.74**, **19.70**.
2 See **19.75**.
3 See **19.72**.
4 See **19.71**.

LIABILITIES OF MORTGAGEE IN POSSESSION

LIABILITY TO ACCOUNT ON WILFUL DEFAULT BASIS

Application of receipts

19.64 The mortgagee should apply receipts, such as rents or profits from the mortgaged property[1] in:

(a) discharging outgoings relating to the property (such as repairs, taxes, insurance premiums);
(b) paying interest on prior incumbrances;
(c) paying the interest due under the mortgage; and
(d) any surplus may be applied in partial discharge of the principal (although the mortgagee is not bound to accept payment by driblets[2] and he may, if he prefers, hand over the surplus to the mortgagor).

1 See eg *Webb v Rorke* (1806) 2 Sch & Lef 661 at 676; also *Re Betts, ex parte Harrison* (1881) 18 Ch D 127; *Re Knight, ex parte Isherwood* (1882) 22 Ch D 384.

2 *Nelson v Booth* (1858) 3 De G & J 119 at 122; *Wrigley v Gill* [1905] 1 Ch 241 at 254; affd [1906] 1 Ch 165. As to accounts in respect of the surplus, see **35.22** ff, in particular **35.26** and **35.35**.

Liability to account on wilful default basis

19.65 Equity does not allow a mortgagee who as such goes into possession of the mortgaged property to any advantage beyond securing payment of the sums due under the mortgage. The property was mortgaged only as security for the moneys owed to the mortgagee and thus the mortgagee is under an equitable duty to be reasonably diligent in utilising the property to realise the moneys owed, so that the property can then be restored to the mortgagor[1]. The mortgagee is therefore bound to account[2] to the mortgagor, both for the rent and profits actually received and for the rent and profits which, but for his wilful default, he might have received[3]. Accordingly, he must take reasonable care to maximize his return from the property[4]. The account usually directed against the mortgagee in possession is of what he has received, or without wilful default or neglect might have received, from the time of his taking possession. The rule applies whether the possession is of land, tangible property, or of a business[5]. Thus the mortgagee of stock should account for any profit from its sale and repurchase[6]; and the mortgagee of a patent should account for royalties received from it[7]. The rule does not apply where the mortgagee has gone into possession in a different capacity; for instance, as tenant[8], or as agent for a subsequent mortgagee[9], or, in the case of a settled estate, where the mortgagee of the reminder has gone into possession as life tenant[10]. However, where after a second mortgage has been granted, a tenancy is granted to the first mortgagee, the first mortgagee is liable to account to the second mortgagee as mortgagee in possession[11].

1 *Lord Kensington v Bouverie* (1855) 7 De GM & G 134; *Downsview Nominees Ltd v First City Corpn Ltd* [1993] AC 295, [1993] 3 All ER 626; *Raja v Lloyds TSB Bank plc* (2001) 82 P & CR 191.
2 In redemption or other proceedings.
3 *Downsview Nominees Ltd v First City Corpn Ltd*, above, at 315; *Medforth v Blake* [2000] Ch 86 at 99. And see also *Holman v Vaux* (c 1616) Tot 133; *Pell v Blewet* (1603) Tot 133; *Hughes v Williams* (1806) 12 Ves. 493; *Lord Trimleston v Hamill* (1810) 1 Ball & B 377; *Sloane v Mahon* (1838) 1 Dr & Wal 189; *Robertson v Norris* (1859) 1 Giff 428 at 436; *Chaplin v Young* (1864) 33 Beav 330; *Noyes v Pollock* (1886) 32 Ch D 53; *Mobil Oil v Rawlinson* (1981) 43 P & CR 221; *Kennedy v General Credits Ltd* (1982) 2 BPR 9456; *Elders Rural Finance Ltd v Westpac Banking Corpn* (1990) 5 BPR 11790; and (1979) 129 NLJ 334.
He is not obliged to pay any surplus yearly or otherwise: *Western Bank Ltd v Schindler* [1977] Ch 1 at 23, [1976] 2 All ER 393 at 408. See eg *Hughes v Williams* (1806) 12 Ves 493; *Quarrell v Beckford* (1816) 1 Madd 269; *Rowe v Wood* (1822) 2 Jac & W 553; *Williams v Price* (1824) 1 Sim & St 581; *Parkinson v Hanbury* (1867) LR 2 HL 1; *National Bank of Australasia v United Hand-in-Hand Band of Hope Co* (1879) 4 App Cas 391; *Gaskell v Gosling* [1896] 1 QB 669. And see **35.22** ff.
4 *Palk v Mortgage Services Funding plc* [1993] Ch 330 at 338; *Downsview Nominees Ltd v First City Corpn Ltd* [1993] AC 295 at 315.See also *Leach v National Bank of New Zealand* [1996] 3 NZLR 707. He need not speculate or take undue risks: *Hughes v Williams* (1806) 12 Ves 493.
5 *Williams v Price* (1824) 1 Sim & St 581; *Chaplin v Young* (1864) 33 Beav 330; *Mayer v Murray* (1878) 8 Ch D 424; *Bompas v King* (1886) 33 Ch D 279, CA.
6 *Langton v Waite* (1868) LR 6 Eq 165, reversed on a different point (1869) 4 Ch App 402.
7 *Steers v Rogers* [1892] 2 Ch 13, affirmed [1893] AC 232; in that case, the mortgagee was also a co-owner of the patent and was not liable to account for royalties derived from its use of the patent as co-owner.
8 *Page v Linwood* (1837) 4 Cl & Fin 399.
9 See *Re M'Kinley's Estate*(1873) 7 IR Eq 467.
10 *Whitbread v Smith* (1854) 3 De GM & G 727.
11 *Gregg v Arrott* (1835) L & G temp Sugd 246.

To whom liability to account is owed

19.66 The mortgagee's liability to account extends in favour of all those who are interested in the equity of redemption. After receiving notice of a later mortgage[1] the mortgagee in possession becomes liable to account to the later incumbrancer for so much of the surplus rent as he has paid to the mortgagor or his representatives. The mortgagee in possession cannot by any dealing with the estate discharge himself of his liability to account[2]. Thus he will remain liable after a transfer of the mortgage, unless the transfer is made with the consent of the court or the concurrence of the mortgagor[3].

1 *Parker v Calcraft* (1821) 6 Madd 11.
2 *Hinde v Blake* (1841) 11 LJ Ch 26; *Re Prytherch* (1889) 42 Ch D 590. Nor, in the absence of special circumstances, will the court assist him to give up possession by appointing a receiver: *Gloucester County Bank v Rudry Merthyr Steam and House Coal Colliery Co* [1895] 1 Ch 629, but he may relieve himself by appointing a receiver under an express or the statutory power: *Refuge Assurance Co Ltd v Pearlberg* [1938] Ch 687, [1938] 3 All ER 231, CA.
3 *Hall v Heward* (1886) 32 Ch D 430, CA, and see **14.2**.

Amount to be accounted for

19.67 Where a mortgagee enters into receipt of rents he accounts at the rate of the rent reserved[1], assuming they were recoverable with due diligence[2]. Where the mortgagee employs an agent to collect the rents, he must account for all the rents received by that agent and not merely for what the agent has paid to him[3], although the mortgagee would normally be entitled to include reasonable management costs (for example, a rent collector's commission) in the account[4]. If he goes into and remains in occupation himself, he is liable to pay an occupation rent[5]. However, he is not liable to account for a notional rent if his possession is only for the purposes of sale within a reasonable time[6] and nor where he lets the purchaser into occupation prior to completion[7]. His liability to account includes the receipts of any person whom the mortgagee has put into possession without a just title and in derogation of the rights of the mortgagor[8]. If the property is vacant, then if appropriate he should use reasonable diligence to let it at a proper rent[9]. However, he is under no duty to do so if, for instance, that would impede the sale of the property[10], or, by introducing a tenant who would have statutory protection, reduce its long-term value. If the mortgagee in possession has sold the property, he will be liable to account for the proceeds of sale received by him, or those which without wilful default he might have received[11]. The mortgagee is only liable to account for profits arising from the mortgaged property. Thus where the mortgagees were brewers, who profited from the sale of beer to the tenant to whom they had let the mortgaged property, they were not liable to account for those profits[12]. Similarly, a co-owner of a patent who takes a mortgage of his co-owner's share is not bound to bring his profits into account as mortgagee in possession[13].

1 *Lord Trimleston v Hamill* (1810) 1 Ball & B 377 at 385; *Metcalf v Campion* (1828) 1 Mol 238.
2 *Noyes v Pollock* (1886) 32 Ch D 53.
3 *Noyes v Pollock*, above.
4 The mortgagee may not charge for managing the premises himself: *Union Bank of London v Ingram* (1880) 16 Ch D 53, CA; *Comyns v Comyns* (1871) 51 IR Eq 583 at 587-588.
5 *Marriott v Anchor Reversionary Co Ltd* (1861) 3 De GF & J 177 at 193; *Metcalf v Campion* (1828) 1 Mol 238. Unless from its ruinous state, or for any other reason, the property is incapable of making a return: *Marshall v Cave* (1824) 3 LJ OS Ch 57; *Fyfe v Smith* [1975] 2 NSWLR 408, (1979) 129 NLJ 334 (Markson). For the position where the mortgagee has taken possession of an uncompleted building, see *Perry v Walker* (1855) 24 LJ Ch 319; *Midland Credit Ltd v Hallad Pty Ltd* (1977) 1 BPR 9570. See further **19.74** and **19.75**.
6 *Norwich General Trust v Grierson* [1984] CLY 2306. See Law Commission Working Paper no 99, *Land Mortgages*, para 3.25.
7 *Shepard v Jones* (1882) 21 Ch D 469.
8 *National Bank of Australasia v United Hand-in-Hand Band of Hope Co* (1879) 4 App Cas 391, PC.
9 *Blacklock v Barnes* (1725) Cas *temp* King 53; *Palk v Mortgage Services Funding Plc* [1993] Ch 330 at 338.
10 *Downsview Nominees Ltd v First City Corpn Ltd* [1993] AC 295, [1993] 3 All ER 626; *China and South Sea Bank Ltd v Tan Soon Gin* [1990] 1 AC 536, [1989] 3 All ER 839; *Huish v Ellis* [1995] BCC 462

11 *Mayer v Murray* (1878) 8 Ch D 424; *National Bank of Australasia v United Hand-in-Hand Band of Hope Co* (1879) 4 App Cas 391, PC. *Farrar v Farrars Ltd* (1888) 40 Ch D 395 and see **20.23**.
12 *White v City of London Brewery Co* (1889) 42 Ch D 237.
13 *Steers v Rogers* [1893] AC 232, HL.

Evidence of wilful default

19.68 The mortgagee is only liable to manage the property with due diligence, and to take reasonable care to maximise the return. Thus, while it has been said that the mortgagee will be charged with the utmost value the lands are proved to be worth, this liability must be limited by the circumstances of the case. He will not be required to account for more than he has received unless it is proved that, but for his serious default, mismanagement or fraud, he might have received more[1]. The initial burden of showing wilful default is on the mortgagor, or other person alleging it to have occurred[2]. The mortgagor is not entitled to require the mortgagee to prove how much rent he could have got when in possession and involve him in a minute inquiry as to whether some person was ready to have given a greater rent, when he has no facts to suggest that was the case. Likewise, if the mortgagor desires an inquiry into the propriety of the sale or the adequacy of the price, he should make a case in that respect[3]. Wilful default may be evidenced, for example, by the mortgagee's refusal to take, or removal of, a satisfactory tenant[4]; by letting at less than the market rent in return for collateral advantages for himself[5]; or by his making an improper use of his security, such as by allowing the mortgagor himself to take the profits to the prejudice of his other creditors or his trustee in bankruptcy[6]. All the circumstances must be taken into account, thus the mortgagee may be entitled to refuse a higher offer from a credit-worthy person where the tenant in possession is in arrears and by removing him the arrears might have been lost. The mortgagee will normally be entitled to rely on the advice of a property agent[7].

1 *Hughes v Williams* (1806) 12 Ves 493; *Wragg v Denham* (1836) 2 Y & C Ex 117. If there is included in a lease by the mortgagee land not mortgaged to him, but to another who concurred in the lease, there will be an apportionment: *Harryman v Collins* (1854) 18 Beav 11.
2 *Brandon v Brandon* (1862) 10 WR 287.
3 *Mayer v Murray* (1878) 8 Ch D 424; *National Bank of Australasia v United Hand-in-Hand and Band of Hope Co* (1879) 4 App Cas 391, PC. *Farrar v Farrars Ltd* (1888) 40 Ch D 395, and see **20.23**.
4 *Noyes v Pollock* (1886) 32 Ch D 53 at 61; *White v City of London Brewery Co* (1889) 42 Ch D 237, CA.
5 *Hughes v Williams*, above; *Metcalf v Campion* (1828) 1 Mol 238; *White v City of London Brewery Co* (1889) 42 Ch D 237, CA (mortgagees were brewers who let public house with a beer tie).
6 *Loftus v Swift* (1806) 2 Sch & Lef 642 at 656.
7 *Metcalf v Campion* (1828) 1 Mol 238; *Brandon v Brandon* (1862) 10 WR 287.

Mortgagor's duty

19.69 It is the duty of the mortgagor, if he has the opportunity, to give notice to the mortgagee that the mortgaged property can be made more productive and to assist him in making it so. If the mortgagor fails to do this and stands by, and does not object to the mortgagee's conduct, he cannot afterwards charge him with mismanagement[1]. An action of the mortgagee will not be chargeable as a wilful default if the mortgagor (or other interested party) was a party to it; for example, refusing to grant a tenancy to a particular person[2].

1 *Hughes v Williams* (1806) 12 Ves 493; *Metcalf v Campion* (1828) 1 Mol 238; *Brandon v Brandon* (1862) 10 WR 287.
2 *Lord Trimleston v Hamill* (1810) 1 Ball & B 377; *Metcalf v Campion*, above.

LIABILITY FOR DELIBERATE AND NEGLIGENT DAMAGE TO THE PROPERTY

General duty

19.70 A mortgagee in possession is not liable for waste as such[1]. He is, however, under an equitable duty to give back the property uninjured on redemption. Thus the mortgagee must take reasonable care of the property: he will be liable to the mortgagor for negligence resulting in damage to the mortgaged property arising out of his possession of it[2]. For example, he will be liable if mortgaged mines are flooded by improper working[3]; if water pipes are negligently allowed to freeze[4]; if mortgaged chattels are injured by negligent removal[5]; or if loss is caused due to alterations injurious to the value of the property, such as the pulling down of cottages on an estate. As regards agricultural land under cultivation, a mortgagee is liable for damage caused by his own gross negligence[6]. He will be liable if, after an order for possession has been made in his favour, he fails to take reasonable steps to protect the premises (for example, against vandals pending sale), and damage to the premises ensues. The mortgagee will be liable if he is in possession of a mortgaged building lease and does not complete the building or sell the property, causing the leases to be forfeited[7]. The mortgagee is entitled to add to the security reasonable and proper expenses incurred in preserving the property from injury[8].

Any loss cause by deliberate injury to the property[9], or by the negligence of the mortgagee, will be charged in the accounts with interest, either as a capital loss or the lost rent or profits[10]. The mortgagee in possession will be liable to persons other than the mortgagor for loss or injury through nuisance, disrepair etc in the same way as any other person with control of property[11]. The following are examples of the specific application of those principles.

1 Law of Property Act 1925, ss 85 (2), 86 (2), 87 (1), Sch 1, Pt VII, paras 1, 2: the demise to the mortgagee is 'without impeachment of waste'. Historically the mortgagee took a legal estate in fee simple, and could not therefore commit waste. Cf *Downsview Nominees Ltd v First City Corpn Ltd* [1993] AC 295 at 315.
2 *Russel v Smithies* (1792) 1 Anst 96; *Palk v Mortgage Services Funding plc* [1993] Ch 330 at 338.
3 *Taylor v Mostyn* (1886) 33 Ch D 226, CA.
4 *Sterne v Victorai & Grey Trust Co* (1984) 14 DLR (4th) 193.
5 *Johnson v Diprose* [1893] 1 QB 512, CA.
6 *Wragg v Denham* (1836) 2 Y & C Ex 117; *Anon* (1823) 1 LJOS Ch 119.
7 *Perry v Walker* (1855) 24 LJ Ch 319; *Taylor v Mostyn*, above. The mortgagee of a debt is liable for its loss, if it becomes irrecoverable through his wilful default: *Williams v Price* (1824) 1 Sim & St 581, but the mortgagee in possession is not obliged to incur the cost and risk of defending doubtful rights in respect of the mortgaged property: *Cocks v Gray* (1857) 1 Giff 77.

8 *Norwich General Trust v Grierson* [1984] CLY 2306. For allowance for outgoings, see **19.82** ff.
9 *Withrington v Banks* (1725) 25 ER 205; *Millett v Davey* (1862) 9 Jur NS 92; *Re Yates* (1888) 38 Ch D 112. He may be prevented from so doing by injunction or by being deprived of possession: *Hanson v Derby* (1700) 2 Vern 392.
10 *Wragg v Denham* (1836) 2 Y & C Ex 117; *Sandon v Hooper* (1843) 6 Beav 246; *Batchelor v Middleton* (1848) 6 Hare 75.
11 For liability to third parties in nuisance and negligence, see (1954) 98 SJ 377.

Timber

19.71 The mortgagee has statutory power to cut and sell timber and other trees ripe for cutting, and not planted or left standing for shelter or ornament, or contract for that to be done within 12 months of the contract, although the power can be excluded or varied by the terms of the mortgage[1]. Apart from statute, the mortgagee of the freehold is entitled to cut timber only where his security is insufficient; otherwise equity will restrain him[2]. The value of the cut timber is to be accounted for as profits from the property.

1 Law of Property Act 1925, s 101 (1) (iv); which may be varied or excluded by the mortgage deed under s 101 (3), (4).
2 *Withrington v Banks* (1725) Cas temp King 30; *Millett v Davey* (1862) 31 Beav 470.

Mines

19.72 A mortgagee may work mines already opened[1] (although he is not obliged to advance more money on them[2]). However, only a mortgagee with an insufficient security may open new mines and quarries and may lease or work abandoned mines; otherwise equity will restrain him[3]. In those circumstances, the mortgagee will only be liable to account for the profits or royalty and not for the value of the minerals raised or the damage caused to the surface[4]. A mortgagee may also be expressly authorised to work mines, in which case he will be allowed the expenses incurred in doing so, with interest[5]. However, where the security is sufficient, the mortgagee has no right to speculate at the mortgagor's expense and the sale of minerals from newly opened mines is a sale of part of the inheritance. Thus, where the security is sufficient, if the mortgagee opens mines or quarries without special authority, he will be charged with his receipts, and will not be allowed the costs of severing the minerals or other expenses[6].

1 *Elias v Snowdon Slate Quarries Co* (1879) 4 App Cas 454.
2 *Rowe v Wood* (1822) 2 Jac & W 553.
3 *Millett v Davey* (1862) 31 Beav 470.
4 *Millett v Davey*, above.
5 *Norton v Cooper* (1854) 25 LJ Ch 121.
6 *Hughes v Williams* (1806) 12 Ves 493; *Thorneycroft v Crockett* (1848) 16 Sim 445.

Business

19.73 Where there is a mortgage of a business as a going concern, the mortgagee may, but is not obliged to, carry on the business with a view to a sale, even if the consequences are to the disadvantage of the mortgagor. If he chooses to do so, he is under a duty to run the business in good faith and for the purposes of repaying the secured debt[1]. He is entitled to be recouped for losses not attributable to his own negligence out of the proceeds of sale of the business[2].

1 *Downsview Nominees Ltd v First City Corpn Ltd* [1993] AC 295, [1993] 3 All ER 626; *AIB Finance Ltd v Debtors* [1998] 2 All ER 929, [1998] 1 BCLC 665; *Yorkshire Bank v Hall* [1999] 1 WLR 1713; *Medforth v Blake* [2000] Ch 86. See **16.13**, n 2.
2 *Bompas v King* (1886) 33 Ch D 279, CA.

LIABILITY TO REPAIR AND MAINTAIN THE PROPERTY AND LIABILITY FOR IMPROVEMENTS

Liability to repair

19.74 The duty of the mortgagee in possession to take reasonable care of the property includes a duty to carry out reasonable repairs[1]. He is not, though, judged by the degree of care which a man is supposed to take of his own property. He will be allowed, in the accounts, the cost of proper and necessary repairs[2] and he ought to do such repairs as can be paid for out of the balance of the rents after his interest has been paid[3]. He should carry out such repairs as are necessary to avoid forfeiture of the property, if they can be discharged from the profits of the property[4]. However, he need not increase his debt by laying out large sums beyond the rents[5]. He need not rebuild ruinous premises[6] and will not be charged with deterioration of the property arising from ordinary decay by lapse of time, unless it was proper and necessary for such decay to be remedied by expending the rents or profits[7].

The mortgagee will be ill-advised to enter into possession merely for the sake of effecting repairs, because on going into possession he will be liable to account on a wilful default basis. If the property is income-producing, the better course is to appoint a receiver and direct him to effect repairs. The well-drafted mortgage will generally contain a covenant by the mortgagor to repair, with power for the mortgagee to enter and effect repairs in case of default; in effecting necessary and proper repairs under this provision, the mortgagee will not be a mortgagee in possession. The terms of the mortgage should contain a covenant by the mortgagor to pay the cost of repairs effected by the mortgagee and a charge of such costs on the mortgaged property.

1 *Richards v Morgan* (1753) 4 Y & C Ex 570; *Palk v Mortagge Services Funding plc* [1993] Ch 330 at 338; *Downsview Nominees Ltd v First City Corpn Ltd* [1993] AC 295 at 315.
2 *Sandon v Hooper* (1843) 6 Beav 246; affd (1844) 14 LJ Ch 120.
3 *Richards v Morgan* (1753) 4 Y & C Ex 570; *Moore v Painter* (1842) 6 Jur 903; *Tipton Green Colliery Co v Tipton Moat Colliery Co* (1877) 7 Ch D 192.
4 *Perry v Walker* (1855) 3 Eq Rep 721.
5 *Moore v Painter* (1842) 6 Jur 903.
6 *Moore v Painter*, above; see also *Perry v Walker* (1855) 24 LJ Ch 319; *Midland Credit v Hallad Pty Ltd* (1977) BPR 9570.
7 *Russell v Smithies* (1794) 1 Anst 96; *Wragg v Denham* (1836) 2 Y & C Ex 117; *Sandon v Hooper* (1843) 6 Beav 246; affd 14 LJ Ch 120.

Improvements

19.75 The mortgagee may, under appropriate circumstances, make improvements[1]. However, they must always be reasonable, having regard to the nature and value of the security[2]. The mortgagee should not improve the property to an extent which prevents the mortgagor from redeeming the property, or makes it more difficult for him to do so[3]. The right of the mortgagee to carry out such works is founded on the principle that the mortgagor, whose right to redeem is only equitable, must repay all that is equitably due. The mortgagee should inform the mortgagor as soon as possible of the necessity or the intention to incur extraordinary expenses. If he does so, and the mortgagor agrees expressly, or by his actions demonstrates consent or acquiescence, the mortgagee need not show that it was reasonable to incur the outlay. The mortgagee will not lose his right to repayment simply because he failed to give prior notice of an improvement, if it was reasonable and beneficial. Conversely, the mortgagor will not be charged the costs of unreasonable expenditure to which he did not consent, merely because he had notice of it. If the property has been sold, the mortgagee will have a stronger claim for repayment than in a redemption action and will be repaid whatever is shown to have been added to the selling value of the property by the expenditure[4].

Thus, in appropriate circumstances, if buildings are incomplete, or have become unfit for use, the mortgagee may complete them or pull them down and rebuild[5]. The rebuilding or repairing may be done in an improved manner and more substantially than before, so long as the work is done providently, and no new or expensive buildings are erected for purposes different from those for which the former buildings were used[6].

1 The distinction between repairs and improvements may in some circumstances be a fine one: see in the landlord and tenant context, Dowding and Reynolds *Dilapidations*, 2nd edn, 2000, Ch 11.
2 *Shepard v Jones* (1882) 21 Ch D 469.
3 See *Sandon v Hooper* (1843) 6 Beav 246; affd (1844) 14 LJ Ch 120; *Southwell v Roberts* (1940) 63 CLR 581.
4 *Shepard v Jones* (1882) 21 Ch D 469; *Matzner v Clyde Securities Ltd* [1975] 2 NSWLR 293. As to estimating the value of improvements to buildings, see *Robinson v Ridley* (1821) 6 Mad 2.
5 *Marshall v Cave* (1824) 3 LJOS Ch 57. See also *Penny v Walker* (1855) 24 LJ Ch 319; *Midland Credit Ltd v Hallad Pty Ltd* (1977) BPR 9570.
6 *Moore v Painter* (1842) 6 Jur 903; *Jortin v South Eastern Rly Co* (1854) 2 Sm & G 48; reversed on other points (sub nom *South Eastern Rly Co v Jortin* (1857) 6 HL Cas 425); *Southwell v Roberts* (1940) 63 CLR 58.

LIABILITY ON FREEHOLD AND LEASEHOLD COVENANTS

19.76 The liability of a mortgagee in possession to the burden of freehold and leasehold covenants affecting the mortgaged land will depend upon general principles applicable to such covenants, bearing in mind that the mortgagee takes possession as mortgagee, and as a successor in title of the mortgagor. A detailed consideration of liability under such covenants is outside the scope of this work[1].

1 See eg 16 *Halsbury's Laws* (4th edn) paras 1345–1359; Preston and Newsom *Restrictive Covenants* (9th edn, 1998); and for leasehold covenants 27 *Halsbury's Laws* (4th edn) para 393.

Freehold covenants

19.77 The burden of a positive freehold covenant will not run at law against a successor in title of the mortgagor[1], although it may be enforceable by certain indirect principles, such as that a mortgagee taking a benefit under a deed may be liable to assume the burdens thereunder[2]. Subject to certain conditions, the burden of restrictive covenants can run in equity and such covenants will in those circumstances be enforceable against a mortgagee by a person who has the benefit thereof[3].

1 *Rhone v Stephens* [1994] 2 AC 310.
2 *Halsall v Brizell* [1957] Ch 169, [1957] 1 All ER 371; *Thamesmead Town v Allotey* [1998] 3 EGLR 97.
3 *Tulk v Moxhay* (1848) 11 Beav 571. In summary, the burden will run where (a) the covenant is negative in nature; (b) the covenant was made for the protection of land retained by the covenantee; (c) the burden of the covenant was intended to run with the covenantor's land; (d) and the burden only runs in equity.

Leasehold covenants

Leases granted before 1 January 1996

19.78 With regard to a mortgagee in possession of a lessor's interest, the obligation under any covenant given by the lessor which refers to the subject matter of the lease will pass with the reversionary estate and the mortgagee will be liable thereunder[1]. A mortgagee in possession of a lessee's interest may be liable under a restrictive covenant entered between landlord and tenant, depending on questions of notice and registration.

Leases granted after 1 January 1996

19.79 Where any landlord covenant of a tenancy is enforceable against the reversioner in respect of any premises demised by the tenancy, it is also enforceable against any mortgagee in possession who is entitled to the rents and profits under the tenancy in respect of those premises[2]. Where any tenant covenant of a tenancy, or any right of re-entry contained in a tenancy, is enforceable against the tenant in respect of any premises demised by the tenancy, it is also enforceable against any mortgagee or chargee in possession of the premises under a mortgage granted by the tenant[3]. The mortgagee will not be liable under a covenant expressed to be personal to the mortgagor or any other person, or a covenant that is unenforceable for want of registration[4].

1 Law of Property Act 1925, s 142.
2 Landlord & Tenant (Covenants) Act 1995, s 15(1), (2).
3 Section 15(4), (6).
4 Section 15(5).

LEASEHOLD ENFRANCHISEMENT[1]

Leasehold Reform Act 1967

19.80 Under the Leasehold Reform Act 1967, where the landlord's mortgagee has gone into possession, the tenant's Notice of Claim to acquire the freehold or an extended lease can be served on either the landlord or the mortgagee[2]. However, all proceedings arising out of the notice which would otherwise have been taken by, or in relation to, the landlord, must be conducted through the mortgagee as if he were landlord Any conveyance to be executed pursuant to the Act must also be executed by the landlord at the direction of the mortgagee, or by the mortgagee in the name and on behalf of the landlord[3]. Where a mortgagee is acting as landlord under those provisions, any compensation which arises or which could have been be recovered by the landlord may be recovered by or awarded to the mortgagee and dealt with as if it were proceeds of sale subject to the mortgage[4]. The mortgagee is also entitled to apply[5] to obtain possession for redevelopment as if he were landlord[6]. Any compensation paid by a mortgagee to the tenant on obtaining possession for redevelopment is to be treated as if it were secured by the mortgage, with the like priority and with interest at the same rate as the mortgage money, except that it is not recoverable from the mortgagor under his personal covenant[7].

1 See generally Hague *Leasehold Enfranchisement* (3rd edn, 1999).
2 Sch 3, para 9(1).
3 Section 25(2).
4 Section 25(4).
5 Under s 17 of the Act.
6 Section 25(2).
7 Section 25(3).

Leasehold Reform, Housing and Urban Development Act 1993

19.81 Under the Leasehold Reform, Housing and Urban Development Act 1993, where the interest of the landlord is subject to a mortgage[1], and the mortgagee is in possession, a relevant notice or a copy of it is regarded as duly given to the landlord if it is given to the mortgagee, but the recipient of the notice must give a copy of it to the mortgagee or the landlord as the case may be. The same applies to a debenture holder's charge[2]. Where a landlord is given a relevant notice or a copy of it and his interest is subject to a mortgage to secure the payment of money, then the landlord must forthwith inform the mortgagee that the notice has been given and give him such further information as the debenture holder's charge may from time to time reasonably require from the landlord[3]. All proceedings arising out of a tenant's notice claiming collective enfranchisement or a new lease[4] which would otherwise have been taken by or in relation to the landlord must be conducted by and through the mortgagee as if he were the landlord[5].

1 Which includes a charge or lien: Sch 2, para 1(1).
2 Sch 2, para 2(5).A debenture holder's charge is a charge, whether floating or not, in favour of the holders of a series of debentures issued by a company or other body of persons, or in favour of trustees for such debenture holders: Sch 2, para 1(1).
3 Sch 2, para 2(6).That does not apply to a debenture holder's charge: Sch 2, para 2(7).
4 Under s 13 or s 42.
5 Sch 2, para 2(1).

OUTGOINGS ALLOWABLE TO MORTGAGEE IN POSSESSION

General rule

19.82 The outgoings which the mortgagee will be allowed to include in the accounts[1] follow from the nature of his rights and liabilities. Thus the mortgagee will be allowed what he has expended in preserving the security: for instance, paying rent to avoid forfeiture of leasehold property; carrying out necessary and proper repairs and improvements[2]; or taking reasonable steps to protect the premises against vandals pending sale. The mortgagee will also be allowed the expenses of obtaining the rents and profits from the property. For example, he will be allowed the amount of compensation payable to an outgoing tenant[3]; the cost of renewing a lease (even if there is no covenant by the mortgagee to renew)[4]; or the expenses of operating a mortgaged mine or business. Where, by statute, the mortgagee in possession is treated as owner, any liability in respect of the premises arising as such will be allowable[5].

1 *Mellick v Mellick* [1939] QSR 251.
2 *Burrowes v Molloy* (1845) 2 Jo & Lat 521; *Brandon v Brandon* (1862) 10 WR 287. With regard to the mortgages of ships, outgoings are not allowed unless incurred with the sanction of the court: *The Fair Haven* (1866) LR 1 A & E 67.
3 *Oxenham v Ellis* (1854) 18 Beav 593.
4 *Woolley v Drage* (1795) 2 Anst 551, but he cannot compel the mortgagor to renew.
5 Eg for notices under the Highways Acts: *Maguire v Leigh-on-Sea UDC* (1906) 95 LT 319; under the Public Health Act 1936: *Davies v Law Mutual Building Society* (1971) 219 Estates Gazette 309; under the London Building Acts (Amendment) Act 1939: *Solomons v R Gertzenstein Ltd* [1954] 2 QB 243, [1954] 2 All ER 625; for the rating surcharge under s 17A and B of the General Rate Act 1967; *Banister v Islington London Borough Council* (1972) 71 LGR 239 (see (1976) 40 Conv (NS) 222 (I'Anson Banks)); *Westminster City Council v Haymarket Publishing Ltd* [1981] 2 All ER 555, [1981] 1 WLR 677, CA.

Agents and commission

19.83 If the mortgagee in possession manages the property via his agent or employees, he may charge for the agent's or employees' salary[1]. However, the mortgagee in possession is generally not allowed anything for personal care or trouble in receiving rents, even though he might have appointed an agent or receiver, since upon taking possession he becomes quasi-owner of the property[2]. The mortgagor and mortgagee can, though, expressly agree that a commission should be allowed to the mortgagee[3]. A solicitor-mortgagee may charge remuneration, whether or not there is an agreement for remuneration[4]. While the mortgagee will be allowed the expenses of a sale of the mortgaged property or part of it[5], a commission will be allowed only if it constitutes a valid collateral advantage[6].

1 *Union Bank of London v Ingram* (1880) 16 Ch D 53, CA. The mortgagee may agree with the mortgagor for the appointment of a receiver to be paid by the latter, or may appoint one under the statutory power (see **18.4** and Chapter 18 generally).
2 *Bonithon v Hockmore* (1685) 1 Vern 316; *Nicholson v Tutin (No 2)* (1857) 3 K & J 159; *Cholmondeley v Clinton* (1820) 2 Jac & W 1, 184 at 191; *Leith v Irvine* (1833) 1 My & K 277; *Robertson v Norris* (1857) 1 Giff 421; *Comyns v Comyns* (1871) 5 IR EQ 583 at 587-588.
3 See **28.11** and **28.12**. Even before the change of policy introduced by *Biggs v Hoddinott* [1898] 2 Ch 307, CA, it was recognised that some such agreements might be binding: *Eyre v Hughes* (1876) 2 Ch D 148.
4 Solicitors Act 1974, s 58.
5 *Farrer v Lacy, Hartland & Co* (1885) 31 Ch D 42, CA.
6 See **28.11**, **28.12** and **35.54**; and see *Browne v Ryan* [1901] 2 IR 653. The general prohibition extends to the partnership of which the mortgagee is a member: *Mattison v Clarke* (1854) 3 Drew 3; *Furber v Cobb* (1887) 18 QBD 494 at 509. The rule is otherwise where the mortgagee is employed to sell by the court: *Arnold v Garner* (1847) 2 Ph 231.

Outgoings in the accounts

19.84 All allowable outgoings will be added to the principal debt and, like it, carry interest. Where such sums are laid out by a subsequent mortgagee in possession, they will not be allowed as against a first mortgagee[1].

1 *Landowners West of England and South Wales Land, Drainage and Inclosure Co v Ashford* (1880) 16 Ch D 411.

EXTINCTION OF MORTGAGOR'S TITLE

19.85 When a mortgagee has been in possession of the mortgaged land as mortgagee for 12 years, he will thereby extinguish the title of the mortgagor or any person claiming through him, including the title of a subsequent mortgagee[1]. The time required to extinguish the title of the mortgagor may be extended in the case of disability, acknowledgment, part payment, fraud or mistake[2].

Where a registered proprietor of a charge has acquired a title under the Limitation Act 1980, he can execute a declaration in the prescribed form that the right of redemption is barred[3]. Subject to furnishing evidence in support of his application[4], he will then be entitled to be registered as proprietor of the land with the same consequences[5] as if he had been a purchaser for valuable consideration of the land under the power of sale[6]. This right is only exercisable subject to any entry to the contrary on the register and subject to the right of any person appearing on the register to be a prior incumbrancer. The enlargement of mortgage terms and vesting declarations where the land is not registered are considered in Chapter 28[7].

1 Limitation Act 1980, ss 16, 17. As to registered land, see Land Registration Act 1925, sections 34 (2), 75 and see *Re Statutory Trusts Declared by Section 105 of the Law of Property Act 1925 affecting the Proceeds of Sale of Moat House Farm, Thurlby* [1948] Ch 191, sub nom *Young v Clarey* [1948] 1 All ER 197.
2 See **16.44–16.56**.
3 Land Registration Rules 1925, r 149 (1), Sch, Form 52.
4 Rule 149 (2), (3).
5 Land Registration Act 1925, s 34 (4).
6 Section 34 (2).
7 See **28.94**.

MORTGAGEE'S RIGHT TO POSSESSION OF PERSONAL CHATTELS AND SHIPS

TAKING POSSESSION OF PERSONAL CHATTELS COMPRISED IN A BILL OF SALE (BILLS OF SALE AMENDMENT ACT 1882)

Grounds for seizure or taking possession

19.86 Section 7 of the Bills of Sale Act (1878) Amendment Act 1882 applies to personal chattels assigned as security under a bill of sale. It provides that such chattels may only be seized or taken possession of by the grantee on the following grounds[1]:

(a) if the grantor defaults in payment of the sum or sums of money secured by the bill at the time provided for payment, or in the performance of any covenant or agreement contained in the bill of sale and necessary for maintaining the security;
(b) if the grantor becomes a bankrupt, or suffers the goods, or any of them, to be distrained for rent, rates or taxes;
(c) if the grantor fraudulently removes, or suffer to be removed, the goods or any of them, to be removed from the premises;
(d) if the grantor fails (without reasonable excuse), upon demand in writing by the grantee, to produce to him his last receipts for rent, rates and taxes;
(e) if execution is levied against the goods of the grantor under any judgment at law.

1 A bill of sale in the form of the Schedule to the Act (and see s 9), together with s 7, gives the grantee an implied power of sale for the causes in s 7: *Watkins v Evans* (1887) 18 QBD 386.

Grantor's right to apply to the court for relief

19.87 However, within five days from the seizure or taking possession of any chattels on any of the above grounds, the grantor may apply to the High Court[1], and if the court is satisfied that by payment of money or otherwise the relevant ground of seizure no longer exists, it may restrain the grantee from removing or selling the chattels, or may make such other order as may seem just[2]. The power of the court to order delivery up of possession of seized goods on payment of principal, interest and costs, depends on whether the seizure has been made for the purpose of realising, or only for the purpose of protecting, the security. In the former case, delivery up will be ordered under the general rule that a mortgagee who takes steps to realise is estopped from declining to receive payment; in the latter, if the date of payment has not arrived, redemption will not be forced on the mortgagee[3].

1 Or to a Judge thereof in chambers.
2 As to the effect of provisions in the bill which conflict with the above restrictions on seizure, see **5.28–5.33**.
3 *Ex p Cotton* (1883) 11 QBD 301; *Ex p Wickens* [1898] 1 QB 543 ; *Ex p Ellis* [1898] 2 QB 79. On possession of chattels, see *Park v Brady* [1976] 2 NSWLR 329.

Construction of the grounds

19.88 The five excepted cases are strictly construed. As to cause (1), where a loan is repayable by instalments, then in default of the payment of one instalment, the grantee is entitled to seize possession of the chattels for the whole debt, even though the bill contains no provision making the whole sum payable in default of any one instalment[1]. As to cause (2), a grantor becomes bankrupt within the meaning of the subsection only where he commits an act of bankruptcy which is followed by an adjudication; any provision in a bill to the contrary will make the bill void[2]. Entering a composition with creditors does not give cause for seizure; again, any provision in a bill to the contrary will make the bill void[3]. If a landlord does distrain, he is not liable to account to the holder of a bill of sale for any surplus he realises[4]. A grantee of a bill who pays rent to a landlord to avoid distraint of the chattels is entitled to be reimbursed by the grantor[5]. As to cause (3), whether or not the removal is fraudulent would appear to be a question of fact[6]. As to cause (4), where a grantor's rent is a few days overdue, but has not been demanded, and has not in fact been paid, his chattels are not liable to be seized if he fails to produce a receipt[7].

1 *Re Wood, ex p Woolfe* [1894] 1 QB 605.
2 *Re Turner, ex p Attwater* (1876) 5 Ch D 27; *Gilroy v Bowey* (1888) 59 LT 223.
3 *Barr v Kingsford* (1887) 56 LT 861.
4 *Evans v Wright* (1857) 2 H & N 527. On distress generally, see Tanney and Travers (eds) *Distress for Rent* (1st edn, 2000).
5 *Edmunds v Wallingford* (1885) 14 QBD 811; cf *England v Marsden* (1866) Har & Ruth 560
6 See by analogy the cases on what constitutes fraudulent removal of goods under the Distress for Rent Act 1737; *Opperman v Smith* (1824) 4 D & R 33; *John v Jenkins* (1832) 1 Cr & M 227; *Inkop v Morchurch* (1861) 2 F & F 501.
7 *Ex p Cotton* (1883) 11 QBD 301. See also *Ex p Wickens* [1898] 1 QB 543 and *Cartwright v Regan* [1895] 1 QB 900 on what constitutes a demand within the subsection.

Consumer credit agreements[1]

19.89 Paragraph (1) of s 7 of the Bills of Sale Act (1878) Amendment Act 1882 does not apply to a default relating to a bill of sale given by way of security for the payment of money under a regulated agreement under the Consumer Credit Act 1974 to which the need for a default notice[2] applies (a) unless the debtor or hirer has failed to take the action specified in the notice within the specified period; or (b) if, by virtue of s 89 of the 1974 Act, the default is to be treated s not having occurred[3]. Where para 1 of s 7 of the 1882 Act does apply in relation to such a bill of sale, it is the county court, not the High Court, which has jurisdiction to exercise the powers given by the proviso to s 7 (to restrain sale, order the delivery up of possession etc)[4].

1 See generally Chapter 10.
2 See s 87 of the Act: see **10.63**, and see s 129 of the Act for time orders, see **10.79**.
3 Bills of Sale Act 1878 (Amendment) Act 1882, s 7A(1) added by the Consumer Credit Act 1974, Sch 4, para 1.
4 Section 7A(2).

Rights of mortgagee against third parties

19.90 The mortgagee of personal chattels may sue third parties in respect of them, if he had a right to immediate possession at the time when the cause of action against the third party accrued. Prior to the Bills of Sale Act (1878) Amendment Act 1882, the mortgagee had a right to immediate possession if there was an assignment to the mortgagee and that assignment had not been qualified by a clause in the bill giving the mortgagor a right to continue in possession until a failure to pay on demand, or a clause providing that the right to possession only arose at some future point[1].Given that s 7 of the 1882 Act takes away, without any qualification, the right of possession of the mortgagee except in the five specified cases, it is submitted that its effect is to affect the rights of the mortgagee against third parties as if s 7 were a clause of the mortgage qualifying the right to possession. Where a sheriff has taken possession of goods on behalf of a judgment creditor, and interpleads, he will be ordered to withdraw unless the judgment creditor is willing to redeem, or unless the court is satisfied that a sale of the goods would realize a sufficient surplus to satisfy the bill of sale holder[2]. Where the mortgagor delivered chattels to a bailee before they were mortgaged, the mortgagee is entitled to recover them from the bailee. Accordingly, if the mortgagee demands them from the bailee, the bailee is justified in refusing to redeliver the chattel to the mortgagor; his original obligation to do so was changed by the mortgage[3].

1 *Wheeler v Montefiore* (1841) 2 QB 133. Where the mortgagor has wrongfully sold the property, the mortgagee may sue the purchaser, unless the latter is protected by sale in market overt or under the Factors Act 1889 or the Sale of Goods Act 1979: *Cooper v Willomatt* (1845) 1 CB 672.
2 *Stern v Tegner* [1898] 1 QB 37.
3 *European and Australian Royal Mail Co v Royal Mail Steam Packet Co* (1861) 30 LJCP 247.

TAKING POSSESSION OF MORTGAGED SHIPS

Right of mortgagor of ship to retain possession

19.91 In the absence of an agreement to the contrary, the mortgagor of a ship is entitled to retain possession until the debt is payable, unless the ship is being dealt with in such a manner as to impair the security[1]. While the mortgagor is allowed by the mortgagee to retain possession, he has full liberty to deal with the ship, so far as he does so consistently with the sufficiency of the security. The mortgagor is entitled to enter into such contracts as are consistent with the full rights and benefit of ownership and by which he can earn the means of discharging the mortgage debt[2]. The mortgagee can only interfere with such a contract if he can show that it will materially prejudice his security[3]. Thus, where a charter has been taken of a ship from the mortgagor, and the mortgagee is not in possession, the mortgagee is not entitled to interfere with the execution of the charterparty, unless it can be shown to impair the security, in which case he will not be bound by it[4]. For so long as the mortgagee does not interfere, he will be held to have acquiesced in all proper engagements for the ship's use which have been made by the mortgagor. The mortgagor may do all that is proper to keep the ship in an effective condition, so that the ship may also be a source of profit to the mortgagee himself when he takes possession. In contracts for repair, the mortgagor in possession does not have authority to pledge the mortgagee's credit by reason of the relationship of mortgagor and mortgagee[5].

1 *The Blanche* (1887) 58 LT 592; *The Heather Bell* [1901] P 272, CA; *The Myrto* [1977] 2 Lloyd's Rep 243.
2 *Collins v Lamport* (1864) 34 LJ Ch 196; *Keith v Burrows* (1877) 2 App Cas 636, HL.
3 *The Blanche*, above.
4 Where the security is not impaired, the mortgagee will be restrained by injunction from interfering with the operation of the charterparty: *Collins v Lamport* (1864) 34 LJ Ch 196. See also: *The Lord Strathcona* [1925] P 143; *The Manor* [1907] P 339; *Law Guarantee and Trust Society v Russian Bank for Foreign Trade* [1905] 1 KB 815, CA; *The Heather Bell* [1901] P 272, CA; *The Fanchon* (1880) 5 PD 173; Merchant Shipping Act 1995, s 16, Sch 1, para 10.
5 *Tyne Dock Engineering Co Ltd v Royal Bank of Scotland* 1974 SLT 57.

Mortgagor responsible for liabilities of ship prior to mortgagee taking possession

19.92 Where a ship[1] or share is subject to a registered mortgage[2] then:

(a) except so far as may be necessary for making the ship or share available as a security for the mortgage debt, the mortgagee shall not by reason of the mortgage be treated as owner of the ship or share; and

(b) the mortgagor shall be treated as not having ceased to be owner of the ship or share[3]. Thus although, as between the parties to the mortgage, the property in the ship has passed to the mortgagee[4], the mortgagor remains responsible for her liabilities[5] and for all matters connected with her usage[6]. This provision is for the protection of the mortgagee[7].

1 'Ship' includes every description of vessel used in navigation: Merchant Shipping Act 1995, s 313(1).
2 See s 16 and para 7 of Sch 1of the Merchant Shipping Act 1995: a mortgage of a registered ship executed in the prescribed form will be registered by the registrar.
3 Merchant Shipping Act 1995, Sch 1, para 10. See formerly the Merchant Shipping Act 1894, s 34; *The St George* [1926] P 217.
4 *The Blanche* (1887) 6 Asp MLC 272.
5 *Dickinson v Kitchen* (1858) 8 E & B 789; cf *Hudson and Humphrey v Swiftsure (Owners), The Swiftsure* (1900) 9 Asp MLC 65 as to the assumption of liabilities by the mortgagee.
6 *Collins v Lamport* (1864) 34 LJ Ch 196; *Keith v Burrows* (1877) 2 App Cas 636, HL.
7 See the sub-heading of Merchant Shipping Act 1995, Sch 1, para 10. *Law Guarantee and Trust Society v Russian Bank for Foreign Trade* [1905] 1 KB 815, CA.

Right of the mortgagee to take possession

19.93 The circumstances in which the mortgagee is entitled to take possession of a mortgaged ship are primarily determined by the terms of the mortgage[1]. Further, the mortgagee is entitled to take possession of the ship if the acts of the mortgagor materially impair the security of the mortgagee, such that they are inconsistent with its sufficiency[2], or if the mortgagor defaults on the sums due under the mortgage. Thus, a mortgagee is entitled to take possession where the mortgagor risks the ship becoming burdened with maritime liens with priority over the mortgage, without prospect of the mortgagor being able to discharge them[3].

The mortgagee can take possession constructively, by clearly asserting his intention to assume rights of ownership[4]. Alternatively, he can take actual possession through a claim in rem for the arrest of the ship by the Admiralty Marshal[5], or by himself putting a person in possession of her.

1 See *The Maule* [1997] 1 WLR 528, PC (right of sale).
2 See eg *Collins v Lamport* 34 LJ Ch 196 at 200, per Lord Westbury; *The Blanche* (1887) 58 LT 592; *The Fanchon* (1880) 5 P 173; *The Manor* [1907] P 339.
3 *The Manor* [1907] P 339.
4 *The Benwell Tower* (1895) 8 Asp MLC 13; *Beynon v Godden* (1878) 3 Ex D 263; *Rusden v Pope* (1868) LR 3 Exch 269.
5 The Admiralty jurisdiction of the High Court may be invoked: Supreme Court Act 1981, ss 20(2)(a), 20(2)(c), 20(7)(c), 21(2); *The St Meriel* [1963] P. 247; *The Acrux* [1965] P. 391. See further *Halsbury's Laws* (4th edn reissue, Admiralty).

Right to control of ship

19.94 Upon the taking of possession, the statutory provision that (for the benefit of the mortgagee) the mortgagor is to retain the character of owner, will cease to operate[1]. A registered mortgagee in possession is entitled to exercise complete control over the ship, for instance by dismissing the master[2].

1 *The Blanche* (1887) 58 LT 592; *The Manor* [1907] P 339; *Law Guarantee and Trust Society v Russian Bank for Foreign Trade* [1905] 1 KB 815, CA. As to what constitutes injury to the security, see also: *The Myrto* [1977] 2 Lloyd's Rep 243; *The Lord Strathcona* [1925] P 143; *The Heather Bell* [1901] P 272, CA; *The Celtic King* [1894] P 175; *Laming & Co v Seater* (1889) 16 R 828; *Cory Bros & Co v Stewart* (1886) 2 TLR 508; *The Fanchon* (1880) 5 PD 173; *The Maxima* (1878) 4 Asp MLC 2; *Keith v Burrows* (1877) 2 App Cas 636, HL; *The Cathcart* (1867) LR 1 A & E 314; *The Innisfallen* (1866) LR 1 A & E 72; *Collins v Lamport* (1864) 34 LJ Ch 196; *Dickinson v Kitchen* (1858) 8 E & B 789; *De Mattos v Gibson* (1858) 5 Jur NS 347; *The Highlander* (1843) 2 Wm Rob 109; *Brigs v Wilkinson* (1827) 7 B & C 30; *Baker v Buckle* (1822) 7 Moore CP 349; *Jackson v Vernon* (1789) 1 Hy Bl 114.

2 *The Fairport* (1884) 10 PD 13.

Right to earnings of ship

19.95 On taking possession, the mortgagee is entitled to enjoy any contractual rights arising from any agreement made by the mortgagor for the use of the ship[1]. Unless there is an agreement to the contrary, the mortgagor is not entitled to the earnings of the ship until the mortgagee takes possession[2]; but on taking possession, the mortgagee is entitled to all earnings falling due thereafter[3]. However, since the right to receive the earnings of the ship, whether freight or passage money, does not pass to him by way of assignment of the freight (unless it is specially assigned as incident to the ownership of the vessel), he must take possession, or assert his right by some corresponding act (such as by requiring payment from the charterer), before it has been paid to the mortgagor[4]. Once the freight has been paid to the mortgagor, the mortgage itself will not entitle the mortgagee to recover it[5]. The mortgagee is entitled to the gross freight, that is without any deduction for sums due from the mortgagor to the charterer, and without any deduction for sums expended in supplying the ship, unless incurred upon the mortgagee's authority[6]. If the mortgagee has paid expenses for which the ship was liable in order to obtain possession of her, he may recover them from the person who incurred, but neglected, to pay them[7].

1 *Stellar Chartering and Brokerage Inc v Efibanca-Ente Finanziario SpA, The Span Terza (No 2)* [1984] 1 WLR 27, HL; *Gumm v Tyrie* (1865) 6 B & S 298, Ex Ch.

2 *Keith v Burrows* (1877) 2 App Cas 636, HL; *The Benwell Tower* (1895) 8 Asp MLC 13; *Anderson v Butler's Wharf Co Ltd*(1879) 48 LJ Ch 824; *Liverpool Marine Credit Co v Wilson* (1872) 7 Ch App 507; *Wilson v Wilson* (1872) LR 14 Eq 32; *Rusden v Pope* (1868) LR 3 Exch 269; *Brown v Tanner* (1868) 3 Ch App 597.

3 *Cato v Irving* (1852) 5 De G & Sm 210; *Brown v Tanner* (1868) 3 Ch App 597; *Liverpool Marine Credit Co v Wilson* (1872) 7 Ch App 507 at 511; *Keith v Burrows* (1877) 2 App. Cas. 636; the mortgagee of ship shares is similarly entitled to his share thereof: *Alexander v Simms* (1854) 18 Beav 80; affd 5 De GM & G 57; *Essarts v Whinney* (1903) 9 asp MLC 363. The mortgagee will not be entitled to freight where he takes possession after the freight has been earned: *Shillito v Biggart* [1903] 1 KB 683; and would not seem to be entitled where the goods have been landed, but a lien retained pending payment: *Belfast Harbour Commissioners v Lawther and Marine Investment Society, The Edward Cardwell* (1865) 12 LT 677. See also *Anderson v Butler's Wharf Co Ltd* (1879) 48 LJ Ch 824.

4 *Wilson v Wilson* (1872) LR 14 Eq 32; *Keith v Burrows*, above, and see *Beynon v Godden* (1878) 3 Ex D 263, CA, and 10th edn of this work, p 519.

5 *Gardner v Cazenove* (1856) 1 H & N 423; *Willis v Palmer* (1860) 7 CBNS 340.

6 *The Troubador* (1866) LR 1 A & E 302; *El Argentino* [1909] P 236; *Tanner v Phillips* (1872) 42 LJ Ch 125. Even in the hands of the mortgagee, the produce is liable for the expenses of the voyage in which it was earned: *Alexander v Simms* (1854) 18 Beav 80; affd 5 De GM & G 57. The lien within the Admiralty jurisdiction of the High Court (see the Supreme Court Act 1981, s 20) does not take priority to his claims, unless, apparently, he had expended money by leave of the court: *The Lyons* (1887) 57 LT 818.

7 *Johnson v Royal Mail Steam Packet Co* (1867) LR 3 CP 38.

Mortgagee's liabilities

19.96 On taking possession, the mortgagee becomes liable for expenses arising from the future use of the ship[1]. He will also be liable to perform contractual obligations incurred by the mortgagor prior to the mortgage, of which he had notice, if they relate to the future, do not injure the security and are the kind of obligations incurred by a person with apparent ownership and control of a ship[2]. A shipwright is entitled to enforce his possessor lien against the mortgagee for such repairs as are made at the mortgagee's direction when in possession[3].

1 *Re Litherland, ex p Howden* (1842) 2 Mont D & De TG 574.
2 *Johnson v Royal Mail Steam Packet Co* (1867) LR 3 CP 38; *Williams v Allsup* (1861) 10 CBNS 417. See also *The Lord Strathcona* [1925] P 143; *Law Guarantee and Trust Society v Russian Bank for Foreign Trade* [1905] 1 KB 815, CA; *The Celtic King* [1894] P 175; *De Mattos v Gibson* (1858) 5 Jur NS 347.
3 *Williams v Allsup* (1861) 10 CBNS 417; *The Skipwith* (1864) 10 Jur NS 445.

Prudent use pending sale

19.97 Every registered mortgagee has the power, if the mortgage money or any part of it is due, to sell the ship or share in respect of which he is registered and to give effectual receipts for the purchase money[1]. However, the mortgagee of a ship in possession is not bound to sell disadvantageously, where the sale would not realise the moneys secured by the mortgage. Thus if he cannot reasonably or prudently sell, he is entitled to employ the ship as would a prudent owner in the exercise of his sound discretion, while awaiting a favourable opportunity to sell her[2]. The mortgagee should not, though, use her so as to put her to unusual risk, or injure her value. Thus he does not have an unlimited right to send her to any distance, or to employ her for an indefinite time at the mortgagor's cost for repairs, wages, insurance and other disbursements and risks; nor to risk involving her in speculative adventures; nor to improperly manage her[3]. A mortgagee may properly refuse to enter into a charter party for the employment of the ship in a voyage of a speculative character.

1 Merchant Shipping Act 1995, Sch 1, para 9. Where two or more mortgagees are registered in respect of the same ship or share, a subsequent mortgagee is not entitled to sell the ship or share without the concurrence of every prior mortgagee, or under an order of a court of competent jurisdiction: s 9(2).The mortgagor and mortgagee can agree to limit the powers of sale: *Brouard v Dumaresque* (1841) 3 Moo PCC 457; *Dickinson v Kitchen* (1858) 8 E & B 789.
2 *European and Australian Royal Mail Co v Royal Mail Steam Packet Co* (1858) 4 K & J 676; *Haviland Routh & Co v Thompson* (1864) 3 M 313; *Marriott v Anchor Reversionary Co* (1861) 30 LJ Ch 571, (1861) 3 De GF & J 177.
3 *European and Australian Royal Mail Co v Royal Mail Steam Packet Co*, above; *Marriott v The Anchor Reversionary Co* (1861) 30 LJ Ch 571, (1861) 3 De GF & J 177. As to damages for loss of profit where a mortgagee is restrained from using the ship, see *De Mattos v Gibson* (1860) 1 John & H 79; but on that case see now *Port Line Ltd v Ben Line Steamers Ltd* [1958] 2 QB 146, [1958] 1 All ER 787, and see *Swiss Bank Corpn v Lloyds Bank Ltd* [1982] AC 584; affd [1982] AC 584, [1981] 2 All ER 449, HL.

TAKING POSSESSION UNDER MORTGAGES OF CHOSES IN ACTION

19.98 Where there is a mortgage of an interest in a trust fund, then in order to take possession the mortgagee must give the trustees notice to pay over the income to him — mere notice to the trustees of the assignment is not in itself equivalent to taking possession of the interest[1]. Where a mortgaged reversionary interest falls into possession, the mortgagee is not entitled to receive the whole of the mortgagor's interest, but only so much as suffices to discharge the principal, interest, and costs due on the mortgage[2]. The mortgagor of a patent can sue for infringement without joining the mortgagee even where the latter is registered as assignee[3].

1 *Re Pawson's Settlement, Higgins v Pawson* [1917] 1 Ch 541.
2 *Hockey v Western* [1898] 1 Ch 350, CA.
3 *Van Gelder, Apsimon & Co v Sowerby Bridge United District Flour Society* (1890) 44 Ch D 374, CA.

Chapter 20

The mortgagee's power of sale out of court

20.1 Under most mortgages, the property comprised in the security may, in certain circumstances, become liable to be sold for the purpose of discharging the debt[1]. The power of the creditor to sell the property himself is considered in this chapter; sale by judicial process is considered in Chapter 21[2].

1 There are some exceptional cases where sale is not available as a remedy, see eg mortgages to secure an advance under the Small Dwellings Acquisition Acts prior to the 1985 amendments (see **20.54**), mortgages by a housing authority where the authority has become entitled to exercise a power of sale within any pre-emption period (see **20.55**).
2 On the Law Commission's proposals as to the mortgagee's remedy of sale, see *Transfer of Land Mortgages* (1991) (Law Com no 204) paras 7.5–7.25.

THE POWER OF SALE

20.2 The mortgagee may have a power of sale as a legal incident of the security[1], under an express power[2], or under a statutory power[3].

1 See **20.3–20.4**.
2 See **20.5**.
3 See **20.6**.

POWER OF SALE AS A LEGAL INCIDENT OF THE SECURITY

Mortgages of chattels and choses in action

20.3 The mortgagee of a personal chattel (when possession has been delivered to him[1]), of stocks and shares, of a policy of insurance, or other chose in action, has an implied power of sale as a legal incident of his security[2]. This right is exercisable where the mortgagor has acted so as to imperil the security; on non-payment on the day fixed for payment; or, where no day has been fixed, after a proper demand and notice[3], and the lapse of a reasonable time[4]. The mortgagee of chattels who sells under either a special or an implied power, is bound to account for the proceeds, to pay over to the owner the surplus purchase-money beyond his demand and the necessary charges and expenses and to return any unsold part of the security to the debtor. If the mortgagee attempts to dispose of the money so as to prejudice any person entitled to receive it, he may be ordered to pay it into court and a receiver may be appointed of the proceeds of any part of the property which may remain unsold[5]. The mortgagor's right of redemption ceases on a contract to sell made after the power of sale has arisen[6].

1 *Re Morritt, ex p Official Receiver* (1886) 18 QBD 222, CA. See **19.86**.
2 *Wilson v Tooker* (1714) 5 Bro Parl Cas 193; *Lockwood v Ewer* (1742) 2 Atk 303; *Kemp v Westbrook* (1749) 1 Ves Sen 278; *Re Morritt, ex p Official Receiver* (1886) 18 QBD 222 at 223; *McHugh* v *Union Bank of Canada* [1913] AC 299; *The Odessa* [1916] 1 AC 145 at 159. As to sale by mortgagees of stocks and shares, see *Stubbs v Slater* [1910] 1 Ch 632, CA.
3 *France v Clark* (1883) 22 Ch D 830; affd 26 Ch D 257, CA; *Re Morritt, ex p Official Receiver*, above. A mistake as to the amount does not invalidate the notice: *Stubbs v Slater*, above; and see *Harrold v Plenty* [1901] 2 Ch 314. See also **20.15**. If shares are sold without notice the mortgagor is entitled to set off the value of the shares on the day preceding the date of the master's certificate in an action on the account: see *Ellis & Co's Trustee v Dixon-Johnson* [1925] AC 489, HL.
4 *Deverges v Sandeman, Clark & Co* [1902] 1 Ch 579, CA; cf *Re Harrison and Ingram, ex p Whinney* (1905) 54 WR 203.
5 *Wilson v Tooker*, above.
6 *The Ningchow* (1916) 31 TLR 470.

Real property

20.4 By contrast, there is no implied power of sale as a legal incident of the security in the case of mortgaged real property. There is no right at common law or in equity for the mortgagee to sell the mortgaged property free from the equity of redemption, unless he does so with the mortgagor's concurrence. In the absence of an express or statutory power, he is only entitled to sell the property subject to the equity of redemption, that is to sell his mortgage[1].

1 See generally Chapter 14.

EXPRESS POWER OF SALE

20.5 To remedy the lack of a legal or equitable right to sell free from the equity of redemption, it became common from the early nineteenth century[1] to insert an express power of sale in the mortgage, until the introduction of a statutory power of sale by Lord Cranworth's Act 1860[2]. The statutory power of sale now contained in the Law of Property Act 1925 has rendered the inclusion of an express power of sale unnecessary. However, there is nothing in ss 101 or 103 of the Law of Property Act 1925 which restricts express powers conferred on the mortgagee by the mortgage deed itself and the mortgagee is entitled to extend or vary the statutory power of sale by express provisions in the deed[3].

An express power of sale is not affected by an arrangement subsequently made between mortgagee and mortgagor for the management of the property[4]. It is not extinguished by an ineffective attempt to exercise it[5]. In a mortgage containing an express power of sale, there is an implied term that the mortgagor will hand over to the mortgagee all deeds necessary to enable the mortgagee to exercise the power of sale, as well as the means of entry to the property[6]. The effect of the exercise of the power is the same as the effect of the exercise of the statutory power of sale.

1 *Clarke* v *Royal Panopticon* (1857) 4 Drew 26 at 30; *Stevens* v *Theatres Ltd* [1903] 1 Ch 857 at 860.
2 Expanded by the Conveyancing Act 1881 (s 1(2)); see also Conveyancing Act 1911.
3 *The Maule* [1997] 1 WLR 528 at 532-533; Law of Property Act 1925, s 101(3).
4 Eg under which a receiver is to grant leases, but is to permit the mortgagor to receive the rents till default: *King v Heenan* (1853) 3 De GM & G 890.
5 *Henderson v Astwood* [1894] AC 150 at 162, PC.
6 *NRMA Insurance* v *Individual Homes* (1988) 92 FLR 1 ACT.

STATUTORY POWER OF SALE

The statutory power

20.6 Where (a) a mortgage is made by deed[1] (which will apply to all legal mortgages), and (b) the mortgage money[2] has become due[3], the mortgagee[4] has a statutory power of sale under s 101(1)(i)[5] of the Law of Property Act 1925, to the same extent as if a power in the following terms had been conferred by the mortgage deed:

> 'A power... to sell, or to concur with any other person in selling, the mortgaged property, or any part thereof[6], either subject to prior charges or not, and either together or in lots, by public auction or by private contract, subject to such conditions respecting title or evidence of title, or other matter[7], as the mortgagee thinks fit, with power to vary any contract for sale, and to buy in at an auction, or rescind any contract for sale, and to re-sell, without being answerable for any loss occasioned thereby[8].'

The power is included only if and as far as a contrary intention is not expressed in the mortgage deed. It has effect subject to the terms of the mortgage deed and may be modified thereby[9].

The power is to sell the mortgaged property or any part thereof[10], that is the property over which the mortgage deed purports to extend and operate[11]. Where there are several properties included in the mortgage, the mortgagee is entitled to sell all of them, notwithstanding the sale of one or more only would raise sufficient to discharge the mortgage[12]. The statutory power extends to fixtures[13], but there is no power to sell timber or fixtures apart from the land[14].

By reference to a collateral security, for instance a mortgage of an insurance policy, an express power of sale may be extended to property comprised in that security[15]. However, since the statutory power is only applicable where the mortgage is by deed, it seems doubtful whether it will extend to such a collateral security made by writing only, unless there is an agreement that it shall be incorporated[16]. Where there is a collateral security by a mortgage by a person other than the mortgagor, the exercise of the power of sale may involve the operation of the doctrine of contribution[17] between the principal mortgagor and the third party.

1 The power applies to any mortgage of any property made by deed, save those to which the Bills of Sale Acts apply (1878, 1882) (see **5.12** ff and **19.86** ff; *Calvert* v *Thomas* (1887) 19 QBD 204); and to debentures issued by a statutory public utility company: *Blaker v Herts and Essex Waterworks Co* (1889) 41 Ch D 399; and see *Deyes v Wood* [1911] 1 KB 806 at 8181, CA.

2 That is money or money's worth secured by a mortgage: Law of Property Act 1925, s 205 (1) (xvi). See generally *Bevham Investments Pty Ltd v Belgot Pty Ltd* (1982) 149 CLR 494.

3 That is, if the legal date for redemption (if any) has passed, or any instalment of the mortgage debt under an instalment mortgage has fallen due: see *Payne v Cardiff RDC* [1932] 1 KB 241. The power may effectively be excluded before a specified date: *Twentieth Century Banking Corpn Ltd* v *Wilkinson* [1977] Ch 99 (no power of sale where principal not yet due, even though interest in arrears), in which case the mortgagee may be able to claim a sale by order of the court: see Chapter 21, and see *Western Bank Ltd v Schindler* [1977] Ch 1, [1976] 2 All ER 393, CA.

4 The power is applicable to a registered chargee; see Land Registration Act 1925, s 34 (1) (see **4.13**) and *Lever Finance Ltd v Needleman's Property Trustee* [1956] Ch 357, [1956] 2 All

ER 375. Where there was before 1926 a mortgage of an undivided share of land, the statutory power applies to the corresponding share of the proceeds of sale under the statutory trusts: Law of Property Act 1925, s 102.

5 Replacing Conveyancing Act 1881, s 19 (which itself replaced Lord Cranworth's Act 1860).

6 See *Champagne Perrier-Jouet SA v H H Finch Ltd* [1982] 3 All ER 713, [1982] 1 WLR 1359 and nn 10–14, below. The mortgagee does not have the power to sever fixtures from the property and sell them separately, unless there is an express or implied term of the mortgage to that effect: *Re Yates* (1888) 38 Ch D 112.

7 See *Property and Bloodstock Ltd v Emerton* [1968] Ch 94 at 117–118, 122, [1967] 3 All ER 321 at 328, 331, CA. The reference to 'other matter' would not, it is submitted, permit an instalment sale of the property. For this, there should be express provision: see the Appendix. The mortgagee could of course grant a new mortgage to the purchaser, but the mortgagee would have to account to the original mortgagor for the price. Where the mortgage permits an instalment sale the mortgagee is bound to account for the instalments as they are received not the whole purchase price: *Wright v New Zealand Farmers Co-operative Association of Canterbury Ltd* [1939] AC 439, [1939] 2 All ER 701, PC.

8 Apart from such a provision a power of sale is not extinguished by an abortive attempt to sell: *Henderson v Astwood* [1894] AC 150 at 162, PC.

9 Law of Property Act 1925, s 101 (3). For forms, see 28 *Forms and Precedents* (5th edn, 1999 reissue) Mortgages and the Appendix. It applies only so far as a contrary intention is not expressed therein: Law of Property Act 1925, s 101 (4). The mere fact that the mortgage contains an express power exercisable at a future date does not show a contrary intention so as to negative the earlier exercise of the statutory power: *Life Interests etc, Corpn v Hand-in-Hand Fire and Life Insurance Society* [1898] 2 Ch 230.

10 See s 101 (1) (i).

11 *Re White Rose Cottage* [1964] Ch 483 at 496.

12 Cf *Ross v Victoria Permanent Property Investment and Building Society* (1882) 8 VLR (E) 254, where there were different lands held under different mortgages with different mortgagees; but the court would sanction a sale in one lot if this were to the benefit of the mortgagor; see **20.25**.

13 Law of Property Act 1925, ss 88 (4), 89 (4); see **20.40** and **20.41**; **20.45**, n 3 and n 3 above,.

14 *Cholmeley v Paxton* (1825) 3 Bing 207; *Re Yates* (1888) 38 Ch D 112, CA; *Hunter v Hunter* [1936] AC 222 at 248, 249, HL; *Kay's Leasing Corpn Pty Ltd v CSR Provident Fund Nominees* [1962] VR 429. For forms of conveyance under the statutory power of sale, see 28 *Forms and Precedents* (5th edn, 1999 reissue) Mortgages.

15 *Ashworth v Mounsey* (1853) 2 CLR 418.

16 *Re Thompson and Holt* (1890) 44 Ch D 492 at 499.

17 For the doctrine of contribution, see **26.2**.

Incidental statutory powers

20.7 Section 101(2) of the Law of Property Act 1925[1] confers the following powers as incidents of the statutory power:

(a) a power to impose or reserve or make binding, as far as the law permits, by covenant, condition, or otherwise, on the unsold part of the mortgaged property or any thereof, or on the purchaser and any property sold, any restriction or reservation with respect to building on or other user of land, or with respect to mines and minerals, or for the purpose of the more beneficial working thereof, or with respect to any other thing;

(b) a power to sell the mortgaged property, or any part thereof, or all or any mines and minerals apart from the surface:
   (i) with or without a grant or reservation of rights of way, rights of water, easements, rights and privileges for or connected with building or other purposes in relation to the property remaining in mortgage or any part thereof, or to any property sold; and
   (ii) with or without an exception or reservation of all or any of the mines

and minerals in or under the mortgaged property, and with or without a grant or reservation of powers of working, way-leaves, or rights of way, rights of water and drainage and other powers, easements, rights, and privileges for or connected with mining purposes in relation to the property remaining unsold or any part thereof, or to any property sold; and

(iii) or without covenants by the purchaser to expend money on the land sold[2].

At any time after the power of sale has become exercisable, the person entitled to exercise it may demand and recover from any person (other than a person having in the mortgaged property an estate, interest or right in priority to the mortgage), all the deeds and documents relating to the property or to the title thereto, which a purchaser under the power of sale would be entitled to demand and recover for him[3].

The mortgagee is not answerable for any involuntary loss happening in or about the exercise or execution of the statutory power of sale, or any trust connected therewith, nor (where the mortgage is executed after 31 December 1911) of any power or provision contained in the mortgage deed[4]. The statutory power of sale does not affect the right of foreclosure[5].

1 These powers were first conferred by s 4 of the Conveyancing Act 1911, which came into force on 1 January 1912 and, accordingly, while in general the statutory powers apply to mortgages executed after 31 December 1881 (see Law of Property Act 1925, s 101 (5)), these powers are restricted, as above stated, to mortgages executed after 31 December 1911.

2 Before the Conveyancing Act 1911, there was power to sell the surface and minerals separately only with the leave of the court and the requirement of leave is preserved as to mortgages made before 1 January 1912, and see Law of Property Act 1925, s 92; *Re Hirst's Mortgage* (1890) 45 Ch D 263.

3 Law of Property Act 1925, s 106 (4). See also *NRMA Insurance* v *Individual Homes* (1988) 92 FLR 1 ACT as to an implied term to similar effect under an express power.

4 Section 106 (3). The first part of this clause reproduces s 21 (6) of the Conveyancing Act 1881. The latter part reproduces an amendment made by the Act of 1911.

5 Law of Property Act 1925, s 106 (2). This is in accordance with the law as to express powers of sale: *Wayne v Hanham* (1851) 9 Hare 62, but after order nisi and pending foreclosure absolute, the mortgagee cannot sell without the leave of the court: *Stevens v Theatres Ltd* [1903] 1 Ch 857. See **16.11** and **22.30**.

MORTGAGES OF SHIPS

20.8 In the case of mortgages of ships, the rights and duties of the parties are 'overwhelmingly dominated by contract'[1]. The mortgage will almost invariably contain an express power of sale.

The Merchant Shipping Act 1995 also gives a registered mortgagee[2] of a ship the power, if the mortgage money or any part of it is due, to sell the ship or any share in the ship in respect of which he is registered and to give effectual receipts for the purchase money[3]. However, the Act provides that where two or more mortgages are registered in respect of the same ship or share of a ship, a subsequent mortgagee shall not, except under an order of the court of competent jurisdiction, sell the ship or share of a ship without the concurrence of every prior mortgagee[4].

Further, the mortgagee of a personal chattel has an implied power of sale as a legal incident of his security[5].

1 *The Maule* [1997] 1 WLR 528 at 533, PC, per Lord Lloyd of Berwick; [1997] LMCLQ 329 (A Clarke).
2 See Merchant Shipping Act 1995, Sch 1, para. 7.
3 Merchant Shipping Act 1995, Sch 1, para 9(1). See *The Maule* [1997] 1 WLR 528 at 532, PC, for the differences between power of sale under the Merchant Shipping Act 1995 and the Law of Property Act 1925, ss 101–103. For damages for improper sale after tender of debt, see *Fletcher and Campbell v City Marine Finance* [1968] 2 Lloyd's Rep 520. For an order for sale, see *The Basildon* [1967] 2 Lloyd's Rep 134.
4 Merchant Shipping Act 1995, Sch 1, para 9(2). The provisions of para 9 follow s 35 of the Merchant Shipping Act 1894.
5 See **20.3**.

THOSE ENTITLED TO EXERCISE THE POWER OF SALE

Devolution of the power

20.9 The statutory power of sale is exercisable by persons deriving title under the original mortgagee[1], which appears to be sufficient to ensure the devolution of the power. It is also provided that it is exercisable by any person for the time being entitled to receive and give a good discharge for the purchase money[2]. An express power is exercisable only by the persons who are designated for that purpose by the power[3], it will normally be sufficient to make it exercisable by persons deriving title under the mortgagee[4]. A transferee can take advantage of a right to sell forthwith existing at the date of the transfer[5]. A receiver may sell, either as delegate of the mortgagee[6], or under an express power of sale in favour of the receiver in the mortgage. A power of attorney given to an agent of the mortgagee to sell land belonging to the donor does not give authority to exercise the donor's power of sale as mortgagee[7].

1 Law of Property Act 1925, s 205 (1) (xvi).
2 Section 106 (1), but this does not confer the power of sale on an agent with a power of attorney to receive and give a good discharge for the purchase money: *Re Dowson and Jenkin's Contract* [1904] 2 Ch 219, CA.
3 *Re Crunden and Meux's Contract* [1909] 1 Ch 690 at 695.
4 An assign of a mortgagee cannot sell under an express power unless the power is expressed to be given to the mortgagee and his assigns: *Re Rumney and Smith* [1897] 2 Ch 351, CA.
5 *Bailey v Barnes* [1894] 1 Ch 25 at 32, CA.
6 Law of Property Act 1925, s 109 (3); see **18.10**.
7 *Re Dowson and Jenkin's Contract* [1904] 2 Ch 219.

Right of sale as between successive incumbrancers

20.10 Where there are successive mortgages, the first mortgagee can exercise his power of sale without the concurrence of the subsequent mortgagees, although he will have to account to them for the surplus (if any) of the purchase money[1]. Where a first mortgagee, after making preliminary arrangements (but without a binding contract) for an advantageous sale of the property, bought up the interest of the second mortgagee at a reduced sum the court refused to set aside the sale[2]. A second or subsequent mortgagee may sell subject to the first or prior mortgages[3]. Alternatively he may sell free of prior incumbrances by arranging for them to be discharged out of the proceeds of sale. In the latter case, the concurrence of the prior mortgagees or application to the court to allow payment into court[4] is necessary.

1 See **20.47**. As to notice requiring payment, see **11.6**. In practice a first mortgagee will often give a second mortgagee an opportunity of taking a transfer of the first mortgage.

2 *Dolman v Nokes* (1855) 22 Beav 402.
3 See *Manser v Dix* (1857) 8 De GM & G 703.
4 Under Law of Property Act 1925, s 50; as to the amount to be paid in see s 50(1), *Milford Haven Rly and Estate Co Mowatt* (1884) 28 Ch D 402: *Re Wilberforce's Trusts* [1915] 1 Ch 94: see also Law of Property Act 1925, s 101(1); see **28.74**.

WHEN THE POWER IS EXERCISABLE

WHEN AN EXPRESS POWER IS EXERCISABLE

20.11 Where an express power is granted, it will arise after due notice or on the happening of some specified event. Provision is usually made that the power shall not be exercised until the expiration of notice to the mortgagor, so that he may have a further opportunity of paying off the debt. While it has been said that a power to sell without notice is of an oppressive character, a provision as to notice is not, however, essential[1]. Thus, in the case of a shipping mortgage, where the parties had expressly agreed that the mortgagees should have the power to sell the vessel in the event of a non-financial default, even though no sum of money had become due under the loan agreement, the mortgagees were not obliged to give notice accelerating repayment of the loan before exercising their power of sale. Although a sale without giving the borrowers sufficient notice to allow them to redeem the ship would be unlawful, the mere presence of a power to sell without notice does not render the whole power invalid[2]. Sometimes non-payment on demand is the only preliminary — in such a case the mortgagor must be allowed a reasonable time to fulfill the demand[3].

1 *Miller v Cook* (1870) LR 10 Eq 641. Hence it is a breach of the duty by a solicitor, who becomes the mortgagee to his client, to omit a stipulation for notice in an express power of sale, without taking care that the client has a full explanation of the circumstances: *Cockburn v Edwards* (1881) 18 Ch D 449, CA, but this does not apply to a mortgage for securing money presently payable, for payment of which the solicitor is giving time: *Pooley's Trustee v Whetham* (1886) 33 Ch D 111, CA.
2 *The Maule* [1997] 1 WLR 528 at 533.
3 *Rogers* v *Mutton* (1862) 7 H & N 733.

WHEN THE STATUTORY POWER IS EXERCISABLE

When the power is exercisable

20.12 As considered above, the statutory power *arises* (in the absence of contrary terms in the deed) when the mortgage is made by deed and the mortgage money is due[1]. Once it has arisen, s 103 of the Law of Property Act 1925 provides that the mortgagee shall not *exercise* the statutory power unless and until:

(a) notice[2] requiring payment of the mortgage money[3] has been served on the mortgagor or one of two or more mortgagors and default has been made in payment of the mortgage money, or of part thereof, for three months after such service[4]; or
(b) some interest under the mortgage is in arrear and unpaid for two months after becoming due[5]; or
(c) there has been a breach of some provision contained in the mortgage deed or in the Act[6], or in an enactment replaced by the Act, and on the part of the mortgagor, or of some person concurring in making the mortgage, to be

observed or performed[7], other than and besides a covenant for payment of the mortgage money or interest thereon[8].

These restrictions on the exercise of the statutory power may be, and commonly are, modified or excluded[9]. The mortgagee's power of sale survives any disclaimer of the mortgaged property by the mortgagor's liquidator or trustee in bankruptcy (even if, as a fee simple, it thereupon escheats to the crown and is terminated)[10].

1 See the Law of Property Act 1925; **20.6**.
2 As to the requirements where a notice is necessary, see **20.13** ff.
3 Ie money or money's worth secured by a mortgage: Law of Property Act 1925, s 205 (1) (xvi). See generally *Bevham Investments Pty Ltd v Belgot Pty Ltd* (1982) 149 CLR 494.
4 Ie after actual service, not after the time fixed by the notice for payment: *Barker v Illingworth* [1908] 2 Ch 20.
5 This includes an instalment expressed to be for principal and interest combined: *Walsh v Derrick* (1903) 19 TLR 209, CA; *Payne v Cardiff RDC* [1932] 1 KB 241. A capitalisation clause may make this inapplicable: see *Davy v Turner* (1970) 21 P & CR 967. Where a mortgagee has gone into possession and has received rents to an amount sufficient to keep down the interest, he cannot be allowed to say that interest is in arrear: *Cockburn v Edwards* (1881) 18 Ch D 449 at 456, 463, CA; *Wrigley v Gill* [1906] 1 Ch 165, CA.
6 Eg failure to fulfil the requirements for the statutory power of leasing: *Public Trustee v Lawrence* [1912] 1 Ch 789.
7 On the difference between such a covenant and a covenant for payment of the mortgage money, see *Bevham Investments Pty Ltd v Belgot Pty Ltd* (1982) 149 CLR 494.
8 Where the statutory or express power to sell or appoint a receiver is exercisable by reason of the mortgagor's bankruptcy, it is not to be exercised without the leave of the court: Law of Property Act 1925, s 110 (1); *Re Huddersfield Building Society* [1940] WN 247. As to other restrictions, under the Rent Act etc, see **16.22** ff. As to estoppel, see *Braithwaite v Winwood* [1960] 3 All ER 642, [1960] 1 WLR 1257. As to where the default has been put right, see *Hughes v Birks* [1958] EGD 341. For sale under a mortgage securing an advance under the Small Dwellings Acquisition Acts, see **20.54**. For vesting orders by housing authorities, see **20.55**.
9 Law of Property Act 1925, s 101(3).
10 *Hindcastle Ltd* v *Barabara Attenborough Associates* [1997] AC 70; *SCMLLA Properties Ltd v Gesso Properties Ltd* [1995] BCC 793.

WHERE NOTICE REQUIRING PAYMENT OF THE MORTGAGE MONEY MUST BE GIVEN

Requirement for notice

20.13 When exercising the statutory power, the second ground contained in s 103 (that some interest is in arrear and unpaid for two months after becoming due) is the one usually relied on; a notice requiring payment is then not required. However, where the ground in s 103(i) is relied on, notice must be served on the mortgagor[1]. Notice is also often required under an express power of sale[2].

1 See **20.12**.
2 See **20.11**.

To whom notice should be given

20.14 Where there are two or more mortgagors, s 103(i) provides that notice need only be served on one of them. In s 103(i), 'mortgagor' includes, unless the context otherwise requires, any person deriving title under the original mortgagor or entitled to redeem a mortgage according to his estate interest or right in the mortgaged property[1]. Where an express power required notice to be given to the mortgagor or his assigns, it was held that a subsequent mortgagee should be served, but it was doubted whether notice also had to be given to the mortgagor[2]. On that basis, it would appear that notice may be given to the mortgagor or to any of the incumbrancers. However, the wording of s 103 (i) is somewhat different and it seems proper to give the notice to the mortgagor and at least the first subsequent incumbrancer[3] and, where a subsequent mortgagee is selling, to give notice to the mortgagor and prior mortgagees.

1 Law of Property Act 1925, s 205 (1) (xvi). If the mortgagor is dead, the notice should be served on his personal representatives as long as the equity of redemption remains in them: *Gill v Newton* (1866) 14 WR 490.
2 *Hoole v Smith* (1881) 17 Ch D 434.
3 See Woolstenholme and Cherry's *Conveyancing Statutes* (13th edn) vol 1, p 211. To ascertain the subsequent incumbrancers search should be made for mortgages registered under the Land Charges Act 1972 or registered or protected under the Land Registration Act 1925.

Form of notice

20.15 The object of the notice is to guard the rights of the mortgagor. If this object is substantially attained, the court will not minutely criticise the exact terms of the notice[1]. The purpose of the notice is to identify the debt, rather than the quantum[2]; a notice is not bad if it overstates the principal[3]. Under the statutory power, the notice may be in the form of demand for immediate payment, with an intimation that if the money is not paid before the expiration of three months from the date of service, the mortgagee will proceed to sell[4]. It is also equally effective if it is a notice to pay at the end of that period[5]. Where notice is given pursuant to an express power, the mortgagor must be given the period of warning required by the terms of the power[6]. If in an express power the length of notice is not specified, a reasonable notice must be given. Notice to pay on the day on which notice is given is not reasonable[7]. Where a notice declared the intention to sell when a proper interval had elapsed from the date of the notice, but the sale was not made until the expiration of the proper interval after the service or delivery of the notice, the sale was held good[8]. The power of sale may not be exercised until the required notice period has expired. However, an agreement for sale may be made before the expiration of the notice, if the agreement is conditional upon the power becoming exercisable and if the price is then proper[9].

1 See generally *Barns v Queensland National Bank Ltd* (1906) 3 CLR 925; Croft *Mortgagee's Power of Sale*, para 29. See also *Mannai Investment Co Ltd* v *Eagle Star Life Assurance Co Ltd* [1997] AC 749 (error in landlord and tenant notice).
2 *Indrisie v General Credits Ltd* [1985] ACLD 242.
3 *Clyde Properties Ltd v Tasker* [1970] NZLR 754; *Banbury Foods Pty Ltd v National Bank of Australasia Ltd* (1984) 153 CLR 491; see **17.6**, n 13.
4 For form, see 28 *Forms and Precedents* (5th edn, 1999 reissue) Mortgages and the Appendix.
5 *Barker v Illingworth* [1908] 2 Ch 20.
6 *Metters v Brown* (1863) 33 LJ Ch 97.
7 *Massey v Sladen* (1868) LR 4 Exch 13; *Ronald Elwyn Lister Ltd v Dunlop Canada Ltd* (1982) 135 DLR (3d) 1; *Bunbury Foods Pty Ltd v National Bank of Australasia Ltd* (1984) 153 CLR 491. As to notice where the mortgage is an equitable mortgage of stocks and shares, see *Stubbs v Slater* [1910] 1 Ch 632, CA.
8 *Metters v Brown* (1863) 33 LJ Ch 97.

9 *Major v Ward* (1847) 5 Hare 598 at 604; *Farrar v Farrars Ltd* (1888) 40 Ch D 395 at 412, CA.

Service of notice

20.16 The service of a notice required or authorised to be served by the Law of Property Act 1925, is regulated by s 196 of that Act[1]. In that case:

(a) the notice must be in writing;
(b) the notice is sufficient, even if it is only addressed to the mortgagor by that designation without his name, or generally to the person interested without any name, and notwithstanding that any person to be affected by the notice is absent, under disability[2], unborn or unascertained[3];
(c) the notice is sufficiently served if it is left at the last-known place of abode or business of the mortgagor[4], or is affixed or left for him on the mortgaged premises[5];
(d) it is also sufficiently served if sent by registered post, and if not returned through the post as undelivered[6].

1 The provisions of the section extend to notices under instruments coming into operation after 1925, unless a contrary intention appears; but not to notices in court proceedings; sub-ss (5), (6).
2 *Tracey v Lawrence* (1854) 2 Drew 403 (infancy); *Robertson v Lockie* (1846) 15 LJ Ch 379 (mental incapacity).
3 This does not seem to cover the case where there is no person in existence on whom notice could be served, eg where the mortgagor has died intestate, and no administrator has been appointed: *Parkinson v Hanbury* (1860) 1 Drew & Sm 143; on appeal 2 De GJ & S 450; affd LR 2 HL 1.
4 *Cannon Brewery Co Ltd v Signal Press Ltd* (1928) 139 LT 384. In *Van Harlaam v Kasner* [1992] 2 EGLR 59, where the tenant was in prison, service through the letterbox of the vacant premises was sufficient. See also *Henry Smith's Charity Trustees* v *Kyriakov* [1989] 2 EGLR 110.
5 It is sufficient to fix it to the door of the residence: *Major v Ward* (1847) 5 Hare 598 at 604.
6 It is also sufficiently served if sent by recorded delivery service: Recorded Delivery Service Act 1962, s 1; and see *Re 88 Berkeley Road NW9, Rickwood v Turnsek* [1971] Ch 648, [1971] 1 All ER 254; *Stephenson & Sons* v *Orca Properties* [1989] 2 EGLR 129.

Withdrawal and waiver of notice

20.17 Once a notice has been given it cannot be withdrawn without the consent of the mortgagor[1], but it can be waived[2]. Thus a subsequent assent to the sale by an interested person, and an agreement by him to join in the conveyance, will operate as a waiver of the notice[3]. If, after the demand, the sale is stopped on receipt of a cheque for the amount due under the mortgage, but the cheque is afterwards dishonoured, the right of sale and the running of the notice having been only suspended, revive, and the power may be exercised without giving a new notice[4].

1 *Santley v Wilde* [1899] 1 Ch 747, reversed on a different point [1899] 2 Ch 474, CA; see also *Kinch* v *Bullard* [1998] 4 All ER 650, [1999] 1 WLR 423.
2 *Walsh v Derrick* (1903) 19 TLR 209, CA; *Barns v Queensland National Bank Ltd* (1906) 3 CLR 925; *Blakely v Teal Investments Ltd* (1982) NZLJ 242 (unqualified acceptance of interest without more does not necessarily waive the notice). See generally Croft *Mortgagee's Power of Sale*, para 33.
3 *Selwyn v Garfit* (1888) 38 Ch D 273, CA; *Re Thompson and Holt* (1890) 44 Ch D 492; but see *Forster v Hoggart* (1850) 15 QB 155.
4 *Wood v Murton* (1877) 47 LJ QB 191.

Costs of notice

20.18 A mortgagee is entitled to add to the security the costs incurred in the preparation and service of all proper notices[1].

1 As to mortgagee's right to costs, see Chapter 36.

EXERCISE OF POWER OF SALE WHERE MORTGAGOR A COMPANY IN LIQUIDATION

20.19 In a compulsory winding up, any disposition of the company's property after the commencement of the winding up is void, unless the court orders otherwise[1]. However, a sale under a mortgage does not fall within this provision, the object of which is to prevent the dissipation of the company's assets. The relevant disposition, in such case, is the mortgage, which precedes the winding up, and not the sale under the mortgage[2].

1 Insolvency Act 1986, s 127. See *Re Tramway Building & Construction Co Ltd* [1988] Ch 293; *Re Fairway Graphics Ltd* [1991] BCLC 468.
2 *Sowman v David Samuel Trust Ltd* [1978] 1 All ER 616, [1978] 1 WLR 22; *Barrow v Chief Land Registrar* (1977) Times, 20 October; and see (1977) Conv NS 83 (Millett), 443 (the reference to s 74(2) of the Law of Property Act 1925 in the reply of Mr Millett (as he then was) is presumably intended to be to s 74(3)). See also *Industrial Development Authority v Moran* [1978] IR 159; *Re Margart Pty Ltd* (1985) 9 ACLR 269. The liquidator will have to join in the conveyance in the absence of a power of attorney; and see generally *Williams on Title* (4th edn) p 227 and Supplement. On the form of receipt and covenants to be given by a liquidator, see [1983] Conv 177. See also *Re Margart Pty Ltd* [1985] BCLC 314; *Re French's Wine Bar Ltd* (1987) 3 BCC 173.

PROTECTION OF PURCHASER

Protection of purchaser against irregularities in the exercise of the power

20.20 Formerly it was the practice to insert in mortgages a clause expressly protecting the purchaser against irregularities in the exercise of the power[1]. However nowadays a purchaser will not be concerned to inquire whether the power of sale has become exercisable (that is, whether the three conditions in s 103 of the Law of Property Act 1925 have been fulfilled, or whether there is some other irregularity or impropriety in the exercise of the power), since in the case of a sale under the statutory power the purchaser is protected by the provisions of s 104 of the Law of Property Act 1925[2].

Section 104(2) provides that where a conveyance is made in exercise of the power of sale conferred by the Act[3], the title of the purchaser is not impeachable on the grounds:

(a) that no case had arisen to authorise the sale; or
(b) that due notice was not given; or
(c) that leave of the court, when required, was not obtained[4]; or
(d) that the power was otherwise improperly or irregularly exercised[5].

Thus a purchaser is not, either before or upon the conveyance[6], concerned to see or inquire whether a case has arisen to authorise the sale, or due notice has been given, or the power is otherwise properly and regularly exercised[7]. Any person damnified (that is, caused loss or injury) by an unauthorised, or improper, or irregular exercise of the power has a remedy in damages against the person exercising the power[8]. Section 104(3) provides that a conveyance on sale by a mortgagee, made after the commencement of the Act, shall be deemed to have been made in exercise of the power of sale conferred by the Act unless a contrary intention appears[9].

However, the purchaser must still satisfy himself that the power of sale has arisen (that is, that the requirements of s 101(1) have been fulfilled[10]), for otherwise the mortgagee will have no statutory power to sell at all[11]. He would only have the power to transfer his mortgage and not the mortgaged property free from the equity of redemption.

1 Unless excused by the terms of the conditions of sale, or of the power, the mortgagee was bound to obtain for a purchaser of the mortgaged property proper evidence of the facts which entitle him to exercise the power of sale. His unsupported statutory declaration, being the evidence of an interested person, was not sufficient for the purpose: *Hobson v Bell* (1839) 2 Beav 17; *Re Edwards and Rudkin to Green* (1888) 58 LT 789. A covenant by the mortgagor that he will join in the sale is for the benefit of the mortgagee only and the purchaser cannot require such concurrence: *Corder v Morgan* (1811) 18 Ves 344.

2 Replacing s 21 (2) of the Conveyancing Act 1881. Under a similar express provision, it was held a sale to a bona fide purchaser without notice was good, though the security had been satisfied: *Dicker v Angerstein* (1876) 3 Ch D 600.

3 Or any enactment it replaced.

4 Where the mortgage was made after the commencement of the Act. Accordingly the purchaser is not concerned to see whether the Rent Acts apply to the property. This was not in the Conveyancing Acts 1881 to 1911. Irregularities had arisen through a failure to obtain orders giving leave to sell under the Courts (Emergency Powers) Acts 1914 to 1919, and the Increase of Rent and Mortgage Interest (Restrictions) Act 1920, s 7; see *Anchor Trust Co v Bell* [1926] Ch 805.

5 Whether the mortgage was made before or after the commencement of the Act.

6 These words reproduce the amendment made by the Conveyancing Act 1911, s 5 (1), in order to get over *Life Interest and Reversionary Securities Corpn v Hand-in-Hand Fire and Life Insurance Society* [1898] 2 Ch 230, where it was held that the vendor could not rely on the Conveyancing Act 1881, s 21 (2), as precluding inquiry by the purchaser before conveyance and see *Holohan v Friends Provident and Century Life Office* [1966] IR 1; *Forsyth v Blundell* (1973) 129 CLR 477 at 502.

7 Section 104(2). See *Bailey v Barnes* [1894] 1 Ch 25 at 35. For building societies selling under the Building Societies Act 1986, see [1982] Conv 246.

8 See also *Platts v TSB Bank plc* [1998] 2 BCLC 1. For involuntary loss, see the Law of Property Act 1925, s 106(3). It has been held that the reference to a remedy in damages does not create a special statutory remedy, nor does it refer to a common law action for damages, but is a reference to the mortgagor's right in equitable proceedings to hold the mortgagee to account on the footing of wilful default: *McGinnis v Union Bank of Australia Ltd* [1935] VLR 161, but the Australian courts have not accepted the principle established in *Cuckmere Brick Co Ltd v Mutual Finance Ltd* [1971] Ch 949, [1971] 2 All ER 633, CA; see (1981) 55 ALJ 559 (Tyler); and see *General Credits (Finance) Pty Ltd v Stryakovich* [1975] Qd R 352. In the case of loss caused by a sale by the mortgagee at an undervalue (see **20.23**), the normal measure of damages would be the difference between the market value and the sale price: *Cuckmere Brick Co Ltd* v *Mutual Finance Ltd* [1971] Ch 949; *Standard Chartered Bank Ltd* v *Walker* [1982] 1 WLR 1410; *Skipton Building Society v Stott* [2000] 2 All ER 779, [2000] 1 All ER (Comm) 257, sub nom *Stott v Skipton Building Society* [1999] All ER (D) 1408, CA. See also *Brutan Investments Pty Ltd v Underwriting and Insurance Ltd* (1980) 58 FLR 289; *Sterne* v *Victoria & Grey Trust Co* (1984) 14 DLR (4th) 193; *Wood v Bank of Nova Scotia* (1980) 112 DLR (3d) 181.

9 See *Re White Rose Cottage* [1965] Ch 940, [1965] 1 All ER 11, CA. Under the Conveyancing Act 1881, s 21 (2), the conveyance in order that the purchaser might get the protection of the statute had to be made 'in professed exercise of the power of sale'. This is no longer necessary.

10 Ie that the mortgage was made by deed and the mortgage money is due.
11 See *Bailey v Barnes* [1894] 1 Ch 25.

Limits of the protection

20.21 Subsection 104(2) has two aspects. First, it deals with the effect of the conveyance[1] on sale and the title of the purchaser after the conveyance. Although the purchaser's title is expressed to be unimpeachable, and it would appear that the only remedy of anyone injured by an improper exercise of the power of sale is the one in damages specified in the subsection, the immunity for a purchaser is not as absolute as it might seem from the words of the subsection[2]. Secondly, it deals with the investigation of title by the purchaser prior to conveyance. The subsection provides that a purchaser is not 'concerned to see or inquire' whether the power of sale is properly exercised. It does not provide, as was usual in express powers of sale before the Conveyancing Act 1881, that a purchaser shall not be affected by knowledge that the notice required by the power had not been given and other similar provisions. Although a purchaser may not be 'concerned to inquire' whether the exercise of the power of sale is proper, he may, of course, obtain actual notice of the impropriety of the sale without inquiry, or be deemed to have constructive notice of the impropriety from those circumstances of which he has knowledge. Perhaps because of the form of the subsection, with the initial unimpeachability part linked to the latter part by the conjunction 'and' (thus importing the limitation in the latter part into the first part)[3], it now appears to be generally accepted[4] that the conveyance may be set aside if the purchaser takes with knowledge of any impropriety in the sale[5]. That appears to be the case whether the knowledge is actual[6] or constructive (in the sense of what would have come to the purchaser's knowledge had he not shut his eyes to suspicious circumstances, rather than the usual sense related to failure to inquire) notice[7]. Since inquiries might lead to a purchaser having notice of an irregularity in the exercise of the sale, then, subject to the point about constructive notice referred to, it is probably better for him to refrain from making any inquiries in relation to the mortgage.

1 Which includes an assignment of leasehold land: Law of Property Act 1925, s 205 (1) (ii).
2 (1983) 127 Sol Jo 487, 488 (Davey).
3 An alternative construction is that the first part of the subsection, dealing with the effect of the conveyance and stating that the purchaser's title shall not be impeachable, cannot be cut down by the latter part (whatever that part might mean) which deals with the purchaser's position *prior* to conveyance.
4 See Croft *Mortgagee's Power of Sale* paras 183–187; Sykes *The Law of Securities* (4th edn) pp 117–120; Fairest *Mortgages* (2nd edn, 1980) pp 95–96; Wylie *Irish Land Law* pp 591–592; [1988] Conv 317 (HWW); [1989] Conv 412 (Robinson); and also *Pasquarella* v *National Australia Finance Ltd* [1987] 1 NZLR 312 at 315-318.
5 *Selwyn v Garfitt* (1888) 38 Ch D 273; *Waring (Lord) v London and Manchester Assurance Co Ltd* [1935] Ch 310 at 318, CA; *Northern Developments (Holdings) Ltd v UDT Securities* [1977] 1 All ER 747, [1976] 1 WLR 1230; *Holohan v Friends Provident and Century Life Office* [1966] IR 1; *Forsyth v Blundell* (1973) 129 CLR 477. See eg *Jenkins v Jones* (1860) 2 Giff 99 (a case under an express power of sale; selling despite principal and instalment having been tendered). To uphold the title of a purchaser who had notice of impropriety or irregularity in the exercise of the power of sale would be to convert the provisions of the statute into an instrument of fraud: *Bailey v Barnes* [1894] 1 Ch 25 at 30, per Stirling J, but note that this statement was made in relation to s 21 (2) of the Conveyancing Act 1881, which is reproduced in the first part only of s 104(2).
6 On express powers, see *Jenkins v Jones* (1860) 2 Giff 99; *Parkinson v Hanbury* (1860) 1 Drew & Sm 143 (this point was not considered on appeal); *Selwyn v Garfit* (1888) 38 Ch

D 273, CA (where, in each case, a purchaser with actual notice was not protected by the express relieving provision).

7 *Holohan v Friends Provident Century Life Office*, above (where the combination of s 21 (2) of the Conveyancing Act 1881 and s 5 (1) of the Conveyancing Act 1911 are equivalent to s 104 (2)); *Bailey v Barnes*, above (where both actual and constructive notice were considered); but s 21 (2) of the Conveyancing Act 1881 has no equivalent of the latter part of s 104 (2) and the constructive notice aspect was founded upon s 3 (1) of the Conveyancing Act 1882 which was a general provision restricting constructive notice (not specifically related to a purchaser on a mortgagee sale and which formed the basis of the Law of Property Act 1925, s 199(1); as to which, see **24.27**)), and see *Forsyth v Blundell* (1973) 129 CLR 477 at 499–503, and at first instance sub nom *Associated Securities Ltd v Blundell* (1971) 19 FLR 17.

MODE OF SALE: THE MORTGAGEE'S RIGHTS AND DUTIES

GENERAL NATURE OF MORTGAGEE'S RIGHTS AND DUTIES[1]

20.22 The power of sale is given to the mortgagee for his own benefit, to enable him the better to realise his debt[2]. Accordingly, his own interests come before those of the mortgagor[3]. The mortgagee is not a trustee of his own power of sale for the mortgagor[4] and nor is he under a general duty of care to the mortgagor[5]. He can, therefore, act in his own interests in deciding whether or not to exercise his power of sale[6]. If the mortgagee does decide to exercise his power of sale, he can likewise act in his own interest in deciding when to exercise it[7], subject to his duty to obtain the best price reasonably obtainable[8]. He is entitled to sell even though a sale (or the time, or the terms, of the sale) may be disadvantageous to the mortgagor[9].

However, while the mortgagee may look to his own interests, he must nevertheless pay some regard to the interests of the mortgagor. Thus, the mortgagee owes a general duty in equity to the mortgagor and to others with an interest in the equity of redemption (including subsequent incumbrancers) to act in good faith and to use his powers for proper purposes[10]. Insofar as consistent with the mortgagee's right to put his own interests first, the mortgagee must act fairly towards the mortgagor. Where their interests conflict, he is not entitled to act in a manner which unfairly prejudices or wilfully and recklessly sacrifices the interests of the mortgagor[11]. Depending on the particular facts and circumstances of the case, he may also owe other duties in equity; the equitable obligations are flexible and will be adjusted to fit the requirements of the time[12].

Subject to those duties, the court will not inquire into his motives for exercising (or not exercising) the power of sale[13]. While the court may interfere with the exercise of the power at the instance of those interested in the proceeds of sale[14], it will not interfere merely to prevent its exercise contrary to the wishes of the mortgagor. Nor, it has been said[15], will the court interfere (except on terms of payment of the mortgage debt), because the mortgagee is seeking some collateral object and not merely the payment of his debt[16]. An equitable mortgagee, whether selling under the statutory power or a power of attorney, owes the same duty as the legal mortgagee[17]. The mortgagee is not answerable for any involuntary loss happening in the exercise of the statutory power of sale or of any power or provision in the mortgage deed[18].

Although there is no reason, in principle, why a mortgage deed cannot provide that, in the exercise of the power of sale, the mortgagee should be able to act as an absolute beneficial owner and in such manner as he, in his absolute discretion, thinks fit[19], such clauses will be narrowly construed in application of the *contra proferentem* rule[20]. However, given that the mortgagee's duties are in equity, and not in tort or contract, the Unfair Contract Terms Act 1977 will have no application to such clauses[21].

A receiver is equally subject to the above duties of the mortgagee[22]. The circumstances in which a mortgagee may be liable for the actions of a receiver, and the additional duties to which a receiver is subject, have been considered in Chapter 18[23].

1 For the law in Australia, see (1998) 6 APLJ 1-20 (Kelly). For similar duties owed in relation to the appointment of a receiver, see **18.6** and **18.9**.

2 *Warner v Jacob* (1882) 20 Ch D 220 at 224; *Palk v Mortgage Services Funding plc* [1993] Ch 330 at 337; *Re Potters Oils Ltd* [1986] 1 WLR 201 at 206

3 *Palk v Mortgage Services Funding plc* [1993] Ch 330 at 337; *Re Potters Oils Ltd* [1986] 1 WLR 201 at 206. And see eg *Warner v Jacob* (1882) 20 Ch D 220 at 234; *Farrar v Farrars Ltd* (1888) 40 Ch D 395 at 398; *Palmer v Barclays Bank Ltd* (1971) 23 P & CR 30; *Lake Apartments Ltd v Bootwala* (1973) 37 DLR (3d) 523; *Forsyth v Blundell* (1973) 129 CLR 477 at 483, 494. Also Law Commission Working Paper no 99, *Land Mortgages*, para 3.71.

4 *Colson v Williams* (1889) 58 LJ Ch 539 at 540; *Kennedy v De Trafford* [1897] AC 180; *Bishop v Bonham* [1988] 1 WLR 742 at 749; *Cuckmere Brick Co Ltd v Mutual Finance Ltd* [1971] Ch 949 at 965, 969, [1971] 2 All ER 633 at 643, 647, CA. See also *Frost Ltd v Ralph* (1981) 1115 DLR (3d) 612 at 622; *Suskind v Bank of Nova Scotia* (1984) 10 DLR (4th) 101 at 107-108; *Commercial & General Acceptance Ltd v Nixon* (1981) 152 CLR 491 at 494, 502, 515; *Halifax Property Corpn Pty Ltd v GIFC Ltd* (1987) 4 BPR 9708 at 9710. Cf *Yarrangah Pty Ltd v National Australia Bank Ltd* (1999) 9 BPR 17061 at 17062, suggesting a mortgagee may be a trustee of his power of sale in some circumstances; and *Sterne v Victoria & Grey Trust Co* (1984) 14 DLR (4th) 193; *Hospital Products Ltd v United States Surgical Corpn* (1984) 156 CLR 41 at 102. For consideration of nineteenth century authorities and the policy then applied, see *Australia and New Zealand Banking Group Ltd v Comer* (1993) 5 BPR 11748 at 9710; and also *Marquis of Cholmondley v Clinton* (1817) 2 Mer 171; *Robertson v Norris* (1857) 1 Giff 421. See also generally Waters *The Constructive Trust* Ch III.

5 *Downsview Nominees Ltd v First City Corpn* [1993] AC 295 at 315. See also **18.6** (appointment of a receiver).

6 *China and South Sea Bank Ltd v Tan Soon Gin* [1990] 1 AC 536; *Routestone Ltd v Minories Finance Ltd* [1997] BCC 180 at 187; and even if professionally advised to sell: *Lloyds Bank plc v Bryant* [1996] NPC 31. See also *Mailman v Challenge Bank Ltd* (1991) 5 BPR 11721.

7 *China and South Sea Bank Ltd v Tan Soon Gin* [1990] 1 AC 536; *Reliance Permanent Building Society v Harwood-Stamper* [1944] Ch 362 at 372, [1944] 2 All ER 75 at 80, per Vaisey J; *Cuckmere Brick Co v Mutual Finance Ltd*, above, at 965, 969; 644, 646; *Re Potters Oils Ltd (No 2)* [1986] 1 All ER 890, [1986] 1 WLR 201. Cf *Standard Chartered Bank Ltd v Walker* [1982] 1 WLR 1410 at 1415; *Wood v Bank of Nova Scotia* (1979) 10 RPR 156, affd (1980) 112 DLR (3d) 181; *Suskind v Bank of Nova Scotia* (1984) 10 DLR (4th) 101.

8 See **20.23**. The mortgagee is not bound to postpone the sale in the hope of obtaining a better price later: *Tse Kwang Lam v Wong Chit Sen* [1983] 3 All ER 54, [1983] 1 WLR 1349, PC; and see *Australian and New Zealand Banking Group Ltd v Bangadilly Pastoral Co Pty Ltd* (1978) 139 CLR 195; *Bank of Cyprus (London) Ltd v Gill* [1979] 2 Lloyd's Rep 508, CA; *Commercial and General Acceptance Ltd v Nixon* (1981) 152 CLR 491, but he must allow sufficient time to permit proper advertising etc so that the best price obtainable may be obtained: *Standard Chartered Bank Ltd v Walker* [1982] 3 All ER 938, [1982] 1 WLR 1410, CA. Delay might be required if there were very clear signs that the property market was improving rapidly and substantially: *Dimmick v Pearce Investments Pty Ltd* (1981) 43 FLR 235; and see *Bank of Cyprus (London) Ltd v Gill*, above. The mortgagee need not give the mortgagor time to try and sell: *Bank of Cyprus (London) Ltd v Gill*, above.

9 See *Farrar v Farrars Ltd* (1888) 40 Ch D 395 at 411; *Sterne v Victoria & Grey Trust Co* (1984) 14 DLR (4th) 193.

10 *Cuckmere Brick Co Ltd v Mutual Finance Ltd* [1971] Ch 949, [1971] 2 All ER 633; *Burgess v Auger* [1998] 2 BCLC 478 at 482; *Yorkshire Bank v Hall* [1999] 1 WLR 1713 at 1728. See also *Robertson v Norris* (1857) 1 Giff 421 at 424-425; *Australia & New Zealand Banking Corpn Ltd v Banagadilly Pastoral Co Pty Ltd* (1978) 139 CLR 193 at 201.

11 *Palk v Mortgage Services Funding plc* [1993] Ch 330; *Forsyth v Blundell* (1973) 129 CLR 477 at 494, per Walsh J; and see *Kennedy v de Trafford* [1897] AC 180 at 185; *Predeth v Castle Phillips Finance Co Ltd* (1986) 279 Estates Gazette 1355, CA; noted at [1986] Conv 442 (Thompson); and also *Barns v Queensland National Bank Ltd* (1906) 3 CLR 925; *Pendlebury*

v Colonial Mutual Life Assurance Society, Ltd (1912) 13 CLR 676; *Henry Roach (Petroleum) Pty Ltd v Credit House (Victoria) Pty Ltd* [1976] VR 309; *Commercial and General Acceptance Ltd v Nixon* (1981) 152 CLR 491. Some overseas jurisdictions specifically require the selling mortgagee to have regard to the interests of the mortgagor: see eg Transfer of Land Act (Vic) 1958, s 77 (1); *Goldcel Nominees Pty Ltd v Network Finance Ltd* [1983] 2 VR 257.

12 *Medforth v Blake* [2000] Ch 86, [1999] 3 All ER 97.

13 See *Belton v Bass, Ratcliffe and Gretton Ltd* [1992] 2 Ch 449 at 465.

14 *Jarrett v Barclays Bank Ltd* [1947] Ch 187, [1947] 1 All ER 72, CA; and see *Clark v National Mutual Life Association of Australasia Ltd* [1966] NZLR 196.

15 *Nash v Eads* (1880) 25 Sol Jo 95, CA, per Sir George Jessell (considered in *Australia & New Zealand Banking Corpn Ltd v Comer* (1993) 5 BPR 11748 at 11751-11752); and see *Belton v Bass, Ratcliffe and Gretton* [1922] 2 Ch 449 at 465–466.

16 Subject to the mortgagee's duty to exercise its power of sale for proper purposes and in good faith.

17 See *Palmer v Barclays Bank Ltd* (1971) 23 P & CR 30.

18 Where the mortgage was executed after 31 December 1911: Law of Property Act, s 106(3) (following s 21(6) of the Conveyancing Act 1881 as amended by the Conveyancing Act 1911).

19 *Bishop v Bonham* [1988] 1 WLR 742 at 752. In the same way as trustees' administrative powers are commonly extended. This would not exclude a fraudulent exercise of the power of sale, but should exclude claims for the negligent exercise of the power of sale: see (1981) 55 ALJ 559, 572 (Tyler) and see *American Express International Banking Corpn v Hurley* [1985] 3 All ER 564 at 571, per Mann J. And see Law Commission Working Paper no 99, Land Mortgages, para 3.71.

20 *Bishop v Bonham* [1988] 1 WLR 742 at 753-754; *American Express International Banking Corpn v Hurley* [1985] 3 All ER 564; *McManus v Royal Bank* (1983) 47 CBR (NS) 252; *Standard Chartered Bank v Walker* [1982] 1 WLR 1410. As to construction of exemption clauses generally, see *Ailsa Craig Fishing v Malvern Fishing* [1983] 1 WLR 964; *George Mitchell Ltd v Finney Lock Seeds Ltd* [1983] 2 AC 803.

21 *Yorkshire Bank v Hall* [1999] 1 WLR 1713; *Medforth v Blake* [2000] Ch 86; *Raja v Lloyds TSB Bank Ltd* [2001] EWCA Civ 210, (2001) 82 P & CR 191.

22 *Medforth v Blake* [2000] Ch 86; *Standard Chartered Bank Ltd v Walker* [1982] 3 All ER 938, [1982] 1 WLR 1410, CA; *American Express International Banking Corpn v Hurley* [1985] 3 All ER 564 and see *Kernohan Estates Ltd v Boyd* [1967] NI 27; *Expo International Pty Ltd v Chant* [1979] 2 NSWLR 820. The handling of rents and profits by a receiver will be subject to less rigorous surveillance by equity than that by a mortgagee in possession: *Refuge Assurance Co Ltd v Pearlberg* [1938] Ch 687 at 691–692; *Yorkshire Bank plc v Hall* [1999] 1 WLR 1713 at 1728, per Robert Walker, LJ.

23 See **18.6–18.9**.

DUTY TO OBTAIN BEST PRICE REASONABLY OBTAINABLE

20.23 If the mortgagee decides to exercise his power of sale, he is under a specific duty to take reasonable care to obtain the best price reasonably available at the time, which will normally equate with the current market value[1]. This duty arises in equity, rather than in tort or contract[2]. The same duty is owed to other mortgagees[3] and a guarantor of the mortgage debt[4] but not to a tenant at will of the mortgaged property[5], and not, where the mortgagor is a trustee, to a beneficiary of that trust[6]. The same duty is owed whether the power of sale is statutory, express, or under a power of attorney[7]. The mortgagee will not be adjudged to be in default unless he is plainly on the wrong side of the line[8].

A mortgagee, who is selling, need not consult the mortgagor nor subsequent incumbrancers and does not limit his freedom of action by electing to keep them informed of the progress of negotiations[9]. A mortgagee is not under a duty to obtain the best available price where it co-operates with the mortgagors to effect a sale at a lower price, because such a sale is more satisfactory to the mortgagors for other reasons[10].

The burden of proof is on the mortgagor, or other person seeking to set aside the sale, to prove breach of this duty by the mortgagee[11]. In view of the sufficient equity in the property required by most mortgagees, a sale at just above the sum to discharge the mortgage may be looked at carefully by the court, but that is not to say that there may not be occasions when that sum is the proper price or true market value. The fact a property has been repossessed by a mortgagee may often cause the property to sell at a reduced price[12]. The fact that the property is resold shortly after the mortgagee sale for a substantially higher price is a matter of suspicion[13]. Often, however, an alleged undervalue will merely be the difference in the opinions of several valuers[14]. Where the property is subject to a right of pre-emption binding on the mortgagee, there is nothing more the mortgagee can do than offer the property to the person with the benefit of the right[15], or, possibly, depending on the wording of the right, foreclose, rather than sell.

The mortagee should follow up the possibility of a sale at a higher price[16]. To accept less in a private sale than a prospective purchaser, with means, has indicated he would bid at a proposed auction may be a breach of the mortgagee's duty; the mortgagee has to balance a higher offer, which is not firm, against a lower firm offer which will be withdrawn if not accepted within a specified period[17]. If possible, interested parties should be put in a position where they are required to compete with one another[18]. However, once a binding contract for sale has been made, the mortgagee is bound to complete that sale even though a higher offer is made[19]. Such an offer can put the mortgagee in a difficult position, because, if it is a serious and realistic one, it may give rise to an argument that the mortgagee has not obtained the best price reasonably obtainable. However, there is nothing the mortgagee can do about this, unless he can properly get out of the contract and the offer is still open. A mortgagee who has contracted to sell, but before the land has become vested in the purchaser has properly rescinded, and who later sells at a lower price, is only accountable for the purchase money received[20].

It was formerly provided by statute that where the mortgagee was a building society, it was required, in exercising any power of sale, to obtain the best price reasonably obtainable[21]. However, with effect from 1 December 1997, any rule of law requiring a mortgagee to take reasonable care to obtain a proper price or true market value has effect as if that, and corresponding earlier enactments, had not been enacted[22].

1 *Downsview Nominees Ltd v First City Corpn Ltd* [1993] AC 295 ((1994) 45 NILQ 61 (Fealy)); [1996] JBL 113 (Lightman J); *Tse Kwong Lam v Wong Chit Sen* [1983] 3 All ER 54, [1983] 1 WLR 1349 at 1355. It has been suggested that this is simply part of the mortgagee's duty to act in good faith: *Forsyth v Blundell* (1973) 129 CLR 477 at 481; see also *Frost v Ralph* (1980) 115 DLR (3d) 612; *Medforth v Blake* [2000] Ch 86. See also *Cuckmere Brick Co Ltd v Mutual Finance Ltd* [1971] Ch 949 at 966 ('proper price' per Cross and Cairns LJJ; 'the true market value' per Salmon LJ); and *Palk v Mortgage Services Funding plc* [1993] Ch 330 at 338; *Matthie v Edwards* (1846) 2 Coll 465 at 480; *Palmer v Barclays Bank Ltd* (1971) 23 P & CR 30; *Barclays Bank v Thienel* [1978] 2 EGLR 116; *Bank of Cyprus (London) Ltd v Gill* [1979] 2 Lloyd's Rep 508, CA; *Standard Chartered Bank Ltd v Walker* [1982] 1 WLR 1410; *American Express International Banking Corpn v Hurley* [1985] 3 All ER 564. It has also been applied, with qualification, in New Zealand: (*Downsview Nominees Ltd v First City Corpn Ltd* (above) was an appeal to the PC from the NZCA) see *Re Blastclean Services Ltd* (1985) 2 NZCLC 99, 282; *Alexandre v New Zealand Breweries Ltd* [1974] 1 NZLR 497, NZCA; *ANZ Banking Group (NZ) Ltd v Gibson* [1981] 2 NZLR 513; *Sullivan v Darkin* [1986] 1 NZLR 214 at 218; in Canada: see eg *McHugh v Union Bank of Canada* [1913] AC 299 at 311; *Gulf and Fraser Fishermen's Union v Calm C Fish Ltd* [1975] 1 Lloyd's Rep 188, BCCA; *Canadian Imperial Bank of Commerce v Haley* (1979) 100 DLR (3d) 470, NBSC; *Bank of Nova Scotia v Barnard* (1984) 9 DLR (4th) 575; in Ireland: see *Holohan v Friends Provident and Century Life Office* [1966] IR 1; and in the Cayman Islands: see *Becker v Bank of Nova Scotia* [1986] LRC (Comm) 638, CA. It has not been applied in Australia:

see the cases referred to in (1975) 53 ALJ 172 (Butt); (1981) 55 ALJ 559 at 572 ff (Tyler); and *Commercial and General Acceptance Ltd v Nixon* (1981) 152 CLR 491; *Goldcel Nominees Pty Ltd v Network Finance Ltd* [1983] 2 VR 257; *Citicorp Australia Ltd v McLoughney* (1984) 35 SASR 375; *Cachalot Nominees Pty Ltd v Prime Nominees Pty Ltd* [1984] WAR 380, SCWA; and see (1983) 57 ALJ 238 (Butt). See also **20.22**, n 8.

2 *Downsview Nominees Ltd v First City Corpn Ltd* [1993] 2 AC 295 at 315; see also *Parker-Tweedale v Dunbar Bank plc* [1991] Ch 12 at 18-19; *Palk v Mortgage Services Funding plc* [1993] Ch 330 at 338; *AIB Finance Ltd v Debtors* [1998] 1 BCLC 665 CA; *Medforth v Blake* [2000] Ch 86 at 102; *Raja v Lloyds TSB Bank Ltd* [2001] EWCA Civ 210 (explaining *Bishop v Bonham* [1988] 1 WLR 742); and [1990] Conv 431 (Beatty). Cases in which the duty has been put in tort (eg *Knight v Lawrence* [1993] BCLC 215) would therefore appear to be incorrect.

3 The mortgagee having an interest in the equity of redemption: *Tomlin v Luce* (1889) 43 Ch D 191. See also *National Westminster Finance New Zealand Ltd v United Finance and Securities Ltd* [1988] 1 NZLR 226; *Suskind v Bank of Nova Scotia* (1984) 10 DLR (4th) 101; *Alliance Acceptance Co Ltd v Graham* [1974–75] 10 SASR 220 (SASC) (third mortgagee obtained injunction restraining sale); *Cuckmere Brick Co Ltd v Mutual Finance Ltd* [1971] Ch 949; *Midland Bank Ltd v Joliman Finance Ltd* (1967) 203 Estates Gazette 1039 (second mortgagee against selling first mortgagee). For assignment of the right to sue for an alleged sale by a mortgagee at an undervalue by a trustee in bankruptcy to a former bankrupt, see *Martin v Lewis* [1985] ACLD 630.

4 See *China v South Sea Bank v Tan* [1990] 1 AC 536 at 544, 545; *Medforth v Blake* [2000] Ch 86 at 98; *Yorkshire Bank v Hall* [1999] 1 WLR 1713 at 1728. Also *Standard Chartered Bank Ltd v Walker* [1982] 3 All ER 938, [1982] 1 WLR 1410, CA, doubting *Barclays Bank Ltd v Thienel* (1978) 247 Estates Gazette 385 and *Latchford v Beirne* [1981] 3 All ER 705; *American Express International Banking Corpn v Hurley* [1985] 3 All ER 564; *Clark v UDC Finance Ltd* [1985] 2 NZLR 636; *Canadian Imperial Bank of Commerce v Haley* (1979) 100 DLR (3d) 470, NBSC. See [1981] Conv 329 (Davies and Palmer); (1978) 52 ALJ 581 (JGS); (1979) 53 ALJ 102–3 (correspondence). In Australia the duty has been expressed as one to creditors of the mortgagor generally: see *Expo International Pty Ltd v Chant* [1979] 2 NSWLR 820, and see per Milmo J in *Latchford v Beirne* [1981] 3 All ER 705 at 709; but this case was doubted in *Standard Chartered Bank Ltd v Walker*, above.

5 *Jarrett v Barclays Bank* [1947] Ch 187, [1947] 1 All ER 72.

6 *Parker-Tweedale v Dunbar Bank plc* [1991] Ch 12; consider also *Hayim v Citibank NA* [1987] AC 730 at 748.

7 For sale under power of attorney, see *Alexandre v New Zealand Breweries Ltd* [1974] 1 NZLR 497.

8 *Cuckmere Brick Co Ltd v Mutual Finance Ltd* [1971] Ch 949 at 969; see eg *Minah v Bank of Ireland* [1995] EGCS 144.

9 *G Merel & Co Ltd v Barclays Bank* (1963) 107 Sol Jo 542. A failure to do so may sometimes be an indication of a lack of good faith: *Australia and New Zealand Banking Group Ltd v Bangdilly Pastoral Co Pty Ltd* (1978) 139 CLR 195; *Goldcel Nominees Pty Ltd v Network Finance Ltd* [1983] 2 VR 257.

10 *Merchantile Credit Co Ltd v Clarke* (1995) 71 P & CR D18, CA.

11 *Haddington Island Quarry Co Ltd v Huson* [1911] AC 727, PC; *Australia and New Zealand Banking Group Ltd v Bangadilly Pastoral Co Pty Ltd* (1978) 139 CLR 195. As to the standard of evidence required, see also *Hausman v O'Grady* (1988) 42 DLR (4th) 119 at 131-132; affd 57 DLR (4th) 480 (cogent evidence required); *McKean v Mahoney* [1988] 1 Qd R 628 at 634-635 (mortgagor not required to produce evidence of would-be purchasers at a higher price).

12 *Canadian Imperial Bank of Commerce v Whitman* (1985) 12 DLR (4th) 326.

13 *Bank of Cyprus (London) Ltd v Gill*, above; *Predeth v Castle Phillips Finance Co Ltd* (1986) 279 Estates Gazette 1355, CA; noted at [1986] Com 442 (Thomson). Also see *Midland Bank Ltd v Joliman Finance Ltd*, above.

14 *Cottenham Park Developments Ltd v Cohen* (1967) 202 Estates Gazette 917; *Sinfield v Sweet* [1967] 3 All ER 479, [1967] 1 WLR 1489; *Pallant v Porter* (1972) 233 Estates Gazette 391; *Waltham Forest London Borough v Webb* (1974) 232 Estates Gazette 461; *Johnson v Ribbins* (1975) 235 Estates Gazette 757.

15 *First National Securities Ltd v Chiltern District Council* [1975] 2 All ER 766; *Williams v Wellingborough Borough Council* [1975] 3 All ER 462, [1975] 1 WLR 1327, CA. For rights of pre-emption on a sale by a local authority and for vesting orders under the Housing Act 1985, see **20.55**. For shares subject to pre-emption rights, see *Hunter v Hunter* [1936] AC 222, HL; *Champagne Perrier-Jouet SA v HH Finch Ltd* [1982] 3 All ER 713, [1982] 1 WLR 1359.

16 *Australia and New Zealand Banking Group Ltd v Bangadilly Pastoral Co Pty Ltd* (1978) 139 CLR 195.
17 *Forsyth v Blundell* (1973) 129 CLR 477; *Midland Bank Ltd v Joliman Finance Ltd*, above. On exploiting the competition, see *Brutan Investments Pty Ltd v Underwriting and Insurance Ltd* (1982) 39 ACTR 47; *Dimmick v Pearce Investments Pty Ltd* (1981) 43 FLR 235. See also *Goldcel Nominees Pty Ltd v Network Finance Ltd* [1983] 2 VR 257; *Johnson v Ribbins* (1975) 235 Estates Gazette 757; *Davey v Durrant* (1857) 1 De G & J 535.
18 *Forsyth v Blundell* (1973) 129 CLR 477.
19 *Casey v Irish Intercontinental Bank Ltd* [1979] IR 364; cf a sale by a liquidator which was subject to the approval of the court: *Van Hool McArdle Ltd v Rohan Industrial Estates Ltd* [1980] IR 237.
20 *Wright v New Zealand Farmers' Co-operative Association of Canterbury Ltd* [1939] AC 439, [1939] 2 All ER 701, PC. Even though the rescission is technically proper, a mortgagor could argue that any reasonable vendor would have waived the default, etc. Whether there is any merit in such argument will depend on the circumstances.
21 Building Societies Act 1986, s 13 (7), Sch 4, para 1. *Reliance Permanent Building Society v Harwood-Stamper* [1944] Ch 362, [1944] 2 All ER 75; *Cotterill v Steyning and Littlehampton Building Society* [1966] 2 All ER 295; *Cuckmere Brick Co Ltd v Mutual Finance Ltd* [1971] Ch 949, [1971] 2 All ER 633, CA.
22 Building Societies Act 1997, s 12(2), brought into force by the Building Societies Act 1997 (Commencement No 3) Order 1997, SI 1997/2668. See **12.76**.

MODE OF SALE

20.24 The above duties on the part of the mortgagee give rise to particular obligations in relation to the manner in which the sale is carried out.

Property included in sale

20.25 Where the mortgagor is running a business on the mortgaged property and the mortgagee has taken possession of premises, or put a receiver in to manage them, and then decides to exercise his power of sale, the mortgagee should consider how the combined assets can be realised most profitably[1]. It may be appropriate to include in the sale of commercial premises any goodwill[2] and licences[3]. Where the security consisted of a farm and a milk quota, and the mortgagee had no power to sell the quota separately without the co-operation of the mortgagor, the mortgagee was free to decide whether it preferred the simple course of selling the land so it carried the quota, or taking the risk of trying to arrange a separate sale of the quota in co-operation with the mortgagor. The mortgagee owed no duty to the mortgagor in making that decision — the limit of its duty was to obtain a proper market price for the land when sold in circumstances where it would carry the quota with it[4]. Where there are several properties or items in the security, the mortgagee, in selling what he does sell, must not deliberately destroy the value of the whole or the set, so that, for example, he could not properly sell seven of a set of eight antique chairs[5]. The mortgagee does not have the power to sever fixtures from the property and sell them separately, unless there is an express or implied term of the mortgage to that effect[6]. Mortgagees may join in selling together different properties, or different interests in the same property, where it is clearly beneficial to do so, but they must see that the purchase money is properly apportioned by their own valuers before the completion of the purchaser[7].

1 *AIB Finance Ltd v Debtors* [1997] 2 BCLC 354; *AIB Finance Ltd v Debtors* [1998] 1 BCLC 665, CA; *Medforth v Blake* [2000] Ch 86 at 102.
2 *Holohan v Friends Provident and Century Life Office* [1966] IR 1.
3 *Palmer v Barclays Bank Ltd* (1971) 23 P & CR 30. *Alexandre v New Zealand Breweries Ltd*

[1974] 1 NZLR 497, NZCA. In *Bank of Cyprus (London) Ltd v Gill* [1979] 2 Lloyd's Rep 508; affd [1980] 2 Lloyd's Rep 51, CA, the bank had acted properly in closing down the hotel. For fixtures, see **20.6**, nn 13, 14, **20.40** and **20.41**.
4 *Huish v Ellis* [1995] BCC 462.
5 *Champagne Perrier-Jouet SA v H H Finch Ltd* [1982] 3 All ER 713 at 725, [1982] 1 WLR 1359 at 1372 per Walton J.
6 *Re Yates* (1888) 38 Ch D 112.
7 *Hiatt v Hillman* (1871) 19 WR 694; *Re Cooper and Allen's Contract* (1876) 4 Ch D 802. See **20.6**, n 12.

Preparing the property for sale

20.26 When selling tenanted property which would realise a much higher price with vacant possession, the mortgagee should, in appropriate cases, attempt to obtain vacant possession[1]. The mortgagee will be in breach of his duty where a receiver appointed by him fails to serve rent review notices in time, reducing the value of the reversion on sale[2].

1 *Holohan v Friends Provident and Century Life Office* [1966] IR 1. If he does not, he is also likely to be in breach of his vendor's obligation to give vacant possession on completion.
2 *Knight* v *Lawrence* [1993] BCLC 215.

Manner of sale

20.27 The mortgagee will need to consider whether a sale by auction, or tender, or by private treaty would be more appropriate, where appropriate seeking expert advice[1]. Sale by auction is the usual method[2]. Although sale by auction does not necessarily prove the validity of a transaction[3], generally the mortgagee can safely accept the highest bid for a properly described and advertised property at a properly publicised auction[4]. The auction must be held in reasonable conditions[5]. Whatever the mode of sale, it should be properly advertised[6]. Advertisements must be sufficient in number and content and location to reach the appropriate market and, in the case of an auction, sufficiently in advance to permit prospective purchasers to attend[7]. Inquiries by potential purchasers should be properly dealt with. All material planning permissions known to the mortgagee should be advertised in good time before the sale[8]. The particulars of sale should be free from misstatement[9]. A low reserve at an auction is a matter for suspicion[10]. The disclosure of a reserve price to an intending purchaser may be a breach of the mortgagee's duty[11].

1 *Tse Kwong Lam v Wong Chit Sen* [1983] 1 WLR 1349 at 1357, 1359. See also *National Westminster Finance New Zealand Ltd v United Finance and Securities Ltd* [1988] 1 NZLR 226.
2 The sale must be by auction where the advance was made under the Small Dwellings Acquisition Acts, see **20.54**. See also *Frost v Ralph* (1980) 115 DLR (3d) 612; *Swerus v Central Mortgage Registry of Australia Pty Ltd* (1988) NSW Conv R 55.407.
3 *Tse Kwong Lam v Wong Chit Sen* [1983] 3 All ER 54, [1983] 1 WLR 1349, PC, and see *Bank of Cyprus (London) Ltd v Gill* [1979] 2 Lloyd's Rep 508, CA; *Australia and New Zealand Banking Group Ltd v Bangadilly Pastoral Co Pty Ltd* (1978) 139 CLR 195; *Forsyth v Blundell* (1973) 129 CLR 477. There is no legal duty simpliciter for a mortgagee on sale to negotiate with the highest bidder nor to treat with the mortgagor if he be the highest bidder: *Stoyanovich v National Westminster Finance* (1984) 3 BPR 9310, SCNSW.
4 *Cuckmere Brick Co Ltd v Mutual Finance Ltd* [1979] Ch 949 at 965, [1971] 2 All ER 633 at 643 respectively, per Salmon LJ. For a startling example, see *Bank of Montreal v Allender Investments Ltd* (1983) 4 DLR (4th) 340.
5 *Standard Chartered Bank Ltd v Walker* [1982] 3 All ER 938, [1982] 1 WLR 1410, CA.
6 *American Express International Banking Corpn v Hurley* [1985] 3 All ER 564; *Skipton Building*

Society v Stott [2000] 2 All ER 779, [2000] 1 All ER (Comm) 257, [1999] All ER (D) 1408. See also *Pendlebury v Colonial Mutual Life Assurance Society Ltd* (1912) 13 CLR 676; *Henry Roach (Petroleum) Pty Ltd v Credit House (Vic) Pty Ltd* [1976] VR 309; *Commercial and General Acceptance Ltd v Nixon* (1981) 152 CLR 491; *McKean v Maloney* [1988] 1 Qd R 628; *National Westminster Finance New Zealand Ltd v United Finance and Securities Ltd* [1988] 1 NZLR 226. Cf *Davey v Durrant* (1857) 1 De G & J 535 at 560.

7 *Australian and New Zealand Banking Group Ltd v Bangadilly Pastoral Co Pty Ltd* (1978) 139 CLR 195; *Commercial and General Acceptance Ltd v Nixon* (1981) 152 CLR 491; *Standard Chartered Bank Ltd v Walker* [1982] 3 All ER 938, [1982] 1 WLR 1410, CA.

8 *Cuckmere Brick Co Ltd v Mutual Finance Ltd*, above; *Alexandre v New Zealand Breweries Ltd* [1974] 1 NZLR 497, NZCA; *Palmer v Barclays Bank Ltd* (1971) 23 P & CR 30; *Brutan Investments Pty Ltd v Underwriting and Insurance Ltd* (1980) 39 ACTR 47; *Commercial and General Acceptance Ltd v Nixon* (1981) 152 CLR 491. See also *National Westminster Finance New Zealand Ltd v United Finance and Securities Ltd* [1988] 1 NZLR 226 (failure of mortgagee to advertise potential to convert building by sub-division).

9 *Wolf v Vanderzee* (1869) 17 WR 547; *Tomlin v Luce* (1889) 43 Ch D 191; *Cuckmere Brick v Mutual Finance* [1971] Ch 949; *Medforth v Blake* [2000] Ch 86 at 99.

10 *Dimmick v Pearce Investments Pty Ltd* (1981) 43 FLR 235.

11 *Barns v Queensland National Bank Ltd* (1906) 3 CLR 925 at 944; *Australian and New Zealand Banking Group Ltd v Bangadilly Pastoral Co Pty Ltd*, above; *Goldcel Nominees Pty Ltd v Network Finance Ltd* [1983] 2 VR 257; *Tse Kwong Lam v Wong Chit Sen* [1983] 1 WLR 1349 at 1358; *Reid v Royal Trust Corpn of Canada* (1985) 20 DLR (4th) 223.

Conditions of sale

20.28 The mortgagee should avoid the use of unnecessarily stringent conditions of sale. Conditions commonly used by conveyancers are, as a general rule, safe for mortgagees. They will not, however, be restrained from adding such further conditions, adapted to the state of the title, as may be reasonably used in the disposal of his property by a prudent owner, anxious to protect himself against the risk and expense of litigation. It is as much for the benefit of the mortgagor as of the mortgagee to avoid that risk. The proper avoidance of such risk will outweigh the possible diminution in the number and value of the biddings which may be caused by the conditions[1].

1 *Hobson v Bell* (1839) 2 Beav 17; *Kershaw v Kalow* (1855) 1 Jur NS 974; *Falkner v Equitable Reversionary Society* (1858) 4 Drew 352. See *Cragg v Alexander* [1867] WN 305, as to improper conditions on sale of a reversion, and see generally as to conditions on the exercise of the statutory power, Law of Property Act 1925, s 101 (1) (i); **20.6**.

Time of sale

20.29 As stated above[1], it is for the mortgagee to choose the time of sale. The mortgagee is not, therefore, obliged to wait until the market picks up[2], or until the mortgagor's circumstances have improved so as to enable him to discharge the mortgage debt[3]. However, this does not absolve the mortgagee from his duty to fairly and properly expose the property to the market, in order to obtain the best price reasonably available. Thus a mortgagee was liable where it sold a property by privately negotiated contract at a 'crash sale valuation', to achieve an immediate disposal, rather than offering it at an open market value[4].

1 See **20.22.**

2 *Cuckmere Brick v Mutual Finance* [1971] Ch 949 at 965; *Reliance Permanent Building Society v Harwood-Stamper* [1944] Ch 362 at 372; *Bank of Cyprus (London) Ltd v Gill* [1980] 2 Lloyd's Rep 51; *Predeth v Castle Phillips Finance Co Ltd* [1986] 2 EGLR 144; [1986] Conv 442 (MP Thompson). In *Standard Chartered Bank v Walker* [1982] 1 WLR 1410 Lord

Denning suggested at 1415, that it was at least arguable that in choosing the time of sale the mortgagee must exercise a reasonable duty of care; it is submitted that is incorrect, in view of the mortgagee's entitlement to put first his own interests in realising his security.
3 *Routestone Ltd v Minories Finance Ltd* [1997] BCC 180.
4 *Predeth v Castle Phillips Finance Co Ltd* [1986] 2 EGLR 144; [1986] Conv 442 (MP Thompson).

Advice as to the sale

20.30 It may well be appropriate to take specialist advice as to the sale, for example, with regard to valuation, as to the most appropriate mode of sale, as to how best to advertise and as to the appropriate reserve price[1]. The more unusual the property, the more likely a failure on the part of the mortgagee to seek such advice would put him in breach of his duty[2]. However, a mortgagee does not relieve himself of his duty by placing the sale in the hands of reputable agents[3]. Where a mortgagee allowed the mortgagor to attempt to sell the property himself, it was not an implied term of the loan agreement that the mortgagee would not seek to impose unreasonable conditions on the mortgagor in the conduct of any sale and nor did the mortgagee owe any duty to advise on the sale with reasonable skill and care, as it did not give advice as part of its banking activities, and gave the mortgagor a choice about the sale[4].

1 *American Express International Banking Corpn v Hurley* [1985] 3 All ER 564; *Pitman v Top Business Systems* [1984] BCLC 593 at 597; *Tse Kwong Lam v Wong Chit Sen* [1983] 1 WLR 1349 at 1357, 1359.
2 *American Express International Banking Corpn v Hurley* [1985] 3 All ER 564.
3 *Downsview Nominees Ltd v First City Corpn Ltd* [1993] AC 295 at 312; see also *Medforth v Blake* [2000] Ch 86 at 99; *Tomlin v Luce* (1889) 43 Ch D 191 at 194. And see per Cross LJ in *Cuckmere Brick Co Ltd v Mutual Finance Ltd* [1971] Ch 949 at 973 and 649 respectively; and (not so firmly) Salmon LJ at 969 and 646 and Cairns LJ at 980, 655; and also *Commercial and General Acceptance Ltd v Nixon* (1981) 152 CLR 491; *Sterne v Victoria and Grey Trust Co* (1985) 14 DLR (4th) 193; *McKean v Maloney* [1988] 1 Qd R 628. Cf *Routestone Ltd v Minories Finance Ltd* [1997] 1 EGLR 123. For the liability of the agent to the mortgagor, see *Garland v Ralph Pay & Ransom* (1984) 271 Estates Gazette 106; *Predeth v Castle Phillips Finance Co Ltd* (1986) 279 Estates Gazette 1355, CA; noted in [1986] Conv 442 (Thompson); cf *Routestone Ltd v Minories Finance Ltd* [1997] 1 EGLR 123 at 124. See also *Lightman and Moss on the Law of Receivers and Administrators of Companies*, 7-040–7-043.
4 *Morgan v Lloyds Bank plc* [1998] Lloyd's Rep Bank 73, CA.

Receipt of the purchase money

20.31 A mortgagee or his auctioneer may accept the purchaser's cheque for the deposit and, if it is dishonoured, the mortgagee is not liable for the costs of an abortive sale, but may add them to his security[1]. The property may be sold upon terms that part or even the whole of the purchase money shall remain on mortgage, where the mortgagee takes the risk and charges himself in account with the mortgagor with the whole purchase money[2]. With respect to the receipt by the mortgagee of the purchase money, the Law of Property Act 1925 provides that the receipt in writing of a mortgagee[3] shall be a sufficient discharge for any money arising under the power of sale conferred by the Act, or any money or securities comprised in his mortgage, or arising thereunder, and a person paying or transferring the same to the mortgagee shall not be concerned to inquire whether any money remains due under the mortgage[4].

1 *Farrer v Lacy, Hartland & Co* (1885) 25 Ch D 636, affd 31 Ch D 42, CA.
2 *Davey v Durrant* (1857) 1 De G & J 535; *Thurlow v Mackenson* (1868) LR 4 QB 97; *Farrar*

v Farrars Ltd (1888) 40 Ch D 395, CA; *Kennedy v De Trafford* [1897] AC 180, HL; *Belton v Bass, Ratcliffe and Gretton Ltd* [1922] 2 Ch 449; *Northern Developments (Holdings) Ltd v UDT Securities Ltd* [1977] 1 All ER 747, [1976] 1 WLR 1230.

3 Where first and second mortgagees have power to sell and give receipts, they may concur in the sale, the one giving a receipt for so much of the purchase money as will discharge his debt and the other for the balance; *M'Carogher v Whieldon* (1864) 34 Beav 107.

4 Law of Property Act 1925, s 107 (1).

Ships

20.32 The mortgagee of a ship owes the same duty of care in relation to the sale as any other mortgagee[1]. The first step taken by the mortgagee in exercising his power of sale will usually be entering into possession of the ship. Alternatively, he may seek the arrest of the ship in a mortgage claim, followed by an order for appraisement and sale[2]. A sale following arrest is usually by the direction of the court, but in exceptional cases the court might permit the mortgagee to sell[3].

1 See *Gulf and Fraser Fishermen's Union v Calm C Fish Ltd* [1975] 1 Lloyd's Rep 188, BCCA.

2 See, generally, *British Shipping Laws* vol 1.

3 See *The Monmouth Coast* (1922) 12 Ll L Rep 22.

MORTGAGEE MAY NOT PURCHASE

20.33 A sale pursuant to the power of sale must be a real sale. Therefore the mortgagee 'cannot sell to himself either alone or with others, or to a trustee for himself, nor to any one employed by him to conduct the sale'[1], unless the sale is made by the court and he has obtained leave to bid[2]. 'For a sale by a person to himself is no sale at all, and a power of sale does not authorise the donee of the power to take the property subject to it at a price fixed by himself, even though such price be the full value'[3]. The same rule applies to any officer of the mortgagee, or the solicitor or other agent who is acting for the mortgagee in the matter of the sale[4], and to a servant of the mortgagee[5]. However, it does not apply to a solicitor who acted in the creation of the mortgage, but not in the matter of the sale[6]. The rule does not apply to an execution creditor[7].

A sale by a person to a corporation of which he is a member, or a company in which he holds shares is not, either in form or in substance, a sale by a person to himself[8], and is therefore permissible if proper in other respects[9]. Nevertheless, such a sale might be restrained or set aside or ignored[10] on the ground that the mortgagee had not acted in good faith[11], or failed to take reasonable precautions to obtain the best price reasonably obtainable[12]. Further, in view of the conflict of interest and duty involved, the burden of proof is reversed, so that it is incumbent on the mortgagee, if a claim is made against him, to prove that he acted in good faith, or took reasonable care to obtain the best price[13]. As a matter of precaution, it might therefore be advisable in such circumstances to seek a sale by the court. A sale by several co-mortgagors to one of their number is similarly capable of being a real sale[14] and a mortgagee may sell to a subsequent mortgagee, provided the latter has not used his position as mortgagee to get an undue advantage or has otherwise acted in bad faith[15].

1 *Farrar v Farrars Ltd* (1888) 40 Ch D 395 at 409; *Martinson v Clowes* (1882) 21 Ch D 857; on appeal 52 LT 706, CA; *Hodson v Deans* [1903] 2 Ch 647; *Australia and New Zealand Banking Group Ltd v Bangadilly Pastoral Co Pty Ltd* (1978) 139 CLR 195, [1989] Conv 336 (Robinson).

2 *Downes v Grazebrook* (1817) 3 Mer 200; *National Bank of Australasia v United Hand-in-Hand etc, Co* (1879) 4 App Cas 391, PC; *Farrar v Farrars Ltd*, above; *Palk* v *Mortgage Services Funding plc* [1993] Ch 330, [1993] 2 All ER 481; *Williams v Wellingborough Borough Council* [1975] 3 All ER 462, [1975] 1 WLR 1327, CA There is now a provision under the Housing Act 1985 allowing a housing authority mortgagee to vest the property in itself with the approval of the court: see **20.55**).

If the mortgagee is a trustee, he will not have leave to bid if the beneficiary objects, unless attempts to sell to others have failed: *Tennant v Trenchard* (1869) 4 Ch App 537. A way around the rule stated above may be to obtain a money judgment on the personal covenant and then purchase the property on a sale on the execution of that judgment: *Simpson v Forrester* (1973) 47 ALJR 149, 46 ALJ 469, 47 ALJ 544 (Barber).

3 *Farrar v Farrars Ltd* (1888) 40 Ch D 395 at 409; *Martinson v Clowes* (1882) 21 Ch D 857; on appeal 52 LT 706, CA; *Hodson v Deans* [1903] 2 Ch 647.

4 *Martinson v Clowes*, above; *Parnell v Tyler* (1833) 2 LJ Ch 195 (solicitor's clerk): *Hodson v Deans*, above.

5 *Sewell v Agricultural Bank of Western Australia* (1930) 44 CLR 104.

6 *Nutt v Easton* [1899] 1 Ch 873; affd on another point [1900] 1 Ch 29, CA.

7 *Stratford v Twynam* (1822) Jac 418. See n 2, above.

8 *Farrar v Farrars Ltd*, above, at 409, and see *Australian and New Zealand Banking Group Ltd v Bangadilly Pastoral Co Pty Ltd* (1978) 139 CLR 195; *Goldcell Nominees Pty Ltd v Network Finance Ltd* [1983] 2 VR 257; [1984] Conv 143 (Jackson).

9 *Tse Kwong Lam v Wong Chit Sen* [1983] 1 WLR 1349.

10 See *Henderson v Astwood* [1894] AC 150, PC.

11 *Farrar v Farrars Ltd*, above; *Hodson v Deans*, above.

12 *Tse Kwong Lam v Wong Chit Sen* [1983] 3 All ER 54, [1983] 1 WLR 1349, PC.

13 *Tse Kwong Lam v Wong Chit Sen* [1983] 1 WLR 1349.

14 *Kennedy v De Trafford* [1897] AC 180, HL; followed in *Re Nunes and District Registrar for the District of Winnipeg* (1972) 21 DLR (3d) 97.

15 *Parkinson v Hanbury* (1860) 1 Drew & Sm 143; *Shaw v Bunny* (1864) 33 Beav 494; affd 2 De GJ & Sm 468; *Kirkwood v Thompson* (1865) 2 Hem & M 392; *Flower & Sons v Pritchard* (1908) 53 Sol Jo 178; *Kennedy v De Trafford* [1897] AC 180; *Nunes v District Registrar of Winnipeg Land Titles Office* [1971] 5 WWR 427, 21 DLR (3d) 97; *Rajah Kishendatt Ram v Rajah Mumtaz Ali Khan* (1879) LR 6 Ind App 145 at 160 PC.

STOPPING OR SETTING ASIDE THE SALE

STOPPING THE SALE[1]

Before contract

20.34 The mortgagee will be restrained from exercising his power of sale if, before there is a contract for the sale of the mortgaged property[2], the mortgagor tenders to the mortgagee or pays into court the amount claimed to be due[3]. The amount due for that purpose is the amount which the mortgagee claimed to be due to him for principal, interest and costs[4] unless, on the face of the mortgage, the claim is excessive[5], in which case the amount claimed less such excess must be tendered or paid[6].

1 On issue estoppel, see *Helmville Ltd v Astilleros Expanoles SA, The Jocelyne* [1984] 2 Lloyd's Rep 569 (decision of Belgian court that sale not at undervalue binding on English court).

2 *Waring (Lord) v London and Manchester Assurance Co Ltd* [1935] Ch 310; *Property and Bloodstock Ltd v Emerton* [1968] Ch 94, [1967] 3 All ER 321, CA; *National & Provincial Building Society v Ahmed* [1995] 2 EGLR 127; and in some jurisdictions, at any time before conveyance: see *Camp-Wee-Gee-Wa for Boys Ltd v Clark* (1971) 23 DLR (3d) 158; *Re Hal Wright Motor Sales Ltd and Industrial Development Bank* (1975) 8 OR (2d) 76. It is sometimes said that the equity of redemption is terminated by the contract (see eg *National & Provincial Building Society v Ahmed* (above)). However if an unconditional contract goes off or the

condition of a conditional contract does not take effect, the equity of redemption becomes exercisable again. Accordingly suspension is, it is submitted, the better description. See also **20.45**, nn 1–2.

3 *Jones v Matthie* (1847) 16 LJ Ch 405; *Warner v Jacob* (1882) 20 Ch D 220; *Duke v Robson* [1973] 1 All ER 481, [1973] 1 WLR 267; *Inglis v Commonwealth Trading Bank of Australia* (1972) 126 CLR 161, HC; *Morton* v *Sunscorp Finance Ltd* (1987) 8 NSWLR 325 at 335; *Yarrangh Pty Ltd* v *National Australia Bank Ltd* (1999) 9 BPR 17061 at 17062.

4 *Hill v Kirkwood* (1880) 28 WR 358; *Hickson v Darlow* (1883) 23 Ch D 690, CA; *Macleod v Jones* (1883) 24 Ch D 289, CA. A tender at the sale of principal and interest, though without costs, has been held to be sufficient: *Jenkins v Jones* (1860) 2 Giff 99.

5 *Hickson v Darlow* (1883) 23 Ch D 690; cf *Deverges v Sandeman, Clark & Co* [1902] 1 Ch 579, CA, and where the mortgagee was, at the time of the mortgage, the mortgagor's solicitor, the court fixed the sum which if considered would cover the advance: *Macleod v Jones* (1883) 24 Ch D 289.

6 See *Armor Coatings (Marketing) Pty Ltd v General Credits (Finance) Pty Ltd* (1978) 17 SASR 259.

After contract

20.35 If the mortgagee has, in exercise of his power of sale, already entered into a contract for the sale of the property, the court will not, upon tender of the money due under the mortgage, interfere to stop the completion of the sale by conveyance unless the sale is improper, since his equity of redemption is suspended during the currency of the contract[1]. Assuming that the mortgagee is otherwise acting properly, the mortgagee will not be restrained from exercising his power of sale because the amount due is in dispute[2].

1 *Waring (Lord) v London and Manchester Assurance Co Ltd* [1935] Ch 310; *Property and Bloodstock Ltd v Emerton* [1968] Ch 94, [1967] 3 All ER 321, CA; *Duke v Robson* [1973] 1 All ER 481; *National & Provincial Building Society v Ahmed* [1995] 2 EGLR 127 but a contract for sale by the mortgagee at a lesser price than the mortgagor has been offered may be evidence that the mortgagee has not obtained the proper price, and see [1986] Conv 441 at 444, where Thompson suggests that the mortgagee might be liable to the mortgagor for failing to exercise reasonable care to avoid causing damage to the mortgagor.

2 *Gill v Newton* (1866) 14 WR 490. Although, where the mortgagor is a company, the presentation of a winding-up petition is not in general a ground for stopping the sale, an interim injunction may be granted where the mortgagee had himself presented the petition: see *Re Cambrian Mining Co Ltd, ex p Fell* (1881) 50 LJ Ch 836. A counterclaim will not prevent the right to sale where it has arisen, see in particular *Barclays Bank plc v Tennet* [1984] CA Transcript 242; and **19.2**, n 8.

INJUNCTION TO RESTRAIN SALE

20.36 After contract and before completion, the mortgagor will be able to obtain an interim injunction to restrain the sale if he can show an arguable case that the power of sale has not been properly exercised: either because the conditions for its exercise (for example, a notice[1]), have not been satisfied, or because the price is an undervalue[2]. If the mortgagee has exercised his powers improperly, and the purchaser has knowledge of the facts, the purchaser cannot obtain a right superior to the right of the mortgagor. The mortgagee and the purchaser may then both be restrained from completing the sale[3]. The same applies even where, at the date of the contract, the purchaser was unaware of the impropriety of the sale[4]. A mortgagee will be restrained if a subsequent incumbrancer has brought an action to redeem and his right to do so has been denied[5].

There is some uncertainty whether injunctive relief is only available where the mortgagee has not acted properly *and* the actual sale would be liable to be set aside[6]. However, since whether or not the completed sale will be set aside will depend on various factors, including matters appertaining to the purchaser, that would not appear to be a wholly satisfactory basis for determining an issue between mortgagor and mortgagee prior to completion. Although it cannot be said that there is any direct modern authority on the point, there are sufficient dicta in the cases to suggest that an injunction is an available remedy in all instances where the power of sale has not been properly exercised[7]. If the court considers that it is appropriate to prevent a transfer from being registered, the proper course is to grant an injunction against the transferee, restraining him from applying for registration, or ordering him to withdraw any application already made. It is not appropriate to grant an injunction against the Chief Land Registrar[8].

It has commonly been said that payment into court[9] is a condition of a grant of an injunction to restrain a sale by a mortgagee[10]. This is merely an aspect of the general rule that the mortgagor must offer to redeem before he can bring the mortgagee before the court[11]. Thus, payment into court is required where the mortgagor seeks to restrain the mortgagee selling prior to any contract for sale having been made and where the mortgagee is acting properly. However, it seems that the mortgagor need not offer to redeem where the mortgagee is not exercising his powers in good faith[12], nor otherwise acting improperly. It seems that if after the contract the mortgagor is alleging that the power of sale has not arisen, or, there has been a lack of good faith, there is likewise no need for any payment into court; but a payment in is necessary if the mortgagee is seeking to stop the sale for any other reason[13].

1 See *Selwyn v Garfit* (1888) 38 Ch D 273, CA.
2 See *Shercliff v Engadine Acceptance Corpn Pty Ltd* [1978] 1 NSWLR 729.
3 *Forsyth v Blundell* (1973) 129 CLR 477 at 497.
4 *Forsyth v Blundell*, above, at 497–499.
5 *Rhodes v Buckland* (1852) 16 Beav 212.
6 See *Waring (Lord) v London and Manchester Assurance Co Ltd* [1935] Ch 310; *Property and Bloodstock Ltd v Emerton* [1968] Ch 94, [1967] 3 All ER 321, CA; *Duke v Robson* [1973] 1 All ER 481; *National & Provincial Building Society* v *Ahmed* [1995] 2 EGLR 127.
7 See eg *Duke v Robson* [1973] 1 All ER 481 at 488, [1973] 1 WLR 267 at 274; *Henry Roach (Petroleum) Pty Ltd v Credit House (Vic) Pty Ltd* [1976] VR 309. See, generally, the cases referred to and the comment in Croft *Mortgagee's Power of Sale* pp 122–125, and see *Mediservices Pty Ltd v Stocks and Realty Pty Ltd* [1982] 1 NSWLR 516; *Clarke v Japan Machines (Australia) Pty Ltd (No 2)* [1984] 1 Qd R 421; *Development Consultants Ltd v Lions Breweries Ltd* [1981] 2 NZLR 247, NZ CA.
8 *National & Provincial Building Society v Ahmed* [1995] 2 EGLR 127.
9 Or undertaking to pay: *United Builders Pty Ltd v Commercial Banking Co of Sydney Ltd* [1975] Qd R 357.
10 See eg **20.34**, n 3; but the condition may be excluded by the terms of the relevant legislation: see *Mediservices Pty Ltd v Stocks and Realty Pty Ltd* [1982] 1 NSWLR 516.
11 See **29.2**. In *Clarke v Japan Machines (Australia) Pty Ltd (No 2)* [1984] 1 Qd R 421 it was expressed to be an application of the maxim 'he who seeks equity to equity must do equity'.
12 *Murad v National Provincial Bank* (1966) 198 Estates Gazette 117.
13 It may be that the requirement to pay into court applies only to interim applications. In *Harvey v McWatters* (1948) 49 SRNSW 173 at 177, Sugerman J said that the rule operates to supplement the ordinary requirement of an undertaking as to damages on an interim application, in which case it can have no application where a final order is sought: see *Mediservices Pty Ltd v Stocks & Realty Pty Ltd*, above. The matter of payment in seems to be more of an issue in Australasia than England (see the Australasian cases mentioned above).

SETTING THE SALE ASIDE

20.37 The statutory provisions relating to the protection of the purchaser and the mortgagor's remedy in damages against the mortgagee for loss cause by an improper sale have been considered above[1]. In those cases where the purchaser is not protected, because he has actual or constructive notice of the impropriety in the sale, the mortgagor can have the sale set aside, if he seeks relief promptly, with the result that he recovers his equity of redemption[2]. Alternatively, the conveyance may be treated as operating only on a transfer of the mortgage and of the debt secured by it and not as a transfer of the mortgagor's interest[3]. Since the mortgagor's claim to impeach a sale by the mortgagee is a mere equity, it will be defeated by a purchaser for value of any legal or equitable interest without notice of the irregularity[4].

1 See **20.20** ff.
2 *Nutt v Easton* [1900] 1 Ch 29, CA; *Belton v Bass, Ratcliffe and Gretton Ltd* [1922] 2 Ch 449; *Tse Kwong Lam* v *Wong Chit Sen* [1983] 1 WLR 1349 at 1359-1360.
3 See *Selwyn v Garfit* (1888) 38 Ch D 273, CA; *Latec Investments Ltd v Hotel Terrigal Pty Ltd* (1965) 113 CLR 265, 274–275; considered in *Forsyth v Blundell* (1973) 129 CLR 477.
4 *Latec Investments Ltd v Hotel Terrigal Pty Ltd* (1965) 113 CLR 265 (Aus HC).

EFFECT OF SALE AND CONVEYANCE

EFFECT OF CONTRACT FOR SALE

20.38 The power of sale is effectively exercised as soon as there is an enforceable contract for sale of the mortgaged property, even if it is merely conditional. The equity of redemption is suspended once the contract is made and extinguished upon conveyance[1].

1 *Lord Waring* v *London & Manchester Assurance Co Ltd* [1935] Ch 310; *Property & Bloodstock Ltd v Emerton* [1968] Ch 94; *National & Provincial Building Society v Ahmed* [1995] 2 EGLR 127. See also *Re Sarlis & Anderson* (1984) 7 DLR (4th) 227; *Chia v Rennie* (1997) 8 BPR 15601. As to stopping a sale, see **20.34** ff.

MORTGAGEE'S POWER TO CONVEY

Power of the mortgagee to convey

20.39 Section 104(1) of the Law of Property Act 1925 provides that a mortgagee exercising the statutory power of sale has the power by deed to convey the property sold, for such estate and interest therein as he is by the Act authorised to sell or convey[1] or may be the subject of the mortgage. The land is conveyed free from all estate, interests, and rights to which the mortgage has priority[2], but subject to all estates, interests, and rights which have priority to the mortgage[3]. The mortgagee is empowered by s 101 of the Law of Property Act 1925 to convey not only the mortgage term but, in freehold mortgages, the fee simple and, in leasehold mortgages, the nominal reversion.

1 Cf the wording in the Conveyancing Act 1881, s 21(1) (considered in earlier editions). See *Re White Rose Cottage* [1965] Ch 940, [1965] 1 All ER 11, CA.

2 *Duke v Robson* [1973] 1 All ER 481, [1973] 1 WLR 267. See also *Lyus v Prowsa Developments Ltd* [1982] 1 WLR 1044 at 1047-1048; *McKean v Mahoney* [1988] 1 Qd R 628.
3 Law of Property Act 1925, s 104(1). As to the effect of the conveyance on equitable interests, see Law of Property Act 1925, s 2 (2) (i), (iii); and as to implied covenants for title, Law of Property Act 1925, s 76 (1) (f).

EFFECT OF THE CONVEYANCE

Effect of conveyance with mortgages of freehold property

20.40 As regards mortgages of freehold property, s 88 of the Law of Property Act 1925 provides that where an estate in fee simple has been mortgaged by the creation of a term of years absolute limited thereout, or by a charge by way of legal mortgage, and the mortgagee sells under his statutory or express power of sale, then:

(a) the conveyance by him shall operate to vest in the purchaser the fee simple in the land conveyed subject to any legal mortgage having priority to the mortgage in right of which the sale is made and to any money thereby secured and thereupon;
(b) the mortgage term or the charge by way of legal mortgage and any subsequent mortgage term or charges merges or is extinguished as respects the land conveyed.

Such conveyance may, as respects the fee simple, be made in the name of the estate owner in whom it is vested[1].

Thus, whether the mortgage was made by demise or by a charge by way of legal mortgage, the purchaser obtains the fee simple free from the mortgage term or the charge, regardless of whether the mortgagee conveys in his own name or in the name of the mortgagor. The conveyance will be subject to any prior legal mortgage—whether it was by demise or legal charge—but it extinguishes all subsequent mortgage terms and legal charges, as well as the mortgagor's equity of redemption[2]. The interests of subsequent incumbrancers and the mortgagor are overreached, that is transferred to the mortgage money[3].

Section 88(5) of the Law of Property Act 1925 provides that in the case of a sub-mortgage by sub-demise of a long term (less a nominal period) itself limited out of an estate in fee simple[4], the provisions of s 88 operate as if the derivative term, if any, created by the sub-mortgage had been limited out of the fee simple, so as to enlarge the principal term and extinguish the derivative term created by the sub-mortgage and to enable the sub-mortgagee to convey the fee simple or acquire it by foreclosure, enlargement or otherwise. This assumes that the sub-mortgagee is exercising the power of sale conferred by the head mortgage and the effect is that the head term is enlarged into the fee simple and the derivative term is extinguished. Hence the purchaser takes the fee simple free both from the head mortgage term and the sub-mortgage term.

1 These last words have been described as a statutory power of attorney: see (1977) 41 Conv (NS) 443, and see Law of Property Act 1925, s 9 (1). The recipient of a grant towards the repair or maintenance of a property does not dispose of his interest in the property for the purposes of s 2(1) of the Local Authorities (Historic Buildings) Act 1962 when the property is sold by a mortgagee in the exercise of his power of sale: *Canterbury City Council v Quine* [1987] 2 EGLR 172. For forms of conveyance by a mortgagee, see 28 *Forms and Precedents* (5th edn, 1999 reissue) Mortgages. Where the mortgage includes

fixtures or personal chattels the statutory power of sale extends to the absolute or other interest therein affected by the charge; sub-s (4), but the fixtures cannot be sold apart from the land: *Re Yates, Batcheldor v Yates* (1888) 38 Ch D 112, CA; see **20.6**, n 6.

The section applies to a mortgage whether created before or after the commencement of the Act, and to a mortgage term created by the Act, but does not operate to confer a better title to the fee simple than would have been acquired if the same had been conveyed by the mortgage (being a valid mortgage) and the restrictions imposed by the Act in regard to the effect and creation of mortgages were not in force and all prior mortgages (if any), not being merely equitable charges, had been created by demise or by charge by way of legal mortgage: sub-s (6). As to a sale of registered land, see Land Registration Act 1925, s 34(4); see **4.16**.

2 The provision in s 4(1) of the Matrimonial Homes Act 1983, that a contract for sale of a dwelling house affected by a charge of the spouse under the Act which has been registered in accordance with s 2 of the Land Charges Act 1972 or s 2(8) of the 1983 Act include a term requiring cancellation of the registration before completion.

3 Law of Property Act 1925, s 2(1)(iii); see *Duke v Robson* [1973] 1 WLR 267.

4 See Law of Property Act 1925, s 85(2).

Effect of conveyance with mortgages of leasehold property

20.41 In relation to mortgages of leasehold property, s 89 of the Law of Property Act 1925 similarly provides that where a term of years absolute has been mortgaged by the creation of another term of years absolute limited thereout or by a charge by way of legal mortgage, and the mortgagee sells under his statutory or express power of sale:

(a) the conveyance by him operates to convey to the purchaser not only the mortgage term, if any, but also (unless expressly excepted with the leave of the court) the leasehold reversion affected by the mortgage, subject to any legal mortgage having priority to the mortgage in right of which the sale is made and to any money thereby secured; and thereupon

(b) the mortgage term, or the charge by way of legal mortgage and any subsequent mortgage term or charge merges in such leasehold reversion or is extinguished (unless expressly excepted with the leave of the court).

Such conveyance may, as respects the leasehold reversion, be made in the name of the estate owner in whom it is vested[1]. Where a licence to assign is required on a sale by a mortgagee, such licence shall not be unreasonably refused[2].

Thus a mortgagee of leaseholds by sub-demise can vest in the purchaser both the mortgage sub-term and the nominal reversion: the mortgage term thereupon merges in the nominal reversion and the conveyance operates as an assignment of the lease. The interests of subsequent incumbrancers and the mortgagor are again overreached. This can be prevented if the court allows the nominal reversion to be excepted from the operation of the conveyance and in that case only the mortgage sub-term will pass[3].

The section takes effect without prejudice to any prior incumbrance or trust affecting the original term. It does not apply where the mortgage term does not comprise the whole of the land included in the leasehold reversion, unless the rent (if any) payable in respect of that reversion has been apportioned as respects the land affected, or the rent is of no money value or no rent is reserved, and unless the lessee's covenants and the conditions (if any) have been apportioned either expressly or by implication, as respects the land affected. For this purpose it is sufficient that there has been an equitable apportionment, that is, an apportionment made by agreement between the owners of the several parts of the premises, but without the consent of the lessor[4].

Section 89(5) of the Law of Property Act 1925 provides that in the case of a sub-mortgage by demise of a term (less a nominal period) itself limited out of a leasehold reversion, the provisions of s 89 operate as if the derivative term created by the sub-mortgage had been limited out of the leasehold reversion and so as (subject as aforesaid) to merge the principal mortgage term therein as well as the derivative term created by the sub-mortgage and to enable the sub-mortgagee to convey the leasehold reversion or acquire it by foreclosure, vesting or otherwise. This differs from the technical effect of a conveyance by a sub-mortgage of freeholds, in that the head mortgage term is not enlarged into the original term and the derivative term then extinguished, but instead both the head and derivative mortgage terms are merged in the original term. However, the effect in each case is identical—the purchaser obtains the whole estate of which the mortgagor could dispose[5].

1 See **20.40**, n 1.
2 See **19.7**, n 10. Where, in the case of leasehold property, the landlord's consent to any assignment of the balance of the term of the lease is required, the mortgagee will not be able to effect a valid assignment without such consent.
3 The Act does not suggest the grounds on which the nominal reversion should be excepted. The object would be to prevent the purchaser becoming liable on the covenants in the lease and these might in certain circumstances be so onerous as to justify the intervention of the court.
4 Law of Property Act 1925, s 89(6), as amended by Law of Property (Amendment) Act 1926, Sch. Section 89(4) corresponds to s 88 (4) as to fixtures and personal chattels and, with the additions mentioned in the text, s 89 (6) corresponds with s 88(6).
5 The provision above mentioned, that the statutory power of sale shall include the power of selling the fee simple or the leasehold reversion (s 101 (6)), is complementary to the provisions as to conveyance.

Sale by proprietor of registered charge

20.42 The powers of the proprietor of a charge have already been considered[1]. Subject to an entry on the register to the contrary, the proprietor has all the powers of a legal mortgagee[2], but he only has these powers when he has been registered as the proprietor[3]. The Land Registration Act provides for the completion of the sale by registration and the cancellation of the charge[4].

1 See **4.13** ff.
2 Land Registration Act 1925, s 34 (1).
3 *Lever Finance Ltd v Needleman's Trustee* [1956] Ch 375, [1965] 2 All ER 378. There is a difficulty when a second mortgagee of registered land following a mortgage by deposit sells. A purchaser can insist upon him procuring his registration as proprietor of the charge, but this will require the co-operation of the depositee of the land certificate: see Land Registration Act 1925, s 110 (5); the alternative suggested by that subsection of procuring a disposition from the proprietor of the land should be avoided (see *Re White Rose Cottage* [1965] Ch 940, [1965] 1 All ER 11, CA).
4 Land Registration Act 1925, s 34 (4), and for the merger of any mortgage term: sub-s (5).

Sale by equitable mortgagee

20.43 An equitable mortgagee, where the mortgage is made by deed, may be able to convey the legal estate in the property. It was held, in a decision under the Conveyancing Act 1881[1], that the equitable mortgagee can only convey his equitable interest[1]. However, dicta in a more recent case, relying on a difference in wording between the 1881 Act and the 1925 Act, suggest that the equitable mortgagee can convey the legal estate[2]. Because of the uncertainty on the point, it is necessary to extend the equitable mortgagee's power of sale. This can be done by inserting additional powers in the terms of the mortgage deed by means of the two devices mentioned above[3]. First, the mortgagee or his assigns can be given power to convey the legal estate by a power of attorney inserted in the deed[4]. Secondly, by a clause inserted in the deed, the mortgagor can declare that he holds the legal estate on trust for the mortgagee and give the mortgagee power to appoint himself (or his nominee) as trustee in the mortgagor's place. That will enable the mortgagee to vest the legal estate in himself or a purchaser[5].

In the case of an equitable mortgage not made by deed, there is no statutory power of sale[6]. If the mortgagee wishes to sell, he must therefore apply to the court, which will be able to vest in him a legal term of years, so he can sell as if he were a legal mortgagee[7].

1 *Re Hodson and Howes' Contract* (1887) 35 Ch D 668, CA.
2 *Re White Rose Cottage* [1965] Ch 940 at 951, [1965] 1 All ER 11 at 15, CA, per Lord Denning MR, and see per Wilberforce J at [1964] Ch 483 at 494–496, [1964] 1 All ER 169 at 176–177. These statements to the contrary are obiter, for the conveyance was not construed as an exercise of the mortgagee's power of sale, but as a transfer by the mortgagor with the mortgagee's concurrence. Harman LJ relied on the power of attorney for the conveyance of the legal estate: [1965] Ch 940 at 956, [1965] 1 All ER 11 at 18.The phrase 'the subject of the mortgage' is, however, the same in the 1881 and the 1925 Acts.
3 See **3.102** and **3.103** (trust of the legal estate and power of attorney).
4 The sale can be made under the power of attorney without the formality of a legal charge being first called for: *Re White Rose Cottage* [1965] Ch 940 at 955–956, [1965] 1 All ER 11 at 18. See the Powers of Attorney Act 1971, as amended, for the regulation of powers of attorney.
5 See Trustee Act 1925, s 40.
6 Law of Property Act 1925, s 101.
7 Under s 91 (2) of the Law of Property Act 1925; see **21.5**. If the court orders a sale it may vest a legal term of years in the mortgagee so that he can sell as if he were a legal mortgagee: s 90(1) of the Law of Property Act 1925, see **21.6**. Also s 91(7); *Oldham v Stringer* (1884) 51 LT 895.

Sale by receiver[1]

20.44 A receiver may sell, either as delegate of the mortgagee[2], or under an express power of sale in favour of the receiver in the mortgage. In the latter case, the mortgagor will have to convey the property, unless the receiver is given power of attorney to execute deeds in the name of the mortgagor[3]. If the mortgagor becomes bankrupt, his trustee must join in any sale by the receiver in the absence of a power of attorney. On a mortgagor-company going into liquidation, the same principles apply[4]. While in a compulsory winding up any disposition of the company's property after the commencement of the winding up is void, unless the court orders otherwise[5], a sale under a mortgage does not fall within this provision, the object of which is to prevent the dissipation of the company's assets. The relevant disposition, in such case, is the mortgage, which precedes the winding up, and not the sale under the mortgage[6].

1 See **18.10**.
2 Law of Property Act 1925, s 34(1).
3 For forms, see 28 *Forms and Precedents* (5th edn, 1999 reissue) Mortgages; and generally *Williams on Title* (4th edn) pp 226, 227 and Supplement.

4 For the power of an administrator of a company to dispose of property of the company which is subject to a security as if the property were not subject to the security, see Insolvency Act 1986, s 15; **23.8**.
5 *Re Fairway Graphics Ltd* [1991] BCLC 468.
6 See also the Australian case of *Re Margart Pty Ltd* [1985] BCLC 314; *Re French's Wine Bar Ltd* (1987) 3 BCC 173.

PROCEEDS OF SALE

TRUST OF SALE MONEYS

20.45 A sale[1] destroys the equity of redemption in the mortgaged property and constitutes the mortgagee exercising the power of sale a trustee of the surplus proceeds of sale, if any, for the interested persons according to their priorities[2]. Formerly the mortgagee would sometimes be declared trustee of the proceeds of sale by the mortgage deed itself[3], now such trusts are declared by s 105 of the Law of Property Act 1925. The trust under s 105 arises as soon as the proceeds of sale are received. Even if the mortgagor is liable to account to the mortgagee for the surplus under another claim, the surplus does not form part of the mortgage debt and the mortgagee is required by s 105 to hold it in trust for the mortgagor. This will apply where a mortgage is obtained by fraud, if the mortgagee elects to affirm the mortgage and exercise his power of sale[4]. As regards the mortgagor, an express trust and, it is submitted, the statutory trust, applies only to the surplus and cannot be enforced by him for any other purpose[5].

Where the statutory trust is not imposed, such as where the sale is under an express power, and the mortgage deed merely declares that the mortgagee shall apply the purchase money in a manner stated, or where the sale is under another statute which contains no special provision for the application of the purchase money[6], a constructive trust arises and the mortgagee becomes a constructive trustee of the surplus as soon as it is shown that there is a surplus[7]. Whether the trust is statutory, express or constructive, time will not run against the person or persons entitled to the surplus, if the selling mortgagee retains the surplus or converts it to his own use[8].

1 It is suspended by a contract for sale: see **20.34**, n 2. Where a contract for sale is rescinded prior to the land becoming vested in the purchaser, the mortgagee is not accountable to the mortgagor for the purchase money he has not received: *Wright v New Zealand Farmers' Co-operative Association of Canterbury Ltd* [1939] AC 439, [1939] 2 All ER 701, PC.
2 *South Eastern Rly Co v Jortin* (1857) 6 HL Cas 425; *Rajah Kishendatt Ram v Rajah Mumtaz Ali Khan* (1879) LR 6 Ind App 145, PC; and see Law of Property Act 1925, s 105; Waters *The Constructive Trust*, pp 203 ff. The mortgagee is trustee of the proceeds of sale, even where the statutory provisions are silent as to the mortgagee's status: *Adams v Bank of New South Wales* [1984] 1 NSWLR 285, NSW CA.
3 *Gouthwaite v Rippon* (1838) 8 LJ Ch 139. If the mortgagee wrongly severs fixtures from the property and sells them separately, the proceeds of sale are treated as proceeds of sale of the mortgaged property: *Re Rogerstone Brick & Stone Co Ltd* [1919] 1 Ch 110; *Re Penning, ex p State Bank of South Australia* (1989) 89 ALR 417; see **20.6**, nn 6, 13–14.
4 *Halifax Building Society v Thomas* [1996] Ch 217; [1996] RLR 92 (P Jaffey); cf also *Lonrho plc v Fayed (No 2)* [1992] 1 WLR 1 and *Westdeutsche Landesbank Girozentrale* v *Islington London Borough Council* [1996] AC 669 for consideration of the circumstances in which a constructive trust may be imposed.
5 *Banner v Berridge* (1881) 18 Ch D 254; *Warner v Jacob* (1882) 20 Ch D 220.
6 Eg the Merchant Shipping Act 1995 and see *The Benwell Tower* (1895) 72 LT 664.
7 *Banner v Berridge*, above; *Charles v Jones* (1887) 35 Ch D 544; *Adams v Bank of New South Wales* [1984] 1 NSWLR 285, NSW CA; for the mortgagee's duty to account, see **35.19**.
8 Limitation Act 1980, s 21 (1) (b). See also *Thorne v Heard* [1895] AC 495, HL.

ORDER OF APPLICATION OF SALE MONEYS

Order of application

20.46 Section 105 of the Law of Property Act 1925 provides that the order of application of any surplus arising from a sale under an exercise of the statutory power[1] is as follows:

(a) in discharge of prior incumbrances to which the sale is not made subject, if any, or payment into court under the Act of a sum to meet any prior incumbrance[2];
(b) in payment of all costs, charges and expenses properly incurred by him as incident to the sale or any attempted sale[3], or otherwise;
(c) in discharge of the mortgage money, interest[4] and costs[5] and other money, if any, due under the mortgage;
(d) by paying the residue of the money received to the person entitled to the mortgaged property, or authorised to give receipts for the proceeds of its sale[6].

If the proceeds of sale are not sufficient to satisfy his debt, the mortgagee can sue the mortgagor on the personal covenant for the deficiency[7]. The mortgagee of a reversionary interest is not entitled to receive the whole of the mortgagor's interest when it falls in, but only so much as to discharge the principal, interest and costs due on the mortgage[8].

Money received by a mortgagee under his mortgage or from the proceeds of securities comprised in his mortgage, including, for example, proceeds from the exercise of an express power of sale, must be applied in the same manner, save that the costs, charges, and expenses payable include those properly incurred in recovering and receiving the money or securities and of conversion of securities into money[9].

1 The direction as to application of the proceeds of sale applies, with an adaptation as to costs, to other money received by a mortgagee, eg the proceeds of sale arising on a sale under an express power of sale: Law of Property Act 1925, s 107 (2). Expenses include building improvements: *Network Finance Ltd v Deposit & Investment Co Ltd* [1972] QWN 19, 46 ALJ 413.

2 Under the Law of Property Act 1925, s 50; see **28.74**. For preferential payments on a winding up, see **8.19**.

3 *Matzner v Clyde Securities Ltd* [1975] 2 NSWLR 293.

4 *Quaere* whether early repayment discount (see **3.25**, n 11) should be allowed.

5 If a mortgagor unsuccessfully impeaches a sale by a first mortgagee, the latter is not allowed to add the costs of defending such action to his mortgage debt against a second mortgagee: *Re Smith's Mortgage, Harrison v Edwards* [1931] 2 Ch 168.

6 These words seem to be incorrect, the person entitled to the property at the time of division of the surplus being in strictness the purchaser and the person authorised to give receipts for the proceeds of sale being the mortgagee who exercises the power, but practically the meaning is clear. The surplus is to be paid to the subsequent incumbrancer, if any, or to the mortgagor or his successors in title.

7 The rule that a mortgagee disables himself from suing for the debt by putting it out of his power to reconvey does not apply to a sale under a power given by the mortgage: *Re McHenry, Barker's Claim* [1894] 3 Ch 290. The mortgage debt remains a specialty debt: see **16.29** and **17.7**.

8 *Re Bell, Jeffrey v Sayles* [1896] 1 Ch 1, CA; *Hockey v Western* [1898] 1 Ch 350, CA; *Re Lloyd, Lloyd v Lloyd* [1903] 1 Ch 385 at 403, CA.

9 Law of Property Act 1925, s 107(2).

Subsequent incumbrancers

20.47 Where there are subsequent incumbrancers[1], the surplus proceeds should be paid to the incumbrancer next in order[2]; he will in turn hold it on trust, to discharge first the money due to him and thereafter to pass on any balance to the next incumbrancer or, if none, to the mortgagor. Where there is more than one mortgage of the same property, the mortgagees can ordinarily (in the absence of an express term in the mortgage to the contrary) vary the order of priority of their mortgages without the mortgagor's consent and a mortgagee can apply the proceeds of sale in accordance with that altered priority[3].

If the first mortgagee has notice[4] of any subsequent incumbrance, he is liable to any subsequent incumbrancer if he pays the proceeds to the mortgagor[5]. Where the title to the mortgaged property is unregistered, the mortgagee should therefore search the Charges Register for any subsequent incumbrances, since registration is deemed to constitute notice[6]. That should not apply where the mortgaged property is registered land, since registration is not deemed to constitute notice.

1 With enforceable claims: *Matthews (C & M) Ltd v Marsden Building Society* [1951] Ch 758, [1951] 1 All ER 1053, CA. Eg a bank claiming under a lien: *Greendon Investments v Mills* (1973) 226 Estates Gazette 1957. For mortgages and charges rendered invalid on insolvency or liquidation, see **13.2** ff and **23.35** ff.

2 *Re Thomson's Mortgage Trusts* [1920] 1 Ch 508, but Eve J admitted that the matter was not free from doubt. The alternative is that the selling mortgagee distributes the surplus between those entitled (see as to mortgages of reversions, **20.46**, n 8), but this will involve the selling mortgagee in the state of accounts between each subsequent mortgagee and the mortgagor. It is submitted that the proper course for the selling mortgagee is, as in *Re Thomson's Mortgage Trusts*, above, it was held he was obliged to do, namely to pay over the surplus to the next incumbrancer, but see *Matthews (C & M) Ltd v Marsden Building Society*, above.

3 *Cheah Theam Swee v Equiticorp Finance Group Ltd* [1992] 1 AC 472, [1991] 4 All ER 989.

4 Eg by registration in the Land Charges Register: Law of Property Act 1925, s 198(1). For constructive notice, see Law of Property Act 1925, s 199 (1). A registered chargee who is selling should search the register of title. Actual notice should be given by a second or subsequent mortgagee: see **11.6**. See *Thorne v Heard and Marsh* [1895] AC 495 at 501 as to whether knowledge of the mortgagee's solicitor acquired in another capacity constitutes notice to the mortgagee.

5 *West London Commercial Bank v Reliance Permanent Building Society* (1885) 29 Ch D 954 at 962, CA. This liability is not dependent on the registration of the subsequent mortgage. For the costs of payment over, see **36.39**, n 5.

6 Law of Property Act 1925, s 198(1); but see *Rignall Developments Ltd v Halil* [1988] Ch 190.

Person entitled to the equity of redemption

20.48 Where there are no subsequent incumbrancers the surplus must be paid over to the mortgagor[1], or other person entitled to the equity of redemption. If the equity of redemption is held upon a trust of land, the surplus should be paid to the trustees[2]; the same will apply where a husband was the sole legal owner and mortgagor, but the court has subsequently declared that the beneficial interest in the mortgaged property is held by the husband and his wife as tenants in common[3]. In cases of difficulty, the money can be paid into court[4]. Where the mortgaged land is settled land, any surplus, as capital money, must be paid to not fewer than two trustees or a trust corporation[5]. Where the mortgagee under a fixed charge exercises the statutory power of sale over the assets of a company which goes into liquidation, the surplus proceeds of sale are payable to the liquidator rather than the preferential creditors[6].

A mortgagor's interest in surplus proceeds of sale following a sale of the mortgaged property by the mortgagee under his statutory power of sale is an equitable chose in action and is included in the mortgagor's personal estate. Thus, if the mortgagor's personal estate is subject to a writ of sequestration[7] the interest is subject to the writ. The mortgagee is bound to pay over the surplus proceeds to the sequestrators and does not need the protection of a specific court order before paying over the surplus[8].

1 See *Re G L Saunders Ltd* [1986] BCLC 40 for conflict between liquidator and preferential creditors. Where the mortgagor has by his will given his realty and personalty to different persons and has died questions may arise as to who is entitled to the surplus proceeds of sale. If the sale took place during the mortgagor's life the surplus goes as personalty (*Re Grange, Chadwick v Grange* [1907] 2 Ch 20); after his death, as realty.
2 The money is capital money and must be paid to not fewer than two trustees or to a trust corporation: Law of Property Act 1925, s 27(2); Trustee Act 1925, s 14.
3 Accordingly it will be necessary for another trustee to be appointed to receive the money: see (1967) 31 Conv (NS) 259 (Poole). The mortgage in this case would seem to be valid; see *Re Morgan's Lease, Jones v Norsesowicz* [1972] Ch 1, [1971] 2 All ER 235, doubting *Weston v Henshaw* [1950] Ch 510 (unauthorised mortgage by tenant for life as absolute owner invalidated by s 18 of the Settled Land Act 1925; and **12.89** ff. There is no corresponding provision under the Law of Property Act 1925). See further (1969) 33 Conv (NS) 240 (Garner).
4 *Re Walhampton Estate* (1884) 26 Ch D 391; Trustee Act 1925, s 63. And see generally CPR Pts 36 and 37.
5 Or into court: Settled Land Act 1925, s 18 (1) (b), (c).
6 *Re G L Saunders* [1986] BCLC 40; as to rights of preferential creditors see also *Re H & K (Medway) Ltd* [1997] 2 All ER 321, [1997] 1 WLR 1422.
7 See CPR Sch 1, Ord 46, r 5(1).
8 *Bucknell v Bucknell* [1969] 2 All ER 998, [1969] 1 WLR 1204. See also *Eckman* v *Midland Bank* [1973] QB 519, [1973] 1 All ER 609; *Messenger Newspapers Group Ltd v National Graphical Association* [1984] 1 All ER 293.

Charging orders and garnishee orders

20.49 A properly protected execution creditor with a charging order is in the same position as an equitable chargee[1] and, accordingly, the mortgagee who has exercised the power of sale may insist on paying over the whole balance to such a person where there is no intermediate incumbrance. Where a garnishee order nisi has been obtained against the mortgagee by a judgment creditor of the mortgagor, and there are no intermediate mortgages, any surplus will be bound by the order[2]. If there are intermediate mortgages or charges, the order will usually have been made subject to the rights thereunder[3] and, in any event, the order cannot give the judgment creditor priority over such incumbrances[4]. Under an order absolute the debt is subject to all rights attaching to it in the hands of the garnishee[5]. The surplus in the hands of a mortgagee who has realised his security cannot be attached by a garnishee order against the mortgagor obtained by a judgment creditor of a subsequent mortgagee before the sale[6]. It is necessary to obtain a garnishee order after the sale against the first mortgagee.

1 Charging Orders Act 1979, s 3 (4). See **2.18**.
2 Even if the surplus exceeds the judgment debt, unless the order is restricted to such amount as will satisfy the judgment debt: *Joachimson v Swiss Bank Corpn* [1921] 3 KB 110 at 121, CA, and see **2.29**.

3 CPR Sch 1, RSC Ord 49, r 6.
4 *Badeley v Consolidated Bank* (1888) 38 Ch D 238, CA. Cf *Vacuum Oil Co Ltd v Ellis* [1914] 1 KB 693, CA.
5 *Norton v Yates* [1906] 1 KB 112 at 121.
6 *Chatterton v Watney* (1881) 17 Ch D 259, CA.

Ships

20.50 A court sale in Admiralty proceedings in rem transfers the mortgagee's contractual or statutory rights to the proceeds of sale in court[1]. The Merchant Shipping Act 1995 contains no express directions as to the disposal of the purchase money[2]. On the principles already considered[3], the selling mortgagee holds any surplus from the proceeds of sale for subsequent mortgagees (if any) and the owner.

1 *The Queen of the South* [1968] 1 Lloyd's Rep 182 at 192.
2 See also *The Benwell Tower* (1895) 72 LT 664.
3 See **20.45**, **20.47**.

Payment by mistake

20.51 If, by a mistake, the mortgagee pays over to a subsequent incumbrancer, or to the mortgagor, more than he should have, he may claim repayment[1]. In cases of difficulty, or if there is a dispute as to whether or not there is a subsequent incumbrance (for example, where the mortgagor contests the validity of the second mortgage) the surplus should be paid into court or, if so requested, put on deposit pending a settlement of the dispute[2].

1 *Weld-Blundell v Symott* [1940] 2 KB 107, [1940] 2 All ER 580, and see also **28.58**.
2 For a dispute as to the entitlement of surplus proceeds of sale see *Samuel Keller (Holdings) Ltd v Martins Bank Ltd* [1970] 3 All ER 950, [1971] 1 WLR 43, CA.

Statute-barred surplus

20.52 If the rights of the mortgagor and his successors have become statute-barred, the mortgagee may keep the surplus[1].

1 *Re Statutory Trusts Declared by Section 105 of the Law of Property Act 1925 affecting the Proceeds of Sale of Moat House Farm, Thurlby* [1948] Ch 191, sub nom *Young v Clarey* [1948] 1 All ER 197.

INTEREST AFTER SALE

20.53 Upon the sale being completed, interest ceases to run against the mortgagor, unless agreed to the contrary[1]. The mortgagee is then allowed a reasonable time to do his sums to ascertain any surplus. A period of 28 days will, generally, be adequate for this purpose[2]. Thereafter interest in equity will run on the surplus. This has been stated to be a matter of the court's discretion, rather than entitlement, but the practice is to allow interest in most cases[3]. The old cases refer to interest at 4 per cent per annum[4] but, probably, now the appropriate rate is what is obtainable on deposit accounts with banks or building societies. Alternatively, it may be appropriate to have an inquiry as to the return the mortgagee has obtained on the surplus[5].

1 *West v Diprose* [1900] 1 Ch 337 at 340.
2 The appropriate searches (see **20.47**) should have been made previously and the amount due under the mortgage easily obtainable, since details will have been required in any possession proceedings. Usually the only outstanding matters will be the fees and disbursements of the sale itself.
3 See *Eley v Read* (1897) 76 LT 39, CA; cf *Mathison v Clark* (1855) 25 LJ Ch 29.
4 *Eley v Read* (1897) 76 LT 39 at 40, CA, per Lord Esher MR; affd sub nom *Read v Eley* (1899) 80 LT 369, HL.
5 See, generally, *Coote on Mortgages* (9th edn) vol 2, p 945; and **35.42**. See also *Bartlett v Barclays Bank Trust Co (No 2)* [1980] Ch 515, [1980] 2 All ER 92.
See *Matthew v T M Sutton Ltd* [1994] 1 WLR 1455 for consideration of the principles in the context of a surplus retained by a pawnbroker; also *Bartlett v Barclays Bank Trust Co Ltd (No 2)* [1980] Ch 515, [1980] 2 All ER 92, as to interest payable where a trustee has retained trust monies.

ADVANCES MADE UNDER THE SMALL DWELLINGS ACQUISITION ACTS

20.54 These Acts were repealed by the Housing (Consequential Provisions) Act 1985 and no new advances can be made[1].

Where default[2] is made in complying with any of the statutory conditions[3] other than that as to residence[4], then, whether or not the statutory condition as to residence has been complied with, the local authority may either take possession of the house or order the sale of the house without taking possession[5]. In the case of the breach of any condition other than that of punctual payment of the principal and interest of the advance, the authority must, previously to taking possession or ordering a sale, by notice in writing delivered at the house and addressed to the proprietor[6], call on the proprietor to comply with the condition. If the proprietor (a) within 14 days after the delivery of the notice gives an undertaking in writing to the authority to comply with the notice, and (b) within two months after the delivery of the notice complies with it, the authority is not entitled to take possession or, as the case may be, order a sale[7]. In the case of the bankruptcy of the proprietor of the house, or in the case of a deceased proprietor's estate falling to be administered in accordance with an order under s 421 of the Insolvency Act 1986[8], the local authority may either take possession of the house, or order the sale of the house without taking possession, and must do so except in pursuance of some arrangement to the contrary with the trustee in bankruptcy[9].

Where a local authority orders a sale of a house without taking possession they shall cause it to be put up for sale by auction and shall retain out of the proceeds of sale (a) any sum due to them on account of the interest or principal of the advance, and (b) all costs, charges and expenses properly incurred by them in or about the sale of the house, and shall pay over the balance (if any) to the proprietor[10]. If the local authority are unable at the auction to sell the house for such a sum as will allow of the payment out of the proceeds of sale of the interest and principal of the advance then due to the authority, and the said costs charges and expenses, they may take possession of the house in the manner provided by Sch 18 to the Housing Act 1985[11], but shall not be liable to pay any sum to the proprietor[12].

1 Section 3, Sch 1. For details for the form of mortgage made under the Acts prior to the Housing Act 1985, see the 9th edition. For details of the provisions applicable to mortgages made under the Acts pursuant to the Housing Act 1985, see s 456, Sch 18, para 2.
2 See *Alnwick RDC v Taylor* [1966] Ch 355, [1966] 1 All ER 899.

3 See Housing Act 1985, Sch 18.
4 In which case the authority may take possession: Housing Act 1985, Sch 18, para 5(1); see **19.15**. The statutory conditions as to residence has effect for a period of three years from the date when the advance was made, or from the date on which the house was completed, whichever was the later: Sch 18, para 2 (2). The condition as to residence may be dispensed with or suspended: para 3. For the meaning of residence, see para 9 (1).
5 Paragraph 5 (1).
6 For the meaning of proprietor, see para 9 (3).
7 Paragraph 5 (2).
8 See Insolvency Act 1985, s 228; as amended by Insolvency Act 1985, s 235(1), Sch 8, para 39 and Insolvency Act 1986, s 439(2), Sch 14.
9 Paragraph 5 (3).
10 Paragraph 7 (1).
11 See **19.15**.
12 Paragraph 7 (2). The proprietor is personally liable for the repayment of any sum due in respect of the advance until he ceases to be the proprietor by reason of a transfer made with the permission of the local authority: para 4. For list of advances and accounts to be kept by the local authority, see para 8. See *Re Brown's Mortgage* [1945] Ch 166, [1945] 1 All ER 397; *Re Caunter's Charge* [1960] Ch 491, [1959] 3 All ER 669.

VESTING ORDER UNDER THE HOUSING ACT 1985

Vesting of mortgaged property in housing authority

20.55 As considered above, a mortgagee cannot sell the mortgaged property to himself in purported exercise of the power of sale[1]. However, in the case of housing authorities, special statutory provision has been made for an authority as mortgagee to vest the property in itself with the approval of the court[2]. The power arises where:

(a) there has been a disposal of a house by a housing authority;
(b) the authority is a mortgagee of the house;
(c) the conveyance or grant contains a pre-emption provision[3] in favour of the authority; and
(d) within the period which the pre-emption provision has effect the authority becomes entitled as mortgagee to exercise the power of sale conferred by s 101 of the Law of Property Act 1925 or the mortgage deed.

The authority may then, if the county court gives it leave to do so, by deed vest the house in itself for the estate and interest in the house which is the subject of the mortgage and which the authority would be authorised to sell or convey on exercising its power of sale, freed from all estates, interests and rights to which the mortgage has priority, but subject to all estates, interests and rights which have priority to the mortgage[4]. On the vesting of the house, the authority's mortgage term or charge by way of legal mortgage and any subsequent mortgage term or charge, merges or is extinguished as respects the house[5].

1 See **20.33**.
2 See *Williams v Wellingborough Borough Council* [1975] 1 WLR 1327 for the situation prior to s 452 of the Housing Act 1985.
3 See Housing Act 1985, s 452 (2).
4 Housing Act 1985, s 452 (1), Sch 17, para 1 (1). For application for leave, see Sch 17, para 1 (2); for conditions for adjournment or postponement of the execution of the vesting deed, see para 1 (3).
5 Housing Act 1985, Sch 17, para 2 (1). For registration of the authority as proprietor under the Land Registration Acts 1925 to 1971, see para 2 (2).

Protection of subsequent transferee

20.56 Where the authority conveys the house, or part of it, to a person (a) the transferee need not be concerned to inquire whether any of the provisions of Sch 17 of the Housing Act 1985 were complied with, and (b) his title is not impeachable on the ground that the house was not properly vested in the authority or that those provisions were not complied with[1].

1 Housing Act 1985, Sch 17, para 2 (3). Cf Law of Property Act 1925, s 104 (2); **20.20**. Section 107 (1) of the Law of Property Act 1925 (see **20.31**, n 4) applies to money payable under the Schedule as it applies to money arising under the power of sale conferred by that Act; para 3 (4). For the value of the house and the appropriation by the authority of a fraud representing that value and interest and the application of that fund, see para 3 (1), (2), (3).

For modifications of the Schedule provisions in the case of a conveyance or grant before 8 August 1980, see para 4.

Chapter 21

Judicial sale

21.1 The mortgagee's power to sell the security out of court has been considered in Chapter 20; in this chapter the court's power to order a sale is considered.

THE COURT'S INHERENT JURISDICTION TO ORDER SALE

Alternative to foreclosure

21.2 The strict right of a legal mortgagee was foreclosure, and he had no general right to a sale[1]. However, the court had the power to order a sale of the property where foreclosure was not available as a remedy or, in certain circumstances, as an alternative to foreclosure. Thus the court would order a sale rather than foreclosure if (as was commonly the case) the value of the property exceeded the mortgage debt, or if there were other incumbrancers interested in the property. Where a charge gave a right of foreclosure on the ground that it implied an agreement to execute a legal mortgage, the remedy was prima facie restricted to foreclosure[2]. However, if it were a mere charge without such agreement, then the remedy was sale[3], and if the agreement were to execute a legal mortgage with a power of sale, the court might order sale as an alternative remedy[4].

1 *Tipping v Power* (1842) 1 Hare 405. See also *Moore v Morton* [1886] WN 196.
2 *Pryce v Bury* (1853) 2 Drew 41. See also *Tipping v Power* (1842) 1 Hare 405; *Manton Parabolic Pty Ltd* (1985) 2 NSWLR 361.
3 See the cases referred to at **22.3**, n 6, but debenture holders are entitled to foreclosure: *Sadler v Worley* [1894] 2 Ch 170.
4 *Lister v Turner* (1846) 5 Hare 281; *Seton* (7th edn) 1976. As to waiver by the mortgagee of his right to the legal security and a claim to sale under the charge, see *Kennard v Futvoye* (1860) 2 Giff 81; *Matthews v Goodday* (1861) 8 Jur NS 90.

Deficient security

21.3 There were also other cases in which, for special reasons connected with the subject matter of the security, sale was the proper remedy. Thus the legal or equitable mortgagee had a general right to a sale where the security was, or was thought to be, scanty or deficient[1]. The mortgagee of a reversion was entitled to a sale on account of the unproductive nature of the security[2], as well as being entitled to foreclosure[3].

1 *Dashwood v Bithazey* (1729) Mos 196; *Earl of Kinnoul v Money* (1767) 3 Swan 202, and see *Daniel v Skipwith* (1787) 2 Bro CC 155; *Lloyds Bank Ltd v Colston* (1912) 106 LT 420.
2 *How v Vigures* (1628) 1 Rep Ch 32.
3 *Slade v Rigg* (1843) 3 Hare 35; *Wayne v Hanham* (1851) 9 Hare 62. Sale is the proper remedy, rather than foreclosure, when the mortgagee is in conflicting positions, as where he becomes executor of the mortgagor or trustee of the mortgaged property: *Lucas v Seale* (1740) 2 Atk 56; *Tennant v Trenchard* (1869) 4 Ch App 537.

Requirement for mortgagee's consent

21.4 No sale can be made of mortgaged property under the court's inherent jurisdiction as against a mortgagee with a paramount title, save with his express consent — without that consent, the sale can only be subject to his mortgage[1]. If he is a party to the action he will be required at once to consent or refuse[2]; the sale can than be directed free from the mortgagee's security if he concurs, but subject to it if he does not.

1 *Wickenden v Rayson* (1855) 6 De GM & G 210. See also *Tipping v Power* (1842) 1 Hare 405. As to the interest which will be allowed to the mortgagee, see *Re Fowler, Bishop v Fowler* (1922) 128 LT 620.
2 *Jenkins v Row* (1851) 5 De G & Sm 107.

SECTION 91 OF THE LAW OF PROPERTY ACT 1925

THE POWER TO ORDER A SALE

21.5 Section 91 of the Law of Property Act 1925[1], which reproduces earlier legislation[2], makes provision for the sale of mortgaged property[3] in a claim for redemption or foreclosure. Any person entitled to redeem mortgaged property may have a judgment or order for sale instead of for redemption in a claim brought by him either for redemption alone, or for sale or redemption in the alternative[4]. The court[5] may direct a sale of the mortgaged property in any claim[6] for foreclosure, redemption, or sale, or for the raising and payment in any manner of mortgage money, on the request of the mortgagee, or of any person interested either in the mortgage money or in the right of redemption[7]. It may do so notwithstanding that: (a) any other person dissents; or (b) the mortgagee or any person so interested does not appear in the claim[8]. The order for a sale may be made on an interim application before trial[9], or at any time before foreclosure absolute[10]. The court need not allow any time for redemption or for payment of any mortgage money[11]. It may order sale on such terms as it thinks fit, including the deposit in court of a reasonable sum fixed by the court to meet the expenses of sale and to secure performance of the terms[12]. In a claim brought by a person interested in the right of redemption and seeking a sale, the court may, on the application of any defendant, direct the claimant to give such security for costs as the court thinks fit, give the conduct of the sale to any defendant and give such directions as it thinks fit respecting the costs of the defendants or any of them[13]. In any case falling within s 91 the court may, if it thinks fit, direct a sale without previously determining the priorities of incumbrancers[14]. The court has the power, in favour of a purchaser, to make a vesting order conveying the mortgaged property, or appoint a person to do so, subject or not to any incumbrance, as it may think fit[15].

1 See [1994] Conv 11 (Adams); (1998) 18 LS 279 (Dixon).

2 Conveyancing Act 1881, s 25.
3 'Mortgaged property' includes the estate or interest which a mortgagee would have had the power to convey if the statutory power of sale were applicable: s 91(6). This subsection was introduced so that a sale might have the same conveyancing effect as a sale by the mortgagee under his power of sale: see Law of Property Act 1925, ss 88, 89 (as to which, see **20.40** and **20.41**).
4 Section 91(1).
5 See Law of Property Act 1925, s 203 (3).
6 On s 91 (2) generally, see *Twentieth Century Banking Corpn Ltd v Wilkinson* [1977] Ch 99, [1976] 3 All ER 361. *Quaere* whether the applicant for sale must establish that he had a right to foreclose: ibid; and see Law Commission Working Paper no 99, *Land Mortgages*, para 3.53. Given the wide terms of the section, and the fact that any interested person may apply, it would seem not.
7 See *Rhymney Valley District Council v Pontygwindy Housing Association Ltd* [1976] LS Gaz R 405. A person claiming a beneficial interest in the property is entitled to apply for an order for sale: *Halifax Building Society v Stansfield* [1993] EGCS 147, CA.
8 Section 91(2).
9 *Woolley v Colman* (1882) 21 Ch D 169.
10 *Union Bank of London v Ingram* (1882) 20 Ch D 463, CA; *Weston v Davidson* [1882] WN 28; *Industrial Development Bank v Lees* (1971) 14 DLR (3d) 612, but if only foreclosure has been claimed and the mortgagor does not appear, sale will not be ordered unless he has had notice of the mortgagee's intention to ask for a sale in lieu of foreclosure: *South Western District Bank v Turner* (1882) 31 WR 113. See also **22.47** and **22.57** ff. For an application for an order made to have effect as if it had been made on an earlier date to give effect to an existing contract, see *Manton v Parabolic Pty Ltd* [1985] ACLD 629.
11 Section 91(2).
12 Section 91(2).
13 Section 91(3).
14 But the order may be accompanied by an inquiry as to priorities: see *Paine v Edwards* (1862) 6 LT 600.
15 Section 91(7).

Equitable mortgages

21.6 In the case of an equitable mortgage, the court may create and vest a mortgage term in the mortgagee to enable him to carry out the sale as if the mortgage had been made by way of legal mortgage[1]. With regard to the realisation of equitable mortgages by the court, s 90 of the Law of Property Act 1925 provides that where an order for sale is made by the court in reference to an equitable mortgage on land (not secured by a legal term of years absolute or by a charge by way of legal mortgage) the court may, in favour of a purchaser, make a vesting order conveying the land, or alternatively may appoint a person to convey the land or create and vest in the mortgagee a legal term of years absolute to enable him to carry out the sale, as the case may require, in like manner as if the mortgage had been created by deed by way of legal mortgage pursuant to the Act. Such an order is without prejudice to any incumbrance having priority to the equitable mortgage, unless the incumbrancer consents to the sale. The power under s 90 applies to equitable mortgages made before or after 1926, but not to a mortgage which has been overreached.

1 This provision applies to an equitable mortgage, whether accompanied by an agreement to execute a legal mortgage or not: *Oldham v Stringer* (1884) 33 WR 251. It is particularly important in the case of an equitable mortgage not made by deed, where there is no statutory power of sale: see **20.43**.

County court jurisdiction

21.7 The county court has jurisdiction under ss 90 and 91 where the amount owing in respect of the mortgage or charge at the commencement of the proceedings does not exceed £30,000[1].

1 Section 91(8), as inserted by the County Courts Act 1984, s 148(1), Sch 2, Pt II, para 3(1), (3); figure substituted by the High Court and County Courts Jurisdiction Order 1991 (SI 1991/724), Art 2(8), Sch. For the jurisdiction of the county court by agreement, see County Courts Act 1984, s 24.

EXERCISE OF THE COURT'S DISCRETION

The court's discretion

21.8 Section 91(2) does not give the parties an absolute right to require a sale, it merely gives the court the power to direct a sale[1]. The court's discretion under s 91(2) is unfettered, but must be exercised judicially having due regard to all interests concerned[2]. In exercising its discretion the court is not limited to considering financial matters, but can also take into account social considerations[3]. The older cases under s 91 were mainly concerned with judicial sale as an alternative to foreclosure; recent cases have concerned disputes between mortgagor and mortgagee as to whether the property should be sold at all — and who should have the conduct of any sale — different considerations apply in each case[4].

1 *Brewer v Square* [1892] 2 Ch 111; cf *Clarke v Pannell* (1884) 29 Sol Jo 147.
2 *Palk v Mortgage Services Funding plc* [1993] Ch 330; (1992) 136 Sol Jo 1000 (Cottell); [1993] Conv 59 (Martin).
3 *Polonski v Lloyd's Bank Mortgages Ltd* (1997) 31 HLR 721.
4 *Palk v Mortgage Services Funding plc* [1993] Ch 330.

On mortgagor's application, as alternative to mortgagee's power of sale[1]

21.9 The fact that the mortgagee has a power of sale which has become exercisable does not prevent an order being made[2]. However, it is not appropriate for the court to order a sale under s 91(2) at the mortgagor's request where the mortgagee is taking active steps to obtain possession and enforce its security under its own power of sale[3]. The discretion of the court to order a sale will almost always be refused where the mortgagee can demonstrate some tangible benefit of which he will be denied if a sale is ordered. Thus, the court will rarely exercise its discretion against the mortgagee's wishes if the proceeds of sale would not discharge the mortgage debt, leaving an unsecured shortfall, whilst a rise in property prices, or an income from the property, would enable the debt to be discharged if the sale is postponed[4]. However, the court ordered a sale, despite the mortgagee's objection, where the sale proceeds would not discharge the mortgage debt, but where the mortgagor had good social reasons for wanting to move house, and had always previously acted in a financially responsible manner[5]. A sale was also ordered where there would have been a continuing shortfall between the mortgage interest and the income available to pay that interest, while a sale would have substantially reduced the mortgage debt. If a sale had been refused, the only prospect of recouping the increasing debt would have been if there was a substantial rise in house prices generally in the future; if the mortgagees wished to proceed on the basis of such an expectation, it was appropriate that they, not the mortgagor, should bear the risk by purchasing the property themselves[6].

1 (1998) 18 LS 279.
2 *Brewer v Square* [1892] 2 Ch 111.
3 *Cheltenham & Gloucester Building Society v Karusz* (1996) 29 HLR 597, CA, disapproving *Barrett v Halifax Building Society* (1996) 28 HLR 634. Further, the mortgagee's possession proceedings will often be in the county court, whilst the mortgagor will have to make his under s 91(2) in the High Court if the amount owing in respect of the mortgage or charge at the commencement of the proceedings exceeds £30,000.
4 *Cheltenham and Gloucester Building Society v Karusz* (1996) 29 HLR 597, CA; *Barrett v Halifax Building Society* (1996) 28 HLR 634.
5 *Polonski v Lloyd's Bank Mortgages Ltd* (1997) 31 HLR 721.
6 *Palk v Mortgage Services Funding plc* [1993] Ch 330.

Judicial sale to render purchaser's title unimpeachable

21.10 The court will not, save in exceptionable circumstances, make an order for sale under s 91(2) so as to make the sale unimpeachable, where the mortgagee's own power of sale is exercisable and where a party with an adverse interest wishes to impeach it. However, such exceptional circumstances existed where the prospects of the mortgagor successfully impeaching the sale were utterly remote, but its conduct justified the apprehension that it would threaten proceedings against the mortgagee to spoil the sale, so that the mortgagee's statutory power of sale would be of no practical use[1].

1 *Arab Bank plc v Marchantile Holdings Ltd* [1994] Ch 71.

Sale in lieu of foreclosure[1]

21.11 The court will prefer to order a sale rather than foreclosure where there is a reasonable equity in the property, as it will usually be unwilling to give the mortgagee a windfall profit[2]. Evidence as to the value of the security as against the mortgage debt should therefore be before the court[3]. The mortgagor or subsequent mortgagees should have the chance of obtaining the surplus likely to be realised upon a sale, provided that the first mortgagee is secured against loss[4]. Thus, a sale may be ordered on the terms that the subsequent mortgagee or the mortgagor asking for a sale pay into court a sum sufficient to secure the first mortgagee against loss[5]. Such terms will be required where the security is deficient, or where the mortgagor's expectation of a surplus is based only on a speculative rise in value[6]. Where the mortgaged property was in several places, and could not be sold as a whole, and part was more valuable than others, the risk of selling merely the most valuable part, and leaving the mortgagee saddled with the worthless part, was a good reason for refusing a sale requested by the second mortgagee[7]. A sale was refused where the security was deficient and it was not for the benefit of either party that the expense of a sale or attempted sale should be incurred[8]. A sale was also refused where vacant possession of the property could not be given[9].

Where sale is sought as an alternative to foreclosure then, rather than an immediate sale being directed, the order will usually provide that the sale shall not take place until three months from the order determining the amount due, so as to give the mortgagor an opportunity of redeeming[10]. The opportunity to redeem should normally be given if there is evidence of the solvency of the mortgagor[11]; however, an immediate sale may be ordered where the property is small and the security deficient[12]. An order for sale may also be postponed for a short time to give interested persons a chance to redeem, for example tenants of the mortgaged property who were not parties to the proceedings[13].

1 See further Chapter 22, **22.47** ff, for the terms on which sale in lieu of foreclosure may be ordered and as to the terms of the order.
2 See eg *Twentieth Century Banking Corpn Ltd v Wilkinson* [1977] Ch 99, [1976] 3 All ER 361; *Rhymney Valley District Council v Pontygwindy Housing Association Ltd* [1976] LS Gaz R 405.
3 *Smithett v Hesketh* (1890) 44 Ch D 161 at 163.
4 *Hurst v Hurst* (1852) 16 Beav 372.
5 *Norman v Beaumont* [1893] WN 45. A sale has been refused where the defendant requesting it would not give security: *Cripps v Wood* (1882) 51 LJ Ch 584.
6 *Hurst v Hurst*, above; *Merchant Banking Co of London v London and Hanseatic Bank* (1886) 55 LJ Ch 479.
7 *Provident Clerks' Mutual, etc Association v Lewis* (1892) 62 LJ Ch 89.
8 *Lloyds Bank Ltd v Colston* (1912) 106 LT 420.
9 *Silsby v Holliman* [1955] Ch 552, [1955] 2 All ER 373 (mortgagee statutory tenant).
10 *Green v Biggs* (1885) 52 LT 680; *Jones v Harris* [1887] WN 10. The order will, in a suitable case, be limited to the sale of so much of the property as will be sufficient to satisfy the amount due: *Wade v Wilson* (1882) 22 Ch D 235. For forms of order, see 28 *Atkin's Court Forms* (1997 issue); *Seton* (7th edn) vol 3.
11 *Hopkinson v Miers* (1889) 34 Sol Jo 128.
12 *Oldham v Stringer* (1884) 33 WR 251; *Williams v Owen* (1883) 27 Sol Jo 256; or a short interval may be fixed: *Charlewood v Hammer* (1884) 28 Sol Jo 710.
13 *Rhymney Valley District Council v Pontygwindy Housing Association Ltd* [1976] LS Gaz R 405.

Conduct of the sale

21.12 The conduct of the sale will usually be given to the mortgagor since it is to his interest to obtain as high a price as possible[1]. In those circumstances, the mortgagor need not generally give security for the costs of the sale, since he will himself be liable for them[2]. Where the proceeds of sale are likely to be insufficient to discharge the mortgage debt, the mortgagee should be given conduct of the sale[3]. Since the sale is by order of the court, the mortgagee can buy the property where the court gives permission[4]. A sale may be made out of court, but the reserve price must be fixed in court and the purchase money paid into court[5]. The party having the conduct of the sale are in the position of ordinary vendors and are not liable for the fraud or other improper acts of other parties to the claim, such as those who make fictitious bids at auction to raise the sale price[6]. An order for sale does not prevent the creditor pursuing his other remedies, for example presenting and prosecuting a bankruptcy petition against the mortgagor[7].

1 *Davies v Wright* (1886) 32 Ch D 220; *Christy v Van Tromp* [1886] WN 111; *Cheltenham and Gloucester plc v Krausz* [1997] 1 WLR 1558. If not to him, then to the mortgagee last in priority: *Norman v Beaumont* [1893] WN 45, but the first mortgagee may be given the conduct: *Re Jordan* (1884) 13 QBD 228; *Hewitt v Nanson* (1858) 28 LJ Ch 49. See further **22.48**.
2 *Davies v Wright*, above; *Manchester and Salford Bank v Scowcroft* (1883) 27 Sol Jo 517; *Wooley v Colman* (1882) 21 Ch D 169; but the court may require this to be done: *Brewer v Square*, above. For estate agents' and auctioneers' remuneration, see *Practice Direction* [1983] 1 All ER 160, [1983] 1 WLR 86. As to security for expenses where a sale is ordered in lieu of foreclosure, see further **22.49**.
3 *Cheltenham and Gloucester plc v Krausz* [1997] 1 WLR 1558.
4 *Ex p Marsh* (1815) 1 Madd 148; *The Wilsons* (1841) 1 Wm Rob 173; *Palk v Mortgage Services Funding plc* [1993] Ch 330; *Polonski v Lloyd's Bank Mortgages Ltd* (1997) 31 HLR 721.
5 *Woolley v Colman* (1882) 21 Ch D 169, 51 LJ Ch 854; *Davies v Wright* [1892] 2 Ch 111; *Brewer v Square*, above. The reserve price should, if the mortgagee does not consent to the sale, be fixed at a sum sufficient, if practicable, to cover the amount due to him: *Woolley*

v Colman, above. As to sales by order of court, see CPR Sch 1, RSC Ord 31; and *Cumberland Union Banking Co v Maryport Hematite Iron and Steel Co* [1892] 1 Ch 92.
6 *Union Bank of London v Munster* (1887) 37 Ch D 51 (so-called 'puffers').
7 *Re Kelday, ex p Meston* (1888) 36 WR 585.

TRUSTS OF LAND AND APPOINTMENT OF TRUSTEES ACT 1996

The power to order a sale

21.13 Any person with an interest in a property subject to a trust of land may make an application to the court for an order for its sale[1]. That enables an equitable chargee of the share of a co-owner of land to apply for an order for sale[2]. In determining an application for such an order, the matters to which the court must have regard include:

(a) the intentions of the person or persons (if any) who created the trust;
(b) the purposes for which the property subject to the trust is held;
(c) the welfare of any minor who occupies or might reasonably be expected to occupy any land subject to the trust as his home; and
(d) the interest of any secured creditor of any beneficiary[3].

The court should also have regard to the circumstances and wishes of any beneficiaries of full age and entitled to an interest in possession in the property subject to the trust or, where there is a dispute, of the majority, according to the value of their combined interests[4].

1 Trusts of Land and Appointment of Trustees Act 1996, s 14.
2 See cases on the similar powers under the now repealed s 30 of the Law of Property Act 1925: *First National Securities Ltd v Hegerty* [1985] QB 850 at 867; *Midland Bank plc v Pike* [1988] 2 All ER 434; *Lloyds Bank plc v Byrne* [1993] 1 FLR 369 at 370.
3 Trusts of Land and Appointment of Trustees Act 1996, s 15.
4 Section 15(3); *Mortgage Corpn v Shaire Ltd* [2001] 3 WLR 639, [2000] 1 FLR 973; *Bank of Ireland Home Mortgages v Bell* [2001] 3 FCR 134, CA.

Exercise of the court's discretion under s 30 of the Law of Property Act 1925

21.14 The statutory predecessor of s 15 was s 30 of the Law of Property Act 1925. Where a chargee sought an order for sale under s 30, the normal rule was that, save in exceptional circumstances, his voice would prevail over the interests of a spouse or children in occupation[1]. The same applied where the sale was sought by a trustee in bankruptcy[2]. The fact that the spouse may have had an overriding interest was irrelevant to an application for sale under the section[3]. However, the court was less willing to order a sale where there was a subsisting collateral purpose of the trust other than the provision of a matrimonial home. Thus, where the sole owner of a property had transferred it into the joint names of her daughter and herself for no consideration, but on condition it would never be sold in her lifetime, an application by the mortgagee of the daughter's interest for an order for sale was refused[4]. Exceptionally an order for sale was refused in the exercise of the court's discretion where, although the charge had been validly registered, it had been altered by the mortgagee's solicitors prior to registration; an order for sale would have rewarded unmeritorious conduct[5]. The court was entitled to take into account similar matters to those it would take into account under s 36 of the Administration of Justice Act 1970[6]. It was inappropriate to make an order for sale without first determining the extent of subrogated rights nor, where the claim was for possession and sale, whether it was appropriate to adjourn the claim under s 36(2) of the Administration of Justice Act 1970[7].

1 *Lloyds Bank v Byrne* [1993] 1 FLR 369; *Mortgage Corpn Ltd v Shaire* [2000] 1 FLR 973.
2 *Re Citro* [1991] Ch 142; *Lloyds Bank plc v Byrne* [1993] 1 FLR 369; *Re Zandfarid v BCCI* [1996] 1 WLR 1420.
3 *Bank of Baroda v Dhilllon* (1997) 30 HLR 845.
4 *Abbey National plc v Moss* (1993) 26 HLR 249.
5 *Halifax Mortgage Services Ltd v Muirhead* (1997) 76 P & CR 418, CA.
6 *Bank of Baroda v Dhilllon* (1997) 30 HLR 845.
7 *Halifax Mortgage Services Ltd v Muirhead* (1997) 76 P & CR 418, CA.

Exercise of the court's discretion under s 15 of the 1996 Act

21.15 Section 15 has changed the law from that which applied under s 30[1]. The court now has greater flexibility as to how it exercises its discretion. It is able, if appropriate, to exercise its discretion more in favour of families in occupation rather than mortgagees: while s 15 specifies the interest of a chargee as one of four factors to be taken into account by the court, there is no suggestion that it is to be given any more importance than the interest of the children residing in the house. Although regard may still be had to the cases decided under s 30, they must therefore be treated with caution and in many cases they are unlikely to be of great, let alone decisive, assistance[2].

A powerful consideration in the exercise of the court's discretion will be whether the creditor is receiving proper recompense for being kept out of his money, where its repayment is overdue[3]. Thus it was plainly wrong for the court to refuse a sale where the debt exceeded what would be realised on a sale, was increasing, and where by refusing a sale the court would have condemned the mortgagee to wait indefinitely for its money[4]. However, where a mortgagee had a 25 per cent equitable interest in a long-standing family home, the court was prepared to refuse a sale if the equitable interest was converted into a loan of 25 per cent of the value of the house, and the mortgagor's former co-habitee could pay interest on the loan at 1 per cent above an appropriate bank base rate, which was somewhat below the market rate[5]. In addition to the matters specified in s 15, the court may wish to consider factors such as:

(a) the respective percentage interests in the property of the mortgagee and any occupiers of the property;
(b) whether, if a sale is refused, proper provision can be made for the mortgagee to have some control of repairs to the property and be able to keep it properly insured;
(c) whether the accommodation provided by the property is excessive for the needs of relevant occupiers;
(d) the sum which any occupiers would receive if the property were sold and whether that would enable them to secure other accommodation;
(e) the earning ability of relevant occupiers and their ability to pay a proper return to a mortgagee;
(f) and any hardship caused by forcing a long-standing resident of the property to move elsewhere[6].

1 *Mortgage Corpn Ltd v Shaire* [2000] 1 FLR 973 (disapproving *TSB Bank plc v Marshall* [1998] 3 EGLR 100 CC); [2000] Conv, 315 (Pascoe); *Bank of Ireland Home Mortgages v Bell* [2001] 3 FCR 134, CA.
2 *Mortgage Corpn Ltd v Shaire*, above; *Bank of Ireland Home Mortgages v Bell*, above.
3 *Mortgage Corpn Ltd v Shaire*, above.
4 *Bank of Ireland Home Mortgages v Bell*, above.
5 *Mortgage Corpn Ltd v Shaire*, above.
6 *Mortgage Corpn Ltd v Shaire*, above.

REGISTERED LAND

21.16 In the case of a registered charge under the Land Registration Act 1925, the registered proprietor of the charge has all the powers conferred by law on a legal mortgagee[1]. He is entitled to foreclosure or sale of the land charged in the same manner and under the same circumstances in and under which he might enforce the same if the land had been demised to him by way of mortgage, subject to a proviso for cesser on payment of the money at the appointed time. A sale by the court shall operate and be completed by registration in the same manner, as nearly as may be (but subject to any alterations on the register affecting the priority of the charge), as a transfer for valuable consideration by the proprietor of the land at the time of the registration of the charge would have operated or been completed and, as respects the land transferred, the charge and all incumbrances and entries inferior thereto shall be cancelled[2].

1 Section 34 (1). The section provides expressly for the completion of an order for foreclosure by the registration of the proprietor of the charge as the proprietor of the land: sub-s (3).
2 Law of Property Act 1925, s 34(4).

ORDER FOR SALE OF LAND BELONGING TO A BANKRUPT

UNDER THE TRUSTS OF LAND AND APPOINTMENT OF TRUSTEES ACT 1996

21.17 Section 335A of the Insolvency Act 1986 provides that any application by a trustee of a bankrupt's estate for an order for sale under s 14 of the 1996 Act must be made to the court with jurisdiction in relation to the bankruptcy[1]. The provisions of s 15 of the 1996 Act (specifying certain matters to which the court must have regard) do not apply to such an application[2]. On such an application the court must make such order as it thinks just and reasonable, having regard to:

(a) the interests of the bankrupt's creditors[3];
(b) where the application is made in respect of land which includes a dwelling house which is or has been the home of the bankrupt or the bankrupt's spouse or former spouse:
  (i) the conduct of the spouse or former spouse, so far as contributing to the bankruptcy;
  (ii) the needs and financial resources of the spouse or former spouse, and
  (iii) the needs of any children; and
(c) all the circumstances of the case other than the needs of the bankrupt[4].

Where such an application is made after the end of the period of one year beginning with the first vesting of the bankrupt's estate in a trustee[5], the court shall assume, unless the circumstances of the case are exceptional[6], that the interests of the bankrupt's creditors outweigh all other considerations[7]. It is an abuse of process for the trustee to make an application for sale for the sole benefit of a secured creditor, where the secured creditor could make an application himself[8].

1 Insolvency Act 1986, s 335A(1); inserted by s 25(1), Sch 3, para 23 of the Trusts of Land and Appointment of Trustees Act 1996.
2 This represents a different approach from that which applied under the now repealed s 30 of the Law of Property Act 1925, under which the court adopted precisely the same approach in a case where one of the co-owners was a bankrupt and in a case where one of the co-owners had charged his interest: see *Re Citro* [1991] Ch 142; *Lloyds Bank v Byrne* [1993] 1 FLR 369; *Zandfarid v BCCI* [1996] 1 WLR 1420; *Mortgage Corpn Ltd v Shaire* [2000] 1 FLR 973. See **21.14**.
3 Including both secured and unsecured creditors: *Judd v Brown* [1998] 2 FLR 360, [1998] Fam Law 514;
4 Insolvency Act 1986, s 335A(2). The creditors have an interest in an order for sale even if the sale proceeds will only be sufficient to discharge the expenses of the bankruptcy: *Eric Bowe v Bowe* [1998] 2 FLR 439, [1998] Fam Law 515.
5 Under Ch IV of Part IX of the Insolvency Act 1986.
6 As to exceptional circumstances, see *Judd v Brown* [1998] 2 FLR 360, [1998] Fam Law 514; *Eric Bowe v Bowe* [1998] 2 FLR 439, [1998] Fam Law 515; *Re Raval* [1998] 2 FLR 718, [1998] Fam Law 590.
7 Insolvency Act 1986, s 335A(3).
8 *Judd v Brown* [1998] 2 FLR 360, [1998] Fam Law 514; *Re Ng (a bankrupt)* [1998] 2 FLR 386, [1998] Fam Law 515.

UNDER THE INSOLVENCY RULES 1986

Power to order sale of mortgaged land

21.18 The ordinary process in bankruptcy is by sale and the Insolvency Rules 1986 provide a mortgagee with a special power of sale[1]. Any person claiming to be the legal or equitable mortgagee[2] of land[3] belonging to a bankrupt may apply to the court for an order directing that the land be sold[4]. The court, if satisfied as to the applicant's title, may direct accounts to be taken and enquiries made to ascertain: (a) the principal, interest and costs due under the mortgage[5], and (b) where the mortgagee has been in possession of the land or any part of it, the rents and profits, dividends, interest or other proceeds received by him or on his behalf. Pursuant to that process, the court can give directions with respect to any mortgage (whether prior or subsequent) on the same property, other than the applicant's[6]. For the purpose of the accounts and inquiries, and for making title to the purchaser, the court can order the parties to give evidence, to produce documents relating to the bankrupt's estate, to clarify any matter in dispute in the proceedings or give any additional information (in relation to which CPR Pt 18 applies)[7]. If the court is satisfied that there ought to be a sale, it may order that the land, or any specified part of it be sold[8]. It also has the power to order that any party bound by the order who is in possession of any part of the land, or who is receiving rents or profits from it, should deliver up possession to any person nominated by the court, including the purchaser[9].

1 Rules 6.197–6.199.
2 The mortgagee need not rely on his special power of sale and is entitled to apply to the court for an order for sale in his general character of mortgagee: *Re Cook, ex p Hodgson* (1821) 1 Gl & J 12; *Ex p Bacon* (1832) 2 Deac & Ch 181; *Re Medley, ex p Barnes* (1838) 3

Deac 223. If the property is bought in by the trustee, the mortgagee, by applying for a second sale, waives all claims against the trustee for any difference in the amount of biddings between the first and second sales *Re Moore, ex p Baldock* (1832) 2 Deac & Ch 60.
3 Which includes any interest in, or right over, land: Insolvency Rules 1986, r 6.197(1).
4 Insolvency Rules 1986, r 6.197(1).
5 It has been said that an order for sale cannot be objected to on the ground that the period has not expired before which, under the terms of the mortgage, the debt could not be called in, on the basis that such a provision has reference to the mortgagee's remedies at the date of the security, when he could rely on the bankrupt as well as the security to rely upon; he cannot be deprived both of interest and of his right to sell: *Re Theobald, ex p Bignold* (1838) 3 Mont & A 477.
6 Insolvency Rules 1986, r 6.197(2).
7 Rule 6.197(3); as amended by the Insolvency (Amendment) (No 2) Rules 1999, SI 1999/1022, r 3, Sch, para 2.
8 Rule 6.198 (1).
9 Rule 6.198(1).

Court to be satisfied of the applicant mortgagee's title

21.19 Before considering whether to exercise its discretion to order a sale, the court must first be satisfied of the applicant mortgagee's title[1]. Thus there can be no sale where the security is inoperative for want of compliance with some legal formality[2]; nor where the mortgagee cannot prove for the deficiency, for instance where the bankrupt is only a purchaser of the equity of redemption, whose covenant for repayment does not make him personally liable for the debt to the mortgagee[3]; nor where the title to the mortgaged property is hampered in some way, for instance where it consists of a share of partnership property subject to a right of pre-emption and the taking of partnership accounts is necessary to ascertain its value[4].

1 Insolvency Rules 1986 r 6.197(2).
2 *Re Swann, ex p Miller* (1849) 3 De G & Sm 553 (enrolment); eg s 2 of the Law of Property (Miscellaneous Provisions) Act 1989.
3 *Re Stockdale, ex p Keightley* (1849) 3 De G & Sm 583. See **17.5**.
4 *Re Borrow, ex p Broadbent* (1834) 1 Mont & A 635; *Re Jackson, ex p Attwood, Spooner & Co* (1834) 2 Mont & A 24.

Mortgaged leaseholds

21.20 The right to an order for sale of a mortgaged leasehold is not affected by a lessee's covenant not to assign without the licence of the lessor[1], although that used to be the case if the lease was determinable on the committal of an act of bankruptcy[2]. On an application for an order for sale of a leasehold, the mortgagee will not be ordered to indemnify the trustee against any breach of the covenants, since the trustee had the option of disclaiming the lease[3].

1 See *Doe d Goodbehere v Bevan* (1815) 3 M & S 353 at 360.
2 *Re Champney, ex p Sherman* (1820) Buck 462.
3 *Re Collins, ex p Fletcher* (1832) 1 Deac & Ch 318; see **23.45**.

Sub-mortgage

21.21 If a mortgagee who has made a sub-mortgage becomes bankrupt, the sub-mortgagee may obtain a sale of the bankrupt's interest in the original security[1]. If the original security was for an uncertain sum, there must first be an inquiry as to the amount due, although permission will be given to enter a claim for the full amount due to the sub-mortgagee pending the inquiry. If after the sub-mortgage the original mortgagee has bought the equity of redemption and the trustee rejects it, the sub-mortgagee may include it in his sale, and the trustee will be bound to convey to the purchaser[2].

1 *Re Wright, ex p Mackay* (1841) 1 Mont D & De G 550; *Re Moore, ex p Powell* (1847) De G 405.
2 *Re Watts, ex p Tuffnell* (1834) 1 Mont & A 620.

Charges by deposit of deeds

21.22 Since 27 September 1989, it has no longer been possible to create charges by the deposit of deeds[1]. In the case of such charges created before that date, a deposit of deeds is not necessary to enable the equitable mortgagee to obtain an order for sale[2], nor is a memorandum of deposit. However, if the mortgagee has no memorandum, he must produce clear evidence in support of his debt — his mere allegation will not stand against the sworn evidence of the bankrupt[3]. If the deposit was made by the solicitor of the bankrupt, it must be shown that he had authority to make it[4]. Likewise, the right to a sale is not affected either by an imperfection in the memorandum, or in the deposit, provided the intention to complete the security is shown. Thus the court has ordered the sale of a freehold property and a leasehold property, where although the deposit of the deeds relating to both was complete, the memorandum related to one only[5] and, conversely, where both properties were specified in the memorandum, but only the deeds relating to one were deposited[6]. The right to a sale is not affected by an arrangement made subsequent to the security, between the mortgagor and a third person, under which the latter acquires an interest in the mortgaged property[7]. If an equitable mortgagee takes a legal mortgage with notice of the bankruptcy, his right to a sale under the equitable mortgage is only suspended and revives when the legal security is declared to be inoperative[8].

1 Law of Property (Miscellaneous Provisions) Act 1989, s 2; *United Bank of Kuwait plc v Sahib* [1997] Ch 107.
2 *Re Blew, ex p Jones* (1835) 4 Deac & Ch 750.
3 Hence, where the bankrupt denied by his affidavit that the security was for past as well as for present and future advances, the order for sale was prefaced by a declaration that the deposit was for present and future advances only, and the order reserved the proceeds after payment of such advances and gave liberty to apply for the purpose of proving the mortgagor's allegation: *Re Cowderoy, ex p Martin* (1835) 2 Mont & A 243.
4 *Re Hood, ex p Coleman* (1840) 4 Deac 242.
5 *Re Evans, ex p Robinson* (1832) 1 Deac & Ch 119.
6 *Re Leathes, ex p Leathes* (1833) 3 Deac & Ch 112.
7 *Re Draper, ex p Booth* (1832) 2 Deac & Ch 59.
8 *Re Emery, ex p Harvey* (1839) 3 Deac 547.

Other incumbrancers

21.23 The mortgagee who applies for a sale should bring all incumbrancers before the court[1]. The court can require particular persons to join in the sale or conveyance and require the payment of the purchase money into court, or to trustees or others[2].

1 *Re Smithies, ex p Burt* (1840) 1 Mont D & De G 191.
2 Insolvency Rules 1986, r 6.198(3)(e) and (f). Formerly, where there were several incumbrancers, the concurrence of all was necessary, and if they did not concur, the court could only sell subject to the rights of those who dissented: *Ex p Jackson* (1800) 5 Ves 357; *Re Watts, ex p Wright* (1837) 3 Mont & A 49.

Factors affecting the exercise of the court's discretion to order a sale

21.24 The court has a discretion as to whether to order sale of the security[1]. A sale may be refused if it would be disadvantageous to the bankrupt's estate. Thus, the court may decide not to order a sale if it would cause injury to other parts of the bankrupt's estate, such as where there is a charge over fixtures in a property which is itself not subject to the security[2]. A sale may also be refused where there is a dispute over whether the property is subject to other incumbrances[3], although the court can now require the payment of the purchase money into court, or to trustees or others, pending the resolution of such disputes[4]. If there is a dispute in respect of part only of the property, the court may order sale of the other part[5], although it will need to consider whether such a sale would realise proportionately less than a sale of the whole. Similarly, where only one partner becomes bankrupt, a sale may be ordered of his separate estate where that is mortgaged for a partnership debt, though there will be no proof against his estate[6].

There will be no order for sale if the security is open to suspicion of any taint. Thus formerly a sale was refused on the ground of usury[7] and where the money could not properly be secured by mortgage[8]. A sale was refused where the lender had notice of a trust, but lent the money to the trustee for his own purpose[9]. Where the bankruptcy follows very soon after the mortgage, the court may require evidence that the security was not made in contemplation of bankruptcy, as a fraudulent preference[10]. In such circumstances, the application may be ordered to stand over pending an inquiry into the existence and circumstances attending the creation of the debt and deposit and to enable the trustee to apply for a delivery of the deeds[11].

1 Insolvency Rules 1986, r 6.198(1).
2 *Re Clarke, ex p Sykes* (1849) 18 LJ Bcy 16.
3 *Re Francis, ex p Bignold* (1836) 1 Deac 515.
4 Insolvency Rules 1986, r 6.198(3)(e) and (f). Formerly, where there were several incumbrancers, the concurrence of all was necessary and, if they did not concur, the court could only sell subject to the rights of those who dissented: *Ex p Jackson* (1800) 5 Ves 357; *Re Watts, ex p Wright* (1837) 3 Mont & A 49.
5 *Re Price, ex p Wace* (1842) 2 Mont D & De G 730.
6 *Re Ireland, and Harrison, ex p Lloyd* (1838) 3 Mont & A 601.
7 *Re Jarmain, ex p Nunn* (1836) 1 Deac 393.
8 *Re Clark, ex p Wake* (1837) 2 Deac 352.
9 *Ex p Turner* (1745) 9 Mod Rep 418.
10 *Re Clark, ex p Wake*, above; *Re Walker, ex p Ainsworth* (1838) 2 Deac 563; *Re Davy, ex p Dewdney* (1835) 4 Deac & Ch 181; *Re Leach, ex p Morgan* (1840) 1 Mont D & De G 116; *Re Lindon, ex p Clouter* (1843) 3 Mont D & De G 187; but see *Re Ogbourne, ex p Heathcote* (1842) 2 Mont D & De G 711. As to fraudulent preferences, see **23.38**.
11 Insolvency Act 1986, s 313 (1) and see Insolvency Rules 1986, r 6.237. For the rights of occupation of the bankrupt and the bankrupt's spouse, see Insolvency Act 1986, sections 336–338; and see **12.132**, n 3; (1987) 137 NLJ 310, 347 (Bailey and Berry).

Conduct of sale

21.25 Generally, the trustee is given the conduct of the sale[1]. The court can permit the person with conduct of the sale to act in such manner as he thinks fit; or can give directions as to the conduct of the sale[2]. Such directions can include:

(a) appointing the person having the conduct of the sale;

(b) fixing the manner of sale (whether by contract conditional on the court's approval, private treaty, public auction or otherwise);
(c) settling the particulars and conditions of sale;
(d) obtaining evidence of the value of the property, and fixing a reserve or minimum price;
(e) requiring particular persons to join in the sale and conveyance;
(f) requiring the payment of the purchase money into court, or to trustees or others; and
(g) if the sale is to be by public auction, fixing the security (if any) to be given by the auctioneer, and his remuneration[3].

On an auction sale by the direction of the court, the court may also direct that the mortgagee can appear and bid on his own behalf[4].

1 As a general rule, where the security is sufficient, the conduct of the sale will be given to the trustee; but where the security is insufficient, to the mortgagee: *Re Jordan, ex p Harrison* (1884) 13 QBD 228.
2 Insolvency Rules 1986, r 6.197(2).
3 Rule 6.198(3).
4 Rule 6.198 (4).

Proceeds of sale

21.26 The proceeds of sale shall be applied:

(a) in payment of the expenses of the trustee (of and occasioned by the application to the court, of the sale and attendance at the sale and of any costs arising from the taking of accounts, and making of enquiries[1]); and
(b) in payment of the amount found due to any mortgagee, for principal, interest and costs[2].

The balance, if any, shall be retained by or paid to the trustee[3]. Where the proceeds of the sale are insufficient to pay in full the amount found due to any mortgagee, he is entitled to prove as a creditor for any deficiency and to receive dividends rateably with other creditors, but not so as to disturb any dividend already declared[4].

1 As directed by the court under r 6.197.
2 Insolvency Rules 1986, r 6.199(1). The mortgagee's costs will include his costs of defending the security (*Re Hofmann, ex p Carr* (1879) 11 Ch D 62, CA), but not of negotiating the loan or preparing the mortgage deed: *Wales v Carr* [1902] 1 Ch 860. For the better taking of inquiries and accounts, and making a title to a purchaser, all parties may be examined by the court and must produce documents on oath: r 197 (3); and the court may order inquiries and accounts to be taken in like manner as in the Chancery Division: r 6.197 (4).
3 Insolvency Rules 1986, r 6.199(1).
4 Insolvency Rules 1986, r 6.199(2).

CHARGING ORDERS[1]

21.27 A charge imposed by a charging order made under the Charging Orders Act 1979 has the like effect and is enforceable in the same courts and in the same manner as an equitable charge created by the debtor by writing under his hand[2]. The remedy under an equitable charge under hand is sale[3]. Proceedings to enforce a charging order by sale of the property charged can be brought in the

Chancery Division[4] of the High Court, in accordance with CPR Pt 8 and CPR Sch 1, RSC Ord 88, r 5A; and in the county court in accordance with CPR Sch 2, CCR 31.4. The witness statement or affidavit in support of the originating summons must contain the matters referred to in CPR Sch 1, RSC Ord 88, r 5A (2) in the High Court and the matters referred to in CPR Sch 2, CCR 31.4(1) in the county court.

Since the proceedings will be for sale only of 'the property charged', they will be of limited value to a creditor where the property charged is the beneficial interest of one of two or more co-owners. A sale of the beneficial interest of one co-owner is not only likely to be impracticable, but is also likely to realise far less than an equivalent share in the value of the property as a whole. Thus a person entitled to a charging order will normally prefer to apply under s 14 of the Trusts of Land and Appointment of Trustees Act 1996[5] to:

(a) identify the charging order sought to be enforced and the subject matter of the charge;
(b) specify the amount in respect of which the charge was imposed and the balance outstanding at the date of the affidavit;
(c) verify, so far as is known, the debtor's title to the property charged;
(d) identify any other incumbrances on the property charged stating, so far as is known, the names and addresses of the incumbrancers and the amounts owing to them;
(e) set out the plaintiff's proposals as to the manner of sale of the property charged together with estimates of the gross price which would be obtained on a sale in that manner and of the costs of such a sale; and
(f) where the property charged consists of land in respect of which the plaintiff claims delivery of possession—
    (i) give particulars of every person who to the best of the plaintiff's knowledge is in possession of the property charged or any part of it; and
    (ii) state, in the case of a dwelling house, whether a land charge of Class F has been registered, or a notice or caution pursuant to s 2(7) of the Matrimonial Homes Act 1967, or a notice pursuant to s 2(8) of the Matrimonial Homes Act 1983 has been entered and, if so, on whose behalf, and whether he has served notice of the proceedings on the person on whose behalf the land charge is registered or the notice or caution entered.

1 See generally **2.12** ff.
2 Charging Orders Act 1979, s 3 (4); CPR Sch 1, RSC Ord 50; CPR Sch 2, CCR Ord 31.
3 *Tennant v Trenchard* (1869) 4 Ch App 537, although the court may also appoint a receiver.
4 Supreme Court Act 1981, s 61(3)(b).
5 See **21.13 ff**. As to his power to do so, see *Thames Guaranty Ltd v Campbell* [1985] QB 210 at 239; *First National Securities Ltd v Hegerty* [1985] QB 850; *Harman v Glencross* [1986] Fam 81, [1986] 1 All ER 545; applied in *Midland Bank plc v Pike* [1988] 2 All ER 434.

UNDER THE CIVIL PROCEDURE RULES, IN PROCEEDINGS RELATING TO LAND

21.28 In any proceedings relating to land, the court may order the land, or part of it, to be sold[1]. An application in existing proceedings for such an order should be made in accordance with CPR Pt 23. The court can make any directions it considers appropriate for giving effect to the order, including:

(a) appointing a party or other person to conduct the sale;
(b) for obtaining evidence of the value of the land;
(c) as to the manner of the sale;
(d) settling the particulars and conditions of the sale;
(e) fixing a minimum or reserve price;
(f) as to the fees and expenses to be allowed to an auctioneer or estate agent;
(g) for the purchase money to be paid into court, or to trustees or any other person; and
(h) for the result of the sale to be certified[2]. In practice it may order a sale 'in such manner as the parties may agree, or, in default of agreement, as the court may direct'. The court can refer any matter of title to conveyancing counsel[3].

Where the court has made an order under CPR 40.16 for land to be sold and a party wishes to bid for, tender or offer to buy the land, he should apply for permission to do so[4]. An application for permission to bid must be made before the sale takes place. If the court gives permission to all parties to make bids or offers, it may appoint an independent person to conduct the sale[5]. The rules make provision for the certification of the sale result[6] and for the fees and expenses of auctioneers and estate agents[7].

1 CPR 40.16.
2 CPR 40DPD, para. 2.
3 CPR 40.18; CPR 40DPD, para 6.1–6.6.
4 CPR 40DPD, para 3.1.
5 CPR 40DPD, para 3.1.
6 CPR 40DPD, para 4.1–4.3.
7 CPR 40DPD, para 5.1–5.4.

PROVISION FOR SALE OF LAND FREE FROM INCUMBRANCES

21.29 Where land subject to any incumbrance[1] is sold, any party to the sale may apply[2] to the court for a direction under[3] s 50 of the Law of Property Act 1925 for the discharge of incumbrances. The directions the court may give on such an application include a direction for the payment into court of a sum of money that the court considers sufficient to meet, first, the value of the incumbrance and, secondly, further costs, expenses and interest that may become due on or in respect of the incumbrance[4]. Where payment into court has been made in accordance with a direction under s 50(1), the court may declare the land to be freed from the incumbrance and make any order it considers appropriate for giving effect to an order made under CPR 40.16 or relating to the money in court and the income thereof.

1 Which has the same meaning as in s 205(1) of the Law of Property Act 1925; CPR 40DPD, para 1.1.
2 An application under s 50 should be made under CPR Pt 23 if made in existing proceedings, or otherwise by Pt 8 claim form: CPR 40DPD, para 1.5.
3 CPR 40DPD, para 1.2.
4 CPR 40DPD, para 1.3; s 50(1) of the Law of Property Act 1925 contains provisions relating to the calculation of these amounts.

MARITIME SECURITIES

The power to order sale

21.30 The Admiralty Court of the Queen's Bench Division of the High Court has the power to order the sale of a ship in a claim in rem at any stage of the proceedings[1]. While a sale by the Admiralty Marshal may involve additional costs and delays when compared to the exercise of the mortgagee's power of sale, it has the benefit that the mortgagor can have no complaint against the mortgagee as to the mode of sale or the sale price and the purchaser will obtain a clean title to the ship[2].

1 In all cases of salvage, damages, necessaries, wages, or bottomry: *The Tremont* (1841) 1 Wm Rob 163; *The Lady Tahilla* [1967] 1 Lloyd's Rep 591 at 601; *The Myrto* [1977] 2 Lloyd's Rep 243 at 259; see **20.8**. See Admiralty Jurisdiction and Proceedings Practice Direction (pursuant to CPR Pt 49), para 8.1(1). The court has no power to order a sale in a claim *in personam*: *The Lady Tahilla*, above.

2 See *The Acrux* [1962] 1 Lloyd's Rep 405. For a fuller discussion of such benefits, and the circumstances in which an order may be made, see *Meeson on Admiralty Jurisdiction and Practice* (2nd edn, 2000) para 10-213 ff.

When sale will be ordered

21.31 An order for sale will not normally be made unless the res is under arrest and in the hands of the court[1], although where it is not already under arrest an order for arrest, appraisement and sale may be made if there are special circumstances[2]. A sale may be made on the defendant's application[3]. Sale is not ordered at the instance of a bottomry bondholder, until the court is satisfied by perusal of the bond that is duly executed and with maritime risk. The court has the power to make an order for the appraisement and sale of the ship whilst the claim is pending, which the court may make to avoid the costs of maintaining the arrest being incurred, or where the property is perishable[4].

1 *The Wexford* (1888) 13 PD 10; *The Ricuna* 1974 Fo 380 (unreported).

2 *The Berriz* 1905 Fo. 497.

3 *The Westport* [1965] 1 WLR 796.

4 *The Myrto* [1977] 2 Lloyd's Rep 243.

The order for sale

21.32 An order for sale before judgment may only be made by the Admiralty Judge[1]. Unless the Admiralty Court orders otherwise, an order for sale will be in Form No ADN14[2]. In giving directions for sale, the Admiralty Court may fix a time within which notice of claims against the proceeds of sale must be filed and the time and manner in which notice of that time must be advertised[3]. Any party with a judgment against the property or proceeds of sale may at any time after that specified time apply to the Admiralty Court for the determination of priorities[4]. The application notice must be served on all persons who have filed a claim against the property. Unless otherwise ordered by the Admiralty Judge, only he may make a determination of priorities[5]. Payment out of the proceeds of sale will be made only to judgment creditors and in accordance with the determination of priorities or as the Admiralty Court may otherwise order[6].

1 Admiralty Jurisdiction and Proceedings Practice Direction, para. 8.1(2).
2 Paragraph 8.1(3).
3 Paragraph 8.1(4).
4 As to priorities in maritime securities, see 10th edn, pp 515 ff.
5 Paragraph 8.2.
6 Paragraph 8.3.

Sale in foreign currency

21.33 In order to obtain the best sale price, the Admiralty Marshal can sell the property at a price in a foreign currency[1]. When proceeds of sale are paid into court by the Marshal and such payment is in a foreign currency, the funds will be placed on one day call interest-bearing account, unless otherwise ordered by the court. An application to place foreign currency on longer term deposit, unless made at the same time as the application for sale or other prior application, may be made to the Admiralty Registrar. Notice of the placement of foreign currency in an interest-bearing account must be given to all parties interested in the fund by the party at whose instance the foreign currency is invested. Any interested party who wishes to object to the mode of investment of foreign currency paid into court may apply to the Admiralty Registrar for directions[2].

1 *The Halcyon the Great* [1975] 1 WLR 515, [1975] 1 Lloyd's Rep 518.
2 Admiralty Jurisdiction and Proceedings Practice Direction, para 8.4.

Chapter 22

Foreclosure[1]

THE RIGHT TO FORECLOSE[2]

THE NATURE OF FORECLOSURE

22.1 Equity grants the mortgagor an equitable right to redeem after the legal date for redemption has passed. Foreclosure is the process by which the mortgagor's equitable right to redeem is extinguished, together with the equity of redemption of all persons claiming through him, including subsequent incumbrancers. By granting an equitable right to redeem, equity interfered with the bargain made between the parties to the mortgage; foreclosure marks the limit of equity's indulgence to the mortgagor. The court removes the stop it has itself put on[3]. There can generally[4] be no foreclosure except by an order of the court[5]. The mortgagee may bring a claim for foreclosure, asking that the equity of redemption of the mortgagor and all persons claiming through him, is extinguished, so as to vest the mortgaged property absolutely in the mortgagee. If the relief is granted, the mortgage is said to be foreclosed. The mortgagee is thereupon entitled to be the absolute owner of the property in both law and equity[6].

Foreclosure was formerly a mortgagee's primary remedy, but it is now rarely sought or granted[7]. The vast majority of mortgages made today are building society mortgages and the only relief the society will want to seek from the court will be an order for possession, so that it can sell with vacant possession under its power of sale; it will not normally want to have the property vested in itself. There is also a lack of finality in an order for foreclosure[8]. However, foreclosure is still an appropriate remedy in the case of an equitable mortgage by deposit of title deeds unaccompanied by any deed or document giving a power of sale (although it has not been possible to create a mortgage by that means since 27 September 1989)[9]. Whenever foreclosure is sought, if there are other incumbrancers interested in the property or if the value of the property exceeds the mortgage debt, the court will, if requested, usually order a sale, rather than foreclosure[10].

1 In Canada foreclosure remains a principal remedy. According to the Report of the Committee on the Enforcement of Judgment Debts (the Payne Committee) 1969, Cmnd 1309, para 1360, there had been a revival in the popularity of foreclosure as a remedy. Notwithstanding the Administration of Justice Act 1970 as extended by the Administration of Justice Act 1973 (see **19.51** ff), there are cases when foreclosure is ordered (eg where there would be a deficiency on a sale and see eg *Lord Marples of Wallasey*

v Holmes (1975) 31 P & CR 94), but the court is usually reluctant to make a foreclosure order where the result would be a windfall profit for the mortgagee. The remedy has been replaced in the Republic of Ireland by judicial sale and has been abolished in New Zealand (see Property Law Act 1952, s 89). See, generally, (1979) 129 NLJ 33 (Markson). For the Law Commission's recommendation for the abolition of foreclosure, see Report *Transfer of Land — Land Mortgages* 1991 (Law Com no 204) paras. 7.26–7.27. On foreclosure generally, see also *Falconbridge on Mortgages* (4th edn) Chs 24–26. For the court's power to authorise a sale under s 91 of the Law of Property Act 1925, having the effect of an order for foreclosure but without the attendant technicality and delay, and preserving the mortgagor's liability on the personal covenants for any shortfall, see *Palk v Mortgage Services Funding plc* [1993] Ch 330, [1993] 2 All ER 481 and **21.5** ff.

2 For the periods of limitation applicable to foreclosure actions, see **16.36** ff.

3 *Carter v Wake* (1877) 4 Ch D 605 at 606, per Jessel MR.

4 The dismissal of an action for redemption is equivalent to foreclosure: *Cholmley v Countess of Oxford* (1741) 2 Atk 267; and see **29.26** ff.

5 *Re Farnol, Eades, Irvine & Co* [1915] 1 Ch 22 at 24; *Ness v O'Neill* [1916] 1 KB 706 at 709.

6 See *Heath v Pugh* (1881) 6 QBD 345 at 360; Law of Property Act 1925, s 88(2), 89(2); see further, **25.58** and **22.59**.

7 *Palk v Mortgage Services Funding plc* [1993] Ch 330 at 336, per Sir Donald Nicholls V-C. The general public still often thinks of the mortgagee's remedies in terms of foreclosure, see, eg *Alliance Perpetual Building Society v Belrum Investments Ltd* [1957] 1 All ER 635, [1957] 1 WLR 720. There was a brief period of popularity in the 1960s and 1970s for jurisdictional reasons: see Law Com no 204, paras 7.26–7.27.

8 See **22.65** ff on reopening the foreclosure.

9 See s 2 Law of the Property (Miscellaneous Provisions) Act 1989; *United Bank of Kuwait plc v Sahib* [1997] Ch 107; and **3.84**, **3.87** and **3.90** ff.

10 See **21.2**, **21.11** and **22.47** ff, and see Law Commission Working Paper no 99, *Land Mortgages*, paras 3.50 ff.

THE LEGAL MORTGAGEE'S RIGHT TO FORECLOSE

22.2 The right to foreclose arises once payment is due at law, since that is when the equitable right to redeem arises; until then, there is nothing to extinguish by foreclosure[1]. Payment is due at law upon the legal date for redemption[2] or upon some earlier default, where the mortgage provides for the debt to be paid upon breach — for example, failure to pay interest[3] or an instalment of the principal debt[4]. Where no date is fixed for payment, the debt is payable after demand or notice[5]. If the mortgagor fails to pay what is due at law, the mortgagee is entitled to bring a claim for foreclosure, unless he has by agreement restricted his right to do so until some specified occurrence[6]. The right to foreclosure exists, although the mortgagee has recovered part of the debt, so long as he has not been fully paid[7]. A mortgagee does not waive his right to foreclose simply by accepting a late payment[8]. However, if the mortgagee proceeds for personal payment after foreclosure absolute, the effect is to re-open the foreclosure[9]. The right to foreclose is not affected by the fact that the mortgagee also has a power of sale[10], although the court may order a sale of the property as an alternative to foreclosure[11]. Where there are successive mortgages, each legal mortgagee has a right to foreclosure and to get in the legal estate of the mortgagor, subject only to prior mortgages. The circumstances in which foreclosure will or may be reopened are considered below[12].

Foreclosure is not confined to mortgages of land: the right to foreclose is available in respect of chattels[13], stocks and shares[14], insurance policies[15], pensions[16], debentures[17], reversionary interests[18], a share in a partnership[19], ships or shares in a ship[20] and other choses in action[21]. A proprietor of a registered charge has all the powers of a legal mortgagee[22]. The court will not order foreclosure against the Crown; it will instead direct a sale and rely upon the Crown to convey the property[23].

1 *Williams v Morgan* [1906] 1 Ch 804. See generally **16.10**.
2 As to default under the proviso for redemption, see **16.10**.
3 *Keene v Biscoe* (1878) 8 Ch D 201; *Twentieth Century Banking Corpn Ltd v Wilkinson* [1977] Ch 99, [1976] 3 All ER 361.
4 *Kidderminster Mutual Benefit Building Society v Haddock* [1936] WN 158.
5 See **17.6**.
6 *Ramsbottom v Wallis* (1835) 5 LJ Ch 92. As to restrictions by agreement on the mortgagee's right to foreclose, see *Seaton v Twyford* (1870) LR 11 Eq 591.
7 A foreclosure will not, however, be made in respect of interest only: *Drought v Redford* (1827) 1 Mol 572.
8 *Keene v Biscoe* (1878) 8 Ch D 201; *Stanhope v Manners* (1763) 2 Eden 197; cf *Re Taaffe's Estate*(1864) 14 IrChR 347; *Langridge v Payne* (1862) 2 John & H 423; *Seal v Gimson* (1914) 110 LT 583.
9 *Lockhart v Hardy* (1846) 9 Beav 349; *Palmer v Hendrie* (1859) 27 Beav 349.
10 *Wayne v Hanham* (1851) 9 Hare 62; *Hutton v Sealy* (1858) 27 LJ Ch 263.
11 *Moore v Morton* [1886] WN 196; and see **21.2**, **21.11** and **22.47** ff.
12 See **22.65** ff.
13 *Harrison v Hart* (1726) 2 Eq Cas Abr 6; *Tancred v Potts* (1749) 2 Fonbl Eq 261n.
14 *General Credit and Discount Co v Glegg* (1883) 22 Ch D 549 at 555.
15 *Re J Kerr's Policy* (1869) LR 8 Eq 331.
16 *James v Ellis* (1871) 19 WR 319.
17 *Sadler v Worley* (1894) 2 Ch 170.
18 *Slade v Rigg* (1843) 3 Hare 35; *Wayne v Hanham* (1851) 9 Hare 62; cf *Stamford, Spalding and Boston Banking Co v Ball* (1862) 4 De GF & J 310, where the terms of the mortgage provided otherwise.
19 *Redmayne v Forster* (1866) LR 2 Eq 467.
20 *The Buttermere* 24 July 1883 (Folio 211); see *Meeson on Admiralty Jurisdiction and Practice* (2nd edn, 2000) para. 10-184.
21 *General Credit and Discount Co v Glegg* (1883) 22 Ch D 549; *Harrold v Plenty* [1901] 2 Ch 314; *Stubbs v Slater* [1910] 1 Ch 632, CA; *Adelaide Building Co Pty Ltd v ABC Investments Pty Ltd* (1990) 8 ACLC 445.
22 Land Registration Act 1925, s 34(1); and see **4.13**.
23 *Hancock v A-G* (1864) 10 Jur NS 557; *Bartlett v Rees* (1871) LR 12 Eq 395. See also *Scott v Robarts* (1856) 4 WR 499; *Rogers v Maule* (1841) 1 Y & C Ch Cas 4; *Prescott v Tyler* (1837) 1 Jur 470. For the former practice of allowing the mortgagee to enjoy the property until the Crown redeemed, see *Hodge v A-G* (1838) 3 Y & C Ex 342; *Lutwich's Case*, cited 2 Atk 223.

EQUITABLE MORTGAGE OR CHARGE

22.3 Where an equitable mortgage is accompanied by an agreement, express or implied, on the part of the mortgagor to execute a legal mortgage, there is a right to foreclosure. Since 27 September 1989 it has no longer been possible to create a mortgage by the deposit of title deeds[1]. However, in respect of a mortgage by deposit made before that date, the depositee of title deeds is entitled to foreclosure, where the deposit was accompanied by an agreement to execute a legal mortgage[2]. The right is available even where there was a simple deposit or memorandum without an agreement to execute a mortgage[3], unless the terms of the agreement exclude the right to a legal mortgage[4]. The deposit is of itself evidence of an agreement to make a legal security, which the court will carry into effect against the mortgagor or any who claim under him with actual or constructive notice of the deposit[5]. However, an equitable chargee cannot foreclose, because there is in his case no agreement to make a legal security nor any estate in him[6].

1 See Law of Property (Miscellaneous Provisions) Act 1989, s 2; *United Bank of Kuwait plc v Sahib* [1997] Ch 107; and **3.84**, **3.87** and **3.90** ff.

2 *Perry v Keane, Perry v Partridge* (1836) 6 LJ Ch 67; *Cox v Toole* (1855) 20 Beav 145; *Underwood v Joyce* (1861) 7 Jur NS 566.
3 *Pryce v Bury* (1854) LR 16 Eq 153n; *Redmayne v Forster* (1866) LR 2 Eq 467; *James v James* (1873) LR 16 Eq 153.
4 *Sporle v Whayman* (1855) 20 Beav 607.
5 *Birch v Ellames* (1794) 2 Anst 427; *Ex p Wright* (1812) 19 Ves 255; *Parker v Housefield* (1834) 2 My & K 419.
6 *Re Owen* [1894] 3 Ch 220; *Shea v Moore* [1894] 1 IR 158; *Tennant v Trenchard* (1869) 4 Ch App 537 at 542; *United Travel Agencies Pty Ltd v Cain* (1990) 20 NSWLR 566; *Croydon (Unique) Ltd v Wright* [2000] 2 WLR 683 at 702A, per Butler-Sloss LJ.

FORM OF PROCEEDINGS

JURISDICTION OF HIGH COURT AND COUNTY COURT

22.4 A county court has all the jurisdiction of the High Court to hear and determine proceedings for foreclosure of any mortgage where the amount owing in respect of the mortgage does not exceed £30,000[1]. The county court has jurisdiction where the amount originally owing exceeded that limit, but has subsequently been reduced below it[2]. The jurisdiction of the county court may be extended by agreement[3]. Although the High Court does not have jurisdiction to hear and determine proceedings in which the mortgagee under a mortgage of land which consists of or includes a dwelling-house situated outside Greater London, that does not apply to a claim for foreclosure (or sale) in which a claim for possession of the mortgaged property is also made[4]. However, the claim for foreclosure must be a genuine one, and not a mere device to evade the jurisdiction of the county court[5]. Where the claim is for possession as well as for foreclosure, the claimant must also comply with the rules as to jurisdiction and procedure governing a claim for possession[6].

1 County Courts Act 1984, s 23(c). For transfer from the High Court to the county court, see County Courts Act 1984, s 40.
2 *Shields, Whitley and District Amalgamated Model Building Society v Richards* (1901) 84 LT 587.
3 County Courts Act 1984, s 24(1).
4 Section 21(3), (4).
5 *Trustee of Manchester Unity Life Insurance Collecting Society v Sadler* [1970] 2 All ER 410, [1974] 1 WLR 770; *Marples v Holmes* (1975) 31 P & CR 94; *PB Frost v Green* [1978] 2 All ER 206, [1978] 1 WLR 949.
6 See **19.28** ff.

FORM OF CLAIM

HIGH COURT

22.5 In the High Court a claim for foreclosure should be brought as a Part 8 claim[1], unless it appears that there is a dispute of fact (for instance a claim by a mortgagor that he is not bound by the mortgage due to undue influence), in which case the Part 7 procedure may be used[2].

1 See CPR Pt 8BPD A.1(3): foreclosure claims would generally have been brought by originating summons before 26 April 1999. (They were also Part 8 claims by virtue of

CPR Pt 8BPD A.1(1) from 26 April 1999 until CPR Sch 1, RSC Ord 88 was revoked from 15 October 2001.)

2 CPR 8.1(2)(a), 8.8(1)(a); Chancery Guide 21.3. For the position where possession is also sought, see CPR Pt 55 and **19.28** ff.

COUNTY COURT

22.6 In the county court, proceedings for the foreclosure of any mortgage may be commenced only in the court for the district in which the land or any part of the land is situated[1]. Most foreclosure proceedings would have been brought by originating summons before 26 April 1999 and thus must now be brought by Part 8 claim form[2], unless it appears that there is a dispute of fact, in which case the Part 7 procedure may be used[3].

1 CPR Sch 2, CCR Ord 4, r 3.
2 CPR 8B-PD B.1(3)(b).
3 CPR 8.1(2)(a), 8.8(1)(a): but not where possession is also sought: CPR Pt 55 and **19.28** ff.

NECESSARY PARTIES TO A CLAIM

22.7 The claimant must join as parties (a) those interested in the security[1], and (b) those interested in the equity of redemption[2].

1 See **22.8** ff.
2 See **22.12** ff.

PERSONS INTERESTED IN THE SECURITY

The holder of the security

22.8 The person in whom the legal interest in the security becomes vested is a necessary party to a claim for foreclosure[1]. That is the case whether it becomes vested in him under the mortgage[2], or by assignment[3], or where he is only a trustee for the persons entitled to the mortgage money[4]. Such a person is a necessary party because a reconveyance will be required should the mortgagor redeem[5], and, in the case of a judgment for foreclosure, because the legal interest is to be protected by the judgment[6]. While a transferee of a mortgage may bring the claim[7], he is subject to the state of the accounts between the mortgagor and the mortgagee at the date of the transfer and also to any equities then existing in favour of the mortgagor[8].

1 *Bartle v Wilkin* (1836) 8 Sim 238; *Smith v Chichester* (1842) 2 Dr & War 393.
2 *Wood v Williams* (1819) 4 Madd 186.
3 *Wetherell v Collins* (1818) 3 Madd 255 and the original mortgagee must be joined in an action by a sub-mortgagee: *Norrish v Marshall* (1821) 5 Madd 475.
4 A trustee of the legal estate in the security having no adverse rights may properly be, and to save expenses to the mortgagor, ought to be, a co-plaintiff: *Smith v Chichester* (1842) 2 Dr & War 393 at 404; unless he refuses, or is likely to refuse, and then he should be made a defendant: *Browne v Lockhart* (1840) 10 Sim 420.

5 See form of foreclosure order, **22.30, 22.32**.
6 The rule is not affected by the present automatic effect of a receipt on the discharge of the mortgage.
7 *Platt v Mendel* (1884) 27 Ch D 246 at 247.
8 Unless the mortgagor was a party to the transfer: see **14.2**.

Personal representatives

22.9 On the death of a mortgagee[1], or a transferee of the mortgage, the debt and security devolve upon his personal representatives. They are entitled to bring a claim for foreclosure until the mortgage has been transferred to a beneficiary or a transferee for value[2].

1 Assuming he has not transferred the mortgage.
2 See **14.23**. As to representation by trustees and personal representatives, see **29.10, 29.19**.

Co-mortgagees

22.10 Where there are co-mortgagees[1] they may institute proceedings jointly. If some of the co-mortgagees are unwilling to be joined as claimants, or have done some act precluding them from claiming in that capacity, one co-mortgagee can claim by himself, provided he makes all the others defendants[2]. A mortgagee who is only entitled to part of the mortgage money cannot sue alone and obtain foreclosure of a corresponding part of the mortgaged property[3].

1 As to co-mortgagees, see **12.2**.
2 *Davenport v James* (1847) 7 Hare 249; *Remer v Stokes* (1856) 4 WR 730; *Luke v South Kensington Hotel Co* (1879) 11 Ch D 121, CA. Unless the advance is made on a joint account (which will usually be the case: see **14.24**, above), the mortgagees are tenants in common of the mortgage money and, on the death of one, his representatives are necessary parties: *Vickers v Cowell* (1839) 1 Beav 529.
3 *Palmer v Earl of Carlisle* (1823) 1 Sim & St 423.

Subsequent incumbrancers

22.11 Subsequent incumbrancers may foreclose the mortgagor and incumbrancers subsequent to themselves, without joining the incumbrancers prior to themselves, since the interests of the latter will not be adversely affected. While the subsequent mortgagees will be unable in those circumstances to redeem all prior incumbrancers in the same claim, which may be inconvenient, that is not considered unjust given that they knowingly lent money upon property that was already incumbered[1]. Likewise, prior incumbrancers are not necessary parties to claims by subsequent creditors for the sale of the mortgaged property, since the sale will be subject to those incumbrances[2]. A judgment creditor may proceed against a receiver and the owner of the mortgaged property for satisfaction out of surplus rents by a former judgment directed to be paid to the owner, without making prior incumbrancers parties[3].

1 *Rose v Page* (1829) 2 Sim 471; *Brisco v Kenrick* (1832) 1 LJ Ch 116; *Richards v Cooper* (1842) 5 Beav 304; and see *Slade v Rigg* (1843) 3 Hare 35. Under special circumstances however, it may be necessary for the second mortgagee to join the first: see eg *Lord Kensington v Bouverie* (1852) 16 Beav 194, (1859) 7 HLC 557, HL.

2 *Delabere v Norwood* (1786) 3 Swan 144n; *Parker v Fuller* (1830) 1 Russ & M 656.
3 *Lewis v Lord Zouche* (1828) 2 Sim 388. If a receiver of the general proceeds of the estate is asked for, the presence of the prior incumbrancers is necessary, since there is an inference with their interests: *Gibbon v Strathmore* (1841) cited Calvert on *Parties in Suits in Equity* (2nd edn, 1847) p 16, unless, of course, the order is to be without prejudice to the prior incumbrancers, and in an action by later incumbrancers against a receiver appointed by the prior incumbrancers, and the mortgager who had covenanted to keep down the incumbrances according to their priorities, the prior incumbrancers had to be joined: *Ford v Rackham* (1853) 17 Beav 485; and see *Re Lord Annaly, Crawford v Annaly* (1891) 27 LR Ir 523.

PERSONS INTERESTED IN THE EQUITY OF REDEMPTION

22.12 The judgment in a claim for foreclosure gives the opportunity of redeeming to all persons interested in the equity of redemption. In default of their doing so, they are foreclosed. Hence all such persons must be parties, or be sufficiently represented by persons who are parties[1].

1 *Tylee v Webb* (1843) 6 Beav 552 at 557; *Gedye v Matson* (1858) 25 Beav 310; *Audsley v Horn* (1858) 26 Beav 195; *Caddick v Cook* (1863) 32 Beav 70; *Griffith v Pound* (1890) 45 Ch D 553 at 567. As to foreclosure where there are rights of contribution and indemnity between co-mortgagors, see *Gee v Liddell* [1913] 2 Ch 62.

Owner of equity of redemption

22.13 The mortgagor himself, while he remains owner of the equity of redemption, and any subsequent owner for the time being of the equity of redemption, must be parties, however remote his chance of redeeming may be[1]. If the equity of redemption is held jointly, all the joint owners must be parties. Where a second mortgagee brings a claim to redeem the first mortgagee, the mortgagor is a necessary party since, on redemption the claim will become a claim for foreclosure against him[2]. The original mortgagor is not a necessary party to an action for foreclosure between a sub-mortgagee and sub-mortgagor[3], but where a sub-mortgagee seeks to foreclose the original mortgagor, the original mortgagee must be joined[4].

1 *Moore v Morton* [1886] WN 196.
2 See **29.9**.
3 See 3 Seton's *Judgments and Orders* (7th edn) p 2011.
4 *Hobart v Abbot* (1731) 2 P Wms 643.

Surety who has given security

22.14 Where there is a principal debtor and a surety, and each has mortgaged his own property, the surety mortgagor is a necessary party to a claim for foreclosure against the principal debtor. The reason is that the surety has the right to redeem and to thereby prevent his own estate from being burdened to a greater amount than the amount which the estate of his principal is insufficient to satisfy[1]. However, a surety is not a necessary party where he is only bound by a personal covenant, unless he has paid off part of the debt[2].

1 *Stokes v Clendon* (1790) 3 Swans 150n; *Gee v Liddell* [1913] 2 Ch 62; *Re A Debtor (No 24 of 1971), ex p Marley v Trustee of Property of Debtor* [1976] 2 All ER 1010, [1976] 1 WLR 952;

Re Thompson (1976) 8 ALR 479, and similarly, where a mortgage of the estate of a married woman is in effect a security for the husband's debt (as to which, see **26.7**), he is a necessary party: see *Hill v Edmonds* (1852) 5 De G & Sm 603; and **22.36**, n 1. See generally **22.36**.

2 *Newton v Earl of Egmont* (1831) 4 Sim 574; *Gedye v Matson* (1858) 25 Beav 310.

Several properties subject to a mortgage

22.15 A mortgagee is not generally entitled to foreclose part only of the mortgaged property, since the whole of the property is liable for the debt. Where several properties are subject to a mortgage and they are subsequently disposed of or incumbered separately, all those interested in the equities of redemption of all the properties, and the incumbrancers thereon, must be made parties. Thus if two properties are subject to a mortgage and the mortgagor subsequently mortgages the equity of redemption of one of them to a second mortgagee, and sells that of the other to a third person, the original mortgagee must join both the second mortgagee and the purchaser if he wishes to foreclose—he is not entitled to foreclose either of the properties alone, since each is equally liable to the debt. The same rule applies where the original equity of redemption has been sold in lots[1]; where several distinct properties are subject to the mortgage; and even, where there is a right to consolidate, where the mortgagee holds securities for distinct debts of the mortgagor, whether the securities are by the same or by different instruments[2].

1 *Peto v Hammond* (1860) 29 Beav 91. As to an allegation by the purchaser that he is assignee for valuable consideration without notice of the mortgage, see *Payne v Compton* (1837) 2 Y & C Ex 457; and see *Hall v Heward* (1886) 32 Ch D 430, CA.

2 *Ireson v Denn* (1796) 2 Cox Eq Cas 425 and see *Payne v Compton*, above. The above paragraph was quoted in *Rushton v Industrial Development Bank* (1973) 34 DLR (3d) 582, SC of Can.

Trustee in bankruptcy

22.16 The trustee in bankruptcy of the mortgagor is the proper party to claims in respect of his interest. The bankrupt will be bound by a judgment against him[1]. However, if the trustee disclaims any interest and is prepared for the equity of redemption to be released, he need not be required to attend the hearing, unless by his disclaimer he admits having an interest in the property[2]. If the mortgagor has parted with his interest before the bankruptcy, the trustee should not be joined. Hence he should not be joined where the equity of redemption was settled by the mortgagor for valuable consideration before his bankruptcy[3].

1 Hence the mortgagor should not be made a party: see *Kerrick v Saffery* (1835) 7 Sim 317; not even if charges of fraud or other charges are made which are not particularly directed to matters on which relief is sought: *Lloyd v Lander* (1821) 5 Madd 282.

2 *Thompson v Kendall* (1840) 9 Sim 397; *Collins v Shirley* (1830) 1 Russ & M 638; see *Melbourne Banking Corpn v Brougham* (1879) 4 App Cas 156, PC, and a bankrupt cannot appeal even though a right of redemption has been given him by the judgment and it is alleged that there is a surplus: *Re Leadbitter* (1878) 10 Ch D 388, CA; *Re Austin, ex p Sheffield* (1879) 10 Ch D 434, CA; and see *Re A Debtor, ex p Debtor v Dodwell (Trustee)* [1949] Ch 236, [1949] 1 All ER 510.

3 *Steele v Maunder* (1844) 1 Coll 535. If the mortgagee has valued his security, the trustee can redeem at the valuation and the order must show this: *Knowles v Dibbs* (1889) 37 WR 378. The form of the order allows for an amendment of proof: *Hayes and Harlington UDC v Williams' Trustee* [1936] Ch 315.

Personal representatives and trustees

22.17 On the death of the mortgagor, or a transferee of the equity of redemption, the mortgaged property devolves upon his personal representatives. They are thus necessary parties, unless they have conveyed or assented to the vesting of the property in some other person[1]. The personal representatives must be parties if the mortgagee is asking for a sale of the property and the security is deficient[2]. It is generally sufficient for property subject to a trust to be represented by the trustees and for an estate under administration to be represented by the executors and administrators. It is generally unnecessary to join any of the beneficiaries as defendants[3].

1 Administration of Estates Act 1925, ss 1(1), 3; CPR 19.8; see **14.23**.
2 See *Daniel v Skipwith* (1787) 2 Bro CC 155.
3 CPR Sch 1, RSC Ord 15, r 14; and see Administration of Justice Act, 1985, s 47 for the power to make judgments binding upon persons interested in the estates of deceased persons or in trusts, who are not before the court; see **29.10** ff. As the same applies to trustees for creditors and debenture trustees where the debentures are secured by a trust deed. For death and bankruptcy in the course of proceedings, see **29.14**.

Equity of redemption subject to a settlement

22.18 Under the Settled Land Act 1925[1] the fee simple subject to the mortgage term is vested in the tenant for life or, where there is no tenant for life or the tenant for life is an infant, in the statutory owners, who hold on trust for all persons beneficially entitled. It is therefore sufficient to join only the holder of the legal estate in the first instance; if necessary, directions for adding other parties will be given[2].

1 With certain minor exceptions, it has not been possible to create new settlements under the Settled Land Act 1925 after 1996: Trusts of Land and Appointment of Trustees Act 1996, s 2.
2 See **29.10** ff.

Subsequent incumbrancers

22.19 The first[1], or any subsequent[2] mortgagee or incumbrancer, whether of a legal[3], or equitable[4] estate, who commences a claim for foreclosure or sale[5], must make every incumbrancer whose security is subsequent to his own a party to the claim. The subsequent incumbrancers are entitled to have their successive rights of redemption preserved and to be able to protect their interests on the taking of the accounts[6].

1 *Adams v Paynter* (1844) 1 Coll 530; *Tylee v Webb* (1843) 6 Beav 552 and, generally, persons interested in the entire equity of redemption, not being *cestuis que trust* who are represented by a trustee, are necessary parties. Thus partners of the mortgagor, who have a right of pre-emption over his mortgaged share, are necessary parties to an action to foreclose the security: *Redmayne v Forster* (1866) LR 2 Eq 467.
2 *Johnson v Holdsworth* (1850) 1 Sim NS 106.
3 *Adams v Paynter*, above.
4 *Tylee v Webb*, above.
5 *Burgess v Sturges* (1851) 14 Beav 440; *Ormsby v Thorpe* (1808) 2 Mol 503.

6 See *Graves v Wright* (1842) cited in 1 Dr & War 193. Where debentures are a second charge and are not secured by a trust deed, it is necessary in an action by the first mortgagee to enforce his security, for all debenture holders to be defendants, or for an order to be made that one or more shall represent the class: *Wallace v Evershed* [1899] 1 Ch 891. A representation order is made under CPR 19.6–19.7. In *Griffith v Pound* (1890) 45 Ch D 553 and *Westminster Bank Ltd v Residential Properties Improvement Co Ltd* [1938] Ch 639, [1938] 2 All ER 374, it was held that all the debenture holders must be joined: cf *Re Wilcox & Co, Hilder v Wilcox & Co* [1903] WN 64. If there are trustees, the trustees will be made parties: *Cox v Dublin City Distillery Co Ltd (No 3)* [1917] 1 IR 203, CA.

Judgment creditors

22.20 The rule that subsequent incumbrancers are necessary parties applies to a judgment creditor who has obtained a charging order on the land of the debtor[1].

1 *Earl of Cork v Russell* (1871) LR 13 Eq 210. For charging orders, see **2.12** ff; and CPR Sch 1, RSC Ord 50; CPR Sch 2, CCR. Ord 31.

Notice of a subsequent incumbrance received pending the hearing of the claim

22.21 If, pending the hearing of the claim, the claimant receives notice of a subsequent incumbrance, the subsequent incumbrancer should be added as a defendant[1]. Where the claimant receives no notice of such a subsequent incumbrance, it may be stated, but (from the imperfect character of the early reports) with caution:

(a) that if the claimant obtains his judgment without having received notice, the judgment will bind the subsequent incumbrancer as to the accounts, if taken in good faith, but not his right of redemption[2]. He may, however, be joined even after judgment is pronounced[3],
(b) collusion or other fraud will also give the subsequent incumbrancer a right to open the accounts, if he claims there are particular errors[4]; but he will not have a right to unravel the accounts merely by making general allegations of fraud and collusion, if the fraud and collusion are denied[5].

If the mortgagor acts with fraudulent or vexatious conduct, creating subsequent incumbrances with the view of shielding himself from foreclosure, that may excuse the mortgagee from making the owners of such securities parties to the claim[6].

1 See *Moser v Marsden* [1892] 1 Ch 487 at 490, CA.
2 *Cockes v Sherman* (1676) Freem Ch 13; and semble in *Lomax v Hide* (1690) 2 Vern 185; and *Godfrey v Chadwell* (1707) 2 Vern 601, but *Morret v Westerne* (1710) 2 Vern 663, seems contra as to accounts. In *Greswold v Marsham* (1685) 2 Cas in Ch 170, a judgment creditor was held to be bound, because he had not given notice of his incumbrance.
3 *Keith v Butcher* (1884) 25 Ch D 750; *Re Parbola Ltd, Blackburn v Parbola Ltd* [1909] 2 Ch 437, following *Campbell v Holyland* (1877) 7 Ch D 166.
4 See **35.3**.
5 *Needler v Deeble* (1677) 1 Cas in Ch 299; *Cockes v Sherman*, above.
6 *Yates v Hambly* (1742) 2 Atk 237; and see *Smith v Chichester* (1842) 2 Dr War 393 at 404.

STATEMENTS OF CASE AND EVIDENCE

THE RELIEF SOUGHT

Payment, foreclosure or sale

22.22 Where the mortgagee is suing for foreclosure only, the claim should be for an account to be taken of the sums due to the mortgagee under the mortgage (the mortgagee should set out full details of the principal, interest and costs[1] he claims to be due) and for the mortgage to be enforced by foreclosure[2]. If the mortgaged land is registered, the claim should refer to the registered instrument of charge as well as the contemporaneous mortgage by deed, but rectification of the register need not be claimed[3]. It is usual to claim payment of the total amount outstanding, and, in default of payment, foreclosure or sale; but the court is entitled to order a sale whether or not it is expressly claimed[4].

1 If the mortgagee claims costs, charges, and expenses beyond his costs of action, he must make out a special case for them at the hearing: *Bolingbroke v Hinde* (1884) 25 Ch D 795. On accounts and costs, see Chapters 35 and 36.
2 For forms see 28 *Atkin's Court Forms* (1997 issue), Mortgages.
3 *Weymouth v Davis* [1908] 2 Ch 169.
4 Law of Property Act 1925, s 91. See **21.5**, **21.11**. *Dymond v Croft* (1876) 3 Ch D 512; *Farrer v Lacy, Hartland & Co* (1885) 31 Ch D 42, CA; and CPR 16.2(5).

Possession

22.23 If the mortgagee is in possession, he will ask for an account of rents and profits received[1] and for the allowance of any special expenses[2]. If the mortgagee is not in possession, and believes that there may be difficulty in obtaining it, he can claim for possession although it is not necessary to do so[3]. A claim for foreclosure includes a claim for possession, and delivery of possession may be ordered against the mortgagor even though not expressly sought as relief[4]. That is the case even if the mortgagor does not appear at the hearing of the claim[5]; but it will not be ordered without notice where it has not been claimed[6]. An order for possession may be made after foreclosure absolute[7], even though it was not sought in the claim[8].

1 See **35.26** and generally **35.22** ff.
2 See **36.33**, **36.35** and Chapter 36 generally.
3 For the difference between a genuine foreclosure action and a disguised possession action, see **19.30**. For the jurisdictional and procedural requirements to which a possession claim is subject, see **19.28** ff.
4 *Manchester and Liverpool Bank v Parkinson* (1889) 60 LT 258; and CPR 16.2(5). See, however, the requirements of CPR Pt 55.
5 *Salt v Edgar* (1886) 54 LT 374.
6 *Le Bas v Grant* (1895) 64 LJ Ch 368.
7 *Keith v Day* (1888) 39 Ch D 452, CA.
8 *Jenkins v Ridgley* (1893) 41 WR 585.

Equitable mortgagee

22.24 In the case of an equitable mortgage created by the deposit of title deeds[1], the mortgagee should claim not only foreclosure, but also a declaration that his deposit operated as a mortgage, that in default of payment of what is found due the mortgagor is a trustee of the legal estate for him and that the mortgagor should convey the estate to him[2].

1 It has not been possible to create such mortgages since the coming into force of s 2 of the Law of Property (Miscellaneous Provisions) Act 1989 on 27 September 1989: *United Bank of Kuwait v Sahib* [1997] Ch 107, [1996] 3 All ER 215.
2 *Marshall v Shrewsbury* (1875) 10 Ch App 250 at 254.

MATTERS TO BE PROVED

22.25 The witness statement in support of a Part 8 claim, or, where the action is commenced by Part 7, the particulars of claim, should contain the following matters[1]:

(a) full particulars of the mortgage, including the amount of the advance or other debt and any further advances, the covenant for repayment, or other circumstances giving rise to the liability (such as any covenants breached by the mortgagor), the rate of interest, details of the mortgaged property and nature of the security, the proviso for redemption or cesser, and any other relevant covenants. A copy of the mortgage deed should be attached. In the case of a mortgage by the deposit of title deeds, or an equitable lien, the relevant factual circumstances should be set out;
(b) where the claimant is not the original mortgagee, the relevant transfers or devolutions;
(c) the default under the proviso for redemption or cesser giving rise to the mortgagee's right to foreclose (normally that following the redemption date the debt is still outstanding), or the breach giving rise to the right to foreclose during the term of a loan;
(d) all other matters relevant to the taking of any account or ascertaining the amount due to the mortgagee[2].

For the matters which must be proved, and the additional procedural requirements, where, in addition to foreclosure, payment of moneys secured by the mortgage is claimed, see Chapter 17[3], and where possession is also claimed, see Chapter 19[4].

1 See also general requirements of CPR Pt 8 or Pt 7 and Pt 16; and 28 *Atkin's Court Forms* (1997 Issue), Mortgages.
2 Eg where the mortgagee has valued the security in the mortgagor's bankruptcy: *Sanguinetti v Stuckey's Banking Co (No 2)* [1896] 1 Ch 502; or where the mortgagee is in possession, or has incurred special expenses: *Binnington v Harwood* (1825) Turn & R 477; or that a receiver has been appointed. Witness statements or affidavits of due execution of mortgages or charges are no longer required on applications for foreclosure nisi unless the court directs otherwise: *Practice Direction* [1969] 2 All ER 639, [1969] 1 WLR 974; although the practice direction has been replaced by the omnibus Chancery Guide, which makes no specific provision as to witness statements of due execution, the same practice should apply.
3 See **17.8** ff.
4 See **19.28** ff.

POWERS OF ADJOURNMENT

22.26 The court's statutory powers to adjourn, suspend or stay a claim for foreclosure under s 36 of the Administration of Justice Act 1970 and s 8 of the Administration of Justice Act 1973 have been considered in Chapter 19[1]. In summary, where the claim is for foreclosure alone, the court may adjourn the proceedings; where the claim is for foreclosure and possession, the court may adjourn the proceedings, or may stay or suspend execution of the order for possession, or postpone the date for the delivery of possession[2].

1 See **19.51** ff.
2 Section 8(3) of the Act of 1973.

THE FORECLOSURE ORDER NISI

22.27 If the court is satisfied that the claimant is entitled to an order for foreclosure, it will initially make an order for foreclosure nisi, that is an order that the mortgagor will be foreclosed unless he redeems by a specified date. The order should provide for the following matters.

ACCOUNTS AND INQUIRIES AND INCIDENTAL MATTERS

Incidental matters

22.28 The order nisi in a claim for foreclosure or sale should be prefaced by a declaration that the security is valid, where that has been in dispute[1]. It should, where necessary, declare the rights and priorities of the various incumbrancers and any person who has a paramount claim on the property, or order an inquiry into such matters[2]. It should provide for any other incidental matters (again, where appropriate by ordering inquiries).

1 *Holmes v Turner* (1843) 7 Hare 367n and form; *Faulkner v Daniel* (1843) 3 Hare 199, establishing judgment debt: *Carlon v Farlar* (1845) 8 Beav 526.
2 *Jones v Griffith* (1845) 2 Coll 207.

Accounts and inquiries

22.29 It is necessary in a foreclosure claim to ascertain the amount of the mortgagor's debt. The mortgagor may admit the amount of the debt and interest, or it may be satisfactorily proved at the hearing. If not, the order should direct that accounts be taken, together with any necessary inquiries[1]. If payment is also claimed, it may be necessary to have two accounts taken, since the amount to be paid to redeem and the amount due under the covenant for payment will not necessarily be the same[2]. Where the mortgagee has been in possession, his receipts should be accounted for in payment first of interest and then of the principal debt[3] and, where necessary, rests made[4]. There should be added to the amount of the mortgagee's own debt any sums paid for the redemption of preceding incumbrancers, any sums to which the mortgagee is entitled for improvements[5] and all payments by the mortgagee for the protection of his security or the mortgaged property[6]. Any special matter affecting the account, such as a valuation of a security in bankruptcy, ought to be stated in the claim and referred to in the judgment[7].

1 For form of foreclosure judgment by consent without account, see *Boydell v Manby* (1842) 9 Hare App liii. For accounts, see Chapter 35.
2 See *Farrer v Lacy, Hartland & Co* (1885) 31 Ch D 42 for the amounts due under the covenant for payment.
3 See *Thorneycroft v Crockett* (1848) 2 HL Cas 239, and see **28.47**. As to form where a receiver has been in receipt of rents and profits, see *Simmons v Blandy* [1897] 1 Ch 19.
4 See **35.33** ff, **35.39**.
5 See **19.75**.
6 See **19.82**.
7 *Sanguinetti v Stuckey's Banking Co (No 2)* [1896] 1 Ch 502.

FORM OF FORECLOSURE ORDER NISI

General nature of order

22.30 The foreclosure order nisi orders the mortgagor to pay the amount required to redeem the mortgage within a specified time[1]. The order should also, where claimed, order payment on the personal covenant. A consent order may be made if the debt exceeds the value of the property, and there is no subsequent incumbrance[2]. During the period allowed for redemption a mortgagee can only exercise his power of sale with the permission of the court[3].

1 The time allowed for redemption is considered at **22.39** ff.
2 *Bakker v Chambri Ltd (No 2)* (1986) 4 BPR 972617.
3 *Stevens v Theatres Ltd* [1903] 1 Ch 857; *Marshall v Miles* (1971) 13 DLR (3d) 158; cf *Petranick v Dale* (1973) 33 DLR (3d) 389 (where the foreclosure order had not been entered up), and see **16.11**, **20.7**.

Price of redemption

22.31 The sum to be paid to redeem the mortgage is the same whether the claim is the mortgagee's for foreclosure, or the mortgagor's for redemption[1]. The terms of the order, and the course of proceedings, are in substance no different whether it is the owner who is seeking to clear his property from incumbrances, or the first[2], or a subsequent[3] mortgagee seeking to get possession of the property in satisfaction of his debt[4].

1 *Du Vigier v Lee* (1843) 2 Hare 326; *Watts v Symes* (1851) 1 De GM & G 240. For redemption claims, see Chapter 29.
2 *Barnes v Fox, Seton* (7th edn) p 1907.
3 *Jackson v Brettall, Seton* (7th edn) p 1908.
4 *Dunstan v Patterson* (1847) 23 Ph 341. See observations, *Watts v Symes* (1851) 1 De GM & G 240 at 242.

If payment is made

22.32 If the mortgagor pays the amount required to redeem within the specified time, the order should provide:

(a) for the mortgagee, upon receiving an endorsed receipt as defined in s 115 of the Law of Property Act 1925, for the reconveyance of the mortgaged property to the mortgagor as specified in that section[1];

(b) to return all deeds and other documents relating to the property[2];
(c) and, if the mortgagee is in possession, for him to deliver possession of the mortgaged property to the mortgagor[3].

The same applies to any other person entitled to redeem. Where the person redeeming is a later mortgagee and the judgment is for personal payment by the mortgagor, the claimant mortgagee should be ordered to assign the benefit of the judgment to the redeeming party, with permission to enforce it in the name of the claimant upon giving him a sufficient indemnity[4].

1 See Law of Property Act 1925, s 115.
2 To avoid unnecessary expense in the preparation of documents for reconveyance should the mortgagor fail to redeem, the order must provide (a) that the mortgagor must give seven days' clear notice of his intention to attend and redeem, and (b) if no such notice is given but the mortgagor in fact attends at the appointed time and place then at the option of the mortgagee the time for redemption must be extended for one week: *Practice Directions* [1955] 1 All ER 30, [1955] 1 WLR 36; although the practice directions have been replaced by the omnibus Chancery Guide, which contains no comparable provision, it is not believed there has been any change in practice.
3 *Yates v Hambly* (1742) 2 Atk 360; *Arthur v Higgs* (1856) and *Evans v Kinsey* (1855), *Seton* (7th edn, 1887). As to the practice where the mortgagee refuses a proper tender, see *Bank of New South Wales v O'Connor* (1889) 14 App Cas 273 at 283, PC.
4 *Greenough v Littler* (1880) 15 Ch D 93.

If payment is not made

22.33 If the mortgagor fails to pay the redemption sum within the specified time, the order should provide for the mortgagee to be entitled to a foreclosure order absolute, whether the mortgage is legal or equitable, foreclosing the mortgagee of, and debarring him from, all equity of redemption[1]. In the case of an equitable mortgage, if the mortgagor fails to pay, he will be ordered to convey or surrender the mortgaged property to the mortgagee free from incumbrances[2]; where a conveyance cannot be obtained in that manner, the mortgagor will be declared to be a trustee of the property for the mortgagor and a vesting order made under s 44 of the Trustee Act 1925[3]. If possession is claimed, the order should also provide for possession to be given in default of payment[4]. Likewise, if in a claim for redemption the mortgagor fails to pay the amount necessary to redeem, the claim will be dismissed and that will have the effect of foreclosure[5].

1 See *Dymond v Croft* (1876) 3 Ch D 512; *Greenough v Littler* (1880) 15 Ch D 93; *Lees v Fisher* (1882) 22 Ch D 283, but it seems that if, for any reason, the judgment to account, instead of being made in the usual manner, proceeds upon the undertaking of the mortgagor to pay what shall be found due, the mortgagee, relying upon this undertaking, cannot avail himself of the right to foreclose if default is made in the payment: *Dunstan v Patterson* (1847) 2 Ph 341. As to the order where, in an action by a mortgagee of shares in a company to enforce his security, the company unsuccessfully disputes the security on the ground that the shares have been forfeited for non-payment of calls, see *Watson v Eales* (1857) 23 Beav 294. See also **22.57**.
2 *Holmes v Turner* (1843) 7 Hare 367n; *Footner v Sturgis* (1852) 5 De G & Sm 736; *Pryce v Bury* (1853) 2 Drew 41. Where the estate has already been sold by the mortgagee under his power of sale, see *Re Smith's Mortgage Account* (1861) 9 WR 799. Where the mortgagor was a company, and it had been dissolved before conveyance, a vesting order could be obtained: *Re Nos 56* and *58, Albert Rd, Norwood* [1916] 1 Ch 289. See now Law of Property Act 1925, s 181; *Re Wells, Swinburne-Hanham v Howard* [1933] Ch 29, CA; *Re Strathblaine Estates Ltd* [1948] Ch 228, [1948] 1 All ER 162.
3 As to vesting orders, see **28.76** ff. If a sale is ordered, the proceeds should be ordered to be paid to the credit of the sums due; or alternatively there can be an order for permission

to apply for directions as to how the sums should be applied. A vesting order may be made in favour of the purchaser, or the court may create and vest in the mortgagee a legal term of years to enable him to carry out the sale: Law of Property Act 1925, s 90.

4 *Wood v Wheater* (1882) 22 Ch D 281. The court has jurisdiction to order possession even where it is not claimed in the statements of case: *Salt v Edgar* (1886) 54 LT 374; CPR 16.2(5) See **22.23**.

5 See **29.26**.

SUCCESSIVE MORTGAGES

Successive foreclosures

22.34 Where there are successive mortgages, the order should be on the basis that the second mortgagee, as the first assignee of the equity of redemption, fills the place and acquires the rights of the mortgagor[1]. It is thus the second mortgagee who has the first right to redeem, upon payment of what is due to the first mortgagee; in default of payment, he is foreclosed. If the second mortgagee is foreclosed, an account is then taken of the first mortgagee's subsequent interest and costs. The third mortgagee may then redeem upon payment of those sums in addition to the amount originally found due — in default of payment, he is in turn foreclosed[2]. This process is carried on with all the successive incumbrancers, until the mortgagor or ultimate owner of the equity of redemption alone remains. He may in turn then redeem in like manner, in default of which he will be foreclosed. The subsequent incumbrancers must be foreclosed absolutely before foreclosure may be claimed against the mortgagor[3]. Once the mortgagor is foreclosed, the first mortgagee is entitled to the property free from all incumbrances. A subsequent incumbrancer can bring an action for foreclosure against the mortgagor or any incumbrancers subsequent to himself, without affecting the prior incumbrancers[4]. Where there are several incumbrancers, and the mortgagor's action for redemption is dismissed (which is generally equivalent to foreclosure[5]), the last incumbrancer becomes quasi mortgagor and the others become first and subsequent incumbrancers according to their priorities[6].

1 Thus, in taking the account the second mortgagee may assert such equity as the mortgagor himself might have to exclude any particular item: *Mainland v Upjohn* (1889) 41 Ch D 126.

2 In *Bingham v King* (1866) 14 WR 414, a later mortgagee, who verified the amount of his debt by affidavit, obtained an order for payment, without taking a formal account, out of surplus proceeds of sale paid in by the first mortgagee; creditors, however, being allowed time to dispute the account.

3 *Whitbread v Lyall* (1856) 8 De GM & G 383; *Webster v Patteson* (1884) 25 Ch D 626.

4 *Rose v Page* (1829) 2 Sim 471.

5 See **29.26**.

6 *Cottingham v Earl of Shrewsbury* (1843) 3 Hare 627. As to whether successive periods for redeeming will be allowed to the successive incumbrancers, or whether one time only will be limited for redemption, see **22.40–22.41**.

Successive redemptions

22.35 The operation of successive foreclosures described above proceeds on the assumption that none of the successive incumbrancers has exercised their rights of redemption. If, however, the second mortgagee redeems the first, then proceedings are then for foreclosure between him and any subsequent incumbrancers and the mortgagor. Thus, if the second mortgagee redeems the first, the order should provide for an account to be taken of what is due to the second mortgagee, as the person redeeming, first on his own security, and secondly for the sums he has paid to the first mortgagee, together with interest and costs[1]. The third mortgagee will then be entitled to redeem upon paying the second mortgagee the total of those sums, in default of which he is foreclosed according to the process described above. If the third mortgagee redeems the second, then the order should provide for an account to be taken of what is due to the third mortgagee, in respect of his own security and of what he has paid to the second mortgagee; the next incumbrancer, or the mortgagor or other ultimate owner of the equity of redemption, may in turn redeem upon payment of those sums. Eventually, the property will remain in the hands of the last of the incumbrancers who redeems, or the mortgagor, free from all the debts which affected it[2].

1 See **35.52**.
2 As to costs where an intermediate mortgagee redeems the first, who also holds a later mortgage, see *Mutual Life Assurance Society v Langley* (1886) 32 Ch D 460, CA. As to an action by a later mortgagee of two estates, subject to separate mortgages, see *Pelly v Wathen* (1849) 7 Hare 351–363; on appeal (1851) 1 De GM & G 16; *Hallett v Furze* (1885) 31 Ch D 312.

MORTGAGE BY SURETY

22.36 Where there is a principal debtor and a surety, and each has mortgaged his own property, the order should be framed so as to give the surety the full benefit of his rights against the property of the principal debtor. Thus, the right of redemption is given to both and it is ordered that if the money is paid by the principal debtor the properties shall be conveyed to their respective owners, but if the money is paid by the surety, both properties are conveyed to him. In the latter case, the surety holds the property which belonged to his principal subject to redemption by him. If neither principal nor surety redeems, then the equities of both their properties are foreclosed[1]. No relief will be given against a surety beyond the express terms of his contract. Thus, his mortgage of a reversionary interest will not be subject either to sale or foreclosure, if its operation is limited to the application of the proceeds when it falls into possession[2].

1 *Beckett v Micklethwaite* (1821) 6 Madd 199; *Seton* (7th edn) 2088. See *Aldworth v Robinson* (1840) 2 Beav 287, which also provides for redemption as between the principal and the surety.

For an order where a wife and husband had mortgaged her estates for the husband's debts, and, after a second security on the whole property to another incumbrancer, the husband became insolvent, see *Hill v Edmonds* (1852) 5 De G & Sm 603. The estate of the husband or wife, as the case may be, will be indemnified out of the estate of the other of them for whose benefit the money was raised: *Wilkinson v Beale* (1823) 1 LJOS 89; *Grays v Dowman* (1858) 27 LJ Ch 702, and see **26.7.**

For form of decree where mortgagee had a mortgage of property belonging to A and B for money advanced to them in different proportions, and another mortgage of the separate property of A, and of his interest in the joint property, to secure his separate debt, see *Higgins v Frankis* (1846) 10 Jur 328.

2 *Stamford, etc, Banking Co v Ball* (1862) 4 De GF & J 310.

JUDGMENT IN RESPECT OF A SUB-MORTGAGE

22.37 In the case of a sub-mortgage, where the sub-mortgagee brings a claim for foreclosure against the mortgagor and the mortgagee, the order should direct an account, first, of what is due to the mortgagee, and secondly, of what is due to the sub-mortgagee. Upon payment to the sub-mortgagee of the sum due to him, not exceeding the sum due to the mortgagee, and on payment of any residue to the mortgagee, each will give a statutory receipt. In case of default the mortgagor is foreclosed. In that case, the mortgagee must pay to the sub-mortgagee all the sums due to him, including subsequent interest and costs, for which the sub-mortgagee will give a statutory receipt; in default of payment the mortgagee will be foreclosed[1].

1 *Seton* (7th edn) p 2009; and see pp 2010, 2011. Directions to give statutory receipts have been substituted above for the former directions to convey.

MIXED MORTGAGES OF LAND AND CHATTELS

22.38 Where the mortgage is of land, but there is also a simple assignment of stock or other personal chattels[1], or of a policy of assurance, the proper order is for sale of the chattel security in the first instance and then for foreclosure in respect of any shortfall. The reason is to avoid the foreclosure being opened by the subsequent sale of the chattels or policy[2].

1 For forms of judgment on mortgages of stock and chattels, see *Seton* (7th edn) pp 1923 ff; and on a mortgage by one of the partners in a mine where the other partners have a right of pre-emption, see *Redmayne v Forster* (1866) LR 2 Eq 467. For judgment on a mortgage of a pension, see *James v Ellis* [1870] WN 269, 24 LT 12; *Seton* (7th edn) p 1925.
2 Where the assignment of the policy is followed by provisions which indicate that the mortgagee shall have the benefit of the policy moneys, foreclosure only may be ordered: *Dyson v Morris* (1842) 1 Hare 413; though this would be liable to be opened, if the mortgagee should afterwards resort to the moneys to become payable on the policy (which he was allowed to retain for that purpose) to cover the amount for which the estate might be insufficient. Hence, where a mortgage of a policy or other future thing in action is made as a collateral security, no provisions should be inserted which may affect the mortgagee's right to an immediate sale of the thing in action, and thereby abridge the remedy against the primary security also, and see **22.66**. As to bringing the value of the collateral security into account, see *De Lisle v Union Bank of Scotland* [1914] 1 Ch 22, CA.

THE TIME ALLOWED FOR PAYMENT

SIX MONTHS ALLOWED TO MORTGAGOR

22.39 It is the usual practice to allow the mortgagor six months to redeem by paying the debt, the period being calculated from the date of the order fixing the amount of the debt[1]; the same period is usually allowed for the mortgagor to pay his debt to the mortgagee on the personal covenant[2]. The master's order must nominate the time and place for redemption; this should be the office of the mortgagee's solicitors if it is within five miles of the Royal Courts of Justice, or such other place as may be agreed between the parties and recorded in the order. In all other cases the place of redemption shall be recorded as Room 136 of the Royal Courts of Justice[3]. An equitable mortgagee will usually be given the same time whether the judgment is for foreclosure or sale[4], although under the statutory jurisdiction to order a sale less than six months may be given, or an immediate sale directed.

1 *Platt v Mendel* (1884) 27 Ch D 246 at 258.
2 *Platt v Mendel* (1884) 27 Ch D 246. If the mortgagor is entitled to a set-off, the court may give him the benefit of his set-off and, upon payment by him into court of the principal and interest, the foreclosure may be suspended until both accounts have been taken: *Dodd v Lydall* (1841) 1 Hare 333. Where the mortgage debt is payable by instalments, the order will direct payment of the amount certified to be already due, and will declare, if necessary, that the mortgagee has a charge in respect of the unpaid instalments and will give him permission to apply for the purpose of giving effect to it: *Greenough v Littler* (1880) 15 Ch D 93; *Nives v Nives* (1880) 15 Ch D 649. See also *Cheltenham & Gloucester Building Society v, Grattridge* (1993) 25 HLR 454, CA.
3 *Practice Direction* [1955] 1 All ER 30, [1955] 1 WLR 36 (the room has been changed since 1955). It is immaterial that the person who attends on behalf of the mortgagee to receive payment of the debt is not furnished with a power of attorney, if no one in point of fact attends on behalf of the mortgagor to pay: *Cox v Watson* (1877) 7 Ch D 196; *King v Hough* [1895] WN 60.
4 *Parker v Housefield* (1834) 2 My & K 419; *Price v Carver* (1837) 3 My & Cr 157 at 163; *King v Leach* (1842) 2 Hare 57; *Lister v Turner* (1846) 5 Hare 281 at 293; *Lloyd v Whittey* (1853) 17 Jur 754; and although the security is given for a debt which does not carry interest: *Meller v Woods* (1836) 1 Keen 16. A judgment creditor, when he has obtained a charging order under the Charging Orders Act 1979, is in the position of an equitable mortgagee (**2.18**) and the judgment debtor has the usual six months.
Whether the Bankruptcy Court can order foreclosure has been questioned. If it can, the period of six months is proper to be allowed although the trustee has no assets except the equity of redemption: *Re Hart, ex p Fletcher* (1878) 9 Ch D 381, (1879) 10 Ch D 610. Probably it has no such jurisdiction. The proper course is for the mortgagee to bring a foreclosure action in the Chancery Division: see **22.5**; Supreme Court Act 1981, s 61(1). The direction for 'payment within six months after the date of the certificate' being a matter which would have been inserted by the registrar as part of a usual order, may be added by way of correction of the judgment, on application: *Bird v Heath* (1848) 6 Hare 236; see CPR 40.12; 40-PD-004 (the 'slip' rule).

SUCCESSIVE INCUMBRANCERS

Former practice

22.40 Where there are successive incumbrancers, the right to redeem is exercisable by them in succession and ultimately by the mortgagor. Formerly it was the practice to give the incumbrancers successive periods within which to redeem, six months for the first: successive periods of three months for each of the subsequent incumbrancers[1] and a final three months after the last incumbrancer's time for payment was allowed to the mortgagor[2]. However, the rule was never universally applied. Thus, the rule did not apply where there were several judgment creditors entitled to a charge on land; they were allowed only a single period of three months, as if their orders formed only a single incumbrance[3]. Only one period of redemption was allowed where several incumbrances were created on the same day[4], where several persons entitled to redeem claimed under the same instrument (even in cases, as with a tenant for life and remainderman, where their periods of enjoyment were different)[5] and where there was any other good reason for a single period, such as the existence of a very small margin for subsequent incumbrancers[6]. Only one period for redemption was ordered where some or all of the defendants to a foreclosure action did not appear at the hearing, since giving successive periods would have fixed their priorities in their absence[7]. Similarly, only a single period was ordered where there were questions of priority between subsequent incumbrancers. The successive periods could not be ordered without determining the questions of priority, but the claimant first mortgagee was not interested those questions and it was unnecessary to determine it in his action. Thus, the order provided for only one period of redemption, without prejudice to the order of the later incumbrancers amongst themselves[8].

1 See *Titley v Davies* (1743) 2 Y & C Ch Cas 399n; *Beevor v Luck* (1867) LR 4 Eq 537; *Lewis v Aberdare and Plymouth Co* (1884) 53 LJ Ch 741.
2 *Seton* (7th edn) p 1907; although the mortgagor should not, by incumbering the equity of redemption, obtain a further right to redeem: *Platt v Mendel* (1884) 27 Ch D 246 at 248.
3 *Radcliff v Salmon* (1852) 4 De G & Sm 526; *Stead v Banks* (1852) 5 De G & Sm 560; *Bates v Hillcoat* (1852) 16 Beav 139.
4 *Long v Storie* (1854) 23 LJ Ch 200.
5 *Beevor v Luck*, above, and only one period was allowed to members of a building society, to whom an estate purchased by their trustees had been allotted: *Peto v Hammond* (1861) 30 Beav 495; and see *Loveday v Chapman* (1875) 32 LT 689.
6 *Cripps v Wood* (1882) 51 LJ Ch 584.
7 *Doble v Manley* (1885) 28 Ch D 664. This is done whether the statement of claim alleges that the defendants are entitled, or only claim to be entitled, to charges upon the property: *Doble v Manley; Smithett v Hesketh* (1890) 44 Ch D 161 at 164.
8 *Bartlett v Rees* (1871) LR 12 Eq 395; *General Credit and Discount Co v Glegg* (1883) 22 Ch D 549; *Lewis v Aberdare and Plymouth Co*, above; *Tufdnell v Nicholls* (1887) 56 LT 152. In case more than one of several persons entitled to redeem at the same time should be then prepared to redeem, permission is given to apply to the court without giving notice to the claimant and without prejudice to any question as to the rights of the defendants as between themselves: see forms of judgment, in *Edwards v Martin* (1859) 28 LJ Ch 49; *Bartlett v Rees*, above. See *Biddulph v Billiter Street Offices Co* (1895) 72 LT 834, applying *Jennings v Jordan* (1881) 6 App Cas 698 at 711, HL.

Current practice

22.41 The former practice of allowing successive periods is now largely obsolete and the current practice is to fix only one period for redemption[1]. However, successive periods will be ordered under special circumstances — the onus is on the subsequent incumbrancers to show why it would be appropriate for the current practice to be departed from[2].

1 *Smith v Olding* (1884) 25 Ch D 462; *Mutual Life Assurance Society v Langley* (1884) 26 Ch D 686; *Platt v Mendel* (1884) 27 Ch D 246 at 258; *Smithett v Hesketh* (1890) 44 Ch D 161.
2 In *Berlin v Gordon* [1886] WN 31, where the mortgage was of a reversionary interest, which was likely soon to fall in, one additional period of a month was allowed; and see *Mutual Life Assurance Society v Langley*, above, where one additional period of three months was allowed; and *Smithett v Hesketh*, above, where two such additional periods were allowed. *Platt v Mendel* (1884) 27 Ch D 246.

ENLARGING THE TIME FOR PAYMENT

Discretion to enlarge time

22.42 Although the foreclosure order nisi will have specified a particular date for payment of the sum required to redeem the mortgage, the court has a discretion to either postpone the date for payment before that day arrives, or to open the foreclosure after the day has passed without payment[1]. The person entitled to redeem may either make a special application[2], or apply at the hearing of the mortgagee's application to make the foreclosure absolute[3]. The court will not normally exercise that discretion in a claim for redemption[4], as opposed to a claim for foreclosure, because in such a claim the mortgagor has come to the court for relief, professing that he has the money to discharge the debt, whereas in a foreclosure action he redeems by compulsion[5]. The court can enlarge the time for paying the redemption sum more than once, if there are good reasons for doing so — relief has been given three, and even four times in succession. Further enlargements of time have been granted even where the time fixed by previous orders of enlargement has been expressed to be peremptory and even though the mortgagor has undertaken not to ask for any further time[6]. The enlargement granted upon the first application is usually six months and it does not appear that any longer enlargement has been granted at any one time. Subsequent enlargements have granted additional periods of three to six months, according to the circumstances.

1 See *Campbell v Holyland* (1877) 7 Ch D 166 at 171, where Jessel MR observed that the final foreclosure order was 'form only, just as the original deed was form only'; *Ingham v Sutherland* (1890) 63 LT 614.
2 For forms of application, see 28 *Atkin's Court Forms* (1997 issue). The application should be in accordance with CPR Pt 23.
3 *Clay v* —— (1745) 9 Sim 317n; *Lee v Heath* (1747) 9 Sim 306n; *Alden v Foster* (1842) 5 Beav 592.
4 See **29.24**.
5 *Novosielski v Wakefield* (1811) 17 Ves 417.
6 *Anon* (1740) Barn Ch 221; *Edwards v Cunliffe* (1816) 1 Madd 287.

Reasons for enlargement

22.43 The time is not enlarged as of course, even upon the first application. Some reason must be given, although a very strong one is not usually necessary[1]. For example, the mortgagor may have used his best endeavours to find an assignee without success, but there may be a reasonable prospect of getting the money if an enlargement time is granted. It may be that negotiations for raising the money are actually pending[2]. The magnitude of the principal debt, and of the arrears of interest, are circumstances to which weight will be given[3]. A purchaser of the equity of redemption whilst the claim is pending will not generally be granted further time[4]. Upon subsequent applications, something more than the above excuses is necessary, for instance, evidence that such steps have been taken that the money is likely to be forthcoming[5]. A strong case of unexpected delay or difficulty must be made out to support a third or fourth application. If there are challenges as to the amount fixed as the amount due and the original time fixed for payment is likely to expire before objections are heard, the court will enlarge the time on the usual application; a new day will be appointed even if the mortgagor omits to make such an application. An extension may be granted even after the objections have been overruled[6]. Where an order has been made for payment to several mortgagees who are entitled on a joint account, and one dies before the day fixed for payment, the survivors are not entitled to the benefit of the order and a new day for payment will be appointed[7].

1 See also CPR 3.9 as to the court's power to grant relief from a failure to comply with the requirements of any court order.
2 *Nanny v Edwards* (1827) 4 Russ 124; *Eyre v Hanson* (1840) 2 Beav 478; *Quarles v Knight* (1820) 8 Price 630. Under the usual circumstances of an application by the mortgagor by reason of his being unable to raise the money in time, it is necessary to show that the estate is an ample security for the debt: *Eyre v Hanson*, above; *Edwards v Cunliffe* (1816) 1 Madd 287; *Nanny v Edwards*, above; *Anon* (1740) Barn Ch 221. This fact was formerly stated in the order: *Geldard v Hornby* (1841) 1 Hare 251.

Where, however, a necessity for enlarging the time has arisen from the opening of the account by the act of the mortgagee, the order will be made, although the security appears on the evidence to be of doubtful sufficiency; but care will be taken that nothing is added by the delay to the amount of the debt: *Geldard v Hornby*.

3 Cf the position where arrears have been allowed to increase: *Holford v Yate* (1855) 1 K & J 677.

4 *Re Parbola Ltd, Blackburn v Parbola Ltd* [1909] 2 Ch 437.

5 *Edwards v Cunliffe* (1816) 1 Madd 287. See *Campbell v Moxhay* (1854) 18 Jur 641, where one reason for refusing an extension was that the application was in violation of an express agreement.

6 *Renvoize v Cooper* (1823) 1 Sim & St 364.

7 *Blackburn v Caine* (1856) 22 Beav 614; *Kingsford v Poile* (1859) 8 WR 110; *Browell v Pledge* [1888] WN 166.

Terms of enlargement

22.44 The court has a discretion as to the terms of the enlargement. The order will commonly be in terms that the time for payment of the principal debt is enlarged, upon condition that the mortgagor must pay the mortgagee the amount certified to be due for interest and costs on the mortgage on or before the day originally fixed for payment of the principal[1]. However, if there is likely to be difficulty in paying the interest and costs on the date originally fixed for payment, for instance because there is only a short time between the hearing of the application for enlargement and the original date for payment, the court may order enlargement on terms that the interest and costs are paid within a month, or some other appropriate time from the date of the order[2]. If there is any doubt as to the sufficiency of the security, the court will also impose a condition that the mortgagee pays immediately the interest which will accrue down to the day fixed for the ultimate payment of the mortgage debt[3].

1 *Edwards v Cunliffe* (1816) 1 Madd 287; *Seton* (7th edn) pp 1911 ff, but where the large sum of £8,000 was due for interest, the first order was made on payment of £3,000 only on account of interest: *Holford v Yate* (1855) 1 K & J 677; and see *Forrest v Shore* (1884) 32 WR 356. The general condition of payment of interest will not be relaxed by reason of the infancy of the person entitled to redeem; *Coombe v Stewart* (1851) 13 Beav 111.

2 *Eyre v Hanson* (1840) 2 Beav 478; *Geldard v Hornby* (1841) 1 Hare 251.

3 *Geldard v Hornby*, above. The condition for payment of interest and costs will not be imposed where the foreclosure is opened by reason of the mortgagee's own acts: see *Buchanan v Greenway* (1849) 12 Beav 355.

Where right to redeem is in dispute

22.45 Where the right to redeem is in dispute, and it is likely that an appeal will not be resolved until after the date fixed for payment, the court will generally order the mortgagor to pay the principal, arrears of interest and the costs of the action, as appropriate, into court by the date fixed for payment and perhaps consent to the appointment of a receiver[1]. The amount paid in will be ordered to be invested at the risk of the applicant[2] and if the dividends or any interest are ordered to be paid to the mortgagee, it will be upon his undertaking to repay the same if the judgment is reversed.

1 *Monkhouse v Bedford Corpn* (1810) 17 Ves 380; *Finch v Shaw, Colyer v Finch* (1855) 20 Beav 555; and see *Holford v Yate* (1855) 1 K & J 677.

2 *Finch v Shaw*, above; see now generally CPR Pt 36.

DISCHARGE OF ORDER NISI

22.46 The mortgagee can discontinue the foreclosure proceedings in accordance with CPR Part 38[1] and have the order nisi discharged, if, for example, the property market has improved so as to make sale preferable to foreclosure. The mortgagor's consent to the discontinuance is not necessary[1]. The mortgagee can also apply for sale in lieu of foreclosure[2], at any time in foreclosure proceedings. However, it may be easier to discontinue the proceedings and sell under a statutory or express power of sale, rather than have to prove a case for sale.

1 *Hang Seng Bank Ltd v Yeung Sau-min* [1986] HKLR 273, in which the comment in the White Book under RSC Ord 21 based upon *Stevens v Theatres Ltd* [1903] 1 Ch 857, that the plaintiff would not be allowed to discontinue without the consent of the mortgagor, was stated not to be supported by Farwell J's judgment in that case. See also CPR 38.2, 38.3.

2 See **22.47**, **21.2**, **21.5**, **21.11**.

ORDER FOR SALE IN LIEU OF FORECLOSURE

Sale in lieu of foreclosure

22.47 The court's power to order a sale in lieu of foreclosure, and the circumstances in which such an order may be made, have been considered in Chapter 21[1]. Where a sale in lieu is ordered, the order should be that in default of payment by the specified date the property comprised in the security shall be sold and the proceeds applied in discharge of the sums due[2]. Where the court orders sale in lieu under its inherent jurisdiction, it will generally allow the same period of six months for payment as it would allow in a foreclosure order nisi[3]. In cases under the statutory jurisdiction, the court is not restricted as to the time for payment, but will usually allow three months[4].

1 See **21.2**, **21.5**, **21.11**. As to the right of the mortgagee to the benefit of goodwill, see pxxx; and as to his right to prevent the use by the assignee of the mortgagors of a trade name included in the security, see *Beazley v Soares* (1882) 22 Ch D 660. If it appears that the property is deficient, foreclosure may be directed even after an order for sale: *Lloyds Bank Ltd v Colston* (1912) 106 LT 420.

2 For forms of order, see 28 *Atkin's Court Forms*. In an action for sale by a second mortgagee, the court in Ireland refused to order the first mortgagee to lodge the deeds in court, since he was willing to produce them and let copies be taken under Conveyancing Act 1881, s 16: *Armstrong v Dickson* [1911] 1 IR 435 (now Law of Property Act 1925, s 96 (1). See **3.74**).

Where an order for sale has been made, the mortgagee will not as a rule be allowed to sell out of court under his express power: *Re Claire* (1889) 23 LR Ir 281; and certainly cannot do so without leave: *Stevens v Theatres Ltd* [1903] 1 Ch 857; and see **16.11**, n 8; but an order for sale obtained by a second mortgagee does not prevent a sale by a first mortgagee who is not a party to the action: *Duff v Devlin* [1924] 1 IR 56.

3 *Lloyd v Whittey* (1853) 22 LJ Ch 1038.

4 See **21.11** and **22.39**. A shorter period, such as one month, may be fixed: *Stains v Rudlin* (1852) 9 Hare App 53n (margin); *Smith v Robinson* (1853) 1 Sm & G 140; see *Lloyd v Whittey*, above; or an immediate sale directed. Formerly this was not done where the owner of the equity of redemption did not appear at the hearing though he had appeared in the action: *Smith v Robinson*, above: but under the present law the order may be made though any of the persons interested do not appear in the action: Law of Property Act 1925, s 91(2), **21.5**.

As to ordering an immediate sale, see cases cited **21.11**, n 12.

Conduct of sale

22.48 The conduct of a sale in lieu of foreclosure is given to the person who has the most interest in getting the best price, that is, the mortgagor; or if he does not wish to conduct the sale, the mortgagee lowest in priority[1]. Permission may be given to the mortgagee to bid at the sale[2]. If the mortgagee becomes the purchaser, and his principal and interest exceed the purchase money, he may be let into possession as from a date earlier than that fixed by the contract[3].

1 See, generally, **21.12**.
2 *Ex p Marsh* (1815) 1 Madd 148; *The Wilsons* (1841) 1 Wm Rob 173; see also *Palk v Mortgage Services Funding Plc* [1993] Ch 330; *Polonski v Lloyds Bank Mortgages Ltd* (1997) 31 HLR 721. It will be refused until other ways of selling have failed, if the mortgagee is also a trustee, and objection is made by *cestuis que trust; Tennant v Trenchard* (1869) 4 Ch App 537, but if he has the conduct of the sale, some other person will be appointed for that purpose: *Domville v Berrington* (1837) 2 Y & C Ex 723; see *Re Laird, ex p M'Gregor* (1851) 4 De G & Sm 603.
3 *Bates v Bonnor* (1835) 7 Sim 427.

Security for expenses

22.49 Where the mortgagor is given conduct of the sale, he need not generally give security for the costs of the sale, since he will himself be liable for them[1]. However, otherwise the court may order a sale in lieu of foreclosure on terms that a reasonable sum (fixed by it) is paid into court by the mortgagor to meet the expenses of the sale and secure the performance of the terms subject to which the order is made[2]. The court may then order the property to be sold if the deposit is paid into court by the date specified (usually within a short time, such as a week, of the order specifying the amount of the deposit); but provide that if the mortgagor fails to pay in the deposit, or if no sale has been effected within six months from the date of the order, then the mortgagor should be foreclosed[3].

1 *Davies v Wright* (1886) 32 Ch D 220; *Manchester & Salford Bank v Scowcroft* (1883) 27 Sol Jo 517; *Woolley v Colman* (1882) 21 Ch D 169, 51 LJ Ch 854. Cf *Brewer v Square* [1892] 2 Ch 111. See **21.12**.
2 Law of Property Act 1925, s 91(2); **21.11–21.12**. In a case in which a sale was ordered after decree for foreclosure, a sufficient amount was paid in to indemnify a later mortgagee, who had bought in several incumbrances, to the extent of his entire advances: *Laslett v Cliffe* (1854) 2 Sm & G 278. The deposit being made for the indemnity of the mortgagee, it will be applied in discharge of his costs of the sale, if it proves abortive: *Corsellis v Patman* (1867) LR 4 Eq 156.
3 *Bellamy v Cockle* (1854) 18 Jur 465.

Equitable interests bound

22.50 The rights of equitable incumbrancers on the estate (whether they are claimants, or defendants, or simply included in the order), are bound by an order for sale in lieu of foreclosure, in the same manner as the equity of redemption is bound by an order for foreclosure[1]. Thus a purchaser who has obtained a conveyance[2] of the legal estate, takes the property discharged from all claims, and is not entitled to any release from the equitable incumbrancers[3].

1 See **22.33**.
2 For a vesting order etc in favour of the purchaser, see Law of Property Act 1925, s 90, and see **21.6**.

3 *Keatinge v Keatinge* (1843) 6 I Eq R 43; *Webster v Jones* (1844) 6 I Eq R 142. Although a sale is made by consent of all parties, yet an investment of the purchase money in court is not at the risk of the mortgagee: *Tompsett v Wickens* (1855) 3 Sm & G 171. Neither is the investment made for his benefit, so that he cannot claim accumulations arising from the purchase moneys, unless they have been carried to his separate account: *Irby v Irby* (1855) 22 Beav 217 and see *R v De la Motte* (1857) 2 H & N 589, and as to distribution of a fund comprising the proceeds of the mortgaged land and other moneys, see *Taylor v Waters* (1836) 1 My & Cr 266.

ORDER ABSOLUTE FOR FORECLOSURE

ENTITLEMENT TO AN ORDER ABSOLUTE

Foreclosure order absolute on mortgagor's failure to pay at the appointed time

22.51 The foreclosure order nisi will provide for the mortgagor to be foreclosed if he fails to pay the required sum at the time appointed by the order[1]. If the mortgagor fails to pay the amount found to be due at the specified time and place, the mortgagee is entitled to have the order for foreclosure in the original order made absolute as a matter of course. That is the case whether the security was legal or equitable[2]. The application should be made in accordance with CPR Part 23; the mortgagee is entitled to make it without notice to the mortgagor[3]. The witness statement in support should give evidence that (a) the mortgagee or his agent attended at the time and place appointed for payment, but that payment was not made; and that (b) the money has not been paid subsequently. Evidence of the former should be by the person who attended at the specified time and place, evidence of the latter should be made by all the mortgagees in the jurisdiction (if there are more than one)[4]. The final order of foreclosure must be obtained before an account is taken of subsequent interest and costs and a time appointed for the exercise of the next right of redemption[5].

1 *Edwards v Cunliffe* (1816) 1 Madd 287; *Eyre v Hanson*, above.
2 *Lees v Fisher* (1882) 22 Ch D 283, CA.
3 For form of application, see 28 *Atkin's Court Forms* (1997 issue). The foreclosure order nisi need not be served on the mortgagor: *Lancashire & Yorkshire Reversionary Interest Co Ltd v Crowe* (1970) 114 Sol Jo 435; but see now CPR 23.4 and Practice Direction.
4 *Kinnaird v Yorke* (1889) 60 LT 380; *Docksey v Else* (1891) 64 LT 256; *Barrow v Smith* (1885) 33 WR 743; and see *Frith v Cooke* (1885) 52 LT 798; *Practice Directions* [1955] 1 All ER 30, [1955] 1 WLR 36; and now Chancery Guide.
5 *Whitbread v Lyall* (1856) 8 De GM & G 383; and if great delay takes place in obtaining it, the court will require an explanation and the owner of the equity of redemption must be served: *Prees v Coke* (1871) 6 Ch App 645. No order absolute may be made where the mortgagor has died during the course of proceedings, pending a grant of probate or letters of administration: *Aylward v Lewis* [1891] 2 Ch 81. Application should be made in accordance with CPR 19.8 to join or appoint the personal representative or a person to represent the estate. As to whether there is any need to obtain a supplementary order to give the added defendant power to redeem see (1947) 97 LJ News 313 at 328. If the mortgagor becomes bankrupt during the proceedings, his trustee must be joined.

Attendance by the mortgagee at the time and place fixed for payment

22.52 If the mortgagee attends at the time and place appointed for payment by his agent, the agent should have an appropriate power of attorney, or other appropriate authority, to receive the money, or an order absolute may be refused[1].

However, orders absolute have been made where the formalities have not been strictly complied with: as where the mortgagee attended for only part of the time fixed for payment; where the mortgagee did not attend at the place fixed for payment at all[2]; and where the mortgagee's agent attended without a power of attorney, but the mortgagor did not attend[3].

1 *Gurney v Jackson* (1853) 1 Sm & G App xxvi.
2 *Lechmere v Clamp (No 3)* (1862) 31 Beav 578; *London Monetary, etc, Society v Bean* (1868) 18 LT 349; *Postlethwaite v Tavers* [1871] WN 173; *Cox v Watson* (1877) 7 Ch D 196. In *Bernard v Norton* (1864) 3 New Rep 701; 10 LT 183, following *Anon* (1844) 1 Coll 273, an order absolute was made, though the mortgagee attended during a part only of the time fixed; and this appears to be sufficient; but in *Lechmere v Clamp*, above, Lord Romilly said that the alleged order in *Anon*, above, did not exist or could not be found.
3 *Lechmere v Clamp*, above; *London Monetary, etc, Society v Bean*, above; *Cox v Watson*, above; *Hart v Hawthorne* (1880) 42 LT 79; *Macrea v Evans* (1875) 24 WR 55; *King v Hough* [1895] WN 60.

FORM OF ORDER FOR FORECLOSURE ABSOLUTE[1]

Order for foreclosure

22.53 The order for foreclosure absolute should include reference to the order for foreclosure nisi, details of accounts ordered and sums found to be due, the time and place appointed for payment and any subsequent enlargements of the time for payment, the mortgagee's evidence of attendance at the specified time and place and the mortgagor's non-payment. It should order that the mortgagor be debarred from and foreclosed of all equity of redemption of, in or to the mortgaged property.

1 See 28 *Atkin's Court Forms* (1997 issue).

Orders for possession

22.54 If appropriate, an order for possession should be included. An order for possession may be made even if it was not claimed in the proceedings, but will not in those circumstances be made on a without notice basis[1].

1 See cases cited at **22.23**, nn 4-8; and CPR 16.2(5); and see *Withall v Nixon* (1885) 28 Ch D 413. The order for delivery of possession should contain a description of the property as in the mortgage: *Thynne v Sarl* [1891] 2 Ch 79. For the procedural requirements as to a claim for possession, see **19.28** ff. The order for foreclosure absolute does not by itself entitle the mortgagee to a writ of possession: *Wood v Wheater* (1882) 22 Ch D 281. The order for possession is inserted for convenience in order to avoid multiplicity of proceedings. If it were omitted the mortgagee would have to take separate proceedings to recover possession, and such proceedings would be based, not on the mortgagor's default (the effect of which is exhausted by the foreclosure), but on the mortgagee's own title as owner of the land: *Wood v Smallpiece* [1942] Ch 190, [1942] 1 All ER 252, CA.

Orders for the delivery of deeds

22.55 In a foreclosure claim there is generally no need to order the mortgagor to deliver the deeds, since the mortgagee will already have the deeds in his possession, having obtained them either from the mortgagor upon the making of the security, or from another incumbrancer whom he has redeemed. However, where all the deeds are not already in the mortgagee's custody, the order should order the delivery of the deeds[1]. The mortgagee's right does not in general extend to deeds which affect only the equity of redemption of the mortgaged property, although delivery of them may be ordered under special circumstances, such as where the possession of them by another person might affect the title[2].

1 *Holmes v Turner* (1843) 7 Hare 367n.
2 *Greene v Foster* (1882) 22 Ch D 566. As to delivery of the register on a sale of a ship by the Admiralty Court, see *The Tremont* (1841) 1 Wm Rob 163.

Orders for transfer and delivery of mortgaged stock and licences

22.56 Similar orders may be made for transfer of mortgaged stock[1] and for the delivery of the licence along with possession of a mortgaged public-house[2].

1 *Ricketts v Ricketts* [1891] WN 29.
2 *Crowley v Fenry* (1888) 22 LR Ir 96. For possession in a foreclosure action, see **22.23**, **22.54**.

EFFECT OF ORDER FOR FORECLOSURE ABSOLUTE

WHEN FORECLOSURE TAKES EFFECT

22.57 It is only the order absolute for foreclosure which has the effect of making the mortgage real estate and causing the quality of personalty to be lost; it does not, in that respect, relate back to the earlier order nisi or the judgment for an account[1].

1 *Thompson v Grant* (1819) 4 Madd 438. A release after judgment of foreclosure is equivalent to an absolute foreclosure by order: *Reynoldson v Perkins* (1769) Amb 564. See also **22.33**.

EFFECT OF ORDER FOR FORECLOSURE ABSOLUTE OF MORTGAGES OF FREEHOLD LAND

22.58 Prior to 1926, freeholds were usually mortgaged by conveyance of the fee simple. Thus upon the extinguishment of the equity of redemption by the order absolute for foreclosure, the freehold legal estate would be left vested in the mortgagee[1]. However, by the Law of Property Act 1925 freeholds can no longer be mortgaged by conveyance of the freehold, but only by (a) a demise for a term of years absolute, subject to a provision for cesser on redemption, or (b) a charge by deed expressed to be by way of legal mortgage[2], and mortgages existing on 1 January 1926 were converted into mortgages by demise. Hence, in order that the position of the mortgagee should not be prejudiced, it was necessary to provide that the foreclosure should operate automatically to vest the fee simple in the mortgagee, with the consequent merger of the mortgage term. Section 88(2) of the Law of Property Act 1925 provides that where an estate in fee simple has been mortgaged by the creation of a term of years absolute or by a charge by way of legal mortgage, then where any mortgagee obtains an order for foreclosure absolute, the order shall operate to vest the fee simple in him (subject to any legal mortgage having priority to the mortgage in right of which the foreclosure is obtained and to any money thereby secured). Thereupon the mortgage term, if any, will thereby be merged in the fee simple and any subsequent mortgage term or charge by way of legal mortgage bound by the order shall thereupon be extinguished.

A similar necessity arises when the mortgagee has acquired a title under the Limitation Act 1980, free from the equity of redemption[3]. Accordingly, s 88(3) of the Law of Property Act 1925 allows such a mortgagee to enlarge the mortgage term into a fee simple under the provisions of s 153 of the Act of 1925, discharged from any legal mortgage affected by the title so acquired. In the case of a chargee by way of legal mortgage, such a mortgagee may by deed declare that the fee simple is vested in him, discharged from any legal mortgage affected by the title so acquired, and fee simple will vest accordingly.

In the case of a sub-mortgage of a freehold mortgage, the same result is arrived at by providing, in effect, that the sub-mortgage term shall be extinguished and the principal term be enlarged into the fee simple, so as to enable the sub-mortgagee to acquire the fee simple by foreclosure or enlargement[4].

1 The mortgagor's equitable interest was in effect transferred to the mortgagee: *Heath v Pugh* (1881) 6 QBD 345 at 360; on appeal 7 App Cas 235, HL. The mortgagee held the mortgaged property as absolute owner and as real property, not personalty: *Thompson v Grant* (1819) 4 Madd 438; *Re Loveridge, Pearce v Marsh* [1904] 1 Ch 518 at 523.
2 Section 85(1).
3 See **19.85**.
4 Section 88 (5), see **20.40**. For acquisition of title under the Limitation Act 1980, see **19.85**.

EFFECT OF FORECLOSURE OF LEASEHOLD MORTGAGES

22.59 Section 89 of the Law of Property Act 1925 makes corresponding provision with regard to leasehold mortgages. Thus, where a term of years absolute has been mortgaged by the creation of another term of years absolute, or by a charge by way of legal mortgage, s 89(2) provides that where any mortgagee obtains an order for foreclosure absolute, the order shall, unless it otherwise provides, operate (without giving rise to a forfeiture for want of a licence to assign) to vest the leasehold reversion affected by the mortgage and any subsequent mortgage term in him, subject to any legal mortgage having priority to the mortgage in right of which the mortgage is obtained and to any money thereby secured, and thereupon the mortgage term and any subsequent mortgage term or charge by way of legal mortgage bound by the order shall, subject to any express provision to the contrary contained in the order, merge in such leasehold reversion or be extinguished.

Similarly, where a mortgagee has acquired a leasehold title under the Limitation Act 1980, free from the equity of redemption, s 89(3) provides any such mortgagee, or the persons deriving title under him, may by deed declare that the leasehold reversion affected by the mortgage and any mortgage affected by the title so acquired shall vest in him, free from any right of redemption which is barred, and the same shall (without giving rise to a forfeiture for want of a licence to assign) vest accordingly. Thereupon the mortgage term, if any, and any other mortgage term or charge by way of legal mortgage affected by the title so acquired shall, subject to any express provision to the contrary contained in the deed, merge in such leasehold reversion or be extinguished.

Provision is made in respect of leasehold sub-mortgages similar to that in the case of freehold sub-mortgages. In effect the sub-mortgage term and also the principal mortgage term are extinguished and the sub-mortgagee becomes entitled to the term created by the lease[1].

1 Section 89 (5); see **20.41**. For acquisition of title under the Limitation Act 1980, see **19.85**.

FORECLOSURE OF REGISTERED LAND

22.60 Where registered land is foreclosed, s 34(3) of the Land Registration Act 1925 provides that the order for foreclosure is completed by the registration of the proprietor of the charge (or such other person as may be named in the foreclosure order absolute for that purpose) as the proprietor of the land and by the cancellation of the charge and of all incumbrances and entries inferior[1] to it. Such registration operates in like manner and with the same consequences as if the proprietor of the charge (or such other person named in the foreclosure order absolute) had been a purchaser for valuable consideration of the land under a subsisting power of sale[2].

1 'For the purposes of this section an incumbrance or entry on the register shall not be deemed to be inferior to the charge in right of which title is made if the incumbrance or other interest is given the requisite priority by statute or otherwise': sub-s (6).
2 As to the extinction of the right of redemption under the Limitation Act 1980, see s 34 (2). As to the effect of a sale under the power of sale, s 34 (4), (5). As to making the necessary entry in the register, see Land Registration Rules 1925, r 147.

FORECLOSURE OF AN EQUITABLE MORTGAGE

22.61 A foreclosure order absolute of an equitable mortgage should contain a direction for conveyance of the legal estate. Where a conveyance cannot be obtained in this way, the mortgagor will be declared to be a trustee for the mortgagee and a vesting order made under s 44 of the Trustee Act 1925[1].

1 See **28.78**; *Lechmere v Clamp (No 2)* (1861) 30 Beav 218, *Lechmere v Clamp (No 3)* (1862) 31 Beav 578; *Re Cuming* (1869) 5 Ch App 72; *Re Crowe's Mortgage* (1871) LR 13 Eq 26; *Re D Jones & Co's Mortgage* (1888) 59 LT 859; *Jones v Davies* 1940 WN 174. It was held in *Smith v Boucher* (1852) 1 Sm & G 72, that the vesting order could not be inserted in the judgment for foreclosure, but required a separate application, but there seems to be no objection to including it in the judgment under appropriate circumstances. The former device for getting in a nominal reversion by vesting declaration is not now required: see **3.4–3.5**; and see *British Empire, etc, Assurance Co v Sugden* (1878) 47 LJ Ch 691.

TRUST PROPERTY

22.62 Where any property vested in trustees by way of security becomes by an order for foreclosure, or by virtue of the statutes of limitation, discharged from the right of redemption, then it is held by the trustees in trust:

(a) to apply the income from the property in the same manner as interest paid on the mortgage debt would have been applicable; and

(b) if the property is sold, to apply the net proceeds of sale, after payment of costs and expenses, in the same manner as repayment of the mortgage debt would have been applicable[1].

1 Section 31(1) of the Law of Property Act 1925, as amended by the Trusts of Land and Appointment of Trustees Act 1996. The subsection operates without any prejudice to any rule of law relating to the apportionment of capital and income between tenant for life and remainderman: s 31(2). As to disposition of the net rents where the mortgage is a trust mortgage, see *Re Horn's Estate, Public Trustee v Garnett* [1924] 2 Ch 222.

CHATTELS

22.63 Sections 88(4) and 89(4) of the Law of Property Act 1925 provide that where a mortgage of freehold or leasehold property includes fixtures or chattels personal, then any right to foreclosure, as well as any statutory power of sale or any right to take possession, will extend to the absolute or other interest therein affected by the charge.

STAMP DUTY ON FORECLOSURE ORDER

22.64 The foreclosure order absolute is deemed by statute to be a conveyance on sale of the property[1], and must be stamped accordingly. The duty is chargeable by reference to the outstanding principal debt and interest[2], but is not to exceed the duty payable on an amount equal to the value of the property foreclosed[3]. The appropriate certificate of value should be referred to in the witness statement in support of the application, so that it can be stated in the order; it will then be conclusive for determining the amount of stamp duty payable. A conveyance pursuant to a duly stamped order is exempt from ad valorem stamp duty[4].

1 Finance Act 1898, s 6. The section is declaratory of the law, and thus retrospective: *Re Lovell and Collard's Contract* [1907] 1 Ch 249. A similar conclusion had been reached by the courts: *Huntington v IRC* [1896] 1 QB 422; *IRC v Tod* [1898] AC 399. The order is not a transfer for valuable consideration, so as to confer an unimpeachable title in the case of registered land: *Re de Leeuw, Jakens v Central Advance, etc, Corpn* [1922] 2 Ch 540 at 555 (see **13.48**).
2 Stamp Act 1891, s 57; *IRC v Liquidators of Glasgow City Bank* (1881) 8 R (Ct of Sess) 389.
3 Finance Act 1898, s 6, proviso (a).
4 Finance Act 1898, s 6, proviso (b).

REOPENING THE FORECLOSURE

DISCRETION TO REOPEN THE FORECLOSURE

Conditions of reopening foreclosure

22.65 The conditions for the enlargement of time are stricter when the application is made after the day fixed for payment has passed, but before an order absolute[1], and more so when the application is made after the order absolute[2], so that the foreclosure has to be reopened in order to grant the enlargement of time[3]. First, the applicant must come with reasonable promptness, having regard to the nature of the property and other circumstances[4]. Secondly, he must account satisfactorily for his failure to pay at the proper time and must repay all expenditure incurred by the mortgagee since the order absolute[5]. Thirdly, he must show that he will be able to redeem if further time is given, and, if thought fit, give security for costs in case he fails to do so[6]. The foreclosure may be opened against a purchaser if the purchase is made shortly after the order absolute and with notice of matters which would affect the mortgagee's right to an absolute title; but not where the purchaser bought a considerable time after the date of the order absolute, and without notice of facts which would lead the court to interfere[7].

1 *Patch v Ward* (1867) 3 Ch App 203 at 212.
2 Where the plaintiffs were the public officer and the estate trustees of an insurance society, and the defendant wished to open the foreclosure after final order and the appointment of new trustees in the place of two of the trustees who had died after the final order, the proper course was for the defendant to apply to the new trustees to allow themselves to be added as plaintiffs; and if they refused, to apply under RSC Ord 15, r 6, to have them added as defendants: *Pennington v Cayley* [1912] 2 Ch 236.
3 As to reopening the foreclosure, see *Cocker v Bevis* (1665) 1 Cas in Ch 61; *Ismoord v Claypool* (1666) 9 Sim 317n; *Nanfan v Perkins* (1766) 9 Sim 308n; *Crompton v Earl of Effingham* (1782) 9 Sim 311n; *Jones v Cresswicke* (1839) 9 Sim 304; *Booth v Creswicke* (1841) Cr & Ph 361. Foreclosure was opened in favour of the heir of the mortgagor, where the latter had been foreclosed by his own consent: *Abney v Wordsworth* (1701) 9 Sim 317n. The order is that the entry of the order absolute shall be vacated and the order discharged on condition of payment on the new day appointed; but on non-payment the order absolute is to stand: *Booth v Creswicke*, above; *Ford v Wastell* (1848) 2 Ph 591; *Thornhill v Manning* (1851) 1 Sim NS 451. The foreclosure cannot be opened as to some only of the parties to the action: *Patch v Ward* (1862) 4 Giff 96.
4 *Campbell v Holyland* (1877) 7 Ch D 166; *Hang Seng Bank Ltd v Mee Chong Investment Co Ltd* [1970] HKLR 94 (nine months delay—reopening refused).
5 *Thornhill v Manning* (1851) 1 Sim NS 451 at 456; *Coombe v Stewart* (1851) 13 Beav 111.
6 *Bird v Gandy* (1715) 7 Vin Abr 45, pl 20; (*Thornhill v Manning* (1851) 1 Sim NS 451; *Coombe v Stewart* (1851) 13 Beav 111; and see *Stevens v Williams* (1851) 1 Sim NS 545.
7 *Campbell v Holyland*, above, but an order was refused in *Re Power and Carton's Contract* (1890) 25 LR Ir 459.

Exercise of discretion to reopen the foreclosure

22.66 Whether the court will reopen the foreclosure, and the terms on which it will do so, depend upon the circumstances of each case. The foreclosure has been reopened in the following circumstances:

(a) where there was an expectation that the money would be ready to redeem, for instance where there was a contract for sale;
(b) where there was a bona fide belief from facts known to the mortgagee that a negotiation was so far complete as to make a tender of the money unnecessary;
(c) where there was some ignorance or mistake as to the state of the proceedings, or the day fixed for payment[1];
(d) where there was some irregularity in the proceedings before the order absolute;
(e) where the mortgagor, or the person charged with payment of the money fell ill, or was accidentally unable to travel;
(f) where there was poverty, but which could be shown to be only temporary; and
(g) where the property had a special value for the mortgagor[2].

Time was also enlarged for redemption of a policy of life assurance where the life insured fell in after the day fixed for payment, but before foreclosure absolute[3]; and where the mortgagor had not understood the effect of the orders nisi and absolute, and there was a great discrepancy between the amount owing under the mortgage (£3,000) and the value of the mortgaged property (more than £6,000)[4]. However, the foreclosure was not reopened where there had been an irregular act, done under what might have been fairly considered to be a correct view of the law rather than fraudulent motives, but the order absolute had been made[5]. The court is generally unwilling to open a foreclosure where it has been made by consent, or after long acquiescence, especially if buildings or other improvements, or settlements have been made on the faith of the order; such relief has been refused after six years[6]. The discharge of an order absolute has been refused with costs, even where there was evidence that the order was obtained by surprise during negotiations between the parties, and notwithstanding evidence by the tenant in possession that he was willing to purchase the estate for more than twice as much as was due in the security[7].

1 *Collinson v Jeffery* [1896] 1 Ch 644.
2 See the cases cited in **22.65**, and see *Joachim v M'Douall* (1798) 9 Sim 314n; *Ford v Wastell* (1847) 6 Hare 229; *Campbell v Holyland* (1877) 7 Ch D 166.
3 *Beaton v Boulton* [1891] WN 30.
4 *Lancashire and Yorkshire Reversionary Interest Co Ltd v Crowe* (1970) 114 Sol Jo 435. The relevant date for determining the value of the property and the mortgage debt is the date of the order for foreclosure absolute: *Patch v Ward* (1867) 3 Ch App 203; *Hang Seng Bank Ltd v Mee Cheong Investment Co Ltd* [1970] HKLR 94.
5 *Patch v Ward* (1867) 3 Ch App 203.
6 *Took v Bishop of Ely* (1705) 15 Vin Abr 476; *Lant v Crisp* (1719) 15 Vin Abr 467; *Fleetwood v Jansen* (1742) 2 Atk 467; and see *Thornhill v Manning* (1851) 1 Sim NS 451; *Jones v Kendrick* (1727) 2 Eq Cas 602. Acquiescence in a judgment for foreclosure does not necessarily preclude a subsequent action for redemption founded on new matter and, notwithstanding the foreclosure, the plaintiff will have the benefit at the hearing of an equity which may arise upon his redemption action; *Fleetwood v Jansen*, above.
7 *Jones v Roberts* (1827) M'Cle & Yo 567.

REOPENING THE FORECLOSURE AS OF RIGHT

22.67 There are circumstances in which the mortgagor is entitled as of right to have the foreclosure reopened.

Receipt of rents by the mortgagee or receiver

22.68 The foreclosure will be reopened as a matter of course where the mortgagee[1], or the receiver appointed in the claim[2], receives rents between the date of the fixing of the amount due and the date fixed for redemption. In those circumstances, a fresh account will be taken and a new day fixed for redemption, unless in the original order the mortgagee agreed to be charged with a sum in respect of rents in the receiver's hands, or which might come to his hands prior to the order absolute, and the amount so received does not exceed the sum so fixed[3]. However, the foreclosure will not be reopened where rents are received between the day fixed for redemption and the date of the order absolute[4]. Nor will foreclosure be reopened on the ground that the receiver appointed by the court has made a mistake in his accounts[5].

1 *Garlick v Jackson* (1841) 4 Beav 154; *Buchanan v Greenway* (1849) 12 Beav 355; *Patch v Ward* (1867) 3 Ch App 203 at 208; *Prees v Coke* (1871) 6 Ch App 645; *Allen v Edwards* (1873) 42 LJ Ch 455.
2 *Jenner-Fust v Needham* (1886) 32 Ch D 582, CA; *Peat v Nicholson* (1886) 54 LT 569; and see *Seton* (7th edn) p 1914.
3 *Barber v Jeckells* [1893] WN 91; *Simmons v Blandy* [1897] 1 Ch 19. For form of such judgment, see *Lusk v Sebright* [1894] WN 134; and see *Ellenor v Ugle* [1895] WN 161, where the order absolute was allowed on certain conditions, the rents received by the receiver being insufficient to pay out-of-pocket expenses and remunerations, and a new day will not be fixed if the original judgment directed that any party might apply in chambers for payment or transfer to him of any money which might come to the hands of the receiver or be paid into court: *Colman v Llewellin* (1886) 34 Ch D 143, CA. In that case the order absolute may provide for payment of the money to the mortgagee; *Colman v Llewellin*. It seems, however, that this latter direction will only be inserted in the judgment in special cases: *Cheston v Wells* [1893] 2 Ch 151.
4 *Prees v Coke*, above, at 650; *Webster v Patteson* (1884) 25 Ch D 626; *National Permanent Building Society v Raper* [1892] 1 Ch 54.
5 *Ingham v Sutherland* (1890) 63 LT 614.

Suing mortgagor for payment

22.69 If the mortgagee sues the mortgagor on his covenant for payment after the foreclosure, claiming that the property is insufficient to satisfy the mortgage debt, that will open the foreclosure and the mortgagor will be entitled to redeem[1]. If, however, the mortgagee no longer has the property under his control (as where he has sold it to a third party), so that he could not on redemption restore it to the mortgagor, then he is not entitled to sue the mortgagor[2], nor a guarantor of the mortgagor's personal covenant[3]. However, the mortgagee will not be prevented from suing where he is unable to restore the property in consequence of an act for which he is not responsible; for instance, where a superior landlord has forfeited and where the mortgagee was not liable to pay the rent or perform the covenants[4]. Nor will the mortgagee be prevented from suing on the personal covenant where the mortgagee's inability to restore the property is the result of a sale by him under his power of sale[5].

1 *Dashwood v Blythway* (1729) 1 Eq Cas Abr 317, pl 3; *Perry v Barker* (1803) 8 Ves 527; *Lockhart v Hardy* (1846) 9 Beav 349; and the mortgagor has this right even though he has assigned the equity of redemption, though—under the former system of reconveyance—the reconveyance would be made subject to such equity for redemption as was vested in any person other than himself; *Kinnaird v Trollope* (1888) 39 Ch D 636 at 645. See also *Canada Permanent Trust Co v King Art Developments Ltd* (1985) 12 DLR (4th) 161 at 173.
2 *Perry v Barker* (1806) 13 Ves 198 at 205; *Lockhart v Hardy*, above; *Palmer v Hendrie* (1859) 27 Beav 349, *Palmer v Hendrie (No 2)* (1860) 28 Beav 341; *Walker v Jones* (1866) LR 1 PC 50 at 62; *Kinnaird v Trollope*, above; *Ellis & Co's Trustee v Dixon-Johnson* [1924] 1 Ch 342 at 351; on appeal [1924] 2 Ch 451 at 470, CA; affd [1925] AC 489, HL; *Gordon Grant & Co Ltd v Boos* [1926] AC 781; *Rushton v Industrial Development Bank* (1973) 34 DLR (3d) 582; *Campbell Sharp Ltd v Caisse Populaire de St Boniface* (1984) 9 DLR (4th) 32 at 35.
3 *Lloyds and Scottish Trust Ltd v Britten* (1982) 44 P & CR 249.
4 *Re Burrell, Burrell v Smith* (1869) LR 7 Eq 399.
5 See **17.7**.

Sale under the power of sale

22.70 The mortgagee can still sell and make a title under his power of sale after the foreclosure. However, in that case, although the purchaser gets a good title and the actual property cannot be restored, the foreclosure is reopened as regards the purchase money and the mortgagee will have to account for that to the mortgagor[1].

1 *Watson v Marston* (1853) 4 De GM & G 230; *Re Alison, Johnson v Mounsey* (1879) 11 Ch D 284, CA; *Stevens v Theatres Ltd* [1903] 1 Ch 857 (and see **16.11**, n 8; **22.47**, n 2 for the need for leave during the period for redemption). Apparently this is not the result of a mere agreement to sell under the power of sale; *Watson v Marston*, above, at 240. The fact that the mortgagee has referred to the mortgage in his will as if the debt were still subsisting is not a ground for opening the foreclosure, but the property will pass according to his actual interest: *Took v Bishop of Ely* (1705) 15 Vin Abr 476, note to pl 1; *Silberschildt v Schiott* (1814) 3 Ves & B 45; *Le Gros v Cockerell* (1832) 5 Sim 384.

Reopening foreclosure for fraud or collusion

22.71 The foreclosure will also be reopened if the judgment has been obtained by false evidence[1], or other fraudulent or collusive[2] practice, in the same way as other judgments will be set aside in such circumstances[3]. However, actual fraud and contrivance, and not merely constructive fraud, must be shown for the purpose[4].

1 *Loyd v Mansell* (1722) 2 P Wms 73.
2 *Harvey v Tebbutt* (1820) 1 Jac & W 197.
3 *Gore v Stacpoole* (1813) 1 Dow 18; *McIlkenny v Chief Constable of the West Midlands Police* [1980] QB 283, 333; for the case of perjury by an officer or employee, see *Re Odyssey (London) Ltd* [2001] Lloyd's Rep IR 1, CA.
4 *Patch v Ward* (1867) 3 Ch App 203.

Chapter 23

Insolvency of mortgagor

RIGHT OF MORTGAGEE TO EXERCISE ORDINARY REMEDIES

GENERAL RIGHT OF MORTGAGEE TO ENFORCE HIS SECURITY IN THE USUAL MANNER

23.1 After the bankruptcy of the mortgagor, the mortgagee may in general take proceedings to enforce his security in the usual manner[1]. Although there is power for a judge of any Division of the High Court, on his own motion, to order the transfer of enforcement proceedings to the Chancery Division[2], a transfer is unlikely to be ordered unless a bankruptcy point is involved[3]. The same rule applies in the winding up of companies[4]. The mortgagee is, in fact, independent of the bankruptcy or winding-up proceedings, and his claim is to enforce a claim, not against the bankrupt or the company, but to his own property. However, the Insolvency Act 1986 imposes significant restrictions on the exercise of a mortgagee's remedies in the case of companies subject to an administration order[5].

1 *Re Wherly, ex p Hirst* (1879) 11 Ch D 278; see *Re Hutton (A Bankrupt)* [1969] 2 Ch 201, [1969] 1 All ER 936. Where the statutory, or an express, power to sell or appoint a receiver is made exercisable by reason of the mortgagor being adjudicated a bankrupt, such power is not to be exercised only on account of the adjudication without the leave of the court: Law of Property Act 1925, s 110 (1), as amended by Insolvency Act 1985, s 235, Sch 10, Pt III. For circumstances in which the court might intervene to stay proceedings against a trustee in bankruptcy prior to the Insolvency Act 1986 and its statutory predecessors see: *Re Chidley, Re Lennard* (1875) 1 Ch D 177, CA; *Re Woods, ex p Ditton* (1876) 1 Ch D 557, CA; *Re Sparke, ex p Cohen* (1871) 7 Ch App 20; *Re Taylor and Rumboll, ex p Rumboll* (1871) 6 Ch App 842; *Re Hall, ex p Rocke* (1871) 6 Ch App 795; *Re Wherly, ex p Hirst* (1879) 11 Ch D 278. See *Re Evelyn, ex p General Public Works and Assets Co Ltd* [1894] 2 QB 302.

2 Insolvency Rules 1986, r 7.15.

3 See under earlier legislation, *Re Champagne, ex p Kemp* [1893] WN 153. Where proceedings have been commenced before the bankruptcy, they will generally be continued in the court in which they were commenced and, unless a bankruptcy point is involved or the costs would be less in the bankruptcy court, there should not be a transfer: see *Re Hutton*, above. In a possession action there is no need to join the trustee (see **19.32**, n 6) and the costs will be less if he is not involved.

4 *Re David Lloyd & Co, Lloyd v David Lloyd & Co* (1877) 6 Ch D 339, CA; and see *Campbell v Compagnie Générale de Bellegarde* (1876) 2 Ch D 181, but the secured creditor is not obliged to realise his security. He may instead petition to wind up the company without first realising the security: *Re Alexanders Securities Ltd (No 2)* [1983] 2 Qd R 597, (1983) 8 ACLR 434.

5 See **23.66** ff.

SAVING OF RIGHTS OF SECURED CREDITORS IN BANKRUPTCY

23.2 Section 285 of the Insolvency Act 1986 provides that at any time when proceedings on a bankruptcy petition are pending or an individual has been adjudged bankrupt, the court may stay any claim, execution or other legal process against the property or person of the debtor or, as the case may be, of the bankrupt[1]. Any court in which proceedings are pending against any individual may, on proof that a bankruptcy petition has been presented in respect of that individual or that he is an undischarged bankrupt, either stay the proceedings or allow them to continue on such terms as it thinks fit[2]. After the making of a bankruptcy order no person who is a creditor of the bankrupt in respect of a debt provable in the bankruptcy shall:

(a) have any remedy against the property or person of the bankrupt in respect of that debt; or
(b) before the discharge of the bankrupt, commence any claim or other legal proceedings against the bankrupt, except with the leave of the court and on such terms as the court may impose, subject to ss. 346 (enforcement procedures) and 347 (limited right to distress)[3].

However, it is specifically provided that this does not affect the right of a secured creditor of the bankrupt to enforce his security[4]. Thus a secured creditor who does not choose to come in under the bankruptcy can use his ordinary remedies for enforcing his security[5], but he cannot at the same time retain his security and prove for the value of his debt. He can only prove for the deficiency after allowing for the security[6].

Similarly, s 286 of the Insolvency Act 1986 provides that where an interim receiver has been appointed[7], then during the period between the appointment and the making of a bankruptcy order on the petition, or the dismissal of the petition, no creditor of the debtor may commence any claim or other legal proceedings against the debtor except with the leave of the court and on such terms as the court may impose. However, an exception is again made in the case of a secured creditor[8].

1 Section 285(1).
2 Section 285(2).
3 Section 285(3). If after the making of a bankruptcy order proceedings are commenced without leave, the court can on a subsequent application grant leave with retrospective effect: *Re Saunders (a bankrupt)* [1997] Ch 60, [1997] 3 All ER 992.
4 The section follows Bankruptcy Act 1914, s 7(2). For restrictions on proceedings against a company in liquidation, see Insolvency Act 1986, ss 126, 130 (2). For the effect of an administration order, see **23.6** ff. For the definition of secured creditor, see **23.3**.
5 *White v Simmons* (1871) 6 Ch App 555. If he proves, the proof is subject to the rule that there cannot be two proofs for one debt. Thus mortgagees of a policy of insurance, the mortgagor having covenanted in the mortgage to pay the premiums, cannot in the bankruptcy of the mortgagor at the same time value the policy and prove on the value of the covenant: *Deering v Bank of Ireland* (1886) 12 App Cas 20, HL.
6 Insolvency Rules 1986, rr 4.88(1), 6.109 (1). Thus the creditor cannot retain his security and at the same time prove on a promissory note, part of the consideration for which consists of arrears of interest on the secured debt: *Re Clark, ex p Clark* (1841) 1 Mont D & De G 622; and where a mortgagor assigns the equity of redemption and covenants to discharge the debt, and the mortgage proves in his bankruptcy, a proof by the assignee on the covenant is a double proof and is not allowed: *Re Hoey, ex p Hoey* (1918) 88 LJ KB 273; see *Re Oriental Commercial Bank, ex p European Bank* (1871) 7 Ch App 99; *Re Rushton*

(a Bankrupt), ex p National Westminster Bank Ltd v Official Receiver [1972] Ch 197, [1971] 2 All ER 937. However, a secured creditor is entitled to apply his security in discharge of whatever liability he thinks fit, so he can appropriate proceeds of sale first in discharge of non-preferential debts: *Re William Hall (Contractors) Ltd* [1967] 2 All ER 1150, [1967] 1 WLR 948. See also **23.10**.

7 Under the Insolvency Act 1986, s 286.

8 Section 286 (6).

Definition of secured creditor

23.3 For the purposes of the Insolvency Act, a 'secured creditor' is a creditor (that is, in relation to a bankrupt, a person to whom any of the bankruptcy debts is owed) who holds any security for the debt (whether a mortgage, charge, lien or any other security) over any property of the person by whom the debt is owed[1]. The question whether a creditor has a mortgage, charge, lien or other security will be determined in accordance with the nature of these securities[2]. Liens which create a secured creditor for the purposes of the Act include solicitors', bankers' and brokers' liens[3], maritime liens[4] and vendors' liens.

The definition of secured creditors is such as to include a charge arising under process of execution[5]. However, as regards execution against the goods or land of a debtor, the creditor is not entitled, as against the official receiver or trustee of the bankrupt's estate, to retain the benefit of the execution or any sums paid to avoid it, unless the execution was completed or the sums were paid before the commencement of the bankruptcy[6]. An execution against goods is completed by seizure and sale, or by the making of a charging order[7]. Execution against land is completed by seizure[8], by the appointment of a receiver or by the making of a charging order[9]. Equitable execution by the appointment of a receiver of an interest other than in land is not within these provisions, but since it cannot be made in such terms as to create a charge in favour of the creditor, it does not make him a secured creditor[10]. The provisions also apply to an attachment of debts; an attachment of a debt is completed by receipt of the debt[11]. If, therefore, the judgment creditor has not received the debt before the commencement of the bankruptcy, he is not a secured creditor, and the trustee is entitled to the debt[12].

1 Insolvency Act 1986, s 383 (1), (2), but security does not include a lien on books, papers or other records, except to the extent that they consist of documents which give a title to property and are held as such: s 383 (4); and in liquidation, see ss 246, 248. For loss of security by a secured creditor, see eg *Re Falconer* [1981] 1 NZLR 266.

2 A wife's beneficial interest in property by virtue of contributions to improvements under the Matrimonial Proceedings and Property Act 1970, s 37 does not apply to the period after bankruptcy. The section only applies between husband and wife and does not apply between wife and a third party: *W A Samuels Trustee v Samuels* (1973) 233 Estates Gazette 149.

3 *Brandao v Barnett* (1846) 12 Cl & Fin 787; *Jones v Peppercorne* (1858) John 430; *Re Keever* ([1967] Ch 182, [1966] 3 All ER 631; *Re Capital Fire Insurance Association* (1883) 24 Ch D 408 (company insolvency cases).

4 *Re Rio Grande do Sul Stemaship Co* (1877) 5 Ch D 282; *Re Australian Direct Steam Navigation Co* (1875) LR 20 Eq 325 (company insolvency cases).

5 *Re Printing and Numerical Registering Co* (1878) 8 Ch D 535 (a company insolvency case). For charging orders see *Re Hutchinson, ex p Hutchinson* (1885) 16 QBD 515 (shares) and *Haly v Barry* (1868) 3 Ch App 452. For a garnishee order, see *Re Stanhope Silkstone Collieries* (1879) 11 Ch D 160; *Re National United Investment Corpn* [1901] 1 Ch 950 (company insolvency cases). But not a mere judgment creditor, nor one who has not completed the process of execution (but see *Hall v Richards* (1961) 108 CLR 84; nor a garnishee order nisi). For charging orders on land, see **2.12** ff.

6 Insolvency Act 1986, s 346 (1). On liquidation, see Insolvency Act 1986, s 183 (1).
7 Under s 1 of the Charging Orders Act 1979; see **2.12** ff.
8 Execution is completed by delivery of the land to the execution creditor, although the sheriff has not made a return to the writ: *Re Hobson* (1886) 33 Ch D 493.
9 Insolvency Act 1986, s 346 (5). On liquidation, see Insolvency Act 1986, s 183 (3).
10 See **2.21**.
11 Insolvency Act 1986, s 346 (5) (c); on liquidation, s 183 (3) (c).
12 *Re Trehearne, ex p Ealing Local Board* (1890) 60 LJ QB 50, CA; *Re Bagley* [1911] 1 KB 317, CA. Payment of the amount of the debt into court by the garnishee is not a receipt by the judgment creditor so long as a third party is claiming it: *Butler v Wearing* (1885) 17 QBD 182 and see also *George v Tompson's Trustee* [1949] Ch 322, [1949] 1 All ER 554.

POWER TO STAY OR RESTRAIN PROCEEDINGS AGAINST COMPANY IN WINDING UP

23.4 Section 126(1) of the Insolvency Act 1986 provides that at any time after the presentation of a winding-up petition, and before a winding-up order has been made, the company, or any creditor or contributory, may:

(a) apply to the court in which any claim or proceeding is pending for a stay of those proceedings, where the proceedings are against the company in the High Court or Court of Appeal in England and Wales or Northern Ireland; and
(b) may, where any other claim or proceeding is pending against the company, apply to the court having jurisdiction to wind up the company to restrain further proceedings in the claim or proceeding.

The court to which such an application is made may (as the case may be) stay, sist or restrain the proceedings on such terms as it thinks fit. Similarly s 130(2) of the Insolvency Act 1986 provides that when a winding-up order has been made, or a provisional liquidator has been appointed, no claim or proceeding shall be proceeded with or commenced against the company or its property, except by leave of the court and subject to such terms as the court may impose. It appears that retrospective leave may be granted on an application following the issue of proceedings[1].

However, the court is very unwilling to interfere with the rights of a mortgagee by refusing him leave under s 130(2) to proceed with a claim to enforce his security following a winding-up order. The court will need to be persuaded that there is some special ground for refusing the mortgagee that to which he is entitled. It will hardly ever interfere with the mortgagee's legal rights without requiring a payment into court, or some other security for the mortgage debt[2].

1 In *Re National Employers Mutual General Insurance Association Ltd (in liquidation)* [1995] 1 BCLC 232, [1995] BCC 774, it was held by Rattee J that retrospective leave could not be granted. However, in *Re Saunders (a bankrupt)* [1997] Ch 60, [1997] 3 All ER 992, a bankruptcy case concerning s 285(3) of the Insolvency Act 1986, Lindsay J conducted a comprehensive review of the authorities, on the basis of which he declined to follow *Re National Employers Mutual General Insurance Association Ltd.*
2 *Re David Lloyd & Co, Lloyd v David Lloyd & Co* (1877) 6 Ch D 339, CA; *Re Longdendale Cotton Spinning Co* (1878) 8 Ch D 150; *Re Henry Pound, Son and Hutchins Ltd* (1889) 42 Ch D 402, CA; *Re Joshua Stubbs Ltd, Barney v Joshua Stubbs Ltd* [1891] 1 Ch 475, CA; *Strong v Carlyle Press* [1893] 1 Ch 268, CA; *The Zafiro* [1960] P 1, [1959] 2 All ER 537.

CIRCUMSTANCES WHERE THE COURT WILL RESTRAIN A MORTGAGEE

23.5 While, historically, the court has generally been reluctant to restrain a mortgagee or other secured creditor in the exercise of his legal remedies[1], the court has restrained claims which are contrary to equitable principles, or the provisions of bankruptcy law[2]. Thus the court restrained a mortgagee from pursuing an claim for foreclosure which had been commenced after the trustee in bankruptcy had made an advantageous contract for the sale of the property; the mortgagee was ordered to concur in the sale and give up the deeds to the property upon his being paid the full amount that was due to him[3]. The court prevented a creditor from suing a trustee in bankruptcy on a bill of sale, where the latter disputed its validity[4]. However, the court refused to intervene in a claim by a mortgagee which involved questions which did not affect the administration of the estate in bankruptcy[5]. The court also refused to interfere with the rights of an execution creditor who had seized goods before the petition in bankruptcy[6].

1 *Re Wherly, ex p Hirst* (1879) 11 Ch D 278. See *Re Evelyn, ex p General Public Works and Assets Co Ltd* [1894] 2 QB 302.
2 *Re Chidley, Re Lennard* (1875) 1 Ch D 177, CA.
3 *Re Woods, ex p Ditton* (1876) 1 Ch D 557, CA. The court will generally order sale rather than foreclosure where the latter would produce a windfall for the mortgagee: see **21.2** and **21.11**.
4 *Re Sparke, ex p Cohen* (1871) 7 Ch App 20.
5 *Re Taylor and Rumboll, ex p Rumboll* (1871) 6 Ch App 842.
6 *Re Hall, ex p Rocke* (1871) 6 Ch App 795.

RESTRICTIONS ON ENFORCING CHARGES AND SECURITIES WHERE COMPANY SUBJECT TO ADMINISTRATION ORDER[1]

Restrictions on enforcing charges and securities

23.6 The purpose of an administration order is to achieve, if possible, the survival and rehabilitation of the company as a going concern, or a more advantageous realisation of the company's assets than would be likely to ensue from a winding-up order. During the period beginning with the presentation of a petition for an administration order[2], and ending with the making of such an order, or the dismissal of the petition, amongst other restrictions, (a) no steps may be taken to enforce any charge on or security over the company's property and (b) no proceedings and no execution or other legal process may be commenced or continued, and no distress may be levied against the company or its property, except with the leave of the court and subject to such terms as the court may impose[3]. During the period for which an administration order is in force, amongst other restrictions, (a) no steps may be taken to enforce any security over the company's property, and (b) no other proceedings and no execution or other legal process may be commenced or continued, except with the consent of the administrator or the leave of the court, and subject, where the court gives leave, to such terms as the court may impose[4].

1 See, generally, see *Corporate Insolvency, Law and Practice* (2nd edn, 2001), Ch 4.
2 Where a petition for an administration order is presented at a time when there is an administrative receiver of the company and the person by or on whose behalf of the receiver was appointed has not consented to the making of the order, the period shall be deemed not to begin unless and until that person so consents: s 10 (3).

3 Insolvency Act 1986, s 10 (1). See *Lingard,* p 140, but the leave of the court is not required for the appointment of an administrative receiver of a company nor for the carrying out by such receiver of any of his functions: s 10 (2).
4 Insolvency Act 1986, s 11(3)(c).

Exercise of the court's discretion

23.7 The court has a general discretion to give leave to a secured creditor to enforce its security and must have regard to all the circumstances[1]. The burden of obtaining leave rests on the creditor[2]. The purpose of the prohibition in s 11 is to assist the company, under the management of the administrator, to achieve the purposes for which the administration order was made; the purpose of the power to give leave is to enable the court to relax the prohibition where it would be inequitable for the prohibition to apply. The court must balance those factors[3]. So far as possible, the administration procedure should not be used to prejudice those who were secured creditors when the administration order was made. Thus it will normally be a sufficient ground for granting leave if significant loss would be caused to the secured creditor by refusing leave[4]. An important consideration will be whether the applicant for leave is fully secured; if he is, delay in enforcement is likely to be less prejudicial than in cases where his security is insufficient[5]. Thus the court refused leave where there was evidence that the administrator would achieve a sale of the property within a reasonable time, which would enable the secured creditor's debt to be discharged in full, but required the administrator to return to court in two months if a binding contract for sale had not then been reached[6]. The court also refused leave to a secured creditor to enforce its security where it would have appointed a receiver, which would inevitably have resulted in the costs of the receivership being added to its security[7]. Leave may be refused where the purpose of the administration order would be frustrated by granting leave[8]. It behoves a secured creditor to make his position clear to the administrator at the start of the administration, and, if it becomes necessary, to apply to the court promptly[9]. Thus leave for a creditor to enforce a security was refused where he had stood by and taken advantage of the administrator's operations over some months and where the granting of leave would have prevented the administrator obtaining his approved objective[10]. It may be appropriate for leave to be given, even where no criticism could be made of the administrator[11]. Where there is a dispute over the existence, validity or nature of the security which the applicant is seeking leave to enforce, it is not for the court on that application to adjudicate upon the issue, unless the issue raises a short point of law which it is convenient to determine without further ado. Otherwise, the court needs to be satisfied only that the applicant has a seriously arguable case[12].

1 *Re Atlantic Computer Systems plc* [1992] Ch 505, [1992] 1 All ER 476, [1991] BCLC 606, [1990] BCC 859,CA; *Re Meesan Investments* (1988) 4 BCC 788.
2 *Re Atlantic Computer Systems plc* above.
3 *Re Atlantic Computer Systems plc* above.
4 *Re Atlantic Computer Systems plc* above; *Bristol Airport v Powdrill* [1990] Ch 744, (1990) BCC 130; *Scottish Exhibition Centre Ltd v Mirestop Ltd* [1993] BCC 529. For an example of where the court made a detailed examination of the actual losses which would be suffered by lessors of chattels, see: *Re David Weeks Access Ltd* [1993] BCC 175.
5 *Re Atlantic Computer Systems plc* [1992] Ch 505, [190] BCC 859, CA.
6 *Re Meesan Investments* (1988) 4 BCC 788; the same terms were imposed in *Royal Trust v Buchler* [1989] BCLC 130.
7 *Royal Trust v Buclher* [1989] BCLC 130.
8 *Re Sibec Developments Ltd* [1993] BCC 148.

9 *Re Atlantic Computer Systems plc* [1992] Ch 505, [1990] BCC 859, CA.
10 *Bristol Airport v Powdrill* [1990] Ch 744, (1990) BCC 130.
11 *Re Meesan Investments* (1988) 4 BCC 788; *Royal Trust v Buchler* [1989] BCLC 130.
12 *Re Atlantic Computer Systems plc* [1992] Ch 505, [1990] BCC 859, CA.

Power of administrator to dispose of property as if not subject to security

23.8 Where the court is satisfied, on the application of an administrator of a company, that the disposal of any property of the company subject to a security[1] would be likely to promote the purposes of the administration order[2], the court may by order authorise the administrator to dispose of the property as if it were not subject to the security[3]. It is a condition of such an order that (a) the net proceeds of disposal, and (b) if those proceeds are less than the amount determined by the court to be the net amount which would be realised on a sale of the property in the open market by a willing vendor, then such sums as may be required to make good the deficiency, must be applied towards discharging the sums secured by the security[4]. In the case of two or more securities, such sums must be applied towards discharging the sums secured by those securities in the order of their priorities[5]. The court gave the administrator leave to sell property subject to a fixed charge as if it were not subject to the security where, although the sale proceeds of the security would have been insufficient to discharge the debt, the shortfall would have been discharged by the sale of other assets of the company[6].

1 That is, any security other than a floating charge, for which the section makes separate provision: s 15(1), (3). For the distinction between fixed and floating charges, see *Re Armagh Shoes Ltd* [1984] BCLC 405; *Re Keenan Bros Ltd* [1986] BCLC 242; *Re New Bullas Trading Ltd* [1994] BCC 36.
2 The disposal should help achieve a proposal which either has been, or will be, put to the creditors, see *Re Consumer & Industrial Press Ltd (No 2)* (1987) 4 BCC 72; *Re T & D Industries plc* [2000] 1 BCLC 471.
3 Insolvency Act 1986, s 15(1).
4 Section 15(5).
5 Section 15(6).
6 *Re ARV Aviation Ltd* (1988) 4 BCC 708.

APPLICATION TO THE BANKRUPTCY COURT FOR AN ORDER FOR SALE

23.9 The ordinary process in bankruptcy is by sale, and the Insolvency Rules 1986 provide a mortgagee with a special power of sale, which is considered in Chapter 21[1].

1 Rules 6.197–6.199; see **21.18** ff. There is also power to order the sale of land belonging to a bankrupt under s 14 of the Trusts of Land etc Act 1996: see **21.17** ff.

MORTGAGEE'S RIGHT TO PROVE

PROOF IN A BANKRUPTCY

Right to prove

23.10 As stated above, a secured creditor who does not choose to come in under the bankruptcy is entitled to use his ordinary remedies for enforcing his security[1].

However, he cannot at the same time retain his security and prove for the value of his debt. He can only prove for the deficiency after allowing for the security[2].

1 *White v Simmons* (1871) 6 Ch App 555; see **23.2**. If he proves, the proof is subject to the rule that there cannot be two proofs for one debt. Thus mortgagees of a policy of insurance, the mortgagor having covenanted in the mortgage to pay the premiums, cannot in the bankruptcy of the mortgagor at the same time value the policy and prove on the value of the covenant: *Deering v Bank of Ireland* (1886) 12 App Cas 20, HL.

2 Insolvency Rules 1986, rr 4.88(1), 6.109 (1). Thus the creditor cannot retain his security and at the same time prove on a promissory note, part of the consideration for which consists of arrears of interest on the secured debt: *Re Clark, ex p Clark* (1841) 1 Mont D & De G 622; and where a mortgagor assigns the equity of redemption and covenants to discharge the debt, and the mortgage proves in his bankruptcy, a proof by the assignee on the covenant is a double proof and is not allowed: *Re Hoey, ex p Hoey* (1918) 88 LJ KB 273; see *Re Oriental Commercial Bank, ex p European Bank* (1871) 7 Ch App 99; *Re Rushton (a Bankrupt), ex p National Westminster Bank Ltd v Official Receiver* [1972] Ch 197, [1971] 2 All ER 937. But a secured creditor is entitled to apply his security in discharge of whatever liability he thinks fit, so he can appropriate proceeds of sale first in discharge of non-preferential debts: *Re William Hall (Contractors) Ltd* [1967] 2 All ER 1150, [1967] 1 WLR 948.

Security must be on debtor's own property

23.11 A debt is secured for the purposes of the Insolvency Act 1986 to the extent that the person to whom the debt is owed holds any security for the debt (whether a mortgage, charge, lien or other security) over any property of the person by whom the debt is owed[1]. Thus the security which constitutes the creditor a secured creditor must be on the property of the debtor. It is only in such a case that the creditor is within the rule that he must deduct the value of his security and prove for no more than the difference[2]. The principle is that a man is not allowed to prove against a bankrupt's estate and to retain a security which, if given up, would go to augment the estate against which he proves[3]. The exception to the rule as to election is so well established that it has been said to be almost a maxim in bankruptcy, that 'a security is never to go in reduction of proof, unless it belongs to the estate against which the proof is tendered'[4].

The are numerous cases to which the exception applies: for example, where the wife's estate is mortgaged to secure the debt of the husband, or where one partner mortgages his separate estate to secure a debt due from the partnership[5]. For this purpose, the joint and separate estates of partners are considered as distinct estates and a joint creditor having a security upon the separate estate of one of the partners can prove against the joint estate for the full amount of his debt without giving up his security and vice versa[6]. The exception from the rule against retainer and full proof does not apply where it is in appearance only that the security belongs to a separate estate. Thus the exception did not apply where the joint debt was secured by shares in a company which, although joint property, were in the separate names of the joint debtors, in compliance with a rule of the company that no shares should be held jointly[7]. Likewise, where real estate bought with joint funds is used jointly, and mortgaged to secure a joint debt, it could not be contended that because the conveyance was made to the partners as tenants in common, there was, for the purpose of this exception, a security upon the separate estate of each tenant in common[8].

1 Section 383(2) of the Insolvency Act 1986.

2 *Re Howe, ex p Brett* (1871) 6 Ch App 838. 'The question is whether, in substance, apart from technicality, the creditors held a security upon property of the bankrupt at the time they made their proof': at 840.

3 *Re Turner, ex p West Riding Union Banking Co* (1881) 19 Ch D 105 at 112, CA; *Re Dutton, Massey & Co, ex p Manchester and Liverpool District Banking Co* [1924] 2 Ch 199.
4 *Re Wyatt, ex p Adams* (1837) 3 Mont & A 157.
5 *Re Hicklin, ex p Hedderly* (1842) 2 Mont D & De G 487; *Re Hart, ex p Caldicott* (1884) 25 Ch D 716. The procedure for proving a debt of a partnership or partner now follows that for insolvent companies. For a case where the subject matter of the security had become vested in the creditor, so that he was not a 'secured creditor', see *Re Hallett, ex p Cocks, Biddulph & Co* [1894] 2 QB 256, CA.
6 *Re Bell, ex p Peacock* (1825) 2 Gl & J 27; *Re Brettell, ex p Bowden* (1832) 1 Deac & Ch 135; *Re Plummer and Wilson, ex p Shepherd* (1841) 2 Mont D & De G 204, 1 Ph 56; *Rolfe and Bank of Australasia v Flower & Co* (1865) LR 1 PC 27 at 47; *Re Fraser, Trenholm & Co* (1868) 4 Ch App 49. As to allowing amendment where a separate security has been by mistake deducted, see *Couldery v Bartrum* (1881) 19 Ch D 394, CA.
7 *Re Clarke, ex p Connell* (1838) 3 Deac 201; *Re Collie, ex p Manchester and County Bank* (1876) 3 Ch D 481, CA; see *Re Cooksey, ex p Portal & Co* (1900) 83 LT 435.
8 *Re Burgess, ex p Free* (1827) 2 Gl & J 250.

Voting

23.12 A secured creditor is entitled to vote only in respect of the balance (if any) due to him after deducting the value of his security[1]. If he votes in respect of his whole debt, he will be deemed to have surrendered his security, unless the court on application is satisfied that the omission to value the security has arisen from inadvertence[2].

1 Insolvency Rules 1986, r. 6.93 (4); in liquidation, see r 4.67 (4).
2 As to inadvertence, see *Re Maxson, ex p Trustee* [1919] 2 KB 330. If the creditor votes in respect of a specific sum and does not include further liability also covered by the mortgage, and there is no inadvertence, he will be taken to have surrendered the mortgage to the extent of the whole liability: *Re Pawson* [1917] 2 KB 527.

Rules as to proof

23.13 The Insolvency Rules 1986 contain specific provision for secured creditors proving in a bankruptcy[1]. Non-compliance with the Rules excludes the creditor from all share in any dividend[2]. The following is a summary of the relevant Rules[3].

1 Under Chapter 9 of the Act.
2 Insolvency Act 1986, s 322 (1); Insolvency Rules 1986, rr 6.96 ff; for liquidation, see Insolvency Rules 1986, rr 4.73 ff.
3 For the case where the petitioning creditor is himself a secured creditor, the Insolvency Act 1986 provides that he must in his petition either state that he is willing to give up his security for the benefit of the creditors, or that the petition is not made in respect of the secured part of the debt. In the latter case he may be admitted as a petitioning creditor to the extent of the balance of the debt after deducting the estimated value: s 269. The surrender of the security vests the interest in it in the trustee. The security is not merged in the equity of redemption for the benefit of a subsequent mortgagee: *Cracknall v Janson* (1877) 6 Ch D 735; and similarly where the trustee redeems: *Bell v Sunderland Building Society* (1883) 24 Ch D 618.

General procedure

23.14 Chapter 8 of the Act deals with the general procedure for proving[1]. There is provision for the trustee to supply forms for proving[2]; and detailed requirements as to the contents of the proof are set out in r 6.98. If a secured creditor does not either realise or surrender his security, he must state in his proof, besides the other matters specified, particulars of any security held, the date when it was given and the value which the creditor puts upon it[3]. The trustee can require a claim of debt to be verified by affidavit[4]. There is provision for the cost of proving[5]. The trustee must allow proofs to be inspected[6]. Certain requirements must be fulfilled in relation to the proof of a licensed moneylender[7]. There is provision for the transmission of proofs on the appointment of a trustee[8], for the admission or rejection of proofs for dividend[9], for an appeal against a decision on proof[10], for the withdrawal or variation of a proof[11] and for the expunging of a proof by the court[12].

1 Rule 6.96 defines the meaning of 'prove'.
2 Rule 6.97.
3 This applies even where the security was given for bills of exchange which have been negotiated by the creditor and which he has had to pay in full: *Baines v Wright* (1885) 16 QBD 330, CA. The estimate need not be the true estimate, but the trustee will be entitled to redeem at the amount estimated: *Re Lacey, ex p Taylor* (1884) 13 QBD 128. If a mortgagee has postponed his security to enable the debtor to raise more money, he will be entitled to prove for the amount which he would have received out of the security if he had not consented to postpone it: *Re Chappell, ex p Ford* (1885) 16 QBD 305, CA. For the operation of the provisions relating to valuing security in relation to a statutory demand, see *Platts v Western Trust and Savings Ltd* [1993] 22 LS Gaz R 38, [1993] NPC 58.
4 Rule 6.99.
5 Rule 6.100.
6 Rule 6.101.
7 Rule 6.102.
8 Rule 6.103.
9 Rule 6.104.
10 Rule 6.105.
11 Rule 6.106.
12 rule 6.107.

What may be proved for

23.15 Rules 6.108 to 6.114 deal with the quantification of the claim made in the proof. If a secured creditor realises his security, he may prove for the balance of his debt, after deducting the amount realised. If a secured creditor voluntarily surrenders his security for the general benefit of creditors, he may prove for his whole debt, as if it were unsecured[1]. The right to prove for interest is considered in detail below[2].

1 Rule 6.109. If he does so, he cannot afterwards change his mind and rely on his security: *Re O'D, ex p Robinson* (1885) 15 LR Ir 496. Surrender of the security and proof for the whole debt does not discharge a surety, since he is considered to contract with reference to the provisions of the bankruptcy legislation: *Rainbow v Juggins* (1880) 5 QBD 422.
2 See **23.22** ff.

Value of security

23.16 A secured creditor may, with the agreement of the trustee or the leave of the court, at any time[1] alter the value which he has, in his proof of debt, put upon his security[2]. However, if a secured creditor (a) being the petitioner, has in the petition put a value on his security, or (b) has voted in respect of the unsecured balance of his debt, he may re-value his security only with leave of the court[3].

1 See r. 6.117 (2), below. Apparently the creditor cannot amend after he has by notice put the trustee to his election whether he will redeem and the trustee has elected to do so: *Re*

Sadler, ex p Norris (1886) 17 QBD 728, CA; see *Re Fanshawe, ex p Le Marchant* [1905] 1 KB 170; *Re Small* [1934] Ch 541; *Re Becher* [1944] Ch 78.

2 Rule 6.116 (1). The amendment will be allowed in a proper case, notwithstanding the opposition of a subsequent mortgagee: *Re Arden, ex p Arden* (1884) 14 QBD 121; *Baines v Wright* (1885) 16 QBD 330, CA.

3 Rule 6.116 (2).

Surrender for non-disclosure

23.17 If a secured creditor omits to disclose his security in his proof of debt, he must surrender his security for the general benefit of creditors, unless the court, on application by him, relieves him from the effect of that rule on the ground that the omission was inadvertent or the result of honest mistake[1]. If the court grants that relief, it may require or allow the creditor's proof of debt to be amended, on such terms as may be just[2].

1 As to inadvertence, see *Re Maxson, ex p Trustee* [1919] 2 KB 330.

2 Rule 6.116.

Redemption by trustee

23.18 The trustee may at any time[1] give notice to a creditor whose debt is secured that he proposes, at the expiration of 28 days from the date of the notice, to redeem the security at the value put upon it in the creditor's proof. The creditor then has 21 days (or such longer period as the trustee may allow) in which, if he so wishes, to exercise his right to re-value his security[2]. If the creditor revalues his security, the trustee may only redeem at the new value. If the trustee redeems the security, the cost of transferring it is borne by the estate. A secured creditor may at any time[3], by a notice in writing, call on the trustee to elect whether he will or will not exercise his power to redeem the security at the value then placed on it; and the trustee then has six months in which to exercise the power to determine not to exercise it[4].

1 Before foreclosure: *Knowles v Dibbs* (1889) 60 LT 291. Judgment for foreclosure against the trustee in bankruptcy and subsequent incumbrancers should show that the trustee was entitled to redeem at the valuation, but subsequent incumbrancers only at the full amount of the first mortgagee's debt: *Knowles v Dibbs*; see *Sanguinetti v Stuckey's Banking Co (No 2)* [1896] 1 Ch 502.

2 With the leave of the court, where r 6.115 (2) applies.

3 Without prejudice to his right to commence a foreclosure action: *Knowles v Dibbs*, above. A mortgagee whose rights are barred by the Limitation Act 1980 cannot give an effective notice under this rule: *Cotterell v Price* [1960] 3 All ER 315, [1960] 1 WLR 1097.

4 Rule 6.117.

Test of security's value

23.19 The trustee may, if he is dissatisfied with the value which a secured creditor puts on his security (whether in his proof or by way of revaluation[1]), require any property comprised in the security to be offered for sale. The terms of the sale should be such as may be agreed, or as the court may direct. If the sale is by auction, the trustee on behalf of the estate, and the creditor on his own behalf, may appear and bid. However, those provisions do not apply if the security has been revalued and the revaluation has been approved by the court[2].

1 Under r 6.117.

2 Rule 6.118.

Realisation of security by creditor

23.20 If a creditor who has valued his security subsequently realises it (whether or not at the instance of the trustee), then (a) the net amount realised is substituted for the value previously put by the creditor on the security, and (b) that amount is treated in all respects as an amended valuation made by him[1].

1 Rule 6.119. But the excess is applicable to the mortgagee's general costs: *Re Johnston, Millar v Johnston* (1888) 23 LR Ir 50; cf *Société Générale de Paris v Green* (1883) 8 App Cas 606, HL, as to allowance of interest on the assessed value.

Surety

23.21 Where a surety becomes surety for the whole of the debt, but his liability is limited to a specified sum, he does not on paying that sum acquire a right of proof in priority to the creditor. Consequently the creditor can still prove for the full debt and the surety cannot prove until the creditor has been fully paid. However, if the surety is a surety for part of the debt and pays that part, he succeeds *pro tanto* to the right of proof of the creditor[1]. A surety who has not been called upon to pay is nevertheless under a contingent liability in respect of which he can prove[2]. A surety is not discharged by the surrender of the security[3].

1 *Re Sass, ex p National Provincial Bank of England* [1896] 2 QB 12; *Barclays Bank Ltd v TOSG Trust Fund Ltd* [1984] 1 All ER 628, CA; affd [1984] AC 626, [1984] 1 All ER 1060, HL.
2 *Re Paine, ex p Read* [1897] 1 QB 122; *Re Herepath and Delmar* (1890) 38 WR 752; *Re Blackpool Motor Car Co Ltd, Hamilton v Blackpool Motor Car Co Ltd* [1901] 1 Ch 77; *Re Fenton, ex p Fenton Textile Association Ltd* [1931] 1 Ch 85, CA, but where a surety had covenanted to keep up the premiums on a policy mortgaged by the principal debtor and to pay interest so long as any principal remained due and the mortgagor had agreed to indemnify him, and the mortgagee valued his security and proved for the deficiency in the bankruptcy of the mortgagor, the surety was not allowed to prove under the indemnity in respect of either head of liability, since the policy had been realised and the debt extinguished by the bankrupt: *Re Moss, ex p Hallett* [1905] 2 KB 307. The decision was based also on the prohibition of double proof: see **23.2**, n 6. On set-off see *MS Fashions Ltd v Bank of Credit and Commerce International SA (No 2)* [1993] 3 All ER 769, [1993] 3 WLR 220, not following *MS Fashions Ltd v Bank of Credit and Commerce International SA* [1993] Ch 425, [1993] BCLC 280; *Re Charge Card Securities Ltd* [1987] Ch 150, [1986] 3 All ER 289; see also *Day and Dent Constructions Pty Ltd v North Australian Properties Pty Ltd* (1982) 150 CLR 85.
3 *Rainbow v Juggins* (1880) 5 QBD 422.

Proof for interest[1]

Where agreement provides for interest

23.22 Where a bankruptcy debt bears interest, that interest is provable as part of the debt, except in so far as it is payable in respect of any period after the commencement of the bankruptcy[2]. In distributing the bankrupt's estate, any surplus remaining after the payment of preferential and ordinary debts must be applied in paying interest on those debts in respect of the periods during which they have been outstanding since the commencement of the bankruptcy[3]. Where the mortgage contains provisions for the capitalisation of interest, those are to be applied in quantifying the claim, although not in respect of interest payments falling due after the commencement of the bankruptcy.[4]

1 For background to the new rules, see Cork Report, Ch 31.

2 Insolvency Act 1986, s 322 (2).
3 Section 328 (4). The interest on preferential debts ranks equally with interest on other debts: s 328(4). The rate of interest is the greater of (a) the rate specified in s 17 of the Judgments Act 1838 at the commencement of the bankruptcy, and (b) the rate applicable to that debt apart from the bankruptcy: s 328(4).
4 *Re Amalgamated Investment and Property Co Ltd* [1985] Ch 349.

Where no provision for interest

23.23 Where interest is not previously reserved or agreed by the transaction, the Insolvency Rules[1] provide that the creditor's claim may include interest on the debt for periods before the bankruptcy order, in the following circumstances:

(a) if the debt is due by virtue of a written instrument and payable at a certain time, interest may be claimed for the period from that time to the date of the bankruptcy order;
(b) if the debt is due otherwise, interest may only be claimed if, before the presentation of the bankruptcy petition, a demand for payment was made in writing by or on behalf of the creditor, and notice was given that interest would be payable from the date of the demand to the date of payment and chargeable at a rate not exceeding that provided for by the Rules.

In the latter case, interest may only be claimed for the period from the date of the demand to that of the bankruptcy order. In each case, the rate of interest to be claimed is the rate specified in s 17 of the Judgments Act 1838 on the date of the bankruptcy order.

1 Rule 6.113, as amended by the Insolvency (Amendment) Rules 1987, SI 1987/1919, r 3(1), Sch, Pt 1, para 112.

General principles of bankruptcy law as to interest

23.24 The above provisions only apply to the proof of debts. Thus they do not interfere with the creditor's right to payment out of the security of all interest which falls due under its terms[1]. If, however, the security is deficient and the creditor has to prove for any part of his debt, he must do so in accordance with those provisions. A secured creditor cannot increase the amount of his proof by applying the proceeds of realisation of his security to payment of interest accruing after the date of the bankruptcy order[2]. Apart from the express provisions of the Insolvency Act, it is a general principle of proof that interest which accrues after the date of the bankruptcy order cannot be proved for[3]. If a debt is payable by instalments which include principal and interest, the rule is applied to the part which represents interest[4].

1 See Insolvency Act 1986, s 285 (4).
2 *Re Bulmer* (1853) 3 De G M & G 218; *Re Bonacino, ex p Discount Banking Co* (1894) 10 R 147, 1 Mans 59; *Re Hall (William) (Contractors) Ltd (In Liquidation)* [1967] 2 All ER 1150, [1967] 1 WLR 948.
3 *Re Flood and Lott, ex p Lubbock* (1863) 4 De GJ & Sm 516; *Re Savin* (1872) 7 Ch App 760 at 764, but the creditor can set off profits realised from the security since the winding up against interest accrued during the same period: *Re London, Windsor and Greenwich Hotels Co, Quartermaine's Case* [1892] 1 Ch 639; see also *Re Savin* (1872) 7 Ch App 760. As to the mode of proof for interest when a debt is payable at a future time, see Insolvency Rules 1986, rr 4.94 and 6.114 and r 11.13 for discount; and under the earlier legislation, see *Re*

Browne and Wingrove, ex p Ador [1891] 2 QB 574, CA; in that case the history of the law as to proof for interest in bankruptcy was considered.

4 *Re Phillips, ex p Bath* (1882) 22 Ch D 450, but if the fixed instalment includes a premium, as well as principal and interest, the premium can be proved for: *Re Phillips, ex p Bath* (1884) 27 Ch D 509, CA.

Administration of insolvent estates of deceased persons

23.25 The above provisions of the Insolvency Act 1986 apply with minor modifications to the administration in bankruptcy of the insolvent estates of deceased persons dying before the presentation of a bankruptcy petition[1]. For that purpose, the estate of a deceased person is insolvent if, when realised, it will be insufficient to meet in full all the debts and other liabilities to which it is subject[2]. Likewise, where the estate of a deceased person is insolvent and is being administered otherwise than in bankruptcy, the same provisions as apply under the law of bankruptcy with respect to the assets of individuals adjudged bankrupt apply to the administration of the estate as to the respective rights of secured and unsecured creditors, to debts and liabilities provable, to the valuation of future and contingent liabilities and to the priorities of debts and other payments[3].

1 See Administration of Insolvent Estates of Deceased Persons Order 1986, SI 1986/1999 (which came into force on 29 December 1986), para 4(1), made under Insolvency Act 1986, s 412.

2 See Insolvency Act 1986, s 421(4). This is a matter of fact; if there is any uncertainty, the administration should proceed on the basis that the estate is insolvent until the debts and liabilities are discharged: see *Re Pink, Elvin v Nightingale* [1927] 1 Ch 237 at 241; *Re Hopkin, Williams v Hopkins* (1881) 18 Ch D 370 at 377.

3 See Administration of Insolvent Estates of Deceased Persons Order 1986, SI 1986/1999, para 4(1), made under Insolvency Act 1986, s 412.

PROOF IN A WINDING UP

Procedure for proving in a winding up

23.26 The procedure for proving[1] in a winding up is very similar to the procedure for proving in a bankruptcy[2]. The following is a summary of the relevant rules. Specific provision is again made for secured creditors[3].

1 Rule 6.96 defines the meaning of 'prove'.

2 See **23.10** ff. It is dealt with in Chapter 9 of the Act.

3 For the definition of 'secured creditor' see **23.2** above.

General procedure

23.27 There is provision for the supply of forms by the trustee[1], for the supply of forms of proof by the liquidator to creditors[2], and for the detailed requirements as to the contents of the proof[3]. A secured creditor must state in his proof, besides the other matters specified, particulars of any security held, the date when it was given and the value which the creditor puts upon it[4].

The liquidator has the power to call for clarification or substantiation of any of the details provided in the creditor's proof[5] and to require a claim of debt to be verified by affidavit[6]. There is provision for the cost of proving[7], for the liquidator to allow proofs to be inspected[8], for the transmission of proofs on the appointment of a liquidator[9], and for the transmission of all proofs to any new liquidator appointed[10]. The Rules provide for the admission or rejection of proofs for dividend[11], for an appeal against a decision on proof[12], for the withdrawal or variation of a proof[13], and for the expunging of a proof by the court[14].

1 Rule 4.73.
2 Rule 4.74.
3 Rule 4.75.
4 Rule 4.75 (1)(g). This applies even where the security was given for bills of exchange which have been negotiated by the creditor and which he has had to pay in full: *Baines v Wright* (1885) 16 QBD 330, CA. The estimate need not be the true estimate, but the trustee will be entitled to redeem at the amount estimated: *Re Lacey, ex p Taylor* (1884) 13 QBD 128. If a mortgagee has postponed his security to enable the debtor to raise more money, he will be entitled to prove for the amount which he would have received out of the security if he had not consented to postpone it: *Re Chappell, ex p Ford* (1885) 16 QBD 305, CA.
5 Rule 4.76.
6 Rule 4.77.
7 Rule 4.78.
8 Rule 4.79.
9 Rule 4.80.
10 Rule 4.81.
11 Rule 4.82.
12 Rule 4.83.
13 Rule 4.84.
14 Rule 4.85.

What may be proved for

23.28 Rules 4.86 to 4.94 deal with the quantification of the claim made in the proof. If a secured creditor realises his security, he may prove for the balance of his debt, after deducting the amount realised[1]. If a secured creditor voluntarily surrenders his security for the general benefit of creditors, he may prove for his whole debt, as if it were unsecured[2]. The right to prove for interest is considered in detail below[3].

1 A secured creditor is entitled to appropriate the amount realised between various debts he is owed by the company as he thinks fit, including between preferential and non-preferential claims (*Ex Parte Hunter* (1801) 6 Ves 94; *Re Fox and Jacobs* [1894] 1 QB 438) and proveable and non-proveable claims (*Re Foster* (1875) LR 20 Eq 767; *Re William Hall (Contractors) Ltd* [1967] 2 All ER 1150, [1967] 1 WLR 948); and see also *Re H E Thorne & Son* [1914] 2 Ch 438. However, a creditor with several securities for several debts may not apply surplus proceeds from the realisation of one security to a deficit on another: *Re Newton* (1836) 2 Deac 66.
2 Rule 4.88.
3 See **23.34**.

Value of security

23.29 A secured creditor may, with the agreement of the liquidator or the leave of the court, at any time alter the value which he has put upon his security in his proof of debt[1]. However, if a secured creditor (a) being the petitioner, has in the petition put a value on his security, or (b) has voted in respect of the unsecured balance of his debt, he may revalue his security only with leave of the court[2].

1 Rule 4.95 (1).
2 Rule 4.95 (2).

Surrender for non-disclosure

23.30 If a secured creditor omits to disclose his security in his proof of debt, he must surrender his security for the general benefit of creditors, unless the court, on application by him, relieves him from that obligation on the ground that the omission was inadvertent or the result of honest mistake[1]. If the court grants that relief, it may require or allow the creditor's proof of debt to be amended, on such terms as may be just[2].

1 Rule 4.96 (1). See *Re Henry Lister & Co Ltd* [1892] 2 Ch 417; *Re Burr* (1892) 67 LT 232; *Re Safety Explosives Ltd* [1904] 1 Ch 226; *Re Rowe* [1904] 2 KB 489.
2 Rule 4.96 (2).

Redemption by liquidator

23.31 The liquidator may at any time give notice to a creditor whose debt is secured that he proposes, at the expiration of 28 days from the date of the notice, to redeem the security at the value put upon it in the creditor's proof[1]. The creditor then has 21 days (or such longer period as the liquidator may allow) in which, if he so wishes, to exercise his right to revalue his security[2]. If the creditor revalues his security, the trustee may only redeem at the new value. If the liquidator redeems the security, the cost of transferring it is payable out of the assets[3]. A secured creditor may at any time, by a notice in writing, call on the liquidator to elect whether he will or will not exercise his power to redeem the security at the value then placed on it and the liquidator then has six months in which to exercise the power or determine not to exercise it[4].

1 Rule 4.97 (1).
2 Rule 4.97 (2); with the leave of the court, where r 4.95 (2) applies.
3 Rule 4.97 (3).
4 Rule 4.97 (4).

Test of security's value

23.32 The liquidator may, if he is dissatisfied with the value which a secured creditor puts on his security (whether in his proof or by way of revaluation[1]), require any property comprised in the security to be offered for sale[2]. The terms of the sale should be such as may be agreed, or as the court may direct. If the sale is by auction, the liquidator on behalf of the estate, and the creditor on his own behalf, may appear and bid.

1 Under r 4.98.
2 Rule 4.98 (1).

Realisation of security by creditor

23.33 If a creditor who has valued his security subsequently realises it (whether or not at the instance of the liquidator), (a) the net amount realised must be substituted for the value previously put by the creditor on the security; and (b) that amount must be treated in all respects as an amended valuation made by him[1].

1 Rule 4.99.

Interest

23.34 The same general principles apply in a winding up as apply in a bankruptcy[1]. Under s 189 of the Insolvency Act 1986, interest is payable on any debt proved in the winding up, including so much of any such debt as represents interest on the remainder[2]. Any surplus remaining after the payment of debts proved in a winding up shall, before being applied for any other purpose, be applied in paying interest on those debts in respect of the periods during which they have been outstanding since the company went into liquidation[3]. All interest paid under those provisions ranks equally, whether or not the debts on which it is payable rank equally[4]. The rate of interest payable under s 189 in respect of any debt ('the official rate') is whichever is the greater of (a) the rate specified in s 17 of the Judgments Act 1838 on the day on which the company went into liquidation, and (b) the rate applicable to that debt apart from the winding up[5].

In provisions analogous to those in bankruptcy, the Insolvency Rules provide that where a debt proved in the liquidation bears interest, that interest is provable as part of the debt, except in so far as it is payable in respect of any period after the company went into liquidation[6]. In the following circumstances the creditor's claim may include interest on the debt for periods before the company went into liquidation, even though not previously reserved or agreed[7]:

(a) if the debt is due by virtue of a written instrument, and payable at a certain time, interest may be claimed for the period from that time to the date when the company went into liquidation[8];
(b) if the debt is due otherwise, interest may only be claimed if, before that date, a demand for payment of the debt was made in writing by or on behalf of the creditor and notice given that interest would be payable from the date of the demand to the date of payment[9].

In the latter case, interest may only be claimed for the period from the date of the demand to that of the company's going into liquidation, at a rate not exceeding that provided by the Act[10]. In each case, the rate of interest to be claimed is the rate specified in s 17 of the Judgments Act 1838 on the date when the company went into liquidation[11].

1 See **23.22** ff.
2 Section 189 (1).
3 Section 189 (2).
4 Section 189 (3).
5 Section 189 (4).
6 Rule 4.93 (1); r. 4.93 was amended by the Insolvency (Amendment) Rules 1987, SI 1987/1919, r 3(1), Sch, Pt 1, para 59.
7 Rule 4.93 (2).
8 Rule 4.93 (3).
9 Rule 4.93 (4).
10 Rule 4.93 (5).
11 Rule 4.93 (6).

TRANSACTIONS WHICH ARE VOID OR CAN BE SET ASIDE UPON BANKRUPTCY OR A WINDING UP

BANKRUPTCY

Restrictions on dispositions of property after presentation of the petition

23.35 Section 284 of the Insolvency Act 1986 provides that where a person is adjudged bankrupt any disposition of property, including any mortgage or charge, made by that person in the period beginning with the day of the presentation of the bankruptcy order and ending with the vesting of the bankrupt's estate in a trustee, is void, except to the extent that it is or was made with the consent of the court, or is or was subsequently ratified by the court[1]. Such a disposition is void notwithstanding that the property is not, or would not be, comprised in the bankrupt's estate; but the section does not apply to any disposition made by a person of property held by him on trust for any other person[2]. Section 284(4) provides that the section does not give a remedy against any person:

(a) in respect of any property or payment which he received before the commencement of the bankruptcy in good faith, for value and without notice that the petition had been presented; or
(b) in respect of any interest in property which derives from an interest in respect of which there is, by virtue of sub-s (4), no remedy.

However, where after the commencement of his bankruptcy the bankrupt has incurred a debt by reason of the making of a payment which is void under s 284, that debt is deemed for the purposes of the Act to have been incurred before the commencement of the bankruptcy unless (a) the debtor had notice of the bankruptcy before the debt was incurred, or (b) it is not reasonably practicable for the amount of the payment to be recovered from the person to whom it was made[3].

1 Section 284(1) and (3). For the previous law, see Bankruptcy Act 1914, s 45; *Re Simms* [1930] 2 Ch 22.
2 Section 284(6).
3 Section 284(5).

Transactions at an undervalue

23.36 Section 339 of the Insolvency Act 1986[1] provides that where a bankrupt has, at a relevant time, entered into a transaction at an undervalue, the trustee of the bankrupt's estate can apply to the court for an order restoring the position to what it would have been if that transaction had not been entered into[2]. An individual enters into a transaction at an undervalue with a person if:

(a) he makes a gift to that person or he otherwise enters into a transaction with that person on terms that provide for him to receive no consideration;
(b) he enters into a transaction with that person in consideration of marriage; or
(c) he enters into a transaction with that person for a consideration the value

of which, in money or money's worth, is significantly less than the value, in money or money's worth, of the consideration provided by the individual[3].

The mere creation of a security in respect of an existing debt does not deplete the debtor's assets and therefore does not amount to consideration in money or money's worth[4]. The transfer of an interest in the equity of redemption in a mortgaged property in return for the assumption of liability under the mortgage is capable of involving a transaction at an undervalue, or an element of 'bounty', if the respective consideration given is unequal[5]. The relevant time for the purposes of a transaction at an undervalue is the period of five years ending with the day of the presentation of the bankruptcy petition on which the individual is adjudged bankrupt[6]. However, the first three years of that period are not relevant unless the individual is insolvent at that time, or becomes insolvent in consequence of the transaction; but those requirements are presumed to be satisfied, unless the contrary is shown, in relation to any transaction at an undervalue which is entered into by an individual with a person who is an associate of his (otherwise that by reason only of being his employee)[7]. For those purposes, an individual is insolvent if (a) he is unable to pay his debts as they fall due, or (b) the value of his assets is less than the amount of his liabilities, taking into account his contingent and prospective liabilities.

1 See *Re MC Bacon* [1990] BCLC 324 for consideration of the similar provisions of s 238 of the Insolvency Act 1986, concerning transactions at an undervalue granted by a company; and see *National Bank of Kuwait v Menzies* [1994] 2 BCLC 306.
2 Section 339(1)–(2).
3 Section 339(3).
4 *Re MC Bacon* above; see also *National Bank of Kuwait v Menzies* above.
5 *Re Kumar (a bankrupt)* [1993] BCLC 548.
6 Section 341(1).
7 Section 341(2).

Transactions defrauding creditors

23.37 Where transactions have been entered at an undervalue for the purpose of putting assets beyond the reach of creditors, or otherwise prejudicing their interests, ss. 423 and 424 of the Insolvency Act 1986 give the court power to restore the position to that which it would have been if the transaction had not been entered into and to protect the interests of persons who are victims of the transaction[1]. Where a mortgagor granted a lease of the mortgaged property to his wife, at full market rate, but the surrender value of the lease (due to its detrimental effect on the freehold value of the property) was greater in value than the consideration provided by the wife, the transaction was set aside under s 423[2].

1 See *Arbuthnot Leasing International Ltd v Havelet Leasing Ltd (No 2)* [1990] BCC 636; *Moon v Franklin* [1996] BPIR 196; *Chohan v Saggar* [1992] BCC 306.
2 *Agricultural Mortgage Corpn plc v Woodward* [1995] 1 BCLC 1; see also *Barclays Bank v Eustice* [1995] 2 BCLC 630; *National Westminster Bank plc v Jones* [2001] 1 BCLC 98.

Preferences

23.38 Section 340 of the Insolvency Act 1986[1] provides that where a bankrupt has, at a relevant time, given a preference to any person, the trustee of the bankrupt's estate can apply to the court for an order restoring the position to what it would have been if that preference had not been given[2]. An individual gives a preference to a person if:

(a) that person is one of the individual's creditors or a surety or guarantor for any of his debts or other liabilities; and
(b) the individual does anything or suffers anything to be done which has the effect of putting that person into a position which, in the event of the individual's bankruptcy, will be better that the position he would have been in if that thing had not been done[3].

Under previous legislation, it was held that giving a security or additional security for an existing debt, or allowing a creditor to perfect a security when he is out of time to do so, might well amount to a preference[4]. The court must not make an order under the section in respect of a preference unless the individual who gave it was influenced in deciding to give it by a desire to produce in relation to that person the effect of putting that person into a position which, in the event of the individual's bankruptcy, would be better than the position he would have been in if that thing had not been done[5]. Desire for that purpose is subjective[6]. However, such an influence will be presumed, unless the contrary is shown, where the person to whom the preference was given was an associate of the individual giving the preference[7]. The fact that something has been done in pursuance of an order of the court does not, without more, prevent it constituting the giving of a preference[8]. The relevant period in the case of a preference which is not a transaction at an undervalue, and which is given to a person who is an associate of the individual, is two years ending with the day of the presentation of the bankruptcy petition on which the individual is adjudged bankrupt and, in the case of any other preference which is not a transaction at an undervalue, the period of six months ending with that day[9]. However, that time is not relevant unless the individual is insolvent at that time, or becomes insolvent in consequence of the preference, but those requirements are presumed to be satisfied, unless the contrary is shown, in relation to any preference at an undervalue which is entered into by an individual with a person who is an associate of his (otherwise that by reason only of being his employee)[10]. For those purposes, an individual is insolvent if (a) he is unable to pay his debts as they fall due, or (b) the value of his assets is less than the amount of his liabilities, taking into account his contingent and prospective liabilities[11].

1 See *Re MC Bacon* [1990] BCLC 324 for consideration of the similar provisions of s 239 of the Insolvency Act 1986, concerning preferences granted by a company.
2 Section 340(1)–(2).
3 Section 340(3).
4 *Sir William Henry Peat v Gresham Trust* [1934] AC 252; see also *Re Jeavons* (1873) 8 Ch App 643; *Re Thompson* (1877) 7 Ch D 138; but given that the test under the old legislation was different, these should be considered with caution: see *Re MC Bacon,* above, at 335, which considers the circumstances in which a debenture granted by a company may constitute a preference under the similar provisions of s 239 of the Insolvency Act 1986.
5 Section 340(4).
6 *Re MC Bacon* [1990] BCLC 324.
7 Section 340(5).
8 Section 340(6).
9 Section 341(1).
10 Section 341(2).
11 Section 341(3).

Orders where there has been a transaction at an undervalue or a preference

23.39 Section 342 of the Insolvency Act 1986 gives the court extensive powers as to the orders it can make to restore the position where there has been a transaction at an undervalue or a preference. In particular, the court can release or discharge (in whole or in part) any security given by the individual.

LIQUIDATION

Avoidance of property dispositions

23.40 Section 127 of the Insolvency Act 1986 provides that in a winding up by the court, any disposition[1] of the company's property made after the commencement of the winding up is, unless the court orders otherwise, void.

1 Which would include a mortgage or charge: see eg Law of Property Act 1925, s 205(1)(ii).

Transactions at an undervalue

23.41 Where an administration order is made in relation to a company, or the company goes into liquidation, and the company has at a relevant time entered into a transaction at an undervalue, section 238 of the Insolvency Act 1986 provides that the administrator or liquidator can apply to the court for an order restoring the position to what it would have been if the company had not entered into the transaction[1]. A company enters into a transaction at an undervalue with a person if:

(a) the company makes a gift to that person or otherwise enters into a transaction with that person on terms that provide for the company to receive no consideration; or
(b) the company enters into a transaction with that person for a consideration the value of which, in money or money's worth, is significantly less than the value, in money or money's worth, of the consideration provided by the individual[2].

The mere creation of a security in respect of an existing debt does not deplete a company's assets, and therefore does not amount to consideration in money or money's worth[3]. However, the court shall not make such an order in respect of a transaction at an undervalue if it is satisfied (a) that the company which entered into the transaction did so in good faith and for the purposes of carrying on its business, and (b) that at the time it did so there were reasonable grounds for believing that the transaction would benefit the company. The relevant time for the purposes of a transaction at an undervalue is the period of two years ending with the onset of insolvency, or at a time between the presentation of a petition for the making of an administration order in relation to the company and the making of such an order on that petition[4]. However, those periods are not relevant unless at the time the company was unable to pay its debts within the meaning of s 123 of the Act, or became unable to pay its debts within the meaning of that section in consequence of the transaction; but those requirements are presumed to be satisfied, unless the contrary is shown, in relation to any transaction at an undervalue entered into with a person connected with the company[5]. For the purposes of the section, the onset of insolvency is the date of the presentation of the petition on which the administration order was made, or the date of the commencement of the winding up[6].

1 Section 238(1)–(3); see generally *Re MC Bacon* [1990] BCLC 324.
2 Section 238(4).
3 *Re MC Bacon* [1990] BCLC 324.
4 Section 240(1).
5 Section 240(2).
6 Section 240(3).

Transactions defrauding creditors

23.42 Where transactions have been entered at an undervalue for the purpose of putting assets beyond the reach of creditors, or otherwise prejudicing their interests, ss. 423 and 424 of the Insolvency Act 1986 give the court power to restore the position to that which it would have been if the transaction had not been entered into, and to protect the interests of persons who are victims of the transaction[1].

1 See *Arbuthnot Leasing International Ltd v Havelet Leasing Ltd (No 2)* [1990] BCC 636; *Moon v Franklin* [1996] BPIR 196; *Chohan v Saggar* [1992] BCC 306.

Preferences

23.43 Where an administration order is made in relation to a company, or the company goes into liquidation, and the company has at a relevant time given a preference to any person, s 239 of the Insolvency Act 1986 provides that the administrator or liquidator can apply to the court for an order restoring the position to what it would have been if the preference had not been given[1]. A company gives a preference to a person if:

(a) that person is one of the company's creditors or a surety or guarantor for any of its debts or other liabilities; and
(b) the company does anything or suffers anything to be done which has the effect of putting that person into a position which, in the event of the company going into liquidation, will be better that the position he would have been in if that thing had not been done[2].

The court must not make an order under the section in respect of a preference unless the company which gave it was influenced in deciding to give it by a desire to produce in relation to that person the effect of putting that person into a position which, in the event of the company's bankruptcy, will be better than the position he would have been in if that thing had not been done[3]. Desire is subjective, and a company will not be taken to desire all the necessary consequences of its acts, as there are acts which a company may have to carry out, which although not in its interests, could be regarded as the unavoidable price of obtaining a sought after advantage. Thus where a company had no choice but to grant a creditor security if it wanted to continue to trade, the debenture was not void as a preference[4]. However, such an influence will be presumed, unless the contrary is shown, where the person to whom the preference was given was connected with the company (otherwise then by reason only of being its employee)[5]. The fact that something has been done in pursuance of an order of the court does not, without more, prevent it constituting the giving of a preference[6]. The relevant period in the case of a preference which is given to a person who is connected with the company is two years ending with the onset of insolvency, and in the case of any other preference, the period of six months ending with the onset of insolvency[7]. However, those periods are not relevant unless at the time the company was unable to pay its debts within the meaning of s 123 of the Act, or became unable to pay its debts within the meaning of that section in consequence of the transaction; but those requirements are presumed to be satisfied, unless the contrary is shown, in relation to any transaction at an undervalue entered into with a person connected with the company[8]. For the purposes of the section, the onset of insolvency is the date of the presentation of the petition on which the administration order was made, or the date of the commencement of the winding up[9].

1 Section 239(1)–(3); see generally *Re MC Bacon* [1990] BCLC 324.
2 Section 239(4).
3 Section 239(5).
4 *Re MC Bacon* [1990] BCLC 324; and see also *Re Ledingham-Smith* [1993] BCLC 635; *Re Fairway Magazines Ltd* [1993] BCLC 643; *Weisgard v Pilkington* [1995] BCC 1108.
5 Section 239(6).
6 Section 239(7).
7 Section 240(1).
8 Section 240(2).
9 Section 240(3).

Extortionate credit transactions[1]

23.44 Just as the court may reopen an extortionate credit agreement with a company upon the application of a liquidator or an administrator[2], the court has jurisdiction to reopen an extortionate credit agreement with a bankrupt made not more than three years before the commencement of the bankruptcy upon the application of the trustee in bankruptcy[3].

1 See further *Corporate Insolvency, Law and Practice* (2nd edn, 2001), paras 14.15–14.19.
2 Insolvency Act 1986, s 244, see **8.15**.
3 Insolvency Act 1986, s 343; for extortionate credit bargains under the Consumer Credit Act 1974, see **10.83** ff.

DISCLAIMER AND VESTING ORDERS

Disclaimer[1]

23.45 The Insolvency Act 1986 empowers a liquidator or a trustee in bankruptcy to disclaim onerous property[2]. Specific provision is made for leaseholds[3]. Disclaimer is made by notice in the prescribed manner[4]. A copy of the notice of disclaimer must be sent or given to a mortgagee of the disclaimed property[5]. A disclaimer of a leasehold does not take effect until due notice has been given, and either (a) no application for a vesting order is made within 14 days, or (b) where such an application has been made, the court directs that the disclaimer is to take effect[6]. Generally, the leave of the court is not required for disclaimer[7]. Where leave is required, the decision to disclaim is simply the exercise of one of the powers of management or distribution conferred on the liquidator (or trustee) by the 1986 Act. In the absence of bad faith or perversity, the court will not interfere with the decision to disclaim[8].

1 For a detailed consideration of disclaimer of the property of an insolvent company, see *Corporate Insolvency, Law and Practice*, (2nd edn, 2001), paras 14.26–14.39.
2 See ss 178–181, 315–321.
3 Insolvency Act 1986, ss 179, 317.
4 Insolvency Rules 1986, rr 4.187, 6.178, Forms 4.53, 6.61.
5 Insolvency Rules 1986, r 4.188(2); r 6.179(2).
6 Insolvency Act 1986, s 317.
7 Leave is not required for a liquidator. A trustee in bankruptcy requires leave for after-acquired property and personal property of the bankrupt exceeding reasonable replacement value: Insolvency Act 1986, s 315 (4).
8 *Re Hans Place* [1993] BCLC 768; [1992] 2 EGLR 179. (For the law prior to the Insolvency Act 1986 see *Re Parker and Parker (No 1), ex p Turquand* (1884) 14 QBD 405; *Re Müller, ex p Buxton* (1880) 15 Ch D 289, CA. *Re Clarke, ex p East and West India Dock Co* (1881) 17 Ch D 759; *Re Katherine et Cie Ltd* [1932] 1 Ch 70; *Re Gee, ex p Official Receiver* (1889) 24 QBD 65).

Vesting order

23.46 The court may, on the application of the mortgagee within three months of whichever is the earlier of (a) his becoming aware of the disclaimer, or (b) receiving notice of the disclaimer, make an order for the vesting of the property in him on such terms as it thinks fit[1].

In the case of disclaimed leasehold property this will not be done except upon the terms of making the mortgagee:

(a) subject to the same liabilities and obligations as the company or bankrupt was subject to under the lease in respect of the property at the date when the winding up was commenced or the bankruptcy petition was presented; or
(b) if the court thinks fit, subject only to the same liabilities and obligations as if the lease had been assigned to the mortgagee at that date[2].

Thus, in the case of leasehold property, ordinarily the mortgagee will take the property subject, not only to future, but also to past liabilities to the lessor. However, in the court's discretion, an order may be made in the alternative form, that is limiting his liabilities to such as he would have incurred as assignee, if the court considers that he will obtain no undue advantage and that no injustice will be done to the lessor[3]. In either event (if the case so requires) the vesting order may be made as if the lease had comprised only the property comprised in the order; and in a proper case the order will include the whole of the property in the lease, even though not subject to the mortgage[4]. A mortgagee may be put to his election as to whether or not to take a vesting order. Where, in the case of leasehold property, ss 182(1) or 321(1) apply, and a person claiming under the bankrupt or the company as underlessee or mortgagee declines to accept an order under those sections, that person is excluded from all interest in the property[5].

1 For the procedural requirements see Insolvency Act 1986, ss. 181, 182, 320, 321; Insolvency Rules 1986, rr 4.194, 6.186. Where a vesting order is made in respect of registered land

the order must direct the alteration of the register in favour of the person in whom the property is vested and on receipt of the order the registrar must alter the register accordingly: Land Registration Act 1925, s 42 (2), as amended by Insolvency Act 1985, s 235, Sch 8, para 5 (2) (b); and Insolvency Act 1986, s 439 (2), Sch 14.

2 Insolvency Act 1986, ss 182, 321, see Insolvency Rules 1986, rr 4.194, 6.186.

3 *Re Carter and Ellis, ex p Savill Bros Ltd* [1905] 1 KB 735, CA; *Re Walker, ex p Mills* (1895) 64 LJ QB 783. And see *Re A E Realisations (1985) Ltd* [1987] 3 All ER 83, [1987] BCLC 486.

4 *Re Holmes, ex p Ashworth* [1908] 2 KB 812; Insolvency Act 1986, s 182(2), s 321(2).

5 Insolvency Act 1986, ss 182(4), 321(4). See also *Re Finley, ex p Clothworkers' Co* (1888) 21 QBD 475; *Re Baker, ex p Lupton* [1901] 2 KB 628, CA. In *Re Smith, ex p Hepburn* (1890) 25 QBD 536 it was held that where, in order to escape this liability, the mortgagees by sub-demise assigned their sub-term to a man of straw as trustee for themselves, they were nevertheless required to accept a vesting order or lose their security.

TRUSTEE MAY APPLY FOR CHARGE ON BANKRUPT'S HOME

23.47 Where any property is comprised in the bankrupt's estate which consists of an interest in a dwelling house which is occupied by the bankrupt, his spouse or his former spouse, and the trustee is, for any reason, unable for the time being to realise the property, the trustee may apply to the court for an order imposing a charge on the property for the benefit of the bankrupt's estate[1]. If such an order is made, the benefit of the charge is comprised in the bankrupt's estate. It is enforceable, up to the value from time to time of the property secured, for the payment of any amount which is payable, otherwise than to the bankrupt, out of the estate and of interest on that amount at the prescribed rate[2]. The terms of the charge to be imposed must be agreed between the trustee and the bankrupt or, failing agreement, must be settled by the court[3]. The court order[4] must provide for the property subject to the charge to cease to be comprised in the bankrupt's estate, and subject to the charge (and any prior charge), to vest in the bankrupt[5]. The charge has the same effect and is enforceable in the same manner as an equitable charge created by the bankrupt under his hand[6].

1 Insolvency Act 1986, s 313 (2). The rate of interest prescribed is the rate specified in s 17 of the Judgments Act 1838 on the day on which the charge is imposed and the rate so applicable shall be stated in the court's order imposing the charge: Insolvency Rules 1986, r 6.237 (5).

2 Insolvency Act 1986, s 313(2). The rate of interest prescribed is the rate specified in s 17 of the Judgments Act 1838 on the day on which the charge is imposed and the rate so applicable shall be stated in the court's order imposing the charge: Insolvency Rules 1986, r 6.237 (5).

3 Insolvency Rules 1986, r 6.237 (4).

4 For terms of the order, see Insolvency Rules 1986, r 6.237 (6).

5 Insolvency Act 1986, s 313 (3). The date for the revesting of the property, subject to the charge, in the bankrupt will generally be the date of the registration of the charge in accordance with s 3 (2) of the Charging Orders Act 1979: Insolvency Rules 1986, r. 6.237 (6) (f), (7). The trustee may call a final meeting of creditors under Insolvency Act 1986, s 331 where a charging order has been made under s 313: Insolvency Act 1986, s 332.

6 Charging Orders Acts 1979, s 3 (4), applied, together with s 3 (1), (2), (5) and (6) by the Insolvency Act 1986, s 313 (4).

DISCHARGE FROM BANKRUPTCY

23.48 Subject to certain exceptions, a first time bankrupt will be automatically discharged three years after the commencement of the bankruptcy, or two years where a certificate for the summary administration of the bankrupt's estate has been issued[1]. Generally, discharge releases the bankrupt from all the bankruptcy debts, but it does not affect the right of any secured creditor of the bankrupt to enforce his security for the payment of a debt from which the bankrupt is released[2].

1 For discharge, see, generally, Insolvency Act 1986, ss 279, 280. For annulment, see s 282, and see Insolvency Rules, Chaps 21, 22.

2 Insolvency Act 1986, s 281 (2) and see *Lamont v Bank of New Zealand* [1981] 2 NZLR 142 (while there was no longer any debt, that in no way affected the secured creditor's powers of realisation of the security; on realisation the secured creditor was entitled to include interest due until the date of realisation).

PART VI

PRIORITIES OF MORTGAGES

Chapter 24

Priorities of mortgages

PRIORITIES GENERALLY

How questions of priorities arise

24.1 If successive advances have been made on the security of the same property by different mortgages it may, for one reason or another, be necessary to discover the order in which the mortgages rank. A mortgagor may have contrived to borrow sums in excess of the value of the security; or the mortgaged property, though at first sufficient to support the debts of all the mortgagees, may have depreciated in value. Of course, the mortgagees have their remedy by way of the personal covenant for repayment made by the mortgagor, but the sale of the mortgaged property may be the only satisfactory method of recovering the sum lent, since the other property of the mortgagor may be of little value. Each mortgagee is then entitled to be satisfied out of the proceeds of sale in full in the order of the priority of the mortgages[1].

A question of priorities may also arise between a mortgagee and, eg, a tenant whether created before or after the grant of the mortgage[2] or a beneficial owner of the property[3].

1 In addition to the question of order of payment, the rules as to priority also determine which one of several subsequent mortgages is entitled to the title deeds on the discharge of a prior mortgage, which one of several mortgages can requisition a transfer instead of a reconveyance and how a mortgage will be affected in an action for redemption or foreclosure.

2 See **19.16–19.27**.

3 This is dealt with in **24.74**. As to priorities of mortgages of ships and aircraft, see **6.9** ff and **6.24** ff respectively.

General

24.2 The principles which applied before 1926 with respect to the priorities of legal and equitable mortgages of, and other interests in, land are not abrogated by the Law of Property Act 1925[1]. The legislation of 1925 had a substantial effect on the former rules which governed the priority of mortgages but that Act does not repeal with regard to mortgages of the legal estate, either the rule 'qui prior est tempore, potior est jure'[2], or the rule of equity giving superiority to the legal title. Nor does the Act affect any question arising out of or consequent upon any omission to obtain or any other absence of possession by any person of documents relating to a legal estate in land[3]. The statutory provisions dealing with priority assume the continuing validity of the former rules. A mortgagee taking a legal estate still has priority over an earlier equitable incumbrance of which he had no notice when he made his advance[4] and a legal mortgagee may by his conduct in relation to the deeds either lose his priority over an earlier equitable incumbrance or be postponed to a subsequent incumbrance. The operation of these rules is, however, largely modified by the statutory provisions with respect to registered land[5]; in the case of unregistered land, the registration as land charges at the Land Charges Register of puisne mortgages, equitable mortgages and general equitable charges, such registration being deemed to constitute actual notice[6] and the registration of charges by companies[7]. The statutory provisions do not, however, affect:

(a) priorities between unregistered charges of registered land, which are still governed by the rule that the first in time prevails[8];
(b) priority between mortgages of equitable interests, which are still governed by the rule in *Dearle v Hall*[9];
(c) the right of the mortgagor to set aside the mortgage procured by the wrongdoing of the debtor, where the mortgagee must rely on the defence of bona fide purchaser for value without notice; or
(d) the existence of any agreement[10] between the incumbrancers modifying the ordinary rules of priorities[11].

The priority of incumbrances post 1925 will depend on one or more of the following considerations:

(a) Prima facie the legal estate gives priority over equitable incumbrances earlier in date, provided it has been acquired for value and without notice of the earlier incumbrance. Notice may be actual, constructive or statutory.
(b) Apart from the effect given to the legal estate, incumbrances rank in order of time in accordance with the maxim 'qui prior est tempore, potior est jure'.
(c) The priority of an incumbrance under rules (a) and (b) may be lost by the conduct of the incumbrancer, usually in relation to the custody of the title deeds.
(d) In certain cases a mortgagee can tack further advances as against a subsequent incumbrancer.
(e) In cases governed by a system of registration of incumbrances, the priority under rules (a) and (b) may be altered in two ways:
    (i) incumbrances may rank in order of registration and registered incumbrances may rank before those which are not registered[12];
    (ii) an unregistered incumbrance may be void as against a purchaser for value.

In addition, there are certain other statutory priority provisions, eg relating to insolvency[13] or bills of sale[14], which determine priorities.

The former classification of mortgages for the purposes of priorities—which distinguished mortgages of interests in land, and mortgages of an equitable interest in pure personalty (bills of sale being subject to statutory provisions)—was abandoned by the 1925 property legislation. Instead of determining whether the mortgage itself is legal or equitable, the governing consideration is now whether the property of the mortgagor which has been given as security is legal or equitable. The appropriate classification is that of legal and equitable mortgages of a legal estate, and mortgages of an equitable interest, whether in land or personalty[15].

1 *Beddoes v Shaw* [1937] Ch 81, [1936] 2 All ER 1108.
2 He who is earlier in time is stronger in law. See *Brace v Duchess of Marlborough* (1728) 2 P Wms 491 at 495; *Wilmot v Pike* (1845) 5 Hare 14 at 22; *Barclays Bank Ltd v Bird* [1954] Ch 274 at 280; *Assaf v Fuwa* [1955] AC 215 at 230; *Macmillan Inc v Bishopsgate Trust (No 3)* [1995] 1 WLR 978 at 1000.
3 Law of Property Act 1925, s 13.
4 See **24.22**.
5 The Land Registration Act 1925 creates a priority system for registered charges (s 29) and to this extent the former rules are superseded, but as regards other charges of registered land the former rules are still, in limited circumstances, applicable.
6 Law of Property Act 1925, s 198. An unregistered land charge is void against a purchaser for value (Land Charges Act 1972, s 4(5)) and not capable of prejudicially affecting a purchaser by notice (Law of Property Act 1925, s 199). See **24.27**.
7 See **12.15** ff.
8 *Mortgage Corpn Ltd v Nationwide Credit Corpn Ltd* [1994] Ch 49 at 56, [1993] 4 All ER 623 at 628, CA, per Dillon LJ. See also **24.71**.
9 (1823) 3 Russ 1 (see **24.90** ff).
10 Which may be express (see **24.123**) or implied (see **24.74** in respect of the postponement of the rights of a beneficial co-owner).
11 As to priority agreements, see **24.123**.
12 The requirement for the registration of bills of sale, see **5.12** ff and for company charges, see **12.15** ff.
13 See **8.19** ff.
14 See **24.120**.
15 For a detailed discussion of the priority of legal mortgages of land after 1925, dealing particularly with the effects of registration and the relationship between the Land Charges Act 1925 (now the Land Charges Act 1972) and the Law of Property Act 1925, see (1941) 7 CLJ 243 (Megarry). See Law Commission Working Paper no 99, Land Mortgages, paras 3.14 ff.

MORTGAGES OF THE LEGAL ESTATE: UNREGISTERED LAND

Introduction

24.3 The issue of priority in unregistered land as between competing mortgagees requires a consideration of whether the mortgage has been granted with the protection of the title deeds. The issue of priority also turns on whether the mortgage is legal[1] or equitable. If the mortgagee of the legal estate, whether the mortgage is legal[2] (by deed) or equitable (not by deed), does not possess the title deeds he must, in order to maintain his priority over subsequent purchasers (including a second mortgagee), register the mortgage as a land charge at the Land Charges Registry[3]. A mortgagee who is protected by the possession of the title deeds cannot register the charge[4] but his priority is protected, where the mortgage is a legal mortgage, by the priority accorded to a legal mortgage[5], or in the case of an equitable mortgage, the absence of the title deeds providing notice to a subsequent purchaser of the existence of the earlier charge. The security which is conferred by the possession of the title deeds is not, unlike registration as a land charge, absolute, as priority may be postponed in light of the mortgagee's conduct with respect to the title deeds[6].

1 Most first legal mortgages of unregistered land are likely to give rise to a requirement for registration at the HM Land Registry. A legal mortgage of an unregistered freehold or

long leasehold made with the deposit of the title deeds and executed after 1 April 1998 triggers a requirement of first registration: Land Registration Act 1925, s 123A(2)-(3). A mortgage of a leasehold interest triggers the requirement for registration only if the lease has more the 21 years unexpired at the date of the dealing.
2 As to what constitutes a legal or equitable mortgage, see **1.7** ff and **1.17** ff.
3 As to mortgages requiring registration, see **24.4**.
4 See **24.4** and the definition of puisne mortgages.
5 See **24.22** ff.
6 See **24.48** ff. This is so whether the mortgage accompanied by the title deeds is legal or equitable.

Puisne mortgages and equitable mortgages

24.4 The Land Charges Act 1972[1] provides for the registration[2] of certain legal and equitable mortgages[3] in the Land Charges Register. For this purpose a distinction is made between mortgages and charges depending on whether they are protected by a deposit of deeds or not. Registrable land charges[4] include:

(a) a 'puisne mortgage', which is defined as being a 'legal mortgage not being a mortgage protected by a deposit of documents relating to the legal estate affected'[5];
(b) equitable mortgages or charges[6], not protected by a deposit of documents relating to the legal estate affected[7] and not included in any other class of land charge[8]. Equitable mortgages arising or affecting an interest arising under a trust of land[9] or a settlement[10] are not registrable. 'Protected' in this context means protected by a deposit of deeds at the time of the creation of the mortgage. Such a mortgage does not become registrable if the mortgagee parts with the deeds[11].

In this regard:

(a) there may be a succession of legal mortgages, with (usually) the first mortgagee holding the deeds, in which case all the other legal mortgages will be puisne mortgages alternatively;
(b) the deeds may be deposited by way of equitable mortgage[12]. In that event any legal mortgages that may exist will be puisne mortgages; and, further,
(c) there may be equitable mortgages not protected by deposit of documents.

Thus there are—for the purposes of registration—four kinds of securities:

(a) legal mortgages accompanied by title deeds;
(b) puisne mortgages, ie legal mortgages not accompanied by title deeds;
(c) equitable mortgages accompanied by title deeds;
(d) equitable mortgages not accompanied by title deeds.

1 Brought into force on 29 January 1973 by SI 1972/2058. It replaced the Land Charges Act 1925.
2 In the Land Charges Register. The Land Registry keeps the following registers (Land Charges Act 1972, s 1(1)): (a) a register of land charges; (b) a register of pending actions; (c) a register of writs and orders affecting land; (d) a register of deeds of arrangement affecting land; and (e) a register of annuities.
3 Also registrable are estate contracts, that is, contracts by an estate owner (or by a person entitled at the date of the contract to have a legal estate conveyed to him) to convey or create a legal estate, including options to purchase, rights of pre-emption (Land Charges Act 1972, s 2(1)(4)(iv). The statutory right of a spouse to occupy the matrimonial home

is registrable as a charge on the legal estate: Family Law Act 1996, s 31(3): see **12.134**. Charges of registered land are not subject to the Land Charges Act 1972: Land Charges Act 1972, s 14. Registration under the Companies Act 1985 of land charges created by companies is dealt with at **12.15** ff.

4 The register of land charges is arranged in classes A, B, C, D, E, and F. Class C, which is relevant for present purposes, is as follows (Land Charges Act 1972, s 2(4):

'A Class C land charge is any of the following (not being a local land charge), namely—
(i) a puisne mortgage;
(ii) a limited owner's charge;
(iii) a general equitable charge;
(iv) an estate contract;

and for this purpose—
(i) a puisne mortgage is a legal mortgage which is not protected by a deposit of documents relating to the legal estate affected;
...
(iii) a general equitable charge is any equitable charge which—
(a) is not secured by a deposit of documents relating to the legal estate affected; and
(b) does not arise or affect an interest arising under a trust of land or a settlement; and
(c) is not a charge given by way of indemnity against rents equitably apportioned or charged exclusively on land in exoneration of other land and against the breach or non-observance of covenants or conditions; and
(d) is not included in any other class of land charge;
(iv) an estate contract is a contract by an estate owner or by a person entitled at the date of the contract to have a legal estate conveyed to him to convey or create a legal estate, including a contract conferring either expressly or by statutory implication a valid option to purchase, a right of pre-emption or any other like right.'

5 Land Charges Act 1972, s 2 (4), Class C(i). Part of the deeds may be held by one mortgagee and part by another. Quaere whether 'protected' under the Act means protected by all the deeds: see (1950) 13 MLR 534 (Hargreaves).

6 Section 2 (4), Class C(iii).

7 Section 2 (4), Class C(iii)(a).

8 Section 2 (4), Class C(iii)(d);*Thomas v Rose* [1968] 3 All ER 765, [1968] 1 WLR 1797; *Georgiades v Edward Wolfe Co Ltd* [1965] Ch 487, [1964] 3 All ER 433, CA; *Williams v Burlington Investments Ltd* (1977) 121 Sol Jo 424, HL; *Property Discount Corpn Ltd v Lyon Group Ltd* [1981] 1 All ER 379, [1981] 1 WLR 300, CA. Such a charge will be overreached on a conveyance to a purchaser who complies with the overreaching machinery: Law of Property Act 1925, s 27.

9 Land Charges Act 1972, s 2 (4), Class C(iii)(b); *Re Rayleigh Weir Stadium* [1954] 2 All ER 283, [1954] 1 WLR 786. Such a charge will be overreached on a conveyance to a purchaser who complies with the overreaching machinery: Law of Property Act 1925, s 27.

10 Land Charges Act 1972, s 2 (4), Class C(iii)(b); Such a charge will be overreached on a conveyance to a purchaser who complies with the overreaching machinery: Law of Property Act 1925, s 27.

11 See (1941) 7 CLJ 249 (Megarry). See Law Commission Report Transfer of Land — Land Mortgages, 1991 (Law Com no 204, paras 3.18-3.19, 3.30-3.34). Cf 32 *Halsbury's Laws* (4th edn, reissue) para 461, fn 7 and para 484, fn 2. As to the possible effect on priority of the mortgagee failing to retain the deeds, see **24.48** ff.

12 Note that since 27 September 1989 an equitable mortgage cannot be created by mere deposit of deeds: see **3.100**.

Registration as land charges

Legal mortgages accompanied by title deeds

24.5 Securities in division (a) do not require to be registered[1].

1 See the definition of puisne mortgage in **24.4**, n 5.

Equitable mortgages accompanied by title deeds

24.6 Securities in division (c) above probably do not require to be registered. However, it has been suggested that securities in division (c) are registrable as estate contracts[1].

1 Land Charges Act 1972, s 2 (4), Class C (iv). See the discussion at **3.106**.

Puisne mortgages, ie legal mortgages not accompanied by title deeds and equitable mortgages not accompanied by title deeds

24.7 Securities in divisions (b) and (d) above require to be registered as land charges in Class C (i) (puisne mortgage) and Class C (iii) (general equitable charge) respectively[1]. Further, the priority of securities in division (d) depends on the order in which they are registered[2].

1 As to the failure to register (which renders the unprotected mortgage void against a purchaser for value of any interest in the land), see **24.10** ff.
2 Section 97 of the Law of Property Act 1925. See **24.11** ff.

Registration equates to notice

24.8 Under the Law of Property Act 1925, s 198(1)[1], registration[2] of an incumbrance in any of these registers kept under the Land Charges Act 1972 constitutes actual notice[3]. Hence, the legal estate will not avail a subsequent legal mortgagee, as he will be deemed to take with notice of any registered charge. Land charges affecting registered land cannot be registered[4].

1 As amended by the Local Land Charges Act 1975, s 17, Sch 1. The section provides:

> '**198** (1) The registration of any instrument or matter in any register kept under the Land Charges Act 1972 or any local land charges register shall be deemed to constitute actual notice of such instrument or matter, and of the fact of such registration, to all persons and for all purposes connected with the land affected, as from the date of registration or other prescribed date and so long as the registration continues in force.
> (2) This section operates without prejudice to the provisions of this Act respecting the making of further advances by a mortgagee, and applies only to instruments and matters required or authorised to be registered in any such register'.

The Law of Property Act 1969, s 24 (the commencement date of which was 1 January 1970) provides that the question whether a buyer has knowledge of a registered land charge prior to contract is to be determined by reference to his actual knowledge without regard to s 198. Therefore, the buyer is not required by law to make pre-contract land charge searches. Section 24 does not apply to local land charges nor registered land. Note the section applies only as between vendor and purchaser. The owner of the registered land charge, however, remains protected: registration constitutes notice to the whole world.

2 The registration of a land charge is effected in the name of the estate owner whose estate is intended to be affected (Land Charges Act 1972, s 3 (1)): Land Charges Rules 1974; see *Barrett v Hilton Developments Ltd* [1975] Ch 237, [1974] 3 All ER 944, CA; *Property Discount Corpn Ltd v Lyon Group Ltd*, above. As to the name, see *Oak Co-operative Building Society v Blackburn* [1968] Ch 730, [1968] 2 All ER 117, CA; *Diligent Finance Co Ltd v Alleyne* (1972) 23 P & CR 346; *Standard Property Investment v British Plastics Federation* (1985) 53 P & CR 25. An error in the name registered does not invalidate the registration if the name given may fairly be called a version of the name, but a person who searches in the correct name is protected even if it fails to reveal an entry: *Oak Co-Operative Building Society v Blackburn* [1968] Ch 730. The expenses of registration of, inter alia, a Class C (iii) (but not C (iv) or D (i)) land charge form part of the land charge: Land Charges Act 1972,

s 3 (4). If it is not created by an instrument, eg a vendor's lien, short particulars of the effect of the charge must be registered with the application to register the charge: Land Charges Act 1972, s 3 (5).

3 In the case of registered land, corresponding protection is obtained by notice, caution etc; see Land Registration Act 1925, s 59.

4 Land Charges Act 1972, s 14 (1). Where an instrument executed on or after 27 July 1971 conveys, grants or assigns an estate in land and creates a land charge which would otherwise require to be registered under the Land Charges Act it is not to be registered if the instrument in question gives rise to the need for compulsory registration of the land under the Land Registration Act 1925; Land Charges Act 1972, s 14 (3).

Vacating the registration

24.9 Registration may be vacated pursuant to an order of the court[1]. The court also has an inherent power to order a registration to be vacated[2]. Where there is no dispute, cancellation is effected by the registrar on the application of the person who applied for registration[3].

1 Section 1(6) of the Land Charges Act 1972.

2 *Heywood v BDC Properties Ltd (No 2)* [1964] 1 All ER 180, [1964] 1 WLR 267; revsd on another point [1964] 2 All ER 702, [1967] 1 WLR 971, CA; *Price Bros (Somerford) Ltd v Kelly Homes (Stoke-on-Trent) Ltd* [1975] 3 All ER 369, [1975] 1 WLR 1512, CA; *Northern Developments (Holdings) Ltd v UDT Securities Ltd* [1977] 1 All ER 747; *Haslemere Estates Ltd v Baker* [1982] 3 All ER 525 at 534; *Bromley London Borough v THI Crystal Palace Ltd and United Cinemas International* [1996] NPC 51, Ch D.

3 See Land Charges Act 1972, s 16 (1) (b); Land Charges Rules 1974. Difficulties sometimes arise on the sale of property which is no longer subject to a mortgage but in relation to which there is an outstanding land charge registration. An entry on the register may be rebutted by the production of the mortgage in respect of which the entry was made duly discharged: see Law Society's Digest (3rd supplement), Opinion No 136. Where the entry is removable by the vendor and cancellation is not effected before completion he should on completion hand over the charge duly discharged (unless it relates also to other property) together with the necessary forms for removal of the entry: Law Society's Digest, Opinion No 139.

Effect of non-registration of puisne mortgages and equitable charges

24.10 The Land Charges Act 1972 provides that a land charge of Class C[1] (other than an estate contract) created or arising on or after 1 January 1926, shall be void as against a purchaser[2] of the land charged with it, or of any interest in such land, unless the land charge is registered in the appropriate register before the completion of the purchase[3]. 'Purchaser' means 'any person (including a mortgagee or lessee) who, for valuable consideration, takes any interest in land or in a charge on land'[4]. There is no requirement that the consideration be adequate; it may be nominal[5]. This provision as to the effect of non-registration does not apply to mortgages or charges created by instruments necessitating registration under the Land Registration Act 1925 or to mortgages or charges of registered land[6]. The subsection only relates to mortgages capable of registration as land charges, namely, puisne mortgages—that is, legal mortgages not protected by a deposit of documents (Class C (i))—and equitable charges, also not secured by deposit of documents (Class C (ii), (iii), and Class D (i)), and is confined to mortgages which affect a legal estate. Thus it includes a legal and an equitable mortgage created by an estate owner (where not accompanied by deposit of deeds), but not a mortgage or charge of an equitable interest[7].

If a subsequent mortgagee has notice (that is, notice actual or constructive in the ordinary sense as opposed to statutory actual notice arising from registration) of an unregistered charge which should have been registered, he is not prejudicially affected by it[8], whether or not he is a purchaser in good faith[9], and so he has priority over the unregistered incumbrance notwithstanding that he may be in fact well aware of it. An unregistered land charge is void only against a purchaser and the position as between the parties to the charge is unaffected by non-registration if the mortgaged property is sold. Although the interest in land created by the charge ceases to subsist because it cannot subsist without the property to which it attaches and is ousted by the absolute interest which the purchaser acquires, the mortgagee remains entitled to a security interest in the proceeds of sale[10].

1 Land Charges Act 1972, s 2(4),Class C. See **24.4**, n 4 for the terms of this subsection.
2 Section 17.
3 Section 4(5). The effect of these provisions is to exclude the equitable doctrine of notice. Statutes which declare the priority between registered instruments in effect give them priority over unregistered instruments. Otherwise the object of registration would be defeated: see *Black v Williams* [1895] 1 Ch 408 as to the shipping register, but registration will not give priority if the intention of the instrument is only to pass the actual interest of the grantor. Thus a deed of assignment for the benefit of creditors does not by registration acquire priority over an earlier unregistered mortgage: *Jones v Barker* [1909] 1 Ch 321; and see *Chang Khiaw Bank Ltd v United Overseas Bank Ltd* [1970] AC 767, PC; *Security Trust Co v Royal Bank of Canada* [1976] AC 503, [1976] 1 All ER 381, PC.
4 Section 17 (1) and see *McCarthy & Stone Ltd v Julian S Hodge & Co Ltd* [1971] 2 All ER 973, [1971] 1 WLR 1547; *Wroth v Tyler* [1974] Ch 30, [1973] 1 All ER 897; *Midland Bank Trust Co Ltd v Green* [1981] AC 513, [1981] 1 All ER 153, HL. For priority pitfalls, see (1974) 124 NLJ 286 (Hayton).
5 *Midland Bank Trust Co Ltd v Green* [1981] AC 513, HL (consideration of £500 given for farm worth £40,000).
6 See Land Charges Act 1972, s 14(2) and (3).
7 The priorities of mortgages of equitable interests in land are governed by the rules in *Dearle v Hall*, as extended by s 137 of the Law of Property Act 1925: see **24.90** ff.
8 Law of Property Act 1925, s 199(1)(i).
9 *Midland Bank Trust Co Ltd v Green* [1981] AC 513, HL, and see *Diligent Finance Co Ltd v Alleyne* (1972) 23 P & CR 346.
10 *Buhr v Barclays Bank plc* [2001] EWCA Civ 1223, [2001] 31 EG 103 (CS), CA and **3.66**. On a solicitor's liability for a failure to register a mortgage and the limitation period, see *Bell v Peter Browne & Co* [1990] 2 QB 495, CA.

Priority of registrable mortgages

24.11 Registration of puisne mortgages and equitable charges, hereinafter referred to as land charges has, therefore, the following effect:

(a) Registered land charges rank in order of registration[1].
(b) An unregistered land charge is valid as between the parties to it[2].
(c) A later legal land charge does not by virtue of the legal estate prevail over an earlier registered equitable land charge[3].
(d) The owner of a registered land charge (the chargee) which does not cover further advances cannot tack a further advance made after registration of a later land charge; nor, unless he has registered a fresh land charge, can he set it up against a later land charge whether registered or not, but when the registered land charge covers further advances, the chargee can tack by virtue of the contract[4].

(e) A later land charge, whether registered or not, has priority over an earlier unregistered land charge even though it was taken with actual notice of the earlier unregistered land charge[5].

(f) The Law of Property Act 1925, s 97, enacts expressly that registered land charges rank in order of registration; s 4 (5) of the Land Charges Act 1972, provides that a puisne mortgage or general equitable charge created or arising after 1925 shall be void as against a purchaser of the land charged with it, or of any interest in such land, unless the land charge is registered in the appropriate register before the completion of the purchase. Difficulties may occur in reconciling these provisions where several mortgages are made before any or all are registered and then some or all are registered. A circulus inextricabilis may arise[6]. It seems that s 97 is to be read subject to s 4 (5)[7] and the doctrine of subrogation resorted to if more than two competing mortgages are involved[8].

(g) The parties may by arrangement made between themselves vary the order of priorities[9]; this is done by a deed of postponement.

1 Law of Property Act 1925, s 97.
2 See **24.10**.
3 Because as the later chargee has notice—by the registration—of the earlier charge, he is postponed: *Williams v Burlington Investments Ltd* (1977) 121 Sol Jo 424, HL.
4 See **24.88**. This is a case where the rule that registration constitutes notice is excluded.
5 See s 4 (5), (6). This does not impose the condition that a purchaser shall himself be registered. And see **24.10** as to the effect of non-registration of a land charge.
6 As to which see **24.14**.
7 See (1943) 7 CLJ 243 (Megarry); for a contrary view (1950) 13 MLR 534–535 (Hargreaves).
8 See *Benham v Keane* (1861) 1 John & H 685 at 710–712; *Re Wyatt, White v Ellis* [1892] 1 Ch 188 at 208–209; cf *Re Weniger's Policy* [1910] 2 Ch 291 and see (1961) 71 Yale LJ 53 (Gilmore); (1968) 32 Conv (NS) 325 (Lee). See Law Commission Working Paper no 99, Land Mortgages, para 3.12.
9 See **24.123**.

Priority as between registerable mortgages

24.12 The priority of registrable mortgages inter se depends on a combination of s 97 of the Law of Property Act 1925 and s 4(5) of the Land Charges Act 1972.

All registered

24.13 Where all the mortgages are registrable and are duly registered priority is simple. As registration equates to actual notice[1], each subsequent incumbrance takes subject to the earlier registered charge. This is so albeit the earlier mortgage is equitable only.

1 Law of Property Act 1925, s 198.

All unregistered

24.14 The decisive factor is that by s 4(5) of the Land Charges Act 1972 a registrable charge is void against a later mortgage unless it is registered before completion of the later transaction[1]. Even if the first mortgage is legal and the second equitable, the first loses priority to the second as the first is void as against the second for want of registration.

The position is not as clear where the registration of the mortgages does not immediately follow creation so that the order of registration does not correspond to the order of creation. Suppose that:

A takes a mortgage without the title deeds on 1 October;

B takes a mortgage without the title deeds on 2 November;

A is registered on 3 November;

B is registered on 4 November;

C takes a mortgage without title deeds on 5 November and registers.

Whether the mortgages are legal or equitable the order of priority is B-A-C. B has obtained priority over A as at the date of creation of B's mortgage it was void as against B by reason of the provisions of s 4(5) of the Land Charges Act 1972. A's mortgage is not void as against C for it was registered as at the date of the completion of C's mortgage. If neither A nor B were registered at the date of the completion of C's mortgage, C would have priority over both thus reversing the maxim 'qui prior est tempore, potior est jure'. The general opinion is that it is considered that the argument that A should rank first in reliance on s 97[2] of the Law of Property Act is incorrect. To agree with it requires one to accept that A's mortgage is to take precedence over the very charge in respect of which it has been declared void by statute. One cannot give priority to something which ex hypothesi has no existence as against B.

If C's mortgage were granted before the registration of B's mortgage but A was registered after the completion of B's mortgage but before C's mortgage was complete, a possible circulus inextricabilis arises. C has priority over B (lack of registration at the date of completion of C's mortgage) but B has priority over A (lack of registration at the date of completion of B's mortgage) who has priority over C (A's mortgage being registered at the date of completion of C's mortgage). A solution to this problem may be had by recourse to the doctrine of subrogation, which will have the effect of transferring to one of the creditors the rights of another but only to the extent that that other has priority over the other creditors. Thus the court may order that C be paid to the extent of B's claim against A (for B has priority over A and C has priority over B); that A be paid in full; payment then be made of the balance due to C and finally payment of any balance to B. The difficulty with this solution is that there is no logical point at which to commence the process of subrogation. Subrogation is a rough and ready method of solving the difficulty. The point of commencement is entirely arbitrary[3]. It might be more just in a case where there value of the asset is insufficient to satisfy the mortgagees to order a payment pari passu, ie a distribution of the proceeds according to the proportion of their respective amounts of the total advances.

1 See **24.10**.
2 Which requires every registrable mortgage to rank according to its date of registration. The argument for the rejection of Land Charges Act 1972, s 4(5) is put forward in (1950) 13 MLR at 534-535.
3 The election to take the mortgages in order of the date of creation subrogating the last to the earliest would appear to accord with authority: Megarry and Wade *The Law of Real Property* (6th edn) p 1276 citing (1961) 71 Yale LJ 53.

Priority of incumbrances accompanied by deeds

24.15 As has been seen a mortgage, whether legal or equitable, which is protected or secured by deposit of deeds, is incapable of registration as a land charge[1]. It is considered that 'protected' (or 'secured') within the statutory wording[2] means originally 'protected' (or 'secured') for otherwise the mortgage would fluctuate between being registrable or unregistrable depending on the mortgagee parting with and regaining the title deeds[3]. A mortgage may be valid if only some or one of the material documents of title to the property have been deposited[4], although a complete title is not thereby shown to the debtor's interest in the property[5]. It follows that if part of the material documents are deposited with one person, and part with another, each may have a good security[6]. In practice only one mortgagee will hold the deeds.

The 1925 legislation does not prejudicially affect the right or interest of any person arising out of or consequent on the possession by him of any documents relating to a legal estate in land, nor affect any question arising out of or consequent upon any omission to obtain or any other absence of possession by any person of any documents relating to a legal estate in land[7]. It should be remembered, with regard to this provision, that a first mortgagee has a right to the possession of the title deeds[8], whether the mortgage be by demise, sub-demise or charge by way of legal mortgage[9]. Thus, questions of priority, so far as they depend on the possession of the deeds, are subject to the same considerations as before 1926[10]. No priority is expressly conferred by statute on a mortgagee who holds the deeds[11]. However, there is nothing in the Law of Property Act 1925[12] to repeal with regard to mortgages of the legal estate the rule 'qui prior est tempore, potior est jure', or the rule of equity giving superiority to the legal title. Accordingly the possession of the title deeds will usually give him priority over other subsequent mortgages, whether legal or equitable: over later unregistrable legal mortgages because the legal mortgagee will have notice of the earlier mortgage by reason of the absence of the deeds[13]; over unregistrable equitable mortgages because the possession of the deeds will give him the better equity[14]. His priority is, however, subject to the rules as to the loss of priority by fraud[15] or gross negligence[16] and (where the first mortgage is equitable) by reliance upon the plea of bona fide purchaser without notice[17]. Thus in this regard it is still the case that it matters whether the mortgage is legal or equitable. A mortgagee who has possession of the title deeds will however be bound by registrable charges registered at the Land Charges Register[18].

As between equitable incumbrancers the mere possession of the title deeds is not enough to give a subsequent incumbrancer priority over an earlier one: there must be some default on the part of the earlier incumbrancer so as to make the equities unequal[19]. If the possession of the title deeds is an essential part of the earlier incumbrancer's security, the same considerations arise as in the case of a legal mortgagee, and if having got in the deeds allows them by negligence or design to be again, without sufficient reason, in the mortgagor's possession he will be postponed to a subsequent incumbrancer to whom they are delivered[20].

1 Land Charges Act 1972, s 2 (4), Class C (i), (iii), but see **24.6**.
2 Section 2(4) Class C, (i), (iii).
3 See (1940) 7 CLJ 249 (R E Megarry).
4 Re *Daintry, ex p Arkwright* (1864) 3 Mont D & De G 129; *Lacon v Allen* (1856) 3 Drew 579.
5 *Ex p Wetherell* (1805) 11 Ves 398; *Robert v Croft* (1857) 24 Beav 223; affd (1857) 2 De G & J 1.
6 *Robert v Croft* above.

7 Law of Property Act 1925, s 13.
8 In general a first mortgagee will have a charge by way of legal mortgage and will hold the deeds (see Law of Property Act 1925, ss 85 (1) proviso, and 86(1) proviso, and he will have unquestioned priority; but the priorities of other incumbrancers will usually depend on registration or its absence and on the effect of registration as actual notice. See further **3.70**.
9 See Law of Property Act 1925, ss 85 (1), 86 (1).
10 See *Beddoes v Shaw* [1937] Ch 81, [1936] 2 All ER 1108.
11 Section 13 of the Law of Property Act 1925 though it prevents the Act from prejudicing rights arising out of the possession of deeds, does not appear to exclude ss 197 and 198, so as to make a search unnecessary on making an advance secured with a deposit of the deeds.
12 See the changes in tacking, **24.83** ff.
13 See **24.17** and **24.22** ff.
14 While a mortgagee accompanied by a deposit of all the deeds would prevail over an earlier unregistered but registrable mortgage — for this would be a puisne mortgage or an equitable charge and would be void against him — yet he is not safe if any material deed happens to be outstanding (see n 4); and this circumstance deprives this non-registrable form of security of the complete protection afforded by registration.
15 As to which see **24.50**.
16 As to which see **24.51** ff.
17 As to which see **24.19** and **24.22**.
18 See further **24.21**. If both mortgagees have title deeds so as to be non-registrable under the Land Charges Act priority will be governed by the date of creation.
19 See **24.58**.
20 See **24.58**.

Priority between unregistrable and registerable mortgages

First mortgage is unregistrable[1]

24.16 As has been mentioned, it is provided by the Law of Property Act 1925[2] that the Act shall not prejudicially affect the right or interest of any person arising out of or consequent on the possession by him of any documents relating to a legal estate in land, nor affect any question arising out of or consequent upon any omission to obtain or any other absence of possession by any person of any documents relating to a legal estate in land. Thus where one of the competing mortgages is protected by the deposit of title deeds regard is to be had to the pre-1926 law[3]. The principles under the pre-1926 law were that a legal mortgage was preferred to an equitable one; that mortgages ranked in order of creation, subject to the preference to the legal mortgage; but either of these principles may be displaced by fraud[4], negligent conduct with reference to the deeds[5] and (where the first is equitable) the plea of bona fide purchaser for value[6].

1 Under the Land Charges Act 1972. As to registration, see **24.4**.
2 Section 13.
3 It should be noted that the priority of a second registrable mortgage is not dependent on registration for priority as against the first. The absence of registration may render it void as against a subsequent (third) mortgage.
4 See **24.50**.
5 See **24.51** ff.
6 See **24.22**.

If both mortgages are legal mortgages

24.17 Priority is accorded to the first in time. This arises by the application of the maxim 'qui prior est tempore, potior est jure' but furthermore the mortgagee has the deeds and thus the second mortgagee will take with notice of the earlier mortgage. Priority may be lost by the first if there is fraud or gross negligence with respect to the deeds.

If the first is legal and the second is equitable

24.18 The first acquires priority by the force of the legal estate and the maxim 'qui prior est tempore, potior est jure'. The mortgagee's conduct with respect to the deeds may cause an earlier legal mortgage to be postponed a later equitable one[1].

1 See **24.49** ff.

If the first is equitable and the second is legal

24.19 Priority is principally dependent on the question of the extent to which the second legal mortgage has notice of the first. Regard is to be had to the doctrine of actual and constructive notice and in particular the provisions of s 199 of the Law of Property Act 1925[1]. The first mortgage ought to have priority over the second as the second should be put on notice of the first by the absence of the deeds and if no enquiry is made about the deeds the second takes with constructive notice of the first in any event[2].

1 See **24.27** ff.
2 As to constructive notice see **24.56**.

Both mortgages are equitable

24.20 Under the pre-1926 law priority was governed by the maxim 'qui prior est tempore, potior est jure'. This maxim still applies[1]. A prior equitable incumbrance with possession of the deeds may be postponed to a later mortgage by the fraud or negligence of the earlier incumbrancer[2].

1 *Beddoes v Shaw* [1937] Ch 81.
2 See **24.58**.

Second mortgage is unregistrable[1]

24.21 Priority is not dependent on the pre-1926 law but only on a consideration of s 97 of the Law of Property Act 1925 and s 4(5) of the Land Charges Act 1972. If the first mortgage (whether legal or equitable) is registered at the date of completion of the second, the first has priority, as the first ranks according to the date of registration in accordance with s 97 and furthermore s 198 of the Law of Property Act provides that registration under the Land Charges Act shall constitute actual notice to all persons and for all purposes connected with the land affected[2]. If the first is not registered at the date of the second the second will obtain priority as by s 4(5) the first is as against the second void for want of registration.

1 Under the Land Charges Act 1972. As to registration, see **24.4**.
2 If the absence of the deeds by the first mortgagee was due to his gross negligence it is

scarcely probable that it can be argued that despite the registration the first might, by virtue of s 13 of the Law of Property Act 1925 be postponed to the second in accordance with the principles of the pre-1926 law: (1940) CLJ 259 (Meggary).

LOSS OF PRIORITY: NOTICE

PRIORITY OF THE LEGAL MORTGAGEE OF LAND

Bona fide purchaser for value of the legal estate

24.22 In English law the order of priority between two competing interests in the same property depends primarily on whether they are legal or merely equitable interests. Where both interests are equitable or both legal, the basic rule is that 'where the equities are equal, the first in time prevails', ie the two interests rank in the order of their creation. The absence of notice of the earlier interest by the party who acquired the later interest is irrelevant, even if he gave value. Where, however, the first is equitable and the second is legal the position is different. It was formerly the foundation of the law as to priorities of mortgages that a mortgagee who had the legal estate should prevail over all other incumbrancers of whose securities he had no notice when he made his advance[1]. A bona fide purchaser[2] for value[3] who obtains the legal estate at the time of his purchase without notice, actual or constructive, of a prior equitable right is entitled to priority in equity as well as at law[4]. He must in order to obtain priority have acquired the legal estate and the question of notice is normally tested at the time when he obtained it. The legal estate may be the fee simple, a legal term of years or a legal mortgage[5].

It is sufficient if the purchaser has the legal estate transferred to a trustee or nominee for him. If neither he nor his nominee has notice of the prior equitable interest, he will take free from it, for he has the better right to the legal estate[6] This is so even though the prior equitable interest itself confers the right to acquire the legal estate[7]. It matters not that the purchaser of the legal estate has notice of an equitable interest created subsequent to contract of purchase, for his equitable interest has priority as first in time over any later equitable interest and the conveyance merely carries out the contract.

1 Bac Abr *Mortgage*, E3. The doctrine of the prevalence of the legal estate was based by Lord Hardwicke on the circumstance of the jurisdiction in law and equity being administered by different courts and it was a consequence of the superior efficacy allowed in equity to the common law and legal titles. In his view, no such doctrine could have arisen if law and equity had been administered in the same jurisdiction: Lord Hardwicke LC in *Wortley v Birkhead* (1754) 2 Ves Sen 571 at 573. It might have been thought, therefore, that on the fusion of the jurisdictions at common law and in equity by the Judicature Acts 1873 and 1875, the doctrine would have disappeared and the equitable rule would have prevailed. The distinction, however, continued, and the doctrine of the prevalence of the legal estate remained, subject to the changes introduced by the Law of Property Act 1925, and the Land Charges Act 1925 (now the Land Charges Act 1972).

2 'Purchaser' includes a mortgagee: *Brace v Duchess of Marlborough* (1728) 2 P Wms 491; *Pilcher v Rawlins* (1872) 7 Ch App 259.

3 'Value' means any consideration in money or money's worth or marriage: *Wormald v Maitland* (1866) 35 LJ Ch 69 at 73; *Salih v Atchi* [1961] AC 778.

4 *Pilcher v Rawlins* (1872) 7 Ch App 259 at 269.

5 *Kingsworth Finance Co Ltd v Tizard* [1986] 1 WLR 783.

6 *Wilkes v Bodington* (1707) 2 Vern 599; *Stanhope v Earl Verney* (1761) 2 Eden 81; *Taylor v London and County Banking Co* [1901] 2 Ch 231 at 262, 263; *McCarthy & Stone Ltd v Julian S*

Hodge & Co Ltd [1971] 2 All ER 973, [1971] 1 WLR 1547; *Macmillan Inc v Bishopsgate Investment Trust plc (No 3)* [1995] 1 WLR 978 at 1001.

7 For, in accordance with the general rule, a purchaser of a legal estate without notice of a prior equitable interest takes free from it, albeit the equitable interest confers a right to call for the legal estate: *Graham v Skipper* (1885) 55 LJ Ch 263.

The subsequent acquisition of the legal estate

24.23 A purchaser without notice who at the time of the purchase fails to obtain either a legal estate or the better right to one will nevertheless prevail over a prior equity if, without being party to a breach of trust, he subsequently gets in a legal estate, even if he then has notice of the equity[1]. The doctrine is a form of tacking[2], or 'quasi-tacking'[3]. The doctrine does not apply where the owner of the later equitable interest acquires the legal estate from a person who commits a breach of trust in conveying it to him and he has actual or constructive notice of the breach at the time of the transfer[4]. If the mortgagee gets in the legal estate at the time of his advance and has no notice that it was affected by a trust, the legal estate protects him[5]. He cannot avail himself of it against the beneficiaries, if he gets it in afterwards, and has notice of the trust when he got it in. In that case he takes subject to the rights of the beneficiaries and becomes a trustee for them[6]. If, at the time of the advance, the mortgagee has notice of an equity affecting the title of the mortgagor, he takes subject to that equity, since he cannot claim a better title than the mortgagor[7]. A trustee is entitled to the advantage of a legal estate vested in him to protect an advance made by him on the share of a beneficiary and it would prevail over a prior incumbrance on the share of which he has no notice[8].

1 *Blackwood v London Chartered Bank of Australia* (1874) LR 5 PC 92 at 111 where Lord Selborne LC said:

> 'There is nothing more familiar than the doctrine of equity that a man, who has bona fide paid money without notice of any other title, though at the time of the payment he, as purchaser, gets nothing but an equitable title, may afterwards get in a legal title, if he can, and may hold it; though during the interval between the payment and the getting in the legal title he may have had notice of some prior dealing inconsistent with the good faith of the dealing with himself.'

See Megarry and Wade *The Law of Real Property* (6th edn) para 5.014 as to whether the subsequent acquisition of the legal estate is truly an exception to the rule that the purchaser must take a legal estate before receiving notice.

2 In a contest between two equitable mortgagees of land before 1926, it was sometimes possible for the later mortgagee to gain priority over the earlier by acquiring a legal mortgage *which had priority to both.* This was known as 'tacking', and more particularly as the 'tabula in naufragio' (or plank in a shipwreck). If, for example, an owner mortgages his land by a first legal mortgage to A to secure an advance of £1,000, and then by successive second and third equitable mortgages to B and C to secure advances of £2,000 each, the land being worth only £3,000 (the shipwreck), and afterwards C acquired A's legal mortgage (the plank) by redeeming it and obtaining a transfer of the legal estate, he could 'tack' his own advance of £2,000 to the £1,000 secured by the legal mortgage and enforce his security for the full £3,000. The result might be to squeeze out B altogether. The only requirement was that C must have had no notice of B's equitable mortgage at the time when he advanced his money; if he had notice he could not tack. But, if he had no notice when he advanced his money, it was immaterial that he had notice before he redeemed A and acquired the legal estate. The doctrine in relation to mortgages was abolished by s 94(3) of the Law of Property Act 1925. The abolition of the doctrine of tacking does not affect the doctrine of bona fide purchaser for value of a legal estate. As to tacking, see **24.75** ff.

3 *Macmillan Inc v Bishopsgate Investment Trust plc (No 3)* [1995] 1 WLR 978 at 1002. A lender who discharges an earlier mortgage is entitled to be subrogated to the rights of the creditor whose secured debt is paid and therefore inherits the priority accorded to the security: *Boscawen v Bajwa* [1996] 1 WLR 328, CA; *Banque Financière de la Cité v Parc (Battersea) Ltd* [1999] 1 AC 221, HL. Where the later incumbrancer is subrogated the mortgage is not kept alive but the party who has the right of subrogation has the same rights as if it had been kept alive and assigned to him. See further **24.89**.

4 *Harpham v Shacklock* (1881) 19 Ch D 207 at 214, Jessel MR. In order to affect the purchaser, the trust must be in favour of the person against whom the priority is claimed and not a third party: *Taylor v Russell* [1891] 1 Ch 8 at 29.

5 *Pilcher v Rawlins* (1872) 7 Ch App 259 at 269.

6 *Taylor v Russell* [1892] AC 244; *Taylor v London and County Banking Co* [1901] 2 Ch 231; *Perham v Kempster* [1907] 1 Ch 373. See *McCarthy & Stone Ltd v Julian S Hodge & Co Ltd* [1971] 2 All ER 973. Contra, if the mortgagees are entitled to suppose that the trusts are at an end: *Pearce v Bulteel* [1916] 2 Ch 544 and see the statement of the doctrine by Wright J in *Powell v London and Provincial Bank* [1893] 1 Ch 610 at 615. It seems to be an open point whether, to be defeated, the mortgagee must not only know of the trust but also that the conveyance to him is in breach of trust: see *Mumford v Stohwasser* (1874) LR 18 Eq 556 at 563; and see *Carter v Green* (1857) 3 K & J 591 at 640–641; and Sykes, *The Law of Securities* (5th edn) pp 392–392; cf (1976) 92 LQR 528, 556 (Goode); (1977) 93 LQR 324 (Donaldson); (1977) 93 LQR 487 (Goode).

7 *Cookson v Lee* (1853) 23 LJ Ch 473, where, upon a purchase of trust property by the solicitor of the trustees being set aside, a mortgage of the property by that solicitor to a mortgagee who had notice of the relationship failed also.

8 *Phipps v Lovegrove* (1973) LR 16 Eq 80; *Newman v Newman* (1885) 28 Ch D 674.

Mere equities

24.24 The purchase of the legal estate is not necessary in order to avoid mere equities. The purchaser of an equitable interest will take free of mere equities of which he has no notice at the date of the transfer[1].

1 See Megarry and Wade, *The Law of Real Property* (6th edn) paras 5.012-5-013. See *Latec Investments Ltd v Hotel Terrigal Pty Ltd* (1965) 113 CLR 265.

Circumstances in which notice is relevant to priority

24.25 Under the present law, the importance of the legal estate has diminished in consequence of the extent to which priority is now determined by the order of registration and of the statutory effect given to registration as constituting 'actual notice'. Registration of mortgages has become the most important method of determining priority. Registration of any matter in any register kept under the Land Charges Act 1972 or in any local land charges register is deemed to constitute constructive notice of the instrument or matter[1]. If the mortgage is a registrable land charge under the Land Charges Act 1972 and has not been registered, it is void against a purchaser of the land charged with it[2] and notice of it, whether actual or constructive, by the purchaser, is irrelevant[3]. However, as has been seen[4], an incumbrancer who has possession of the title deeds cannot register the charge. His priority is usually guaranteed by the deeds[5]. Notice is irrelevant where both competing mortgages are registrable under the Land Charges Act 1972[6] or where the second but not the first is protected by a deposit of deeds[7]. Nor is notice relevant to the priority of registered charges of registered land. Notice is relevant however to the determination of priorities where the first mortgage but not the second is protected by the deposit of deeds[8].

1 Law of Property Act 1925, s 198.
2 Land Charges Act 1972, s 4(5). See **24.10**.
3 Section 199(1)(i); *Diligent Finance Co Ltd v Alleyne* (1972) 23 P & CR 346; *Lloyds Bank plc v Carrick* [1996] 4 All ER 630, 73 P & CR 314, CA.
4 See **24.5** and **24.6**.
5 As to the priority conferred by the possession of the deeds, see **24.15**.
6 As to which see **24.13**.
7 As to which see **24.21**. As the first will be registrable as a puisne mortgage and priority will depend on registration.
8 As to which see **24.16** ff and in particular **24.19**.

SUCCESSORS IN TITLE

24.26 Where a legal mortgagee has gained priority over an earlier equitable incumbrance owing to want of notice, he may transfer his security with the like advantage to a transferee with notice, for otherwise his right of disposition would be fettered[1]. This rule does not apply where the transfer is made voluntarily in order to avoid the effect of notice[2], or to a transfer in breach of a fiduciary relationship[3].

1 *Lowther v Carlton* (1741) 2 Atk 242; *Kettlewell v Watson* (1882) 21 Ch D 685 at 707; *Wilkes v Spooner* [1911] 2 KB 473, CA.
2 *Merry v Abney* (1663) 1 Cas in Ch 38; *Coote v Mammon* (1724) 5 Bro Parl Cas 355.
3 *Re Stapleford Colliery Co, Barrow's Case* (1880) 14 Ch D 432; *Gordon v Holland* (1913) 82 LJ PC 81.

SECTION 199 OF THE LAW OF PROPERTY ACT 1925

24.27 The doctrine of equity regarding notice is now regulated by statute. By s 199(1) of the Law of Property Act 1925[1] it is provided that the purchaser[2] shall not be prejudicially affected by notice of any instrument or matter:

(a) capable of registration under the Land Charges Act 1972 which is void or not enforceable as against him under that Act by reason of its non-registration[3]; or
(b) unless:
  (i) it is within his own knowledge; or
  (ii) it would have come to his knowledge if such inquiries and inspections had been made as ought reasonably to have been made by him[4]; or
(c) it has, in the same transaction with respect to which a question of notice to the purchaser arises[5]:
  (i) come to the knowledge of his counsel, as such, or of his solicitor or other agent, as such[6]; or
  (ii) would have come to the knowledge of his solicitor or other agent, as such, if such inquiries and inspections had been made as ought reasonably to have been made by the solicitor or other agent[7].

Thus it is clear from the statutory provision that a purchaser is affected by notice in three cases:

(a) where he has actual knowledge of the equity;

(b) where he has failed to make proper inquiries which would have revealed the equity — constructive notice;
(c) where his agent has actual or constructive notice of the equity — imputed notice.

1 In the earlier editions of this work it was said that 'The object of these provisions is to get rid of some of those extensions of the law of notice which have gradually arisen out of the somewhat refined reasonings of courts of equity, and which operated with much harshness, but in applying the Act it will often be as necessary as before to consider what constitutes "knowledge", either in the person to be affected by notice, or in his agent "as such", when agency exists; whether the knowledge has been acquired in the same transaction; and what inquiries and inspections ought reasonably to have been made.'
2 Including a mortgagee: Land Charges Act 1972, s 17. See **24.22**, n 2.
3 Law of Property Act 1925, s 199 (1) (i) and the Land Charges Act 1972 s 18(6).
4 Section 199(1)(ii). This subsection does not exempt a purchaser from any liability under, or any obligation to perform or observe, any covenant, condition, provision or restriction contained in any instrument under which his title is derived, mediately or immediately; and such liability or obligation may be enforced in the same manner and to the same extent as if that paragraph had not been enacted: s 199(2).
5 Thus knowledge of the solicitor acquired in relation to a previous transaction is not imputed to the mortgagee. See **24.40**.
6 As to the effect of the statutory restriction see *Halifax Mortgage Services Ltd (formerly BNP Mortgages Ltd) v Stepsky* [1996] Ch 207, [1996] 2 All ER 277, CA; *Barclays Bank plc v Thomson* [1997] 4 All ER 816, [1997] 1 FLR 156, CA; *National Westminster Bank plc v Beaton* (1997) 30 HLR 99, 74 P & CR D19, CA, which are considered in **24.40** ff.
7 The statutory provisions dealing with notice have no application, even by analogy, to registered land: *Williams and Glyn's Bank Ltd v Boland* [1981] AC 487 at 504, [1980] 2 All ER 408 at 412, per Lord Wilberforce.

ACTUAL NOTICE

24.28 The 1925 Act[1] refers to the matter or thing being within the purchaser's or his agent's 'own knowledge'. Knowledge may be taken to imply, and to be equivalent to, what is commonly known as actual notice. Actual notice may be oral as well as written.[2] It may be effected by the delivery of a document which shows the nature and extent of the claim[3]. It is not necessary that it should have been given for the purpose of making a transaction valid. If it is actually given, the object for which it was given is not material[4].

The notice must be distinct. If written notice has not been given, evidence of casual conversations will be insufficient. It must be shown that such an intelligent apprehension of the fact has been acquired as would induce a reasonable man or an ordinary man of business to act upon the information, and to regulate his conduct by it in the matter[5]. There must be clear evidence of notice, for suspicious circumstances are insufficient[6]. It seems that it matters not from whom the knowledge was acquired[7] although it has been said that it ought to be given by a person interested in the property[8]. There is some authority for the view that forgetfulness does not deprive the purchaser of notice of the equity[9]. However, it has been suggested that if a person has genuinely forgotten something he will not be fixed with notice of it[10].

Actual notice is equally effectual whether it is received by the incumbrancer himself or by a solicitor[11] or other agent[12] employed by him in the matter of the mortgage. Notice to a director is not necessarily notice to the company[13].

Actual notice of an incumbrance is constructive notice of matters which the intending mortgagee would have discovered if he had made inquiries as to the incumbrance[14].

1 Section 199(1)(ii)(a); s 199(1)(iii)(a).
2 *Browne v Savage* (1859) 4 Drew 635. Notice may also be statutory: the Law of Property Act 1925, s 198 provides that land charges registered in the Land Charges Register constitute 'actual notice' and this is so albeit the purchaser does not in fact know of it.
3 *Baille v M'Kewan* (1865) 35 Beav 177.
4 *Smith v Smith* (1833) 2 Cr & M 231; *Richards v Gledstanes* (1861) 3 Giff 298; affd 31 LJ Ch 142.
5 *Ford v White* (1852) 16 Beav 120; *Edwards v Martin* (1865) LR 1 Eq 121; *Saffron Walden, etc, Building Society v Rayner* (1880) 14 Ch D 406.
6 *Whitfield v Fausset* (1750) 1 Ves Sen 387; *West v Reid* (1843) 2 Hare 249.
7 *Lloyd v Banks* (1868) 3 Ch App 488.
8 Sugd *V & P* (14th edn) p 755.
9 *Rignall Developments Ltd v Halil* [1988] Ch 190 at 201-202; *Eagle Trust plc v SBC Securities Ltd* [1993] 1 WLR 484 at 494; *Polly Peck International plc v Nadir (No 2)* [1992] 4 All ER 769 at 781. None of these decisions was concerned with the question whether an incumbrance bound a purchaser of land.
10 *Re Montagu's Settlement Trusts* [1987] Ch 264 at 284; *El Ajou v Dollar Land Holdings plc* [1993] 3 All ER 717 at 743.
11 Law of Property Act 1925, s 199(1)(ii). See **24.44**.
12 Law of Property Act 1925, s 199(1)(ii). See **24.40** ff. However, the first question is whether, apart from the statutory restriction, notice to a solicitor or agent would be imputed to the principal: see *Bouts v Stenning* (1892) 8 TLR 600; *Kettlewell v Watson* (1882) 21 Ch D 685 at 707; cf *Sharpe v Foy* (1868) 4 Ch App 35; *Sankey v Alexander* (2)(1874) 9 IR Eq 259 at 259n, 300, Ir CA. See also *El Ajou v Dollar Land Holdings plc* [1994] 2 All ER 685, CA; *Halifax Mortgage Services Ltd (formerly BNP Mortgages Ltd) v Stepsky* [1996] Ch 1, [1995] 4 All ER 656 (affd on different grounds [1996] Ch 207, [1996] 2 All ER 277, CA); *Barclays Bank plc v Thomson* [1997] 4 All ER 816, [1997] 1 FLR 156, CA; *National Westminster Bank plc v Beaton* (1997) 30 HLR 99, 74 P & CR D19, CA. See further 16 *Halsbury's Laws*, Equity (reissue) para 769. As to an agent's knowledge binding his principal see *Blackburn, Low & Co v Vigors* (1887) 12 App Cas 531 at 538, HL; *Muir's Executors v Craig's Trustees* 1913 SC 349.
13 *El Ajou v Dollar Land Holdings plc* [1994] 2 All ER 685, CA. See also *Bank of Ireland v Cogry Spinning Co Ltd* [1900] 1 IR 219 at 248; *Re David Payne & Co Ltd, Young v David Payne & Co Ltd* [1904] 2 Ch 608, CA.
14 *Taylor v Baker* (1818) 5 Price 306; *Penny v Watts* (1849) 1 Mac & G 150; *Montefiore v Browne* (1858) 7 HL Cas 241. As to the doctrine of constructive notice generally see **24.29** ff.

CONSTRUCTIVE NOTICE

24.29 Implied, or constructive, notice is knowledge which the courts impute to a person[1]. The knowledge is presumed to exist or to have been communicated[2]. The presumption is so strong that it cannot be allowed to be rebutted. Accordingly, a person who is proved to have known facts, from which a court or an impartial person would properly draw a certain inference will not be allowed to escape from notice by saying that he did not draw the natural inference from the facts[3]. It is a presumption adopted for the prevention of fraud. It extends to matters affecting the title to property and to circumstances which would entitle persons to equitable priorities or change the character of rights depending upon want of notice. It does not extend to matters which relate merely to the motives and object of the parties, or to the consideration upon which the matter in hand is founded[4].

1 Notice is either actual or constructive: the one kind being a question of fact, the other arising from construction of law: Co Litt 309 b. The term 'actual notice' is used in the Law of Property Act 1925, ss 197, 198.
2 *Hewitt v Loosemore* (1851) 9 Hare 449; *Plumb v Fluitt* (1791) 2 Anst 432.

3 *Re Douglas, ex p Snowball* (1872) 7 Ch App 534 and see *McCarthy & Stone Ltd v Julian S Hodge & Co Ltd* [1971] 2 All ER 973, [1971] 1 WLR 1547.
4 Per Lord Chelmsford in *Eyre v Burmester* (1862) 10 HL Cas 90.

When constructive notice to be obtained

24.30 To be effectual, notice must be obtained before the completion of the transaction. It will be good if given before the execution of the deed although the money has already been paid, because the payment and execution are but parts of the same transaction[1]. Similarly, notice will be good if received before payment, though security has been given by the execution of the conveyance for perhaps after notice the consideration will not be paid[2].

1 *Wigg v Wigg* (1739) 1 Atk 382 at 384.
2 *Tourville v Naish* (1743) 3 P Wms 307; *Hardingham v Nicholls* (1745) 3 Atk 304.

When constructive notice is implied

24.31 A mortgagee has constructive notice of a prior incumbrance:

(a) when, on advancing his money, he omits to make inquiries which, having regard to the state of the title known to him, are usual inquiries for a purchaser to make and which would have led him to a knowledge of the prior incumbrance; and
(b) when he has reason to suspect a prior incumbrance and wilfully or fraudulently avoids receiving actual notice of it.

The first ground is based on the presumption of law that a purchaser has investigated the title of the property which he purchases and has examined whatever forms a link in that title[1]. The second is based on an obvious principle of equity and, in these circumstances, notice may be imputed to the mortgagee although he acts in the matter, not personally, but by an agent[2].

1 *Jones v Smith* (1841) 1 Hare 43; *Berwick & Co v Price* [1905] 1 Ch 632; *Kemmis v Kemmis* [1988] 1 WLR 1307. If there is anything else on the title that would put a professional man on inquiry, a mortgagor cannot set up the defence that he had no professional adviser: *Berwick & Co v Price*, above.
2 *Espin v Pemberton* (1859) 3 De G & J 547. Notice to him who transacts is notice to him for whom he transacts: *Merry v Abney* (1663) 1 Cas in Ch 38. The infancy of the principal makes no difference: *Toulmin v Steere* (1817) 3 Mer 210. As to agency see **24.40** ff.

Constructive notice through non-inquiry

Inquiries which should be made

24.32 The statutory test for constructive notice is that the 'instrument or matter or any fact or thing' would have come to the knowledge of the person against whom notice is sought to be established 'if such inquiries and inspections had been made as ought reasonably to have been made by him'[1]. The inquiries which are reasonable are those which ought to have been made as a matter of prudence, having regard to what is usually done for the purpose of obtaining good title by careful men of business, advised by a competent lawyer[2], in similar circumstances[3]. Where a person has actual notice that the property with which he is dealing is charged or otherwise affected, generally , it is his duty to inquire into the extent and nature of the charges. He must not assume that the reference is only to charges which are already known to him[4]. If there is no actual notice that the property is affected, and no turning away from the knowledge of facts which the circumstances would suggest to a prudent mind, there will be no constructive notice[5]. If the inquiries which ought to have been made would not in any event have revealed the matters of which constructive notice is sought to be fixed the mortgagee is unaffected by them[6].

1 Law of Property Act 1925, s 199(1)(ii).
2 *Berwick & Co v Price* [1905] 1 Ch 632 and see also **24.31**, n 1 and *Northern Bank Ltd v Henry* [1981] IR 1 at 18.
3 *Bailey v Barnes* [1894] 1 Ch 25 at 35, per Lindley LJ, CA; *Berwick & Co v Price* [1905] 1 Ch 632; *Woolwich plc v Gomm* (1999) 79 P & CR, CA , reviewing and applying *Bailey v Barnes.* The inquiries which are reasonable are equivalent to those which a purchaser should make according to the practice of conveyancers; and see *Agra Bank Ltd v Barry* (1874) LR 7 HL 135; *McCarthy & Stone Ltd v Julian S Hodge & Co Ltd* [1971] 2 All ER 973, [1971] 1 WLR 1547; *Re Fuller & Co Ltd, O'Connor v McCarthy* [1982] IR 161 (bank fixed with constructive notice by failure to enquire whether there was any litigation pending or threatened in respect of the property offered as security); *Kingsnorth Trust Ltd v Tizard* [1986] 2 All ER 54, [1986] 1 WLR 783; (1986) 136 NLJ 771 (Luxton); and the cases referred to in n 2.
4 *Jones v Williams* (1857) 24 Beav 47: the omission to make inquiry so obviously tends to fraud that the purchaser is affected with notice, even though the omission does not proceed from fraudulent motives.
5 *Plumb v Fluitt* (1791) 2 Anst 432; *Evans v Bicknell* (1801) 6 Ves 174; *Jones v Smith* (1841) 1 Hare 43; affd (1843) 1 Ph 244. See *Agra Bank Ltd v Barry* (1874) LR 7 HL 135; *English and Scottish Mercantile Investment Co v Brunton* [1892] 2 QB 700 (where the mortgagee's solicitor knew that the mortgaging company had issued debentures, but was told that they did not affect the property proposed to be mortgaged to his client); *Re Castell and Brown Ltd, Roper v The Company* [1898] 1 Ch 315; *Re Valletort Sanitary Steam Laundry Co Ltd, Ward v The Company* [1903] 2 Ch 654; *Re Bourne, Bourne v Bourne* [1906] 2 Ch 427.
6 *Kemmis v Kemmis* [1988] 1 WLR 1307 at 1317, CA.

Inquiries necessary to ascertain title

24.33 An intending mortgagee must satisfy himself that the mortgagor has at least a prima facie title. It is not sufficient for him merely to put the question 'is this your property?'[1]. He will be deemed to have notice of all facts which he would have learned upon a proper investigation of the title, under a contact containing no restriction of his rights in that respect[2]. If, therefore, he does not ask for the title deeds, he will be affected with notice of the rights of an undisclosed mortgagee in whose custody they are[3]. A fortiori, if knowing[4] that the deeds are in deposit, or that the person with whom he deals is indebted, and has given security to another, and that the title deeds are not forthcoming[5], he abstains from seeking information as to their actual position.

The notice will not affect the purchaser if he afterwards purchases other lands under a title independent of the instrument of which he had notice, though that instrument may have actually related to him as he is being neither presumed to take notice of, nor be bound to remember, more than is necessary to make out his title[6].

The fact that the mortgagee does not employ a solicitor, and is himself ignorant of the law, is immaterial[7].

1 *Mulville v Munster and Leinster Bank* (1891) 27 LR Ir 379.
2 *Re Nisbet and Potts' Contract* [1905] 1 Ch 391; on appeal [1906] 1 Ch 386. See also *Re Cox and Neve* [1891] 2 Ch 109 at 117. A vendor may be called upon, under an open contract, to show a title for the last 15 years: Law of Property Act 1925, s 44 (1), as amended by the Law of Property Act 1969, s 23. The purchaser is entitled to require a good root of title at least 15 years old. The root of title may be longer eg 30 years, in which case the purchaser will have constructive notice of equitable interests from that date. A good root of title must commence with a document which deals with the whole legal and equitable interest in the land and describes the property adequately and contains nothing to throw doubt on the title: Megarry and Wade *The Law of Real Property* (6th edn) paras 12.075-12.076. If the purchaser's rights in respect of the root of title are restricted by the contract of sale to a shorter period, he is deemed to have notice of any equitable rights appearing on the title which he would have discovered if he had investigated the title for the whole period.
3 *Berwick & Co v Price* [1905] 1 Ch 632; per Joyce J at 638. See *Kennedy v Green* (1834) 3 My & K 699; *Jones v Smith*, above; *Hewitt v Loosemore* (1851) 9 Hare 449; *Lloyd's Banking Co v Jones* (1885) 29 Ch D 221; *Oliver v Hinton* [1899] 2 Ch 264.
If A claims priority over B on the ground that B took with notice of A's earlier security, the onus lies on A to prove such notice and it is not sufficient to show that the deeds were in the hands of A if, irrespective of the security, he was the person entitled to hold them: *Re Hardy, ex p Hardy* (1832) 2 Deac & Ch 393. Possession of deeds by a solicitor is in the ordinary course of business and does not call for inquiry: *Bozon v Williams* (1829) 3 Y & J 150.
4 *Birch v Ellames* (1794) 2 Anst 427; *Hiern v Mill* (1806) 13 Ves 114.
5 *Whitbread v Jordan* (1835) 1 Y & C Ex 303.
6 *Hamilton v Royse* (1804) 2 Sch & Lef 315.
7 *Berwick & Co v Price*, above, and a person will be affected with notice of an instrument brought to his actual knowledge, though it be inartistically expressed, if the meaning is so plain that an unprofessional person would not be misled: *Davies v Davies* (1841) 4 Beav 54.

Of whom inquiries should be made

24.34 Where notice may depend on the result of inquiries, these should not be made of the mortgagor if there are better means of information[1]. Inquiry only of those against whose possible fraud the inquiries are intended to be a safeguard is, in general, not sufficient. If the mortgagee has inquired honestly and to the best of his means, he will not be prejudiced because he has been misled by false information[2]. If he fails to make inquiry at all he cannot seek to excuse his failure by relying on the fact that if he had asked he would probably have been met with an excuse for the non-production of the deeds[3].

1 *Taylor v Baker* (1818) 5 Price 306; *Broadbent v Barlow* (1861) 3 De GF & J 570.
2 *Jones v Smith* (1841) 1 Hare 43; *Jones v Williams* (1857) 24 Beav 47; *Hipkins v Amery* (1860) 2 Giff 292. See also **24.37**, nn 7 and 8 and **24.38**, n 1.
3 *Jones v Williams* (1857) 24 Beav 47 at 62. As to the provision of a reasonable excuse for non-production, see **24.57**.

Notice from form of conveyance

24.35 Notice may also arise from the nature or form of a conveyance. Thus, a purchaser has notice of a prior title by the concurrence in the conveyance to him of persons interested under that title. Though a peculiarity in a deed, such as the unusual position of a signature or the manner of engrossing it, ought to cause inquiry, it will not lead to notice of a defect in the title with which it is not connected.

Notice of equities

24.36 The rule under consideration is not confined to plain recitals of matters of fact. A purchaser will generally be bound by the particulars, and even sometimes by the equities, arising out of an important or peculiar transaction recited or referred to in a deed or abstract, of which he has notice, and concerning which transaction it becomes his duty to inquire. Thus notice will be imputed of the particulars of a trust, of the existence of which there is actual notice[1]. There will be no notice of an equity which the usual inquiry into title would not discover. Thus, a purchaser from a trustee will not have notice of negligence or other matter amounting to breach of trust in connection with the sale[2]. Notice, however, will arise where the matter depends upon the application of a clear equitable doctrine. Hence notice of the reservation of an equity of redemption is notice of the mortgage title, if the court is of opinion that the equity still subsists[3]. Where, however, the construction of a deed is so uncertain, and the equity so doubtful, that the decision of the court could not be known, a purchaser for valuable consideration, denying actual notice, will not be affected[4].

1 *Malpas v Ackland* (1827) 3 Russ 273; provided, that is, the notice is clear: see *London and Canadian etc Co v Duggan* [1893] AC 506 and see *Lacey v Ingle* (1847) 2 Ph 413 (notice imputed to mortgagee of contract for sale that prior incumbrancers had claims on the purchase money).
2 *Borrell v Dann* (1843) 2 Hare 440.
3 *Hansard v Hardy* (1812) 18 Ves 455.
4 *Parker v Brooke* (1804) 9 Ves 583. See also *Bovey v Smith* (1682) 1 Vern 144.

Notice of deeds

Deeds affecting title

24.37 Actual notice of an instrument which must necessarily affect the title is constructive notice of its contents and of everything to which it refers[1]. Thus, notice of a lease is notice of all covenants in it whether usual or unusual, provided the purchaser has a fair opportunity of ascertaining its provisions[2]. Generally, a purchaser who is provided with an instrument for the express purpose of examination in the transaction[3], or for whose inspection it is left open for examination in the transaction[4], has actual or constructive notice of its contents, though the nature of the contents may have been misrepresented.

A purchaser is bound by a mortgage, though not particularly specified, if the deed, subject to or under which he claims, shows the existence of prior mortgages[5]. There will be full notice of an incumbrance as against a person who takes subject to it although, in the recital of it, it is inaccurately or not completely described[6]. There is no notice where a representation is made, concerning the mortgage deed, which is calculated to mislead and to disarm inquiry[7]; nor where an imperfect or erroneous statement has been made as to the contents of a deed[8].

In cases of fraud, it would seem that none but the parties to a deed is affected by the constructive notice of the fraud[9].

1 *Jones v Smith* (1843) 1 Ph 244 at 253.
2 *Grosvenor v Green* (1858) 28 LJ Ch 173; *Hyde v Warden* (1877) 3 Ex D 72; *Re White and Smith's Contract* [1896] 1 Ch 637.

3 *Cosser v Collinge* (1832) 3 My & K 283.
4 *Crofton v Ormsby* (1806) 2 Sch & Lef 583.
5 *Eland v Eland* (1839) 1 Beav 235; *Farrow v Rees* (1840) 4 Beav 18.
6 *Hope v Liddell* (1855) 21 Beav 183 and see *Gibson v Ingo* (1847) 6 Hare 112.
7 *Drysdale v Mace* (1854) 2 Sm & G 255; affd 5 De GM & G 103.
8 *Re Bright's Trusts* (1856) 21 Beav 430.
9 *Read v Ward* (1739) 7 Vin Abr 119 pl 2.

Deeds not necessarily affecting title

24.38 While notice of a deed which must of necessity affect the title is constructive notice of its contents, this is not so with other deeds. Mere notice of some other document is not notice of its contents so long as the person who has notice acts honestly and is not guilty of gross negligence. Thus, a purchaser is not affected with notice of the contents of a document if told that it does not affect the property and he honestly believes this statement[1]. A purchaser is not affected with notice of matters appearing upon an abstract or a deed which merely leave room for suspicion of what the purchaser cannot know to be, and which may not be, true[2]. However, cases of this kind depend very much on their own circumstances and that which will not affect one man will be abundantly sufficient to affect another[3].

1 *Jones v Smith* (1843) 1 Ph 244 at 257. See *Finch & Shaw* (1854) 18 Jur 935; affd sub nom *Colyer v Finch* (1856) 5 HL Cas 905; *Lloyds Banking Co v Jones* (1885) 29 Ch D 221 at 230; as to debentures, see *English and Scottish Mercantile Investment Co v Brunton* [1892] 2 QB 700; *Re Valletort Sanitary Steam Laundry Co, Ward v The Company* [1903] 2 Ch 654; *Wilson v Kelland* [1910] 2 Ch 306.
2 See *M'Queen v Farquhar* (1805) 11 Ves 467 at 482; *Dodds v Hills* (1865) 2 Hem & M 424.
3 *Jones v Smith* (1841) 1 Hare 43 at 55.

Notice by occupation

24.39 Where a person other than the person with apparent title is in actual occupation[1] or in receipt of the rents of the land, notice of such occupation or receipt is constructive notice of the estate, interest or rights of the occupier or recipient[2]. Thus, eg where a tenant is in occupation, the purchaser is put on inquiry as to the terms of the holding and has constructive notice of the tenant's rights[3]. It is not sufficient to make inquiry solely of the vendor[4]. The mortgagee should ask a tenant in occupation for a copy of his tenancy agreement, but is not obliged to make further inquiry and is entitled to assume that the document represents the agreement between tenant and mortgagor[5]. Where, however, the tenant is paying rent to a person claiming adversely to the vendor, the purchaser is not, as between himself and such claimant, bound to inquire to whom the rent is paid and he does not have constructive notice of the title of the person receiving the rent[6]. If, however, he inquires and finds that rent is being paid to an adverse claimant he has constructive notice of that person's rights[7]. The principle of the doctrine is that the purchaser is not justified in assuming the possession of the occupier to be that of the apparent owner, but is bound to inquire into the nature of his interest. Thus the notice equally arises, whether the property is described to the purchaser as occupied by the person alone who claims the interest in question, or by him and his undertenants[8].

Inquiry should be made of the spouse of the vendor if in occupation[9], but need not be made of children of the vendor, since their occupation is that of their parents[10]. Where the property to be charged is owned by a company and occupied by its director, the mortgagee is not required to inquire about the rights in the mortgaged property of the director if he negotiates the loan on behalf of the company mortgagor[11].

A mortgagee is not prejudicially affected by notice of the registrable but unregistered interest of a person in occupation, such as an estate contract[12], or a claim for a property adjustment order[13]. The equitable interests of a person in occupation under a trust of land may be overreached where the mortgage is granted by at least two trustees of the trust and capital money arising on the mortgage is paid to them or by their direction[14].

Even though a purchaser or mortgagee may have constructive notice of an occupier's right, the occupier may be estopped by his conduct from asserting it[15].

1 Ie physical presence, not some entitlement in law: *Williams and Glyn's Bank Ltd v Boland* [1981] AC 487 at 505, [1980] 2 All ER 408 at 413. See [1990] CLJ 277 at 315-320.

2 *Williams and Glyn's Bank Ltd v Boland* [1981] AC 487, [1980] 2 All ER 408, HL; *Kingsnorth Trust Ltd v Tizard* [1986] 2 All ER 54, [1986] 1 WLR 119, CA; and see *Hodgson v Marks* [1971] Ch 892, [1971] 2 All ER 684, CA. The doctrine of notice has no application in the context of registered land. As regards registered land, occupation as a fact may protect rights, if the person in occupation has rights: Land Registration Act 1925, s 70(1)(g); *Williams and Glyn's Bank Ltd v Boland* [1981] AC 487, [1980] 2 All ER 408. Although a vendor's lien is an overriding interest in land, if the agreement is that the outstanding balance of the purchase price is to be secured by a charge on the property the lien never comes into existence, for it is, by agreement being replaced by the charge: *Nationwide Anglia Building Society v Ahmed* (1995) 70 P & CR 381, CA.

3 *Barnhart v Greenshields* (1853) 9 Moo PCC 18 at 32 and see *Hegeman v Rogers* (1972) 21 DLR (3d) 272. Where the property is in the possession of a partnership, a mortgagee from one partner has constructive notice of the title of the firm: *Cavander v Bulteel* (1873) 9 Ch App 79.

4 *Hodgson v Marks* [1971] Ch 892, [1971] 2 All ER 684, CA.

5 *Smith v Jones* [1954] 2 All ER 823, [1954] 1 WLR 1089.

6 *Barnhart v Greenshields*, above; *Hunt v Luck* [1902] 1 Ch 428 at 432; *Green v Rheinberg* (1911) 104 LT 149, CA; *Smith v Jones* [1954] 2 All ER 823, [1954] 1 WLR 1089; and *Latec Investments Ltd v Hotel Terrigal Pty Ltd* (1965) 113 CLR 265.

7 *Bailey v Richardson* (1852) 9 Hare 734; *Barnhart v Greenshields*, above; *Hunt v Luck*, above, at 433.

8 *Bailey v Richardson*, above, and see *Crofton v Ormsby* (1806) 2 Sch & Lef 583; *Hanbury v Litchfield* (1833) 2 My & K 629; *Miles v Langley* (1831) 1 Russ & M 39; affd (1831) 2 Russ & M 626.

9 See *Williams and Glyn's Bank Ltd v Boland* [1981] AC 487, [1980] 2 All ER 408, HL; *Hodgson v Marks* [1971] Ch 892, [1971] 2 All ER 684, CA (disapproving *Caunce v Caunce* [1969] 1 All ER 722 at 727–728, [1969] 1 WLR 286 at 293, per Stamp J). If , for example, a husband is sole legal owner of land, but his wife has an equitable interest in the property by reason of some contribution to the costs of its acquisition, any purchaser will be bound by her interest unless it was disclosed after proper inquiry of her. However, it is likely that the wife as beneficial co-owner will be postponed on the basis that knowing of the proposal to obtain the advance upon the security of the property she impliedly consented to being postponed to the mortgagee: see **24.74**.

10 *Hypo-Mortgage Services Ltd v Robinson* [1997] 2 FCR 422, [1997] 2 FLR 71,CA.

11 *Midland Bank Ltd v Farmpride Hatcheries Ltd* [1981] 2 EGLR 147, CA.

12 *Lloyds Bank plc v Carrick* [1996] 4 All ER 630, 73 P & CR 314, CA. As to the irrelevance of notice of unregistered mortgages which are registrable pursuant to the Land Charges Act 1972, see **24.10**, n 8.

13 *Whittingham v Whittingham* [1979] Fam 9, [1978] 3 All ER 805, CA.

14 Law of Property Act 1925, ss 2, 27 (both as amended); *City of London Building Society v Flegg* [1988] AC 54,[1987] 3 All ER 435, HL.

15 *Midland Bank Ltd v Farmpride Hatcheries Ltd* [1981] 2 EGLR 147, 260 Estates Gazette 493, CA. See on estoppel **24.59**.

IMPUTED NOTICE

Notice must be received in the same transaction

24.40 The principal may be affected by notice received through his agent[1], but under s 199 of the Law of Property Act 1925[2] the effect of notice to the agent, whether actual or constructive, is confined to notice received in the same transaction as that with respect to which the question arises[3]. Thus the principal is unaffected where the notice is acquired by a solicitor, subsequently instructed both by the mortgagor and the mortgagee, in a previous transaction when acting only for the mortgagor, albeit one closely connected with the transaction in which notice to the principal arises[4]. A solicitor, like any other agent, may be instructed specifically to act for a party for one particular purpose but not to act for him generally for other purposes. It is only knowledge which he acquires when carrying out that part of the transaction in which he is instructed to act as agent which is to be imputed to the party who for that purpose is his principal[5]. Where, therefore, the mortgagee's solicitor was instructed by the mortgagee to register the charge, the agent's knowledge that the guarantor, the mortgagor's wife, had not been adequately advised was not to be imputed to the mortgagee, as the solicitor had not been appointed to ensure that the charge was effective against the wife[6].

1 Otherwise notice might always be avoided by employing agents: *Sheldon v Cox* (1764) Amb 624. The doctrine is not confined to notice received through solicitors: *Merry v Abney* (1663) 1 Cas in Ch 38.
2 For the terms of which, see **24.27**.
3 *Re Cousins* (1886) 31 Ch D 671; *Thorne v Heard* [1895] AC 495, HL; *Magee v UDC Finance Ltd* [1983] NZLR 438. Where the agent who effected the earlier mortgage himself becomes second mortgagee, it is probably the case that he will be unable to deny notice of the earlier mortgage: see *Perkins v Bradley* (1842) 1 Hare 219. See generally Nield (2000) Conv 196.
4 *Halifax Mortgage Services Ltd v Stepsky* [1996] Ch 207, CA. See also n 2.
5 *Midland Bank plc v Serter* (1995) 71 P & CR 264, [1995] 1 FLR 1034, CA. See also *Barclays Bank plc v Thomson* [1997] 4 All ER 816 at 828, 829.
6 *Midland Bank plc v Serter* (1995) 71 P & CR 264, [1995] 1 FLR 1034,CA.

'As such'

24.41 The notice must be received by the agent in his capacity as such. Information acquired by the agent informally at a funeral service rather than in the course of the transaction is not acquired by the agent 'as such'[1]. Notice acquired by the agent in an earlier but closely related transaction than that upon which he was instructed by the mortgagee, is not notice acquired 'as such' by the agent[2]. If a solicitor is advising a signatory to the mortgage albeit at the request of the mortgagee and at the same time acting for the mortgagee in a ministerial capacity at completion, the solicitors in advising the signatory are acting exclusively for the signatory, not the lenders, and knowledge acquired by solicitors whilst tendering independent advice to a signatory does not come to them as agents as such for the mortgagee[3].

1 *Société Générale de Paris v Tramway Union Co Ltd* (1885) 14 QBD 424 (claim to shares by executors) Cotton LJ said: 'Where notice to the board is necessary, it is not essential that notice should be given formally, but notice to be effectual must be information given or coming to them as directors, or in a matter relating to the interests of their company. But

here the information given to the secretary was given to him, not as secretary to the company, but as a relation of the deceased, and not with reference to the affairs or business of the company, but as explanatory of the state of the affairs of the deceased'. See also *Rock Permanent Benefit Building Society v Kettlewell* (1956) 168 Estates Gazette 397, where notice acquired by the mortgagee's solicitor as a result of his being the mortgagor's brother was not imputed.

2 *Halifax Mortgage Services Ltd v Stepsky* [1996] Ch 207, CA . Knowledge received by the solicitors acting on behalf of the mortgagor that he had misrepresented the true purpose of the loan to the proposed mortgagee was not to be imputed to the mortgagee upon the appointment of the mortgagor's solicitor to act for them in the transaction. The solicitor was not appointed until one week after the information had been communicated to the solicitors by the mortgagor and accordingly it could not be said that, at the time of the receipt of the communication to the solicitors, they were acting as agents of the mortgagee in the transaction in which the question of notice arose. The information was not received 'as such' within in the terms of the Law of Property Act 1925, s 199(1)(ii)(b). *Halifax Mortgage Services Ltd v Stepsky* was approved in *Royal Bank of Scotland v Etridge (No 2)* [1998] 4 All ER 705, CA. The Court of Appeal in *Halifax Mortgage Services Ltd v Stepsky* did not deal with the issue which was considered at length by the judge at first instance as to whether knowledge acquired by a common solicitor is to be imputed to both mortgagor and mortgagee. On this issue, see **24.44**, n 5.

3 *Midland Bank plc v Serter* (1995) 71 P & CR 264, [1995] 1 FLR 1034, CA; *Barclays Bank plc v Thomson* [1997] 4 All ER 816 at 828, 829 ; *National Westminster Bank plc v Beaton* (1997) 30 HLR 99, 74 P & CR D19, CA; *Royal Bank of Scotland v Etridge (No 2)* [2001] UKHL 44, [2001] 4 All ER 449 at [77], [176]–[179], HL. If the common solicitor is retained to do more than act in a ministerial capacity, notice of the agent, eg of the undue influence of the mortgagor over his wife acting as guarantor, may be imputed to the mortgagee. For a detailed treatment of constructive notice of the equity to set aside the transaction on the ground of undue influence, see **13.31** ff.

Constructive notice of agent through lack of inquiry

24.42 If the fact of which notice is sought to be imputed to the principal would have come to the agent's knowledge if he had undertaken reasonably prudent inquiries, the agent will have constructive notice of it and as such the fact will be imputed to the principal. The statutory test for constructive notice is that the 'instrument or matter or any fact or thing' would have come to the knowledge of the person against whom notice is sought to be established 'if such inquiries and inspections had been made as ought reasonably to have been made by him'[1]. The inquiries which are reasonable are those which ought to have been made as a matter of prudence, having regard to what is usually done by careful men of business in similar circumstances[2]. The mortgagee does not have to act as a suspicious lender would act but only as a reasonably prudent lender would act[3]. The instructions given by the principal to the agent do not affect the question of whether the agent has actual or constructive notice of a matter which can be imputed to the principal; the statutory formula imposes an objective standard as to what inquiries ought to be undertaken by the agent and does not depend on the particular instructions given[4]. If a fact ought to have been discovered by the mortgagee if it had undertaken appropriate inquiries the mortgagee cannot say that it does not have the relevant knowledge because it ought to have been discovered by its agent or solicitor. That is because the effect of the statute is to impute to the mortgagee knowledge which should have been acquired by the reasonably prudent mortgagee instructing a solicitor[5].

1 Law of Property Act, 1925, s 199(1)(ii)(b).

2 *Bailey v Barnes* [1894] 1 Ch 25, CA; *Woolwich plc v Gomm* (1999) 79 P & CR 61. See also **24.32**.

3 *Woolwich plc v Gomm* (1999) 79 P & CR 61.
4 *Woolwich plc v Gomm*. Although the terms of the retainer are relevant to the question whether the knowledge of the agent has come to him as such in the same transaction as that in respect of which notice of the fact is sought to be imputed: see **24.40**.
5 *Woolwich plc v Gomm* above.

Relation of principal and agent

24.43 The relation of principal and agent must subsist at the time of the transaction. But actual retainer of a person as agent seems unnecessary; for even where the person to be affected knows nothing of the matter until after its completion, if he then acts upon or adopts it, he thereby makes the agent his agent ab initio. If the agent is employed in part only of the transaction, notice arises of whatever came to his knowledge during his agency[1]. A solicitor is not an agent for the purpose of receiving notice of an incumbrance on or other dealings with the security, merely because he was employed to invest the money[2].

1 *Bury v Bury* (1748) Sudg V & P (11th edn) App No 25. For the case of a bank manager who is agent for his bank, see *Re Macnamara* (1884) 13 LR Ir 158.
2 *Saffron Walden Second Benefit Building Society v Rayner* (1880) 14 Ch D 406.

Solicitor as agent

24.44 Notice to a solicitor in and affecting a transaction in which he is engaged on behalf of a client is notice to the client[1]. The solicitor's knowledge that another member of the firm acted for the other party will not be imputed to his client unless the facts are so compelling as to put him on inquiry[2]. Where both parties employ the same solicitor the knowledge of the mortgagor will not be notice to the mortgagee[3]. There is a conflict of authority as to whether the knowledge acquired by a solicitor employed by both parties instructed in the same transaction is to be imputed to both. The older cases suggest that it would[4] whereas more recent authority suggests that any notice the common solicitor acquires affecting the same transaction will not, generally, be imputed to both[5].

1 *Magee v UDC Finance Ltd* [1983] NZLR 438.
2 *B v B (P Ltd intervening) (No 2)* [1995] 2 FCR 670, [1995] 1 FLR 374.
3 *Re Cousins* (1886) 31 Ch D 671, and the same principle applies where the same person acts as officer of two companies: *Re Hampshire Land Co* [1896] 2 Ch 743; *Mid-Glamorgan County Council v Ogwr Borough Council* (1994) 68 P & CR 1 at 10; *El Ajou v Dollar Land Holdings plc* [1994] 2 All ER 685 at 698, per Nourse LJ, cf Hoffmann LJ at 704. It has been said that if the mortgagor, being a solicitor himself, prepares the security, and no other solicitor is employed, the mortgagor will still be the mortgagee's solicitor; and it makes no difference that the mortgagee pays him nothing for his services, because it is the nature of the transaction that all the expenses should be borne by the mortgagor: *Kennedy v Green* (1834) 3 My & K 699; *Hewitt v Loosemore* (1851) 9 Hare 449; cf *Espin v Pemberton* (1859) 3 De G & J 547; *Kettlewell v Watson* (1884) 21 Ch D 685, but if the mortgagee employs no solicitor, it will not be assumed, in the absence of evidence, that the mortgagor's solicitor acted for him: *Atterbury v Wallis* (1856) 2 Jur NS 1177.
4 *Dryden v Frost* (1838) 3 My & Cr 670; *Meyer v Charters* (1918) 34 TLR 589; and see *Lloyds Bank Ltd v Marcan* [1973] 3 All ER 754, [1973] 1 WLR 1387, CA.
5 *Halifax Mortgage Services Ltd v Stepsky* [1996] Ch 1 affirmed on other grounds [1996] Ch 207. For a short summary of the facts see **24.41**, n 2. The reasoning would appear to be that as the disclosure of the subject matter of the notice to the party to whom it is sought to impute notice would be contrary to the interests of the other party, the solicitor is in a

position where his interests conflict and as such negates the duty of the agent to disclose the notice to the principal. (The Court of Appeal declined to endorse or reject this reasoning deciding the matter by reference to the Law of Property Act 1925, s 199, as to which see **24.40** and **24.41**. See also *Birmingham Midshires Mortgage Services v Mahal* (1996) 73 P & CR D7; *Barclays Bank plc v Thomson* [1997] 4 All ER 816 at 828/829; *National Westminster Bank plc v Beaton* (1997) 30 HLR 99; *Leamington Spa BC v Verdi* (1997) 75 P & CR D16. All of these cases concerned the question of imputed notice in the context of a common solicitor acting for the mortgagee and a surety of the mortgagor's liabilities.) Cf *El Ajou v Dollar Land Holdings* [1994] 2 All ER 685 at 702.

Fraud of agent

24.45 Notice to the agent is not imputed to the principal where the transaction effected by the agent is itself founded in fraud. The exclusion of imputed notice where the agent has acted fraudulently is based upon the fact that the agent is presumed not to have passed on knowledge of facts which would have revealed his fraud[1]. This rule is not altered by the statute; otherwise an agent, under its shelter, might use the knowledge which he acquired in one transaction for the purpose of committing a fraud in another. It is otherwise, however, where the matter is not connected with the fraud[2]. The burden of proof is upon the client to show the probability of non-communication of the fact by the agent[3].

1 See *Kennedy v Green* (1834) 3 My & K 699; *Cave v Cave* (1880) 15 Ch D 639; *Rhodes v Moules* [1895] 1 Ch 236. In *Espin v Pemberton* (1859) 3 De G & J 547 at 554, Lord Chemlsford LC put the exclusion on the basis that the fraud of the agent broke off the relation of principal and agent and went beyond the scope of authority and therefore prevented the possibility of imputing the knowledge of the agent to the principal. See also Watts (2001) 117 LQR 300.

2 See *Le Neve v Le Neve* (1747) 3 Atk 646; *Hewitt v Loosemore* (1851) 9 Hare 449; *Bradley v Riches* (1878) 9 Ch D 189.

3 *Thompson v Cartwright* (1836) 33 Beav 178.

CONSTRUCTIVE NOTICE OF THE RIGHTS OF THE SIGNATORY TO THE MORTGAGE TO SET IT ASIDE

24.46 If the mortgagee knows of certain facts which put him on inquiry as to the possible existence of the rights of a signatory to the mortgage to set aside the transaction and he fails to make such inquiry or take such other steps as are reasonable to verify whether such earlier right does or does not exist, he will have constructive notice of what he would have discovered if he had made reasonable inquiry. If he does make reasonable inquiry and the results of the inquiries are such as to allay suspicion, he takes free from the rights of the signatory. The circumstances in which the mortgagee is put on inquiry and the steps he has to take to take free of the signatory's right to set aside the transaction has recently been considered by the House of Lords[1].

1 *Royal Bank of Scotland v Etridge (No 2)* [2001] UKHL 44, [2001] 4 All ER 449, HL. A detailed treatment of this subject is to be found at **13.22–13.36**.

SALES BY THE COURT

24.47 Before 1882 notice operated in a transaction under the direction of the court, just as in any other case, for the court did not warrant the validity of titles, but only employed its officer to investigate them[1]. The Law of Property Act 1925[2] provides that an order of the court[3] under any statutory or other jurisdiction shall not, as against a purchaser[4], be invalidated on the ground of want of jurisdiction, or of want of any concurrence, consent, notice or service, whether the purchaser has notice of any such want or not. This section has effect with respect to any lease, sale or other act under the authority of the court[5] and purporting to be in pursuance of any statutory power notwithstanding any exception in such statute. This provision does not render an order binding on any estate or interest which, having regard to the terms and scope of the order, was not intended to be bound. It does not enable the court to sell and give a title to the property of A when it supposed that it was selling the property B[6]. It seems to follow that such an order would not protect a purchaser against an incumbrance, of which he had notice, if the court had no notice of it, and there was nothing in the order which suggested that the incumbrancer was intended to be bound. It is also considered that it protects only completed transactions and would not be available for a purchaser with regard to anything to be done in the future in cases where there has been fraud, although the purchaser had no notice of it[7]. On the other hand, where the court purports to bind a third party by the order, a purchaser will be protected, even though the order is on the face of it 'ultra vires'[8].

1 *Toulmin v Steere* (1817) 3 Mer 210; distinguished in *Re Howard's Estate* (1892) 29 LR Ir 266.
2 Section 204. The Act of 1925 reproduces s 70 of the Conveyancing Act 1881. The section applies to all orders made before or after the commencement of the Act.
3 'Court' means the High Court and the county courts, where those courts respectively have jurisdiction: s 203 (3). The grant of administration by the Probate Division is an 'order of court': *Hewson v Shelley* [1914] 2 Ch 13. As to judicial sale, see Chapter 21.
4 'Purchaser' means a purchaser in good faith for valuable consideration and includes 'a ... mortgagee': s 205 (1) (xxi).
5 It seems that if the court merely authorises the exercise of a statutory power out of court, the order only brings the power into force and enables the donee of the power, eg tenant for life, to bind the beneficiaries; it does not affect persons claiming under a paramount title: see Wolstenholme and Cherry *Conveyancing Statutes* (13th edn) vol 1, p 335.
6 *Jones v Barnett* [1900] 1 Ch 370.
7 See *Eyre v Burmester* (1862) 10 HL Cas 90; *Heath v Crealock* (1874) 10 Ch App 22; and cf *Pilcher v Rawlins* (1872) 7 Ch App 259.
8 *Re Hall-Dare's Contract* (1882) 21 Ch D 41; *Mostyn v Mostyn* [1893] 3 Ch 376.

LOSS OF PRIORITY: FRAUD AND GROSS NEGLIGENCE

POSTPONEMENT OF LEGAL MORTGAGEE

24.48 A legal mortgagee may by his conduct forfeit the priority which his legal estate gives him over an earlier equitable incumbrancer; and he may even, despite his holding the legal estate, be postponed to a subsequent equitable incumbrancer. Since 1926 the circumstances in which a mortgagee's priority may be lost by his conduct with respect to the title deeds is limited. Priority is principally governed by registration[1]. The mortgagee's conduct with the deeds is relevant only where the mortgage is unregistrable as being one accompanied by the title deeds.

1 See **24.3** ff.

First mortgage legal, subsequent mortgage equitable

24.49 The legal mortgagee will usually have priority by reason of the priority conferred upon a mortgage of a legal estate. The legal mortgagee will be postponed to a subsequent equitable incumbrancer if, owing to his conduct in regard to the deeds, it has been possible for the subsequent incumbrance to be created so that it would be inequitable to allow him to rely on his priority[1].

1 *Cottey v National Provincial Bank of England Ltd* (1904) 48 Sol Jo 589, 20 TLR 607; *Walker v Linom* [1907] 2 Ch 104; cf *Hudston v Viney* [1921] 1 Ch 98 and see *Tsang Chuen v Li Po Kwai* [1932] AC 715, PC. See Law Commission Working Paper No 99, Land Mortgages, para 3.16.

Postponement by fraud

24.50 Actual fraud is an obvious ground for postponement[1] and a mortgagee will be postponed to a subsequent incumbrance which has been created through his own fraud. Thus if the mortgagee has assisted in a fraud which has given rise to the creation of a subsequent equitable mortgage without notice of the prior legal mortgage, the prior legal interest will be postponed[2]. The principle also extends to the fraud of the mortgagee's solicitor although in such a case it must be shown that, at the time of the fraud, the relation of solicitor and client subsisted; it is not sufficient that it had previously subsisted[3].

1 *Birch v Ellames* (1794) 2 Anst 427 (legal mortgage antedated so as to validate it in bankruptcy and no inquiry made as to the object of a prior deposit of the deeds).
2 *Peter v Russell* (1716) 1 Eq Cas Abr 321; *Northern Counties of England Fire Insurance Co v Whipp* (1884) 26 Ch D 482 at 494.
3 *Finch v Shaw, Colyer v Finch* (1854) 19 Beav 500; affd sub nom *Colyer v Finch* (1856) 5 HL Cas 905. See also *Peter v Russell* (1716) 1 Eq Cas Abr 321.

Postponement by 'gross' negligence

24.51 The negligence which will cause an earlier legal mortgagee to be postponed may consist of failure to get the title deeds into the mortgagee's possession, or parting with them after they have been in his possession. The expression 'gross negligence' has been used to describe the degree of negligence required to postpone the mortgage. It is an expression which is incapable of precise definition[1]. In *Oliver v Hinton*[2] it was used to indicate a degree of negligence which made it unjust to enforce the natural order of priority. It was described in *Hudston v Viney*[3] as follows:

> 'It must at least be carelessness of so aggravated a nature as to amount to the neglect of precautions which the ordinary reasonable man would have observed, and to indicate an attitude of mental indifference to obvious risks'.

Fraud and negligence, even when it is gross negligence, are of a different nature, the one importing a design to commit the fraud, the other an omission due to carelessness or want of thought or attention[4]. The idea that there must be fraud has been dropped[5]. To postpone the legal mortgagee it is sufficient that there has been gross negligence on his part[6].

1 In *Wilson v Brett* (1843) 11 M & W 113 at 115 it was said that 'gross' added nothing but a 'vituperative epithet'.

2 [1899] 2 Ch 264, CA. In *Walker v Linom* [1907] 2 Ch 104, Parker J said:

> 'Any conduct on the part of the holder of the legal estate in relation to the deeds which would make it inequitable for him to rely on his legal estate against a prior equitable estate of which he had no notice ought also be sufficient to postpone him to a subsequent equitable estate the creation of which has only been rendered possible by the possession of deeds which but for such conduct would have passed into the possession of the owner of the legal estate.'

3 [1921] 1 Ch 98 at 104, per Eve J.
4 *Northern Counties Fire Insurance Co v Whipp* (1884) 26 Ch D 482 at 494, CA, per Fry LJ.
5 In *Evans v Bicknell* (1801) 6 Ves 174 at 189, Lord Eldon used the phrase 'gross negligence that amounts to evidence of a fraudulent intent'. In *Northern Counties Fire Insurance Co v Whipp*, above, a case in which a mortgagee had parted with the deeds, Fry LJ stated that fraud was required both for failing to obtain the deeds and to retain them. *Clarke v Palmeer* (1882) 21 Ch D 124 (no finding of fraud where mortgagee had failed to retain deeds and was duly postponed) and *Walker v Linom* [1907] 2 Ch 104 (failure by trustees to discover that settlor had retained a deed which enabled him to effect mortgage, trustees held negligent but not dishonest but postponed to subsequent mortgagee) are both consistent with the view that gross negligence alone is sufficient. It is now accepted by the textbook writers that gross negligence is sufficient: see *Coote on Mortgages* (9th edn) p 1341; Waldock *The Law of Mortgages* (2nd edn) pp 395–397; Sykes *The Law of Securities* (5th edn) pp 396-397.
6 See *Hunt v Elmes* (1860) 2 De GF & J 578; *Ratcliffe v Barnard* (1871) 6 Ch App 652, CA.

Obtaining deeds

24.52 A first legal mortgagee is entitled to possession of the deeds of the mortgaged property[1]. A legal mortgagee who does not acquire the deeds now constitutes a puisne mortgage and is required to register the same at the Land Charges Registry in order to maintain his priority[2]. It was formerly the case that a legal mortgagee who was entitled to the deeds could be postponed if he failed to exercise due diligence to obtain the deeds. Thus, a failure by the legal mortgagee to ask for the deeds resulted in his postponement to a subsequent equitable owner who exercised due diligence in inquiring for the deeds[3]. This was not the case if the mortgagee had asked for the deeds and had been given a reasonable excuse for their non-production[4] nor if he received some of the deeds reasonably believing them to be all[5]. A legal mortgagee was said not to be guilty of negligence in omitting to give notice of his mortgage, which was expressly granted subject to an earlier equitable mortgage, who held the deeds, with the result that the prior equitable mortgage was paid off and a new equitable mortgage created without notice of the legal mortgage[6].

1 Law of Property Act 1925, ss 85(1) proviso and 86(1) proviso (and see **3.69** ff). Thus, where a purchaser of land took a conveyance, but allowed the vendor to retain the deeds, and the vendor then mortgaged the land and delivered the deeds to the mortgagee, the purchaser was held to be entitled to recover the deeds from the mortgagee: *Harrington v Price* (1832) 3 B & Ad 170; see *Smith v Chichester* (1842) 2 Dr & War 393; and cf *Hunt v Elmes*, above (leasehold).
2 See **24.4**.
3 *Clarke v Palmeer* (1882) 21 Ch D 124; *Walker v Linom* [1907] 2 Ch D 104.
4 As to the provision of a reasonable excuse see **24.57**.
5 *Colyer v Finch* (1856) 5 HL Cas 905; *Hunt v Elmes* (1860) 2 De GF & J 578; *Northern Counties of England v Whipp* (1884) 26 Ch D 482 at 492.
6 *Grierson v National Provincial Bank of England* [1913] 2 Ch 18.This case would not arise now as the legal mortgagee would be a puisne mortgage in respect of which priority is determined by registration.

Custody of deeds

24.53 If the legal mortgagee having obtained possession of the deeds, returns them to the mortgagor[1], with the result that a subsequent mortgage or other disposition of the estate is accepted on the faith of the deeds, the legal mortgagee will lose his priority[2]. The same principles apply in cases in which the mortgagee has had, but has afterwards given up, or otherwise lost, the possession of the title deeds. If, under the circumstances, it can be inferred that he did this fraudulently, or if 'gross negligence' can be imputed to him, he will be postponed, not only in favour of the particular incumbrancer, who by the legal mortgagee's conduct has been induced to advance money on the estate, but also in favour of all later incumbrances, who, after making proper inquiries as to the deeds, have lent their money in ignorance of the original security[3].

1 It is not considered that the legal mortgagee, upon parting with the deeds, converts his mortgage into a puisne mortgage requiring registration as a land charge, so that if not registered it would be void as against a subsequent incumbrancer, see **24.4**, n 11.
2 *Commonwealth of Australia v Platzer* [1996] QLR 237.
3 *Perry-Herrick v Attwood* (1857) 2 De G & J 21; *Clarke v Palmer* (1882) 21 Ch D 124.

Delivery of deeds for raising money

24.54 This class of case depends not strictly on negligence, but upon the estoppel arising out of the circumstance that the legal mortgagee has enabled the mortgagor to represent himself as unincumbered owner. The mortgagee has by delivery of the deeds to the mortgagor either expressly or impliedly conferred on him authority to deal with the property. If the third party is unaware of any limitation on the authority so represented he will take free of it. Thus, where the first mortgagee delivered the deeds to the mortgagor for the express purpose of creating a security up to a limited amount, which was to have precedence to his own, and the mortgagor raised a larger sum, the first mortgage was postponed to the whole sum so raised[1]. Similarly, where the owner of property delivered the deeds to an agent in order to raise money up to a specified amount, and the agent raised money in excess of that amount and misappropriated the excess, the owner could only redeem on payment of the full amount raised[2]. The mortgagee was also postponed where he delivered the deeds to the mortgagor, in order to make a second mortgage, upon the faith that the mortgagor would disclose the first mortgage, which he omitted to do[3].

1 *Brocklesby v Temperance Permanent Building Society* [1895] AC 173, HL.
2 *Brocklesby v Temperance etc Society*, above; *Rimmer v Webster* [1902] 2 Ch 163.
3 *Briggs v Jones* (1870) LR 10 Eq 92; see *Re Lambert's Estate* (1884) 13 LR Ir 234.

Where legal mortgagee not postponed

24.55 The legal mortgagee is not, however, required to guarantee the safety of the deeds, and if in spite of his having taken proper precautions for their custody, they come into the hands of the mortgagor and are used by him for creating a subsequent incumbrance, the legal mortgagee will not be postponed[1]. Nor will he be postponed if he hands the deeds to the mortgagor upon his requesting them for a reasonable purpose[2]. If the purpose for which the deeds have been deposited is only temporary, the mortgagee will be postponed if he omits within a reasonable time to ensure the return of the deeds[3].

The mortgagee will not be postponed if the deeds come to the mortgagor's hands by the wrongful act of a third person to whom the mortgagee had properly delivered them[4]. Nor will he be postponed where it cannot be discovered by what means the deeds come back into the mortgagor's possession, provided there is nothing to show that he was enabled by the first mortgagee to commit the fraud. The mere possession of the deeds by the mortgagor, without evidence that he got them through the neglect or fraud of the mortgagee, is not enough to postpone the latter[5].

1 *Northern Counties of England Fire Insurance Co v Whipp* (1884) 26 Ch D 482, CA.
2 Eg that the mortgagor wants the deeds to enable him to grant a building lease advantageous to the estate: *Peter v Russell* (1716) 2 Vern 726 and see *Martinez v Cooper* (1826) 2 Russ 198; *Hall v West End Advance Co* (1883) Cab & El 161. As to the suggestion that on the legal mortgagee parting with the deeds his mortgage would become a puisne mortgage and would require to be registered as a land charge, so that if not registered it would be void as against a subsequent incumbrancer, see **24.4**, n 11.
3 *Waldron v Sloper* (1852) 1 Drew 193; dist'd in *Re Vernon, Evans & Co* (1886) 33 Ch D 402; and see *Dowle v Saunders* (1864) 2 Hem & M 242.
4 *Taylor v London and County Banking Co* [1901] 2 Ch 231.
5 *Allen v Knight* (1847) 11 Jur 527.

First mortgage equitable, subsequent mortgage legal

24.56 It is possible although unlikely that notwithstanding the fact that the equitable mortgagee holds the title deeds he may be postponed to a later legal incumbrancer. Where there is an earlier equitable mortgage, the priority of the legal mortgagee depends primarily on his taking without notice of it[1]. When the mortgagee who is taking a legal mortgage has notice[2] that there is a subsisting equitable charge, his title is subject to it, and if he is told that the charge has been cleared off, he must verify this; otherwise he takes his mortgage at his own risk[3]. The conduct which will postpone a legal mortgagee to a prior equitable incumbrancer of which he had no notice may be either actual fraud or gross negligence. Where the equitable incumbrance precedes the legal mortgage, gross negligence is the negligence described by Lindley MR in *Oliver v Hinton*[4] of such a type as would render it unjust to deprive the prior incumbrancer of his priority. Thus, a legal mortgagee will be postponed to a prior equitable incumbrancer who holds the deeds, if he has not investigated the title at all[5], or has not inquired for the deeds[6], or, having inquired, has accepted an insufficient reason for their non-production[7] or has failed to obtain the deeds through the deceit of the mortgagor, eg where the mortgagor assures the mortgagee that he has delivered to him all the deeds[8].

1 In *Snell's Equity* (13th edn) para 4.37, it is suggested that the application of the principle of postponement by reason of the gross negligence of the legal mortgagee is unnecessary 'since the legal owner will be postponed by the doctrine of constructive notice in failing to make such investigations as a prudent purchaser ought to have made'.
2 As to notice, **24.27** ff.
3 *Jared v Clements* [1903] 1 Ch 428.
4 [1899] 2 Ch 264, CA. See **24.51**.
5 *Oliver v Hinton* [1899] 2 Ch 264.
6 *Hewitt v Loosemore* (1851) 9 Hare 449; *Berwick & Co v Price* [1905] 1 Ch 632; especially if the abstention from inquiry was to avoid having knowledge of a prior incumbrance: *Ratcliffe v Barnard* (1871) 6 Ch App 652. The failure to inquire for the deeds or the inability of the mortgagor to produce the deeds would amount to constructive notice of the earlier equitable charge: see **24.33**. He does not have constructive notice of the earlier incumbrance

where having made a request for the deeds he is given a reasonable excuse for their non-production: see **24.57** as to the provision of a reasonable excuse.

7 As to the provision of a reasonable excuse which will not adversely affect priority see **24.57**.

8 *Roberts v Croft* (1857) 2 De G & J 1; *Hunt v Elmes* (1860) 2 De GF & J 578; *Dixon v Mucklestone* (1872) 8 Ch App 155, and see *Ratcliffe v Barnard*, above; *Colyer v Finch*, above.

Reasonable excuse

24.57 If a reasonable excuse has been given for the non-production of the deeds the legal mortgagee will not lose his priority[1]. The question, what is a reasonable excuse, must always be decided in the light of the particular circumstances of the case. Where the mortgagee, a farmer, took a legal mortgage of a leasehold interest from a solicitor but failed to obtain possession of the lease, which in fact had already been deposited with the claimant, on the mortgagor's excuse that he was then busy but he would give it to him at another time, the mortgagee was not postponed to the claimant[2]. In some cases, however, false statements as to the place or nature of the custody of the deeds have been held not to relieve the person who accepts them for notice of the real facts, when by inquiry the truth could easily have been discovered[3].

1 *Hewitt v Loosemore* (1851) 9 Hare 449; *Espin v Pemberton* (1859) 4 Drew 333. This principle applies equally to competing equitable interests in registered land: *Barclays Bank Ltd v Taylor* [1974] Ch 137,CA.

2 *Hewitt v Loosemore*, above.

3 *Maxfield v Burton* (1873) LR 17 Eq 15; *Spencer v Clarke* (1878) 9 Ch D 137: but see *Agra Bank Ltd v Barry* (1874) LR 7 HL 135.

POSTPONEMENT OF EQUITABLE INCUMBRANCER

Date of creation

24.58 As between equitable incumbrancers, the prima facie rule is that the incumbrancers rank in order of time, 'qui prior tempore potior est jure'[1]. When two equitable interests are of the same quality, so that neither can be said to be superior to the other, the fact that the incumbrancer who is the later in time has possession of the deeds may give him the better equity and cause the earlier incumbrance to be postponed[2]. The mere possession of the title deeds is not enough to give a subsequent incumbrancer priority over an earlier one[3]. There is inequality of the interest only when there has been some default on the part of the prior equitable incumbrancer in respect of the deeds, and in effect he is postponed by reason of his default or negligence[4].

It has been seen that gross negligence may postpone a legal mortgagee[5]. The negligence which will postpone an equitable incumbrancer appears never to have been described in these terms and a distinction has been drawn between the gross negligence which will postpone a legal mortgagee and the slighter negligence which will postpone a prior equitable mortgagee to a later[6]. The question in the latter case is whether the earlier incumbrancer has acted in such a way that he is not justified in insisting on his prima facie priority[7]. According to the modern view, however, this amounts to the test for the negligence which will postpone a legal mortgagee. It is such negligence as would render it unjust to deprive the prior equitable incumbrancer of his priority[8]. It would seem, therefore, that there is no difference between the tests for the two cases and in each the question is whether the conduct of the legal mortgagee or the equitable mortgagee has been such as will justifiably deprive him of the priority given to him either by the possession of the legal estate or by his being first in time[9].

Accordingly, the prior equitable incumbrancer was postponed where the deeds were left in the possession of the mortgagor, because he thereby enabled the mortgagor to deal with the property as if it were free from incumbrance[10]. The prior equitable incumbrancer was, similarly, postponed where, without adequate reason, he parted with the deeds after he had them in his possession[11]. It was otherwise where there was no default attributable to the prior incumbrancer[12]. Where notice by an equitable mortgagee is not required to be given for his own protection, the omission to give notice is not a ground for postponing him, although the notice might have prevented the creation of a subsequent incumbrance[13].

1 *Rice v Rice* (1853) 2 Drew 73 at 78. For the modern application of the same rule to things in action and equitable interests in land, see Law of Property Act 1925, s 137 (1).
2 See *Rice v Rice* (1854) 2 Drew 73 at 81, per Kindersley V-C. See also *McCarthy and Stone Ltd v Julian S Hodge & Co Ltd* [1971] 2 All ER 973, [1971] 1 WLR 1547; *Heid v Reliance Finance Corpn Pty Ltd* (1984) 154 CLR 326. The mere possession of the title deeds is not enough to give a subsequent incumbrancer priority over an earlier one: *Evans v Bicknell* (1801) 6 Ves 174 at 183.
3 *Evans v Bicknell* (1801) 6 Ves 174 at 183. An equitable mortgage by the simple deposit of deeds cannot now be created, see **3.90–3.100**. If the earlier equitable incumbrance constitutes a general equitable charge for the purposes of the Land Charges Act 1972, s 2(4) (as to which see **24.4**. The statutory wording is to be found in n 4) priority is maintained by registration.
4 *Farrand v Yorkshire Banking Co* (1888) 40 Ch D 182; *Flinn v Pountain* (1889) 58 LJ Ch 389. Where an option holder had failed to protect the option at the Land Registry that in itself would not be a reason for postponing the equitable interest as against a subsequent equitable incumbrancer. However, as the option holder had entered into a wholly artificial transaction to give the world the impression that the land owner, subject to the option, was the unencumbered owner to deal with it as he pleased, the equities were not equal and the option holder was postponed to the later equitable incumbrance: *Freeguard v Royal Bank of Scotland plc* (1998) 79 P & CR 81,CA. As to priorities where the title to land is registered see **24.69** ff.
5 See **24.51**.
6 *Farrand v Yorkshire Banking Co* (1888) 40 Ch D 182. Applied in *Mortgage Corpn Ltd v Nationwide Credit Corpn Ltd* [1994] Ch 49.
7 *Kettlewell v Watson* (1882) 21 Ch D 685; *National Provincial Bank of England v Jackson* (1886) 33 Ch D 1.
8 See **24.51**.
9 This view was most emphatically expressed by Kay J in *Taylor v Russell* [1891] 1 Ch 8 at 17. His judgment was reversed by the Court of Appeal ([1891] 1 Ch 24), but on another point, and the question of negligence as between rival equities was not discussed. In the House of Lords ([1892] AC 244 at 262) Lord Macnaghten referred to the point, but only to say that he was not convinced of the correctness of Kay J's view. See also *Taylor v London and County Banking Co* [1901] 2 Ch 231 at 260, per Stirling LJ. Since priorities are now mainly determined by registration, the question is unlikely to be determined. See Law Commission Working Paper no 99, Land Mortgages, para 3.16. See also (1998) 18 NZ Univ L Rev 46 (for a more restricted approach as to the postponement of the earlier equitable interest).
10 *Layard v Maud* (1867) LR 4 Eq 397. This case would not arise today as a mortgage unaccompanied by the deposit of the title deeds will be registrable as either a pusine mortgage or a general equitable charge under the Land Charges Act 1972. See **24.4**.
11 *Waldron v Sloper* (1852) 1 Drew 193.
12 *Allen v Knight* (1847) 5 Hare 272; *Re Castell and Brown Ltd* [1898] 1 Ch 315.
13 *Union Bank of London v Kent* (1888) 39 Ch D 238.

LOSS OF PRIORITY: ESTOPPEL

24.59 The priority conferred by the possession of the legal estate or the date of creation operate to the advantage of a mortgagee only if the equities are in other respects equal. A person entitled to a charge over an interest in property who has, knowingly or unknowingly, allowed or encouraged a subsequent incumbrancer to assume to his detriment that his security has priority may be estopped from asserting priority if it would be unconscionable to do so[1]. Thus, where an equitable incumbrancer acts in such a way as to enable the owner of the land to represent that the incumbrance no longer exists, as where, for instance, the incumbrancer executes a conveyance containing a receipt for the money due to him, although it is not in fact paid[2] his priority may be postponed. This is in accordance with the doctrine of estoppel by representation, recognised both at law and in equity, namely, that where one by his words or conduct causes another to believe the existence of a certain state of things, and induces him to act on that belief, and the latter in so doing alters his own position, the former cannot aver against him the existence of a different state of things[3]. A representation as to the non-existence of the earlier legal mortgage may arise where the legal mortgagee has returned the deeds in order to enable the mortgagor to raise further moneys[4]. If, for instance, the first mortgagee leaves the deeds in the possession of the mortgagor, who requires them for the purpose of raising a further advance, on the understanding, however, that the existence of the prior mortgage will be disclosed, and the mortgagor conceals the prior incumbrance, the mortgagee will not, as against third parties, be able to claim that the mortgagor was acting in excess of his authority[5].

1 *Taylors Fashions Ltd v Liverpool Victoria Trustees Ltd* [1982] QB 133n at 151-152. As to the postponement on the basis of estoppel of a beneficial co-owner and of a vendor seeking to rely on a lien for the purchase moneys, see **24.74** and **24.68** respectively.
2 *Rice v Rice* (1853) 2 Drew 73; *Lloyds Bank Ltd v Bullock* [1896] 2 Ch 192; *Rimmer v Webster* [1902] 2 Ch 163 at 175; *Jared v Clements* [1903] 1 Ch 428.
3 *Pickard v Sears* (1837) 6 Ad & El 469 per Lord Denham CJ. See also *Kettlewell v Wilson* (1884) 26 Ch D 501; *Cannock v Jauncey* (1857) 27 LJ Ch 57.
4 See **24.54** and *Commonwealth Bank v Platzer* [1996] QCA 237.
5 *Perry-Herrick v Attwood* (1857) 2 De G & J 21; *Northern Counties of England Fire Insurance Co v Whipp* (1884) 26 Ch D 482. See Farwell J in *Rimmer v Webster* [1902] 2 Ch 163 at 173; 'When ... the owner is found to have given the vendor or borrower the means of representing himself as the beneficial owner, the case forms one of actual authority apparently equivalent to absolute ownership, and involving the right to deal with the property as owner, and any limitations on this generally must be proved to have been brought to the knowledge of the purchaser or mortgagee.'

CONCLUSION

24.60 Throughout the many and various instances of cases in which the mortgagee may lose his priority, whether it be a legal mortgagee to a prior or even subsequent equitable incumbrancer, or an equitable incumbrancer to another, and whether the grounds of such loss be actual fraud, negligence, misrepresentation or estoppel, there runs the principle that priority may be lost if the conduct of the mortgagee, who prima facie has priority, is such that it would be unjust, on the particular facts and in relation to one or more of the foregoing heads, to postpone another mortgagee whose claim is more deserving of merit.

PRIORITY BETWEEN EQUITABLE INCUMBRANCES

Rule of priority in time

24.61 Subject to the statutory effect of registration[1], equitable incumbrances rank in order of date of creation, provided the equities are otherwise equal[2]. This is in accordance with the maxim 'qui prior est tempore, potior est jure' and has been justified on the ground that the first equitable incumbrancer has a vested interest which cannot be displaced except for strong reasons[3]. The rule is also a consequence of the principle that a mortgagor cannot grant more than he is justly entitled to. Hence, after he has diminished his ownership by the grant of an equitable mortgage, a second equitable mortgage is necessarily subject to the first[4].

1 See the discussion at **24.4–24.12**.
2 See *Rice v Rice* (1854) 2 Drew 73 at 78; *Capell v Winter* [1907] 2 Ch 376 at 381.
3 See *Willoughby v Willoughby* (1756) 1 Term Rep 763 at 773, per Lord Hardwicke C; *Cory v Eyre* (1863) 1 De GJ & Sm 149 at 167, per Turner LJ.
4 *Phillips v Phillips* (1862) 4 De GF & J 208 at 215, per Lord Westbury C; *Cave v Cave* (1880) 15 Ch D 639; *Latec Investments Ltd v Hotel Terrigal Pty Ltd (in Liquidation)* (1965) 113 CLR 265; *McCarthy & Stone Ltd v Julian S Hodge & Co Ltd* [1971] 2 All ER 973, [1971] 1 WLR 1547.

Contemporaneous instruments

24.62 Where several instruments have been executed on the same day, priority will follow the order of execution, subject to any contrary intention appearing on the deeds, and an inquiry may be directed to ascertain the times of execution if uncertain[1].

1 *Gartside v Silkstone and Dodworth Coal Co* (1882) 21 Ch D 762.

Operation of the rule

24.63 In accordance with the above rule, the claim of an equitable mortgagee will prevail against the solicitor of the mortgagor into whose hands the deeds subsequently come and the solicitor cannot thereby acquire any lien for his costs[1]. Moreover, where the mortgagor made two securities by depositing part of the deeds with one person and part with another, the former had preference[2].

1 *Molesworth v Robbens* (1845) 2 Jo & Lat 358; *Smith v Chichester* (1842) 2 Dr & War 393; *Pelly v Wathen* (1851) 1 De GM & G 16.
2 *Roberts v Croft* (1857) 24 Beav 223; see *Dixon v Mucklestone* (1872) 8 Ch App 155.

Rule applies to equitable interests generally

24.64 The rule is not confined to priority as between equitable incumbrances, but applies to equitable interests generally[1]. A mere equity to set aside a deed will, however, be postponed to an actual equitable interest created for valuable consideration under the deed[2].

1 An equitable mortgagee by deposit of deeds was postponed to a prior purchaser, whose purchase (without negligence on his part) has not been completed: *Flinn v Pountain* (1889) 58 LJ Ch 389; *McCarthy & Stone Ltd v Julian S Hodge & Co Ltd*, above. An equitable mortgage by a deposit of deeds alone cannot now be created: see **3.90–3.100**.

2 *Roddy v Williams* (1845) 3 Jo & Lat 1; *Hiorns v Holton* (1852) 16 Beav 259; *Phillips v Phillips*, above; *French v Hope* (1887) 56 LJ Ch 363, but see *Latec Investments Ltd v Hotel Terrigal Pty Ltd*, above.

The better equity prevails[1]

24.65 The rule as to priority in time is subject to the important qualification that the equities of the rival incumbrancers are in other respects equal. Equality means here the non-existence of any circumstances which affects the conduct of one of the rival claimants and makes it less meritorious than that of the other[2]. Thus, in one case[3], a vendor conveyed without receiving the purchase money, but a receipt was indorsed on the conveyance and the title deeds delivered to the purchaser. The purchaser then created a mortgage by deposit of the deeds and absconded. It was held that the indorsement of the receipt and the possession of the title deeds gave the mortgagee the better equity and he had priority over the vendor's lien. However, in a case in which the first incumbrancer is postponed on the ground of negligence, the better equity of a later incumbrancer is usually founded on the negligence of the first[4].

1 On the theoretical basis for granting priority—whether the basis is in the doctrine of estoppel or a more general principle of the better equity, see *Heid v Reliance Finance Corpn Pty Ltd* (1984) 154 CLR 326, 339 ff.

2 *Bailey v Barnes* [1894] 1 Ch 25, per Lindley LJ, and see *McCarthy & Stone Ltd v Julian S Hodge & Co Ltd* [1971] 2 All ER 973, [1971] 1 WLR 1547. See also **24.58**.

3 *Rice v Rice*, above.

4 In *Bradley v Riches* (1878) 9 Ch D 189, Fry J said that priority might be displaced by showing either fraud on the part of the earlier mortgagee, or a better equity in the later, but, on another view, there appears to be no real alternative. As to postponement on the ground of negligence, see **24.58**.

Mortgages in breach of trust

24.66 The question of the values of rival equities arises where a trustee creates an equitable mortgage in breach of trust. The courts of this country[1] have held that the interest of the beneficiary is of the same quality as the interest of the equitable mortgagee, and being prior in time it prevails[2], provided the beneficiary has no reason to suspect want of good faith on the part of the trustee. The fact that the beneficiary has created the trust for his own purposes, and has allowed the deeds to remain in the custody of the trustee, is not negligence so as to postpone him[3]. It makes no difference that the mortgaged property belongs partly to the trustee himself[4]. This will be so, however, only where the deeds have in the first place come into the possession of the trustee. If he negligently omits to get them in, and is postponed on this ground, the beneficiary is postponed also[5].

If the transaction is authorised by the trust, and the deed contains a proper receipt clause, the equitable title taken under the trustee will prevail[6]. But this will not be so when, the trustee having power to sell only, the transaction, while in form a sale, is, in substance, a mortgage[7].

If trustees invest the trust fund upon property which, by the terms of the purchase, becomes subject to an obligation, the beneficiaries are bound by the obligation, though the transaction was a breach of trust, so long as they claim the benefit of the purchase[8]. Where the trustee improperly invests the trust fund in the purchase of land the beneficiaries are entitled to follow it into the land. This right is not a mere equity, but gives them an equitable interest in the land, so that they will not be postponed to an equitable incumbrancer under the trustee without notice[9].

The above principles have no application to the case of negotiable instruments, the legal interest in which passes by indorsement or delivery free from all equities, unless the transferee has notice[10].

1 In Ireland, it has been held that the mortgagee has the better equity: see *Re Bobbett's Estate* [1904] 1 IR 461; *Scott v Scott* [1924] 1 IR 141.
2 *Cave v Cave* (1880) 15 Ch D 639; *Coleman v London County and Westminster Bank Ltd* [1916] 2 Ch 353 at 361; *Walker v Linom* [1907] 2 Ch 104 at 114 ff. Similarly, where a personal representative charges the estate for his own purposes, the estate has priority over the mortgagee: *Re Morgan, Pillgrem v Pillgrem* (1881) 18 Ch D 93.
3 *Carrit v Real and Personal Advance Co* (1889) 42 Ch D 263.
4 *Cory v Eyre* (1863) 1 De GJ & Sm 149 at 169; *Bradley v Riches* (1878) 9 Ch D 189.
5 *Walker v Linom* [1907] 2 Ch 104. An equitable mortgagee accompanied by a deposit of earlier title deeds will retain his priority over a mortgagee by deposit of the subsequent deeds, if he was led by the mortgagor to believe that they were the whole of the deeds: *Roberts v Croft* (1857) 2 De G & J 1; *Dixon v Muckleston* (1872) 8 Ch App 155.
6 *Lloyds Bank v Bullock* [1896] 2 Ch 192.
7 *Capell v Winter* [1907] 2 Ch 376.
8 *New London and Brazilian Bank v Brocklebank* (1882) 21 Ch D 302.
9 *Cave v Cave* (1880) 15 Ch D 639.
10 See *London Joint Stock Bank v Simmons* [1892] AC 201; *Jameson v Union Bank of Scotland* (1914) 109 LT 850.

Mortgagee from defaulting trustee

24.67 The right of trustees to be indemnified out of the trust property in respect of the liabilities incurred in the exercise of their office is to be preferred to any charge created by the beneficiary[1]. However, since a defaulting trustee, who also has a beneficial interest, cannot share in the trust estate till his own default has been made good, a mortgagee from him is in the same position and will be postponed to claims of the beneficiaries[2].

1 *Re Exhall Coal Co* (1860) 35 Beav 449, but the trustee cannot set up against an assignee of the beneficiary a debt to him incurred by the beneficiary after notice: *Re Pain, Gustavson v Haviland* [1919] 1 Ch 38.
2 *Doering v Doering* (1889) 42 Ch D 203, for the application of the same principle to derivative interests.

Rights as between equitable mortgagee and unpaid vendor[1]

24.68 As soon as a binding contract for the sale of land is entered into the vendor has a lien on the property for the purchase money and a right to remain in possession of the property until the money is paid. The lien does not arise on completion but on exchange of contracts. It is discharged on completion to the extent that the purchase money is paid[2]. Even if the vendor executes an outright conveyance of the legal estate in favour of a purchaser and delivers the title deeds to him, he still retains an equitable lien on the property to secure the payment of any part of the purchase money which remains unpaid. The lien is not excluded by the fact that the conveyance contains an express receipt for the purchase money. Where, however, an unpaid vendor hands to the purchaser the title deeds with a conveyance containing a receipt for the purchase money, he thereby enables the purchaser to represent himself as the owner of the property and he will be postponed to an equitable mortgagee from the purchaser who obtains the deeds[3]. The lien arises by operation of law and does not depend on the subjective intention of the parties[4]. Thus it is irrelevant to the existence of the lien that the vendor is unaware that equity confers upon him a lien for the purchase price[5]. The lien is excluded where its retention would be inconsistent with the provision of the contract of sale or with the nature of the transaction between the parties. Thus it is excluded where on completion the vendor receives all he bargained for. If, therefore, the agreement is that the outstanding balance of the purchase price is to be secured by a charge on the property the lien never comes into existence, for it is by agreement replaced by the charge[6]. This is so notwithstanding the fact that the vendor's lien is void for want of registration as a land charge under the Land Charges Act[7]. The vendor may be taken to have agreed to postpone his lien. Thus where the vendor enabled the purchaser to deal with the estate as an absolute owner free from the lien the vendor was taken to agree to a postponement of his priority so as to be unable to assert the lien against the sub-purchasers[8]. If the unpaid vendor remains in possession as tenant to the purchaser, there is no notice to a subsequent incumbrancer of his lien for unpaid purchase money[9].

A vendor's lien is registrable as a land charge at the Land Charges Register[10]. It is void against a purchaser for value of an interest in the land subject to the lien[11]. For the purposes of registered land a vendor's lien is an overriding interest[12].

1 See also **2.39–2.47**.
2 *Re Birmingham* [1959] Ch 523, cited with approval in *London and Cheshire Insurance Co Ltd v Laplagrene Co* [1971] Ch 499 at 514.
3 *Rice v Rice* (1854) 2 Drew 73; *Smith v Evans* (1860) 28 Beav 59. A prior incumbrancer who has been induced by misrepresentation to release his security will not, however, necessarily be postponed: *Beckett v Cordley* (1784) 1 Bro CC 353.
4 *Barclays Bank plc v Estates and Commercial Ltd* [1997] 1 WLR 415, 74 P & CR 30, CA.
5 *Barclays Bank plc v Estates and Commercial Ltd*, above.
6 *Nationwide Anglia Building Society v Ahmed* (1995) 70 P & CR 381, CA. See also the earlier decisions of *Capital Finance Co Ltd v Stokes* [1969] 1 Ch 261 and *Congresbury Motors Ltd v Anglo-Belge Finance Co Ltd* [1971] Ch 81.
7 *Capital Finance Co Ltd v Stokes* [1969] 1 Ch 261 and *Congresbury Motors Ltd v Anglo-Belge Finance Co Ltd* [1971] Ch 81.
8 *Kettlewell v Watson* (1884) 26 Ch D 501, CA.
9 *White v Wakefield* (1835) 7 Sim 401 at 417.
10 As a general equitable charge within Class C(iii), Land Charges Act 1972, s 2(4); *Uziell-Hamilton v Keen* (1971) 22 P & CR 655. See also [1997] Conv 336 at 342.
11 Land Charges Act 1972, s 4(5). See **24.10**.
12 *Nationwide Anglia Building Society v Ahmed* (1995) 70 P & CR 381, CA.

MORTGAGES OF THE LEGAL ESTATE: REGISTERED LAND

Registered charges

24.69 By s 29 of the Land Registration Act 1925, charges on registered land rank in the order in which they are entered on the register, rather than according to the order in which they are created.

This, however, is subject to other arrangements[1], made between the parties, and the order of priority may be varied, provided the variation appears on the register[2]. Such variation may be made by a clause in the instrument of charge providing for the charges to rank either equally, or otherwise in a manner different from the rule in s 29. An alteration in priorities can be made after the registration of the charge by further deed. It requires the consent of the proprietor of the registered land and of the proprietors of all registered charges (if any) of equal or inferior priority, affected by the alteration. The alteration is completed by entry on the register[3]. A subsequent registered charge has priority to any prior charge not registered or protected on the register[4].

1 As to agreements altering the priorities, see **24.123**.
2 A may be estopped from denying that B's charge takes priority on the basis of a representation that B's charge should rank before his own, on which B had acted to his detriment. See *Nationwide Anglia Building Society v Ahmed* (1995) 70 P & CR 381 at 390.
3 Land Registration Act 1925, s 31; Land Registration Rules r 150: Form 51.
4 Sections 20, 23; see *De Lusignan v Johnson* (1973) 230 Estates Gazette 499. A constructive trust may prevail over the provisions of the legislation: see *Lyus v Prowsa Developments Ltd* [1982] 2 All ER 953, [1982] 1 WLR 1044.

Lien by deposit of land certificate

24.70 Prior to the commencement of the Law of Property (Miscellaneous Provisions) Act 1989[1], it was possible to create a mortgage of unregistered land by deposit of the title deeds with the lender[2]. In respect of registered land, the equivalent was the lien which could be created by deposit of the land certificate[3]. After 26 September 1989, such a charge is only valid if it complies with the requirements for a written document incorporating the terms agreed by the parties and signed by them[4]. In respect of liens created by deposit of the land certificate prior to 3 April 1995, where a notice of deposit has been given to the Registrar, it will operate as a caution under s 54 of the Land Registration Act 1925[5], which would protect any further dealings with the land[6]. However, after 3 April 1995, it is no longer possible to apply for the entry of a notice of deposit of the land certificate[7] and if a lien has been validly created, priority will only be obtained by the entry of a notice under s 49(1) of the Land Registration Act 1925.

1 26 September 1989.
2 See **3.90** ff.
3 Section 66; **3.91**.
4 Law of Property (Miscellaneous Provisions) Act 1989, s 2; *United Bank of Kuwait v Sahib* [1997] Ch 107.
5 Land Registration Rules 1925, r 239.
6 Although the entry of a caution does not regulate the priority of the interest protected — see below.
7 Land Registration Rules 1995 (SI 1995/140), r 4.

Unregistered mortgages of registered land

24.71 A mortgage off the register may be created, by deed or otherwise, and such a mortgage takes effect in equity and should be protected by a notice or a caution. However, priority over a subsequent registered charge cannot be conferred either by entering a caution[1], or even a notice[2]. Accordingly, in relation to equitable mortgages, priority is determined, prima facie, by the order of creation rather than the date of protection, subject to the exception of gross carelessness or inequitable conduct[3].

1 *Clark v Chief Land Registrar* [1993] Ch 294.
2 *Mortgage Corpn Ltd v Nationwide Credit Corpn Ltd* [1994] Ch 49.
3 See *Barclays Bank Ltd v Taylor* [1974] Ch 137, [1973] 1 All ER 752, CA, *Williams & Glyn's Bank Ltd v Boland* [1981] AC 487 at 504, [1980] 2 All ER 408 at 412, per Lord Wilberforce (the law as to notice as it may affect purchasers of unregistered land has no application even by analogy to registered land). For the confused state of priorities of mortgages of registered land see [1966] CLP 26 (Ryder); (1971) 35 Conv (NS) 122, 168 (Robinson); (1974) 124 NLJ 634 (Robinson): Law Commission Report Transfer of Land — Land Mortgages 1991 (Law Com no 204, para 3.22). Under systems of title registration, the system of registration generally replaces the former rules of equitable priorities (see eg *Farrier-Waimak Ltd v Bank of New Zealand* [1965] AC 376, [1964] 3 All ER 657, PC) and failure to use the system's methods of protection may lead to loss of priority against a subsequent unregistered or protected equitable mortgage: see *Lapin v Abigail* (1930) 44 CLR 166 (on appeal *Abigail v Lapin* [1934] AC 491, PC). See also *Freeguard v Royal Bank of Scotland* (1998) 79 P & CR 81. See also *Abbey National Building Society v Cann* [1991] 1 AC 56, HL; *Lloyds Bank plc v Rosset* [1991] 1 AC 107, HL. For the priority point in relation to a mortgage and other interests in registered land, see *Paddington Building Society v Mendelsohn* (1985) 50 P & CR 244; [1986] Conv 57 at 58–59 (Thompson).

Tacking further advances

24.72 Section 94 of the Law of Property Act 1925, which abolishes the doctrine of tacking in general, whilst providing for tacking in cases where the mortgage is originally made to cover further advances, applies only to unregistered land. The equivalent provision in relation to registered land is s 30 of the Land Registration Act 1925[1]. Apart from this, a further advance can only be safely made after searching the register and it must be protected by a new registered charge or an alteration of the existing charge[2]. This will then take its place in due order according to the register[3].

1 See **24.88**.
2 See **24.88**.
3 See **24.69**.

PRIORITY BETWEEN MORTGAGEE AND TENANT

24.73 Questions of priority often arise between a mortgagee and a tenancy whether granted before of after the mortgage. This subject is dealt with at **19.16–19.27**.

PRIORITY BETWEEN MORTGAGEE AND BENEFICIAL CO-OWNER

24.74 The interest of a beneficial co-owner of property, being an undivided share in land, can take effect only in equity. A disposition of the legal estate to, for instance, a mortgagee, will overreach the trust of land pursuant to which the undivided shares are held[1]. Overreaching arises out of and is a corollary of the exercise of a trust power to sell[2]. The sale must, however, be in accordance with the trust powers and the requirements of the Law of Property Act 1925. If the purchase moneys, including an advance by a mortgagee, is paid to at least two trustees[3] or a trust corporation, the purchaser takes free from the equitable interest whether or not he has notice of it[4]. Where moneys are advanced to acquire property, the mere fact that a person is contributing to the purchase price does not however confer priority upon him in preference to the mortgagee as, albeit the purchase moneys may be paid only to a sole trustee, normally the husband in whose sole name the property is to be transferred, the transfer and the mortgage are to be regarded as taking place simultaneously so there is no scintilla temporis in which the co-owner is able to gain priority[5]. By borrowing money for the security of which he is contractually bound to grant a mortgage to the lender eo instante with the execution of the conveyance in his favour, the legal owner cannot in reality ever be said to have acquired even for a scintilla temporis the unencumbered fee simple or leasehold estate in land whereby he could grant interests having priority over the mortgage[6].

Most problems arise where an advance is made subsequent to the acquisition. If the occupier is aware that the sole trustee and legal owner is raising money on the security of the property the beneficial co-owner will be estopped from claiming priority to the mortgagee[7]. The imputed intention to postpone the equitable interest to that of the mortgagee continues to apply to any mortgage replacing the first, at least up to the sum secure[8] under the first and this is so whether or not the equitable co-owner knew of the second mortgage[9]. Alternatively, the second replacement mortgage is to be viewed as being subrogated to the rights of the first[10]. In light of these decisions and the approach taken by the courts to acquisition mortgages, mortgagees are conferred a considerable degree of protection against trust beneficiaries. A mortgagee it would appear is only at risk to being postponed in his priority over a beneficial co-owner where he is dealing with a sole trustee and the beneficial co-owner is genuinely unaware of the proposed advance. Such a risk may be avoided by obtaining a waiver of priority[11].

The equitable interest of the co-owner may be postponed to that of the mortgagee by express agreement[12]. However, in many cases this device has proved inadequate, not least because occupiers who have given such consent have sought to claim that it has been vitiated by duress or undue influence[13].

Where the title to the land is unregistered, the question of whether the mortgagee has priority over the beneficial interest of the co-owner depends on whether he has notice of it[14]. Where the title to the land is registered the rights of every person in occupation[15], including the right of a beneficial co-owner of property to occupy the property, constitute an overriding interest[16]. The rights of the occupier can be avoided and priority obtained only if enquiry is made of the occupier and such rights are not disclosed[17]. Enquiries of someone other than the occupier, eg the spouse, is insufficient[18]. The occupier must be in occupation at the date of the transfer in order to obtain protection[19].

1 The beneficial interests overreached are shifted from the land and attach to the capital monies arising on the disposition: (1986) 49 MLR 345 (Thompson); (1986) 136 NLJ 208 (Hayton); (1986) 136 NLJ 771 (Luxton); [1986] Conv 309 (Sparkes).

2 *State Bank of India v Sood* [1997] Ch 276, CA; overreachable rights consist of those interests readily converted into the capital proceeds arising upon the disposition: *Birmingham Midshires Mortgage Service Ltd v Sabherwal* (1999) 80 P & CR 256, CA.

3 Where the legal title is vested in one person only but held on an implied trust for himself and another, normally the spouse, the mortgagee is of course unaware of the need to pay the capital moneys to two trustees.

4 Law of Property Act 1925, ss 2(1)(ii) and 27(2) (as amended by Law Property (Amendment) Act 1926, Sch; Trusts of Land and Appointments of Trustees Act 1996, s 25(1), Sch 3); *City of London Building Society v Flegg* [1988] AC 54, HL. Payment to fewer than two trustees or a trust corporation does not effect an overreaching of the beneficial interest under the trust of land either in registered or unregistered land. However, s 27 requires payment to two trustees only where capital moneys arise on the disposition of the legal estate. The requirement for payment to two trustees does not arise if no capital money arises on the disposition, eg where the money has been paid in advance or is drawn down subsequently as in the case of an overdraft facility: *State Bank of India v Sood* [1997] Ch 276, CA.
5 *Abbey National Building Society v Cann* [1991] 1 AC 56, HL.
6 At 102, per Lord Jauncey.
7 *Bristol and West Building Society v Henning* [1985] 1 WLR 778, CA (unregistered land); *Paddington Building Society v Mendlesohn* (1985) 50 P & CR 244, CA (registered land); *Skipton Building Society v Clayton* (1993) 66 P & CR 223 at 229, CA.
8 Including accrued interest.
9 *Equity & Law Home Loans v Prestidge* [1992] 1 WLR 137, CA.
10 *Castle Phillips Finance v Piddington* [1995] 1 FLR 783.
11 See **24.123**.
12 An alternative has been to require the beneficial owner to sign a licence agreement in which it is acknowledged that the occupation of the land does not arise by virtue of any beneficial entitlement but only as licensee: *Kemmis v Kemmis* [1988] 1 WLR 1307 at 1335.
13 *Barclays Bank plc v O'Brien* [1994] 1 AC 180, HL. See **13.22** ff.
14 *Kingsworth Finance Co Ltd v Tizard* [1986] 1 WLR 783. As to the entitlement of a spouse to register at the Land Charges Registry their 'matrimonial home rights' under the Family Law Act 1996 as a charge on the estate of interest of other, see **12.132–12.139**.
15 As to what constitutes 'occupation' for the purposes of the section see *Strand Securities Ltd v Caswell* [1965] Ch 958, CA.
16 Land Registration Act 1925, s 70(1)(g); *William and Glyn's Bank v Boland* [1981] AC 487, HL. Protection of the minor interest may also be obtained by registration, eg by way of a caution or a restriction.
17 Land Registration Act 1925, s 70(1)(g); *Hodgson v Marks* [1971] Ch 892; *Kling v Keston Properties* (1985) 49 P & CR 212 at 220.
18 *William and Glyn's Bank v Boland* [1981] AC 487, HL.
19 *Abbey National Building Society v Cann* [1991] 1 AC 56, HL; *Lloyds Bank plc v Rossett* [1991] 1 AC 107, HL.

TACKING

PRE 1926

24.75 Prior to 1926, there were two forms of tacking available to a mortgagee: tacking further advances and the 'tabula in naufragio'.

Tacking further advances[1]

24.76 Firstly, where a legal mortgagee desired to lend more money on the same security at a later date, and at the time of the further advance had no notice of a second mortgage, his legal estate gave priority to the further advance[2]. This doctrine, known as the tacking of further advances would also apply to an equitable mortgagee, where the intervening incumbrancer agreed to the further transaction, or if the prior mortagee made express provision for the extension of the security to further advances. However, in the case of both an equitable and a legal mortgagee, if he has notice, at the time of making the further advance, of an intervening incumbrance, he will not be able to take advantage of the doctrine.

1 There is no difference in substance between a further advance and a re-advance. A re-advance is a further advance after the original principal sum has been reduced and within the monetary limits of the original advance.
2 See (1958) 22 Conv (NS) 44 (Rowley), but quaere whether the principle does depend on the doctrine of estates in land: see *Matzner v Clyde Securities Ltd* [1975] 2 NSWLR 293.

Former conditions for tacking further advances

Priority of the legal estate

24.77 The first way in which a mortgagee could tack further advances arose where the mortgagee did not have notice of the intervening incumbrance. If this was the case, the mortgagee could still tack where he had the legal estate, because of the special value that was attached to it. However, it was not essential that the legal estate should be vested in him — it was sufficient if he had the best right to call for it[1]. It was also sufficient if he had a partial interest in the legal estate, such as a term of years, or a security which might be used at law, such as a judgment[2]. His claim, however, depended on the continued holding of the legal estate and he lost the right to tack if he parted with that estate[3]. Further, it was necessary that he should hold both securities in his own right[4] and that he should have an equal equity with the mesne incumbrancer[5].

1 *Wilkes v Bodington* (1707) 2 Vern 599; *Ex p Knott* (1806) 11 Ves 609. Thus, an incumbrancer in whose favour a declaration of trust of the legal interest had been made (*Stanhope v Earl Verney* (1761) 2 Eden 81; *Wilmot v Pike* (1845) 5 Hare 14; *Taylor v London and County Banking Co* [1901] 2 Ch 231 at 263; but see *McCarthy & Stone Ltd v Julian S Hodge & Co Ltd* [1971] 2 All ER 973, [1971] 1 WLR 1547), or who, having the best right to call for a transfer of that interest, had done some act short of obtaining a transfer, but equivalent to an act of ownership (*Ex p Knott*, above, at 618; *Fourth City Mutual Benefit Building Society v Williams* (1879) 14 Ch D 140) was, for the purpose of tacking, in the same position as if he actually held the legal estate.
2 *Brace v Duchess of Marlborough*, above; *Re Russell Road Purchase-Moneys* (1871) LR 12 Eq 78.
3 *Rooper v Harrison* (1855) 2 K & J 86.
4 *Morret v Paske* (1740) 2 Atk 52; *Barnett v Weston* (1806) 12 Ves 130; see *Shaw v Neale* (1858) 6 HL Cas 581.
5 *Lacey v Ingle* (1847) 2 Ph 413 at 419; *Rooper v Harrison*, above.

The legal estate might be got in either at the time of the later incumbrance which it was desired to tack, or subsequently: *Willoughby v Willoughby* (1756) 1 Term Rep 763; *Brace v Duchess of Marlborough*, above; *Cooke v Wilton* (1860) 29 Beav 100, and similarly, where a prior mortgagee acquired a later incumbrance, he must have had no notice of the mesne incumbrance at the time of such acquisition: *Bedford v Backhouse* (1730) 2 Eq Cas Abr 615; *Morret v Paske*, above.

Where a subsequent mortgagee acquired a prior mortgage it was immaterial whether the first mortgagee, from whom the legal estate was got in, had at that time notice of the mesne incumbrance, hence a second mortgagee could not protect himself by giving notice to the first mortgagee: *Peacock v Burt* (1834) 4 LJ Ch 33; that is, the first mortgagee could prefer which of the subsequent incumbrances he pleased; but this doctrine, though apparently accepted, was disapproved: *Bates v Johnson* (1859) John 304 at 314; *West London Commercial Bank v Reliance Permanent Building Society* (1885) 29 Ch D 954. But while it was essential that there should be no notice of the mesne incumbrance at the time of the advance, the subsequent mortgagee could tack notwithstanding that he had notice when he got in the legal estate: *Blackwood v London Chartered Bank of Australia* (1874) LR 5 PC 92 at 111. He could not, however, avail himself of a legal estate it if were got in with notice that the conveyance was a breach of trust: *Saunders v Dehew* (1692) 2 Vern 271; *Taylor v Russell* [1891] 1 Ch 8, CA; on appeal, [189] AC 244, HL at 261, per Lord Macnaghten; *Bailey v Barnes* [1894] 1 Ch 25; but see *Pilcher v Rawlins* (1872) 7 Ch App 259. Nor could he avail himself of a legal estate if it were got in from a satisfied mortgagee, since such a mortgagee was a trustee for the equitable incumbrancers according to their priorities: *Prosser v Rice* (1859) 28 Beav 68 at 74; *Taylor v Russell* [1892] AC 244 at 259, HL; and the trustee of the mortgagor could not make use of the legal estate to alter the priorities: *Ledbrook v Passman* (1888) 57 LJ Ch 855.

Agreement

24.78 Irrespective of the priority given to the legal estate, there were two situations, prior to 1926, where the right to tack further advances was said to derive from agreement. The first, and most straightforward, was where the intervening incumbrancer agreed. This applied to both legal and equitable mortgagees who wished to tack a further advance. The operation of the doctrine in this scenario was simply a matter of contract between the respective incumbrancers[1].

The second was where a mortgage was made to cover further advances. This occurred when the first mortgage was expressed to cover the advance made at the time and also further advances. In such a case the mortgagee could, by virtue of the contract, tack a further advance to the original advance as against a subsequent mortgagee who had not got the legal estate, provided that, at the time of the further advance, he had no notice of the subsequent mortgage and a mortgage to secure a current account was on the same footing[2]. If a further advance was made either by a legal mortgagee[3], or by an equitable mortgagee with the best right to the legal estate, and this further advance was made without notice of the intervening mortgage, it might be tacked and priority resulted in such a case from the superiority attached to the legal estate. If, however, the contract expressly provided for the extension of the security to cover further advances, the device of tacking might be used by either a legal or an equitable mortgagee. Notice of a subsequent mortgage prevented the first mortgagee from gaining priority for advances subsequently made, and it was decided that the same rule applied even where the first mortgage contained a covenant to make further advances[4]. Accordingly, whenever a mortgagee (legal or equitable) had notice of a subsequent incumbrance, he could not tack further advances against it.

1 For priority agreements, see **24.123**.

2 *Hopkinson v Rolt* (1861) 9 HL Cas 514; *Calisher v Forbes* (1871) 7 Ch App 109; see *Re Weniger's Policy* [1910] 2 Ch 291 at 295.

3 *Wyllie v Pollen* (1863) 3 De GJ & Sm 596.

4 *West v Williams* [1899] 1 Ch 132, CA. The extension of the rule as to notice, via *Hopkinson v Rolt*, above, to the case where tacking was based on agreement, rather than the superiority of the legal estate, shows an increasing restriction by the courts of this form of tacking. Originally it was held that where the second mortgagee took with notice that the first mortgage was to cover further advances, the first mortgagee might tack advances made subsequently to the second mortgage and it was folly of the second mortgagee with notice to take such a security: *Gordon v Graham* (1716) 2 Eq Cas Abr 598. This was overruled by *Hopkinson v Rolt*, above, see *London and County Banking Co v Ratcliffe* (1881) 6 App Cas 722, HL; *Bradford Banking Co v Briggs, Son & Co Ltd* (1886) 12 App Cas 29, HL; *Union Bank of Scotland v National Bank of Scotland* (1886) 12 App Cas 53, HL; *Matzner v Clyde Securities Ltd* [1975] 2 NSWLR 293; *Central Mortgage Registry of Australia Ltd v Donemore Pty Ltd* [1984] 2 NSWLR 128.

The principle that notice of a subsequent incumbrance prevents a first mortgagee from gaining priority for further advances applies also to a company claiming a lien on shares of a member for debts incurred after it has received notice of an incumbrance on the shares (*Bradford Banking Co v Briggs*, above) and applies also to mortgages of ships (*The Benwell Tower* (1895) 72 LT 664).

Tabula in naufragio

24.79 The second form of tacking was known as the 'tabula in naufragio'[1]. This applied where[2], after a legal mortgage to A, and subsequently, an equitable mortgage to B, there was a third mortgage to a different person, C, who made his advance without notice of the second mortgage. If C then took a transfer of A's mortgage, he would have priority, in respect of both the first and the third mortgages. In other words, by tacking the third mortgage to the first, he could squeeze out the second[3]. It is quite possible, in this situation, for C to have lent sums in excess of the equity remaining in the property, after the mortgage to B, since he would have been unaware of this mortgage.

1 This expression was attributed to Hale CJ; see *Brace v Duchess of Marlborough* (1728) 2 P Wms 491; *Wortley v Birkhead* (1754) 2 Ves Sen 571; but the acquisition of the legal estate in part of a security did not protect any more of the subsequent incumbrance than was charged upon that part: *Marsh v Lee*, above.
2 See also the example given in **24.23**, n 2.
3 *Marsh v Lee* (1670) 2 Ventr 337; *Brace v Duchess of Marlborough* (1728) 2 P Wms 491; *Wortley v Birkhead* (1754) 2 Ves Sen 571; the court would not take from the third mortgagee the legal protection of an honest debt: *Belchier v Renforth* (1764) 5 Bro Parl Cas 292; *Blackwood v London Chartered Bank of Australia* (1874) LR 5 PC 92, per Lord Selborne C at 111.

Conditions for the operation of the tabula in naufragio

24.80 Again, it was necessary for the mortgagee who wished to tack in this way to have had no notice of the prior equitable mortgage when he advanced his money[1]. However, if he had no notice at the time of the advance, it was immaterial that he may have obtained notice prior to obtaining the legal estate[2].

1 *Bates v Johnson* (1859) Johns 304.
2 *Taylor v Russell* [1892] AC 244.

Tacking against surety

24.81 The mortgagee might also, perhaps, tack a further advance as against a surety if the contract of guarantee did not affect his right to make further advances[1], and might certainly do so where he had no notice that the surety was merely a surety[2], but where he had notice of an intermediate charge, then, as he could not tack as against that charge, it was held that he could not in general tack as against the surety's right to the benefit of his security on payment of the first advance alone[3].

1 *Williams v Owen* (1843) 13 Sim 597; *Farebrother v Wodehouse* (1856) 23 Beav 18; dissented from in *Forbes v Jackson* (1882) 19 Ch D 615; but followed in *Nicholas v Ridley* [1904] 1 Ch 192. This case was, however, decided by the Court of Appeal on other grounds: at 205.
2 *Re Toogood's Legacy Trusts* (1889) 61 LT 19; *Nicholas v Ridley*, above.
3 *Drew v Lockett* (1863) 32 Beav 499; *Forbes v Jackson*, above; *Leicestershire Banking Co Ltd v Hawkins* (1900) 16 TLR 317.

Tacking unsecured debts

24.82 Although as against mesne incumbrances tacking was allowed only where the debt to be tacked was incurred on the credit of the estate, and this applied also as against the mortgagor[1] and persons claiming under him inter vivos[2] yet, after the death of the mortgagor, such debts could be tacked against his successors in title to the equity of redemption, so far as the land was assets in their hands for the payment of the unsecured debt[3]. This, however, was allowed only to enable the mortgagee to recover his whole debt in one proceeding and so avoid circuitry of action. It was not tacking in the full sense, so as to disturb the priorities and enable the mortgagee to exclude a mesne incumbrancer[4].

1 *Challis v Casborn* (1715) Prec Ch 407.
2 *Coleman v Winch* (1721) 1 P Wms 775; *Richardson v Horton* (1843) 7 Beav 112.
3 *Heams v Bance* (1748) 3 Atk 630; *Coleman v Winch*, above; *Thomas v Thomas* (1856) 22 Beav 341.
4 *Pile v Pile* (1875) 23 WR 440; see *Morret v Paske* (1740) 2 Atk 52; *Irby v Irby* (1855) 22 Beav 217. As to the extension of the liability of real estate to simple contract debts, with the extension also of this right of tacking, see the Administration of Estates Act 1833, now repealed and reproduced by the Administration of Estates Act 1925, s 32.

POST 1925

24.83 The doctrine of tacking is now contained in s 94 of the Law of Property Act 1925 in respect of unregistered land and s 30 of the Land Registration Act 1925 in respect of registered land.

Unregistered land

24.84 Section 94(1) of the Law of Property Act 1925 sets out three instances in which a prior mortgagee is entitled to make further advances to rank in priority to subsequent mortgages:

(a) where there is an agreement with the intervening incumbrancer;
(b) where the mortgagee has no notice of the subsequent mortgages at the time when the further advance is made;
(c) where the mortgage imposes an obligation on the mortgagee to make a further advance, even if he has notice of the subsequent mortgage.

The first scenario, (a), leaves the previous law unchanged and is based on the agreement between the parties inter se[1].

As for (b), this actually extends the doctrine, in that under the former law, if the prior mortgage did not cover further advances, the further advance could only be tacked by virtue of the legal estate. Accordingly, a prior mortgagee, though he is only an equitable mortgagee and though his mortgage is not expressed to cover further advances, may tack a further advance provided he has no notice of the subsequent mortgage. This extension will be effective if the subsequent mortgage is not registered but, if it is registered, the registration will constitute notice.

In retaining the requirement for the absence of notice, actual or constructive, s 94(1)(b) preserves the doctrine in *Hopkinson v Rolt*[2]; but, provided he searched the register at the time when the original mortgage was created, he need not search it again on making further advances[3].

Under s 94(1)(c), the mortgage will be made expressly for securing the further advance[4]. The right to tack does not depend on the possession of the legal estate. Formerly it would have depended on the contract; now it depends on the statute, but the effect of notice has been altered. Formerly the prior mortgagee could not tack a further advance made after notice of a subsequent mortgage, even though he was under an obligation to make it[5]. Now he can perform his contract and tack the further advance notwithstanding notice.

1 For priority agreements, see **24.123**.
2 See above. See also *Bank of Western Australia v Connell* (1996) 16 WAR 483; *R & I Bank of Western Australia v Cash Resources* (1993) 11 WAR 536.
3 Under the former law, when tacking depended upon the contract in the original mortgage, and that mortgage covered only further advances up to a specified limit, any advance beyond the limit could be tacked only by virtue of the legal estate, if the mortgagee had it: see *Hopkinson v Rolt*, above. Under s 94 (1) tacking depends neither on the legal estate nor on the contract and under that subsection an advance beyond the limit can be tacked provided a new security is taken, and provided, of course, there is no notice; but the benefit of sub-s (2) can probably be obtained only where the further advance is within the authorised limit. A mortgage 'made expressly for securing a current account or other further advances' appears to refer to the account or advance as authorised by the mortgage. See generally (1958) 22 Conv (NS) 44 (Rowley); and **24.85**.
4 For the meaning of further advance, see **24.76**, n 1.
5 *West v Williams* [1899] 1 Ch 132, CA.

Current accounts, etc

24.85 Under s 94(1)(b), the practical effect, if it stood alone, would be to abolish the former facilities for obtaining further advances in particular where the mortgage to cover such advances is a mortgage to secure a current account with a bank. Since registration of a subsequent mortgage constitutes notice[1], no cheque drawn against the account while it was in debit could safely be honoured and no advance could otherwise be made to a customer, without fresh search in the appropriate register. Accordingly, the rule that registration constitutes notice is excluded by sub-s (2) in cases where the prior mortgage 'was made expressly for securing a current account or other further advances'. This preserves the former law as to mortgages of this nature.

1 Law of Property Act 1925, s 198 and see **24.8**.

Limits to tacking under s 94

24.86 Under s 94, a mortgagee cannot tack further advances if he has notice, actual or constructive, of a subsequent mortgage, unless his own mortgage contains an obligation to make further advances, even if the mortgage was expressed to be security for any further advances which he might choose to make. Where a subsequent mortgagee has registered his mortgage, that registration will amount to notice and, unless the original mortgage contained an obligation to make further advances, will prevent the original mortgagee from tacking.

Apart from these express situations, in which a mortgagee has the right to tack further advances, the right to tack has been abolished — s 94(3). Accordingly, the doctrine of tabula in naufragio has been abolished[1].

1 Ie in the context of mortgages at least: see *McCarthy & Stone Ltd v Julian S Hodge & Co Ltd* [1971] 2 All ER 973, [1971] 1 WLR 1547. See also *Macmillan v Bishopsgate Trust* [1995] 1

WLR 978 (and [1996] 1 WLR 387, CA), in which Millett J discussed the doctrine in the context of successive interests in shares. Reference was made to the decision in *Dodds v Hills* (1865) 2 Hem & M 424, in which it was held that a transferee of shares can defeat an intervening equitable interest by registering the shares even if he has notice of the intervening interest at the time of registration, as long as he did not have such notice at the time of acquisition. It was considered that this was an example of a residual role for the doctrine of tabula in naufragio, otherwise abolished by s 94.

Effect of rule in Clayton's Case

24.87 Where a prior mortgage is made to cover a current account with a bank and notice of a subsequent mortgage is received, the rule in *Clayton's Case*[1] applies if the account continues to be operated upon. Subsequent payments into the account are credited to the overdraft existing at the time of the notice[2] and, in effect, these are for the benefit of the subsequent mortgagee. He takes subject only to the overdraft at that time and the reduction of the overdraft correspondingly improves his security. This result can be avoided by the bank closing the account and, if it thinks fit, allowing the mortgagor to open a new account into which future payments will be made.

1 (1816) 1 Mer 572, and see **28.56**.
2 *Deeley v Lloyds Bank Ltd* [1912] AC 756, HL; see *Re Chute's Estate* [1914] 1 IR 180.

Registered land — Land Registration Act 1925, s 30

24.88 Registered charges on registered land are excluded from s 94 of the Law of Property Act 1925[1] and further advances on the security of such charges are subject to s 30 of the Land Registration Act 1925. This provides that where a registered charge is made for securing further advances[2], the registrar must give to the proprietor of the charge, at his registered address, notice by registered post of any intended entry which may prejudicially affect the priority of the advance made under the charge and the proprietor of the charge is not affected by any such entry unless the advance is made after the date when the notice ought to have been received[3]. If the registrar fails to give such notice, and the proprietor of the charge suffers loss in relation to a further advance, he is entitled to an indemnity under the Land Registration Act, as if there were an error in the register[4].

Where the proprietor of a charge is under an obligation, which is duly noted on the register, to make a further advance, a subsequent registered charge shall take effect subject to any further advance made pursuant to that obligation. Where there is no obligation to make further advances and a further advance is made after registration of a subsequent charge, the further advance will not have priority, unless the subsequent chargee agrees to postpone his charge[5].

1 Section 94(4).
2 The fact that the charge is to secure further advances should be shown in a prominent position on the form (so that there is no chance of the Registry overlooking the point): see (1974) 118 SJ 889. For a proposal that the registrar should not be under an obligation to give notice, see Law Commission Report, Law Com no 204, 1991, paras 9.1-9.5.
3 See *Lloyd v Nationwide Anglia Building Society* [1996] EGCS 80.
4 See Land Registration Act 1925, s 83.
5 The postponement is not, it is submitted, an alteration within s 31 of the Land Registration Act 1925 and, therefore, does not have to be by deed in Form 51 under r 150. If s 31 is

applicable, the subsequent chargee would be bound by any postponement to which he agreed even if not by deed on the ground of estoppel, but the position of the transferee from the subsequent registered chargee would be uncertain. The section provides a means of alteration of charges by deed in Form 51 and completion of the alteration by entry on the register (sub-s (3)). If the prior chargee has failed to use the method provided it can be argued that he should lose priority for his further advance against a transferee from the subsequent chargee (whether with notice of the further advance or not), because there is no entry of the further advance on the register. Section 33 of the 1925 Act, dealing with transfer of charges, does not cover the whole ground of s 114 of the Law of Property Act 1925 (so arguably, save in so far as s 33 is inconsistent with s 114, s 114 applies and the transferee steps into the shoes of the transferor—see **4.19**). Subsection (5) of s 33 provides that the vesting of any term in the transferee on registration under sub-s (4) has the same effect as if the transferee had been registered as transferee for valuable consideration of the term and this is *subject to any entry to the contrary on the register*. It can be argued that this reference to 'any entry' etc means that if there is no entry of the further advance on the register, the transferee will take with priority to it.

SUBROGATION

24.89 A lender may obtain priority by being subrogated to the rights of an earlier incumbrancer. If the moneys advanced by a lender are used to discharge a security he will be subrogated to the rights under that security and obtain priority over incumbrances subsequent to that security, if (a) the subsequent incumbrancer has been enriched at the lender's expense; (b) such enrichment was unjust; and (c) there are no policy reasons of denying a remedy[1].

1 *Boscawen v Bajwa* [1996] 1 WLR 328, CA; *Banque Financière de la Cité v Parc (Battersea) Ltd* [1999] 1 AC 221, HL. Where the later incumbrancer is subrogated the mortgage is not kept alive but the party who has the right of subrogation has the same rights as if it had been kept alive and assigned to him. See further **14.22**.

MORTGAGES OF EQUITABLE INTERESTS: THE RULE IN *DEARLE v HALL*

THE RULE

Priority by order of notice

24.90 This rule applies where property is held by a trustee, or other person having legal control of property. While notice to the trustees of an assignment of an equitable interest does not affect the validity of the assignment itself[1], the priority of successive assignments depends upon the order in which notice of the disposition is given to the trustee. This is known as the rule in *Dearle v Hall*[2].

Under the rule, if the assignee of an equitable interest in property to which the rules applies[3] fails to give notice of the assignment to the trustees, and a later assignee or chargee gives notice, the interest of the later assignee prevails over the earlier interest. The rule applies equally when the equitable owner has died and his personal representative makes an assignment[4]. If notice of two or more assignments is received by the trustees on the same day, the assignments rank in order of their dates[5]. If notice is delivered at business premises after business hours, it is treated as having been given at the time at which in the ordinary course of business, it would be opened and read, that is, on the following day[6]. If two assignees rank equally in point of time, they share the fund rateably[7]. The rule applies to dispositions generally, save that a mere declaration of trust made by the beneficiary need not be notified, for this leaves the interest still in his hands, and the sub-beneficiary can assert his right only through him[8].

Where a mortgage is made to cover further advances, and notice of this mortgage has been given to the trustees, further advances probably need not be notified[9]; but a further advance should not be made without inquiring of the trustees whether notice of a subsequent incumbrance has been received[10]. Where the mortgage does not cover further advances, notice of any further charge must be given to the trustees[11]. Where the security is on an interest in a trust fund which is in two parts, part of which is in court, and the remainder is in the hand of the trustees, notice to the trustees will only relate to that part of the fund which is in their hands. Therefore, a stop order[12] should be obtained by the assignee in relation to the part of the fund which is in court[13].

1 *Bell v London and North Western Rly Co* (1852) 15 Beav 548; *Re Lowes' Settlement* (1861) 30 Beav 95; *Donaldson v Donaldson* (1854) Kay 711; *Ward v Duncombe* [1893] AC 369 at 392; *Gorringe v Irwell India Rubber etc Works* (1886) 34 Ch D 128, CA.

2 (1828) 3 Russ 1. For a consideration of this case and *Warner Bros Records Inc v Rollgreen Ltd* [1976] QB 430, [1975] 2 All ER 105, CA, see (1975) 39 Conv (NS) 261 (Kloss). The burden of showing absence of notice is on those who claim against an earlier security: *Re Stevens, ex p Stevens* (1834) 4 Deac & Ch 117. The rule in *Dearle v Hall* has no application where in fact the assignor has no beneficial interest he can effectively assign: see *B S Lyle Ltd v Rosher* [1958] 3 All ER 597, [1959] 1 WLR 8.

3 For property to which this rule applies, see **24.92** ff. On tracing and book debts, see (1980) 96 LQR 90 (McLauchlan).

4 *Re Freshfield's Trusts* (1879) 11 Ch D 198; *Montefiore v Guedalla* [1903] 2 Ch 26.

5 *Calisher v Forbes* (1871) 7 Ch App 109; *Johnstone v Cox* (1881) 16 Ch D 571; (1882) 19 Ch D 17.

6 *Re Dallas* [1904] 2 Ch 385 at 395, CA.

7 *Re Metropolitan Rly Co etc, ex p Kent* (1871) 19 WR 596.

8 *Hill v Peters* [1918] 2 Ch 273.

9 *Calisher v Forbes* (1871) 7 Ch App 109; *Re Weniger's Policy* [1910] 2 Ch 291. See *West v Williams* [1899] 1 Ch 132, CA. Perhaps the Law of Property Act 1925, s 94, is confined to land, but this is not clear (see sub-s (4)).

10 *Calisher v Forbes* (1871) 7 Ch App 109; *Re Weniger's Policy* [1910] 2 Ch 291. See *West v Williams* [1899] 1 Ch 132, CA. Perhaps the Law of Property Act 1925, s 94, is confined to land, but this is not clear (see sub-s (4)).

11 *Re Weniger's Policy*, above, at 296.

12 As to stop orders, see **24.115**.

13 *Mutual Life Assurance Society v Langley* (1886) 32 Ch D 460, CA.

Origin of the rule

24.91 When the rule was first introduced in *Dearle v Hall*[1], the bankruptcy rules then in force required notice to be given in the case of an assignment of a chose in action, in order to take the property out of the order and disposition of the assignor[2]. 'The legal holders', it was said by Plumer MR, 'are converted into trustees for the new purchaser, and are charged with responsibility towards him; and the cestui que trust is deprived of the power of carrying the same security repeatedly into the market, and of inducing third persons to advance money on it under the erroneous belief that it continues to belong to him absolutely, free from incumbrance, and that the trustees are still trustees for him, and for no-one else.' Lord Lyndhurst C, said: 'The act of giving the trustee notice is, in a certain degree, taking possession of the fund; it is going as far towards equitable possession as it is possible to go; for, after notice is given, the trustee of the fund becomes a trustee for the assignee who has given him notice'[3]. It has been pointed out that, in many of the subsequent cases, the facts have not been as clear or as simple as those of the leading cases and it has become necessary to ascertain the principles on which the rule is based[4]. In some cases, the giving of notice in respect of a chose in action has been likened to the delivery of a chose in possession. In others, courts have emphasised the necessity of preventing frauds by beneficiaries who create successive incumbrances without disclosing the earlier ones. It is said, however, that the real foundation of the judgment of Plumer MR lay in the duty of the assignee to do all that he could to obtain the possession of the subject-matter of the assignment. 'He must do that which is tantamount to obtaining possession by placing every person who has an equitable or legal interest in the matter under an obligation to treat it as his property'[5]. The importance of the matter lay in the avoidance of the application of the rule that assignments of equitable interests rank in order of time[6], and this was done by treating the omission of the first assignee to give notice, so leaving the assignor free to deal with the property over again—enabling him to gain a 'false and delusive credit'—as negligence sufficient to postpone him[7]. Lord Herschell (with whom Lord Hannen agreed) said in *Ward v Duncombe*[8] that the leading consideration in *Dearle v Hall* for laying down the rule was that any other decision would facilitate fraud by the cestui que trust and cause loss to those who might have used every precaution before parting with their money. In *Ward v Duncombe*, Lord Macnaghten expressed doubt as to whether there is any satisfactory principle upon which the doctrine rests. He went on to express the view[9] that in seeking to extend the doctrine beyond the sphere of bankruptcy, the courts had 'gone perilously near legislating'. Indeed, he concluded, while parliament had modified the rules relating to bankruptcy, 'the rule in *Dearle v Hall*, founded in great measure on the bankruptcy law as it existed sixty years ago, remains unaltered, and it is beyond the power of any court to alter it' and the rule 'has on the whole produced at least as much injustice as it has prevented'.

1 (1828) 3 Russ 1.
2 Under the Bankruptcy Act 1914, s 38 the order and disposition clause applied only to business debts. This reputed ownership doctrine was abrogated by the Insolvency Act 1985, s 130 (see now s 283 of the IA 1986 for the definition of the bankrupt's estate) following recommendations in the Report of the Review Committee on Insolvency Law (Cmnd 8558) and the proposals in the White Paper 'A Revised Framework for Insolvency Law' (Cmnd 9175).
3 *Dearle v Hall*, above at 58. In *Ward v Duncombe* [1893] AC 369, Lord Macnaghten took exception to the statement that notice 'converts' the trustee of the fund into a trustee for the person who gives the notice: 'The trustee of the fund is trustee for the persons entitled to the fund, whether he knows their names or not. The notice, no doubt, places him under a direct responsibility to the person who gives the notice … but before notice is given he is just as much a trustee for the persons rightfully entitled as he is after he receives the notice.'
4 *Ward v Duncombe* [1893] AC 369.
5 *Dearle v Hall*, above, at 23. For a full account (from which the above paragraph is taken) of the development of the rule, see (1895) LQR 337 ff (Firth).
6 See **24.2**.
7 *Dearle v Hall*, above, at 22.
8 [1893] AC 369 at 378.
9 [1893] AC 369 at 393.

PROPERTY TO WHICH THE RULE APPLIES

Prior to 1926

24.92 Before 1926, the rule in *Dearle v Hall* was confined to equitable interests in personal property. It did not apply to equitable interests in land[1], including leaseholds[2], although it did apply where the interest in land could only reach the beneficiary or assignee in the form of money, to arise from a trust for sale of land present[3]. Furthermore, it did not apply to a mortgage debt, for although the debt was a chose in action, the mortgagee was treated as having an 'interest in land', where the debt was secured on the land[4]. Moreover, where the assignor of a chattel cannot deliver possession, the assignee must protect himself against subsequent assignees by giving such notice as goes as far as possible towards taking possession. Otherwise the subsequent assignee, by obtaining possession, will have priority[5].

The rule does not apply where the security consists of a bill of exchange, promissory note payable to order, or other negotiable instrument[6], whether indorsed or not by the debtor[7]. Nor does it apply to shares in a company which is precluded by its constitution from receiving notices of trusts[8].

1 Whether the rule formerly applied to moneys subject to a trust for investment in land, or to capital moneys arising under the Settled Land Acts was not clear.
2 *Jones v Jones* (1838) 8 Sim 633; *Wilmot v Pike* (1845) 5 Hare 14; *Rooper v Harrison* (1855) 2 K & J 86 at 103; *Re Richards, Humber v Richards* (1890) 45 Ch D 589; *Ward v Duncombe* [1893] AC 369 at 390; *Wiltshire v Rabbits* (1844) 14 Sim 76; *Union Bank of London v Kent* (1888) 39 Ch D 238.
3 *Re Wyatt, White v Ellis* [1892] 1 Ch 188 at 195; on appeal, *Ward v Duncombe* [1893] AC 369 at 390, HL; *Lloyds Bank v Pearson* [1901] 1 Ch 865; *Gresham Life Assurance Society v Crowther* [1915] 1 Ch 214. The same applies to future trusts for sale — *Lee v Howlett* (1856) 2 K & J 531; *Arden v Arden* (1885) 29 Ch D 702.
4 *Jones v Gibbons* (1804) 9 Ves 407.
5 *Daniel v Russell* (1807) 14 Ves 393.
6 As to the effect on title where instruments are 'negotiable', see *London Joint Stock Bank v Simmons* [1892] AC 201.
7 *Re Gibbs, ex p Price* (1844) 3 Mont D & De G 586: the incumbrancer may have an equity to have the security indorsed by the debtor or his assignees; but the debtor may ignore a notice given by the assignee of the consideration for the note or bill if the assignor is still the holder of the instrument itself: *Bench v Shearman* [1898] 2 Ch 582.
8 *Société Générale de Paris v Walker* (1885) 11 App Cas 20.

Extension to equitable interests in land — Law of Property Act 1925, s 137[1]

24.93 Section 137(1) of the Law of Property Act 1925 provides that the rule in *Dearle v Hall* applies (with modifications) to dealings with equitable interests in land in relation to dispositions made on or after 1 January 1926. 'Dealings' include dispositions by operation of law[2].

1 For examples of the rule in *Dearle v Hall* being applied, see *Rhodes v Allied Dunbar Pension Service Ltd* [1988] 1 All ER 524, [1987] 1 WLR 1703 and *E Pfeiffer Weinkellerei-Weineinkauf v Arbuthnot Factors* [1988] 1 WLR 150, [1987] BCLC 522; *Lloyds Bank v Messologides*.
2 Section 137(10). For the connection between s 137 and the Land Charges Act 1972, see [1993] Conv 22 (Howell).

Locality of fund

24.94 The rule applies where the legal holder of the fund is in England. Thus it applies to all dealings in English trust funds settled by English trust instruments, the trustees of which are in England, although the assignor is domiciled abroad, and even though, according to his lex domicilii, notice to trustees is unnecessary[1].

1 *Kelly v Selwyn* [1905] 2 Ch 117.

Life policies

24.95 Special provision with respect to life policies is made by the Policies of Assurance Act 1867. No assignment of a policy of life assurance confers on the assignee a right to sue for the policy moneys until written notice of the assignment has been given to the assurance company at their principal place, or one of their principal places, of business, and the date on which the notice is received regulates the priority of all claims under any assignment[1]. However, notwithstanding this provision, a subsequent assignee does not by giving notice first obtain priority over a previous assignment of which he has notice[2]. The company must, upon request in writing by the person giving notice, acknowledge in writing the receipt of the notice[3], but an instrument of deposit, not operating as an assignment of the policy, will not be construed as an assignment as against the company by reason of their accepting notice of it and giving a receipt; and in such a case the company may refuse payment of the policy on the death of the assured until the consent of his representatives has been obtained[4].

A mere agreement to execute a mortgage of a policy is not an assignment within the Act and notice of it to the company will not give priority over an earlier equitable mortgagee, who has given no notice[5]. Also, where a solicitor has a lien for costs on a policy of insurance in his possession, a subsequent assignee cannot gain priority by giving notice[6].

1 Section 3; see *English and Scottish Mercantile Investment Co v Brunton* [1892] 2 QB 700.
2 *Newman v Newman* (1885) 28 Ch D 674.
3 Section 6, and see **7.15**.
4 *Crossley v City of Glasgow Life Assurance Co* (1876) 4 Ch D 421; *Webster v British Empire Mutual Life Assurance Co* (1880) 15 Ch D 169.
5 *Spencer v Clarke* (1878) 9 Ch D 137.
6 *West of England Bank v Batchelor* (1882) 51 LJ Ch 199.

Shares in companies

24.96 Under s 360 of the Companies Act 1985, no notice of a trust is to be entered on the register of companies, and therefore, the rule in *Dearle v Hall* cannot apply between a company and those who are beneficially interested in its shares. However, the directors of a company will be personally liable if they allow shares which, to their knowledge, are affected by equitable rights, to be faudulently transferred so as to destroy such rights[1]. Nevertheless, even though notice given to the company does not affect the priority of equitable claims in respect of registered shares, such a notice is not inoperative for all purposes and the receipt of notice by a company of a charge upon some of its shares will prevent the company from availing itself, as against those shares, of any lien under its articles of association for a debt to the company incurred subsequently to its receipt of the notice[2].

Where the security consists of shares in a public company or undertaking, if the security is made by the directors and secretary for the purposes of the company, no further notice will be necessary[3].

Until a person is registered as a shareholder, his title to the shares is equitable only, and subsequent equitable titles rank in order of time, unless postponed by conduct in relation to the share certificate[4].

It would seem that the possession by the mortgagee of the share certificates is sufficient to preserve that mortgagee's priority as against subsequent incumbrancers[5].

1 *Société Générale de Paris v Tramways Union Co* (1884) 14 QBD 424, CA; affirmed without reference to this point, *sub nom Société Générale de Paris v Walker* (1885) 11 App Cas 20, HL.
2 *Bradford Banking Co v Briggs, Son & Co* (1886) 12 App Cas 29, HL, applying the principle of *Hopkinson v Rolt* (1861) 9 HL Cas 514; *Champagne Perrier-Jouet SA v H H Finch Ltd* [1982] 3 All ER 713, [1982] 1 WLR 1359, and see **7.25**.
3 *Re Shelley, ex p Stewart* (1864) 4 De GJ & Sm 543.
4 See *Moore v North-Western Bank* [1891] 2 Ch 599.
5 *Colonial Bank v Whinney* (1886) 11 App Cas 426.

OPERATION OF THE RULE

Rule is independent of conduct

24.97 While in its inception the rule was an application of the general principle that a prior incumbrancer may be postponed to a subsequent incumbrancer on the ground of negligence, and was based on the consideration that, by the omission to give notice, the subsequent incumbrancer was misled, it has now ceased to depend upon the conduct of the incumbrancers, or on the subsequent incumbrancer's being in fact misled, and has become an absolute rule that, as between equitable incumbrancers, priority depends solely on notice[1]. It is therefore immaterial that the subsequent incumbrancer made no inquiry of the trustee before he took his security[2]; or that the earlier incumbrancer was prevented from giving notice, because he was not aware of the assignment to himself[3]; or that the security was such that notice could not effectually be given[4]; or that at the date of the earlier assignment there was no trustee to whom notice could be given[5].

1 *Ward v Duncombe* [1893] AC 369 at 391; *Re Dallas* [1904] 2 Ch 385 at 414, CA; see *Lloyds Bank v Pearson* [1901] 1 Ch 865 at 872–873.
2 *Meux v Bell* (1841) 1 Hare 73 at 84–86; *Re Brown's Trusts* (1867) LR 5 Eq 88 at 89.
3 *Re Lake* [1903] 1 KB 151.
4 *English and Scottish Mercantile Investment Trust Ltd v Brunton* [1892] 2 QB 1 at 8: of course, it makes no difference that the earlier incumbrancer has agreed not to give notice.
5 *Re Dallas* [1904] 2 Ch 385 at 397, 415, 417–418; as to giving notice in such a case by memorandum indorsed on the trust deed, see Law of Property Act 1925, s 137 (4), see **24.113**.

Assignees who are not within the rule

24.98 The rule does not apply to a statutory assignee, since he cannot have been misled by the absence of notice[1]. Hence a trustee in bankruptcy cannot, by giving notice, obtain priority over a mortgage made before the bankruptcy[2]. He takes the property subject to all equities to which it would be liable in the hands of the bankrupt[3] and, generally, the rule does not apply in favour of persons who are not allowed to put themselves in a better position than the assignor, such as a voluntary assignee[4], or a judgment creditor who has obtained a charging order[5], or a garnishee order[6], or equitable execution by the appointment of a receiver[7]. A judgment creditor seeks whatever security he can get in respect of credit already given; he is not making a decision about whether to lend money in the first place. Therefore, he has no reason to make any enquiries of the trustees[8]. Another reason why the rule does not apply to a judgment creditor is that the debtor receives no consideration from the judgment creditor at the time the charge is created, and the rule does not assist a volunteer[9].

1 *Re Anderson, ex p New Zealand Official Assignee* [1911] 1 KB 896.
2 *Re Wallis, ex p Jenks* [1902] 1 KB 719; but the trustee should give notice in order to perfect his title and, if he does so, he will have priority over a subsequent assignee from the bankrupt: *Mercer v Vans Colina* [1900] 1 QB 130n; *Re Beall, ex p Official Receiver* [1899] 1 QB 688. Otherwise he will be postponed to a subsequent assignee for value without notice of the bankruptcy, who gives notice or obtains a stop order, eg *Palmer v Locke* (1881) 18 Ch D 381.
3 *Re Atkinson* (1852) 2 De GM & G 140; see *Re Garrud, ex p Newitt* (1881) 16 Ch D 522.
4 *West v Williams* [1899] 1 Ch 132, CA.
5 *Scott v Lord Hastings* (1858) 4 K & J 633.
6 *Re Marquis of Anglesey, De Galve v Gardner* [1903] 2 Ch 727 at 732.
7 *Arden v Arden* (1885) 29 Ch D 702; *Re Marquis of Anglesey etc*, above.
8 *United Bank of Kuwait v Sahib* [1997] Ch 107, per Chadwick J.
9 *United Bank of Kuwait v Sahib*, above.

Effect of notice of prior incumbrance

24.99 The subsequent assignee cannot gain priority by giving notice to the trustees if, at the time when he took his security, he had notice of the first assignment[1]; but if he had no notice at that time, receiving notice afterwards does not prevent him from obtaining priority by serving notice before the first assignee does so. Indeed, it is in just this situation that an incumbrancer would be moved to gain his priority by giving notice[2].

1 *Re Holmes* (1885) 29 Ch D 786. But see [1999] Conv 311 (de Lacy) for the view that this 'second limb' of the rule, ie that the assignee must have no notice of the first assignment, is superfluous, and that none of the authorities cited in support of this rule, including *Re Holmes*, actually support this proposition.
2 *Mutual Life Assurance Society v Langley* (1886) 32 Ch D 460, CA.

Bankruptcy of assignor

24.100 The effect of the creation of an incumbrance by the bankrupt on after-acquired property is governed by the Insolvency Act 1986, s 307[1]. Such an incumbrance will be subject to the interest of the trustee in bankruptcy if the trustee serves a notice on the bankrupt claiming the property within 42 days of the first knowledge of the property by the trustee[2], unless the incumbrancer is in good faith, for value and without notice of the bankruptcy[3] or is a banker entering into the transaction in good faith and without such notice[4].

1 To some extent altering the previous law laid down in *Hunt v Fripp* [1898] 1 Ch 675; *Re Benrend's Trust, Surman v Biddell* [1911] 1 Ch 687.
2 Sections 307 (1), 309.
3 Section 307 (4) (a).
4 Section 307 (4) (b).

Assignment of mortgage

24.101 It is not necessary in order to complete the title of an assignee of a mortgage, or of a sub-mortgage, either of land or personal estate, to give notice to the original mortgagor of the assignment of the mortgage debt, because the debt is incident to the property which forms the security, and cannot be taken from the assignee without payment[1], but so long as the original mortgagor has no notice of the assignment, his payments on account of the debt to his original mortgagee will discharge him[2].

An equitable charge on land is an equitable interest within s 137 of the Law of Property Act 1925 and an assignment of it requires to be protected by notice to the estate owner of the land.

1 *Jones v Gibbons* (1804) 9 Ves 407; see *Re Reay, ex p Barnett* (1845) De G 194.
2 *Re Lord Southampton's Estate, Allen v Lord Southampton* (1880) 16 Ch D 178.

TO WHOM NOTICE SHOULD BE GIVEN

To the legal holder of the fund

24.102 Ordinarily, notice must be given to the person having the legal interest in or control over the property which is the subject of the security[1]. Usually this is a personal representative or trustee. In the case of a debt, or of other property depending on an obligation to pay money, such as a policy of insurance, it is the debtor or person under obligation[2]. In the case of a legacy, notice must be given to the executor[3]. If the legacy is a trust legacy, then, after assent by the executor in favour of the trustees, notice must be given to the trustees. If the subject of the legacy is held by trustees under a prior instrument, and an assignment is made before assent, notice must be given to the executor, and when the assent is given, notice of the assent and of the assignment should be given to the trustees of the prior instrument, but if the assignment is made after assent, notice should be given to the trustees of the prior instrument, and not to the executor[4]. The notice must be given to the trustees personally or to an agent expressly or impliedly authorised to receive it on their behalf. Unless their solicitor has such authority, notice to him is not effectual[5]. A notice served on an agent so authorised will be binding, though the agent, in compliance with the direction of his principal, has not forwarded the notice to him[6]. The holder of, or other person having any control over, the property concerning which the notice is given, is bound to accept the notice[7]; and if he disregards it and parts with the fund, he may be compelled to make it good to the person entitled, but he is not bound to inform the giver of the notice that he himself has a charge upon the fund[8].

1 If there are prior incumbrances, notice to a prior mortgagee only affects priorities in that it prevents a prior mortgagee from tacking a further advance: *Re Weniger's Policy* [1910] 2 Ch 291.
2 *Gardner v Lachlan* (1838) 4 My & Cr 129; as to a policy of insurance, see **24.95**. If the debt is due from a company in liquidation notice should be given to the liquidator: *Re Breech-Loading Armoury Co, Wragge's Case* (1868) LR 5 Eq 284.
3 See *Re Dallas* [1904] 2 Ch 385, CA, but it would seem that notice to an executor who renounces is ineffective: *Re Wasdale, Brittin v Partridge* [1899] 1 Ch 163.
4 *Holt v Dewell* (1845) 4 Hare 446.
5 *Saffron Walden Second Benefit Building Society v Rayner* (1880) 14 Ch D 406, CA; *Arden v Arden* (1885) 29 Ch D 702 at 709.
6 *Re Hennessey* (1842) 2 Dr & War 555. As to notice to an agent who, as assignor, has an interest in withholding communication of it, see *Re Dallas*, above, and as to notice to a company through an interested officer, see *Re Hennessey*, above; *Re Sketchley, ex p Boulton* (1857) 1 De G & J 163; and cf *Bartlett v Bartlett* (1857) 1 De G & J 127. Where it is necessary to give notice to a company or association it makes no difference that they have no rules or provisions applicable to the receipt of such notices: *Williams v Thorp* (1828) 2 Sim 257; or that they do not require notices to be given of assignments: *Re Loosemore, ex p Patch* (1843) 12 LJ Bcy 44.
7 *Williams v Thorp*, above; *Re Hennessey*, above.
8 *Re Lewer, ex p Wilkes* (1876) 4 Ch D 101.

Derivative settlements

24.103 Where notice is given to a trustee, this must be the trustee who is immediately responsible to the assignor. Thus in the case of a security on an interest under a derivative settlement, the notice should be given to the trustees of that settlement, and not to the trustees of the original settlement, notwithstanding that the fund is still vested in them. The trustees of the derivative settlement are bound in due course to get in the fund and it is to them that the assignee will look for payment. In other words, there is no priority between assignees of interests under the derivative settlement and the trustees of the original settlement[1].

1 *Stephens v Green* [1895] 2 Ch 148, CA; in accordance with *Holt v Dewell*, above.

As to equitable interests in land

24.104 By s 137(2), the persons to whom notice is to be given under s 137 are:

(a) In the case of a dealing with an equitable interest in settled land, capital money or securities representing capital money, the trustees of the settlement. Where the equitable interest is created by a derivative or subsidiary settlement, the trustees of that settlement.
(b) In the case of a dealing with an equitable interest in land subject to a trust of land, or the proceeds of sale of such land, the trustees.
(c) In any other case of a dealing with an equitable interest in land, the estate owner of the land in question.

However, this provision does not apply where the money or securities are in court, in which case a stop order should be obtained[1].

1 See **2.12** and **24.115**.

Trustee's title

24.105 In order that the notice may be effectual, the person to whom it is given must at the time be trustee for the assignor[1]. This requires:

(a) That he shall be a duly constituted trustee[2]. Thus notice to an administrator is ineffectual unless he has obtained a grant of administration; and so, it seems, is notice to an executor who afterwards renounces without having acted, or to a trustee who disclaims[3].
(b) There must be under his control property in which the assignor has an actual interest, that is, the fund must be in the hands of the holder on behalf of the assignor, and priority will follow the dates of the notices after it is in his hands[4].

The fact, however, that at the time of the several assignments there was no trust fund and no trustee in existence does not prevent the rule in *Dearle v Hall* from applying and priorities will be regulated in accordance with notices given after the fund has come into existence, and there is a person who has legal control over it[5], but where notices have only been given before this time, the order in date of the incumbrances prevails[6].

Prior to the enactment of the Law of Property Act 1925, it was held that where a trustee had acquired knowledge of an incumbrance before his appointment and this had continued to operate on his mind after his appointment, the priority of the incumbrance would be protected against a subsequent incumbrance of which notice was given after his appointment[7]. However, the present requirement of written notice under s 137(3) of the Law of Property Act 1925[8] implies that such notice must, now, be given after the trustee's appointment.

1 *Dearle v Hall* (1828) 3 Russ 1 at 58; *Meux v Bell* (1841) 1 Hare 73 at 87; *Ward v Duncombe* [1893] AC 369 at 387, 389, 392, HL; *Stephens v Green* [1895] 2 Ch 148 at 158, CA; *Re Dallas* [1904] 2 Ch 385, CA.
2 See *Webster v Webster* (1862) 31 Beav 393.
3 *Re Dallas*, above; *Re Kinahan's Trusts* [1907] 1 IR 321.
4 Thus in a series of Army cases it was held that notice to an Army agent of an assignment by an officer of money payable to him on retirement was only effective if at the time the agent had in his hands money either credited to the officer, or at least specifically available for him: *Somerset v Cox* (1864) 33 Beav 634; *Yates v Cox* (1868) 17 WR 20; *Boss v Hopkinson* (1870) 18 WR 725; *Addison v Cox* (1872) 8 Ch App 76; *Addison v Cox* (1874) 30 LT 253; or, perhaps, only if given after the retirement had been gazetted: *Earl of Suffolk and Berkshire v Cox* (1867) 36 LJ Ch 591; *Johnstone v Cox* (1881) 19 Ch D 17. As to these cases, see *Re Dallas*, above, at 418.

Where there were two sets of trustees, one of an annuity, and the other of a term by which the annuity was secured, notice of a prior incumbrance to one of the trustees of the annuity was held binding, although the trustees of the term had no notice: *Wise v Wise* (1845) 2 Jo & Lat 403.

5 *Re Dallas*, above, and it was the same where, the assignor being himself the sole trustee, no effective notice could be given: *Re Dallas* at 401–402; see *Phipps v Lovegrove* (1873) LR 16 Eq 80.
6 *Buller v Plunkett* (1860) 1 John & H 441. The rule has been applied to an attachment in the

Mayor's Court, London, against a fund before it has reached the trustee's hands: *Webster v Webster* (1862) 31 Beav 393.

7 *Ipswich Permanent Money Club Ltd v Arthy* [1920] 2 Ch 257.

8 See **24.11**.

Effect of notice to one trustee

24.106 Where notice is given to one trustee, that is sufficient for the purposes of securing priority against subsequent incumbrancers as long as that trustee remains in office. The subsequent incumbrancer has a duty to enquire of all trustees, and, therefore, should learn of the prior interest[1]. However, the trustee to whom notice has been given is not bound to answer when faced with a request by a potential incumbrancer, and the latter proceeds at his own risk. If the trustee does answer, he must answer correctly; otherwise he will be liable to indemnify the mortgagee[2].

If notice is only given to one trustee, and that trustee dies after a subsequent incumbrancer has given notice of his assignment to all trustees, the priority of the first incumbrancer is not lost by virtue of that death[3]. However, where the subsequent incumbrancer acquires his interest after the death of the one trustee who had notice of the prior incumbrance, the subsequent mortgagee can obtain priority by giving notice to the surviving trustees[4].

1 *Smith v Smith* (1833) 2 Cr & M 231; *Willes v Greenhill* (1861) 4 De GF & J 147.

2 *Low v Bouverie* [1891] 3 Ch 82, CA; unless, indeed, the answer has been obtained by the concealment by the inquiring party of a material fact, eg that he had already applied to the trustee's solicitors who were considering what advice they should give: *Porter v Moore* [1904] 2 Ch 367.

3 *Ward v Duncombe* [1893] AC 369.

4 *Timson v Ramsbottom* (1837) 2 Keen 35. In *Ward v Duncombe* [1893] AC 369, this was accepted as correct by Lord Herschell, but Lord Macnaghten was inclined to allow more weight to the fact that the rule had been complied with, and less to the continuing effect of the notice on the apparent control of the mortgagor. 'It may be,' he said, 'that when an assignee or mortgagee has once discharged that duty [of giving notice] he has done all that the rule requires of him … and that he is not, on a change of trustees, to be deprived of his pre-existing equitable title by the diligence or by the happy thought of a subsequent incumbrancer.' In *Ward v Duncombe* it was not necessary to decide this point. Notice of an assignment had been given to one of two trustees, A. During his life notice of a second assignment was given to both trustees. It was held that the subsequent death of A did not deprive the first assignees of the priority they had already acquired over the second assignees in his life-time, but the doctrine of *Timson v Ramsbottom* was followed in *Re Phillips' Trusts* [1903] 1 Ch 183, and an assignee after the death of A, who gave notice to the existing trustees, had priority over the assignee who gave notice to A alone, since the effect of his notice had ceased on A's death: see also the statement of the law by Byrne J in *Freeman v Laing* [1899] 2 Ch 355 at 359.

Effect of notice to all trustees

24.107 On the other hand, where the mortgagee has given notice to all the trustees, he has done all that is required of him to secure priority. He is not bound to watch for changes in the trusteeship and give fresh notices from time to time; and he is entitled to priority over a subsequent assignee who has taken his assignment after the death or retirement of all the first trustees and who gives notice to the new trustees[1].

1 *Re Wasdale, Brittin v Partridge* [1899] 1 Ch 163. Similarly, if an assignee gives notice to all the trustees and the fund is afterwards paid into court, he has priority over a subsequent assignee who takes his assignment without notice of the prior assignment after the payment into court and obtains a stop order: *Livesey v Harding* (1856) 23 Beav 141; *Re Marquis of Anglesey, De Galve v Gardner* [1903] 2 Ch 727 at 732.

The doctrine that notice given to one of several trustees secures priority only while he is living leads to complications if there are successive incumbrancers, A, B, and C, and, there being two trustees, X and Y. A gives notice to X only; B gives notice to X and Y; and C, taking his security after the death of X, gives notice to Y. Thus, while A by reason of his notice to X ranks before B, and B by reason of his notice to Y, ranks before C, yet C ranks before A because A's notice as against C is exhausted by the death of X. The solution of the difficulty is, it seems, to be found by subrogating C to A to the extent of A's charge; then comes B, his position not being disturbed; then C takes the balance, if any, of his charge; and A comes last: *Re Wyatt, White v Ellis* [1892] 1 Ch 188 at 209; see *Benham v Keane* (1861) 1 John & H 685; argument in *Taylor v London and County Banking Co* [1901] 2 Ch 231 at 244; *Re Weniger's Policy* [1910] 2 Ch 291 at 296.

So, where, for any reason, out of securities in the above order, B has priority over A, and C over B, but as between A and C, A retains priority, if the fund available is not more than B's security will exhaust, it will be paid first to C, to the extent of the debt for which he has priority over B, and the balance to B, but it seems that if the fund is more than enough for B all further sums received by C will be for the benefit of A: *Benham v Keane* (1861) 1 John & H 685; affd (1861) 3 De GF & J 318; *Re Lord Kensington, Bacon v Ford* (1885) 29 Ch D 527.

Duties of trustees to answer inquiries

24.108 Under s 137 of the Law of Property Act 1925, subject to the payment of costs, the trustees are obliged to produce the notice to anyone interested in the beneficial interest[1]. Where the statute does not apply, however, the trustees are under no obligation to inform a potential incumbrancer of equitable interests. If the trustee decides to answer the inquiry, his duty is limited to giving an honest answer to the best of this actual knowledge and belief[2]. However, if a trustee makes a negligent misstatement that there is no prior incumbrance, he may be liable for economic loss flowing from such a statement, under the *Hedley Byrne & Co Ltd v Heller & Partners Ltd*[3] line of authority.

1 Section 137(8).
2 *Low v Bouverie* [1891] 3 Ch 82; *Ward v Duncombe* [1893] AC 369.
3 [1964] AC 465.

Duties of trusties as to custody of notice

24.109 Section 137(8) provides that the trustees from time to time of a settlement shall be entitled to custody of a written notice served under that section and that any written notice received by the trustees should be handed to over to new trustees[1]. However, although new trustees are obliged to inquire as to the property which is comprised in the trusts and, also, to look amongst the trust documents and papers, in order to discover what notices there are of incumbrances affecting the trust[2], there is no duty to inquire of the old trustees as to notices received[3].

1 See also *Re Booth's Settlement Trusts* (1853) 1 WR 444.
2 *Hallows v Lloyd* (1888) 39 Ch D 686.
3 *Phipps v Lovegrove* (1873) LR 16 Eq 80.

Service on trust corporation

24.110 Section 138 of the Law of Property Act 1925 makes provision for the nomination of a trust corporation in order to relieve trustees of their obligations in respect of the receipt of notices[1] of dealings affecting real or personal property. The court has jurisdiction, on the application of any person interested, to make a nomination in default of such a nomination by the trustees. Once a corporation has been nominated for this purpose, the name of the corporation must be endorsed on the trust instrument by the person who has custody of it. If, where a trust corporation is acting, a notice is given to a trustee, he must forthwith deliver or post it to the trust corporation and, until received by the corporation, it does not affect any priority[2]. A trust corporation appointed in accordance with s 138 must keep a register of notices of dealings[3] and may require the applicant to pay a fee in accordance with a prescribed rate before making an entry in the register[4]. Subject to the payment of the fee, the trust corporation must permit any person who would, if the corporation had been the trustee, have been entitled to inspect notices served on the trustee, to inspect the register and any notices held by the corporation[5]. Further, subject to the payment of a fee, the trust corporation must reply to all inquiries respecting notices in the same circumstances as if it had been the trustee of the trust instrument.

1 As to 'trust corporation', see Law of Property Act 1925, s 205 (1) (xxviii); Law of Property (Amendment) Act 1926, s 3; Public Trustee (Custodian Trustee) Rules 1975, and see further as to the nomination of a trust corporation, s 138(5), (6).
2 This does not seem to avoid the necessity of obtaining a stop order should the funds, at the time of the assignment, be in court: see **24.115**.
3 Section 138(7).
4 Section 138(8).
5 Section 138(9).

FORM OF NOTICE

24.111 By s 137(3) of the Law of Property Act 1925, notice must be in writing if it is to secure priority[1]. This applies to both real and personal property[2].

1 This provision does not alter the law as to the effect of notice to only one of several trustees. The only alteration in the law is as to the form of the notice. Verbal notice, or knowledge acquired incidentally, is not enough to satisfy the rule in *Dearle v Hall*. The notice must be in writing — see *Smith v The Owners of the Steamship 'Zigurds'* [1934] AC 209.
2 Prior to 1925, no written or formal notice was necessary, it was simply necessary to show that the trustee had such knowledge of the transaction, however acquired, as an ordinary man of business would act upon: *Lloyds v Banks* (1868) 3 Ch App 488; *Re Worcester, ex p Agra Bank* (1868) 3 Ch App 555 at 559; *Re Dallas* [1904] 2 Ch 385 at 399, CA, but it was not correct to say that incumbrances ranked not in the order of notices given by the incumbrancers, but of accidental knowledge obtained by the trustees: *Arden v Arden* (1885) 29 Ch D 702 at 708. Formerly, if the assignee was himself one of the trustees, the knowledge which he had of his own security gave him priority over subsequent assignments made during his life (*Browne v Savage* (1859) 4 Drew 635). It followed that if, before the fund came to the hands of the trustee, incumbrances were created in favour of A and then of the trustee, A could not secure priority. For notice by him would not operate until the trustee received the fund and, when this happened, the notice of his own security would attach and would give him priority: *Somerset v Cox* (1864) 33 Beav 634; *Roxburghe v Cox* (1881) 17 Ch D 520; see *Re Goddard, Hooker v Buckley* (1912) 57 Sol Jo 42, CA, but notice, though ineffectual to give priority over the trustee's existing charge, prevented the trustee from acquiring any new charge or right of set-off, and he was, from that time, bound to

withhold all further payments on account of the mortgagor unless made with the mortgagee's consent: *Stephens v Venables* (1862) 30 Beav 625; *Re Pain, Gustavson v Haviland* [1919] 1 Ch 38.

Apart from the question of notice, the priority of the holder of the fund extends not only to actual charges, but to all rights of lien, set-off, and other equities existing between him, or the estate out of which the fund is payable, and the person entitled to the fund subject to the incumbrances: *Webster v Webster* (1862) 31 Beav 393; *Stephens v Venables*, above; *Roxburghe v Cox*, above; see *Willes v Greenhill*, above. If the assignor was a trustee, the knowledge which he had of the security did not operate as notice to him, whether he was one of several trustees (*Lloyds Bank v Pearson* [1901] 1 Ch 865) or sole trustee (*Re Dallas* [1904] 2 Ch 385 at 401–402, CA). Thus, where the assignor was sole trustee, no effectual notice could be given: *Phipps v Lovegrove* (1873) LR 16 Eq 80; and where he was one of several trustees, it was a question whether notice to him and the other trustees would be a good notice to all the existing trustees so as to survive changes in the trusteeship: see *Willes v Greenhill* (1860) 29 Beav 376 (No 1), 387 (No 2); on appeal (1861) 4 De GF & J 147. In such a case a memorandum of the assignment should now be indorsed on the trust instrument: **24.113**.

Notice of assignment is notice of contents

24.112 As a general rule trustees to whom notice of an assignment is given have notice of all the contents of the deed. Thus, notice of a general charge by the deed is sufficient and the trustees and subsequent assignees must satisfy themselves as to the extent of the charge[1]. However, if a notice in general terms is incomplete, or erroneous, it does not necessarily give notice of the real contents of the deed, such as where the deed comprises two funds held under one settlement and the notice specifies only one fund as being affected, that notice will not be sufficient notice of the other fund[2]; and similarly, if the notice states that only sum A is charged on the assignor's interest, while sum B is also charged, the notice is only effective as to sum A, unless the charge of sum B is merely ancillary[3].

1 *Re Bright's Trusts* (1856) 21 Beav 430 at 434.
2 *Re Bright's Trusts*, above; *Mutual Life Assurance Society v Langley* (1886) 32 Ch D 460 at 474, CA.
3 *Re Bright's Trusts*, above.

Indorsement on trust instrument

24.113 Section 137(4) of the Law of Property Act 1925 provides that where, in relation to any dealing with an equitable interest in real or personal property:

(a) the trustees are not persons to whom a valid notice of the dealing can be given; or
(b) there are no trustees to whom a notice can be given; or
(c) for any other reason a valid notice cannot be served, or cannot be served without unreasonable cost or delay;

a purchaser of the interest may require that a memorandum of the dealing be indorsed on or annexed to the trust instrument and that the instrument be produced to him as proof that the memorandum has been indorsed on it. Once indorsed in this way, the memorandum has the same effect as notice given to trustees who would be qualified to receive it at the time the memorandum is indorsed[1].

In the case of settled land, the memorandum should be indorsed on the trust instrument, and not the vesting instrument, and in the case of land held on trust for sale, on the instrument whereby the equitable interest is created: sub-s (5). Where the trust is created by statute or by operation of law, or in the other cases where there is no trust instrument, the indorsement will be made on the instrument under which the equitable interest is acquired, or which is evidence of the devolution thereof; in particular, where the trust arises by reason of an intestacy, the letters of administration or probate in force when the dealing was effected are to be deemed the trust instrument: sub-s (6). Probate will be the appropriate instrument in cases of partial intestacy.

1 Where the fund is not a fund in court and consists of any government stock, and any stock of any body (other than a building society) incorporated within England and Wales, stock of any body incorporated outside England and Wales or of any state or territory outside the United Kingdom, being stock registered in a register kept at any place within England and Wales, units of any unit trust in respect of which a register of the unit holders is kept at any place within England and Wales, and there is no trustee—if, for instance, the sole trustee is dead and there is no legal personal representative—priority can be secured by serving on the Bank of England or the company a stop notice: see RSC Ord 50, rr 11, 12; and **2.27**.

As to giving an ordinary notice of equitable rights in shares to a limited company, see **24.96**. It may be necessary to have recourse to a stop notice, where, for instance, there is no trust instrument on which a memorandum can be indorsed.

TRUST INTERESTS IN REGISTERED LAND

24.114 The provisions of ss 137 and 138 of the Law of Property Act 1925 and the rule in *Dearle v Hall* now apply to registered land as they apply to unregistered land. As regards certain dealings with trust interests in registered land prior to 1 January 1987, a system corresponding to the nomination of a trust corporation was enacted by s 102 of the Land Registration Act 1925, such dealings being protected by priority cautions registered in the Minor Interests Index[1]. However all these provisions were abolished by s 5 of the Land Registration Act 1986[2]. As regards priority cautions registered before the repeal of s 102, it is no longer necessary to search the Minor Interests Index which has been abolished. Priority cautions registered before the repeal of s 102 rank in terms of priority in accordance with the date when the trustees or other persons appropriate to receive it, received the notice of the entry of the priority caution[3]. Where a trust corporation has been nominated under s 138(4) of the Law of Property Act 1925, the trustees of the settlement are under a duty to deliver notice of the entry as soon as practicable after the commencement of the Act to the trust corporation[4]. Compensation is payable by the Land Registry to any person who suffers a loss by reason of the operation of s 5 of the Land Registration Act 1986[5].

1 For the operation of s 102, see 9th edn of this work, pp 477–480.
2 The Land Registration Act 1986 came into effect on 1 January 1987, Land Registration Act 1986 (Commencement) Order 1986, SI 1986/2117.
3 Section 5 (2) (a). Trustees and registered proprietors received notice of an entry of a priority caution under r 229(1) of the Land Registration Rules 1925.
4 Section 5 (2) (b).
5 Section 5 (3), (4), subject to the Land Registrar's right to enforce against the trustees the right which the person indemnified would have been entitled to enforce.

FUNDS IN COURT

Stop orders[1]

24.115 When a fund is in court, an incumbrancer on it can secure priority by obtaining a stop order[2]. This will be as effectual for the purpose as notice in other cases[3]. A stop order gives priority even though another assignee has given notice before the stop order was obtained[4], provided the mortgagor claims directly under the trustees whose trust is being administered by the court[5].

The stop order will not give priority over a prior mortgagee of whose mortgage the party obtaining the stop order had notice when he made his advance, although such prior mortgagee may have omitted to obtain a stop order himself[6]. Where, however, the second incumbrancer was ignorant of the prior mortgage when he made his advance, he will get priority by means of a stop order even though he has notice of the prior mortgage at the time the stop order is obtained[7]. Like notice, the stop order applies only to the particular charge in respect of which it is obtained, although it is granted against the whole fund[8]. Apparently a stop order will not affect funds paid into court after its date unless those funds are named in the order[9].

1 For charging orders on funds in court, see **2.12** ff.
2 CPR, Sch 1, RSC Ord 50, r 10; see **2.28**. The application is made under CPR Pt 23, by application notice in pending proceedings and by claim form if there are no pending proceedings. Where an order to show cause has been made in relation to funds in court (including securities in court) and a copy thereof has been served on the Accountant General, no disposition by the judgment debtor of any interest to which the order relates, made after the making of that order, shall, so long as the order remains in force, be valid as against the judgment creditor: RSC Ord 50, r 6(1). Notice of the stop order should be given to all persons who have obtained similar orders on the fund: *Hulkes v Day* (1840) 10 Sim 41. A stop order cannot be obtained on a fund in court in respect of a mortgage of costs not yet ordered to be paid: *Lord v Colvin* (1862) 2 Drew & Sm 82. Where securities are not in court the procedure is by way of stop notice: see RSC Ord 50, rr 11 ff; and see **2.27**.
3 *Greening v Beckford* (1832) 5 Sim 195; *Swayne v Swayne* (1848) 11 Beav 463; *Warburton v Hill*, above; *Montefiore v Guedalla* [1903] 2 Ch 26. Where an assignee who has obtained a stop order assigns his interest, his assignee should obtain a stop order: *Wheatley v Bastow* (1855) 3 WR 296; on appeal (1855) 7 De GM & G 261, 3 WR 540.
4 *Pinnock v Bailey* (1883) 23 Ch D 497.
5 *Stephens v Green* [1895] 2 Ch 148, and see *Re Bell* (1886) 54 LT 370; *Re Dallas* [1904] 2 Ch 385 at 403, CA; *Re Seager Hunt* [1906] 2 Ch 295.
6 *Re Hamilton's Windsor Ironworks, ex p Pitman and Edwards* (1879) 12 Ch D 707 at 711; *Re Holmes* (1885) 29 Ch D 786; *Montefiore v Guedalla*, above.
7 *Timson v Ramsbottom* (1837) 2 Keen 35.
8 *Re Dallas* [1904] 2 Ch 385 at 395, CA.
9 *Timson v Ramsbottom*, above at 49.

Carrying share to new account

24.116 If, after the stop order has been obtained, the share is carried over to the account of the mortgagor and his incumbrancers, a stop order obtained by a later mortgagee will not affect the priority of him who obtained the first, though, it seems, it would be otherwise if the fund were carried over to the account of the mortgagor alone[1].

1 *Mutual Life Assurance Society v Langley* (1886) 32 Ch D 460; *Ward v Royal Exchange Shipping Co, ex p Harrison* (1887) 58 LT 174.

Stop orders on same day

24.117 When several stop orders have been obtained on the same day, a prior notice by one of the assignees will give priority to his claim[1]; or, perhaps, the claims rank in order of their dates[2], and where none of the assignees has obtained a stop order, notice to the trustees may be effectual to determine priority[3].

1 *Macleod v Buchanan* (1864) 4 De GJ & Sm 265. The order should state whether capital or income, or both, are affected. If it does not, recourse may be had to any part of the order to ascertain its operation: *Mack v Postle* [1894] 2 Ch 449.
2 *Shaw v Hudson* (1879) 48 LJ Ch 689.
3 *Lister v Tidd* (1867) LR 4 Eq 462; *Mutual Life Assurance Society v Langley*, above.

Incumbrance at payment in

24.118 When a person who has a lien upon a fund, of which he is the holder, pays it into court, he should state his claim and obtain a stop order; otherwise he may lose his priority as against a creditor without notice of the lien, who gets such an order[1], but if, before conversion and payment into court of the proceeds of incumbered property, an incumbrancer has completed his title by giving notice to the holder, his priority will not be affected by a stop order obtained by another claimant[2].

1 *Swayne v Swayne* (1848) 11 Beav 463.
2 *Brearcliff v Dorrington* (1850) 4 De G & Sm 122; *Livesey v Harding* (1856) 23 Beav 141; see *Re Marquis of Anglesey, De Galve v Gardner* [1903] 2 Ch 727 at 732.

Bankruptcy of beneficiary

24.119 If there is no fund in court which could be the subject of a stop order before the bankruptcy of the assignor, and the assignee has given notice, he will have a better right than the bankruptcy trustee to the fund when brought into court[1]. If the trustee himself makes the advance, the fund being in court, he should obtain a stop order, so that any other person who proposes to make an advance may ascertain if the fund is incumbered[2], and a trustee in bankruptcy must protect himself by a stop order[3].

1 *Day v Day* (1857) 1 De G & J 144.
2 *Elder v Maclean* (1857) 5 WR 447; see *Mutual Life Assurance Society v Langley*, above.
3 *Stuart v Cockerell* (1869) LR 8 Eq 607; *Palmer v Locke* (1881) 18 Ch D 381; and see **24.115**.

BILLS OF SALE (MORTGAGES OF CHATTELS)

Priority according to order of registration

24.120 Section 10(3) of the Bills of Sale Act 1878 provides that where two or more bills of sale are given comprising in whole, or in part, any of the same chattels, they shall rank in order of their registration.

Consequently, the holder of a later registered bill of sale does not, by taking possession of the goods, obtain priority over the holder of an earlier registered bill[1], and although the language of this subsection appears to be applicable only to questions of priority between earlier and later registered bills of sale, it provides in effect that registered bills of sale shall have priority over such as are unregistered, so far as the latter have any force[2], and an unregistered bill of sale will be void as against an execution creditor, though the latter had notice of it when his debt was contracted[3], but under the Bills of Sale Act (1878) Amendment Act 1882, all unregistered bills of sale given by way of security are ipso facto void[4].

1 *Re Middleton, ex p Allen* (1870) LR 11 Eq 209.
2 *Conelly v Steer* (1881) 7 QBD 520; *Lyons v Tucker* (1881) 7 QBD 523. For priority between the holder of a registered bill of sale and the unpaid vendor of the goods mortgaged, see *Bunbury Foods Pty Ltd v National Bank of Australasia Ltd* [1985] WAR 126.
3 *Edwards v Edwards* (1876) 2 Ch D 291.
4 Accordingly, a prior unregistered absolute bill of sale is not defeated by a subsequent registered bill given as security for money, since the grantor was not the true owner at the date of the later bill (Bills of Sale Act (1878) Amendment Act 1882, s 5): *Tuck v Southern Counties Deposit Bank Ltd* (1889) 42 Ch D 471.

Chattels

24.121 Where the equitable incumbrancer of chattels has completed his title by giving notice[1], he will have priority over the subsequent judgment creditor without notice, who has sued out his fi fa. It has, therefore, been held that a judgment creditor had no right to take in execution a ship and cargo, as against prior equitable mortgagees (under a security made whilst the ship was at sea), who had sent notice of the assignment to the master and had received immediate possession of the property from him upon the termination of the voyage[2].

1 See **5.1**.
2 *Langton v Horton* (1842) 1 Hare 549. It was intimated (at 560) that if the prior equitable title was incomplete, the claim of a subsequent judgment creditor as well as that of a subsequent equitable purchaser, might prevail, but this would be contrary to the principle stated above. The judgment creditor takes subject to any prior equity.

MORTGAGES AND CHARGES BY COMPANIES

24.122 Legal and equitable mortgages or charges by a company must be registered in the Companies Register[1]. Those mortgages or charges capable of registration under the Land Charges Act 1972[2] must also be registered under that Act[3]. Where the title to land is registered the charge[4] must also be registered under the Land Registration Act to confer protection against a subsequent disposition of the land including a subsequent charge. The registrar of the Land Registry is not concerned with any mortgage, charge, debenture, debenture stock, trust deed for securing the same, or other incumbrance created or issued by a company unless the same is registered or protected by caution or otherwise under the Land Registration Act[5]. Thus a purchaser from a company chargor will take free of any unprotected charge albeit the same may be registered as a company charge.

A floating charge not containing a restriction against subsequent dealing does not have priority over a subsequent fixed legal or equitable charge, even if taken with notice of the earlier charge[6]. If the floating charge does contain a restriction against dealing the subsequent chargee takes subject to the earlier charge only if he has notice of the restriction. Knowledge of the charge is not knowledge of the restrictive clause[7].

1 See **12.15–12.40** for the requirement and effect of registration and the consequences of non-registration.
2 As to which see **3.107** and **24.4**. A charge secured by the deposit of title deeds need be concerned only with registration under the company charges registration system.
3 However, a floating charge of a company need not be registered at the Land Charges Registry if registered in the company charges register. Such regisatration has effect as if registered under the Land Charges Act: Land Charges Act 1972, s 3 (7), (8).
4 A floating charge is not exempt from the need for protection, either by notice or caution: Land Registration Act 1925, ss 49 and 54. See **8.11**.
5 Section 60.
6 *Re Hamilton's Windsor Ironworks, ex p Pitman and Edwards* (1879) 12 CD 707. See generally, Floating Charges and Priorities (1974) 38 Conv 315; Goode *Legal Problems of Credit and Security* (2nd edn), pp 84-92; Gough *Company Charges* (2nd edn), Ch 12. As to floating charges, see **8.8**.
7 See generally **8.9**.

PRIORITY AGREEMENTS

24.123 It is quite common for a prior lender to agree to be postponed, either wholly or in respect of a particular asset, to a subsequent lender. Whatever the priority by operation of law the parties may agree between themselves, unless agreed otherwise with the mortgagor, a different order of priorities[1]. Although a mortgagor who wishes to have the secured debts satisfied in a particular order can require a specific term to be inserted in the mortgage preventing the priorities of the mortgages from being altered, a reference in the first mortgage to the charge being a first charge merely describes the nature of the security and confers no contractual right on the mortgagor to have that debt satisfied first[2]. A mortgagee of registered land cannot, however, gain priority over an existing protected or statutory tenant in occupation of a dwelling house by inducing him to sign a form of consent[3].

Postponement by agreement is effected by a deed of postponement or priority agreement as a separate document or included in a substantive transaction[4]: careful drafting is required. Any problems that arise are usually as to the construction of the extent of the postponement[5]. Special attention should be given to the consequences of insolvency. For example, lending banks or other lending institutions may agree to rank equally, in which case the fact that some of the lenders have floating, rather than fixed, charges and are therefore subject to the priority of preferential creditors, should be given attention[6].

One particular type of arrangement is the so-called subordination clause. For example, where a loan is made to a company which is part of a group, it is common to provide that other loans made by other members of the group to the borrowing company shall be subordinated to the outside lender[7].

1 *Cheah Theam Swee v Equiticorp Finance Group Ltd* [1992] 1 AC 472, PC. The parties may agree priorities whether the land is registered or unregistered land. As to the effect of an agreement postponing a fixed charge to a floating charge see *Re Portbase Clothing Ltd* [1993] Ch 388, [1993] 3 All ER 829.
2 *Cheah Theam Swee v Equiticorp Finance Group Ltd* [1992] 1 AC 472, PC.

3 *Woolwich Building Society v Dickman* [1996] 3 All ER 204, 72 P & CR 470, CA.
4 For forms, see 28 *Forms and Precedents* (5th edn, 1999 reissue) Mortgages. For the postponement of a wife's charge under the Family Law Act 1996, see the Appendix.
5 See eg *ANZ v National Mutual Life Nominees Ltd* (1977) 137 CLR 252; *Ashfield Land (Bartlett Court) Ltd v B Ratcliffe (Gloucester) Ltd* (11 May 2000, unreported), Ch D, issue as to whether the deed of priority contained a limit on the postponement of the priority.
6 See generally, Lingard *Bank Security Documents* (3rd edn) pp 337 ff.
7 On subordination clauses generally, see Goode *Commercial Law* (2nd edn) pp 663–666; Goode *Legal Problems of Credit and Security* (2nd edn) pp 23, 24 and 95-98; Gough *Company Charges* (2nd edn) pp 1035-1045 and see *Re Woodroffes (Musical Instruments) Ltd* [1986] Ch 366, [1985] 2 All ER 908; *AG v Mcmillan and Lockwood Ltd (In Rec and Liq)* [1991] 1 NZLR 53, NZCA; (1989) NZLJ 224 and (1991) NZLJ 39; [1987] 15 Aus Bus LR 80; [1989] LMCLQ 49 (Watts).
Where a bank gives an assurance that a mortgage held by it will be postponed to a mortgage in favour of a subsequent creditor and the latter relies on the bank's assurance, the bank is liable in negligence for the creditor's loss: *Federal Savings Credit Union Ltd v Hessian* (1980) 98 DLR (3d) 488, NSSC.

OTHER STATUTORY CHARGES

Charging orders

24.124 The court can for the purposes of enabling a judgment creditor to enforce his judgment make a charging order on the debtor's property[1]. A charging order so made has the same effect as an equitable charge in writing created by him[2]. The Land Charges Act 1972 and the Land Registration Act 1925 apply in relation to charging orders[3] as they apply in relation to other orders or writs issued or made for the purposes of enforcing judgments[4]. In the case of unregistered land, a charging order over the legal estate is registrable[5] but not over a beneficial interest alone[6]. If it is not registered it is void against a purchaser[7] of the land[8]. In the case of registered land, a charging order may be protected by notice, if it is one which in the case of unregistered land may be protected by registration under the Land Charges Act 1972, or by caution.[9] A caution registered to protect a charging order confers no priority[10].

It seems that such a charge takes effect subject to any prior mortgages, whether legal or equitable, affecting the estate or interest charged[11]. The rule in *Dearle v Hall*[12] does not relate to a judgment creditor.

1 Charging Orders Act 1979. For a detailed treatment of charging orders, see **2.12–2.20**.
2 Section 3(4).
3 Made pursuant to the Charging Orders Act 1979, as well as the Criminal Justice Act 1988 or the Drug Trafficking Act 1994.
4 Charging Orders Act 1979, s 3(2).
5 Land Charges Act 1972, s 6(1),(1A)(as added). It is registrable in the register of writs and orders affecting land. Registration is effective for five years but may be renewed: s 6(1)(c).
6 A charging order over the debtor's beneficial interest is not registrable: see Land Charges Act 1972, s 6(1)(c) and *Perry v Phoenix Assurance plc* [1988] 1 WLR 940.
7 'Purchaser' is defined as meaning any person (including a mortgagee or lessee) who, for valuable consideration, takes any interest in land or in a charge on land: Land Charges Act 1972, s 17.
8 Section 6(4).
9 Land Registration Act 1925, s 49(1)(g)(as amended), s 54(1)(as amended), s 59(1), s 6.
10 *Clark v Chief Land Registrar* [1994] Ch 370, [1994] 4 All ER 96, CA; *United Bank of Kuwait plc v Sahib* [1997] Ch 107, [1996] 3 All ER 215, CA.
11 *Whitworth v Gaugain* (1846) 1 Ph 728; *Legg v Mathieson* (1860) 2 Giff 71; *Kinderley v Jervis*

(1856) 22 Beav 1; *Eyre v M'Dowell* (1861) 9 HL Cas 619; *Wickham v New Brunswick and Canada Rly Co* (1865) LR 1 PC 64; *Chung Khiaw Bank Ltd v United Overseas Bank* [1970] AC 767, [1970] 2 WLR 858. Where the title to land is unregistered it is not considered that the chargee would obtain priority as against an unregistered puisne mortgage or general equitable charge (as to which see **24.4**) not least because the chargee cannot be described as a 'purchaser' within the LCA 1972, s 17 (see n 7).

12 *Dearle v Hall* (1828) 3 Russ 1.

Local land charges[1]

24.125 Local land charges consist principally of charges and restrictions imposed pursuant to various statutory powers by local authorities, water authorities, government departments or some other statutory body to secure a liability arising under statute, eg financial charges in favour of a local authority under the Public Health Acts and Highway Acts[2]. Such charges must be registered with the appropriate registering authority[3]. This applies equally to registered land[4]. Registration is deemed to constitute actual notice of the instrument or matter which is required to be registered under the local land charges register[5]. A local land charge, of the type creating a financial charge, when registered, takes effect as if it had been created by a deed of charge by way of legal mortgage, but without prejudice to the priority of the charge[6]. Statutory charges on 'the land' or 'the premises' confer priority both over existing and future incumbrances[7].

Failure to register a local land charge in the appropriate local land charges register does not affect the enforceability of the charge, but gives a purchaser who suffers any loss thereby, or by a defective official search certificate, a right to compensation[8]. Where the interest is subject to a mortgage the mortgagee may claim, but no compensation is payable in respect of the mortgagee's interest as distinct from the mortgaged property[9]. The nature, effect and priority of a statutory charge depends on the provisions of the statute in question[10].

1 See generally, *Garner's Local Land Charges* (12th edn).

2 For definition see Local Land Charges Act 1975, ss 1 (inclusion), 2 (exclusion) and the Acts referred to in Sch 1 of the 1975 Act. The Local Land Charges Act 1975 came into force on 1 August 1977: SI 1977/984. It replaced the Land Charges Act 1925, s 15 and other legislation.

3 Local Land Charges Act 1975, ss 5, 6. Registration is against the land affected: s 5(3). Registers are kept by each London Borough, the Common Council of the City of London and elswhere by each district council: s 3(1),(3).

4 By a notice or caution or other prescribed entry: Land Registration Act 1925, s 59 (2). Unless and until registered or protected on the register they take effect as overriding interests: Land Registration Act 1925, s 70(1)(i). Thus the charge albeit not registered will be binding on a purchaser. However, charges to secure money are not enforceable until registered: s 59(2) proviso. See Ruoff and Roper *Registered Conveyancing* (looseleaf).

5 Law of Property Act 1925, s 198 as amended by the Local Land Charges Act 1975, s 17(2), Sch 1.

6 Local Land Charges Act 1975, s 7.

7 *Paddington Borough Council v Finucane* [1928] Ch 567; *Bristol Corpn v Virgin* [1928] 2 KB 622; *Westminster City Council v Haymarket Publishing Ltd* [1981] 2 All ER 555, [1981] 1 WLR 677, CA.

8 Local Land Charges Act 1975, s 10.

9 Section 11.

10 See generally in respect of registered land, Ruoff and Roper *Registered Conveyancing* (looseleaf) para 23-33.

Improvement of Land Acts

24.126 Under the Improvement of Land Acts 1864 and 1899 and other statutes[1], money may be raised for the improvement of land and secured by charge upon it[2]. Such charges must, where the title to land is unregistered, be registered as land charges[3] at the Land Charges Register or they are void against purchasers of the land charged[4]. Where the title to land is registered the charge, if not registered, is protected by notice or caution[5]. Subject to the necessity for registration, charges under the Improvement of Land Act 1864 have priority both over existing and future incumbrances[6].

1 Lands Improvement Company's Acts 1853 to 1969.
2 See **12.109**.
3 As a Class A charge, see the Land Charges Act 1972, ss 2(2) and 4(1)–(4).
4 See the Land Charges Act 1972, ss 2(1),(2)(a), 4(2).
5 Land Registration Act 1925, s 49(1)(c), 59(2), Land Registration Rules 1925, r 155.
6 See the Improvement of Land Act 1864, s 59. See also **12.110**.

PART VII

INCIDENCE OF THE MORTGAGE DEBT

Chapter 25

Incidence on the death of the mortgagor

Formerly personal estate primarily liable

25.1 Formerly, as between the personal representatives of a deceased mortgagor, and the heir or devisee of the whole or part of mortgaged land, the mortgagor's personal property was primarily liable to the debt. The mortgagor's personal property exonerated the mortgaged land, which was treated only as collateral security[1].

1 See earlier editions of this work. For exoneration, see Chapter 26.

Mortgaged property now primarily liable

25.2 By a series of statutes, known as Locke King's Acts[1], now repealed, but reproduced and extended to mortgaged personal estate by the Administration of Estates Act 1925, the old rule was reversed. As between the persons entitled to the mortgagor's property, the mortgaged property, real or personal, is now the primary fund for the payment of the debt. The Administration of Estates Act 1925 provides:

> **35** (1) Where a person dies[2] possessed of, or entitled to, or, under a general power of appointment (including the statutory power to dispose of entailed interests) by his will disposes of, an interest in property[3], which at the time of his death is charged with the payment of money, whether by way of legal mortgage, equitable charge[4] or otherwise (including a lien for unpaid purchase money[5]), and the deceased has not by will, deed, or other document[6] signified a contrary or other intention, the interest so charged shall, as between the different persons claiming through the deceased[7], be primarily liable for the payment of the charge; and every part of the said interest, according to its value, shall bear a proportionate part of the charge on the whole thereof[8].
>
> (2) Such contrary or other intention shall not be deemed to be signified—
> (a) by a general direction for the payment of debts or of all the debts of the testator out of his personal estate, or his residuary real and personal estate, or his residuary real estate; or
> (b) by a charge of the debts upon any such estate;
>
> unless such intention is further signified by words expressly or by necessary implication referring to all or some part of the charge.

(3) Nothing in this section shall affect the right of a person entitled to the charge to obtain payment or satisfaction thereof either out of the other assets of the deceased or otherwise[9].

1 Real Estate Charges Acts 1854, 1867 and 1877.
2 The section applies whether the mortgagor dies testate or intestate.
3 Previous distinctions between different types of 'property' no longer exist as 'property' is defined to include 'a thing in action and any interest in real or personal property': Administration of Estates Act 1925, s 55 (1) (xvii).
4 Including an equitable charge by deposit, whether or not accompanied by a memorandum: *Pembrooke v Friend* (1860) 1 John & H 132; *Coleby v Coleby* (1866) LR 2 Eq 803; *Davis v Davis* (1876) 24 WR 962 (but note that it is not now possible to create a charge by mere deposit: Law of Property (Miscellaneous Provisions) Act 1989, s 2; *United Bank of Kuwait plc v Sahib* [1997] Ch 107). The Administration of Estates Act 1925 extends to every equitable charge, whether created by statute or however enforceable. Hence it applies to a charge for estate duty (*Re Bowerman, Porter v Bowerman* [1908] 2 Ch 340; *Re Wilson* [1916] 1 Ch 220) and a charging order on land (*Re Anthony, Anthony v Anthony* [1892] 1 Ch 450), but not to a general charge by the testator upon his real estate in aid of his personalty for payment of debts or legacies until the amount of the charge has become accurately defined: *Hepworth v Hill* (1862) 30 Beav 476.
5 This extension was introduced by s 2 of the Act of 1867. It includes a vendor's lien under a contract to create and sell ground rents: *Re Kidd, Brooman v Withall* [1894] 3 Ch 558; and a lien of a company: *Re Turner, Tennant v Turner* [1938] Ch 593, [1938] 2 All ER 560; *Re Birmingham* [1959] Ch 523, [1958] 2 All ER 397.
6 For a case where a contrary intention was signified by documents other than the will, see *Re Campbell, Campbell v Campbell* [1893] 2 Ch 206. See also *Re Nicholson, Nicholson v Boulton* [1923] WN 251; *Re Wakefield, Gordon v Wakefield* [1943] 2 All ER 29, CA; *Re Birmingham*, above.
7 The provision is only intended for the benefit of the beneficiaries inter se. See *Re Fison's Will Trusts* [1950] Ch 394, [1950] 1 All ER 501.
8 Unless the will shows a contrary intention each property charged, whether real or personal estate, contributes rateably to the payment of the charge: *Lipscomb v Lipscomb* (1868) LR 7 Eq 501; *Trestrail v Mason* (1878) 7 Ch D 655; *Re Newmarch, Newmarch v Storr* (1878) 9 Ch D 12, CA; *Re Major* [1914] 1 Ch 278. Value in this context means probate value: *Re Cohen* [1960] Ch 179, [1959] 3 All ER 740. Where several properties, each separately mortgaged, are devised to the same devisee, all the mortgages are consolidated in favour of the personal estate: *Re Baron Kensington, Earl of Longford v Baron Kensington* [1902] 1 Ch 203.
9 This provision is for the exclusive benefit of the mortgagee: *Lipscomb v Lipscomb*, above.

Contrary intention

25.3 The effect of sub-s (2)[1] is that a 'contrary intention' is not shown by a mere charge of, or direction for, the payment of the testator's debts out of his personal estate, or out of his other real estate; or out of a mixed fund, in aid of his personal estate, or in exoneration of his real or other real estate; or by a combination of those expressions[2]. Where there are several properties comprised in one charge the fact that a specific devise is made of one of the properties, while the other passes under a residuary devise, does not indicate a contrary intention[3].

A contrary intention is shown by a direction to pay mortgages out of a special fund[4]. In one case, a direction to pay debts out of the residue 'except the mortgage debts, if any, on' Blackacre implied that other mortgage debts were to be paid out of residue[5]. In another, a direction to pay 'trade debts' out of residuary personal estate was sufficient to exonerate real estate, the title deeds of which were subsequently deposited with the testator's bankers to secure an overdrawn trade account[6]. Where there are several properties comprised in one charge an indication that one property was intended to form a primary security and the other a secondary security will constitute a contrary intention[7]. The intention to exonerate must be signified by words referring clearly to the mortgage debt.

The intention to exonerate the mortgaged estate extends only to the value of the fund or property made liable by the testator. If that fund or property is insufficient, the residue must be borne by the mortgaged estate, though there may be other property which is liable by law to the testator's debts, eg, the general personal estate[8].

1 For the origin of sub-s (2)(a) see the 10th edition of this work at p 524.
2 *Re Newmarch, Newmarch v Storr* (1878) 9 Ch D 12, CA; *Re Rossiter, Rossiter v Rossiter* (1879) 13 Ch D 355; *Elliott v Dearsley* (1880) 16 Ch D 322. Nor was it shown even where the testator directed payment out of a specific fund of *all and every liability* which he might have incurred during his lifetime: *Re Hooper, Ashford v Brooks* [1892] WN 151.
3 *Re Neeld* [1962] Ch 643, [1962] 2 All ER 335, CA; overruling *Re Biss, Heasman v Biss* [1956] Ch 243, [1956] 1 All ER 89.
4 *Allie v Katah* [1963] 1 WLR 202, PC.
5 *Re Valpy, Valpy v Valpy* [1906] 1 Ch 531.
6 *Re Fleck, Colston v Roberts* (1888) 37 Ch D 677; see *Re Valpy, Valpy v Valpy*, above.
7 *Lipscomb v Lipscomb* (1868) LR 7 Eq 501; *Leonino v Leonino* (1879) 10 Ch D 460; *Re Athill, Athill v Athill* (1880) 16 Ch D 211, CA.
8 *Re Birch, Hunt v Thorn* [1909] 1 Ch 787, explaining *Allen v Allen* (1862) 30 Beav 395 at 403; *Re Fegan, Fegan v Fegan* [1928] Ch 45.

Where Act does not apply

25.4 The Act will not apply in a number of situations:

(a) where land belonging to a partner had been mortgaged to secure a partnership debt and, at the time of the partner's death, the partnership assets were sufficient to answer all the debts of the partnership[1];
(b) where a testator gave his son the option of purchasing the land at a fixed price; the price so fixed was taken to be for the land free from incumbrances[2];
(c) where the testator was a surety for the debt and the debt was paid off by the principal debtor after the testator's death[3].

Where the Act does not apply (or where the necessary contrary intention is shown) the devisee of the mortgaged land is entitled as against the remaining beneficiaries to have the mortgaged property vested in him unencumbered.

1 *Re Ritson, Ritson v Ritson* [1899] 1 Ch 128, CA.
2 *Re Wilson, Wilson v Wilson* [1908] 1 Ch 839; *Re Fison's Will Trusts* [1950] Ch 394, [1950] 1 All ER 501.
3 *Re Hawkes, Reeve v Hawkes* [1912] 2 Ch 251 (obiter: on the facts the testator was a principal debtor). For another situation where the Act did not apply, on facts which are unlikely to recur today, see *Re Williams, Cunliffe v Williams* [1915] 1 Ch 450.

Chapter 26

Incidence as between different properties

Liabilities of different properties

26.1 Where a mortgage includes properties belonging to different owners, each property may have to contribute its share of the common burden, or one property may be entitled to be exonerated by the other. There may also be a claim to exoneration where, though only a single property is mortgaged, the debt is primarily the debt of someone other than the owner of the property. The incidence of the debt is also varied by marshalling. The remainder of this chapter explains these concepts.

CONTRIBUTION[1]

The doctrine of contribution

26.2 The doctrine of contribution is typically resorted to where several properties charged with a single debt devolve into different ownerships. The doctrine rests upon the principle that a fund, which is equally liable with another to pay the debt, shall not escape because the creditor has been paid out of that other fund alone.

If several properties are mortgaged for, or subject equally to, one debt and are devised to different persons (and not to the same person[2]) the several properties will contribute rateably to the debt. For this purpose they are valued subject to any other incumbrance by which they are affected. The rule applies whether the properties belong to one or to several owners[3]. It also applies if a single owner of several properties, having mortgaged one of them, charges his land with, or devises it in trust for, payment of his debts[4]. It does not matter that one of the properties passes by a specific and the other by a residuary devise[5].

The right of contribution extends to sureties who are liable for the same debt and whose liabilities are contemporaneous[6].

The right of contribution between properties so charged is not affected by the Administration of Estates Act 1925, s 35[7]. Nor does this section affect the liability of real and personal estate to contribute rateably, when both are included in the same security[8].

It is to be emphasised that the right of contribution depends upon it being shown that as between mortgagor and mortgagee it was intended that the several funds should be equally liable. Different facts will produce different results. So, in one case, property was mortgaged for a repayment of a sum and later mortgaged together with another property for repayment of the original sum and a further advance. It was held that the first was to bear its own debt alone, but that both properties were to contribute rateably to the later debt (the value of the first property for this purpose being its value minus the first debt)[9]. But if there is a succession of loans given and securities taken over time, which the parties treat as in effect a single transaction, all will be charged rateably[10].

The requirement for the doctrine to apply that each property should be equally liable also means that there will be no contribution where one party is subject to a specific charge, and the other is subject merely to a general lien for the debt[11]. Nor will the doctrine apply if one property is surety or collateral security for another[12].

In questions of liability, the use of the word 'collateral' does not imply that the security so called is secondary to another and the absence of a special provision that one property shall be resorted to before another is relevant[13].

1 See generally on the doctrine of contribution *Wolmershausen v Gullick* [1893] 2 Ch 514; *Albion Insurance Co Ltd v Government Insurance Office of New South Wales* (1969) 121 CLR 342.
2 *Stronge v Hawkes* (1853) 4 De GM & G 186.
3 See *Aldrich v Cooper* (1803) 8 Ves 382; *Johnson v Child* (1844) 4 Hare 87. For contribution (or marshalling) in respect of settlement of debts of a group of companies, see *Brown v Cork* [1985] BCLC 363, CA.
4 *Carter v Barnadiston* (1718) 1 P Wms 505; *Irvin v Ironmonger* (1831) 2 Russ & M 531; *Middleton v Middleton* (1852) 15 Beav 450.
5 *Gibbins v Eyden* (1869) LR 7 Eq 371; *Sackville v Smyth* (1873) LR 17 Eq 153; *Re Smith, Hannington v True* (1886) 33 Ch D 195, dissenting from *Brownson v Lawrence* (1868) LR 6 Eq 1.
6 *Duncan, Fox & Co v North and South Wales Bank* (1879) 11 Ch D 88; and see (1880) 6 App Cas 1. As to co-sureties, see *Scholefield Goodman & Sons v Zyngier* [1986] AC 562, [1985] 3 All ER 105, PC, in which *D & J Fowler (Australia) Ltd v Bank of New South Wales* [1982] 2 NSWLR 879 was doubted.
7 *Sackville v Smyth*, above; notwithstanding *Brownson v Lawrence*, above; and see *Re Smith, Hannington v True*, above. For s 35, see **25.2**.
8 *Lipscomb v Lipscomb* (1868) LR 7 Eq 501; *Trestrail v Mason* (1878) 7 Ch D 655, and see *Re Dunlop, Dunlop v Dunlop* (1882) 21 Ch D 583 at 590, CA. As to foreclosure where there are rights of contribution and indemnity between co-mortgagors, see *Gee v Liddell* [1913] 2 Ch 62.
9 *Lipscomb v Lipscomb*, above; *De Rochefort v Dawes* (1871) LR 12 Eq 540.
10 *Leonino v Leonino* (1879) 10 Ch D 460; and see *Flint v Howard* [1893] 2 Ch 54, CA.
11 *Re Dunlop, Dunlop v Dunlop*, above.
12 *Marquis of Bute v Cunynghame* (1826) 2 Russ 275; *Stringer v Harper* (1858) 26 Beav 33.
13 *Re Athill, Athill v Athill* (1880) 16 Ch D 211, CA. For policies avoided by suicide, see **7.19**.

Where contribution excluded

26.3 The right of contribution may be prevented by the right of marshalling from being applied against a property which is liable to other creditors of the debtor, if that other property is the only security of the other creditors[1].

Further, if one of several properties charged with the payment of debts is expressly made liable to the payment of a mortgage debt to which it is subject, it will not be liable to contribute with other properties to the general charge[2].

1 *Bartholomew v May* (1737) 1 Atk 487. As to marshalling, see **26.8**. On the analogy of contribution to marshalling see *Finance Corpn of Australia Ltd v Bentley* [1991] ACL Rep

295 NSWCA (citing *Banner v Berridge* (1881) 18 Ch D 254); *Finance and Investment Pty Ltd v Van Kempen* (1986) 6 NSWLR 305, CA.
2 *Wisden v Wisden* (1854) 2 Sm & G 396.

EXONERATION

Where one owner personally liable

26.4 The doctrine of contribution may be displaced by the doctrine of exoneration. If the mortgagor of two properties, who is personally liable upon the covenant to repay, assigns one property, X, and retains the other, Y, X is no longer treated as equally liable with Y to bear the debt, unless the assignment is expressly made subject to the mortgage[1]. X is said to be exonerated. The duty of the mortgagor to discharge his own personal liability makes the property in his hands the primary fund for payment. So, too, where it has passed to one of his personal representatives. The consequences of exoneration are that if the mortgagor or his personal representatives have paid the debt, there is no equity to compel contribution from X[2]. Further, if the mortgagee enforces the debt against X, the assignee of that property is entitled to be exonerated at the expense of Y[3]. This is so whether the assignment of X was for valuable consideration or was voluntary[4].

1 *Re Mainwaring's Settlement Trusts, Mainwaring's Trustee in Bankruptcy v Verden* [1937] Ch 96, [1936] 3 All ER 540, CA.
2 *Re Darby's Estate, Rendall v Darby* [1907] 2 Ch 465.
3 *Re Best, Parker v Best* [1924] 1 Ch 42.
4 *Ker v Ker* (1869) 4 IR Eq 15. As to an exchange, see *Kirkham v Smith* (1749) 1 Ves Sen 258; and as to the effect of a sale by the court, *Lloyd v Johnes* (1804) 9 Ves 37 at 64. If a person, bound to elect between two properties, has mortgaged one of them before election, and afterwards elects to take the other, the first must be taken subject to the mortgage, but will be exonerated by the other: *Rumbold v Rumbold* (1796) 3 Ves 65.

Assignment of one property free from mortgage

26.5 If the mortgagor has assigned both properties, each to a different assignee, neither assignee is personally liable and the above justification for exoneration will not apply. Where, however, the first assignment (that of X) was to a purchaser for value and contained a covenant against incumbrances, or for further assurance, this is a ground for giving preferential treatment to X. In such a case, the assignee of X will be entitled to exoneration out of Y[1]. This is so albeit that his claim, being only equitable, will not be enforceable against a purchaser of the legal estate in Y for value and without notice[2]. It is the same where, on the assignment of X, the mortgagor represented that it was free from incumbrances[3], but it seems that this ground of exoneration is not available for a voluntary assignee[4].

1 *Re Jones, Farrington v Forrester* [1893] 2 Ch 461 at 470; see *Averall v Wade* (1835) L & G temp Sugd 252; *Hughes v Williams* (1852) 3 Mac & G 683; *Chappell v Rees* (1852) 1 De GM & G 393; *Re Roddy's Estate, ex p Fitzgerald* (1861) 11 I Ch R 369; *Re Roche's Estate* (1890) 25 LR Ir 271.
2 *Ocean Accident and Guarantee Corpn Ltd and Hewitt v Collum* [1913] 1 IR 337.
3 *M'Carthy v M'Cartie (No 2)* [1904] 1 IR 100 at 115; see *Finch v Shaw, Colyer v Finch* (1854) 19 Beav 500.
4 *Tighe v Dolphin* [1906] 1 IR 305; and see *Stronge v Hawkes* (1859) 4 De G & J 632.

Paramount mortgage

26.6 Where properties X and Y have become vested in an owner, A, subject to a mortgage which he did not create, but to which his title is subject, and he assigns X, whether for value or not, here again the first ground for displacing the principle of equality fails. Hence, if A pays off the mortgage, he is entitled to contribution from X[1], unless he assigned X on the footing that it was free from incumbrances, so as to entitle it to exoneration on the second ground[2].

1 *Ker v Ker* (1869) 4 IR Eq 15; and see *Re Darby's Estate, Rendal v Darby* [1907] 2 Ch 465.
2 See cases in **26.5**, n 1.

Mortgage for another's debt

26.7 A person who has mortgaged his property to secure the debt of another is presumed in the absence of other evidence to be only a surety and is entitled to be exonerated by the principal debtor. The same is true where jointly-owned property is mortgaged to secure money raised for the benefit of one joint owner. A great many of the cases illustrating the application of exoneration in such cases are examples of wives mortgaging their solely or jointly-owned property for their husband's benefit. The cases in question largely date from the Victorian era and before[1] and depended on inferences to be drawn as to the intentions of spouses in social conditions then obtaining. These conditions have now changed[2]. What is more, a lender seeking to enforce such a mortgage by a wife in modern conditions might well find recent developments in the law of undue influence mean that his mortgage is voidable at the wife's election[3].

Nonetheless, in a case where the mortgage is valid, the possibility of exoneration remains. The principle has been held[4] to be that where jointly-owned property is charged to secure the debts of only one of the joint owners then in the absence of a shared contrary intention, the other joint owner, being in the position of a surety, is entitled not only as between the two joint owners but also as between him or herself and the creditor, to have the secured indebtedness discharged so far as possible out of debtor's interest in the property. On the facts of that case, which concerned a broken marriage, the jointly-owned matrimonial home was mortgaged to secure an overdraft account. Payments made out of that account for the benefit of the joint household were not subject to the equity of exoneration and were to be deducted as much from the wife's share of the matrimonial home as the husband's. However, payments out of the account for the husband's business, and for his mistress, could not be charged to the wife's share, which was to that extent exonerated[5].

1 Discussed in the 10th edn of this work at pp 528–529.
2 *Re Pittortou* [1985] 1 All ER 285; [1985] 1 WLR 58.
3 For these developments, see **13.22** ff.
4 *Re Pittourtou*, above.
5 See also *Paget v Paget* [1898] 1 Ch 470; *Hall v Hall* [1911] 1 Ch 487.

MARSHALLING

Principle of marshalling

26.8 The doctrine of marshalling rests upon the principle that a creditor who has the means of satisfying his debt out of several funds shall not, by the exercise of his right, prejudice another creditor whose security comprises only one of the funds.

If the owner of two properties[1], X and Y, mortgages them both to A, and then mortgages one of them, Y , to B, B may require the securities to be marshalled. In other words, B may require that A's mortgage shall be discharged from property X so far as possible, and property Y, or so much as is not required for A's mortgage, be left to satisfy B's mortgage[2]. This principle applies to all securities, whether mortgages, charges[3], or liens, but does not apply where the creditor's right against the second fund is merely a right of set-off[4].

However, the doctrine applies only against the owner of the two properties, and not between the creditors inter se. The principle does not, in other words, interfere with the right of a creditor with several securities to resort to whichever he chooses. However, if, in the example, A did satisfy the whole of his debt from property Y, B would be subrogated to A's rights against X[5].

The principle of marshalling is not such as to confer an equitable right of property on a party to whom the right is available. It is no more than a right to seek from the court an equitable remedy in certain circumstances[6].

1 The doctrine applies to all types of property. For insurance policies, see *Heyman v Dubois* (1871) LR 13 Eq 158; *Bank of New South Wales v City Mutual Life Assurance Society Ltd* [1969] VR 556; *Commonwealth Trading Bank v Colonial Mutual Life Assurance Society Ltd* (1970) 26 FLR 338, [1970] Tas SR 120. The doctrine only operates in relation to securities given by the debtor not, eg, to a collateral security given by the debtor's company or by some relative: *Re O'Leary, ex p Bayne* (1985) 61 ALR 674.

2 *Lanoy v Duke of Athol* (1742) 2 Atk 444; *Aldrich v Cooper* (1803) 8 Ves 382; *Baldwin v Belcher, Re Cornwall* (1842) 3 Dr & War 173; *Tidd v Lister* (1852) 10 Hare 140 at 157; on appeal (1854) 3 De GM & G 874; *Gibson v Seagrim* (1855) 20 Beav 614; *Lawrence v Galsworthy* (1857) 3 Jur NS 1049; *Re Roddy's Estate* (1861) 11 I Ch R 369; *Webb v Smith* (1885) 30 Ch D 192, CA; *Bank of New South Wales v City Mutual Life Assurance Society Ltd*, above; *Commonwealth Trading Bank v Colonial Mutual Life Assurance Society Ltd*, above; *Victoria and Grey Trust Co v Brewer* (1971) 14 DLR (3d) 28; *Butler Engineering Ltd v First Investors Corpn Ltd* [1986] 1 WWR 469; *Mir Bros Projects Pty Ltd v Lyons* [1978] 2 NSWLR 505. See *Re Chute's Estate* [1914] 1 IR 180, where a bank mortgage for an overdraft was treated as paid off in accordance with the rule in *Clayton's Case* (1816) 1 Mer 572, as applied in *Devoynes v Noble, Deeley v Lloyds Bank Ltd* [1912] AC 756, see **28.50**. In *Lanoy v Duke of Athol*, above, it was said that the second mortgage must be taken without notice of the first, but this does not seem to be material: *Flint v Howard* [1893] 2 Ch 54 at 74, CA; but cf *Re Lawder's Estate* (1861) 11 I Ch R 346; *Re Roddy's Estate*, above; *Re Roche's Estate* (1890) 25 LR Ir 271.

3 *Lanoy v Duke of Athol*, above; *Rancliffe v Parkyns* (1818) 6 Dow 149 at 214.

4 *Trimmer v Bayne* (1803) 9 Ves 209; *Sproule v Prior* (1826) 8 Sim 189; *Webb v Smith*, above.

The doctrine has been applied, notwithstanding s 35 of the Administration of Estates Act 1925 (as to which see **25.2**) so as to entitle rentchargees under a will, whose rentcharges were to be created out of mortgaged land, to have the land sold, reserving the rentcharges, and then to have any deficiency made good out of the personal estate: *Re Fry, Fry v Fry* [1912] 2 Ch 86, following and applying *Buckley v Buckley* (1888) 19 LR Ir 544. It has also been applied by analogy where a broker pledged his customer's securities with his own, so that, on the broker's bankruptcy, and a sale by the pledgee of the customer's securities, the customer was entitled, as against the trustee in bankruptcy, to the benefit of the broker's securities: *Re Burge, Woodall & Co, ex p Skyrme* [1912] 1 KB 393.

5 *Mason v Bogg* (1837) 2 My & Cr 443; *Wallis v Woodyear* (1855) 2 Jur NS 179; *Dolphin v Aylward* (1870) LR 4 HL 486 at 500–501; *The Chioggia* [1898] P 1 distinguishing *The Edward Oliver Investors Corpn Ltd* (1867) LR 1 A & E 379, where the claimant was first mortgagee of three properties A, B and C; the defendant was second mortgagee of C; a sale of A and B alone would have produced a substantial deficiency, but a sale of all three properties would have produced a substantial balance. The second mortgagee was permitted to pay the first mortgagee the difference between the value of A and B and the first mortgage moneys and was subrogated to the first mortgage in respect of C. As to the case where the only fund to which the subsequent mortgagee could resort has been applied for the first creditor's debt by order of the court, see *Gwynne v Edwards* (1825) 2 Russ 289n.

A mortgagee may resort to funds not comprised in his security where, eg, that has been swept away by a landlord under a distress for rent: *Re Stephenson, ex p Stephenson* (1847) De G 586; and see *Aldrich v Cooper* (1803) 8 Ves 382.

6 *Commonwealth Trading Bank v Colonial Mutual Life Assurance Society Ltd* [1970] Tas SR 120 where the defendant was first mortgagee of land and of one of its own life policies. The bank was second mortgagee of the land. On default by the mortgagor, the defendant sold the land for more than its debt and reassigned the policy to the mortgagor. The bank claimed, unsuccessfully, that the defendant held the policy in trust for it.

No marshalling to injury of third incumbrancer

26.9 Equity will not marshall securities where in aiding one incumbrancer, it would injure another[1]. Thus, if properties X and Y are mortgaged first to A and then X is mortgaged to B, and Y to C, A may resort for his whole debt either to X or Y. If A is compelled by B to take his debt exclusively from Y, X will be left free for B. But this would be at the expense of C. Equity will not permit this result. For even if C had notice when he took his security, he had notice only than that A had security over Y[2]. He ought not therefore to lose the benefit of his security to B, who claims under no contract against that property. B having lent his money on property X only, and having taken no charge upon or covenant respecting Y, has against property Y merely a potential equity of marshalling. The subsequent security given to C prevents this equity from fully arising and B has no equity to prevent the mortgagor from charging property Y to C. In such a case, therefore, A would be required to look to both his securities, rateably according to their value, leaving the residue of each to satisfy the subsequent incumbrancer, to whom it was specifically mortgaged[3]. However, if C's mortgage is expressed to be subject to and after satisfaction of both the previous mortgages, B can marshal against C[4].

1 *Aldrich v Cooper* (1803) 8 Ves 382; *Averall v Wade* (1835) Ll & G *temp* Sugd 252; *Dolphin v Aylward* (1870) LR 4 HL 486 at 500–501; *Victor Investment Corpn v Fidelity Trust Co* (1973) 41 DLR (3d) 65, SC of Can.

2 A purchaser is not bound to take notice of all the equities arising out of a particular deed or action: *Averall v Wade*, above; *Shalcross v Dixon* (1836) 7 LJ Ch 180, but cf *Webb v Smith* (1885) 30 Ch D 192 at 202, CA.

3 *Barnes v Racster* (1842) 1 Y & C Ch Cas 401; *Bugden v Bignold* (1843) 2 Y & C Ch Cas 377; *Titley v Davies* (1843) 2 Y & C Ch Cas 399; and see *Gibson v Seagrim* (1855) 20 Beav 614; *Liverpool Marine Credit Co v Wilson* (1872) 7 Ch App 507; *Flint v Howard* [1893] 2 Ch 54, CA; and *Moxon v Berkeley Mutual Benefit Building Society* (1890) 59 LJ Ch 524; *Baglioni v Cavalli* (1900) 49 WR 236. In *Re Archer's Estate* [1914] 1 IR 285, under similar circumstances, marshalling of the first mortgagee's security in favour of the second mortgagee was allowed; but in *Smyth v Toms* [1918] 1 IR 338, this was considered to be opposed to *Barnes v Racster*, above, and the first mortgagee's debt was apportioned between his two securities.

4 *Re Mower's Trusts* (1869) LR 8 Eq 110.

In whose favour the doctrine applies

26.10 The doctrine of marshalling applies in favour of a subsequent mortgagee of one of the properties subject to the original mortgagee's security, and it applies generally in favour of persons taking under the mortgagor by assignment, whether for value or not. Thus, if, subsequently to the mortgage, the mortgagor settles one of the mortgaged properties, the mortgage debt will be thrown as far as possible on the other[1].

A surety is entitled to the benefit of marshalling[2]. As in the case of the mortgagee's right to hold several securities[3], his equity of marshalling overrides the right of the surety to have the benefit of all securities for the debt which he has discharged. However, a surety can by contract with the mortgagor prevent the mortgagor from conferring upon a later mortgagee the ordinary right to have the securities marshalled[4].

If a consignee or other agent pledges his principal's goods with his own for his own debt, the pledgee will be compelled to resort in the first instance to the agent's goods[5].

The doctrine does not apply in favour of the mortgagor himself or his trustee in bankruptcy, or his personal representatives, or persons who do not take by assignment or charge or conveyance an actual interest in one of the properties. Thus, it does not apply in favour of unsecured creditors[6], or in favour of a judgment creditor[7], unless he has obtained a charge on the estate[8].

1 *Hales v Cox* (1863) 32 Beav 118; *Aldridge v Forbes* (1839) 9 LJ Ch 37; *Anstey v Newman* (1870) 39 LJ Ch 769; *Mallott v Wilson* [1903] 2 Ch 494; but see *Re Lysaght's Estate* [1903] 1 IR 235.
2 *Heyman v Dubois* (1871) LR 13 Eq 158, and see *Re Westzinthus* (1833) 5 B & Ad 817.
3 See **27.10.**
4 *South v Bloxam* (1865) 2 Hem & M 457. This case was considered in *New Zealand Loan and Mercantile Agency Co Ltd v Loach* (1912) 31 NZLR 292.
5 *Broadbent v Barlow* (1861) 3 De GF & J 570; *Re Holland, ex p Alston* (1868) 4 Ch App 168; followed in *Re Stratton, ex p Salting* (1883) 25 Ch D 148, CA.
6 *Anstey v Newman*, above.
7 See *Averall v Wade* (1835) L & G temp Sugd 252 at 262; *Re Stephenson, Solomon v Trustees Executors & Agency Co of New Zealand* (1911) 30 NZLR 145; *Williamson v Loonstra* (1973) 34 DLR (3d) 275, BCSC.
8 *Re Fox* (1856) 5 I Ch R 541.

Against whom the doctrine is applied

26.11 The doctrine applies against the mortgagor[1], and persons claiming under him otherwise than by assignment or charge. Hence it applies against his trustee in bankruptcy[2], and his personal representatives[3], and against a judgment in his favour[4] and, a fortiori, his simple contract creditors. It also applies against the wife of the mortgagor who has charged her own property to secure the prior—that is, the double—creditors' debt[5].

1 *Haynes v Forshaw* (1853) 11 Hare 93.
2 *Baldwin v Belcher, Re Cornwall* (1842) 3 Dr & War 173; *Re Tristram, ex p Hartley* (1835) 1 Deac 288; *Re Holland, ex p Alston* (1868) 4 Ch App 168; *Heyman v Dubois* (1871) LR 13 Eq 158; see *Re Stephenson, ex p Stephenson* (1847) De G 586.
3 *Flint v Howard* [1893] 2 Ch 54 at 73, CA. The right to marshal formerly existed against the heir: *Lanoy v Duke of Athol* (1742) 2 Atk 444 at 446.
4 *Gray v Stone* (1893) 69 LT 282.
5 *Tidd v Lister* (1854) 3 De GM & G 857.

Marshalling excluded by exoneration

26.12 In accordance with the rule that marshalling will not be applied to the prejudice of the rights of third persons, it will not be applied to its full extent against persons claiming part of the property by assignment or charge, whether for value[1], or as volunteers[2], unless the other part had already been disposed of with a right to exoneration against the double creditor's mortgage[3]. Ordinarily it will be subject to apportionment of the first mortgage debt between the two parts of the property[4].

1 *Barnes v Racster* (1842) 1 Y & C Ch Cas 401; *Flint v Howard* [1893] 2 Ch 54 at 73, CA.
2 *Dolphin v Aylward* (1870) LR 4 HL 486 at 501.
3 As to such right of exoneration, **26.4**.
4 So far as *Finch v Shaw* (1854) 19 Beav 500; aff sub nom *Colyer v Finch* (1856) 5 HL Cas 905 at 922, and *Haynes v Forshaw* (1853) 11 Hare 93 suggest that the subsequent alienation of another part is necessarily subject to marshalling, they appear to be contrary to *Barnes v Racster*, above.

Maritime securities

26.13 Maritime securities will be marshalled so far as may be consistent with the rules of maritime priority. This qualification enables the owner of a cargo which is included in a bottomry bond, with the ship and freight, to resist a claim to throw the debt upon the cargo for the purpose of leaving the ship and freight to satisfy the debt of another bondholder, whose security was confined to them. By maritime law the cargo is not liable until the ship and freight are exhausted[1].

Demands for wages, pilotage, and towage, to which the ship and freight are liable pro rata, will not be thrown upon the freight, for the benefit of a bondholder on the ship only, so as to prejudice the owner of the cargo, by diminishing the residue of the freight which would otherwise be available for another incumbrancer upon the cargo[2]. Nor will the equity be applied where both funds are not under the control of the court. Therefore, seamen will not be compelled to proceed on their personal remedy for wages against the shipowner, that the ship may be left to satisfy the bondholder[3].

1 *The Priscilla* (1859) 1 Lush 1; *The Edward Oliver* (1867) LR1 A & E 379.
2 *The La Constancia* (1846) 2 Wm Rob 460.
3 *The Arab* (1859) 5 Jur NS 417.

Pleading

26.14 It is not necessary to frame the statements of case in a claim expressly for marshalling[1]. When the court sees at any time that one class of creditors will be deprived of their debts by the claims of another class upon their fund, it will, without being called upon, direct the assets to be marshalled[2].

1 See CPR 16.2(5).
2 *Gibbs v Ougier* (1806) 12 Ves 413; *Westpac Banking Corpn v Daydream Island Pty Ltd* [1985] 2 Qd R 330. See now Supreme Court Act 1981, s 49(2).

Chapter 27

Consolidation

Nature of consolidation

27.1 The mortgagee's right of consolidation is an equitable right. It may arise where a mortgagee holds several distinct mortgages by the same mortgagor. If the legal dates for redemption have passed[1], the mortgagee may within certain limits, and against certain persons entitled to redeem all or some of the mortgages, consolidate them, ie decline to be redeemed as to any, unless he is redeemed as to all[2]. The conditions in which the right will arise are discussed below. The principle is that, redemption being an equitable right, the person who redeems must on his part do equity towards the mortgagee, and redeem him entirely. It would be inequitable for the mortgagor to redeem one of his securities, leaving the mortgagee exposed to the risk of deficiency on the other[3].

A right of consolidation may also be expressly agreed between mortgagor and mortgagee in which case there will be no need to rely on the equitable doctrine. Rules or mortgages of building societies generally include a provision to the effect that the mortgagor shall not be entitled to redeem a mortgage without at the same time redeeming every other security on any other property for the time being in mortgage to the society by the mortgagor and a like provision is common in land mortgages.

The term consolidation is sometimes used in another sense. Where there are several mortgages subsisting between the same persons it may be convenient to treat the mortgages as one. A deed effecting such an arrangement is often called a deed of consolidation[4].

1 Or the mortgage moneys have otherwise become due; eg in an instalment mortgage on default.

2 Consolidation is an application of the rule that he who seeks equity must do equity (*Chesworth v Hunt* (1880) 5 CPD 266 at 271), and is a condition which can only be imposed on the equitable right to redeem which arises after default in payment, not on the contractual right to redeem on the day fixed for payment: *Cummins v Fletcher* (1880) 14 Ch D 699 at 708, CA; *Mills v Jennings* (1880) 13 Ch D 639 at 646, CA; *Minter v Carr* [1894] 3 Ch 498 at 501, CA; *Browne v Cranfield* (1925) 25 SRNSW 443 at 446–447.

The doctrine has been applied, but probably improperly, where they were several mortgages on the same property: *Re Salmon, ex p Trustee* [1903] 1 KB 147 (but cf *Snell's Equity* (30th edn) p 501, n 59). The Law Commission has recommended the abolition of the doctrine of consolidation: see Report 'Transfer of Land – Land Mortgages' (1991) Law Com No 204, para 6.44. For the conditions for consolidation, see below.

3 *Jennings v Jordan* (1881) 6 App Cas 698 at 700, HL; *Mills v Jennings*, above; *Griffith v Pound* (1890) 45 Ch D 553 at 560. The mortgagee is entitled to consolidate, whether the action is by a person who is actively seeking the aid of equity to redeem, or in a foreclosure

action, in which the mortgagor can redeem only upon the same terms as if he were suing for redemption; or in bankruptcy, whether the application to the court is by the mortgagee himself or not: *Tribourg v Lord Pomfret* (1773) Amb 733; *Re Loosemore, ex p Berridge* (1843) 3 Mont D & De G 464; *Watts v Symes* (1851) 1 De GM & G 240; *Selby v Pomfret* (1861) 3 De GF & J 595; notwithstanding *Holmes v Turner* (1843) 7 Hare 367n; *Smeathman v Gray* (1851) 15 Jur 1051. The mortgagor cannot insist upon consolidation as against the later mortgagee of two properties, of which there are prior mortgages to different persons. Either of such persons may be redeemed separately by the later mortgagee, notwithstanding the mortgagor's objection: *Pelly v Wathen* (1849) 7 Hare 351; affd (1851) 1 De GM & G 16.

4 For forms, see 28 *Forms and Precedents* (5th edn, 1999 reissue) Mortgages. Such deeds are often made by parent and subsidiary companies in favour of banks or financial institutions and contain cross guarantees and charges.

Statutory exclusion of consolidation

27.2 In practice the doctrine of consolidation was found to cause hardship to persons dealing with mortgaged estates and it was abolished by s 17 of the Conveyancing Act 1881, as to securities dated after that year, unless a contrary intention was expressed in the mortgage deeds or one of them. This provision was reproduced in the Law of Property Act 1925:

> **93** (1) A mortgagor seeking to redeem any one mortgage is entitled to do so without paying any money due under any separate mortgage made by him, or by any person through whom he claims, solely on property other than that comprised in the mortgage which he seeks to redeem.
>
> This subsection applies only if and as far as a contrary intention is not expressed in the mortgage deeds or one of them[1].
>
> (2) This section does not apply where all the mortgages were made before the first day of January, eighteen hundred and eighty-two.
>
> (3) Save as aforesaid nothing in this Act, in reference to mortgages, affects any right of consolidation or renders inoperative a stipulation in relation to any mortgage made before or after the commencement of this Act reserving a right to consolidate.

1 An undertaking by an equitable mortgagee to execute a legal mortgage, with all such powers and provisions and in such form as the mortgagee may require, does not entitle the latter to have the above section negatived: *Whitley v Challis* [1892] 1 Ch 64, CA; *Farmer v Pitt* [1902] 1 Ch 954.

Where the right of consolidation is to be preserved, it is usual to provide expressly that the section shall not apply to the security: see 28 *Forms and Precedents* (5th edn, 1999 reissue) Mortgages; and see the Appendix, but a clause providing for the preservation of the right of consolidation is equally effective: *Hughes v Britannia Permanent Benefit Building Society* [1906] 2 Ch 607 at 611. A clause excluding the statute contained in the first of several mortgages will preserve the right to consolidation although it is not contained in the subsequent mortgages: *Re Salmon, ex p Trustee* [1903] 1 KB 147, and a clause in a subsequent mortgage is effective as to previous mortgages: *Griffith v Pound* (1890) 45 Ch D 553.

In the leasehold enfranchisement context, for the purpose of determining the amount payable in respect of a mortgage on the landlord's estate the person entitled to the mortgage is not permitted to exercise any right of consolidation: Leasehold Reform Act 1967, s 12(3); Leasehold Reform, Housing and Urban Development Act 1993, Sch 8, para 3.

Conditions for consolidation

27.3 Where the statute is excluded, certain conditions must be met for the right to arise. It is necessary that the mortgages shall have been created by the same mortgagor, and that all the securities—with an exception as to the exercise of the power of sale—shall be in existence when the claim to consolidate is made. The legal dates for redemption must have passed (because consolidation is an equitable doctrine). However, the securities need not have been originally made to the same mortgagee, nor need they be of the same nature. Further discussion of these conditions follows.

Same mortgagor

27.4 The mortgages must originally have been made by the same mortgagor[1]. Thus, there can be no consolidation of a security given by a person for his own debt, with one given by him and another for their joint debt[2], and a mortgage by three cannot be consolidated with a prior mortgage by two of the same persons, though the equity of redemption belonged to all three[3]. For the mortgagee has no right to go behind the mortgagor and inquire into equitable interests for the purpose of consolidation[4].

1 *Cummins v Fletcher* (1880) 14 Ch D 699, CA; *Sharp v Rickards* [1909] 1 Ch 109; notwithstanding *Beevor v Luck* (1867) LR 4 Eq 537; and see *Marcon v Bloxam* (1856) 11 Exch 586; *Coronzo Pty Ltd v Total Australia Ltd* {1987] 2 Qd R 11 at 20.

2 *Re Raggett, ex p Williams* (1880) 16 Ch D 117, CA.

3 *Re Raggett, ex p Williams*, above.

4 *Sharp v Rickards* [1909] 1 Ch 109; and a mortgagee with several securities is not entitled to the discharge of both debts against a person who happens to be engaged with another in one mortgage only, though his co-mortgagor may have pledged another property to the same mortgagee: see *Jones v Smith* (1794) 2 Ves 372; *Aldworth v Robinson* (1840) 2 Beav 287; *Higgins v Frankis* (1846) 15 LJ Ch 329; *Bowker v Bull* (1850) 1 Sim NS 29.

Where a tenant for life had charged the estate in exercise of a power reserved to him, and had mortgaged the charge with other property to a second mortgagee, it was held that the remainderman might redeem the latter without paying off the whole debt, on the ground that the burden of the whole redemption would in effect be an increase, by so much, of the charge, making the estate of no value to those in remainder, but it was intimated that there was a distinction between the cases of the mortgagor and of the remainderman: *Lord Kensington v Bouverie* (1854) 19 Beav 39; affd (1859) 7 HL Cas 557. As to mortgages of different interest in the same land, see *Jones v Griffith* (1845) 2 Coll 207. For the form of an order for redemption where they were successive mortgages, first, of the entirety of land, and then of undivided shares, and the mortgages of the entirety and of one of the shares were assigned to the same person, see *Thorneycroft v Crockett* (1848) 2 HL Cas 239. The case was treated as if the securities on the undivided shares were charges on different estates, but now the entirety would be vested in trustees on a trust of land.

Securities in existence

27.5 The securities must be in existence at the time when consolidation is claimed. Hence a surplus on one mortgage cannot be retained to meet a deficiency on a mortgage which has ceased to exist through the determination of its subject matter, such as a lease[1] or a life interest[2]. However, this does not apply where a security has ceased to exist through realisation (eg sale by the mortgagee) and hence the mortgagee's right is not affected by his selling one of the estates under his power of sale[3].

1 *Re Raggett, ex p Williams* (1880) 16 Ch D 117, CA.

2 *Re Gregson, Christison v Bolam* (1887) 36 Ch D 223. See *Brecon Corpn v Seymour* (1859) 26 Beav 548.

3 *Selby v Pomfret* (1861) 1 John & H 336; *Cracknall v Janson* (1879) 11 Ch D 1, CA.

Different mortgagees

27.6 The securities need not have all been made to the same mortgagee. It is sufficient that they are united in the same person when consolidation is claimed[1]. But a mortgage to one person and a mortgage to the same person and another on a joint account cannot be consolidated[2].

The mortgagee may consolidate, though the mortgages were granted to trustees for him, and even where they are made to different sets of trustees[3]. If the mortgages are made to different mortgagees, one of whom takes an assignment from the other of his security, the assignee may consolidate, whether he had an interest which entitled him to require an assignment (as where he was surety for that debt[4]), or not[5].

A mere equitable interest in the securities will enable the mortgagee to hold them both, the right not being founded upon any principle connected with the legal estate[6].

1 *Tweedale v Tweedale* (1857) 23 Beav 341; *Vint v Padget* (1858) 2 De G & J 611; *Selby v Pomfret* (1861) 3 De GF & J 595; *Jennings v Jordan* (1881) 6 App Cas 698 at 700, HL; *Pledge v White* [1896] AC 187, HL.
2 *Riley v Hall* (1898) 79 LT 244. An assignment can be taken after the bankruptcy of the mortgagor, though the holder of an original security taken after notice of the insolvency of the mortgagor will not, in bankruptcy, be allowed to gain a preference by consolidating it with an earlier security for another debt: *Re Softley, ex p Hodgkin* (1875) LR 20 Eq 746.
3 *Tassell v Smith* (1858) 2 De G & J 713.
4 *Tweedale v Tweedale*, above.
5 *Vint v Padget*, above, followed in *Pledge v White*, above; and see *Re Salmon, ex p Trustee* [1903] 1 KB 147.
6 *Watts v Symes* (1851) 1 De GM & G 240; *Neve v Pennell* (1863) 2 Hem & M 170; and see *Re Loosemore, ex p Berridge* (1843) 3 Mont D & De G 464; where the rule was applied in bankruptcy by directing an account of what was due upon all the securities.

Securities may be of different natures

27.7 The mortgagee may consolidate securities of different natures, eg an assignment of personal property with a mortgage upon freeholds and leaseholds[1]. However, the surplus produced by a sale of goods included in a bill of sale cannot be held by the grantee of the bill of sale against an execution creditor, on the ground that the former holds a mortgage of other property from the same grantor. Such a claim is considered to be inconsistent with the definition of a bill of sale and with the provision as to setting out the consideration and other matters in the Bills of Sale Act 1878[2].

1 *Watts v Symes* (1851) 1 De GM & G 240; and see *Spalding v Thompson* (1858) 26 Beav 637; *Tassell v Smith* (1858) 2 De G & J 713; *Re McDonald* (1972) 28 DLR (3d) 380 (ancillary chattel mortgage).
2 *Chesworth v Hunt* (1880) 5 CPD 266; and a fortiori under the Bills of Sale Act (1878) Amendment Act 1882.

Against whom consolidation can be enforced

27.8 So long as there is no severance in the titles to the equities of redemption in the mortgaged properties, the right of consolidation is not affected by any change of ownership, whether by devolution on death, sale, mortgage, or otherwise[1]. Also, where property is mortgaged to different mortgagees, and the mortgages later vest in the same person, that person may still consolidate, notwithstanding that the vesting occurred after the change of title to the equities of redemption[2]; and with notice of such change[3]. However, this will only be the case if the mortgages were all made while the properties belonged to the original mortgagor[4].

1 *Re Breeds, ex p Alsager* (1841) 2 Mont D & De G 328; *Selby v Pomfret* (1861) 3 De GF & J 595; *Margrave v Le Hooke* (1690) 2 Vern 207.

2 Thus the right of consolidation exists where the mortgages become united after the bankruptcy of the mortgagor; *Selby v Pomfret*, above; *Re Salmon, ex p Trustee* [1903] 1 KB 147; or after the sale or further mortgage of both properties as one transaction to the same person: *Tweedale v Tweedale* (1857) 23 Beav 341; *Vint v Padget* (1858) 2 De G & J 611; *Pledge v White* [1896] AC 187, HL.

3 *Vint v Padget*, above. For the suggestion that a right of consolidation should be registered as a land charge (general equitable charge, Class C (iii)), see (1948) 92 Sol Jo 736, but quaere whether the right of consolidation amounts to a charge.

4 See *Squire v Pardoe* (1891) 40 WR 100; see also **27.4**.

No consolidation attaches after severance of equities

27.9 Where the title to the equities of redemption has been severed, the right of consolidation cannot be enforced unless it had already arisen prior to the severance. Thus, if the mortgagor assigns his equity in the first property, and then mortgages the second property, the assignee will take free of the mortgagee's right to consolidate. However, if the mortgages were made prior to the assignment of the equity in the first property, the assignee takes subject. The principle is that the assignee of one property takes subject to the possibility of existing mortgages being consolidated, but the mortgagor cannot by any subsequent dealing prejudice the rights of his assignee[1]. The purchaser of the equity of redemption therefore takes subject only to the equities which existed at the date of the conveyance to him and is not affected by possibilities of equities, which are dependent upon future and uncertain dealings with the property. For the same reason, there is no right of consolidation against the assignee where the properties were originally mortgaged to different mortgagees and the mortgages vest in the same person only after the separation of the equities of redemption of the different properties[2].

1 *Harter v Colman* (1882) 19 Ch D 630; *Mutual Life Assurance Society v Langley* (1886) 32 Ch D 460. There can be no consolidation after an assignment in bankruptcy: *Eastern Canada Savings and Loans Co v Campbell (No 2)* (1971) 19 DLR (3d) 231.

2 *Jennings v Jordan* (1881) 6 App Cas 698, HL; *Hughes v Britannia Permanent Benefit Building Society* [1906] 2 Ch 607, and see *Baker v Gray* (1875) 1 Ch D 491; *Minter v Carr* [1894] 3 Ch 498, CA. In *Andrews v City Permanent Benefit Building Society* (1881) 44 LT 641, a first mortgagee was allowed to consolidate against a second mortgagee who had notice of an express covenant for consolidation in the first mortgage. That case was not cited in *Hughes v Britannia Permanent Benefit Building Society*, above, the facts of which were substantially the same, where the claim to consolidate was rejected as being contrary to the principle of *Hopkinson v Rolt* (1861) 9 HL Cas 514 (see **24.75** ff), ie such a right of consolidation is treated as a right to tack further advances, so that the first mortgagee cannot consolidate mortgages created after he has received notice of the second mortgage.

As to the effect on consolidation of a consent by a second mortgagee to the first mortgagee making further advances in priority to himself, see *Bird v Wenn* (1886) 33 Ch D 215. As to the effect of a voluntary settlement on consolidation, apart from the Law of Property Act 1925, s 173 (2) (as to which, see **13.9** ff), see *Re Walhampton Estate* (1884) 26 Ch D 391.

Extent of right of consolidation

27.10 Subject to the above restrictions, a mortgagee may assert his right to consolidate even against a purchaser or mortgagee of the equity of redemption in one of the mortgaged properties who took without notice of the other mortgage[1]. Where a mortgagee of Blackacre and Whiteacre asserted a right to consolidate against a later mortgagee of Whiteacre, by refusing consent to a sale thereof by the latter under his power of sale unless he was paid out of the proceeds the total secured against both properties, the later mortgagee was taken to have paid that sum out of his own money. He was therefore subrogated to the first mortgagee's security over Blackacre and was in turn entitled to consolidate that security with others he enjoyed over other property of the mortgagor[2].

The right of consolidation overrides the right of the surety for one of the debts, who discharges it, to have the full benefit of the security for that debt[3], unless there is a special contract that the surety's right shall have priority, or unless fraud or misrepresentation against the surety has affected the rights of the mortgagee. A contract in the surety's favour will not be inferred from the mere fact that the suretyship extends only to one of the debts, and that he refused to be bound for the other[4].

1 *Ireson v Denn* (1796) 2 Cox Eq Cas 425; *Neve v Pennell* (1863) 2 Hem & M 170; *Cracknall v Janson* (1879) 11 Ch D 1, CA; *Neve v Pennell*, above; *Bovey v Skipwich* (1671) 1 Cas in Ch 201; *Titley v Davies* (1743) 2 Y & C Ch Cas 399n.
2 *Cracknall v Janson*, above.
3 See **26.10**.
4 *Farebrother v Wodehouse* (1856) 23 Beav 18, compromised on appeal (1857) 26 LJ Ch 240 (doubted in *Re Butlers Wharf Ltd* [1995] 2 BCLC 43). Cf *Nicholas v Ridley* (1904) 89 LT 234; affd [1904] 1 Ch 192.

Registered charges

27.11 By s 25 (3) of the Land Registration Act 1925, any provision in a charge which purports to affect any registered land or charge other than that in respect of which the charge is to be expressly registered is void. Rule 154 (1) of the Land Registration Rules 1925 provides that where a charge, whether affecting the whole or a part of the land comprised in a title, reserves the right to consolidate, it shall not on that account only be registered against any other land than that expressly described in it. Rule 154 (2) states that where the right reserved is to consolidate with a specified charge, on an application in writing made to register the right in respect of a specified charge, the registrar shall require the production of the land certificates[1] of all the titles affected and, on the production thereof, shall enter in the register a notice that the specified charges are consolidated.

The Registry view of these provisions is that s 25 of the Act does not operate to make void a clause in a charge of registered land which excludes s 93 of the Law of Property Act, for otherwise r 154 would be without meaning. Nor is a right of consolidation contained in a mortgage or charge dependent upon a notice under the Rules, although such a notice has its value[2].

1 An obvious slip for charge certificates.
2 Ruoff and Roper *Registered Conveyancing* para 23–41, where the practice is also set out. Note that before any entry as to consolidation can be made, all relevant charge certificates must be produced: Land Registration Rules 1925, r 154 (2).

PART VIII

DISCHARGE OF THE MORTGAGE

Chapter 28

Redemption

THE NATURE OF THE RIGHT OF REDEMPTION

The rights of redemption

28.1 A mortgagor enjoys two distinct rights to redeem the mortgage. The first is the contractual right, provided for expressly in the mortgage itself, and invariably expressed to be exercisable only at a certain time (usually the expiry of six months from the date of the mortgage). The second right is the equitable right, which is of much more importance in practice. The latter right may be exercised at any time after the contractual date, but only in accordance with conditions laid down by equity[1].

Both rights must be distinguished from the mortgagor's equity of redemption, which is discussed below.

The contractual right to redeem used to take the form of a proviso or condition in the mortgage to the effect that, if the mortgagor or his representative should pay to the mortgagee the principal sum, with interest at the rate fixed, on a certain day, the mortgagee, or the person in whom the estate was vested, would, at the cost of the person redeeming, reconvey to him or as he should direct[2]. This is still the practice in the case of a mortgage effected by an assignment of the mortgagor's interest[3]. A proviso for reconveyance was no longer appropriate after 1925 for a legal mortgage of land, which has to be made by demise[4] (or charge by deed expressed to be by way of legal mortgage). Statute provides that the term ceases on repayment[5]. However, in order to define the rights of the mortgagor and the mortgagee, a proviso is inserted expressly stating that the term will cease at the date fixed[6].

1 For historical discussion of the equitable right see *Medforth v Blake* [2000] Ch 86. For the question whether a mortgagor may repay the debt without being required to redeem the mortgage, see 10th edn of this book, pp 543–544.
2 See **1.7**.
3 Eg where the property mortgaged is a chose in action or an equitable interest in realty or personalty. For forms, see 28 *Forms and Precedents* (5th edn, 1999 reissue) Mortgages.
4 See **3.3**.
5 Law of Property Act 1925, ss 5, 116. See **28.54** and **28.56**.
6 See Law of Property Act 1925, ss 85(1) and 86(1). The right of redemption arises, without being expressly conferred, whenever property has been conveyed as a security for the payment of money (see **1.9**), and where the nature of the transaction is doubtful, it can be inquired into by the court; see **1.12**.

A mortgagor of chattels can still redeem even after the mortgagee has seized the goods, so long as the goods are in the mortgagee's possession: *Johnson v Diprose* [1893] 1 QB 512, CA.

The equity of redemption

28.2 Where a mortgage is effected by assignment or demise, then upon non-payment by the appointed time, the estate of the mortgagee at law becomes absolute and irredeemable. However, equity does not give to the mortgagor merely a right to redeem after the contractual date for redemption. From the outset of the mortgage, equity regards the mortgagor as the 'true' owner of the land, subject to the mortgage[1]. This equity of redemption is itself an interest in property, which has been described as an estate[2], and as an interest[3] or equitable right[4] inherent in the land. Its existence (unlike the equitable right to redeem) pre-dates the contractual redemption date[5]. The equity is assignable, chargeable and devisable — even at law[6] — and subsists until extinguished by, for example, sale or foreclosure, notwithstanding that the mortgagee's interest may in the meantime have become absolute.

In the case of legal mortgages of land after 1925, a legal estate remains in the mortgagor. This has led to suggestions[7] that since the mortgagor has a freehold estate he cannot have an equitable estate co-extensive with it, so that the equity of redemption subsists only as a right in equity to redeem the property, the right being attached to the mortgagor's legal estate. The better view, however, is that there is no such merger[8].

1 *Re Wells, Swinburne-Hanham v Howard* [1933] Ch 29, CA.
2 *Casborne v Scarfe* (1738) 1 Atk 603; *Re Wells, Swinburne-Hanham v Howard* [1933] Ch 29, CA.
3 *Lloyd v Lander* (1821) 5 Madd 282.
4 *Pawlett v A-G* (1667) Hard 465 at 469.
5 *Kreglinger v New Patagonia Meat and Cold Storage Co Ltd* [1914] AC 25 at 48, HL.
6 *Pawlett v A-G*, above; *Fawcet v Lowther* (1751) 2 Ves Sen 300 (it was subject to gavelkind and other customs which affected the ordinary legal ownership).
7 32 *Halsburys Laws* para 503.
8 Turner, *Equity of Redemption (Cambridge Studies in English Legal History)* pp 186–187; Waldock, *The Law of Mortgages* (2nd edn) p 205.

ASSIGNMENT OF EQUITY OF REDEMPTION

The right to assign[1]

28.3 In the absence of statutory[2] or other express provision to the contrary, the mortgagor is free to deal with the equity of redemption. Where, as in the case of a legal mortgage of land, the mortgagor retains a legal estate, the same proposition applies.

However, under most institutional mortgages the mortgagor is restrained from transferring the land without the lender's consent[3] and many other mortgages similarly so provide[4]. Such a restraint, which lasts only while the mortgage exists, is not objectionable as a clog on the equity[5]. The reason for the restraint is that burden of the covenant for payment does not run with the equity of redemption (or the mortgagor's legal estate)[6]. There is, therefore, a danger from the lender's point of view on a long term mortgage that if the borrower could freely dispose of the property, he might disappear leaving the lender to his security rights alone. In a falling market this would expose the lender to a loss.

Consent to a transfer of the equity is usually forthcoming on terms of the transferee entering into a covenant for payment with the lender[7]. A transfer without consent, where consent is required, does not in itself, in the case of unregistered land, invalidate the transfer, but will be a breach of the terms of the mortgage. The mortgage will usually provide that in such an event the lender shall have the right to call in the mortgage moneys, together with his other remedies.

In the case of registered land where the restraint is protected by a restriction, this will be to the effect that without an order of the registrar no transfer is to be registered without the consent thereto of the lender, so without the prior consent there can be no registered dealing with the land. Depending on the terms of the restraint provision in the mortgage, it may be possible to avoid the restraint by a transfer of the equitable interest or interests in the property[8]. This will not usually assist where an independent purchaser of the property is involved, but may be of some use where, eg a husband wishes to transfer his interest to his wife.

1 On the right to assign see *Casborne v Scarfe* (1838) 1 Atk 603; *Sibbles v Highfern Pty Ltd* (1987) 164 CLR 214. See now Law Commission Report no 204, para 6.31.
2 Eg in respect of advances made under the Small Dwellings Acquisition Acts: see now Housing Act 1985, s 456, Sch 18, para 4 (2), (3); see **28.4**.
3 For sale of equity of redemption on building society mortgages, see **28.4**.
4 See the Appendix.
5 See **28.6**.
6 See **17.5**.
7 See eg *Esso Petroleum Co Ltd v Alstonbridge Properties Ltd* [1975] 3 All ER 358, [1975] 1 WLR 1474. See the Appendix. In *Chelsea and Walham Green Building Society v Armstrong* [1951] Ch 853, [1951] 2 All ER 250, where there was a registered transfer of the equity and a covenant by the transferee with the building society which was not a party to the transfer it was held that the society could sue on the covenant.
8 See *Spellman v Spellman* [1961] 2 All ER 498 at 501, CA.

Form of assignment[1]

28.4 The mortgaged property is conveyed or otherwise transferred subject to the mortgage[2]. If the mortgagee is party to the assignment, there will normally be a release of the original mortgagor and this release should be extended to the covenants for title implied in the mortgage[3] and the assignee will enter into fresh covenants with the mortgagee. If the mortgagee is not party to the assignment, the assignee should covenant with the assignor to pay the principal and interest payable under the mortgage, to observe and perform the other covenants in the mortgage and to indemnify the assignor[4].

1 See 28 *Forms and Precedents* (5th edn, 1999 reissue) Mortgages; and the Appendix. On solicitors' liability, see [1982] Conv 331–333 (JEA).
2 On covenants for title by the assignor, see Law of Property (Miscellaneous Provisions) Act 1994, s 3(1), (3) and see **3.39**. For discussion in relation to the covenants which these provisions replaced, see [1982] Conv 254–5; and by joint assignors [1983] LS Gaz 1693; [1984] LS Gaz 628.
3 See Precedents for the Conveyancer, Form 16–A3; and for registered land, Form 17–A5; [1982] Conv 252–255 (JEA).
4 The burden of the covenant for payment does not run with the equity of redemption, see **17.5**.

THE TIME FOR REDEMPTION

Usual time for redemption

28.5 Even where the principal and interest are repayable by instalments a mortgage is usually made redeemable at the expiration of six months from its date[1]. The date for redemption should be the same as the date (if any) fixed by the covenant for payment[2]. It should be expressed in a legal mortgage so that the time when the right to foreclosure arises can be ascertained[3]. For the same reason a provision for redemption is sometimes included in a legal charge but, in the absence of such a provision, it is generally accepted that the right of the legal chargee to foreclose arises by implication at the date fixed in the covenant for payment[4].

When a time is fixed for redemption (and provided the time fixed is unobjectionable[5]) a mortgage is not redeemable until that time has arrived[6]. A mortgagee may take objection to an action to redeem at an earlier day even though the mortgagor tenders interest during the whole intervening period[7], but if the mortgagee has taken steps to recover payment by taking possession of the property or otherwise he cannot object[8].

Where no date for redemption is specified and the debt is repayable on demand by the mortgagee, the mortgagor may, it seems, redeem at any time, and this is apparently so even where the mortgagee has covenanted not to call the mortgage in until a specified date[9]. Where no date for redemption is specified but the covenant for repayment specifies a date for repayment, the mortgage can only be redeemed before that date on terms set by the mortgagee. Where there is no date for redemption but the covenant for repayment provides for instalment payments, whether redemption is postponed depends upon the form of the covenant. If there is a direct covenant[10], usually the borrower cannot redeem until the date for payment of the final instalment[11]. In any event the mortgagor cannot redeem while there are contingent liabilities secured by the mortgage capable of arising[12].

The mortgage may expressly provide for redemption at any time, on payment of the principal together with, for example, three months' interest thereon and all costs, charges and expenses due to the mortgagee and the costs of redemption, or after a specified period of notice or upon payment of interest in lieu of notice. Institutional mortgages sometimes permit redemption whenever the interest rate is varied.

1 See the Appendix.
2 See **3.25**.
3 See **3.41**.
4 See **3.41**.
5 See **28.6**.
6 Cited in *Hyde Management Services Pty Ltd v FAI Insurances Ltd* [1979] Qd R 98; affd (1979) 144 CLR 541.
7 *Brown v Cole* (1845) 14 Sim 427; and see *Harding v Tingey* (1864) 34 LJ Ch 13; *Hyde Management Services Pty Ltd v FAI Insurances Ltd*, above. For statutory exceptions see Chapter 34, Discharge or Modification by Statute.
8 *Bovill v Endle* [1896] 1 Ch 648; *Ex p Wickens* [1898] 1 QB 543 at 548, CA; *Re Mangan, ex p Andrew* [1983] ACLD 528: cf *Re Tori and McMahon* [1977] Qd R 256, affd (1977) 51 ALJ 586.
9 *GA Investments Pty Ltd v Standard Insurance Co Ltd* [1964] WAR 264, where it was held that the only notice required was for such period as would enable the mortgagee to receive the money and bank it, and see *Encyclopedia of Banking Law* vol 1 E(455). The difference between this and the previous case is that specifying a date for redemption indicates

that the mortgage is not a temporary investment (see 'the investment theory' in relation to the six months' rule, **28.33**).
10 See **3.25**.
11 *De Borman v Makkofaides* [1971] EGD 909. *Re Tori and McMahon*, above, is a special case as the mortgage was interest free and not to be regarded as an investment.
12 *Re Rudd & Son Ltd* (1986) 2 BCC 98, 955. And see *Estoril Investments Ltd v Westpac Banking Group* (1993) ACL Rep 295 NSW 24.

Postponement of redemption

28.6 The right of redemption[1], while it cannot be altogether done away with by the original contract[2], may be postponed by a covenant that during a certain time the mortgage shall remain irredeemable[3]. The mere length of time of any postponement is not in itself an objection to the enforceability of such a covenant, although it may well be an important consideration. So long as the essential requirements of a mortgage transaction are observed, and oppressive and unconscionable terms are not imposed, the court will not interfere[4]. The essential requirements of a mortgage transaction are not observed where the right of redemption is rendered illusory. The nature of the interest mortgaged is relevant in this respect. Where it is freehold or a long term of years is still outstanding, subject to the other conditions of not being oppressive or unconscionable, a long postponement may be unobjectionable[5]. On the other hand, where the interest mortgaged is a short term of years a postponement for as long as, or nearly as long as, the remainder of the term will render the equity of redemption illusory[6].

As to oppressive and unconscionable terms, relevant considerations are the absence of a corresponding restraint on the mortgagee, ie there is nothing to prevent him calling the mortgages in[7], the size of loan[8], the character and bargaining power of the parties—companies or individuals[9], the circumstances surrounding the loan[10] and, perhaps, the circumstances surrounding the claim that the postponement is invalid[11].

The doctrine of restraint of trade applies to mortgages. A postponement which might by itself be valid may thereafter be unenforceable if accompanied by an unreasonable restraint of trade during the postponement period[12].

If a provision for postponement is invalid, it is invalid as much against the assign of the mortgagor as against the mortgagor himself[13].

The mortgagee is entitled to the benefit of a valid postponement provision against a subsequent mortgagee, who took his security with notice of the covenant and who will not be allowed during the stipulated period to redeem the prior mortgage[14]. If he takes without notice, the equity of redemption also still seems to be bound in his hands by the covenant of the mortgagor who can give to another no better equity against the first mortgagee than he had himself.

A mortgage may be validly irredeemable for an uncertain period, when, for example, it is made to secure an annuity, or as in an indemnity against future liabilities, or for any other object not capable of immediate pecuniary valuation[15] and in certain cases statute permits the postponement of redemption[16]. The rule against perpetuities does not apply to a postponement provision[17].

1 Strictly the contractual right to redeem, but a restriction on the contractual right must necessarily affect the equitable right.
2 See **28.8**.
3 For consumer credit agreements, see s 94 of the Consumer Credit Act 1974 (right to complete payments ahead of time), s 113 (which puts a security in relation to a regulated agreement in the same position) and s 173 (contracting out forbidden): and **10.53**. Some

jurisdictions have a general statutory right to accelerate repayment: see eg New Zealand Law of Property Act 1952, s 81 (2); New South Wales Conveyancing Act 1919, s 93.

4 *Knightsbridge Estates Trust Ltd v Byrne* [1938] Ch 741, [1938] 2 All ER 444, Luxmoore J, revsd [1939] Ch 441, [1938] 4 All ER 618, CA; affirmed on other grounds [1940] AC 613, [1940] 2 All ER 401, HL. Note the distinction drawn by Sir Wilfred Greene MR between the equitable right to redeem and the contractual right. A direct covenant for repayment by a specified number of instalments or over a specified number of years may operate as a postponement; see *De Borman v Makkofaides* [1971] EGD 909; and the Appendix.

5 A postponement of 40 years in the case of freehold was considered unobjectionable in *Knightsbridge Estates Trust Ltd v Byrne*, above, CA. No opinion was expressed on this point in the House of Lords, in which the case was decided on the grounds that debentures may be irredeemable: see **28.6**, n 16.

The following periods have been held unobjectionable: five or seven years (*Teevan v Smith* (1882) 20 Ch D 724 at 729, CA); five years (*Biggs v Hoddinott* [1898] 2 Ch 307, CA); 14 years (*Williams v Morgan* [1906] 1 Ch 804); and see *Re Fortesque's Estate* [1916] 1 IR 268, CA (ten years). Such arrangements are supported on the ground that the contract is valuable to both parties—the mortgagee being sure of a continuing security and the mortgagor being freed from the expense and trouble of seeking new lenders. In *Multiservice Bookbinding Ltd v Marden* [1979] Ch 84, [1978] 2 All ER 489 the borrower appears to have accepted the validity of a ten years postponement.

6 *Fairclough v Swan Brewery Co Ltd* [1912] AC 565, PC (mortgage of term of 17½ years postponing redemption until last six weeks of term); *Davis v Symons* [1934] Ch 442, explained in *Knightsbridge Estates Trust Ltd v Byrne* [1939] Ch at 461–462, [1938] 4 All ER at 629 (mortgage of insurance policies maturing before end of postponement period); *Santley v Wilde* [1899] 2 Ch 474, CA (mortgage of ten years residue of term with covenant to pay one-third of net profits of rents derived from underleases—mortgage security for loan and for the payments under the said covenant) must be contrasted with these cases. It was criticised in *Noakes & Co Ltd v Rice* [1902] AC 24, HL, by Lords Macnaghten and Davy (although the criticism was on the basis that the case concerned a collateral advantage) and it seems impossible to support the decision. It has also been suggested by Dr J H C Morris that the transaction was not one of mortgage but a partnership agreement to share in the profits: Waldock *Law of Mortgages* (2nd edn) 187. And see *Bevham Investments Pty Ltd v Belgot Pty Ltd* (1982) 149 CLR 494.

7 *Williams v Morgan* [1906] 1 Ch 804; *Morgan v Jeffreys* [1910] 1 Ch 620; *Davis v Symons*, above, at 448. Quaere whether this consideration survived the supposed rejection of the test of reasonableness by *Knightsbridge Estates Trust Ltd v Byrne*, above.

8 *Knightsbridge Estates Trust Ltd v Byrne* [1939] Ch 441 at 455, [1938] 4 All ER 618 at 625, CA, per Sir Wilfred Greene MR. In that case the loan was £310,000 and the parties were a property company and the trustees of a friendly society bargaining at arm's length.

9 *Samuel v Jarrah Timber and Wood Paving Corpn* [1904] AC 323 at 327, HL, per Lord Macnaghten.

10 See *Knightsbridge Estates Trust Ltd v Byrne* [1939] Ch 441 at 454, [1939] 4 All ER 618 at 624, per Greene MR.

11 In *Knightsbridge Estates Trust Ltd v Byrne* interest rates had generally declined below the rate specified in the mortgage. This was no doubt why the mortgagor was seeking redemption. A restraint on redemption for 20 years and within 12 months' notice after that time, where the mortgagee was the solicitor of the mortgagor was rejected as oppressive in *Cowdry v Day* (1859) 1 Giff 316 and see *Talbot v Braddill* (1683) 1 Vern 183 at 394; *Morgan v Jeffreys*, above.

12 *Esso Petroleum Co Ltd v Harper's Garage (Stourport) Ltd* [1968] AC 269, [1967] 1 All ER 699, HL (21 years unreasonable, five years reasonable); *Re Petrol Filling Station, Vauxhall Bridge Road, London, Rosemex Service Station v Shell-Mex and BP* (1968) 20 P & CR 1; *Texaco Ltd v Mulberry Filling Station* [1972] 1 All ER 513, [1972] 1 WLR 814. The five years rule of thumb for petrol supply restraints was considered in *Alec Lobb (Garages) Ltd v Total Oil (GB) Ltd* [1985] 1 All ER 303, [1985] 1 WLR 173, CA. By virtue of the Supply of Beer (Loan Ties, Licensed Premises and Wholesale Prices) Order 1989, SI 1989/2258 a loan by a brewery which includes a tie cannot after 1 May 1990 prevent the repayment of the loan except by requiring more than three months' notice (art 2(3)(a)).

13 *Mehrban Khan v Makhna* (1930) LP 57 Ind App 168, PC at 172.

14 *Lawless v Mansfield* (1841) 1 Dr & War 557.

15 *Fleming v Self* (1854) 3 De GM & G 997. And see *Richards v Commercial Bank of Australia* (1971) 18 FLR 95. For a detailed survey of what in the USA are called 'dragnet clauses'

see *Estoril Investments Pty Ltd v Westpac Banking Corp* (1993) ACL Rep 295 NSW 24, per Young J.

16 A company may issue perpetual debentures: Companies Act 1985, sections 193, 744; and see *Knightsbridge Estates Trust Ltd v Byrne* [1940] AC 613, [1940] 2 All ER 401, HL. Certain agricultural mortgages and charges may be made irredeemable (see **9.7** ff, and the Agriculture Act 1967, s 28 (8) (to secure loan for amalgamation, etc)).

17 *Knightsbridge Estates Trust Ltd v Byrne* [1939] Ch 441 at 463, [1938] 4 All ER 618 at 631.

OTHER AGREED RESTRICTIONS ON THE RIGHT TO REDEEM

'Breaking' the mortgage

28.7 In many cases where redemption is postponed the terms of the mortgage also provide that if there is any default on the part of the mortgagor in the payment of interest or instalments for a specified period the whole of the mortgage moneys shall become due. Accordingly if the mortgagor has the means to redeem he has merely to default and then tender the mortgage moneys, but this cannot be done if the mortgagee has the choice of treating the default as making the mortgage moneys due or not.

Once a mortgage, always a mortgage

28.8 While redemption may be postponed, if the above-mentioned conditions are satisfied, it cannot be extinguished by any covenant or agreement made at the time of the mortgage[1] as part of the mortgage transaction[2]. This has been summarised in the rule 'once a mortgage, always a mortgage'[3]. Hence an agreement confining the right of redemption to any given period, such as the life of the mortgagor, or to any specified class of persons, such as to the mortgagor alone, will be invalid[4].

Nor will an agreement made at the time of the loan not to sue for redemption or for discharge of the equity of redemption upon some event or condition be allowed[5]; nor a separate covenant that if the mortgagee shall think fit, the mortgagor will convey to him so much of the estate as shall be of the value of the mortgage money at so many years' purchase[6].

An option granted to the mortgagee as part of the mortgage transaction to purchase the mortgaged property will not be enforceable, at all events if the purchase price is a fixed one[7]. The position is otherwise when the option relates to property other than the mortgaged property.

Where the mortgaged property is leasehold and the lease contains an option to renew or to purchase the reversion and the mortgagee exercises the option, the mortgagor is entitled on redemption to have the renewed lease or the reversion transferred to him, subject to payment of the proper expenses involved in exercising the option[8].

1 *Fairclough v Swan Brewery Co Ltd* [1912] AC 562. For the statutory exceptions, see **28.6**, n 16.

2 *Alec Lobb (Garages) Ltd v Total Oil (GB) Ltd* [1983] 1 All ER 944 at 965, [1983] 1 WLR 87 at 98, on appeal [1985] 1 All ER 303, [1985] 1 WLR 173.

3 *Newcomb v Bonham* (1681) 1 Vern 7; *Spurgeon v Collier* (1758) 1 Eden 55.

4 *Howard v Harris* (1683) 1 Vern 33 and 190; *Salt v Marquess of Northampton* [1892] AC 1, HL.

5 *Toomes v Conset* (1745) 3 Atk 261; *Vernon v Bethell* (1762) 2 Eden 110; *Salt v Marquess of Northampton*, above.

6 *Jennings v Ward* (1705) 2 Vern 520, as explained in *Biggs v Hoddinott* [1898] 2 Ch 307 at 315, 323, CA.

7 *Samuel v Jarrah Timber and Wood Paving Corpn* [1904] AC 323, HL, (1944) 60 LQR 191 (Williams); see also *Lewis v Frank Love Ltd* [1961] 1 All ER 446, [1961] 1 WLR 261 (option contained in assignment of mortgage; this was not really a case of a simple transfer, but more of a new loan. This case was applied in *Jones v Morgan* [2001] EWCA Civ 995, [2001] NPC 66; *Bannerman, Brydone Folster & Co v Murray* [1972] NZLR 411; *Re Supreme Court Registrar to Alexander Dawson Inc* [1976] 1 NZLR 615. An option granted before the mortgage was made and not part of the mortgage transaction would be enforceable: *London and Globe Finance Corpn Ltd v Montgomery* (1902) 18 TLR 661 (where it was held that the transaction was not a mortgage). Where, on a sale, part of the purchase moneys are left on mortgage, a covenant for pre-emption is good if part of the contract for sale: *Davies v Chamberlain* (1909) 26 TLR 138, CA; and see *Orby v Trigg* (1722) 9 Mod Rep 2. A right of pre-emption is not subject to the same objection as an option since the mortgagor cannot be compelled to sell and see *Re Petrol Filling Station, Vauxhall Bridge Road, London, Rosemex Service Station v Shell Mex and BP Ltd* (1968) 20 P & CR 1.

Where the mortgage and the option to purchase were part of a vendor and purchaser arrangement and where the option was given to prevent the property coming into the hands of a competitor it has been held that the option was enforceable: see *Re Moore and Texaco Canada* [1965] CLY 2548, and so the option is, probably, valid where it is part of the sale price of the property, but a mortgagee cannot sell to himself in exercise of his power of sale in accordance with an option or right of pre-emption: see *Williams v Wellingborough Borough Council* [1975] 3 All ER 462, [1975] 1 WLR 1327, CA. The clog rule in relation to options was reviewed in *Westfield Holdings Ltd v Australian Capital Television Pty Ltd* [1992] ACL Rep 295 NSW 10. On the liability of a solicitor for failure to advise in this context see *Bannerman, Brydone and Folster & Co v Murray*, above.

8 *Nelson v Hannam* [1943] Ch 59, [1942] 2 All ER 680, CA. Whether or not a mortgagee could stipulate to have the benefit of an option transferred to him as something collateral to a mortgage transaction was left open.

Release of equity of redemption

28.9 A mortgagee cannot at the time, or as a part, of the mortgage transaction, stipulate in advance for the extinguishment of the equity of redemption if the debt is not paid by a certain time. However, the equity of redemption may be released under a separate transaction[1]. The rule which prohibits a trustee from buying the trust property from his beneficiary, does not apply to a purchase of the equity of redemption by the mortgagee from the mortgagor, since they are regarded for such a purpose as on the ordinary footing of vendor and purchaser, until the contrary is shown by the person impeaching the deed[2]. There are thus no special rules applicable to the purchase of the equity of redemption by a mortgagee. The only significance of the relationship of mortgagor and mortgagee is that it affords to the unscrupulous mortgagee the opportunity to take an unfair advantage of the mortgagor. It is for this reason that the court will scrutinise the transaction with care[3].

The right of redemption will not be defeated, however, if the release was obtained by fraud or oppression, such as would invalidate a sale between an ordinary vendor and purchaser or, if by means of the influence of his position, the mortgagee has obtained the purchase at a nominal or insufficient price. Undervalue alone will not be sufficient to impeach the release[4]. The validity of the release may also be impeached for other reasons[5].

When the release is of an interest in land it must be in writing[6].

1 *Reeve v Lisle* [1902] AC 461, HL; but see *Lewis v Frank Love Ltd* [1961] 1 All ER 446, [1961] 1 WLR 261. *Lewis v Frank Love Ltd* has been applied to invalidate an agreement for the

transfer of part of the mortgaged property to the mortgagee reached some four years after the mortgage and without duress or unconscionability: see *Jones v Morgan* [2001] EWCA Civ 995, [2001] NPC 66. The court held on the facts that the later transaction was in effect part of a remortgage of the remainder of the property.
2 *Alec Lobb (Garages) Ltd v Total Oil (GB) Ltd* [1983] 1 All ER 944 at 965, [1983] 1 WLR 87 at 99, per Peter Millett QC.
3 *Alec Lobb (Garages) Ltd v Total Oil (GB) Ltd* [1983] 1 All ER 944 at 965, [1983] 1 WLR 87 at 99, per Peter Millett QC.
4 *Knight v Marjoribanks* (1849) 2 Mac & G 10; *Ford v Olden* (1867) LR 3 Eq 461; *Melbourne Banking Corpn v Brougham* (1882) 7 App Cas 307, PC.
5 Eg if it were made by a person without power to make it, or if there was no release of the covenant for payment of the debt.
6 Law of Property Act 1925, s 53; Law of Property (Miscellaneous Provisions) Act 1989, s 2 (for releases after 1 January 1990).

Lease to mortgagee

28.10 During the subsistence of the relation of mortgagor and mortgagee the mortgagee may not take a lease from the mortgagor upon terms which are, as regards the mortgagor, improvident[1], but this objection does not lie against an occupation lease for a short term at a fair rent[2].

1 *Webb v Rorke* (1806) 2 Sch & Lef 661; *Morony v O'Dea* (1809) 1 Ball & B 109; *Hickes v Cooke* (1816) 4 Dow 16, HL.
2 *Gubbins v Creed* (1804) 2 Sch & Lef 214; *Hicks v Cooke*, above; *Alec Lobb (Garages) Ltd v Total Oil (GB) Ltd* [1983] 1 All ER 944, [1983] 1 WLR 87.

Collateral advantages and clogs on the equity of redemption

28.11 The principle 'once a mortgage, always a mortgage' has already been discussed. However, it is unlawful not only to exclude the right to redeem, or postpone it to the point where it is illusory, or provide for it to be extinguished after a period or on the happening of an event. It is also unlawful for a mortgagee by a stipulation forming part of the mortgage transaction to prevent the mortgagor getting back on redemption exactly what he mortgaged[1]. This is the rule that there must be no clogs on the equity of redemption[2]. Thus a mortgagor who mortgages a free-house to a brewery is entitled on redemption to get back a free-house, and not one with a brewery tie[3].

The rule against clogs does not itself preclude the mortgagor from stipulating for an advantage which does not affect the property, or which affects the property but ceases on redemption. Such a clause is challengeable, if at all, only on other grounds. What is more, a condition which is expressed to obtain beyond redemption under the rule against clogs merely ceases to be enforceable on redemption. The clause will be valid until redemption, unless it is challengeable on some other ground.

If an advantage is not a clog, on what grounds may it be challenged? It is, of course, common for mortgage transactions to give to the mortgagee some advantage additional to the mortgagor's covenant to repay together with interest. However, when the charging of interest was prohibited by the usury laws, the courts were astute to strike down advantages which they regarded as disguised interest. Even after the charging of interest was permitted, it was for a time said that a mortgagor was not entitled to more than the principal, interests and costs. Additional advantages came to be known as collateral advantages, and were unlawful. Now that the severity of the old rule has been relaxed[4], the difficulty is to distinguish between those advantages which are consideration for the loan[5], and therefore lawful, and those which are collateral.

If the provision is contained in an agreement forming a separate transaction from the mortgage[6] or, if, although contained in the mortgage deed, it is independent of the mortgage[7], the special rules relating to collateral advantages do not apply and the validity of the stipulation must be determined on general principles. If, however, the stipulation can be construed as a term of the mortgage, the rule is that such a stipulation will not be enforceable[8] if it is either (a) unfair and unconscionable, or (b) in the nature of a penalty clogging the equity of redemption, or (c) inconsistent with or repugnant to the contractual and equitable right to redeem[9].

Relevant considerations in determining unfairness or unconscionability are the character and bargaining power of the parties—company or individual[10], the circumstances of the loan—commercial transaction or private loan[11], the quantum of consideration[12], the benefits to the mortgagor[13], the nature of the security[14], the nature and duration of the restriction (if any) on the mortgagor's right to deal freely with the mortgaged property and other property of the mortgagor[15], whether the borrower was advised by solicitors[16] and the terms of the collateral advantage[17]. A collateral advantage (as opposed to a clog affecting the property itself) is not, it seems, invalid merely because it is to endure after redemption[18]. It has been held that a stipulation will not be struck down for unconscionability unless the conscience of the stronger party is affected[19].

There are a number of miscellaneous rules associated with the rule against clogs and collateral advantages. Thus, a provision that a land mortgage may not be redeemed without also redeeming an associated chattel mortgage has been held not to be a clog[20]. A collateral advantage may affect the mortgaged property[21], or be personal to the mortgagor[22] (though a clog probably must purport to affect the mortgaged property). An enforceable collateral advantage, if in substance a restrictive covenant, may bind not only on the mortgagor but also on his assigns and tenants provided the general rules for the running of the burden of a restrictive covenant are met[23]. The special rules relating to collateral advantages apply to a debenture with a floating charge[24], but debenture holders may, if it is so provided, share in surplus assets although they have been paid off[25].

The doctrine of restraint of trade applies to collateral advantages, so that a restriction which is not invalidated by the test applicable to mortgages may be invalid for other reasons[26].

1. *Cheah Theam Swee v Equiticorp Finance Group Ltd* [1992] 1 AC 472 at 476.
2. The rule has been described as a useless appendix to the law, in a case where (somewhat suprisingly) the Court of Appeal then applied it in arguably novel circumstances: see per Lord Phillips MR in *Jones v Morgan* [2001] EWCA Civ 995, [2001] NPC 66. The Law Commission has recommended abolition of the rule against clogs and its replacement with a statutory jurisdiction: Law Com Rep, 204 Pt VIII. See also Devonshire (1997) 5 APLJ 21.
3. *Noakes & Co Ltd v Rice* [1902] AC 24.
4. By *Biggs v Hoddinot* [1898] 2 Ch 307.
5. *Santley v Wilde* [1899] 2 Ch 474, CA.
6. Whether or not a stipulation forms part of the mortgage is determined by the intention of the parties; *Kreglinger v New Patagonia Meat and Cold Storage Co Ltd* [1914] AC 25 at 61, per Lord Parker. The question is not one of form but of substance: at 39 per Lord Haldane; and see *Re Supreme Court Registrar to Alexander Dawson Inc* [1976] 1 NZLR 615 but the form may be the best evidence of the intention: at 43 per Lord Haldane. Cf *Jones v Morgan*, above.
7. The collateral advantage was independent in *De Beers Consolidated Mines Ltd v British South Africa Co* [1912] AC 52, HL; see *Kreglinger v New Patagonia Meat and Cold Storage Co*

Ltd, above, at 44 per Lord Haldane; *Re Petrol Filling Station, Vauxhall Bridge Road, London, Rosemex Service Station Ltd v Shell Mex and BP Ltd* (1968) 20 P & CR 1. See Law Commission Report (1991) No 204, Land Mortgages, proposing that in the case of a protected mortgage a postponement of the right to redeem should be void, unless the mortgaged property includes non-residential premises, in which case the postponement will be subject to the court's jurisdiction to set aside or vary the mortgage terms. This jurisdiction will replace the present equitable jurisdiction in relation to postponements of and clogs upon the equity and will apply to all types of mortgage. See Report, para 6.42 to 6.43 and Pt VIII.

8 So long, it seems, as the mortgagor has offered to repay the mortgage: see *Esso Petroleum Co Ltd v Harper's Garage (Stourport) Ltd* [1968] AC 269 at 299, [1967] 1 All ER 699 at 708, HL; *Amoco Australia Pty Ltd v Rocca Bros Motor Engineering Co Pty Ltd* [1975] AC 561, [1975] 1 All ER 968, PC.

9 *Kreglinger v New Patagonia Meat and Cold Storage Co Ltd*, above, at 61, per Lord Parker; and see *Knightsbridge Estates Trust Ltd v Byrne* [1939] Ch 441 at 457, [1938] 4 All ER 618 at 629, CA; *Cityland and Property (Holdings) Ltd v Dabrah* [1968] Ch 166, [1967] 2 All ER 639; *Multiservice Bookbinding Ltd v Marden* [1979] Ch 84, [1978] 2 All ER 489. In the latter case Browne-Wilkinson J did not think that Goff J by his reference to 'unreasonable' in the *Cityland* case had intended to cut down the effect of the *Kreglinger* and *Knightsbridge Estates* cases.

10 See eg *Cityland and Property (Holdings) Ltd v Dabrah* [1968] Ch 166 at 180, [1967] 2 All ER 639 at 647; *Multiservice Bookbinding Ltd v Marden* [1979] Ch 84 at 111, [1978] 2 All ER 489 at 502. In the latter case, where the amount of principal and interest payable was linked to the rate of exchange of the Swiss franc to the pound sterling, the judge compared the effect of the Swiss franc 'up lift' on the principal and interest to the rate of the capital growth of the premises.

11 See above.

12 *Esso Petroleum Co Ltd v Harper's Garage (Stourport) Ltd* [1968] AC 269 at 300, 323, [1967] 1 All ER 699 at 708–709, 723; *Alec Lobb (Garages) Ltd v Total Oil (GB) Ltd* [1985] 1 All ER 303 at 310, [1985] 1 WLR 173 at 179, CA.

13 *Amoco Australia Pty Ltd v Rocca Bros Engineering Co Pty Ltd* [1975] AC 561 at 579, [1975] All ER 968 at 978; *Alec Lobb (Garages) Ltd v Total Oil (GB) Ltd* [1985] 1 All ER 303 at 310, [1985] 1 WLR 173 at 179, CA.

14 In *Kreglinger v New Patagonia Meat and Cold Storage Co Ltd*, above, the security was a floating charge.

15 In *Bradley v Carritt* [1903] AC 253, HL and *Noakes & Co Ltd v Rice* [1902] AC 24, HL, the restriction was perpetual. In *Kreglinger v New Patagonia Meat and Cold Storage Co Ltd*, above, it was for five years.

16 *Multiservice Bookbinding Ltd v Marden* [1979] Ch 84, at 111, [1978] 2 All ER 489 at 502. On undue influence, see **13.23**.

17 In *Kreglinger v New Patagonia Meat and Cold Storage Co Ltd*, above, the right granted to the mortgagee to purchase the mortgagor's sheepskins was on the terms that the mortgagee should pay a price equal to the best price offered by any other person. Quaere whether the result would have been the same had the price not been such.

18 Cf *Noakes & Co Ltd v Rice*, above.

19 *Crédit Lyonnais Bank Nederland NV v Burch* [1997] 1 All ER 144, CA.

20 *Re Macdonald and Cowtin* (1972) 28 DLR (3d) 380.

21 As in *Biggs v Hoddinott*, above.

22 As in *Bradley v Carritt*, above.

23 *John Bros Abergarw Brewery Co v Holmes* [1900] 1 Ch 188; *Bradley v Carritt*, above; cf *Reeve v Lisle* [1902] AC 461, HL; *Davies v Chamberlain* (1909) 26 TLR 138, CA.

24 *De Beers Consolidated Mines Ltd v British South Africa Co* [1912] AC 52, HL.

25 *Re Cuban Land Co (1911) Ltd* [1921] 2 Ch 147.

26 *Esso Petroleum Co Ltd v Harper's Garage (Stourport) Ltd*, above; *Alec Lobb (Garages) Ltd v Total Oil (GB) Ltd* [1985] 1 All ER 303, [1985] 1 WLR 173, CA (where finance was raised, in effect, by lease and leaseback rather than mortgage). See (1969) 86 LQR 229 (Heydon); and see **28.6**, n 12. As to the possibility that solus ties may breach Art 81 of the Treaty of Rome, see *Courage Ltd v Crehan* [1999] 2 EGLR 145.

Bonuses, premiums and costs[1]

28.12 A provision for the payment by the mortgagor on redemption of a premium, bonus or other such sum is probably not automatically invalid, but is to be determined as to its validity in the same way as any other collateral advantage[2]. An exception might be where the premium required is so large as to make the right of redemption illusory. In such a case, the stipulation would, it is submitted, fall to be treated in the same way as an unlawful postponement of the right[3].

Mortgage loans made at a fixed rate of interest commonly provide for penalties payable by the mortgagor on early redemption. Depending on the wording of the provision, such a device may be permissible under a special rule relating to a mortgagee's entitlement to interest in lieu of notice of redemption[4]. This is considered below. Subject to this, the lawfulness of such redemption penalties would appear to be measurable against the above factors. It is anticipated that the redemption penalties of most institutional lenders are likely to be found to be lawful[5].

Likewise, a provision that a mortgage shall be redeemable only on payment of a larger sum than that advanced is not necessarily bad[6]. The sum may be larger than that advanced because a sum representing interest has been added to the advance[7] (ie at the beginning of the mortgage as opposed to a redemption penalty) or because the principal is index-linked[8]. A premium may be justifiable if it is in lieu of interest (so long as it represents interest at a reasonable rate[9]), or where the security is of a hazardous nature[10]. That the premium as well as the loan (and not merely the balance of the loan) shall become payable forthwith on default is a relevant factor[11].

If the provision is unreasonable it will not be payable, but interest on the principal sum advanced at a rate fixed by the court will be payable. The rate chosen will depend on the facts of the case[12].

In taking the account in a redemption action[13] the court will allow to the mortgagee a bonus or commission[14] actually deducted by him as a commission on making the advances provided the deductions were made as part of the mortgage contract under a bargain deliberately entered into by the parties on equal terms without improper pressure, unfair dealing or undue influence. The commission will be regarded as part of the consideration for the facility[15]. If it is not deducted at the time of the advance it will be subsequently allowed in taking account of what is due to the mortgagee or under the head of just allowance[16].

A reasonable sum may be deducted from the advance, but be allowed in the taking of accounts, in respect of a service charge[17]. Additional interest by way of 'commission' on unpaid instalments may be allowed if at a reasonable rate[18].

A solicitor-mortgagee can charge his costs, or those of the firm of which he is a member, for work done in negotiating a loan, deducing and investigating title, and preparing and completing a mortgage, against the security[19].

1 For the judicial control of extortionate credit bargains under ss 137–140 of the Consumer Credit Act 1974, see **10.83** ff. And on insolvency, see **8.15** and **13.14** ff.

2 *Kreglinger v New Patagonia Meat and Cold Storage Co Ltd*, above; *Cityland and Property (Holdings) Ltd v Dabrah* [1968] Ch 166, [1967] 2 All ER 639; *Multiservice Bookbinding Ltd v Marden* [1979] Ch 84, [1978] 2 All ER 489. For Law Commission recommendations, see **28.11**, n 7.

3 *Cityland and Property (Holdings) Ltd v Dabrah*, above.

4 See **28.34**.

5 But cf *Falco Finance Ltd v Gough* (1999) 17 Tr LR 526; Wurtzburg & Mills *Building Society Law* para 6.68 on the impact of para 2(b) of Sch 2 to the Unfair Terms in Consumer Contracts Regulations 1999. See also **3.50**.

6 *Potter v Edwards* (1857) 26 LJ Ch 468 (loan of £700 and premium of £300 held good); *Mainland v Upjohn* (1889) 41 Ch D 126; *C J Belmore Pty Ltd v AGC (General Finance) Ltd* [1976] 1 NSWLR 507.

7 *Cityland and Property (Holdings) Ltd v Dabrah*, above. Such sums added to the advance are commonly known as premiums.
8 *Multiservice Bookbinding Ltd v Marden*, above.
9 *Cityland and Property (Holdings) Ltd v Dabrah*, above. Inter alia, the nature of the security and the means of the borrower are relevant as to the reasonableness of the rate. In *Cityland*, where the premium was held unreasonable, the premium amounted to 57 per cent of the loan and could not be claimed to be in lieu of interest because interest was also claimed, but had it been in lieu of interest it would have represented interest at 19 per cent, or 38 per cent taking into account that on default it became payable forthwith.
10 *Potter v Edwards*, above; *Mainland v Upjohn*, above. See the review of these cases in *Cityland and Property (Holdings) Ltd v Dabrah*, above.
11 *Cityland and Property (Holdings) Ltd v Dabrah*, above; *Wanner v Caruana* [1974] 2 NSWLR 301; *O'Dea v Allstates Leasing System (WA) Pty Ltd* (1983) 57 ALJR 172; *Re Mangan, ex p Andrew* [1983] ACLD 528; *Van Kempen v Finance and Investment Pty Ltd* [1984] ACLD 697. For early repayment discount, see **28.13**.
12 *Cityland and Property (Holdings) Ltd v Dabrah*, above. However, in that case, no evidence of prevailing market rates was adduced. In fact the premium represented interest at 9½ per cent non-reducing over six years. Non-reducing rates are common in private mortgages and indeed any but institutional mortgages and 9½ per cent non-reducing was at the date of the decision far from being an exceptional rate. Hire-purchase rates are often higher. Day-to-day balances are exceptional. Even building societies lend on yearly balances. For a consideration of such mortgages, see the Report of the Committee on the Enforcement of Judgment Debts (the Payne Committee) 1969, Cmnd 3909, paras 1355–1358 ff.
13 As to which see Chapter 29.
14 In the case of building societies the Building Societies Act 1986, restricts commissions to directors, etc: see s 67 (as amended by the Building Societies Act 1997). For the nature of a premium, see *Re Phillips, ex p Bath* (1884) 27 Ch D 509, CA.
15 *Mainland v Upjohn*, above; *Biggs v Hoddinott* [1898] 2 Ch 307.
16 *General Credit and Discount Co v Glegg* (1883) 22 Ch D 549; *Bucknell v Vickery* (1891) 64 LT 701, PC.
17 *Wallingford v Mutual Society* (1880) 5 App Cas 685, HL; *Protector Endowment Loan and Annuity Loan Co v Grice* (1880) 5 QBD 592, CA. The costs of setting up the mortgage are, of course, greater at the start, though the charge will usually be spread evenly over the prospective term of the mortgage.
18 *General Credit and Discount Co v Glegg* (1883) 22 Ch D 549; *Bucknell v Vickery* (1891) 64 LT 701, PC.
19 Solicitors Act 1974, s 58.

Early repayment discount

28.13 For the type of mortgage where the interest is calculated for a fixed term and added to the principal as a premium, the mortgage should provide for an early repayment discount[1]. The absence of such may result in the premium being void as an unreasonable collateral advantage[2]. For regulated agreements under the Consumer Credit Act 1974, regulations provide for a rebate on early settlement[3] and these provisions will apply equally to any security provided in relation to a regulated agreement[4].

1 This is usually done by reference to a scheduled table or to the rule of 78 (a formula whereunder a sum of interest is spread over the period of a loan so that, in general terms, the interest is at a constant rate over the period and reducing. It is not advisable to provide for a discount based simply on the proportion of the term expired, because, although the interest element will have been spread evenly over the term of the mortgage, the interest is in fact greater in the early part of the term.
2 *Cityland and Property (Holdings) Ltd v Dabrah* [1968] Ch 166, [1970] 2 All ER 639; see **28.11**. Subject thereto there would appear to be no entitlement to a discount: see *Harvey v Municipal Permanent Investment Building Society* (1884) 26 Ch D 273, CA; *Wadham Stringer Finance Ltd v Meaney* [1980] 3 All ER 789, [1981] 1 WLR 39; Goode, *Payment Obligations*

in Commercial Transactions pp 51-53. The position is not like that in hire purchase where the owner is claiming damages against the hirer on default: see Goode *Hire-Purchase Law and Practice* (2nd edn, 1970) pp 399 ff.

3 Section 95. Consumer Credit (Rebate on Early Settlement) Regulations 1983 (SI 1983/1562; amended SI 1989/596).

4 Section 113. For a discussion on early settlement rebate in the consumer credit context, see the Crowther Report (1971) paras 5.4.4. and 6.7.6. ff.

PERSONS ENTITLED TO REDEEM

Mortgagor and his successors in title

28.14 The right to redeem is attached to the interest of the mortgagor, and is exercisable by him and also by those taking the whole of his interest, whether by assignment inter vivos, or by devolution on death. The right also belongs to those who have only a partial interest in the property[1].

1 *Pearce v Morris* (1869) 5 Ch App 227; *Tarn v Turner* (1888) 39 Ch D 456, CA (but cf *Re Australia and New Zealand Banking Group Ltd v Devine Holdings Ltd* [1991] ACL Rep 295, Qd FC (short term lessee not entitled to redeem). For loss of the right to redeem, see **28.83** ff.

Assignee of property subject to mortgage

28.15 The assignee of mortgaged property can redeem, even if a volunteer[1] and even if a voluntary assignment contains a power of revocation, so long as it is not acted upon. The assignee of one of two properties comprised in the same mortgage cannot insist on redeeming that property only, and cannot be compelled to do so, his right being to redeem the whole[2].

On assignment the mortgagor ceases to be entitled to redeem. However, his right to do so revives if he is sued for the mortgage debt (for which, in the absence of express provision, he remains liable after the assignment). He is then, in effect, a surety for the assignee[3] and he may redeem notwithstanding that the assignee has created fresh charges in favour of the mortgage[4].

The right to redeem extends also to a limited interest granted by the mortgagor, such as that of a lessee under a lease which is not binding on the mortgagee and which the mortgagee refuses to recognise[5]. It does not, however, extend to a statutory tenant under the Rent Acts[6].

1 *Rand v Cartwright* (1664) 1 Cas in Ch 59; *Howard v Harris* (1683) 1 Vern 190 at 193; *Carpentaria Investments Pty Ltd v Airs and Arnold* [1972] 1 Qd R 436; *Bunbury Foods Pty Ltd v National Bank of Australasia Ltd* [1985] WAR 126.

2 *Mutual Life Assurance Society v Langley* (1886) 32 Ch D 460, CA; *Hall v Heward* (1886) 32 Ch D 430, CA.

3 *Kinnaird v Trollope* (1888) 39 Ch D 636 at 645.

4 See above.

5 *Tarn v Turner*, above, at 465. Cf *Australia and New Zealand Banking Group Ltd v Devine Holdings Pty Ltd* [1991] ACL Re 295, Qd FC.

6 *Britannia Building Society v Earl* [1990] 2 All ER 469, [1990] 1 WLR 422.

Title by adverse possession

28.16 Where an adverse possessor has gained a title against the mortgagor, but not against the mortgagee, so that the mortgagor's title is extinguished and a new title created in the adverse possessor, there is in effect an assignment of the equity of redemption and he can redeem[1].

1 *Fletcher v Bird* (1896), decided by Hawkins J (afterwards Lord Brampton). A report of the judgment was given in the Appendix to the 6th edn of this work, p 1025 (cited in *Lee v Wansey* (1963) 81 WN (Pt 1) (NSW) 24).

Bankrupts

28.17 The bankruptcy of the mortgagor operates to vest the mortgaged property in the trustee and, as in the case of a voluntary assignment, the mortgagor ceases to be entitled to redeem[1]. The right to redeem passes to the trustee and, if the mortgagee comes in under the bankruptcy, it is exercisable in accordance with the Insolvency Rules 1986. If the mortgagee values his security for the purpose of proving in the bankruptcy, the trustee may redeem the security upon giving 28 days' notice at the value put upon it by the mortgagee[2], subject to the mortgagee's right to revalue[3] and subject to the trustee's right to have the property sold if he considers that the value put upon it by the remortgagee is excessive[4]. If, however, the mortgagee relies on his security, and remains outside the bankruptcy, the trustee cannot redeem except on the ordinary terms[5].

1 *Spragg v Binkes* (1800) 5 Ves 583.
2 Insolvency Rules 1986, r 6.117. A secured creditor may call upon the trustee to elect whether to exercise this power within six months, r 6.117 (4).
3 Rule 6.117 (2), revaluation of a security is governed by r 6.115.
4 Rule 6.118.
5 Where the mortgagee is the petitioning creditor and values his security for the purpose of the petition, it has been held that the trustee cannot claim to redeem at this value: *Re Vautin, ex p Saffery* [1899] 2 QB 549; *Re Lacey, ex p Taylor* (1884) 13 QBD 128. The point was left open by the Court of Appeal in *Re Button, ex p Voss* [1905] 1 KB 602, where it was held that for the purpose of proof the petitioning creditor would not, in the absence of mistake as to value, be allowed to depart from his estimate.

Bona vacantia

28.18 On the intestacy of the person entitled to the mortgaged property, in the absence of persons entitled as next of kin the property passes to the Crown as *bona vacantia*[1]. Where a corporation has executed a mortgage and later has been dissolved at a time when it was still entitled to the equity of redemption, the mortgaged property passes to the Crown as *bona vacantia*[2].

1 Administration of Estates Act 1925, s 46 (1) (vi); see now Intestates' Estates Act 1952, s 4 and Sch 1.
2 *Re Wells, Swinburne-Hanham v Howard* [1933] Ch 29, CA; Companies Act 1985, s 654.

Later mortgagee: 'redeem up; foreclose down'

28.19 A later mortgagee is entitled to redeem, but his right is not, as in the case of the mortgagor and the assignee of the mortgaged property, an absolute right[1]. If the right has to be asserted in a redemption action, the court will require the later mortgagee to redeem not only the prior mortgage, but all mortgages standing between his interest and that of the prior mortgagee (though not mortgages which are themselves prior to the interest of the prior mortgagee, to which the later mortgagee will in any event take subject). The court will also require the mortgagee seeking redemption to foreclose against the mortgagor and all mortgagees ranking after the redeeming mortgagee[2]. The reason is that the account taken in the redemption action will affect the amounts available to the owners of all interests ranking subsequent to that of the mortgage sought to be redeemed. Yet it is unreasonable to require the owners of those interests to be joined merely for the purposes of the account. Accordingly, the court insists that all interests be settled in the one action: 'redeem up; foreclose down'.

This requirement is strict. For example, if the later mortgagee has, by covenant, agreed with the mortgagor not to foreclose prior to a certain date, he cannot insist that, upon paying off the prior mortgagee, the latter shall assign the mortgage to him. Because the later mortgagee is unable to seek relief against the mortgagor by reason of his covenant, he may not seek to redeem the prior mortgagee and the action will fail[3].

However, the later mortgagee is not, in such a case, altogether without remedy. The court will restrain the first mortgagee from depriving him of his right by a sudden sale of the property, where it appears that the sale is about to be made for that purpose[4]. Moreover, the rule does not justify the first mortgagee in refusing to be redeemed except in an action. He should, without the necessity for judicial proceedings, accept payment from the second mortgagee and thereupon effect a transfer of the first mortgage[5].

1 *Teevan v Smith* (1882) 20 Ch D 724 at 729, CA.
2 *Fell v Brown* (1787) 2 Bro CC 276; 'The natural decree is that the second mortgagee shall redeem the first mortgagee, and that the mortgagor shall redeem him or stand foreclosed': *Palk v Lord Clinton* (1805) 12 Ves 48 at 58; *Farmer v Curtis* (1829) 2 Sim 466; *Teevan v Smith*, above.
3 *Rhodes v Buckland* (1852) 16 Beav 212.
4 See above.
5 *Smith v Green* (1844) 1 Coll 555 at 563.

Creditors

28.20 A judgment creditor, save in the cases mentioned below, cannot redeem. A charging order in favour of a judgment creditor of a mortgagor may be made on the mortgagor's land[1]. Such an order has the like effect as an equitable charge created by the debtor by writing under his hand[2] and takes effect subject to every liability under which the debtor holds it[3]. The chargee is therefore in the same position as the subsequent mortgagee dealt with above.

A further mode of execution is that of the appointment by the court of a receiver by way of equitable execution against a mortgagor's estate or interest in land[4]. A judgment creditor who has obtained such an order and registered it may redeem[5]. The receiver holds the property subject to prior incumbrances, but the judgment creditor can obtain a sale of the interest of the debtor in the land without redeeming prior incumbrances[6].

A judgment creditor has been allowed to make a payment to save an estate, where the representatives of the debtor omitted to do so[7].

The general creditors of the mortgagor cannot generally redeem[8], but under special circumstances this may be allowed. An example is where it is necessary for enabling them to obtain the benefit of an order of the court[9]. If creditors can make out that the trustees to whom the mortgaged property has been assigned for their benefit are colluding with the mortgagee to prevent the recovery of their claim, or that the trustees were called on to redeem and refused to do so, or that they themselves are unsafe, it seems they may redeem[10]. If the bankruptcy trustee refuses to bring an action to redeem for the benefit of the estate it seems that the creditor may do so under peril of costs[11], but liberty to redeem will be given to the trustee first and then to the claimant.

1 Charging Orders Act 1979, ss 1, 2 (2) (a). See **2.12**.
2 Section 3 (4). As to protection of such orders by registration, see Land Charges Act 1972, ss 6, 17 and Land Registration Act 1925, ss 49(1)(g), 59 (1); Charging Orders Act 1979, s 3 (2), (3). In *Perry v Phoenix Assurance plc* [1988] 1 WLR 940 it was held that a charging order against an undivided share in land could not be registered under the Land Charges Act 1972. Quaere: whether this decision has survived the Trusts of Land and Appointment of Trustees Act 1996. A list of charges similar in effect to charging orders is at s 49(1)(g) of the Land Registration Act 1925.
3 See **24.124**.
4 Supreme Court Act 1981, s 37; CPR, Pt 50 and Sch 1, RSC Ord 51. Such an appointment requires registration; see **28.19**, n 5 and **2.21**.
5 *Earl of Cork v Russell* (1871) LR 13 Eq 210.
6 *Wells v Kilpin* (1874) LR 18 Eq 298; *Beckett v Buckley* (1874) LR 17 Eq 435.
7 *Blagrave v Clunn* (1706) 2 Vern 576; *Frederick v Aynscombe* (1739) 1 Atk 392.
8 *Beckett v Buckley*, above.
9 *Christian v Field* (1842) 2 Hare 177.
10 *Troughton v Binkes* (1801) 6 Ves 573; *White v Parnther* (1829) 1 Knapp 179 at 229.
11 *Francklyn v Fern* (1740) Barn Ch 30 at 32.

Devolution on death

28.21 On the death of the mortgagor, the mortgaged property, and with it the right to redeem, devolves on his personal representatives[1], and is exercisable by them until, by assent or conveyance, the equity becomes vested in the devisee or other person entitled.

1 Administration of Estates Act 1925, ss 1, 3.

Where mortgaged property is settled or held on trust

28.22 In the case of settled land[1] the legal estate is vested in the tenant for life or statutory owners as trustee for all parties interested[2]. Where the mortgage affects the legal estate the right of redemption is primarily in the tenant for life as estate owner. The case is within the general rule that, for the purposes of redemption, the trustees represent their beneficiaries, and the beneficiaries should not seek to redeem on their own account unless the trustees are improperly refusing to do so[3].

In the case of land subject to a trust of land the legal estate is vested in the trustees and the general rule stated in the previous paragraph applies.

Where a mortgage has been made of a limited interest, such as a mortgage by the tenant for life of his life interest, this will be subject to redemption by the mortgagor and those claiming under him in the ordinary way.

1 No new settlements of land may be created after 1 January 1997: see Trusts of Land and Appointment of Trustees Act 1996, s 2.
2 Settled Land Act 1925, ss 16, 107 (1).
3 *Troughton v Binkes* (1801) 6 Ves 573 at 575; *Mills v Jennings* (1880) 13 Ch D 639, CA. An alternative would appear to be for the beneficiaries to seek an order under s 14 of the Trusts of Land and Appointment of Trustees Act 1996. For the power of trustees to

redeem, see s 6 of that Act. The old cases establish that a remainderman could not redeem without the consent of the tenant for life: *Ravald v Russell* (1830) You 9; *Raffety v King* (1836) 1 Keen 601; *Prout v Cock* [1896] 2 Ch 808. This is still probably so now that the tenant for life has the legal estate (in pre-1997 settlement).

Persons under disability

28.23 Land which is, by instrument made prior to 1 January 1997[1], limited in trust for an infant for an estate in fee simple or term of years absolute is for the purposes of the Settled Land Act 1925, settled land[2], and the right of redemption will be in the trustees in whom the land is vested. Where land is so limited by instrument made after that date it will be held on a trust of land, though the result is the same[3].

Where the right of redemption is vested in a patient it is exercised by the Court of Protection on his behalf[4].

1 The date on which the Trusts of Land and Appointment of Trustees Act 1996 came into force.
2 Settled Land Act 1925, s 1 (1) (ii) (d).
3 Trusts of Land and Appointment of Trustees Act 1996, s 2 and Sch 1, para 1.
4 Mental Health Act 1983, s 96.

Co-owners

28.24 Where, by reason of a tenancy in common, land is held on trust for the co-owners[1], and where there is a trust of land arising by reason of a joint tenancy[2], the primary right of redemption is in the trustees. Subject thereto one co-owner may redeem the whole debt[3].

1 Law of Property Act 1925, sections 1 (6), 34; Sch 1, Pt IV. Trusts of Land and Appointment of Trustees Act 1925, s 5 Sch 2, para 7.
2 Law of Property Act 1925, s 36.
3 *Marquis of Cholmondeley v Lord Clinton* (1820) 2 Jac & W 1; *Waugh v Land* (1815) Coop G 129; *Hall v Heward* (1886) 32 Ch D 430, CA. For partners, see *Hegeman v Rogers* (1972) 21 DLR (3d) 272, referring to *Re Pollard's Estate* (1863) 3 De GJ & Sm 541; *Cavander v Bulteel* (1873) 9 Ch App 79.

Sureties

28.25 The right to redeem belongs also to a person who is under liability for the mortgage debt[1], or whose property is subject to the debt[2]. Thus a surety, if he pays the debt himself, or if the mortgagor refuses to pay, is entitled to redeem[3]. If a third person has brought property of his own into the security he is entitled to redeem in order to protect his property. Thus a wife who has mortgaged her own property for her husband's debt, and in aid of a mortgage of his property, is entitled to redeem the husband's property[4].

1 *Green v Wynn* (1869) 4 Ch App 204.
2 *Gedye v Matson* (1858) 25 Beav 310.
3 This is by virtue of his right to avail himself of all the creditor's securities. The surety does not have the right to redeem, if he has given up his right to subrogation: *Royal Trust Co Mortgage Corpn v Nudnyk Holdings Ltd* (1974) 4 OR (2d) 721.
4 *Dixon v Steel* [1901] 2 Ch 602; *Re Thompson* (1976) 8 ALR 479. See **12.132** ff.

Spouse in occupation under Family Law Act 1996

28.26 Where a spouse is entitled under s 30 of the Family Law Act 1996[1] to occupy a dwelling house or any part thereof and makes any payment in or towards satisfaction of any liability of the other spouse in respect of mortgage repayments affecting the dwelling house, the person to whom the payment is made may treat it as having been made by that other spouse[2]. Although under this provision the mortgagee is not obliged to treat the payment as having been made by the other spouse, under another provision[3] such payment shall be as good as if made by the other spouse. It appears, therefore, that the occupying spouse can initiate the redemption of the mortgage. Under other provisions of the Act where the house is subject to mortgage and the mortgagee brings an action to enforce the security, the occupying spouse may apply to be made a party to the action[4] and in that manner, upon payment of the mortgage moneys, can obtain the redemption of the mortgage.

1 See **28.25**, n 4.
2 Family Law Act 1996, s 30(5).
3 Section 30(3). See *Hastings and Thanet Building Society v Goddard* [1970] 3 All ER 954, [1970] 1 WLR 1544, CA, and see **12.138**.
4 Family Law Act 1996, s 55, and for notice of proceedings, where the rights of occupation are protected, see s 56.

Reservation of redemption to third party

28.27 The present system of legal mortgage under which the proviso for reconveyance is replaced by a proviso for cesser[1] is inconsistent with a reservation of redemption to a third party[2], but should occasion arise for pursuing the matter reference should be made to the principles set out in earlier editions of this work.

1 See **3.41**.
2 See eg *Plomley v Felton* (1888) 14 App Cas 61 at 65, PC.

REDEMPTION OF BUILDING SOCIETY MORTGAGES

Generally[1]

28.28 The right of borrowers to redeem a building society mortgage are the same as under any other mortgage[2] and will be on the terms set out in the mortgage deed and in the rules of the society. A society must set out in its rules the conditions upon which a borrower can redeem[3], but a member[4] is not merely a mortgagor. He is liable to have his rights altered by an alteration of the rules and thereby to have his right of redemption postponed[5].

1 The distinction between terminating and permanent building societies is not made by the Building Societies Act 1986 (as amended by the Building Societies Act 1997). Owing to the repeal of s 106 of the Building Societies Act 1962 by the Building Societies Act 1986, Sch 19, a terminating society as such can not now exist. For the redemption of mortgages granted by terminating societies, see the 9th edn of this work at pp 534–535.
2 *Provident Permanent Building Society v Greenhill* (1878) 9 Ch D 122.
3 Building Societies Act 1986, Sch 2, para 3 (4), Item 5.
4 Schedule 2, para 5 (as amended by the Building Societies Act 1997).

5 *Bradbury v Wild* [1893] 1 Ch 377. The society, if it insists that a mortgagor shall only redeem subject to his liabilities as a shareholder, must prove his membership.

Future interest and fines

28.29 Although a mortgage provides for retention out of the proceeds of sale under the power of sale of all subscriptions, fines and other moneys[1] which should then be due, or should become due, in respect of the loan during the remainder of the period over which the repayment of the principal and interest was spread, this does not authorise retention in respect of interest after repayment of principal[2]. This would also apply to redemption, but a member cannot redeem without paying fines which are properly due from him[3].

In the absence of special contract members of building societies are entitled to redeem by paying up the amount remaining due on their securities and so put an end to their connection with the society. They are not bound to remain members for the purpose of sharing any loss that may have been sustained by the society[4].

1 See *Bailes v Sunderland Equitable Industrial Society Ltd* (1886) 55 LT 808.
2 *Re Goldsmith, ex p Osborne* (1874) 10 Ch App 41; *Matterson v Elderfield* (1869) 4 Ch App 207.
3 *Parker v Butcher* (1867) LR 3 Eq 762.
4 *Re West Riding of Yorkshire Permanent Building Society, ex p Pullman* (1890) 45 Ch D 463 (where the members had obtained a statutory receipt before the commencement of the winding up). Where there is a special contract, advanced members must on redemption pay their proper proportion of losses sustained by the society: *Re West of Yorkshire Permanent Building Society* (1890) 43 Ch D 407.

Liability on dissolution of society

28.30 Where a society is being wound up or dissolved by consent a borrowing member shall not be liable to pay any amount other than one which at that time is payable under the mortgage or other security by which his indebtedness to the society is secured. Hence advanced members cannot be required to pay the balance owing on their securities except in accordance with their contracts so they can continue to pay by instalments[1].

1 *Kemp v Wright* [1895] 1 Ch 121; Building Societies Act 1986, s 92 (as amended by the Act of 1997).

REDEMPTION ON COMPULSORY PURCHASE

28.31 The Lands Clauses Consolidation Act 1845 provides that the promoters of an undertaking to which that Act is applied by their special Act may purchase or redeem the interest of the mortgagee of any lands required for the purposes of the special Act, whether they shall have previously purchased the equity of redemption or not, and whether the mortgagee shall be entitled in his own right or in trust; and whether he be in possession by virtue of the mortgage or not, and whether the mortgage affect the lands solely or jointly with any other lands not required for the purposes of the special Act[1].

When this procedure is adopted the authority may redeem at once on payment of principal, interest and costs, with six months' additional interest, or may give six months' notice to pay, unless there is a current notice of intention to redeem by the mortgagor. Then either immediately or at the expiration of either of such notices, the mortgagee must reconvey on payment or tender of principal, interest and costs, the interest including any additional interest which the circumstances require[2]. If the mortgagee fails to reconvey, or to adduce a good title, the authority may deposit in the Supreme Court the amount due and vest the estate and interest of the mortgagee in themselves by deed poll[3].

Where the mortgaged land is of less value than the mortgage debt, the value of the lands or compensation to be paid must be settled between the mortgagee and the person entitled to the equity of redemption on the one part and the acquiring authority on the other or, failing agreement, determined by the Lands Tribunal[4]. When agreed or determined, it is to be paid by the authority in settlement of the debt so far as it will extend[5] and upon payment or tender the mortgagee must reconvey all his interest in the and to the authority or as it directs[6].

Similar provisions to those mentioned above apply if the mortgagee fails to reconvey or adduce a good title[7]. The payment to the mortgagee or into court must be accepted by the mortgagee in satisfaction of his debt so far as it will extend and will be a full discharge of the land from all money due thereon[8]. All rights and remedies possessed by the mortgagee against the mortgagor by virtue of any bond, covenant or obligation, other than the right to the mortgaged land, remain in force in respect of so much of the debt as has not been satisfied by the payment to the mortgagee or into court[9].

Further provisions of the Acts apply where part only of the mortgaged land is required by the acquiring authority and that part is of less value than the mortgage debt and the mortgagee does not consider the remaining part of the land a sufficient security for the money charged thereon or he is not willing to release the part so required[10].

If in any of the cases mentioned above there is in the mortgage deed a time limited for payment of the principal money thereby secured, and the mortgagee is required to accept payment of his mortgage money or of part thereof at a time earlier than the time so limited, the acquiring authority must pay to the mortgagee, in addition to the sum paid off, all costs and expenses properly incurred by him in respect of, or which shall be incidental to the reinvestment of, the sum paid off. If the rate of interest secured by the mortgage is higher than that which can reasonably be expected to be obtained on reinvesting the money, at the time when the mortgage is paid off, regard being paid to the current rate of interest, the mortgagee will be entitled to receive from the acquiring authority, in addition to the principal and interest, compensation in respect of the loss to be sustained by him by reason of the mortgage money being prematurely paid off[11]. The amount of the compensation is to be ascertained, in case of difference, or in other cases of disputed compensations by the Lands Tribunal[12]. Until payment or tender of the compensation the authority is not entitled, as against the mortgagee, to possession of the mortgaged land[13].

1 Section 108. See also the Compulsory Purchase Act 1965, Pt 1. These provisions are supplementary only to the general provisions of the respective Acts and do not exclude the right of mortgagees as owners to recover compensation for severance or other injurious affection: *R v Middlesex (Clerk of the Peace)* [1914] 3 KB 259.

In the absence of any express provision between the parties a mortgagee is entitled to a notice to treat even though the acquiring authority is negotiating only with the mortgagor and leaving him to discharge the mortgage: *Cooke v LCC* [1911] 1 Ch 604 (but see the more limited view of this case taken in *Shewu v Richmond upon Thames and Hackney London Boroughs* (1999) 79 P & CR 47). Unless the mortgagee agrees to the acquiring authority treating only with the mortgagor, the authority must take care that his interest is provided for, otherwise it will be restrained from carrying out the works on the mortgaged land until the mortgage has been redeemed or the appropriate compensation paid to the mortgagee: *Ranken v East and West India Docks and Birmingham Junction Rly Co* (1849) 12 Beav 298. If the authority purchases land from the mortgagor, the mortgagor must give notice to redeem: *Re Spencer-Bell to London and South Western Rly Co and Metropolitan District Rly Co* (1885) 33 WR 771.

2 Lands Clauses Consolidation Act 1845, s 108; Compulsory Purchase Act 1965, s 14 (2), (3).

3 Lands Clauses Consolidation Act 1845, s 109 (as amended by the Administration of Justice Act 1965, s 17, Sch 1); Compulsory Purchase Act 1965, ss 14 (4), (5), (6), 28 (2). For costs see Lands Clauses Consolidation Act 1845, s 80, as amended by Administration of Justice Act 1965, Sch 1; considered in earlier editions.

4 Lands Clauses Consolidation Act 1845, s 110; Compulsory Purchase Act 1965, s 15 (1).

5 Lands Clauses Consolidation Act 1845, s 110; Compulsory Purchase Act 1965, s 15 (2).

6 Lands Clauses Consolidation Act 1845, s 110; Compulsory Purchase Act 1965, s 15 (3). Where by reason of the confirmation of a CPO a mortgagor is unable to sell the property and discharge a mortgage thereon, the Lands Tribunal has no jurisdiction to determine compensation for additional interest paid in the meantime: *Shewu v Richmond upon Thames and Hackney London Boroughs* (1999) 79 P & CR 47.

7 Lands Clauses Consolidation Act 1845, s 111; Compulsory Purchase Act 1965, sections 15 (4), 28 (2).

8 Lands Clauses Consolidation Act 1845, s 111 (as amended by the Administration of Justice Act 1965, s 17, Sch 1); Compulsory Purchase Act 1965, sections 15 (6), 25 (1); Administration of Justice Act 1982, s 75, Sch 9, Pt 1.

9 Lands Clauses Consolidation Act 1845, s 111; Compulsory Purchase Act 1965, s 15 (7).

10 Lands Clauses Consolidation Act 1845, ss 112, 113; Compulsory Purchase Act 1965, s 16.

11 Lands Clauses Consolidation Act 1845, s 114; Compulsory Purchase Act 1965, s 17 (1).

12 Lands Clauses Consolidation Act 1845, s 114; Compulsory Purchase Act 1965, s 17 (2).

13 Lands Clauses Consolidation Act 1845, s 114; Compulsory Purchase Act 1965, ss 14 (2), (3), 16 (5). For mortgagee's costs, see Lands Clauses Consolidation Act 1845, s 80, as amended by the Administration of Justice Act 1965, Sch 1. For the rare cases where it will be necessary to consider these provisions, see the 8th edn of this work; and notes to RSC Ord 62, r 2 in the Supreme Court Practice (not reproduced in the replacement volume, Civil Procedure CPR Pt 50, Sch 1).

REDEMPTION OF CHARGING ORDERS

28.32 A charge imposed by a charging order has the like effect as an equitable charge created by the debtor in writing under hand[1]. The court making the order may at any time on application of the debtor or any person interested in any property to which the order relates make an order discharging or varying the charging order[2]. The grounds on which the court may discharge a charging order include that the judgment debt has been satisfied[3], including interest and costs whether or not expressly stated in the order[4], or that the order should never have been made absolute[5].

1 Charging Orders Act 1979, s 3(4).
2 Section 3(5).
3 CPR Part 50, Sch 1, RSC Ord 50, r.7(2).
4 *Ezekiel v Orakpo* [1997] 1 WLR 340.
5 *Howell v Montey* (1990) 61 P & CR 18.

PAYMENT OF THE DEBT

NOTICE TO PAY OFF

Notice before payment

28.33 After default by the mortgagor to repay on the appointed day, the mortgagee is generally entitled to notice before his security is discharged by payment. The reason for this was said to be that the mortgagor having lost his estate at law, and being only entitled to redeem in equity, had to do equity by allowing a reasonable opportunity for the mortgagee to find a new investment for his money[1]. Six months' notice is treated as a reasonable and proper time[2], though modern mortgages usually provide for an express period of notice. However, if the mortgagee demands his money, or (with the qualifications mentioned below) takes proceedings to realise his security notice will be unnecessary[3], whether the time for payment has arrived or not[4]. It is the same where the mortgagee has taken possession, this also being in effect a demand for payment[5]. Where money is in court and the mortgagor applies for payment out to the mortgagee and himself, the mortgagee is entitled to six months' notice[6]. Also, where judgment has been given in a foreclosure action appointing a specific date for redemption, the mortgagor cannot redeem before without paying interest up to that day, for the judgment has settled the rights of the parties[7].

As we have seen[8], where no date for redemption is specified and the debt is repayable on demand, the mortgagor may redeem at any time without paying interest.

1 The mortgagor does not lose his estate, but will have lost his contractual right to redeem. For the position where there is no specific redemption date, see **28.5**.
2 *Cromwell Property Investment Co Ltd v Western and Toovey* [1934] Ch 322. The six months rule is too firmly established to be disregarded and any change to the rule should not be made by the court: *Friend v Mayer* [1982] VR 941, FC, per Sir John Young CJ. For a form of notice, see the Appendix.
3 *Smith v Smith* [1891] 3 Ch 550; *Edmondson v Copland* [1911] 2 Ch 301.
4 *Bovill v Endle* [1896] 1 Ch 648.
5 *Bovill v Endle*, above; for other instances where notice is unnecessary, see *Matson v Swift* (1841) 5 Jur 645; *Re Fowler, Bishop v Fowler* (1922) 128 LT 620; *Re Moss, Levy v Sewill* (1885) 31 Ch D 90; *Re Alcock, Prescott v Phipps* (1883) 23 Ch D 372, CA; *Hill v Rowlands* [1897] 2 Ch 361, CA.
6 *Smith v Smith*, above.
7 *Hill v Rowlands*, above. Cf *Soloway v Sheahan* (1972) 21 DLR (3d) 388.
8 See **28.5**.

Interest in lieu of notice

28.34 By a rule of practice the mortgagee is entitled to six months' interest in lieu of notice[1]. The mortgagee cannot claim interest in lieu of notice where he has waived the right to it by his own action[2].

1 *Browne v Lockhart* (1840) 10 Sim 420 at 424; *Johnson v Evans* (1889) 61 LT 18, CA. Quaere: whether this would survive the Unfair Terms in Consumer Contracts Regulations 1994 (SI 1994/3159, reg 4(4), Sch 3, para 1(e)).
2 *Banner v Berridge* (1881) 18 Ch D 254.

When rule as to notice applies

28.35 The rule that a mortgagee, who has taken no steps to call in or realise his mortgage, is entitled to six months' notice or to six months' interest in lieu of notice, did not apply to equitable mortgages by deposit, with or without memorandum, these being presumed to be a mere temporary security[1]. It is no longer possible to create a mortgage by mere deposit[2]. Otherwise the rule applies not only to securities upon realty, but upon things in action and other personalty wherever the nature of the security might make it necessary for the mortgagor to take proceedings for redemption.[3]

The rule also applies where the security is naturally discharged by an event which does not depend on the will of the debtor, or by the falling in of a policy of insurance which constitutes the security[4].

A mortgagee can require fresh notice, or interest in lieu of notice, where the money is not paid on the expiration of the first notice, whether it was given by himself or the mortgagor[5]. Six months is again the reasonable and proper period[6], unless, where the first notice was given by the mortgagor, there is some reasonable explanation for his failure to pay[7], in which case a shorter period, such as three months, will be allowed.

1 *Fitzgerald's Trustee v Mellersh* [1892] 1 Ch 385, for where the mortgage debt is repayable on demand.
2 Law of Property (Miscellaneous Provisions) Act 1989, s 2, *United Bank of Kuwait plc v Sahib* [1997] Ch 107.
3 *Smith v Smith* [1891] 3 Ch 550.
4 *Smith v Smith*, above, and where a railway company purchased land compulsorily, it was held that the mortgagee was entitled to insist on six months' interest in lieu of notice from the vendor: *Spencer-Bell to London and SW Rly Co* (1885) 33 WR 771.
5 *Bartlett v Franklin* (1867) 36 LJ Ch 671; cf *Edmondson v Copland* [1911] 2 Ch 301.
6 *Re Moss* (1885) 31 Ch D 90.
7 *Cromwell Property Investment Co Ltd v Western and Toovey* [1934] Ch 322.

Missing mortgagee

28.36 Where the mortgagee is missing it will not be possible to give him notice. In such circumstances it may be possible to commence redemption proceedings seeking substituted service and asking the court to appoint a person to execute a statutory receipt or other discharge on payment of the mortgage moneys into court. Alternatively if the property is to be sold the procedure under s 50 of the Law of Property Act 1925[1] may be adopted, where all the moneys have been repaid and there is evidence of that fact no further action is necessary[2].

In some other jurisdictions[3] there is special provision for the payment of the mortgage moneys into court where the person entitled to receive the mortgage moneys is out of the jurisdiction, cannot be found or is unknown or it is uncertain who is entitled to the moneys.

1 See **28.74** and **28.75**, and for vesting orders under s 44 of the Trustee Act 1925 see **28.76**.
2 See **28.56**.
3 Eg NSW Conveyancing Act 1919, s 98 (see *Wayne v Kusznierz* [1973] 2 NSWLR 799); Qld Property Law Act 1974, s 101 (see *Re Losa* [1982] Qd R 381); NZ Property Law Act 1952, s 102A (*Murphy v New Zealand Newspapers Ltd* [1983] NZLR 255).

TENDER AND PAYMENT

Effect of tender of amount due[1]

28.37 Upon the contractual date of redemption or upon the expiration of the notice of intention to redeem, the mortgagee is taken to know the amount due to him. If he unjustifiably refuses to accept an unconditional tender of all that is due, it will be at his own risk as to the costs of any necessary redemption action[2]. A qualified refusal will be justified if an unusual form of discharge is tendered with the money, for the mortgagee is entitled to a reasonable time to be advised whether such a document is proper for him to execute and a draft should have been sent to him beforehand[3].

The mortgagor is entitled to know how much he is liable to pay and this is provided by the mortgagee in what is now commonly called a redemption statement. The mortgagor has the right to know how the redemption figure is arrived at[4]. If the mortgagee extorts more than is due, the overpayment may be recovered by the mortgagor as money had and received by the mortgagee to his use[5] or, alternatively, money paid by mistake[6], or alternatively, by the imposition of a constructive trust[7]. If the redemption figure supplied is less than the amount actually due, the mortgagee may claim the deficiency, subject to any issue of estoppel or change of position[8].

An action in trespass to goods for deeds deposited by way of equitable mortgage of land cannot be supported prior to actual repayment, the proper remedy of an equitable mortgagor being an action of redemption[9]. Likewise the obligation to provide a redemption statement arises not in contract or tort, but is simply a rule of equity[10]. So if a mortgagor tenders the amount owing, the mortgagee is under an obligation to accept it. But if he does not, while there may be costs consequences in a redemption action, there is no claim at law for (eg) a lost sale of the mortgaged property. The mortgagor's remedies are in the Law of Property Act 1925, ss 50 and 91(2)[11].

Interest ceases to run upon the mortgage debt from the time at which a proper tender of the whole amount due is shown to have been made[12], provided that from the time of the tender the money was kept ready by the mortgagor and no profit was afterwards made from it. Upon proof to the contrary interest will still run[13]. The money should be paid into court if there are proceedings pending in which this can be done or put on deposit, the mortgagor accounting for the interest thereon to the mortgagee[14]. There must be an actual tender of the money due[15]. The court will not stay the interest on proof of a proposal by the mortgagor to set off against the mortgage sums due to him from the mortgagee on another account between them[16].

At law, payment into court of the sums tendered is an essential element of the defence of tender before action[17]. However, a tender to stop mortgage interest need not be such as would afford a defence of tender at law[18].

1 A tender does not eliminate the debt. This section considers only the effect of tender in the context of the right to redeem.

2 *Harmer v Priestly* (1853) 16 Beav 569; *Bank of New South Wales v O'Connor* (1889) 14 App Cas 273, PC.

3 *Webb v Crosse* [1912] 1 Ch 323.

4 See *Cityland and Property (Holdings) Ltd v Dabrah* [1968] Ch 166 at 172–173, [1967] 2 All ER 639 at 641–642. For the right of the debtor under a regulated agreement under the Consumer Credit Act 1974 to know the amount and rate of the total charge for credit (s 60 (1) (b)), the amount remaining payable (ss 77, 78) and the settlement figure (s 97), see **10.37** and **10.48** ff.

5 *Astley v* Reynolds (1731) 2 Stra 915; Close *v Phipps* (1844) 7 Man & G 586; *Fraser v Pendlebury* (1861) 10 WR 104; *Mobil Oil Canada Ltd v Rural Municipality of Storthoaks (No 3)* [1973] 6 WWR 644.

6 The old distinction between mistakes of fact and of law has been largely abrogated by *Kleinwort Benson Ltd v Lincoln City Council* [1999] 2 AC 349 (but see Virgo *Principles of the Law of Restitution* (Oxford 1999) p 162).

7 *Westdeutsche Landesbank Girozentrale v Islington London Borough Council* [1996] AC 669, [1996] 2 All ER 961. But moneys paid under protest under threat (made in good faith) of legal process (eg winding up) are not recoverable: Goff and Jones *The Law of Restitution* (5th edn 1998) p 312.

8 See the bank cases, where a customer has been credited in error and would have acted differently if he had not believed he were richer than in fact he was: see *United Overseas Bank v Jiwani* [1977] 1 All ER 733, [1976] 1 WLR 964; and *Avon County Council v Howlett* [1983] 1 All ER 1073, [1983] 1 WLR 605, CA. The importance of estoppel as a bar to recovery by the mortgagee is less important now in the light of the acceptance in English law of the defence of change of position: see *Lipkin Gorman v Karpnale Ltd* [1991] 2 AC 548. An estoppel can be asserted by a mortgagor or by his solicitor who has given a professional undertaking to a purchaser to procure the discharge of the mortgage, the latter being more likely to succeed than the former. For the binding effect of statements given under the Consumer Credit Act 1974; see s 172 of that Act and **10.47** ff.

9 *Bank of New South Wales v O'Connor*, above. As to the effect of a statutory receipt see **28.57**.

10 *Downsview Nominees Ltd v First City Corpn Ltd* [1993] AC 295; *China and Southsea Bank v Tan Soon Gin* [1990] 1 AC 536.

11 *Equatorial Corp plc v Shah* [1996] NPC 172.

12 *Bank of New South Wales v O'Connor*, above; *Rourke v Robinson* [1911] 1 Ch 480; *Edmondson v Copland* [1911] 2 Ch 301; *Graham v Seal* (1918) 88 LJ Ch 31, CA; *Estoril Investments Pty Ltd v Westpac Banking Corpn* (1993) ACL Rep 295 NSW 24, per Young J citing the text. Executors who refuse a proper tender on the ground that they have not proved the will can demand no further interest, because they are entitled to receive the money before probate: *Austen v Dodwell's Executors* (1729) 1 Eq Cas Abr 318 pl 9.

13 *Gyles v Hall* (1726) 2 P Wms 378.

14 *Kinnaird v Trollope* (1889) 42 Ch D 610; *Edmondson v Copland*, above; *Barratt v Gough-Thomas* [1951] 2 All ER 48.

15 *Bishop v Church* (1751) 2 Ves Sen 371. An assertion of willingness to pay is not enough: *Devon Nominees Ltd v Hampstead Holdings Ltd* [1981] 1 NZLR 477.

16 *Garforth v Bradley* (1755) 2 Ves Sen 675. See also *Samuel Keller (Holdings) Ltd v Martins Bank Ltd* [1970] 3 All ER 950, [1971] 1 WLR 43, CA.

17 CPR 37.3.

18 *Webb v Crosse* [1912] 1 Ch 323.

Where tender dispensed with

28.38 The conduct of the creditor may amount to a dispensation with the tender. A mere claim of more than is due will not have this effect, but if by claiming too much, or setting up two different claims, one of which is wrongful, he so conducts himself as to show that a tender of the amount properly due would not be accepted, it will be a dispensation[1].

1 *Scarfe v Morgan* (1838) 4 M & W 270; *Kerford v Mondel* (1859) 28 LJ Ex 303.

Time of tender

28.39 The payment must be tendered at a proper time and place, in sufficient money, with proper formalities, and by and to the proper person. The fixing of a special time and place for payment is unusual today. If a certain hour is fixed, an attendance before the beginning of the next hour will be sufficient[1] and to satisfy an order to pay money between certain specified hours it is not necessary to attend during the whole period[2]. Where a tender was not made on time, but was properly made later, an attempted sale on the ground of default was set aside[3].

1 *Knox v Simmons* (1793) 4 Bro CC 433.
2 *Bernard v Norton* (1864) 10 LT 183.
3 *Camp-Wee-Gee-Wah for Boys Ltd v Clark* (1971) 23 DLR (3d) 158.

Place of tender

28.40 Unless a particular place is agreed upon, a personal tender is generally necessary. If a particular place is fixed by the deed or by a notice by the mortgagor and there are no circumstances making that choice of place unreasonable, an effective tender may be made there[1]. The mortgaged land itself is not the place for payment, the charge being a sum in gross and not a rent issuing out of the land[2].

It may be sufficient to tender the money at the mortgagee's house, or last place of abode, though it does not appear that the tender was made to him, or even that he was within the house. This can be done, for instance, where the mortgagee is deliberately keeping out of the way to avoid the tender[3].

In the case of debentures it is usual to provide by the debenture that the principal money and interest shall be paid at the bank or registered office of the company. In the absence of such a provision the company is bound to seek out the debenture holder in order to pay him[4].

1 *Gyles v Hall* (1726) 2 P Wms 378. The place of tender may be implied: *Shallay Holdings Pty Ltd v Griffith Cooperative Society Ltd* [1983] 1 VR 760.
2 *Phipps v Earl of Anglesea* (1721) 5 Vin Abr 209 pl 8.
3 See *Manning v Burges* (1663) 1 Cas in Ch 29.
4 *Fowler v Midland Electric Corpn for Power Distribution Ltd* [1917] 1 Ch 656, CA.

Legal tender

28.41 The tender must be a legal tender[1].

1 As to tender generally, see 9(1) *Halsbury's Laws* (4th edn) (reissue), Contract, paras 971 ff. On 'jingle' money, see *Leeward Holdings Ltd v Douglas* [1982] NZLR 532. A debt is not discharged on delivery of a cheque: *Official Solicitor to the Supreme Court v Thomas* [1986] 2 EGLR 1. On post-dated cheques, see *Brien v Dwyer* (1979) 141 CLR 378. When a loan is made in foreign currency, the borrower is entitled to redeem in that currency, notwithstanding that it may have depreciated in value: *British Bank for Foreign Trade Ltd v Russian Commercial and Industrial Bank* (1921) 38 TLR 65; *Russian Commercial and Industrial Bank v British Bank for Foreign Trade* [1921] 2 AC 438.

Production of the money

28.42 Generally the money should be actually produced[1], but actual production may be dispensed with by the express declaration or equivalent act of the creditor if the tender is otherwise sufficient[2]. So that if the creditor refuses to authorise his agent to take the money, or to take it himself, the tender will be good[3].

1 For it was said that though the creditor may at first refuse, yet the sight of the money

may tempt him to take it, and see *Powney v Blomberg* (1844) 8 Jur 746 (tender by letter insufficient).
2 *Dickinson v Shee* (1801) 4 Esp 67; *Thomas v Evans* (1808) 10 East 101.
3 *Robarts v Jeffreys* (1830) 8 LJOS Ch 137.

Tender must be unconditional

28.43 A tender will be bad if it is made on condition, as, for instance, that the mortgagee should give a receipt to the effect that the payment discharges the balance due[1]. It is otherwise where the creditor refuses to give a receipt because he wrongfully asserts that the tenderer should pay more[2]. A tender will not be invalidated because it reserves to the tenderer the right to tax the mortgagee's costs and to review his account[3].

1 *Evans v Judkins* (1815) 4 Camp 156.
2 *Cole v Blake* (1793) Peake 238.
3 *Greenwood v Sutcliffe* [1892] 1 Ch 1, CA.

Who may make a tender

28.44 The persons entitled to redeem[1] are, of course, able to make a good tender of the mortgage money. However, a good tender cannot be made by a stranger, or, generally, by anyone not entitled to the equity of redemption[2].

1 See **28.14** ff.
2 *Pearce v Morris* (1869) 5 Ch App 227. An agent may, of course, pay for his principal, and if a solicitor pays off his client's mortgage, he is considered to have paid it as his agent: *Ward v Carttar* (1865) 35 Beav 171. An agent who has exceeded his authority in tendering the whole amount due will be allowed to stand by subrogation in the place of the mortgagee; *Butler v Rice* [1910] 2 Ch 277.

To whom the tender may be made

28.45 The tender, to be effective, must be made to the person named for the purpose in the mortgage deed, if any, or to the person or persons legally entitled to receive the money and to reconvey the estate[1].

Money will be well tendered to the executors of the mortgagee, though the day fixed arrives before they have proved the will[2].

The mortgagor will not be discharged by payments to the agent of the mortgagee, unless the agent has authority to receive the money on the mortgagee's behalf. However, where a solicitor produces a deed having in the body thereof, or endorsed thereon, a receipt for consideration money or other consideration, the deed being executed or the receipt signed by the person entitled to give a receipt, the agent has statutory authority to receive the money on the mortgagee's behalf[3].

A trustee may authorise any person[4] to receive trust money as their agent under s 11 of the Trustee Act 2000. This includes money due under a loan by the trustees secured on a mortgage. Where, immediately before the Act came into force (on 1 February 2001), a solicitor is appointed to receive trust moneys under the statutory procedure in s 23(3) of the Trustee Act 1925[5] he is to be treated as having been authorised under s 11 of the Act of 2000[6].

Subject to the statutory exception there is no power in the mortgagee's solicitor or agent to receive either the principal or the interest of the mortgage debt merely by virtue of his possession of the security[7] or to receive the principal merely by virtue of an authority to receive the interest[8].

1 Co Litt 210 and see *Cliff v Wadsworth* (1843) 2 Y & C Ch Cas 598.
2 *Austen v Dodwell's Executors* (1729) 1 Eq Cas Abr 318 pl 9.
3 Law of Property Act 1925, s 69. A forged reconveyance will not satisfy this provision: *Jared v Walke* (1902) 18 TLR 569.
4 Subject to restrictions in the Trustee Act 2000, s 12.
5 Now repealed: see Trustee Act 2000, s 40(3) and Sch 4. The old procedure involved the trustee permitting the solicitor to have the custody of and produce a deed with a receipt in the body thereof or endorsed thereon.
6 Trustee Act 2000, s 40(2), Sch 3 para 5(6).
7 *Jared v Walke*, above.
8 *Withington v Tate* (1869) 4 Ch App 288; *Bonham v Maycock* (1928) 138 LT 736 and see *Martin v Diamantikos* [1964] VR 593. It may be inferred that the mortgagee treated his solicitor as his agent to receive the interest, as where, after receiving interest by his hands, the mortgagee allowed arrears to accumulate without applying to the mortgagor for payment: *Kent v Thomas* (1856) 1 H & N 473.

Payment to joint creditors

28.46 Although a joint debt was discharged at law by payment to one joint creditor[1], yet the receipt of one joint creditor for a mortgage debt, without evidence of any special authority to receive it, would not discharge the security in equity[2], the interest of the creditors being then treated as a tenancy in common. So if one of the joint creditors died, his representatives were entitled in equity to his share of the debt[3]. It therefore became usual to insert in mortgages to trustees, or other persons whose interests were intended to survive, a provision that the receipt of the survivors or survivor should be a good discharge for the debt; and it was considered that, if such a security had been acted upon by the mortgagees, the clause would operate, although the deed was not actually executed by them. Such a clause is no longer necessary, it being provided by the Law of Property Act 1925 that where the advance is expressed to be made by several persons out of moneys belonging to them on a joint account, or the mortgage is made to more persons than one jointly, the receipt in writing of the survivors or the last survivor of them, or of the personal representative of the last survivor, is a complete discharge for the money, notwithstanding any notice to the payer of a severance of the joint account[4].

1 *Husband v Davis* (1851) 10 CB 645.
2 *Powell v Brodhurst* [1901] 2 Ch 160. See *Re Losa* [1982] Qd R 381, but see now for the effect of a receipt, *Edwards v Marshall-Lee* (1975) 119 Sol Jo 506, (1976) 40 Conv (NS) 102; see **28.58**.
3 *Petty v Styward* (1631) 1 Eq Cas Abr 290; *Vickers v Cowell* (1839) 1 Beav 529.
4 Section 111, replacing s 61 of the Conveyancing Act 1881. See **14.24**.

APPROPRIATION OF PAYMENTS[1]

Appropriation to principal or interest

28.47 Where the debtor claims to be discharged by reason of payments which were not specifically allocated as between principal or interest, the rule is that such a payment should be applied in the first place to reduce the interest, before any part of the principal is discharged[2].

1 For the appropriation of payments in respect of two or more regulated agreements under the Consumer Credit Act 1974, see s 81 of that Act.
2 *Chase v Box* (1702) Freem Ch 261; and see *Parr's Banking Co Ltd v Yates* [1898] 2 QB 460 at 466, CA; *Wrigley v Gill* [1906] 1 Ch 165, CA. This passage was cited in *Re Mangan, ex p Andrew* [1983] ACLD 528 and see *Falk v Haugh* (1935) 53 CLR 163 where the rule is expressed as affording only a presumption in the absence of any actual or express appropriation by the debtor or the creditor.

Appropriation by debtor

28.48 However, the debtor is entitled at the time of payment to declare towards which debt he pays the money[1] and, when he has so declared, the destination of the payment cannot be changed[2].

1 *Mills v Fowkes* (1839) 5 Bing NC 455; *Re Walsh, ex p Deputy Federal Comr of Taxation* (1982) 42 ALR 727; *Re Mangan, ex p Andrew* [1983] ACLD 528.
2 *Hammersley v Knowlys* (1798) 2 Esp 666; *Simson v Ingham* (1823) 2 B & C 65. Entries made by the debtor in his own books are not sufficient evidence of the particular appropriation of money paid on a general account: *Manning v Westerne* (1707) 2 Vern 606, and see *Wrout v Dawes* (1858) 25 Beav 369.

Appropriation by creditor

28.49 Where at the time of payment the debtor fails to declare the debt towards which the money was paid, he cannot afterwards do so[1]. The right of appropriation is then with the creditor who may allocate the payment to the debt for which he has the least available security[2]. However, when the creditor by himself or his authorised agent has accepted the payment on a particular account, he cannot afterwards change the appropriation without the debtor's consent[3].

The creditor may appropriate the payment to a debt at any time after payment and before action brought or account settled between him and his debtor[4]. The creditor's written memorandum may be used after his death as evidence of his intention[5], and the accounts kept by a mortgagee have been used as evidence against himself of a continuing agreement to apply rents in payment of interest, not only during the time covered by the accounts, but until the mortgagor had notice to the contrary[6].

When the debtor becomes bankrupt, the creditor's right of appropriation accrues to him and is fixed at the bankruptcy and must be regulated by the state of the account at that time[7].

1 *Wilkinson v Sterne* (1744) 9 Mod Rep 427.
2 *Mackenzie v Gordon* (1839) 6 Cl & Fin 875 and see *Re William Hall (Contractors) Ltd (In Liquidation)* [1967] 2 All ER 1150, [1967] 1 WLR 948; *Tucuba Pty Ltd v AGC (Advances) Ltd* [1991] ACL Rep 295 NSW 13.
3 *Kershaw v Kirkpatrick* (1878) 3 App Cas 345.
4 *Blackburn Building Society v Cunliffe, Brooks & Co* (1882) 22 Ch D 61 at 71, CA, affd *Cunliffe, Brooks & Co v Blackburn Benefit Building Society* (1884) 9 App Cas 857, HL.
5 *Wilkinson v Sterne*, above; *Simson v Ingham* (1823) 2 B & C 65.
6 *Cockburn v Edwards* (1881) 18 Ch D 449, CA, and see *Wrigley v Gill* [1906] 1 Ch 165, CA.
7 *Re Bulmer ex p Johnson* (1853) 3 De Gm & G 218.

The rule in *Clayton's Case*

28.50 Where there is a current account, but not otherwise[1], and there has been no appropriation by either party, the general presumption—known as the rule in *Clayton's Case*[2]—is that the moneys are intended to be applied in discharge of the items of the debt consecutively[3]. The rule is said to be a rule of practice and convenience but neither its acclaim nor its application has been universal[4]. The rule applies in favour of a purchaser or subsequent mortgagee of property mortgaged to a bank to secure a current account, unless the bank mortgage imposes an obligation on the bank to make further advances, where the bank has notice of the sale or subsequent mortgage[5], unless there is evidence to show that the bank did not intend to appropriate payments in discharge of the balance due at the date of the purchase or subsequent mortgage[6].

The presumption is liable to be rebutted by evidence of a different intention[7] and the rule does not apply where the interest of a surety raises an obligation against the creditor to discharge the debt for which he is liable[8].

Bank mortgages to secure overdraft facilities generally expressly exclude the operation of the rule in *Clayton's Case* by including therein a declaration that the security is to be a continuing one[9] and where the mortgage does not impose an obligation on the bank to make further advances the operation of the rule can be avoided in the case of a subsequent mortgage by ruling off the mortgagor's account and passing future transactions through a separate account.

1 *Cory Bros & Co v Turkish SS Mecca (Owners), The Mecca* [1897] AC 286, HL.
2 *Devaynes v Noble, Clayton's Case* (1816) 1 Mer 529.
3 *Clayton's Case*, above; and see *Bodenham v Purchas* (1818) 2 B & Ald 39.
4 *Barlow Clowes International Ltd (in liq) v Vaughan* [1992] 4 All ER 22 at 43, per Leggatt LJ. This case contains a useful discussion of the rule, and of alternative methods of apportionment.
5 *London and County Banking Co v Ratcliffe* (1881) 6 App Cas 722, HL.
6 *Deeley v Lloyds Bank Ltd* [1912] AC 756, HL.
7 *Deeley v Lloyds Bank Ltd*, above; *Cory Bros & Co v Turkish SS Mecca (Owners), The Mecca*, above, and see *Re Sherry, London and County Banking Co v Terry* (1884) 25 Ch D 692, CA; *Fahey v MSD Spiers Ltd* [1975] 1 NZLR 240, PC; *Barlow Clowes International Ltd (in liq) v Vaughan*[1992] 4 All ER 22, CA; and see (1993) 4 JBFLP (Russell) on tracing and contributory mortgages.
8 *Pearl v Deacon* (1857) 24 Beav 186; *Kinnaird v Webster* (1878) 10 Ch D 139.
9 For form, see 4(1) *Forms and Precedents* (5th edn, 2000 reissue) Banking.

DISCHARGE OF THE MORTGAGE

Mortgagee's duty

28.51 Upon the debt being paid off[1] the mortgagor is entitled to have the mortgaged property restored to him free from the mortgagee's security. Under the pre-1926 method of creating mortgages the mortgagor's estate or interest was conveyed to the mortgagee and upon payment off it was the duty of the mortgagee to reconvey the property to the mortgagor[2]. The repayment of the debt was made against the reconveyance of the property and the handing back of the deeds and strictly these should be simultaneous transactions[3]. As previously stated[4], a tender of the amount due for principal, interest and costs conditionally upon the mortgagees then and there executing a reconveyance and handing over the deeds was a good tender, so that if it was refused, interest stopped running.

This assumed that the mortgagee had had a reasonable opportunity of approving the conveyance[5], or that for any other reason no delay was necessary[6]. A reasonable time had to be allowed for obtaining the execution of the deed, especially when the conveying parties were not the persons to whom the tender was made[7].

Payment and reconveyance being thus related, it was considered that the mortgagee's action for foreclosure implied an offer to reconvey on redemption[8]. The mortgagee could not refuse on redemption to reconvey the mortgaged property to the mortgagor, or those claiming under him, and had no right to dispute the mortgagor's title. Under both the former and present system of mortgages the mortgagee will not be allowed to deal with the property in such a way that the property cannot be restored to the mortgagor on discharge of the debt[9]. This does not apply where the property has been sold by the mortgagee under his power of sale[10], or where he contracted to sell it under such power[11], or where he has been evicted by title paramount[12] and the mortgagee may claim to retain the property on the ground of a future contingent claim upon it[13].

Under the former system of creating mortgages after payment the mortgagee became constructively a trustee for the mortgagor. There was an implied trust to surrender the estate to the person entitled to demand it[14] and in the meantime the mortgagor in possession was tenant at will to the mortgagee for the purposes of limitation of actions[15]. Now after payment the mortgage term generally becomes a satisfied term and ceases[16]. A satisfied mortgagee is bound to take care that the security gets back to the mortgagor, or to someone to whom he authorises it to be transferred[17].

1 A surety was not entitled to redeem where the charge embraced contingent liabilities of the principal debtor: *Re Rudd & Son Ltd* [1986] 2 BCC 98 at 955. It is not enough that the borrower has a counterclaim for an equal or greater amount. And see *Estoril Investments Ltd v Westpac Banking Group* (1993) ACL Rep 295 NSW 24. See further on the relation between payment and re-conveyance *Samuel Keller (Holdings) Ltd v Martins Bank Ltd* [1970] 3 All ER 950, [1971] 1 WLR 43, CA.

2 *Graham v Seal* (1918) 88 LJ Ch 31, CA. As to delivery of deeds, see **28.80**.

3 *Graham v Seal*, above.

4 See **28.1**.

5 *Wiltshire v Smith* (1744) 3 Atk 89; *Graham v Seal*, above.

6 *Rourke v Robinson* [1911] 1 Ch 480.

7 *Webb v Crosse* [1912] 1 Ch 323.

8 *Matthews v Antrobus* (1879) 49 LJ Ch 80.

9 *Tasker v Small* (1837) 3 My & Cr 63 at 70; *Thornton v Court* (1854) 3 De GM & G 293; *Walker v Jones* (1866) LR 1 PC 50; *Kinnaird v Trollope* (1888) 39 Ch D 636.

10 *Rudge v Richens* (1873) LR 8 CP 358.

11 *Property and Bloodstock Ltd v Emerton* [1968] Ch 94, [1967] 3 All ER 321, CA (even if the mortgaged property is leasehold and the landlord's consent to an assignment is required), and see *Lord Waring v London and Manchester Assurance Co Ltd* [1935] Ch 310; *Duke v Robson* [1973] 1 All ER 481, [1973] 1 WLR 267.

12 *Re Burrell, Burrell v Smith* (1869) LR 7 Eq 399.

13 See *Brecon Corpn v Seymour* (1859) 26 Beav 548; *Chilton v Carrington* (1854) 15 CB 95.

14 *Pearce v Morris* (1869) 5 Ch App 227 and see *Holme v Fieldsend* [1911] WN 111. If the mortgagee refused to reconvey after payment, the mortgagor could obtain a declaration that the mortgagee was trustee for the mortgagor and an order that the registrar convey the property to him or a vesting order: see **28.76** ff.

15 *Sands to Thompson* (1883) 22 Ch D 614.

16 Law of Property Act 1925, ss 5, 116. See **28.56** ff.

17 *Magnus v Queensland National Bank* (1888) 37 Ch D 466, CA.

Mortgagee can be required to transfer mortgage

28.52 The mortgagor is entitled to require the mortgagee to transfer the mortgage to a third party instead of taking a reconveyance to himself. The Law of Property Act 1925[1] provides as follows:

> **95** (1) Where the mortgagor[2] is entitled to redeem[3], then, subject to compliance with the terms on compliance with which he would be entitled to require a reconveyance or surrender, he is entitled to require the mortgagee, instead of reconveying or surrendering, to assign the mortgage debt and convey the mortgaged property to any third person[4], as the mortgagor directs; and the mortgagee is bound to assign and convey accordingly[5].
>
> (2) The rights conferred by this section belong to and are capable of being enforced by each incumbrancer, or by the mortgagor, notwithstanding any intermediate incumbrance[6]; but a requisition of an incumbrancer prevails over a requisition of the mortgagor, and, as between incumbrancers, a requisition of a prior incumbrancer prevails over a requisition of a subsequent incumbrancer.
>
> (3) The foregoing provisions of this section do not apply in the case of a mortgagee being or having been in possession[7].
>
> ...
>
> (5)[8] This section applies to mortgages made either before or after the commencement of this Act, and takes effect notwithstanding any stipulation to the contrary.

Subsection (2), which entitles the mortgagor to call for a transfer even if there is a second mortgage[9], does not justify the first mortgagee in disregarding notice of the second mortgage, and where he has such notice, he should not transfer without the consent of the second mortgagee[10]. The subsection throws upon the mortgagee the burden, to which before the Act of 1882 he was not subject, of determining which among several other incumbrancers is entitled to priority.

1 Reproducing the Conveyancing Act 1881, s 15 (with an addition made by the Conveyancing Act 1882, s 12). Previously the mortgagee was bound only to reconvey to the owner of the equity of redemption: *James v Biou* (1819) 3 Swans 234.

2 'Mortgagor' includes any person from time to time deriving title under the original mortgagor or entitled to redeem the mortgage: see Law of Property Act 1925, s 205 (1) (xvi). It includes second and later mortgagees: *First Chicago Australia Ltd v Loyebe Pty Ltd* [1980] 2 NSWLR 703 and also an alter ego of the original mortgagor such as his personal representative and trustee in bankruptcy: *First Chicago*.

3 Every mortgagor is entitled to redeem, unless he is precluded by a special term in the mortgage from exercising his right: see **28.6**. As to a transfer so as to keep alive the rights of other persons interested in the equity of redemption, see *Alderson v Elgey* (1884) 26 Ch D 567.

4 Ie a person other than the original mortgagor named in the mortgage: *First Chicago Australia Ltd v Loyeby Pty Ltd*, above. Cf *Ley v Scarff* (1981) 146 CLR 56; *Corozo Pty Ltd v Wetspac Banking Corp* [1988] 2 Qd R 481.

5 This applies also to an equitable mortgagee or chargee and the holder of a lien: Law of Property Act 1925, s 205 (1) (xvi); and see *Everitt v Automatic Weighing Machine Co* [1892] 3 Ch 506.

6 This overrules *Teevan v Smith* (1882) 20 Ch D 724, CA, and see *First Chicago Australia Ltd v Loyebe Pty Ltd*; and see (1981) 55 ALJ 692 (Butt).

7 A mortgagee in possession is exempted from the obligation to transfer because he cannot in this way rid himself of his liability to account as mortgagee in possession: *Hall v Heward*

(1886) 32 Ch D 430 at 435, CA; and see *Re Prytherch, Prytherch v Williams* (1889) 42 Ch D 590; *Gaskel v Gosling* [1896] 1 QB 669 at 691, CA. He may only do so if he transfers under an order of the court.

8 Subsection (4) relates to a different matter, namely the mortgagee's right to possession, and is out of place in this section.

9 Where there is a second mortgage sub-s (1) by itself does not entitle the mortgagor to call for a transfer, for it operates only where the mortgagor is entitled to require a conveyance and if there is a second mortgage the reconveyance should be to the second mortgagee: *Teevan v Smith*, above.

10 *Re Magneta Time Co Ltd, Molden v The Company* (1915) 84 LJ Ch 814; and see *Corbett v National Provident Institution* (1900) 17 TLR 5. The correctness of this statement was confirmed in *Ley v Scarff* (1981) 146 CLR 56; and see (1981) 55 ALJ 692 (Butt).

Reconveyance formerly necessary

28.53 Before the Law of Property Act 1925, the reconveyance of property which had been mortgaged by conveyance of the whole estate of the mortgagor, whether freehold or leasehold, and whether legal or equitable, was effected by a regrant or reassignment to the owner of the equity of redemption. Where the mortgage had been made by a demise for a term of years the reconveyance was effected by a surrender of the term. In the case of equitable mortgages created by deed, the ordinary form of reconveyance was usually adopted, but this was technically unnecessary since the mere receipt of the debt put an end to the mortgagee's interest[1]. Nor was it necessary in the case of freehold[2] mortgages by demise, since the term ceased on payment of the debt by virtue of the Satisfied Terms Act 1845.

In the case of mortgages to unincorporated building societies s 5 of the Building Societies Act 1836 avoided the necessity of an actual reconveyance by making a receipt indorsed on the mortgage operate to revest in the mortgagor the mortgagee's estate in the mortgaged property and substantially the same provision was later applied to incorporated building societies[3].

1 See *Firth & Sons Ltd v IRC* [1904] 2 KB 205.

2 But not leasehold mortgages: *Re Moore and Hulm's Contract* [1912] 2 Ch 105.

3 Building Societies Act 1874, s 42; and see now Building Societies Act 1986, Sch 2A, para 2 (amended by the Building Societies Act 1997). Similar provisions were later applied to friendly and industrial and provident societies: see Friendly Societies Act 1974, s 57, Sch 4; Industrial and Provident Societies Act 1965, s 33.

Unregistered land: extension of automatic reconveyance to all mortgages

28.54 This device of automatic reconveyance by indorsed receipt was extended generally to mortgages of unregistered land[1] by the Law of Property Act 1925, which provides:

> **115** (1) A receipt endorsed on, written at the foot of, or annexed to, a mortgage[2] for all money thereby secured[3], which states the name of the person who pays the money[4] and is executed[5] by the chargee by way of legal mortgage or the person in whom the mortgaged property[6] is vested and who is legally entitled to give a receipt for the mortgage money[7], shall operate, without any reconveyance, surrender or release—
>
> (a) Where a mortgage takes effect by demise or subdemise, as a surrender of the term, so as to determine the term or merge the same in the reversion immediately expectant thereon;

(b) Where the mortgage does not take effect by demise or subdemise, as a reconveyance thereof to the extent of the interest which is the subject matter of the mortgage, to the person who immediately before the execution of the receipt was entitled to the equity of redemption;

and in either case, as a discharge of the mortgaged property from all principal money and interest secured by, and from all claims under the mortgage[8], but without prejudice to any term or other interest which is paramount to the estate or interest of the mortgagee or other person in whom the mortgaged property was vested.

(2) Provided that where by the receipt the money appears to have been paid by a person who is not entitled to the immediate equity of redemption[9], the receipt shall operate as if the benefit of the mortgage had by deed been transferred to him; unless—

(a) it is otherwise expressly provided[10]; or
(b) the mortgage is paid off out of capital money, or other money in the hands of a personal representative or trustee properly applicable for the discharge of the mortgage, and it is not expressly provided that the receipt is to operate as a transfer[11].

(3) Nothing in this section confers on a mortgagor a right to keep alive a mortgage paid off by him, so as to affect prejudicially any subsequent incumbrancer; and where there is no right to keep the mortgage alive, the receipt does not operate as a transfer[12].

This section does not affect the right of any person to require a reassignment, surrender, release, or transfer to be executed in lieu of a receipt: sub-s (4)[13]. The receipt may be in the form in the Third Schedule to the Act, with such variations and additions as may be deemed expedient: sub-s (5)[14]. Where the mortgage consists of a mortgage and a further charge or of more than one deed it is sufficient for the purposes of the section if the receipt refers either to all the deeds whereby the mortgage money secured and for the time being owing, and is indorsed on, written at the foot of, or annexed to, one of the mortgage deeds: sub-s (7). The section applies to the discharge of a charge by way of legal mortgage: sub-s (8). Building and friendly societies may employ a statutory receipt under the provisions of this section: sub-s (9)[15]. The section does not apply to the discharge of a charge or incumbrance registered under the Land Registration Act 1925: sub-s (10). In view of the words 'in whom the mortgaged property is vested' in sub-s (1) a statutory receipt is in appropriate to discharge an equitable mortgage.

1 For mortgages of registered land, see below.
2 Not a transfer thereof, unless the transfer contains a further charge, when sub-s (7) will apply. As to mortgages of personalty, see **28.66**.
3 Semble, secured at the date of repayment. See the statutory form of receipt which includes the balance remaining owing: Law of Property Act 1925, Sch 3.
An indorsed receipt cannot be used where only part of the mortgage money is repaid and in such a case if no part of the security is discharged an ordinary receipt should be used. Nor can a statutory receipt be used where a mortgage deed is lost. In that case a release or surrender is necessary.
4 For where the receipt does not name the payer, see *Edwards v Marshall-Lee* (1975) 119 Sol Jo 506; see **28.56**.
5 It need only be under hand: (*Simpson v Geoghegan* [1934] WN 232, (1934) 78 Sol Jo 930), unless made by a building society (see **28.57**).
6 Ie the property remaining subject to the mortgage at the date of the receipt: sub-s (11).
7 Thus a trustee is legally entitled to give a receipt for moneys payable to him under a trust: Trustee Act 1925, s 14. The receipt of the trustees for the time being gives a good discharge unless the mortgage expressly provides that the money is not advanced on a

joint account: Law of Property Act 1925, ss 111–113. A receipt by personal representatives of the mortgagee or a transferee should be made by all the proving personal representatives, but the fact that it was made by only one or some of the proving personal representatives does not constitute an objection to the title in the case of a mortgage by demise since on payment the mortgage term becomes satisfied: see Law of Property Act 1925, ss 5, 116; see **28.56** ff. Where the mortgagee is a mental patient the Court of Protection has power to make an order for the discharge of a mortgage security vested in a patient: see Mental Health Act 1983, s 95. For the practice in respect of applications for such an order, see Heywood and Massey's *Court of Protection Practice* (12th edn) pp 173–177.

8 For the effect of the receipt on the personal liability of the mortgagor, see **28.58**.

9 An express statement to the effect is not necessary: *Simpson v Geoghegan*, above.

10 See *Pyke v Peters* [1943] KB 242. A mortgagee cannot object to signing a receipt which includes the statement that the receipt does not operate as a transfer: *Hartley v Burton* (1868) 3 Ch App 365 at 366.

11 Where the holder of the equity of redemption is not the original mortgagor, the fact that the person paying the mortgage money is the holder of the equity of redemption should be made to appear in the receipt, where it is intended to extinguish the mortgage, unless (a) or (b) of sub-s (2) apply: see *Cumberland Court (Brighton) Ltd v Taylor* [1964] Ch 29, [1963] 2 All ER 536. See (1971) 69 LS Gaz 175 (Adams).

12 Where there is a second mortgage, the second mortgagee is the person entitled to the immediate equity of redemption. Hence if the mortgagor pays off the mortgage and takes a receipt showing that he is not so entitled this will operate prima facie as a transfer of the mortgage to him. A mortgagor cannot, however, keep a mortgage alive in his own favour as against his own creditors: *Otter v Vaux* (1856) 6 De GM & G 638, see **32.8**; sub-s (3) preserves this rule.

13 In the absence of express provision therefor a mortgagor may not be able to require a reassignment, where a statutory receipt is applicable (but see **28.56**), but in some cases a receipt will not be appropriate or sufficient: see *Nelson v Hannam and Smith* [1943] Ch 59, [1942] 2 All ER 680, CA (where the mortgagee of leasehold land had exercised an option to purchase the reversion). Where there is a second mortgagee a surrender by a first mortgagee should be to the second mortgagee and not to the borrower: *Hosking v Smith* (1888) 13 App Cas 582 at 589, HL. On a partial redemption a statutory receipt cannot be employed: see **28.54**, n 3.

Quaere whether a statutory receipt may be employed where a right of consolidation exists, since the receipt will not be 'for all money thereby secured'.

14 For the abolition of stamp duty on discharge and transfer etc of a mortgage, see Finance Act 1971, s 64.

In a receipt given under the section covenants 'as mortgagee' are implied, subject to any interest which is paramount to the mortgagee: sub-s (6). These covenants include a covenant that the mortgagee has not incumbered. Accordingly, where there has been a sub-mortgage a statutory receipt may not be appropriate (see **15.6**). For forms of statutory receipt, see 1 *Forms and Precedents* (5th edn) Acknowledgments and Receipts; and the Appendix.

15 As an alternative to the special forms of receipt applicable thereto, as to which, see Building Societies Act 1986, para 2, Sch 2A and **28.57**, and Friendly Societies Act 1974, s 57. It seems that the effect of the amendment made to sub-s (9) by the Industrial and Provident Societies Act 1965, s 77 (1), Sch 5 is that industrial and provident societies may use only the form contained in the Industrial and Provident Societies Act 1965. For discussion of s 115(9) see **28.57**.

Receipt operating as a transfer

28.55 In order that the receipt may operate as a transfer[1] it must state the name of the person paying the mortgage money and it must appear by the receipt that the person making the payment is not entitled to the immediate equity of redemption. A statement that the payer is not so entitled is sufficient, but such a statement is not necessary[2].

If the land is settled land[3] and there is no second mortgage, the tenant for life will be entitled to the immediate equity of redemption and, if the payment is made by the trustees out of capital moneys, it is not paid by the persons entitled to the immediate equity of redemption and prima facie would operate as a transfer. In effect, however, it is on the same footing as regards the discharge of the mortgage as a payment by a mortgagor and where this fact appears it does not operate as a transfer unless expressly so provided[4]. Where the mortgage money is paid by the tenant for life a statutory receipt would, it seems, not operate as a transfer, since the money has been paid by the person entitled to the immediate equity of redemption. Accordingly in such a case a transfer of the mortgage should be employed[5].

Where the land is subject to a trust of land the legal estate therein is in the trustees who are accordingly the persons entitled to the immediate equity of redemption (if there is no second mortgage). If the mortgage money is paid by the beneficiary it is not paid by the persons entitled to the immediate equity of redemption and prima facie a receipt in such circumstances would operate as a transfer.

1 Under s 115, sub-s (2). As to transfer of mortgages, see Part IV.
2 *Simpson v Geoghegan* [1934] WN 232, (1934) 78 Sol Jo 930, and see *Pyke v Peters* [1943] KB 242; *Cumberland Court (Brighton) Ltd v Taylor* [1964] Ch 29, [1963] 2 All ER 536.
3 There can be no new settlements of land after 1 February 1997: see Trusts of Land and Appointment of Trustees Act 1996, s 2. A disposition of land which would formerly have taken effect under the Settled Land Act 1925 now takes effect as a trust of land.
4 See s 115, sub-s (2), exception (b). A note appended to the statutory form of receipt says that in such a case the receipt should state that the payers are paying the money out of a fund applicable to the discharge of the mortgage. A similar case may arise, as sub-s (2) suggests, where payment is made by a personal representative, but usually a personal representative who pays off a mortgage is entitled to the immediate equity of redemption by devolution from the mortgagor.
5 In such circumstances prima facie merger does not follow: see **32.2** ff.

Cessation of mortgage terms on payment

28.56 The Law of Property Act provides:

> **5** (1) Where the purposes of a term of years, created or limited at any time out of freehold land, become satisfied either before or after the commencement of this Act (whether or not that term either by express declaration or by construction of law becomes attendant upon the freehold reversion), it shall merge in the reversion expectant thereon and shall cease accordingly[1].
>
> (2) Where the purposes of a term of years created or limited, at any time, out of leasehold land, become satisfied after the commencement of this Act, that term shall merge in the reversion expectant thereon and shall cease accordingly[2].
>
> (3) Where the purposes are satisfied only as respects part of the land comprised in a term, this section shall have effect as if a separate term has been created in regard to that part of the land[3].
>
> **116** Without prejudice to the right of a tenant for life or other person having only a limited interest in the equity of redemption to require a mortgage to be kept alive by transfer or otherwise, a mortgage term shall, when the money secured by the mortgage has been discharged, become a satisfied term and shall cease[4].

Section 116 covers the same ground as s 5. It assumes that the mortgage has been finally discharged, that is, that the term has become a satisfied term. In that

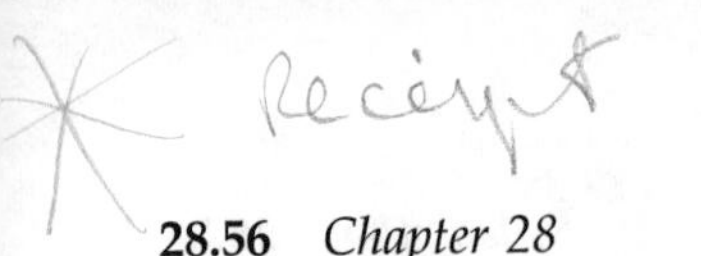

case it cannot be kept alive and so complicate the title to the land. The effect of the cessation of the mortgage term on payment is that evidence of payment is sufficient to discharge a mortgage by demise. Thus an ordinary receipt is as effective as a statutory receipt, and a simple receipt is, apparently, sufficient to discharge a mortgage by way of legal charge[5]. But, except in the case of registered charges[6], it is not the practice to discharge legal mortgages of land by an ordinary receipt. However, in certain cases, the discharging effect of a simple receipt may usefully be relied upon where, for example, there has been a reconveyance to the wrong person (and there is no question of a statutory receipt operating as a transfer) or after repayment, but before execution of a discharge, the mortgagee has disappeared.

The relationship of ss 115 and 116 is a matter of some uncertainty. In a previous edition of this work it was stated that the provision for automatic reconveyance by indorsed receipt is not required where the mortgage term ceases on payment and that a surrender of the term in such circumstances is unnecessary and indeed is inoperative[7]. In relation to sub-s (4) of s 115 it has been suggested that in the absence of express provision for reassignment etc a mortgagor has no right thereto when a statutory receipt is applicable[8]. The basis for this suggestion cannot logically be limited to s 115 (4), but must also apply to the right to the statutory receipt itself. Section 115 (4) assumes the existence of the right to a reassignment, etc, and in spite of the provisions of the Satisfied Terms Act 1845, on the discharge of a mortgage by demise it was usual to effect a reconveyance by a surrender of the term. Moreover it is difficult to see the point of the detailed provisions as to statutory receipts if they are not to be employed in every case where a simple receipt would suffice. From the mortgagor's point of view the statutory receipt with its implied covenants for title[9] is the better discharge and it is submitted that no special provision for a statutory receipt is required. Nor is any special provision required for a reassignment etc[10].

1 This reproduces s 2 of the Satisfied Terms Act 1845. As to satisfaction of a mortgage term, see *Anderson v Pignet* (1872) 8 Ch App 180 at 188–189.
2 This extends the same principle to sub-terms, and thus overrules *Re Moore and Hulm's Contract* [1912] 2 Ch 105, but only where the mortgage has been paid off after 31 December 1925. Where the sub-term was already a satisfied term at that date it merged in the reversion and ceased but without prejudice to any protection which it afforded to the reversioner: Law of Property Act 1925, Sch 1, Pt II, para 1.
3 This was new and enables the term to be kept alive in part of the land only.
4 As to the prevention of merger when a person with a limited interest in land becomes absolutely entitled to the benefit of a charge on it, see **32.4**. The effect of this automatic cessation of the mortgage term on a legal current account mortgage (such as a bank mortgage) appears to be that the mortgage would cease to be supported by a legal term as soon as, under the rule in *Clayton's Case* (see **28.5**), or otherwise, the account was in credit, but the mortgage would continue as an equitable security for further advances: see *Jones v Consolidated Investment Assurance Co* (1858) 26 Beav 256 at 259; *London and County Banking Co v Ratcliffe* (1881) 6 App Cas 722 at 737, HL, but this effect is in practice avoided by provision in the mortgage that the security shall be a continuing security.
5 *Edwards v Marshall-Lee*; see (1975) 119 Sol Jo 506; (1976) 40 Conv (NS) 102.
6 See **28.59**.
7 7th edn, p 631.
8 *Key and Elphinstone* (15th edn) vol 2, p 284, para (8); 27 *Forms and Precedents* (5th edn, 1997 reissue) Mortgages.
9 Law of Property Act 1925, s 115 (6).
10 In practice the statutory receipt is employed wherever appropriate, save in the case of a mortgage debenture where a simple receipt is used. If the mortgagor insists on a re-assignment etc where a statutory receipt would be appropriate, he must pay the costs.

Building society receipts

28.57 A building society mortgage may be discharged on repayment of the mortgage debt either under the Law of Property Act 1925 or the Building Societies Act 1986[1].

The Law of Property Act 1925 provides:

> **115** (9) The provisions of this section relating to the operation of a receipt shall (in substitution for the like statutory provision relating to receipts given by or on behalf of a building, society) apply to the discharge of a mortgage made to any such society, provided that the receipt is executed in the manner required by the statute relating to the society.

The requirement that the receipt be executed in the manner required by the society's statute has been largely superseded by para 1 of Sch 2A to the Building Societies Act 1986[2] which provides:

> (1) When all money intended to be secured by a mortgage given to a building society has been fully paid or discharged, the society may endorse on or annex to the mortgage one or other of the following—
> (a) a receipt in the prescribed form signed by any person acting under the authority of the board of directors;
> (b) a reconveyance of the mortgaged property to the mortgagor;
> (c) a reconveyance of the mortgaged property to such person of full age, and on such trusts (if any), as the mortgagor may direct.
>
> (2) Where in pursuance of sub-paragraph (1) above a receipt is endorsed on or annexed to a mortgage, not being a charge or incumbrance registered under the Land Registration Act 1925, the receipt shall operate in accordance with s 115 (1), (3), (6) and (8) of the Law of Property Act 1925 (discharge of mortgages by receipt) in the like manner as a receipt which fulfils all the requirements of sub-s (1) of that section.
>
> (3) Section 115 (9) of the Law of Property Act 1925 shall not apply to a receipt in the prescribed form endorsed or annexed by a building society in pursuance of sub-paragraph (1) above; and in the application of that subsection to a receipt so endorsed or annexed which is not in that form, the receipt shall be taken to be executed in the manner required by the statute relating to the society if it is signed as mentioned in sub-paragraph (1) (a) above.
>
> (4) The foregoing sub-paragraphs shall, in the case of a mortgage of registered land, have effect without prejudice to the operation of the Land Registration Act 1925 or any rules in force under it.

The 'prescribed forms' are laid down in rules made by the Chief Registrar of Friendly Societies[3]. The principal difference between the two forms of statutory receipt is that under the Law of Property Act, but not under the Building Societies Act, the receipt must state the name of the person who pays the money. A receipt under the Building Societies Act 1986, whether or not in the prescribed form, therefore cannot operate as a transfer of the mortgage to someone who pays off the debt, not being entitled to the immediate equity of redemption. A receipt in the prescribed form operates only in accordance with s 115(1), (3), (6) and (8) of the 1925 Act and the transfer provisions are in s 115(2). An informal receipt under the 1986 Act takes effect under s 115(9) of the 1925 Act, which expressly refers only to discharge and not transfer. Nor do the provisions of s 115(4) and (7) apply to a receipt under the 1986 Act in the prescribed form; and the only provisions of s 115 which apply to an informal receipt under the 1986 Act are those relating to the *operation* of a receipt (s 115(9)).

1 As to friendly societies and industrial and provident societies, see **28.54**, n 14.
2 Essentially re-enacting Building Societies Act 1962, s 37, which removed a number of difficulties which previously existed arising out of s 115 of the Law of Property Act 1925 and s 42 of the Building Societies Act 1874; see para 2 of the Lord Chancellor's Memorandum on the Consolidation of Certain Enactments relating to Building Societies, dated 15 February 1962 (HL 39; HC 117).
3 Sch 2A, para 3. The forms are in the Schedule to the Building Societies (Prescribed Forms of Receipt) Regulations 1997, SI 1997/2869.

Effect of receipt on mortgagor's liability

28.58 The effect of the statutory receipt[1] is, inter alia, to discharge the mortgaged property from all principal money and interest secured thereby and from all claims under the mortgage[2]. Nothing is said about the debt. Two late nineteenth century cases[3] concerning receipts by building societies under previous building societies' legislation[4] support the proposition that the receipt also releases the mortgagor from all liability in respect of the debt. This view has been followed in a twentieth century county court decision[5]. The statutory form receipt[6] contains an acknowledgment that the chargee has received the sum of £X representing the [aggregate] [balance remaining owing in respect of the] principal money secured by the charge etc. The problem arises where, in the event, through some miscalculation or otherwise, the money paid is less than the correct amount due. There would appear to be no reason in principle, subject to the precise wording used in the receipt and questions of estoppel[7], why (whatever the method of discharge[8]) the underpaid lender should not be able to recover the balance moneys due[9] either under the personal covenant, or as money had and received[10].

If the receipt has been delivered only as an escrow, the mortgagee may show that the mortgage has not been paid off[11].

1 For the effect of the redemption statement, see **28.37**.
2 Law of Property Act 1925, s 115 (1); see **28.54**.
3 *Harvey v Municipal Permanent Investment Building Society* (1884) 26 Ch D 273, especially at 286, per Cotton LJ; *London and County United Building Society v Angell* (1896) 65 LJQB 194; and see also *Priestley v Hopwood* (1864) 10 LT 646, a decision upon the wording of the particular Building Society Rules.
4 The decisions in the above cases could be said to turn on the special wording of the current building societies legislation, under which the effect of the receipt was stated to be to vacate the mortgage or debt. Cf the wording in the Law of Property Act 1925, s 115.
5 *Erewash Borough Council v Taylor* [1979] CLY 1831 (referred to in *Lombard North Central plc v Stobart* [1990] CCLR 53, CA).
6 Law of Property Act 1925, Sch 3, Form No 2.
7 See *Erewash Borough Council v Taylor*, above.
8 For overpayment, see **28.37**.
9 *State Bank of New South Wales v Berowra Waters Pty Ltd* (1986) 4 NSWLR 398; *Groongal Pastoral Co Ltd v Falkiner* (1924) 35 CLR 157; *Associated Securities Ltd v Perry* [1978] Qd R 13; *Perpetual Trustees Estate and Agency Co of NZ Ltd v Morrison* [1980] 2 NZLR 447; *Grundy v Ley* [1984] 2 NSWLR 567; *Marac Finance Ltd v Dyer* (1990) ANZ Conv 276, NZHC.
10 *Hartl v Cowen* [1983] ACLD 144.
11 *Lloyds Bank Ltd v Bullock* [1896] 2 Ch 192.

Discharge of registered and noted charges etc

28.59 The discharge of a charge registered under the Land Registration Act 1925 is effected by notification on the register. The Land Registration Act 1925 provides:

> **35** (1) The registrar shall, on the requisition of the proprietor of any charge, or on due proof of the satisfaction (whole or partial) thereof, notify on the register in the prescribed manner, by cancelling or varying the original entry or otherwise, the cessation (whole or partial) of the charge, and thereupon the charge shall be deemed to have ceased (in whole or part) accordingly.
>
> (2) On the notification on the register of the entire cessation of a registered charge whether as to the whole or part only of the land affected thereby, the term or sub-term implied in or granted by the charge or by any deed or alteration, so far as it affects the land to which the discharge extends, shall merge and be extinguished in the registered estate in reversion without any surrender.

As previously stated, s 115 of the Law of Property Act 1925 does not apply to the discharge of a charge or incumbrance registered under the Land Registration Act 1925[1].

The discharge of a registered charge must comply with the Land Registration Rules 1925, the material rules being as follows[2]:

> **151**(1) Subject to rule 151A, a discharge of a registered charge shall be in form DS1.
>
> (2) Subject to rule 151A, a release of part of the land from a registered charge shall be in form DS3.
>
> (3) Any discharge or release in form DS1 or DS3 shall be executed as a deed or authenticated in such other manner as the Registrar may approve.
>
> (4) Notwithstanding paragraphs (1) and (2) above and rule 151A, the Registrar shall be entitled to accept act upon any other proof of satisfaction of a charge as he may deem sufficient.
>
> (5) Subject to rule 85B[3], an application to register a discharge in Form DS1 shall be made on form AP1 or Form DS2 and an application to register a release in Form DS3 shall be made on Form AP1.

Rule 151A contains elaborate provision for the Registrar by notice to provide for applications to be made by alternative non-documentary means and for discharges or releases effected pursuant to applications made under such arrangements to have the same effect as in the case of applications made under r 151[4]. The object of the rule is to reduce delays arising from the fulfilment by the vendor's solicitor of his usual undertaking to discharge outstanding mortgages on completion. Where documentary means are used, the procedure requires an engrossed form of discharge (DS1) to travel between the vendor's solicitor, the lender and the purchaser's solicitor. Rule 151A allows for electronic notifications of discharge to speed matters up ('ENDs'). The Chief Land Registrar has issued notices to a number of particular named lenders allowing them to take advantage of this facility. Under the r 151A procedure, the vendor's solicitor undertakes to pay off the amount outstanding under the charge from the proceeds of sale and to arrange for the lender to transmit an END to the Registry. The solicitor arranges this by sending a Land Registry Form END 1 to the lender with the mortgage monies. The vendor's solicitor must then apply to the Registry in the usual way on Form AP1 or DS 2. On receipt of the application, and the END, the Registry cancels the entry relating to the charge.

Apart from ENDs, where the lender is a bank, the Registrar is normally willing under his power under r 151(4) to accept other methods of authentication to accept a form of discharge or release signed by a general manager, assistant general manager, a branch manager or someone of comparable rank[5].

In the case of a building society, Form DS1 or DS3 should be executed under seal in accordance with the rules of the Society[6]. The Registrar again may accept a statutory receipt indorsed on or annexed to the charge either in the Law of Property Act 1925 form[7] or that prescribed by the Chief Registrar of Friendly Societies[8]. A similar position obtains in respect of friendly societies, or industrial and provident societies[9].

The same rules apply where a person is registered as proprietor of a charge created prior to first registration[10] and to a registered sub-charge[11].

If the charge certificate is not already on deposit at the Land Registry, it must be delivered up for cancellation[12].

Where a mortgage existing at the time of first registration has merely been noted on the register[13] and has not been substantively registered, the registrar will, on proof to his satisfaction of the discharge of the incumbrance, notify such discharge , either by cancelling the original entry or by noting the fact, as he thinks fit[14]. The appropriate proof is a sufficient release or discharge executed by the person named in the document as having the benefit of the noted incumbrance. Form DS1 is not applicable.

Mortgage cautions may be withdrawn in the same manner as other cautions[15] or vacated, subject to the requisite evidence being furnished to the registrar of the discharge of the mortgage[16].

A notice of deposit or notice of intended deposit may be withdrawn from the register on a written request or consent signed by the person entitled to the lien created by the deposit, or notice of intended deposit, or his successor in title— accompanied in either case by the land certificate, or charge certificate[17].

1 Section 115(10).
2 No fee is payable for registering the discharge of a registered charge: Land Registration Fees Order 2001, Sch 4(5), para 11.
3 This deals with applications by electronic means.
4 The Building Societies Act 1986, Sch 2A takes effect subject to these rules: see Sch 2A, para 1(4). The Land Registration Rules 1925 used to contain special provision for the discharge of building society mortgages, but these have been revoked (Land Registration (Charges) Rules 1990, r 5): but see below.
5 Ruoff and Roper, *Registered Land* para 24-19.
6 Building Societies Act 1986, Sch 2, para 3.
7 Law of Property Act 1925, s 115, Sch 3 Form 2.
8 Under the Building Societies Act 1986, Sch 2A, para 3. See Sch to the Building Societies (Prescribed Form of Receipt) Rules 1997, SI 1997/2869.
9 See Ruoff and Roper, para 24-19.
10 Land Registration Rules 1925, rr 161, 162.
11 Rule 164 (1).
12 Rule 267.
13 Under Land Registration Act 1925, s 49(1)(c).
14 Land Registration Act 1925, s 46; Land Registration Rules, rr 201, 203.
15 Land Registration Rules 1925, r 68; in Form WCT.
16 Rule 224 (1), now Building Societies Act 1986, Sch 4, para 2.
16 Rule 224 (2). For cancellation of notice, see r 204.
17 Rule 246. Form 86 is the relevant form.

Discharge of statutory mortgage

28.60 A statutory mortgage may be surrendered or discharged by the prescribed form of receipt[1].

1 Law of Property Act 1925, s 120, Sch 4, Form No 5.

Discharge of equitable mortgages

28.61 The statutory receipt is inapplicable[1]. A mortgage of an equitable interest is discharged by a reassignment of the interest.

In the case of an equitable mortgage by mere deposit[2] a simple receipt may be employed. Where the deposit is accompanied by a written agreement or deed of charge a separate receipt should be used, but a mere cancellation of the document suffices[3].

If the mortgage is a mortgage of an equitable interest in land, capital money, or settled funds, notice of the receipt should be given to the trust corporation, if any, nominated to receive notices, or, if none, to the trustees or estate owner[4].

1 Because the mortgage has no legal estate which needs to be reconveyed. See (1962) 26 Conv (NS) pp 449–453 (Rowley). For a form of simple receipt, see 1 *Forms and Precedents* (5th edn) Acknowledgments and Receipts, and the Appendix.
2 A mortgage can no longer be created by mere deposit: Law of Property (Miscellaneous Provisions) Act 1989, s 2.
3 For partial release, see **30.5**.
4 Law of Property Act 1925, ss 137, 138.

Debentures

28.62 Where the debenture does not create a legal charge on land, it may be discharged by a simple receipt, indorsed on the debenture[1] or separately. A statutory vacating receipt[2] may be used for a debenture creating a specific legal charge, but, as indicated above[3], a simple receipt will be sufficient. For registered land, the appropriate method, mentioned above[4], should be use[5].

1 For a form, see 1 *Forms and Precedents* (5th edn) Acknowledgments and Receipts. In *Scottish and Newcastle plc, Petitioners* [1993] BCC 634 the Court of Session held that the Companies Acts did not contain any mandatory provisions as to how a debenture should be discharged.
2 See **28.54**.
3 See **28.56**.
4 See **28.59**.
5 The registration at the Companies Registry will require cancellation by the official form of declaration of satisfaction and, where appropriate, any land charge registration will require cancellation.

Mortgages, charges and orders registered as land charges

28.63 The registration of a land charge may be vacated pursuant to an order of the court or a judge thereof[1].

1 Land Charges Act 1972, s 1 (6). The County Court has jurisdiction if the amount secured by the charge does not exceed £30,000 (s 1(6A)).

Discharge of registered shipping mortgages

28.64 The method of automatic reconveyance by endorsed receipt is applied to shipping mortgages. Thus, the Merchant Shipping Act 1995 provides that where any registered mortgage has been discharged, the registrar shall, on the production of the mortgage deed and such evidence of the discharge as may be prescribed, cause an entry to be made in the register to the effect that the mortgage has been discharged[1].

Under the predecessors to these provisions, it was held that entry when made is conclusive as to the discharge of the mortgage which cannot be revived by an entry on the register that the former entry was erroneous where the priorities or other mortgagees are affected[2]. The registrar has no power to erase entries of mortgages[3].

1 Schedule 1, para 13. For the prescribed evidence see Merchant Shipping (Registration of Ships) Regulations 1993, SI 1993/3138, reg 62(1).
2 *Bell v Blyth* (1868) 4 Ch App 136. Where they are not so affected the court may order a receipt endorsed on a mortgage by mistake to be set aside: *The Rose* (1873) LR 4 A & E 6.
3 *Chasteauneuf v Capeyron* (1882) 7 App Cas 127, PC, but he may be ordered to do so by the court, see eg *Burgis v Constantine* [1908] 2 KB 484, CA.

Discharge of registered aircraft mortgages

28.65 No special form is prescribed for the discharge of such mortgages. The registration of a mortgage will be marked 'discharged' if a copy of the document of discharge or receipt for the mortgage money or of any document which shows to the satisfaction of the Civil Aviation Authority that the mortgage has been discharged together with the prescribed fee and the prescribed form is received[1]. There is now no *obligation* to inform the Civil Aviation Authority of the discharge of a mortgage[2].

1 Mortgaging of Aircraft Order 1972, SI 1972/1268, reg 9, as inserted by the Mortgaging of Aircraft (Amendment) Order 1981, SI 1981/611.
2 This change was effected by the Mortgaging of Aircraft (Amendment) Order 1981, SI 1981/611.

Discharge of mortgages of personalty

28.66 It has been doubted whether the Law of Property Act 1925, s 115, applies to mortgages of choses in action or pure personalty. It is submitted however that a statutory receipt under s 115 is effectual to discharge such mortgages with the exception of bills of sale mentioned below. Nevertheless such mortgages are generally discharged by reassignment[1].

1 For a form of reassignment, see 1 *Forms and Precedents* (5th edn) Acknowledgments and Receipts. Notice of the reassignment should be given to those to whom notice of the mortgage was given.

Reassignment of life policies

28.67 A statutory receipt may be used to reassign a life policy, the subject of a legal mortgage and in the case of a building society mortgage the receipt under para 4 of Sch 2A to the Building Societies Act 1986 may be used, but a simple receipt is acceptable. However, the printed forms of a mortgage of a life policy of banks and building societies and other institutional lenders usually provide for an express reassignment[1]. Notice of the discharge should be given to the insurance company. An equitable mortgage of a life policy may be discharged by redelivery and the cancellation of the memorandum of deposit, if any.

1 For a form of receipt and reassignment, see 1 *Forms and Precedents* (5th edn) Acknowledgments and Receipts.

Discharge of bills of sale

28.68 A Master of the Supreme Court may order a memorandum of satisfaction to be written upon any registered copy of a bill of sale upon the prescribed evidence being given that the debt (if any), for which such bill of sale was made or given, has been satisfied or discharged[1]. The prescribed evidence is a consent, signed by the person entitled to the benefit of the bill of sale, which must be verified by affidavit. If the consent cannot be obtained, the application is made by originating summons supported by evidence as to the satisfaction or discharge of the debt.

1 Bills of Sale Act 1878, s 15; CPR Pt 50, Sch 1, RSC Ord 95, r 2.

Discharge of consumer credit securities

28.69 The Consumer Credit Act 1974 does not make any special provision for the discharge of securities provided in relating to a regulated agreement. The general provisions of the 1974 Act as regards early payment by the debtor, the appropriate notice and statements apply to the agreement[1] and the mortgagee is required to give information to the mortgagor on request[2].

1 Sections 94 ff; see also **10.53**.
2 Section 110; see also **10.66**.

Discharge of collateral security

28.70 The various types of collateral security have already been mentioned[1]. A further charge by a mortgagor is discharged in the usual form by a statutory receipt endorsed on the principal mortgage referring to the further charge or to the aggregate amount of the mortgage money secured by both deeds (Law of Property Act 1925, s 115 (7)). Where there is a principal debtor and a surety and payment is made by the principal debtor (there being separate mortgages) both mortgages should be discharged by statutory receipt. Where payment is made by the surety he is entitled to a discharge of his own mortgage and a transfer of the mortgage of the principal debtor[2]. However, where there are not separate mortgages (where, for example, the principal debtor does not charge any of his property but the surety does, or where both principal debtor and surety each charges his property in one deed) then, on payment by the surety he is entitled (in the first case) to an assignment of the personal debt of the principal debtor (the mortgage being discharged) and (in the second case) to a transfer of the security created by the principal debtor (the security created by the surety being released).

1 See **1.23**.
2 See **31.9**.

The mortgagor's right to policies

28.71 It has been seen that the mortgagor is entitled to have back on redemption the property which is strictly comprised in the mortgage, free from clogs or collateral advantages accruing to the mortgagee. In many cases, a further question arises whether he is entitled also to a policy which has been effected as a collateral security.

If the relation of debtor and creditor exists between the parties, and it has been agreed, or can be inferred, that the debtor was obliged to pay the premiums and that the policy is effected as a security or indemnity, the policy or the balance of the insurance money, after discharge of the debt, will be the debtor's. It is immaterial in such a case that the premiums were not actually paid by the debtor, if he has been charged with them in account by the creditor and has not disputed his liability to pay them[1]. If the mortgagor refuses to pay premiums, and they are discharged by the mortgagee, the mortgagor may yet be entitled to the policy if he should later pay a sum in respect of the advances for the premiums with interest[2].

If the policy is not taken out under an arrangement with the debtor, but is effected entirely by the creditor for his own protection, he alone is interested in it. The mere fact that the creditor has charged the debtor with the premiums in his accounts, if there is no evidence that the debtor was aware of the fact, or that he had agreed to pay them, will not give him a right to the policy[3].

The mortgagor will also take the benefit of the insurance if there is an agreement, express or to be inferred[4], to that effect. If the agreement is that the mortgagor may elect to take the benefit of the policy, the mortgagee will not be obliged to keep up payments after the mortgagor has elected. However, the mortgage may not dispose of the policy for his own benefit, whether before or after the election[5].

If a lessee mortgages his interest, the benefit of a fire insurance, effected in the names of himself and the lessor, with a provision that the money payable under the policy should be applied in restoring the premises, passes under the mortgage, whether or not it is mentioned in it. So where the mortgagee spent money restoring the premises after the fire, he was entitled to require the mortgagor to join with the lessor in signing a joint receipt to the insurance office for the money[6]. A mere covenant by the mortgagor with the mortgagee to effect an insurance, does not imply that the mortgagee shall have the benefit of the insurance, either in discharge of the debt or in the restoration of the property, if there is no stipulation to that effect[7].

1 *Holland v Smith* (1806) 6 Esp 11; *Lea v Hinton* (1854) 5 De GM & G 823; *Morland v Isaac* (1855) 20 Beav 389; *Freme v Brade* (1858) 2 De G & J 582; *Re Storie's Will Trusts* (1859) 1 Giff 94; *Courtenay v Wright* (1860) 2 Giff 337.
2 *Drysdale v Piggott* (1856) 8 De GM & G 546; *Salt v Marquess of Northampton* [1892] AC 1 at 16, HL.
3 *Bruce v Garden* (1869) 5 Ch App 32.
4 *Gottlieb v Cranch* (1853) 4 De GM & G 440.

5 Even before election: *Hawkins v Woodgate* (1844) 7 Beav 565.
6 *Garden v Ingram* (1852) 23 LJ Ch 478.
7 *Lees v Whiteley* (1866) LR 2 Eq 143.

Solicitor's undertaking to discharge mortgage[1]

28.72 Where a mortgage is to be discharged out of the proceeds of the sale of the mortgaged property, it is common for completion to take place upon the undertaking of the vendor's solicitor[2] to discharge the mortgage and to forward the discharged mortgage to the purchaser's solicitor within a specified period[3]. The risk of liability under the undertaking ought to be considered by the maker, as he may be ordered by the court to implement his undertaking[4] and the liability may be grater than would at first sight appear by virtue of the reservation of a power of consolidation[5]. The risk to the purchaser's solicitor, in accepting such undertaking, to a negligence claim must also be considered[6]. For the procedure for complying with an undertaking to discharge, reference should be made to specialist works on conveyancing[7].

1 See (1961) 25 Conv (NS) 259. For undertakings in discharge of registered charges, see (1976) 120 SJ 406, 433, 454.
2 Who should seek the vendor's authority to give the undertaking; see *Holmes v Kennard* (1985) 49 P & CR 292; (1985) 128 Sol Jo 824, CA; [1985] Conv 293 (Price).
3 For Law Society recommended form, see Law Society Conveyancing Handbook (2001) para 4.2.11. Cf Land Registration Rules 1926, r 151A, discussed at **28.59**.
4 *United Mining and Finance Corpn Ltd v Becher* [1910] 2 KB 296; *Re Mallows* (1960) 176 Estates Gazette 1117 (undertaking to cancel entries to puisne mortgages as land charges); and see *Re a Solicitor (Lincoln)* [1966] 3 All ER 52; *Silver and Drake v Baines* [1971] 1 QB 396, [1971] 1 All ER 473, CA; *John Fox v Bannister King & Rigbeys* [1988] QB 925n; [1987] 1 All ER 737, [1987] 3 WLR 480n, CA; *Udall v Capri Lighting Ltd* [1988] QB 907; [1987] 3 All ER 262; [1987] 137 NLJ Rep 293, CA. The Law Society's Adjudication Committee construes an undertaking to procure the discharge of 'all mortgages' as referring to all mortgages regardless of whether the solicitor giving the undertaking knows of the existence of the mortgage and that an answer to a requisition on title that 'the usual undertaking will be given' is equivalent to giving a formal undertaking (1987) 84 LSoc Gaz 1622; (1987) 84 LSoc Gaz 3470 (Paine)). These principles were applied by Warner J in *Bray v Stuart A West & Co* [1989] NLJR 753 where it was held that a reply to a requisition on title that 'we will give our undertaking to discharge all subsisting charges' was an undertaking even though no formal undertaking was actually given. Further the undertaking was construed to cover a statutory charge imposed by a local authority. This case was followed by Judge Maddocks sitting as a Judge of the Chancery Division in *Redrow v Ramsbottom and Lord* (unreported December 1991) where a reply to a requisition that 'the usual undertaking will be given' was treated as an actual undertaking. Judge Maddocks rejected an argument that the 'usual undertaking' could not extend to a mortgage in favour of a bank, rather than a building society, and held that the undertaking required a solicitor to procure the discharge of the mortgage even if the mortgage secured more than the purchase price.
The Law Society's Indemnity Policy covers a solicitor's personal liability for undertakings of this nature. However, not all employed solicitors are covered by this or similar policies. Considerable thought should be given before accepting an undertaking from an employed solicitor in a substantial matter where there is doubt as to the employer's solvency.
5 There is little or no danger in the case of the private vendor and the single mortgage, but the position may be otherwise in the case of a developer vendor who may have several mortgages on foot. See further on undertakings (1970) 67 LS Gaz 753; (1971) 35 Conv (NS) 3; (1971) 115 SJ 684 (Aldridge); (1973) 70 LS Gaz 1346, 1360 (Adams); (1980) 77 LS Gaz 259; [1985] Conv 10; and correspondence in (1976) 118 Sol Jo 406 at 433, 454.
6 See *Edward Wong Finance Co Ltd v Johnson Stokes & Master* [1984] AC 296, PC, [1984] Conv 86; and see *Al-Kandari v JR Brown & Co* [1987] QB 514, [1987] 2 All ER 302.
7 Eg Law Society's *Conveyancing Handbook 2001*, paras 4.2.10 ff.

Costs of redemption

28.73 On this topic, see **36.41**.

DISCHARGE UNDER OVERREACHING POWERS

Discharge on payment into court

28.74 Where land subject to any incumbrance, whether immediately realisable or payable or not, is sold or exchanged by the court, or out of court, the court may, if it thinks fit, on the application on any party to the sale or exchange, direct or allow payment into court of such a sum as, when invested in government securities, would in the court's view be sufficient, by means of the dividends thereof, to keep down or otherwise provide for that charge, together with any additional sum to meet further costs, expenses and interest or any other contingency[1]. Thereupon the court may declare the land freed from the incumbrance and make any order for conveyance, or vesting order, proper for giving effect to the sale or exchange, and give directions for the retention and investment of the money in court and for the payment or application of the income thereof[2]. The court may declare all other land, if any, affected by the incumbrance (besides the land sold or exchanged) to be freed from the incumbrance[3].

Payment of money into court effectually exonerates therefrom the person who makes the payment[4].

1 See Law of Property Act 1925, s 50, replacing, with amendments, s 5 of the Conveyancing Act 1881, and s 1 of the Conveyancing Act 1911.
2 Section 50 (2). See *Re Uplands* [1948] WN 165.
3 Section 50 (3); and see *Re Wilberforce* [1915] 1 Ch 94; *Lidco Investments Ltd v Hale* (1971) 219 Estates Gazette Digest 715, and see **28.51**, n 14.
4 Law of Property Act 1925, s 203 (1).

Discharge under overreaching conveyance

28.75 By s 2 of the Law of Property Act 1925[1] certain sorts of conveyance to a purchaser of a legal estate in land can overreach (ie shift from the land to the purchase money) any equitable mortgage affecting the estate whether or not the purchaser has notice. Section 2 does not apply to an equitable mortgage protected by deposit of documents[2]. The sorts of conveyance in question are the subject of detailed provision in s 2, but include an overreaching conveyance under powers conferred on a tenant for life or trustees of a settlement, and a conveyance under a trust of land. The trust of land may be either a trust of land already existing or a trust of land created for the express purpose of overreaching the incumbrance[3]. In either case in order that it may have the overreaching effect, the trustees must be either two or more individuals approved or appointed by the court or the successors in office of the individuals so approved or appointed; or a trust corporation[4]. Whether the sale is made under a trust of land or under the statutory powers of the Settled Land Act, the land is conveyed free from the equitable incumbrance[5].

1 As amended by the Trusts of Land and Appointment of Trustees Act 1996.
2 Law of Property Act 1925, ss 2 (3) and 13; Settled Land Act 1925, s 21 (2). An unprotected equitable mortgage may be overreached even if registered as a general equitable charge.

3 Section 2(2).
4 Law of Property Act 1925, s 2 (2), as amended by the Law of Property (Amendment) Act 1926.
5 It is the duty of the trustees to provide for the incumbrance out of the proceeds of sale and unless the incumbrance can be immediately paid off they must allow for a proper margin. The principle is the same as in ascertaining the amount to be paid into court, but the trustees do not have the advantage of an order of the court in fixing the amount.

VESTING ORDERS

Vesting orders in case of trustees and patients

28.76 Since a receipt or other evidence that the mortgage money has been paid shows that the mortgage term has ceased, it should rarely be necessary to obtain a vesting order or order for conveyance on discharge of the mortgage. However, a vesting order[1] may be required where a mortgagee is a trustee, or a patient or both. Such orders can be made under the Trustee Act 1925 and the Mental Health Act 1983, the main distinctions being that the order is made under the Mental Health Act where the mortgagee is a patient and the mortgage belongs to him beneficially; generally, under either Act where a patient is a trustee; and under the Trustee Act if the mortgagee is a trustee who is not a patient.

1 As to vesting orders where an order for sale is made in reference to an equitable mortgage of land, see Law of Property Act 1925, s 90, and see also **21.6**.

Mortgagee beneficially entitled to mortgage to property

28.77 The judge[1] has power to make such orders and give such directions and authorities as he thinks fit relating to his functions with respect to the property and affairs of a patient[2], and in particular for the control (with or without the transfer or vesting of the property or the payment into or lodgment in court of money or securities) and management of any property of the patient[3].

1 One or more judges of the Supreme Court nominated to act for the purposes of Pt VII of the Mental Health Act 1983, s 93 (1).
2 Ie under s 95 of the Act. For the definition of patient, see s 94.
3 Mental Health Act 1983, s 96 (1) (a).

Mortgagee-trustee

28.78 The Trustee Act 1925 provides as follows:

> **41** (1)[1] The court[2] may, whenever it is expedient to appoint a new trustee or new trustees, and it is found inexpedient, difficult, or impracticable so to do without the assistance of the court, make an order appointing a new trustee or new trustees either in substitution for or in addition to any existing trustee or trustees, or although there is no existing trustee.
>
> In particular and without prejudice to the generality of the foregoing provision, the court may make an order appointing a new trustee in substitution for a trustee who is ...[3] incapable by reason of mental disorder within the meaning of the Mental Health Act 1983, of exercising his functions as trustee, or is a bankrupt, or is a corporation which is in liquidation or has been dissolved.

44 In any of the following cases, namely—

(i) Where the court appoints or has appointed a trustee, or where a trustee has been appointed out of court under any statutory or express power;

(ii) Where a trustee entitled to or possessed of any land or interest therein, whether by way of mortgage or otherwise, or entitled to a contingent right therein, either solely or jointly with any other person—

(a) is under disability; or

(b) is out of the jurisdiction of the High Court; or

(c) cannot be found[4], or, being a corporation, has been dissolved;

(vii) Where any land or any interest therein is vested in a trustee whether by way of mortgage or otherwise, and it appears to the court to be expedient;

the court[5] may make an order (in this Act called a vesting order) vesting the land or interest therein in any such person, in any such manner, and for any such estate or interest as the court may direct, or releasing or disposing of the contingent right to such person as the court may direct[6]:

Provided that—

(a) Where the order is consequential on the appointment of a trustee the land or interest therein shall be vested for such estate as the court may direct in the persons who on the appointment are the trustees; and

(b) Where the order relates to a trustee entitled or formerly entitled jointly with another person, and such trustee is under disability or out of the jurisdiction of the High Court or cannot be found, or being a corporation has been dissolved, the land, interest, or right shall be vested in such other person who remains entitled, either alone or with any other person the court may appoint.

Section 51 provides for vesting orders as to stock and things in action being made by the court under similar circumstances[7].

54 (1) Subject to the provisions of this section, the authorities having jurisdiction under Part VII of the Mental Health Act 1983, shall not have power to make any order, or give any direction or authority, in relation to a patient who is a trustee if the High Court has power under this Act to make an order to the like effect.

(2) Where a patient is a trustee and a receiver appointed by the said authority is acting for him or an application for the appointment of a receiver has been made but not determined, then, except as respects a trust which is subject to an order for administration made by the High Court, the said authority shall have concurrent jurisdiction with the High Court in relation to—

(a) mortgaged property of which the patient has become a trustee merely by reason of the mortgage having been paid off;

(b) matters consequent on the making of provision of the said authority for the exercise of a power of appointing trustees or retiring from a trust[8].

1 As amended by the Mental Health Act 1983, s 148, Sch 4.

2 Ie the High Court (see Trustee Act 1925, s 67) and also the county court where the amount or value of the estate or fund does not exceed the county court limit (see Trustee Act 1925, s 63A, inserted by the County Courts Act 1984, s 148 (1), Sch 2, para 1). The current county court limit is £30,000.

3 The words 'convicted of felony' were repealed by the Criminal Law Act 1967, Sch 3.

4 Since, after repayment, the mortgagee is trustee for the mortgagor, s 44 may be used in a case where there is proof of repayment but no receipt and the mortgagee has disappeared. Section 59 of the Trustee Act 1925 enables the court to give judgment in the absence of a trustee.

5 Ie the High Court (see Trustee Act 1925, s 67) and also the county court where the amount or value of the estate or fund does not exceed the county court limit (see Trustee Act 1925, s 63A, inserted by the County Courts Act 1984, s 148 (1), Sch 2, para 1). The current county court limit is £30,000.

6 By s 49 a vesting order operates as a conveyance made by the appropriate conveying parties or, under s 50, the court may, if it is more convenient, appoint a person to convey.

See also Law of Property Act 1925 ss 2(1)(iv), 9(1)(a), (2) for the effect of a vesting order in respect of a legal estate in land.

7 By sub-s (6) the provisions of the Act as to vesting orders apply to shares in ships registered under the Merchant Shipping Act 1995 as if they were stock. See s 58 as to the persons who may apply under the Act.

8 Substituted for the original; see now Mental Health Act 1983, s 148, Sch 4.

DELIVERY OF THE DEEDS

Registered land

28.79 In the typical case of a mortgage of registered land, the mortgagee will not have the title deeds. The mortgagee will have its charge certificate as its document of title and the mortgage itself will be registered as a charge both on its own account and in the charges register of the mortgagor's title. Thus in most cases the law concerning the obligation on a mortgagee to deliver up the title deeds is of largely historical interest (though the mortgagee should co-operate in the cancellation of the charge[1]). However, it may still apply to some mortgages of unregistered land and (by definition) to mortgages by deposit.

1 See **28.59**.

Duty of mortgagee to have the deeds ready

28.80 Where the mortgage is to be paid off in accordance with notice given on either side, it is the duty of the mortgagee to see that the title and mortgage deeds are available on the day fixed[1]. The mortgagor is entitled to demand these documents, even where the mortgagee has settled the mortgage moneys by a memorandum endorsed on the deeds[2]. This right extends to previous mortgages, assignments and reconveyances made between the same parties, or their representatives, before the redeemed mortgage[3]. Where several mortgages on distinct properties have been transferred by a single deed, one of the mortgagors who seeks to redeem singly is entitled to have the deed of transfer delivered to him, upon his covenanting to produce it[4].

Where the mortgage is redeemed on only part of the property, and the mortgagee is entitled to retain the deeds by virtue of his title to the remainder, he ought also to covenant with the redeeming party for production[5].

1 *Lord Midleton v Eliot* (1847) 15 Sim 531, and the mortgagee is not liable on account of delivering the deeds to the person not having the best right thereto, unless he has notice of the better right: Law of Property Act 1925, s 96 (2); *Corbett v National Provident Institution* (1900) 17 TLR 5. To avoid the necessity of search by the mortgagee, this subsection was amended by the Law of Property (Amendment) Act 1926, so as to exclude notice implied by registration.

2 *Dobson v Land* (1851) 4 De G & Sm 575 at 581.

3 *Hudson v Malcolm* (1862) 10 WR 720 and a mortgagee or transferee of a mortgage, though he is entitled to keep a copy of the draft for his own protection until the transaction is completed, has no right to keep copies of the mortgage or transfer after his is paid off. Whatever copies he has are, as a general rule, copies paid for by the mortgagor and must be delivered up to him when he pays off the mortgage: *Re Wade and Thomas* (1881) 17 Ch D 348.

4 *Capper v Terrington* (1844) 1 Coll 103.

5 *Yates v Plumbe* (1854) 2 Sm & G 174.

Loss of the title deeds

28.81 The mortgagee will not be deprived of the benefit of his security by reason of the loss of the title deeds, if the court is satisfied that a security was effected and that they have really been lost[1].

If the title deeds of a property have been lost by, or stolen from, the mortgagee or his agent, the court, either in a redemption or foreclosure action, will direct appropriate inquiries as to what deeds or documents were delivered to the mortgagee and their whereabouts[2]. The costs of such an action will fall on the mortgagee[3], and the same result follows where he has to sue a third party for them[4].

1 *Baskett v Skeel* (1863) 11 WR 1019.
2 *Smith v Bicknell* (1805) cited 3 Ves & B 51n; *Stokoe v Robson* (1814) 3 Ves & B 51; *Bentinck v Willink* (1842) 2 Hare 1.
3 *James v Rumsey* (1879) 11 Ch D 398; *Caldwell v Matthews* (1890) 62 LT 799.
4 *James v Rumsey*, above. Where the failure to produce the deeds was due to an adverse claim by an attorney, an account was ordered to be taken of the principal, interest and costs, the amount to be paid into and remain in the bank until the deeds could be secured and a reconveyance had: *Schoole v Sall* (1803) 1 Sch & Lef 176.

Indemnity and compensation by mortgagee

28.82 If the deeds are certified to be lost, or are known to have been destroyed or fraudulently disposed of by the mortgagee or his agent, the mortgagor will be entitled to an inquiry as to what indemnity or security ought to be given in respect of the loss[1] and also as to what ought to be allowed as a sufficient compensation for the damage done to the estate by the loss or destruction of the deeds[2].

The mortgagee will also be directed to deliver, upon oath, attested copies of such of the documents destroyed of which attested copies can be made or had.

If it is found, or appears, that the deeds were stolen, an indemnity will be ordered[3]. But in the absence of fraud or collusion, no liability arises for compensation, whether the deeds were in the possession of the mortgagee himself, or of his solicitor or agent in whose custody he might properly have left them had they been his own[4].

If the result of the inquiry is merely that the deeds are not to be found, it seems that an indemnity[5] only, and no compensation, will be directed. The court will assume in favour of the mortgagee that the deeds were stolen, or have gone missing without any wrongdoing or negligence on the part of the mortgagee[6].

There is authority for the proposition that a mortgagee is not liable in negligence for the loss of the title deeds[7], although there is some older authority to the contrary[8].

1 *Lord Midleton v Eliot* (1847) 15 Sim 531; *James v Rumsey* (1879) 11 Ch D 398; and see as to bond of indemnity, *Caldwell v Matthews* (1890) 62 LT 799.
2 *Hornby v Matcham* (1848) 16 Sim 325. This compensation is given in respect of the expense to arise on future dealings with the estate in getting office copies of the order and other proceedings in the action, which must thenceforth form part of the title; and not as speculative damages for injury occasioned by the absence of the deeds at a sale; and the amount of the compensation will be set off against the principal and interest due on the security: *Brown v Sewell* (1853) 11 Hare 49; *James v Rumsey*, above, and see *Macartney v Graham* (1831) 2 Russ & M 353, where the document lost was a bill of exchange and only an indemnity was given.
3 *Shelmardine v Harrop* (1821) 6 Madd 39. See form of bond of indemnity in *Stokoe v Robson* (1814) Ves & B 51, and *James v Rumsey*, above, at 400, 401.

4 *Jones v Lewis* (1751) 2 Ves Sen 240; and see *Woodman v Higgins* (1850) 14 Jur 846.
5 The indemnity must be given even in the absence of negligence: *James v Rumsey*, above.
6 *Smith v Bicknell* (1805) cited Ves & B 51n, *Stokoe v Robson*, above; *Lord Midleton v Eliot*, above.
7 *Browning v Handiland Group Ltd* (1978) 35 P & CR 345, Rubin J relying on *Bank of New South Wales v O'Connor* (1889) 14 App Cas 273 at 282, per Lord MacNaghten, PC; and *Gilligan and Nugent v National Bank Ltd* [1901] 2 IR 513. Sed quaere.
8 *Brown v Sewell*, above; *Hornby v Matcham*, above. Where compensation is given, it is given not under any implied covenant for safe custody, but under the general jurisdiction of the court in accident; *Gilligan and Nugent v National Bank Ltd*, above.

LOSS OF THE RIGHT OF REDEMPTION

Generally

28.83 The right of redemption may be lost by release of the right to the mortgagee by the mortgagor[1], by entry into a contract for the sale of the land by the mortgagee under his power of sale[2], upon foreclosure[3] and by extinguishment by lapse of time under the Limitation Act 1980.

1 See Chapter 30.
2 See Chapter 20; *National & Provincial Building Society v Ahmed* [1995] NPC 88, CA.
3 See Chapter 22.

EXTINGUISHMENT OF THE EQUITY OF REDEMPTION BY LAPSE OF TIME[1]

Mortgages of land

28.84 The Limitation Act 1980 provides:

> **16**[2] When a mortgagee of land[3] has been in possession[4] of any of the mortgaged land for a period of 12 years, no action to redeem the land of which the mortgagee has been so in possession shall be brought after the end of that period by the mortgagor or any person claiming through him[5].

Further:

> **29** (4)[6] Where a mortgagee is by virtue of the mortgage in possession of any mortgaged land and either—
> (a) receives any sum in respect of the principal or interest of the mortgage debt; or
> (b) acknowledges the title of the mortgagor, or his equity of redemption;
> an action to redeem the land in his possession may be brought at any time before the expiration of 12 years from the date of the payment or acknowledgment.

1 See, generally, 28 *Halsbury's Laws* (4th edn) paras 919 ff; Preston and Newsom *Limitation of Actions* (4th edn) para 6.1.1 and 6.4.4 and see **19.49**. These provisions are not contrary to the Human Rights Act 1998: *Pye JA (Oxford) v Graham* [2000] Ch 676, [2000] 3 WLR 242.
2 Replacing Limitation Act 1939, s 12.
3 See *Re Midleton's Settlement, Lord Cottesloe and Lloyd v A-G and Earl of Midleton* [1947] 1 Ch 583, [1947] 2 All ER 134, CA; affd *sub nom Earl of Midleton v Baron Cottesloe* [1949] AC 418, [1949] 1 All ER 841, HL; *Bank of Ireland v Domvile* [1956] IR 37; *Smith v Hill* (1878) 9 Ch D 143.
4 See *Lord Advocate v Lord Lovat* (1880) 5 App Cas 273 at 288, HL; *Kirby v Cowderoy* [1912] AC 599, PC.

5 The terms of the mortgage may provide for redemption beyond the 12 year period: *Alderson v White* (1857) 2 De G & J 97 at 109.
6 Replacing Limitation Act 1939, s 23 (3).

Effect of expiration of limitation period

28.85 Subject to s 18 of the Limitation Act 1980 (settled land and land held on trust) and s 75 of the Land Registration Act 1925 (registered land) at the expiration of the 12 year period the title of the mortgagor is extinguished[1]. If the mortgagee sells after being in possession for 12 years he may keep the whole of the proceeds of sale[2]. In such a case he should sell as mortgagee unless the mortgage term has been enlarged[3].

1 Limitation Act 1980, s 17, replacing Limitation Act 1939, s 16. As also is that of a subsequent mortgagee: *Re Statutory Trust Declared by Section 105 of the Law of Property Act 1925 affecting the Proceeds of Sale of Moat House Farm Thurlby* [1948] Ch 191, sub nom *Young v Clarey* [1948] 1 All ER 197. On the Real Property Limitation Act 1883, see *Addison v Billion* [1983] 1 NSWLR 586.
2 *Young v Clarey*, above.
3 See **28.94**.

Possession by mortgagee

28.86 To gain the benefit of the statute, the mortgagee must enter and continue in possession solely as mortgagee[1]. If he enters as purchaser of a life tenancy of settled land, the statute will not, during the continuance of his interest, run against the remainderman[2].

Where the mortgaged property is leasehold the receipt by the mortgagee of the rent reserved thereout for 12 years amounts to adverse possession of the land[3].

1 See *Park v Brady* [1976] 2 NSWLR 329.
2 *Hyde v Dallaway* (1843) 2 Hare 528. A life tenant holds the legal estate as trustee and cannot set up his possession against the remainderman.
3 Limitation Act 1980, Sch I, para 8 (3) (b) and see *Ward v Carttar* (1865) LR 1 Eq 29; *Markwick v Hardingham* (1880) 15 Ch D 339, CA.

When time begins to run

28.87 The statute will generally begin to run from the date of the mortgagee's entry into possession[1], but the terms of the deed and the circumstances of the case may start the period running at another time. Indeed it is common for institutional lenders to postpone the right of possession until an even of default, to prevent time running.

1 *Re Metropolis and Counties Permanent Investment Building Society, Gatfield's Case* [1911] 1 Ch 698.

Disabilities

28.88 The provisions of the Limitation Act 1980, relating to disability apply to the disability of the mortgagor who seeks to redeem[1].

1 Section 28 and see s 32 (fraud and mistake).

Acknowledgment and part payment

28.89 As indicated above s 29 (4) of the Limitation Act 1980 deals with the fresh accrual of an action to redeem on acknowledgment or part payment. The formal provisions as to acknowledgments and part payments are set out in s 30[1].

An acknowledgment must be in writing and signed by the mortgagee or other person claiming through him, or by his agent. It must be given to the mortgagor or his successor in title or his agent[2]. It cannot be given to the mortgagor after his title has ceased[3].

Where the mortgagee has entered into possession accounts of his receipt of rents are not a sufficient acknowledgment, unless kept for or communicated to the mortgagor or his agent[4].

Payments in respect of the mortgage debt must be made to the mortgagee or his agent[5]. Receipt of the rents and profits by the mortgagee while in possession is not a receipt of any sum in respect of the mortgage debt and accordingly not a part payment[6].

Where there are first and second mortgages in favour of two sets of trustees and a member of both sets receives the rents and applies them for over 12 years in paying off the capital and interest of the first mortgage, time will not run against the second mortgagees, for when the hand to pay and the hand to receive the money due to the first mortgagees is the same, time does not run[7].

1 See **16.44** ff. An acknowledgment or part payment made after the statutory period is ineffective, see **16.59**.
2 *Trulock v Robey* (1841) 12 Sim 402; *Lucas v Dennison* (1843) 13 Sim 584.
3 Eg after his bankruptcy: *Markwick v Hardingham* (1880) 15 Ch D 339.
4 *Re Alison, Johnson v Mounsey* (1879) 11 Ch D 284, and see *Wilson v Walton and Kirkdale Permanent Building Society* (1903) 19 TLR 408; *Re Metropolis and Counties Permanent Investment Building Society, Gatfield's Case* [1911] 1 Ch 698.
5 As to part payment, see **16.44** ff.
6 *Harlock v Ashberry* (1882) 19 Ch D 539. Payment of the rents and profits to the mortgagee by a receiver appointed by him constitutes part payment: *Berwick & Co v Price* [1905] 1 Ch 632 at 642.
7 *Hodgson v Salt* [1936] 1 All ER 95; cf *Bowring-Hanbury's Trustee v Bowring-Hanbury* [1943] Ch 104, [1943] 1 All ER 48, CA.

Acknowledgment by one of several mortgagees

28.90 Where two or more mortgagees are by virtue of the mortgage in possession of the mortgaged land, an acknowledgment of the mortgagor's title or of his equity of redemption by one of the mortgagees shall only bind him and his successors in title and shall not bind any other mortgagee or his successors[1]. Where the mortgagee by whom the acknowledgment is given is entitled to a part of the mortgaged land and not to any ascertained part of the mortgage debt, the mortgagor shall be entitled to redeem that part of the land on payment, with interest, of the part of the mortgage debt which bears the same proportion to the whole of the debt as the value of the part of the land bears to the whole of the mortgaged land[2].

1 Limitation Act 1980, s 31 (3).
2 Section 31 (4). See Preston and Newsom *Limitation of Actions* (4th edn) para 9.3.

Acknowledgment to one of several mortgagors

28.91 Where there are two or more mortgagors, and the title or right of redemption of one of the mortgagors is acknowledged as aforesaid, the acknowledgment shall be deemed to have been made to all the mortgagors[1].

1 Limitation Act 1980, s 31 (5).

Redemption of personalty

28.92 There is no corresponding enactment barring actions to redeem mortgages of pure personalty[1] and the 12 year period is not adopted by analogy. The right of redemption is only barred upon equitable grounds, such as the acquiescence of the mortgagor in the extinction of the right of redemption, or the alteration of the position of the mortgagee[2]. As in other cases of the enforcement of equitable demands after the lapse of time, it is a question of the balance of justice and injustice in granting the remedy or withholding it. Although mere length of time may bar the remedy, this is on the ground that to allow redemption would be unjust. There is no hard and fast rule that 20 years will be sufficient for the purpose, but probably there will be a difficulty in establishing a right to redeem after this period[3].

1 See the 5th Interim Report of the Law Revision Committee, 1936, Cmnd 5334, p 15. Cf, for example, NSW: see *Park v Brady* [1976] 2 NSWLR 329.
2 *Weld v Petre* [1929] 1 Ch 33, CA.
3 *Weld v Petre*, above at 53, 54, per Lawrence LJ.

Mortgage of land and personalty

28.93 Where a mortgage comprises both land and personalty, if the equity of redemption is barred as regards the land, it is barred as to the personalty also, because the right of redemption of the properties is indivisible[1].

1 *Charter v Watson* [1899] 1 Ch 175.

Enlargement of mortgage term into fee simple

28.94 Where a mortgagee of freehold property has acquired a title under the Limitation Acts, he, or the persons deriving title under him, may enlarge the mortgage term into a fee simple under the statutory power for that purpose[1] discharged from any legal mortgage affected by the title so acquired. Likewise a chargee by way of legal mortgage may by deed declare that the fee simple is vested in him so discharged and the same vests accordingly[2].

Similarly, where a mortgagee of leasehold property has acquired a title under the Limitation Acts, he, or the persons deriving title under him, may by deed declare that the leasehold reversion affected by the mortgage and any term affected by the title so acquired shall vest in him, free from any right of redemption which is barred, and the same vests accordingly. Such a vesting is not a breach of covenant in the lease not to assign the term without licence or consent. Thereupon the mortgage term, if any, and any other mortgage term or charge by way of legal mortgage affected by the title so acquired shall, subject to any express provision to the contrary contained in the deed, merge in such leasehold reversion or be extinguished[3].

A long term, originating in an old mortgage by demise, the equity of redemption of which has become barred by the Limitation Acts, is occasionally encountered and the above provisions permit such a term to be enlarged. It must, of course, be ascertained that the conditions of s 153 of the Law of Property Act 1925 are satisfied.

1 Law of Property Act 1925, s 153.
2 Section 88 (3).
3 Section 89 (3). As to the declaration by a registered chargee that the right of redemption is barred, see Land Registration Act 1925, s 34 (2); see **19.85**.

Subsequent incumbrancer

28.95 Where a subsequent mortgagee's right of action against the mortgagor is barred he cannot claim to redeem a prior incumbrancer[1].

1 *Cotterell v Price* [1960] 3 All ER 315.

Chapter 29

Redemption claims

INSTITUTION OF PROCEEDINGS[1]

High Court

29.1 Claims for the redemption of mortgages are assigned to the Chancery Division[2]. A claim for redemption is a Part 8B Practice Direction claim[3]. The claimant must use the Part 8 claim form[4]. The claim form must state where the mortgaged property is situated[5] and must otherwise comply with the requirements of Part 8[6]. Among other things, therefore, the claimant must file and serve any written evidence on which he intends to rely when he files and serves his claim form[7]. Any witness statement in support should set out particulars of the mortgage and all the material facts showing the plaintiff's right to redeem. Any special circumstances, such as that the defendant mortgagee has been in possession, should be stated.

The Part 8 procedure is mandatory in redemption claims, and proceedings must (inconveniently) be brought by this means even if there is a dispute of fact. A measure of relief is afforded by provision allowing a defendant in his acknowledgement of service to state his belief that the Part 8 procedure should not be used because of a substantial dispute of fact[8]. The court may then order the claim to continue as though commenced under Part 7.

1 See, generally, 28 *Atkin's Court Forms* (2nd edn, 1997 reissue), Mortgages.
2 Supreme Court Act 1981, s 61, Sch 1 and see RSC Ord 88.
3 CPR 8BPD, para A.1(1) and Table; CPR 50, Sch 1 and RSC Ord 88, r 1, 3.
4 Paragraph A.3.
5 CPR 50, Sch 1 and RSC Ord 88, r 3(2)(a).
6 CPR 8BPD, para A.2(1).
7 CPR 8.5.
8 CPR 8.8.

Offer to redeem

29.2 As a general rule the mortgagor is not entitled to bring the mortgagee before the court except for the purpose of redemption[1]. Hence a mortgagee cannot be made a party to a claim relating to the mortgage unless there is expressly or by implication an offer to redeem[2].

This rule does not apply where the object of the proceedings is to obtain the construction of the mortgage deed[3], or where the equity of redemption has become subject to trusts which provide for the payment of the mortgage debt and the mortgagee is made a party to a claim relating to the trusts[4]. It does not apply where the mortgagor's claim is for sale and not redemption[5], or to restrain the mortgagee from an improper sale of the mortgaged property[6].

1 *Tasker v Small* (1837) 3 My & Cr 63; *Jeffreys v Dickson* (1866) 1 Ch App 183; *National Bank of Australasia v United Hand-in-Hand Band of Hope Co* (1879) 4 App Cas 391, PC. Redemption is the only relief to which a subsequent incumbrancer is entitled against the prior mortgagee: *Gordon v Horsfall* (1847) 5 Moo PCC 393 at 426.

2 *Troughton v Binkes* (1801) 6 Ves 573; *Balfe v Lord* (1842) 2 Dr & War 480; *Dalton v Hayter* (1844) 7 Beav 313; *Gordon v Horsfall*, above; *Harding v Tingey* (1864) 10 Jur NS 872; *Hughes v Cook* (1865) 34 Beav 407. See *Russian Commercial and Industrial, Bank v British Bank for Foreign Trade Ltd* [1921] 2 AC 438. There must be an offer to redeem even though the claimant is a trustee, because the mortgagee is not interested in the trust: *M'Donough v Shewbridge* (1814) 2 Ball & B 555. This is the case even though part of trust property has been improperly included in the mortgage, see *Eaton v Hazel* (1852) 1 WR 87. As to the extent of the offer, see *Grugeon v Gerrard* (1840) 4 Y & C Ex 119. As a general rule an offer made in a statement of case cannot be revoked: *Davis v Duke of Marlborough* (1819) 2 Swan 108 at 134; *Bazzelgetti v Battine* (1821) 2 Swan 156n. An offer to redeem made under a mistake as to the amount secured on the property was enforced in *Holford v Burnell* (1687) 1 Vern 448, but this would hardly be so now, at least if the other party knew or suspected the mistake (see *Commission for the New Towns v Cooper (Great Britain) Ltd* [1995] Ch 259, [1995] 2 All ER 929). The court may in its discretion refuse to enforce the offer where it would be unjust to do so: *Knight v Bowyer* (1858) 2 De G & J 421; or where it is so limited in its terms as not to be strictly applicable to the state of affairs which has resulted from the hearing of the cause: *Pelly v Wathen* (1849) 7 Hare 351. As to enforcing payment where there has been no offer to redeem, see *Hollis v Bulpett* (1865) 12 LT 293.

Where the claim was framed for redemption, an offer to redeem, if not made expressly, might be added by amendment: *Palk v Lord Clinton* (1805) 12 Ves 48.

3 *Re Nobbs, Nobbs v Law Reversionary Interest Society* [1896] 2 Ch 830.

4 *Jeffreys v Dickson*, above. Similarly if the claim relates to different property, which has been conveyed in trust to exonerate the mortgaged property, and the claim cannot proceed without joining the mortgagee, he may be joined without any offer to redeem him: *Dalton v Hayter*, above. The prior mortgagee, if he is a necessary party in respect of accounts, may waive the redemption of his security. If he does so the judgment should be prefaced by a statement that he consents not to be redeemed, and to allow his debt to remain a charge on the estate: *Lord Kensington v Bouverie* (1854) 19 Beav 39.

5 Under the Law of Property Act 1925, s 91; see **21.5**.

6 *Murad v National Provincial Bank* (1966) 198 Estates Gazette 117.

Claim to impeach mortgage

29.3 It has been held that where the claim is brought to impeach the mortgage and is framed solely for this purpose, with no claim for redemption, then if the claim fails and the validity of the mortgage is established the claimant cannot obtain an order for redemption in those proceedings but must start afresh[1]. An exception was said to apply where the defendant had not relied solely on his title as mortgagee, but had, for example, alleged that he was absolute owner[2]. In such a case the mortgagor could claim to set aside the mortgage, or, in the alternative, if it is valid, to redeem[3].

However, modern rules of court would seem to have reversed this technical rule[4].

1 *Martinez v Cooper* (1826) 2 Russ 198; *Johnson v Fesenmeyer* (1858) 25 Beav 88; *Crenver etc Mining Co Ltd v Willyams* (1866) 35 Beav 353.

2 *National Bank of Australasia v United Hand-in-Hand band of Hope Co*, above.

3 See *Hunt v Worsfold* [1896] 2 Ch 224, but formerly, it seems, this was not allowed: see *Ernest v Partridge* (1863) 1 New Rep 425.
4 CPR 1.1, 16.2.5, 17.

Claim for redemption

29.4 A claim may be treated as a redemption claim although it involves a claim to set aside a sale by the mortgagee[1]. However redemption will not be ordered in a claim for possession against the purchaser unless the claim includes specifically a prayer for redemption[2].

Again, modern rules of court would seem to allow for greater flexibility[3].

In a claim for redemption the claimant is entitled to disclosure in the usual way[4]. It is thought that he can therefore have disclosure of the mortgagee's securities[5], of the amount claimed to be due[6] and of the names of incumbrancers[7].

1 *Powell v Roberts* (1869) LR 9 Eq 169; see *Inman v Wearing* (1850) 3 De G & Sm 729.
2 *Murugaser Marimuttu v De Soysa* [1891] AC 69, PC.
3 See **29.3**, n 4.
4 CPR 31.
5 *West of England and South Wales Bank v Nickolls* (1877) 6 Ch D 613.
6 *Bridgwater v De Winton* (1863) 33 LJ Ch 238; *Beavan v Cook* (1869) 17 WR 872; *Elmer v Creasy* (1873) 9 Ch App 69.
7 *Union Bank of London v Manby* (1879) 13 Ch D 239, CA, and see Law of Property Act 1925, s 96 (1), see **3.74**. If a trustee who lends money on mortgage is a solicitor (an ordinary part of whose duty it is to lay out money for his clients), he is not bound to disclose the names of his beneficiaries, or to produce documents relating to the transactions, if he cannot do it without a breach of professional confidence, notwithstanding any inconvenience which may arise to the claimant: *Jones v Pugh* (1842) 1 Ph 96.

Effect of foreclosure on claim for redemption

29.5 Possession under a judgment of foreclosure is a good defence to a claim to redeem, if the rights of the claimants or of those under whom they claim are concluded by the judgment. The qualification applies although the mortgagee on foreclosure had no notice of other incumbrances. Accordingly, the defence will not defeat a claim by subsequent incumbrancers, who were not parties to the claim by which the foreclosure was effected[1]. Under particular circumstances, however, the foreclosure may be opened, and a new right will be given to redeem[2].

The foreclosure cannot be pleaded until the final order has been obtained[3] for up to that time the estate retains the quality of a mortgage and was not deviseable by the will of the mortgagee made before the date of the order absolute[4].

1 *Nichols v Short* (1713) 2 Eq Cas Abr 608, 15 Vin Abr 478. A party to a claim in which a judgment of foreclosure has been made is bound by it, though it was made in the absence of a person whose interest was not disclosed by the statements of case: *Bromitt v Moor* (1851) 9 Hare 374. A mortgagor who was defendant in that capacity to a foreclosure claim was bound by the judgment in that claim in respect of his interest in another capacity, though the other interest did not appear in the statements of case: *Goldsmid v Stonehewer* (1859) 9 Hare App xxxviii. However, it seems that if a person whose interest has been foreclosed in a claim to which he was a party becomes afterwards entitled to another interest in the same estate, derived from a person who was not a party to that claim, the owner of the newly-acquired interest may bring his claim for redemption, notwithstanding the former judgment and foreclosure, but the pleadings ought to state the former proceedings in the foreclosure claim: *Bromitt v Moor*, above.
2 See **22.65**.

3 *Senhouse v Earl* (1752) 2 Ves Sen 450; see *Quarrell v Beckford* (1816) 1 Madd 269.
4 *Thompson v Grant* (1819) 4 Madd 438.

Joinder of causes of action

29.6 A mortgagor formerly could not in the same claim seek redemption of one and foreclosure of another mortgage[1]. A mortgagor was also entitled effectively to strike out a claim, which, besides redemption, sought a general administration of the personal estate of the deceased mortgagor, and a declaration of the rights of devisees and legatees[2]. The practice in these matters is now governed by the Civil Procedure Rules, which allow a plaintiff to unite in the same claim, and in the same Particulars of Claim, several causes of action, subject to the power of the court or judge to make orders for separate trials or separate disposal of the claims[3].

1 *Plumbe v Plumbe* (1841) 4 Y & C Ex 345.
2 *Pearse v Hewitt* (1835) 7 Sim 471.
3 CPR 3.1 and 7.3.

County court

29.7 A county court has all the jurisdiction of the High Court to hear and determine proceedings for redemption of any mortgage where the amount owing in respect of the mortgage[1] does not exceed the county court limit[2]. The proceedings must be taken in the court within the district of which the land or any part thereof is situated[3].

Proceedings for redemption in the county court may, it appears, be commenced by a claim form under CPR Part 7 or Part 8, depending on whether the claim involves a substantial dispute of fact[4].

1 Ie owing at the time of the claim: *Shields, Whitley and District Amalgamated Model Building Society v Richards* (1901) 84 LT 587.
2 County Courts Act 1984, s 23 (c). The current limit is £30,000: County Courts Jurisdiction Order 1981. The county court may be given extended jurisdiction by written agreement between the parties: County Courts Act 1984, s 24.
3 CPR 50, Sch 2; CCR Ord 4, r 3. For forms, see 28 *Atkin's Court Forms* (2nd edn, 1997 issue and Supplement), Forms 42 to 44.
4 Cf the position in the High Court, discussed above. A redemption claim is not a claim for the recovery of land (and CPR 55 does not therefore apply). Nor would such a claim have been brought by originating application prior to 26 April 1999. For these reasons the correct procedure depends on the matters stated in the text: see CPR 8BPD, para B.1; CCR 1981, Ord 3 rr 1, 4; CPR 8.1(2)(a). The difference in procedure between the High Court and county court may be inadvertent.

PARTIES TO THE CLAIM

PERSONS INTERESTED IN THE EQUITY OF REDEMPTION

Persons entitled to redeem

29.8 All persons entitled to redeem[1] and all persons interested in the security[2] are necessary parties to a redemption claim. The rule requiring the presence of all parties is based on the right of the mortgagee to account once and for all, which can only be done if the account is taken in the presence of all parties who could demand an account[3]. A person entitled to redeem cannot be omitted because his interest is very small[4]. An exception to the rule applies as regards beneficiaries under a trust and persons interested in the estate of a deceased person[5]. Additionally, the court will not stop redemption on account of the absence of a party who cannot be found if the mortgagee is not prejudiced[6].

1 See also **22.12**. The person who seeks redemption must show a good right to redeem, for the mortgagee is entitled to retain the property against all persons save those with a paramount title. If the Defendant can show that the title is vested in someone other than the claimant, the latter will not even be allowed to redeem at his own risk: *Lomax v Bird* (1683) 1 Vern 182; see *Francklyn v Fern* (1740) Barn Ch 30. But an application to strike out a redemption claim, on the ground of lack of title in the Claimant, was held bad, where the mortgagor had parted with his interest in the security to an assignee for whose benefit he was seeking redemption, though the assignee must be a party to such a claim: *Winterbottom v Taybe* (1854) 2 Drew 279.

If the right to redeem is dependent on the validity of an instrument, there will be no declaration as to the terms of redemption until the question of validity has been settled: *Blake v Foster* (1813) 2 Ball & B 387. The court will act upon a prima facie title shown by the plaintiff, however complicated, if it is supported by satisfactory evidence and is contradicted only by a mere allegation of an adverse claim. The only matter determined is the right of redemption, the judgment for which will not hinder an adverse claimant from asserting his title in another proceeding: *Lloyd v Wait* (1842) 1 Ph 61.

2 See **29.16**.

3 *Palk v Lord Clinton* (1805) 12 Ves 48.

4 *Hunter v Maclew* (1846) 5 Hare 238. So when legal tenancy in common existed, the owners of all the undivided shares had to be parties: *Bolton v Salmon* [1891] 2 Ch 48.

5 See below.

6 *Faulkner v Daniel* (1843) 3 Hare 199 at 212. The rule that the court must have all interested parties before it is only a prima facie rule: *Re Richerson, Scales v Heyhoe (No 2)* [1893] 3 Ch 146.

Owner of equity of redemption

29.9 The mortgagor himself, or the owner (or all of the joint owners) for the time being of the whole of the equity of redemption, must be parties in every claim in which the question of redemption arises between mortgagees. This is because after giving permission to the later mortgagee to redeem the first, the court will order that the former in turn may be redeemed by the mortgagor and in default the latter will be foreclosed[1]. If the mortgagor were not party to the claim, his right of redemption would remain open and the first mortgagee would be exposed to another claim[2]. The mortgagor, however, need not be joined in a redemption claim between the mortgagee and his derivative or sub-mortgagee. The assignee of the equity of redemption stands in the place of the mortgagor for the purpose of this rule.

The owner of the equity of redemption of one of two properties comprised in the same mortgage cannot sue for redemption of the one property separately[3].

1 The mortgagor must also be a party to a claim in which the validity of the mortgage is contested: *Thompson v Baskerville* (1688) 3 Rep Ch 215; and see *Stackhouse v Countess of Jersey* (1861) 1 John & H 721.

2 *Fell v Brown* (1787) 2 Bro CC 276; *Palk v Lord Clinton* (1805) 12 Ves 48; and see *Ramsbottom v Wallis* (1835) 5 LJ Ch 92; *Caddick v Cook* (1863) 9 Jur NS 454.

3 *Hall v Heward* (1886) 32 Ch D 430, CA.

Representation of beneficiaries by trustees, etc

29.10 As regards beneficiaries and persons interested in the estate of a deceased person it is sufficient for proceedings to be commenced by or against the trustees or personal representatives, leaving it to the court to direct beneficiaries to be joined as parties if necessary[1]. Thus proceedings can be commenced by or against fiduciary mortgagors alone, leaving it to the court in each case to add beneficiaries if the circumstances require that they should be separately represented[2].

1 CPR 50, Sch 1; RSC Ord 15, r 14; for county courts, see County Courts Act 1984, s 76.
2 The practice was formerly as follows: Where trustees were suing for redemption they represented the trust estate if, in fact they had, like executors, complete power over the estate, or had under their control funds applicable for redemption: *Mills v Jennings* (1880) 13 Ch D 639, CA; *Re Cooper, Cooper v Vesey* (1882) 20 Ch D 611; and where the beneficiaries were infants, or the shares have been resettled, the court did not require separate representation of the infants or of persons interested under the derivative settlement: *Goldsmid v Stonehewer* (1859) 9 Hare App xxxviii and see *Watts v Lane* (1901) 84 LT 144.
If the trustees were also executors, it was unnecessary to join the beneficiaries: *Re Mitchell, Wavell v Mitchell* (1892) 65 LT 851 (explaining *Wavell v Mitchell* (1891) 64 LT 560): *Re Booth and Kettlewell's Contract* (1892) 67 LT 550. The former cases may still furnish guidance as to the manner in which the discretion of the court as to adding parties will be exercised, but they do not govern the initiation of proceedings.

Where beneficiaries are necessary parties

29.11 Although trustees now represent the persons beneficially interested in the mortgaged property yet where such beneficiaries are many and fluctuating, and questions arise between the trustees as to the proper mode of protecting their interests, some or all ought to be parties[1].

1 See *Minn v Stant* (1851) 15 Beav 49; *Re De Leeuw, Jakens v Central Advance and Discount Corpn* [1922] 2 Ch 540.

Personal representatives

29.12 Aside from the Civil Procedure Rules[1], the executor or administrator is the necessary and proper person to sue for redemption[2]. However, where an administrator is appointed to act only during the minority of an executor[3], the court will probably exercise its power to add parties if, but not unless[4], the beneficiaries might suffer from the limited power of the administrator[5].

1 See **29.10**, n 1.
2 See the Administration of Estates Act 1925, ss 1 (1), 3 (1) as amended by Trusts of Land and Appointment of Trustees Act 1996, s 25(2), Sch 4.
3 See Non-contentious Probate Rules 1987, r.32.
4 *Faulkner v Daniel* (1843) 3 Hare 199 at 208; *Davis v Chanter* (1848) 2 Ph 545; *Maclean v Dawson (No 3)* (1859) 27 Beav 369.
5 As in *Ellis v Deane* (1827) Beat 5; *Clough v Dixon* (1841) 10 Sim 564; *Groves v Lane* (1852) 16 Jur 854. The authority of an administrator *durante minore* is, while it lasts, the same as that of an ordinary administrator: *Re Cope, Cope v Cope* (1880) 16 Ch D 49.
Where the mortgagor dies during the course of the proceedings his personal representative should seek an order under CPR 19.2 to carry on the proceedings.

Creditors under deed of arrangement

29.13 Unless the trustees have some interest distinct from the creditors[1], they represent the creditors for the purpose of claims relating to the property comprised in the deed[2].

1 Though the creditors had no right of redemption apart from the trustees (*Troughton v Binkes*) (1801) 6 Ves 573) they may, in this exceptional case, be parties.
2 See *Morley v Morley* (1858) 25 Beav 253.

Assignment of equity during claim

29.14 In case of an assignment, creation or devolution of any estate or title during the currency of a claim, the claim is not rendered invalid, but may be continued by or against the person to or upon whom such estate or title has come or devolved. In case of a transmission of interest or liability new parties may be added if it becomes necessary or desirable so the court can resolve the matters in dispute in the proceedings[1]. There is no rule preventing an assignee from enforcing the assignment in separate proceedings against the assignor, merely by reason of the assignment having been made during the currency of a claim relating to the property[2]. If, therefore, pending a claim for redemption, the equity of redemption is assigned by the mortgagor, the assignee will be bound[3].

The power to add parties under the CPR would appear to be exercisable whether or not the assignee consents, if the addition of the assignee is desirable[4]. In particular, it will be desirable to joint an assignee who takes a legal interest, because, although the legal interest will be bound in his hands, so as to make him a trustee for the person entitled under the order, unless he is joined, he cannot be compelled to reconvey[5].

1 CPR 19.2.
2 Co Litt 102 b; *Metcalfe v Pulvertoft* (1813) 2 Ves & B 200; *Bishop of Winchester v Paine* (1805) 11 Ves 194, and as to adjusting the rights of an assignee of a later mortgagee after judgment for foreclosure *nisi* by which his assignor's interest is bound, see *Booth v Creswicke* (1837) 8 Sim 352.
3 *Garth v Ward* (1741) 2 Atk 174; *Eades v Harris* (1842) 1 Y & C Ch Cas 230 at 234; *Patch v Ward* (1867) 3 Ch App 203 at 208. The rule applies as well to assignments which affect the whole equitable estate or interest in question in the claim as to those by which one of several parties assigns his or her separate interest: *Eades v Harris*, above.
4 *Campbell v Holyland* (1877) 7 Ch D 166. Under the RSC, the court could, on the application of the mortgagee, stay the redemption proceedings unless the assignee of the equity of redemption was made a party: *Three Rivers District Council v Governor of the Bank of England* [1996] QB 292.
5 *Bishop of Winchester v Paine*, above; *Barry v Wrey* (1827) 3 Russ 465. In *Coles v Forrest* (1847) 10 Beav 552, the legal interest appears to have been assigned.

Involuntary alienation

29.15 An involuntary assignee who takes during the currency of a claim will not be bound if not a party to the proceedings. Therefore where the mortgagor becomes bankrupt, or a judgment creditor obtains a charge on the property, the trustee in bankruptcy[1] or the creditor[2] should be joined as a party.

1 *Wood v Surr* (1854) 19 Beav 551.
2 *Re Parbola Ltd, Blackburn v Parbola Ltd* [1909] 2 Ch 437.

PERSONS INTERESTED IN THE SECURITY

The holder of the security

29.16 The person in whom the legal interest in the security becomes vested, whether originally by the mortgage[1], or by assignment[2], and though he is only a trustee for the persons entitled to the mortgage money[3], is a necessary party to a claim for redemption[4] so that a reconveyance may be obtained[5].

A purchaser seeking specific performance of a contract to acquire the equity of redemption may not make the mortgagee either of a legal[6], or an equitable[7] interest, a party to a claim. The mortgagee has no interest in the contract and performance of the decree will not affect his security or interfere with his remedies[8].

Neither the mortgagor[9] nor the mortgagee[10] is allowed to dispute the title of the other. However, if the mortgagor's title is impeached by a claim, the mortgagee, having an obvious interest in supporting the mortgagor's title ought to be joined[11].

1 *Wood v Williams* (1819) 4 Madd 186.
2 *Wetherell v Collins* (1818) 3 Madd 255. The mortgagor will not be allowed in a redemption claim to contest the mortgagee's title before redeeming: *Smith v Valence* (1655) 1 Rep Ch 90.
3 A person who claims to be interested in part of a mortgage debt vested in another is sufficiently represented by the latter in a claim to set aside the security and should not be made a party: *Emmet v Tottenham* (1864) 10 Jur NS 1090. As to a trustee who has not been fully discharged from the trust by the appointment of a successor, see *Adams v Paynter* (1844) 1 Coll 530.
The trustee of the legal interest in the security having no adverse rights may properly be, and to save expense to the mortgagor ought to be, a co-plaintiff: *Smith v Chichester* (1842) 2 Dr & War 393; unless he refuses, or is likely to refuse, and then he should be made a defendant: *Browne v Lockhart* (1840) 10 Sim 420.
4 *Wetherell v Collins*, above.
5 The rule is not affected by the present automatic effect of a receipt on the discharge of the mortgage. The mortgagee is not a necessary party to a claim brought by the mortgagor in possession to prevent injury to the mortgaged property: *Fairclough v Marshall* (1878) 4 Ex D 37; see **19.4**.
6 *Tasker v Small* (1837) 3 My & Cr 63.
7 *Hall v Laver* (1838) 3 Y & C Ex 191.
8 It is the same where one has agreed to purchase a property which is afterwards mortgaged: *Long v Bowring* (1864) 33 Beav 585. Both cases are based on the principle that he who claims a right to redeem must first have acquired the mortgagor's title to a reconveyance: *Franklyn v Fern* (1740) Barn Ch 30 at 32.
9 *Darcy v Callan* (1836) 1 Jo Ex Ir 614.
10 *Wroe v Clayton* (1839) 9 LJ Ch 107; *Roberts v Clayton* (1796) 3 Anst 715.
11 *Copis v Middleton* (1818) 2 Madd 410. Cf *Hitchins v Lander* (1807) Coop G 34, where the validity of a lease was in dispute and the lessor's mortgagee was held to be a necessary party. As to pleading a paramount title to a claim for redemption, see *Meder v Birt* (1726) Gilb Rep in Eq 185.

Purchasers from the mortgagee

29.17 The purchaser under a power of sale in a mortgage is not a necessary party to a claim by the mortgagor against the mortgagee to recover the surplus purchase money[1]. However, where the mortgagee allowed a stranger to work the mortgaged land for coal, which the stranger sold, it was proper for the stranger to be joined as a party to a redemption claim. The stranger was in possession of the value of part of the mortgaged property and, though the mortgagor could not redeem the property in specie, he was entitled to an account for its value[2].

1 *Minn v Stant* (1851) 15 Beav 49.
2 *Hood v Easton* (1856) 2 Jur NS 917.

Transferee of mortgage

29.18 Ordinarily, where the mortgage has been assigned, and the mortgagor sues for redemption, the mortgagee need not be a party in respect of the accounts[1]. If the mortgagor is not a party to the assignment, and had no notice of it, the assignee is bound by all the equities subsisting between mortgagee and mortgagor. He cannot therefore afterwards object to a settlement of the account between the mortgagor and mortgagee arrived at prior to the assignment[2]. Where the mortgagor is a party the terms of the assignment may be such as to amount to an admission by all parties of the sums due[3].

An old exception (unlikely to be encountered today) was where the mortgagee had entered into possession and the mortgagor sought an account of receipts in excess of the dent. In such a case the mortgagee, notwithstanding the assignment, must be joined with the assignee, so that he may account for what he received in his time[4].

If only part of the security has been assigned to a derivative mortgagee for a less sum than the original debt, then upon a claim for redemption, the original mortgagee, as well as the assignee, must be a party for he claims an interest, viz a right to redeem the assignee and prevent another account[5].

1 *Anon* (1680) Freem Ch 59, 2 Eq Cas Abr 594.
2 *Hill v Adams* (1740) 2 Atk 39; *Chambers v Goldwin* (1804) 9 Ves 254, at 269; *Norrish v Marshall* (1821) 5 Madd 475. See **14.21**, above.
3 *Anon* (1680) Freem Ch 59; *Car v Boulter* (1697) Freem Ch 217.
4 *Anon*, above. It has been suggested that this case was overruled by *Chambers v Goldwin*, above, but Lord Eldon's observations in that case did not extend to the circumstances in the text. *Lowther v Carlton* (1741) Barn Ch 358, 2 Atk 139 is also authority for the proposition in the text.
5 *Norrish v Marshall*, above; *Hobart v Abbot* (1731) 2 P Wms 643; *Re Burrell, Burrell v Smith* (1869) LR 7 Eq 399. If in such case the objection of the absence of the original mortgagee is not taken until the hearing, the case will be allowed to proceed without him, if he is called and gives evidence that he has been paid off what he was owed and retains no interest: *Norrish v Marshall*, above.

Personal representatives

29.19 Both the mortgage debt and the estate or interest of the mortgagee in the mortgaged property devolve on his death upon his personal representatives. They are the persons to represent the security in a redemption claim unless by transfer or assent or other means they have divested themselves of their title[1].

Where a mortgagee has no legal personal representative, who (if existing), would be a necessary defendant, the court may now appoint someone to represent the estate[2].

1 Administration of Estates Act 1925, ss 1 (1), 3 (1), as amended by Trusts of Land and Appointment of Trustees Act 1996, s 25(2), Sch 4.
2 Administration of Justice Act 1985, s 50. When the mortgagee dies during the course of the proceedings, they should be carried on against his personal representatives or his estate: CPR 19.2.

Mortgages to several

29.20 If a mortgage of land is made to several persons they necessarily, under the present law, take the mortgage term jointly, since land cannot be held in undivided shares[1]. They may, however, be either joint tenants or tenants in common of the mortgage money. If they are joint tenants—that is, if the money belongs to them on a joint account—then, on the death of one, the survivors or survivor are entitled to the mortgage money and the personal representatives of the deceased mortgagee need not be joined in a redemption claim. If they are tenants in common, the personal representatives should be joined, even though the mortgaged land vests in the survivors or survivor[2]. However, this will be so only if the mortgage expresses that the money is advanced by or belongs to the mortgagees in stated sums or shares. If the advance is expressed to be made out of moneys belonging to the mortgagees on a joint account, or if the mortgage is simply made to the mortgagees jointly, then they are deemed to be joint tenants[3].

1 See **12.2**.
2 *Vickers v Cowell* (1839) 1 Beav 529.
3 Law of Property Act 1925, s 111; see **14.24**.
If payment is made to one joint mortgagee during the lifetime of the others, this is a good discharge of the debt at law: but the equitable rule prevails and the security is only discharged to the extent of the payee's beneficial interest at the time (if any), although he is ultimately the last survivor in the joint account: *Matson v Dennis* (1864) 4 De GJ & Sm 345; *Powell v Brodhurst* [1901] 2 Ch 160.

Claim to redeem by subsequent mortgagee: 'redeem up, foreclose down'

29.21 In the case of successive mortgages a later mortgagee must make all mortgagees subsequent to himself, as well as the mortgagor, parties in a claim to redeem the mortgage immediately prior to his mortgage[1]. If he seeks to redeem any other prior mortgage he must make parties all mortgagees between himself and the mortgagee whom he seeks to redeem[2].

1 *Fell v Brown* (1787) 2 Bro CC 276; *Johnson v Holdsworth* (1850) 1 Sim NS 106 at 109; *Farmer v Curtis* (1829) 2 Sim 466; *Rose v Page* (1829) 2 Sim 471; *Ramsbottom v Wallis* (1835) 5 LJ Ch 92; *Richards v Cooper* (1842) 5 Beav 304; *Slade v Rigg* (1843) 3 Hare 35; *Teevan v Smith* (1882) 20 Ch D 724, CA. See **28.19**.
2 *Teevan v Smith*, above.

THE JUDGMENT

Order for redemption

29.22 The common form of order for redemption directs that an account taken of what is due to the mortgagee under the mortgage[1], including his assessed costs of the redemption claim, and orders that the mortgagor pay to the mortgagee within six months[2] from the date of the master's certificate the amount certified to be due and that upon his doing so the mortgagee shall to surrender or give a statutory receipt and deliver the deeds to the mortgagee[3].

1 The judgment will be prefaced by a declaration that the right of redemption is subsisting, if this has been in dispute: *Holmes v Turner* (1843) 7 Hare 367n note and form; *Faulkner v Daniel* (1843) 3 Hare 199; *Carlon v Farlar* (1845) 8 Beav 526.

It declares, where necessary, the rights and priorities of the various incumbrancers (*Jones v Griffith* (1845) 2 Coll 207), and the order may be made without prejudice to the rights of incumbrancers between themselves.

Special directions may have to be given for the account. Where the mortgagee has been in possession the order directs as against the mortgagee an account of the rents and profits (see **35.26**). To the amount due to the mortgagee are added all sums to which he may be declared to be entitled for improvements (see **19.75**), or for payments in respect of or for the protection of his security, or the property (see **16.4**). If the order for redemption is made after tender, the account is directed of what was due on the date of the tender with consequential directions to meet the alternative results of the amount due exceeding or not exceeding the amount ordered: *Greenwood v Sutcliffe* [1892] 1 Ch 1.

The mortgagor in a claim for redemption against the mortgagee and his sub-mortgagee can have the estate discharged on payment into court of the amount found due to the mortgagee without waiting for the settlement of the accounts and inquiries between the mortgagee and sub-mortgagee: *Lysaght v Westmacott* (1864) 33 Beav 417. And as to an order in a redemption claim by a second mortgagee, where a later mortgagee subsequently made a sub-mortgage, see *Booth v Creswicke* (1837) 8 Sim 352.

2 Ie calendar months: Law of Property Act 1925, s 61(a) and CPR 2.10.

3 For forms of order, see 28 *Atkin's Court Forms* (2nd edn, 1997 reissue and Supplement), Form 80, and see **22.27** ff.

Successive mortgages

29.23 Where there are successive mortgages, the judgment proceeds on the principle that the second mortgagee, as the first assignee of the equity of redemption, steps into the shoes of and acquires the rights of the mortgagor[1]. He therefore enjoys the first right to redeem on payment of what is due to the first mortgagee; but, in default of payment, he is foreclosed. This process is carried on as to all the successive mortgagees, until the mortgagor alone remains, when he may likewise redeem, or, in default, stand foreclosed.

The judgment provides for the exercise of the rights by directing that in case the second mortgagee shall redeem the first, an account shall be taken of what is due to second mortgagee on his own security, and of the sums he has paid to the first mortgagee, with interest thereon[2] and costs. On payment of the aggregate of these sums the third mortgagee has permission to redeem the second mortgagee, in default of which he is foreclosed. Accounts will continue in this way until, eventually, the mortgagor is at liberty to redeem. Upon non-payment to the last person to be redeemed of what the latter has paid to the prior mortgagee and of his own principal, interest and costs, all later mortgagees and the mortgagor stand absolutely foreclosed. The property becomes that of the mortgagee who cleared off the rest free from any mortgages[3].

1 Thus, in taking the account the second mortgagee may assert such equity as the mortgagor himself might have to exclude any particular item: *Mainland v Upjohn* (1889) 41 Ch D 126.

2 See **35.48** ff.

3 As to costs where an intermediate mortgagee redeems the first, who holds a later mortgage, see *Mutual Life Assurance Society v Langley* (1886) 32 Ch D 460. As to a claim by a later mortgagee of two properties, subject to separate mortgages, see *Pelly v Wathen* (1849) 7 Hare 351; affd (1851) 1 De GM & G 16; *Hallett v Furze* (1885) 31 Ch D 312.

Extension of time for payment

29.24 The time for payment will not generally be extended in a claim for redemption[1], but in special circumstances the time for payment may be extended[2].

1 *Novosielski v Wakefield* (1811) 17 Ves 417; *Faulkner v Bolton* (1835) 7 Sim 319.
2 *Novosielski v Wakefield*, above; *Collinson v Jeffrey* [1896] 1 Ch 644. As to extension of time, see **22.42**; CPR 3.1(2)(a).

DISMISSAL OF THE CLAIM FOR REDEMPTION

Evidence of non-payment

29.25 The claim for redemption will be dismissed, on application in private, upon production of the certificate of the amount due and of an witness statement showing attendance and non-payment of the money[1] even though, after the time fixed for payment, the mortgagor has tendered the principal and interest, with an additional sum for interest, to the day of tender[2]. The court, however, may extend time for payment[2].

1 *Stuart v Worrall* (1785) 1 Bro CC 581; *Proctor v Oates* (1740) 2 Atk 140; *Newsham v Gray* (1742) 2 Atk 287.
2 *Faulkner v Bolton* (1835) 7 Sim 319. For a form of order, see 28 *Atkin's Court Forms* (2nd edn, 1997 reissue and Supplement), Form 81.

Dismissal operates as foreclosure

29.26 Dismissal of the claim to redeem, by reason of default in payment of the money, or for any other cause than for want of prosecution, operates as a judgment of foreclosure[1]. The mortgagor admits by his claim the title of the mortgagee and the debt. Therefore if he does not discharge it, it is an abuse of process for him to bring another claim for the same purpose. Where a claim for redemption fails, rules of court provide for the mortgagee to obtain possession in the same action[2].

If a claim to redeem an equitable mortgage is dismissed, this does not have the effect of a foreclosure, because the mortgagee does not get the relief which he would have in a foreclosure claim, viz a conveyance[3]. Where a legal mortgagor issued a claim for redemption, and in his defence the mortgagee refused to redeem save on terms for the discharge of another security, the mortgagor, by discontinuing his claim was not taken to admit the other debt[3]. Though the second alleged mortgage was equitable, the same result would apparently follow if it were legal.

1 *Cholmley v Countess of Oxford* (1741) 2 Atk 267; *Bishop of Winchester v Paine* (1805) 11 Ves 194; *Hansard v Hardy* (1812) 18 Ves 455; *Inman v Wearing* (1850) 3 De G & Sm 729. See *Garth v Ward* (1741) 2 Atk 174; *Wood v Surr* (1854) 19 Beav 551.

In the case of successive mortgages, if the mortgagor is the plaintiff, the effect of excluding his interest is that the last incumbrancer becomes quasi-mortgagor, the prior mortgagees ranking according to their priorities: *Cottingham v Earl of Shrewsbury* (1843) 3 Hare 627 at 637.
2 CPR 50, Sch 1; RSC Ord 88, r 7.
3 *Marshall v Shrewsbury* (1875) 10 Ch App 250.

Right to redeem refused

29.27 The claim will be dismissed at the hearing if the right to redeem is rejected by the court. A dismissal was upheld on appeal where the claimant had claimed an absolute right to redeem upon certain terms and the court below had found that he had no equity to redeem upon those terms[1].

So a claim for redemption, by a person who is subject to the same equities as the mortgagor, will be dismissed as against a defendant, who, as between himself and the mortgagor, is not liable to be foreclosed by incumbrancers on the estate, having prior rights to such defendant[2].

The claim for redemption will also be dismissed if, at the hearing, the plaintiff refuses to ask for any accounts[3]. This may happen when the plaintiff, being a later mortgagee, finds that the security is wholly insufficient.

1 *Seagrave v Pope* (1852) 1 De GM & G 783.
2 Thus, where A was a mortgagor, B and C incumbrancers, and X tenant in tail in remainder, whose estate, as between himself and A was not liable to the incumbrances of B and C (having been exonerated therefrom by A's covenant), a claim by E, a subsequent judgment creditor of A, was dismissed against A, because E was not in the position of a purchaser for valuable consideration without notice, but was subject to the same equities as A and could not compel X to pay off B and C: *Hughes v Williams* (1852) 3 Mac & G 683, but, semble, that X should first have had a permissive right to redeem. See *Chappell v Rees* (1852) 1 De GM & G 393, where the same principle was applied in a claim by the assignee of the insolvent mortgagor and covenantor.
3 *Gibson v Nicol* (1846) 9 Beav 403.

Disclaiming defendants

29.28 It is the practice to dismiss the claim as against defendants who disclaim all interest in the mortgaged premises, where such defendants are able to make and do make a complete and valid disclaimer and, provided the disclaimer is complete, it will be valid whether it was made before or after the commencement of the claim[1].

1 *Aldworth v Robinson* (1840) 2 Beav 287; *Thompson v Kendall* (1840) 9 Sim 397; *Silcock v Roynon* (1834) 2 Y & C Ch Cas 376; *Lock v Lomas* (1851) 15 Jur 162; and semble also in *Ford v Earl of Chesterfield* (1853) 16 Beav 516; *Vale v Merideth* (1854) 18 Jur 992; *Thorneycroft v Crockett* (1848) 2 HL Cas 239.

COSTS

29.29 For the costs of redemption proceedings, see Chapter 36.

Chapter 30

The release of the debt or security

Generally

30.1 The whole or part of the debt or the security may be released, either before or after the date for repayment, upon the payment of the whole or part of the loan or without such payment.

Release of the debt

30.2 By releasing the debt the security for the debt is released[1]. To be binding a release of a debt must generally be made for consideration[2], or by deed. While an alleged release or forgiveness of the debt cannot be established merely by showing that the creditor had expressed an intention to release the debt[3] yet where the creditor has so acted that the debtor has done acts by which his position has been altered, the creditor will not be allowed to enforce his security[4]. Moreover, a declaration of present forgiveness of the debt, though only verbal and unsupported by consideration may be effective to release the debt, if it is accompanied by the delivery of the deeds to the debtor[5]. If the mortgagee declares himself a trustee of the mortgaged premises for the mortgagor, this will be equivalent to release[6].

A release of the debt is usually encountered on the disposition of the whole of the equity of redemption, either on sale, or, for example, on its transfer to new trustees. The purchaser or other assignee of the equity of redemption is not liable on the covenant for payment[7], and the mortgagor remains liable, but the assignee will be liable to indemnify the mortgagor, even if there is no express indemnity covenant[8]. On a disposition of the equity of redemption the mortgagee may release the mortgagor or his successor in title from the mortgage debt in consideration of a covenant by the purchaser or donee, or, for example, the new trustees, for payment and to observe and perform the mortgagor's covenants in the mortgage deed. The release and covenant may be included in the transfer or be effected by a separate document[9].

1 Shep Touchst Prest 342; *Cowper v Green* (1841) 7 M & W 633.
2 See eg *Taylor v Manners* (1865) 1 Ch App 48.
3 If the intention is there and the mortgagee cancels the mortgage this is as much a release as cancelling a bond.
4 *Yeomans v Williams* (1865) LR 1 Eq 184. This will be more readily applied to the release of interest than principal, because the intention to release the latter would probably be evidenced by the giving up of the security.

5 Or where the debtor becomes the creditor's personal representative: *Strong v Bird* (1874) LR 18 Eq 315. So long as the intention to forgive continued until the creditor's death: *Re Wale, Wale v Harris* [1956] 3 All ER 280, [1956] 1 WLR 1346.
6 *Re Hancock, Hancock v Berrey* (1888) 57 LJ Ch 793.
7 *Re Errington* [1894] 1 QB 11 and see **17.5**.
8 *Waring v Ward* (1802) 7 Ves 332 and see **17.5**.
9 For release of debts by will, see 50 *Halsbury's Laws* (4th edn, reissue) para 536. The appointment of a debtor as executor may extinguish the cause of action in debt, but the executor may remain liable under an equitable obligation to account to those interested in the estate for the amount of the debt; see *Stamp Duties Comr v Bone* [1977] AC 511, [1976] 2 All ER 354, PC.

Release of the security

30.3 It has been seen[1] that on payment of the mortgage moneys, a mortgage term becomes a satisfied term and, so it seems, a legal charge is discharged. Therefore, where the whole of the mortgage moneys are paid, strictly speaking no further documentation is required though it is desirable from the practical point of view of proof of the intent to discharge.

In the case of a mortgage by demise, for an express release or surrender a deed is required to convey the legal estate[2]. However, there may be an implied, informal surrender, where, for example, the mortgagee hands back the mortgage deed and treats the mortgage as at an end[3].

The form of the release of property secured by legal mortgage depends on the circumstances[4]. Usually it is made for value to enable the mortgagor to sell the property. In such circumstances where the land is registered land, the requirements to be observed to effect a discharge have already been discussed[5]. In other cases, the mortgagee may join in the conveyance rather than making a statutory receipt, where that is appropriate, or a separate deed of surrender or release followed by the conveyance. Where the mortgagee joins in the conveyance, unless the property, if any, remaining in mortgage is sufficient security for the mortgage debt, he will usually require the whole or part of the purchase money to be paid to him in discharge or reduction of the mortgage debt.

Where a sale of the property to be released is not contemplated a statutory receipt should be used if the release is in consideration of the repayment of the moneys secured by the mortgage, but otherwise a deed of surrender, where the mortgage was by demise or sub-demise, or release, in the case of charge, will be appropriate[6].

1 See **28.56**.
2 Law of Property Act 1925, s 52.
3 *Haigh v Brooks* (1839) 10 Ad & El 309.
4 For forms, see 28 *Forms and Precedents* (5th edn, 1999 reissue) Mortgages.
5 See **28.59**.
6 Debentures are released in the appropriate manner according to what sort of charge had been created, ie specific legal charge, equitable charge or floating charge (as to the latter, see **30.41**, n 1). Application should be made to the Companies Registry on the official form for entry of release. Any land charge registration in respect of the mortgage should be cancelled (see **28.62**).

Release of security under equitable mortgage

30.4 Such a mortgage does not create any legal estate or interest in favour of the mortgagee and no formal deed of release is required. A release of the whole of such property may be effected by the cancellation of the mortgage or a simple receipt. The release of part of equitably mortgaged property is generally effected by a written statement or letter from the mortgagee that he has no charge on the particular property[1].

1 See (1962) 26 Conv (NS) pp 449–453 (Rowley). For property subject to a floating charge a letter of non-crystallisation from some officer of the company or its solicitor suffices.

Partial discharge of security by trustee-mortgagees

30.5 A trustee-mortgagee may release part of his security on receipt of the whole of the purchase money produced thereby[1].

1 *Re Morell and Chapman's Contracts* [1915] 1 Ch 162. A purchaser or part of mortgaged lands who has notice that the mortgagees are trustees should not accept a conveyance from such trustee-mortgagees without satisfying himself that the security will not be substantially impaired, see Williams on *Vendor and Purchaser* (4th edn) pp 655, 656, but see Law of Property Act 1925, s 113 (see **14.16**).

Partial discharge of leasehold property

30.6 The statutory provisions as to the realisation of leasehold mortgages[1] do not apply where the mortgage term does not comprise the whole of the land included in the leasehold reversion, unless the rent (if any) payable in respect of that reversion has been apportioned, either legally or informally, as respects the land affected, or the rent is of no money value or no rent is reserved, and unless the lessee's covenants and the conditions (if any) have been apportioned either expressly or by implication, as respects the land affected[2]. Accordingly a release should never be executed as to part of mortgaged leaseholds without such apportionment.

1 See Law of Property Act 1925, s 89.
2 Section 89 (6) as amended.

Release of part of land affected from a judgment

30.7 A partial release does not affect the judgment charge as respects any land not specifically released[1].

1 Law of Property Act 1925, s 71.

Lost security

30.8 Where the mortgage deed has been lost and but for that fact a statutory receipt would have been appropriate, a release or surrender will be necessary.

Release of surety[1]

30.9 The fact that a creditor accepts further security from the principal debtor does not release the surety[2], but a surety is entitled to the benefit of collateral security[3]. A release of the collateral security will release the surety[4].

1 See **31.6**.
2 *Twopenny v Young* (1824) 3 B & C 208; *Eyre v Everett* (1826) 2 Russ 381 at 384.
3 *Dixon v Steel* [1901] 2 Ch 602.
4 *Pearl v Deacon* (1857) 1 De G & J 461.

Release of collateral security

30.10 For discharge of collateral security, see **28.70**.

Chapter 31

Waiver

WAIVER GENERALLY

Nature of waiver

31.1 As regards the debt itself a waiver is ineffectual unless it amounts to a release[1], but the rights of the creditor under his security may be varied by the waiver, provided he is cognisant of his rights[2]. Waiver may be express or implied.

1 A mere waiver signifies nothing more than an expression of intention not to insist on the right and as such is unenforceable: *Stackhouse v Barnston* (1805) 10 Ves 453, but the plaintiff's conduct may be such as to estop him from asserting the continuance of the liability: *Yeomans v Williams* (1865) LR 1 Eq 184.

2 *Vyvyan v Vyvyan* (1861) 30 Beav 65; *Peyman v Lanjani* [1985] Ch 457, [1984] 3 All ER 703, CA.

Express waiver

31.2 The extent of an express waiver is governed by the language used. If the waiver is clearly limited to part of the security, the mortgagee's rights over the remainder of the security will be unaffected. Accordingly, where a mortgagee surrendered his legal interest in a leasehold security to enable the mortgagor to provide another security, but stipulated that the surrender was without prejudice to any other security he might have for his debt, he and his assignee were held to be still entitled to the benefit of the covenants in the mortgage; the legal interest only, and not the covenants, being within the operation of the surrender[1]. If the waiver is on the face of it clearly a general one, it will not be restricted on the representation of one of the parties that a more limited one was intended[2].

1 *Greenwood v Taylor* (1845) 14 Sim 505; varied sub nom *A-G v Cox, Pearce v A-G* (1850) 3 HL Cas 240.

2 *Drought v Jones* (1840) 4 Dr & War 174.

Implied waiver

31.3 As stated above, there can only be a waiver if the creditor is aware of his rights[1]. The court will not be anxious to imply waiver from a mere omission, or other circumstances, from which the intention cannot fairly be inferred[2]. Thus, where it was provided by the mortgage deed that, as between the mortgagor and his surety, a certain part of the security given by the principal should be primarily liable to the debt, without mentioning the rest, it was held that the surety upon paying off the debt had not lost, by the omission, the right to a transfer of the whole security[3].

1 *Vyvyan v Vyvyan* (1861) 30 Beav 65.
2 The sale by a mortgagee of mortgaged chattels discharged a collateral security of land in *Greenberg v Rapport* (1970) 10 DLR (3d) 737.
3 *Bowker v Bull* (1850) 1 Sim NS 29. See **31.9**.

Taking additional security

31.4 If a creditor, having a security on the funds of his debtor for part of his debt, takes another security on the same funds for his whole debt, the earlier debt remains in force and may be separately dealt with[1]. Similarly, where a creditor who enjoys a security upon the debtor's funds, acting either on behalf of himself and another creditor or jointly with another creditor, takes a security for both debts on the same funds the separate security remains in force and may be separately dealt with. Where the surety pays off the debt or interest in arrears and his payment has been included in the security of a subsequent mortgagee (the surety having taken a note from the latter to that effect) an intention by the surety to take an additional security, and not a waiver of his old right, is to be inferred[2].

1 See *Miln v Walton* (1843) 2 Y & C Ch Cas 354 (a case dealing with a lien on the freight of a ship which arose from the discounting of bills of exchange).
2 *Beckett v Booth* (1708) 2 Eq Cas Abr 595; and see *Martin v Sedgwick* (1846) 9 Beav 333.

Taking substituted security

31.5 When it is contended that the benefit of a security has been waived by the acceptance of another security in its place, it is for the owner of the estate to show that it was discharged by the taking of the new security and not for the creditor to disprove the substitution of the new security for the old. The mere acceptance of a personal security for interest in arrear, or other charge whether express or implied, is therefore not a waiver of the original security, even if a receipt is given for the amount[1]. The absence of any mention of the original security, and the reservation of interest at a different rate from that which was secured by it, have been treated as evidence that the new security was taken by way of substitution[2].

1 *Barret v Wells* (1700) Prec Ch 131; *Hardwick v Mynd* (1793) 1 Anst 109; *Curtis v Rush* (1814) 2 Ves & B 416; *Saunders v Leslie* (1814) 2 Ball & B 509. *Quaere*, as against a purchaser for value for a subsequent interest in the estate on the faith of an assurance (supported by the receipt) that no interest was due; see *Kemmis v Stepney* (1828) 2 Mol 85.
2 *Re Brettle, Brettle v Burdett* (1864) 2 De GJ & Sm 244.

WAIVER AGAINST SURETIES[1]

Variation of the terms of the mortgage

31.6 The creditor may by various acts or omissions waive or lose his right against the surety for the principal debtor. In particular, it is a general rule that a surety is discharged by the creditor dealing with the principal debtor or a co-surety in a manner at variance with the contract the performance of which the surety had guaranteed[2].

This, for instance, will happen where, without the surety's consent, and without reserving his rights against him[3], the creditor gives the debtor further time for payment of the debt[4]. Time is only given within this rule if there is a binding agreement arrived at for good consideration[5]. The rule does not apply when time is given after judgment has been obtained against both the principal debtor and the surety[6]. A consolidation of mortgages given by the principal debtor, with the fixing of a later date for payment, operates as a giving of time and discharges the surety[7]. The surety may also be discharged by the mortgagee consenting to the surrender of a leasehold interest which formed part of the security with the guarantor's consent[8].

The reason for the discharge of the surety in such a case is either that the contract for which the surety became responsible has been altered, and that he cannot be made responsible for another and different contract[9], or that the giving of time alters the rights of the surety against the debtor[10]. A release of the surety extends to any security he has given[11].

The surety is also released if there has been a material alteration in his position by operation of law[12].

As previously stated in view of the effect of a variation of the terms of the mortgage on the obligations of the surety a guarantee usually contains a provision reserving, inter alia, the right of the creditor to give time to the debtor and such a provision is effective to prevent waiver[13].

A material change in a head contract does not discharge a guarantee of the performance of sub-contracts to which the person giving the guarantee is not a party[14].

1 See 20 *Halsbury's Laws* (4th edn reissue) paras 197 ff.

2 *Ward v National Bank of New Zealand* (1883) 8 App Cas 755; *Re Wolmershausen* (1890) 62 LT 541 and see *Lep Air Services Ltd v Rollsowin Investments Ltd* [1971] 3 All ER 45, [1971] 1 WLR 934, CA; affd sub nom *Moschi v Lep Air Services Ltd* [1973] AC 331, [1972] 2 All ER 393, HL. Sometimes the rule has been applied strictly without regard to the question whether the surety is prejudiced or not and even though the alteration is for his benefit: *Blest v Brown* (1862) 4 De GF & J 367; *Polak v Everett* (1876) 1 QBD 669; but there is an exception where it is evident without inquiry that the alteration is unsubstantial, or that it cannot be otherwise than beneficial to the surety; and then he is not discharged: *Holme v Brunskill* (1878) 3 QBD 495 at 505, per Cotton LJ; *Chatterton v Maclean* [1951] 1 All ER 761; and see *Winstone Ltd v Bourne* [1978] 1 NZLR 94.

3 *Wyke v Rogers* (1852) 1 De GM & G 408. The creditor's rights can be reserved when time is given: *Re Renton, ex p Glendinning* (1819) Buck 517; and this is effectual although the surety is not informed: *Webb v Hewitt* (1857) 3 K & J 438. A general reservation is usually included in the guarantee. See further below.

4 *Samuell v Howarth* (1817) 3 Mer 272; *Bank of Ireland v Beresford* (1818) 6 Dow 233; *Oakeley v Pasheller* (1836) 10 Bli NS 548; *Overend, Gurney & Co v Oriental Finance Corpn* (1874) LR 7 HL 348.

5 *Rouse v Bradford Banking Co* [1894] AC 586 at 594, per Lord Herschell, LC.

6 *Re a Debtor (No 14 of 1913)* [1913] 3 KB 11.

7 *Bolton v Buckenham* [1891] 1 QB 278, CA; *Bolton v Salmon* [1891] 2 Ch 48.

8 See *Dowling v Ditanda Ltd* (1975) 236 Estates Gazette 485.

9 *The Harriett* (1841) 1 Wm Rob 182, per Dr Lushington.

10 *Browne v Carr* (1831) 7 Bing 508, per Tindal CJ, and see *Samuell v Howarth*, above, at 278, per Lord Eldon. The right lost is that of subrogation to the creditor's rights against the debtor upon the surety paying the creditor on the date for repayment. See also Glanville Williams *Joint Obligations* (1949) 123 and Cardozo *The Nature of the Judicial Process* (1932) pp 152–154.

11 *Bolton v Salmon*, above; see *Hodgson v Hodgson* (1837) 2 Keen 704, but where a surety

guaranteed the sufficiency of the principal debtor's security for part of the debt, and paid a sum of money in discharge of his guarantee, the security not being delivered up, it was not released, but remained as security for the balance; *Waugh v Wren* (1862) 7 LT 612.

12 *Mortgage Insurance Corpn Ltd v Pound* (1894) 64 LJQB 394, per Wright J; on appeal (1895) 64 LJQB 394, CA; revsd (1895) 65 LJQB 129, HL.

13 *Cowper v Smith* (1838) 4 M & W 519; *Union Bank of Manchester Ltd v Beech* (1865) 3 H & C 672; *Perry v National Provincial Bank of England* [1910] 1 Ch 464; *British Motor Trust Co Ltd v Hyams* (1934) 50 TLR 230, but see *Burnes v Trade Credits Ltd* [1981] 2 All ER 122, [1981] 1 WLR 805, PC; (1981) 131 NLJ 883 (Wilkinson). For discussion of such clauses in the landlord and tenant context see *Selous Street Properties v Oronel Fabrics* [1984] 1 EGLR 50; *West Horndon Industrial Park v Phoenix Timber Group* [1995] 1 EGLR 77; *Howard de Walden Estates v Pasta Place* [1995] 1 EGLR 79.

14 *Town of Truro v Toronto General Insurance Co* (1973) 38 DLR (3d) 1; *Metropolitan Properties Co (Regis) Ltd v Bartholomew* (1995) 72 P & CR 304, [1996] 1 EGLR 85.

Release of principal debtor

31.7 Where the creditor gives the debtor an absolute release of the debt (as opposed to an agreement not to sue[1]), the surety is discharged. Because the debt ceases to exist at law, the creditor cannot reserve any right against the surety[2]. It is the same where the creditor releases the principal debtor and accepts another person as debtor in his stead, so that there is a novation of the contract[3]. However, a release by operation of law, eg in bankruptcy, does not release the surety[4].

Again it is usual to insert in a guarantee a provision permitting the creditor to compound with the principal debtor without affecting the guarantor's liability[5].

1 But query this distinction in the light of *Johnson v Davies* [1999] Ch 117.

2 *Webb v Hewitt* (1857) 3 K & J 438; *Bateson v Gosling* (1871) LR 7 CP 9, per Willes J; *Perry v National Provincial Bank of England*, above; aliter, where, although the principal debtor is released, the debt remains: *Perry v National Provincial Bank of England*, above.

3 *Commercial Bank of Tasmania v Jones* [1893] AC 313.

4 Insolvency Act 1986, s 281 (7). The surety is released by a deed of composition voluntarily entered into between the creditor and the principal debtor: *Re Renton, ex p Glendinning* (1819) Buck 517 at 520. A voluntary arrangement under statute will not necessarily discharge a surety: *RA Securities Ltd v Mercantile Credit Co Ltd* [1995] 3 All ER 581, [1994] BCC 598. For a review of the authorities, see *Johnson v Davies*, discussed below.

5 For forms, see 28 *Forms and Precedents* (5th edn, 1999 reissue) Mortgages.

Release of co-surety

31.8 A release of one co-surety may or may not discharge the other. The matter formerly depended in part on whether the release could be construed as a covenant not to sue one of the joint and several debtors, or instead as a release of the debt. This approach no longer obtains. Where liability is joint and several it is a question of construction of the agreement with the co-surety to see whether the creditor intended to preserve his right against the other co-surety[1]. It has now been held that the same approach applies where the liability is joint only[2]. Where liability is several only, it is believed that the same approach applies, but the court will be slow to construe an agreement with one several debtor as releasing others[3].

1 *Watts and Tolstoy v Aldington* (1993) Times, 16 December.

2 *Johnson v Davies* [1999] Ch 117.

3 *Ex p Crisp* (1744) 1 Atk 133; *Aldrich v Cooper* (1803) 8 Ves 382; *Ward v National Bank of New Zealand* (1883) 8 App Cas 755. The principles are the same where judgment has been obtained for the joint and several obligations: *Re EWA* [1901] 2 KB 642; cf *Re a Debtor (No 14 of 1913)* [1913] 3 KB 11.

Surety's right to securities

31.9 A surety is entitled to the benefit of every security which the creditor has against the principal debtor, the whole or any part of whose debt he has discharged[1]. This right is not merely inchoate until the surety is called upon to pay, but is complete throughout[2]. The creditor is bound to hold and preserve the securities for the benefit of the surety[3] so that on payment of the debt he may receive them unimpaired[4], whether the surety was or was not aware of the existence of the securities[5] and although they were taken by the creditor after the contract of suretyship[6]. It makes no difference that the surety may have taken a particular indemnity upon other property, if he has done so without knowledge of the security held by the creditor, which was available for his own indemnity[7].

A surety for a limited sum only has, on payment of that sum, all the rights of the creditor in respect of that amount and is therefore entitled to a share in any security held by the creditor for the whole of the debt[8].

The restriction on the creditor in dealing with his securities only applies when he has notice of the suretyship. Thus, if he accepts the liability of two co-debtors without knowing that, while they are both principal debtors towards him, they stand in the relation of principal and surety between themselves, he is not affected by the restriction until he has notice of the rights of the surety. To these rights, subject to his own claims, he must then give effect[9].

The right of the surety extends to all equities which the creditor whose debt he has discharged could have enforced, not merely against the principal debtor, but against all who claim under him[10].

This right of the surety to the benefit of the creditor's securities was affirmed by the Mercantile Law Amendment Act 1856. A surety who pays the debt is entitled to have all the securities held by the creditor assigned to him and to stand in the place of the creditor, and use all remedies and, if need be, upon a proper indemnity, use his name in any proceeding in order to obtain from the principal debtor, or any co-surety, or co-debtor, indemnity for the payment he has made[11].

1 *Goddard v Whyte* (1860) 2 Giff 449. A surety who takes security from the principal debtor holds it not for his exclusive benefit, but for the benefit of himself and his co-sureties: *Berridge v Berridge* (1890) 44 Ch D 168. For the effect of a voluntary payment, see (1976) 92 LQR 188 (Birks and Beatson); *Owen v Tate* [1976] QB 402, [1975] 2 All ER 129, CA.
2 *Dixon v Steel* [1901] 2 Ch 602.
3 *McColl's Wholesale Pty Ltd v State Bank of New South Wales* [1984] 3 NSWLR 365. For the creditor's liability to the surety in the exercise of the power of sale, see **20.23**, and see, generally, *Bauer v Bank of Montreal* (1980) 110 DLR (3d) 424, SC of Can; (1986) 1 Banking & Finance Law Review (Carswell, Canada) 73 (Kent).
4 *Pledge v Buss* (1860) John 663; *Pearl v Deacon* (1857) 24 Beav 186.
5 *Lake v Brutton* (1856) 8 De GM & G 440.
6 *Forbes v Jackson* (1882) 19 Ch D 615.
7 *Lake v Brutton*, above, and see *Brandon v Brandon* (1859) 3 De G & J 524. Though, under different circumstances, a person who had made his own interest in the mortgaged property liable to the debt was held to have lost his right against the principal security, by taking from the principal debtor by way of indemnity a security upon other property: *Cooper v Jenkins* (1863) 32 Beav 337.

8 *Goodwin v Gray* (1874) 22 WR 312.
9 *Duncan, Fox & Co v North and South Wales Bank* (1880) 6 App Cas 1; *Rouse v Bradford Banking Co* [1894] AC 586; *Nicholas v Ridley* [1904] 1 Ch 192.
10 See *Drew v Lockett* (1863) 32 Beav 499; also *Praed v Gardiner* (1788) 2 Cox Eq Cas 86.
11 Mercantile Law Amendment Act 1856, s 5. The statute applies to a co-debtor as well as to a surety; and see *Brown v Cork* [1985] BCLC 363.

Failure of creditor to preserve securities

31.10 The surety being thus interested in the mortgaged estate, the neglect of the creditor to preserve the securities for his benefit will result in the release of the surety, either entirely or to the extent of the lost fund[1]. The creditor cannot, as against the surety, apply the security in payment of any other debt than that for which the surety was liable[2].

However, the creditor is under no obligation not to assign the securities or the debt. Upon such an assignment the creditor's obligation to preserve the securities attaches upon the assignee, who also acquires the rights of the creditor against the surety. Those rights are not lost by the neglect of the assignee to give notice of the assignment to the surety; though by omitting to give notice he will risk the consequences of a payment by the surety to the assignor. Nonetheless, if, through the neglect of the creditor or his assignee to enforce or protect the security, the benefit of it is lost to the surety, he is discharged[3].

It is usual to insert in the guarantee a provision to prevent the release of securities discharging the surety[4].

1 Cf the absolute discharge where the terms of the principal contract are varied to the surety's disadvantage. Where securities are released the surety is released only to the extent of the loss of his security. The wasteful application of the principal debtor's estate by the creditor will release the surety: *Mutual Loan Fund Association v Sudlow* (1858) 5 CBNS 449. Similarly if the creditor instead of proving, as he ought to do, under the bankruptcy of the debtor, without notice to the surety, releases the trustee and the bankrupt's estate in consideration of a conveyance of the equity of redemption: *Pledge v Buss* (1860) Johns 663. But the creditor may choose the time to sell the security. If the creditor refuses the surety's request to sell the security, the surety should pay off the debtor and take over the security: *China and South Sea Bank Ltd v Tan Soon Gin* [1990] 1 AC 536, [1989] 3 All ER 839, PC; *Downsview Nominees v First City Corpn Ltd* [1993] AC 295, [1993] 3 All ER 626, PC. Both these cases were applied in *Equitorial Corpn plc v Shah* [1996] NPC 172.
2 *Pearl v Deacon* (1857) 24 Beav 186.
3 *Taylor v Bank of New South Wales* (1886) 11 App Cas 596; *Buckeridge v Mercantile Credits Ltd* (1981) 147 CLR 654.
4 See **31.7**, n 5. The whole of this paragraph was quoted in *Dowling v Ditanda Ltd* (1975) 236 Estates Gazette 485 and see *Buckerridge v Mercantile Credit Ltd* (1981) 147 CLR 654.

WAIVER OF VENDOR'S LIEN

Effect of taking security

31.11 The lien of a vendor of land for unpaid purchase money will under certain circumstances either not arise or, if it has arisen, will be regarded as having been surrendered. In either case the lien is said to be waived. The question whether there has been a waiver usually arises when the vendor has accepted other security for the purchase money. But the simple rule that the taking of any security shall be regarded as a substituted security and exclude the lien has not been adopted and it depends upon the circumstances of each case whether the proper inference is that the lien was intended to be reserved, or whether the vendor intended to rely on the other security[1]. The burden of proof that the lien has been waived is on the purchaser[2].

1 *Mackreth v Symmons* (1808) 15 Ves 329 at 350; *Cood v Cood and Pollard* (1822) 10 Price 109; *Thames Iron Works Co v Patent Derrick Co* (1860) 1 John & H 93. For the vendor's lien, see **2.39**, and note the subrogation cases referred to at **2.45**. Cf *Banque Finance de la Cite v Parc (Battersea) Ltd* [1999] 1 AC 221.
2 *Hughes v Kearney* (1803) 1 Sch & Lef 132 at 135; *Mackreth v Symmons*, above.

Taking personal security

31.12 The lien is not generally destroyed by the vendor taking a promissory note, bill of exchange, or other negotiable instrument for the purchase money, since these are only modes of payment[1]; nor by the vendor taking a bond[2] or covenant for payment of the purchase money, even though a surety joins[3].

It does not matter that the conveyance contains a receipt for the purchase money[4]. A note may be given, not to supersede the lien, but for the purpose of ascertaining the debt, and countervailing the receipt[5].

1 *Hughes v Kearney*, above; *Grant v Mills* (1813) 2 Ves & B 306; *Nairn v Prowse* (1802) 6 Ves 752; *Gunn v Bolckow, Vaughan & Co* (1875) 10 Ch App 492 (as to chattels).
2 *Winter v Anson* (1827) 3 Russ 488; *Collins v Collins (No 2)* (1862) 31 Beav 346; *Pell v Midland Counties and South Wales Rly Co* (1869) 20 LT 288.
3 *Elliott v Edwards* (1802) 3 Bosx & P 181; cf *Cood v Cood and Pollard*, above.
4 *Winter v Lord Anson*, above.
5 *Nairn v Prowse*, above at 759.

Taking a mortgage

31.13 If it appears by direct agreement, or can be clearly inferred from the circumstances, that the vendor intended to rely upon the alternative security only, and not upon the land, then the lien will be gone[1]. The taking of security for part of the purchase money by mortgage of part of the estate and by bond[2], and the taking of a mortgage for part and of a note payable on demand for the residue of the purchase money[3], have been held to show an intention to abandon the lien[4]. This is apparently because a charge for part of the money shows an intention not to charge the residue.

The lien has also been held to be lost by taking, a special security over stock which was sufficient or probably sufficient to cover the purchase money. On the facts, the intention of the parties was that the stock was pledged so that the purchaser could take the land free of the lien[5]. On the same principle, a mortgage upon another property of the purchaser may have a like effect, if the intention is to burden one property, so that the other might be unencumbered[6].

However, the above are probably no more than cases on their facts. The true principle to be applied in determining whether the lien is excluded is to ask whether there was anything in the transaction or documents giving effect to it which would lead to the conclusion that the parties must have intended to exclude the existence of the vendor's unpaid lien. The parties' intention is to be ascertained objectively and it is thought that the courts will be less ready to infer the exclusion of a lien than in the past[7].

1 *Winter v Lord Anson*, above at 492. See *Frail v Ellis* (1852) 16 Beav 350, and *Re Taylor, Stileman and Underwood* [1891] 1 Ch 590; *Re Molton Finance Ltd* [1968] Ch 325, [1967] 3

All ER 843, CA; *Capital Finance Co Ltd v Stokes* [1969] 1 Ch 261, [1968] 3 All ER 625, CA; *Security Trust Co v Royal Bank of Canada* [1976] AC 503, [1976] 1 All ER 381, PC; and see **2.46**. For a discussion of the relationship of a lien and a mortgage see (1970) 33 MLR 131 (Sunnucks).

2 *Capper v Spottiswoode* (1829) Taml 21.

3 *Bond v Kent* (1692) 2 Vern 281.

4 An inference said by Lord Eldon in *Mackreth v Symmons*, above at 348, not to be conclusive. It seems that the mere retention by the vendor of the title deeds does not waive or exclude his lien: *Wreforde v Lethern* (1824) 2 LJ OS Ch 173.

5 *Nairne v Prowse*, above.

6 See *Mackreth v Symmons*, above at 348.

7 *Barclays Bank plc v Estates and Commercial Ltd* [1997] 1 WLR 415 at 425, per Millett LJ.

Circumstances excluding lien

31.14 It has been held that there is no lien where the consideration for sale is the security itself and not a sum secured; where, for example, land is granted in consideration of the purchaser's covenant to pay an annuity to the vendor[1]; or where an express stipulation for the protection of the vendor has been substituted for the lien[2]; or a special mode of payment has been agreed upon[3]; or where payment was to be made within two years after a resale[4]; or where the object of the purchase[5], or nature of the consideration[6], is inconsistent with the existence of a lien, and the vendor will lose his lien if he is a party to a subsequent mortgage which is inconsistent with it[7]. Where the vendor enabled a sub-sale to be made as though it did not exist, the lien was postponed to the sub-purchaser but was not lost and could be enforced against the head-purchaser[8].

1 *Parrott v Sweetland* (1835) 3 My & K 655; cf *Dixon v Gayfere, Fluker v Gordon* (1857) 1 De G & J 655 at 659.

2 *Re London and Lancashire Paper Mills Co* (1888) 58 LT 798.

3 *Re Brentwood Brick and Coal Co* (1876) 4 Ch D 562. But see the explanation of this case in *Barclays Bank plc v Estates and Commercial Ltd*, above.

4 *Re Parkes, ex p Parkes* (1822) 1 Gl & J 228; cf *Re Patent Carriage Co, Gore and Durant's Case* (1866) LR 2 Eq 349.

5 *Earl Jersey v Briton Ferry Floating Dock Co* (1869) LR 7 Eq 409.

6 *Re Albert Life Assurance Co, ex p Western Life Assurance Society* (1870) LR 11 Eq 164 (the consideration being the taking over of debts and engagements).

7 *Cood v Cood and Pollard*, above.

8 *Kettlewell v Watson* (1884) 26 Ch D 501 (as analysed in *Barclays Bank plc v Estates and Commercial Ltd*, above); see *Smith v Evans* (1860) 28 Beav 59.

Lien for part of consideration

31.15 It has been held that where the unpaid purchase consideration consisted partly of a gross sum due on bonds which the purchaser had undertaken, but had failed to pay, and partly of liability for annuities, against which the purchaser had undertaken to indemnify the vendor, there was a lien as to the gross sum but not as to the annuities[1].

1 *Mackreth v Symmons*, above.

Where contract not completed

31.16 The vendor loses his lien if by his own act or default the contract is not completed[1].

1 *Oxenham v Esdaile* (1828) 2 Y & J 493; *Esdaile v Oxenham* (1824) 3 B & C 225; *Dinn v Grant* (1852) 5 De G & Sm 451. For the loss of the lien of a vendor of goods, see previous editions of this work.

Chapter 32

Merger

MERGER OF CHARGES

Merger of estates[1]

32.1 Merger of estates took place at law when two estates in land, which were held in the same legal right[2], became united in the same person. The lesser estate (in legal terms) was then swallowed up or merged in the greater. In equity merger depended on intention and the equitable rule now prevails. There is no merger by operation of law of any estate[3] the beneficial interest in which would not be deemed to be merged or extinguished in equity[4].

1 See, generally, as to merger, 16 *Halsbury's Laws* (4th edn, reissue) paras 883 ff; 32 *Halsbury's Laws* (4th edn, reissue) paras 874 ff. Snell *Equity* (30th edn) Ch 26.
2 *Re Redcliffe, Radcliffe v Bewes* [1892] 1 Ch 227, CA, but see Challis *Real Property* (3rd edn) p 92; and *Jones v Davies* (1861) 7 H & N 507.
3 Ie a fee simple or term of years; Law of Property Act 1925, s 1 (1).
4 Law of Property Act 1925, s 185, replacing Judicature Act 1873, s 25 (4). This applies only to the merger of estates: *Capital and Counties Bank Ltd v Rhodes* [1903] 1 Ch 631 at 648, CA.

Merger of charges

32.2 Analogous to the merger of estates at law was the extinguishment, or merger in equity of a charge on land where the absolute ownership of the charge and the land were united in the same person. In an appropriate case the charge would be regarded as merged for the benefit of the land[1].

In equity the test for merger was not the mere union of interests, but the intention of the owner and the equitable rule now prevails[2]. The usual circumstance in which an owner acquires the benefit of a charge is by paying off the sums due to the mortgagee. The question in such a case is whether the charge was paid off for the benefit of the land, or whether the owner intended to preserve the charge against the land for his benefit. Only in the former case will there be a merger. The owner's intention might be actual, evidenced by declaration, or by circumstances at the time of the union of interests or subsequently during his life[3]. If there is no evidence of actual intention, the court will presume that the owner intends merger or not according to whether it is for his benefit. When there is no advantage to him in the subsistence of the charge, then the prima facie rule operates and the charge is extinguished[4].

The result, where an equitable mortgagee purchases the equity of redemption, may be to subject him to agreements made by the mortgagor such as an agreement to grant a lease[5].

1 *Earl of Buckinghamshire v Hobart* (1818) 3 Swan 186 at 199; *Re French-Brewster's Settlements, Walters v French-Brewster* [1904] 1 Ch 713; cf *Re Simmons, Dennison v Orman* (1902) 87 LT 594.
2 See now Supreme Court Act 1981, s 49 (1), under which, in any conflict or variance between the rules of equity and the rules of common law, the rules of equity prevail.
3 The presumption of intention as to merger arises on the death of the person entitled both to the estate and the charge and this intention is to be collected from all the circumstances which existed at that period, including his acts prior to his decease and all the facts affecting his position down to and at the time of his decease: *Swinfen v Swinfen (No 3)* (1860) 29 Beav 199 at 204.
4 *Forbes v Moffatt* (1811) 8 Ves 384; *Thorne v Cann* [1895] AC 11 at 18, HL.
5 *Smith v Phillips* (1837) 1 Keen 694 (considered in *Rust v Goodale* [1957] Ch 33, [1956] 3 All ER 373); *O'Loughlin v Fitzgerald* (1873) 7 IR Eq 483.

Analagous situations

32.3 Merger, then, is a question of intention. A charge will not merge in the security if that was not what was intended. Where someone with no interest in the property pays off the mortgage (otherwise than by way of gift to the mortgagor), a situation analogous to non-merger may result. Unless the payer intended to make an unsecured loan to the mortgagor, the payer will be subrogated to the rights of the mortgagee. Strictly speaking, the mortgage is not preserved. However, the payer has the same rights against the mortgagor as if it were[1].

Thus in one case[2] a company made an unsecured loan to another, to be used to discharge a first mortgage over property owned by the second company. The first company made the loan knowing of second charges over the property in favour of other companies in the same group as the second company, to secure intra-group loans. However, the first company had received a letter from the group holding company undertaking that the holders of the later charges would not seek to recover their loans until the first company had been paid. The House of Lords held that though the first mortgage was discharged, legal relations between the first company and the owners of the later charges were to be regulated as though the first charge was still on foot, to prevent the unjust enrichment of the owners at the first company's expense.

By similar means, a co-owner who consents to the first mortgage, but not to a subsequent mortgage designed to pay off the first, cannot set up her interest in priority to the subsequent mortgage[3].

1 See *Banque Financière v Parc (Battersea) Ltd* [1999] 1 AC 221. Cf *Castle Philips Finance Ltd v Piddington* (1994) 70 P & CR 592; *Bankers Trust v Namdar* [1997] EGCS 20; *Halifax Mortgage Services Ltd v Muirhead* (1997) 76 P & CR 418.
2 *Banque Financière de la Cité v Parc (Battersea) Ltd* [1999] 1 AC 221.
3 *Equity and Law Home Loans Ltd v Prestidge* [1992] 1 WLR 137; *Locabail v Waldorf Investment Corpn* [1999] NLJR 1793.

Where limited owner acquires charge

32.4 Where a tenant for life or other limited owner becomes entitled to the charge, the presumption is that there is no merger. The result of merger would be that the limited owner would have paid off the charge for the benefit of the remaindermen, and this is not to be presumed[1]. Hence the merger only results where the tenant for life shows an intention that the charge shall be extinguished for the benefit of the remaindermen[2]. The burden of proof is on those who claim to have the estate exonerated[3] and this is so even when the remainderman is the child of the tenant for life[4].

1 For the same reason, where a person entitled to the equity of redemption of an estate which is jointly mortgaged together with another pays off the mortgage, it will be kept alive in his favour: *Taws v Knowles* [1891] 2 QB 564 at 572, CA.
2 *Wyndham v Earl of Egremont* (1775) Amb 753; *Williams v Williams-Wynn* (1915) 84 LJ Ch 801.
3 *Countess of Shrewsbury v Earl of Shrewsbury* (1790) 3 Bro CC 120 at 127; *Burrell v Earl of Egremont* (1844) 7 Beav 205.
4 *Re Harvey, Harvey v Hobday* [1896] 1 Ch 137; though in such a case the smallest indication that the tenant for life meant to pay the money himself will prevent his representatives from obtaining repayment.

Evidence of intention

32.5 Evidence of intention may be direct or may be inferred from the attendant circumstances. Moreover, since the intention may be formed at any time during the life of the owner, so long as his ownership both of the land and the charge continue[1], it is necessary to consider the circumstances not only at the time when the union of interests first occurs, but also subsequently. Parol evidence may be used[2].

The clearest way of causing or preventing merger is by an express declaration in the instrument which effects the union of the charge and the estate.

An express assignment of the charge to the owner or to a trustee for him, while it affords some evidence of an intention against merger, is neither necessary nor sufficient for that purpose[3]. Where it is accompanied by a declaration of trust[4], the intention of preventing merger should be clearly and unequivocally stated. Indeed, where there is such an instrument the court may conclude that the intention to exclude merger, had it existed, would have been expressed in such an instrument and be accompanied by a declaration of trust of the charge[5].

Any dealing in relation to the property which indicates that the owner considers the charge to be existing can be used as evidence against merger[6], but the owner cannot set up the charge after he has disposed of the land whether by sale[7], mortgage[8], or settlement[9] on the footing that it is free from the charge. An intention in favour of merger may be inferred if the owner of the land disposes of it by will, making no mention of the charge (unless there are other charges to which the devise is subject and which are also not mentioned) and using language calculated to exclude the existence of any charge on the estate[10], or other circumstances showing that it was not treated as subject to any charge[11].

A charge, though merged, may be treated as existing for the purpose of liability to death duties[12].

1 See above.
2 *Astley v Miller* (1827) 1 Sim 298 at 345.
3 *Hood v Phillips* (1841) 3 Beav 513 at 518; *Parry v Wright* (1823) 1 Sim & St 369; affd (1828) 5 Russ 142.
4 See *Bailey v Richardson* (1852) 9 Hare 734.
5 An intention against merger might be inferred, eg where the owner declared a trust in favour of his personal representatives, but see *Tyrwhitt v Tyrwhitt* (1863) 32 Beav 244; *Re Gibbon, Moore v Gibbon* [1909] 1 Ch 367.

6 *Hatch v Skelton* (1855) 20 Beav 453; *Re Gibbon, Moore v Gibbon*, above.
7 *Bulkeley v Hope* (1855) 1 K & J 482 at 487; *Re Gibbon, Moore v Gibbon*, above.
8 *Tyler v Lake* (1831) 4 Sim 351; *Re Gibbon, Moore v Gibbon*, above.
9 *Gower v Gower* (1783) 1 Cox Eq Cas 53.
10 *Hood v Phillips*, above; *Swinfen v Swinfen (No 3)* (1860) 29 Beav 199; *Re Lloyd's Estate* [1903] 1 IR 144.
11 *Pitt v Pitt* (1856) 22 Beav 294.
12 *Swabey v Swabey* (1846) 15 Sim 106, 502; *Re French-Brewster's Settlements, Walters v French-Brewster* [1904] 1 Ch 713.

Where no evidence of intention, benefit of owner prevails

32.6 Where there is no evidence of the conduct or acts of the owner of the estate or the evidence is neutral, it will be presumed that the owner intended what was most beneficial to him[1]. The circumstances, therefore, that the estate is subject to debts and legacies, or other charges, to which the charge in question is paramount (even though the liability for debts and legacies is not significant); the uncertainty whether the estate will be sufficient to bear all its burdens; and other matters which make it better for the owner of the estate to preserve then merge the charges, will be taken as grounds for presuming his intention to do so[2].

1 *Adams v Angell* (1876) 5 Ch D 634, CA; *Thorne v Cann* [1895] AC 11, HL; *Liquidation Estates Purchase Co v Willoughby* [1896] 1 Ch 726. The owner of an estate who buys up an incumbrance at less than its full value is entitled to hold it for full value against subsequent incumbrancers: *Davis v Barrett* (1851) 14 Beav 542 and see *Ghana Commercial Bank v Chandiram* [1960] AC 732, [1960] 2 All ER 865, PC.
2 *Forbes v Moffatt* (1811) 18 Ves 384; *Whiteley v Delaney* [1914] AC 132, HL.

Circumstances affecting merger

32.7 The intention to merge will not be imputed to an owner on account of dealings with the estate, which are explicable on the basis that the owner was ignorant of his rights. An example is where a tenant for life, who was also executor, paid off certain charges on the settled estate, under circumstances which showed his belief that he was bound to do so in his capacity as executor and residuary legatee of the settlor[1]. On the other hand, a mortgagor who, as one of the executors and residuary legatees of the mortgagee, is treated as having in his hands the amount owing on the mortgage will be also treated as having intended to discharge the mortgage out of his share of the residue[2].

1 *Burrell v Earl of Egremont* (1844) 7 Beav 205; *Connolly v Barter* [1904] 1 IR 130.
2 *Re Greg, Fordham v Gregg* [1921] 2 Ch 243.

Keeping prior mortgages on foot. The rule in *Otter v Lord Vaux*[1]

32.8 Where the owner of land creates successive mortgages upon it he is not allowed to pay off the first mortgage and then rely on it against the subsequent incumbrancers. The reason is that for a mortgagor to attempt to rely on the first mortgage against later mortgages would be to derogate from his bargain with the later mortgagees[2]. Accordingly a statutory indorsed receipt cannot operate in his favour as a transfer[3]. However, a purchaser of the equity of redemption, not being himself liable on the mortgage, is not subject to this restriction.

Depending on his intention, such a person may prevent the merger of the first mortgage[4].

1 *Otter v Lord Vaux* (1856) 6 De G M & G 638, preserved by s 115(3) of the Law of Property Act 1925. Applied *Sussman v AGC (Advances) Ltd* [1991] ACL Rep 295 NSW 14; *Rogers v Resi-Statewide Corpn Ltd* (1991) 101 ALR 377.
2 *Otter v Lord Vaux* (1856) 6 De GM & G 638 at 642; *Re W Tasker & Sons Ltd, Hoare v W Tasker & Sons Ltd* [1905] 2 Ch 587, CA (a company, paying off some of its debentures, cannot keep them alive against others of the same series ranking *pari passu*; except for the purpose of reissue: Companies Act 1985, s 194); *Morrison v Guaranty Trust Co of Canada* (1972) 28 DLR (3d) 458 (husband and wife mortgagors—wife who pays off mortgage cannot keep it alive); *Cochrane v Cochrane* [1985] 3 NSWLR 403. When a mortgagor becomes bankrupt (and so is released from the debt), and subsequently buys the first mortgage, it seems he can keep it on foot: *Re Howard's Estate* (1892) 29 LR Ir 266, and it is considered that a purchase by the mortgagor, after several bona fide mesne transfers, might be set up, since the mortgagor would not then be found paying into the hand of the prior mortgagee money which he is bound by his contract to pay in discharge of his debt: *Otter v Lord Vaux*, above.
3 Law of Property Act 1925, s 115 (3). See **28.54**.
4 *Adams v Angell*, above; *Whiteley v Delaney*, above, and see *Parkash v Irani Finance Ltd* [1970] Ch 101, [1969] 1 All ER 930; *Re H & S Credits Ltd, Tucker v Roberts* [1969] Qd R 280.

The doctrine of *Toulmin v Steere*[1]

32.9 Sir William Grant MR in this case suggested that even a purchaser of the equity of redemption, not liable on the mortgage, could not preserve a charge for his own benefit. This can no longer be regarded as a correct statement of the law[2]. In every case the question is one of intention[3] and all that *Toulmin v Steere* should be treated as deciding is that if there is no evidence of actual intention to the contrary then the mortgage which is paid off will merge and the subsequent mortgagees will be advanced. Thus, while the decision stands, the purchaser of the equity of redemption is not entitled to the benefit of the presumption that he intended what was for his benefit. However, where there are intermediate mortgages the court will readily find an intention against merger[4].

1 (1817) 3 Mer 210.
2 *Whiteley v Delaney*, above.
3 *Adams v Angell*, above; *Minter v Carr* [1894] 3 Ch 498.
4 *Toulmin v Steere* was considered in, inter alia, the following cases: *Watts v Symes* (1851) 1 De GM & G 240; *Stevens v Mid-Hants Rly Co, London Financial Association v Stevens* (1873) 8 Ch App 1064, CA; *Adams v Angell*, above; *Thorne v Cann*, above; *Liquidation Estates Purchase Co v Willoughby*, above; *Manks v Whiteley* [1911] 2 Ch 448, [1912] 1 Ch 735, CA; and *Whiteley v Delaney*, above. It may be that the attitude of a modern court to questions of merger will reflect the principles obtaining in determining whether an unpaid vendor's lien has been waived. As to this see **31.13**.

Cases of merger

32.10 Sometimes, however, the circumstances show an intention that the charge which is paid off shall merge. If, for example, a mortgagee takes a conveyance of the equity of redemption, in consideration of the debts due to himself and the other mortgagees, whom he covenants to pay, prima facie the mortgagee's own debt will merge in favour of the other mortgagees[1].

1 *Brown v Stead* (1832) 5 Sim 535 and see *Parry v Wright* (1828) 5 Russ 142, doubted in *Stevens v Mid-Hants Rly Co*, above at 1069.

Effect of bankruptcy

32.11 The giving up by a mortgagee of his security for the benefit of the creditors in the mortgagor's bankruptcy puts the trustee in the mortgagee's place and does not destroy the security so as to let in subsequent incumbrancers[1]. Where the trustee purchases the first mortgage, he only has the rights of a transferee as against subsequent incumbrancers[2]. The trustees of a deed for the benefit of creditors, by which all the real and personal estate of the debtor has been conveyed to them, do not thereby become owners of the estate, so as to cause the merger of a judgment assigned to them by one of the creditors[3].

1 *Cracknall v Janson* (1877) 6 Ch D 735.
2 *Bell v Sunderland Building Society* (1883) 24 Ch D 618.
3 *Squire v Ford* (1851) 9 Hare 47.

MERGER OF LOWER IN HIGHER SECURITY

General rules

32.12 The benefit of the security will be lost by merger in a security of a higher nature. Thus a simple contract debt merges in a specialty debt[1]—that is, a contract under seal, such as a bond or covenant—and both a simple contract debt and a specialty debt merge in a judgment[2].

The same principle has been applied where an informal equitable mortgage—such as a mortgage by deposit of deeds—has been followed by a formal mortgage, so that the equitable mortgage is extinguished and the formal mortgage stands as security only for the sums it is expressed to cover, although these do not include all sums which were secured by the deposit[3]. An original mortgage will not, however, be merged in a new mortgage on the same property taken as security for the old debt and further advances[4].

1 *Owen v Homan* (1851) 3 Mac & G 378; *Price v Moulton* (1851) 10 CB 561 (but see *Stamps Comrs v Hope* [1891] AC 476, PC); *Saunders v Milsome* (1866) LR 2 Eq 573; *Re European Central Rly Co, ex p Oriental Financial Corpn* (1876) 4 Ch D 33, CA, but a taking of a mortgage will not merge a simple contract debt if a contrary intention appears; *Bank of Victoria v Looker* (1896) 21 VLR 704. *Barclays Bank Ltd v Beck* [1952] 2 QB 47, [1952] 1 All ER 549, CA. For merger of the vendor's lien in a mortgage to the vendor, see the cases cited in **31.13**, n 1.

It is not uncommon for certain mortgages, usually second mortgages to hire-purchase and finance companies, to contain as a schedule to the deed a promissory note. In order to prevent merger of the personal remedy on the promissory note either no covenant for payment should be inserted in the mortgage, or, if inserted, it should be accompanied by a declaration against merger. For a form of mortgage to secure due payment of bills of exchange, see 28 *Forms and Precedents* (5th edn, 1999 reissue) Mortgages. The question as to whether there has been a merger or not is relevant in considering an action on the covenant for payment, for if the promissory note etc has merged in the mortgage the action must be commenced in the Chancery Division, whilst if there has not been a merger the lender can, it is submitted, sue for payment in the Queen's Bench Division on the promissory note and ignore the mortgage. Moreover if separate liability under the promissory note remains any action by the court in discharging or varying the mortgage may not affect the liability under the promissory note.

2 *Ward v Liddaman* (1847) 10 LT OS 225, but not while the debt remains unsatisfied, so as to prevent the creditor from making the debtor bankrupt in respect of it: *Re Mostyn, ex p Griffiths* (1853) 3 De GM & G 174. The obtaining of a judgment for the mortgage debt does not, while the judgment remains unsatisfied, prevent the mortgagee from enforcing his security: *Lloyd v Mason* (1845) 4 Hare 132.

3 *Vaughan v Vanderstegen* (1854) 2 Drew 289.
4 *Tenison v Sweeney* (1844) 1 Jo & Lat 710; *Re James, ex p Harris* (1874) LR 19 Eq 253, and see generally on the merger of an earlier equitable mortgage in a later legal mortgage, *Farrier-Waimak Ltd v Bank of New Zealand* [1965] AC 376, [1964] 3 All ER 657, PC.

Effect of judgment on mortgage interest

32.13 On the above principle a covenant in a mortgage for payment of principal is merged in a judgment obtained on the covenant and the interest runs on the judgment at the statutory rate[1]. If the mortgage provides for a higher rate, the right to recover the difference between the higher rate and the judgment rate depends on the form of the covenant for payment of interest and the nature of the proceedings—whether the claim is against the mortgagor personally, or is against the mortgaged property[2]. Special rules govern the position in respect of mortgages regulated under the Consumer Credit Act 1974[3].

If the effect of the covenant for payment of interest is that interest is to be payable so long as any principal money shall be due on the covenant for payment of principal, then it is extinguished in the judgment together with the latter covenant. On judgment being obtained principal is no longer due on the covenant since it is gone[4]. The principal is thenceforth due on the judgment. The interest covenant is considered to have this effect where it provides for payment of interest until the principal is repaid[5], or so long as the principal or any part thereof remains unpaid[6].

A covenant of this nature is said to be ancillary to the main covenant and the excess of interest cannot be recovered in proceedings against the mortgagor personally. Where the interest covenant is not merely ancillary, but is an independent covenant, it is not extinguished in the judgment and the excess of interest can be recovered in personal proceedings. A covenant for payment of interest so long as any principal remains due on the security is an independent covenant, since the principal is equally due on the security whether it is owing on the covenant or the judgment. Consequently under a covenant in this form the excess interest can be recovered in personal proceedings[7].

In proceedings in which the mortgagee's claim is against the property, the full interest provided for by the mortgagee is recoverable whether the interest covenant is independent or ancillary[8].

1 See **35.47**.
2 See *Mercantile Credits Ltd v McDowell* [1980] 2 NSWLR 101.
3 *Director General of Fair Trading v First National Bank Ltd* [2000] QB 672, [2000] 2 WLR 1353.
4 *Economic Life Assurance Society v Usborne* [1902] AC 147, HL. The speech of Lord Davey in this case comments on and explains the authorities mentioned below prior to that case, and see *Elders Trustee & Executor Co Ltd v Eagle Star Nominees Ltd* [1987] ACLD 32, SCNSW; *Re Mangan, ex p Andrew* (1994) 123 ALR 633.
5 *Re European Central Rly Co, ex p Oriental Financial Corpn* (1876) 4 Ch D 33, CA.
6 *Re Sneyd, ex p Fewings* (1883) 25 Ch D 338, CA.
7 *Popple v Sylvester* (1882) 22 Ch D 98; *Mercantile Credits Ltd v McDowell* [1980] 2 NSWLR 101. For a form of independent covenant, see the Appendix.
8 *Lowry v Williams* [1895] 1 IR 274, CA; *Aman v Southern Rly Co* [1926] 1 KB 59 at 73. This is so in foreclosure and redemption, and also whenever an account has to be taken between mortgagee and mortgagor.

Where the mortgage allows for a higher rate than 4 per cent up to the day fixed for payment, but there is no provision for future interest, the judgment of Lord Davey in *Economic Life Assurance Co v Usborne* appears to assume that the full rate will run, but, in the past, only 5 per cent has been allowed; see *Wallington v Cook* (1878) 47 LJ Ch 508.

Conditions of merger of the security

32.14 It is a necessary condition for merger of a lower in a higher security that the remedy given by the higher shall be co-extensive with that under the inferior security. Therefore, if several persons are indebted on a joint and several note, and some only of them execute a mortgage, the liability on the note will not merge in the covenant in the mortgage[1]. Nor will there be any merger unless the securities are vested in the same person[2]; and the debt comprised in each security must be the same[3]. There will be no merger if the higher security is ineffectual[4].

1 *Boaler v Mayor* (1865) 19 CBNS 76; *Westmorland Green and Blue Slate Co v Feilden* [1891] 3 Ch 15.
2 *Bell v Banks Drinkwater* (1841) 3 Man & G 258.
3 *Holmes v Bell* (1841) 3 Man & G 213; *Norfolk Rly Co v M'Namara* (1849) 3 Exch 628.
4 *Re Emery, ex p Harvey* (1839) Mont & Ch 261; *Vibart v Coles* (1890) 24 QBD 364, CA; cf *Capital Finance Co Ltd v Stokes*, see **2.47**.

Merger prevented by intention

32.15 Merger of a lower in a higher security may be prevented by an expressed or an implied intention to the contrary[1]. A recital in the security that it is given by way of further or collateral security will prevent merger both at law and in equity[2] and an intention against it may be sufficiently shown from the nature of the transaction, or the acts of the parties. Thus where a reversionary lease was deposited as security, and the debtor afterwards purchased the lease in possession and deposited it with the same lender as security for another sum, it was held that there was no merger[3].

1 *General Credits (Finance) Pty Ltd v Brushford Pty Ltd* [1975] 2 NSWLR 308.
2 *Twopenny v Young* (1824) 3 B & C 208; *Stamps Comrs v Hope* [1891] AC 476, PC; *Barclays Bank Ltd v Beck*, above.
3 *Re Dix, ex p Whitbread* (1841) 2 Mont D & De G 415, and see *Locking v Parker* (1872) 8 Ch App 30.

Chapter 33

Destruction or loss of the property and repudiation

Security lost with the property

33.1 The benefit of a security may be lost by the destruction, or loss, of the property of which it is the subject[1]. In the case of mortgaged leaseholds loss could occur through forfeiture[2], but not by surrender[3]. Where the buildings on land are destroyed the rules with regard to insurance moneys will generally apply[4].

Though the security is lost the liability of the mortgagor under the personal covenant will remain and the mortgagee, in appropriate cases, may have a claim against a third party[5].

1 *Story on Bailment* (9th edn) s 363. As to the loss of the security in the case of mortgages of ships captured in war, see *The Marie Glaeser* [1914] P 218. The total loss or destruction of the ship, but nothing less, will discharge the condition of a bottomry bond: *Stephens v Broomfield, The Great Pacific* (1869) LR 2 PC 516.
2 See **3.6**.
3 See **3.16**. On frustration of leases, see *National Carriers Ltd v Panalpina (Northern) Ltd* [1981] AC 675, [1981] 1 All ER 161, HL.
4 See **3.44** ff. For the effect of the impossibility of fulfilling a covenant in a mortgage, see *Moorgate Estates Ltd v Trower and Barstow* [1940] Ch 206, [1940] 1 All ER 195.
5 *London and South of England Building Society v Stone* [1983] 3 All ER 105, [1983] 1 WLR 1242, CA.

Change of nature of property

33.2 The right of the owner of property generally, and therefore of one who has a security thereon, is not destroyed by the mere transmutation of its subject matter into a different form without his assent[1].

1 *Story on Bailment* s 363.

Repudiation

33.3 It is not clear whether a mortgage may be terminated by one party treating himself as discharged by reason of the other's breach of the mortgage terms. Traditionally, the contractual concept of repudiation has not applied to transactions creating interests in land. However, in a number of cases in the landlord and tenant context, the contrary has been decided or assumed[1].

However, there will rarely be an advantage to a mortgagee in treating the mortgage as discharged, for he will lose his security. A mortgagor will rarely be in a position to allege a repudiatory breach. Even if he were, the consequence would seem to be that he would have to pay back the advance at once, so it would seldom be to his advantage to do so.

1 *Hussein v Mehlman* [1992] 2 EGLR 87; *Chartered Trust plc v Davies* [1997] 2 EGLR 83; *Nynehead Developments Ltd v Fireboard Containers Ltd* [1999] 1 EGLR 7.

Chapter 34

Discharge or modification by statute

UNDER THE HOUSING ACTS

34.1 Formerly, where a housing authority compulsorily acquired a house which was unfit for human habitation, or a house was vacated pursuant to a closing or demolition order[1], the Housing Act 1985, Part XVII provided for the payment of compensation at site value to the owner of a relevant interest in the property[2]. Where that interest was subject to a mortgage, special provision was made for the discharge of the mortgage by the court, which could impose terms as to payment[3].

Those provisions have been repealed for orders made after 31 March 1990[4]. Instead, where a closing order or demolition order is made in respect of premises, and there is a mortgagee in possession, the housing authority must pay to the mortgagee compensation assessed by reference to the diminution in the compulsory purchase value of the mortgagee's interest arising from the making of the order[5]. Where the mortgagee is not in possession, the procedure for discharge of the mortgage, and the compensation payable, are the same as in other cases of compulsory purchase[6].

1 Under Housing Act 1985, ss 264, 265.
2 Section 585.
3 Section 591. For details, see the previous edition of this book.
4 See Local Government and Housing Act 1989, ss 165(1), 194(4) and Sch 9, Pt IV, para 76; Sch 12, Pt II; Local Government and Housing Act 1989 (Commencement No 5 and Transitional Provisions) Order 1990, SI 1990/431.
5 1985 Act, ss 584A, 602. Compulsory purchase value means the amount which would be due under the Land Compensation Act 1961 (s 584A(4)).
6 See below.

UNDER THE LEASEHOLD REFORM ACT 1967

Purposes of the Act

34.2 The Act entitles tenants of houses held on long leases at low rents to acquire the freehold or an extended lease[1]. Part I of the Act, which comprises all but two of the sections of the Act, deals with enfranchisement and extension of long leaseholds. Enfranchisement and extension may affect mortgages of both the landlord's and the tenant's estate.

1 For other Acts giving a right of enfranchisement, see Law of Property Act 1925, s 153, and the Places of Worship (Enfranchisement) Act 1920. The latter Act is amended by the 1967 Act.

Discharge of mortgages on landlord's estate

34.3 Where a tenant has exercised his right to acquire the freehold, the landlord is bound to make to the tenant a grant of the house and premises for an estate in fee simple absolute, subject to the tenancy and to tenant's incumbrances[1], but otherwise free of incumbrances[2]. Express provision is made by the Act for the automatic discharge of a mortgage affecting the landlord's interest. A conveyance made in pursuance of the landlord's obligation shall as regards any charge[3] on the landlord's estate (however created or arising) to secure the payment of money or the performance of any other obligation by the landlord or any other person, not being a charge subject to which the conveyance is required to be made or which would be overreached apart from the relevant provision[4], be effective to discharge the house and premises from the charge, and from the operation of any order made by a court for the enforcement of the charge, and to extinguish any term of years created for the purpose of the charge, and shall do so without the persons entitled to or interested in the charge or in any such order or term of years becoming parties to or executing the conveyance[5].

Where the conveyance to the tenant is effective to discharge the mortgage it is the duty of the tenant to apply[6] the price payable for the house and premises[7], in the first instance in or towards the redemption of the mortgage (and, if there are more than one, then according to their priorities), and if any amount so payable is not so paid nor paid into court in accordance with the provision in respect thereof[8] then, for the amount in question, the house and premises shall remain subject to the charge[9]. For the purpose of determining the amount payable in respect of any mortgage the person entitled thereto is not permitted to exercise any right of consolidation[10]. The mortgagee may be required to accept three months' or any longer notice of the intention to pay the whole or part of the principal secured by the mortgage, together with interest to the date of payment, notwithstanding that the terms of the mortgage make other provision or no provision as to the time and manner of payment, but the mortgagee will be entitled, if he so requires, to receive such additional payment as is reasonable in the circumstances in respect of the costs of reinvestment or other incidental costs and expenses and in respect of any reduction in the rate of interest obtainable on reinvestment[11].

The mortgagee need not be a party to execute the conveyance[12], but he may join in the conveyance for the purpose of discharging the house and premises from the mortgage without payment or for a less payment than that to which he would otherwise be entitled, and, if he does so, the persons to whom the price ought to be paid should be determined accordingly[13]. As the mortgage is only discharged if the mortgagee is wholly, or where the purchase price is not sufficient, partially satisfied, or if payment is made into court[14], the enfranchising tenant will need to satisfy a subsequent purchaser that payment was in fact made and he should accordingly demand from the mortgagee a formal discharge, where the mortgage is paid in full, or a formal release of the security, where there is only a partial payment, or that the mortgagee join in the conveyance to acknowledge receipt of the whole amount owing to him, or the whole of the purchase money, if that is less, and if the mortgagee refuses to do so, the tenant will be entitled to pay into court the amount of the payment to be made in respect of the mortgage[15].

Where the house and premises are discharged from a mortgage (without the obligations secured thereby being satisfied by the receipt of the whole or part of the price) the discharge of the house and premises does not prejudice any right or remedy for the enforcement of these obligations against other property comprised in the same or any other security, nor prejudice any personal liability as principal or otherwise of the landlord or any other person[16].

1 A charge on the landlord's estate to secure the payment of money or the performance of any other obligation is not treated as a tenant's incumbrance by reason only of the grant of the tenancy being subsequent to the creation of the charge and not authorised as against the persons interested in the charge (and the mortgagee is treated as having duly concurred in the grant of the tenancy for the purpose only of validating it despite the charge on the grantor's estate), but the mortgage is treated as a tenant's incumbrance if the tenancy was granted after 1 January 1968 (the appointed day), and it has not by the time of the conveyance become binding on the mortgagee: Leasehold Reform Act 1967, s 12(8).

2 Leasehold Reform Act 1967, s 8 (1).

3 A debenture holder's charge, whether a floating charge or not, in favour of trustees for such debenture holders is not a charge for this purpose. It is automatically discharged by the conveyance, the provision as to payment of the purchase price to the person(s) entitled to the benefit of the charge do not apply and the charge is to be disregarded in determining priorities, but a charge in favour of trustees for debenture holders which at the date of the conveyance is a specific and not a floating charge is a charge for this purpose; s 12 (5), and a specific charge under a single debenture or in favour of a single debenture holder would appear to be a charge for this purpose.

4 A conveyance executed under the landlord's obligation to enfranchise (a) has effect under s 2 (1) of the Law of Property Act 1925 to overreach any incumbrance capable of being overreached under that section as if, where the interest conveyed is settled land, the conveyance were made under the powers of the Settled Land Act 1925, and as if the requirements of s 2 (1) as to payment of the capital money allowed any part of the purchase price paid or applied in accordance with ss 11 to 13 of the Leasehold Reform Act 1967, to be so paid or applied; (b) shall not be made subject to any incumbrance capable of being overreached by the conveyance, but shall be made subject (where they are not capable of being overreached) to rentcharges redeemable under ss 8-10 of the Rentcharges Act 1977 and those falling within paragraphs (c) and (d) of s 2(3) of that Act (estate rentcharges and rentcharges implied under certain easements), except as otherwise provided by s 11 of the Leasehold Reform Act 1967: Leasehold Reform Act 1967, s 8 (4). Section 11 (as amended by the Rentcharges Act 1977, s 17 (1), Sch 1, para 4 (1)) relates to exoneration from, or redemption of, rentcharges (which were abolished by the 1977 Act) etc, and s 13 relates to payment into court in respect of mortgages, etc: see **34.4**.

5 Leasehold Reform Act 1967, s 12 (1).

6 If the tenant is himself entitled to the mortgage he can retain the appropriate amount in respect thereof: s 12 (3).

7 Less any amount paid out for the redemption of a rentcharge: s 12 (9).

8 See **34.4**.

9 Section 12 (2).

10 Section 12 (3).

11 Section 12 (4). The additional payment is presumably payable by the enfranchising tenant.

12 Section 12 (1).

13 Section 12 (7).

14 Section 12 (2).

15 Under s 13, above.

16 Section 12 (6), but see s 36 as to relief in respect of mortgages, etc on landlord's estate, **34.5**.

Payment into court in respect of mortgages, etc

34.4 The enfranchising tenant may pay into court on account of the price for the house and premises[1] the amount, if known, of the payment to be made in respect of the mortgage or, if that amount is not known, the whole of the price or such less amount as the tenant thinks right in order to provide for that payment in the following circumstances:

(a) because for any reason difficulty arises in ascertaining how much is payable in respect of the mortgage;
(b) because a person who is or may be entitled to receive payment cannot be found or ascertained;
(c) because any such person refuses or fails to make out a title, or to accept payment and give a proper discharge, or to take any steps reasonably required of him to enable the sum payable to be ascertained or paid;
(d) because a tender of the sum payable cannot, by reason of complications in the title to it or the want of two or more trustees or for other reasons, be effected, or not without incurring or involving unreasonable costs or delay[2].

The tenant must pay the purchase price[3] into court if before execution of the conveyance written notice is given to him:

(a) that the landlord or person entitled to the benefit of a charge on the house and premises so requires for the purpose of protecting the rights of persons so entitled, or for reason related to any application made or to be made under s 36 of the Act[4], or to the bankruptcy or winding up of the landlord; or
(b) that steps have been taken to enforce any charge on the landlord's interest in the house and premises by the bringing of proceedings in any court, as by the appointment of a receiver or otherwise[5].

Payment into court of the correct amount automatically discharges the mortgage, but if less than the correct amount is paid in the discharge is not total[6]. The difficulty of satisfying a subsequent purchaser as to the discharge mentioned previously[7] applies also in the case of payment into court.

1 Less the amount for the redemption of any rentcharge: s 13 (4).
2 Leasehold Reform Act 1967, s 13 (1), (2).
3 See n 1.
4 See above.
5 Leasehold Reform Act 1967, s 13 (3). Where payment is to be made into court by reason only of such a notice and the notice is given with reference to proceedings in a court specified in the notice other than the county court, payment must be made into the court so specified: s 13 (3).
6 Section 12 (1), (2).
7 See **34.3**.

Relief in respect of mortgages, etc on landlord's estate

34.5 In certain cases the landlord or a second or subsequent mortgagee will be able to apply to the court[1] for such order as the court thinks proper for the purpose of avoiding or mitigating any financial hardship that might otherwise be caused by the rights conferred on tenants by the Leasehold Reform Act 1967[2]. The mortgage must affect the estate of the immediate or a superior landlord of a house held at the passing of the Act (27 October 1967) on a long tenancy not having more than 20 years unexpired, or on a long tenancy capable of being determined within 20 years by notice given by the landlord[3]. The application may be made in the following circumstances:

(a) where the landlord proposes during the tenancy (including any extension thereof under the Act) to sell or realise any property which is subject to the charge, or a tenant of the house has given notice of his desire to have the freehold[4];
(b) where during the tenancy (including any such extension) the mortgagee has taken any steps to enforce the charge or demanded payment of the sum thereby secured or, if the house or any other property subject to the mortgage is subject also to another mortgage created or arising before 27 October 1967, the person entitled to the benefit of the other mortgage has taken any steps to enforce the other mortgage or demanded payment of the sum thereby secured[5].

If the application is made by the landlord the court may make an order providing for all or any of the following:

(a) for discharging or modifying any liability in respect of the sum secured by the charge, whether of the landlord or of persons liable jointly with him or as surety for him;
(b) for discharging or modifying the terms of the charge whether as respects the house or any other property subject to the mortgage, or the terms of any collateral charge;
(c) for restricting the exercise of any right or remedy in respect of any such liability or charge[6].

If the application is made by the second or subsequent mortgagee the court may make an order providing for all or any of the following:

(a) for discharging or modifying the terms of any prior charge, whether as respects the house or any other property subject to the charge;
(b) for restricting the exercise of any right or remedy in respect of any prior charge on the house or other property subject to the charge[7].

In either case any order may be made either conditionally or subject to such terms and conditions, including conditions with respect to the payment of money, as the court may think just and equitable to impose[8].

1 The county court: s 20 (1), but where steps are taken in a court other than the county court to enforce a mortgage or recover any sum thereby secured, that other court has the like powers in relation to that or any other mortgage as the county court, or, if an application for relief is pending in the county court, the other court may suspend the proceedings for enforcement etc on such terms as it thinks just, or direct that the proceedings for enforcement etc be transferred to the county court: s 36 (5).
2 Leasehold Reform Act 1967, s 36.
3 Section 36 (1) (a), (b).
4 Section 36 (2) (a).
5 Section 36 (2) (b).
6 Section 36 (2).
7 Section 36 (3).
8 Section 36 (4).

UNDER THE LEASEHOLD REFORM, HOUSING AND URBAN DEVELOPMENT ACT 1993

34.6 Chapter I of the 1993 Act gives to most lessees of flats in a residential building who hold long leases at a low rent the right collectively to acquire at market value the freehold of their building. Chapter II gives to most individual lessees of residential flats holding long leases at a low rent the right individually to extend their lease for 90 years beyond the term date of their present lease[1].

Lessees exercising their rights under Chapter I do so through a nominee purchaser[2]. Where any interest is acquired by the nominee purchaser pursuant to Chapter I of the Act[3] the conveyance is effective as regards certain mortgages to discharge the interest from the mortgage and from the operation of any court order for the enforcement of the mortgage and to extinguish any term of years created for the purposes of the mortgage. The conveyance has this effect whether or not the persons entitled to or interested in the mortgage are parties to, or execute, the conveyance[4]. The mortgages discharged under this section of the Act are those to secure the payment of money or the performance of any other obligation by the person from whom the interest is acquired or any other person and which would not overreached apart from the section[5]. Notwithstanding the provision for statutory discharge, it is open to the nominee purchaser and the owner of the reversion or other relevant landlord[6] to agree that the interest shall be acquired subject to the mortgage.

Where a conveyance is effective under Chapter I to discharge a mortgage to secure money, it is the duty of the nominee purchaser to apply the consideration payable for the interest in question[7] in the first instance in or towards the redemption of any such mortgage (and if there are more than one then according to their priorities). If he fails to do so, or to pay the money into court[8], the relevant interest remains subject to the mortgage as regards the amount in question and to that extent the provisions in the Act for discharge do not apply[9]. These provisions do not apply to a charge in favour of debenture holders or trustees therefor and such a charge is disregarded in determining priorities, unless (in the case of a charge in favour of trustees) by the date of the conveyance the charge has become a specific and not a floating charge[10].

If the purchase price is paid over by the nominee purchaser but the amount is insufficient to satisfy the obligations secured by the mortgage, the mortgage will be discharged but without prejudice to any right or remedy for the enforcement of those obligations against other property comprised in the same or any other security or any personal liability of the landlord or any other person[11].

The Act makes provision for determining the amount due under the mortgage for the above purposes. In particular, the mortgagee may not consolidate the mortgage with a separate mortgage on other property. If the reversioner or relevant landlord, or a participating tenant, is himself a mortgagee in respect of an interest to be acquired under Chapter I, the mortgage ranks for payment as though a stranger were entitled to it. Notwithstanding the expressed terms of the mortgage, a mortgagee can be required to accept three months or longer notice of intention to redeem, but is entitled in return to interest down to the date of payment and other compensation[12].

The Act lists circumstances which, if they give rise to difficulty in making payment, allow the nominee purchaser, instead of paying money to the mortgagee or other person entitled, to pay the money into court. These are:

(a) if for any reason difficulty arises in ascertaining how much is payable in respect of the mortgage;
(b) the person entitled to be paid cannot be found or his identity cannot be ascertained;
(c) that person refuses or fails to make out a title or to accept payment or give a proper discharge or to take any steps reasonably required of him to enable the sum payable to be ascertained and paid;
(d) a tender of the sum payable cannot, by reason of complications in the title to it or want of two or more trustees or for other reasons, be effected, or not without incurring or involving unreasonable expense or delay[13].

The sum to be paid into court on account of the consideration payable for the relevant interest is the amount, if known, of the payment to be made in respect of the mortgage, or, if that amount is not known the whole of that consideration or such lesser amount as the nominee purchaser thinks right in order to provide for that payment[14].

The nominee purchaser must also pay the whole or part of the consideration into court, if before the execution of the relevant conveyance, a landlord or person entitled to the benefit of a mortgage on the relevant interest, by notice requires him to do so. The purposes for which a notice may be given are the protection of the rights of the persons entitled to the benefit of the mortgage or for reasons related to the bankruptcy or winding up of the landlord. A notice may also be given where steps have been taken to enforce the mortgage by court proceedings, or by appointment of a receiver, or otherwise[15].

As a matter of good practice, where a mortgage is discharged pursuant to a payment by the nominee purchaser, the mortgagor should seek from the mortgagee a formal discharge of the mortgage[16].

On the grant of an extension lease under Chapter II, different considerations apply. There is no discharge of a mortgage of the landlord's interest. Instead, where the landlord's interest is subject to a mortgage, the Act provides that the lessee is entitled to an extension lease notwithstanding that the original lease was granted subsequent to the mortgage and not authorised by those entitled to the mortgage. The extension lease itself is deemed to be authorised against such persons and is binding on them[17]. An exception applies where the original lease was granted after 1 November 1993, is granted subsequent to a mortgage of the landlord's interest and does not bind the persons interested in the mortgage, In such a case, the extension lease will not be deemed to bind those persons[18].

Where an extension lease is granted, the landlord must deliver a counterpart of it to the mortgagee[19]. If he fails to do so, the mortgagee may treat him as having breached the mortgage[20]. Further, the landlord must takes steps to comply with the mortgage to ensure that the lease is not liable to be defeated by the mortgagee[21].

The Act makes separate provision for the case where the lessee's interest is subject to a mortgage. The existing lease is surrendered on the grant of the extension lease, but the new lease takes effect subject to the mortgage in substitution for the existing lease. The terms of the mortgage automatically apply to the new lease[22]. Again, the lessee must deliver the new lease to the mortgagee within one month of its return from the Land Registry[23].

1 For details see Hague *Leasehold Enfranchisement* (3rd edn) (1999) Chs 20-23 (collective enfranchisement) and Ch 29 (individual right to extension lease).
2 Leasehold Reform Housing and Urban Development Act 1993, s 15.
3 Including superior leasehold interests and other interests in the premises listed in s 2(1).

4 Section 35(1)(a), (b).
5 Section 35(1)(b).
6 Ie owner of a superior leasehold interest to be acquired with the freehold: see s 9(2A).
7 If the interest charged is a superior lease, the nominee purchaser need apply to the discharge of the mortgage only the funds payable in respect of that separate interest.
8 See below.
9 Schedule 8, para 2(1), (2).
10 Schedule 8, para 2(3), (4).
11 Schedule 8, para 5.
12 Schedule 8, para 3(1), (2), (3).
13 Schedule 8, para 4(1), (2).
14 Schedule 8, para 4(1), (2).
15 Schedule 8, para 3, which makes provision for the court into which the sum should be paid.
16 See *Hague*, above, para 13-06.
17 Section 58(1).
18 Section 56(2).
19 Section 58(3).
20 Section 58(6).
21 Section 58(7).
22 Section 58(4).
23 Section 58(5).

UNDER THE RENT ACT 1977

Variation of the terms of regulated mortgages

34.7 As to this, see **16.26**.

UNDER THE CONSUMER CREDIT ACT 1974

Refusal of enforcement order, etc

34.8 As to this, see **10.55** ff.

UNDER THE LANDS CLAUSES ACT

Redemption on compulsory purchase

34.9 As to this, see **28.31** ff.

UNDER THE LANDLORD AND TENANT ACT 1987

Redemption on compulsory purchase of landlord's interest

34.10 The legislation entitles qualifying tenants of blocks of flats to apply to the court for an acquisition order[1] and contains provision for the discharge of mortgages on the landlord's interest, if such order is made[2].

Where a landlord has made a disposal of an interest in premises to which Part I of the Landlord and Tenant Act 1987 applies, but has not first served a notice offering to dispose of the interest to a majority of qualifying tenants, those tenants may require the purchaser by notice to dispose of that interest to them.

If the interest has at any time since the original disposal become subject to any charge or mortgage, then unless the court otherwise directs, the instrument by virtue of which the property is disposed of by the purchaser operates to discharge the property from that charge or mortgage[3].

1 Landlord and Tenant Act 1987, Pt III. See (1987) 137 NLJ 843 (Madge).
2 Section 32, Sch 1.
3 Section 12B(5)(a). See generally Radevsky and Clarke *Tenants' Right of First Refusal* (Butterworths, 2001).

PART IX

ACCOUNTS AND COSTS

Chapter 35

Accounts

ACCOUNTS GENERALLY BETWEEN MORTGAGOR AND MORTGAGEE

WHO IS BOUND BY THE ACCOUNTS

Accounts prima facie binding on all parties

35.1 An account taken between the mortgagee and mortgagor, whether it is taken in or out of court, is prima facie binding not only on the parties to it, but on other persons interested in the equity of redemption. It is binding, therefore, on a subsequent incumbrancer[1]. Accounts taken in an action by a subsequent incumbrancer against the mortgagor and the prior incumbrancer bind the mortgagor as to the amount of the debt due to the prior incumbrancer, so long as the judgment remains unimpeached[2].

1 *Needler v Deeble* (1677) 1 Cas in Ch 299; *Williams v Day* (1680) 2 Cas in Ch 32; *Wrixon v Vize* (1842) 2 Dr & War 192; affd (1842) 3 Dr & War 104.

2 *Farquharson v Seton* (1828) 5 Russ 45. An account taken in court between the mortgagee and the tenant for life of the estate will bind the person entitled to the vested remainder, though he was no party to the action, as well as a contingent remainderman, though not *in esse* when the accounts were taken: *Allen v Papworth* (1731) 1 Ves Sen 163; and see *Wrixon v Vize*, above. Under the present law the tenant for life would, as estate owner, represent the remainderman.

Sureties are bound by the accounts of a receiver appointed by the court, where the accounts are regularly passed: *Mead v Lord Orrery* (1745) 3 Atk 235. Where an insolvent was party to an action, he was bound by the accounts although the person who represented his estate was absent: *Byrne v Lord Carew* (1849) 13 I Eq R 1.

When accounts not binding

35.2 The account is only binding when the parties to it represent both sides of the account. Hence the mortgagor, or a person claiming under him, is not bound by accounts taken in his absence between the mortgagee and a transferee of the mortgage[1] and accounts taken in an action are not binding upon co-defendants, as between themselves, except so far as the relief sought by the claimant required that such accounts should be taken as between those defendants. In the case, for example, of a simple action to redeem against several incumbrancers, any accounts taken will not be binding as between them[2] as it is unnecessary for the purposes of the judgment to take the accounts between the subsequent incumbrancers.

1 *Earl Macclesfield v Fitton* (1683) 1 Vern 168; *Mangles v Dixon* (1852) 3 HL Cas 702 at 737.
2 *Cottingham v Earl of Shrewsbury* (1843) 3 Hare 627 at 638. See also *North West Water v Binnie & Partners* [1990] 3 All ER 547.

Inference with settled accounts

35.3 A settled account[1], although prima facie binding on the parties to it and on other persons interested in the equity of redemption, and although in the ordinary course not liable to be disturbed[2], may under special circumstances be either reopened altogether, or may be subjected to possible alteration in respect of particular items only. In the former case the order is that the settled account shall be opened and set aside and a new account taken; in the latter case, that the settled account is to stand, but that any of the parties are to be at liberty 'to surcharge and falsify any of the items and charges therein'[3]. Moreover, when an account is admitted to contain an error, it can be 'purged' by setting off against that error an error shown to have been made in another account, in favour of the person prejudiced by the first error[4].

1 A settled account is sometimes referred to as a stated account, but the meaning is the same. The account is stated between the parties, or stated by one side and agreed to by the other. The reservation in an account of 'errors excepted' does not prevent it from being considered as settled; and such an account will be taken to be settled where the balance is carried over to a new account: *Johnson v Curtis* (1791) 3 Bro CC 266, and as to settled accounts, see *Parkinson v Hanbury* (1867) LR 2 HL 1 at 12; and as to when an account rendered will be deemed to have been agreed to, see *Sherman v Sherman* (1692) 2 Vern 276; *Hunter v Belcher* (1864) 2 De GJ & Sm 194.
2 *Newen v Wetten* (1862) 31 Beav 315.
3 'If any of the parties can show an omission for which credit ought to be given, that is a surcharge; or if anything is inserted that is a wrong charge, he is at liberty to show it, and that is falsification': *Pit v Cholmondeley* (1754) 2 Ves Sen 565 at 566. It has been said that for accounts to be falsified they must contain charges in the nature of fraud, not merely charges which may be regarded as excessive: *Heighington v Grant* (1845) 1 Ph 600 at 601, per Lord Lyndhurst LC, but a charge might be so excessive as to be improper and fraudulent in equity, though there was no actual fraud.
4 *Lawless v Mansfield* (1841) 1 Dr & War 557.

Re-opening of the account

35.4 Where the reopening of the account is claimed, either fraud or specific error must be alleged and proved[1]. The account will be opened altogether in case of fraud and this notwithstanding the lapse of a great number of years[2].

Moreover, apart from fraud, it will be reopened if the relation of the parties, or the manner in which the settlement took place, or the nature of the error proved, shows that the settlement ought not to be considered as an act binding on the parties who signed it and that it would be inequitable for the accounting party to take advantage of it[3].

The accounts will be more readily opened where the relationship of solicitor and client exists[4], 'provided, that is, excessive charge or error is shown'[5]; but unless fraud, or error amounting to evidence of fraud, in the bill of costs which forms the subject of the security, is relied on, the specific items alleged to be erroneous[6] must be identified and proved.

The account may also be reopened if it contains errors of considerable extent both in number and amount. If a fiduciary relation exists between the parties, where, for instance, the accounting party is an agent or a trustee, fewer errors will be required for the making of such an order[7].

A single error of large amount has been made the ground for reopening the whole account[8], but ordinarily it will be sufficient to give leave to surcharge and falsify[9].

Where the person objecting to the account was not one of the parties to it, collusion between such parties will also be a ground for opening it[10].

1 *Needler v Deeble* (1677) 1 Cas in Ch 299; *Knight v Bampfield* (1683) 1 Vern 179; *Dawson v Dawson* (1737) West temp Hard 171; *Taylor v Haylin* (1788) 2 Bro CC 310; *Johnson v Curtis* (1791) 3 Bro CC 266.

2 *Vernon v Vawdrey*, above (23 years); *Allfrey v Allfrey* (1849) 1 Mac & G 87 (17 years). See *Drew v Power* (1803) 1 Sch & Lef 182 at 192; *Chambers v Goldwin*, above, at 265; *Davis v Spurling* (1829) Taml 199; *Clarke v Tipping* (1846) 9 Beav 284; *Cheese v Keen* [1908] 1 Ch 245 at 252. In *Wharton v May* (1799) 5 Ves 27, the account was reopened for fraud, notwithstanding the vouchers had been destroyed by general consent.

3 *Coleman v Mellersh*, above, at 314; *Re Webb, Lambert v Still* [1894] 1 Ch 73 at 84.

4 *Lewes v Morgan* (1817) 5 Price 42; *Morgan v Evans* (1834) 3 Cl & Fin 159; *Ward v Sharp* (1884) 53 LJ Ch 313.

5 *Re Webb, Lambert v Still* [1894] 1 Ch 73; *Cheese v Keen* [1908] 1 Ch 245 where, however, only liberty was given to tax and to surcharge and falsify.

6 A general allegation of error will be sufficient if it is admitted by the solicitor: *Matthews v Wallwyn* (1798) 4 Ves 118 at 125; but otherwise specific items must be alleged and proved to be erroneous; the account is not reopened on the mere relationship of solicitor and client: *Morgan v Higgins* (1859) 1 Giff 270 at 277. See *Waters v Taylor* (1837) 2 My & Cr 526; *Lewes v Morgan* (1829) 3 Y & J 230 at 394. In *Blagrave v Routh* (1856) 2 K & J 509; affd (1856) 8 De GM & G 620, the claim to open the account was precluded by length of time and acquiescence.

7 *Williamson v Barbour* (1877) 9 Ch D 529, but although the errors are numerous and important, yet if there has been a great lapse of time, and the books and documents have been lost, the court may decline to open the account altogether and give leave only to surcharge and falsify: *Millar v Craig* (1843) 6 Beav 433. In a foreclosure action the mortgagor can set up a claim to reopen an account by way of defence in the same way as if the claim had been made by counterclaim: *Eyre v Hughes* (1876) 2 Ch D 148.

8 *Pritt v Clay* (1843) 6 Beav 503.

9 *Gething v Keighley* (1878) 9 Ch D 547; save in case of fraud and fiduciary relationship: *Williamson v Barbour*, above.

10 *Sherman v Cox* (1674) 3 Rep Ch 83, where it was said that an account should bind, unless the plaintiff proved a great collusion.

Liberty to surcharge and falsify

35.5 Liberty to surcharge and falsify will be given merely on the ground of error in the account[1], but it is essential that at least one error shall be specifically charged and proved[2]. This also is sufficient since, if one error has been proved, it may be expected that, upon investigation, others will be discovered[3]. The error may be either of fact or of law[4].

It appears not to have been decided whether, where there are several distinct accounts, in some only of which errors are alleged and proved, all become liable to be surcharged and falsified[5].

1 *Vernon v Vawdrey* (1740) 2 Atk 119; *Chambers v Goldwin* (1804) 9 Ves 254 (commission on consignment improperly charged); *Langstaffe v Fenwick* (1805) 10 Ves 405 (commission on personal collection of rents by mortgagee); *Daniell v Sinclair* (1881) 6 App Cas 181 (compound instead of simple interest charged by common mistake); see *Wrixon v Vize* (1842) 2 Dr & War 192 at 203.

The amount of the error, it has been said, is immaterial. The court looks at the principle involved. Thus relief has been given upon an error of only a few shillings: *Lewes v Morgan* (1817) 5 Price 42 at 86; *Lawless v Mansfield*, above, at 616. One would not, however, expect any error to be de minimis.

For overpayment of surplus proceeds of sale by first mortgagee, see *Weld-Blundell v Synott* [1940] 2 KB 107, [1940] 2 All ER 580; and see **20.45** ff.

2 *Parkinson v Hanbury* (1867) LR 2 HL 1 at 12; see *Chambers v Goldwin*, above, but particular statements of error are only necessary where the object of the action is to impeach a settled account and not where an account is prayed and no settled account is proved, though the pleading suggests the existence of a settled account. In such a case liberty will be given to surcharge and falsify, if upon inquiry any settled account is found to exist, whether specific errors have been charged or not: *Kinsman v Barker* (1808) 14 Ves 579; *Lawless v Mansfield*, above. If a settled account is proved, as set up by the pleadings, and no error shown by the plaintiff, the action will be dismissed: *Endo v Caleham* (1831) You 306; *Drew v Power* (1803) 1 Sch & Lef 182; *Lawless v Mansfield*, above.

3 *Coleman v Mellersh* (1850) 2 Mac & G 309 at 314.

4 *Roberts v Kuffin* (1741) 2 Atk 112; *Langstaffe v Fenwick*, above; *Daniell v Sinclair*, above, at 190.

5 *Lawless v Mansfield*, above; and see *Chambers v Goldwin*, above, where, however, the commission complained of extended to all the accounts.

Special circumstances affecting the accounts

35.6 Any special circumstance or fact affecting the amount due from the mortgagor to the mortgagee in a foreclosure action, such as a valuation of the security in bankruptcy, should be pleaded or brought to the attention of the court before the usual foreclosure judgment is made, in order that a direction may be given that, in taking the accounts, regard shall be had to such special circumstance or fact. If this is not done at the trial, no such question can be raised subsequently on taking the account[1].

1 *Sanguinetti v Stuckey's Banking Co (No 2)* [1896] 1 Ch 502.

Where proof of accounts to be given

35.7 In an action for an account, evidence may be called to demonstrate that the right to an account has arisen where the defendant has not in terms conceded it. The right is then a matter of evidence[1]. Convenience would normally, however, dictate that evidence as to the state of the accounts should not be allowed at such a hearing, because the account should be taken altogether in any subsequent proceedings[2].

The court may decide any question on the accounts at the further hearing, on the certificate and merits[3].

1 *Tomlin v Tomlin* (1841) 1 Hare 236 at 245. In a question as to accounts which had been kept by a creditor in the position of a trustee, but which were always open to the inspection of the debtor, the books were admitted as prima facie evidence of the amount of all moneys received and paid by the creditor, with liberty to surcharge and falsify: *Ogden v Battams* (1855) 1 Jur NS 791; and an account book of a deceased mortgagee, containing entries against interest, has been admitted as evidence on behalf of his executors: *Hudson and Humphrey v Owners of Swiftsure* (1900) 82 LT 389.

2 *Walker v Woodward* (1826) 1 Russ 107; *Law v Hunter* (1826) 1 Russ 100.

3 *Burne v Robinson* (1844) 1 Dr & Wal 688; *Skirrett v Athy* (1811) 1 Ball & B 433.

ACCOUNTS AGAINST THE MORTGAGOR

Mortgagee's right to an account

35.8 Whether the action is for foreclosure or redemption[1] the mortgagee is entitled to an immediate account[2] of his principal, interest, and costs, including:

(a) costs, charge, and expenses properly incurred in relation to the debt and security;
(b) the costs of litigation properly undertaken by the mortgagee; and
(c) the costs of the redemption or foreclosure proceedings[3].

The mortgagee is also entitled to have a day fixed for:

(a) payment or foreclosure; and
(b) all moneys for which the deed is expressly declared to be a security, or which carry interest, or are otherwise of the nature of principal as, for instance, fines secured to a building society, may be claimed as principal[4].

An assignee or subsequent incumbrancer of the equity of redemption stands in the position of the mortgagor as to accounts[5].

Foreclosure will not be ordered without such an account if the mortgagor insists on it, even where the mortgagee swears at the hearing that the money due to him is many times more than the value of the estate, but in that case the court will reserve the costs of the account[6].

1 *Du Vigier v Lee* (1843) 2 Hare 326; *Sober v Kemp* (1847) 6 Hare 155.
2 *Pearse v Hewitt* (1835) 7 Sim 471. The provisions as to the taking of accounts are set out at CPR 40PD-002. The account is taken by the master or district judge: CPR 40PD-010.
3 See *Re Wallis, ex p Lickorish* (1890) 25 QBD 176, CA; see Chapter 36.
4 *Blackford v Davis* (1869) 4 Ch App 304; *Provident Permanent Building Society v Greenhill* (1878) 9 Ch D 122. Where the mortgage is limited to a stated sum, this means that amount of principal, exclusive of interest and costs: *White v City of London Brewery Co* (1889) 42 Ch D 237, CA. A current account is not necessarily closed by the appointment of a receiver: *Yourell v Hibernian Bank Ltd* [1918] AC 372, HL. See *National Bank of Greece SA v Pinios Shipping* [1990] 1 AC 637, [1990] 1 All ER 78, HL.
5 *Melbourne Banking Corpn v Brougham* (1882) 7 App Cas 307, PC; *Mainland v Upjohn* (1889) 41 Ch D 126.
6 *Taylor v Mostyn* (1883) 25 Ch D 48.

Evidence of the debt

35.9 The production of the security is prima facie evidence of the existence of the debt[1] and if payment is acknowledged in the usual manner by the deed, and sworn to by the mortgagee, he need not prove the payment of the consideration money by other evidence, even against a purchaser of the estate, especially after some time has elapsed[2].

An account stated for the purposes of a security in respect of which the debtor is entitled to the protection of the court, such as a *post obit* security, is not conclusive against him[3], and where there is an uncertainty as to the amount of principal due, either because it is shown that the sum mentioned in the security was not advanced, but that only a running security was intended to be made[4], or by reason of the making of further advances[5], an inquiry may be directed to ascertain the amount lent under or on the credit of the mortgage security. If there is no evidence of the amount really lent, the mortgagor will be charged to the extent of his own admissions only[6].

1 *Piddock v Brown* (1734) 3 P Wms 288. The realisation of a surety's securities may be equivalent to a further advance to the principal debtor: *Re Smith, Lawrence v Kitson* [1918] 2 Ch 405.
2 *Goddard v Complin* (1669) 1 Cas in Ch 119; *Holt v Mill* (1692) 2 Vern 279; *Hampton v Spencer* (1693) 2 Vern 287.

3 *Tottenham v Green* (1863) 32 LJ Ch 201, and where there are manifest signs of fraud there must be proof of actual payment: *Piddock v Brown*, above. See as to proving consideration for a bond debt: *Whitaker v Wright* (1843) 2 Hare 310.
4 *Melland v Gray* (1843) 2 Y & C Ch Cas 199.
5 *Gordon v Graham* (1716) 2 Eq Cas Abr 598, 7 Vin Abr 52, pl 3.
6 *Melland v Gray*, above. Entries in the books of a deceased person, who was the solicitor of the mortgagor at the date of the mortgage, to the effect that he had received the money and had paid it over to the mortgagor, are admissible as evidence of payment of the mortgage money: *Clark v Wilmot* (1841) 1 Y & C Ch Cas 53; and see *Smart v Williams* (1694) Comb 247 (book of bursar of a college).

Where the debt is for costs

35.10 In the case of a mortgage given to a solicitor by his client to secure the amount of a bill of costs, the court will assume, after several years have elapsed, that the business charged for was actually done. However, the particular way in which the court considers such transactions will cause it to direct an inquiry as to the fairness of the charges, although at the time of executing the security the client had assented to the bill[1]. Where money has been lent by the solicitor to the client, the security is not conclusive proof of the actual advance and this must be proved by other evidence[2].

1 *Wragg v Denham* (1836) 2 Y & C Ex 117.
2 *Lewes v Morgan* (1829) 3 Y & J 394; *Lawless v Mansfield* (1841) 1 Dr & War 557; *Gresley v Moulsey* (1862) 3 De GF & J 433.

Payments on account of debt

35.11 The assignee of the security will be bound to allow payments made by the mortgagor to the original mortgagee after, but without notice of, the assignment[1], but payments of principal made to the mortgagee's solicitors, if the solicitors had no special authority to receive such payments, will not be allowed the mortgagor[2].

1 *Williams v Sorrell* (1799) 4 Ves 389; *Re Lord Southampton's Estate, Allen v Lord Southampton* (1880) 16 Ch D 178; *Bickerton v Walker* (1885) 31 Ch D 151 at 158; *Turner v Smith* [1901] 1 Ch 213; cf *Dixon v Winch* [1900] 1 Ch 736, where there was collusion, and that a mortgagor may be debarred from claiming credit in respect of moneys realised under an earlier mortgage which he has allowed to be outstanding, see *Re Ambrose's Estate* [1913] 1 IR 506; affd [1914] 1 IR 123.
2 *Withington v Tate* (1869) 4 Ch App 288.

Accounting for rents: legal mortgage

35.12 Subject to statutory restriction, a legal mortgagee is generally entitled to take possession immediately upon execution of the mortgage[1]. So long as he abstains from taking possession, neither the mortgagor, remaining in possession[2], nor his assignees in bankruptcy, nor a person holding under a mere voluntary trust for the mortgagor (and whose possession may therefore be considered to be that of the mortgagor[3]), is bound to account to the mortgagee for the rents[4].

As regards tenancies created before the mortgage or created by the mortgagor after the mortgage under an express or statutory power, the mortgagee, being entitled to the reversion, may require payment to himself of all arrears of rent existing when he goes into possession, whether falling due before or after the mortgage was granted[5]. A mortgagee is not bound by a collateral agreement between the mortgagor and a tenant under a lease created before 1 January 1996 and before the mortgage, but if he takes as mortgagee with knowledge that the land is used for a particular purpose, he cannot object to that user[6].

In the case of a lease made after the mortgage, the mortgagee can give notice to the tenant to pay the rent to him if the tenant has attorned to the mortgagee or the lease was made under the mortgagor's statutory power[7].

1 See Chapter 19.
2 *Higgins v York Buildings Co* (1740) 2 Atk 107; *Drummond v Duke of St Albans* (1800) 5 Ves 433; *Ex p Wilson* (1813) 2 Ves & B 252; *Ex p Calwell* (1828) 1 Mol 259.
3 *Hele v Lord Bexley* (1855) 20 Beav 127; *Flight v Camac* (1856) 4 WR 664.
4 This rule applies also to the owner of an estate in possession, keeping down the interest of charges on the estate, just as to an ordinary mortgagor: *Earl of Clarendon v Barham* (1842) 1 Y & C Ch Cas 688; see **35.60**, and the mortgagee of a rentcharge during the life of a tenant for life, who has not entered into possession, is not an assign of the mortgagor within the Apportionment Act and cannot have payment of the arrears of his rentcharge out of the apportioned part of the rents to the death of the tenant for life: *Re Marquis of Anglesey's Estate, Paget v Anglesey* (1874) LR 17 Eq 283; *Yorkshire Banking Co v Mullan* (1887) 35 Ch D 125. If, however, the mortgagee is dispossessed by the mortgagor's collusion with the tenants, and his persuasion to attorn to him, he ought to account for the rents upon coming to redeem: *Mead v Lord Orrery* (1745) 3 Atk 235; and see *Goodman v Kine* (1845) 8 Beav 379.
5 As to tenancies created before 1 January 1996 see the Law of Property Act 1925, s 141(3); *London and County (A&D) Ltd v Wilfred Sportsman Ltd* [1971] Ch 764; *Kataria v Safeland plc* [1998] 1 EGLR 39, CA. As to tenancies granted on or after 1 January 1996 see the Landlord and Tenant (Covenants) Act 1995, s 15(1). See **19.78** and **19.79**.
6 *Thomas v Jennings* (1896) 66 LJQB 5; *Moreland v Richardson* (1857) 24 Beav 33. In relation to tenancies granted on or after 1 January 1996, a mortgagee in possession is bound by a covenant that falls to be complied with by the landlord even if contained in a collateral agreement: Landlord and Tenant (Covenants) Act 1995 s 15(3).
7 Where attornment is required, this is not conclusively shown by the tenant merely continuing in possession after receipt of the notice: *Towerson v Jackson* [1891] 2 QB 484; diss from *Underhay v Read* (1887) 20 QBD 209, and *Brown v Storey* (1840) 1 Man & G 117, and the attornment of the tenant will not set up the mortgagee's title by relation to the time of the notice: *Evans v Elliott* (1838) 9 Ad & El 342; *Hickman v Machin* (1859) 4 H & N 716.

Accounting for rents: equitable mortgage

35.13 The right of an equitable mortgagee, who is not in possession, to rents does not arise until he is entitled to possession[1]. Often that will be upon an order for sale being made[2]. From the date of the application upon which an order for sale is made he is entitled to the rent[3], even though an inquiry as to the date of his security forms part of the order[4].

If, however, by any means the equitable mortgagee should get into lawful possession[5], he will be entitled, just as a legal mortgagee in the same circumstances, to the rents from the date of his possession[6], and to growing crops which he severs from the soil[7] and he will not be made to refund them upon the making of the order[8]. In the same way, if rent is paid to an equitable mortgagee by a tenant who is under no mistake of fact, but knows that the rent is claimed by a mere equitable mortgagee, the tenant cannot demand it back[9].

1 See **19.6**. An equitable mortgagee is not entitled to rents (which are payable to a legal reversioner), because such a mortgage creates no privity of estate between the mortgagee

and the tenant entitling the mortgagee to claim the rent. Accordingly an equitable mortgagee has no right to direct a tenant of the mortgagor to pay the rent to him.

In bankruptcy, where a legal mortgagee has not entered or given notice to the tenants, an order for sale is not treated as equivalent to notice and he takes the rents only from the sale: *Re Tombs, ex p Living* (1835) 1 Deac 1; *Re Medley, ex p Barnes* (1838) 3 Mont & A 497. Payments under licence to dig brick earth, held to belong to the mortgagee as rent in arrear: *Re Brindley, ex p Hankey* (1829) Mont & M 247.

2 Eg under the Law of Property Act 1925, s 91; see **21.5**.

3 *Re Norman, ex p Burrell* (1838) 3 Mont & A 439; *Re Birks, ex p Carlon* (1837) 3 Mont & A 328; *Re Pearson, ex p Scott* (1838) 3 Mont & A 592; *Re Postle, ex p Bignold* (1834) 2 Mont & A 16.

4 *Re Teesdale, ex p Thorpe* (1838) 3 Mont & A 441; *Re Harvey, ex p Bignold* (1827) 2 Gl & J 273; *Re Feaver, ex p Smith* (1844) 3 Mont D & De G 680.

5 If, for example, the mortgagee entitles him to possession.

6 *Re Postle, ex p Bignold* (1835) 4 Deac & Ch 259.

7 *Re Gordon, ex p Official Receiver* (1889) 61 LT 299.

8 *Re Freeman, ex p Williams* (1865) 13 WR 564.

9 *Finck v Tranter* [1905] 1 KB 427.

Growing crops

35.14 A mortgagee who has not taken possession is not entitled to growing crops which have been removed by the mortgagor between the time of demand and recovery of possession. A legal or equitable mortgagee has a right to all crops growing on the premises when he takes possession[1], unless the mortgagor can claim them as emblements under an express contract of tenancy[2] and the mortgagor and persons claiming under him will be restrained from removing the crops[3].

1 *Re Gordon*, above.

2 *Re Skinner, ex p Temple* (1822) 1 Gl & J 216; *Re Phillips, ex p National Mercantile Bank* (1880) 16 Ch D 104; *Official Trustee in Bankruptcy v Westpac Banking Corpn Ltd* (1987) 77 ALR 677.

3 *Bagnall v Villar* (1879) 12 Ch D 812.

Improvements

35.15 A mortgagor can have no allowance for money spent by him on the estate, all improvements enuring for the benefit of the mortgagee[1].

1 *Norris v Caledonian Insurance Co* (1869) LR 8 Eq 127.

Where receiver in possession

35.16 A receiver is entitled to rents in arrear at the time of his appointment[1], but if the mortgagor is in possession, he is liable to pay an occupation rent only from the date of the demand by the receiver[2].

If a mortgagee is restrained from taking possession, and a receiver is appointed adversely to him, the receiver will be charged an occupation rent on an undertaking to be answerable in damages[3]. Where a receiver is in possession in an action to which the mortgagee is not a party, a mortgagee out of possession will not be entitled to the rents paid by the tenants to the receiver even after notice given them by the mortgagee as it is necessary, first, to apply to the court to discharge the receiver[4].

From the time of the discharge of a receiver appointed in an action to which the mortgagee is not a party, or of the application for it, the mortgagee may be considered to be in possession and to be entitled to the rents[5].

1 See *Re Ind Coope & Co Ltd, Fisher v Ind Coope & Co* [1911] 2 Ch 223, but where the produce of crops was shipped to the consignees of the mortgagor, but was not converted prior to the appointment of a receiver on behalf of the mortgagee, the mortgagor was not obliged to give any account of it: *Codrington v Johnstone* (1838) 1 Beav 520.
2 *Yorkshire Banking co v Mullan* (1887) 35 Ch D 125.
3 *Re Joyce, ex p Warren* (1875) 10 Ch App 222.
4 See Chapter 18.
5 *Thomas v Brigstocke* (1827) 4 Russ 64. As to payments by a receiver to a first mortgagee in excess of the interest to which he is entitled, see *Law v Glenn* (1867) 2 Ch App 634. As to payment of rents to a mortgagee by sequestrators under a sequestration for contempt, see *Walker v Bell* (1816) 2 Madd 21, and cases cited there; *Tatham v Parker* (1855) 1 Jur NS 992; *Re Hoare, Hoare v Owen* [1892] 3 Ch 94.

ACCOUNTS AGAINST THE MORTGAGEE AND HIS ASSIGNS

Purchase of mortgage debt under par

35.17 When the amount of the debt owing on the mortgage has been established, the mortgagor cannot claim the benefit of a purchase of the security by a transferee for less than that amount. As a general rule, the bona fide purchaser of an incumbrance for less than is due upon it, or than it is worth, whether he is a creditor of the mortgagor[1], or a stranger[2], is entitled, both against the mortgagor or his representatives[3] and other incumbrancers[4], to be paid all that is due on the purchased security[5]; there is also no right against a bona fide purchaser for an account of what he has paid for his purchase. The rule depends upon the principle that the assignee stands in the place of his assignor and, as the assignor might have assigned to the assignee for no consideration, it is only just that the measure of the allowance should be what was due and not what was paid. The assignee taking the risk should also have the benefit of the bargain, neither the mortgagor, nor any subsequent incumbrancer having any equity to deprive him[6].

The rule is, however, different if the purchaser of the incumbrance is a person in whom the estate charged with the incumbrance has become vested subject also to other liabilities of the former owner, as (formerly) the heir-at-law, or executor of the owner[7], or if he is a person standing in any confidential relation with the mortgagor, by reason of which his interest and his duty are in conflict, for example as guardian[8], trustee[9], counsel[10], or agent[11]. Similarly, if a tenant for life bought a mortgage on the inheritance for less than is due, he does so for the benefit of the estate[12] and a surety of the mortgagor liable upon a contract of indemnity is under an obligation, if he can make terms with the creditor, to treat the settlement as a payment of the debt and to give his principal the benefit of the arrangement[13]. In each case, no more will be allowed in account than they have paid for the incumbrance[14], with interest at the legal or current rate, if that is less than the interest reserved[15].

Even if the fiduciary relation has ceased, a former trustee will be allowed no more than he has paid, unless he has entered into a fair contract with the persons interested or can show that there was no fraud or concealment, or that he has not taken any advantage of information acquired in the character of trustee[16].

1 *Morret v Paske* (1740) 2 Atk 52; *Darcy v Hall* (1682) 1 Vern 49.
2 *Davis v Barrett* (1851) 14 Beav 542; *Anon* (1707) 1 Salk 155.
3 *Phillips v Vaughan* (1685) 1 Vern 336; *Ascough v Johnson* (1688) 2 Vern 66.
4 *Morret v Paske*, above.
5 So, if the reversioner in fee, not being the original mortgagor of an estate which is subject to several charges, purchases the first for less than is due upon it, he may hold it for all that is due, and the later incumbrancers will have no account against him, nor any equity to make the purchased security stand only for the price which he paid for it: *Davis v Barrett*, above.
6 *Anon* (1707) 1 Salk 155; and see *Dobson v Land* (1851) 4 De G & Sm 575.
7 *Braithwaite v Braithwaite* (1685) 1 Vern 334; *Morret v Paske*, above. There was formerly an exception when the purchaser had bought to protect the inheritance to which he was himself entitled: *Darcy v Hall*, above.
8 *Powell v Glover* (1721) 3 P Wms 251n.
9 *Morret v Paske*, above; see also *Baskett v Cafe* (1851) 4 De G & Sm 388.
10 *Carter v Palmer* (1842) 8 Cl & Fin 657, HL.
11 *Hobday v Peters* (1860) 28 Beav 349; *Morret v Paske*, above.
12 See *Hill v Browne* (1844) Drury temp Sug 426.
13 *Reed v Norris* (1837) 2 My & Cr 361.
14 But though the purchase is made by a person, who, under ordinary circumstances, would be allowed no more than he paid yet, if it was made under the advice of a later incumbrancer, who did not disclose the fact that he, and not the purchaser, would reap the benefit of it, the full sum due will be allowed to the assignee: *Bayly v Wilkins* (1846) 3 Jo & Lat 630.
15 *Carter v Palmer*, above. The rule did not, however, extend to a tenant in common, as there was no fiduciary relation between him and his co-tenants: *Kennedy v De Trafford* [1896] 1 Ch 762.
16 *Carter v Palmer*, above; *Ex p James* (1803) 8 Ves 337; *Coles v Trecothick* (1804) 9 Ves 234 at 247. A mortgagee, after payment of his mortgage debt, has been said (*Baldwin v Banister* (1718) 3 P Wms 251n; but see *Dobson v Land*, above) to be a trustee within the rule, but he hardly seems to be within the principle; unless, perhaps, he is a mortgagee in possession, holding over after payment. From the record of *Baldwin v Banister*, Reg Lib A 1717, 609, it would seem that the point did not arise.

Transferee takes subject to state of accounts

35.18 The transferee of the mortgage is bound by the state of accounts between the mortgagor and mortgagee[1]. Therefore, even though the transferee may not have had notice, by indorsements on the deeds or otherwise, that part of the debt has been discharged, he cannot claim under his assignment any more than is really due as between the mortgagor and the mortgagee[2], without reference to what was paid on the assignment[3] and is subject to have the whole account taken[4].

The mortgagee who transfers his mortgage does not get rid of his liability to future accounts by virtue of the assignment, but may be decreed to account, both before[5] and after the assignment[6], the reason for this being that the mortgagee must be responsible for the person to whom he assigns the mortgagor's estate, but he is not answerable if he assigns by the direction of the court[7].

1 See **35.1**.
2 *Porter v Hubbart* (1673) 3 Rep Ch 78; *Matthews v Wallwyn* (1798) 4 Ves 118; *Chambers v Goldwin* (1804) 9 Ves 254; *Mangles v Dixon* (1852) 3 HL Cas 702; *Elders Rural Finance Ltd v Westpac Banking Corpn* (1988) 4 BPR 9383.

The transferee of a mortgage will not be bound by a statement in the deed as to the amount due on the security, notwithstanding a special receipt clause to the effect that part of the sum is for costs, the amount of which is to be afterwards adjusted: *Re Forsyth* (1865) 11 Jur NS 213; on appeal (1865) 11 Jur NS 615.
3 *Turner v Smith* [1901] 1 Ch 213; *De Lisle v Union Bank of Scotland* [1914] 1 Ch 22, CA. It is assumed that the mortgagor was not a party to the assignment. If he were a witness,

it should be pleaded that he knew and agreed to the contents of the deed: *Jamieson v English* (1820) 2 Mol 337.

4 It seems that if redemption is sought after a great length of time, or after the dismissal of a former action to redeem, or several assignments, the account will be taken against an assignee in possession only from the time of his purchase; prior to which the profits will be set against the interest: *Pearson v Pulley* (1668) 1 Cas in Ch 102.

5 Notwithstanding the mortgagee has been in possession and has accounted with the assignee: *Venables v Foyle* (1661) 1 Cas in Ch 2.

6 *Venables v Foyle*, above; 1 Eq Ca Ab 328, pl 2; *Hall v Heward* (1886) 32 Ch D 430, CA.

7 *Hall v Heward*, above.

Accounting for proceeds of sale[1]

35.19 On a sale of the mortgaged property by the mortgagee under his power of sale, the mortgagor (and a second[2] and subsequent mortgagee, at least if there is a surplus[3]), is entitled to an account of the proceeds[4].

If, in addition to the mortgage debt, there is another account between mortgagor and mortgagee, the mortgagee will be treated as having received the money on the mortgage account and not on the other account, provided this is in accordance with the nature of the transaction[5].

If the mortgagor sells, and the mortgagee adopts the contract, the mortgagee as between himself and the purchaser stands in the mortgagor's place and must bear the loss occasioned by the insolvency of a person to whom the deposit has been paid[6]. As between the mortgagee and the mortgagor, however, if the mortgagee has consented to the sale upon the terms that he shall be paid out of the purchase money, his execution of the conveyance and signature of the receipt will discharge the purchaser but will not discharge the mortgagor if the money is misappropriated by his agent without the mortgagee's default, though the agent may have also acted for the mortgagee[7].

1 A party cannot, as it were, have little bits of accounts. There is one account and one account only and the issue is what is owed and what is not owed. The declaratory procedure cannot be used to get declarations about little bits of accounts, because the proceedings may become, in relation to a total account, otiose: *Colin D Young Pty Ltd v Commercial and General Acceptance Ltd* (24 August 1982, unreported), NSWCA (but see (1982) NSW Conv R 55–097), referred to in *Adams v Bank of New South Wales* [1984] NSWLR 285, NSWCA. *Project Research Pty Ltd v Permanent Trustee of Australia Ltd* (1990) 5 BPR 11; *Estoril Investments Pty Ltd v Westpac Banking Corpn* (1983) ACL Rep 295 NSW 24.

2 *Adams v Bank of New South Wales*, above.

3 On the basis of there being a trust of the purchase money: see **20.45** ff.

4 The account between the mortgagor and the first mortgagee does not create an estoppel between the first mortgagee and a second mortgagee: *Weld-Blundell v Synott* [1940] 2 KB 107, [1940] 2 All ER 580.

5 *Young v English* (1843) 7 Beav 10; *Johnson v Bourne* (1843) 2 Y & C Ch Cas 268.

6 *Rowe v May* (1854) 18 Beav 613.

7 *Barrow v White* (1862) 2 John & H 580.

Over-payments of interest

35.20 Where interest on the mortgage has been paid in excess of what was due, the over-payments will be treated as payments on account of principal[1].

1 *Re Carroll's Estate* [1901] 1 IR 78, but it is otherwise where interest has been paid on money which is afterwards found not to be included in the mortgage, and this will not be taken to have been paid on account of the principal: *Blandy v Kimber (No 2)* (1858) 25 Beav 537.

Sale by mortgagee of shares

35.21 Mortgagees of stocks or shares, who sell the securities in their hands, may apparently (contrary to the general rule) purchase themselves, but they must take them at the market price of the day and cannot credit the debtor with less than that price, on the speculation that if the securities had come together into the market, the price would have fallen[1].

1 *Stubbs v Lister* (1841) 1 Y & C Ch Cas 81.

ACCOUNTS AGAINST THE MORTGAGEE IN POSSESSION

Accounts extend to wilful default[1]

35.22 The mortgagee's duties[2] are rendered onerous by the fact that he is liable on the footing of 'wilful default'[3]. The account usually directed against the mortgagee in possession, either of tangible property or of a business[4] is, therefore, an account of what he has or without wilful default might have received from the time of his taking possession. This will include the receipts of any person whom the mortgagee has put into possession without a just title and in derogation of the rights of the mortgagor[5].

If the mortgagee in possession has sold the property, the account will extend to the proceeds of sale received by him, or which without wilful default he might have received; but (if no special case is made[6]) there will not be an inquiry into the propriety of the sale or the adequacy of the price[7].

1 For the liability of the mortgagee in possession to account, see **19.64**. Where a mortgagee has been in possession, in any settlement of accounts between the mortgagee and mortgagor, tax payable on interest due is allowed as money received on account of interest: see *Hollis v Wingfield* [1940] Ch 336, [1940] 1 All ER 531, CA. And see [1979] Conv 345 (Stannard).

2 The mortgagee's duties are duties in equity: *Medforth v Blake* [2000] Ch 86; *Yorkshire Bank v Hall* [1999] 1 All ER 879, [1999] 1 WLR 1713. As such, any action for breach is not an action on a specialty and is not subject to the 12 year limitation period under s 8(2) of the Limitation Act 1980: *Raja v Lloyds TSB Bank Ltd* [2001] EWCA Civ, 210, 82 P & CR 191, CA.

3 *Downsview Nominees Ltd v First Corpn Ltd* [1993] AC 295 at 315, per Lord Templeman. See *Lord Trimleston v Hamill* (1810) 1 Ball & B 377 at 385; *Sloane v Mahon* (1838) 1 Dr & Wal 189 at 192, 195; *Mobil Oil Co Ltd v Rawlinson* (1982) 43 P & CR 221 at 224; *Medforth v Blake* [2000] Ch 86 at 99B. The handling of rents and profits by a receiver is not subject to the same rigorous surveillance of equity as that by a mortgagee in possession: *Refuge Assurance Co Ltd v Pearlberg* [1938] Ch 687 at 691-692; *Yorkshire Bank plc v Hall* [1999] 1 WLR 1713 at 1728, per Robert Walker LJ.

4 *Williams v Price* (1824) 1 Sim & St 581; see *Chaplin v Young* (1864) 33 Beav 330. As to his position, if he becomes a partner in the business, see *Rowe v Wood* (1822) 2 Jac & W 553 at 556, 558. As to receipt of rents by mistake, see *Forster v Forster* [1918] 1 IR 95.

5 *National Bank of Australasia v United Hand-in-Hand Band of Hope, Co* (1879) 4 App Cas 391.

6 See **20.22** ff.

7 *Mayer v Murray* (1878) 8 Ch D 424; *Farrar v Farrars Ltd* (1888) 40 Ch D 395; *Meredith v Davis* (1933) 33 SRNSW 334. It has been said that the case of an account against a mortgagee is the only instance in which the court directs an account on the footing of wilful default without any special case made for the purpose: *Lord Kensington v Bouverie* (1855) 7 De GM & G 134 at 156; although a purchaser, whose purchase has been set aside and ordered to stand as a security, is within the rule: *Adams v Sworder* (1864) 2 De GJ & Sm 44.

As to how possession is obtained, see Chapter 19.

Possession must be as mortgagee

35.23 A mortgagee who is in possession of the mortgaged property will not be liable to account as mortgagee in possession unless he entered as mortgagee. The court will not treat possession as being held by the mortgagee as such unless it is satisfied that he took possession in his capacity of mortgagee, without reasonable ground for believing himself to hold in any other capacity[1]. The following have, for example, been held not to be in possession as mortgagee in possession:

(a) a person who, having a lien on property, takes possession thinking himself to be purchaser[2];
(b) a mortgagee who has possession as tenant[3];
(c) a person who entered possession under a forfeiture, and not as mortgagee, where his possession was acquiesced in[4];
(d) a mortgagee who lawfully uses the property for purposes unconnected with the mortgage[5];
(e) the assignee of a tenant for life during the life estate[6].

1 *Gaskell v Gosling* [1896] 1 QB 669 at 691.
2 *Parkinson v Hanbury* (1867) LR 2 HL 1.
3 *Page v Linwood* (1837) 4 Cl & Fin 399.
4 *Blennerhassett v Day* (1812) 2 Ball & B 104 at 125.
5 *Re Colnbrook Chemical and Explosives Co, A-G v Colnbrook Chemical and Explosives Co* [1923] 2 Ch 289. Where the creditor entered as receiver under a power of attorney and afterwards becomes mortgagee, he was still treated for the purpose of accounting as receiver: *Lord Trimleston v Hamill* (1810) 1 Ball & B 377.
6 *Whitbread v Smith* (1854) 3 De GM & G 727 at 741; *Lord Kensington v Bouverie* (1855) 7 De GM & G 134 at 156.

Attornment by mortgagor

35.24 It has been said that the attornment of the mortgagor, if in actual occupation, as tenant to the mortgagee (although only by virtue of an attornment clause in the mortgage deed) makes the mortgagee liable as mortgagee in possession to subsequent incumbrancers[1], but that view has not been accepted[2] and the ordinary relation of mortgagor and mortgagee continues[3]. In any case, the mortgagee is not liable on this ground to account as mortgagee in possession to the mortgagor[4].

1 *Re Stockton Iron Furnace Co* (1879) 10 Ch D 335 at 357, and see *Re Kitchin, ex p Punnett* (1880) 16 Ch D 226; *Re Betts, ex p Harrison* (1881) 18 Ch D 127; *Green v Marsh* [1892] 2 QB 330 at 336.
2 *Stanley v Grundy* (1883) 22 Ch D 478.
3 *Re Knight, ex p Isherwood* (1882) 22 Ch D 384 at 392.
4 *Re Betts, ex p Harrison*, above.

Inquiry as to possession

35.25 In case of doubt the court will grant an inquiry as to the fact of possession. The inquiry will be as to whether the mortgagee has been in possession of the rents and profits as mortgagee. If he has, the account is directed to be taken against him as mortgagee in possession, including wilful default[1].

Admission of possession, though contrary to the fact, has been held to make the mortgagee liable to account on that footing[2].

1 *Dobson v Lee* (1842) 1 Y & C Ch Cas 714. No special direction as to wilful default is necessary.
2 *Parker v Watkins* (1859) John 133. As to the liability of the guardian of an infant who takes an assignment of a mortgage on the infant's estate, see *Bishop v Sharp* (1704) 2 Vern 469; but the infant's estate would now be vested in trustees.

Account of rents and profits

35.26 The mortgagee who takes possession of the mortgaged estate is required to be diligent in realising the amount due on the mortgage so that the estate may be redelivered to the mortgagor[1]. He is liable to account for the rents and other profits during his possession[2] and if he remains in occupation himself he is liable to pay an occupation rent. If the mortgagee does not remain in possession himself, the mortgagee cannot simply leave the property empty, perhaps waiting for an improvement in the market, but must let the property at a 'proper market rent'[3], unless a letting might hinder or interfere with an intended sale of the property[4].

The mortgagee's liability to account extends in favour of all those who are interested in the equity of redemption, including second and later mortgagees and any guarantor or surety of the mortgage loan[5] and the mortgagee cannot by any dealing with the estate discharge himself of this liability[6]. After receiving notice of a later mortgage, the mortgagee in possession becomes liable to account to the subsequent mortgagee for so much of the surplus rent as he has paid to the mortgagor or his representatives, but so long as the mortgagee in possession was without notice, the subsequent mortgagee cannot call upon him or the mortgagor for an account of the historic rents[7].

1 *Lord Kensington v Bouverie* (1855) 7 De GM & G 134 at 157; see *Langton v Waite* (1869) 4 Ch App 402. As to the different nature of the possession of a person who holds under a receivership deed, see *Lord Kensington v Bouverie*, above.
2 See *Gould v Tancred* (1742) 2 Atk 533, and he is bound, if required by a request for further information in a redemption action, to set out in his answer such particulars as will sufficiently show the state of the account, what is due to him, and what securities he holds for the debt: *Elmer v Creasy* (1873) 9 Ch App 69; *West of England and South Wales, Bank v Nickolls* (1877) 6 Ch D 613.

In taking the account the Limitation Act is no bar where the relation of mortgagor and mortgagee is subsisting, because the mortgagor having a right to get back the value of his property, every time must be brought into account: *Hood v Easton* (1856) 2 Giff 692; on appeal, (1856) 2 Jur NS 917, but where the mortgagee is claiming under a tenant for life and is called to account after his death by the remainderman, there being no fiduciary relation, the account will only be carried back through the six years limited by the statute: *Hickman v Upsall* (1876) 4 Ch D 144, and see *Forster v Forster* [1918] 1 IR 95.
3 *Palk v Mortgage Services Funding plc* [1993] Ch 330 at 338, per Nicholls V-C.
4 *Downsview Nominees Ltd v First City Corpn Ltd* [1993] AC 295.
5 *Tomlin v Luce* (1889) 41 Ch D 573 at 575-576; on appeal (1889) 43 Ch D 191 at 194, per Cotton LJ; *Cuckmere Brick Co Ltd v Mutual Finance Ltd* [1971] Ch 949 at 966, per Salmon LJ; *National Westminster Finance New Zealand Ltd v United Finance & Securities Ltd* [1988] 1 NZLR 226 at 234; *China and South Sea Bank Ltd v Tan Soon Gin* [1990] 1 AC 536 at 544, per Lord Templeman. Cf, *Parker-Tweedale v Dunbar Bank Plc* [1991] Ch 12.
6 *Hinde v Blake* (1841) 11 LJ Ch 26.
7 *Maddocks v Wren* (1680) 2 Rep Ch 209; *Berney v Sewell* (1820) 1 Jac & W 647; *Parker v Calcraft* (1821) 6 Madd 11; *Archdeacon v Bowes* (1824) 13 Price 353 at 368; *Holton v Lloyd* (1827) 1 Mol 30. After redemption, where the mortgagee has died, a claim in respect of profits during his possession should not be made in a creditor's action, but by proceedings to correct the redemption judgment: *Shoobridge v Woods* (1843) 8 Jur 27.

Equitable possession

35.27 A subsequent mortgagee's action to enforce his claim (the prior mortgagee being made a party), amounts to an equitable possession of the rents and binds the surplus rents in the hands of the prior mortgagee until the dismissal of the action, even though it is not prosecuted[1]. The mortgagee must account for whatever he may receive after the order to account[2] despite the fact that the practice is to direct the account without future words.

It is said that the mortgagee is not bound to account to a subsequent mortgagee for the profits received after foreclosure, although he had notice of the claim before judgment[3].

1 *Parker v Calcraft* (1821) 6 Madd 11.
2 *Bulstrode v Bradley* (1747) 3 Atk 582.
3 *Bird v Gandy* (1715) 7 Vin Abr 45 pl 20. A judgment creditor can obtain a charge on the property giving him a right to a sale (see **2.12**), but according to the former practice—which, it may be presumed, continues—he must submit to account as a mortgagee in possession, as the price of the relief sought: *Bull v Faulkner* (1847) 1 De G & Sm 685; see *O'Brien v Mahon* (1842) 2 Dr & War 306; but he will not be liable to this form of account unless he has actually obtained possession under his claim to the exclusion of the mortgagor: *Kingston v Cowbridge Rly Co* (1871) 41 LJ Ch 152; see *Hele v Lord Bexley* (1853) 17 Beav 14.

Amount of rents to be accounted for

35.28 Where a mortgagee enters into receipt of rents he accounts at the rate of the rent reserved[1]. Where he enters into actual possession, it has been said that he will be charged with the utmost value the lands are proved to be worth[2]. The mortgagee's liability is limited by the circumstances of the case and he will not usually be required to account for more than he has received, unless it is proved that, but for his gross default, mismanagement, or fraud, he might have received more[3].

1 *Lord Trimleston v Hamill* (1810) 1 Ball & B 377 at 385; *Metcalf v Campion* (1828) 1 Mol 238.
2 *Lord Trimleston v Hamill*, above.
3 *Hughes v Williams* (1806) 12 Ves 493; *Wragg v Denham* (1836) 2 Y & C Ex 117. If there is included in a lease by the mortgagee land not mortgaged to him, but to another who concurred in the lease, there will be an apportionment: *Harryman v Collins* (1854) 18 Beav 11. See **19.65** ff.

Occupation rent

35.29 If the mortgagee has been in actual occupation of the whole or some part of the property, he may be charged an occupation rent, but his occupation must be stated in the statements of case[1]. An inquiry as to the fact of occupation may be directed, if it is not admitted, and any necessary directions will be given for ascertaining the amount of rent to be fixed. No rent will be charged if the property has no rental value or during such time as the property was incapable of making any return[2] because of its dilapidated state or otherwise.

1 *Trulock v Robey* (1846) 15 Sim 265; *Shepard v Jones* (1882) 21 Ch D 469, CA. See *Fee v Cobine* (1847) 11 I Eq R 406.
2 *Fyfe v Smith* [1975] 2 NSWLR 408. If the mortgagee has expended money in permanent improvements, these will not increase the occupation rent, unless the expenditure is allowed

him in his accounts: *Bright v Campbell* (1885) 54 LJ Ch 1077; see **19.75**; *Marshall v Cave* (1824) 3 LJOS Ch 57.

If the mortgagee has sold the estate, the admission of the purchaser into possession before the stipulated time will not make the mortgagee liable for occupation rent, though he may have admitted him upon terms which raise a claim for wilful default; *Shepard v Jones*, above.

Where a lease by the mortgagor to the mortgagee has been set aside, the mortgagee will be charged with the rent reserved by the lease if a fair one: see *Gubbins v Creed* (1804) 2 Sch & Lef 214; *Webb v Rorke* (1806) 2 Sch & Lef 661.

Where rents collected by agent

35.30 Where the mortgagee employs an agent to collect the rents[1], he must account for all the rents received by that agent and not merely for what the agent has paid to him. The death of the agent and consequent difficulty of proving what the agent received is no answer[2].

1 Unless collected by the mortgagor as the mortgagee's agent: *Dallimore v Oriental Bank Corpn* (1875) 1 VLR (Eq) 13.
2 *Noyes v Pollock* (1885) 30 Ch D 336.

Accounts of mines

35.31 The mortgagee in possession who without special authority opens mines or quarries will be charged with his receipts, but will not be allowed the costs of severing the produce or other expenses. The mortgagee has no right to speculate at the mortgagor's expense and the act is a sale of part of the inheritance[1]. A mortgagee with an insufficient security may, however, open new mines, or may lease or work abandoned mines, and will be only liable to account for the profits or royalty and not for the value of the ore raised or the damage caused to the surface[2].

If the mortgagee is specially authorised to work the mines, he will be allowed the expenses incurred in doing so, with interest[3].

If the mortgagee comes into possession of open mines, he cannot be called upon to speculate by working them, however likely it may be that the mines will be improved by a large expenditure[4]. He is not bound to advance more than a prudent owner and cannot be charged with mismanagement if he omits to do so. By way of contrast, a mortgage of a colliery was prima facie a mortgage of it as a going concern and passed the right to work the mines[5].

1 *Hughes v Williams* (1806) 12 Ves 493; *Thorneycroft v Crockett* (1848) 16 Sim 445. See *Taylor v Mostyn* (1886) 33 Ch D 226; and *Hood v Easton* (1856) 2 Giff 692, where a mortgagee, without authority to work mines, authorised strangers to work them; doubted on appeal, (1856) 2 Jur NS 917. As to inquiries with respect to the working of mines, see *Mulhallen v Marum* (1843) 3 Dr & War 317; *Thorneycroft v Crockett*, above.
2 *Millett v Davey* (1862) 31 Beav 470.
3 *Norton v Cooper* (1854) 25 LJ Ch 121.
4 *Rowe v Wood* (1820) 2 Jac & W 553.
5 *Gloucester County Bank v Rudry Merthyr Steam and House Coal, Colliery Co* [1895] 1 Ch 629, distinguishing *Whitley v Challis* [1892] 1 Ch 64. As to where the mortgagee is also a lessee of the mines with certain restrictions on working pillars, see *Taylor v Mostyn*, above, and where there is a mortgage of a business as a going concern, the mortgagee in possession is entitled to be recouped losses (not attributable to negligence) out of the proceeds of the sale of the estate: see *Bompas v King* (1886) 33 Ch D 279 (a block of residential flats).

Repairs and improvements, etc

35.32 For allowances to the mortgagee for certain repairs and permanent improvements, etc, see **19.74** and **19.75**.

TAKING ACCOUNTS WITH RESTS

Form of accounts

35.33 The usual mode of taking accounts against the mortgagee in possession is to set out the total amount of rents and profits received by, or found to be chargeable to him, against the whole amount due upon the mortgage debt and to apply them in discharge successively of the interest of the mortgage debt, and of money advanced for costs and improvements, and then of the principal[1]. This is only done, however, in arriving at the final result, when the account could, if necessary, be shown as a complete debtor and creditor account. In practice, the account is taken in a series of separate accounts:

(a) an account of principal, interest and costs;
(b) an account of moneys expended by the mortgagee in repairs and permanent improvements, with interest from the date of expenditure; and
(c) an account of rents and profits.

The balance is arrived at by adding the result of accounts (a) and (b), and subtracting what the mortgagee has to account for under (c)[2]. If, during the currency of the account, a part of the mortgaged property is sold, the net proceeds are credited to the mortgagor in account (a), first in payment of interest due, and then in reduction of principal, and the interest is correspondingly reduced; but account (b) is not further affected[3].

The result of taking this continuous account is that if the rents and profits exceed the interest, the mortgagee benefits. The mortgagee does not apply the excess in reduction of principal, with consequent reduction of subsequent interest, but keeps it in hand paying no interest on it, while interest is running all the time on the undiminished principal. If, however, the rents and profits are less than the interest, the mortgagor benefits, as the deficiency is a further debt due from him, but it does not carry interest[4].

1 *Webb v Rorke* (1806) 2 Sch & Lef 661; *Union Bank of London v Ingram* (1880) 16 Ch D 53.
2 See *Thorneycroft v Crockett* (1848) 2 HL Cas 239; *Wrigley v Gill* [1905] 1 Ch 241 at 253; affd [1906] 1 Ch 165, CA. Account (3) includes all sums which the mortgagee has received—or, in a case of wilful default, is treated as having received (see **35.26**)—by virtue of the mortgage, whether rents and profits or accidental payments, such as fines: see *Thompson v Hudson* (1870) LR 10 Eq 497 at 498; *Union Bank of London v Ingram*, above; *Cockburn v Edwards* (1881) 18 Ch D 449 at 456, CA.
3 *Wrigley v Gill*, above; *Ainsworth v Wilding* [1905] 1 Ch 435; cf *Thompson v Hudson*, above.
4 See *Union Bank of London v Ingram*, above.

Accounts with rests

35.34 Where the receipts of the mortgagee are more than sufficient to cover the interest a different method may be adopted, known as taking the account with rests. A balance in the account is struck at stated intervals[1] and the surplus to the credit of the mortgagor is applied in reduction of principal[2].

1 See *Montreal Trust Co v Hounslow Holdings Ltd* (1972) 22 DLR (3d) 503.
2 See *Thorneycroft v Crockett*, above. It has been said that this method applies only in the case of real estate: *Robinson v Cumming* (1742) 2 Atk 409; but there appears to be no reason for so restricting it. Under an account with rests an occupation rent for which the mortgagee is liable must be brought in: *Donovan v Fricker* (1812) Jac 165; *Wilson v Metcalfe* (1826) 1 Russ 530; but not a rent payable by the mortgagee when he is in occupation as tenant, and not as mortgagee in possession: *Page v Linwood* (1837) 4 Cl & Fin 399. See **35.29**.

When accounts taken with rests

35.35 It is not a matter of course for rests to be made against a mortgagee in possession[1]. The order must expressly direct that the accounts shall be taken with rests[2] and special circumstances justifying the direction must be alleged and proved[3].

The reason why rests are not the normal method of taking the accounts is said to be that the mortgagee is not bound to accept payment by 'driblets', but is entitled to have the account taken as whole and is entitled not to be treated as repaid until that account has been taken[4]. As a result, to direct the account to be with rests penalises the mortgagee[5] and will not generally be directed unless the mortgagee went into possession where there were no arrears of interest due, or no material arrears of interest due, or the annual rents greatly exceed the interest[6]. Rests will also be directed where the mortgagee denies that he took possession as mortgagee and sets up an adverse title[7].

The fact that arrears of interest are or are not due at the time of taking possession is not, however, altogether decisive upon the question of rests and the circumstances of the particular case will be considered.

Consequently, rests will not be directed against the mortgagee, even though he would otherwise fall within the general rule[8]:

(a) if the mortgagee has been driven by the acts of others to take possession; or
(b) has been harassed by litigation and put to consequential cost (even though the costs have afterwards been ordered to be paid to him by his opponent) and the mortgagee's own conduct has been free from harshness or vexation; or
(c) in the case of leaseholds, where the security is endangered by non-payment of ground-rent or insurance or through want of repairs.

1 *Gould v Tancred* (1742) 2 Atk 533; *Davis v May* (1815) 19 Ves 383; *Donovan v Fricker* (1821) Jac 165; *Scholefield v Ingham* (1838) Coop Pr Cas 477; see *Wrigley v Gill*, above.
2 *Fowler v Wightwick* (1810) 1 Madd 14; *Webber v Hunt* (1815) 1 Madd 13; *Wrigley v Gill*, above. Any special matter affecting the accounts must be brought forward at the trial and dealt with in the judgment: *Sanguinetti v Stuckey's Banking Co (No 2)* [1896] 1 Ch 502, CA; and see *Taylor v Mostyn* (1886) 33 Ch D 226, CA.
3 Traditionally, the special case for rests must be made on the pleadings where the action is by writ: *Neesom v Clarkson* (1845) 4 Hare 97; see *Blackford v Davis* (1869) 4 Ch App 304 at 308; otherwise, it must appear on the claim form or the mortgagor's affidavit.
4 *Nelson v Booth* (1858) 3 De G & J 119 at 122; *Wrigley v Gill* [1905] 1 Ch 241 at 254, but this is not a sufficient ground for adopting an unnatural mode of taking the account. That mode is a tradition which the court in England had not yet had the courage to abandon. It is otherwise in Ireland, where rests are made half-yearly without special direction; but not at intermediate periods: *Graham v Walker* (1847) 11 I Eq R 415.

5 See *Wrigley v Gill* [1905] 1 Ch 241 at 254.

6 *Uttermare v Stevens* (1851) 17 LTOS 115. That rests will usually be directed if interest was not in arrear, see also *Shepard v Elliot* (1819) 4 Madd 254; *Nelson v Booth* (1858) 3 De G & J 119; but not where it was in arrear: *Stephens v Wellings* (1835) 4 LJ Ch 281; *Finch v Brown* (1840) 3 Beav 70; *Wilson v Cluer* (1840) 3 Beav 136. Where interest was to be paid half-yearly, and there was a half-year's interest due when the mortgagee entered, this was sufficient to save him from annual rests: *Moore v Painter* (1842) 6 Jur 903. Where the mortgagee takes possession after bills have been indorsed to him for the arrears of interest, and the bills become due and are dishonoured after possession taken, the interest is considered to be in arrear at the time of taking possession, and no rests will be made: *Dobson v Land* (1851) 4 De G & Sm 575. That a great excess of rents over interest will make the mortgagee liable to rests, see also *Thorneycroft v Crockett* (1848) 2 HL Cas 239; *Carter v James* (1881) 29 WR 437, but rests will not be directed on the ground of a slight excess: *Gould v Tancred*, above, see *Baldwin v Lewis* (1835) 4 LJ Ch 113; *Nelson v Booth*, above.

7 *Incorporated Society in Dublin v Richards* (1841) 1 Dr & War 258 at 290, 334; *Montgomery v Calland* (1844) 14 Sim 79; *National Bank of Australasia v United Hand-in-Hand Band of Hope Co* (1879) 4 App Cas 391 at 409, PC; *Wrigley v Gill* [1905] 1 Ch 241 at 254; see *Douglas v Culverwell* (1862) 4 De GF & J 20 (sale treated as mortgage).

8 *Horlock v Smith* (1844) 1 Coll 287; *Patch v Wild* (1861) 30 Beav 99; and see *Nelson v Booth*, above.

Circumstances subsequent to taking possession

35.36 The circumstances when the mortgagee took possession usually determine his liability to rests. If interest was in arrear and rests were not directed, he will not, without special reason, become liable to rests after the arrear has been paid off[1]. If, however, after the mortgagee has taken possession, there is a settled account by which it appears that either no interest is due or that any interest due has been satisfied as interest by being turned into principal, and the mortgagee continues in receipt of rents more than sufficient to satisfy the interest of such principal, the settlement is considered as a rest made by the parties. From that point, the mortgagee will be treated as a mortgagee who takes possession with no interest in arrear and will be subject to annual rests[2].

1 *Finch v Brown*, above; see *Davis v May*, above; *Latter v Dashwood* (1834) 6 Sim 462; *Scholefield v Lockwood (No 3)* (1863) 32 Beav 439.

2 *Wilson v Cluer* (1840) 3 Beav 136. If rests have been directed in a redemption action which is abandoned, they will also be directed in a foreclosure action afterwards commenced by the mortgagee, though no case for them is then made: *Morris v Islip* (1855) 20 Beav 654.

Intervals of rests

35.37 The order for accounts with rests usually directs that the rests shall be made at stated intervals: half-yearly or yearly. As long as principal remains due, the excess of rents and profits over interest and expenses at each interval is struck off the principal and the account is then carried on upon the footing of the reduced principal[1].

An alternative method is to direct that rests shall be made from time to time whenever the mortgagee has an excess of rents and profits over interest in his hands. If this is combined with a direction for annual rests, a rest should be made at the date when the mortgagee has this excess in his hands, although in the interval between the annual rests, and from this date the subsequent annual rests will be computed[2].

1 This is the effect of an order substantially in the form in *Yates v Hambly* (1742) 2 Atk 360 at 362: 'Take an account of what shall be coming due on account of rents and profits, to be applied in the first place in payment of interest and principal, and make annual rests: and in taking such account make all just allowances': cited in *Webber v Hunt* (1815) 1 Madd 13 at 14; see *Wilson v Cluer*, above; *Thorneycroft v Crockett* (1848) 2 HL Cas 239 at 256.

2 *Binnington v Harwood* (1825) Turn & R 477.

Account when debt paid off

35.38 As soon as no principal remains due, the effect of the order is to charge the mortgagee with compound interest on the excess of rents and profits over outgoings at each rest[1]. Generally, if the mortgagee has been paid off his interest and principal out of rents and profits and nevertheless continues in possession, he becomes a debtor to the mortgagor in respect of subsequent receipts. Annual rests will then be directed in the account against him, although no rests were directed in the original order for accounts[2].

1 This is expressly stated in the order in *Cotham v West* (1839) 1 Beav 380. Reg Lib: 'Take an account etc, and in taking the said account, make annual rests of the clear balance, and compute interest on such respective balances at £5 per cent; and in making such annual rests, except the first, include in the balance then stated, the interest of each preceding balance, so as to charge the defendant with compound interest thereon.' The usual rate, in the past, was £4 per cent: *Ashworth v Lord* (1887) 36 Ch D 545 at 552. The order in *Cotham v West* is the basis of the form now in use. Presumably, a higher rate of interest would be allowed today: see **35.55**. See also *Raphael v Boehm* (1805) 11 Ves 92; affd (1807) 13 Ves 407, 590; *Heighington v Grant* (1840) 5 My & Cr 258.

2 *Wilson v Metcalfe* (1826) 1 Russ 530; *Wilson v Cluer*, above; *Uttermare v Stevens* (1851) 17 LTOS 115; *Ashworth v Lord* (1887) 36 Ch D 545, and this may be done where the mortgagee becomes overpaid during the action, though he will not be charged with interest on the surplus received prior to the date of the certificate: *Lloyd v Jones* (1842) 12 Sim 491.

An action for an account where the mortgagee was satisfied more than six years ago is really for redemption and therefore not barred in six years: *Ocean Accident and Guarantee Corpn Ltd and Hewitt v Collum* [1913] 1 IR 337.

Receipts after certificate

35.39 It would seem that where money has been received after the date of the master's certificate, which represents corpus of the mortgaged property, no further account is required[1]. However, if, after that date and before the day fixed for redemption, the mortgagee varies the amount by receiving rent or other moneys in the nature of income[2], the accounts must be carried on and a new day fixed for redemption[3]—usually the expiration of a month from the date originally named. The receipt of rent after default and before the affidavit of default, does not make a further account necessary[4].

1 *Welch v National Cycle Works Co* (1886) 55 LT 673, CA.

2 Cf *Welch v National Cycle Works Co*, above, *Lacon v Tyrrell* (1887) 56 LT 483.

3 *Jenner-Fust v Needham* (1886) 32 Ch D 582; *Garlick v Jackson* (1841) 4 Beav 154; *Alden v Foster* (1842) 5 Beav 592; *Ellis v Griffiths* (1844) 7 Beav 83; *Prees v Coke* (1871) 6 Ch App 645. For exceptions to this rule, see **22.65** ff. This extension of the time for redemption is not, as in the case of an extension granted on the application of the mortgagor, dependent on the mortgagor paying forthwith arrears of interest and costs: *Buchanan v Greenway* (1849) 12 Beav 355. The mortgage accounts by affidavit for the amount received: *Oxenham v Ellis* (1854) 18 Beav 593. Where a receiver has been appointed by the court, a further account may be avoided by inserting in the order for foreclosure *nisi* liberty to apply in private for payment of any moneys in his hands: *Coleman v Llewellin* (1886) 34 Ch D 143,

CA; and see *Smith v Pearman* (1888) 36 WR 681, but perhaps this will only be done under special circumstances: *Cheston v Wells* [1893] 2 Ch 151. For another form of order intended to avoid a further account where a receiver has been appointed, see *Simmons v Blandy* [1897] 1 Ch 19, following *Barber v Jeckells* [1893] WN 91.

4 *Constable v Howick* (1858) 5 Jur NS 331; *National Permanent Mutual Benefit Building Society v Raper* [1892] 1 Ch 54.

ACCOUNTS OF INTEREST

THE RIGHT TO INTEREST

Interest on mortgage debts

35.40 Contrary to the general rule as to loans[1], interest is payable upon mortgage debts even though it is not expressly reserved and although the mortgage is only equitable[2]. Interest is payable on a charge by mere deposit of title deeds[3] and, generally, where the principal sum is a charge on specified property[4]. Where, however, the contract provides expressly for reconveyance upon payment of the principal, interest will not be payable[5] unless the deed also contains an express or implied agreement for payment of interest[6].

Interest arises on mortgages from day to day[7]. The person who takes the income of the security is entitled to the interest to the time of his death or other termination of his estate.

1 *President of India v La Pintada Cia Navigacion SA* [1985] AC 104, [1984] 2 All ER 773; but see now Supreme Court Act 1981, s 35A; County Courts Act 1984, s 69 (power to award interest on debts and damages).

2 *Anon* (1813) 4 Taunt 876; *Re Every, ex p Hirtzel* (1858) 3 De G & J 464; *Re Kerr's Policy* (1869) LR 8 Eq 331; *Cityland and Property (Holdings) v Dabrah* [1968] Ch 166, 182; *Re Drax, Savile v Drax* [1903] 1 Ch 781. Cf, interest is also payable where the payment of interest is not provided for on a loan secured by an equitable charge: *Al-Wazir v Islamic Press Agency Inc* (31 July 2001), CA.

3 *Anon*, above; *Carey v Doyne* (1856) 5 I Ch R 104; *Re Kerr's Policy*, above; notwithstanding the doubt expressed in *Ashton v Dalton* (1846) 2 Coll 565.

4 *Lippard v Ricketts* (1872) LR 14 Eq 291; *Re Drax, Saville v Drax* [1903] 1 Ch 781, CA; *Mendl v Smith* (1943) 112 LJ Ch 279, but interest may not be allowed in addition to a premium: see *Cityland and Property (Holdings) Ltd v Dabrah* [1968] Ch 166 at 182, [1967] 2 All ER 639 at 648; see **28.12**. As to the limitation on the arrears recoverable, see **16.33**. And see *NZI Capital Corpn Ltd v Child* (1991) 23 NSWLR 481.

A power to charge land with a sum of money carries power to charge it also with interest: *Kilmurry v Geery* (1713) 2 Salk 538.

A charge of debts by will, upon real estate, does not entitle simple contract creditors to interest, unless the debtor has given to the debts the quality of specialities in his lifetime, as by making a schedule of debts and creating a trust term for payment: *Stewart v Noble* (1788) Vern & Scr 528; *Barwell v Parker* (1751) 2 Ves Sen 364.

A mortgagee will be allowed no interest upon a debt which would have been satisfied but for his wrongful or inequitable act, during such time as the debt has thereby remained unsatisfied: see *Thornton v Court* (1854) 3 De GM & G 293 at 301.

As to the right of creditors to interest under a deed of trust executed by the debtor for their benefit, see *Jenkins v Perry* (1838) 3 Y & C Ex 178.

For rests, see **35.35**.

5 *Thompson v Drew* (1855) 20 Beav 49. See *Re Lane, ex p Hodge* (1857) 26 LJ Bcy 77; and cf *Ashwell v Staunton* (1861) 30 Beav 52; *Mendl v Smith* (1943) 169 LT 153.

6 *Ashwell v Staunton*, above. See *Re King, ex p Furber* (1881) 17 Ch D 191.

7 *Wilson v Harman* (1755) 2 Ves Sen 672; *Re Rogers' Trusts* (1860) 1 Drew & Sm 338; Apportionment Act 1870.

Interest after day for redemption

35.41 Where the security does not expressly provide for payment of interest after the time fixed for redemption, interest will still be recoverable, not on the contract, but as damages for the detention of the debt and, therefore, only to the extent of the damages claimed[1]. To avoid payment of subsequent interest, the mortgagor must be prepared to pay at the day fixed and must give notice that he will do so. If, by the default of the mortgagor, the principal is not paid on the day of redemption, the mortgagor will be liable to pay subsequent interest even if it is provided that interest is only to be paid until the day of redemption or that interest is not to be paid after the day of redemption[2].

In fixing the amount of subsequent interest the court will consider, but will not be entirely guided by, the agreement between the parties as to the rate payable during the term. In the past, the court would be inclined to cut the rate down if it exceeded 5 per cent[3].

1 *Price v Great Western Rly Co* (1847) 16 M & W 244; *Morgan v Jones* (1853) 8 Exch 620; *Cook v Fowler* (1874) LR 7 HL 27; *Re European Central Rly Co, ex p Oriental Financial Corpn* (1876) 4 Ch D 33, CA; *Re Roberts, Goodchap v Roberts* (1880) 14 Ch D 49, CA; *Goldstrom v Tallerman* (1886) 18 QBD 1, CA; *Mellersh v Brown* (1890) 45 Ch D 225; see also *Re Horner, Fookes v Horner* [1896] 2 Ch 188; *London, Chatham and Dover Rly Co v South Eastern Rly Co* [1893] AC 429, HL, and *Mathura Das v Raja Narindar Bahadur Pal* (1896) 12 TLR 609, PC.
2 *Price v Great Western Rly Co*, above; *Gordillo v Weguelin* (1877) 5 Ch D 287, CA.
3 *Re Roberts, Goodchap v Roberts*, above; *Mellersh v Brown*, above. See *Re King, ex p Furber* (1881) 17 Ch D 191. In *Wallington v Cook* (1878) 47 LJ Ch 508, the interest was cut down from 60 to 5 per cent, but a more realistic rate would now be allowed, see *Cityland and Property (Holdings) Ltd v Dabrah* [1968] Ch 166, [1967] 2 All ER 639; *Wallersteiner v Moir (No 2)* [1975] QB 373, 508n, [1975] 1 All ER 849; *Bartlett v Barclays Bank Trust Co, Ltd (No 2)* [1980] Ch 515, [1980] 2 All ER 92; [1982] Conv 93 (JTF); *International Military Services Ltd v Capital and Counties plc* [1982] 2 All ER 20, [1982] 1 WLR 575; and see **35.35**.

Interest on money retained

35.42 The mortgagee may be liable to pay interest on money in his hands arising from the security. For example, where, being mortgagee in possession, he holds over and receives rents after the mortgage debt has been paid[1] or where, though not in possession, there is a balance due from him and he improperly resists redemption[2] or where, after a sale under his power, he retains the surplus[3].

1 *Ashworth v Lord* (1887) 36 Ch D 545, and see **35.38**.
2 *Smith v Pilkington* (1859) 1 De GF & J 120.
3 *Charles v Jones* (1887) 35 Ch D 544 (interest allowed at 4 per cent per annum).

Interest on expenditure

35.43 The court allows the mortgagee interest, in certain cases, upon money which he has laid out for the benefit of the estate or the support of his security. Such payments are treated as further advances and the rate is generally that which is payable on the original loan. Interest will be allowed upon:

(a) fines paid by the mortgagee for the renewal of leases upon which the estate is held, even though there is no covenant by the mortgagor for renewal[1];
(b) premiums on life policies, which form part of the security[2];

(c) money laid out in supporting the mortgagor's title where it has been impeached[3];
(d) money laid out in the redemption of land tax[4]; and
(e) money laid out in lasting improvements or otherwise for the benefit of the estate, where the principal so laid out is allowed[5].

Interest will not be allowed upon costs ordered to be paid by the mortgagor, unless the mortgagee has been given permission to add them to his security. If the mortgagee is given permission to add the costs to his security he will be allowed to charge interest from the date of the taxing master's certificate[6].

1 5 Bac Abr 736; *Manlove v Bale and Bruton* (1688) 2 Vern 84; *Lacon v Mertins* (1743) 3 Atk 1; *Woolley v Drag* (1795) 2 Anst 551.
2 *Bellamy v Brickenden* (1861) 2 John & H 137. As to interest on premiums paid by a surety, see *Hodgson v Hodgson* (1837) 2 Keen 704.
3 *Godfrey v Watson* (1747) 3 Atk 517.
4 *Knowles v Chapman* (1815) 3 Seton's Judgment & Orders 7th edn 1905.
5 *Quarrell v Beckford* (1816) 1 Madd 269; *Webb v Rorke* (1806) 2 Sch & Lef 661. As to sums expended by the mortgagee in the working of mines, where he was authorised by the deed to work them, see **35.31**.
It is not the practice generally to allow interest upon money expended by the mortgagee in repairs, although it has sometimes been done: Seton (7th edn) 1906.
6 *Eardley v Knight* (1889) 41 Ch D 537, and payment of interest on costs will be directed where they have been paid under an order of the court which declared the person paying them to be entitled to an indemnity for so doing: *Wainman v Bowker* (1845) 8 Beav 363.

Payment of interest in bankruptcy

35.44 A mortgagee who realises his security can, notwithstanding the bankruptcy of the mortgagor, apply the proceeds in payment of principal, interest, and costs in full. However, if the mortgagee claims to prove in the bankruptcy (either on abandoning his security or assessing it or realising it and proving for the balance) he can only claim interest up to the date of the making of the bankruptcy order unless there is a surplus[1].

1 *Ex p Badger* (1798) 4 Ves 165; *Re Lancaster, ex p Kensington* (1835) 2 Mont & A 300; *Re Savin* (1872) 7 Ch App 760 at 764; *Re Phillips, ex p Bath* (1882) 22 Ch D 450, CA; *Re London, Windsor and Greenwich Hotels Co, Quartermaine's Case* [1892] 1 Ch 639, and see Insolvency Act 1986, ss 322 (2), 338 (4).
Under special circumstances, as where the mortgagee at the request of the trustee has postponed the sale for the purpose of getting a better market, or has made some other special agreement with him, interest after the bankruptcy will be allowed: *Re Lancaster, ex p Kensington*, above, distinguished in *Re Savin*, above, but it may be doubted whether this could be done under the present law.

Neglect to claim interest

35.45 If a prior mortgagee does not take possession and the interest falls into arrear, a subsequent mortgagee cannot redeem without paying the whole interest[1]. This is said to be the case even though the prior mortgagee let the interest run in arrear with an ill intent to get the estate, but will not be the case if there is fraud or collusion[2]. The neglect, without fraud, of the incumbrancer to demand interest from the tenant for life, or to require him to pay head rents will not prejudice the right against the remainderman[3].

1 *Aston v Aston* (1750) 1 Ves Sen 264.
2 *Bentham v Haincourt* (1691) Prec Ch 30, 1 Eq Cas Abr 320 pl 2.
3 *Loftus v Swift* (1806) 2 Sch & Lef 642; *Roe v Pogson* (1816) 2 Madd 457; *Wrixon v Vize* (1842) 2 Dr & War 192; affd (1842) 3 Dr & War 104; *Hill v Browne* (1844) Drury temp Sug 426; *Makings v Makings* (1860) 1 De GF & J 355.

INTEREST ON SPECIALTY AND JUDGMENT DEBTS

Bond covering mortgage debt

35.46 Generally, bond debts carry no interest, either at law or in equity, beyond the amount of the penalty, which is taken to represent by the agreement of the parties the ultimate amount of the debt[1]. If, however, there is a bond and also a mortgage to secure the same sum together with all interest that may accrue due, interest will be carried under the mortgage beyond the penalty of the bond: the amount of the penalty is not to prejudice the mortgage[2]. In such cases, it makes no difference whether the mortgage precedes or follows the bond. Interest will also be given in such a case where the mortgagor is a surety, since the creditor may make the mortgage as available as if it were given by the principal debtor.

By contrast, a trust for payment of bond debts out of the proceeds of real estate, together with the interest due and to accrue due to the day of payment, will not carry interest beyond the penalties of the bonds. As, under the general rule, interest does not accrue due beyond the penalties, the trust will be satisfied by payment of interest to the amount of the penalties[3].

1 *Hatton v Harris* [1892] AC 547.
2 *Clarke v Lord Abingdon* (1810) 17 Ves 106.
3 *Hughes v Wynne* (1832) 1 My & K 20; *Clowes v Waters* (1852) 16 Jur 632.

Judgment debts

35.47 Historically, apart from special circumstances interest was not allowed on a judgment debt[1]. Under the Judgments Act 1838[2], judgment debts bear interest at the statutory rate[3] from the entering up of the judgment[4] until satisfaction[5]. Judgments of a court exercising its equitable jurisdiction have the effect of judgments at law[6].

Where an order for the administration of the estate of a deceased person has been made, provision is made under the Civil Procedure Rules that, if a debt does not carry interest, the creditor is entitled to interest at the same rate from the date of the judgment for administration but only after payment of costs, debts and the interest on such debts as by law carry interest[7].

1 *Lewes v Morgan* (1829) 3 Y & J 394; *Gaunt v Taylor* (1834) 3 My & K 302; as to the power of the court to allow interest, see *Burland v Earle* [1905] AC 590.
2 Judgments Act 1838, s 17 (as amended).
3 As prescribed by order made under statutory instrument from time to time. Generally, a county court judgment or order carries interest at the same rate as a High Court judgment if it is for the payment of not less than £5,000: see the County Court (Interest on Judgment Debts) Order 1991, SI 1991/1184, arts 1, 2, 5 (arts 1, 5 as amended). The interest rate has been 8 per cent since 1 April 1993: Judgment Debts (Rate of Interest)

Order 1993, SI 1993/564. Interest is not payable on a county court judgment which grants a mortgagee a suspended order for possession of a dwelling house: see art 2(3)(b)(ii).

4 Ie the date on which judgment was pronounced: *Parsons v Mather and Platt Ltd* [1977] 2 All ER 715, [1977] 1 WLR 855.

5 Section 17; county court judgments do not come within s 17; see *R v Essex County Court Judge* (1887) 18 QBD 704; *Sewing Machines Rentals Ltd v Wilson* [1975] 3 All ER 553, [1967] 1 WLR 37, CA.

6 Judgments Act 1838, s 18. Where the amount due is to be ascertained by inquiry, interest is payable under this section only from the date when the amount is ascertained by the master's certificate: *A-G v Lord Carrington* (1843) 6 Beav 454.

7 CPR Sch 1 RSC 44.9. Where the debt accrues due after the judgment, interest runs from the due date: *Re Salvin, Worseley v Marshall* [1912] 1 Ch 332; cf *Lainson v Lainson (No 2)* (1853) 18 Beav 7. As to the effect on interest of merger of the debt in the judgment, see **32.13**.

CAPITALISATION OF INTEREST

Interest on arrears not allowed apart from contract

35.48 Interest upon arrears, or upon fines for non-payment of principal and interest, is not allowed by the court where there is no contract for it[1]. As a result, in a mortgage to bankers to secure a specific sum at a fixed rate of interest, it is not open to the bank, in the absence of express contract, to charge compound interest on this sum or to include it in the general banking account[2]. Where, however, the mortgage is given to the bank to secure the balance of a current account, there is an implied contract for payment of compound interest with yearly or even half-yearly rests[3].

Before the abolition of the usury laws there could be no payment of such interest by virtue of an original stipulation in the mortgage deed. At that time it was essential that the interest should first be due, before any agreement to turn it into principal would hold good[4]. Such a contract is now valid where there is no question of fraud or oppression[5] and a provision in the mortgage for capitalisation of overdue interest will be supported[6].

1 *Procter v Cooper* (1700) Prec Ch 116; *Thornhill v Evans* (1742) 2 Atk 330; *Parker v Butcher* (1867) LR 3 Eq 762; *Daniell v Sinclair* (1881) 6 App Cas 181, PC; *Domaschenz v Standfield Properties Pty Ltd* (1977) 16 SASR 56.

2 *Lloyds Bank plc v Voller* [2000] 2 All ER (Comm) 978, CA; *Stewart v Stewart* (1891) 27 LR Ir 351; and see *Mosse v Salt* (1863) 32 Beav 269; and *London Chartered Bank of Australia v White* (1879) 4 App Cas 413 at 424, PC.

3 *Crosskill v Bower* (1863) 32 Beav 86; *National Bank of Australasia v United Hand-in-Hand Band of Hope Co* (1879) 4 App Cas 391 at 400, PC. A bank which is otherwise entitled to charge compound interest, does not cease to be so entitled by closing a client's account after a demand for repayment of a loan: *National Bank of Greece SA v Pinios Shipping Co* [1990] 1 AC 637, [1990] 1 All ER 78, HL.

4 *Lord Ossulston v Lord Yarmouth* (1707) 2 Salk 449; *Broadway v Morecraft* (1729) Mos 247; *Re Mills, ex p Champion* (1792) 3 Bro CC 436; *Ex p Bevan* (1803) 9 Ves 223; *Morgan v Mather* (1792) 2 Ves 15; *Mainland v Upjohn* (1889) 41 Ch D 126 at 136. Capitalised interest was payable, if so provided by a subsequent agreement: see *Ex p Bevan*, above.

5 *Clarkson v Henderson* (1880) 14 Ch D 348.

6 *Wrigley v Gill* [1906] 1 Ch 165, CA; *CJ Belmore Ltd v AGC (General Finance) Ltd* [1976] 1 NSWLR 507. Where, however, the mortgagee goes into possession and has net rents in his hands sufficient to keep down the interest he is bound to apply them to that purpose: *Wrigley v Gill*, above. For a form of capitalisation clause, see 28 *Forms and Precedents* (5th edn, 1999 reissue) Mortgages.

Effect of capitalisation

35.49 The capitalisation of income does not mean that such interest becomes capital for all purposes, for example, income tax[1] or priority payment on liquidation[2]. The capitalisation clause may also prevent money being due for the purposes of the exercise by the mortgagee of the power of sale[3].

1 *Re Morris, Mayhew v Halton* [1922] 1 Ch 126, CA; *IRC v Oswald* [1945] AC 360, [1945] 1 All ER 641, HL; and see Chapter 37.
2 *Bank of New South Wales v Brown* (1983) 151 CLR 514.
3 Though a capitalisation clause has the effect of increasing the total amount of interest payable that does not mean that there is a variation in the rate of interest chargeable under the original loan: *Imperial Life Assurance Co of Canada v Efficient Distributors Ltd* [1992] 2 AC 85, [1992] 2 WLR 503, PC.

Capitalisation after mortgage

35.50 After the mortgage a mere notice by the mortgagee to the mortgagor is not sufficient to turn arrears of interest into principal. In order for that to happen there must be a distinct assent to the demand or an agreement otherwise made. Such an agreement must be made fairly and is generally, and most properly, made upon the advance of fresh money[1].

1 *Tompson v Leith* (1858) 4 Jur NS 1091; *Thornhill v Evans*, above, but such an agreement, when made in favour of the first mortgagee, will not hold against later incumbrancers of whom he made in favour of the first mortgagee, will not hold against later incumbrancers of whom he had notice: *Digby v Craggs* (1763) Amb 612.

Capitalisation on transfer of mortgage

35.51 Arrears of interest will be capitalised on the transfer of a mortgage if the transfer is made with the concurrence of the mortgagor[1]. Arrears of interest will not be capitalised where the mortgage is transferred without the mortgagor's concurrence[2] unless, it seems, the mortgagor first refuses either to pay off the debt or to join in the transfer[3].

The privity or assent of the mortgagor to the account is not sufficient to change the interest into principal, even if the mortgagor signs the account. This is because no intent is shown to alter the nature of that part of the debt which consists of interest[4]. On the other hand, conversion may take place on the mere written consent of the mortgagor or person entitled to redeem without his being actually a party to the assignment or on the inference of his consent arising from his acts or from his acquiescence[5].

1 *Ashenhurst v James* (1745) 3 Atk 270; *Earl of Macclesfield v Fitton* (1683) 1 Vern 168; *Matthews v Wallwyn* (1798) 4 Ves 118; *Chambers v Goldwin* (1804) 9 Ves 254; *Mangles v Dixon* (1852) 3 HL Cas 702 at 737.
2 *Cottrell v Finney* (1874) 9 Ch App 541, and even where the transferee of a mortgage, by payment of arrears of interest and costs, had preserved the estate from a forced sale, it appears to have been assumed that he should only have his principal without interest: *Cottrell v Finney*; though apparently he should have had interest on the salvage principle.
3 *Anon* (1719) Bunb 41.
4 *Brown v Barkham* (1720) 1 P Wms 652.
5 Thus, where interest had been paid for many years upon an ascertained balance of principal and interest, reported due at the date of a decree for sale, the court inferred an

agreement that interest should be paid as the price of forbearance to enforce the sale: *M'Carthy v Llandaff* (1810) 1 Ball & B 375; and see *Ashenhurst v James*, above.

As to the form of judgment where it is denied that anything was due at the time of the assignment, see *Matthews v Walwyn*, above.

Capitalisation under foreclosure order

35.52 Interest is also, in effect, capitalised in working out foreclosure in an action by a first mortgagee against subsequent mortgagees and the mortgagor. If successive periods of redemption are directed, the second mortgagee is first given the chance of redeeming on payment of the sum certified to be due to the first mortgagee for principal, interest and costs. If he fails to redeem, the direction is that subsequent interest shall be computed and this computation is made, not on the principal due, or on principal and costs, but on the total amount originally certified to be due, such amount being treated as one consolidated sum[1]. As a result, for the purpose of the further account the interest due to the first mortgagee is capitalised and made to bear interest.

Where interest runs on the whole sum found due by a certificate, it runs only from the date when the certificate becomes binding and up to that time on the principal only[2].

1 *Elton v Curteis* (1881) 19 Ch D 49, per Fry J. For the previous practice and the distinction between the case in which the subsequent mortgagee, having paid the mortgagee above him, is in his turn to be redeemed by the next below him, and the case in which the subsequent mortgagee has been foreclosed for default in payment see 9th edn, p 632, footnote (*l*).

2 *Jacob v Earl of Suffolk* (1728) Mos 27.

THE RATE OF INTEREST ALLOWED

Lower rate on punctual payment

35.53 It is a well-settled, if not an intelligible rule, that if the mortgagee wishes to stipulate for a higher rate of interest in default of punctual payment, he must reserve the higher rate as the interest payable under the mortgage and provide for its reduction in case of punctual payment[1]. The mortgagee cannot achieve his aim by reserving the lower rate and making the higher the penalty for non-payment at the appointed time because, it is said, such an agreement is a penalty[2] and relievable in equity[3].

Where the provision for reduction of interest is in a general form, the mortgagor cannot have the benefit of it unless he strictly performs the condition. The mortgagor will have no relief after the time of payment has passed[4] and, if the mortgagee has taken possession by reason of the mortgagor's default, the mortgagee will also be entitled to the higher rate of interest reserved[5] even if there was no interest in arrear when he took possession and although he did so by arrangement with the mortgagor[6]. If, however, it is provided that as often as interest shall be paid within the limited time, the lower rate shall be accepted, or some equivalent words are used pointing to any payment of interest, the mortgagor will not, by a single breach of the condition, lose his right to the benefit of it on future payments, but only upon that particular occasion[7].

1 *Strode v Parker* (1694) 2 Vern 316; *Jory v Cox* (1701) Prec Ch 160; *Walmesley v Booth* (1741) 2 Atk 25. *Lordsvale Finance plc v Bank of Zambia* [1996] QB 752, [1996] 3 All ER 156. As to the restriction on increasing the rate of interest under the Rent Act, see **16.22** ff.

2 Nomine poena.
3 *Holles v Wyse* (1693) 2 Vern 289; *Strode v Parker*, above; *Nicholls v Maynard* (1747) 3 Atk 519; *Wallingford v Mutual Society* (1880) 5 App Cas 685 at 702, HL; *CJ Belmore Pty Ltd v AGC (General Finance) Ltd* [1976] 1 NSWLR 507. In *Brown v Barkham* (1720) 1 P Wms 652, the higher rate was allowed as the price of the mortgagee's forbearance.
4 *Bonafous v Rybot* (1763) 3 Burr 1370; *Jory v Cox*, above; *Stanhope v Manners* (1763) 2 Eden 197. There will be no relief in equity under an agreement not to call in a mortgage on punctual payment of interest, though it be but two or three days in arrear: *Hicks v Gardner* (1837) 1 Jur 541; *Leeds and Hanley Theatre of Varieties v Broadbent* [1898] 1 Ch 343, CA; *Maclaine v Gatty* [1921] 1 AC 376, HL. A trustee is justified in accepting the lower rate, after the higher rate has become payable by the strict terms of the contract, it being the usual course to treat interest paid under such circumstances as having been paid within the time fixed: *Booth v Alington* (1856) 26 LJ Ch 138.
5 *Union Bank of London v Ingram* (1880) 16 Ch D 53; *Cockburn v Edwards* (1881) 18 Ch D 449 at 463, CA; *Bright v Campbell* (1889) 41 Ch D 388. All explained in *Wrigley v Gill* [1906] 1 Ch 165, CA.
6 *Bright v Campbell*, above.
7 *Stanhope v Manners*, above. See *Burrowes v Molloy* (1845) 2 Jo & Lat 521; *Wayne v Lewis* (1855) 3 WR 600.

Commission on unpaid instalments

35.54 A contract to pay a percentage on unpaid instalments for the interval between the time fixed for and that of actual payment, under the name of a 'commission', has been allowed as not being in the nature of a penalty[1]. So has a similar payment on the renewal of promissory notes[2]. The mortgagee of a ship may also contract for a commission on any cash advance remaining unpaid for two months[3].

1 *General Credit and Discount Co v Clegg* (1883) 22 Ch D 549.
2 *Buckness v Vickery* (1891) 64 LT 701 (2 per cent).
3 *The Benwell Tower* (1895) 72 LT 664.

Rate of interest allowed by the court

35.55 Where no rate of interest is fixed by the parties the court can fix it[1]. This has also been decided to be the proper rate where an absolute conveyance has been cut down to a security on principles analogous to those formerly applied in cases of usury[2]. In the case of further advances, or of money allowed in the nature of further advances, the interest is generally given at the same rate as upon the moneys originally lent[3].

1 See the notes to CPR Pt 7. *Ashwell v Staunton* (1861) 30 Beav 52; *Mendl v Smith* (1943) 169 LT 153. Cf *Re Kerr's Policy* (1869) LR 8 Eq 331; *Re Drax, Savile v Drax* [1903] 1 Ch 781, CA (4 per cent per annum allowed); *Cityland and Property (Holdings) Ltd v Dabrah* [1968] Ch 166, [1967] 2 All ER 639 (7 per cent per annum); *Congresbury Motors Ltd v Anglo-Belge Finance Co Ltd* [1970] Ch 294, [1969] 3 All ER 545 (5 per cent); *Finance and Investment Pty Ltd v Van Kempen* (1986) 6 NSWLR 305, CA. But see now *Wallersteiner v Moir (No 2)* [1975] QB 373, 508n, [1975] 1 All ER 849; *Bartlett v Barclays Bank Trust Co Ltd (No 2)* [1980] Ch 515, [1980] 2 All ER 92; [1982] Conv 93 (JTF).
2 See *Douglas v Culverwell* (1862) 4 De GF & J 20; *Re Unsworth's Trusts* (1865) 2 Drew & Sm 337.
3 *Woolley v Drag* (1795) 2 Anst 551. It has, however, been directed to be computed after the rate current in a foreign country where the money was expended, the current rate there being less than the interest reserved by the mortgage: *Quarrell v Beckford* (1816) 1 Madd 269 at 281; and see *Badham v Odell* (1742) 4 Bro Parl Cas 349.

Variation in rate of interest

35.56 An unwritten agreement to reduce the rate of interest on a mortgage is good; but in the absence of evidence or presumption of such an agreement, the difference between the rate reserved and that actually paid must be made good[1]. So, if a higher rate than is reserved is paid, the excess may be deducted on discharge of the mortgage[2].

1 *Lord Milton v Edgworth* (1773) 5 Bro Parl Cas, 313; *Gregory v Pilkington* (1856) 26 LJ Ch 177; *Re Venning* (1947) 63 TLR 394, CA, and note the doctrine of estoppel as enunciated in *Central London Property Trust Ltd v High Trees House Ltd* [1947] KB 130. For variation of mortgages, see **3.30**.
2 *Tyler v Manson* (1826) 5 LJ OS Ch 34.

WHEN INTEREST CEASES TO RUN[1]

Notice to pay off mortgage

35.57 The mortgagee is entitled to six months' interest from the date of the notice to him of the intended discharge of the security. If the payment is not made at the time fixed, the mortgagee is entitled to a new notice, or to six months' additional interest from the time of actual payment[2]. The mortgagee will not, however, be entitled to such interest if he has demanded payment or taken proceedings to recover payment, even though, pending the proceedings, notice of payment has been given to and accepted by him[3]. If, therefore, the mortgagee sells he can charge interest only up to the completion of the purchase. The same rule applies if the interest is payable in advance and the mortgagee sells before the day of payment[4].

If the mortgage cannot be discharged at the time fixed, for example by reason of the inability of the mortgagee to produce the deeds or if he omits to attend at the time and place fixed for payment in a redemption of foreclosure action, the mortgagee will be allowed no interest beyond that day. Where, however, the mortgagee's omission to attend arose from a mistake and the mortgagor also neglected to attend, the mortgagee was not compelled to wait another six months, but a new time was fixed for payment at the end of ten days[5].

1 For early repayment, see **10.53** and **28.13**.
2 See **28.34**.
3 *Bartlett v Franklin* (1867) 15 WR 1077; *Re Alcock, Prescott v Phipps* (1883) 23 Ch D 372, CA. Where the mortgagee consents in an administration action to a sale of the mortgaged property, he will have interest for six months from the date of the consent, if the mortgage is discharged before the end of that time, but if it is not, interest runs to the time of payment: *Day v Day* (1862) 31 Beav 270.
4 *Banner v Berridge* (1881) 18 Ch D 254; and see *Van Kempen v Finance and Investment Pty Ltd* [1984] ACLD 697; (1986) 6 NSWLR 293; on appeal sub nom *Finance and Investment Pty Ltd v Van Kempen* (1986) 6 NSWLR 305, CA.
5 *Lord Midleton v Eliot* (1847) 15 Sim 531; *Hughes v Williams* (1853) Kay App iv, and form of order there; *James v Rumsey* (1879) 11 Ch D 398.

Interest ceases on tender

35.58 Subject to the above, interest will cease to run upon the mortgage debt from the time at which a proper tender of the whole amount due is shown to have been made[1] or upon payment into court[2].

1 On tender, see **28.37**. If the right to redeem is disputed, and an inquiry becomes necessary, the mortgagee is not to lose his interest, pending the inquiry, although a tender has been made: *Sharpnell v Blake* (1737) 2 Eq Cas Abr 604.
2 *CJ Belmore Ltd v AGC (General Finance) Ltd* [1976] 1 NSWLR 507.

Purchase by mortgage

35.59 Upon a purchase by the mortgagee of the mortgaged estate, where the mortgagee takes possession but completion is deferred for a long time, it may be inferred that there was a set-off of the mortgage debt against the purchase money at the time of taking possession and that interest reserved by the contract on the purchase money runs only on the balance[1].

1 *Wallis v Bastard* (1853) 4 De GM & G 251 and as to set-off against the mortgage of sums due to persons claiming under the mortgagor, see *Pettat v Ellis* (1804) 9 Ves 563; and in bankruptcy, *Re Barker, ex p Penfold* (1851) 4 De G & Sm 282; *Re Penfold, ex p Ramsbottom* (1835) 4 Deac & Ch 198.

INCIDENCE AS BETWEEN TENANT FOR LIFE AND REMAINDERMAN[1]

Tenant for life bound to keep down interest

35.60 A tenant for life of a mortgaged estate is bound to keep down the interest of the charge during his life to the extent of the rents and profits of the mortgaged property[2] and also of any other property comprised in the settlement under which he is life tenant[3]. This duty subsists in favour of the reversioner and gives no right to the incumbrancer[4].

It is for the reversioner to see that the duty is performed[5]. If it is neglected, the reversioner[6] or, it seems, the next tenant for life[7], may commence an action to make the rents available and may compel the tenant for life to account for what has accrued. The reversioner has an equity to have the estate recouped out of the future income accruing to the tenant for life[8].

1 No settlement created after 1 January 1997 is a settlement for the purposes of the Settled Land Act 1925 and no settlement is deemed to be made under that Act after that date: Trusts of Land and Appointment of Trustees Act, s 2(1). Strict settlements in existence on 1 January 1997 continue to exist until there is no relevant property: s 2(4). 'Relevant property' is defined in s 67(1) of the Act.
2 *Revel v Watkinson* (1748) 1 Ves Sen 93; *Amesbury v Brown* (1750) 1 Ves Sen 477; *Faulkner v Daniel* (1843) 3 Hare 199; *Burges v Mawbey* (1823) Turn & R 167 at 174; *Lord Kensington v Bouverie* (1855) 7 De GM & G 134, and in an administration action he must keep down the interest upon all debts charged upon the estate from the testator's death: *Marshall v Crowther* (1874) 2 Ch D 199. The tenant for life is not exempted from this liability by the possession of an absolute power of appointment, by virtue whereof he is able, like the tenant in tail, to make the estate his own: *Whitbread v Smith* (1854) 3 De GM & G 727 at 741, and a tenant in fee subject to an executory devise over is under the same liability: *Butcher v Simmonds* (1876) 35 LT 304. So also are the assignee and judgment creditor of the tenant for life: *Scholefield v Lockwood* (1863) 9 Jur NS 1258.
3 *Frewen v Law Life Assurance Society* [1896] 2 Ch 511; *Honywood v Honywood* [1902] 1 Ch 347.
4 *Re Morley, Morley v Saunders* (1869) LR 8 Eq 594.
5 *Caulfield v Maguire* (1845) 2 Jo & Lat 141 at 160.
6 *Lord Penrhyn v Hughes* (1799) 5 Ves 99 at 106; *Lord Kensington v Bouverie* (1859) 7 HL Cas 557 at 575; *Makings v Makings* (1860) 1 De GF & J 355; but cf *Scholefield v Lockwood* (1863) 4 De GJ & Sm 22 at 31; 'A tenant for life has all his lifetime to pay off the arrears of interest, and he cannot be charged with neglect of duty, neither does any right arise as to

the remainderman, until death or insolvency of the tenant for life.' There seems to be no other authority for this view of the law.

7 *Reven v Watkinson*, above.

8 *Waring v Coventry* (1834) 2 My & K 406. As to the application after a testator's death of rents in respect of separate mortgaged properties, the interest being in arrear at his death and the share in his estate settled, see *Re Coaks, Coaks v Bayley* [1911] 1 Ch 171.

If a mortgagee who has allowed the interest to fall into arrears purchases the estate of the tenant for life, the surplus rents received after the purchase beyond the current interest of the mortgage must be applied in discharge of the arrears and the mortgagee cannot charge the arrears upon the inheritance, for the vendor under whom he claims was bound to keep down the interest: *Lord Penrhyn v Hughes*, above. So as to a purchaser who actually pays off the arrears: *Whitbread v Smith* (1854) 3 De GM & G 727 at 741.

Tenant in tail not so bound

35.61 The adult tenant in tail of an incumbered estate is not obliged to keep down the interest on the charge because, having, or being able by his own act to acquire, full power over the estate, neither the issue in tail nor the remainderman has any equity to call for an indemnity against the arrears of interest accrued during the possession of their predecessor[1]. On the other hand, if the tenant in tail dies without barring the entail after keeping down the interest or taking an assignment of the mortgage (in which case he is considered to have paid himself the interest out of the rents and profits), the issue in tail have the benefit and the personal representatives of the tenant in tail have no equity to charge the reversion with interest accrued during his life[2].

1 *Chaplin v Chaplin* (1733) 3 P Wms 229 at 235; *Burges v Mawbey* (1823) Turn & R 167.

2 *Amesbury v Brown* (1750) 1 Ves Sen 477. An infant tenant in tail, being unable to make the estate his own, was in the position of a tenant for life: *Sarjeson v Cruise* (circ 1750) cited in *Amesbury v Brown*, above, at 480; *Sergison v Sealey* (1742) 2 Atk 412; *Burgess v Mawbey*, above, at 177, but now the legal estate would be vested in the trustees of the settlement as statutory owners and, ordinarily, they would keep down the interest out of rents and profits.

Successive tenants for life

35.62 Where there are successive tenants for life, each is bound to keep down the interest on incumbrances which accrues in his own time[1]. In so far as the rents and profits are insufficient for this purpose or, so far as through the insolvency of the first tenant for life the interest is not kept down, the interest is charged on the reversion[2].

1 *Caulfield v Maguire* (1845) 2 Jo & Lat 141. The suggestion made in *Lord Penrhyn v Hughes* (1799) 5 Ves 99 at 106 that the tenant for life in remainder must bear the arrears of interest which accrued in the time of a previous tenant for life, has not been accepted.

2 *Sharshaw v Gibbs* (1854) Kay 333, and where arrears which had accrued, through insufficiency of rents, during the lifetime of one tenant for life were discharged by the trustees of a subsequent life estate, they were thrown on the reversion: *Sharshaw v Gibbs*.

Variation of incidence

35.63 The incidence of the interest may be varied by the special circumstances. As a consequence, if the reversioner stands by and allows the rent to be received by the tenant for life and not applied in payment of interest, the reversion will be charged and the reversioner cannot afterwards establish a claim against the estate of the tenant for life on the ground that the rents were sufficient[1]. On the other hand, the conduct of the tenant for life in keeping down out of his own moneys so much of the interest as the estate cannot pay and without informing the remainderman of the deficiency, may show that he intended to exonerate the estate so that there is no charge on the remainder[2].

1 *Lord Kensington v Bouverie* (1854) 19 Beav 39 at 54.
2 *Lord Kensington v Bouverie* (1859) 7 HL Cas 557.

Possession under paramount title

35.64 It seems that the tenant for life is not excused by the fact that a portion of the estate was, during part of his time, in the possession of another under a paramount title, for example a jointress under a prior settlement. The tenant for life must discharge the arrears which accrued in the time of the paramount estate out of the additional rents received at its expiration[1] and, to liquidate such arrears, he must furnish all the rents, if necessary, during the whole of his life. This is, however, apparently subject to the equity that if the settlor of the estate is *in loco parentis* to the tenant for life and the tenant for life is not otherwise provided for, a reasonable maintenance shall be allowed him out of the rents and profits[2].

1 *Revel v Watkinson* (1748) 1 Ves Sen 93; *Tracy v Lady Hereford* (1786) 2 Bro CC 128.
2 *Revel v Watkinson*, above; and *Butler's Case* cited there at 95.

Direction to receiver to keep down interest

35.65 The order of the court directing a receiver to keep down the interest of incumbrances, does not amount to an appropriation of the rents and profits to that purpose, so as to make the rights of the parties where the interest has not been paid or applied for the same as if interest had been actually paid. The order is partly made in justice to the incumbrancers and partly for the benefit of the estate, in case the incumbrancers should proceed in respect of their unpaid interest. If they do not, however, apply for it, they are presumed to be content with their security for principal and interest, and the estate remains burdened with the arrears, for which there is no equity against the surplus rents paid over by the receiver[1].

1 *Bertie v Earl of Abingdon* (1817) 3 Mer 560.

Chapter 36

Costs

GENERAL RIGHT OF MORTGAGEE TO COSTS

Rule in absence of contractual provision

Basic entitlement to recover costs out of the mortgaged property

36.1 A mortgagee's right to costs arises out of the particular relationship between him and the mortgagor. Therefore, even in the absence of a stipulation regulating the recovery of costs in the security document, a mortgagee is entitled to reimburse himself out of the mortgaged property for all costs, charges and expenses reasonably and properly incurred in enforcing or preserving the security[1]. Because the process of enforcement or preservation often makes it necessary for the mortgage to take or defend proceedings, the right to costs extends to the costs of litigation reasonably and properly undertaken by the mortgagee[2]. In this regard, the following three propositions may be stated[3]:

(a) the mortgagee's costs, reasonably and properly incurred, of proceedings between himself and the mortgagor or his surety are allowable[4];
(b) allowable also are the mortgagee's costs, reasonably and properly incurred, of proceedings between himself and a third party where what is impugned is the title to the estate[5];
(c) but where a third party impugns the title to the mortgage, or the enforcement or exercise of some right or power accruing to the mortgagee thereunder, the mortgagee's costs of the proceedings, even though they be reasonably and properly incurred, are not allowable[6].

The first and second propositions have together been called the general rule and the third (which does not depend on the cause of action on which the third party relies) has been called the exception to the rule[7]. The distinction between the second and third categories of case is that in the former the mortgagee acts directly for the benefit of the equity of redemption as much as for that of the security, the proceedings being in substance between the third party on the one hand and the mortgagee and mortgagor together on the other (with each having a concern to assert or defend his separate estate or interest in the property), whereas in the latter the benefit is directly for the mortgagee and at most only indirectly for the mortgagor[8]. The consequence of the third proposition is that a mortgagee is not entitled to the costs of defending his title to the mortgage against persons other than the owner of the equity of redemption—as distinguished from defending the title to the estate—and generally he will not have the costs of litigation concerning the mortgaged property arising out of the wrongful act of a stranger[9].

Although there is something to be said for the complaint that the exception to the rule is illogical, no good reason has been be shown for overruling it; where there is a question as to which of two innocent parties ought to bear costs which have been run up by the wrongful and improvident actions of a third party, a line will have to be drawn somewhere[10]. That line has been drawn so as to preclude in general recovery by the mortgagee of the costs of litigation concerning the mortgaged property arising out of the wrongful act of a stranger to the mortgage.

1 *R v Chambers* (1840) 4 Y & C Ex 54; *Wade v Ward* (1859) 4 Drew 602; *Cotterell v Stratton* (1874) LR 17 Eq 543 & (1872) LR 8 Ch App 295; *Parker-Tweedale v Dunbar Bank plc (No 2)* [1991] Ch 26, CA; *Gomba Holdings (UK) Ltd v Minories Finance Ltd (No 2)* [1993] Ch 171, CA. See also *Central Mortgage and Housing Corpn v Johnson* (1971) 20 DLR (3d) 622; *Elders Trustees & Executor Co Ltd v Eagle Star Nominees Ltd* (1986) 4 BPR 9205; *Elders Trustee and Executor Co Ltd v EG Reeves Pty Ltd* (1988) 84 ALR 734; *Project Research Pty Ltd v Permanent Trustee of Australia Ltd* (1990) 5 BPR 11.

The right is treated as an implied term of the mortgage contract: *Re Wallis, ex p Lickorish* (1890) 25 QBD 176 at 180 & 181, CA; or at least it rests 'substantially on contract': *Cotterell v Stratton* (1872) 8 Ch App 295 at 302.

2 *Parker-Tweedale v Dunbar Bank plc (No 2)* [1991] Ch 26, CA.

3 See *Parker-Tweedale v Dunbar Bank plc (No 2)* [1991] Ch 26, CA.

4 *Detillin v Gale* (1802) 7 Ves 583, 32 ER 234; *Dryden v Frost* (1838) 3 My & Cr 670, [1835-42] All ER Rep 390; *National Provincial Bank of England v Games* (1886) 31 Ch D 582, CA; *Re Leighton's Conveyance* [1937] Ch 149, CA.

5 *Detillin v Gale* (1802) 7 Ves 583, 32 ER 234; *Dryden v Frost* (1838) 3 My & Cr 670, [1835-42] All ER Rep 390; *National Provincial Bank of England v Games* (1886) 31 Ch D 582, CA; *Re Leighton's Conveyance* [1937] Ch 149, CA.

6 *Doe d Holt v Roe* (1830) 6 Bing 447; *Owen v Crouch* (1857) 5 WR 545; *Parker v Watkins* (1859) John 133, 70 ER 369; *Re Smith's Mortgage, Harrison v Edwards* [1931] 2 Ch 168; *Re Leighton's Conveyance* [1937] Ch 149, CA.

7 *Parker-Tweedale v Dunbar Bank plc (No 2)* [1991] Ch 26, CA.

8 *Parker-Tweedale*, above.

9 This passage (in the previous edition) was cited with approval in *Parker-Tweedale v Dunbar Bank plc (No 2)*, above.

10 *Parker-Tweedale v Dunbar Bank plc (No 2)*, above.

Scope of entitlement: costs, charges and expenses

Generally

36.2 The first proposition covers all nature of proceedings between mortgagee and mortgagor. The classic examples are proceedings for payment, sale, foreclosure or redemption, but nowadays the most common are those for possession of the mortgaged property preliminary to an exercise of the mortgagee's statutory power or sale out of court[1].

The mortgagee will be allowed the costs of obtaining[2] or recovering[3] possession of the mortgaged property, of recovering the mortgage debt, whether against the mortgagor[4] or a surety, and despite the fact that the fruits of the claim are lost by the surety's insolvency[5]. A like position obtains in relation to the costs of taking out administration to the mortgagor or to a person interested under his will[6] as a necessary party, if required for recovery of the mortgage debt[7].

In relation to the second proposition, the mortgagee's right extends to costs incurred (or any deficiency, where some of those costs have been recovered from a third party) in asserting or defending the mortgagor's title to the property[8], or in defending the title of the mortgaged property against the mortgagor and persons claiming under him[9].

The mortgagee's above entitlement to all costs, charges, and expenses reasonably and properly incurred in ascertaining or defending his rights[10], preserving the security, or recovering the mortgage debt (as well as the right to costs of foreclosure or redemption claims) is founded on the principle that the mortgagee ought to be indemnified to the extent to which he acts reasonably as mortgagee[11]. The 'costs' referred to in the rule are the costs of litigation outside the claim in which the costs, charges and expenses are allowed and properly such costs come under 'charges and expenses'[12].

The owner of a share of an estate and his incumbrancers have but one set of costs, which is received by the first incumbrancer[13].

1 *Parker-Tweedale v Dunbar Bank plc (No 2)* [1991] Ch 26, CA.

2 *Wilkes v Saunion* (1877) 7 Ch D 188. See *Halsall v Egbunike* (1963) 107 Sol Jo 514 (where the mortgagor was legally aided).

3 *Millar v Major* (1818) Coop temp Cott 550; *Lewis v John* (1838) 9 Sim 366; *Sandon v Hooper* (1843) 6 Beav 246, 250 (where *plaintiff* appears to be a mistake for *defendant*); on appeal (1844) 14 LJ Ch 120; *Horlock v Smith* (1844) 1 Coll 287; *Owen v Crouch* (1857) 5 WR 545.

4 *National Provincial Bank of England v Games* (1886) 31 Ch D 582, CA, where *Ellison v Wright* (1827) 3 Russ 458 was preferred to *Lewis v John* (1838) 9 Sim 366 and *Merriman v Bonner* (1864) 12 WR 461, so far as the latter two cases throw doubt on the first on the ground that the costs are not incurred in relation to the mortgage security.

5 *Ellison v Wright* (1827) 3 Russ 458. This is so, although the contract of suretyship is subsequent to the mortgage: *Sachs v Ashby & Co* (1903) 88 LT 393.

6 *Ramsden v Langley* (1705) 2 Vern 536.

7 *Hunt v Fownes* (1803) 9 Ves 70. The costs of administration incurred by the mortgagor's personal representative without the request of the mortgagee do not have priority over the mortgage: *Saunders v Dunman* (1878) 7 Ch D 825.

8 *Sandon v Hooper*, above; *Sclater v Cottam* (1857) 5 WR 744. In estimating the value of his security in the bankruptcy of the mortgagor, the mortgagee may bring into account costs expended in properly defending a claim brought against him in respect of his title to the mortgaged property: *Re Hofmann, ex p Carr* (1879) 11 Ch D 62 (in which the mortgagee was allowed the costs of defending proceedings resulting from the inclusion by the mortgagor in the mortgage of property which the mortgagor did not own).

9 *Ramsden v Langley*, above, *Samuel v Jones* (1862) 7 LT 760; see *Clark v Hoskins* (1868) 37 LJ Ch 561 at 569; *Re Baldwin's Estate* [1900] 1 IR 15. The right to add costs to the security applied where the mortgagor sued as a 'poor person' (against whom no costs order could, by statute, be made): *Re Leighton's Conveyance* [1937] Ch 149, [1936] 3 All ER 1033, CA. This was because the statutory provisions did not impinge upon the right of a party to recover costs by means not involving payment.

See *Sinfield v Sweet* [1967] 1 WLR 1489 for an unsuccessful attempt to make the mortgagor personally liable for costs to avoid the limitations imposed in legal aid cases. See also *Saunders v Anglia Building Society (No 2)* [1971] AC 1039, HL; *Maker v Network Finance Ltd* [1982] 2 NSWLR 503.

10 *Dryden v Frost* (1838) 3 My & Cr 670.

11 *Detillin v Gale* (1802) 7 Ves 583; 'The owner coming to deliver the estate from that incumbrance he himself put upon it, the person having that pledge is not to be put to expense with regard to that.'A mortgagee does not in terms contract for costs, but the rule is that all costs which he, being mortgagee, properly incurs in relation to his security, are to be allowed to him': *National Provincial Bank of England v Games* (1886) 31 Ch D 582 at 592, CA. See also *Elders Trustees & Executor Co Ltd v Eagle Star Nominees Ltd* (1986) 4 BPR 920.

The basing of the right to costs on an implied term of the mortgage contract (see above) states this principle in another way.

12 *Re Chennell, Jones v Chennell* (1878) 8 Ch D 492; *Re Beddoe, Downes v Cottam* [1893] 1 Ch 547.

13 *Remnant v Hood (No 2)* (1860) 27 Beav 613; *Equitable Reversionary Interest Society v Fuller* (1861) 1 John & H 379; *Ward v Yates* (1860) 1 Drew & Sm 80.

Particular instances

36.3 A mortgagee who has commenced a foreclosure claim, pending a claim to administer the mortgagor's estate, is entitled, after being satisfied under the latter, to dismiss his own claim, and to have the costs of it[1].

Where a foreclosure claim is pending when a claim for redemption is brought by a later incumbrancer, the costs of the foreclosure claim will be provided for in the redemption claim[2].

Where there is a right of consolidating mortgages[3], costs incurred in respect of one estate may be added to the debt due upon another, of which redemption is ordered[4]. In the absence of such a right, the costs of proceedings relating to different mortgagees will be borne rateably by the two estates[5].

If one of two mortgagees who advanced the money in separate sums brings a claim for foreclosure, the other being a defendant, the judgment will direct foreclosure on default of payment of the whole debt and the costs of both mortgagees[6].

In a claim to determine priorities the costs usually follow the mortgages[7], but the court has a discretion and can order one or the other of the claimants to pay the costs if a case is made for it[8].

1 *Brooksbank v Higginbottom* (1862) 31 Beav 35, and as to costs on staying proceedings in a foreclosure claim, upon the offer of a later incumbrancer to pay the claimant's debt, see *Jones v Tinney* (1845) Kay App xlv.
2 *Ainsworth v Roe* (1850) 14 Jur 874.
3 *Cotterell v Stratton* (1872) 8 Ch App 295 at 302; *Johnstone v Cox*, above; *Re Love, Hill v Spurgeon* (1885) 29 Ch D 348, CA; *De Caux v Skipper* (1886) 31 Ch D 635, CA.
4 *Batchelor v Middleton* (1848) 6 Hare 75 at 86.
5 *De Caux v Skipper* (1886) 31 Ch D 635, CA.
6 *Davenport v James* (1847) 7 Hare 249. Costs of trustees who hold on trust to sell and pay off the mortgage may have priority over the mortgagee and his judgment creditor: *Clare v Wood* (1844) 4 Hare 81. The mortgagee may add to his debt the costs of his trustee who is made a defendant to a foreclosure claim: *Browne v Lockhart* (1840) 10 Sim 420.
7 With the consequence that each mortgagee add his own costs to his security and that such costs have the same priority as the respective mortgage debts.
8 *Harpham v Shacklock*, above at 215. In a case where the legal mortgagee brought a foreclosure claim and one of the defendants, an equitable mortgagee, unsuccessfully claimed priority, it was held that the legal mortgagee should add its ordinary foreclosure costs to their security and that the equitable mortgagee must pay them the residue of their costs of the claim: *Northern Counties of England Fire Insurance Co v Whipp* (1884) 26 Ch D 482 at 496, CA.

Limitations on entitlement

36.4 However, it is essential to any claim to litigation costs that the proceedings in question were reasonable. Hence the mortgagee will not be allowed the costs of improper, or useless, or unnecessary litigation[1]. The many judicial references to costs 'properly incurred' serve to make it clear that the court will examine the costs, charges and expenses sought to be added to the security and disallow those that it considers have not been 'properly incurred'[2]. See further **36.20**.

1 See *Dryden v Frost* (1838) 3 My & Cr 670, where the mortgagee, having only a title in equity defended a claim by the legal owner for the recovery of the property: *Burke v O'Connor* (1885) 4 Ir Ch R 418, where the mortgagee's claim for rent failed through being brought in the name of the wrong person; *Peers v Ceeley* (1852) 15 Beav 209, where the mortgagee, having sold under his power of sale, sued for specific performance, but lost the claim owing to misdescription. See also *Macken v Newcomen* (1844) 2 Jo & Lat 16.
2 *Parker-Tweedale v Dunbar Bank plc (No 2)* [1991] Ch 26, CA.

Basis of assessment of costs

36.5 The basic rule is that costs in a mortgage claim should be recovered by the mortgagee on the standard basis[1], unless there is a contract between the parties plainly and unambiguously providing for assessment on some other basis (for example, the indemnity basis)[2].

1 *The Kestrel* (1866) LR 1 A & E 78; *Re Queen's Hotel Co Cardiff Ltd, Re Vernon Tin Plate Co Ltd* [1900] 1 Ch 792; *Re Adelphi Hotel (Brighton) Ltd, District Bank Ltd v Adelphi Hotel (Brighton) Ltd* [1953] 2 All ER 498; affd in *Central Mortgage and Housing Corpn v Johnson* (1971) 20 DLR (3d) 622; and see *Jamieson v Gosigil Pty Ltd* [1983] 2 Qd R 117; *ANZ Banking Group (NZ) Ltd v Gibson* [1981] 2 NZLR 513. Cf *Re Griffiths, Jones & Co* (1883) 53 LJ Ch 303, CA, where it was held that, as a general rule, solicitor and client costs (now costs on the indemnity basis) were given (see *Lomax v Hide* (1690) 2 Vern 185). Cf *Re New Zealand Midland Rly Co, Smith v Lubbock* [1901] 2 Ch 357, where it was stated that a claimant in a debenture holder's claim was, as between himself and the mortgagors, only entitled to party and party costs (now costs on the standard basis), but that if the assets were insufficient to pay the debentures in full, then, as between himself and the other debenture holders, he was entitled to solicitor and client costs (now costs on the indemnity basis).

2 *Jamieson v Gosigil Pty Ltd* [1983] 2 QD R 117 at 120.

No personal liability of mortgagor, but costs are added to the debt

36.6 In the absence of an express term, there is no implied obligation upon the mortgagor to pay the costs, charges and expenses so incurred by the mortgagee. Consequently, unless the mortgage so provides, they are not recoverable from the mortgagor personally[1] (except if in the particular case he has become personally liable to pay them)[2].

However, the costs are added to the secured debt[3] and, both as against the mortgagor and other persons interested in the equity of redemption, they are added by the mortgagee to the amount due upon his security[4] and must be paid as a condition of redeeming[5]. With the principal and interest they form a single debt and are payable in the same priority[6].

1 *Re Sneyd, ex p Fewings* (1883) 25 Ch D 338 at 352, CA; *Sinfield v Sweet* [1967] 1 WLR 1489.

2 The mortgagor will be personally liable under his covenant for further assurance for costs incurred by the mortgagee under that covenant: *Langton v Langton* (1854) 18 Jur 1092; reversed, but not on this point (1855) 7 De GM & G 30.

A mortgagor who puts forward an unsustainable defence is personally liable to pay any costs incurred in consequence if the security proves insufficient: *Liverpool Marine Credit Co v Wilson* (1872) 7 Ch App 507, CA. Personal liability also arises where a redemption claim is dismissed because the mortgagor fails to redeem the mortgage: *Mutual Life Assurance Society v Langley* (1886) 32 Ch D 460, CA.

3 'If a mortgagee has expended any sum of money in supporting the right of the mortgagor to the estate, where his title has been impeached, the mortgagee may certainly add this to the principal of his debt, and it shall carry interest': *Godfrey v Watson* (1747) 3 Atk 517 at 518.

4 A provision entitling a mortgagee to add costs to the mortgage debt prevailed over legal aid legislation which provided that where a court made an order for costs against a legally aided person the legal aid authority should pay the costs within a specified limit: *Maker v Network Finance Ltd* [1982] 2 NSWLR 503. See also *Re Leighton's Conveyance* [1937] Ch 149, [1936] 3 All ER 1033, CA.

5 *Frazer v Jones* (1846) 5 Hare 475 at 483; *Dunstan v Patterson* (1847) 2 Ph 341; *Cotterell v Stratton*, above; *Re Sneyd, ex p Fewings*, above; *Re Wallis, ex p Lickorish* (1890) 25 QBD 176, CA.

6 *Barnes v Racster* (1842) 1 Y & C Ch Cas 401; *Johnstone v Cox* (1881) 19 Ch D 17, CA; *Harpham v Shacklock* (1881) 19 Ch D 207 at 215, CA; *Pollock v Lands Improvement Co* (1888) 37 Ch D 661 at 668; *Re Baldwin's Estate* [1900] 1 IR 15. The mere fact that the mortgage contains a declaration that the 'total amount to be recovered by the mortgagees

under these presents shall not exceed' so much, does not preclude the mortgagee from adding arrears of interest and costs beyond that sum, since the proviso is construed to relate exclusively to principal: *White v City of London Brewery Co* (1889) 42 Ch D 237, CA.

Application to equitable mortgages and charges

36.7 The principle that a mortgagee can recover from the mortgaged property his costs, charges and expenses properly incurred applies equally in relation to equitable mortgages, including mortgages by deposit (whether with or without a memorandum of deposit) and charges[1].

1 *Connell v Hardie* (1839) 3 Y&C Ex 582; *R v Chambers* (1840) 4 Y & C Ex 54; *Wade v Ward* (1859) 4 Drew 602; *Cotterell v Stratton* (1874) LR 17 Eq 543; *Ezekiel v Orakpo* [1997] 1 WLR 340, CA. See also *Central Mortgage and Housing Corpn v Johnson* (1971) 20 DLR (3d) 622; *Elders Trustees & Executor Co Ltd v Eagle Star Nominees Ltd* (1986) 4 BPR 9205.
Because the Charging Orders Act 1979, s 3(4) provides that charging order takes effect and is enforceable as an equitable charge, the holder of charging order is similarly entitled to add the costs of enforcing the order (ie obtaining possession and sale) to the security and thus to recover the same out of the proceeds of sale: *Holder v Supperstone* [2000] 1 All ER 473.

Interest on costs

36.8 In the absence of contractual provision, a mortgagee is only entitled to charge interest on his assessed costs if they are directed to be added to the security[1] and then they carry interest from the date when the assessment is completed and a costs certificate issued and not from the date of the judgment[2].

1 *Eardley v Knight* (1889) 41 Ch D 537. In that case the claim was brought by the mortgagor to set aside the mortgage. It was dismissed with costs. On the mortgagee's counterclaim, a foreclosure decree was made. The mortgagee sought to bring into the mortgage account interest on the costs in the foreclosure proceedings. Kay J held that there was no rule that in every foreclosure the mortgagor could not redeem until payment, not only of principal, interest and costs, but also of interest on the costs. He observed that the costs might carry interest if they were charged on the estate (see *Lippard v Ricketts* (1872) LR 14 Eq 291) but that in the case before him under the judgment the costs had to be got from the mortgagor personally and were not charged on the estate.
2 *Eardley v Knight*, above.

Position where contractual provision

Generally

36.9 A mortgage deed may, and almost invariably does, contain express provision regarding the mortgagee's entitlement to recover from the mortgaged property costs incurred by him. Nonetheless, the principle in law that a mortgagee is entitled to add to the secured debt those expenses properly incurred[1] underlies all such contractual provisions[2] and, presumably, is to be borne in mind when interpreting them.

1 As to which, see **36.1**.
2 *Gomba Holdings (UK) Ltd v Minories Finance Ltd (No 2)* [1993] Ch 171, CA.

Specifically

36.10 The express terms in most mortgages generally extend the mortgagee's basic right to reimbursement considered above. It is typical for the instrument to stipulate that:

(a) the mortgagor is personally liable for the payment of costs[1];
(b) the costs are recoverable and to be assessed on the indemnity basis[2];
(c) the mortgagee is entitled to recover the costs of proceedings where a third party impugns the mortgage title or in relation to the enforcement or exercise of a right or power accruing to the mortgagee thereunder[3];
(d) interest will be payable on the costs and expenses added to the security.

Of course, the effect of any given provision necessarily turns upon its true construction for it is always necessary to determine what extent or level of recovery or retention or costs and expenses actually incurred by the mortgagee the mortgage deed permits[4].

1 *Gomba Holdings (UK) Ltd v Minories Finance Ltd (No 2)* [1993] Ch 171, CA.

2 *Gomba Holdings*, above, at 186: 'the reference to "a full indemnity basis" would avoid the risk of [assessment] .... on a standard basis.'

In this context, some expressions have been the subject of apparently conflicting decisions. In *Re Adelphi Hotel (Brighton) Ltd* [1953] 1 WLR 955 Vaisey J held that a clause securing payment of 'all costs, charges and expenses' required those costs to be assessed on the equivalent of what is now the standard basis. That decision was not cited in *Bank of Baroda v Panessar* [1987] Ch 335 in which Walton J held that 'all costs' meant that the costs would be paid on the indemnity basis. To the same effect had been the decision of Glidewell J in *Drummond v S & U Stores Ltd* [1981] 1 EGLR 42, a landlord and tenant case in which the *Adelphi Hotel* case was not followed. Reservations as to the correctness of the decision in *Re Adelphi Hotel (Brighton) Ltd* were expressed by Vinelott J in *Gomba Holdings* at first instance ([1992] BCLC 851 at 856-860) but the Court of Appeal put forward no view on the matter.

It is submitted that the better view is that 'all costs' should entitle the recipient to an assessment on the indemnity basis. This approach derives support from the judgment in another landlord and tenant case, *Fairview Investments Ltd v Sharma* (14 October 1999, unreported, CA). Although no reference was made to the above decisions (except *Gomba Holdings*) Chadwick LJ stated, 'The lessor should have its costs of and incidental to the litigation; and those costs should be [assessed] on an indemnity basis. The indemnity basis is appropriate because the opening words .... require the lessee to pay "all" expenses. The word 'all' does not enable or entitle the lessor to recover costs and expenses which are unreasonably incurred or which are unreasonable in amount .... But to enable the lessor to recover the costs which can properly be recovered, [an assessment] on the indemnity basis is appropriate.'

However, it seems also that subtle differences in language may result in different outcomes: in *Primeridge Ltd v Jean Muir Ltd* [1992] 1 EGLR 273 (a landlord and tenant case) Judge Esyr Lewis QC held that 'all proper costs' meant nothing more than such costs as the receiving party was entitled to recover under a court order or provision in the rules. He considered that the *Adelphi Hotel* case demonstrated that it has to be shown that the contractual provision upon which reliance is placed plainly and unambiguously entitles the party to an order for costs on the indemnity basis. He duly held that the expression with which he was concerned did not and, in so doing, noted that the vital difference between the *Primeridge* and the *Bank Baroda* cases was that the presence of the adjective 'proper'. Note also the impact of the Unfair Terms in Consumer Contracts Regulations 1999, as to which see **3.53**.

3 *Gomba Holdings (UK) Ltd v Minories Finance Ltd (No 2)* [1993] Ch 171 at 186, CA where it was observed that, 'the words, "however incurred" presumably avoid the exclusion of the third category of costs, charges and expenses referred to ... in *Parker-Tweedale v Dunbar Bank plc (No 2)* [1991] Ch 26', ie costs of litigation concerning the mortgaged property arising out of the wrongful act of a stranger to the mortgage.

4 *Gomba Holdings (UK) Ltd v Minories Finance Ltd (No 2)* [1993] Ch 171 at 183–184, CA.

Costs improperly incurred or unreasonable in amount

36.11 It is difficult to contemplate that a mortgage deed would ever be construed as entitling a mortgagee to charge against the mortgaged property, or to require the mortgagor to pay, all costs even if improperly or unreasonably incurred or improper or unreasonable in amount[1]. It would certainly require express terms in the deed to justify such a conclusion. Furthermore, even if the language clearly and unambiguously dictated that result, the enforceability of such a provision would be open to serious question on public policy grounds[2] and, in an appropriate case, under the Unfair Terms in Consumer Contracts Regulations 1999, SI 1999/2083[3].

1 *Gomba Holdings UK Ltd v Minories Finance Ltd (No 2)* [1993] Ch 171 at 187, CA.
2 *Gomba Holdings*, above, at 188.
3 As to which see **3.50**.

Court's jurisdiction to order, disallow and assess costs

Mortgagee not required to obtain order for costs

36.12 Where the mortgagee has a contractual right to recover costs out of the mortgage funds, he is not required to apply for an order those costs and the court is not required to assess such costs[1]. Instead, he may in such circumstances simply add the costs to the mortgage debt. Therefore, it seems that, in the absence of an application by the mortgagor (as to which see below), the court cannot make an order assessing a mortgagee's costs in a case where the mortgagee seeks no costs order, being content (as is customary) simply to rely on his contractual entitlement to add costs to the security[2].

1 CPR 48PD 50.2.
2 See CPR 48.3, 48PD 50.2, 48PD 50.1, 48PD 50.3(5) (discussed below) and *Mortgage Funding Corp plc v Kashef-Hamadani* (23 April 1993, unreported, CA), applied in *Bank of Ireland Home Mortgages Ltd v Bissett* (23 June 1999, unreported, Cty Ct).
Further confirmation appears in CPR 44PD 13.3 which provides that the general rule as to when the court should summarily assess costs does not apply to a mortgagee's costs in mortgage possession proceedings or other proceedings relating to a mortgage unless the mortgagee asks the court to make an order for his costs to be paid by another party.

Mortgagor's right to challenge mortgagee's costs

36.13 However, where the contract entitles the mortgagee to add the costs of litigation relating to the mortgage to the secured sum and/or to require the mortgagor to pay those costs, the mortgagor can apply to the court for a direction that an account of the mortgagee's costs be taken[1]. The mortgagor may then dispute an amount in the mortgagee's account on the basis that it has been unreasonably incurred or is unreasonable in amount[2]. In that event the court may order that the disputed costs are assessed under CPR 48.3[3].

1 CPR 48PD 50.4(1) and 25.1(1)(n).
2 CPR 48PD 50.4(2).
3 CPR 48PD 50.4(3).

Burden of proof and court's powers in relation to costs

36.14 Where the court assesses costs payable under the terms of a contract, the costs so payable are, unless the contract expressly provides otherwise, presumed to be costs which: (a) have been reasonably incurred; and (b) are reasonable in amount, and the court will assess them accordingly[1]. The onus is on the paying party (the mortgagor) to satisfy the court that costs have been unreasonably incurred or are unreasonable in amount, in which case the court may make an order that all or part of the costs payable under the contract (mortgage) shall be disallowed[2].

1 CPR 48.3(1).
2 CPR 48PD 50.1.

Governing principles

36.15 In assessing costs relating to a mortgage the court must adhere to the following principles[1]:

(a) an order for the payment of costs of proceedings by one party to another is always a discretionary order: see s 51 of the Supreme Court Act 1981;
(b) where there is a contractual right to the costs the discretion should ordinarily be exercised so as to reflect that contractual right[2];
(c) the power of the court to disallow a mortgagee's costs sought to be added to the mortgage security is a power that does not derive from s 51 of the Supreme Court Act 1981, but from the power of the courts of equity to fix the terms on which redemption will be allowed[3];
(d) a decision by a court to refuse costs in whole or in part to a mortgagee litigant may be:
    (i) an exercise in the exercise of the s 51 discretion[4];
    (ii) a decision in the exercise of the power to fix the terms on which redemption will be allowed;
    (iii) a decision as to the extent of a mortgagee's contractual right to add his costs to the security; or
    (iv) a combination of two or more of those things[5];
(e) a mortgagee is not to be deprived of a contractual or equitable right to add costs to the security merely by reason of an order for payment of costs made without reference to the mortgagee's contractual or equitable rights and without any adjudication as to whether or not the mortgagee should be deprived of these costs[6].

1 Set out in CPR 48PD 50.3, reflecting those expressed in *Gomba Holdings (UK) Ltd v Minories Finance Ltd (No 2)* [1993] Ch 171 at 194, CA.
2 For example, in particular as to the basis (standard or indemnity) for the assessment of the costs.
3 Although the court's jurisdiction has for a long time been fully established, there was a time when the court seems to have doubted its power to throw costs upon a mortgagee: *Francklyn v Fern* (1740) Barn Ch 30; *Detillin v Gale* (1802) 7 Ves 583. And in *Dunstan v Patterson* (1847) 2 Ph 341 it had been held that a claim by the mortgagor that the mortgagee should pay the costs, ought to be included in the original inquiry, for the court would not attend afterwards to evidence upon the subject.
4 Except that the discretionary power as to costs conferred by s 51 applies to cost 'of an incidental to proceedings' and therefore applies only to litigation costs and does not extend to non-litigation costs: *Gomba Holdings (UK) Ltd v Minories Finance Ltd (No 2)* [1993] Ch 171 at 192, CA.
5 The statements of case in the proceedings or the submissions made to the court may indicate which of the decisions has been made: CPR 48PD 50.3(4).
6 Where an order for assessment of costs on the standard basis has been made without any such adjudication (in circumstances where the court did not purport and intend to deprive the mortgagee of any costs to which it was contractually entitled to add to its security on an indemnity basis) the mortgagee remains entitled on the taking of the account to have its costs assessed on the indemnity basis (and to add such costs to the debt): *Gomba Holdings (UK) Ltd v Minories Finance Ltd (No 2)* [1993] Ch 171 at 194-195, CA. See also *Lomax v Hide* (1690) 2 Vern 185; *Ramsden v Langley* (1705) 2 Vern 536.

Court's discretion and circumstances to be taken into account

36.16 The court has discretion as to:

(a) whether costs are payable by one party to another[1];
(b) the amount of those costs[2];
(c) when the costs are to be paid[3].

If the court decides to make an order about costs the general rule is that the unsuccessful party will be ordered to pay the costs of the successful party, but the court may make a different order[4].

In deciding what order (if any) to make, the court must have regard to all the circumstances including:

(a) the conduct of the parties[5];
(b) whether a party succeeded on part of its case, even if it was not wholly successful[6];
(c) any payment into court or admissible offer to settle drawn to the court's attention[7].

The orders which the court may make include an order that a party must pay:

(a) a proportion of another party's costs[8];
(b) a stated amount in respect of another party's costs[9];
(c) costs from or until a certain date only[10];
(d) costs incurred before proceedings have begun[11];
(e) costs relating to particular steps taken in the proceedings[12];
(f) costs relating only to a distinct part of the proceedings[13]; and
(g) interest on costs from or until a certain date, including a date before judgment[14].

Where practicable, however, the court must make an order under (a) or (c) rather than (f) above[15].

Interim payments on account can be ordered where an order for costs has been made but the costs in question have not yet been assessed[16]. There is also provision for set-off of mutual costs orders in appropriate cases[17].

1 CPR 44.3(1)(a).
2 CPR 44.3(1)(b).
3 CPR 44.3(1)(c).
4 CPR 44.3(2).
5 CPR 44.3(4)(a). See, further, CPR 44.3(5).
6 CPR 44.3(4)(b). For general guidance as to the factors to be taken into account in apportioning costs between a partially successful litigant and his defeated counterpart (ie where one party succeeded overall but lost on a number of issues), see *Antonelli v Allen* [2000] NLJR 1825, Neuberger J; *Scholes Windows Ltd v Magnet Ltd (No 2)* [2000] ECDR 266, N Underhill QC.
7 CPR 44.3(4)(c). This includes Pt 36 offers: see, generally, CPR Pt 36.
8 CPR 44.3(6)(a).
9 CPR 44.3(6)(b).
10 CPR 44.3(6)(c).
11 CPR 44.3(6)(d).
12 CPR 44.3(6)(e).
13 CPR 44.3(6)(f). It appears that there is a judicial trend to make orders for costs which reflect the relative success of a particular party in relation to sub-issues in the litigation: *AEI Rediffusion Music Ltd v Phonographic Performance Ltd* [1999] 1 WLR 1507 at 1522-

1533, CA per Lord Woolf MR; *Shirley v Caswell* [2001] 1 Costs LR 1, [2000] Lloyds Rep PN 955, CA, indicating a departure from the more restricted approach to the award of costs under the previous rules of court as summarised in *Re Elgindata Ltd (No 2)* [1992] 1 WLR 1207 at 1214, CA. Cf *DEG Deutsche Investitions und Entwicklungs Gmbh v Koshy* (17 February 2000, unreported, Rimer J) and *McGhan Medical UK Ltd v Nagor Ltd* (28 March 2001, unreported, R Fysh QC): no requirement to adopt 'an issue based approach' to the question of costs and *Elgindata* still affords at least a good working guide as to the appropriate approach.

Although it is clear from the above cases that a successful party who has failed on some issues may be deprived of the whole or some part of his costs, particularly in a case where the issues on which he was unsuccessful caused a significant increase in the length or cost of the proceedings, it is less apparent whether, in such circumstances, the successful party can be ordered to pay the other side's costs of such issues (unless he acted improperly or unreasonably in advancing them): see the cases cited above and cf *Johnsey Estates (1990) Ltd v Secretary of State for the Environment, Transport and the Regions* [2001] EWCA Civ 535, CA (11 April 2001, unreported). Conflicting approaches emerge: *Elgindata* suggests no such order can be made, whereas *Johnsey* indicates otherwise. The tension now seems to have been resolved: in *Summit Property Ltd v Pitmans (a firm) (Costs)* (19 November 2001, unreported) the Court of Appeal held that the *Elgindata* requirement for there to have been unreasonableness no longer applies; instead the CPR requires the court to be more ready than was formerly the case to make separate costs orders reflecting the outcome of specific issues in order to encourage parties to limit the issues pursued and to discourage a 'no stone unturned' approach to the presentation of cases. In *Summit Property* the Court of Appeal upheld the decision of Park J (in view of the defendant's failure on the main issue, despite success on a point of law) to make an issue-based costs order that the successful defendant do pay 65% of the unsuccessful claimant's costs, with the claimant paying 30% of the defendant's costs.

14 CPR 44.3(6)(g).
15 CPR 44.3(7).
16 CPR 44.3(8).
17 CPR 44.3(9).

Assessment of costs[1]

36.17 On the taking of an account, the quantification of costs should be by way of a detailed assessment[2].

The basis of the assessment (as to which see below) should, it seems, normally correspond with the contractual entitlement of the mortgagee under the mortgage deed[3].

Under the Civil Procedure Rules the two possible bases of assessment are (a) the standard basis and (b) the indemnity basis[4]. The principal difference is that when assessing costs on the standard basis the court will only allow courts which are proportionate to the matters in issue and will resolve any doubt as to whether costs were reasonably incurred or reasonable and proportionate in amount in favour of the paying party[5], whereas on the indemnity basis it will resolve any such doubt in favour of the receiving party[6].

There is a seemingly unresolved difficulty if the contractual entitlement of the mortgagee to costs, charges and expenses does not correspond either to the standard basis or the indemnity basis of assessment. This is because:

(a) CPR 44.4(1) provides that where the court is to assess the amounts of costs, it will assess those costs on the standard basis or on the indemnity basis;
(b) CPR 44.4(4) states that where the court makes an order for costs to be assessed on a basis other than the standard basis or the indemnity basis, the costs will be assessed on the standard basis.

These provisions appear to preclude any direction being given other than for assessment on a standard or indemnity basis[7]. Whether the draftsman of the rules had in mind the possibility that costs might, for contractual reasons, need to be assessed on some other basis than standard or indemnity seems doubtful[8].

The answer to the conundrum may, however, lie in CPR 48.3 and CPR 48PD 50, which deal with the amount of costs where costs are payable pursuant to contract. As noted above, these provisions indicate, albeit without expressly stating this to be the position, that the appropriate basis of assessment in such cases is the indemnity basis[9]. If this was the intention, it is regrettable that it was not more clearly expressed[10]. The rules appear to be capable of leading to curious results, for instance in a case where the mortgage deed is silent as to the basis of assessment of the mortgagee's costs[11].

Fortunately, however, in most cases nowadays the mortgage deed makes it tolerably clear that the mortgagee's contractual right to costs is on the indemnity basis. Therefore, it is to be hoped that the scenario will not occur frequently[12].

1 'Assessment' is the name ascribed by the CPR to the process (formerly known as 'taxation') of quantifying a costs liability.
2 See CPR 44PD 13.3 (which applies unless the mortgagee asks the court to make an order for his costs to be paid by another party) and cf CPR 44.7. For the meaning of 'summary assessment' and 'detailed assessment' see CPR 43.3 and 43.4 respectively.
3 *Gomba Holdings UK Ltd v Minories Finance Ltd (No 2)* [1993] Ch 171 at 191, CA.
4 CPR 44.4(1).
5 CPR 44.4(2).
6 CPR 44.4(3). In that event the onus is on the paying party to demonstrate that the costs were unreasonably incurred or unreasonable in amount; moreover, there is no express requirement of proportionality: CPR 44.4(3) and see CPR 44.5(1).
7 *Gomba Holdings (UK) Ltd v Minories Finance Ltd (No 2)* [1993] Ch 171 at 191, CA.
8 *Ibid.* The 'rules' to which the Court of Appeal was referring were the Rules of the Supreme Court 1965, since superseded by the CPR.
9 See the presumption in CPR 48.3 and CPR 48PD 50.1 and 50.4(2) which put the burden of challenge firmly on the mortgagor.
10 Particularly because the provisions appear to sit uneasily with the general principle stated in *Gomba Holdings* at 191, as to which see n 3 (and the rules committee was clearly aware of that decision, given that CPR 48PD 50.3 is taken word for word from the judgment).
11 Although the presumption in CPR 44.3 is expressed not to apply if 'the contract expressly provides otherwise', there is, it is submitted, a distinction between on the one hand a mortgage deed which refers to 'costs, to be assessed on the standard basis' and one which simply speaks of 'costs' without more. In the former case it may fairly be said that the contract 'expressly provides otherwise' but this is doubtful in the latter case.

If the effect of the CPR is thus potentially to convert a contractual entitlement which, properly construed, is to costs on the standard basis into a right to recover indemnity costs, this is considered surprising and difficult to justify. Furthermore, it is somewhat difficult to reconcile with the principle laid down in *Gomba Holdings* and also CPR 48PD 50.3(2) (which speaks of the court's discretion being exercised 'so as to reflect' (and not exceed) the mortgagee's contractual right to costs).
12 In *Gomba Holdings* the Court of Appeal was satisfied that the mortgagee's entitlement corresponded to the indemnity basis and thus did not need to grapple with the implications of the rules: [1993] Ch 171 at 191.

Costs of mortgagee's solicitor

36.18 A mortgagor who is liable to pay the bill of the mortgagee's solicitor can have it assessed under the Solicitors Act 1974[1]. Where the assessment is applied for by the mortgagor under this section, items which the mortgagor would not be liable to pay as between himself and the mortgagee will be disallowed, even though the solicitor would be entitled to charge them against his client, the mortgagee[2]. There are limitations, however, where the application is made more than a year after delivery of the bill, after judgment for the recovery of the costs has been obtained or after the bill has been paid[3]; in those cases no order shall be made except in special circumstances[4]. The assessment is on the indemnity basis[5].

1 Sections 70 and 71.
2 *Re Longbotham & Sons* [1904] 2 Ch 152, CA, approving *Re Gray* [1901] 1 Ch 239; and see *Re Cohen and Cohen* [1905] 2 Ch 137, CA; *Forsinard Estates Ltd v Dykes* [1971] 1 All ER 1018, [1971] 1 WLR 282.
3 Sections 70(3) and 71(2).
4 Sections 70(3) and 71(2).
5 CPR 48.8(2) and CPR 48PD 54.2(1).

Non-litigation costs

36.19 Whatever the extent of the mortgagee's (contractual or other) right to costs, some means of quantification must be adopted[1]. 'Assessment' is simply the name given to the quantification process whereby the amount of recoverable costs is ascertainable by the court[2]. It is clear that non-litigation costs can be subjected by the court to the process of assessment in just the same way as litigation costs[3].

1 *Gomba Holdings (UK) Ltd v Minories Finance Ltd (No 2)* [1993] Ch 171 at 188, CA.
2 *Gomba Holdings*, above, at 189.
3 *Gomba Holdings*, above, at 189. See also: (a) the definition of 'costs' in CPR 43.2(1)(a); (b) CPR 43.2(2)(b) which provides that the costs to which CPR Pts 44-48 apply include 'costs which are payable by one party to another party under the terms of a contract, where the court makes an order for an assessment of those costs'; (c) CPR 44.3(6)(d) which refers to 'costs incurred before proceedings have begun'.

INSTANCES WHERE RIGHT TO COSTS MAY BE LOST

General examples

36.20 As mentioned above, a mortgagee will not be permitted to recover costs or expenses unreasonably or improperly incurred[1]. The mortgagee may forfeit his entitlement to costs by gross misconduct, or may even have to pay the costs of such a claim in a case where he has acted vexatiously or unreasonably[2]. This will be the case if he has been guilty of such inequitable conduct as amounts to a violation or culpable neglect of his duty under the contract[3].

The jurisdiction either to deprive the mortgagee of costs, or to order him to pay costs, will also be exercised where, even without improper motive, he has caused expenses to be incurred which cannot justly be thrown upon the mortgagor.

The following, drawn from the various authorities, provide examples of instances where one or the other course has been (and might in similar future circumstances well be) adopted[4]:

(a) where the mortgagee sets up an unjust defence[5];
(b) where the mortgagee resists a claim to redeem on the ground of a foreclosure collusively obtained[6];
(c) where the mortgagee resists a just claim to redeem (whether on the basis that the right to redeem has been extinguished or otherwise)[7], in which event the mortgagee is liable for so much of the costs as his improper conduct had caused, though he may be allowed the ordinary costs of redemption[8];
(d) where the mortgagee refuses a proper (and actual) tender, even one made under protest[9];

(e) where the mortgagee fails on tender to execute a reconveyance which has already been approved[10];
(f) where the mortgagee continues to proceed after payment of all that was due[11].

In the last three scenarios the mortgagee so acts on peril of paying the costs incurred after the payment or tender[12], whether it was made before or after the commencement of the claim and whether by the mortgagor or one representing him, or by a later incumbrancer[13].

It should be noted that all the authorities cited in this section (**36.20–36.26**) must now be viewed in the light of the Civil Procedure Rules (as to which see above).

1 *Gomba Holdings (UK) Ltd v Minories Finance Ltd (No. 2)* [1993] Ch 171, CA.
2 *Bank of New South Wales v O'Connor* (1889) 14 App Cas 273 at 278, PC; and see *Meredith v Davis* (1933) 33 SRNSW 334. As regards costs, mortgagees and trustees are on the same footing: *Turner v Hancock* (1882) 20 Ch D 303 at 304.
3 *Cotterell v Stratton* (1872) 8 Ch App 295 at 302; see *M'Donnell v M'Mahon* (1889) 23 LR Ir 283.
4 As to the costs of the mortgagee where the advance is made out of trust moneys, see *Allen v Knight* (1846) 5 Hare 272; *West v Jones* (1851) 1 Sim NS 205.
5 *Mocatta v Murgatroyd* (1717) 1 P Wms 393; *Baker v Wind* (1748) 1 Ves Sen 160; and see *Thornton v Court* (1854) 3 De GM & G 293; *England v Codrington* (1758) 1 Eden 169; *Tomlinson v Gregg* (1866) 15 WR 51; *Tarn v Turner* (1888) 39 Ch D 456, CA, and if the contract under which the mortgagee claims is illegal: *Johnson v Williamhurst* (1823) 1 LJ OS Ch 112; or if he has been guilty of ill conduct in attempting to deprive another of the benefit of his security by a dealing behind his back (*Taylor v Baker* (1818) Dan 71 at 82) he may be refused his costs.
6 *Hall v Heward* (1886) 32 Ch D 430 at 436, CA.
7 See *Squire v Pardoe* (1891) 66 LT 243; *Henderson v Astwood* [1894] AC 150 at 162, PC; *Tomlinson v Gregg* (1866) 15 WR 51.
8 *Harvey v Tebbutt* (1820) 1 Jac & W 197; *Harryman v Collins* (1854) 18 Beav 11; *Whitbread v Smith* (1854) 3 De GM & G 727. But in a case where the mortgagee set up an adverse title and failed, he was ordered to pay the whole costs of the claim: *Roberts v Williams* (1844) 4 Hare 129; *National Bank of Australasia v United Hand-in-Hand Band of Hope Co* (1879) 4 App Cas 391, PC.

As to costs where the mortgagee makes claims which he fails to establish, see *Montgomery v Calland* (1844) 14 Sim 79; *Cockell v Taylor* (1851) 15 Beav 103 at 127; *Green v Briggs* (1849) 6 Hare 632; *West v Jones* (1851) 1 Sim NS 205 at 218; *Gregg v Slater* (1856) 22 Beav 314.
9 *Greenwood v Sutcliffe* [1892] 1 Ch 1, CA; *Fletcher and Campbell v City Marine Finance Ltd* [1968] 2 Lloyd's Rep 510. However, if the mortgagor makes no tender, but only states in his defence that he is willing to pay so much as he considers to be due before the institution of the claim, he will not save the costs, even though there is a dispute and at the hearing he succeeds in establishing his case as to the amount due: *Hodges v Croydon Canal Co* (1840) 3 Beav 86; *Gammon v Stone* (1749) 1 Ves Sen 339. See also *Broad v Selfe* (1863) 9 Jur (NS) 885, where, under the circumstances, no costs were given on either side to the hearing. As to an offer to pay the amount found due upon assessment, see *Sentance v Porter* (1849) 7 Hare 426.

Where a tender has been made and refused, the application that the mortgagee may pay the subsequent costs may be made at the hearing, supported by evidence of the tender and refusal: *Sentance v Porter*, above.
10 *Graham v Seal* (1918) 88 LJ Ch 31, CA. For a case in which a mortgagee who neglected to attend at the appointed time and place for the completion of redemption was refused his costs see *Cliff v Wadsworth* (1843) 2 Y & C Ch Cas 598.
11 *Gregg v Slater* (1856) 22 Beav 314; *Seal v Kemsley* [1883] WN 122, CA.
12 *Shuttleworth v Lowther*, undated, cited 7 Ves 586; *Cliff v Wadsworth* (1843) 2 Y & C Ch Cas 598; *Harmer v Priestley* (1853) 16 Beav 569; *Morley v Bridges* (1846) 2 Coll 621; *Gregg v Slater* (1856) 22 Beav 314, and to save the expense of coming to the court on further consideration, a direction that the mortgagee shall pay the costs, if the sum due does not exceed the tender, may be added to the judgment at the hearing: *Hosken v Sincock* (1865) 11 Jur NS 477.
13 *Smith v Green* (1844) 1 Coll 555 at 564.

When nothing due

36.21 If the mortgagee institutes a foreclosure claim and upon taking the accounts it is shown that nothing was due at the commencement of the proceedings, or if he drives the mortgagor to institute a claim under like circumstances, he must bear the whole expense of the claim[1].

Or if, being a defendant, he denies that he is satisfied, when nothing remains due, he must pay the costs of so much of the proceedings as have been caused by his denial or false suggestion[2]. So where, knowing that he is already overpaid, the creditor contests the mode of taking the accounts and fails[3]; or, having sold the mortgaged property, asserts that the surplus, after paying principal, interest, and costs, is much less than is found due from him on the master's certificate[4]; or refuses to account and the balance is found against him[5]; or causes subsequent proceedings by keeping money and receiving rents, long after his right to receive them as mortgagee in possession has ceased[6], he will be allowed such costs only as arose whilst he filled the character of a creditor and must pay the rest.

A person who, whether his true character is that of a mortgagee or not, places himself in the position of an accounting party, and so undertakes a duty which he cannot perform by reason of the loss of vouchers for sums which he has paid, will not have the costs of taking the accounts[7].

1 *Binnington v Harwood* (1825) Turn & R 477; *Morris v Islip* (1856) 23 Beav 244; *O'Neill v Innes* (1864) 15 I Ch R 527.
2 *Montgomery v Calland* (1844) 14 Sim 79; *Stagg v Frizell* (1846) 3 Jo & Lat 383; *Ashworth v Lord* (1887) 36 Ch D 545; *Kinnaird v Trollope* (1889) 42 Ch D 610.
3 *Skirrett v Athy* (1811) 1 Ball & B 433.
4 *Charles v Jones* (1887) 35 Ch D 544. As to the discretion of the court in such cases, and the mode of its exercise, see *Heath v Chinn* (1908) 98 LT 855.
5 *Tanner v Heard* (1857) 23 Beav 555; *Powell v Trotter* (1861) 1 Drew & Sm 388.
6 *Archdeacon v Bowes* (1824) 13 Price 353. Prima facie, the mortgagee in possession has a right to the costs of a claim instituted to take the account and it is not merely because there is a difficulty in taking it, not occasioned by his misconduct, or because the result is against him, that he will be deprived of his costs: *Stagg v Frizell*, above. Neither will this be done where he is found to have been overpaid, though he has insisted that a large sum remained due to him, if the judgment has been made to include costs in the usual form: *Gilbert v Golding* (1794) 2 Anst 442.
7 *Price v Price* (1845) 15 LJ Ch 13.

Costs due to loss of deeds

36.22 If the mortgagee has lost the title deeds of the estate, he becomes liable for any costs which have been incurred in consequence of such loss. If, therefore, upon the mortgagor's refusal to repay the debt, by reason of the non-production of the deeds and the mortgagee's neglect to give a satisfactory indemnity, a claim is brought for foreclosure[1] or recovery of the land[2], or if the mortgagor sues for redemption[3], and has to accept an indemnity for the loss of the deeds, the costs of any of such claims will fall upon the mortgagee, and in a claim for redemption, the court will not consider whether the indemnity[4] (if any has been offered) should have satisfied the mortgagor, for he is entitled to institute a claim, in order that any person with whom he may thereafter deal respecting the estate may be fully satisfied of the loss, but it is said that, in a foreclosure claim, it will be inquired whether a proper indemnity was offered[5].

1 *Stokoe v Robson* (1815) 19 Ves 385.
2 *Lord Midleton v Eliot* (1847) 15 Sim 531.
3 *Lord Midleton v Eliot*, above; *James v Rumsey* (1879) 11 Ch D 398; *Caldwell v Matthews* (1890) 62 LT 799. The mortgagee must give the indemnity at his own cost: *Lord Midleton v Eliot*, above.
4 See **28.82**.
5 See *Macartney v Graham* (1831) 2 Russ & M 353. So, if the mortgagee has a power of sale, but by reason of the loss of the deeds he is obliged to come for a sale under a judgment, the subsequent incumbrancers are entitled to be paid their costs of the claim out of the purchase money, although the amount of it is insufficient to pay the principal and interest due to the claimant: *Wontner v Wright* (1829) 2 Sim 543.

Unnecessary or unsuccessful proceedings

36.23 It is the duty of the mortgagee so to pursue his remedy as not to incur unnecessary costs. Hence he must bear the cost of proceedings so far as they are mistaken or useless[1] and the court may except from the general costs the costs of a particular issue on which the mortgagee has failed, although the remainder of the claim was justified[2].

The costs incurred by an improper joinder of parties, whether as claimants or defendants, must be paid by the mortgagee[3] as, for instance, in a claim for sale prior annuitants were joined, though the sale should have been made subject to their annuities[4], or where in a like claim subsequent incumbrancers were needlessly made parties[5]. However, it is not a reason for depriving the mortgagee of costs that the person, in respect of whose interest they were incurred, might have been a co-claimant in the claim, because he might have objected to being a claimant[6].

1 Where, for instance, a claim was not originally commenced as, but was turned into a foreclosure claim, the costs incurred before it assumed that form were thrown on the mortgagee: *Smith v Smith* (1815) Coop G 141; *Briant v Lightfoot* (1837) 1 Jur 20; *Philips v Davies* (1843) 7 Jur 52; *Hogan v Baird* (1843) 4 Dr & War 296, and as to costs incurred unnecessarily, see *Marsack v Reeves* (1821) 6 Madd 108; *Ex p Fletcher* (1832) Mont 454; *Cocks v Stanley* (1857) 4 Jur NS 942.
2 *Deeley v Lloyds Bank (No 2)* (1909) 53 Sol Jo 419; and a mortgagee who has neglected to attend at the appointed time and place for the completion of redemption, and has thereby created the difficulty which caused the claim, has been refused his costs: *Cliff v Wadsworth* (1843) 2 Y & C Ch Cas 598.
3 *Pearce v Watkins* (1852) 5 De G & Sm 315 at 317.
4 *Delabere v Norwood* (1786) 3 Swan 144n; and see *Horrocks v Ledsam* (1845) 2 Coll 208.
5 *Cooke v Brown* (1840) 4 Y & C Ex 227.
6 *Browne v Lockhart* (1840) 10 Sim 420; that is, to deprive the mortgagee of the costs of the party joined as a defendant it must be shown, not only that he might have been, but that he was willing to be, a claimant, and that the mortgagee wilfully abstained from so joining him.

Costs of parties added for benefit of mortgagee

36.24 Under special circumstances the mortgagee has been ordered to pay the costs of the defendant in the first instance (even though the security is deficient), and then add them to his debt[1], but otherwise costs of parties whose presence is made necessary by the act of the mortgagor are not generally paid by the mortgagee[2] and the mortgagee will not be ordered to pay such costs. This is so even where the mortgagee has been ordered to pay his own costs of an unsuccessful claim, the determination of which was the object of the claim[3].

1 Eg costs of guardian of infant defendant. See *Harris v Hamlyn* (1849) 3 De G & Sm 470; *Newburgh v Morten* (1851) 15 Jur 166; *Spurgeon v Witham* MR (unreported, 21 December 1855), on petition for costs not provided for by decree, as well as at the hearing; and as to the costs of the trustees of the equity of redemption where a judgment creditor of the mortgagees sues for the purpose of getting a charge on the mortgage debt, see *Clare v Wood* (1844) 4 Hare 81.

2 *Siffken v Davis* (1853) Kay App xxi, appears to be contra, but does not seem intelligible.

3 *Green v Briggs* (1849) 6 Hare 632.

Parties added through mortgagee dealing with the estate

36.25 The mortgagee is entitled to deal with his estate as owner so soon as the day fixed for redemption has passed and his estate has become absolute at law and if he disposes of it so as to make other parties beside himself necessary parties to a redemption[1] or foreclosure[2] claim, as trustees or otherwise, their costs will be paid by him in the first instance and he will add them to his debt[3].

The mortgagee's acts must have been so done as not to burden the estate with unnecessary expense. Therefore if he, or those who represent him, transfer mortgages on separate properties by a single deed, so as to cause a necessity for a covenant for production, either by the person redeeming[4] or by those interested under the assignment in case the former should waive his right to delivery[5], the costs of preparing and perfecting the covenant and attested copies, and of the redeeming parties' application to the court, will fall upon the mortgagee's estate.

The costs of both the mortgagee himself and of a trustee, where either of them are necessary parties by the imprudence of the mortgagee, may be thrown upon the latter[6].

If an assignment of the mortgage security is made after judgment, or, it seems, is made at all *pendente lite*, the mortgagor will not be charged with costs of the supplementary proceedings by which the assignee is brought before the court[7].

1 *Wetherell v Collins* (1818) 3 Madd 255.

2 *Bartle v Wilkin* (1836) 8 Sim 238.

3 *Smith v Chichester* (1842) 2 Dr & War 393; *Bartle v Wilkin*, above, but the costs of incumbrancers on a charge or life estate will be borne by the charge or life estate, not by the inheritance or the estate out of which the charge is raiseable: *Stewart v Marquis Donegal* (1845) 2 Jo & Lat 636, but where the mortgagee has been disallowed or ordered to pay costs, for improper conduct, the mortgagor has been ordered to pay the costs of the mortgagee's trustee and to be repaid by the mortgagee: *Montgomery v Calland* (1844) 14 Sim 79; *Cockell v Taylor* (1851) 15 Beav 103, and it has been said that where an incumbrancer creates a trust for his own purposes, he gets only his own costs and pays those of his trustee; but where he devises or disposes of the charge to several, each, being made a defendant, gets his costs, because all represent but one original incumbrancer: *Galway v Butler* (1819) 1 Mol 13n, but the former part of this proposition seems hardly consistent with the rule stated above as to the rights of the mortgagee. As to the costs of the mortgagee's trustee in bankruptcy, see *Coles v Forrest* (1847) 10 Beav 552.

4 *Capper v Terrington* (1844) 1 Coll 103.

5 *Dobson v Land* (1851) 4 De G & Sm 575–581, but where the mortgagor refused an offer to deliver the deed to him upon his covenanting to produce it, the costs of his application to the court for a reconveyance were thrown upon himself: *Capper v Terrington*, above.

6 For examples of this, see *Shackleton v Shackleton* (1825) 2 Sim & St 242; *S C Anon* (1825) 3 LJOS Ch 141; *Hickson v Fitzgerald* (1826) 1 Mol 14n.

7 *Barry v Wrey* (1827) 3 Russ 465; *Coles v Forrest*, above. Where an order was made in a foreclosure claim to revive against an assignee after decree, it was ordered to be specified that the costs should be paid by the claimant: *James v Harding* (1855) 24 LJ Ch 749. A purchaser *pendente lite* comes into court *pro bono et malo*, and may become liable for the whole costs of the claim: *Anon* (1739) 1 Atk 89.

Where right to costs not lost

36.26 In the absence of a tender by the mortgagor, the mortgagee will neither be ordered to pay, nor forfeit his right to, costs even though he claims (in good faith) more than that to which the court adjudges him to be entitled[1]. The result is the same if the mortgagee stipulates that the accounts required shall be furnished at the cost of the mortgagor where they are of a special nature[2]. Further, the mortgagee will not necessarily have to pay the costs occasioned by a dispute as to fact, even though the eventual result may be against him, for this may not necessarily amount to unreasonable conduct[3]. He may be deprived of costs where his claim, even if made in good faith, is unfounded; however, the position is different where the claim, despite being ultimately unsuccessful, is fairly arguable[4].

1 *Loftus v Swift and St Patrick's Hospital* (1806) 2 Sch & Lef 642 at 657; *Cotterell v Stratton* (1872) 8 Ch App 295; *Re Watts, Smith v Watts* (1882) 22 Ch D 5, CA.
2 *Norton v Cooper* (1854) 5 De Gm & G 728; and see *Project Research Pty Ltd v Permanent Trustee of Australia Ltd* (1990) 5 BPR 11 at 225; *Estoril Investments Ltd v Westpac Banking Group* (1993) ACL Rep 295 NSW 24.
3 *Quarrell v Beckford* (1816) 1 Madd 269; *Wilson v Metcalfe* (1818) 3 Madd 45.
4 See *Credland v Potter* (1874) 10 Ch App 8; *Kinnaird v Trollope* (1889) 42 Ch D 610; *Bird v Wenn* (1886) 33 Ch D 215. In a doubtful case as to the right of foreclosure (*Teulon v Curtis* (1832) 1 You 610), or to redeem (*Kirkham v Smith* (1749) 1 Ves Sen 259), it may be that no costs will be given on either side, but the costs occasioned by an unsuccessful objection to the mortgagee's right to sue may be thrown on the defendant: *Tildesley v Lodge* (1857) 3 Sm & G 543; and so may the costs of a claim which the incumbrancer has been obliged to institute, by reason of subsequent dealings with the estate by the owner of the equity of redemption without giving notice of the charge: *Wise v Wise* (1845) 2 Jo & Lat 403.

Consequences of costs order made against mortgagee

36.27 An order for payment of costs made against a mortgagee is not necessarily an order for personal payment. He may, and indeed frequently will, be allowed to set them off against the amount payable to him in respect of his debt[1] and where the costs of the claim, or part of them, would have been thrown upon a mortgagee, being solvent, yet if he is insolvent (and, therefore, unable to pay), he will not receive any general costs[2].

1 *Banks v Whittall* (1847) 1 De G & Sm 536 at 541; *West v Jones* (1851) 1 Sim NS 205; *Wheaton v Graham* (1857) 24 Beav 483; *Forbes v Jackson* (1882) 19 Ch D 615. As to costs of the mortgagee's executors in a foreclosure claim where the mortgagee had made himself liable to costs in a previous claim, see *Long v Storie* (1852) 9 Hare 542.
2 *Rider v Jones* (1843) 2 Y & C Ch Cas 329.

COSTS OF DISCLAIMING DEFENDANTS IN FORECLOSURE PROCEEDINGS

Rules as to costs

36.28 A defendant for a foreclosure claim may be allowed costs if, having been needlessly made a party, he disclaims any interest in the subject matter of the claim. The right to costs in such circumstances is governed by the following rules[1]:

(a) where a defendant disclaims in such a manner as to show that he never had, and never claimed, an interest at or after the commencement of the claim, he is entitled to his costs against the claimant[2];
(b) if, having an interest, he shows that he disclaimed, or offered to disclaim before the institution of the claim, under circumstances which establish actual notice of the disclaimer against the claimant mortgagee, or which show that with ordinary prudence the mortgagee might have had such notice[3], he is also entitled to his costs[4];
(c) if, having an interest, he allows himself to be made a party to the claim, and does not disclaim or offer to disclaim before claim, he is not entitled to his costs[5];
(d) if, having been properly made a party, he disclaims during the claim and, without waiting to be asked, offers to be dismissed without costs, and is yet brought to the hearing for some special purpose of the claimant, he will have his costs subsequent to the disclaimer or offer[6].

1 *Ford v Earl of Chesterfield* (1853) 16 Beav 516; *Ridgway v Kynnersley* (1865) 2 Hem & M 565; *Earl of Cork v Russell* (1871) LR 13 Eq 210; *Ward v Shakeshaft* (1860) 1 Drew & Sm 269.

2 *Tipping v Power* (1842) 1 Hare 405; *Gabriel v Sturgis* (1846) 5 Hare 97; *Grigg v Sturgis* (1846) 5 Hare 93; *Jones v Rhind* (1869) 17 WR 1091. In this case he is not properly made a party: *Furber v Furber* (1862) 30 Beav 523 at 524. The rule applies where he had an interest, but assigned it before claim: *Glover v Rogers* (1847) 11 Jur 1000; *Hurst v Hurst* (1852) 22 LJ Ch 538; otherwise, if he had only agreed to assign it, the actual transfer not being made till after claim: *Roberts v Hughes* (1868) LR 6 Eq 20; see *Land v Wood* (1823) 1 LJOS Ch 89; and it applies to a trustee under a will who has never acted: *Benbow v Davies* (1848) 11 Beav 369; and to a beneficial devisee who has not accepted the devise: *Higgins v Frankis* (1850) 20 LJ Ch 16.

The disclaimer may be either before or after the commencement of the claim: *Bellamy v Brickenden* (1858) 4 K & J 670; *Day v Gudgen* (1876) 2 Ch D 209. If on being joined the party takes no step in the claim, but states the facts to the claimant's solicitors and asks if he is required to appear or plead, he will have his costs incurred after that communication: *Howkins v Bennet* (1863) 2 Hem & M 567n. Cf *Vale v Merideth* (1854) 18 Jur 992, where a formal and exact disclaimer was insisted on—that the defendant did not and never did claim and that she disclaimed, though an informal disclaimer may be effectual to prevent the personal representative of the defendant being a proper party; and if joined he will have costs: *Ridgway v Kynnersley*, above.

3 See *Ridgway v Kynnersley*, above.

4 *Ford v Earl of Chesterfield*, above, see *Thompson v Kendall* (1840) 9 Sim 397; *Lock v Lomas* (1851) 15 Jur 162. In this case he is prima facie a necessary party; see *Gibson v Nicol* (1846) 9 Beav 403; *Ohrly v Jenkins* (1847) 1 De G & Sm 543; *Staffurth v Pott* (1848) 2 De G & Sm 571; *Buchanan v Greenway* (1848) 11 Beav 58, but if he disclaims before claim he ceases to be a necessary party, and therefore if the disclaimer is known to the claimant, and nevertheless he is made a defendant, this is improper. In cases where the defendant is properly made a party, the mortgagee will have the costs over against the mortgagor. Where the defendant assigns his interest before defence, see *Hawkins v Gardiner* (1854) 17 Jur 780; also *Wright v Barlow* (1851) 5 De G & Sm 43.

5 *Ford v Earl of Chesterfield*, above. To entitle a defendant who has an interest to costs there must be a disclaimer or an offer to disclaim or release: *Lock v Lomas* (1851) 15 Jur 162; *Thompson v Kendall* (1840) 9 Sim 397.

A statement that if he had been applied to he would have released or disclaimed his right, but that no such application was made to him, gives no right to costs, for this shows that the right remains in the defendant; and it is not the duty of the claimant before claim to ascertain from the defendant whether he does or does not claim an interest: *Collins v Shirley* (1830) 1 Russ & M 638; *Cash v Belcher* (1842) 1 Hare 310; *Ford v White* (1852) 16 Beav 120. An untrue averment by the claimant that he has given the defendant an opportunity to disclaim may entitle him to costs: *Gurney v Jackson* (1852) 1 Sm & G 97.

6 *Talbot v Kemshead* (1858) 4 K & J 93; *Dillon v Ashwin* (1864) 10 Jur NS 119; *Jones v Rhind* (1869)17 WR 1091; *Greene v Foster* (1882) 22 Ch D 566 at 569. The disclaimer should be

made immediately on notice of the claim: *Bradley v Borlase* (1858) 7 WR 125. The offer to disclaim need not contain an offer to pay the costs of the disclaimer: *Lock v Lomas*, above, and if, while disclaiming, the defendant pleads and appears to claim his costs, he will have none: *Maxwell v Wightwick* (1866) LR 3 Eq 210; *Lewin v Jones* (1884) 53 LJ Ch 1011, and he will not have costs subsequent to the disclaimer if he appears of his own accord without being required for such special purpose of the claimant: *Gowing v Mowberry* (1863) 11 WR 851; *Lewin v Jones*, above, even though he is served with notice of the subsequent proceedings: *Clarke v Toleman* (1872) 42 LJ Ch 23, disapproving *Davis v Whitmore* (1860) 28 Beav 617.

Representative defendants

36.29 The right of disclaiming defendants, who represent a bankrupt estate, to receive costs is no better than that of any other defendants who disclaim. Thus they have no right, arising out of the office which they fill, to receive costs from the mortgagee, even on terms that he may add them to the debt. Similarly, they have no entitlement to costs on the ground that no assets have been received out of the estate because they stand in the place of the bankrupt, who can give no more right than he had himself[1]. So, if the trustee litigates as a contending party, instead of disclaiming it, he will be left to take his costs out of the bankrupt's estate[2]. The costs even of the Attorney-General, claiming ineffectually on behalf of the Crown, have been refused where the costs would have come out of the mortgaged property[3].

1 *Cash v Belcher* (1842) 1 Hare 310; *Hunter v Pugh* (1839) 1 Hare 307n; *Appleby v Duke* (1842) 1 Hare 303; *Clark v Wilmot* (1843) 1 Ph 276; *Hughes v Kelley* (1843) 3 Dr & War at 482 at 495. The assignee of a bankrupt mortgagor, who by his answer disclaimed all interest in the equity of redemption, and alleged a previous offer to do so, but claimed another interest in the claim, was neither allowed to receive, nor ordered to pay, costs: *Edwards v Jones* (1844) 1 Coll 247.

2 *Rider v Jones* (1843) 2 Y & C Ch Cas 329.

3 *Perkins v Bradley* (1842) 1 Hare 219; see *Kane v Reynolds* (1854) 4 De GM & G 565.

TREATMENT OF PARTICULAR TYPES OF COSTS, CHARGES AND EXPENSES

Costs of preparation of mortgage

36.30 The general costs, charges and expenses which the mortgagee can add to his security do not include the costs of and incidental to preparing the mortgage; these costs are merely a simple contract debt[1]. In practice, such costs are deducted from the initial advance.

Similarly, in the absence of a provision to this effect in the mortgage, the general costs which can be added to the security do not extend to the costs of investigating the mortgagor's title for the purpose of preparing a legal mortgage pursuant to the covenant in that behalf[2].

Further, the solicitor of an intending mortgagee has no claim against the intending mortgagor for the cost of an unsuccessful negotiation for the security or for the costs of investigating the title to the property because there is no implied contract of the part of the borrower to produce a security of any particular degree of safety, or any particular title, as in the case of a contract for sale[3].

1 *Wales v Carr* [1902] 1 Ch 860. An agreement for the payment of the costs of an intending lender does not cover his expenses of obtaining the money: *Re Blakesley and Beswick* (1863)

32 Beav 379. Likewise, an agreement to pay all costs and charges of investigating the title will not cover the interest of money lying idle during the negotiation of the mortgage: *Sweetland v Smith* (1833) 1 Cr & M 585.

2 *National Provincial Bank of England v Games* (1886) 31 Ch D 582, CA.

3 *Rigley v Daykin* (1828) 2 Y & J 83; *Melbourne v Cottrell* (1857) 29 LTOS 293; *Wilkinson v Grant* (1856) 18 CB 319; *Re Cowburn, ex p Firth* (1882) 19 Ch D 419 at 427, CA. For construction of an agreement on the subject, see *St Leger v Robson* (1831) 9 LJOS KB 184.
Where the court authorised a mortgage on an infant's estate and the negotiation went off without any default on the part of the mortgagee, after he had incurred expenses in the examination of the title, the court allowed him his costs out of the infant's estate: *Craggs v Gray* (1866) 35 Beav 166. His costs of preparing the security, including counsel's fees, should, it has been said, be provided for by the order: *Nicholson v Jeyes* (1853) 22 LJ Ch 833.

Costs of completing, transferring and discharging security

36.31 The mortgagee will be allowed to add to the security the costs of preparing a legal mortgage in pursuance of an agreement accompanying a deposit of deeds, including the expenses of such inspection of the deeds as was necessary for preparing it[1]. He will also be permitted to recover the costs of obtaining a stop order if the fund forming the subject of the mortgage is in court and the mortgage authorises the application[2]. Upon a transfer of the mortgage, the transferee can add the costs of the transfer to his security if the mortgagor has been required to pay the debt, or if the interest was in arrear, but not otherwise[3].

However, the mortgagee cannot add to the debt the costs of deeds which are not necessary for the security of the mortgagee, such as a declaration of trust where the mortgagee is a trustee[4] and, on discharge of the mortgage, the mortgagee is not entitled to the costs of making a copy of it, although he may at the mortgagor's cost make a fair copy of the draft security to keep until redemption[5].

1 *National Provincial Bank of England v Games* (1886) 31 Ch D 582, CA; and also the costs of correspondence relating to the legal mortgage: *National Provincial etc.*

2 *Waddilove v Taylor* (1848) 6 Hare 307; unless the application was unnecessary: *Hoole v Roberts* (1848) 12 Jur 108.

3 *Re Radcliffe* (1856) 22 Beav 201; *Bolingbroke v Hinde* (1884) 25 Ch D 795; *Sewell v Bishopp* (1893) 62 LJ Ch 985; *Re Mangan, ex p Andrew* [1983] ACLD 528.

4 *Martin v Baxter* (1828) 5 Bing 160; 2 Moo & P 240.

5 *Re Wade and Thomas* (1881) 17 Ch D 348.

Costs of solicitor-mortgagees in completing mortgage, etc

36.32 In the absence of express agreement[1] a mortgagee cannot charge for work done by himself, although in the course of his business[2], and formerly a solicitor-mortgagee could not charge profit-costs for work done in connection with the mortgage[3], including the costs of a redemption or foreclosure claim[4], but this rule was abolished by the Mortgagees Legal Costs Act 1895[5], which is now replaced by the Solicitors Act 1974.

If a mortgage is made to a solicitor, either alone or jointly[6] with any other person, he, or the firm of which he is a member, shall be entitled to recover from the mortgagor in respect of all business transacted and acts done by him or them in negotiating the loan, deducing and investigating the title to the property, and preparing and completing the mortgage, such usual costs as he or they would have been entitled to receive if the mortgage had been made to a person who was not a solicitor and that person had retained and employed him or them to transact that business and do those acts[7].

1 Formerly an agreement allowing the mortgagee to charge for his personal services was void on the ground that it gave him a collateral advantage: *French v Baron* (1740) 2 Atk 120; *Scott v Brest* (1788) 2 Term Rep 238; *Chambers v Goldwin* (1804) 9 Ves 254 at 271; *Leith v Irvine* (1833) 1 My & K 277; *Broad v Selfe* (1863) 11 WR 1036; *Comyns v Comyns* (1871) 5 IR Eq 583; *James v Kerr* (1889) 40 Ch D 449 at 459; *Field v Hopkins* (1890) 44 Ch D 524 at 530, CA; *The Benwell Tower* (1895) 72 LT 664, but this reason no longer exists, since a collateral advantage is now allowed, though it may only be enforced during the subsistence of the security: *Browne v Ryan* [1901] 2 IR 653; see **28.51**; and see *Maxwell v Tipping* [1903] 1 IR 499; *Bath v Standard Land Co Ltd* [1911] 1 Ch 618.

2 *Barrett v Hartley* (1866) LR 2 Eq 789 (bonuses for managing business); *Mattison v Clarke* (1854) 3 Drew 3; *Furber v Cobb* (1887) 18 QBD 494 at 509, CA (auctioneer); *Arnold v Garner* (1847) 2 Ph 231 (broker), but this rule does not now extend, as was held in *Matthison v Clarke*, above, to prevent a partner from taking remuneration, provided, if there is an agreement, that the mortgagee is excluded from sharing, or if there is no agreement, that his partnership share does not go to his partner: *Re Doody, Fisher v Doody* [1893] 1 Ch 129 at 136, 137, and see *Wellby v Still* [1895] 1 Ch 524; *Eyre v Wyn-Mackenzie* [1894] 1 Ch 218, CA.

3 *Sclater v Cottam* (1857) 5 WR 744; *Re Roberts* (1889) 43 Ch D 52; *Field v Hopkins* (1890) 44 Ch D 524; *Re Wallis, ex p Lickorish* (1890) 25 QBD 176; *Re Doody, Fisher v Doody* [1893] 1 Ch 129.

4 *Stone v Lickorish* [1891] 2 Ch 363. The rule, contrary to the exception made in favour of solicitor trustees (*Cradock v Piper* (1850) 1 Mac & G 664), applied even where the solicitor was only one of several co-mortgagees: *Re Doody, Fisher v Doody*, above.

5 Section 2 (1). Section 2 applied only to mortgages made after the Act: sub-s (2). Section 3 made similar provision where a mortgage has become vested in a solicitor by transfer or transmission and this applied to mortgages made and business done either before or after the Act, but not where judgment was given before the Act: *Eyre v Wynn-Mackenzie*, above; and a solicitor who obtained foreclosure before the Act was not allowed after the Act to recover profit costs: *Day v Kelland* [1900] 2 Ch 745, CA.

6 *Re Norris* [1902] 1 Ch 741.

7 Section 58(1). Subsection (2) contains similar provisions Act where a mortgage has become vested in a solicitor by transfer or transmission. 'Mortgage' includes any charge on any property for securing money or money's worth: s 58(3).

Costs of preserving the security

36.33 The mortgagee is generally entitled to expenditure properly incurred in preserving the security, for example: the payment of rent to avoid the forfeiture of leasehold property; carrying out necessary and proper repairs and improvements; taking reasonable steps to protect the premises against vandals pending sale[1]. He is also entitled to include in the account any premium paid upon renewal of a lease (even if there is no covenant in the original lease by the mortgagee to renew)[2].

The mortgagee will also be allowed the expenses of obtaining the rents and profits from the property and any compensation properly payable to an outgoing tenant[3].

Where sums are expended by a subsequent mortgagee in possession, that mortgagee will not be entitled to the same as against a prior mortgagee[4].

1 *Godfrey v Watson* (1747) 3 Atk 517; *Sandon v Hooper* (1843) 6 Beav 246, affd 4 LJ Ch 120; *Hill v Browne* (1844) Drury *temp* Sug 426; *Burrowes v Molloy* (1845) 2 Jo & Lat 521; *Brandon v Brandon* (1862) 10 WR 287; *White v City of London Brewery Co* (1889) 42 Ch D 237 at 243, CA.

2 *Woolley v Drage* (1795) 2 Anst 551. However, he cannot compel the mortgagor to renew.
3 *Oxenham v Ellis* (1854) 18 Beav 593.
4 *Landowners West of England and South Wales Land Drainage and Inclosure Co v Ashford* (1880) 16 Ch D 411.

Costs of insurance premiums

36.34 Where the mortgage is made by deed, the mortgagee has by virtue of the Law of Property Act 1925[1] a limited power to insure and keep insured the mortgaged property[2]. Further, the premiums paid for any such insurance are a charge on the mortgaged property or estate or interest, in addition to the mortgage money, and with the same priority and with interest at the same rate, as the mortgage money. However, although the premiums are a charge, they cannot be recovered from the mortgagor as a debt, in the absence of a covenant to pay them.

If the security covers a life policy, the mortgagee is allowed to add to the secured debt the premiums paid by him for keeping the policy on foot[3]. This is so even if the mortgagee has covenanted to pay the premiums[4].

If the mortgagee is an insurance company and the mortgage gives them power, they can themselves pay the premiums and add them to the security[5]. However, an issue of a policy as between two branches of the same office will not give the right to charge the premiums[6]. The office can charge the full premiums although their solicitor, as their agent, has received commission[7].

1 Section 101(1)(ii). This power may be varied or extended by the mortgage deed; and the section applies only if and so far as a contrary intention is not expressed in that deed: sub-ss (3), (4).
2 See **3.44**.
3 *Bellamy v Brickenden* (1861) 2 John & H 137; *Gill v Downing* (1874) LR 17 Eq 316.
4 *Shaw v Scottish Widows' Fund Assurance Society* (1917) 87 LJ Ch 76.
5 *Richards v Macclesford* (1841) 10 LJ Ch 329; *Earl Fitzwilliam v Price* (1858) 4 Jur NS 889; see also *Browne v Price* (1858) 4 CBNS 598; 4 Jur NS 882.
6 *Grey v Ellison* (1856) 1 Giff 438.
7 *Leete v Wallace* (1888) 58 LT 577.

Costs of management: agents and commission

36.35 A mortgagee in possession is generally not allowed any remuneration in respect of his personal care or trouble in the collection of rents or management[1]. However, if the mortgagee manages the property by an agent or employee, he may, if he would engage the services of such a person if he owned the property himself, add to the mortgage debt the agent's or employee's salary[2]. Further, the mortgagor and mortgagee can express agree that a commission should be allowed to the mortgagee[3].

1 *Bonithon v Hockmore* (1685) 1 Vern 316; *Nicholson v Tutin (No 2)* (1857) 3 K & J 159; *Cholmondeley v Clinton* (1820) 2 Jac & W 1, 184 at 191; *Leith v Irvine* (1833) 1 My & K 277; *Robertson v Norris* (1857) 1 Giff 421.
2 *Union Bank of London v Ingram* (1880) 16 Ch D 53, CA. In *Bath v Standard Land Co Ltd* [1911] 1 Ch 618, CA it was held that a company mortgagee could use the services of its own directors in connection with the mortgaged property and charge this against the security.
3 *Biggs v Hoddinott* [1898] 2 Ch 307, CA; *Bath v Standard Land Co Ltd* [1911] 1 Ch 618, CA.

COSTS ON SALE

Expenses of the sale

36.36 A mortgagee can add to the security the expenses of a sale[1] and those of an attempted sale[2]. Although credit may have to be given for any loss caused by negligence on the part of the mortgagee, the acceptance by the mortgagee of a cheque for the deposit, which is subsequently dishonoured, is not such negligence as to deprive the mortgagee of his right to the expenses of the abortive sale[3].

1 *White v City of London Brewery Co* (1889) 42 Ch D 237 at 243, CA.
2 *Sutton v Rawlings* (1849) 3 Exch 407; *Farrer v Lacy, Harland & Co* (1885) 31 Ch D 42, CA.
3 Above. See also *Thompson v Rumball* (1839) 3 Jur 53; *Batten v Wedgwood Coal and Iron Co* (1884) 28 Ch D 317. As to expenses where there is a statutory limit, see *McHugh v Union Bank of Canada* [1913] AC 299 at 305, PC.

Costs on sale by court

36.37 The right of a mortgagee to costs extends to the case where the mortgaged property is sold under the order of the court[1]. The order for sale does not of itself alter the rights of the parties, but the purchase money, being considered to be substituted for the property, is treated in the same manner as the property and each incumbrancer will be paid his costs, including the costs of obtaining the direction for payment to him of the proceeds of the sale, together with his principal and interest, according to priority, the later incumbrancer taking nothing until he who is prior has been paid in full[2].

1 The equitable mortgagee is in the same position (though formerly he was not: see earlier editions of this work).
2 *Upperton v Harrison* (1835) 7 Sim 444; *Chissum v Dewes* (1828) 5 Russ 29; *Barnes v Racster* (1842) 1 Y & C Ch Cas 401; *Wild v Lockhart* (1847) 10 Beav 320; *Cook v Hart* (1871) LR 12 Eq 459; *Wonham v Machin* (1870) LR 10 Eq 447; *Leonard v Kellett* (1891) 27 LR Ir 418 at 427.

Account of proceeds

36.38 Where the mortgagee has sold the property he holds the surplus proceeds on trust[1] for the persons entitled to the equity of redemption. Hence a claim by the mortgagor or a second mortgagee for an account is not treated as a redemption claim and is outside the rule which entitles the first mortgagee to costs[2]. Further, if the claim has been occasioned by his refusing to account, or if, on taking the accounts, it is found that a much larger sum is due from him than he admitted, he will either be refused costs or have to pay them[3].

After the accounts have been taken in a foreclosure claim, the court will not reopen the judgment so as to include costs since incurred by the mortgagee in a different claim, in respect of property mortgaged to him, which upon sale proved to be insufficient for payment of the prior incumbrancers[4].

1 *Banner v Berridge* (1881) 18 Ch D 254. See the Law of Property Act 1925, s 105. Though a trustee, the selling mortgagee is, it is submitted, allowed the costs involved in ascertaining any subsequent mortgagees and of payment over.

2 *Parker-Tweedale v Dunbar Bank plc (No 2)* [1991] Ch 26, CA.
3 *Tanner v Heard* (1857) 23 Beav 555; *Charles v Jones* (1887) 35 Ch D 544; *Williams v Jones* (1911) 55 Sol Jo 500.
4 *Barron v Lancefield* (1853) 17 Beav 208, but where costs of recovering possession in ejectment had not been provided for, the court, but not without hesitation, made a subsequent order that those costs and expenses should be added to the principal: *Spurgeon v Witham* MR 21 December 1855. It appeared, however, that little or no opposition was made to the order.

Priority of costs, waiver of priority and administration proceedings

36.39 The mortgagee's right to costs includes the costs of a claim to realise the security by sale[1]. However, the priority for such costs depends upon the object of such claim.

If a mortgagee merely consents to a sale, or is a party to a claim solely with a view to the realisation of his security, his claim against the proceeds is prior to the general costs of the claim[2]. He will, however, be taken to have waived his priority over such costs if, rather than simply relying on his security, he takes advantage of administration proceedings[3] in order to obtain a remedy against the mortgagor's personal estate[4]. However, on the other hand, if the mortgagee commences proceedings to realise the security and also to administer the mortgagor's estate in order to recover any shortfall from that estate, he will be entitled in full to the proceeds of sale, except only the sale expenses[5], in partial discharge of the mortgage debt including costs. In that case the costs of all parties will be paid as in ordinary administration proceedings[6].

Where, however, a later incumbrancer, either by a claim to ascertain the priorities or by proceedings in a dormant claim, is the means of securing and distributing a fund for the benefit of all the incumbrancers, his costs of the claim or proceeding will rank as a first charge and thus be paid before the other charges on the fund, even though the litigation is not an administration claim[7].

A mortgagee's costs may be postponed to an advance made for the protection of the property without notice of the mortgage[8].

1 *Wade v Ward* (1859) 4 Drew 602.
2 *Hepworth v Heslop* (1844) 3 Hare 485; *Armstrong v Storer* (1851) 14 Beav 535; *Wonham v Machin* (1870) LR 10 Eq 447; *Re Johnston, Millar v Johnston* (1888) 23 LR Ir 50; *Hilliard v Moriarty* [1894] 1 IR 316; and see *Crosse v General Reversionary and Investment Co* (1853) 3 De GM & G 698.
3 The ordinary rule in which is that the costs of all necessary parties are a first charge upon the estate.
4 *Re Spensley's Estate, Spensley v Harrison* (1872) LR 15 Eq 16; also *Ford v Earl of Chesterfield (No 3)* (1856) 21 Beav 426.

As to a claim by beneficiaries against the trustees and the mortgagees of the trust fund, see *Bryant v Blackwell* (1851) 15 Beav 44. In a claim for foreclosing a mortgage of a term the mortgagee retained his priority for costs, although by agreement the reversion was included in the sale: *Cutfield v Richards* (1858) 26 Beav 241.

A mortgagee who sues for general administration of his deceased mortgagor's assets on behalf of himself and the other creditors is entitled to the usual judgment in favour of an equitable mortgagee: *Greenwood v Firth* (1842) 2 Hare 241n; *Skey v Bennett* (1843) 2 Y & C Ch Cas 405; and also to that in favour of a general creditor: *Skey v Bennett*, above, but the modern practice is to ask for realisation of the security and payment of the deficiency from the general assets.

5 The expenses of the sale, since they are incurred as much for the benefit of the mortgagee as of other persons interested, are a first charge on the proceeds: *Dighton v Withers* (1862) 31 Beav 423; *Re Oriental Hotels Co, Perry v Oriental Hotels Co* (1871) LR 12 Eq 126; *Batten v Wedgwood Coal and Iron Co* (1884) 28 Ch D 317; *Lathom v Greenwich Ferry Co* (1895) 72 LT 790. The same is true as regards the costs of an abortive sale: *Henderson v Astwood*

[1894] AC 150, PC; *Matzner v Clyde Securities Ltd* [1975] 2 NSWLR 293. Where the mortgagee is a party, he must submit to the costs of sale being paid first: *Re Regent's Canal Ironwork Co, ex p Grissell* (1875) 3 Ch D 411 at 427, CA; and also it would seem, where, without being a party, he consents to the sale.

6 *Tuckley v Thompson* (1860) 1 John & H 126; *Pinchard v Fellows* (1874) LR 17 Eq 421.

7 *White v Bishop of Peterborough* (1821) Jac 402; *Ford v Earl of Chesterfield*, above; *Wright v Kirby* (1857) 23 Beav 463; *Batten, Proffitt and Scott v Dartmouth Harbour Comrs* (1890) 45 Ch D 612; *Re Barne* (1890) 62 LT 922; *Carrick v Wigan Tramways Co* [1893] WN 98.

8 *Myers v United Guarantee and Life Assurance Co* (1855) 7 De GM & G 112.

Rights of subsequent mortgagee to have first mortgagee's costs assessed

36.40 The selling mortgagee's costs will generally be deducted from the proceeds of sale of the mortgaged property before the balance (if any) is paid over to the second mortgagee and, if appropriate, subsequent mortgagee or mortgagees. The subsequent mortgagee who has thus suffered deduction from the moneys payable to him is entitled to have the selling mortgagee's costs assessed as a person (other than the party chargeable with the bill) who has paid or is or was liable to pay the bill either to the solicitor or to the party chargeable with the bill[1]. The right to have a bill assessed implies the right to have a bill prepared and delivered[2].

1 Solicitors Act 1974, s 71(1). See *Re Taylor* (1854) 18 Beav 165; *Re Early* [1897] 1 IR 6, Ir CA; *Debney v Semerdziev* [1982] 2 NSWLR 716, CA; *West v AGC (Advances) Ltd* (1984) 5 NSWLR 610. In some instances 'paid' means paid following the delivery of a bill and is not applicable where no bill has been delivered: *Ex p Farmers' Fertilizers Corpn Ltd* (1916) 16 SRNSW 645; *Debney v Smerdziev*, above.

2 *Debney v Semerdziev*, above.

COSTS OF RECONVEYANCE

General rule

36.41 The costs of reconveyance are borne by the mortgagor, both in ordinary case where the mortgage title has not been changed, or has become vested by transfer or devolution in persons from whom a reconveyance can be obtained[1], and also where there has been a change of title or other event which necessitates special expense, such as the obtaining a vesting order if, for instance, the person who should reconvey is under disability or cannot be found[2], or if the mortgage is vested in a trustee-mortgagee who has absconded[3].

There is an exception where the mortgagee is a mentally disordered person and, in that case, if he is beneficially interested in the mortgage money, the costs of any application for an order for conveyance or vesting are borne by his estate[4]; and if he is a trustee, they are borne by the trust estate[5].

The mortgagor pays the ordinary costs of the reconveyance, where a reconveyance is ordered.

1 *King v Smith* (1848) 6 Hare 473 at 475, and the mortgagor may be liable for the costs of proceedings to obtain delivery of the deeds by the mortgagee's solicitor, who claims a lien on them as against the mortgagee: *Rider v Jones* (1843) 2 Y & CCC 329. As to the costs of an order for delivery of deeds where they have come into court in the course of an administration claim relating to the mortgagee's estate, see *Burden v Oldaker* (1844) 1 Coll 105; *Reed v Freer* (1844) 13 LJ Ch 417.

2 *Ex p Ommaney* (1841) 10 Sim 298; *King v Smith*, above; *Re Stuart, ex p Marshall* (1859) 4 De G & J 317; *Webb v Crosse* [1912] 1 Ch 323.
3 *Webb v Crosse*, above.
4 *Re Lewis, ex p Richards* (1820) 1 Jac & W 264; *Re Townsend* (1847) 2 Ph 348; *Re Biddle* (1853) 23 LJ Ch 23; *Re Rowley* (1863) 1 De GJ & Sm 417. The contrary view in *Re Marrow* (1841) Cr & Ph 142, has not been accepted, though the exception has been admitted with reluctance: see *Re Stuart, ex p Marshall*, above, at 319; and it did not extend to the lunacy of a person taking, on the death of the mortgagee, as formerly his heir at law: *Re Stuart, ex p Marshall*, above; *Re Jones* (1860) 2 De GF & J 554.
5 *Re Townsend* (1850) 1 Mac & G 686; *Re Phillips* (1869) 4 Ch App 629; *Re Jones* (1876) 2 Ch D 70. In general a mortgage made with trust money does not disclose the trust, but it has been held that where the trust appears on the face of the mortgage, these costs fall on the mortgagor: *Re Lewes* (1849) 1 Mac & G 23.

Trustee for mortgagee

36.42 A trustee for the mortgagee is bound to assign according to his direction and, if he refuses to do so, in a plain and simple case (as for instance to a purchaser under a power of sale), he will be made to pay the costs of a claim rendered necessary by his refusal[1].

1 *Hampshire v Bradley* (1845) 2 Coll 34.

Conveyance to equitable mortgagee

36.43 The costs of conveying to the equitable mortgagee upon the foreclosure are not generally provided for by the judgment[1], which simply directs the conveyance to be made. When there is no express covenant by the mortgagor to pay the costs of the conveyance, he is only bound by the terms of the judgment to execute the conveyance when tendered to him, because it is said he has only contracted to vest the estate in the mortgagee who, according to the ordinary practice, prepares and tenders the conveyance for his execution; though since the contract, on an equitable mortgage, is a contract to transfer the legal estate to the mortgagee, the person whose duty it is to make the transfer must pay the expenses of it[2].

1 *Lees v Fisher* (1882) 22 Ch D 283, CA.
2 *Pryce v Bury* (1853) 2 Drew 41; affd (1854) LR 16 Eq 153n.

MISCELLANEOUS

'Just allowances'

36.44 In taking an account as between mortgagor and mortgagee, where the account has been directed by any judgment or order, all 'just allowances' will be made without any direction for that purpose[1]. In general, the charges are treated as just allowances[2], but where it is desired to make any unusual charge, this should be asked for at the hearing and the claim established at the hearing and a special direction will then be inserted in the order[3].

1 *Wilkes v Saunion* (1877) 7 Ch D 188, explaining *Horlock v Smith* (1844) 1 Coll 287.
2 *Blackford v Davis* (1869) 4 Ch App 304.

3 *Rees v Metropolitan Board of Works* (1880) 14 Ch D 372; *Bolingbroke v Hinde* (1884) 25 Ch D 795. See *Waddilove v Taylor* (1848) 6 Hare 307. If necessary, an inquiry as to the costs and charges claimed will be directed: *Merriman v Bonner* (1864) 10 Jur NS 534. Formerly the claim had to be made on the pleadings: *Millard v Magor* (1818) 3 Madd 433; *Ward v Barton* (1841) 11 Sim 534; and it is still advisable to do so where there are statements of case. If the judgment gives no direction, an inquiry may be directed on further consideration: *Thompson v Rumball*, above.

Costs of bottomry bondholder

36.45 The incumbrancer by bottomry has, like a mortgagee, a right to the general costs of enforcing his security. However, the right to the costs of a reference, to ascertain what is due on the bond, will be determined according to the circumstances of each case; although this is done with an inclination to the bondholder, he may nevertheless be condemned in the whole costs of the reference if the result shows that his demand was exorbitant and extortionate[1].

1 *The Eliza* (1842) 1 Wm Rob 328; *The Catherine* (1847) 3 Wm Rob 1; *The Kepler* (1861) Lush 201. These authorities should now be read in the light of the CPR.

Chapter 37

Taxes

INCOME TAX

Taxation of mortgage interest

37.1 In the case of an individual who is the recipient of mortgage interest, and who is not carrying on the business of lending money[1], the interest is chargeable to income tax under Case III of Schedule D[2], and in the case of a company it is subject to corporation tax[3]. Premiums and discounts may be treated as interest, particularly where no interest is payable[4], but if interest is also payable, there is no presumption that the discount or premium is interest[5]. Capitalised interest does not cease to be interest[6].

1 A moneylender is chargeable under Case I of Sch D.
2 Income and Corporation Taxes Act 1988 ('TA') s 18, and see *Dunmore v McGowan* [1978] 2 All ER 85, [1978] 1 WLR 617, CA; *Macpherson v Bond* [1985] 1 WLR 1157. For the tax implications of mortgage uplift (eg as in *Multiservice Bookbinding Ltd v Marden* [1979] Ch 84, [1978] 2 All ER 489), see [1978] Conv 432 (Williams).
3 TA 1988, ss 6 ff.
4 See *IRC v Thomas Nelson & Sons Ltd* 1938 SC 816; *Davies v Premier Investment Co Ltd* [1945] 2 All ER 681.
5 *Lomax v Peter Dixon & Son Ltd* [1943] KB 671, [1943] 2 All ER 255, CA.
6 *IRC v Oswald* [1945] AC 360, [1945] 1 All ER 641, HL.

Deduction of income tax on payment of mortgage interest

37.2 Subject to the exceptional cases mentioned below, mortgage interest is payable gross. The exceptional cases are, first, those payments specified in s 349(2) of the Income and Corporation Taxes Act 1988 and, secondly, loan interest to which the mortgage interest relief at source scheme applies[1]. The exceptions specified in s 349(2) of the Income and Corporation Taxes Act 1970 when mortgage interest is payable under deduction of tax are where yearly interest is paid:

(a) otherwise than in a fiduciary or representative capacity, by a company other than a building society[2] or local authority; or
(b) by or on behalf of a partnership of which a company is a member; or
(c) by any person to another person whose usual place of abode is outside the United Kingdom[3].

These exceptions do not apply to interest payable on an advance from a bank, if at the time when the interest is paid, the person beneficially entitled to the interest is within the charge to corporation tax as respects that interest[4], or to interest paid by a bank in the ordinary course of its business[5].

1 See **37.4**. This category has been virtually eradicated by the Finance Act 1999.
2 Inserted by the Finance Act 1991.
3 TA 1988, s 349(2).
4 Section 349(3)(a).
5 Section 349(3)(b).

Tax relief for mortgage interest

37.3 Formerly, tax relief was given in respect of interest paid on a loan for the purpose of:

(a) purchasing an estate or interest in land, or a caravan or houseboat; or
(b) improving or developing the land; or
(c) paying off another loan where the interest on that loan would, if it had not been repaid, have been eligible for tax relief;

provided that the land, caravan or houseboat was used as the only or main residence of the person by whom the interest was paid[1], either at the time the interest was paid, or if the interest was paid within 12 months of the date on which the loan was made, within that 12-month period[2].

The Finance Act 1999 virtually abolished tax relief for interest on these loans for the purchase of land. The only remnant of this tax relief is in respect of a loan made *before 9 March 1999* as part of a home annuity or home income plan where at least 90 per cent of the amount borrowed was used by the borrower to buy a life annuity on his own life or on the life of the survivor of himself and some other person or persons[3]. In order to be eligible for relief, the following conditions must be satisfied:

(a) the loan must have been made before 9 March 1999[4];
(b) the borrower or the annuitants must have been 65 or over at the time the loan was made;
(c) the loan must be secured on land in the UK or Eire;
(d) the borrower or one of the annuitants must own an interest in that land;
(e) the borrower or each of the annuitants must use the land as his only or main residence at the time the interest is paid;
(f) the interest must be paid by the borrower or by one of the annuitants.

Where a loan is taken out on or after 26 July 1999, as part of a scheme under which the whole or part[5] of the proceeds of the loan was used to defray money applied in paying off a loan which satisfies the above conditions[6], the provisions will apply.

Apart from loans used to purchase a life annuity, the tax relief ceased in relation to other loans taken out for purchasing, developing or improving property. This relief ceased entirely in relation to payments of interest after 5 April 2000, even if such payments fell due before that date, and to payments made before 5 April 2000 (but not before 9 March 1999), which fell due on or after 5 April 2000[7]. The abolition of this relief also applies to a payment made before 5 April 2000 (but not before 9 March 1999), which was made for the purposes of avoiding these provisions.

1 Prior to 5 April 1988, this included the residence of a dependent, relative or former or separated spouse.
2 TA 1988, ss 353-355.
3 Section 365, as amended by the Finance Act 1999, ss 39 and 40.
4 Or, made on or after 9 March 1999 in pursuance of an offer made by the lender before that date, such offer being in writing or evidenced by a note or memorandum made by the lender before that date: TA 1988, s 365(1AA), inserted by Finance Act 1999, s 39(2).
5 Where only part of the proceeds of the new loan were used to defray money applied in paying off the old loan, this provision applies only if, under the scheme, at least 90 per cent of the remaining part of the proceeds of the new loan was applied to the purchase of an annuity by the person to whom the loan was made, ending with his life or with the life of the survivor of two or more persons including him.
6 TA 1988, s 365(1AB).
7 Finance Act 1999, s 38.

Mortgage interest relief at source ('MIRAS')

37.4 The Finance Act 1982 introduced a scheme under which payments of relevant loan interest by a qualifying borrower to a qualifying lender are made net of basic rate income tax[1]. The scheme worked by the payer retaining the basic rate tax so deducted, but being credited by the lender as having paid this sum. The lender would then recover from the Revenue an amount equal to the sum deducted by the borrower. The relief was formerly given for the purchase of land in the UK used wholly or substantially as the main residence of the claimant and for the purchase of a qualifying life annuity secured on the main residence of the borrower or an annuitant. The relief for interest on a residence loan has now been withdrawn for interest paid after 5 April 2000. Relief for interest on an annuity loan is withdrawn for interest in respect of a loan made after 8 March 1999, but continues to be available for interest in respect of a loan made before 9 March 1999[2].

1 Introduced under the Finance Act 1982, ss 26-29. Now contained in TA 1988, ss 369-379.
2 See above.

SOME OTHER TAXES

Capital gains tax

37.5 The conveyance or transfer of an asset by way of security constitutes neither an acquisition nor a disposal by the mortgagee or mortgagor[1]. Therefore, the redemption of the security is neither a disposal nor a reacquisition for capital gains tax purposes. Where the creditor enforces the security, eg by exercising his power of sale, he is not treated, for capital gains tax purposes, as the transferor, but rather, as acting as nominee of the borrower. The same applies where the transfer is effected by a receiver or manager[2]. Where a transfer of an asset which is subject to a mortgage takes place, and the transferee acquires the asset subject to the mortgage, the amount outstanding on the loan is treated as forming part of the consideration given by the transferor and received by the transferee[3].

1 Taxation of Chargeable Gains Act 1992, s 26(1).
2 Section 26(2).
3 Section 26(3).

Inheritance tax

37.6 Inheritance tax is payable on any non-exempt disposition whereby the value of a person's estate is reduced. So, eg, a gratuitous discharge or transfer of a mortgage or a discharge or transfer for less than full value will give rise to a charge[1] where the disposition is on death or where the disponor dies within seven years of the disposition.

The Finance Act 1986 revived certain former estate duty provisions providing for the abatement of certain debts. In relation to a debt or incumbrance incurred or created on or after 18 March 1986, if in determining the value of a person's estate immediately before his death account would be taken of a liability consisting of a debt incurred by him or an incumbrance created by a disposition made by him, that liability shall be subject to abatement to the extent proportionate to the value of any of the consideration given for the debt or incumbrance which consisted of (a) property derived from the deceased; or (b) consideration (not being property derived from the deceased) given by any person who was at any time entitled to, or amongst whose resources there was at any time included, any property derived from the deceased[2].

1 Lifetime transfers are potentially exempt: see Finance Act 1986, s 101, Sch 19, para 1. For the exemption of normal expenditure out of income, see Inheritance Tax Act 1984, s 21. For the annual exemption, see Inheritance Tax Act 1984, s 19. For interest free or cheap loans made out of the transferor's income, see Inheritance Tax Act 1984, s 29.
2 Finance Act 1986, s 103 (1).

Value added tax

37.7 Mortgages as such are exempt from VAT[1]. However, where the mortgagee forecloses, there results a supply from the mortgagor to the mortgagee for the purposes of VAT. Where the mortgagee exercises his power of sale, the disposal, for VAT purposes, is taken to be a supply by the mortgagor, and not the mortgagee[2]. Likewise, when a mortgagee in possession grants a lease of the land, any rent recovered is consideration for a supply by the mortgagor.

1 Under the exemption in the Value Added Tax Act 1994, s 31, Sch 9, Group 5.
2 Value Added Tax Act 1994, Sch 4, para 7.

STAMP DUTIES

Generally

37.8 The ad valorem duties under the head 'Mortgage, Bond, etc' in Sch I of the Stamp Act 1891 were abolished by the Finance Act 1971, s 64[1].

1 See now Finance Act 1999, Sch 13, para 25(a).

Appendix

Basic conveyancing and court forms

This Appendix consists of some basic conveyancing and court forms, the main purpose of which is to illustrate points in the text. The conveyancing forms have been reproduced from *Butterworths Encyclopaedia of Forms and Precedents* (5th edn), volumes 28 (1999 reissue) MORTGAGES and 16(2) (2001 reissue) FAMILY.

CONTENTS

CHARGE BY WAY OF LEGAL MORTGAGE OF FREEHOLDS BY ONE BORROWER TO ONE LENDER: LOAN OF FIXED AMOUNT TO BE REPAID ON FIXED DATE

THIS LEGAL CHARGE is made the .... day of .... BETWEEN

(1) *(name of borrower)* [of *(address)* *(or)* the registered office of which is at *(address)* and the company registration number of which is *(number)*] ('the Borrower') and

(2) *(name of lender)* [of *(address)* *(or)* the registered office of which is at *(address)* and the company registration number of which is *(number)*] ('the Lender')

RECITALS

(1) [The Borrower is the estate owner absolute in possession in respect of the fee simple *(or)* The Borrower is registered at HM Land Registry as proprietor with title [absolute *(or as the case may be)*]] of the property described in the schedule to this deed [subject as mentioned in the schedule but otherwise] free from incumbrances.

(2) The Lender has agreed to lend to the Borrower £......... on condition that its repayment together with interest is secured in the manner set out below.

NOW THIS DEED WITNESSES as follows:

1 Definitions

In this legal charge:

1.1 'the Interest Payment Days' means *(state days for payment)*;

1.2 'the Interest Rate' means [*(for fixed rate)* ......% a year *(or for variable rate)* ......% above the rate of *(specify lending or base rate by which reference to which interest is to be calculated)* from time to time];

1.3 'the Principal' means £.........;

1.4 'the Property' means the property specified in the schedule below and all buildings and fixtures on it; and

1.5 'the Redemption Date' means *(date)*.

2 Payment of principal, interest and costs

In consideration of the Principal now paid by the Lender to the Borrower (receipt of which the Borrower acknowledges) the Borrower covenants with the Lender as set out below.

2.1 Principal

The Borrower covenants with the Lender to pay the Principal to the Lender [free from any legal or equitable right of set-off] on the Redemption Date or, if earlier, immediately [on demand] if:

2.1.1 any interest or other sum payable under this security is not paid within *(number)* days of becoming due; or

2.1.2 the Borrower or any surety fails to comply with any term, condition, covenant or provision of, or to perform any of his obligations or liabilities under, this or any associated or collateral security; or

2.1.3 any representation or warranty given by the Borrower or any surety to the Lender is or becomes incorrect; or

2.1.4 any judgment or order made against the Borrower or any surety by any court is not complied with within *(number)* days; or

2.1.5 the property of the Borrower or any surety becomes subject to any forfeiture or execution, distress, sequestration or other form of process; or

2.1.6 a mortgagee takes possession of or exercises or seeks to exercise any power of sale or of an appointment of a receiver in relation to the property charged by this deed or any other property of the Borrower or of any surety; or

2.1.7 in the case of an individual:

(a) the Borrower or any surety becomes subject to an interim order or makes a proposal for a voluntary arrangement under Part VIII of the Insolvency Act 1986 or enters, or seeks to enter, into any other form of composition or arrangement with his creditors whether in whole or in part; or

(b) a petition is presented for the bankruptcy of the Borrower or any surety; or

(c) the Borrower or any surety dies or becomes of unsound mind; or

2.1.8 in the case of a company:

(a) the Borrower or any surety ceases or threatens to cease to carry on, or disposes or threatens to dispose of, its business or a material part of its business; or

(b) the Borrower or any surety makes a proposal for a voluntary arrangement under Part I of the Insolvency Act 1986 or enters, or seeks to enter, into any other form of composition or arrangement with its creditors whether in whole or in part; or

(c) a petition is presented for the making of an administration order in respect of the Borrower or any surety; or

(d) an administrative receiver is appointed in respect of the whole or any part of the undertaking of the Borrower or any surety; or

(e) a petition is presented in any court or a meeting is convened for the purpose of considering a resolution for the winding up of the Borrower or any surety (except in the case of a reconstruction or amalgamation that has the previous approval in writing of the Lender).

2.2 *Interest*

2.2.1 *Payment*

The Borrower covenants with the Lender to pay to the Lender interest on the Principal (or so much of it as may from time to time remain outstanding) at the Interest Rate, from the date of this deed, by equal *(specify frequency)* payments on the Interest Payment Days, such interest to be payable as well after as before any [demand or] judgment or the [administration or liquidation *(or)* bankruptcy, death or insanity] of the Borrower.

[2.2.2 *Reduction for prompt payment*

Subject to the Borrower having otherwise in all respects and at all times observed and performed his obligations under this deed and to payment being made not later than *(specify period which should be no longer than that specified in clause 2.1.1)* after the due date for payment, the Lender will accept interest from the Borrower at the rate of *(specify reduced fixed or variable rate)* in satisfaction of payment at the Interest Rate.]

[2.2.3 *Capitalisation*

(a) If any interest payable under this security is not paid within *(specify period)* after the due date for payment it shall be capitalised and added to the Principal and be charged on the Property and bear interest from the due date for payment at the Interest Rate and on the Interest Payment Days.
(b) The capitalisation of arrears of interest is to be without prejudice to the Lender's right at any time to enforce payment of the sums concerned as interest in arrear.
(c) The Borrower may on any of the Interest Payment Days pay to the Lender, in addition to the interest then due, all or any part of the Principal representing capitalised arrears of interest.
(d) Otherwise all covenants and provisions contained in this mortgage and all powers and remedies conferred by law or by this mortgage and all rules of law or equity relating to the Principal and interest on it shall equally apply to capitalised arrears of interest and to interest on them.]

2.3 *Costs, charges, expenses and other liabilities*

2.3.1 *Covenant to pay*

The Borrower covenants with the Lender to pay to the Lender on demand, and on a full and unlimited indemnity basis, all costs, charges, expenses and liabilities paid and incurred by the Lender (whether directly or indirectly) in relation to the security constituted by and the obligations owed under and associated with this deed (including all commission, legal and other professional costs and fees and disbursements and VAT on them) together with interest from the date when the Lender becomes liable for them until payment by the Borrower at the Interest Rate, such interest to be payable in the same manner as interest on the Principal.

2.3.2 *Costs included*

Without prejudice to the generality of the provisions of that clause, the Borrower's liability under clause 2.3.1 will include not only those costs, charges, expenses and liabilities that would otherwise be allowable on the taking of an account between a mortgagor and mortgagee but also (and in so far as they are not so allowable) those incurred in relation to or arising out of:
(a) the contemplation and institution of all proceedings and other action in connection with the enforcement, preservation and protection of the security constituted by this deed;
(b) the contemplation and institution of all proceedings and other action (whether against the Borrower or otherwise) for the payment or discharge of the money and liabilities secured by or associated with this deed;
(c) the exercise or contemplated exercise of any power, right or discretion conferred by this deed or by law on the Lender;
(d) any default by the Borrower or any surety in compliance with the obligations imposed by the terms of this security or associated with it;
(e) any impeachment or attempted impeachment of the title of the Lender (whether by the Borrower or by a third party) or of the title of the Borrower; and

(f) the contemplation or doing of any other matter or thing which the Lender considers to be for the benefit or improvement of the security.

3 Legal charge

The Borrower, with [full *(or)* limited] title guarantee, charges the Property to the Lender by way of [first *(or as the case may be)*] legal mortgage with payment or discharge of all money and other obligations and liabilities in this deed covenanted to be paid or discharged by the Borrower or otherwise secured by this deed.

4 Borrower's representations and warranties

The Borrower represents and warrants to the Lender that:

4.1 the present use of the Property is a permitted use within the provisions of the Town and Country Planning Act 1990;

4.2 the Borrower has not before the execution of this deed carried out any operation upon the Property or put the Property to any use which is a development within the provisions of the Town and Country Planning Act 1990 and in respect of which any requisite permission has not been obtained or any valid enforcement order may be made;

4.3 the Borrower has complied with environmental law and, in particular (but without prejudice to the generality of that representation and warranty) that no hazardous or toxic materials, substances, pollutants, contaminants or wastes have at any time before the execution of this deed been released into the environment or deposited, discharged, displaced or disposed of at or near the Property; [and]

4.4 the execution of, and the observance and performance of his obligations under, this mortgage does not and will not contravene any other charge, mortgage, lease, loan facility or other agreement[; and

4.5 the execution of and the observance of its obligations under this mortgage does not and will not contravene any of the provisions of its Memorandum and Articles of Association].

5 Borrower's covenants as to the Property

The Borrower covenants with the Lender as set out below.

5.1 Repair

5.1.1 The Borrower will keep all buildings, fixtures and fittings, services and service media in, on or associated with the Property in good and substantial repair and good working order and condition.

5.1.2 The Borrower will permit the Lender and his representatives at all reasonable times and upon reasonable notice to enter upon the Property or any part of it to inspect the state and condition of the said buildings, fixtures and fittings, services and service media without the Lender becoming liable as mortgagee in possession.

5.1.3 If the Borrower fails to maintain the buildings, fixtures and fittings, services and service media in the requisite state of repair and condition the Lender and his representatives may (but without being bound to do so) at any time thereafter enter upon the Property or any part of it and execute all remedial works that the Lender considers to be necessary and proper without the Lender thereby becoming liable as mortgagee in possession.

5.1.4 The Borrower will on demand repay to the Lender all expenses incurred by the Lender in carrying out inspections and works permitted by this clause together with interest from the date when the Lender becomes liable for the same until repayment by the Borrower at the Interest Rate (such interest to be payable in the same manner as interest on the Principal) all of which money and interest shall be charged on the Property.

5.2 *Alterations*

The Borrower will not without the previous written consent of the Lender (and then only to the extent permitted by and in accordance with any conditions attached to the consent) make any structural or material alteration to, or pull down or remove any or any part of, any buildings, fixtures and fittings, services and service media in or upon or associated with the Property.

5.3 *Insurance*

5.3.1 *Duty to insure*

The Borrower will:

(a) ensure the Property is kept insured for such amount or amounts (including sums in respect of any loss of rent and any professional fees which may be incurred in or about repair, rebuilding or reinstatement), in such name or names, and against loss or damage due to such risks and with such underwriters as the Lender may in each case and from time to time approve; and

(b) make all payments required for this purpose [as and when *(or)* within *(number)* days after] they become due and will when required by the Lender deliver to him the policy of insurance and the receipt for each payment.

5.3.2 *Indemnity for payments by the Lender*

If the Borrower fails to perform any of his obligations under this clause and if the Lender takes out any insurance on the Property or any part of it, the Borrower will on demand repay to the Lender all payments made by him for that purpose and will pay interest at the Interest Rate from the date of payment until repayment on any money not repaid on demand (such interest to be payable in the same manner as interest on the Principal). All such money and interest shall be charged on the Property.

5.3.3 *Application of insurance money*

Any money received under any policy of insurance effected or maintained by the Borrower (whether or not pursuant to his obligations under this clause 5.3) shall, at the option and absolute discretion of the Lender, be applied either in making good the loss or damage in respect of which it was received or in or towards discharge of the money due under this security, and if received by the Borrower will be held on trust for the Lender for this purpose.

5.4 *Outgoings*

The Borrower will punctually pay, and indemnify the Lender against, all rents, rates, taxes, levies, assessments, impositions and outgoings whatsoever (whether governmental, municipal, contractual or otherwise) which may be or may become imposed upon or payable in respect of the Property or any part of it.

5.5 *General covenant to comply with statutes etc*

The Borrower will ensure that any legislation, regulations or bye-laws for the time being in force applicable to the Property [or to the employment of persons in the Property] are complied with in all respects.

5.6 *General covenant to produce notices etc*

5.6.1 The Borrower will immediately produce to the Lender any order, direction, permission, notice or other matter whatever affecting or likely to affect the Property and served upon the Borrower by any third party, and will allow the Lender to make a copy of it.

5.6.2 The Borrower will comply with any such order, direction, permission, notice or other matter without delay or, if the Lender so requires, will make or join with the Lender in making such objections or representations against or in respect of the same as the Lender may request or approve.

5.7 *Specific covenants relating to planning and environmental matters*

5.7.1 *Alteration of present use of the Property*

The Borrower will not use the Property for any purpose other than the present permitted use except with the previous written consent of the Lender and the relevant planning authority and then only to the extent permitted by and in accordance with any conditions attached to such consent. The Borrower will deliver any such consent of the relevant planning authority to the Lender but shall be entitled to a copy of it.

5.7.2 *No development without the Lender's consent*

The Borrower will not without the previous written consent of the Lender (and then only to the extent permitted by and in accordance with any conditions attached to such consent) carry out any operation or use the Property for any use which is a development within the provisions of the Town and Country Planning Act 1990.

5.7.3 *Compliance with conditions of permission for development*

If the Borrower at any time obtains permission for any development of the Property within the provisions of the Town and Country Planning Act 1990 he will comply with all conditions subject to which such permission is granted.

5.7.4 *Compliance with environmental matters*

The Borrower will observe and perform all environmental laws, regulations, directives and codes of practice affecting the Property.

5.7.5 Compliance with notices etc

(a) If any valid enforcement or other notice, claim, order or proposal is made or served by the relevant authority under or by virtue of the Town and Country Planning Act 1990 or the Environmental Protection Act 1990 the Borrower will immediately produce the same to the Lender and allow the Lender to take a copy of it.

(b) The Borrower will at his own expense in all respects comply with the requirements of any such notice, order or proposal without delay and in any event within any time which may be specified for compliance. Alternatively, if the Lender so requires, the Borrower will make or join with the Lender in making such objections or representations as the Lender may request or approve against or in respect of any such notice or order or proposal.

(c) If the Borrower fails to take immediate steps to commence compliance, or fails within the relevant time limit to conclude compliance with any such requirement, the Lender may (but shall not be obliged to) at any time thereafter enter on the Property and execute any works and do anything on the Property necessary to ensure such compliance without the Lender thereby becoming liable as mortgagee in possession and all costs and expenses so incurred by the Lender, with interest on them at the Interest Rate, shall be payable and charged upon the Property as provided by clause 5.1.4.

(d) The Borrower irrevocably appoints the Lender and his substitutes for the time being to be his attorney to apply for and procure on his behalf any licences, permissions or other things from any competent authority necessary for the execution of the works authorised by this clause to be executed by the Lender on the default of the Borrower.

(e) All expenses incurred by the Lender in securing such licences permissions and other things shall be treated as part of the cost of the works and such expenses and interest on them shall be charged upon the Property as provided by clause 5.1.4.

5.8 Specific covenant in relation to compulsory purchase

5.8.1 The Borrower will not without the previous consent in writing of the Lender (and then only to the extent permitted by and in accordance with any conditions attached to that consent) enter into any negotiations with any local or other authority for or consent to the compulsory acquisition of the Property either in whole or in part.

5.8.2 If the Lender so requires the Borrower will permit the Lender to conduct such negotiations and grant such consent on his behalf.

5.8.3 Any compensation payable to or received by the Borrower in respect of the compulsory acquisition of the Property or any part of it will, if so and to the extent required by the Lender, be applied in or towards the discharge of the money due under this security.

5.9 Leasing and disposal

The Borrower must not without the previous consent in writing of the Lender (and then only to the extent permitted by and in accordance with any conditions attached to such consent):

5.9.1 exercise or agree to exercise any power of leasing or of accepting surrenders of leases (whether conferred by statute or otherwise) or vary or agree to vary any lease or tenancy agreement or the amounts payable thereunder; or

5.9.2 otherwise part with or share possession or occupation of or dispose of or deal with the Property or any part of it or any interest in it.

5.10 Compliance with terms of conveyances etc

5.10.1 The Borrower will observe and perform the terms of all conveyances, grants, assignments, contracts and other deeds and documents from time to time affecting the Property and binding on the Borrower.

5.10.2 The Borrower will keep the Lender indemnified against all proceedings and claims on account of any breach of those terms.

5.10.3 All expenses damages and costs incurred by the Lender in relation to any such breach together with interest at the Interest Rate shall be payable and charged upon the Property as provided by clause 5.1.4.

[*5.11 Not to register*

The Borrower must not without the previous consent in writing of the Lender cause or allow any person to be registered under the Land Registration Acts as proprietor of the Property or any part of it.]

[*5.12 Other charges*

The Borrower shall not without the previous consent in writing of the Lender (and then only to the extent permitted by and in accordance with any conditions attached to such consent) create or permit to subsist any mortgage, pledge, charge, incumbrance, lien or other security interest in the Property other than this security.]

6 Lender's powers and rights

6.1 Exercise of statutory powers

6.1.1 Section 103 of the Law of Property Act 1925 shall not apply to this security.

6.1.2 At any time after the money secured by this deed has become due and payable the security shall be immediately enforceable and the power of sale as amended or varied by this deed shall be immediately exercisable in respect of the whole or any part of the Property without the restrictions contained in that Act as to the giving of notice or otherwise.

6.2 Extension of statutory powers

6.2.1 The power of sale conferred upon mortgagees by the Law of Property Act 1925 shall be extended so as to authorise any person exercising it to do so by selling the Property or any part of it in such manner and on such conditions as to payment of the purchase price and otherwise as the Lender may think fit.

6.2.2 By way of extension of the powers contained in the Law of Property Act 1925 sections 99 and 100 the Lender shall at any time or times hereafter (and whether or not he has entered into or is in possession of the Property or has appointed a receiver who is still acting) be entitled to grant or vary or reduce any sum payable under, or accept surrenders of, leases of the Property or any part or parts of it or agree to do so without restriction in such manner and on such terms and conditions as he shall think fit. For the purposes of the exercise of these powers the provisions of the Law of Property Act 1925 sections 99 and 100 shall be deemed to have been enacted with the omission of sections 99(18) and 100(12).

6.2.3 At any time after this security has become enforceable and notwithstanding the appointment of any receiver the Lender may at his absolute discretion exercise any power which a receiver appointed by him could exercise.

[6.2.4 The powers granted or extended by this clause shall be exercisable free from any liability on the part of the Lender or the person exercising them to the Borrower or any other interested person, whether in negligence or otherwise.]

6.3 *Powers in respect of furniture and effects*

6.3.1 At any time after this security has become enforceable the Lender may, as agent for and on behalf of the Borrower and at the expense of the Borrower, remove, store, preserve, sell or otherwise dispose of any livestock or any furniture, effects, chattels or other items situate at or in the Property which are not charged by this mortgage.

6.3.2 The Lender will have no liability to the Borrower for any loss incurred in connection with any such removal, storage, preservation, sale or disposal.

[(*corporate borrowers only*)

6.3.3 The Lender will have the right to set off any such proceeds of sale against the sums due under this security.

or (*individual borrowers only*)

6.3.3 The Lender will pay any net proceeds of any sale (after payment of removal, storage and preservation costs and the costs of the sale) to the Borrower on demand.

[6.3.4 The provisions of this clause are not intended to grant the Lender any rights in, or any charge or security over, any livestock, furniture, effects, chattels or other items or the proceeds of any sale of them so as to constitute this security a bill of sale.]]

6.4 *Power to appoint a receiver*

6.4.1 At any time after this security becomes enforceable, or at the request of the Borrower, the Lender may by writing under hand appoint any person or persons to be a receiver of all or any part of the Property.

6.4.2 The Lender may at any time and from time to time in like manner remove any receiver so appointed and appoint another in his place or appoint an additional person as receiver.

6.4.3 The Lender may, either at the time of appointment or at any time subsequently and from time to time, fix the remuneration of any receiver so appointed.

6.4.4 None of the restrictions imposed by the Law of Property Act 1925 in relation to the appointment of receivers or as to the giving of notice or otherwise shall apply.

6.4.5 Where more than one receiver is appointed they shall have the power to act severally.

6.4.6 Any receiver so appointed shall be the agent of the Borrower for all purposes and the Borrower shall be solely responsible for his acts or defaults and for his remuneration.

6.4.7 Any receiver so appointed shall have all the powers conferred on mortgagees or receivers by the Law of Property Act 1925 (but without the restrictions contained in section 103 of that Act) and on administrative receivers by the Insolvency Act 1986 Schedule 1 except to the extent to which those powers are expressly or impliedly excluded by the terms of this deed. In the event of ambiguity or conflict the terms of this deed will prevail.

6.4.8 In addition any receiver so appointed shall have power at his discretion, to such extent and upon such terms as he may in his absolute discretion think fit, and notwithstanding the [administration or liquidation *(or)* bankruptcy, death or insanity] of the Borrower, to do or omit to do anything which the Borrower could do or omit to do in relation to all or any part of the Property. In particular (but without limitation) any such receiver shall have the power:

(a) to take possession of, collect and get in all or any part of the Property and for that purpose bring any proceedings in the name of the Borrower or otherwise;

(b) to manage or carry on or concur in carrying on any business of the Borrower;

(c) to raise or borrow money (whether from the Lender or otherwise) to rank for payment in priority to this security and with or without a charge on all or any part of the Property;

(d) to sell (whether by public auction or private contract or otherwise), lease, vary, renew or surrender leases or accept surrenders of leases (without needing to observe the provisions of the Law of Property Act 1925 sections 99 and 100) of, or otherwise dispose of or deal with all or any part of, the Property or of rights associated with all or any part of the Property or to concur in so doing whether in the name or on behalf of the Borrower or otherwise;

(e) to seize and sever all or any fixtures at or in the Property [*(where the Borrower is an individual)* other than and except trade machinery as defined by the Bills of Sale Act 1878] and sell the same separately from the Property or its site;

(f) to settle, arrange, compromise or submit to arbitration any accounts, claims, questions or disputes whatsoever which may arise in connection with any business of the Borrower or the Property or in any way relating to this security;

(g) to bring, take, defend, compromise, submit to arbitration or discontinue any actions, suits or proceedings whatsoever whether civil or criminal in relation to the matters referred to in clause 6.4.8(f);

(h) to disclaim, abandon or disregard all or any outstanding contracts of the Borrower and to allow time for payment of any debts either with or without security;

(i) to repair, insure, manage, protect, improve, enlarge, develop, build, complete or reconstruct or replace all or any part of the Property and to apply for and obtain any appropriate permissions approvals consents or licences;

(j) to acquire by purchase lease or otherwise any further property assets or rights;

(k) to appoint, employ and dismiss managers, officers, contractors and agents;

(l) to do (whether in the name of the Borrower or otherwise) all such other acts and things as he may consider necessary or desirable for the preservation, management, improvement or realisation of the Property or as he may consider incidental or conducive to any of the above matters or to the exercise of any of the above powers [and for these purposes the Borrower authorises the receiver to elect to waive exemption under the Value Added Tax Act 1994 Schedule 10 paragraph 2(1) on behalf of the Borrower in respect of the Property].

6.4.9 All money received by any receiver shall be applied by him:

(a) in payment of the costs, charges and expenses of and incidental to the appointment of the receiver and the exercise of all or any of his powers and of all outgoings paid by him (including preferential debts);

(b) in payment to the receiver of such remuneration as may be agreed between him and the Lender at, or at any time and from time to time after, his appointment;

(c) in or towards satisfaction of the amount owing on this security

and the surplus (if any) shall be paid to the Borrower or other persons entitled to it.

6.5 *Right to consolidate*

Section 93 of the Law of Property Act 1925 (restricting the Lender's right of consolidation) shall not apply to this security.

7 Protection of persons dealing with the Lender or a receiver

No person dealing with the Lender or any receiver appointed by him shall be concerned bound or entitled to inquire or be affected by notice as to any of the following matters:

7.1 whether this security has become enforceable;

7.2 whether any power exercised or purported to be exercised under this mortgage has arisen or become exercisable;

7.3 the propriety, regularity or purpose of the exercise or purported exercise of any such power;

7.4 whether any money remains due under the security; or

7.5 the necessity or expediency of the stipulations and conditions subject to which any disposition shall be made;

and the receipt of the Lender or any receiver for any money shall effectually discharge the person paying from such matters and from being concerned to see to the application or being answerable for the loss or misapplication of such money.

8 Indulgence and waiver

The Lender may at any time or times without discharging or diminishing or in any way prejudicing or affecting this security or any right or remedy of the

Lender under this mortgage grant to the Borrower, or to any other person, time or indulgence, further credit, loans or advances or enter into any arrangement or variation of rights or, either in whole or in part, release, abstain from perfecting or enforcing or neglect or fail to perfect or enforce any remedies, securities, guarantees or rights which he may now or subsequently have from or against the Borrower or any other person.

9 Demands and notices

9.1 A demand or notice by the Lender under this mortgage shall be deemed to have been properly served on the Borrower if served personally on [the Borrower *(or)* any one of the directors or the secretary of the Borrower], by first class letter post, telex or fax addressed to the Borrower at or by delivery to [his usual or last known place of abode or business *(or)* its registered office or at any of its principal places of business].

9.2 Service shall be deemed to be effected notwithstanding the [death *(or)* dissolution] of the Borrower:

- 9.2.1 at 10 am on the second business day immediately following the day of posting if given by first class letter post irrespective of the time or date of actual delivery or of lack of delivery,
- 9.2.2 when dispatched if given by telex or fax, and
- 9.2.3 when left at the property concerned if delivered.

9.3 The methods of service described in clause 9.1 are in addition, and without prejudice, to any other method of service prescribed or permitted by law and in particular to the provisions of the Law of Property Act 1925 section 196.

9.4 If the expression 'the Borrower' includes more than one person, service on any one person shall be deemed to constitute service upon all such persons.

10 Validity and severability

10.1 Each of the provisions of this mortgage is severable and distinct from the others and if at any time one or more of such provisions is or becomes invalid, illegal or unenforceable the validity, legality and enforceability of the remaining provisions shall not be affected or impaired.

10.2 If this mortgage is executed by or on behalf of more than one person and any one or more of those persons is not bound by its provisions (whether by reason of lack of capacity or improper execution or for any other reason), the remaining parties shall continue to be so bound as if those who are not bound had not been parties to the security.

[11 Partnerships

This deed is intended to secure the repayment of all money for the time being owing by [*(name of firm)* to the Lender *(or)* the Borrower to *(name of firm)*] and shall have effect accordingly notwithstanding any change in the constitution of *(name of firm)* by reason of the death or retirement or expulsion of any member of it or the introduction of any new member or any change in the style of *(name of firm)*.]

12 Interpretation

12.1 Unless the context otherwise requires:
 12.1.1 the singular includes the plural and vice versa,
 12.1.2 references to persons include references to firms companies or corporations and vice versa, and
 12.1.3 references in the masculine gender include references in the feminine or neuter genders and vice versa.

12.2 Unless the context otherwise requires the expressions 'the Borrower' and ' the Lender' include their respective successors and assigns whether immediate or derivative and where appropriate the survivors or survivor of them.

12.3 All covenants, charges, agreements, undertakings, representations and warranties given or implied in this mortgage by more than one person shall be deemed to have been given jointly and severally by those concerned.

12.4 References to any statutory provision shall be construed as including any statutory modification or re-enactment of it and any order, regulation, directive or code of practice made under it or associated with it.

12.5 The clause headings do not form part of this mortgage and shall not be taken into account in its construction or interpretation.

12.6 Any reference to a clause or a paragraph or a schedule is to one in this mortgage so numbered or named.

13 Governing law and jurisdiction

13.1 This mortgage shall be governed by and construed in accordance with English law.

13.2 It is irrevocably agreed for the exclusive benefit of the Lender that the courts of England are to have jurisdiction to settle any disputes which may arise out of or in connection with this mortgage and that accordingly any suit, action or proceeding arising out of or in connection with this mortgage may be brought in such courts.

13.3 Nothing in this clause shall limit the Lender's right to take proceedings against the Borrower in any other court of competent jurisdiction, nor shall the taking of proceedings in one or more jurisdictions preclude the taking of proceedings in any other jurisdiction, whether concurrently or not.

IN WITNESS etc*)*

[SCHEDULE
The Property

(insert details)]

(signatures (or common seals) of the parties)

(signatures of witnesses)

This precedent is reproduced from *Butterworths Encyclopaedia of Forms and Precedents* (5th edn), volume 28 (1999 reissue) MORTGAGES, Form 2, contributed by Andrew Whittaker, solicitor.

CHARGE BY WAY OF LEGAL MORTGAGE OF FREEHOLDS BY ONE BORROWER TO ONE LENDER: LOAN OF FIXED AMOUNT TO BE REPAID BY EQUAL INSTALMENTS

THIS LEGAL CHARGE is made the .... day of .... BETWEEN

(1) *(name of borrower)* [of *(address) (or)* the registered office of which is at *(address)* and the company registration number of which is *(number)*] ('the Borrower') and

(2) *(name of lender)* [of *(address) (or)* the registered office of which is at *(address)* and the company registration number of which is *(number)*] ('the Lender')

RECITALS

(1) [The Borrower is the estate owner absolute in possession in respect of the fee simple *(or)* The Borrower is registered at HM Land Registry as proprietor with title [absolute *(or as the case may be)*]] of the property described in the schedule to this deed [subject as mentioned in the schedule but otherwise] free from incumbrances.

(2) The Lender has agreed to lend £......... to the Borrower on condition that its repayment together with interest is secured in the manner set out below.

NOW THIS DEED WITNESSES as follows:

1 Definitions

In this legal charge:

1.1 'the Interest Payment Days' means *(state days for payment)* in each year commencing on *(date)*;

1.2 'the Interest Rate' means [*(for fixed rate)* ......% a year *(or for variable rate)* ......% above the rate of *(specify lending or base rate by which reference to which interest is to be calculated)* from time to time];

1.3 'the Principal' means £.........;

1.4 'the Property' means the property specified in the schedule below and all buildings and fixtures on it.

2 Payment of principal, interest and costs

In consideration of the Principal, now paid by the Lender to the Borrower (receipt of which the Borrower acknowledges) the Borrower covenants with the Lender as set out below.

2.1 *Principal*

2.1.1 Payment

The Borrower covenants with the Lender to pay the Principal to the Lender [free from any legal or equitable right of set-off] by equal *(state frequency)* instalments of £......... each on the Interest Payment Days, PROVIDED that if:

(a) any instalment of the Principal is not paid within *(number)* days of becoming due; or

(b) any interest or other sum payable under this security is not paid within *(number)* days of becoming due; or

(c) the Borrower or any surety fails to comply with any term, condition, covenant or provision of, or to perform any of his obligations or liabilities under, this or any associated or collateral security; or

(d) any representation or warranty given by the Borrower or any surety to the Lender is or becomes incorrect; or

(e) any judgment or order made against the Borrower or any surety by any court is not complied with within *(number)* days; or

(f) the property of the Borrower or any surety becomes subject to any forfeiture or execution, distress, sequestration or other form of process; or

(g) a mortgagee takes possession of or exercises or seeks to exercise any power of sale or of an appointment of a receiver in relation to the property charged by this deed or any other property of the Borrower or of any surety; or

(h) in the case of an individual:

 (i) the Borrower or any surety becomes subject to an interim order or makes a proposal for a voluntary arrangement under Part VIII of the Insolvency Act 1986 or enters, or seeks to enter, into any other form of composition or arrangement with his creditors whether in whole or in part; or

 (ii) a petition is presented for the bankruptcy of the Borrower or any surety; or

 (iii) the Borrower or any surety dies or becomes of unsound mind; or

(i) in the case of a company:

 (i) the Borrower or any surety ceases or threatens to cease to carry on, or disposes or threatens to dispose of, its business or a material part of its business; or

 (ii) the Borrower or any surety makes a proposal for a voluntary arrangement under Part I of the Insolvency Act 1986 or enters, or seeks to enter, into any other form of composition or arrangement with its creditors whether in whole or in part; or

 (iii) a petition is presented for the making of an administration order in respect of the Borrower or any surety; or

 (iv) an administrative receiver is appointed in respect of the whole or any part of the undertaking of the Borrower or any surety; or

 (v) a petition is presented in any court or a meeting is convened for the purpose of considering a resolution for the winding up of the Borrower or any surety (except in the case of a reconstruction or amalgamation that has the previous approval in writing of the Lender)

the whole of the balance of the Principal then outstanding shall be immediately due and repayable by the Borrower to the Lender [on demand].

[2.1.2 Power to anticipate instalments

(a) Subject to the provisions of clause 2.1.2(b) the Borrower may, on giving to the Lender at least *(specify period)* previous notice in writing, repay to the Lender in [sums *(or)* multiples] of *(specify amounts)*, on any day on which interest is payable under this deed, the whole or any part of the Principal then owing.

(b) This entitlement to make anticipatory repayments shall only be capable of being exercised if the interest due on the proposed repayment date in respect of the whole Principal for the time being owing is also paid.

(c) In the case of a partial repayment by anticipation the succeeding instalments of principal shall continue to be payable in due course pursuant to the provisions of clause 2.1.1 until the whole of the Principal has been satisfied.]

Insert charging clause and remaining clauses as required

This precedent is reproduced from *Butterworths Encyclopaedia of Forms and Precedents* (5th edn), volume 28 (1999 reissue) MORTGAGES, Form 5, contributed by Andrew Whittaker, solicitor.

CHARGE BY WAY OF LEGAL MORTGAGE OF FREEHOLDS BY ONE BORROWER TO ONE LENDER WITH A SURETY JOINING TO COVENANT FOR PAYMENT BUT WITHOUT CHARGING HIS OWN PROPERTY: LOAN OF FIXED AMOUNT TO BE REPAID ON FIXED DATE

THIS LEGAL CHARGE is made the .... day of .... BETWEEN

(1) *(name of borrower)* [of *(address) (or)* the registered office of which is at *(address)* and the company registration number of which is *(number)*] ('the Borrower')

(2) *(name of surety)* [of *(address) (or)* the registered office of which is at *(address)* and the company registration number of which is *(number)*] ('the Surety') and

(2) *(name of lender)* [of *(address) (or)* the registered office of which is at *(address)* and the company registration number of which is *(number)*] ('the Lender')

RECITALS

(1) [The Borrower is the estate owner absolute in possession in respect of the fee simple *(or)* The Borrower is registered at HM Land Registry as proprietor with title [absolute *(or as the case may be)*]] of the property described in the schedule to this deed [subject as mentioned in the schedule but otherwise] free from incumbrances.

(2) The Borrower and the Surety have requested the Lender to lend the Principal to the Borrower, which the Lender has agreed to do on condition that its repayment together with interest is secured in the manner set out below.

NOW THIS DEED WITNESSES as follows:

1 Definitions

In this legal charge:

1.1 'the Interest Payment Days' means *(state days for payment)*;

1.2 'the Interest Rate' means [*(for fixed rate)* ......% a year *(or for variable rate)* ......% above the rate of *(specify lending or base rate by which reference to which interest is to be calculated)* from time to time];

1.3 'the Principal' means £........;

1.4 'the Property' means the property specified in the schedule below and all buildings and fixtures on it; and

1.5 'the Redemption Date' means *(date)*;

1.6 'the Surety's Liability Limit' means £.........

2 Payment of principal, interest and costs

In consideration of the Principal, now paid by the Lender to the Borrower at the request of the Surety (receipt of which the Borrower and payment of which the Surety respectively acknowledge), the Borrower and the Surety covenant with the Lender as set out below.

2.1 *Principal*

The Borrower and the Surety covenant with the Lender to pay the Principal to the Lender [free from any legal or equitable right of set-off] on the Redemption Date or, if earlier, immediately [on demand] if:

2.1.1 any interest or other sum payable under this security is not paid within *(number)* days of becoming due; or

2.1.2 the Borrower or the Surety or any other surety fails to comply with any term, condition, covenant or provision of or to perform any of his obligations or liabilities under this or any associated or collateral security; or

2.1.3 any representation or warranty given by the Borrower or the Surety or any other surety to the Lender is or becomes incorrect; or

2.1.4 any judgment or order made against the Borrower or the Surety or any other surety by any court is not complied with within *(number)* days; or

2.1.5 the property of the Borrower or the Surety or any other surety becomes subject to any execution, distress, sequestration or other form of process; or

2.1.6 a mortgagee takes possession of or exercises or seeks to exercise any power of sale or of an appointment of a receiver in relation to the property charged by this deed or any other property of the Borrower or the Surety or any other surety; or

2.1.7 in the case of an individual:

(a) the Borrower or the Surety or any other surety becomes subject to an interim order or makes a proposal for a voluntary arrangement under Part VIII of the Insolvency Act 1986 or enters or seeks to enter into any other form of composition or arrangement with his creditors whether in whole or in part; or

(b) a petition is presented for the bankruptcy of the Borrower or the Surety or any other surety; or

(c) the Borrower or the Surety or any other surety dies or becomes of unsound mind; or

2.1.8 in the case of a company:

(a) the Borrower or the Surety or any other surety ceases or threatens to cease to carry on, or disposes or threatens to dispose of, its business or a material part of its business; or

(b) the Borrower or the Surety or any other surety makes a proposal for a voluntary arrangement under Part I of the Insolvency Act 1986 or enters or seeks to enter into any other form of composition or arrangement with its creditors whether in whole or in part; or

(c) a petition is presented for the making of an administration order in respect of the Borrower or the Surety or any other surety; or

(d) an administrative receiver is appointed in respect of the whole or any part of the undertaking of the Borrower or the Surety or any other surety; or

(e) a petition is presented in any court or a meeting is convened for the purpose of considering a resolution for the winding up of the Borrower or the Surety or any other surety (except in the case of a reconstruction or amalgamation that has the previous approval in writing of the Lender).

2.2 *Interest*

2.2.1 *Payment*

The Borrower and the Surety covenant with the Lender to pay to the Lender interest on the Principal (or so much of it as may from time to time remain outstanding) at the Interest Rate from the date of this deed by equal *(specify frequency)* payments on the Interest Payment Days, as well after as before any [demand or] judgment or the [administration or liquidation *(or)* bankruptcy death or insanity] of the Borrower or of the Surety.

[2.2.2 *Reduction for prompt payment*

Subject to the Borrower and the Surety having otherwise in all respects and at all times observed and performed their obligations under this deed and to payment being made not later than *(specify period which should be no longer than that specified in clause 2.1.1)* after the due date for payment the Lender will accept interest on the Principal from the Borrower and the Surety at the rate of *(specify reduced fixed or variable rate)* in satisfaction of payment at the Interest Rate.]

[2.2.3 *Capitalisation*

(a) If any interest payable under this security is not paid within *(specify period)* after the due date for payment it shall be capitalised and added to the Principal and be charged on the Property and bear interest from the due date for payment, such interest to be payable at the Interest Rate on Interest Payment Days.

(b) The capitalisation of arrears of interest will be without prejudice to the Lender's right at any time to enforce payment of the sums concerned as interest in arrear.

(c) The Borrower and the Surety may on any of the days specified in clause 2.2.1 pay to the Lender in addition to the interest then due all or any part of the Principal representing capitalised arrears of interest.

(d) Otherwise all covenants and provisions contained in this mortgage and all powers and remedies conferred by law or by this mortgage and all rules of law or equity relating to the Principal and interest on it shall equally apply to capitalised arrears of interest and to interest on them.]

2.3 *Costs, charges, expenses and other liabilities*

2.3.1 *Covenant to pay*

The Borrower and the Surety covenant with the Lender to pay to the Lender on demand and on a full and unlimited indemnity basis all costs, charges, expenses and liabilities paid and incurred by the Lender (whether directly or indirectly) in relation to the security constituted by and the obligations owed under and associated with this deed (including all commission legal and other professional costs and fees and disbursements, and VAT thereon) together with interest from the date when the Lender becomes liable for the same until payment by the Borrower or the Surety at the Interest Rate, such interest to be payable in the same manner as interest on the Principal.

2.3.2 *Costs included*

Without prejudice to the generality of the provisions of that clause the liability of the Borrower and the Surety under clause 2.3.1 will include not only those costs, charges, expenses and liabilities that would otherwise be allowable on the taking of an account between a mortgagor and a mortgagee but also (and in so far as they are not so allowable) those incurred in relation to or arising out of:

(a) the contemplation and institution of all proceedings and other action in connection with the enforcement preservation and protection of the security constituted by this deed;
(b) the contemplation and institution of all proceedings and other action (whether against the Borrower or the Surety or otherwise) for the payment or discharge of the money and liabilities secured by or associated with this deed;
(c) the exercise or contemplated exercise of any power, right or discretion conferred by this deed or by law on the Lender;
(d) any default by the Borrower or the Surety or any other surety in compliance with the obligations imposed by the terms of this security or associated with it;
(e) any impeachment or attempted impeachment of the title of the Lender (whether by the Borrower or by the Surety or by a third party) or of the title of the Borrower or of the Surety; and
(f) the contemplation or doing of any other matter or thing which the Lender considers to be for the benefit or improvement of the security.

3 Legal charge

The Borrower with [full *(or)* limited] title guarantee charges the Property to the Lender by way of [first *(or as the case may be)*] legal mortgage ('with the payment or discharge of all money and other obligations and liabilities by this deed covenanted to be paid or discharged by the Borrower or the Surety or otherwise secured by this deed.

4 Representations and warranties

The Borrower and the Surety represent and warrant to the Lender that:

4.1 the present use of the Property is a permitted use within the provisions of the Town and Country Planning Act 1990;
4.2 the Borrower has not before the execution of this deed carried out any operation upon the Property or put the Property to any use which is a development within the provisions of the Town and Country Planning Act 1990 and in respect of which any requisite permission has not been obtained or any valid enforcement order may be made;
4.3 the Borrower has complied with environmental law and in particular (but without prejudice to the generality of that representation and warranty) that no hazardous or toxic materials substances pollutants contaminants

or wastes have at any time before the execution of this deed been released into the environment or deposited, discharged, displaced or disposed of at or near the Property;

4.4 the execution of and the observance and performance of their obligations under this mortgage does not and will not contravene any other charge, mortgage, lease, loan facility or other agreement[; and

4.5 the execution of and the observance of their obligations under this mortgage does not and will not contravene any of the provisions of their Memoranda and Articles of Association].

5 Covenants by the Borrower and the Surety as to the Property etc

The Borrower and the Surety covenant with the Lender as follows:

Insert covenants as required

6 Lender's rights

Insert rights as required

7 Protection of persons dealing with the Lender or a receiver

Insert clause as required

8 Liability and incidence of liability of the Borrower and the Surety

8.1 Although as between the Borrower and the Surety the Surety is only a surety for the Borrower, as between the Surety and the Lender the Surety is to be considered a principal debtor for all money and other obligations and liabilities covenanted to be paid or discharged by the Borrower or the Surety under this deed or otherwise secured by this deed.

[8.2 Subject to clause 8.1, the Surety shall not be liable under the covenants by him contained in this deed to pay a larger sum in the aggregate in respect of the Principal interest and costs charges and other expenses than the Surety's Liability Limit.]

Insert further clauses as required

IN WITNESS etc

SCHEDULE
The Property

(insert details)

(signatures (or common seals) of the parties)

(signatures of witnesses)

This precedent is reproduced from *Butterworths Encyclopaedia of Forms and Precedents* (5th edn), volume 28 (1999 reissue) MORTGAGES, Form 9, contributed by Andrew Whittaker, solicitor.

SECOND OR SUBSEQUENT CHARGE BY WAY OF LEGAL MORTGAGE OF FREEHOLDS BY ONE BORROWER TO ONE LENDER: LOAN OF FIXED AMOUNT REPAYABLE ON FIXED DATE

THIS LEGAL CHARGE is made the .... day of .... BETWEEN

(1) *(name of borrower)* of [*(address)* *(or)* the registered office of which is at *(address)* and the company registration number of which is *(number)*] ('the Borrower') and

(2) *(name of lender)* of [*(address)* *(or)* the registered office of which is at *(address)* and the company registration number of which is *(number)*] ('the Lender')

RECITALS

(1) [The Borrower is the estate owner absolute in possession in respect of the fee simple *(or)* The Borrower is registered at HM Land Registry as proprietor with title [absolute *(or as the case may be)*]] of the property described in schedule 1 to this deed subject [as mentioned in schedule 1 and] to the mortgage[s] specified in schedule 2 but otherwise free from incumbrances.

(2) The principal sums secured by the mortgage[s] specified in schedule 2 are still owing with current interest.

(3) The Borrower has requested the Lender to lend him the Principal, which the Lender has agreed to do on having the repayment of it with interest secured in the manner set out below.

NOW THIS DEED WITNESSES as follows:

1 Definitions

In this legal charge:

1.1 'the Interest Payment Days' means *(state days for payment)*;

1.2 'the Interest Rate' means [*(for fixed rate)* ......% a year *(or for variable rate)* ......% above the rate of *(specify lending or base rate by which reference to which interest is to be calculated)* from time to time];

1.3 'the Principal' means £.........;

1.4 'the Property' means the property specified in the schedule below and all buildings and fixtures on it; and

1.5 'the Redemption Date' means *(date)*.

2 Payment of principal, interest and costs

Insert provisions as required

3 Legal charge

The Borrower with [full *(or)* limited] title guarantee charges the Property to the Lender by way of [second *(or as the case may be)*] legal mortgage, subject to the mortgage[s] specified in schedule 2 and to the principal sum[s] and interest and other money secured by them, with payment or discharge of all money and other obligations and liabilities covenanted to be paid or discharged by the Borrower under this deed or otherwise secured by it.

4 Borrowers representations and Borrowers covenants

Insert provisions as required

6 Lender's powers and rights

Insert provisions as required

6.6 *Power to settle with prior mortgagees*

6.6.1 If any proceedings or steps are taken to exercise or enforce any powers or remedies conferred by any incumbrance having priority over this security against the Property, the Lender or any receiver appointed by him may redeem that prior incumbrance or procure the transfer of it to himself and may settle and pass the accounts of any incumbrancer entitled to such prior security.

6.6.2 All the principal money, interest, costs, charges and expenses of and incident to any such redemption or transfer shall be repaid by the Borrower to the Lender on demand with interest at the Interest Rate payable from the date of payment by the Lender until repayment by the Borrower (such interest to be payable in the same manner as interest on the Principal), and until repayment all such sums and interest shall be charged on the Property.

6.6.3 Any accounts settled or passed in connection with any such redemption or transfer shall be conclusive and binding as well between the Lender and any receiver appointed by him on the one hand and the Borrower on the other hand as between such prior incumbrancer and the Borrower.

Insert further clauses as required

IN WITNESS etc

SCHEDULE 1
The Property

(insert details)

SCHEDULE 2
The Prior Mortgages

(insert details)

(signatures (or common seals) of the parties)

(signatures of witnesses)

This precedent is reproduced from *Butterworths Encyclopaedia of Forms and Precedents* (5th edn), volume 28 (1999 reissue) MORTGAGES, Form 14, contributed by Andrew Whittaker, solicitor.

NOTICE OF SECOND MORTGAGE FROM SECOND TO FIRST LENDER

To *(name of first lender)*
of *(address of first lender)*

I now give you notice that by a mortgage dated *(date)* and made between (1) *(name of borrower)* and (2) myself the property comprised in the mortgage dated *(date)* and made between (1) *(name of borrower)* and (2) yourself has been charged to me by way of legal mortgage for securing £......... and interest on it [at the rate of ......% a year].

Dated:

(signature of second lender)

(address of second lender)

This precedent is reproduced from *Butterworths Encyclopaedia of Forms and Precedents* (5th edn), volume 28 (1999 reissue) MORTGAGES, Form 16, contributed by Andrew Whittaker, solicitor.

CHARGE BY WAY OF LEGAL MORTGAGE BY CO-OWNERS OF FREEHOLDS TO ONE LENDER: LOAN OF FIXED AMOUNT REPAYABLE ON FIXED DATE

THIS LEGAL CHARGE is made the .... day of .... BETWEEN:

(1) *(names of mortgagors)* [of *(address(es))* *(or)* the registered office[s] of which [is *(or)* are] at *(address(es))* and the company registration number[s] of which [is *(or)* are] *(number(s))*] ('the Borrowers') and

(2) *(name of lender)* [of *(address)* *(or)* the registered office of which is at *(address)* and the company registration number of which is *(number)*] ('the Lender')

RECITALS

(1) [The Borrowers are the estate owners absolute in possession in respect of the fee simple *(or)* The Borrowers are registered at HM Land Registry as proprietors with title absolute *(or as the case may be)*] of the property described in the schedule to this deed [subject as mentioned in the schedule but otherwise] free from incumbrances.

(2) The Lender has agreed to lend the Principal to the Borrowers on condition that its repayment together with interest is secured in the manner set out below.

Insert clauses as required

This precedent is reproduced from *Butterworths Encyclopaedia of Forms and Precedents* (5th edn), volume 28 (1999 reissue) MORTGAGES, Form 17, contributed by Andrew Whittaker, solicitor.

CHARGE BY WAY OF LEGAL MORTGAGE OF FREEHOLD UNREGISTERED LAND TO CO-MORTGAGEES WHO HAVE ADVANCED ON A JOINT ACCOUNT: LOAN OF FIXED AMOUNT REPAYABLE ON FIXED DATE

THIS LEGAL CHARGE is made the .... day of .... BETWEEN:

(1) *(name of borrower)* [of *(address)* *(or)* the registered office of which is at *(address)* and the company registration number of which is *(number)*] ('the Borrower') and

(2) *(names of mortgagees)* [of *(addresses)* *(or)* the registered offices of which are at *(addresses)* and the company registration numbers of which are *(numbers)*] ('the Lenders')

RECITALS

(1) The Borrower is the estate owner absolute in possession in respect of the fee simple of the property described in the schedule to this deed [subject as mentioned in the schedule but otherwise] free from incumbrances.

(2) The Lenders have agreed to lend the Principal to the Borrower out of money belonging to them on a joint account on condition that its repayment together with interest is secured in the manner set out below.

NOW THIS DEED WITNESSES as follows:

1 Definitions

In this deed:

1.1 'the Principal' means £.........;

Insert other definitions as required

2 Payment of principal, interest and costs

In consideration of the Principal, now paid by the Lenders out of money belonging to them on a joint account to the Borrower (receipt of which the Borrower acknowledges), the Borrower covenants with the Lenders as set out below.

Insert clauses as required

9 Provision relating to co-mortgagees

For the avoidance of doubt the rights powers and remedies granted to the Lenders by this deed or otherwise implied in their favour may only be exercised by them together.

Insert further clauses as required

IN WITNESS etc

(signatures (or common seals) of the parties)

(signatures of witnesses)

This precedent is reproduced from *Butterworths Encyclopaedia of Forms and Precedents* (5th edn), volume 28 (1999 reissue) MORTGAGES, Form 20, contributed by Andrew Whittaker, solicitor.

CHARGE OF THE WHOLE OF THE LAND IN A REGISTERED TITLE BY A BORROWER WHO IS THE REGISTERED PROPRIETOR: SHORT FORM

[HM LAND REGISTRY
LAND REGISTRATION ACTS 1925 to 1986

Administrative area

Title No

Property]

In consideration of .... pounds (£.........) receipt of which is acknowledged I *(name of borrower)* of *(address of borrower)* with [full *(or)* limited] title guarantee charge by way of legal mortgage the land comprised in the title above referred to with the payment to *(name of lender)* of *(address of lender)* on *(date)* of the principal sum of £......... with interest at ......% a year payable [half yearly *(or)* quarterly *(or specify)*] on *(state days for payment)* in each year

(signatures (or common seals) of the parties)

(signatures of witnesses)

This precedent is reproduced from *Butterworths Encyclopaedia of Forms and Precedents* (5th edn), volume 28 (1999 reissue) MORTGAGES, Form 35, contributed by Andrew Whittaker, solicitor.

MEMORANDUM OF DEPOSIT OF TITLE DEEDS AND AGREEMENT TO EXECUTE A LEGAL MORTGAGE TO SECURE A NEW ADVANCE OR AN OUTSTANDING DEBT: SIMPLE FORM UNDER HAND

MEMORANDUM

1 Definitions and interpretation

In this memorandum:

[1.1 'the Advance' means £.........;]

1.2 'the Borrower' means *(name of chargor)* [of *(address)* *(or)* the registered office of which is at *(address)* and the company registration number of which is *(number)*];

1.3 'the Interest Payment Days' means *(state dates for payment)*;

1.4 'the Interest Rate' means the rate of ......% a year;

1.5 'the Lender' means *(name of chargee)* [of *(address)* *(or)* the registered office of which is at *(address)* and the company registration number of which is *(number)*];

1.6 'the Property' means the [freehold *(or)* leasehold] property known as *(insert details)*;

1.7 unless otherwise stated, 'interest' means interest at the Interest Rate payable by equal *(specify frequency)* payments on the Interest Payment Days.

2 Deposit and charge

[The documents of title of the Property have this day been deposited by the Borrower with the Lender to the intent that the Property may be equitably charged, and the Borrower with [full *(or)* limited] title guarantee charges it, with repayment to the Lender of the Advance made by him to the Borrower (receipt of which the Borrower acknowledges) with interest on it from the date of this memorandum.

(or)

In consideration of the Lender forbearing from pressing for immediate repayment of the Debt now owing to him by the Borrower (as the Borrower acknowledges) the documents of title of the Property have this day been deposited by the Borrower with the Lender to the intent that the Property may be equitably charged with repayment to the Lender of the Debt with interest on it from the date of this memorandum.]

3 Borrower to execute legal mortgage on request

The Borrower undertakes (whenever called upon to do so) to make and execute at his own cost a valid legal mortgage in favour of the Lender of the Property or any part of it to secure all sums for the time being owing to the Lender on this security, with interest, in such form and containing such covenants, conditions, powers and provisions as the Lender reasonably requires, but in any event including provisions excluding the Law of Property Act 1925 sections 93 (relating to consolidation) and 99(1) (relating to mortgagors' power of leasing).

4 Repair

The Borrower undertakes to keep all buildings and fixtures on the Property in good and substantial repair and condition.

5 Insurance

The Borrower undertakes to keep all buildings and fixtures on the Property insured against fire and such other risks as the Lender may reasonably require in their full value and, on demand in writing, to produce the receipts for premiums paid in respect of such insurance.

6 Costs

The Borrower undertakes to pay on demand all costs, charges and expenses paid or incurred by the Lender in perfecting or in enforcing this security or in obtaining payment or discharge of the money secured by this security.

Dated: *(date)*

AS WITNESS etc

(signatures of the parties)

This precedent is reproduced from *Butterworths Encyclopaedia of Forms and Precedents* (5th edn), volume 28 (1999 reissue) MORTGAGES, Form 43, contributed by Andrew Whittaker, solicitor.

MEMORANDUM AS A DEED TO ACCOMPANY DEPOSIT OF DEEDS WHERE THE SECURITY IS TO EXTEND TO FURTHER ADVANCES, WITH DECLARATION OF TRUST OF THE LEGAL ESTATE AND EXPRESS RIGHT TO POSSESSION

MEMORANDUM

1 Definitions and interpretation

In this memorandum:

1.1 'the Advance' means £.........;

1.2 'the Borrower' means *(name of chargor)* [of *(address)* *(or)* the registered office of which is at *(address)* and the company registration number of which is *(number)*];

1.3 'the Documents' means the several documents of title specified in the schedule;

1.4 'the Interest Payment Days' means *(state dates for payment)*;

1.5 'the Interest Rate' means the rate of ......% a year;

1.6 'the Lender' means *(name of chargee)* [of *(address)* *(or)* the registered office of which is at *(address)* and the company registration number of which is *(number)*];

1.7 'the Property' means the [freehold *(or)* leasehold] property known as *(insert details)*;

1.8 unless otherwise stated, 'interest' means interest at the Interest Rate payable by equal *(specify frequency)* payments on the Interest Payment Days.

2 Deposit and charge

The Documents have this .... day of .... been deposited by the Borrower with the Lender to the intent that the Property may be equitably charged, and the Borrower with [full *(or)* limited] title guarantee charges it, with the payment to the Lender of:

2.1 the Advance now paid by the Lender to the Borrower (receipt of which the Borrower acknowledges) with interest from the date of this memorandum; and

2.2 all further sums the Lender, while retaining possession of the Documents, from time to time advances to the Borrower with interest from the date of each such advance.

3 Borrower to execute legal mortgage on request

The Borrower undertakes (whenever called upon so to do) to make and execute at his own cost a valid legal mortgage of the Property or any part of it in favour of the Lender to secure all sums for the time being due or to become due to the Lender on this security, with interest, in such form and containing such covenants, conditions, powers and provisions as the Lender reasonably requires but in any event including provisions excluding the Law of Property Act 1925 sections 93 (relating to consolidation) and 99(1) (relating to mortgagors' power of leasing).

4 Borrower to hold legal estate in trust for Lender [coupled with power of attorney]

The Borrower declares and agrees that:

4.1 he will henceforth hold the Property as trustee for executing the charge or mortgage specified in clause 3 in favour of the Lender;

4.2 the statutory power of appointing a new trustee in his place shall be exercisable by the Lender and the persons deriving title under him who shall have full power to make such appointment and to remove the Borrower from such trusteeship at his or their sole and unfettered discretion notwithstanding that none of the events referred to in the statutory power as conditions precedent to its exercise have occurred;

4.3 on any such exercise of the statutory power the party or parties exercising the same may appoint himself or themselves or one of themselves to be the new trustee or trustees; and

[4.4 the Lender and the persons deriving title under him shall be and are irrevocably and by way of security appointed the attorney and attorneys of the Borrower and the persons deriving title under him, in his and their names and on his and their behalf to vest the legal estate in the Property in any purchaser or other person in exercise of the statutory powers conferred on mortgagees free and discharged from all rights of redemption under this memorandum].

5 Possession

The Borrower further agrees and declares that the Lender shall have the same rights to possession of the Property as he would have if the charge created by this deed had been a legal mortgage created by way of demise for the term of 3,000 years.

6 Repair

The Borrower undertakes to keep all buildings and fixtures on the Property in good and substantial repair and condition.

7 Insurance

The Borrower undertakes to keep all buildings and fixtures on the Property insured against fire and such other risks as the Lender may reasonably require in their full value and, on demand in writing, to produce the receipts for premiums paid in respect of such insurance.

[8 Borrower not to register

The Borrower covenants with the Lender that the Borrower will not so long as this security continues cause or allow any person to be registered under the Land Registration Act 1925 or other similar statutory provision as the proprietor of the Property without the consent of the Lender.]

9 Costs

The Borrower undertakes to pay on demand all costs, charges and expenses paid or incurred by the Lender in perfecting or in enforcing this security or in obtaining payment or discharge of the money secured by this security.

10 Interpretation

In this memorandum where the context admits the expressions 'the Borrower' and 'the Lender' include the persons deriving title under each of them respectively.

IN WITNESS etc

SCHEDULE
The Documents

(insert particulars of deposited deeds)

(signatures (or common seals) of the parties)

(signatures of witnesses)

This precedent is reproduced from *Butterworths Encyclopaedia of Forms and Precedents* (5th edn), volume 28 (1999 reissue) MORTGAGES, Form 45, contributed by Andrew Whittaker, solicitor.

MEMORANDUM UNDER HAND CHARGING LANDS WITH REPAYMENT OF A LOAN, WITH PROVISION FOR FURTHER ADVANCES

MEMORANDUM

1 Definitions and interpretation

In this memorandum:

1.1 'the Advance' means £......... made to the Borrower on *(date)*;
1.2 'the Interest Payment Days' means *(state dates for payment)*;
1.3 'the Interest Rate' means the rate of ......% a year;
1.4 'the Lender' means *(name of chargee)* [of *(address)* *(or)* the registered office of which is at *(address)* and the company registration number of which is *(number)*];
1.5 'the Property' means the [freehold *(or)* leasehold] property known as *(insert details)*;
1.6 'the Payment Date' means *(date)*;
1.7 unless the context otherwise requires, 'interest' means interest at the Interest Rate payable by equal *(specify frequency)* payments on the Interest Payment Days.

2 Charge on lands

I *(name of chargor)* of *(address)* with [full *(or)* limited] title guarantee charge the Property with:

2.1 payment to the Lender on the Payment Date of the Advance now paid by him to me (as I acknowledge) together with interest from this date;
2.2 payment of any further sum the Lender may from time to time advance to me to the Lender at the expiration of 6 months after the date of such advance together with interest from the date of such advance; and
2.3 payment to the Lender of interest on all principal money from time to time due under this security.

3 Borrower to execute legal mortgage on request

I undertake (whenever called upon so to do) to make and execute at my own cost a valid legal mortgage in favour of the Lender of the Property or any part of it to secure all sums for the time being due or to become due to the Lender on this security with interest in such form and containing such covenants, conditions, powers and provisions as the Lender reasonably requires but in any event including provisions excluding the Law of Property Act 1925 sections 93 (relating to consolidation) and 99(1) (relating to mortgagors' power of leasing).

4 Repair

I undertake to keep all buildings and fixtures on the Property in good and substantial repair and condition.

5 Insurance

I undertake to keep all buildings and fixtures on the Property insured against fire and such other risks as the Lender may reasonably require in their full value and, on demand in writing, to produce the receipts for premiums paid in respect of such insurance.

6 Costs

I undertake to pay on demand all costs, charges and expenses paid or incurred by the Lender in perfecting or in enforcing this security or in obtaining payment or discharge of the money secured by this security.

Dated *(date)*

SCHEDULE
The Property

(describe property to be charged)

(signatures of the parties)

This precedent is reproduced from *Butterworths Encyclopaedia of Forms and Precedents* (5th edn), volume 28 (1999 reissue) MORTGAGES, Form 46, contributed by Andrew Whittaker, solicitor.

TRANSFER OF MORTGAGE (OTHER THAN A REGISTERED CHARGE OF REGISTERED LAND) BY ORIGINAL MORTGAGEE: SHORT FORM

THIS TRANSFER OF MORTGAGE is made the .... day of .... BETWEEN

(1) *(transferor)* [of *(address)* *(or)* the registered office of which is at *(address)* and the company registration number of which is *(number)*] ('the Lender') and

(2) *(transferee)* [of *(address)* *(or)* the registered office of which is at *(address)* and the company registration number of which is *(number)*] ('the Transferee')

RECITALS

(1) By a mortgage ('the Mortgage') dated *(date of mortgage)* and made between (1) *(mortgagor)* and (2) the Lender the property known as *(describe property)* ('the Property') became security for the repayment of the money mentioned in the Mortgage.

(2) [Of the principal sum of £......... secured by the Mortgage £......... *(or)* The principal sum of £......... secured by the Mortgage] remains due and owing together with interest on it from *(date)* and the Lender has agreed with the Transferee to transfer the benefit of the Mortgage to the Transferee on payment as set out below.

NOW THIS DEED WITNESSES that in consideration of £......... paid by the Transferee to the Lender (receipt of which the Lender acknowledges) the Lender, with [full *(or)* limited] title guarantee, transfers the benefit of the Mortgage to the Transferee.

IN WITNESS etc

(signature (or common seal) of transferor)

(signature(s) of witness(es))

This precedent is reproduced from *Butterworths Encyclopaedia of Forms and Precedents* (5th edn), volume 28 (1999 reissue) MORTGAGES, Form 73, contributed by Andrew Whittaker, solicitor.

NOTICE TO MORTGAGOR BY TRANSFEREE OF TRANSFER OF MORTGAGE

To *(mortgagor)*

of *(address)*

I now give you notice that by a transfer ('the Transfer') dated *(date)* and made between (1) *(mortgagee)* and (2) myself the benefit of the mortgage dated *(date)* and made between (1) yourself and (2) *(mortgagee)* for securing £......... ('the Principal') and interest on it has been transferred to me.

Dated:

(signature of transferee)

(address of transferee)

This precedent is reproduced from *Butterworths Encyclopaedia of Forms and Precedents* (5th edn), volume 28 (1999 reissue) MORTGAGES, Form 89, contributed by Andrew Whittaker, solicitor.

NOTICE OF INTENTION TO PAY OFF ALL MONEY OWING ON MORTGAGE

To *(mortgagee)*
of *(address)*

I, [as solicitor on behalf of *(mortgagor)* of *(address)*] give you notice that [I intend *(or)* *(mortgagor)* intends] to pay off at the expiration of 6 months from the date of the service of this notice all money then owing on the security of a mortgage dated *(date)* and made between (1) [myself *(or)* *(mortgagor)*] and (2) [yourself *or* *(original mortgagee)*].

Dated *(date)*

(signature and address of mortgagor or solicitor)

This precedent is reproduced from *Butterworths Encyclopaedia of Forms and Precedents* (5th edn), volume 28 (1999 reissue) MORTGAGES, Form 134, contributed by Andrew Whittaker, solicitor.

THE LAW SOCIETY'S RECOMMENDED FORM OF UNDERTAKING FOR THE DISCHARGE OF A BUILDING SOCIETY MORTGAGE

(to be addressed to the buyer's solicitors)

In consideration of your today completing the purchase of .... WE HEREBY UNDERTAKE forthwith to pay over to the .... Building Society the money required to redeem the mortgage/legal charge dated .... and to forward the receipted mortgage/legal charge to you as soon as it is received by us from the Building Society.

This precedent is reproduced from *Butterworths Encyclopaedia of Forms and Precedents* (5th edn), volume 28 (1999 reissue) MORTGAGES, Form 142, contributed by Andrew Whittaker, solicitor.

RECEIPT ON DISCHARGE OF STATUTORY LEGAL CHARGE OR MORTGAGE

I *(name)* of *(address)* acknowledge that I have this .... day of .... received the sum of £......... representing the [aggregate *(or)* balance remaining owing in respect of the] mortgage money secured by the [annexed *(or)* above] statutory [legal charge *(or)* mortgage] [and by the further statutory charge dated *(date of further charge)* *(or)* *(specify)*] together with all interest and costs the payment having been made by *(name)* of *(address)* and *(name)* of *(address)* [who is entitled to the immediate equity of redemption]

[This receipt does not operate as a transfer]

AS WITNESS etc

(signature of lender)

This precedent is reproduced from *Butterworths Encyclopaedia of Forms and Precedents* (5th edn), volume 28 (1999 reissue) MORTGAGES, Form 145, contributed by Andrew Whittaker, solicitor.

RECEIPT TO BE ENDORSED ON MEMORANDUM OF DEPOSIT OF TITLE DEEDS OR OTHER EQUITABLE SECURITY

The [undersigned *(name)* sole executor of the] mortgagee *(name)* acknowledges that he has this day received £......... being the full amount of the principal and interest [and costs] now owing on the security of the above instrument.

Date *(date)*

(signature of payee)

This precedent is reproduced from *Butterworths Encyclopaedia of Forms and Precedents* (5th edn), volume 28 (1999 reissue) MORTGAGES, Form 148, contributed by Andrew Whittaker, solicitor.

RELEASE OF PART OF UNREGISTERED PROPERTY COMPRISED IN A LEGAL CHARGE

THIS DEED OF RELEASE is made the .... day of .... BETWEEN

(1) *(mortgagee)* [of *(address)* *(or)* the registered office of which is at *(address)* and the company registration number of which is *(number)*] ('the Lender') and

(2) *(mortgagor)* [of *(address)* *(or)* the registered office of which is at *(address)* and the company registration number of which is *(number)*] ('the Borrower')

RECITALS

(1) By a charge by way of legal mortgage ('the Mortgage') dated *(date of mortgage)* and made between the same parties the property released by this deed together with other property was charged by way of legal mortgage to the Lender to secure repayment to him of £......... with interest on it as expressed in the Mortgage.

(2) The Lender has agreed with the Borrower to release the property described in schedule 1 to this deed ('the Released Property') from the Mortgage on payment of £......... [the principal money owing to the Lender having been reduced to £.........].

[(3) The documents of title specified in schedule 3 ('the Documents') which are now in the possession of the Lender relate as well to the Released Property as to other property comprised in the Mortgage.]

NOW THIS DEED WITNESSES as follows:

1 Release

In pursuance of the above agreement and in consideration of £......... [now paid *(or)* having been repaid before the execution of this deed] by the Borrower to the Lender (receipt of which the Lender acknowledges) the Lender releases the Released Property to the Borrower with [full *(or)* limited] title guarantee, to hold to the Borrower free from the Mortgage and all principal money and interest secured by it and from all claims and demands under or relating to it.

2 Proviso as to lands not released

The Mortgage shall remain in full force and effect with regard to the property described in schedule 2.

[3 Acknowledgement

The Lender acknowledges the right of the Borrower, on payment of all costs properly incurred by the Lender in relation to it, to production of the Documents and to delivery of copies of them.]

IN WITNESS etc

SCHEDULE 1
The Released Property

(insert details)

SCHEDULE 2
The Retained Property

(insert details)

[SCHEDULE 3
The Documents

(insert details)]

(signatures (or common seals) of the parties)

(signatures of witnesses)

This precedent is reproduced from *Butterworths Encyclopaedia of Forms and Precedents* (5th edn), volume 28 (1999 reissue) MORTGAGES, Form 153, contributed by Andrew Whittaker, solicitor.

APPOINTMENT OF RECEIVER OF MORTGAGED PROPERTY UNDER THE LAW OF PROPERTY ACT 1925 BY AGREEMENT NOT EXECUTED AS A DEED

THIS APPOINTMENT is made the .... day of .... BETWEEN

(1) *(mortgagee)* [of *(address) (or)* the registered office of which is at *(address)* and the company registration number of which is *(number)*] ('the Lender') and
(2) *(receiver)* of *(address)* ('the Receiver')

RECITALS

(1) By a mortgage ('the Mortgage') dated *(date)* and made between (1) *(mortgagor)* ('the Borrower') and (2) the Lender the property described in the schedule to this deed ('the Property') was charged in favour of the Lender by way of [legal] mortgage to secure payment of £......... ('the Principal') on *(date for redemption)* and interest on the Principal until payment at the rate of ......% a year.
(2) The Principal is still owing on the security of the Mortgage and [upwards of 3 months have elapsed since service on the Borrower of a notice requiring its payment, with which he has not complied *(or)* and the interest on it at the rate set out above is now in arrear for upwards of 2 months after becoming due *(or) (specify any other breach which is relied upon as having made the Mortgagee's power of sale exercisable)*].

NOW IT IS AGREED as follows:

1 Appointment of receiver

In exercise of the statutory power and any other power enabling him to do so, the Lender appoints the Receiver to be receiver of [[the income *(or)* the rents and profits] of] the Property at a commission of ......% on the gross amount of all money received by him.

[2 Delegation of powers of leasing and accepting surrenders of leases

The powers of leasing and of accepting surrenders of leases conferred on the Lender by sections 99 and 100 of the Law of Property Act 1925 are hereby delegated by the Lender to the Receiver.]

[3 Direction as to insurance

The Receiver shall out of the money received by him insure, and keep insured, any building, effects or property comprised in the Mortgage, being of an insurable nature, whether affixed to the freehold or not, against loss or damage by fire, to the extent to which the Lender might have insured.]

[4 Direction as to ultimate balances

The Receiver shall pay the ultimate balances of income received by him to the Lender in or towards discharge of the principal money owing on the security of the Mortgage.]

AS WITNESS etc

SCHEDULE

The Property

(insert details)

(signature for or on behalf of the lender)

This precedent is reproduced from *Butterworths Encyclopaedia of Forms and Precedents* (5th edn), volume 28 (1999 reissue) MORTGAGES, Form 160, contributed by Andrew Whittaker, solicitor.

APPOINTMENT OF RECEIVER UNDER EXPRESS POWER

THIS APPOINTMENT is made the .... day of .... BETWEEN

(1) *(mortgagee)* [of *(address)* *(or)* the registered office of which is at *(address)* and the company registration number of which is *(number)*] ('the Lender') and

(2) *(receiver)* of *(address)* ('the Receiver')

RECITALS

(1) By a mortgage ('the Mortgage') dated *(date)* and made between (1) *(mortgagor)* ('the Borrower') and (2) the Lender the property described in the schedule to this deed ('the Property') was charged in favour of the Lender by way of [legal] mortgage to secure payment of £......... on *(date)*

(or, if earlier, immediately [on demand] on the happening of the events specified in the Mortgage) and payment or discharge of all other money, obligations and liabilities covenanted to be paid or discharged by the Borrower under the Mortgage or otherwise secured by it.

(2) The money secured by the Mortgage has become due and payable and the security constituted by it enforceable.

NOW IT IS AGREED as follows:

1 Appointment of receiver

The Lender, in pursuance of the powers given to him by the Mortgage and all other powers conferred upon him by statute or otherwise, appoints the Receiver to be the receiver of the Property and all the income of the Property (if any) and to exercise all the powers of a receiver given by the Mortgage or by statute or otherwise.

2 Receiver to be agent of the Borrower

It is declared that the Receiver shall be the agent of the Borrower for all purposes and that the Borrower shall be solely responsible for his acts and defaults.

AS WITNESS etc

SCHEDULE

The Property

(insert details)

(signature of or on behalf of the lender)

This precedent is reproduced from *Butterworths Encyclopaedia of Forms and Precedents* (5th edn), volume 28 (1999 reissue) MORTGAGES, Form 161, contributed by Andrew Whittaker, solicitor.

NOTICE OF APPOINTMENT GIVEN BY THE RECEIVER TO A TENANT

To *(name of tenant)*
of *(address)*

Property:

(insert details)

Lease

(date and parties)

By a mortgage dated *(date)* your landlord *(name)* charged *(property)* to *(mortgagee)* [subject to the rights of occupation created by the terms of the above-mentioned lease].

The power of sale under this charge having arisen and become exercisable, I give you formal notice that I have today been duly appointed receiver of [the income of] the said property as agent of *(mortgagor)*.

I also give you formal notice and demand that all future sums falling due by way of rental or otherwise under the terms of the above-mentioned lease, and any arrears of rent presently subsisting, should be paid to me, in the case of future sums on or before their due dates, and in the case of any arrears, forthwith.

As from the date of this notice *(mortgagor)* can no longer give a good receipt or valid discharge for any sums tendered to him under the terms of the above-mentioned lease.

You should note that in my capacity as receiver I act as agent for *(mortgagor)* who is solely responsible for my acts or defaults. In particular, I neither accept nor assume any personal liability in relation to the said property, the said lease or otherwise.

Dated:

(signature and address of receiver)

This precedent is reproduced from *Butterworths Encyclopaedia of Forms and Precedents* (5th edn), volume 28 (1999 reissue) MORTGAGES, Form 167, contributed by Andrew Whittaker, solicitor.

MORTGAGE BY SMALL TRADER OF LEASEHOLD PREMISES AND THE FIXTURES GOODWILL AND BOOK DEBTS OF A BUSINESS

THIS LEGAL CHARGE is made the .... day of .... BETWEEN

(1) *(mortgagor)* [of *(address) (or)* the registered office of which is at *(address)* and the company registration number of which is *(number)*] ('the Borrower') and

(2) *(mortgagee)* [of *(address) (or)* the registered office of which is at *(address)* and the company registration number of which is *(number)*] ('the Lender')

RECITALS

(1) By the Lease the Landlord demised the Property to the Borrower for the term of *(number)* years from *(date)* at the yearly rent of £......... and subject to the tenant's covenants and the conditions contained in the Lease.

(2) The Borrower is now carrying on the Business on the property described below.

(3) The Lender has agreed to advance the Principal to the Borrower on having repayment of it with [interest *(or)* a sum equal to a share of profits of the Business by way of interest] secured in the manner appearing below.

NOW THIS DEED WITNESSES as follows:

1 Definitions

In this mortgage:

1.1 'the Interest Payment Days' means *(state days for payment)*;

1.2 'the Interest Rate' means [*(for fixed rate)* ......% a year *(or for variable rate)* ......% above the rate of *(specify lending or base rate by which reference to which interest is to be calculated)* from time to time];

1.3 'the Principal' means £.........;

1.4 'the Property' means the property described in schedule 1 below demised by the Lease; and
1.5 'the Redemption Date' means *(date)*;
1.6 'the Lease' means a lease dated *(date)* and made between (1) the Landlord' and (2) the Borrower;
1.7 'the Landlord' means *(lessor)* of *(address)*;
1.8 'the Business' means the business of *(insert details)*;
1.9 'the Accounting Date' means [31 December *(or as required)*];
[1.10 'the Profit Payment Date' [31 January *(or as required)*];]
[1.11 'the Instalments' means *(number)* equal [monthly *(or as required)*] sums of £........., each one to be paid on the first day of each [month *(or as required)*] beginning from *(date)* next [or within *(number)* days from that day]]

[2 Payment of principal and interest

In consideration of the Principal now paid by the Lender to the Borrower (receipt of which the Borrower acknowledges) the Borrower covenants with the Lender that the Borrower will on the Redemption Date pay the Principal to the Lender with interest on it from the date of this deed at the Interest Rate. If the Principal is not paid on that day then, so long as any part of it remains owing, the Borrower will (as well after as before any judgment) pay to the Lender interest at the Interest Rate on the Principal or such part of it as from time to time remains owing by equal [quarterly *(or as required)*] payments on the Interest Payment Days in each year.

(or)

2 Payment of principal and share of profits

In consideration of the Principal now paid by the Lender to the Borrower (receipt of which the Borrower acknowledges) the Borrower covenants with the Lender:
2.1 that he will on the Profit Payment Date next pay the Principal to the Lender together with a sum equal to [10% *(or as required)*] of the net profits of the Business for the year ending on the Accounting Date next;
2.2 that he will on the Profit Payment Date in every subsequent year during the continuance of this security pay to the Lender instead of interest a sum equal to [20% *(or as required)*] of the net profits of the Business for the year ending on the Accounting Date previous.

If the Principal is not repaid on the Profit Payment Date next the Borrower may pay the Principal at any time after that if he pays to the Lender with it a sum bearing the same proportion to [20% *(or as required)*] of the profits of the Business for the preceding year as the period between the date of such repayment and the preceding Profit Payment Date bears to the whole year and also a further sum equal to 50% of the amount paid in lieu of interest in respect of the preceding year, provided that if the Borrower gives the Lender 6 months' previous notice of his intention to repay the Principal this further sum shall not be payable. If the repayment of the Principal is made during the year next after the Profit Payment Date next the sum or sums payable with the Principal shall be calculated having regard to the amount of the sum payable with the Principal on the Profit Payment Date next and also to the proportion which the period from the date of this deed to the Accounting Date next bears to the whole year.]

3 Sub-demise

For the above consideration, the Borrower demises the Property to the Lender, with [full *(or)* limited] title guarantee, to hold to the Lender for the residue of the term granted by the Lease except the last 10 days of it, but subject to the provision for cesser contained in clause 5.

4 Assignment of fixtures goodwill and book debts

For the above consideration, the Borrower assigns to the Lender, with [full *(or)* limited] title guarantee:

4.1 all the trade and tenant's fixtures and fittings on the Property specified in schedule 2,

4.2 the goodwill of the Business, and

4.3 all the book and other debts which now are or may in future become owing to the Borrower in connection with the Business,

to hold to the Lender subject only to the provision for redemption contained in clause 5.

5 Provision for cesser and redemption

If the Borrower, on the [Redemption Date *(or)* Profit Payment Date next], pays to the Lender the Principal with [interest on it as from the date of this deed at the Interest Rate *(or)* the additional sum covenanted to be paid under clause 2], the sub-term created by this deed shall cease and the Lender will at the request and cost of the Borrower reassign the fixtures and fittings, goodwill and book debts to the Borrower or as he directs.

6 Borrower's covenants

The Borrower covenants with the Lender to observe the obligations and restrictions set out below.

6.1 Insurance of buildings

Insert appropriate covenant

6.2 Insurance of fixtures and stock-in-trade

The Borrower will insure and keep insured the fixtures and fittings and stock-in-trade on the Property, in some office approved by the Lender, against loss or damage by fire or aircraft, to their full insurable value, and will on demand produce to the Lender the policy of insurance and the receipt for each premium paid in respect of it.

6.3 Repair and replacement of fixtures

The Borrower will keep the fixtures and fittings in repair and will replace any that may become worn out, or otherwise unfit for use, with others of a similar nature and equal value which shall then be charged with the repayment of the money secured by this deed. The Borrower will not, without the consent in writing of the Lender, remove any such fixtures and fittings except in the case of replacement.

6.4 *Carrying on of the Business*

The Borrower will carry on the Business to the best advantage.

6.5 *Books of account*

The Borrower will:
6.5.1 keep proper books of account of the Business,
6.5.2 have them at all times properly posted up,
6.5.3 permit the Lender or any person appointed for that purpose by the Lender to examine the books at all reasonable times and make copies of or extracts from them, and
6.5.4 give to the Lender all information with regard to the Business which he may reasonably require.

6.6 *Balance sheets*

The Borrower will within 7 days after the Accounting Date in each year sign and transmit to the Lender a just, true and complete balance sheet or statement [audited by an accountant to be named by the Lender] of the results of the previous year's trading in the usual form, so as to show the true state of the Business and the assets, credits and liabilities of it and the amount of profits during the year just ended, and if required verify the same by statutory declaration.

6.7 *Not to register*

Insert appropriate covenant

7 Power of attorney to recover book debts

The Borrower appoints the Lender, and the persons deriving title under the Lender, to be his attorney, in his name and on his behalf to demand, sue for, receive and give effectual discharges for all or any of the book and other debts mortgaged by this deed, but it shall not be incumbent on the Lender to take any steps or to institute any proceedings for recovery of any of the debts assigned by this deed.

[8 Payment by equal instalments

If the Borrower pays the Instalments to the Lender, and with each of them pays one [month's *(or as required)*] interest at the Interest Rate on that sum and on any of the Instalments that for the time being remain unpaid, the Lender will accept the payment of the Instalments in repayment of the Principal and will not enforce the security constituted by this deed so long as the Borrower performs all his obligations under this deed other than in regard to the payment of the Principal [and interest].]

9 Provisos

9.1 Exercise of statutory power of sale

The statutory power of sale shall be exercisable if:

9.1.1 default is made in payment of the Principal for the time being owing on the security of this mortgage for [one month *(or as required)*] after notice requiring payment of it has been served on the Borrower;

9.1.2 any [interest due under this deed *(or)* money payable under this deed instead of interest] is unpaid for *(number)* days after it has become due;

9.1.3 the Borrower fails to observe any of his obligations under this mortgage (other than in regard to the payment of the Principal [and interest]);

9.1.4 any execution is issued against the Borrower, or any distress is levied on his chattels on the Property;

9.1.5 the Borrower, being an individual, dies; or

9.1.6 the Borrower makes default in payment of any negotiable instrument which he is liable to pay.

[9.2 Leasing

Insert appropriate provision]

9.3 Consolidation

Insert appropriate provision

9.4 Partnership

Nothing contained in or to be done in pursuance of this deed shall constitute a partnership between the parties to this deed.

10 Interpretation

Insert appropriate provision

IN WITNESS etc

SCHEDULE 1
The Property

(describe leaseholds to be mortgaged)

SCHEDULE 2
Fixtures and fittings

(describe fixtures and fittings to be mortgaged)

(signatures (or common seals) of the parties)

(signatures of witnesses)

This precedent is reproduced from *Butterworths Encyclopaedia of Forms and Precedents* (5th edn), volume 28 (1999 reissue) MORTGAGES, Form 217, contributed by Andrew Whittaker, solicitor.

MEMORANDUM (NOT EXECUTED AS A DEED) TO ACCOMPANY DEPOSIT OF SECURITIES TO SECURE THE DUE PAYMENT OF BILLS OF EXCHANGE

MEMORANDUM

Note that:

1 *(lender)* [of *(address) (or)* the registered office of which is at *(address)* and the company registration number of which is *(number)*] ('the Lender') having required security, the documents specified in schedule 1 below ('the Documents') have today been deposited by *(borrower)* [of *(address) (or)* the registered office of which is at *(address)* and the company registration number of which is *(number)*] ('the Borrower') with the Lender as security for payment by the Borrower at maturity of the bills of exchange specified in schedule 2 below and interest on the money due on any bill not paid by the Borrower at maturity at the rate of ......% a year by equal quarterly payments on *(state days of payment)* in each year; and

2 the Borrower undertakes on the request of the Lender, but at his own cost, to execute a proper legal mortgage of the property to which the Documents relate in such form as the Lender reasonably requires.

Dated:

SCHEDULE 1
The Documents

(insert details)

SCHEDULE 2
The Bills of Exchange

(insert details)

(signature of borrower)

This precedent is reproduced from *Butterworths Encyclopaedia of Forms and Precedents* (5th edn), volume 28 (1999 reissue) MORTGAGES, Form 235, contributed by Andrew Whittaker, solicitor.

LEGAL CHARGE OF PARTLY-BUILT HOUSE—FULL FORM

THIS LEGAL CHARGE is made the .... day of .... BETWEEN

(1) *(mortgagor)* [of *(address) (or)* the registered office of which is at *(address)* and the company registration number of which is *(number)*] ('the Borrower') and

(2) *(mortgagee)* [of *(address) (or)* the registered office of which is at *(address)* and the company registration number of which is *(number)*] ('the Lender')

RECITALS

(1) [The Borrower is the estate owner in respect of the fee simple absolute in possession of the Property *(or)* The Borrower is registered at HM Land Registry as proprietor of the Property with title [absolute *(or as the case may be)*]] free from incumbrances.

(2) The Borrower [intends *(or)* has begun] to erect upon that property a house

and outbuildings in accordance with the specifications set out in the schedule, at the Prime Cost;

(3) The Borrower has obtained all necessary planning approvals and other consents in respect of the house and buildings.

(4) The Borrower requires an immediate advance of £......... to enable him to [begin *(or)* continue] the erection of the house and outbuildings and may from time to time require further advances for the completion of it.

(5) The Borrower has applied to the Lender to advance to him the Immediate Advance for the above purpose, which the Lender has agreed to do on repayment of it, with interest, being secured in the manner appearing below.

(6) The Lender has also agreed to make further advances to the Borrower if he so requires as provided and on the terms set out below.

NOW THIS DEED WITNESSES as follows:

1 Definitions

In this legal charge:

1.1 'the Interest Payment Days' means *(state days for payment)*;

1.2 'the Interest Rate' means [*(for fixed rate)* ......% a year *(or for variable rate)* ......% above the rate of *(specify lending or base rate by which reference to which interest is to be calculated)* from time to time];

1.3 'the Immediate Advance' means £.........;

1.4 'the Further Advances' means advances of:

1.4.1 £......... when all the walls of the house (both external and internal) are erected and the main timbers and joists for the floors placed in position [to the satisfaction of the Lender's architect];

1.4.2 £......... when the roofs of the house and outbuildings are fully completed and [tiled *(or)* slated] and the outer doors and window frames fitted [to the satisfaction of the Lender's architect]; and

1.4.3 £......... when the house and outbuildings are fully completed [to the satisfaction of the Lender's architect] so as to be fit for occupation;

1.5 'the Property' means *(describe property)*;

[1.6 'the Building Contract' means the building contract dated *(date)* and made between (1) the Borrower and (2) *(builders)*;]

1.7 'the Redemption Date' means *(date)*;

1.8 'the Building Completion Date' means *(date)*;

1.9 'the Prime Cost' means not less than £..........;

1.9 'the Insurance Company' means *(insurance company)*.

2 Immediate advance

The Lender will on the execution of this deed advance to the Borrower the Immediate Advance.

3 Further advances

If the Borrower strictly observes and performs all the agreements, stipulations and conditions on his part contained in this deed, but not otherwise the Lender will advance the Further Advances.

4 Payment of principal and interest

In consideration of the Immediate Advance paid by the Lender to the Borrower (receipt of which the Borrower acknowledges) the Borrower covenants with the Lender as follows:

4.1 The Borrower will repay the Immediate Advance to the Lender on the Redemption Date with interest on it at the Interest Rate.

4.2 The Borrower will repay to the Lender on the first of the Interest Payment Days to happen next after any of the Further Advances is made by the Lender that further advance together with interest on it at the Interest Rate, and all surveyor's and architect's fees and other expenses incurred by the Lender in relation to this security and not repaid to the Lender.

4.3 If the Immediate Advance, or any of the Further Advances, or any such fees and expenses are not repaid to the Lender on the day appointed above for payment of them respectively, the Borrower will thereafter (as well after as before any judgment) pay to the Lender interest at the Interest Rate on the principal sums, fees and expenses from time to time remaining unpaid on the security of this deed, by equal [quarterly *(or as required)*] payments on the Interest Payment Days in each year, until the whole of those sums is repaid.

5 Legal charge

For the above consideration the Borrower, with [full *(or)* limited] title guarantee, charges by way of legal mortgage the Property, and all buildings now or in future to be erected on the Property, with payment in accordance with the covenants contained in this deed of all principal money, interest and other money covenanted by this deed to be paid by the Borrower, subject only to the provision for redemption contained in clause 6.

6 Provision for redemption

If the Borrower pays the Immediate Advance to the Lender on the Redemption Date and pays to the Further Advances and all other sums secured by this deed to him on the days on which the same respectively ought to be paid under this deed, with interest in each case as provided in this deed, the Lender will at the request and cost of the Borrower duly discharge this security.

7 Borrower's covenants

The Borrower covenants with the Lender to observe and perform the obligations and restrictions set out below.

7.1 Insurance of unfinished building and materials

[The Borrower will during the continuance of this security produce, on demand by the Lender, the policy of insurance against fire and otherwise effected in accordance with the Building Contract and the receipt for each premium paid in respect of it.

(or)

7.1.1 The Borrower will, in the joint names of the Borrower and Lender, insure all work executed and materials and goods on the Property against loss and damage by fire, for their full value [plus ......% to cover architect's and surveyor's fees], and will keep the work, materials and goods so insured until the house and outbuildings are fully completed [to the satisfaction of the Lender's architect] so as to be fit for occupation.

7.1.2 The insurance shall be with the Insurance Company, and the policy and premium receipts shall, as and when received by the Borrower, be deposited with the Lender.

7.1.3 If the Borrower fails to secure such insurance the Lender may insure as specified above, and if the Borrower fails to pay any premiums the Lender may pay them, and all premiums and other sums paid by the Lender shall be subject to the provisions of clause 13 below.

7.1.4 All money received under the insurance shall be expended in rebuilding, repairing and replacing the buildings, goods and materials insured. Any money not so expended shall be paid to the Lender and applied in reduction of the principal sums secured by this deed.]

7.2 *Insurance of completed building*

7.2.1 The Borrower will:

(a) immediately on the completion of the house and outbuildings and so long as any money remains unpaid on this security, keep the buildings for the time being comprised in this security insured in the joint names of the Lender and the Borrower against loss or damage by fire or aircraft, to their full insurable value, with the Insurance Company;

(b) make all payments required for that purpose within *(number)* days after they become due; and

(c) when required by the Lender deliver to him the policy of insurance and the receipt for each payment made under it.

7.2.2 If the Borrower fails to perform any of his obligations under this clause 7.2, the Lender may insure the house and buildings or any of them for an amount not exceeding the full insurable value of the house or buildings. All payments, costs and expenses so incurred by the Lender shall be subject to the provisions of clause 13 below.

7.2.3 All money received by virtue of the insurance shall be applied in making good the loss or damage in respect of which it has been received and, in so far as it is not so applied, in reduction of the principal sums secured by this deed.

7.2.4 If at any time the Borrower is entitled to the benefit of an insurance on the house and buildings which is not effected or maintained in pursuance of this obligation, all money received by virtue of that insurance shall, if the Lender so requires:

(a) be applied at the option of the Lender in making good the loss or damage in respect of which it was received, or

(b) be paid to the Lender and be applied by him in reduction of the principal sums secured by this deed.

7.3 *Repair of buildings*

7.3.1 The Borrower will, so long as any money remains unpaid on this security, keep the house and buildings for the time being comprised in this security in good repair, and if the Borrower fails to do so, the Lender may enter on the Property or any part of it and execute such repairs as may be necessary or proper without becoming liable as mortgagee in possession and all payments, costs and expenses including architects' or surveyors' costs incurred by the Lender shall be subject to the provisions of clause 13 below.

7.3.2 To ascertain whether the house and buildings are for the time being in good condition and repair, the Lender may from time to time have them surveyed by a competent surveyor appointed by the Lender. The surveyor may, without rendering the Lender liable as a mortgagee in possession, at all reasonable times enter the house and buildings or any part of them to make a survey of them. The certificate of the surveyor shall be conclusive as to the state of repair of the house and buildings and as to what repairs are necessary and proper.

7.3.3 All costs and expenses incurred under this clause shall be subject to the provisions of clause 13 below.

[7.4 ***Not to register***

The Borrower will not cause or allow any person to be registered under the Land Registration Act 1925 or any similar statutory provision as proprietor of the Property without the consent in writing of the Lender, and the costs and expenses incurred by the Lender of entering any caution against such registration shall be subject to the provisions of clause 13.]

[7.5 ***Compliance with covenants and restrictions***

The Borrower will during the continuance of this security perform and observe all the covenants and restrictions as to building on or use of the Property or any part of it contained in a conveyance dated *(date)* and made between *(parties)* or otherwise validly in force in respect of the Property, and will keep the Lender indemnified against all proceedings, claims, costs and expenses on account of any breach of those covenants or restrictions. Any damages, costs and expenses incurred by the Lender in relation to any such breach shall be subject to the provisions of clause 13.]

8 Completion and use of house

The Borrower further covenants with the Lender as follows:

8.1 Completion of building

The Borrower will diligently proceed with the erection of the house and buildings and complete them fit for occupation [to the satisfaction of the Lender's architect] on or before the Building Completion Date, and will apply all sums advanced by the Lender from time to time under this deed for that purpose and for none other.

8.2 Amount to be spent

The Borrower will expend in the erection of the house and buildings the Prime Cost.

8.3 Use of building

8.3.1 The Borrower will not, without the previous written consent of the Lender, carry out any operation in the house and buildings, or use them for any use, which is a development within the provisions of the Town and Country Planning Act 1990.

8.3.2 If any development to which the Lender has not consented is carried out, all and every or any of the powers and remedies conferred on mortgagees by the Law of Property Act 1925 shall become immediately exercisable by the Lender.

8.4 Notices

The Borrower will immediately produce to the Lender any order, direction, requisition, permission, notice or other matter whatsoever affecting or likely to affect the house, land and buildings served on the Borrower by any third party, and allow the Lender to make a copy of it.

8.5 Development

If the Borrower at any time obtains permission for any development of the house and buildings within the provisions of the Town and Country Planning Act 1990, he will comply with all conditions subject to which the permission is granted.

8.6 Enforcement notices

If any valid enforcement or other notice or order is made or served by a competent authority under or by virtue of the Town and Country Planning Act 1990 requiring the discontinuance of, or imposing conditions on, any use of the house and buildings or any part of them or requiring the removal or alteration of any works or buildings on them, the Borrower will, at his own expense in all respects, comply with the requirements of that notice or order within any time limit specified in it for compliance, or within a period of 3 months from the date of the notice, whichever is the shorter.

8.7 Power to Lender to comply with notices

If the Borrower fails to comply with any requirement of any competent authority made under the Town and Country Planning Act 1990 or any other statute, the Lender may, in so far as it may be necessary to comply with the requirement, enter the house, land and buildings or any part of them on giving the Borrower [14 *(or as required)*] days' previous notice in writing of the intention so to do, and execute any works and do anything necessary to ensure compliance. All costs and expenses so incurred by the Lender shall be subject to the provisions of clause 13.

8.8 Power of attorney

The Borrower irrevocably appoints the Lender and his substitutes for the time being to be his attorney to apply for and procure on his behalf any licences, permissions or other things from any competent authority necessary for the execution of the repairs and other works authorised by this deed to be executed by the Lender on the default of the Borrower. All expenses incurred by the Lender in securing these licences, permissions and other things shall be treated as part of the cost of the repairs and other works, and such expenses, and interest on them, shall be subject to the provisions of clause 13.

9 Modification of power of sale

The power of sale and the power of appointing a receiver conferred on mortgagees by the Law of Property Act 1925 shall, in relation to this security, be modified so that the powers shall be exercisable:

9.1 without the need to give any previous notice to that effect; and

9.2 although no part of the principal sums or interest secured by this deed have become due, if:

- 9.2.1 the Borrower has any judgment or order of any court executed against his property,
- 9.2.2 the Borrower commits any breach of the stipulations contained in this deed on his part to be observed and performed, or
- 9.2.3 any development to which the Lender has not consented is carried out as stated in clause 8.3.

10 Remedies

10.1 If and when the above mentioned power of sale becomes exercisable, the Lender may enter on and take possession of the Property and all buildings and erections and fixtures whatsoever on it. If the house and buildings are then unfinished the Lender may complete them in accordance with any building contract or agreement then in force, but with liberty to agree with the builder or any other person interested in the contract or agreement to any modification of it.

10.2 For the purposes of this clause the Lender may employ an architect, surveyor, contractors, builders, workmen and others and purchase all proper materials as he may in his absolute discretion think fit.

10.3 All money expended by the Lender in pursuance of this clause shall be subject to the provisions of clause 13.

11 Consolidation

The Law of Property Act 1925 section 93 (restricting the Lender's right of consolidation) shall not apply to this security.

12 Leases

During the continuance of this security the Borrower shall not, without the written consent of the Lender, grant or agree to grant any lease or tenancy of the Property or of any part of it, or accept or agree to accept any surrender of a lease or tenancy of it.

13 Charge of expenses

Where any money expended or to be expended by the Lender is stated above to be subject to the provisions of this clause:

13.1 that amount shall be payable by the Borrower to the Lender on demand;

13.2 the Borrower covenants to pay interest from the date of demand until repayment on all amounts not so paid on demand at the Interest Rate;

13.3 all such money and interest on it shall be charged on the Property; and

13.4 the Lender shall, so far as the law allows and subject to any order of the court, be entitled to and receive from the Borrower a full indemnity in respect of all costs and expenses arising under this deed or in any way relating to the charge created by this deed.

14 Interpretation

In this deed where the context so permits:

14.1 the terms 'the Borrower' and 'the Lender' include the persons deriving title under them;

14.2 all references to the Town and Country Planning Act 1990 include all Acts amending or re-enacting the provisions of that Act or to be construed with it for the time being in force, and all orders, plans, regulations, permissions, consents and directions made under or in pursuance of such Acts; and

14.3 any covenant by the Borrower not to do any act or thing includes a covenant not to permit or suffer the doing of that act or thing.

IN WITNESS etc

SCHEDULE
The Plans and Specifications

(set out the plans and specifications relating to the house and outbuildings)

(signatures (or common seals) of the parties)

(signatures of witnesses)

This precedent is reproduced from *Butterworths Encyclopaedia of Forms and Precedents* (5th edn), volume 28 (1999 reissue) MORTGAGES, Form 239, contributed by Andrew Whittaker, solicitor.

TRANSFER BY DEED BY THE PERSONAL REPRESENTATIVE OF THE LENDER TO THE BENEFICIARY ENTITLED TO A MORTGAGE (OTHER THAN A CHARGE OF REGISTERED LAND) ON THE DEATH OF THE LENDER

THIS TRANSFER OF MORTGAGE is made the .... day of .... BETWEEN:

(1) *(personal representative)* of *(address)* ('the Transferor') and

(2) *(beneficiary)* of *(address)* ('the Beneficiary')

RECITALS

(1) By a mortgage ('the Mortgage') dated *(date of mortgage)* and made between (1) *(mortgagor)* and (2) *(mortgagee)* ('the Lender') the property described in the schedule below was [demised to the Lender for a term of 3000 years by

way of legal mortgage *(or)* charged by way of legal mortgage] to secure payment to the Lender of £......... with interest at the rate of ......% a year in the manner set out in the Mortgage.

(2) [The Lender died on *(date of death)* intestate and letters of administration to his estate were granted on *(date)* out of the [Principal *(or) (name)* District Probate] Registry of the Family Division of the High Court to the Transferor *(or)* The Lender died on *(date of death)* having by his will dated *(date)* appointed the Transferor to be the executor, and the Transferor proved the will on *(date)* in the [Principal *(or) (name)* District Probate] Registry of the Family Division of the High Court.

(3) The Transferor has duly paid and discharged all debts funeral and testamentary expenses and inheritance tax payable out of the estate of the Lender.

(4) In the administration of the estate of the Lender the Beneficiary is entitled to have the mortgage transferred to him and the Transferor has agreed to make this transfer accordingly.

NOW THIS DEED WITNESSES as follows:

1 Transfer

In consideration of the above-recited matters the Transferor, with [full *(or)* limited] title guarantee, transfers the benefit of the Mortgage to the Beneficiary.

2 Acknowledgement for production

The Transferor acknowledges the right of the Beneficiary to production of the [letters of administration to the Lender's estate *(or)* probate of the will of the Lender] and to delivery of copies.

IN WITNESS etc

SCHEDULE
The mortgaged property

(describe property subject to the mortgage)

(signature of transferor)

(signatures of witnesses)

This precedent is reproduced from *Butterworths Encyclopaedia of Forms and Precedents* (5th edn), volume 28 (1999 reissue) MORTGAGES, Form 278, contributed by Andrew Whittaker, solicitor.

TRANSFER OF MORTGAGE (OTHER THAN A CHARGE OF REGISTERED LAND) ON APPOINTMENT OF NEW TRUSTEES, TRUST NOT BEING DISCLOSED

THIS TRANSFER OF MORTGAGE is made the .... day of .... BETWEEN

(1) *(names and addresses of previous trustees)* ('the Mortgagees') and

(2) *(names of continuing trustees if any and names and addresses of new trustees)* ('the Transferees')

RECITALS

(1) By a mortgage ('the Mortgage') dated *(date of mortgage)* and made between *(parties)* certain property at *(address)* described in the Mortgage was made security for repayment of £......... ('the Principal'), then lent by the Mortgagees to *(borrower)*, to the Mortgagees in the manner set out in the Mortgage together with interest as mentioned in the Mortgage.

(2) The Principal is still owing on the security of the Mortgage [but all interest has been paid up to *(date) (or)* together with arrears of interest amounting to £.........].

(3) The benefit of the Mortgage now belongs in equity to the Transferees jointly and the Mortgagees have accordingly agreed at the request of the Transferees to execute such transfer of the benefit of the Mortgage as is set out below.

NOW THIS DEED WITNESSES that in consideration of the above-recited matters the Mortgagees, with [full *(or)* limited] title guarantee, transfer to the Transferees the benefit of the Mortgage.

IN WITNESS etc

(signatures of mortgagees)

(signatures of witnesses)

This precedent is reproduced from *Butterworths Encyclopaedia of Forms and Precedents* (5th edn), volume 28 (1999 reissue) MORTGAGES, Form 324, contributed by Andrew Whittaker, solicitor.

MORTGAGE BY DEMISE BY ONE BORROWER TO ONE LENDER: UNREGISTERED LAND

THIS MORTGAGE is made the .... day of .... BETWEEN

(1) *(borrower)* [of *(address) (or)* the registered office of which is at *(address)* and the company registration number of which is *(number)*] ('the Borrower') and

(2) *(lender)* [of *(address) (or)* the registered office of which is at *(address)* and the company registration number of which is *(number)*] ('the Lender')

RECITALS

(1) The Borrower is the estate owner in respect of the fee simple absolute in possession of the property described below free from incumbrances.

(2) The Lender has agreed to lend to the Borrower the Principal on having repayment of it together with interest secured in the manner set out below.

NOW THIS DEED WITNESSES as follows:

1 Definitions

In this mortgage:

1.1 'the Interest Payment Days' means *(state days for payment)*;

1.2 'the Interest Rate' means ......% a year;

1.3 'the Principal' means £.........;

1.4 'the Property' means the property specified in the schedule below and all buildings and fixtures on it;
1.5 'the Redemption Date' means *(date)*;
1.6 'the Insurance Value' means £.........;
1.7 'the Reduced Rate' means ......% a year.

2 Payment of principal and interest

In consideration of the Principal now paid by the Lender to the Borrower (receipt of which the Borrower acknowledges) the Borrower covenants with the Lender to pay the Principal to the Lender on the Redemption Date with interest on it from the date of this deed at the Interest Rate and if the Principal or any part of it is not paid on that date to pay to the Lender (as well after as before any judgment) interest at the Interest Rate on the Principal or such part of it as from time to time remains owing by equal [quarterly *(or as required)*] payments on the Interest Payment Days in each year.

3 Demise

For the above consideration the Borrower, with [full *(or)* limited] title guarantee, demises the Property to the Lender to hold it to the Lender for the term of [3,000 years *(or as required)*] from the date of this deed without impeachment of waste subject to the provision for cesser contained in clause 4.

4 Provision for cesser

If the Borrower pays the Principal to the Lender on the Redemption Date with interest on it from the date of this deed at the Interest Rate the term created by this deed shall cease.

5 Borrower's covenants

The Borrower covenants with the Lender as follows:

5.1 Insurance of buildings

5.1.1 So long as any money remains owing on this security the Borrower will keep the buildings for the time being comprised in this security insured in the name[s] of the Lender [and the Borrower] against loss or damage caused by fire [and by aircraft] [for the Insurance Value at least *(or)* to their full insurable value *(or)* in a sum equal to at least three-quarters of the sum required to restore the buildings if they are totally destroyed] with some insurance office or underwriters approved by the Lender, will make all payments required for the above purpose [as and when *(or)* within *(number)* days after] they become due, and will when required by the Lender deliver to him the policy of insurance and the receipt for each payment.

5.1.2 If the Borrower fails to perform any of his obligations under this clause, and if the Lender then insures the buildings or any of them for a sum not exceeding in the aggregate the Insurance Value, the Borrower will on demand repay to the Lender all payments made by him for that purpose and will pay interest at the Interest Rate from the date of demand until repayment on any money not so repaid on demand. All such money and interest shall be charged on the Property.

[5.1.3 All money that may be received by virtue of any such insurance shall be applied in the first place in making good the loss or damage in respect of which it is received.]

[5.2 *Application of money received from other insurance policies*

If at any time the Borrower is entitled to the benefit of an insurance on the buildings for the time being comprised in this security not effected or maintained in pursuance of his obligation set out in clause 5.1, all money received by virtue of such insurance shall, if the Lender so requires and at his option, either be applied in making good the loss or damage in respect of which it is received or be paid to the Lender and be applied by him in or towards discharge of the Principal.]

5.3 *Repair of buildings*

So long as any money remains owing on this security the Borrower will keep the buildings for the time being comprised in this security in good repair. [If the Borrower fails so to do the Lender may enter upon the premises or any part of them and execute such repairs as [in the opinion of the Lender] may be necessary or proper without thereby becoming liable as mortgagee in possession, and the Borrower will on demand repay to the Lender all the expenses thereby incurred by the Lender and will pay interest at the Interest Rate from the date of demand until repayment on any money not so repaid on demand. All such expenses and interest shall be charged on the Property.]

5.4 *Not to register*

So long as any money remains owing on this security the Borrower will not cause or permit any person to be registered under the Land Registration Act 1925 or any substituted statutory provision as the proprietor of the Property or any part of it without the written consent of the Lender. If the Lender enters a caution against any such registration the costs incurred by him in so doing shall be deemed to have been properly incurred as mortgagee.

6 Provisos

[6.1 *Reduction of rate of interest on punctual payment*

If within *(number)* days after the day on which any [quarterly *(or as required)*] payment of interest ought to be made the Borrower, having complied with all his obligations under this deed other than those relating to the payment of the Principal and interest, pays to the Lender one [quarter's *(or as required)*] interest on the Principal at the Reduced Rate the Lender will accept the payment in satisfaction of payment of interest at the Interest Rate.]

[6.2 *Debt not to be called in for a specified time*

If the Borrower pays each instalment of interest on the Principal within [14 days *(or as required)*] after the day on which it becomes due under the covenant contained in clause 2 (as to which time shall be of the essence of the contract), and complies with all his obligations under this deed other than in regard to the payment of the Principal and interest, the Lender will not take any steps to enforce the payment of the Principal or any part of it during the period of *(number)* years from the date of this deed.]

[6.3 *Mortgage not to be redeemed for a specified time*

The Borrower shall not be entitled to redeem this security during the period of *(number)* years from the date of this deed.]

[6.4 *Restriction on powers of leasing*

The Borrower shall not be entitled to exercise any powers of leasing or accepting surrenders of leases given by any statute except with the consent in writing of the Lender.]

6.5 Consolidation

The Law of Property Act 1925 section 93 (restricting the Lender's right of consolidation) shall not apply to this security.

7 Interpretation

In this deed where the context admits the expressions 'the Borrower' and 'the Lender' shall include the persons deriving title under the Borrower and the Lender respectively.

IN WITNESS etc

SCHEDULE
The Property

(describe the property to be mortgaged)

(signatures (or common seals) of the parties)

(signatures of witnesses)

This precedent is reproduced from *Butterworths Encyclopaedia of Forms and Precedents* (5th edn), volume 28 (1999 reissue) MORTGAGES, Form 340, contributed by Andrew Whittaker, solicitor.

MORTGAGE OF LEASEHOLDS BY SUB-DEMISE: UNREGISTERED LAND

THIS MORTGAGE is made the .... day of .... BETWEEN

(1) *(mortgagor)* [of *(address) (or)* the registered office of which is at *(address)* and the company registration number of which is *(number)*] ('the Borrower') and

(2) *(mortgagee)* [of *(address)* *(or)* the registered office of which is at *(address)* and the company registration number of which is *(number)*] ('the Lender')

RECITALS

(1) By the Lease the Landlord demised the Property to the Borrower for the term of *(number)* years from *(date)* at the yearly rent of £......... and subject to the covenants and conditions binding on the lessee contained in the Lease [and in particular to a covenant not to assign underlet, charge or encumber the demised premises or any part of them without first obtaining the written consent of the Landlord].

(2) The Lender has agreed to advance the Principal to the Borrower on having repayment of it with interest secured in the manner set out below.

[(3) The Landlord has duly given his written consent to the mortgage effected by this deed.]

NOW THIS DEED WITNESSES as follows:

1 Definitions

In this mortgage:

1.1 'the Interest Payment Days' means *(state days for payment)*;

1.2 'the Interest Rate' means [*(for fixed rate)* ......% a year *(or for variable rate)* ......% above the rate of *(specify lending or base rate by which reference to which interest is to be calculated)* from time to time];

1.3 'the Principal' means £.........;

1.4 'the Property' means described in [the schedule *(or)* schedule 1] and all other (if any) the property comprised in and demised by the Lease;

1.5 'the Redemption Date' means *(date)*;

1.6 'the Landlord' means *(lessor)*;

1.7 'the Lease' means the lease dated *(date)* and made between (1) the Landlord and (2) the Borrower.

2 Payment of principal and interest

In consideration of the Principal paid by the Lender to the Borrower (receipt of which the Borrower acknowledges) the Borrower covenants with the Lender to pay the Principal to the Lender on the Redemption Date with interest on it from the date of this deed at the Interest Rate, and if the Principal is not paid on that day then, so long as any part of it remains owing, to pay to the Lender interest at the Interest Rate (as well after as before any judgment) on the Principal or such part of it as from time to time remains owing by equal [half-yearly *(or as required)*] payments on the Interest Payment Days in each year.

3 Demise

For the above consideration the Borrower, with [full *(or)* limited] title guarantee, demises the Property to the Lender, to hold to the Lender [subject to the respective underleases set out in schedule 2 below] for the residue of the term created by the Lease except the last 10 days of the term subject to the provision for cesser contained in clause 4.

4 Provision for cesser

If the Borrower pays the Principal to the Lender on the Redemption Date with interest on it from the date of this deed at the Interest Rate, the sub-term created by this deed shall cease.

5 Borrower's covenants

The Borrower covenants with the Lender as follows:

Insert covenants as to insurance and repair, and not to register, as appropriate

6 Provisos

Insert provisos as required, eg for reduction of rate of interest on punctual payment, restriction on powers of leasing, removal of restrictions on consolidation

[*6.4 Power to sub-demise on sale of leaseholds in lots*

The statutory power of sale shall be extended so as to authorise any person exercising it by selling the Property in lots to carry the sale into effect by a sub-demise of each lot sold to the purchaser of it for the residue of the term created by the Lease less one day at an apportioned rent or by assigning the whole of the Property to one purchaser who will then sub-demise to every other purchaser in the above manner the lot purchased by him, and subject in either case to such covenants and conditions as the person exercising the power thinks fit.]

7 Interpretation

In this deed where the context admits the expressions 'the Borrower' and 'the Lender' include the persons deriving title under the Borrower and the Lender respectively.

IN WITNESS etc

SCHEDULE [1]
The Property

(describe property to be mortgaged)

[SCHEDULE 2
Existing underleases

(give details of subsisting underleases)]

(signatures (or common seals) of the parties)

(signatures of witnesses)

This precedent is reproduced from *Butterworths Encyclopaedia of Forms and Precedents* (5th edn), volume 28 (1999 reissue) MORTGAGES, Form 341, contributed by Andrew Whittaker, solicitor.

SECOND MORTGAGE BY DEMISE OF FREEHOLDS BY ONE BORROWER TO ONE LENDER: UNREGISTERED LAND

THIS MORTGAGE is made the .... day of .... BETWEEN

(1) *(borrower)* [of *(address) (or)* the registered office of which is at *(address)* and the company registration number of which is *(number)*] ('the Borrower') and

(2) *(lender)* [of *(address) (or)* the registered office of which is at *(address)* and the company registration number of which is *(number)*] ('the Lender')

RECITALS

(1) The Borrower is the estate owner in respect of the fee simple absolute in possession of the land described below subject to the First Mortgage by which £......... was secured [by a term of 3,000 years from the date of the First Mortgage *(or)* by a charge by way of legal mortgage] but otherwise free from incumbrances.

(2) The principal sum secured by the First Mortgage is still owing with current interest.

(3) The Lender has agreed to lend to the Borrower the Principal on the repayment of it with interest being secured in the manner set out below.

NOW THIS DEED WITNESSES as follows:

1 Definitions

In this mortgage:

1.1 'the Interest Payment Days' means *(state days for payment)*;

1.2 'the Interest Rate' means [*(for fixed rate)* ......% a year *(or for variable rate)* ......% above the rate of *(specify lending or base rate by which reference to which interest is to be calculated)* from time to time];

1.3 'the Principal' means £.........;

1.4 'the Property' means the property described in the schedule [and shown coloured red on the annexed plan];

1.5 'the Redemption Date' means *(date)*;

1.6 'the First Mortgage' means a mortgage dated *(date)* and made between *(parties)*.

2 Payment of principal and interest

In consideration of the Principal paid by the Lender to the Borrower (receipt of which the Borrower acknowledges), the Borrower covenants with the Lender to pay the Principal to the Lender on the Redemption Date with interest from the date of this deed at the Interest Rate and, if the Principal or any part of it is not paid on that date, to pay to the Lender interest (as well after as before any judgment) at the Interest Rate on the Principal or such part of it as from time to time remains owing by equal [half-yearly *(or)* quarterly] payments on the Interest Payment Days in each year.

3 Demise

For the above consideration the Borrower, with [full *(or)* limited] title guarantee, demises to the Lender the Property, to hold to the Lender for the term of [3,000 years *(or as the case may be)*] and one day from the date of the First Mortgage without impeachment of waste subject to the First Mortgage and to the principal sum and interest secured by it and subject to the provision for cesser in clause 4 below.

4 Provision for cesser

If the Borrower pays the Principal on the Redemption Date with interest at the Interest Rate the term created by this deed shall cease.

5 Borrower's covenants

Insert covenants as to insurance, repair and not to register, as appropriate

6 Provisos

Insert provisos as to reduction of interest rate, not calling in debt, restricting redemption before specified time, restricting leasing, and consolidation as required

6.6 Redemption of the First Mortgage

If any proceeding or step is taken to exercise or enforce any powers or remedies conferred by the First Mortgage against the Property, the Lender may redeem the First Mortgage or procure the transfer of it to himself and may settle and pass the accounts of the First Mortgagee. Any accounts so settled and passed shall be conclusive and binding on the Borrower and all the principal sum, interest, costs, charges and expenses of and incident to such redemption or transfer shall be paid by the Borrower to the Lender on demand with interest at the Interest Rate from the time or respective times of them having been paid or incurred and until payment the Property shall stand charged with the amount so to be paid with the above interest.

7 Interpretation

In this deed where the context admits the expressions 'the Borrower' and 'the Lender' include the persons deriving title under the Borrower and the Lender respectively.

IN WITNESS etc

SCHEDULE
The Property

(describe property to be mortgaged)

(signatures (or common seals) of the parties)

(signatures of witnesses)

This precedent is reproduced from *Butterworths Encyclopaedia of Forms and Precedents* (5th edn), volume 28 (1999 reissue) MORTGAGES, Form 342, contributed by Andrew Whittaker, solicitor.

CHARGING CLAUSE FOR SECOND MORTGAGE OF LEASEHOLD BY DEMISE

2 Demise

For the above consideration the Borrower, with [full *(or)* limited] title guarantee, demises to the Lender all the property described in [the schedule *(or)* schedule 1] and demised by the Lease ('the Property'), to hold to the Lender for the residue of the term granted by the Lease except the last 2 days of the term subject to the First Mortgage [and subject to the respective subsisting underleases specified in schedule 2]

This precedent is reproduced from *Butterworths Encyclopaedia of Forms and Precedents* (5th edn), volume 28 (1999 reissue) MORTGAGES, Form 343, contributed by Andrew Whittaker, solicitor.

POSTPONEMENT OF STATUTORY CHARGE SECURING MATRIMONIAL HOME RIGHTS UNDER THE FAMILY LAW ACT 1996

In consideration of your agreeing to make facilities available to my [husband *(or)* wife] *(spouse)* of *(address)* ('the Borrower') on the security of a charge on [his *(or)* her] estate or interest in *(describe property)* I *(declarant)* agree under the Family Law Act 1996 Schedule 4 paragraph 6 that your charge and all money including interest, charges and further advances intended to be secured by your charge shall rank in priority to the charge to which I am entitled in respect of my matrimonial home rights by virtue of section 31 of that Act.

(date)

(signature of spouse)

This precedent is reproduced from *Butterworths Encyclopaedia of Forms and Precedents* (5th edn), volume 28 (1999 reissue) MORTGAGES, Form 352, contributed by Andrew Whittaker, solicitor.

TRANSFER OF THE WHOLE OF UNREGISTERED FREEHOLD LAND UNDER AN AGREEMENT OR COURT ORDER FOR THE TRANSFER OF THE MATRIMONIAL HOME BY HUSBAND TO WIFE, SUBJECT TO A MORTGAGE, THE HUSBAND REMAINING LIABLE AND THE WIFE INDEMNIFYING HIM

Use Land Registry form TR1
and insert in the panels specified below, the wording shown:

Panel 1 Stamp Duty

It is certified that this transfer falls within category 'H' in the Schedule to the Stamp Duty (Exempt Instruments) Regulations 1987

Panel 3 Property

(address or description) *being the whole of the land described in [a conveyance* or (as the case may be)*] dated* (date) *made between* (parties) *('the Conveyance')*

Panel 5 Transferor

(*husband*)

Panel 6 Transferee

(*wife*)

Panel 9 Consideration

This transfer is not for money or anything which has a monetary value

Panel 10 Title guarantee

[Full *or* limited] title guarantee

Panel 12 Additional provisions

12.1 In this transfer:
- 12.1.1 'the Charge' means a [legal charge *or* mortgage] dated *(date)* made between (1) the Transferor and (2) the Chargee under which £... is owing in respect of principal and unpaid interest
- 12.1.2 'the Chargee' means *(proprietor of charge)* of *(address)*

12.2 This transfer is made pursuant to [an agreement *or* order of the [*(name)* County Court *or* Divorce Registry *or* High Court of Justice Family Division [*(name)* District Registry]]] dated *(date)*

12.3 The property is transferred subject to the Charge

12.4 The Transferee covenants with the Transferor and the Chargee from the date of this transfer to pay the principal interest and any other money due under the Charge and to comply with the Transferor's obligations in the Charge in accordance with its terms and to indemnify the Transferor's estate and effects against all claims and demands arising out of any failure to do so

12.5 The Transferor warrants to the Transferee that the total amount outstanding under the Charge at the date of this transfer is as stated in Panel 12.1.1 and is made up as there detailed

12.6 The property is transferred subject to [and (where appropriate) with the benefit of] the matters contained or referred to in the [Conveyance *or (insert details)*]

[12.7 With the object of giving the Transferor a complete indemnity but not for any other purpose the Transferee covenants with the Transferor from the date of this transfer to observe and perform the covenants and conditions [set out *or* referred to in] [the Conveyance *or (insert details)*] so far as they relate to the property and are capable of being enforced and any breach of them would or could expose the Transferor to liability and to that extent to indemnify the Transferor against all costs claims and demands in respect of any breach of them]

This precedent is reproduced from *Butterworths Encyclopaedia of Forms and Precedents* (5th edn), volume 16(2) (2001 reissue) FAMILY, Form 31, contributed by Alison Hawes, solicitor.

TRANSFER OF THE WHOLE OF REGISTERED FREEHOLD LAND UNDER AN AGREEMENT OR COURT ORDER FOR THE TRANSFER OF THE MATRIMONIAL HOME BY HUSBAND TO WIFE, SUBJECT TO A REGISTERED CHARGE, THE HUSBAND REMAINING LIABLE AND THE WIFE INDEMNIFYING HIM

Use Land Registry form TR1
and insert in the panels specified below, the wording shown:

Panel 1 Stamp Duty

It is certified that this transfer falls within category 'H' in the Schedule to the Stamp Duty (Exempt Instruments) Regulations 1987

Panel 5 Transferor

(*husband*)

Panel 6 Transferee

(*wife*)

Panel 9 Consideration

This transfer is not for money or anything which has a monetary value

Panel 10 Title guarantee

[Full *or* limited] title guarantee

Panel 12 Additional provisions

12.1 In this transfer
- 12.1.1 'the Charge' means the registered charge dated *(date)* registered on *(date)* of which the Chargee is proprietor and under which £... is owing in respect of principal and unpaid interest
- 12.1.2 'the Chargee' means *(proprietor of charge)* of *(address)*

12.2 This transfer is made pursuant to [an agreement *or* order of the [*(name)* County Court *or* Divorce Registry *or* High Court of Justice Family Division [*(name)* District Registry]]] dated *(date)*

12.3 The property is transferred subject to the Charge

12.4 The Transferee covenants with the Transferor and the Chargee from the date of this transfer to pay the principal interest and any other money due under the Charge and to comply with the Transferor's obligations in the Charge in accordance with its terms and to indemnify the Transferor's estate and effects against all claims and demands arising out of any failure to do so

12.5 The Transferor warrants to the Transferee that the total amount outstanding under the Charge at the date of this transfer is as stated in Panel 12.1.1 and is made up as there detailed

12.6 With the object of giving the Transferor a complete indemnity but not for any other purpose the Transferee covenants with the Transferor from the date of this transfer to observe and perform the covenants and conditions contained or referred to in the property [proprietorship] and charges registers of title number *(number)* so far as they relate to the property and are capable of being enforced and any breach of them would or could expose the Transferor to liability and to that extent to indemnify the Transferor against all costs claims and demands in respect of any breach of them]

This precedent is reproduced from *Butterworths Encyclopaedia of Forms and Precedents* (5th edn), volume 16(2) (2001 reissue) FAMILY, Form 32, contributed by Alison Hawes, solicitor.

TRANSFER OF THE WHOLE OF UNREGISTERED FREEHOLD LAND UNDER AN AGREEMENT OR COURT ORDER FOR THE TRANSFER OF THE MATRIMONIAL HOME BY HUSBAND TO WIFE, SUBJECT TO A MORTGAGE, THE HUSBAND BEING RELEASED AND THE WIFE ASSUMING LIABILITY

Use Land Registry form TR1
and insert in the panels specified below, the wording shown:

Panel 1 Stamp Duty

It is certified that this transfer falls within category 'H' in the Schedule to the Stamp Duty (Exempt Instruments) Regulations 1987

Panel 3 Property

(address or description) *being the whole of the land described in [a conveyance* or (as the case may be)*] dated* (date) *made between* (parties) *('the Conveyance')*

Panel 5 Transferor

(husband)

Panel 6 Transferee

(*wife*)

Panel 9 Consideration

This transfer is not for money or anything which has a monetary value

Panel 10 Title guarantee

[Full *or* limited] title guarantee

Panel 12 Additional provisions

12.1 In this transfer
  12.1.1 'the Charge' means a [legal charge *or* mortgage] dated *(date)* made between (1) the Transferor and (2) the Chargee under which £... is owing in respect of principal and unpaid interest
  12.1.2 'the Chargee' means *(proprietor of charge)* of *(address)*
12.2 This transfer is made pursuant to [an agreement *or* order of the [*(name)* County Court *or* Divorce Registry *or* High Court of Justice Family Division [*(name)* District Registry]]] dated *(date)*
12.3 The property is transferred subject to the Charge
12.4 The Chargee releases and discharges the Transferor from all the obligations of the Transferor under the Charge and from all claims and demands arising out of the Charge
12.5 The Transferee covenants with the Chargee from the date of this transfer to pay the principal interest and other money due under the Charge and to comply with the Transferor's obligations in the Charge in accordance with its terms
12.6 The property is transferred subject to [and (where appropriate) with the benefit of] the matters contained or referred to in the [Conveyance *or (insert details)*]
[12.7 With the object of giving the Transferor a complete indemnity but not for any other purpose the Transferee covenants with the Transferor from the date of this transfer to observe and perform the covenants and conditions [set out *or* referred to in] [the Conveyance *or (insert details)*] so far as they relate to the property and are capable of being enforced and any breach of them would or could expose the Transferor to liability and to that extent to indemnify the Transferor against all costs claims and demands in respect of any breach of them]

This precedent is reproduced from *Butterworths Encyclopaedia of Forms and Precedents* (5th edn), volume 16(2) (2001 reissue) FAMILY, Form 33, contributed by Alison Hawes, solicitor.

TRANSFER OF THE WHOLE OF REGISTERED FREEHOLD LAND UNDER AN AGREEMENT OR COURT ORDER FOR THE TRANSFER OF THE MATRIMONIAL HOME BY HUSBAND TO WIFE, SUBJECT TO A MORTGAGE, THE HUSBAND BEING RELEASED AND THE WIFE ASSUMING LIABILITY

Use Land Registry form TR1
and insert in the panels specified below, the wording shown:

Panel 1 Stamp Duty

It is certified that this transfer falls within category 'H' in the Schedule to the Stamp Duty (Exempt Instruments) Regulations 1987

Panel 5 Transferor

(*husband*)

Panel 6 Transferee

(*wife*)

Panel 9 Consideration

This transfer is not for money or anything which has a monetary value

Panel 10 Title guarantee

[Full *or* limited] title guarantee

Panel 12 Additional provisions

12.1 In this transfer
 12.1.1 'the Charge' means a registered charge dated *(date)* registered on *(date)* of which the Chargee under which £... is owing in respect of principal and unpaid interest
 12.1.2 'the Chargee' means *(proprietor of charge)* of *(address)*
12.2 This transfer is made pursuant to [an agreement *or* order of the [*(name)* County Court *or* Divorce Registry *or* High Court of Justice Family Division [*(name)* District Registry]]] dated *(date)*
12.3 The property is transferred subject to the Charge
12.4 The Chargee releases and discharges the Transferor from all the obligations of the Transferor under the Charge and from all claims and demands arising out of the Charge
12.5 The Transferee covenants with the Chargee from the date of this transfer to pay the principal interest and other money due under the Charge and

to comply with the Transferor's obligations in the Charge in accordance with its terms

[12.6 With the object of giving the Transferor a complete indemnity but not for any other purpose the Transferee covenants with the Transferor from the date of this transfer to observe and perform the covenants and conditions contained or referred to in the property [proprietorship] and charges registers of title number *(number)* so far as they relate to the property and are capable of being enforced and any breach of them would or could expose the Transferor to liability and to that extent to indemnify the Transferor against all costs claims and demands in respect of any breach of them]

This precedent is reproduced from *Butterworths Encyclopaedia of Forms and Precedents* (5th edn), volume 16(2) (2001 reissue) FAMILY, Form 34, contributed by Alison Hawes, solicitor.

Index